Ecozones with Sub-ecozones

- Appalachian Plateau (A)
- Great Lakes Plain (B)
- Tug Hill Plateau (C)
- St. Lawrence Plains (D)
- Champlain Valley (E)
- Adirondacks (F)
- Mohawk Valley (G)
- Hudson Valley (H)
- Taconic Highlands (I)
- Hudson Highlands (J)
- Triassic Lowlands (K)
- Manhattan Hills (L)
- Coastal Lowlands (M)

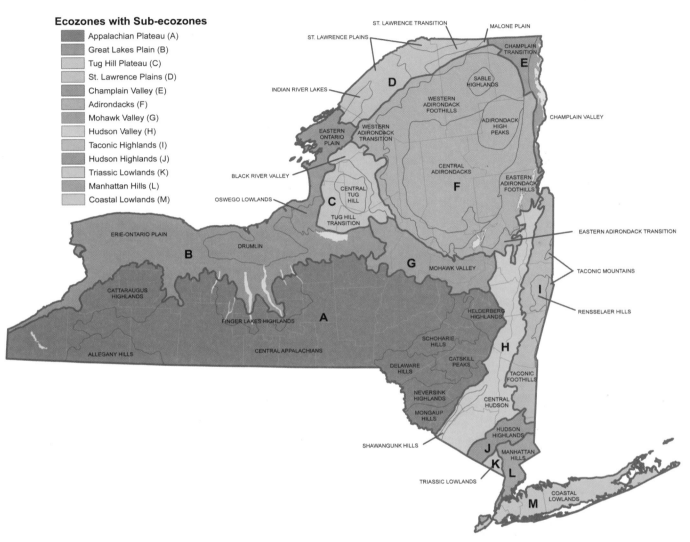

Ecozones and sub-ecozones in New York.

The Second Atlas of Breeding Birds in New York State

PUBLISHED IN ASSOCIATION WITH the New York State Ornithological Association and the New York State Department of Environmental Conservation in cooperation with the New York Cooperative Fish and Wildlife Research Unit at Cornell University, Cornell University Department of Natural Resources, Cornell Lab of Ornithology, and Audubon New York.

The Second Atlas of
BREEDING BIRDS IN NEW YORK STATE

Edited by

KEVIN J. McGOWAN *and* KIMBERLEY CORWIN

©JPB 2005

COMSTOCK PUBLISHING ASSOCIATES *a division of*
CORNELL UNIVERSITY PRESS
Ithaca and London

Major funding for the Breeding Bird Atlas project was provided by the Return a Gift to Wildlife state income tax checkoff. Additional support was provided by the New York State Conservation Fund, the Hudson River Estuary Program, and through New York State Wildlife Grant T-2-1 in cooperation with the U.S. Fish and Wildlife Service Division of Wildlife and Sport Fish Restoration.

Copyright © 2008 by Cornell University

First published 2008 by Cornell University Press

Library of Congress Cataloging-in-Publication Data

The second atlas of breeding birds in New York State / edited by Kevin J. McGowan and Kimberley Corwin.
   p. cm.
 "Published in association with the New York State Ornithological Association and the New York State Department of Environmental Conservation in cooperation with the New York Cooperative Fish and Wildlife Research Unit at Cornell University, Cornell University Department of Natural Resources, Cornell Lab of Ornithology, and Audubon New York."
 Earlier atlas published under title: The atlas of breeding birds in New York State. Ithaca : Cornell University Press, 1988.
 Includes bibliographical references and index.
 ISBN 978-0-8014-4716-7 (cloth : alk. paper)
 1. Birds—New York (State) 2. Birds—New York (State)—Geographical distribution. 3. Birds—New York (State)—Geographical distribution—Maps. I. McGowan, Kevin J. (Kevin James), 1956– II. Corwin, Kimberley, 1969– III. New York State Ornithological Association. IV. New York (State). Dept. of Environmental Conservation. V. New York Cooperative Fish and Wildlife Research Unit. VI. New York State College of Agriculture and Life Sciences. Dept. of Natural Resources. VII. Cornell University. Laboratory of Ornithology. VIII. Audubon New York. IX. Title: 2nd atlas of breeding birds in New York State. X. Title: Atlas of breeding birds in New York State.
 QL684.N7S43 2008
 598.09747--dc22

                                                                        2008015639

Cornell University Press strives to use environmentally responsible suppliers and materials to the fullest extent possible in the publishing of its books. Such materials include vegetable-based, low-VOC inks and acid-free papers that are recycled, totally chlorine-free, or partly composed of nonwood fibers. For further information, visit our website at www.cornellpress.cornell.edu.

Cloth printing   10 9 8 7 6 5 4 3 2 1   Printed in China.

*To the Atlas volunteers, who shared the vision of
creating the next generation of bird distribution
maps in New York State. Without their
commitment and extensive knowledge
this Atlas project would not
have been possible.*

Contents

Foreword by Valerie M. Freer   IX
Acknowledgments   XI
Contributors   XVI

CHAPTER ONE   Introduction and Methodology
KIMBERLEY CORWIN   I

CHAPTER TWO   Summary of Results
KEVIN J. MCGOWAN AND BENJAMIN ZUCKERBERG   15

CHAPTER THREE   Habitats of New York State
GREGORY J. EDINGER AND TIMOTHY G. HOWARD   43

CHAPTER FOUR   Land-Use Changes and Breeding Birds
CHARLES R. SMITH AND PETER L. MARKS   59

CHAPTER FIVE   Ornithology and Birding in New York State
JOHN M. C. PETERSON   69

CHAPTER SIX   Conservation of New York's Breeding Birds
KENNETH V. ROSENBERG AND MICHAEL F. BURGER   75

THE SPECIES ACCOUNTS   85

APPENDIX 1 Rare, Improbable, and Historic Breeders   625
APPENDIX 2 Breeding Season Table   635
APPENDIX 3 Common and Scientific Names of Plants and Animals Referred to in Text   643

Citations for Map Data   645
Literature Cited   647

Index   683

Foreword

The book you are holding represents the fruit of the efforts of over 1,200 people. Its roots first took hold in the fall of 1998, when the late Bob Miller, leader of the Nongame and Habitat Unit in the New York State Department of Environmental Conservation (NYSDEC), organized a meeting of people interested in the idea of conducting a second Atlas project in New York. Bob was instrumental in starting New York's first Breeding Bird Atlas in the late 1970s when the concept of documenting breeding ranges by atlasing was new in North America.

That meeting ten years ago resulted in the formation of the Breeding Bird Atlas 2000 Steering Committee, which represented each of the partnering organizations listed on the title page. Over the next seven years, the hard-working committee met more than 40 times, guiding the project from the design stage through publication. The committee spent considerable time studying techniques used in other atlas projects before making a fundamental decision to use the same field protocols and once again collect data from all blocks, instead of sampling, in order to provide for direct comparison with the first Atlas. We on the committee agreed to update communication and data storage technology, to make the field maps and species distribution maps and data available to anyone interested, to establish levels of careful review of records, and to publish a printed book at the end of the project.

We knew that a major hurdle would be to find capable birders who were willing to work in each of the 5,335 blocks in the state. We relied on the connections and leadership of the New York State Ornithological Association (NYSOA) to identify motivated and skilled regional coordinators who would recruit, guide, and encourage the field workers. The field workers and the outstanding regional coordinators who led them formed the foundation of this project. Because of their efforts we were able to achieve our goal of obtaining coverage of the entire state comparable to that in the first Atlas.

An important early task for the Steering Committee was the selection and hiring of Kimberley Corwin to manage the day-to-day aspects of data collection and management. Ornithologist Kevin McGowan was later employed to analyze the changes in bird distribution evident in the data, and to edit the book, and Kim's role was changed to co-editor. The skills, dedication, and high standards that both have brought to this project are evident in this book.

A key person leading many aspects of the project was John Ozard of the NYSDEC, who from the beginning showed remarkable ability to find a way to do whatever needed to be done. This was often accomplished with the cooperation of Milo Richmond at Cornell University. Bard Prentiss, our volunteer art editor, worked countless hours with the artists and the Technical Art Committee to attain the levels of accuracy and beauty that are evident in this book. His was a labor of love.

A major part of our funding was provided through Return a Gift to Wildlife, donations made on income tax forms by New York State taxpayers. Thank you!

We believe that the highest value of this tremendous project lies not only in the publication of the book but also in the quality (and quantity) of the information that was collected in the field. The 1980–85 database and the 2000–05 database are valuable by themselves, but together they provide a resource unlike any other, one that will increase in value with time. As more researchers make use of these databases, and sound environmental decisions are based on the data they provide, bird populations of the state will benefit.

Valerie M. Freer, Chair
Breeding Bird Atlas 2000 Steering Committee

Acknowledgments

Partnering Organizations

New York State Ornithological Association, Inc.
New York State Department of Environmental Conservation
New York Cooperative Fish and Wildlife Research Unit
Cornell University Department of Natural Resources
Cornell Lab of Ornithology
Audubon New York

Steering Committee

Valerie M. Freer, Chair
Timothy H. Baird
Robert E. Budliger
Michael F. Burger
Kimberley Corwin
Phyllis R. Jones
Berna B. Lincoln
Kevin J. McGowan
Robert L. Miller
John W. Ozard
Bard Prentiss
Milo E. Richmond
Charles R. Smith
Laura A. Sommers

Project Coordinator

Kimberley Corwin

Database Design and Management

John W. Ozard

Technological Support and Map Production

Katherine Barnes
Eryle Bixler
Gerald Colborn
James Daley
Tori Ferro
Sara Frankenfeld
Pete Gradoni
Saikumar Jonnalagadda

Jim McKelvy
Beth O'Pezio
Gerald Rasmussen
Wayne Richter
Laura A. Sommers
Dennis Wischman

Editorial Assistance

Matthew D. Medler
John W. Ozard

Art Editor

Bard Prentiss

Literature Review

Jane Denker Graves

Indexing

Donald A. Windsor

Regional Coordinators

Region 1: Dorothy J. Rosche, Richard C. Rosche
Region 2: Dominic F. Sherony, Robert G. Spahn
Region 3: Bard Prentiss, Dave Russell
Region 4: Chad E. Covey, Bob Donnelly, Thomas Salo
Region 5: Dorothy W. Crumb, Bill Purcell
Region 6: Robert E. Long
Region 7: John M. C. Peterson
Region 8: Mark Fitzsimmons, Jane Denker Graves
Region 9: Michael Bochnik, Barbara Butler, Renee Davis, Valerie M. Freer, Carol A. Weiss
Region 10: Ken Feustel

Records Review Committee

Robert G. Spahn, Chair
Kimberley Corwin
Berna B. Lincoln
Kevin J. McGowan

Richard C. Rosche
Charles R. Smith

Artwork Technical Committee

Bard Prentiss, Chair
Robert F. Andrle
Kevin J. McGowan

Logo Design

Cory Wolcott

Peer Reviewers

David Adams, Daniel R. Ardia, Timothy H. Baird, Guy
Baldassarre, Andrew J. Bernick, Jeffrey Bolsinger, Tom Burke,
Barbara Butler, Anne B. Clark, Ben Clock, Joan E. Collins,
Michael Cooper, Kimberley Corwin, Susan Elbin, Ken Feustel,
Valerie M. Freer, Tom Gavin, Michelle Gibbons, James Gibbs,
Julie Hart, Tom Hodgman, Robin Holevinski, Paul Kerlinger,
Bill Krueger, Sarah Lazazzero, Jillian Liner, Michael Losito,
Barbara Allen Loucks, James D. Lowe, Irene Mazzocchi,
Kevin J. McGowan, Matthew D. Medler, Shaibal S. Mitra,
Sandy Muller, Robert Mulvihill, Michael T. Murphy,
Christopher Nadareski, Paul Novak, Peter E. Nye, Timothy
J. O'Connell, John W. Ozard, Carl Parker, Kathy Parsons,
John M. C. Peterson, Timothy J. Post, Bill Purcell, Milo E.
Richmond, Patricia Riexinger, John Rogers, Thomas Salo,
Michael Schiavone, William Shields, Charles R. Smith, Gerry
Smith, Robert G. Spahn, Scott Sutcliffe, Bryan L. Swift, Rachel
Vallender, David W. Winkler, Matthew A. Young, Steve Young,
John Zarudsky

Authors of Species Accounts

Daniel R. Ardia
    European Starling
Kevin L. Berner
    Eastern Bluebird
Anne B. Clark
    Red-winged Blackbird
Jeremy T. H. Coleman
    Double-crested Cormorant
Joan E. Collins
    Nashville Warbler, Black-throated Blue Warbler,
    Blackburnian Warbler, Mourning Warbler
John Confer
    Blue-winged Warbler, Golden-winged Warbler, Blue-
    winged Warbler x Golden-winged Warbler hybrid
Kimberley Corwin
    White-winged Tern

Scott Crocoll
    Northern Goshawk, Red-shouldered Hawk, Broad-
    winged Hawk, Red-tailed Hawk
Melanie J. L. Driscoll
    House Finch
Valerie M. Freer
    Bank Swallow
Jon S. Greenlaw
    Nelson's Sharp-tailed Sparrow, Saltmarsh Sharp-tailed
    Sparrow, Seaside Sparrow
Ralph S. Hames
    Sharp-shinned Hawk, Cooper's Hawk, Veery, Swainson's
    Thrush, Hermit Thrush, Wood Thrush, Scarlet Tanager
Glenn Johnson
    Spruce Grouse
Heidi Bogner Kennedy
    Least Bittern
Barbara Allen Loucks
    Peregrine Falcon
James D. Lowe
    Sharp-shinned Hawk, Cooper's Hawk, Veery, Swainson's
    Thrush, Hermit Thrush, Wood Thrush, Scarlet Tanager
Irene Mazzocchi
    Black Tern
Donald A. McCrimmon Jr.
    Great Blue Heron, Great Egret, Snowy Egret, Little Blue
    Heron, Tricolored Heron, Cattle Egret, Green Heron,
    Black-crowned Night-Heron, Yellow-crowned Night-
    Heron
Kent McFarland
    Blackpoll Warbler
Kevin J. McGowan
    Canada Goose, Mute Swan, Trumpeter Swan, Gadwall,
    American Wigeon, Blue-winged Teal, Northern Shoveler,
    Northern Pintail, Green-winged Teal, Canvasback,
    Redhead, Ring-necked Duck, Greater Scaup, Lesser
    Scaup, Common Eider, Bufflehead, Hooded Merganser,
    Common Merganser, Red-breasted Merganser, Ruddy
    Duck, Greater Prairie-Chicken, Wild Turkey, Northern
    Bobwhite, Pied-billed Grebe, American White Pelican,
    American Bittern, White-faced Ibis, Black Vulture,
    Turkey Vulture, Merlin, Sandhill Crane, Killdeer, Spotted
    Sandpiper, Upland Sandpiper, Wilson's Snipe, Rock
    Pigeon, Eurasian Collared-Dove, Mourning Dove,
    Passenger Pigeon, Black-hooded Parakeet, Yellow-billed
    Cuckoo, Black-billed Cuckoo, Barn Owl, Great Horned
    Owl, Barred Owl, Northern Saw-whet Owl, Chimney
    Swift, Ruby-throated Hummingbird, Belted Kingfisher,
    Red-headed Woodpecker, Red-bellied Woodpecker,
    Yellow-bellied Sapsucker, Downy Woodpecker, Hairy
    Woodpecker, Northern Flicker, Pileated Woodpecker,
    Eastern Wood-Pewee, Least Flycatcher, Eastern Phoebe,

Great Crested Flycatcher, Western Kingbird, Eastern Kingbird, White-eyed Vireo, Yellow-throated Vireo, Blue-headed Vireo, Warbling Vireo, Philadelphia Vireo, Red-eyed Vireo, Gray Jay, Blue Jay, American Crow, Fish Crow, Common Raven, Skylark, Northern Rough-winged Swallow, Black-capped Chickadee, Tufted Titmouse, Red-breasted Nuthatch, White-breasted Nuthatch, Brown Creeper, Bewick's Wren, House Wren, Winter Wren, Sedge Wren, Marsh Wren, Golden-crowned Kinglet, Ruby-crowned Kinglet, Blue-gray Gnatcatcher, American Robin, Gray Catbird, Northern Mockingbird, Brown Thrasher, Northern Parula, Magnolia Warbler, Yellow-rumped Warbler, Yellow-throated Warbler, Pine Warbler, Palm Warbler, American Redstart, Prothonotary Warbler, Ovenbird, Northern Waterthrush, Common Yellowthroat, Hooded Warbler, Wilson's Warbler, Canada Warbler, Yellow-breasted Chat, Summer Tanager, Eastern Towhee, Chipping Sparrow, Savannah Sparrow, Henslow's Sparrow, Song Sparrow, Northern Cardinal, Rose-breasted Grosbeak, Blue Grosbeak, Indigo Bunting, Dickcissel, Western Meadowlark, Brewer's Blackbird, Common Grackle, Boat-tailed Grackle, Brown-headed Cowbird, Orchard Oriole, Baltimore Oriole, European Goldfinch, House Sparrow

Matthew D. Medler
Glossy Ibis, Black Rail, Clapper Rail, King Rail, Virginia Rail, Sora, Common Moorhen, American Coot, Wilson's Phalarope, Black Skimmer, Long-eared Owl, Common Nighthawk, Whip-poor-will, Purple Martin, Tree Swallow, Cliff Swallow, Barn Swallow

Shaibal S. Mitra
Gull-billed Tern, Roseate Tern, Monk Parakeet, Chuck-will's-widow, Yellow Warbler

Sandy Muller
Black Tern

Mike Murphy
Ring-necked Pheasant

Paul Novak
Loggerhead Shrike

Peter E. Nye
Osprey, Bald Eagle, Golden Eagle, American Kestrel

Carrie Osborne
Swamp Sparrow

John M. C. Peterson
Common Goldeneye, American Three-toed Woodpecker, Black-backed Woodpecker, Olive-sided Flycatcher, Yellow-bellied Flycatcher, Boreal Chickadee, Tennessee Warbler, Cape May Warbler, Bay-breasted Warbler, Lincoln's Sparrow, White-throated Sparrow, Rusty Blackbird

Timothy J. Post
Gray Partridge, Ruffed Grouse, Northern Harrier,

American Woodcock, Alder Flycatcher, Willow Flycatcher, Chestnut-sided Warbler, Black-throated Green Warbler, Black-and-white Warbler, Field Sparrow

Milo E. Richmond
Ring-billed Gull, Herring Gull, Great Black-backed Gull, Common Tern

Christopher C. Rimmer
Bicknell's Thrush, Blackpoll Warbler

Kenneth V. Rosenberg
Cerulean Warbler, Louisiana Waterthrush, Kentucky Warbler

Angelena Ross
Spruce Grouse

Kathryn J. Schneider
Short-eared Owl

Nina Schoch
Common Loon

Charles R. Smith
Eastern Screech-Owl, Acadian Flycatcher, Horned Lark, Carolina Wren, Prairie Warbler, Worm-eating Warbler, Clay-colored Sparrow, Vesper Sparrow, Grasshopper Sparrow, Dark-eyed Junco, Bobolink, Eastern Meadowlark

Gerry Smith
Caspian Tern

Bryan Swift
Wood Duck, American Black Duck, Mallard, Mallard x Black Duck hybrid,

Michael R. Wasilco
Piping Plover, American Oystercatcher, Willet, Laughing Gull, Least Tern, Forster's Tern

Mark Witmer
Cedar Waxwing

Matthew A. Young
Purple Finch, Red Crossbill, White-winged Crossbill, Pine Siskin, American Goldfinch, Evening Grosbeak

The Artwork

All artwork that appears in the book (except for one color painting) are original works commissioned for the Atlas publication.

Sue deLearie Adair
Black-and-white illustrations: Wood Duck, Gadwall, American Wigeon, American Black Duck, Mallard, Mallard x Black Duck hybrid, Blue-winged Teal, Northern Shoveler, Northern Pintail, Green-winged Teal, Common Loon, Pied-billed Grebe, European Starling, Nashville Warbler, Yellow Warbler, Chestnut-sided Warbler, Magnolia Warbler, Black-throated Blue Warbler, Prairie Warbler, Black-and-white Warbler, American Redstart, Ovenbird, Dickcissel

Color habitat paintings: Eastern Kingbird and Eastern Phoebe in the Albany Pine Bush, Chipping and Song sparrows at Saratoga Battlefield

John Perry Baumlin
Black-and-white illustrations: Canvasback, Redhead, Ring-necked Duck, Lesser Scaup, Common Eider, Common Goldeneye, Hooded Merganser, Common Merganser, Red-breasted Merganser, Ruddy Duck, American Bittern, Least Bittern, Great Blue Heron, Great Egret, Snowy Egret, Little Blue Heron, Tricolored Heron, Cattle Egret, Green Heron, Black-crowned Night-Heron, Yellow-crowned Night-Heron, Osprey, Bald Eagle, Northern Harrier, Sharp-shinned Hawk, Cooper's Hawk, Northern Goshawk, Red-shouldered Hawk, Broad-winged Hawk, Red-tailed Hawk, Golden Eagle, American Kestrel, Merlin, Peregrine Falcon, Sandhill Crane, American Woodcock
Color habitat paintings: Raptors in the Susquehanna Valley
Color painting for cover: Merlin

James Coe
Color habitat paintings: Small-footed birds in an Albany evening, Barn and Tree swallows on a dairy farm

Michael DiGiorgio
Black-and-white illustrations: Common Nighthawk, Chuck-will's-widow, Whip-poor-will, Olive-sided Flycatcher, Eastern Wood-Pewee, Yellow-bellied Flycatcher, Acadian Flycatcher, Alder Flycatcher, Willow Flycatcher, Least Flycatcher, Eastern Phoebe, Great Crested Flycatcher, Eastern Kingbird, Loggerhead Shrike, White-eyed Vireo, Yellow-throated Vireo, Blue-headed Vireo, Warbling Vireo, Philadelphia Vireo, Red-eyed Vireo, Yellow-breasted Chat, Summer Tanager, Scarlet Tanager, Red-winged Blackbird, Eastern Meadowlark, Rusty Blackbird, Common Grackle, Boat-tailed Grackle, Brown-headed Cowbird, Orchard Oriole, Baltimore Oriole

Dale Dyer
Black-and-white illustrations: Black-capped Chickadee, Boreal Chickadee, Tufted Titmouse, Red-breasted Nuthatch, White-breasted Nuthatch, Brown Creeper, Carolina Wren, House Wren, Winter Wren, Sedge Wren, Marsh Wren, Golden-crowned Kinglet, Ruby-crowned Kinglet, Blue-gray Gnatcatcher, Northern Cardinal, Rose-breasted Grosbeak, Blue Grosbeak, Indigo Bunting, Bobolink, Purple Finch, House Finch, Red Crossbill, White-winged Crossbill, Pine Siskin, American Goldfinch, Evening Grosbeak, House Sparrow

Robert McNamara
Color habitat paintings: Wrens in a suburban backyard, Warblers in Letchworth State Park

Alan Messer
Black-and-white illustrations: Canada Goose, Mute Swan, Trumpeter Swan, Black Rail, Clapper Rail, King Rail, Virginia Rail, Sora, Common Moorhen, American Coot, Laughing Gull, Ring-billed Gull, Herring Gull, Great Black-backed Gull, Least Tern, Gull-billed Tern, Caspian Tern, Black Tern, Roseate Tern, Common Tern, Forster's Tern, Black Skimmer, Rock Pigeon, Mourning Dove, Monk Parakeet, Yellow-billed Cuckoo, Black-billed Cuckoo
Color habitat paintings: Mute Swan and Mallard on the Hudson River; Piping Plover, Willet, and Black Skimmer on Long Island beach; Laughing Gull and Common Tern at Kennedy Airport; Monk Parakeet and Yellow-billed Cuckoo in Green-Wood Cemetery; Red-eyed and Warbling vireos in Central Park

Daniel Meyer
Color habitat painting: Great Horned Owl and Eastern Screech-Owl in Mixed Woodland

Cynthia J. Page
Black-and-white illustrations: Gray Partridge, Ring-necked Pheasant, Ruffed Grouse, Spruce Grouse, Wild Turkey, Northern Bobwhite, Black Vulture, Turkey Vulture, Barn Owl, Eastern Screech-Owl, Great Horned Owl, Barred Owl, Long-eared Owl, Short-eared Owl, Northern Saw-whet Owl, Chimney Swift, Gray Jay, Blue Jay, American Crow, Fish Crow, Common Raven, Purple Martin, Tree Swallow, Northern Rough-winged Swallow, Bank Swallow, Cliff Swallow, Barn Swallow

Susan Bull Riley
Color habitat paintings: Common Loon and Pied-billed Grebe on an Adirondack lake; Rails at Montezuma National Wildlife Refuge; Pileated and Hairy woodpeckers in a Finger Lakes gorge; Common Raven and Gray Jay in the Adirondacks; Black-capped Chickadee and Red-breasted Nuthatch on an Adirondack peak; Thrushes along a Catskill stream; Cedar Waxwing, Northern Mockingbird, and European Starling in a Finger Lakes vineyard; Northern Cardinal and Indigo Bunting in an old field; Red-winged Blackbird and Bobolink in central New York farmlands

Michael C. Ringer
Color habitat painting: Great Blue Heron along the St. Lawrence River

N. John Schmitt
Black-and-white illustrations: Red-headed Woodpecker, Red-bellied Woodpecker, Yellow-bellied Sapsucker, Downy Woodpecker, Hairy Woodpecker, American Three-toed Woodpecker, Black-backed Woodpecker, Northern Flicker, Pileated Woodpecker

Barry W. Van Dusen
Black-and-white illustrations: Piping Plover, Eastern Bluebird, Blue-winged Warbler, Golden-winged Warbler
Color habitat painting: Wild Turkey and Ruffed Grouse along a woodland edge

John Wiessinger
Black-and-white illustrations: Double-crested Cormorant, Glossy Ibis, Killdeer, American Oystercatcher, Willet, Spotted Sandpiper, Upland Sandpiper, Wilson's Snipe, Wilson's Phalarope, Veery, Bicknell's Thrush, Swainson's Thrush, Hermit Thrush, Wood Thrush, American Robin, Eastern Towhee, Chipping Sparrow, Clay-colored Sparrow, Field Sparrow, Vesper Sparrow, Savannah Sparrow, Grasshopper Sparrow, Henslow's Sparrow, Saltmarsh Sharp-tailed Sparrow, Seaside Sparrow, Song Sparrow, Lincoln's Sparrow, Swamp Sparrow, White-throated Sparrow, Dark-eyed Junco

Color habitat painting: Red Crossbill and Pine Siskin in a spruce plantation

Julie Zickefoose
Black-and-white illustrations: Ruby-throated Hummingbird, Belted Kingfisher, Horned Lark, Gray Catbird, Northern Mockingbird, Brown Thrasher, Cedar Waxwing, Lawrence's Warbler, Brewster's Warbler, Tennessee Warbler, Northern Parula, Cape May Warbler, Yellow-rumped Warbler, Black-throated Green Warbler, Blackburnian Warbler, Yellow-throated Warbler, Pine Warbler, Palm Warbler, Bay-breasted Warbler, Blackpoll Warbler, Cerulean Warbler, Prothonotary Warbler, Worm-eating Warbler, Northern Waterthrush, Louisiana Waterthrush, Kentucky Warbler, Mourning Warbler, Common Yellowthroat, Hooded Warbler, Wilson's Warbler, Canada Warbler

Artist Reference

The following supplied photographs that provided a valuable resource to some of the artists: Al Campanie, Cornell Lab of Ornithology, Frank Dutton, Warren Greene, Rick Kline, Gerry Lemmo, Garth McElroy, Jay McGowan, Kevin J. McGowan, Jeff Nadler, Robert Royse, U.S. Fish and Wildlife Service.

Contributors

The data for the Breeding Bird Atlas were collected by over 1,200 people who spent more than 155,000 hours in the field. The project would not have happened without their interest, talents, and dedication. Here we list the names of volunteers and blockbusters in appreciation of their efforts.

Jan Abernethy
Kenneth P. Able
Norbert L. Ackermann
Sue deLearie Adair
Robert A. Adamo
Carol Adams
Elliott Adams
Marion D. Adams
Morton S. Adams
Jodi Adamson
Dan Albano
Matt F. Albright
Lawrence J. Alden
Ginny Alfano
Karen L. Allaben-Confer
Deborah Allen
Michael Allen
Russell L. Allen
Janet Allison
Larry Alson
Anne D. Altshuler
Andrew R. Andersen
Elaine G. Andersen
Diana F. Anderson
Judith L. Anderson
Rebecca J. Anderson
Richard W. Anderson
Marie Andes-Barberio
Dawn Andrews
Helen M. Andrews
Robert F. Andrle
Richard E. Andrus
Betty J. Armbruster
Linda Armstrong
David Arner
Emily Arter
Sheila Arthur

Robert Asanoma
Mary R. Ashwood
Richard S. Ashworth
Richard Askeland
John P. Askildsen

Marilyn Badger
Paul L. Baglia
David H. Baim
Carol A. Baird
Timothy H. Baird
Faith A. Baker
William W. Baker
Andrew J. Baldelli
John Balint
Thomas C. Barber
William H. Barber
Charles Bares
Beth A. Barker
James Barlow
Christine A. Barnes
Susan C. Barnett
Carol Barrett
Catherine Barrow
Jessie H. Barry
Jim Barry
Richard Barry
Joan C. Bartlett
Michael K. Barylski
Douglas K. Bassett
Frank W. Bassett
Trina B. Bassoff
Hope J. Batcheller
Mary H. Batcheller
Michael S. Batcher
Larry Bates
James Battaglia
Gertrude R. Battaly
Mack Baxter
Kate Beale
Barbara Beall
Kenneth C. Beardsley
Ramona N. Bearor
Douglas Beattie
Marion L. Bee
Susan K. Bell
William C. Benish
Dianne A. Benko
Allen H. Benton
James Benton
Robert J. Berlingeri

Andrew J. Bernick
Nancy Berns
James Berry
Fred J. Bertram
Richard Berube
Adam L. Best
Brenda Best
Luci Betti-Nash
Michael G. Beykirch
Steven L. Biasetti
Lois A. Bingley
Gladys J. Birdsall
John C. Birkett
Orhan Birol
Garvin S. Bixler Jr.
Lisa D. Blackman
Robin Blakesley
Marie Blazonis
Andrew v. F. Block
Andrew M. Blum
Michael C. Bochnik
Bob Boehm
John W. Boettcher
Sue Boettger
William J. Bogacki
Cheryl M. Boise
Isabel H. Bolinger
Jeffrey S. Bolsinger
Frank A. Bonanno
Helen S. Booth
Robert T. Booth
Charles J. Bordonaro
Vicki Boria
William Boria
Arlene D. Borko
Marty Borko
Brenda Borquist
Ronald V. Bourque
Lynn E. Bowdery
Martin Bowman
Brent L. Boyer
Bruce Bozdos
Rick F. Braaten
Lynn Braband
Daniel W. Brauning
Alfred T. Brayton
Alvin R. Breisch
Ariana Breisch
Kirstin Breisch
Marc A. Breslav
Melissa A. Brewer
Sandy Bright
Joseph Brin

Jodi Brodsky
Sharon G. Brody
Elizabeth W. Brooks
Richard Brooks
Angela Broughton
Richard I. Brouse
Gene Brown
Kelley M. Brown
Mark K. Brown
Philip Brown
Stewart H. Brown
Thomas Brown
William P. Brown
Jack M. Brubaker
Stuart A. Buchanan
Carol A. Budd
Robert E. Budliger
Christine A. Budniewski
Raymond C. Budniewski
Kristen A. Buechi
Mary Buehler-Brandt
Mark Buehlman
Joyce A. Burchill
Ken Burdick
Michael F. Burger
Bill Burke
Thomas W. Burke
Doris Burton
Mike Burton
Ron Bussian
Barbara A. Butler
Ryan S. Butryn

Randall T. Caccia
Bruce L. Cady
Carol A. Cady
Mary Ann Cairo
Stephen F. Caldwell
Cynthia V. Campbell
Nancy S. Cannon
David Capen
Gregory L. Capobianco
Joe Carey
Laura A. Carey
Gerianne Carillo
Barbara Carlson
Don A. Carlson
Ruth E. Carlson
Bernard Carr
Ethan Carr
William R. Case

Carol J. Cash
Daniel B. Cash
John Cashier
Carolyn T. Cass
Erik Caster
Sally Castren
Bill Cathy
Bob Cathy
Jean Cathy
Wanda Cawein
James W. Cayea III
Gene Ceccano
Belma Cerosaletti
Sheila S. Cerwonka
Gary C. Chapin
Glen D. Chapman
Malinda Chapman
Gerald Chapple
Nina Chapple
Monika Chas
Binnie B. Chase
Sharon Cheney
Alex Chmielewski
Steve M. Chorvas
Peggy Christensen
Peter B. Christensen
Richard Christensen
Daniel M. Christman
Linda B. Christy
Drew Ciganek
Joan L. Cipriani
Lance Clark
Sylvia Clarke
Anne Clarridge
Jennifer Clement
Richard D. Clements
Claudia B. Cliffel
Linda Clougherty
James Coe
Roger A. Cohn
Elizabeth T. Cole
Russell S. Cole
Joan C. Coleman
Mary A. Collier
Joan E. Collins
Patricia D. Collins
Harry Comstock
John L. Confer
Robert Confer
Greg Coniglio
Kris Conklin
Veronique Connolly
Lorraine M. Connor

Paul F. Connor
Beatrice Conover
Donald L. Coogan Jr.
Dean L. Cook
William E. Cook
Anne B. Cooke
Art Cooley
Christopher M. Cooley
Herb Cooley
Michael F. Cooper
Eileen D. L. Corbett
William Corbett
Janet H. Cordsen
Candace E. Cornell
Scott C. Cornett
Jeff Corser
Kimberley Corwin
Noreen F. Cote
Marc Cousoulis
Chad E. Covey
Salvatore A. Cozzolino
James H. Craft
Don Craig
Daniel E. Crane
Michael Crane
Thomas M. Crepet
Scott T. Crocoll
Ellen Cronan
Dorothy W. Crumb
Martin A. Cuff
Paul T. Culley
Karl E. Curtis
Mary L. Curtis
Nancy Curtis
Bruce E. Cushing
Nancy E. Cusumano
Gregory Cuvelier
Julie Cuvelier
Micheal Czarnecki

Cyndi L. Daigler
Jim Daley
Kathleen E. Dalton
Tom Damiani
Lisa D'Andrea
Nancy D. Danehy
James D'Angelo
Doug Daniels
Mary Jo Daniels
Taddy Dann
Betsy D'Anna

William D'Anna
Dutchie Davidson
Kathryn A. Davino
Donald A. Davis
John S. Davis
Michael A. Davis
Renee Davis
Nancy Davis-Ricci
Peter H. Debes
Patrick Dechon
Leonard J. DeFrancisco
Amy M. DeGaetano
Laura R. DeGaetano
Marcelo Del Puerto
Janet L. Delaney
Charlcie A. Delehanty
Donna V. DeLeon
Emma E. DeLeon
Robert L. DeLeon
Margaret Della Rocco
Tim Demoulin
Dennis Dempsey
David S. Denk
Tom Dent
Michael J. Desha
Roger Desy
Laurie A. Devine
Judy A. Dewitt
Ron Dewitt
Joseph DiCostanzo
Dean DiTommaso
Robert T. Dobson
Jon G. Dombrowski
Luke Donius
Bob Donnelly
Eric C. Donohue
Stephen P. Donohue
Jean M. Dorman
Kris M. Dower
Michael A. Drahms
Michael Drake
Robbyn J. Drake
William Drakert
Brian Drumm
Thomas R. Dudones
Adam Duerr
Jackie L. Duhon
Ethan C. Duke
Edward Dunbar
Kate Dunham

Stephen Eaton
James A. Ebert
Greg Ecker
Donald L. Eddinger
Gregory J. Edinger
James Edson
Marian L. Edson
Kate L. Edwards
Douglas R. Eger
Roberta L. Ehlert
William J. Ehmann
David P. Ellers
Walter Ellison
Paul Emerson
James P. Engel
Nancy A. Engel
Marilyn England
Helen Eno
Mike Ermer
Nancy J. Evans
Darin Everdyke
Brett M. Ewald

Lin Fagan
Richard C.A. Faille
Michael A. Farina
James F. Farquhar III
Peggy Fasciani
Wilmer D. Faux
Michael J. Federice
Margaret R. Ferjet
Lucy T. Fetterolf
Ken Feustel
Suzanne Feustel
Roy C. Fillingham
Frederick Findlay
Peter S. Finlay
Terry L. Finlay
Annette Finney
Tina Finneyfrock
Tom Fiore
Howard Fischer
Martha J. Fischer
Audrey Fishburne
Martha Fisher
Kayla M. Fisk
David E. Fiske
Elizabeth Fitts

Janet T. Fitzpatrick
John Fitzpatrick
Mark Fitzsimmons
Mark D. Fitzsimmons
Henry F. Flamm
Dorothea I. Fleisher
Donna M. Fletcher
Dorothy Fleury
Bob Fogg
Anna M. Forbes
John W. Foster
Jonathan L. Foster
John C. Foust
Kurt A. Fox
Dennis Frame
Laura Francoeur
Walter Franklin
Carolyn D. Fredericks
Kenneth Fredericks
Misha Fredericks
Laurie J. Freeman
Valerie M. Freer
Amy L. Freiman
Kenny Frisch
Gerta Fritz
John J. Fritz
Paul R. Fuhrmann
Douglas J. Futuyma

J. William Gage
Michael F. Galas
Tim Gallagher
Peter F. Galvani
Natalia G. Garcia
Jean A. Gawalt
Liz Gee
Sharon Genaux
Jeff Gerbracht
Ludlow Gere
Richard J. Gershon
James R. Gibbs
Christine Gibson
David H. Gibson
Neil A. Gifford
William G. Gillette
Bruce Gilman
Donna M. Gilmore
Joe Giunta
Michale J. Glennon
Grace Gloeckler
Joanne Goetz

Lorraine Goldsmith
David A. Gooding
Sunny H. Gooding
Kim Goodspeed
Sally Goodwin
Lisa G. Gorn
Margaret Gorton
Scott F. Graber
Judy R. Graham
Robert J. Grajewski
Jane H. Grant
Anthony L. Graves
Esther M. Graves
Jane Graves
Jean M. Green
Jay R. Greenberg
Evelyn Greene
Michael Greenwald
Ruth D. Greenwood
John Gregoire
Sue Gregoire
Julia A. Gregory
Mark Gretch
Rebecca K. Gretton
Susan J. Grieser
Kevin C. Griffith
Ann Grisez
Ted Grisez
Lucretia S. Grosshans
Robert Grover
William C. Grow
Bill Gruenbaum
April Grunspan
Christine M. Guarino
Judith L. Gurley
Robert G. Guthrie
Steven C. Guy
Marsha Guzewich

John H. Haas
Denise A. Hackert-Stoner
Frank Haftl
Robert K. Hagar
Cliff Hagen
Robert Haggett
Estelle M. Hahn
Henry J. Halama
Sunita Halasz
Bert Hall
John W. E. Hall
Millard Hall

Steve Hall
Helen Haller
Betty Hamilton
Michael Hamilton
Thomas M. Hampson
George A. Hanson
Kathleen L. Hanson
Douglas C. Happ
Kathleen Haremza
Paul Haremza
Meena Haribal
Gregory F. Harper
Thomas Harper
Nancy Harple
David W. Harrison
Ronald Harrower
Gregory G. Hartenstein
Mary E. Hartigan
Jack H. Hartwig
Doris Hartz
John R. Hauber
Elva H. Hawken
David J. Hayes
Lois M. Head
Nancy Heaslip
Jack H. Hecht
Andrew D. Heineman
Judith F. Heintz
Roger L. Heintz
Ed Hemminger
Barbara W. Henderson
Diane Henderson
Todd R. Henderson
Derek Hengstenberg
Robert C. Henrickson
Barbara P. Herrgesell
Heather L. Herrmann
Monika J. Herrmann-Kokis
John M. Hershey
Candace Hess
Paul Hess
Erin L. Hewett
Alan C. Hicks
Sue Higgins
Michael Higgiston
Karen Hinderstein
Richard M. Hirschman
David J. Hoag
Robert R. Hoeing
Deuane Hoffman
Judith Hoffman
Ken Hoffman
Jeff Holbrook

Terri Holdsworth
Honey J. Hollen
Christopher V. Hollister
Linda Holmes
Betty J. Hooker
Jim Hooper
Alta H. Hoover
Richard C. Hoppe
Audrey Horbett
Joel L. Horman
Margaret A. Horman
Edwin H.E. Horning
Gordon E. Howard
Linda J. Hoyt
Lisa J. Hoyt
Susan C. Hubbard
Frank Hugar
Gene R. Huggins
Alec Humann
Mary H. Humiston
Dorian E. Huneke
Marilyn Huneke
Anne A. Hungerford
Pamela D. Hunt
Ellen Hurst
Mahlon H. Hurst
Larry Hymes

Suzanne M. Infante
Selma S. Isil

Carolyn D. Jacobs
Florence James
Robert James
Carl A. Jaslowitz
Jesse W. Jaycox
Anne Jeffrey
Marianne Jenkins
Margaret S. Jewett
Tait Johansson
Anne M. Johnson
Glenn Johnson
Jennifer R. Johnson
Marie T. Johnson
Rodney Johnson
Sarah Johnson
Arthur Jones
Patrick Jones
Phyllis R. Jones

Susan Joseph
Thomas R. Judd
David Junkin
Thomas J. Jurczak

Steve Kahl
Mark Kandel
Edward J. Kanze III
Erin Karnatz
Doris Kaufman
J. Edward Kautz
Laura J. Kearns
Rick Kedenburg
Brian W. Keelan
Eileen M. Keenan
Aron Kehlenbeck
Paul N. Keim
Henry B. Keller
Steve Kelling
Maria I. Kelly
Paul J. Kelly
Catherine Kerr
Bernie Kester
Mary C. Key
Douglas P. Kibbe
Teresa J. Kibbe
James Kimball
Erin M. Kinal
Sara V. Kinch
Cynthia G. Kindle
Anne King
Elizabeth B. King
Mark King
Matthew King
Hugh Kingery
Urling Kingery
Deborah Kingsbury
Gail M. Kirch
Betty W. Kirwan
Sylvia Klassen
Catherine Klatt
Lois E. Klatt
David W. Klauber
Harold G. Klein
Brendan Klick
Eileen Kline
Clarence Klingensmith
James A. Kloiber
Alan Klonick
Geo Kloppel
Robert Klose

Gary A. Klue
John Knapp
Suzanne F. Knapp
Frank W. Knight
Ruth H. Knight
Karl Knoecklein
Floyd Knowlton
Nancy Knudsen
Kathleen Koch
Dennis T. Kochem
Patricia Kocinski
Alan L. Koechlein
Margaret Koechlein
Mary Alice Koeneke
Bonnie Koop
Thomas Koopman
William Kratzenstein
Veronika Krause
Heidi E. Kretser
Ward C. Krkoska
Sharon M. Krotzer
William E. Krueger
David H. Kubek
Jay D. Kuhlman
Patricia L. Kuhn
David S. Kunstler
Robert J. Kurtz
Jed M. Kusterer

June LaBell
Charlene LaFever
Ruth M. Lamb
Sandy Lamb
Mary Laura Lamont
James R. Landau
Karen J. Landau
Lynne Landon
Hatti Langsford
Linda N. Lapan
Jan Larsen
Thomas Lathrop
Julie M. Lattrell
Anthony J. Lauro
Leona C. Lauster
Jerry Lazarczyk
Sarah A. Lazazzero
Andy R. Leahy
Rod Leavell
Eileen Leavitt
Thomas LeBlanc
Monica G. LeClerc

Gary N. Lee
Daniel C. Leete
John J. Lehr
Kalista Lehrer
Harold Leidy
Debbie Lemaster
David Lemmon
William K. Lenhart
Lucille Leonard
Robert Leonard
Lorinda Leonardi
Nick Leone
Frank Lescinsky
Gerard C. Letendre
Beverly Letter
Gene Letter
Emanuel Levine
Robert M. Lichorat
Berna B. Lincoln
Stanley R. Lincoln
Vern L. Lindquist
Patricia J. Lindsay
Jillian M. Liner
Kathy A. Linker
Gwendolyn Linn
Doug C. Linstruth
Deborah T. Litwhiler
Eileen Locaino
Joyce LoConti
Audrey L. Loewer
Eileen P. Loiacono
Robert E. Long
Thomas L. Lord
Jeff J. Loukmas
Stacey Low
Daniel A. Lowe
James D. Lowe
Vince Lucid
Ruth Lundin
Kathy A. Luther
Patricia Lutter
George Lyke
Joyce Lyke
Michael K. Lyons

Harrison D. Maas
Richard W. Macdonald
Kevin F. Mack
Theodore D. Mack
Andrew J. Mackie
Brenda Mahnken

Whitney W. Mallam
Kevin M. Malone
James P. Manley Jr.
Barbara A. Mansell
Carol Manske
Mark A. Manske
Bruce J. Manuel
Alan A. Mapes
Jan Marazita
Robert E. Marcotte
Cynthia L. Marino
David W. Mark
Daniel Markham
Barbara M. Marsala
Wendy Marsh
Al Martel
Antonia Martin
Dennis C. Martin
Nancy Martin
Pat Martin
Andrew L. Mason
Lawrence L. Master
Ray Masters
Gintaras Matiukas
Michael J. Matthews
Martin J. Mau
Robert A. Mauceli
Don Mauer
Maeve Maurer
George R. Maxwell
Robert G. May
Adeline Maysick
Irene M. Mazzocchi
Winifred Mc Carley
Brian Mc Donnell
Alice Mc Kale
Jeffrey Mc Mullen
Brian J. McAllister
Mary McCanna
Walter F. McCanna
David A. McCartt
Melanie A. McCormack
Matt McDonald
Kevin H. McGann
Ed McGowan
Jay McGowan
Kevin J. McGowan
Robert T. McGrath
Kathryn L. McIntyre
Thomas J. McKay
William P. McKeever
Malachy McKenna
Chita McKinney

Margaret McKinney
Robert G. McKinney
David A. McLean
Judith L. McMillan
Jeffrey McMullen
Robert McNamara
Deborah A. McNaughton
John P. McNeil
Ken McNichol
Matthew D. Medler
Philip C. Meisner
Ferne F. Merrill
John E. Merrill
Rich Merritt
Jackson Mesick
Steve Mesick
David J. Messineo
Marsha Meyer
Bill Michalek
Karen Michel
Allan J. Michelin
Barbara J. Michelin
Roland Micklem
Gail Mihocko
Janet R. Mihuc
James J. Miles
Marilyn Miles
Michael Militello
Cynthia Miller
Darlene D. Miller
Fred Miller
Jean D. Miller
Joyce A. Miller
Miley Miller
Robert L. Miller
Roger L. Miller
Sandy Miller
William W. Miller
Shorn Mills
Randi S. Minetor
Ann L. Mitchell
Charles W. Mitchell
Frank A. Mitchell
Shaibal S. Mitra
Israel Mizrahi
Michael J. Moccio
Bobbie K. Monroe
John H. Moore
Patsy Moran
Jessica A. Morgan
Michael R. Morgan
Michael M. Morgante
John A. X. Morris

Anne W. Morse
Solon Morse
Terry D. Mosher
Francis D. Mueller
David Muir
Sandy Muller
Sheila A. Mumpton
Ted G. Murin
Frank P. Murphy
Malcolm V. Murphy
Megan A. Murphy
Peter Q. Murphy
Sally Murray

Christopher A. Nadareski
Ronald J. Nagy
Margaret V. Napoleon
David E. Nash
Marjorie Neel
Tina Nelson
Ken K. Neunzig
Lucille Neveu
David S. Newberger
Francis W. Newsome
Dan Nickerson
Joseph A. Nielsen
Elaine Niertit
Vickie L. Nitkiewicz
Daniel K. Niven
Tom Nix
H. Scott Norris
Elaine H. Norton
James C. Norwalk
Paul G. Novak
Jesse Null
Geoffrey J. Nulle
Peter E. Nye
Ida Nystrum

Evan W. Obercian
Kathleen M. O'Brien
Lucille O'Brien
Robert O'Brien
James A. Ochterski
Joseph J. O'Connell
Marilyn O'Connell
David E. Odell
Mary A. O'Dell
Thomas M. O'Donnell

Susan H. Oehser
Robert E. Off
Barbara Olds
Kevin O'Leary
Edward A. Oliver Jr.
Nancy L. Olsen
John Olson
Suzanne Olson
David Olyphant
Elizabeth A. O'Neill
Stephen B. Oresman
Carrie E. Osborne
Paul R. Osgood
Peter V. O'Shea
Nancy L. Ostman
William A. Ostrander
William O'Toole
John W. Ozard

J. Dave Pacey
John R. Pachuta
Rodney R. Pack
Patti A. Packer
John D. Page
Shelley E. Page
Tom Painting
Thomas R. Palmer
Drew Panko
David P. Paradowski
Daniel F. Parker
Frederick B. Parker
Karl Parker
Pat Parker
Amy B. Parr
Gene M. Parsons
Bonnie B. Parton
Mary E. Passage
Eileen M. Patch
Dick Patrick
Gerhard Patsch
James Pawlicki
Robert O. Paxton
Stacy E. Pecor
Jeffrey D. Peil
Patricia I. Pelkowski
Wayne A. Pembroke
Wendi Pencille
Larry Penny
Claudia Perretti
David N. Perrin
Matt J. Perry

Estelle Peterman
Daniel E. Peters
Alan W. Peterson
John M. C. Peterson
Susan F. Peterson
Paul Pfenniger
Sean Phelan
Gerard J. Phillips
Robert Phillips
Bradley A. Pickens
Cheryl Pierce-Berrin
Bob Pinkney
Karen Pinkney
Joseph Robert Pipal
John S. Pipkin
Linda I. Pistolesi
Alan P. Pistorius
Vivian M. Pitzrick
Vincent Plogar
Alicia Plotkin
Sandy Podulka
Carena Pooth
Timothy J. Post
Betsy Potter
Michael E. Powers
Bard V. Prentiss
James J. Previdi
Albert Price
David Prill
Will Pryor
Robyn Puffenbarger
Anne M. Purcell
Bill Purcell
Barbara Putnam

Jim Quackenbush
Linda H. Quackenbush
Rebecca A. Quail
Joan L. Quinlan
Glenn H. Quinn

Lisa Randles
Gary A. Randorf
Tom Rankin
Cynthia Rankus
Paul Rappleyea
Gerald R. Rasmussen
Edward F. Ratajczak
William J. Raup

Jessie Ravage
Katharine A. Ray
Fredrik M. Realbuto
Fred T. Reckner
Louise I. Redden
Timothy S. Redman
Diane L. Reed
Edward Reed
Jeffrey M. Reed
William B. Reeves
Peter M. Regan
Evan Rehm
Christopher R. Reidy
Michelle D. Reidy
Wilfred Relyea
Paul F. Renken
Stephanie M. Restuccia
Barbara C. Reuter
Frances M. Rew
Barbara A. Reynolds
Patricia G. Reynolds
Helen Rice
Stephen D. Rice
Vesta Rice
Bruce E. Richards
George D. Richards
Daniel E. Richardson
Jonathan L. Richardson
Wayne Richter
Evelyn M. Rifenburg
Thomas M. Riley
Chris Rimmer
Gerald R. Rising
Cindy Roach
Dennis Roach
Donald C. Roberson
Margery Robertiello
Chris Roberts
Joan A. Robertson
Raymond J. Robinson
Suzanne R. Robinson
Kenneth J. Roblee
Jon Robson
Frederic Rockefeller
George Rodenhausen
John H. Rogers
Nancy H. Rogers
Wayne P. Rogers
Mandi L. Roggie
Dana C. Rohleder
Matt Romocki
Carolyn Ronald
Dorothy J. Rosche

Richard C. Rosche
Kenneth V. Rosenberg
Charles Rosenburg
Angelena M. Ross
James M. Ross
Jay Ross
Judy A. Ross
Jean E. Rothe
Larry Rousch
Charles A. Rouse
Randy Rowe
Kathy H. Rowland
Larry B. Rowland
George Rowson
Greg Rudio
Peggy A. Rudis
May Ruhl
Margaret Rusk
Bev Ruska
John Ruska
David J. Russell
Joan Russell
Mark D. Russell
Matthew R. Russell
Michael Russell
David M. Rutkowski
Cathy Ryan
Jeanne L. Ryan
Pat Rybke
Warren B. Ryther

Paul E. Saffold
Laura Salmonsen
Jo Salo
Tom Salo
Leslie Saltsman
Eric Salzman
Catherine I. Sandell
Bennett Sandler
Jarrod A. Santora
William Sarbello
Alan F. Sargeant
John Sayles
Audrey Schafer
Susan Scheck
Michael S. Scheibel
Charlie Scheim
Russel Scheirer
Vincent P. Schiappa
Diane Schietinger
Seymour Schiff

Marty Schlabach
Mark T. Schlacter
Ed Schlauch
Charles Schleigh
Lucia Schneck
Kathryn J. Schneider
Nina Schoch
Steven M. Schultz
Stephen H. Schwab
Mose J. Schwartz
Bert Schweigert
Mickey Scilingo
Robert D. Scott
Thomas Scott
Joan Scrocarelli
Kathryn E. Scullion
Gail W. Seamans
Barbara Seeger
Bonnie R. Seegmiller
Linda J. Seifried
William A. Seleen, Jr.
David A. Seyler
Miriam A. Sharick
Kathy A. Sharp
Hollie Y. Shaw
Mary Ann Sheehan
Ed I. Sheidlower
Mary Shepard
Julian Shepherd
Tim L. Shera
Diane L. Sheridan
Mike Sheridan
Dominic F. Sherony
Amy R. Shiffer
Antony E. Shrimpton
Wesley C. Shuart
Ruth M. Shursky
Stephen M. Shursky
Doug Shutters
Fred C. Sibley
Thomas A. Simmons
Howard A. Simonin
Carol U. Sisler
Jack J. Skalicky
Jeanne Skelly
Dan R. Skinner
Cathie B. Slack
Carole A. Slatkin
Judith A. Slein
Nicholas Sly
Charles R. Smith
Gerald A. Smith
Janet Buchanan Smith

Jeffrey H. Smith
Jeffrey S. Smith
Marilyn C. Smith
Pat Smith
Porgy Smith
Rosalyn G. Smith
Sheila Smith
Thomas W. Smith
Raymond M. Soff Jr.
Laura A. Sommers
Casey Southard
Richard Sowinski
Charles C. Spagnoli
Robert G. Spahn
Susan B. Spahn
Dean T. Spaulding
James A. Spencer
Selden J. Spencer
Dave Spier
Diane Spitz
Ray A. Sprague
Susanne Sprague
Jonathon Staller
Ruth Standridge
Cedar B. Stanistreet
Ann C. Stear
Randy Stechert
Laura Stenzler
Richard Stevens
Neil S. Stewart
Michael Stickney
Wesley B. Stiles
Daniel Stoebel
Scott J. Stoner
Carl Strickland
Kathleen Strickland
Paul R. Stringer
Linda A. Strohl
Allan Strong
David B. Strong
Grace Strong
Conrad J. Strozik
Carl Studt
Jerry Sullivan
John J. Sullivan
Kristi Sullivan
Kristy L. Sullivan
Alexander Summers
Robert Sundell
Sally Sutcliffe
Scott Sutcliffe
Thomas D. Sutter
Nancy H. Swanson

Eve M. Sweatman
Tracey Sweeting
Janet L. Swentusky
Bryan L. Swift
William D. Symonds

Theodore Taft
Laurel R. Talbot
Arnold V. Talentino
Winifred Talentino
Basil P. Tangredi
David Tapke
Thomas E. Tasber
Casey Taylor
John Taylor
Stephen Taylor
Eric K. Teed
Hope Tenney
Philip G. Terrie
Christopher T. Tessaglia-Hymes
Diana C. Teta
Dave Tetlow
Michael Tetlow
John Thaxton
Patricia H. Thaxton
Barbara H. Thomas
Linda E. Thomas
Wilford "Bil" J. Thomas
Craig Thompson
Gregory W. Thompson
Molly A. Thompson
Anthony Tierno
Bernice Timmerman
Richard T. Timmerman
Donald J. Timmons
Jane Tofel
Charles Townsend
Jeanne Townsend
John R. Tramontano
Donald L. Traver
Donna B. Traver
Norm J. Trigoboff
Betsy Trometer
Janet E. Trzeciak
Mike Turisk
Ava Turnquist
Sheila Tuttle

Sally Uzunov

Roberta Vallone
Mary Van Buren
Eileen Van Duyne
Denny Van Horn
Alison E. Van Keuren
Melissa E. Van Namee
John J. Van Niel
Marion Van Wagner
Joyce E. Vana
James S. Vanscoy
Regina M. Vanscoy
Kirk Vanstrom
Dorothy Anthony Vecchio
Eugene Vermilyea
Bonnie Vicki
Matt Victoria
Joseph Viglietta
Aaron C. Virgin
Christine G. Vitale
Fred Von Mechow
Thomas Voss
Doris Voyack

George R. Wade
Jeanne A. Waful
Robert M. Wagner
Betty M. Wahl
Robert B. Wakefield
Robert C. Walker
William M. Wallace
Steve Walter
Marybeth Warburton
Irene C. Warshauer
Michael R. Wasilco
Cynthia J. Waterman
Daniel T. Watkins
Ann Watson
Jack Watson
William Watson
Donald Watts
Doris J. Waud

John M. Waud
Gil Weakland
Alyson F. Webber
James S. Webber
Hans W. Weber
Peter G. Weber
John A. Weeks
Jonathon D. Weeks
Robert C. Wei
Joseph G. Weise
Kurt Weiskotten
Carol A. Weiss
Thomas D. Welch
Troy W. Weldy
Lyle E. Welker
Millicent M. Welker
Alan W. Wells
Allison Wells
Daniel L. Wells
Della Wells
Inga Wells
Jeffrey Wells
Kenneth J. Welsh
Beverly J. Whalen
David R. Wheeler
Diane M. Wheelock
Carol Whitby
Owen Whitby
Brian White
Christopher White
Derek J. White
Hollis L. White
Laura M. White
Kathryn Whitehorne
Timothy N. Whitens
Marjorie Whitney
Philip R. Whitney
Susan J. Whitney
Kinsley A. Whittum
Nancy Wicker
Emma May Wightman
Audrey W. Wigley
Fred G. Wilhelm
Glenn Williams
Matthew J. Williams
Jacqueline L. Williamson
Edith V. Wilson
Robert O. Wilson
Donald A. Windsor

Cris L. Winters
Dennis Wischman
Ken Witkowski
James L. Wojewodzki
Karen L. Wolf
Susan K. Wolfe
Glenn A. Wolford
Al Wollin
Colleen L. Wolpert
Bette A. Wood
Russell Wood
David C. Woodruff
John Workman
Marcus Workman
Gary Worthington
Judy Wright
Kyle R. Wright
Harold Wunder
Janet Wunder

William L. Yandik
Fran Yardley-Parks
Peter A. Yoerg
Terry L. Yonker
Matthew A. Young
Robert P. Yunick

Kim Marie Zahno
John D. Zarudsky
Michael A. Zebehazy
Carl G. Zenger
Phyllis S. Zenger
Martha L. Zettel
Mary C. Zimmer
Brian C. Zitani
C. Kendall Zoller
Marion E. Zuefle

Fiesta

comes with warblers,
waves of warblers
moving up the continents

Yellows, Bay-breasteds,
Black-throated Blues, Greens,
Myrtles, Magnolias
flourishing wing-tail skirts of white and yellow,
Redstarts flashing flamenco fans of orange and red,
Chestnut-sideds displaying headdresses of the sun

Then, Blackburnians
flown from flames of Aztec fires,
Prothonotary emblazoned with Inca gold

Maxwell Corydon Wheat Jr.
Reprinted by kind permission of the author.

CHAPTER ONE

Introduction and Methodology

Kimberley Corwin

In the 20 years since the publication of *The Atlas of Breeding Birds in New York State* (Andrle and Carroll 1988), a wave of interest in and use of biological atlases has crossed the country. New York's first Breeding Bird Atlas was among the earliest to be published in the United States and remains one of New York State's most valuable resources of avian data.

As an outgrowth of the widespread recognition of the value of bird atlases, a Northeastern Breeding Bird Atlas Conference was held at the Vermont Institute of Natural Science in 1981. Conference attendees later formed the North American Ornithological Atlas Committee (NORAC) and published the *Handbook for Atlasing North American Breeding Birds* (Smith 1990). NORAC's purpose is to encourage states and provinces to conduct their own atlas projects, by providing standards for doing so, as well as advice and support. NORAC recommends that atlases be updated at 20-year intervals to allow for regular documentation of changes in bird distribution. And so, a second Breeding Bird Atlas project was initiated in New York, with fieldwork beginning in 2000, exactly 20 years after the first Atlas project began.

The goal of this second Atlas was to document the current distribution of the state's avifauna. Efforts were made to conduct fieldwork in a manner consistent with the protocol used for the first Atlas, to allow for comparison between the two datasets. A total of 1,207 individuals submitted data for the second Atlas, resulting in a database of 519,562 records. While the distribution for most species remained similar to that reported in the first Atlas, significant expansions in distribution were seen for many species, and for some in quite a surprising manner. For another group of species, whose populations are known to be declining, the Atlas data document the details of their range contractions.

Planning and Management

Planning for New York State's second Breeding Bird Atlas began in the fall of 1998. An ad hoc committee was formed to lay the groundwork for repeating the state's first Breeding Bird Atlas. The ad hoc committee consisted of representatives from the New York State Department of Environmental Conservation (NYSDEC), the New York State Ornithological Association (NYSOA; at that time the Federation of New York State Bird Clubs), the Cornell Lab of Ornithology, the New York Fish and Wildlife Research Unit at Cornell University, and Audubon New York. These organizations oversaw the work for New York's first Atlas from beginning to end and so were able to contribute their valuable experience. The Breeding Bird Atlas 2000 Steering Committee was formed from the ad hoc committee, and in December 1999 the project coordinator, Kimberley Corwin, was hired. The Steering Committee met several times throughout each year and provided guidance to the project coordinator regarding the management goals and timeline of the project. The project coordinator worked full-time and was responsible for the day-to-day administration of the project.

With help from NYSOA, one or two regional coordinators were recruited in each of ten Atlas Regions of the state. These Atlas Regions are nearly the same as those used by NYSOA for reporting purposes and are the same as those used in the 1980–85 Atlas. Regional coordinators were chosen for their familiarity both with the avifauna of the region and with most of the atlasers who conducted surveys there. This familiarity with the region and depth of knowledge gave them the ability to detect probable errors in identification or in the use of the breeding codes early in the process, and to provide atlasers additional training or help with fieldwork as needed.

Regional coordinators were responsible for overseeing coverage of the blocks in their region. They recruited volunteers through their associations with local birders, by giving presentations to local bird clubs, and through local news media. Regional coordinators assigned blocks to interested volunteers and provided the volunteers with atlasing materials, including data forms, and in some cases, regional newsletters. The *Handbook for Workers*, a booklet that describes the project and how to participate was also provided. Regional coordinators received data sheets annually from the atlasers in their region. Each data sheet was checked for errors before being sent to the project coordinator for entry into the database.

Data for New York State's second Breeding Bird Atlas were collected following the schedule of the first Atlas. Originally five field seasons were planned, 2000–04, but an additional year of field work was added after 2004. Termed a "mop-up" effort, the sixth year of data collection was directed at blocks in a specified order of priority: (1) those with no species, (2) those with fewer than 25 species, and (3) those with fewer than 50 species. Experienced atlasers who expressed an interest in continuing to survey were directed to work in blocks chosen with these priorities in mind. If blocks meeting these priorities were not available near an atlaser who wanted to work, the atlaser was asked to survey specifically for owls and/or wetland species. Regional coordinators did not promote data collection in the sixth year other than as outlined above.

Work toward the publication began as planned in January 2005, at which time Kevin J. McGowan was hired as co-editor. The project coordinator began a transition to co-editor at that time, while overseeing the final year of field work.

Recording Methods and Data Collection

The grid system used in the first Atlas, a metric-based coordinate system known as the Transverse Mercator Grid, was again used to define the basic unit for reporting data in 2000–05 (Figure 1.1). This system divides the 128,402 sq km (49,576 sq mi) area of the state into approximately 1,300 squares, each measuring 10 km × 10 km (6 mi × 6 mi). The squares are numbered sequentially from south to north and from west to east. The atlas reporting unit, a block, is one quarter of this square, and each resulting 5 km × 5 km (3 mi × 3 mi) block is named with the four-digit numeric of its square and a letter, A, B, C, or D.

For the first Atlas project there were 5,335 blocks statewide. For the second Atlas, 2 blocks were removed, leaving the number of blocks to be surveyed at 5,333. The boundary lines for Block 1679A, on the northwestern edge of Niagara County, were drawn incorrectly for the first Atlas. Maps created in 2000 for the second Atlas showed that Block 1679A includes only land that is in Canada. For the first Atlas, Block 6851D on the south shore of Long Island in Suffolk County had only a small amount of sandy beach in its northwestern corner. Twenty years later the sand had shifted and left no land in the block.

As stated, volunteers were provided with an updated *Handbook for Workers*, which explained the objectives of the project, survey techniques, and breeding codes and provided a table of breeding season dates from the first Atlas publication, as well as other information to assist them with atlasing.

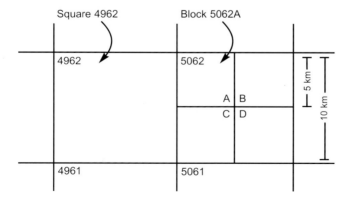

Figure 1.1 Atlas grid system.

Breeding Categories and Codes

Breeding was recorded at three levels, indicating increasing certainty: Possible, Probable, and Confirmed. Within each of these categories are breeding codes that describe the specific behavior observed; these codes are the same as those used in the first Atlas. The following descriptions were given to atlasers:

Possible Breeding

X   Species observed in possible nesting habitat, but no other indication of breeding noted. Singing male(s) present (or breeding calls heard) in breeding season.

Probable Breeding

S   Singing male present (or breeding calls heard) on more than one date at least a week apart in the same place. This is a good indication that a bird has taken up residence if the dates are a week or more apart.

P   Pair observed in suitable habitat in breeding season.

T   Bird (or pair) apparently holding territory. In addition to territorial singing, chasing of other individuals of same species often marks a territory.

D   Courtship and display, agitated behavior, or anxiety calls from adults suggesting probable presence nearby of a nest of young; well-developed brood patch or cloacal protuberance on trapped adult. Includes copulation.

N   Visiting probable nest site. Nest building by wrens and woodpeckers. Wrens may build many nests. Woodpeckers, although they usually drill only one nest cavity, also drill holes just for roosting.

B   Nest building or excavation of a nest hole.

Confirmed Breeding

DD   Distraction display or injury-feigning. Agitated behavior and/or anxiety calls are Probable-D.

UN   Used nest found. Caution: these must be carefully identified if they are to be counted as evidence. Some nests (e.g., Baltimore Oriole) are persistent and very characteristic. Most are difficult to identify correctly.

FE   Female with egg in the oviduct (by bird bander).

FL   Recently fledged young (including downy young of precocious species—waterfowl, shorebirds). This code should be used with caution for species such as blackbirds and swallows, which may move some distance soon after fledging. Recently fledged passerines are still dependent on their parents and are fed by them.

ON   Adult(s) entering or leaving nest site in circumstances indicating occupied nest. *Not* generally used for open-nesting birds. It should be used for hole nesters only when a bird enters a hole and remains inside, makes a changeover at a hole, or leaves a hole after having been inside for some time. If you simply see a bird fly into or out of a bush or tree, and do not find a nest, the correct code would be Probable-N.

FS Adult carrying fecal sac.

FY Adult(s) with food for young. Some birds (gulls, terns, and raptors) continue to feed their young long after they are fledged, and even after they have moved considerable distances. Also, some birds (e.g., terns) may carry food over long distances to their young in a neighboring block. Be especially careful on the edge of a block. Care should be taken to avoid confusion with courtship feeding (Probable-D).

NE Identifiable nest and eggs, bird sitting on nest or egg, identifiable eggshells found beneath nest, or identifiable dead nestling(s). If you find a cowbird egg in a nest, the code is NE for cowbird, and NE for the nest's owner.

NY Nest with young. If you find a young cowbird with other young, the code is NY for cowbird and NY for identified nest owner.

A single Field Card was used for each block for the duration of a season. Observations were recorded on the Field Card during each visit to the block. Dates of observations were not collected during the first Atlas project, but during the second Atlas project, observers were instructed to record the first date and breeding code for an observed species. If a subsequent visit to the block resulted in an observation that allowed the use of a higher breeding code, the lower breeding code and associated date were replaced. At the end of each field season, volunteers transcribed their data from the Field Card to the Annual Summary Form. They then submitted their Annual Summary Forms to the regional coordinator and retained the Field Cards for later data checking and confirmation if necessary.

Notable Species Forms were requested from volunteers for the purpose of collecting additional information on 33 species that are of conservation concern in New York State; biologists in the NYSDEC and the New York Natural Heritage Program created this list of species. In addition, several regional coordinators included other species that are of concern in their own regions. The Notable Species Form was used to collect details on

Species for which Notable Species Forms were requested statewide

Trumpeter Swan	Barn Owl	Cape May Warbler
Ruddy Duck	Long-eared Owl	Yellow-throated Warbler
Pied-billed Grebe	Short-eared Owl	Palm Warbler
American Bittern	Common Nighthawk	Bay-breasted Warbler
Least Bittern	Chuck-will's-widow	Prothonotary Warbler
Spruce Grouse	Whip-poor-will	Kentucky Warbler
Northern Harrier	American Three-toed Woodpecker	Wilson's Warbler
Golden Eagle	Loggerhead Shrike	Yellow-breasted Chat
Black Rail	Sedge Wren	Clay-colored Sparrow
King Rail	Bicknell's Thrush	Henslow's Sparrow
Upland Sandpiper	Tennessee Warbler	Seaside Sparrow

the observation, including a description of the habitat where the observation was made, the behavior of the bird(s), and the exact location of the observation. A block map showing the location of the observation was submitted with the Notable Species Form.

Field Surveying and Coverage

Atlasers agreed to survey one or more blocks and were expected to spend at least eight hours in each block, visiting each habitat represented in the block and including at least one nighttime visit to document nocturnal species. For the first Atlas project, a block was considered to have been adequately surveyed when a total of at least 76 species had been identified from the block and half were confirmed as breeders. This standard of "adequately surveyed" was derived from the experience of the first Vermont Breeding Bird Atlas and was further described by Smith (1982). This same standard was provided to atlasers for the second Atlas project as well, with recognition in both Atlas projects that blocks in some areas of the state, such as the Adirondacks (Region 7) and Long Island (Region 10), might be expected to have fewer species.

The Steering Committee recognized from experience with the first Atlas that the use of paid field workers, called blockbusters, would be necessary to ensure coverage in the remote blocks of some regions, especially the Adirondacks and Catskill Peaks. In the first Atlas, blockbusting was described as a survey method in which a team of two observers worked intensively in June and July, spending 16–20 person-hours in a block, camping overnight to document nocturnal species, and then moving on to the next block. A less structured method of blockbusting was carried out by individuals who were willing to travel to remote areas to conduct surveys as their schedule permitted. Approximately 25 percent of 1980–85 Atlas coverage was completed by blockbusters. Both of these approaches were used in the second Atlas, with blockbusting beginning in 2000 but becoming most intense in the final three years of fieldwork. The effort initially focused on the Adirondacks and Catskills but later extended across the state as needed. About 20 percent of 2000–05 Atlas coverage was completed by blockbusters.

Data Processing and Presentation

The 2000–05 Atlas database holds 519,562 records representing 248 species and three hybrids. The cumulative database, which holds 383,051 records, includes only the highest breeding code for each species reported in each block. The distribution maps that appear in the species accounts in this book were created from the cumulative database. The 1980–85 Atlas database holds 361,595 records and includes only the highest breeding code (cumulative); no database exists for the 1980–85 data that were replaced by records with higher breeding codes.

All breeding data were submitted on one of two data forms:

the Annual Summary Form or the Casual Observation Form. The Annual Summary Form was the standard method of data submission that atlasers used to report all data collected in one block in a single season. The Casual Observation Form was for reporting observations on a single date in a single block and could be used to submit records for as many as 20 species. Both forms were available from regional coordinators or the project coordinator, but a single-page version of the Casual Observation Form could also be printed from the Atlas web site. The Annual Summary Form was not available online because of its large size (four 11 × 14-inch pages) and detailed nature. Online data entry was not available.

Both data forms could be read with an optical scanner and scanning software. One step of the scanning process was an on-screen review by the project coordinator in which handwritten letters and numbers that fell within a questionable range, as determined by the operator of the software, were corrected. The original data forms were consulted when necessary. After the forms were scanned, data went directly into an Oracle database stored on a server at the NYSDEC office in Albany. Data on the server were backed up nightly and hard copies of the database were stored off-site.

The Breeding Bird Atlas web site was launched in 2000 and provided atlasers with a valuable source of information that was not available during the first Atlas project. For the first time, the web site made the 1980–85 species distribution maps available in color. Also available for the first time were lists of species that were reported in each block in 1980–85. Atlasers were encouraged to access the 1980–85 species lists and use them as guidance for finding species in their block. The Steering Committee recognized this recommendation as a potential source of bias but agreed that an atlaser's awareness of what species might be present could lead to more thorough coverage.

The Breeding Bird Atlas web site also provided a way to share data collected during the ongoing 2000–05 Atlas project. Interim distribution maps were first posted on the web site in 2002 and were updated after each field season. Species lists for each block were also available online and were always up-to-date, as queries from the web site generated a list via a direct link to the database. Statewide atlasing progress maps were posted on the web site as well, showing the number of species that had been reported in each block.

Quality Control of Data: Biases and Limitations

Clearly, there is much variability in skill level among a volunteer base of over 1,200 people; eight hours of fieldwork by a skilled observer will result in more species being recorded than the same amount of work by a beginner. These biases are inherent in all atlases, however, and can be assumed for both New York State Atlases. Though the statewide average of time spent in a block was similar in the two Atlases (Table 2.1, see Chapter 2),

this variability among observers must not be discounted when examining changes in distribution. While a record in the database indicates the presence of a species in a block, the absence of a record does not necessarily indicate absence of the species in that block.

Procedures to ensure the integrity of the records in the database were developed early in the project. There are several sources of potential errors in the data. These errors fall into two categories: data collection and interpretation, and data transcription. Data collection and interpretation errors include errors in species identification by the observer, in assignment of breeding status to nonbreeding birds, and in assignment of an incorrect breeding code to an observed behavior. Transcription errors could occur when data from the Field Card were transferred to the Annual Summary Form, and when data from the Annual Summary Form or Casual Observation Form were scanned to the database.

Three levels of quality control, described in detail below, were applied to ensure accuracy of the Atlas database: 1) review by regional coordinators prior to entry of data, 2) review by observers after data entry, and 3) review by the Records Review Committee, convened to evaluate the occasional unlikely or improbable record.

1) Nearly all data were first screened when Annual Summary Forms and Casual Observation Forms were submitted to the appropriate regional coordinator. Regional coordinators checked data forms for the reasonableness of the species recorded, for the correct use of codes, and to see that dates were within the breeding season for the species. The regional coordinator then communicated with the observer to resolve apparent problems before forwarding the forms to the project coordinator. They also ensured that verification was provided when necessary.

2) Data were entered in the fall of each year. Species lists were available online immediately and static species distribution maps were posted online in the early months of the following year. Lists of the records reported by each observer were also printed and mailed to the observer each year with a request to check the data entered against the original Field Card. Errors detected in any of these steps were described on the Data Correction Form, which was then sent to the project coordinator for correction in the database. Copies of all these transactions were provided to the regional coordinators.

3) The Records Review Committee was established by the Steering Committee and began meeting in the final year of scheduled fieldwork. The committee was charged with reviewing all records in the database for reasonableness in three areas: geographic distribution, breeding dates, and use of codes. Prior to each of the three meetings, the Records Review Committee carefully reviewed all species distribution maps. During the meetings, distribution maps with questionable records were projected on a screen and studied by all; the associated database entries were also displayed and examined. Following discussion, questionable records were either retained or discarded, or more

information was sought from the observer and/or the regional coordinator. Notable Species Forms, as described above, were available for study as necessary or were requested if not available. In cases where the date for a record was near the cutoff dates for breeding, the record was left in the database and was to be addressed in the species accounts in the context of all the data for the species. Records for species on the New York State Avian Records Committee (NYSARC) list requiring verification, or for birds new to the state or new to breeding in the state, required documentation and were accepted or rejected based on the determinations of NYSARC. In future Atlas projects, the Records Review Committee recommends that, ideally, review of the data should begin in the first year of the project and be carried out after each year of data collection.

From the experience of the first Atlas, the Records Review Committee thought that the reporting of intentionally defective data and identification errors of significance were minor concerns. There is, in fact, no way to detect simple errors in identification or even fraudulent reports, unless they are truly absurd and unbelievable in the context of historical data. Only a very few such cases were even suspected, and the data from such observers were discarded and the blocks reassigned. A more likely problem with less skilled observers was failing to detect a species that actually was present. In the ideal case, more skilled observers would have been directed to complete all blocks where species were obviously being missed. The reality of this project is that some blocks simply will be missing records for species that are likely present, but the inability of volunteers to identify them could not be corrected due to a lack of more skilled observers to supplement coverage in such blocks.

Observations and Results of Records Review

Most of the errors detected resulted from mistakes made when observers transcribed data from the Field Cards to the Annual Summary Forms or from poor handwriting.

Although the table of breeding season dates provided guidance to volunteers, there remains uncertainty regarding the date at which a species can be considered at least possibly breeding. Early and late breeding dates vary widely across New York. For species whose distributions are changing, making decisions about acceptable dates becomes even more complicated. Regional coordinators and the Records Review Committee strove to be reasonable and consistent in dealing with such records.

Some problems arose with the use of a few breeding codes, particularly Probable-S (singing), Probable-P (pair), Probable-T (holding territory), and Confirmed-ON (occupied nest). Volunteers were reminded of the proper use of breeding code definitions throughout the project, and corrections were made as they were identified. The Records Review Committee then dealt with some of the more obvious mis-uses by changing codes that were inappropriately assigned, for example, reducing Probable-

S to Possible-X (present) for species that do not sing; reducing Probable-P to Possible-X for species where the sexes are indistinguishable; reducing Probable-T to Possible-X for species with no real territorial display; or changing Confirmed-ON records to Confirmed-NE (eggs) for noncavity nesters. Beyond that, the committee agreed that it was of no real value to attempt to detect and repair every possible misuse in the database, especially for common breeding species, so attention was focused largely on uncommon or rare species.

The Species Accounts

Species accounts are included for 241 species and three hybrids that breed in New York. Seventeen additional species are discussed in Appendix 1. The order of the accounts follows the taxonomic order as established by the American Ornithologists' Union Check-List of North American Birds (AOU 1998) and supplements up through the seventh (Banks et al. 2007). The standard reference used for plant names in the accounts is the New York Flora Atlas (Weldy and Werier 2005), and the standard reference for place names is the seventh edition of the New York State Atlas and Gazetteer (DeLorme 2003).

The current (2000–05) distribution map is shown in each species account, with breeding categories indicated by color. A map displaying changes in distribution is also shown for species that were detected as breeders in both Atlases. The change map combines the distribution found during the first and second Atlas surveys without regard for the level of breeding. Gray indicates that the species distribution was unchanged (present in both Atlases), while blue indicates loss (breeding in the first Atlas only) and brown indicates gain (present in the second Atlas only). On both the distribution map and the change map, areas of white show blocks where no records were reported.

Each species account describes the history of the species in the state, including the distribution recorded during the first and second Atlas surveys. For the most part, ecozone terminology (see Chapter 3) is used for these descriptions. The focus of each account is the change in distribution that occurred between the first and second surveys. Suspected reasons for any changes are discussed, as are recommendations for management of the species where necessary.

Where appropriate, species accounts include data from the Breeding Bird Survey (BBS), a nationwide, long-term bird-monitoring program administered by the U.S. Geological Survey and the Canadian Wildlife Service (Sauer et al. 2007). The BBS graphs shown for some species include data from 1966 to 2005 for New York State. The value on the y axis is the adjusted number of birds counted on each route; this is the standard index value calculated for use in BBS analyses. All species trend-line curves are based on Loess regression with a smoothing parameter of 0.5. The data and permission to use them were provided by John Sauer of the Patuxent Wildlife Research Center.

The BBS data for some species are known to have deficiencies. Regional Credibility Measures indicate three levels of caution that should be considered when using these data (see Sauer et al. 2007). Trend lines are shown for all species in the blue (no known deficiency) and yellow categories (known deficiency) and for selected species in the red category. The red category denotes data that have "an important deficiency," particularly one resulting from very low abundance, very small samples, or a very imprecise model. Trend graphs were included for the following species with a red designation: Wild Turkey, Common Loon, Double-crested Cormorant, Upland Sandpiper, Red-headed Woodpecker, Philadelphia Vireo, Fish Crow, Common Raven, Carolina Wren, Marsh Wren, and Henslow's Sparrow. Trend lines for these species are noted as being "BBS red category deficiency." Trend lines are not shown for species with data from fewer than seven routes.

For some species, trend graphs using other data sources are shown. Christmas Bird Count data are used for four owl species: Barn Owl, Eastern Screech-Owl, Great Horned Owl, and Barred Owl. Data from NYSDEC breeding surveys are used for Osprey, Bald Eagle, and Peregrine Falcon.

Descriptive Maps

The maps shown on the following pages illustrate various characteristics of New York State. They were created using ESRI ArcMap v. 9.2 software. The projected coordinate system used was NAD 1983 UTM Zone 18N. The first map (Figure 1.2) is a base map that was used as a template for the remaining maps. The base map includes an arrow indicating north and a scale bar, which for simplicity are not shown on the other maps. Sources used for the creation of the maps are listed in the Citations for Map Data section.

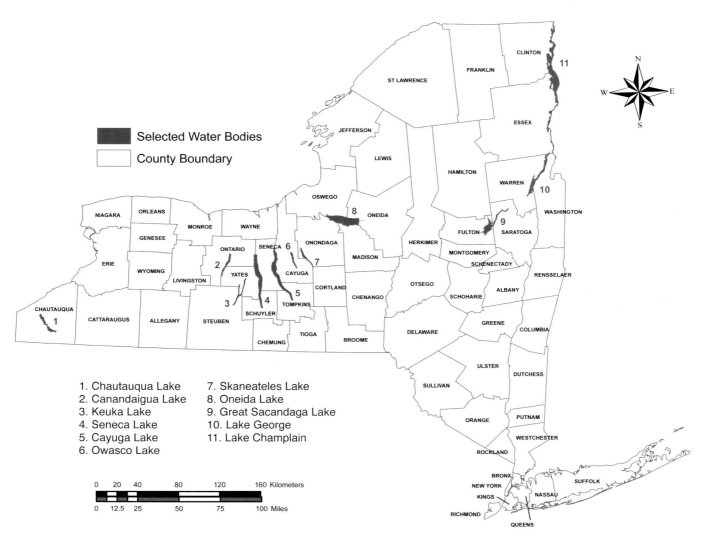

1. Chautauqua Lake
2. Canandaigua Lake
3. Keuka Lake
4. Seneca Lake
5. Cayuga Lake
6. Owasco Lake
7. Skaneateles Lake
8. Oneida Lake
9. Great Sacandaga Lake
10. Lake George
11. Lake Champlain

Figure 1.2 Base map for descriptive maps of New York State (Figures 1.3–1.16) showing county boundaries and major lakes.

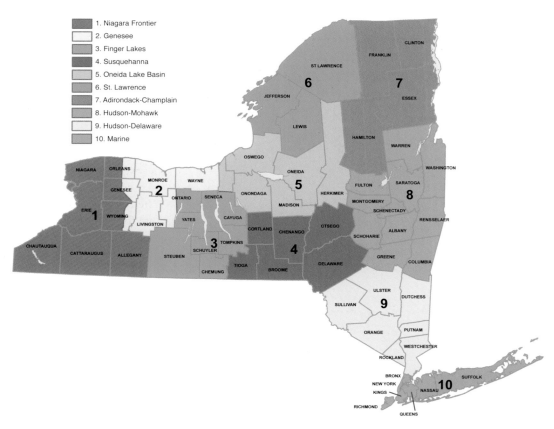

Figure 1.3 New York State Ornithological Association (NYSOA) regions.

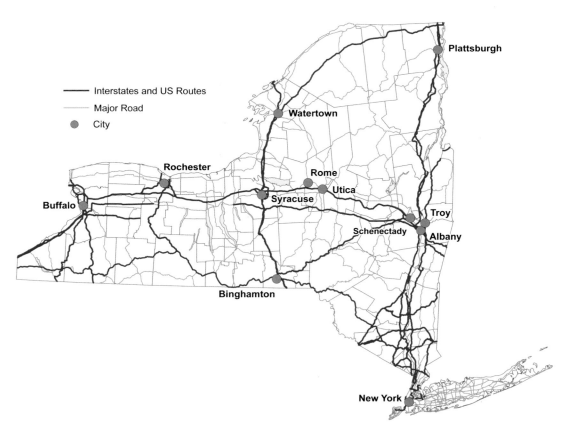

Figure 1.4 Cities and major roads in New York.

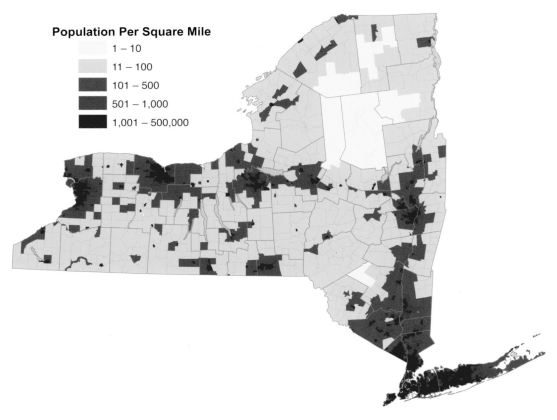

Figure 1.5 Human population per square mile by census tract in New York (2000 census).

Figure 1.6 Selected river systems in New York.

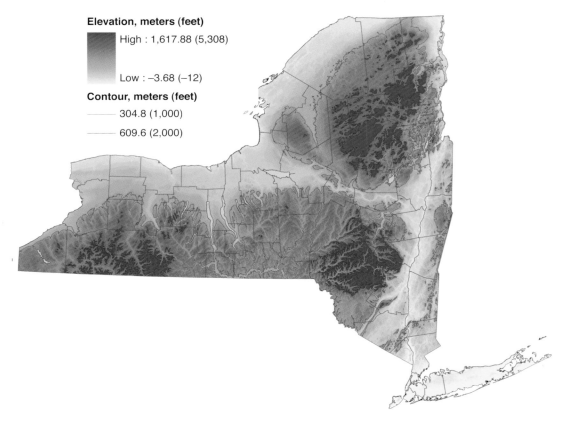

Figure 1.7 Elevation in New York.

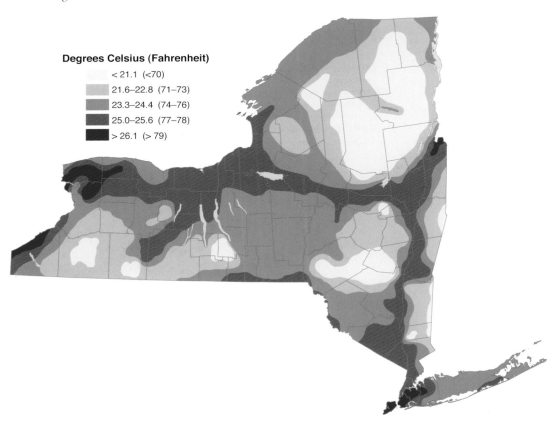

Figure 1.8 Mean July temperature in New York for the period 1905–2005.

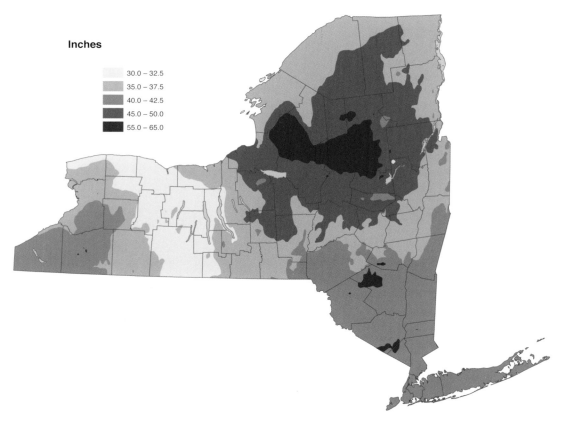

Inches

■ 30.0 – 32.5
■ 35.0 – 37.5
■ 40.0 – 42.5
■ 45.0 – 50.0
■ 55.0 – 65.0

Figure 1.9 Mean annual precipitation in New York for the period 1961–90.

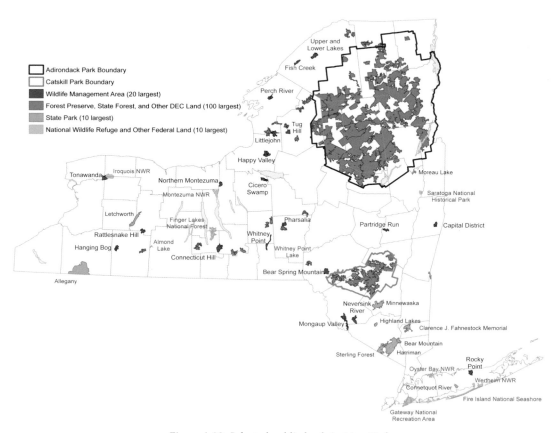

Figure 1.10 Selected public lands in New York.

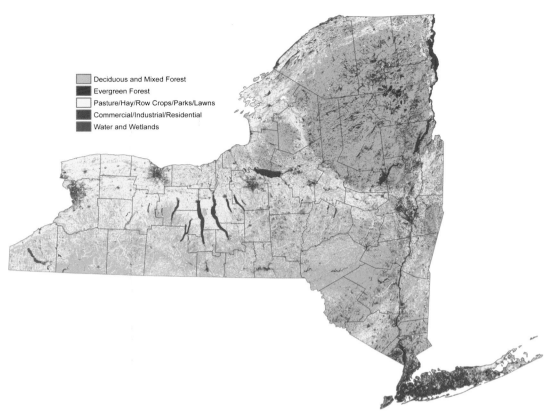

Deciduous and Mixed Forest
Evergreen Forest
Pasture/Hay/Row Crops/Parks/Lawns
Commercial/Industrial/Residential
Water and Wetlands

Figure 1.11 Land-use categories in New York.

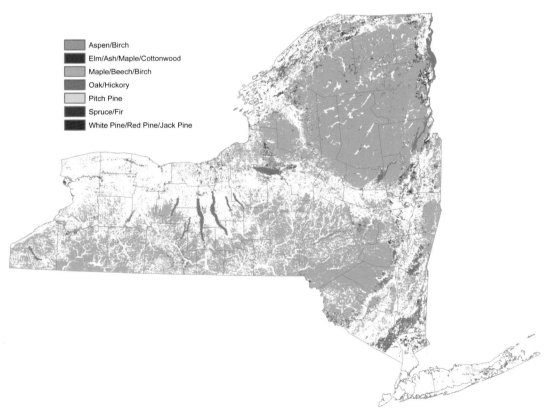

Aspen/Birch
Elm/Ash/Maple/Cottonwood
Maple/Beech/Birch
Oak/Hickory
Pitch Pine
Spruce/Fir
White Pine/Red Pine/Jack Pine

Figure 1.12 Forest types in New York. Excerpt from a larger dataset (Ruefenacht et al. in press),
used with permission of the authors.

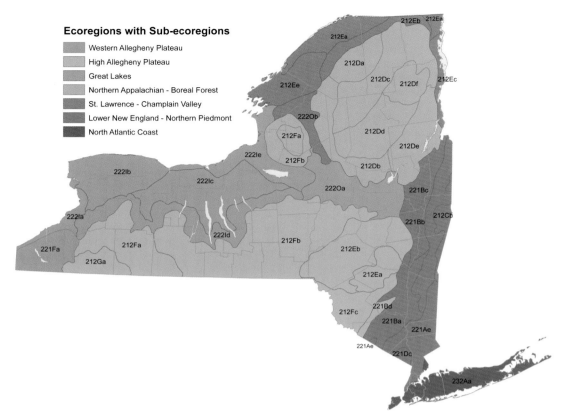

Figure 1.13 Ecoregions and sub-ecoregions in New York.

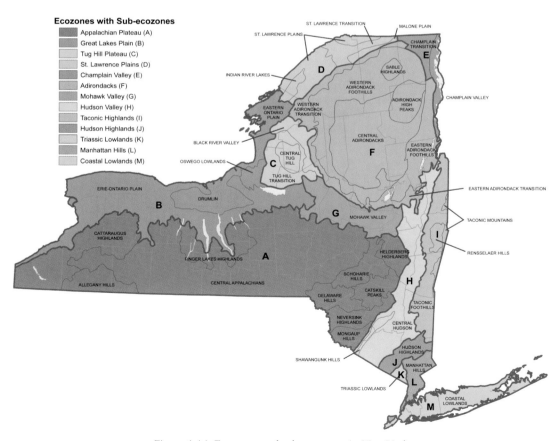

Figure 1.14 Ecozones and sub-ecozones in New York.

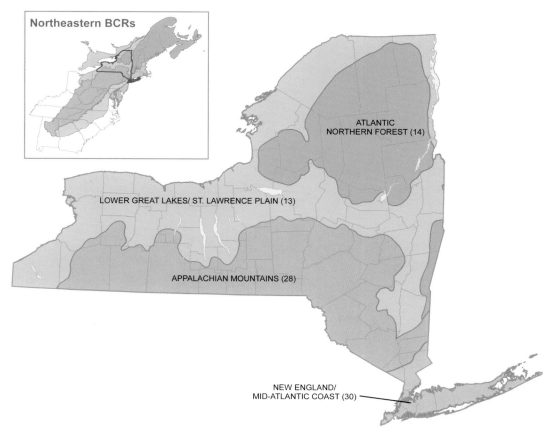

Figure 1.15 Bird Conservation Regions (BCRs) in New York.

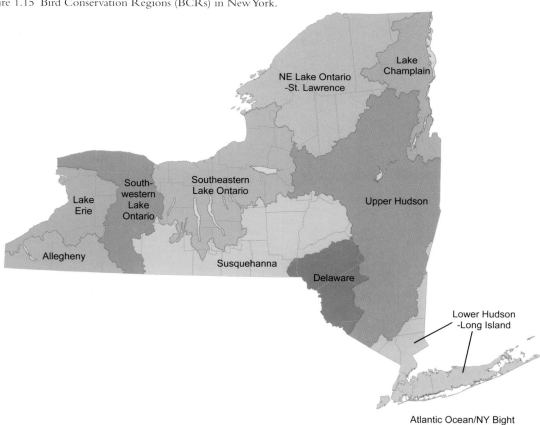

Figure 1.16 Watersheds in New York.

CHAPTER TWO

Summary of Results

KEVIN J. MCGOWAN AND BENJAMIN ZUCKERBERG

Bird distributions might seem static, but they are, in fact, dynamic. Some changes occur over centuries following extensive habitat alterations, such as the massive deforestation of eastern North America (see Chapter 4). Others can be more dramatic, taking just a few decades. It is just this kind of change that breeding bird atlases were designed to monitor, with the understanding that atlas fieldwork will need to be repeated approximately every 20 years. As only a few second breeding bird atlases have been completed throughout the world (e.g., Gibbons et al. 1993, Hustings and Vergeer 2002, Barrett et al. 2003), just how much change is to be expected is unknown. A surprising amount of change took place between the survey periods for the two New York Breeding Bird Atlas projects. A few species were lost, a few were gained, and the distributions of many changed.

Just how well the two Atlas datasets can be compared depends to a large extent on using a similar methodology (Donald and Fuller 1998), but coverage differences can make assessing the validity of apparent changes difficult. As discussed in Chapter 1, the methods used in the two New York Atlas projects were virtually identical. Still, one must be cautious in reading too much into the Atlas data, especially at the smaller scales. In general, the usefulness of atlas data declines as one looks at smaller and smaller areas. Changes evident on a species map might be the results of factors other than actual biological differences in species distribution. Determination of the presence or absence of a species in a block reflects a complex combination of actual presence or absence and the perceived detection of the species by an observer. Detection depends not only on the habitat and the behavior of a particular bird species but also on a host of variables related to the skill and effort expended by the observer. It is likely that a skilled observer can detect essentially all of the birds in a block that sing to proclaim territory, by visiting all habitats at varying times of the day and seasons over a five-year period. As is true of all such large volunteer projects, however, sufficient numbers of highly skilled observers are not available to cover all blocks in such a fashion. Consequently, the observers available and the times covered represent a compromise in an imperfect world. One can hope that the differences in observers, skill, and effort, and consequently the differences in coverage, will not cause systematic biases in the data but rather will be balanced across the state and the project. The likelihood of biased results is greatest when comparisons are made at smaller and smaller spatial scales. Changes within an ecozone might be biologically real, but changes within a single block or county might well be affected by other factors, such as coverage and effort, and any such changes must be interpreted with caution.

"Coverage" is a function of the amount of time spent in a block, during different parts of the season, at various times of the day and night, and in the different habitats available, as well as the skill of the observer. A skilled observer with good hearing can detect more species in a few hours in a block than other observers spending over 100 hours. In addition, coverage can be influenced by other common factors associated with bird studies such as site accessibility (i.e., the presence of roads) and changes in weather. Clearly in such a volunteer project, most of these variables were not quantified and could not have been.

A few differences in coverage between the Atlases are known to the authors and editors. Perhaps most significant is the increased access to the Fort Drum Military Reservation in northeastern Jefferson County on the edge of the Eastern Ontario Plain. Fort Drum blocks were visited only once or a few times during a single year (and some not at all) in the 1980s but were covered very thoroughly during the second Atlas survey. This improved coverage resulted in apparent increases in the breeding distribution of a number of species, including some whose distribution was declining in most other areas. Another known coverage issue is the extensive amount of owling done in Wyoming and Livingston counties for the second Atlas. The exceptional effort there is likely the reason for some of the apparent increases in breeding distribution seen of several owl species in those counties.

In order to analyze changes in effort and species distributions, we aggregated the data in two different ways. We examined the data by Atlas Region, where results could be affected by both geographic and administrative influences. We also examined the data by ecozone (see Chapter 3) to look at geographic factors (in this analysis, the Catskill Peaks and Catskill Highlands sub-ecoregions within the Appalachian Plateau ecozone were included).

Effort Analyses

The total amount of time spent in each block was recorded, and although imperfect, evaluation of this information on effort represents one method of assessing the change in coverage for the two atlas surveys. Although equivalence of time spent in a block does not necessarily represent equivalence of coverage,

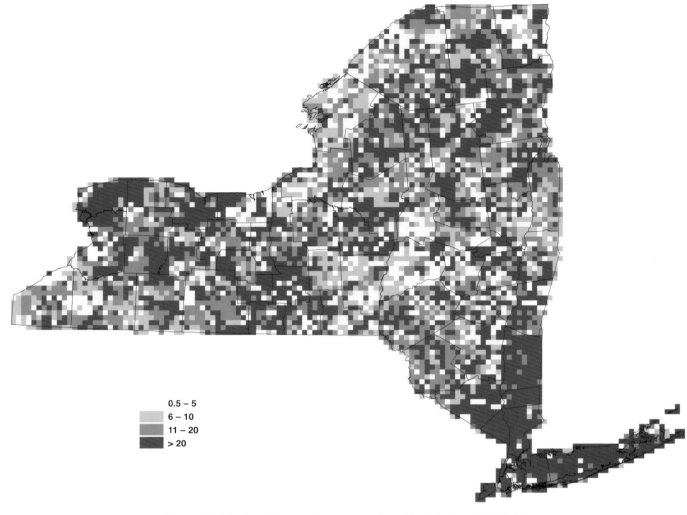

0.5 – 5
6 – 10
11 – 20
> 20

Figure 2.1 Number of person-hours reported per block for the 1980–85 Atlas.

large differences in effort expended might indicate differences in coverage and could point out situations where caution is warranted in making comparisons.

Effort was measured as the number of person-hours spent atlasing per block (the sum of the number of hours spent in each block × the number of people atlasing each block). Effort data were collected for both Atlas projects, although participants were not advised of how the data would be used in either Atlas other than for grant-matching purposes. No detailed guidelines were provided on how to record effort data. Total hours expended per block were not normally distributed in either Atlas, but normality was approximated with a log transformation, and the statistical analyses described here were done only on transformed data.

Was the effort expended in an individual block consistent between the Atlases or did it vary in a meaningful way? The access to or desirability of a particular block might introduce biases that could result in some blocks being over-sampled and others nearly ignored. Maps showing the effort expended per block for each Atlas can be seen in Figures 2.1 and 2.2. A simple correlation of the effort expended per block for the second Atlas and

that logged in the first Atlas (on log-transformed data) gives a statistically significant ($r = 0.245$, $r^2 = 0.060$, $P < 0.001$) but biologically meaningless relationship. Only 6 percent of the variation in the second Atlas was explained by the amount of effort expended in that block during the first Atlas. Although little effort may have been expended for some hard-to-access blocks in both Atlas projects, by and large how much attention a block received was independent in the two Atlases.

If effort is examined as the total number of hours recorded during an Atlas survey, or as the average number of hours spent per block, absolutely more time was invested in the 2000 Atlas survey (Table 2.1). We tested whether average effort per block changed between the Atlas projects, using paired t-tests (i.e., each block compared with itself), and found a significant increase of 1.5 hours expended per block for the second Atlas survey ($t = -8.185$, $df = 5006$, $P < 0.001$). Change in effort varied by region (ANOVA, $F_{9,5130} = 45.773$, $P < 0.001$; Table 2.2, Figure 2.3). Atlas Regions 1, 4, 5, 6, and 8 showed significantly more effort in the recent Atlas; Regions 2, 7, and 9 showed no change; and Regions 3 and 10 showed significant declines. Change in effort also var-

Figure 2.2 Number of person-hours reported per block for the 2000–05 Atlas.

Table 2.1. Effort data for the two Atlas projects

	1980–85	2000–05
No. of blocks with effort data	5,058	5,279
Total effort (no. of person-hours) recorded	140,803	155,381
Average no. of hours/block	27.84	29.43
Standard deviation of mean	33.591	35.807
Maximum	561.8	1,011
Minimum	0.2	0.5
Median	18.0	20.0

ied (ANOVA, $F_{14,5305}$ = 22.326, P < 0.001; Table 2.3, Figure 2.3), with the Appalachian Plateau, Catskill Highlands, Catskill Peaks, Great Lakes Plain, Champlain Valley, Tug Hill Plateau, Mohawk Valley, and Hudson Valley showing significantly more effort per block; the St. Lawrence Plains and Taconic Highlands with no significant change; and the Coastal Lowlands, Manhattan Hills, Triassic Lowlands, and Hudson Highlands showing significantly less effort during the second Atlas project. It is important to re-member that these comparisons represent only change in effort and do not reflect whether the final effort was adequate. For ex-ample, the Manhattan Hills showed the largest change in effort reported, declining an average of 35.3 hours per block, but this region still had the second-highest average effort of any ecozone during the second Atlas survey, at 50.2 hours per block, well above the statewide average. Still, apparent declines in species distributions in the southeastern regions may well have been af-fected by the lower effort during this Atlas survey, and interpreta-tions must be made with caution.

In order to incorporate the known differences in effort into

< −22 (14%)
− 22 to −12 (10%)
−11 to 11 (47%)
12 to 22 (12%)
> 22 (17%)

Figure 2.3 Difference in the number of person-hours reported per block between the two Atlases. Categories represent approximately one-half of one standard deviation of the mean difference.

Table 2.2. Comparison of average effort and species richness for the two Atlas projects by region

Region	No. of blocks	Average effort/block in person-hours (SD)		Statistical significance (paired t-tests on log-transformed data)	Average no. of species/block (SD)		Statistical significance (paired t-tests)
		First Atlas	Second Atlas		First Atlas	Second Atlas	
New York total	5,333	27.8 (33.591)	29.4 (35.807)		67.9 (16.217)	71.8 (16.560)	
1	634	25.0 (30.462)	30.9 (27.504)	$P < 0.001$★★★	63.1 (12.186)	73.9 (12.341)	$P < 0.001$★★★
2	338	31.6 (32.993)	31.9 (29.359)	$P = 0.463$ n.s.	76.2 (14.041)	78.6 (13.627)	$P = 0.003$★★
3	448	28.0 (22.017)	22.1 (25.958)	$P < 0.001$★★★	74.5 (13.378)	74.4 (16.625)	$P = 0.923$ n.s.
4	539	20.5 (26.917)	31.4 (29.444)	$P < 0.001$★★★	76.2 (11.270)	83.1 (8.786)	$P < 0.001$★★★
5	552	19.8 (17.705)	28.7 (22.013)	$P < 0.001$★★★	72.1 (12.744)	78.7 (10.810)	$P < 0.001$★★★
6	587	16.5 (13.177)	19.8 (25.287)	$P = 0.013$★	62.9 (15.278)	69.7 (16.239)	$P < 0.001$★★★
7	690	29.1 (36.013)	30.5 (52.648)	$P = 0.199$ n.s.	61.4 (19.949)	59.6 (19.861)	$P = 0.022$★
8	755	20.3 (21.382)	23.1 (22.937)	$P < 0.001$★★★	65.3 (14.751)	71.1 (13.076)	$P < 0.001$★★★
9	527	45.3 (49.316)	41.8 (41.985)	$P = 0.659$ n.s.	73.2 (13.536)	72.5 (13.749)	$P = 0.266$ n.s.
10	263	69.0 (56.656)	45.4 (66.903)	$P < 0.001$★★★	57.5 (22.724)	54.2 (20.967)	$P < 0.001$★★★

SD, standard deviation; n.s., not significant; ★, significant at $P < 0.05$ level; ★★, significant at $P < 0.01$ level; ★★★, significant at $P < 0.001$ level.

Table 2.3. Comparison of average effort and species richness for the two Atlas projects by ecozone

Ecozone	No. of blocks	Average effort/block in person-hours (SD)		Statistical significance (paired t-tests on log-transformed data)	Average no. of species/block (SD)		Statistical significance (paired t-tests)
		First Atlas	Second Atlas		First Atlas	Second Atlas	
New York total	5,333	27.8 (33.591)	29.4 (35.807)	$P < 0.001$★★★	67.9 (16.217)	71.8 (16.560)	
Appalachian Plateau	1,572	23.5 (27.512)	27.8 (25.872)	$P < 0.001$★★★	73.0 (13.863)	79.6 (12.665)	$P < 0.001$★★★
Catskill Highlands	144	19.2 (17.601)	24.9 (31.333)	$P = 0.012$★★	68.5 (12.562)	74.9 (8.937)	$P < 0.001$★★★
Catskill Peaks	65	21.3 (30.725)	29.5 (22.389)	$P = 0.001$★★	65.6 (13.524)	65.0 (12.610)	$P = 0.750$ n.s.
Great Lakes Plain	858	25.4 (25.352)	33.3 (30.788)	$P < 0.001$★★★	67.7 (14.494)	73.6 (13.846)	$P < 0.001$★★★
St. Lawrence Plains	205	14.8 (14.617)	14.7 (16.994)	$P = 0.833$ n.s.	64.8 (14.485)	67.3 (14.959)	$P = 0.027$★
Champlain Valley	104	26.2 (35.515)	42.5 (99.830)	$P < 0.001$★★★	62.9 (22.750)	72.3 (22.547)	$P < 0.001$★★★
Adirondacks	1,091	25.4 (28.968)	24.4 (31.404)	$P = 0.132$ n.s.	62.2 (17.646)	61.6 (17.299)	$P = 0.277$ n.s.
Tug Hill Plateau	185	18.2 (14.799)	22.0 (25.288)	$P = 0.024$★	70.5 (12.889)	81.0 (10.448)	$P < 0.001$★★★
Mohawk Valley	182	17.8 (19.524)	23.5 (19.349)	$P < 0.001$★★★	67.2 (12.157)	75.1 (10.608)	$P < 0.001$★★★
Hudson Valley	310	35.4 (37.499)	40.2 (40.097)	$P = 0.003$★★	69.8 (13.538)	74.2 (13.233)	$P < 0.001$★★★
Taconic Highlands	226	27.8 (29.183)	26.8 (28.994)	$P = 0.739$ n.s.	69.6 (15.276)	73.3 (12.945)	$P < 0.001$★★★
Hudson Highlands	57	72.0 (44.085)	54.9 (57.283)	$P = 0.004$★★	78.7 (10.874)	72.1 (15.222)	$P = 0.001$★★
Triassic Lowlands	14	65.1 (37.457)	40.6 (33.251)	$P = 0.020$★	66.2 (17.143)	64.8 (11.656)	$P = 0.580$ n.s.
Manhattan Hills	75	85.5 (86.192)	50.2 (46.300)	$P < 0.001$★★★	67.1 (23.491)	63.3 (21.008)	$P = 0.024$★
Coastal Lowlands	246	67.5 (55.047)	44.9 (68.330)	$P < 0.001$★★★	58.8 (22.307)	54.9 (20.616)	$P < 0.001$

SD, standard deviation; n.s., not significant; ★, significant at $P < 0.05$ level; ★★, significant at $P < 0.01$ level; ★★★, significant at $P < 0.001$ level.

interpretations of the change in bird distribution, we calculated a correction factor for the results of the second Atlas. We combined the data from both Atlas projects and generated a regression of effort per block (log-transformed) on species richness in a block. We found a significant relationship that explained nearly 15 percent of the variance ($r = 0.384$, $r^2 = 0.147$, $P < 0.001$). The formula for the line was

$$\text{Number of Species/block} = (16.674 \star \log \text{effort}) + 48.346$$

We entered the average effort expended per block into this formula to calculate predicted average species richness (total number of species) per block for each Atlas project. We then took the difference of these values to get the amount of change in species richness that would be expected based on effort differences alone, 0.405 species per block.

With the assumption that all species are equally detectable (clearly not true, but probably reasonable for a large number of species), the percentage change resulting from effort was applied to the blocks with records of each species to calculate a "corrected" number of blocks. For the statewide calculations, the 0.405-species-per-block increase is the equivalent of a 0.589 percent increase over the average number of species per block found in the first Atlas (67.9, see Table 2.2)—that is, $0.405/67.9 \star 100 = 0.596$. Therefore, one could multiply all of the second Atlas block totals for each species by 0.994 to get a corrected total to use in statistical analyses of significance of change.

Effort did not change identically among ecozones, and species were not randomly distributed among them, so a refinement of these correction factors was made to take ecozones into account. We calculated the species accumulation formulae for each of the ecozones and calculated the change in number of species per block that should result from the recorded effort differences as was described above for the entire state. These values were then used to calculate "corrected" numbers of blocks for each ecozone, which were then summed to give a statewide total for each species for comparison.

Results

The number of species found during the second Atlas survey was close to that reported in the first Atlas: 248 species (plus three named hybrids) for this Atlas, 242 (plus the same hybrids) in the first Atlas (Table 2.4). Breeding was confirmed for 240 species in the second Atlas, compared to 230 in the first. Five species detected during the first Atlas project were not seen during the second one: Greater Scaup, Bufflehead, White-faced Ibis, Black-hooded Parakeet, and Brewer's Blackbird. Of these species, only the Black-headed Parakeet was confirmed nesting during the first Atlas survey (see Appendix 1). Other species that had been confirmed as breeders in the first Atlas but not for the second one are the Canvasback and Loggerhead Shrike. Of all of these "lost" species, only the Loggerhead Shrike represents a significant loss from the avifauna of New York, as the other species were incidental breeders at best. The loss of the shrike is the perhaps inevitable conclusion of a long-term decline of a species that had become rare by the time of the first Atlas project (see the species account for the full story).

Table 2.4 Species found during the two Atlas surveys

Species	No. of blocks detected in 1980–85	No. of blocks detected in 2000–05	Change (%)	Change adjusted for effort (%)
Canada Goose	1,058	3,968	275	273
Mute Swan	218	407	87	86
Trumpeter Swan	0	12		
Wood Duck	1,923	2,789	45	44
Gadwall	114	115	1	0
American Wigeon	42	22	−48	−48
American Black Duck	1,102	728	−34	−34
Mallard	3,175	4,029	27	26
Mallard x American Black Duck hybrid	73	86	18	17
Blue-winged Teal	460	170	−63	−63
Northern Shoveler	19	25	32	31
Northern Pintail	35	10	−71	−72
Green-winged Teal	120	66	−45	−45
Canvasback	1	1	0	−1
Redhead	8	14	75	74
Ring-necked Duck	47	97	106	105
Greater Scaup	2	0	−100	−100
Lesser Scaup	3	2	−33	−34
Common Eider	0	2		
Bufflehead	2	0	−100	−100
Common Goldeneye	24	31	29	28
Hooded Merganser	384	810	111	110
Common Merganser	470	1,104	135	134
Red-breasted Merganser	14	20	43	42
Ruddy Duck	7	18	157	156
Gray Partridge	36	7	−81	−81
Ring-necked Pheasant	1,699	1,069	−37	−37
Ruffed Grouse	3,152	2,579	−18	−19
Spruce Grouse	27	20	−26	−26
Wild Turkey	1,567	3,651	133	132
Northern Bobwhite	236	175	−26	−26
Common Loon	369	528	43	42
Pied-billed Grebe	182	267	47	46
American White Pelican	0	1		
Double-crested Cormorant	22	179	714	709
American Bittern	534	478	−10	−11
Least Bittern	142	129	−9	−10
Great Blue Heron	3,166	3,806	20	20
Great Egret	65	111	71	70

Species	No. of blocks detected in 1980–85	No. of blocks detected in 2000–05	Change (%)	Change adjusted for effort (%)
Snowy Egret	94	58	−38	−39
Little Blue Heron	19	18	−5	−6
Tricolored Heron	11	13	18	18
Cattle Egret	20	7	−65	−65
Green Heron	2,544	2,213	−13	−13
Black-crowned Night-Heron	211	213	1	0
Yellow-crowned Night-Heron	40	29	−28	−28
Glossy Ibis	47	38	−19	−20
White-faced Ibis	1	0	−100	−100
Black Vulture	0	100		
Turkey Vulture	2,147	3,675	71	70
Osprey	335	826	147	145
Bald Eagle	35	445	1,171	1,164
Northern Harrier	930	917	−1	−2
Sharp-shinned Hawk	859	1,440	68	67
Cooper's Hawk	550	1,355	146	145
Northern Goshawk	445	355	−20	−21
Red-shouldered Hawk	702	865	23	23
Broad-winged Hawk	1,944	1,961	1	0
Red-tailed Hawk	3,714	3,955	6	6
Golden Eagle	8	9	13	12
American Kestrel	3,450	2,960	−14	−15
Merlin	0	131		
Peregrine Falcon	17	111	553	549
Black Rail	1	1	0	−1
Clapper Rail	58	56	−3	−4
King Rail	5	5	0	−1
Virginia Rail	458	553	21	20
Sora	241	278	15	15
Common Moorhen	288	192	−33	−34
American Coot	72	79	10	9
Sandhill Crane	0	9		
Piping Plover	75	76	1	1
Killdeer	3,939	3,780	−4	−5
American Oystercatcher	45	68	51	50
Spotted Sandpiper	2,022	1,772	−12	−13
Willet	43	76	77	76
Upland Sandpiper	476	165	−65	−66
Wilson's Snipe	969	991	2	2
American Woodcock	1,926	2,004	4	3
Wilson's Phalarope	0	4		
Laughing Gull	32	6	−81	−81
Ring-billed Gull	38	31	−18	−19
Herring Gull	269	235	−13	−13
Great Black-backed Gull	71	67	−6	−6
Least Tern	87	69	−21	−21
Gull-billed Tern	3	5	67	66
Caspian Tern	3	5	67	66
Black Tern	73	44	−40	−40
White-winged Tern	0	1		
Roseate Tern	19	12	−37	−37

Table 2.4 Species found during the two Atlas surveys (continued)

Species	No. of blocks detected in 1980–85	No. of blocks detected in 2000–05	Change (%)	Change adjusted for effort (%)
Common Tern	122	121	−1	−1
Forster's Tern	2	10	400	397
Black Skimmer	37	25	−32	−33
Rock Pigeon	3,771	3,741	−1	−1
Eurasian Collared-Dove	0	2		
Mourning Dove	4,402	4,803	9	8
Monk Parakeet	3	15	400	397
Black-hooded Parakeet	5	0	−100	−100
Yellow-billed Cuckoo	1,281	1,324	3	3
Black-billed Cuckoo	1,963	2,034	4	3
Barn Owl	126	28	−78	−78
Eastern Screech-Owl	1,125	1,137	1	1
Great Horned Owl	1,968	1,622	−18	−18
Barred Owl	1,075	1,534	43	42
Long-eared Owl	81	48	−41	−41
Short-eared Owl	36	24	−33	−34
Northern Saw-whet Owl	129	146	13	13
Common Nighthawk	477	138	−71	−71
Chuck-will's-widow	21	8	−62	−62
Whip-poor-will	564	241	−57	−58
Chimney Swift	3,124	2,652	−15	−16
Ruby-throated Hummingbird	3,518	4,254	21	20
Belted Kingfisher	3,814	3,595	−6	−6
Red-headed Woodpecker	691	167	−76	−76
Red-bellied Woodpecker	978	2,182	123	122
Yellow-bellied Sapsucker	2,205	3,358	52	51
Downy Woodpecker	4,562	4,683	3	2
Hairy Woodpecker	3,768	4,095	9	8
American Three-toed Woodpecker	22	15	−32	−32
Black-backed Woodpecker	114	127	11	11
Northern Flicker	4,898	4,867	−1	−1
Pileated Woodpecker	2,714	3,491	29	28
Olive-sided Flycatcher	479	316	−34	−34
Eastern Wood-Pewee	4,537	4,346	−4	−5
Yellow-bellied Flycatcher	192	273	42	41
Acadian Flycatcher	162	239	48	47
Alder Flycatcher	1,929	2,805	45	45
Willow Flycatcher	1,932	2,619	36	35
Least Flycatcher	3,818	3,671	−4	−4
Eastern Phoebe	4,283	4,666	9	8
Great Crested Flycatcher	4,305	4,169	−3	−4
Western Kingbird	0	1		
Eastern Kingbird	4,805	4,460	−7	−8
Loggerhead Shrike	24	4	−83	−83
White-eyed Vireo	174	162	−7	−7
Yellow-throated Vireo	1,679	1,561	−7	−8
Blue-headed Vireo	1,892	2,634	39	38
Warbling Vireo	3,133	3,537	13	12
Philadelphia Vireo	46	72	57	56
Red-eyed Vireo	4,984	5,128	3	2

Species	No. of blocks detected in 1980–85	No. of blocks detected in 2000–05	Change (%)	Change adjusted for effort (%)
Gray Jay	95	114	20	19
Blue Jay	5,154	5,177	0	0
American Crow	4,958	5,001	1	0
Fish Crow	210	324	54	53
Common Raven	313	1,879	500	497
Horned Lark	1,105	698	−37	−37
Purple Martin	963	583	−39	−40
Tree Swallow	4,650	4,852	4	4
Northern Rough-winged Swallow	1,564	1,895	21	20
Bank Swallow	1,966	1,421	−28	−28
Cliff Swallow	1,250	1,105	−12	−12
Barn Swallow	4,917	4,629	−6	−6
Black-capped Chickadee	5,149	5,205	1	1
Boreal Chickadee	123	138	12	12
Tufted Titmouse	1,557	3,121	100	99
Red-breasted Nuthatch	1,690	2,306	36	36
White-breasted Nuthatch	4,263	4,393	3	2
Brown Creeper	2,037	2,142	5	5
Carolina Wren	305	1,250	310	308
House Wren	4,396	4,259	−3	−4
Winter Wren	1,210	1,802	49	48
Sedge Wren	57	72	26	26
Marsh Wren	439	461	5	4
Golden-crowned Kinglet	973	1,095	13	12
Ruby-crowned Kinglet	187	175	−6	−7
Blue-gray Gnatcatcher	876	1,039	19	18
Eastern Bluebird	2,460	3,796	54	53
Veery	4,265	4,159	−2	−3
Bicknell's Thrush	39	57	46	45
Swainson's Thrush	704	589	−16	−17
Hermit Thrush	2,088	2,730	31	30
Wood Thrush	4,764	4,428	−7	−8
American Robin	5,189	5,239	1	0
Gray Catbird	4,920	4,743	−4	−4
Northern Mockingbird	1,490	1,635	10	9
Brown Thrasher	3,341	2,337	−30	−30
European Starling	4,622	4,551	−2	−2
Cedar Waxwing	4,915	5,025	2	2
Blue-winged Warbler	1,867	2,189	17	17
Golden-winged Warbler	577	270	−53	−53
Brewster's Warbler	129	118	−9	−9
Lawrence's Warbler	42	39	−7	−8
Tennessee Warbler	27	28	4	3
Nashville Warbler	1,476	1,374	−7	−7
Northern Parula	342	515	51	50
Yellow Warbler	4,580	4,587	0	0
Chestnut-sided Warbler	3,634	3,993	10	9
Magnolia Warbler	1,682	2,119	26	25
Cape May Warbler	18	14	−22	−23
Black-throated Blue Warbler	1,738	1,919	10	10

Table 2.4 Species found during the two Atlas surveys (continued)

Species	No. of blocks detected in 1980–85	No. of blocks detected in 2000–05	Change (%)	Change adjusted for effort (%)
Yellow-rumped Warbler	2,094	2,831	35	34
Black-throated Green Warbler	2,375	3,055	29	28
Blackburnian Warbler	1,712	2,040	19	18
Yellow-throated Warbler	3	5	67	66
Pine Warbler	348	1,113	220	218
Prairie Warbler	731	875	20	19
Palm Warbler	1	43	4,200	4,176
Bay-breasted Warbler	32	12	−63	−63
Blackpoll Warbler	125	115	−8	−9
Cerulean Warbler	279	244	−13	−13
Black-and-white Warbler	2,775	2,756	−1	−1
American Redstart	4,289	4,389	2	2
Prothonotary Warbler	22	11	−50	−50
Worm-eating Warbler	225	223	−1	−1
Ovenbird	4,041	4,411	9	9
Northern Waterthrush	1,134	1,183	4	4
Louisiana Waterthrush	1,055	838	−21	−21
Kentucky Warbler	39	11	−72	−72
Mourning Warbler	1,398	1,460	4	4
Common Yellowthroat	5,175	5,169	0	−1
Hooded Warbler	421	1,035	146	144
Wilson's Warbler	3	2	−33	−34
Canada Warbler	1,684	1,299	−23	−23
Yellow-breasted Chat	122	27	−78	−78
Summer Tanager	3	3	0	−1
Scarlet Tanager	4,299	4,338	1	0
Eastern Towhee	3,758	3,313	−12	−12
Chipping Sparrow	4,870	4,891	0	0
Clay-colored Sparrow	23	69	200	198
Field Sparrow	3,891	3,273	−16	−16
Vesper Sparrow	1,116	564	−49	−50
Savannah Sparrow	3,005	3,070	2	2
Grasshopper Sparrow	822	477	−42	−42
Henslow's Sparrow	348	70	−80	−80
Nelson's Sharp-tailed Sparrow	0	2		
Saltmarsh Sharp-tailed Sparrow	72	61	−15	−16
Seaside Sparrow	48	36	−25	−25
Song Sparrow	5,195	5,168	−1	−1
Lincoln's Sparrow	277	240	−13	−14
Swamp Sparrow	2,893	3,066	6	5
White-throated Sparrow	2,331	1,996	−14	−15
Dark-eyed Junco	2,295	2,828	23	23
Northern Cardinal	3,575	3,896	9	8
Rose-breasted Grosbeak	4,670	4,382	−6	−7
Blue Grosbeak	4	9	125	124
Indigo Bunting	4,264	4,227	−1	−1
Dickcissel	1	5	400	397
Bobolink	3,465	3,178	−8	−9
Red-winged Blackbird	5,061	4,981	−2	−2
Eastern Meadowlark	3,506	2,635	−25	−25

Species	No. of blocks detected in 1980–85	No. of blocks detected in 2000–05	Change (%)	Change adjusted for effort (%)
Western Meadowlark	6	1	−83	−83
Rusty Blackbird	151	117	−23	−23
Brewer's Blackbird	1	0	−100	−100
Common Grackle	5,023	4,932	−2	−2
Boat-tailed Grackle	4	38	850	845
Brown-headed Cowbird	4,519	4,209	−7	−7
Orchard Oriole	223	389	74	73
Baltimore Oriole	4,426	4,276	−3	−4
Purple Finch	3,148	3,165	1	0
House Finch	2,871	3,421	19	18
Red Crossbill	234	84	−64	−64
White-winged Crossbill	209	238	14	13
Pine Siskin	413	419	1	1
American Goldfinch	4,912	5,003	2	1
Evening Grosbeak	250	360	44	43
House Sparrow	4,197	3,935	−6	−7

Species recorded as Confirmed during the second Atlas survey that were not detected during the first survey were Trumpeter Swan, Common Eider, Black Vulture, Merlin, Sandhill Crane, and Wilson's Phalarope. Of these new species, eider and phalarope breeding were rather isolated events, but the others are more significant and represent interesting stories of range expansion that will undoubtedly develop over the years. The crane and swan were found in multiple blocks, and whether they become important members of the New York avifauna remains to be seen. The vulture and falcon, however, are already well established in the state. The Merlin story has developed in several interesting directions, with parallels to changes seen in Merlin populations on the Great Plains in the late 20th century. In addition to these newly confirmed species, the Eurasian Collared-Dove and Nelson's Sharp-tailed Sparrow were recorded as Probable breeders, and the American White Pelican, White-winged Tern, and Western Kingbird as Possible breeders. Species that were seen and not confirmed as breeders for the first Atlas, but were confirmed as breeders during the second Atlas survey include the Caspian Tern, Monk Parakeet, Cape May Warbler, Wilson's Warbler, Summer Tanager, and Dickcissel. Of these, both the Caspian Tern and Monk Parakeet now have significant breeding populations in the state; over 1,400 tern nests were counted in the breeding colony on Little Galloo Island!

The most common species in the state changed little between the two Atlas periods. Of the top 20 most common species, 16 remained the same, with the Eastern Kingbird, Wood Thrush, Rose-breasted Grosbeak, and European Starling dropping out and being replaced by the Mourning Dove, Downy Woodpecker, Eastern Phoebe, and Yellow Warbler (Table 2.5).

Species Richness (number of species per block)

Looking at species richness by block, the ranges seen in the two Atlas projects are comparable, but the average number of species found in a block increased by 3.9, a statistically significant result ($t = -17.442$, $df = 5,319$, $P < 0.001$) (Table 2.6). Species richness data were normally distributed and did not require transformation for statistical tests. The resulting difference of 3.9 species is substantially larger than the 0.4-species increase predicted by the correction for effort, supporting the hypothesis that species richness increased, on average, in New York between the two Atlas periods.

Was species richness consistent within a block for the two Atlas projects? When a generalized map of species richness for the first Atlas period (Figure 2.4) is compared with that for the current Atlas period (Figure 2.5), the patterns look similar but not identical. A regression of the number of species detected in each block showed a much stronger relationship than the comparison of effort in each block ($r = 0.491$, $r^2 = 0.241$, $P < 0.001$), with 24 percent of the variation in species richness in a given block in the second Atlas project explained by the species richness in that block in the first Atlas. In general, blocks with high species richness in the first Atlas remained high in species richness for the second Atlas. This result is to be expected (and hoped for) if species richness varies with region in the state. Looking at this relationship by ecozone, blocks in the Coastal Lowlands and Adirondacks had the lowest species richness in both Atlas projects (Table 2.3, Figures 2.4 and 2.5).

Both the number of species seen per block and the effort expended per block increased for the entire state. The results varied somewhat by ecozone and Atlas regions (Tables 2.2 and 2.3, Figure 2.6). In general, species numbers were up in all re-

Table 2.5 Top 20 species reported during each Atlas survey*

| 1980–85 | | 2000–05 | |
Species	Blocks (%)	Species	Blocks (%)
Song Sparrow	97.4	American Robin	98.2
American Robin	97.2	Black-capped Chickadee	97.6
Common Yellowthroat	97.0	Blue Jay	97.1
Blue Jay	96.6	Common Yellowthroat	96.9
Black-capped Chickadee	96.5	Song Sparrow	96.9
Red-winged Blackbird	94.9	Red-eyed Vireo	96.2
Common Grackle	94.2	Cedar Waxwing	94.2
Red-eyed Vireo	93.4	American Goldfinch	93.8
American Crow	92.9	American Crow	93.8
Gray Catbird	92.2	Red-winged Blackbird	93.4
Barn Swallow	92.2	Common Grackle	92.5
Cedar Waxwing	92.1	Chipping Sparrow	91.7
American Goldfinch	92.1	Northern Flicker	91.2
Northern Flicker	91.8	Tree Swallow	91.0
Chipping Sparrow	91.3	**Mourning Dove**	90.0
Eastern Kingbird	90.1	Gray Catbird	88.9
Wood Thrush	89.3	**Downy Woodpecker**	87.8
Rose-breasted Grosbeak	87.5	**Eastern Phoebe**	87.4
Tree Swallow	87.2	Barn Swallow	86.8
European Starling	86.6	**Yellow Warbler**	86.0

* Species not listed as in the top 20 for both surveys are noted in **bold**.

Table 2.6 Species richness data from the two Atlas surveys

	1980–85	2000–05
No. of blocks with data	5,323	5,332
Total no. of species recorded	242	249
Average no. of species/block	67.9	71.8
Standard deviation of mean	16.217	16.560
Maximum	141	129
Minimum	1	1
Median	68	75

gions of the state, except in the southeastern ecozones (Coastal Lowlands, Hudson Highlands, and Manhattan Hills), where effort was down, and in the highest-elevation regions (Adirondacks and Catskill Peaks), where increases might be the least expected. Species numbers increased even in areas where effort remained the same (e.g., St. Lawrence Plain, Taconic Highlands). In all ecozones the changes in species richness were greater than the value expected on the basis of effort alone, except for the Catskill Peaks, Adirondacks, and Hudson Highlands (Table 2.7). All of the trends shown are consistent with the hypothesis that species richness increased throughout the state, except for the decline in species numbers with similar effort in Atlas Region 7, and no change despite increased effort in the Catskill Peaks where increases might be limited by available habitats. The decline in species numbers in the southeastern regions could be real and might be the result of increasing urbanization and development, or the decline in coverage might be the most important factor. The lack of change in the average number of species recorded per block in the Adirondacks and the Catskill Peaks despite similar and increased effort (respectively) might represent the limitations to colonization of the most inhospitable regions of the state. It is not hard to believe that most blocks included

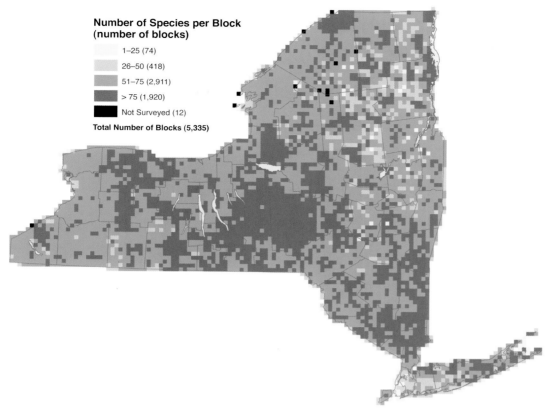

**Number of Species per Block
(number of blocks)**

    1–25 (74)

    26–50 (418)

    51–75 (2,911)

    > 75 (1,920)

    Not Surveyed (12)

Total Number of Blocks (5,335)

Figure 2.4 Species richness by block in the 1980–85 Atlas.

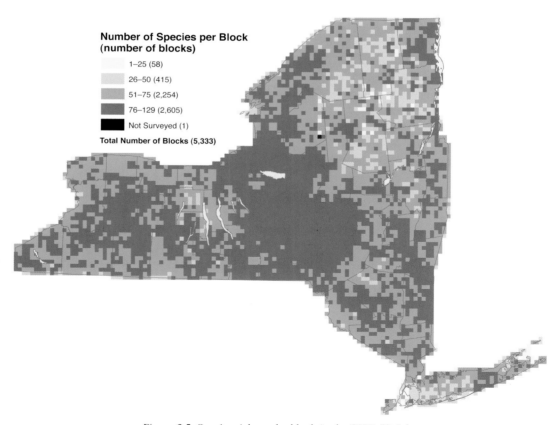

**Number of Species per Block
(number of blocks)**

    1–25 (58)

    26–50 (415)

    51–75 (2,254)

    76–129 (2,605)

    Not Surveyed (1)

Total Number of Blocks (5,333)

Figure 2.5 Species richness by block in the 2000–05 Atlas.

Table 2.7 Differences in species richness per block in each ecozone, observed and expected based on changes in effort

Ecozone	Average effort difference (person-hours/block)	Observed average difference in no. of species/block	Predicted average difference in no. of species/block
New York total	1.5	3.9	0.4
Appalachian Plateau	3.5	6.6	1.2
Catskill Highlands	6.0	6.4	1.8
Catskill Peaks	6.5	−0.5	0.7
Great Lakes Plain	7.9	5.9	1.6
St. Lawrence Plains	−0.3	2.8	0.1
Champlain Valley	18.6	9.4	6.6
Adirondacks	−1.0	−0.6	−0.4
Tug Hill Plateau	3.7	10.4	1.9
Mohawk Valley	6.4	7.9	1.5
Hudson Valley	4.4	4.4	0.9
Taconic Highlands	−0.7	3.6	−0.4
Hudson Highlands	−16.4	−6.5	−2.2
Triassic Lowlands	−27.9	−1.4	−3.1
Manhattan Hills	−38.0	−3.8	−5.2
Coastal Lowlands	−23.4	−4.1	−5.0

more species in the second Atlas survey when one considers the dramatic explosion of Canada Goose, Wild Turkey, Turkey Vulture, Red-bellied Woodpecker, Yellow-bellied Sapsucker, Common Raven, Tufted Titmouse, and Eastern Bluebird, all of which showed increased occurrence by more than 1,000 blocks. Brown Thrasher was the only species for which occurrence declined by more than 1,000 blocks.

Unfortunately, the results in Tables 2.2 and 2.3 are also consistent with the hypothesis that species richness varied with the change in effort, with the exceptions of Region 2 (no change in effort but increased species richness), Region 3 (decreased effort but no change in species richness), Region 7 (no change in effort but a decrease in species richness), the Catskill Peaks (no increase in species despite increased effort), St. Lawrence Plains (increased species despite no change in effort), Taconic Highlands (increased species despite no change in effort), and the Triassic Lowlands (no change in species despite decreased effort). A limited sample of blocks that had less than one-hour difference in coverage between the two Atlas projects is available (*n* = 189). Average effort for this sample was the same for both Atlas projects, 15.5 hours. Average species richness, however, was significantly higher in the data from the second Atlas survey (mean (SD) 1980 = 65.0 (15.509), mean (SD) 2000 = 68.4 (16.168), $t = -3.519$, $P = 0.001$), and the increase was similar to that seen statewide in the full sample.

In conclusion, the increase in number of species seen during the second Atlas survey does not appear to be an artifact of increased effort. Declines in any region or ecozones other than the extreme southeastern part of the state are likely the result of factors other than a decline in sampling effort. Declines seen in the Coastal Lowlands and the lower Hudson Valley and associated highlands, however, must be treated with more caution.

Species Trends

Of the 253 species detected during the two Atlas surveys, 137 species were found in more blocks, 4 in exactly the same number of blocks, and 112 in fewer blocks (Table 2.8). After the adjustments for effort, the data showed that 132 species were found in more blocks, 5 in the same number of blocks, and 116 in fewer blocks. When statistical probability of significance (at $P < 0.001$ because of the large number of blocks) was determined using a two-by-two contingency table (first or second Atlas, present or not present in each block), with the adjusted values, 128 changes were shown to be significant and 125 were not. Of those demonstrating significant changes, 58 species declined and 70 increased. The species showing the largest increases in number of blocks with records, as measured by percentage increase, are listed in Table 2.9, and those showing the largest decreases in number of blocks with records are listed in Table 2.10.

Many of the changes were well known, such as the increases in Canada Goose and Wild Turkey populations, but the extent of their spread in the last 20 years might be surprising to many readers. The increase in Double-crested Cormorant numbers has been widely advertised, so the change map for that species might be anticipated. The change in Common Raven distribution, though, might be a shock for some people. It is interesting to see that many species that were expanding their ranges during the first Atlas period continued to do so (e.g., Red-bellied Woodpecker, Tufted Titmouse, Carolina Wren). Some of those species, such as the Wild Turkey, even expanded into unexpected parts of the state. The stories of many species with a diminishing range have been well known for a while too. Upland Sandpiper, Henslow's Sparrow, and Red-headed Woodpecker have become more and more difficult to find each year. The magnitude of their disappearance is bound to be surprising for some, though. The statewide declines in such widespread species as Brown Thrasher and Canada Warbler are also disheartening, with maps that now look like Swiss cheese, the change maps filled with the blue indicating loss since the first Atlas period.

It is good to see that many of the specific projects that targeted endangered or threatened species seem to have worked. The Bald Eagle, Osprey, and Peregrine Falcon, all of which received considerable help and study by the New York State Department of Environmental Conservation over the years, showed particularly impressive gains.

Approximately half of all of the bird species in New York

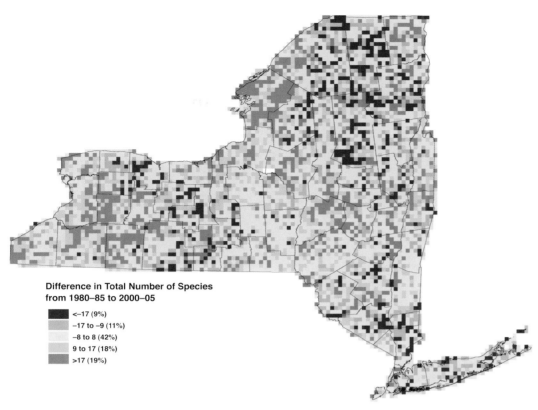

**Difference in Total Number of Species
from 1980–85 to 2000–05**

- <–17 (9%)
- –17 to –9 (11%)
- –8 to 8 (42%)
- 9 to 17 (18%)
- >17 (19%)

Figure 2.6 Difference in species richness by block between the two Atlases. Categories represent approximately one-half of one standard deviation of the mean difference.

Table 2.8 Changes in occurrence between the two Atlas periods, arranged from greatest positive change to greatest loss

Species	No. of blocks with records in 1980–85	No. of blocks with records in 2000–05	Change (%)	Change adjusted for effort (%)
Merlin	0	131		
Black Vulture	0	100		
Trumpeter Swan	0	12		
Sandhill Crane	0	9		
Wilson's Phalarope	0	4		
Common Eider	0	2		
Eurasian Collared-Dove	0	2		
Nelson's Sharp-tailed Sparrow	0	2		
American White Pelican	0	1		
White-winged Tern	0	1		
Western Kingbird	0	1		
Palm Warbler	1	43	4,200	4,176
Bald Eagle	35	445	1,171	1,164
Boat-tailed Grackle	4	38	850	845
Double-crested Cormorant	22	179	714	709
Peregrine Falcon	17	111	553	549
Common Raven	313	1,879	500	497
Forster's Tern	2	10	400	397
Monk Parakeet	3	15	400	397
Dickcissel	1	5	400	397
Carolina Wren	305	1,250	310	308

Species	No. of blocks with records in 1980–85	No. of blocks with records in 2000–05	Change (%)	Change adjusted for effort (%)
Canada Goose	1,058	3,968	275	273
Pine Warbler	348	1,113	220	218
Clay-colored Sparrow	23	69	200	198
Ruddy Duck	7	18	157	156
Osprey	335	826	147	145
Cooper's Hawk	550	1,355	146	145
Hooded Warbler	421	1,035	146	144
Common Merganser	470	1,104	135	134
Wild Turkey	1,567	3,651	133	132
Blue Grosbeak	4	9	125	124
Red-bellied Woodpecker	978	2,182	123	122
Hooded Merganser	384	810	111	110
Ring-necked Duck	47	97	106	105
Tufted Titmouse	1,557	3,121	100	99
Mute Swan	218	407	87	86
Willet	43	76	77	76
Redhead	8	14	75	74
Orchard Oriole	223	389	74	73
Turkey Vulture	2,147	3,675	71	70
Great Egret	65	111	71	70
Sharp-shinned Hawk	859	1,440	68	67
Gull-billed Tern	3	5	67	66
Caspian Tern	3	5	67	66
Yellow-throated Warbler	3	5	67	66
Philadelphia Vireo	46	72	57	56
Eastern Bluebird	2,460	3,796	54	53
Fish Crow	210	324	54	53
Yellow-bellied Sapsucker	2,205	3,358	52	51
American Oystercatcher	45	68	51	50
Northern Parula	342	515	51	50
Winter Wren	1,210	1,802	49	48
Acadian Flycatcher	162	239	48	47
Pied-billed Grebe	182	267	47	46
Bicknell's Thrush	39	57	46	45
Alder Flycatcher	1,929	2,805	45	45
Wood Duck	1,923	2,789	45	44
Evening Grosbeak	250	360	44	43
Common Loon	369	528	43	42
Red-breasted Merganser	14	20	43	42
Barred Owl	1,075	1,534	43	42
Yellow-bellied Flycatcher	192	273	42	41
Blue-headed Vireo	1,892	2,634	39	38
Red-breasted Nuthatch	1,690	2,306	36	36
Willow Flycatcher	1,932	2,619	36	35
Yellow-rumped Warbler	2,094	2,831	35	34
Northern Shoveler	19	25	32	31
Hermit Thrush	2,088	2,730	31	30

Species	No. of blocks with records in 1980–85	No. of blocks with records in 2000–05	Change (%)	Change adjusted for effort (%)
Common Goldeneye	24	31	29	28
Black-throated Green Warbler	2,375	3,055	29	28
Pileated Woodpecker	2,714	3,491	29	28
Mallard	3,175	4,029	27	26
Sedge Wren	57	72	26	26
Magnolia Warbler	1,682	2,119	26	25
Dark-eyed Junco	2,295	2,828	23	23
Red-shouldered Hawk	702	865	23	23
Northern Rough-winged Swallow	1,564	1,895	21	20
Ruby-throated Hummingbird	3,518	4,254	21	20
Virginia Rail	458	553	21	20
Great Blue Heron	3,166	3,806	20	20
Gray Jay	95	114	20	19
Prairie Warbler	731	875	20	19
Blackburnian Warbler	1,712	2,040	19	18
House Finch	2,871	3,421	19	18
Blue-gray Gnatcatcher	876	1,039	19	18
Tricolored Heron	11	13	18	18
Mallard x American Black Duck hybrid	73	86	18	17
Blue-winged Warbler	1,867	2,189	17	17
Sora	241	278	15	15
White-winged Crossbill	209	238	14	13
Northern Saw-whet Owl	129	146	13	13
Warbling Vireo	3,133	3,537	13	12
Golden-crowned Kinglet	973	1,095	13	12
Golden Eagle	8	9	13	12
Boreal Chickadee	123	138	12	12
Black-backed Woodpecker	114	127	11	11
Black-throated Blue Warbler	1,738	1,919	10	10
Chestnut-sided Warbler	3,634	3,993	10	9
Northern Mockingbird	1,490	1,635	10	9
American Coot	72	79	10	9
Ovenbird	4,041	4,411	9	9
Mourning Dove	4,402	4,803	9	8
Northern Cardinal	3,575	3,896	9	8
Eastern Phoebe	4,283	4,666	9	8
Hairy Woodpecker	3,768	4,095	9	8
Red-tailed Hawk	3,714	3,955	6	6
Swamp Sparrow	2,893	3,066	6	5
Brown Creeper	2,037	2,142	5	5
Marsh Wren	439	461	5	4
Mourning Warbler	1,398	1,460	4	4
Tree Swallow	4,650	4,852	4	4
Northern Waterthrush	1,134	1,183	4	4
American Woodcock	1,926	2,004	4	3
Tennessee Warbler	27	28	4	3
Black-billed Cuckoo	1,963	2,034	4	3

Species	No. of blocks with records in 1980–85	No. of blocks with records in 2000–05	Change (%)	Change adjusted for effort (%)
Yellow-billed Cuckoo	1,281	1,324	3	3
White-breasted Nuthatch	4,263	4,393	3	2
Red-eyed Vireo	4,984	5,128	3	2
Downy Woodpecker	4,562	4,683	3	2
American Redstart	4,289	4,389	2	2
Wilson's Snipe	969	991	2	2
Cedar Waxwing	4,915	5,025	2	2
Savannah Sparrow	3,005	3,070	2	2
American Goldfinch	4,912	5,003	2	1
Pine Siskin	413	419	1	1
Piping Plover	75	76	1	1
Black-capped Chickadee	5,149	5,205	1	1
Eastern Screech-Owl	1,125	1,137	1	1
American Robin	5,189	5,239	1	0
Black-crowned Night-Heron	211	213	1	0
Scarlet Tanager	4,299	4,338	1	0
Gadwall	114	115	1	0
Broad-winged Hawk	1,944	1,961	1	0
American Crow	4,958	5,001	1	0
Purple Finch	3,148	3,165	1	0
Blue Jay	5,154	5,177	0	0
Chipping Sparrow	4,870	4,891	0	0
Yellow Warbler	4,580	4,587	0	0
Canvasback	1	1	0	−1
Black Rail	1	1	0	−1
King Rail	5	5	0	−1
Summer Tanager	3	3	0	−1
Common Yellowthroat	5,175	5,169	0	−1
Song Sparrow	5,195	5,168	−1	−1
Northern Flicker	4,898	4,867	−1	−1
Black-and-white Warbler	2,775	2,756	−1	−1
Rock Pigeon	3,771	3,741	−1	−1
Common Tern	122	121	−1	−1
Indigo Bunting	4,264	4,227	−1	−1
Worm-eating Warbler	225	223	−1	−1
Northern Harrier	930	917	−1	−2
European Starling	4,622	4,551	−2	−2
Red-winged Blackbird	5,061	4,981	−2	−2
Common Grackle	5,023	4,932	−2	−2
Veery	4,265	4,159	−2	−3
House Wren	4,396	4,259	−3	−4
Great Crested Flycatcher	4,305	4,169	−3	−4
Baltimore Oriole	4,426	4,276	−3	−4
Clapper Rail	58	56	−3	−4
Gray Catbird	4,920	4,743	−4	−4
Least Flycatcher	3,818	3,671	−4	−4
Killdeer	3,939	3,780	−4	−5

Species	No. of blocks with records in 1980–85	No. of blocks with records in 2000–05	Change (%)	Change adjusted for effort (%)
Eastern Wood-Pewee	4,537	4,346	−4	−5
Little Blue Heron	19	18	−5	−6
Great Black-backed Gull	71	67	−6	−6
Belted Kingfisher	3,814	3,595	−6	−6
Barn Swallow	4,917	4,629	−6	−6
Rose-breasted Grosbeak	4,670	4,382	−6	−7
House Sparrow	4,197	3,935	−6	−7
Ruby-crowned Kinglet	187	175	−6	−7
Brown-headed Cowbird	4,519	4,209	−7	−7
White-eyed Vireo	174	162	−7	−7
Nashville Warbler	1,476	1,374	−7	−7
Yellow-throated Vireo	1,679	1,561	−7	−8
Wood Thrush	4,764	4,428	−7	−8
Lawrence's Warbler	42	39	−7	−8
Eastern Kingbird	4,805	4,460	−7	−8
Blackpoll Warbler	125	115	−8	−9
Bobolink	3,465	3,178	−8	−9
Brewster's Warbler	129	118	−9	−9
Least Bittern	142	129	−9	−10
American Bittern	534	478	−10	−11
Cliff Swallow	1,250	1,105	−12	−12
Eastern Towhee	3,758	3,313	−12	−12
Spotted Sandpiper	2,022	1,772	−12	−13
Cerulean Warbler	279	244	−13	−13
Herring Gull	269	235	−13	−13
Green Heron	2,544	2,213	−13	−13
Lincoln's Sparrow	277	240	−13	−14
American Kestrel	3,450	2,960	−14	−15
White-throated Sparrow	2,331	1,996	−14	−15
Chimney Swift	3,124	2,652	−15	−16
Saltmarsh Sharp-tailed Sparrow	72	61	−15	−16
Field Sparrow	3,891	3,273	−16	−16
Swainson's Thrush	704	589	−16	−17
Great Horned Owl	1,968	1,622	−18	−18
Ruffed Grouse	3,152	2,579	−18	−19
Ring-billed Gull	38	31	−18	−19
Glossy Ibis	47	38	−19	−20
Northern Goshawk	445	355	−20	−21
Louisiana Waterthrush	1,055	838	−21	−21
Least Tern	87	69	−21	−21
Cape May Warbler	18	14	−22	−23
Rusty Blackbird	151	117	−23	−23
Canada Warbler	1,684	1,299	−23	−23
Eastern Meadowlark	3,506	2,635	−25	−25
Seaside Sparrow	48	36	−25	−25
Northern Bobwhite	236	175	−26	−26
Spruce Grouse	27	20	−26	−26
Yellow-crowned Night-Heron	40	29	−28	−28

Species	No. of blocks with records in 1980–85	No. of blocks with records in 2000–05	Change (%)	Change adjusted for effort (%)
Bank Swallow	1,966	1,421	−28	−28
Brown Thrasher	3,341	2,337	−30	−30
American Three-toed Woodpecker	22	15	−32	−32
Black Skimmer	37	25	−32	−33
Lesser Scaup	3	2	−33	−34
Common Moorhen	288	192	−33	−34
Short-eared Owl	36	24	−33	−34
Wilson's Warbler	3	2	−33	−34
American Black Duck	1,102	728	−34	−34
Olive-sided Flycatcher	479	316	−34	−34
Horned Lark	1,105	698	−37	−37
Roseate Tern	19	12	−37	−37
Ring-necked Pheasant	1,699	1,069	−37	−37
Snowy Egret	94	58	−38	−39
Purple Martin	963	583	−39	−40
Black Tern	73	44	−40	−40
Long-eared Owl	81	48	−41	−41
Grasshopper Sparrow	822	477	−42	−42
Green-winged Teal	120	66	−45	−45
American Wigeon	42	22	−48	−48
Vesper Sparrow	1,116	564	−49	−50
Prothonotary Warbler	22	11	−50	−50
Golden-winged Warbler	577	270	−53	−53
Whip-poor-will	564	241	−57	−58
Chuck-will's-widow	21	8	−62	−62
Bay-breasted Warbler	32	12	−63	−63
Blue-winged Teal	460	170	−63	−63
Red Crossbill	234	84	−64	−64
Cattle Egret	20	7	−65	−65
Upland Sandpiper	476	165	−65	−66
Common Nighthawk	477	138	−71	−71
Northern Pintail	35	10	−71	−72
Kentucky Warbler	39	11	−72	−72
Red-headed Woodpecker	691	167	−76	−76
Barn Owl	126	28	−78	−78
Yellow-breasted Chat	122	27	−78	−78
Henslow's Sparrow	348	70	−80	−80
Gray Partridge	36	7	−81	−81
Laughing Gull	32	6	−81	−81
Loggerhead Shrike	24	4	−83	−83
Western Meadowlark	6	1	−83	−83
Greater Scaup	2	0	−100	−100
Bufflehead	2	0	−100	−100
White-faced Ibis	1	0	−100	−100
Black-hooded Parakeet	5	0	−100	−100
Brewer's Blackbird	1	0	−100	−100

Table 2.9 Species showing significant increases between the two Atlas periods, arranged from largest change to smallest

Species	No. of blocks with records in 1980–85	No. of blocks with records in 2000–05	Change (%)	Change adjusted for effort (%)
Merlin	0	131		
Black Vulture	0	100		
Trumpeter Swan	0	12		
Palm Warbler	1	43	4,200	4,176
Bald Eagle	35	445	1,171	1,164
Boat-tailed Grackle	4	38	850	845
Double-crested Cormorant	22	179	714	709
Peregrine Falcon	17	111	553	549
Common Raven	313	1,879	500	497
Carolina Wren	305	1,250	310	308
Canada Goose	1,058	3,968	275	273
Pine Warbler	348	1,113	220	218
Clay-colored Sparrow	23	69	200	198
Osprey	335	826	147	145
Cooper's Hawk	550	1,355	146	145
Hooded Warbler	421	1,035	146	144
Common Merganser	470	1,104	135	134
Wild Turkey	1,567	3,651	133	132
Red-bellied Woodpecker	978	2,182	123	122
Hooded Merganser	384	810	111	110
Ring-necked Duck	47	97	106	105
Tufted Titmouse	1,557	3,121	100	99
Mute Swan	218	407	87	86
Orchard Oriole	223	389	74	73
Turkey Vulture	2,147	3,675	71	70
Great Egret	65	111	71	70
Sharp-shinned Hawk	859	1,440	68	67
Eastern Bluebird	2,460	3,796	54	53
Fish Crow	210	324	54	53
Yellow-bellied Sapsucker	2,205	3,358	52	51
Northern Parula	342	515	51	50
Winter Wren	1,210	1,802	49	48
Acadian Flycatcher	162	239	48	47
Pied-billed Grebe	182	267	47	46
Alder Flycatcher	1,929	2,805	45	45
Wood Duck	1,923	2,789	45	44
Evening Grosbeak	250	360	44	43
Common Loon	369	528	43	42
Barred Owl	1,075	1,534	43	42
Yellow-bellied Flycatcher	192	273	42	41
Blue-headed Vireo	1,892	2,634	39	38
Red-breasted Nuthatch	1,690	2,306	36	36
Willow Flycatcher	1,932	2,619	36	35
Yellow-rumped Warbler	2,094	2,831	35	34
Hermit Thrush	2,088	2,730	31	30
Black-throated Green Warbler	2,375	3,055	29	28
Pileated Woodpecker	2,714	3,491	29	28

Species	No. of blocks with records in 1980–85	No. of blocks with records in 2000–05	Change (%)	Change adjusted for effort (%)
Mallard	3,175	4,029	27	26
Magnolia Warbler	1,682	2,119	26	25
Dark-eyed Junco	2,295	2,828	23	23
Red-shouldered Hawk	702	865	23	23
Northern Rough-winged Swallow	1,564	1,895	21	20
Ruby-throated Hummingbird	3,518	4,254	21	20
Great Blue Heron	3,166	3,806	20	20
Prairie Warbler	731	875	20	19
Blackburnian Warbler	1,712	2,040	19	18
House Finch	2,871	3,421	19	18
Blue-gray Gnatcatcher	876	1,039	19	18
Blue-winged Warbler	1,867	2,189	17	17
Warbling Vireo	3,133	3,537	13	12
Black-throated Blue Warbler	1,738	1,919	10	10
Chestnut-sided Warbler	3,634	3,993	10	9
Ovenbird	4,041	4,411	9	9
Mourning Dove	4,402	4,803	9	8
Northern Cardinal	3,575	3,896	9	8
Eastern Phoebe	4,283	4,666	9	8
Hairy Woodpecker	3,768	4,095	9	8
Red-tailed Hawk	3,714	3,955	6	6
Tree Swallow	4,650	4,852	4	4
Red-eyed Vireo	4,984	5,128	3	2

Table 2.10 Species showing significant decreases between the two Atlas periods, arranged from largest change to smallest

Species	No. of blocks with records in 1980–85	No. of blocks with records in 2000–05	Change (%)	Change adjusted for effort (%)
Loggerhead Shrike	24	4	−83	−83
Laughing Gull	32	6	−81	−81
Gray Partridge	36	7	−81	−81
Henslow's Sparrow	348	70	−80	−80
Yellow-breasted Chat	122	27	−78	−78
Barn Owl	126	28	−78	−78
Red-headed Woodpecker	691	167	−76	−76
Kentucky Warbler	39	11	−72	−72
Northern Pintail	35	10	−71	−72
Common Nighthawk	477	138	−71	−71
Upland Sandpiper	476	165	−65	−66
Red Crossbill	234	84	−64	−64
Blue-winged Teal	460	170	−63	−63
Whip-poor-will	564	241	−57	−58
Golden-winged Warbler	577	270	−53	−53
Vesper Sparrow	1,116	564	−49	−50
Green-winged Teal	120	66	−45	−45
Grasshopper Sparrow	822	477	−42	−42

Table 2.10 Species showing significant decreases between the two Atlas periods, arranged from largest change to smallest (continued)

Species	No. of blocks with records in 1980–85	No. of blocks with records in 2000–05	Change (%)	Change adjusted for effort (%)
Purple Martin	963	583	–39	–40
Ring-necked Pheasant	1,699	1,069	–37	–37
Horned Lark	1,105	698	–37	–37
Olive-sided Flycatcher	479	316	–34	–34
American Black Duck	1,102	728	–34	–34
Common Moorhen	288	192	–33	–34
Brown Thrasher	3,341	2,337	–30	–30
Bank Swallow	1,966	1,421	–28	–28
Eastern Meadowlark	3,506	2,635	–25	–25
Canada Warbler	1,684	1,299	–23	–23
Louisiana Waterthrush	1,055	838	–21	–21
Northern Goshawk	445	355	–20	–21
Ruffed Grouse	3,152	2,579	–18	–19
Great Horned Owl	1,968	1,622	–18	–18
Swainson's Thrush	704	589	–16	–17
Field Sparrow	3,891	3,273	–16	–16
Chimney Swift	3,124	2,652	–15	–16
White-throated Sparrow	2,331	1,996	–14	–15
American Kestrel	3,450	2,960	–14	–15
Green Heron	2,544	2,213	–13	–13
Spotted Sandpiper	2,022	1,772	–12	–13
Eastern Towhee	3,758	3,313	–12	–12
Cliff Swallow	1,250	1,105	–12	–12
Bobolink	3,465	3,178	–8	–9
Eastern Kingbird	4,805	4,460	–7	–8
Wood Thrush	4,764	4,428	–7	–8
Brown-headed Cowbird	4,519	4,209	–7	–7
House Sparrow	4,197	3,935	–6	–7
Rose-breasted Grosbeak	4,670	4,382	–6	–7
Barn Swallow	4,917	4,629	–6	–6
Belted Kingfisher	3,814	3,595	–6	–6
Eastern Wood-Pewee	4,537	4,346	–4	–5
Killdeer	3,939	3,780	–4	–5
Least Flycatcher	3,818	3,671	–4	–4
Gray Catbird	4,920	4,743	–4	–4
Baltimore Oriole	4,426	4,276	–3	–4
Great Crested Flycatcher	4,305	4,169	–3	–4
House Wren	4,396	4,259	–3	–4
Common Grackle	5,023	4,932	–2	–2
Red-winged Blackbird	5,061	4,981	–2	–2

showed significant changes in breeding distribution. Of those, 55 percent had an increase. That the number of species with increased distributions was larger than the number of those with decreased distributions may be a surprise to some people, especially as the general consensus is that global biodiversity is declining at its fastest rate in human history (Millennium Ecosystem Assessment 2005). But changes in diversity can differ at differing spatial scales. Even though global diversity may be declining, increases can be seen at local scales, and in fact, local increases in species richness are common (Sax and Gaines 2003). Data from the second breeding bird atlas conducted in the Netherlands also showed an increase in species richness (Van Turnhout et al. 2007), as was true with the second atlas survey performed in the autonomous community of Catalonia in Spain (Estrada et al. 2004). Both of these European atlases reported increases in the populations of widespread species but the loss of "specialty" species restricted to unusual habitats, something not apparent in New York. Within North America, a recent study using Breeding Bird Survey and Christmas Bird Count data performed by the National Audubon Society found that two-thirds of the species with significant changes in numbers increased and one third declined (Butcher and Niven 2007), indicating that this trend of increasing species richness is not a phenomenon restricted to New York.

The concept of grouping species based on shared environmental requirements, such as breeding habitat and migratory status, can be useful for assessing the potential effects of large-scale environmental change on bird distributions. For example, a decline in the distribution of a single grassland species (e.g., Grasshopper Sparrow) is alarming and may require species-specific management recommendations, but the declining distributions of an entire assemblage of grassland species suggests that larger, more regional approaches to conservation might be necessary. Atlases represent an excellent source of data for detecting changes in entire groups of birds. In addition, the analysis of data on groups of species, rather than individual species, lessens the inherent biases of atlas surveys (e.g., detection problems, changes in effort, and so forth).

To quantify changes in entire groups of birds, we classified 236 species based on their breeding habitat requirements and migratory behavior. We assigned a breeding habitat guild and migratory status to each species based on BBS guild classifications groups (Sauer et al. 1999) and the classification of De-Graaf and Yamasaki (2001). Breeding habitat guild classifications included woodland, scrub-successional, generalist, grassland, wetland–open water, and urban species. Migratory status classifications included resident, short-distance migrant, and long-distance (Neotropical) migrant species.

Of all six breeding habitat groups, only woodland birds demonstrated a significant increase in their average distribution between the two Atlas periods (Wilcoxon Test: $P < 0.001$) while grassland birds showed the only significant decrease (Wilcoxon Test: $P = 0.002$) (Figure 2.7). Scrub-successional, wetland, and urban species showed no significant change in their distribution between the two Atlas periods. Within migratory groups, we found significant increases in the overall distribution of permanent residents (Wilcoxon Test: $P = 0.02$) and short-distance migrants (Wilcoxon Test: $P = 0.02$) (Figure 2.8). Neotropical migrants showed no significant change. These trends suggest that certain regional factors of environmental change may be affecting entire groups of species.

New York State represents a shifting mosaic of habitat types being driven by a 50-year decline in agricultural land area and farmland abandonment (see Chapter 4). Although the rates of reforestation have apparently stabilized over the past 20 years, there can be little doubt that the 20th century witnessed widespread rates of reforestation throughout the northeastern United States. As a group, forest-breeding birds in New York State may be responding to this long-term change in regional habitat availability. Although further research is required, the regeneration of forest on abandoned farmland offers the most logical explanation for the distributional changes being seen in woodland and grassland birds in New York (Askins 1993, Confer and Pascoe 2003, Dettmers 2003). Interestingly, other regions throughout the world have documented this pattern of increasing woodland species and declining grassland or heathland species (Chamberlain and Fuller 2001, Van Turnhout et al. 2007), although the exact causes of these changes are undoubtedly different (e.g., shifting agricultural practices in Britain). Declines in the populations of grassland birds in North America are well known, and the group is frequently cited as of great conservation concern (e.g., Rich et al. 2004, Askins et al. 2007). Chapter 6 discusses in more detail the changes in communities of birds of conservation importance.

It is tempting to ascribe all changes in bird distribution to corresponding changes in habitat availability. As the primeval forests were cut down by European settlers in the 18th and 19th centuries and replaced with farmlands (see Chapter 4), populations of forest birds decreased and those of grassland birds increased. As agriculture was abandoned and farmland reverted to shrubland and then to forest, the grassland birds disappeared and the shrub and forest birds returned. The stories of the history of some of these species in New York are compelling and obvious (see, e.g., the Northern Bobwhite, Pileated Woodpecker, and Horned Lark species accounts), but other changes are not so readily explained. Over many years, patterns emerge, but within the limited time frame of the two Atlas studies, simple explanations for many patterns are difficult to offer. That significant change took place in bird populations in New York during that time is unmistakable. Assigning causation for each story, however, is difficult. The Common Raven is an example. A bird primarily of forests, it became nearly extirpated in New York at the peak of deforestation at the beginning of the 20th century. It has shown a remarkable comeback, being detected in 1,879 blocks (35 percent of all blocks) during this latest Atlas period. Its recovery might be ascribed to the return of forests (accounting for

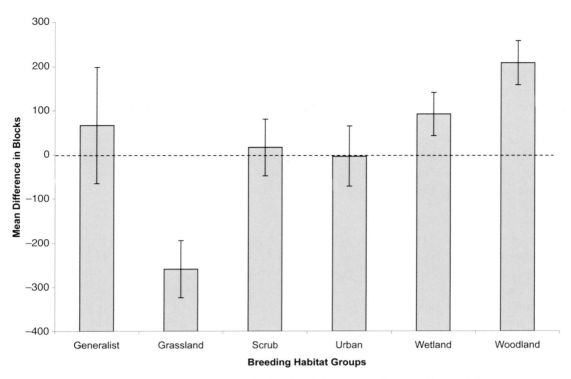

Figure 2.7 Changes in occurrence for breeding habitat groups between the two Atlases.
Bars represent means ± standard error.

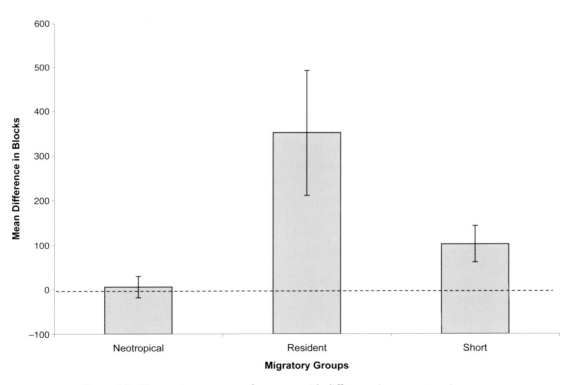

Figure 2.8 Changes in occurrence for groups with different migratory strategies.
Bars represent means ± standard error.

14 percent of land cover in 1900 and 65 percent in 2000, see Chapter 4). However, during the first Atlas project the raven was found in only 313 blocks (6 percent). The 500 percent increase was not matched by an equivalent increase in forest cover. In fact, forest cover does not appear to have increased at all during the time between the two Atlas projects (see Chapter 4), so some other explanation must be sought. Certainly the explosion of Palm Warbler across the bogs in the Adirondacks has nothing to do with changes in habitat availability. Changes in behavior (e.g., increasing tolerance of humans) and larger patterns of population increase and spread are the more likely explanations in these and some other cases.

Differing amounts of change between groups of birds using different migratory stategies may be suggestive of another regional process occurring in the Northeast: climate change. There are few studies documenting the effects that global climate change has on the structure of avian communities, but one might expect warmer winters to lead to declining distributions of long-distance migrants if resident birds benefit from warmer winters and impose increasing competitive pressure on migrants (O'Connor 1990, Lemoine and Böhning-Gaese 2003, Böhning-Gaese and Lemoine 2006). The results of several atlas-based studies in Europe suggest that such shifts are beginning to take place (Lemoine et al. 2007a, b). Could an increasing population of resident birds be a sign of warming winter temperatures in New York and eventually lead to declines in other migrant species? Further research is needed to address this question, but Atlas data and these emerging trends have uncovered several promising avenues for future research.

Atlas Data as a Tool for Monitoring Population Change

Given the significant changes in distributions found between the two Atlas periods, one might ask whether these statewide changes parallel local changes in abundance, and if so, what role do atlases have in monitoring avian population change. This specific question relates to a general theory in macroecology referred to as the abundance-occupancy rule. This rule predicts a positive relationship, both within and among species, between local abundance and regional occupancy, such that distributional changes should be highly correlated with changes in abundance and population size (see review by Gaston et al. 2000). That is, if the population of one species grows and that species becomes more abundant, it would be expected to expand its range too. The abundance-occupancy rule has important implications in wildlife inventorying and monitoring because occupancy data, such as atlas data, are increasingly important for documenting the response of wildlife populations to large-scale threats, such as global climate change and shifting land-use practices. To address this question and test this theory, Zuckerberg (2008) compared New York Atlas results with another avian database that collects

abundance estimates, the North American Breeding Bird Survey (BBS). The BBS is an annual survey providing information on the presence and relative abundance of bird species at state and regional scales (Sauer et al. 2005). Within New York State, there are approximately 198 roadside surveys, each covering 39.4 km (25 mi) (although not every route is surveyed every year). Not all bird species are adequately sampled by roadside surveys, however, and Zuckerberg (2008) limited his analyses to only those species that were detected on more than 14 routes or that had a regional abundance greater than 0.1 bird/route (credibility measures suggested by the BBS).

If Atlas data were closely related to relative abundance (as measured by the BBS), one would expect to find 1) a positive relationship between abundance and distribution in the two separate time periods (1980–85 and 2000–05), 2) a positive relationship between Atlas-documented changes and abundance over the 20-year period, and 3) a consistency in these patterns between breeding habitat and migratory groups. Zuckerberg (2008) found that statewide distributions were indeed significantly positively correlated with relative abundance for 98 and 85 species in the two separate time periods of 1980–85 and 2000–05, respectively. That is, species that were widely distributed in New York tended to be species of high relative abundance, and species with more localized distributions were of low relative abundance. This relationship proved stable over time and was notably consistent between breeding habitat groups, migratory groups, and species of differing phylogenetic origins. Between 1980 and 2005, changes in distribution between the two Atlas periods were highly correlated with long-term abundance trend estimates provided by the BBS for 75 species ($r^2 = 0.88$). For the majority of species in this analysis, changes in their distribution paralleled changes in their relative abundance over the same time period.

Changes in Atlas distributions and abundance data indicate population changes at two different resolutions, and as a consequence, for some species the results may differ. Regression analysis suggests that an abundance trend estimate of 1 percent per year resulted in an average distributional change of 6 percent. Consequently, Atlas data are less likely to detect small fluctuations in population size than are abundance data (Bart and Klosiewski 1989). In addition, 22 of the 24 species showing a lack of concurrence between Atlas and abundance changes showed a negative trend in abundance and an increase in distribution. For example, the Black-throated Blue Warbler showed an increase in its distribution of 10.4 percent but a declining abundance trend of −2.48 percent per year over the same time period. In general, these negative abundance trends were slight and ranged from −0.2 to −2.5 percent per year. This result may suggest a nonlinear relationship where changes in abundance are not reflected in Atlas data until a threshold point is reached or until enough time has lapsed for Atlas data to reflect changes in local abundance. As noted earlier, woodland and resident birds showed the greatest increases in their distributions while grassland species showed the greatest decline; these patterns were mirrored by changes in local abundance. These findings suggest that although exceptions did exist, most changes in occupancy were paralleled by changes in local abundance.

Atlases offer an important tool for setting conservation goals and monitoring animal populations and are a critical supplement to collecting more intensive abundance data for answering questions about population change. Considering the close association between statewide changes and local abundance, Atlas-detected changes are critical for identifying those species that may be facing a troubling scenario of "double jeopardy" in which a species is becoming increasingly rare at both regional and local scales (Lawton 1996, Gaston 1998). Although Atlas data are not a substitute for more intensive surveys of populations, the concurrence of Atlas changes with changes in local abundance provides further support for the use of Atlas data in monitoring avian population changes in New York State.

Hints of Poleward Shifts in Species Distributions within New York State?

An emerging consensus is that species distributions are beginning to move polewards in response to climate change (Parmesan and Yohe 2003, Walther et al. 2005, Thomas et al. 2006). In support of this consensus, researchers have used atlases for measuring the possible response of species to climate change (Thomas and Lennon 1999, Brommer 2004, Shoo et al. 2006). Given its geographic position and trends in regional warming, New York State represents a likely area for distributional shifts in response to climate change. In fact, climate change has been offered as a potential reason for the expanding ranges of several species in New York (e.g., Carolina Wren, Red-bellied Woodpecker, and Tufted Titmouse). If southerly species are expanding their ranges to the north, one could predict that their breeding range in New York would be expanding and should show large and significant increases between the two Atlas periods. Similarly, if northerly species are being forced northward by a warming environment, then those species reaching the southern limit of their breeding range in New York should have decreased distributions. Of the 128 species showing significant changes in distribution (Tables 2.9, 2.10), 26 could be considered northerly species near the southern edge of their range, and 35 considered southerly species near the northern edge of their range. Of the 26 northerly species, 17 had increasing distributions and 9 decreasing distributions. Of the 35 southerly species, 20 had increasing distributions and 15 decreasing distributions. Neither of these is significantly different from the 33:34 increase-decrease ratio of the species more in the middle of their range (Fisher Exact $P = 0.361$). Of course a more refined analysis is needed, given that overall distributional changes may be masking latitudinal shifts in species' range boundaries within New York.

Thomas and Lennon (1999) were the first to propose a methodology of analyzing atlas data for documenting range shifts in response to climate change. Their method emphasized latitudinal shifts in range boundaries for northerly and southerly species while controlling for changes in overall distribution. They hypothesized that increases in distribution would cause southerly species to move northward at their northernmost range boundary and northerly species to move southward at their southernmost range boundary. Alternatively, a decline in distribution would result in a retraction southward of the northern boundary for southerly species and a northward shift of the southern boundary for northerly species. A regression of the change in overall distribution against the change in range boundaries would produce an $X = 0$ intercept value, which if positive, suggests that the range boundaries of these species are moving northward, even when there is no change in their overall distribution. Using this method on Britain's two bird atlases, Thomas and Lennon (1999) found that the northern range margin of southerly species shifted northward by 18.9 km over 20 years, but found no shift for northerly species. Using the same methodology, an analysis of Finland's two atlases produced similar results (Brommer 2004). Hitch and Leberg (2007) also found similar patterns for North American birds but were not able to control for changes in overall distribution because they used BBS data.

If the same approach is employed, do the New York Atlas data support this repeating pattern? Following Thomas and Lennon (1999), Zuckerberg (2008) used the same approach on the Atlas data for New York State. After excluding coastal breeding, ubiquitous, rare, and game species, he classified birds as southerly or northerly based on their average latitudinal position in the first Atlas. He identified 59 southerly and 71 northerly species. For southerly species, he calculated the northern range boundary in each Atlas as the median latitude of the 10 most northerly blocks. For northerly species, he calculated the southern range boundary in each Atlas as the median latitude of the 10 most southerly blocks. The change in range margins of bird species was regressed against changes in distribution. For southerly species, the $X = 0$ intercept was positive and indicated a marginally significant northward shift of 11.5 km ($P = 0.06$). Overall, 27 percent of southerly species showed a significant shift northward in their range boundaries while 20 percent showed a shift southward. For northerly species, the $X = 0$ intercept for northerly species showed a significant shift northward of 7.61 km ($P = 0.02$). Of these northerly species, 30 percent demonstrated a significant shift northward in their range boundaries while 18 percent demonstrated a shift southward. These findings support the general patterns found in other studies and geographic regions, that species distributions are showing signs of a northward shift.

There are a number of reasons to be cautious when interpreting these findings. First, the examination of the effects of climate change on bird distributions in New York is complicated by the geography of the state. The boreal Adirondacks are surrounded on all sides by the more temperate St. Lawrence, Champlain, Hudson, and Mohawk valleys. The higher-elevation Appalachian Plateau is bordered on the north by the warmer

Great Lakes Plain and Mohawk Valley. Consequently, strictly north-south changes in distribution would not necessarily reflect the underlying assumption of expansion of breeding range into formerly less temperate areas. Although changes in temperature may not strike a strict north-south gradient within New York State, birds are likely responding to climate changes occurring throughout the Northern Hemisphere (IPCC 2007). A second confounding factor to simple interpretations is that several regions have experienced changes in effort in the two Atlas projects. A decline or increase in effort (e.g., Champlain Valley: + 62 percent; Coastal Lowlands: −33 percent) may affect the delineation of range boundaries for both northerly and southerly species. Third, New York State represents a partial range analysis. Few of the species included in the study reach the limits of their distribution in New York State. Lastly, the causal effects of climate change on avian distributions are difficult to establish and any conclusions are inferential at best. This limitation is common to many large-scale analyses, however, and understanding the effects of climate change on species distributions relies on systematic trends across diverse species, geographic regions, and scales of study rather than the conclusions of any individual study (Parmesan and Yohe 2003). These findings are more convincing when placed in the context of other studies that have found similar patterns, and highlight the need for future research in analyzing bird distributional changes in New York.

The data from the two New York Atlas projects present the opportunity to ask many other such questions. It is hoped that more people will take advantage of the availability of such a rare resource and search for answers to many more questions that will increase our understanding of the dynamics of bird distribution. The third Atlas project, to be conducted in 20 more years, will undoubtedly provide even more opportunity and make these data even more valuable. We look forward to seeing that come to pass.

CHAPTER THREE

Habitats of New York State

GREGORY J. EDINGER AND TIMOTHY G. HOWARD

New York State's landscape is wonderfully variable. Differences in natural and cultural factors such as land forms and topography, geology, climate, vegetation, and land use contribute to this variety. To understand the patterns of distribution and diversity found throughout the state, and to interpret any changes occurring over time, it is important to use specific and consistent terminology to describe the landscape.

Several landscape classifications are used in New York; one divides the landscape into ecoregions (Figure 1.13) and another into ecozones (Figure 1.14). A third classification, Bird Conservation Regions (Figure 1.15), groups ecologically similar areas for the purpose of bird conservation. The origins and descriptions of all are presented here, along with a description of the ecological communities found in the state.

Ecoregions of New York

In the 1980s and 1990s the Forest Service in the U.S. Department of Agriculture (USDA) developed a framework for classifying and mapping the Earth's landscape, beginning at very broad scales and further dividing each unit into sections with increasingly similar ecological conditions (Bailey 1980, 1995; Cleland at al. 1997). From a statewide perspective, the most useful levels in the hierarchy are perhaps the ecoregional section and subsection. Many environmental factors are used to distinguish among ecoregional sections (often simply called ecoregions) and their subsections, including landform, climate, hydrology, geology, soils, and potential natural vegetation (Keys et al. 1995). These boundaries cross state lines, and because of the consistent way in which they were developed, comparisons among ecoregions or subsections can be made nationwide. The Nature Conservancy (TNC) quickly recognized their value and importance and adopted the ecoregional boundaries for use in its conservation planning efforts (The Nature Conservancy 2000). The seven ecoregions found within New York and their subsections are described below.

The ecoregional map in Figure 1.13 shows the version developed by TNC after Bailey (1980). The descriptions below draw from Keys et al. (1995); Bailey (1980, 1995); Omernik (1987); and the U.S. Environmental Protection Agency (EPA), USDA Forest Service, and TNC web sites. There are seven TNC ecoregions and 34 ecoregion subsections in New York. Subsection

codes (in parentheses) follow the Forest Service's hierarchical classification system.

1) Western Allegheny Plateau (WAP) ecoregion has a glaciated and unglaciated portion. Located in the southwestern-most end of the state, the unglaciated portion is hilly and home to the Allegheny Mountains. The glaciated portion is characterized by low, rounded hills and wetlands. The New York portion includes the following ecoregion subsection:

- Allegheny Plateau (221Fa)

2) High Allegheny Plateau (HAP) ecoregion is defined by a broad series of high-elevation hills that form a plateau rising to 518–640 m (1,700–2,100 ft), extending in the north from the Great Lakes Plain of Lake Ontario to the ridge and valley region of the Central Appalachians to the south, and from the Lake Erie Plain in the west to the Hudson River Valley. The New York portion includes the following ecoregion subsections:

- Catskill Mountains (212Ea)
- Catskill Highlands (212Eb)
- Cattaraugus Highlands (212Fa)
- Central Allegheny plateau (212Fb)
- Eastern Allegheny Plateau (212Fc)
- Allegheny High Plateau (212Ga)
- Kittatinny–Shawangunk Ridges (221Bd)

3) Great Lakes (GL) ecoregion was recently formed during the last glacial advance 14,000 years ago and is characterized by gently rolling, low-level landscapes and flat lake plains. The region's climate is influenced by the Great Lakes and has an astonishingly high level of biodiversity and unique habitats. The New York portion includes the following ecoregion subsections:

- Lake Erie Plain (222Ia)
- Erie–Ontario Lake Plain (222Ib)
- Eastern Ontario Till Plain (222Ic)
- Cattaraugus Finger Lakes Moraine and Hills (222Id)
- Eastern Ontario Lake Plain (222Ie)
- Mohawk Valley (222Oa)

4) Northern Appalachian–Boreal Forest (NAP-BF) ecoregion covers a large portion of northern New York, including most of the Adirondacks and Tug Hill Plateau. The region is defined by matrix forest communities and several large-scale wetland and remote pond complexes. The New York portion includes the following ecoregion subsections:

- Adirondack Hills and Flats (212Da)
- Western Adirondack Foothills (212Db)
- Adirondack Highlands and Lakes (212Dc)
- Central Adirondack Mountains (212Dd)
- Eastern Adirondack Low Mountains (212De)
- Adirondack Peaks (212Df)
- Tug Hill Plateau (212Fa)
- Tug Hill Transition (212Fb)

5) St. Lawrence–Champlain Valley (STL-LC) ecoregion is characterized by mountain streams and deltas and marshes that line the shores of the St. Lawrence River and Lake Champlain. The New York portion includes the following ecoregion subsections:

- St. Lawrence Glacial Marine Plain (212Ea)
- St. Lawrence Till Plain (212Eb)
- Champlain Glacial Lake and Marine Plains (212Ec)
- St. Lawrence Glacial Lake Plain (212Ee)
- Black River Valley (222Ob)

6) Lower New England–Northern Piedmont (LNE-NP) ecoregion lies along the mid to southeastern portion of New York. The limestone valley is defined by low mountains and lakes throughout. The New York portion includes the following ecoregion subsections:

- Hudson Highlands (221Ae)
- Hudson Limestone Valley (221Ba)
- Taconic Foothills (221Bb)
- Hudson Glacial Lake Plains (221Bc)
- Taconic Mountains (212Cb)
- Newark Piedmont (221Dc)

7) North Atlantic Coast (NAC) ecoregion includes marine, estuarine, and coastal components. The region that covers Long Island and Staten Island is characterized by grasslands, shrublands, vast pine barrens, coastal plain ponds and dunes, and extensive salt marshes. The New York portion includes the following ecoregion subsection:

- Long Island Coastal Lowland and Moraine (232Aa)

Ecozones of New York

During the early stages of ecoregional development, researchers at the New York State Department of Environmental Conservation (NYSDEC) mapped the physiographic zones in New York through two efforts: southern and western New York (Dickinson 1979, 1983), and northern New York (Will et al. 1982). Joining the results of these separate works, as done by NYSDEC, provides an excellent overview of the physiography of New York State.

As in the classification of ecoregions, the goal of delineating these ecozones was to depict on a map areas of similar environ-

mental or ecological conditions. With a focus devoted solely to New York State, however, ecozones tend to show slightly finer distinctions than ecoregions. Some ecozones can be considered subzones of major zones, and others as transitions relating to forest and nonforest cover between zones.

The 13 ecozones and their subsections are described below. These ecozones were described in the first Atlas as well and are the primary areas of description used in the accounts in this book. For this Atlas, the organization of the ecozones and sub-ecozones has been modified from earlier treatments; areas have been recalculated, and cover type (e.g., amount of forests, agriculture) percentages were updated using the 2001 National Land Cover Data Set (Homer et al. 2004). A full breakdown, by ecozone, of the area occupied by each cover type is given in Table 3.1. This table provides perspective on the patterns of land use throughout the state and a starting point for investigating land-use change over time. More detailed discussions of physical and cultural features can be found in Dickinson (1979, 1983) and Will et al. (1982), from which these modified ecozone and sub-ecozone descriptions were derived.

(A) Appalachian Plateau

Covering 43,613 sq km (16,839 sq mi), the Appalachian Plateau ecozone is mainly hill country with deeply dissected valleys, but it retains a plateau aspect with more or less flat-topped hills and with a skyline about 610 m (2,000 ft). Elevation ranges from 152 m (500 ft) near the Hudson Valley to over 1,219 m (4,000 ft) in the Catskills. Water erosion largely determined the topography, with glaciers later modifying it. Escarpments exist in some places. Most of the plateau has cold, snowy winters and cool, wet summers. Northern hardwoods cover much of the zone, with oaks abundant especially on south-facing slopes. Beech, sugar maple, basswood, white ash, and black cherry predominate; red oak is the most frequent where oaks occur. Hemlock and white pine are also found, along with many plantations of spruce and pine.

The following sub-ecozones are found within the Appalachian Plateau:

Cattaraugus Highlands

With the exception of the valleys along the boundary with the Great Lakes Plain, the Cattaraugus Highlands sub-ecozone ranges in elevation from 305 to 549 m (1,000–1,800 ft), with a few altitudes in the southeast exceeding 610 m (2,000 ft). Covering 6,407 sq km (2,474 sq mi), and about 47 percent wooded, northern hardwoods predominate, with oaks frequently found on the south slopes. Deep valleys dissect the rather flat-topped uplands. Agricultural activity occupies about 38 percent of the land and is primarily dairying.

Allegany Hills

The Allegany Hills sub-ecozone is 81 percent forested, with northern hardwoods covering the ridges and with more oaks on the south slopes than farther to the north. Allegany State Park covers much of this area, which totals 1,991 sq km (767 sq mi). Altitudes range from 427 m to above 732 m (1,400 to above 2,400 ft). It contains one of the very few areas in the state that was not glaciated. Less land is in agriculture here than in the sub-ecozones to the north and west.

Central Appalachians

Most of the Central Appalachians, the largest sub-ecozone, lies at elevations above 457 m (1,500 ft) and has a few heights reaching 701 m (2,300 ft) and more. It encompasses 23,123 sq km (8,928 sq mi). The economy is dominated by several large urban industrial areas. Overall, the land is 58 percent forested with mixtures of hardwoods, hemlocks in the ravines, and oaks on the south slopes. Agriculture is predominant in areas outside of urban communities, with much of the woodland on farms.

Finger Lakes Highlands

The Finger Lakes Highlands sub-ecozone possesses relatively level uplands dissected by deep valleys. It extends over about 2,864 sq km (1,106 sq mi). Oak forests are most widespread, but there are sections of pure northern hardwoods, hemlock–northern hardwoods, and white pine. About 32 percent wooded, this sub-ecozone has agricultural activity of several kinds on the hills, slopes, and in the valleys. At 46 percent, this sub-ecozone is second in the amount of the landscape devoted to agriculture. Except for the deeper valleys, elevations range generally from 305 to 518 m (1,000–1,700 ft), with a few points over 610 m (2,000 ft).

Helderberg Highlands

Flat hilltops intermixed with steep valleys occur throughout the Helderberg Highlands, a rather small sub-ecozone of about 1,344 sq km (519 sq mi). About 63 percent of the land is forested, which in many places follows the steep, shallow-soil valleys; higher lands are often in fields or shrubs. Oak and pine are found on the slopes, with mixtures of northern hardwoods elsewhere. Dairy farming is common. Elevations in the sub-ecozone, except for the lower east edge bordering the Hudson Valley, range from 274 to 488 m (900–1,600 ft), although there are a few higher peaks, including one near 640 m (2,100 ft).

Neversink Highlands

The Neversink Highlands sub-ecozone contains numerous well-known Catskills resorts. Overall, the sub-ecozone is 74 percent wooded, primarily with northern hardwoods, black cherry, and ash, but with hemlock and white pine in the ravines. Some farming contributes to the economy. The area covers about 1,638 sq km (632 sq mi), with altitudes starting at 183 m (600 ft). Most of the highlands are over 366 m (1,200 ft); maximum local heights range from 457 to 610 m (1,500–2,000 ft), and a few peaks exceed this. Relief is low compared with sub-ecozones to the north.

Mongaup Hills

Relief in the Mongaup Hills sub-ecozone, an area of 957 sq km (369 sq mi), is quite low except in the steep southern ravines. Minimum altitude is 183 m (600 ft), but most of the area is above 305 m (1,000 ft), with a few heights reaching 488 m (1,600 ft). The area is 89 percent wooded, with mixtures of oak and red maple on the original oak–chestnut sites and with hemlock and white pine in pure stands or in mixture with hardwoods. Isolated by mountains and the Delaware Valley, and with poor soil conditions precluding extensive agricultural activities, this sub-ecozone has large amounts of land that are held for recreational purposes.

Schoharie Hills

The Schoharie Hills sub-ecozone, covering 1,954 sq km (754 sq mi), is characterized by rolling uplands cut by deep ravines. The area is 79 percent wooded by oak, pine, hemlock, and northern hardwoods. Minimum altitude is 274 m (900 ft), most elevations are above 610 m (2,000 ft), and some peaks reach 1,219 m (4,000 ft). Dairy farming is the principal activity in the area. This sub-ecozone is sometimes combined with the next two (Delaware Hills and Catskill Peaks) into the Catskill Highlands.

Delaware Hills

Extensive, solid blocks of woodlands characterize the Delaware Hills, a sub-ecozone of about 1,742 sq km (673 sq mi). Forests are mainly young, even-aged hardwoods of sugar maple, white ash, black cherry, and basswood, often with hemlock, and cover about 88 percent of the landscape. Dairying predominates. Elevations are quite variable, ranging from a minimum of 274 m (900 ft) to some peak elevations up to 914 m (3,000 ft).

Catskill Peaks

The Catskill Peaks sub-ecozone is a rugged area of 1,594 sq km (615 sq mi) dominated by erosion-resistant sandstones and few valleys and streams. It is about 96 percent forested (the highest percentage statewide), mainly with northern hardwoods and some spruce and fir. Recreation and forestry are prominent, along with some farming. In the eastern portion along the Hudson Valley zone, altitudes begin at about 152 m (500 ft). In the western part of this sub-ecozone, however, elevations are generally over 610 m (2,000 ft), with many peaks topping 914 m (3,000 ft), the highest being 1,280 m (4,200 ft). Climate is generally cool and winters severe.

(B) Great Lakes Plain

The Great Lakes Plain, covering approximately 19,760 sq km (7,629 sq mi), is a low terrain ecozone with horizontal rock formations. It is essentially a flat plain having little local relief, with the exception of the drumlin area between Rochester and Syracuse. The plain has a simple erosional topography of glacial till, modified by moraines, shoreline deposits, and drumlins. The

Table 3.1 The area occupied by land cover classes★ for the entire state and each ecozone or sub-ecozone, in hectares with percentages in parentheses

	Open Water†	Developed, Open Space	Developed, Low Intensity	Developed, Medium Intensity	Developed, High Intensity	Barren Land	Deciduous Forest
Entire state†	359,277.7 (2.9)	613,683.8 (4.9)	285,759.6 (2.3)	155,285.2 (1.2)	74,940.5 (0.6)	23,466.2 (0.2)	4,626,165.3 (36.9)
Adirondack High Peaks	2,997.9 (1.7)	2,584.4 (1.5)	413.1 (0.2)	58.8 (0)	13.4 (0)	221.0 (0.1)	59,485.4 (33.9)
Allegany Hills	1,946.4 (1)	5,173.8 (2.6)	1,385.6 (0.7)	536.4 (0.3)	82.9 (0)	699.7 (0.4)	144,082.2 (72.4)
Black River Valley	2,062.1 (1.5)	4,170.1 (3)	1,616.9 (1.2)	487.2 (0.4)	182.3 (0.1)	160.3 (0.1)	30,124.9 (21.8)
Catskill Peaks	329.6 (0.2)	2,174.4 (1.4)	224.9 (0.1)	36.4 (0)	8.6 (0)	2.3 (0)	125,697.2 (78.9)
Cattaraugus Highlands	8,049.2 (1.3)	25,902.0 (4)	4,994.8 (0.8)	1,261.0 (0.2)	240.1 (0)	447.7 (0.1)	242,442.9 (37.8)
Central Adirondacks	56,701.5 (6)	8,083.2 (0.9)	960.8 (0.1)	229.2 (0)	42.0 (0)	911.1 (0.1)	488,269.3 (51.7)
Central Appalachians	20,982.1 (0.9)	88,184.2 (3.8)	20,365.3 (0.9)	6,429.2 (0.3)	1,534.0 (0.1)	1,819.1 (0.1)	927,071.5 (40.1)
Central Hudson	21,596.0 (3)	71,255.3 (9.9)	38,055.2 (5.3)	19,694.1 (2.7)	7,401.6 (1)	1,567.7 (0.2)	175,042.2 (24.3)
Central Tug Hill	1,679.3 (1.8)	102.7 (0.1)	4.1 (0)	0 (0)	0 (0)	6.8 (0)	60,353.5 (65.9)
Champlain Transition‡	725.8 (0.6)	3,647.7 (3.2)	1,385.4 (1.2)	288.3 (0.3)	80.9 (0.1)	37.1 (0)	41,629.5 (36.1)
Champlain Valley	1,144.7 (1.5)	4,935.6 (6.5)	3,447.4 (4.6)	1,309.8 (1.7)	410.0 (0.5)	94.8 (0.1)	16,616.7 (22)
Coastal Lowlands‡	5,096.2 (1.4)	70,899.0 (19.3)	66,806.5 (18.2)	64,233.6 (17.5)	36,704.2 (10)	5,811.8 (1.6)	42,957.5 (11.7)
Delaware Hills	3,397.0 (2)	3,921.3 (2.3)	664.7 (0.4)	119.5 (0.1)	22.1 (0)	988.2 (0.6)	125,128.8 (71.8)
Drumlin	4,627.4 (1.6)	16,444.0 (5.8)	4,499.1 (1.6)	1,382.0 (0.5)	434.8 (0.2)	332.1 (0.1)	53,139.9 (18.7)
Eastern Adirondack Foothills	24,087.6 (7)	10,664.1 (3.1)	2,975.0 (0.9)	604.9 (0.2)	121.5 (0)	436.0 (0.1)	108,617.6 (31.5)
Eastern Adirondack Transition	9,676.9 (10.2)	6,601.7 (6.9)	2,890.8 (3)	702.1 (0.7)	238.0 (0.3)	875.3 (0.9)	13,196.7 (13.9)
Eastern Ontario Plain	4,666.0 (1.9)	8,510.5 (3.5)	6,162.2 (2.5)	1,778.0 (0.7)	568.8 (0.2)	333.1 (0.1)	54,203.8 (22.4)
Erie-Ontario Plain‡	71,883.2 (5.2)	109,153.0 (7.9)	77,669.6 (5.6)	30,153.9 (2.2)	13,280.2 (1)	4,829.9 (0.4)	236,136.7 (17.2)
Finger Lakes Highlands	11,238.8 (3.9)	12,842.6 (4.5)	2,792.1 (1)	1,119.2 (0.4)	325.4 (0.1)	104.6 (0)	62,408.0 (21.8)
Helderberg Highlands	1,591.3 (1.2)	6,755.3 (5)	950.0 (0.7)	181.0 (0.1)	50.9 (0)	27.4 (0)	50,846.8 (37.8)
Hudson Highlands	7,465.2 (5.4)	15,177.6 (11)	4,363.0 (3.2)	1,704.9 (1.2)	345.8 (0.3)	206.7 (0.2)	90,749.8 (65.9)
Indian River Lakes	6,379.8 (12.6)	869.3 (1.7)	147.5 (0.3)	12.4 (0)	0.6 (0)	4.0 (0)	19,074.3 (37.6)
Malone Plain‡	191.2 (0.5)	1,157.2 (2.9)	291.9 (0.7)	72.1 (0.2)	16.2 (0)	4.5 (0)	14,097.1 (35.3)
Manhattan Hills	15,891.7 (11.1)	27,560.8 (19.3)	13,563.6 (9.5)	14,307.2 (10)	10,825.6 (7.6)	100.0 (0.1)	42,947.5 (30.1)
Mohawk Valley	6,123.6 (1.4)	22,292.9 (5)	9,000.4 (2)	2,980.4 (0.7)	716.1 (0.2)	106.1 (0)	99,287.6 (22)
Mongaup Hills	3,726.5 (3.9)	2,630.8 (2.7)	328.8 (0.3)	74.4 (0.1)	17.5 (0)	130.1 (0.1)	49,955.0 (52.2)
Neversink Highlands	6,072.0 (3.7)	8,093.3 (4.9)	1,403.6 (0.9)	440.8 (0.3)	144.7 (0.1)	572.2 (0.3)	75,113.0 (45.9)
Oswego Lowlands	457.8 (0.6)	3,459.4 (4.7)	1,023.0 (1.4)	333.4 (0.5)	87.0 (0.1)	146.8 (0.2)	21,404.1 (28.9)
Rensselaer Hills	547.6 (1.1)	1,590.2 (3.2)	250.3 (0.5)	45.8 (0.1)	9.1 (0)	36.0 (0.1)	23,753.3 (48.4)
Sable Highlands	1,352.9 (2.8)	567.6 (1.2)	0.5 (0)	0 (0)	0 (0)	40.0 (0.1)	30,084.7 (62.5)
Schoharie Hills	1,332.8 (0.7)	6,460.7 (3.3)	519.7 (0.3)	78.3 (0)	9.5 (0)	337.8 (0.2)	113,284.0 (58)
Shawangunk Hills	212.7 (0.6)	1,354.5 (3.7)	169.5 (0.5)	56.3 (0.2)	6.4 (0)	13.7 (0)	20,737.0 (56.7)
St. Lawrence Plains‡	5,803.7 (2.3)	9,113.9 (3.7)	3,484.4 (1.4)	894.1 (0.4)	204.0 (0.1)	126.9 (0.1)	76,457.6 (30.7)
St. Lawrence Transition‡	4,249.4 (3.6)	3,025.3 (2.5)	482.2 (0.4)	57.7 (0)	12.6 (0)	51.9 (0)	38,337.8 (32.2)
Taconic Foothills	4,252.0 (1)	18,832.9 (4.6)	6,970.6 (1.7)	2,028.4 (0.5)	326.9 (0.1)	473.8 (0.1)	165,727.6 (40.8)
Taconic Mountains	104.1 (0.3)	1,207.0 (3)	179.0 (0.4)	47.6 (0.1)	5.3 (0)	0.4 (0)	25,826.4 (64.9)
Triassic Lowlands	761.2 (2.7)	11,741.8 (42.4)	3,577.6 (12.9)	1,244.6 (4.5)	410.0 (1.5)	92.4 (0.3)	6,306.9 (22.8)
Tug Hill Transition	3,645.5 (1.6)	2,209.1 (1)	320.4 (0.1)	44.9 (0)	10.1 (0)	86.3 (0)	91,297.8 (40.2)
Western Adirondack Foothills	29,279.0 (3.5)	9,065.2 (1.1)	782.5 (0.1)	130.6 (0)	25.9 (0)	668.2 (0.1)	445,431.3 (54)
Western Adirondack Transition	6,944.5 (2.4)	5,291.6 (1.9)	642.1 (0.2)	138.9 (0)	38.7 (0)	565.9 (0.2)	118,865.6 (41.9)

★ Cover classes follow the NLCD 2001 Land Cover Class Definitions (Homer et al. 2004).

† Although the state boundaries include approximately half of Lake Champlain and portions of Lake Ontario, Lake Erie, and the St. Lawrence River, the numbers presented here exclude these water bodies.

‡ Champlain Transition, Coastal Lowlands, Erie-Ontario Plain, Malone Plain, St. Lawrence Plains, and St. Lawrence Transition have 22.9, 227.6, 10.4, 0.7, 46, and 7.6 ha with "no data," respectively.

Evergreen Forest	Mixed Forest	Shrub/Scrub	Grassland/Herbaceous	Pasture/Hay	Cultivated Crops	Woody Wetlands	Emergent Herbaceous Wetlands
1,068,990.7 (8.5)	957,563.0 (7.6)	382,968.7 (3.1)	123,866.4 (1)	1,744,987.2 (13.9)	1,071,560.6 (8.5)	972,701.5 (7.8)	76,992.3 (0.6)
63,217.7 (36)	35,451.0 (20.2)	949.4 (0.5)	685.5 (0.4)	391.0 (0.2)	799.1 (0.5)	7,761.2 (4.4)	667.4 (0.4)
9,096.7 (4.6)	7,424.7 (3.7)	6,484.6 (3.3)	1,029.2 (0.5)	10,538.0 (5.3)	7,381.6 (3.7)	3,040.9 (1.5)	190.3 (0.1)
10,889.4 (7.9)	3,017.2 (2.2)	12,636.8 (9.1)	4,346.4 (3.1)	34,816.7 (25.2)	18,651.3 (13.5)	14,014.4 (10.1)	1,043.4 (0.8)
9,345.8 (5.9)	17,851.0 (11.2)	157.4 (0.1)	331.2 (0.2)	1,068.9 (0.7)	307.1 (0.2)	1,800.4 (1.1)	65.7 (0)
27,482.3 (4.3)	29,654.5 (4.6)	22,096.5 (3.4)	7,720.5 (1.2)	133,819.0 (20.9)	111,615.9 (17.4)	22,314.2 (3.5)	2,634.4 (0.4)
160,088.6 (16.9)	92,614.3 (9.8)	11,374.2 (1.2)	1,071.4 (0.1)	224.1 (0)	434.4 (0)	115,660.7 (12.2)	8,222.0 (0.9)
144,111.7 (6.2)	276,509.9 (12)	74,428.6 (3.2)	25,178.0 (1.1)	449,711.0 (19.4)	207,637.7 (9)	61,963.6 (2.7)	6,378.9 (0.3)
22,098.5 (3.1)	59,006.0 (8.2)	12,616.3 (1.8)	1,659.9 (0.2)	105,823.0 (14.7)	80,809.6 (11.2)	99,116.1 (13.8)	3,713.9 (0.5)
4,706.5 (5.1)	1,859.2 (2)	4,146.6 (4.5)	870.6 (1)	929.7 (1)	187.6 (0.2)	16,082.2 (17.6)	616.5 (0.7)
16,331.6 (14.2)	6,173.2 (5.4)	5,601.2 (4.9)	5,246.9 (4.6)	9,143.8 (7.9)	8,020.4 (7)	16,311.4 (14.1)	641.7 (0.6)
9,559.7 (12.7)	5,753.2 (7.6)	779.7 (1)	1,551.2 (2.1)	7,536.9 (10)	12,403.3 (16.4)	9,252.4 (12.3)	652.1 (0.9)
18,060.0 (4.9)	8,426.2 (2.3)	3,592.8 (1)	2,534.0 (0.7)	10,915.5 (3)	10,907.6 (3)	7,638.1 (2.1)	12,569.1 (3.4)
9,494.7 (5.5)	18,939.9 (10.9)	779.0 (0.4)	816.8 (0.5)	5,152.0 (3)	1,063.0 (0.6)	3,586.0 (2.1)	120.8 (0.1)
2,574.0 (0.9)	12,796.9 (4.5)	10,307.8 (3.6)	847.7 (0.3)	76,459.1 (26.9)	61,173.2 (21.5)	35,052.5 (12.3)	4,031.2 (1.4)
101,549.3 (29.4)	58,375.6 (16.9)	2,701.1 (0.8)	1,039.2 (0.3)	2,375.2 (0.7)	3,349.0 (1)	26,981.6 (7.8)	950.1 (0.3)
18,680.8 (19.7)	5,780.4 (6.1)	452.2 (0.5)	513.9 (0.5)	4,398.2 (4.6)	3,972.9 (4.2)	26,744.2 (28.1)	330.8 (0.3)
6,244.6 (2.6)	3,281.8 (1.4)	17,977.9 (7.4)	8,562.6 (3.5)	74,061.4 (30.6)	24,866.3 (10.3)	27,095.7 (11.2)	3,623.0 (1.5)
14,296.9 (1)	37,012.0 (2.7)	46,422.9 (3.4)	10,829.8 (0.8)	311,826.7 (22.7)	305,789.6 (22.2)	99,069.0 (7.2)	7,602.6 (0.6)
7,045.7 (2.5)	23,316.9 (8.1)	18,776.9 (6.6)	1,537.4 (0.5)	76,817.8 (26.8)	55,103.5 (19.2)	12,010.1 (4.2)	923.3 (0.3)
14,433.2 (10.7)	19,250.6 (14.3)	541.4 (0.4)	792.2 (0.6)	19,531.9 (14.5)	5,450.2 (4.1)	13,755.7 (10.2)	242.6 (0.2)
3,267.7 (2.4)	1,900.8 (1.4)	933.5 (0.7)	890.4 (0.6)	3,421.8 (2.5)	544.0 (0.4)	5,922.8 (4.3)	735.0 (0.5)
2,199.3 (4.3)	644.0 (1.3)	1,373.3 (2.7)	1,534.2 (3)	5,897.0 (11.6)	923.8 (1.8)	10,979.5 (21.7)	653.0 (1.3)
3,238.7 (8.1)	1,191.9 (3)	1,159.8 (2.9)	855.9 (2.1)	9,598.7 (24)	4,578.8 (11.5)	3,285 (8.2)	184.7 (0.5)
6,339.2 (4.4)	920.7 (0.6)	652.1 (0.5)	310.4 (0.2)	4,516.4 (3.2)	397.9 (0.3)	3,340.6 (2.3)	1,217.2 (0.9)
20,023.1 (4.4)	29,938.4 (6.6)	22,351.6 (5)	10,172.5 (2.3)	110,970.4 (24.6)	74,905.6 (16.6)	40,180.3 (8.9)	1,276.0 (0.3)
10,929.1 (11.4)	24,663.4 (25.8)	407.4 (0.4)	58.5 (0.1)	656.5 (0.7)	175.4 (0.2)	1,743.6 (1.8)	172.5 (0.2)
16,586.6 (10.1)	29,825.8 (18.2)	335.6 (0.2)	639.3 (0.4)	14,499.7 (8.9)	2,366.1 (1.4)	7,502.2 (4.6)	196.5 (0.1)
4,019.0 (5.4)	1,890.9 (2.6)	7,557.9 (10.2)	358.7 (0.5)	14,194.7 (19.2)	4,858.6 (6.6)	13,453.2 (18.2)	777.0 (1)
5,535.5 (11.3)	12,876.9 (26.2)	1,078 (2.2)	29.8 (0.1)	2,619.4 (5.3)	208.4 (0.4)	216.4 (0.4)	265.7 (0.5)
8,095.9 (16.8)	1,510.6 (3.1)	1,319.8 (2.7)	111.3 (0.2)	3.7 (0)	6.8 (0)	4,803.0 (10)	236.2 (0.5)
19,422.4 (9.9)	22,069.3 (11.3)	481.1 (0.2)	1,717.8 (0.9)	20,417.0 (10.4)	4,685.9 (2.4)	4,356.3 (2.2)	237.7 (0.1)
1,974.0 (5.4)	8,186.1 (22.4)	120.2 (0.3)	672.3 (1.8)	875.4 (2.4)	471.7 (1.3)	1,738.2 (4.8)	5.0 (0)
12,669.8 (5.1)	2,639.8 (1.1)	8,051.7 (3.2)	8,895.6 (3.6)	57,432.0 (23.1)	19,373.5 (7.8)	39,793.9 (16)	3,873.2 (1.6)
16,451.5 (13.8)	3,931.7 (3.3)	3,535.9 (3)	3,218.5 (2.7)	11,777.2 (9.9)	4,557.2 (3.8)	27,326.5 (22.9)	2,148.4 (1.8)
33,150.2 (8.2)	14,740.0 (3.6)	18,791.6 (4.6)	806.0 (0.2)	102,819.1 (25.3)	17,699.3 (4.4)	18,541.1 (4.6)	1,469.2 (0.4)
3,363.0 (8.4)	4,400.8 (11.1)	450.3 (1.1)	17.8 (0)	3,342.7 (8.4)	350.2 (0.9)	483.8 (1.2)	30.3 (0.1)
53.1 (0.2)	0 (0)	95.2 (0.3)	35.5 (0.1)	37.1 (0.1)	352.1 (1.3)	2,956.2 (10.7)	47.4 (0.2)
37,620.2 (16.6)	8,757.3 (3.9)	22,025.2 (9.7)	3,930.3 (1.7)	20,099.4 (8.8)	7,325.8 (3.2)	28,808.3 (12.7)	949.7 (0.4)
143,199.4 (17.4)	50,540.3 (6.1)	24,276.0 (2.9)	5,568.7 (0.7)	6,860.0 (0.8)	2,165 (0.3)	101,685.1 (12.3)	5,258.9 (0.6)
51,536.9 (18.2)	14,451.4 (5.1)	15,146.0 (5.3)	6,880.9 (2.4)	19,419.3 (6.8)	5,697.4 (2)	36,327.4 (12.8)	1,995.2 (0.7)

natural vegetation consists of elm–red maple–northern hardwoods, with beech, white ash, basswood, sugar maple, hickory, hemlock, and tulip tree predominating on better drained sites. Farms and orchards predominate, with only about one-fifth of the land forested, mainly in a disrupted pattern. Climate is equable, modified by Lakes Erie and Ontario. Elevations range from 75 m (245 ft) at the Lake Ontario shoreline to about 305 m (1,000 ft), but are mostly under 244 m (800 ft).

The following sub-ecozones are within the Great Lakes Plain:

Erie-Ontario Plain

A large sub-ecozone of the Great Lakes Plain, the Erie-Ontario Plain borders Lakes Erie and Ontario and consists of relatively level terrain that is about 21 percent wooded in disrupted sections. Much of the area is farmland, accounting for about 45 percent of the land. It covers 13,760 sq km (5,313 sq mi). Elevations along the Lake Ontario shore begin at 75 m (245 ft) and along the Lake Erie shore at about 174 m (527 ft). Almost the entire sub-ecozone is lower than 244 m (800 ft).

Drumlin

Prominent oval, elongated drumlins, generally aligned northeast-southwest and composed of glacial deposits, characterize this sub-ecozone, which covers 2,841 sq km (1,097 sq mi). The area is about 24 percent forested and has significant farming (about 48 percent of the land area—the highest in the state). Elevations range from 91 m (300 ft) near Lake Ontario to a maximum of about 244 m (800 ft) above sea level at the summits of drumlins.

Oswego Lowlands

Rolling plains of about 740 sq km (286 sq mi) with elevations varying from 91 to 152 m (300–500 ft) are typical of the Oswego Lowlands, a small lowland sub-ecozone. Lake Ontario exerts a moderating effect conducive to agriculture. Forest types of elm and red maple exist but are not extensive; total forest cover is about 37 percent. Moderately productive muck soils overlie sandstone.

Eastern Ontario Plain

The Eastern Ontario Plain, a nearly level area, ranges in elevation from 76 to 152 m (250–500 ft). Lake Ontario moderates the climate for agriculture and dairying. Elm–red maple and northern hardwoods are the dominant forest types; overall forests cover 26.3 percent of the landscape. The sub-ecozone covers about 2,419 sq km (934 sq mi). Soils are mostly lake sediments over limestone bedrock.

(C) Tug Hill Plateau

The Tug Hill Plateau is an outlier of the Appalachian Plateau. It comprises the hilly Tug Hill Transition sub-ecozone and the largely flat and undulating Central Tug Hill sub-ecozone, and descends to lowlands on all sides.

The following sub-ecozones are within the Tug Hill Plateau:

Tug Hill Transition

The forest type in the low hills of the Tug Hill Transition sub-ecozone is mainly northern hardwoods, with hemlock in the western section. Elevations range between 305 m and 518 m (1,000–1,700 ft). Soils are of low productivity over Hudson River shale. Marginal dairy farms are located mostly in the southern part, and many have been abandoned. Pioneer species and the introduction of state reforestation softwood plantations have replaced many farms in this sub-ecozone of 2,271 sq km (877 sq mi). Forests, wetlands and open water, and agricultural lands cover 61 percent, 15 percent, and 12 percent of the landscape, respectively.

Central Tug Hill

Poorly drained soils are the reason for the large area of wetlands in the Central Tug Hill sub-ecozone, an area covering 915 sq km (353 sq mi). It is mainly flat and rolling terrain, with elevations ranging from 457 to 579 m (1,500–1,900 ft). Large accumulations of snow occur on this isolated plateau from the moisture-laden air of Lake Ontario. Dense forests of cut-over northern hardwoods, spruce, and fir cover 73 percent of the landscape. Severe climate and poor soils have prevented agricultural development, and much privately owned land is used for logging and outdoor recreation.

Black River Valley

A largely agricultural area with some woodlots of northern hardwoods, the Black River Valley occupies about 1,382 sq km (534 sq mi) and has an average elevation of about 305 m (1,000 ft). About 39 percent of the landscape is agricultural by area; 32 percent is forested. It lies between two large second-growth forest regions and old fields with the higher Tug Hill Plateau to the west, the Precambrian Shield on the east, the divide between the Mohawk and Black River drainages on the south, and the escarpment of the Tug Hill Plateau and margin of the flat Eastern Ontario Plain on the north. Rich loam soils cover the limestone bedrock.

(D) St. Lawrence Plains

The lowlands adjacent to the St. Lawrence River make up the St. Lawrence Plains ecozone. Covering 4,587 sq km (1,771 sq mi), this gentle landscape varies from about 76 to 270 m (250–1,000 ft) in elevation. Large wetland complexes are common; indeed, of the five sub-ecozones with the highest area of wetlands and open water, three are found here. Agriculture is also common throughout the gentle terrain of this ecozone.

The following sub-ecozones are within the St. Lawrence Plains:

St. Lawrence Plains

The St. Lawrence Plains sub-ecozone extends over about 2,489 sq km (961 sq mi) and generally is a flat, rolling plain ranging in elevation from 76 to 122 m (250–400 ft). Northern hardwoods are dominant in small woodlots, often in low, swampy areas. Land abandonment has resulted in conversion back to forests, and it possesses more hills and swamp forest with elm and red maple than does the Eastern Ontario Plain. About 37 percent of the landscape is forested, 20 percent wetlands and open water, and 31 percent agricultural. Soils of medium productivity overlie limestone and sandstone. Higher agricultural production distinguishes this area from the transition zones to the north and east.

Indian River Lakes

Encompassed by the St. Lawrence Plains and Eastern Ontario Plain, the Indian River Lakes sub-ecozone, a lowland of 507 sq km (196 sq mi), consists primarily of rolling hills and granite outcrops ranging in elevation from 107 to 152 m (350–500 ft). Precambrian granite and intruding Potsdam sedimentary sandstones underlie the shallow, poorly drained soils. Forests are a transition between northern hardwoods and oak-hickory of more southern affinity and cover about 43 percent of the landscape overall. Glacial lakes, outcrops, and rough terrain prevail in an area of chiefly recreational use.

Malone Plain

Topography in the Malone Plain varies from flat to rolling plains. The area covers about 399 sq km (154 sq mi), with elevations ranging from 122 to 305 m (400–1,000 ft). Aspen, gray birch, and paper birch make up the principal forest type, covering 46 percent of the landscape. Agriculture remains quite extensive (about 36 percent of the land) but is declining as land is abandoned. Clay soils cover sandstone.

St. Lawrence Transition

About 1,192 sq km (460 sq mi) in area and averaging elevations of 122 m (400 ft), the St. Lawrence Transition sub-ecozone has soil of low to medium productivity, with a resulting decrease in farming and increase in state ownership. The area is 49 percent wooded, mainly with aspen, birch, and shrubland.

(E) Champlain Valley

The Champlain Valley ecozone is about 1,907 sq km (736 sq mi) with elevations ranging from about 30 to 550 m (100–1,800 ft), with the higher elevations found in the Champlain Transition sub-ecozone as the land rises toward the northern Adirondacks. Gentle topography and relatively mild seasons combine to make this region attractive to agriculture.

The following sub-ecozones are in the Champlain Valley:

Champlain Valley

A lowland that covers about 754 sq km (291 sq mi), the Champlain Valley sub-ecozone contains natural forests of white pine, northern hardwoods, and pioneer species. Elevations range from 30 to 213 m (100–700 ft). Gentle relief and a rather mild climate owing to its proximity to Lake Champlain are characteristic, with farming prominent. It is bounded on the west and south by the Precambrian Shield and has clay soils derived from sediments of glacial lakes.

Champlain Transition

Lower elevations and gentle topography combined with better soil productivity make the Champlain Transition sub-ecozone attractive for agriculture. It occupies about 1,152 sq km (445 sq mi), with elevations varying from 91 to 366 m (300–1,200 ft) and averaging 213 m (700 ft). Forests cover 55 percent of the landscape and consist primarily of aspen, birch, and northern hardwoods, with some white pine, red spruce, and balsam fir. The greater amount of land use for agriculture here contrasts with ecozones to the west and south, where much land has reverted to second-growth forest.

(F) Adirondacks

The Adirondacks comprise approximately 27,177 sq km (10,493 sq mi), and the land ranges from low hills and lake country to the highest peaks in the state. With the exception of portions of the Champlain Transition and Champlain Valley sub-ecozones, the Adirondack Park Agency Blue Line falls entirely within this ecozone; 39 percent of the land is state-owned.

The following sub-ecozones are within the Adirondacks:

Western Adirondack Transition

Poor soils over Precambrian bedrock, rougher topography, and more severe climate than in the other transition areas characterize the Western Adirondack Transition sub-ecozone. This northern area of 2,839 sq km (1,096 sq mi) now consists mostly of forest (65 percent) and wetlands and open water (16 percent), with lower percentages of agricultural land (8.8 percent) and successional lands (8 percent).

Western Adirondack Foothills

A large area of 8,249 sq km (3,185 sq mi), the Western Adirondack Foothills sub-ecozone is physically similar to the Central Adirondacks and Eastern Adirondack Foothills, but topography is gentler here. Average elevation is 457 m (1,500 ft). Forest types are spruce, balsam fir, and northern hardwoods, occupying about 77 percent of the area. Shrublands occupy an additional 7.8 percent, about the same coverage as agricultural lands, at 8.8 percent. Wetlands are characteristic of the floodplains adjacent to many rivers and streams and make up 16 percent of the total area. Logging here has created more variety in forest composition than in any other forest zone. Paper companies, hunting clubs, and large estates occupy much of the private land. Human settlement is rather low, but density is double that of the Central Adirondacks.

Central Adirondacks

The Central Adirondacks sub-ecozone, a large area of 9,449 sq km (3,648 sq mi), is composed of hills and rounded mountains ranging from 396 to 1,219 m (1,300–4,000 ft) in elevation. Spruce, balsam fir, and northern hardwoods are the main forest components and cover more than 78 percent of the landscape. Over 62 percent of the land is part of the State Forest Preserve, more than in any other ecozone. This fact largely determines land use and human population density. The eastern boundary of this zone represents the separation of the spruce-fir associations from the white pine of the Eastern Adirondack Foothills.

Adirondack High Peaks

Forests in the Adirondack High Peaks sub-ecozone cover about 90 percent of the landscape and often include spruce, balsam fir, and northern hardwoods. Topography in this rugged terrain, which includes the alpine biome, largely determines its use: mostly recreational. About 60 percent of the total area is included in the State Forest Preserve. The sub-ecozone encompasses about 1,757 sq km (678 sq mi), with altitudes ranging from 305 to 1,629 m (1,000–5,344 ft) and averaging 762 m (2,500 ft).

Sable Highlands

An isolated sub-ecozone in the Western Adirondack Foothills, the Sable Highlands region consists of hills and rounded mountains covered by pioneer spruce, balsam fir, and northern hardwoods (82 percent forested in total). Almost a third of the land is state-owned. The area is about 481 sq km (186 sq mi), with altitudes varying from 396 to 1,036 m (1,300–3,400 ft) and averaging 610 m (2,000 ft). Topography and poor soils have determined land use, which is largely recreational.

Eastern Adirondack Foothills

Hills and rounded mountains cover some 3,448 sq km (1,331 sq mi) of the Eastern Adirondack Foothills, with elevations ranging from 152 to 914 m (500–3,000 ft) and averaging 427 m (1,400 ft). White pine, oak, and northern hardwoods typify woodlands, which cover about 78 percent of the landscape. The abrupt eastern margin of the Precambrian Shield marks a change in typical vegetation from the spruce-fir to the west, and it possesses a somewhat milder climate than the Western Adirondack Foothills.

Eastern Adirondack Transition

The rolling plains of the Eastern Adirondack Transition sub-ecozone have a more significant proportion of oak and a higher human population density than do the other transition areas. There is a high degree of land abandonment, and many former agricultural sites have either converted back to forest or con-verted to other human use. Forests account for approximately 40 percent of the landscape, wetlands and open water 39 percent, and developed lands 11 percent. The area is about 951 sq km (367 sq mi), with altitudes extending from 91 to 610 m (300–2,000 ft) and averaging 213 m (700 ft). The bedrock of granites, sandstones, limestones, and acid glacial till is covered by soils of medium to low productivity.

(G) Mohawk Valley

The Mohawk Valley, an area of over 4,503 sq km (1,739 sq mi), is characterized by a valley of variable terrain with soft sedimentary rock overlaid by glacial till. Rolling plains with gentle slopes and low local relief occur, as well as some hills with moderate slopes and higher relief. Elevations range from 152 m (500 ft) to over 518 m (1,700 ft). The narrow inner river valley has elevations averaging 305 m (1,000 ft) below those of the country to the north and south. This zone generally has cooler temperatures than the Great Lakes Plain. Northern hardwoods and associated species predominate, with hemlock stands in some ravines, white pine and cedar in a few swamps, and oaks on the shale slopes. Forested areas are mostly on farms and occupy 33 percent of the land. Manufacturing industries, intensive dairy farming, and a variety of crop farms account for the major uses of land in this area.

(H) Hudson Valley

Rolling plains and hills bound the Hudson Valley, a 7,560 sq km (2,919 sq mi) depression interlaced with long, narrow stream bottomlands. Most elevations are below 152 m (500 ft) and near sea level to the south. Hills and terraces overlie highly folded sedimentary rock. Hills exceeding 305 m (1,000 ft) above sea level rise toward the south. The climate is relatively mild, and the vegetation includes oak–northern hardwoods and white pine. The Albany sand plains support pitch pines and scrub oaks. Oaks are common on south slopes, and red cedar in abandoned fields. Several types of agriculture are practiced, there are major transportation centers, and population density is high, particularly in the north.

The following sub-ecozones are within the Hudson Valley:

Central Hudson

The Central Hudson sub-ecozone, 7,195 sq km (2,778 sq mi) in area, is generally flat to rolling land mostly at elevations below 152 m (500 ft) but with a number of hilltops reaching over 305 m (1,000 ft). Northern and pioneer hardwoods are the most extensive forest types, with some white pine and red cedar. There is a mixture of industry, residential centers, and a variety of farms in the area. Forests, agriculture, and developed lands cover 35.6 percent, 17.3 percent, and 19 percent of the landscape, respectively.

Shawangunk Hills

The Shawangunk Hills sub-ecozone is about 84 percent wooded, with generally high local relief ranging from 122 to 698 m (400–2,289 ft). The area covers only 366 sq km (141 sq mi). Oaks are abundant on upper slopes and ridgetops, while tulip tree, white ash, hard maple, and hemlock, mixed with oak, occur on the lower slopes and better sites.

(I) Taconic Highlands

Terrain in the Taconic Highlands, an area of 4,955 sq km (1,913 sq mi), is rolling near the Hudson Valley and hillier toward the eastern border of the state. Geologically it is a very complex area, with intensely folded and faulted rocks covered with acid till. Woodlands on good soils contain white ash, tulip tree, basswood, sugar maple, black cherry, hemlock, white pine, and red oak. Those on the poorer, shallower soils are scrubby pioneer forests with gray birch, black birch, maple, and red cedar. The northern part of this zone contains successional-growth northern hardwoods, oak, and hickory with large areas of shrubland. Elevation starts at 122 m (400 ft) in the west and gradually trends higher to about 610 m (2,000 ft) along the Massachusetts state line. Maximum height reaches about 853 m (2,800 ft). Agriculture is the chief land use in this ecozone.

The following sub-ecozones are within the Taconic Highlands:

Taconic Foothills

A 40 percent wooded area of rolling terrain, the Taconic Foothills sub-ecozone contains forests that range from scrub pioneer types to old-growth stands of oaks and other hardwoods of a variety of species. It covers an area of 4,066 sq km (1,570 sq mi), and altitudes vary from 122 to over 366 m (400–1,200 ft) on many hilltops on the east. Agriculture is the main land use, but as with the Taconic Highlands, it has decreased and been replaced by old fields and woodlands in various stages of succession. Forests now cover about 53 percent of the landscape, followed by agricultural lands at 29.6 percent.

Rensselaer Hills

Over 86 percent of the Rensselaer Hills, a sub-ecozone of 491 sq km (189 sq mi), is wooded, with spruce and balsam fir common. Elevation begins at 213 m (700 ft), but most of the varied landscape is well above 305 m (1,000 ft). Some hilltops reach 579 m (1,900 ft). Predominately stony soils of low agricultural value have led to a considerable decrease in farming.

Taconic Mountains

The Taconic Mountains sub-ecozone is a very small area of 398 sq km (154 sq mi) in two sections, with rock outcrops and shallow soils of low agricultural quality covering 67 percent of it. Forests are quite extensive, covering about 84 percent of the landscape, and consist of northern hardwoods often mixed with white birch and oak; spruce and fir occur at higher altitudes. Elevation starts near 305 m (1,000 ft), with peaks averaging over 579 m (1,900 ft) and the highest reaching 853 m (2,798 ft).

(J) Hudson Highlands

The Hudson Highlands ecozone covers 1,376 sq km (531 sq mi), and the highlands themselves are steep, rough, and stony from water erosion. Underlying igneous and metamorphic rocks are complex, with many folds and faults. Soils are shallow and acid. Altitudes range from 61 m (200 ft) to a peak of 488 m (1,600 ft), with much of the zone over 213 m (700 ft); maximum local elevations are near 305 m (1,000 ft), but many altitudes are as high as 427 m (1,400 ft). Oak is the natural vegetation, with northern hardwoods much less abundant; about 69.7 percent of the land is forested. Industrialization has spread to many small communities, and there is considerable demand for homes by commuters, which is reflected in the relatively high percentage of lands developed, at 15.7 percent.

(K) Triassic Lowlands

A small ecozone (277 sq km, 107 sq mi) of low relief and gently rolling plains, the Triassic Lowlands includes the Palisades on the east, a large igneous escarpment adjacent to the Hudson River. Soils of glacial till are deep and loamy from the underlying sandstone, limestone, and shale, with intervening lava flows protruding in some places. Only about 23 percent of the land is covered by oak–northern hardwood forest, as much has gone to development, which now covers 61 percent of the landscape. Climate is warm and humid in the summer and mild and wet in the winter. At the base of the Palisades, altitude is near sea level, but most of the area is above 61 m (200 ft), with maximum local elevation being about 183 m (600 ft).

(L) Manhattan Hills

Covering 1,429 sq km (552 sq mi) with elevations ranging from near sea level close to the Hudson River to over 213 m (700 ft) on many hilltops, the Manhattan Hills ecozone has mild wet winters and warm humid summers. Oak and oak–northern hardwoods predominate, with pioneer trees most common as in the Hudson Highlands. Developed lands (residential and industrial) cover 46 percent of the landscape while forests cover 35 percent of the landscape, overall. The country is rolling, there are many rock exposures, and soils vary in type and depth.

(M) Coastal Lowlands

The Coastal Lowlands ecozone, a part of the Atlantic Coastal Plain, has very low relief, with elevations mostly below 61 m (200 ft) but reaching a maximum of 122 m (400 ft). Its area totals 3,674 sq km (1,419 sq mi). Covered by glacial drift, this zone is underlain by sands and clays. The climate is moderated by the ocean. Because of poor soils, scrub oaks dominate the zone, with pitch pine the main conifer, often in mixture. In addition, tulip tree, sweet birch, sugar and red maples, and elm occur. Much of the vegetation of the zone, as well as farmland, is being lost by rapid urban and suburban expansion. Indeed, this zone currently has the highest area of the landscape classified as developed, at 65 percent. Forest cover totals 18.9 percent, the lowest among all ecozones.

Bird Conservation Regions

A classification of physiographic areas was developed for use specifically in the context of bird conservation. Different from the finer-scaled classification of landscape types, Bird Conservation Regions (BCRs) classify larger areas with similar bird communities, habitats, and resource management issues (NABCI 2007). Specific bird conservation plans have been developed for species groups within BCRs nationwide. New York's lands are classified in four BCRs, as shown in Figure 1.15. The four descriptions below are derived from the North American Bird Conservation Initiative web site.

Lower Great Lakes/St. Lawrence Plain (BCR 13)

This BCR covers the low-lying areas to the south of the Canadian Shield and north of various highland systems in the United States. In addition to important lakeshore habitats and associated wetlands, this region was originally covered with a mixture of oak-hickory, northern hardwood, and mixed-coniferous forests. Very little of the forests remains today, primarily owing to agricultural conversion. This is now the largest and most important area of grassland in the Northeast because of agriculture, though much is being converted to urban uses or being lost to succession.

Atlantic Northern Forest (BCR 14)

The nutrient-poor soils of northernmost New England and the Adirondacks support spruce-fir forests on more northerly and higher sites and northern hardwoods elsewhere. Virtually all of the world's Bicknell's Thrush breed on mountaintops in this region. Beaver ponds and shores of undisturbed lakes and ponds provide excellent waterfowl breeding habitat.

Appalachian Mountains (BCR 28)

The rugged terrain in this BCR is generally dominated by oak-hickory and other deciduous forest types at lower elevations and by various combinations of pine, hemlock, spruce, and fir in higher areas. While flatter portions are in agricultural use, the majority of most segments of this region are forested.

New England/Mid-Atlantic Coast (BCR 30)

This area has the densest human population of any region in the country. Much of what was formerly cleared for agriculture is now either in forest or in residential use. The highest-priority birds are in coastal wetland and beach habitats.

Natural and Cultural Ecological Communities of New York

While ecoregions and ecozones describe landscape patterns at a relatively broad scale, one can regularly notice patterns in the way plants and animals occur in landscapes at a much finer scale as well. Walking to a pond's edge, one will see different species living there than at the rock outcrop on the side of a nearby hill. Chances are good that at another pond, one will see some of the same species seen at the last pond. As these "species communities" are found at this relatively fine scale, many patches of different community types occur within a single subsection or ecozone. Natural communities have been mapped at specific locations throughout the state, such as the New York State Wildlife Management Areas and State Parks, but not statewide. A full classification of all the communities in the state has been developed, however, and is presented by Edinger et al. (2002). This classification provides a common language for enthusiasts and researchers alike to share information about sites and habitats throughout the state.

The list of ecological communities provided below is from the New York Natural Heritage Program's draft revision of *Ecological Communities of New York State* (Edinger et al. 2002). An earlier list of ecological communities was included in the first Atlas as Appendix B. That appendix was derived from Reschke (1990), the precursor to the work of Edinger et al. (2002).

The primary objective of this classification is to identify all of the natural and cultural ecological communities found in New York. Together, these communities constitute the full ecological and biotic array of the state. It is intended to serve a variety of needs, among them a consistent means of describing wildlife habitats. A community, as used herein, is defined as a reoccurring assemblage of populations of all the resident organisms that share a common environment. Each community is conceived as being based on its dominant and characteristic species, as well as on its most apparent and significant environmental features.

This classification is organized into seven systems, each of which is divided into subsystems. Below, we define each system and subsystem, with the most apparent identification features, and list the natural communities within these groups. The classification is based on literature review, field surveys, and discussions with ecologists, naturalists, and wildlife biologists. This list provides an iterative means of identifying the many ecological communities used by New York's breeding birds.

I. Marine System. The marine system consists of open ocean overlying the continental shelf, the associated coastline that is exposed to wind and waves, and shallow coastal bays that are saline because they lack significant freshwater inflow. The limits extend from mean high water seaward, beyond the limits of rooted vascular vegetation. Salinity usually exceeds 30 parts per thousand (ppt) ocean-derived salts, with little or no dilution except outside the mouths of estuaries (Cowardin et al. 1979), where it can range as low as 18 ppt in New York (Edinger et al. 2002).

A. Marine Subtidal. This subsystem includes the area below the lowest tide that is permanently flooded with tidal water.

1. Marine deepwater community
2. Marine eelgrass meadow

B. Marine Intertidal. This subsystem includes the area between the highest tide level and the lowest tide level; the substrate is periodically exposed and flooded by semidiurnal tides (two high tides and two low tides per tidal day) (Edinger et al. 2002).

1. Marine intertidal mudflats
2. Marine intertidal gravel/sand beach
3. Marine rocky intertidal

C. Marine Cultural. This subsystem includes communities that are either created and maintained by human activities, or modified by human influence to such a degree that the physical conformation of the substrate or the biological composition of the resident community is substantially different from the character of the substrate or community as it existed prior to human influence (Edinger et al. 2002).

1. Marine submerged artificial structure/reef
2. Marine dredge spoil shore
3. Marine riprap/artificial shore

II. Estuarine System. The estuarine system consists of deepwater tidal habitats and adjacent tidal wetlands that are usually semi-enclosed but have open, partly obstructed, or sporadic access to open ocean or tidal fresh water, and in which ocean water is at least occasionally diluted by freshwater runoff. The limits extend from the upstream limit of tidal influence seaward to an imaginary line closing the mouth of a river or bay. Salinity is usually less than 30 ppt ocean-derived salts but can range from hyperhaline (>40 ppt) to oligohaline (0.5–5.0 ppt) (Cowardin et al. 1979, Edinger et al. 2002).

A. Estuarine Subtidal. This subsystem includes the area below the lowest tide; the substrate is permanently flooded with tidal water; it is continuously submerged.

1. Tidal river

2. Saltwater tidal creek
3. Freshwater tidal creek
4. Brackish subtidal aquatic bed
5. Freshwater subtidal aquatic bed

B. Estuarine Intertidal. This subsystem includes the area between the highest tide level and the lowest tide level; the substrate is periodically exposed and flooded by semidiurnal tides (two high tides and two low tides per tidal day). Some areas are only irregularly exposed at low tide, while other areas are only irregularly flooded at high tide. Semidiurnal submergence, warm water, copious deposits of mud, and varying salinity make the intertidal estuarine communities extreme and specialized habitats (Edinger et al. 2002).

1. Brackish meadow
2. Salt shrub
3. High salt marsh
4. Salt panne
5. Low salt marsh
6. Coastal salt pond
7. Brackish interdunal swales
8. Brackish tidal marsh
9. Brackish intertidal mudflats
10. Brackish intertidal shore
11. Freshwater tidal swamp
12. Freshwater tidal marsh
13. Freshwater intertidal mudflats
14. Freshwater intertidal shore

C. Estuarine Cultural. This subsystem includes communities that either are created and maintained by human activities, or are modified by human influence to such a degree that the physical conformation of the substrate or the biological composition of the resident community is substantially different from the character of the substrate or community as it existed prior to human influence (Edinger et al. 2002).

1. Estuarine submerged structure
2. Estuarine water chestnut bed
3. Estuarine channel/artificial impoundment
4. Estuarine ditch
5. Estuarine impoundment marsh
6. Estuarine reedgrass marsh
7. Estuarine dredge spoil shore
8. Estuarine riprap/artificial shore

III. Riverine System. The riverine system consists of linear aquatic communities of flowing, nontidal waters with a discrete channel, with persistent emergent vegetation sparse or lacking, but may include areas with abundant submerged or floating-leaved aquatic vegetation. The riverine communities in this classification are distinguished primarily by position of the stream in the watershed and water flow characteristics (Edinger et al. 2002).

    A. Natural Streams. This subsystem includes streams in which the stream flow, morphometry, and water chemistry have not been substantially modified by human activities, or the native biota are dominant. The biota may include some introduced species (e.g., stocked or accidentally introduced fishes); however, the introduced species are not usually dominant in the stream community as a whole (Edinger et al. 2002).

        1. Rocky headwater stream
        2. Marsh headwater stream
        3. Confined river
        4. Unconfined river
        5. Backwater slough
        6. Intermittent stream
        7. Coastal plain stream
        8. Deepwater river
        9. Spring

    B. Riverine Cultural. This subsystem includes communities that either are created and maintained by human activities, or are modified by human influence to such a degree that stream flow, morphometry, water chemistry, or the biological composition of the resident community are substantially different from the character of the stream community as it existed prior to human influence. No biotic riverine cultural types have been noted. New York Natural Heritage is currently unaware of examples of streams without physical or chemical alterations that have become dominated by exotic biota such as water chestnut and Eurasian water milfoil (Edinger et al. 2002).

        1. Riverine submerged structure
        2. Riverine water chestnut bed
        3. Acidified stream
        4. Canal
        5. Ditch/artificial intermittent stream
        6. Industrial effluent stream

IV. Lacustrine System. The lacustrine system consists of ponded waters situated in topographic depressions or dammed river channels, with persistent emergent vegetation sparse or lacking, but including any areas with abundant submerged or floating-leaved aquatic vegetation. The lacustrine communities in this classification are distinguished primarily by trophic state, alkalinity, annual cycles of thermal stratification, circulation, morphometry (size and shape of the lake basin and drainage area; water permanence), and water chemistry (including salinity) (Edinger et al. 2002).

    A. Natural Lakes and Ponds. This subsystem includes the Great Lakes, and inland lakes and ponds in which

the trophic state, morphometry, and water chemistry have not been substantially modified by human activities, or the native biota are dominant. The biota may include some introduced species (e.g., non-native macrophytes, stocked or accidentally introduced fishes); however, the introduced species are not usually dominant in the lake or pond community as a whole (Edinger et al. 2002).

        1. Great Lakes deepwater community
        2. Great Lakes aquatic bed
        3. Great Lakes exposed shoal
        4. Bog lake
        5. Oligotrophic dimictic lake
        6. Mesotrophic dimictic lake
        7. Eutrophic dimictic lake
        8. Summer-stratified monomictic lake
        9. Winter-stratified monomictic lake
        10. Meromictic lake
        11. Marl pond
        12. Inland salt pond
        13. Oxbow lake
        14. Coastal plain pond
        15. Oligotrophic pond
        16. Eutrophic pond

    B. Lacustrine Cultural. This subsystem includes communities that either are created and maintained by human activities, or are modified by human influence to such a degree that the trophic state, morphometry, water chemistry, or biological composition of the resident community are substantially different from the character of the lake community as it existed prior to human influence (Edinger et al. 2002).

        1. Lacustrine submerged structure
        2. Acidified lake
        3. Cultural eutrophic lake
        4. Lacustrine water chestnut bed
        5. Farm pond/artificial pond
        6. Reservoir/artificial impoundment
        7. Quarry pond
        8. Artificial pool
        9. Industrial cooling pond
        10. Sewage treatment pond

V. Palustrine System. The palustrine system consists of nontidal, perennial wetlands characterized by emergent vegetation. The system includes wetlands permanently saturated by seepage, permanently flooded wetlands, and wetlands that are seasonally or intermittently flooded (these may be seasonally dry) if the vegetative cover is predominantly hydrophytic and soils are hydric. Wetland communities are distinguished by their plant composition (hydrophytes), substrate (hydric soils), and hydrologic regime (frequency of flooding) (Cowardin et al. 1979, Edinger et al. 2002).

A. Open Mineral Soil Wetlands. This subsystem includes wetlands with less than 50 percent canopy cover by trees. In this classification, a tree is defined as a woody plant usually having one principal stem or trunk, a definite crown shape, and characteristically reaching a mature height of at least 5 m (16 ft) (Driscoll et al. 1984). The dominant vegetation may include shrubs or herbs. Substrates range from mineral soils or bedrock to well-decomposed organic soils (muck). Fluctuating water levels allow enough aeration of the substrate to allow plant litter to decompose, so there is little or no accumulation of peat (Edinger et al. 2002).

1. Deep emergent marsh
2. Shallow emergent marsh
3. Shrub swamp
4. Cobble shore wet meadow
5. Inland calcareous lake shore
6. Inland noncalcareous lake shore
7. Coastal plain pond shore
8. Sinkhole wetland
9. Maritime freshwater interdunal swales
10. Pine barrens vernal pond
11. Pine barrens shrub swamp

B. Open Peatlands. This subsystem includes peatlands with less than 50 percent canopy cover by trees. The dominant vegetation may include shrubs, herbs, or mosses. Substrates range from coarse fibrous or woody peat, to fine-grained marl and organic muck. Peat layer should be at least 20 cm deep (Edinger et al. 2002).

1. Inland salt marsh
2. Sedge meadow
3. Marl pond shore
4. Marl fen
5. Rich sloping fen
6. Rich graminoid fen
7. Rich shrub fen
8. Medium fen
9. Inland poor fen
10. Alpine sliding fen
11. Coastal plain poor fen
12. Sea-level fen
13. Perched bog
14. Patterned peatland
15. Dwarf shrub bog
16. Highbush blueberry bog thicket

C. Forested Mineral Soil Wetlands. This subsystem includes seasonally flooded forests, and permanently flooded or saturated swamps. These forests and swamps typically have at least 50 percent canopy cover by trees. For the purposes of this classification, a tree is defined as a woody plant usually having one principal stem or trunk, a definite crown shape, and characteristically reaching a mature height of at least 5 m (16 ft).

1. Floodplain forest
2. Red maple–hardwood swamp
3. Red maple–black gum swamp
4. Red maple–sweetgum swamp
5. Silver maple–ash swamp
6. Vernal pool
7. Perched swamp white oak swamp
8. Hemlock-hardwood swamp
9. Spruce-fir swamp

D. Forested Peatlands. This subsystem includes peatlands with at least 50 percent canopy cover by trees. Substrates range from coarse woody or fibrous peat to fine-grained marl and organic muck (Edinger et al. 2002).

1. Inland Atlantic white cedar swamp
2. Coastal plain Atlantic white cedar swamp
3. Red maple–tamarack peat swamp
4. Pitch pine–blueberry peat swamp
5. Northern white cedar swamp
6. Rich hemlock–hardwood peat swamp
7. Black spruce–tamarack bog

E. Palustrine Cultural. This subsystem includes communities that either are created and maintained by human activities, or are modified by human influence to such a degree that the physical conformation of the substrate, the hydrology, or the biological composition of the resident community is substantially different from the character of the substrate, hydrology, or community as it existed prior to human influence (Edinger et al. 2002).

1. Reverted drained muckland
2. Impounded marsh
3. Impounded swamp
4. Reedgrass marsh
5. Purple loosestrife marsh
6. Dredge spoil wetland
7. Mine spoil wetland
8. Water recharge basin

VI. Terrestrial System. The terrestrial system consists of upland habitats. These habitats have well-drained soils that are dry to mesic (never hydric), and vegetative cover that is never predominantly hydrophytic (wet), even if the soil surface is occasionally or seasonally flooded or saturated. In other words, this is a broadly defined system that includes everything except aquatic, wetland, and subterranean communities (Edinger et al. 2002).

A. Open Uplands. This subsystem includes upland communities with less than 25 percent canopy cover by trees; the dominant species in these communities are shrubs, herbs, or cryptogammic plants (mosses, lichens, and such). Three distinctive physiognomic types are included in this subsystem. Grasslands include communities that are dominated by grasses and sedges; they may include scattered shrubs (never more than 50 percent cover by shrubs), and scattered trees (usually less than one tree per acre, or three trees per hectare). Meadows include communities with forbs, grasses, sedges, and shrubs codominant; they may include scattered trees. Shrublands include communities that are dominated by shrubs (more than 50 percent cover by shrubs); they may include scattered trees (Edinger et al. 2002).

1. Sand beach
2. Great Lakes dunes
3. Maritime beach
4. Maritime dunes
5. Maritime shrubland
6. Maritime heathland
7. Maritime grassland
8. Hempstead Plains grassland
9. Riverside ice meadow
10. Riverside sand/gravel bar
11. Shoreline outcrop
12. Calcareous shoreline outcrop
13. Cobble shore
14. Alvar shrubland
15. Alvar grassland
16. Alvar pavement-grassland
17. Alpine meadow
18. Cliff community
19. Calcareous cliff community
20. Shale cliff and talus community
21. Maritime bluff
22. Great Lakes bluff
23. Riverside/lakeside bluff
24. Rocky summit grassland
25. Successional fern meadow
26. Successional blueberry heath
27. Successional northern sandplain grassland
28. Successional old field
29. Successional shrubland

B. Barrens and Woodlands. This subsystem includes upland communities that are structurally intermediate between forests and open-canopy uplands. Several physiognomic types are included in this subsystem. Savannas are communities with a sparse canopy of trees (25–60 percent cover), and a ground layer that is either predominantly grassy or shrubby (these will be called, respectively, grass-savanna and shrub-savanna). Woodlands include communities with a canopy of stunted or dwarf trees (less than 4.9 m or 16 ft tall), and wooded communities occurring on shallow soils over bedrock with numerous rock outcrops. The term "barrens" is commonly applied to both savannas and woodlands (e.g., pine barrens) (Edinger et al. 2002).

1. Serpentine barrens
2. Dwarf pine plains
3. Dwarf pine ridges
4. Maritime pitch pine dune woodland
5. Pitch pine–scrub oak barrens
6. Pitch pine–oak–heath woodland
7. Post oak–blackjack oak barrens
8. Pitch pine–heath barrens
9. Boreal heath barrens
10. Sandstone pavement barrens
11. Oak openings
12. Calcareous pavement barrens (nonalvar)
13. Alpine krummholz
14. Limestone woodland
15. Calcareous red cedar barrens
16. Alvar woodland
17. Ice cave talus community
18. Calcareous talus slope woodland
19. Acidic talus slope woodland
20. Shale talus slope woodland
21. Pitch pine–oak–heath rocky summit
22. Red pine rocky summit
23. Spruce-fir rocky summit
24. Red cedar rocky summit
25. Northern white cedar rocky summit
26. Successional red cedar woodland

C. Forested Uplands. This subsystem includes upland communities with more than 60 percent canopy cover by trees; these communities occur on substrates with less than 50 percent rock outcrop or shallow soil over bedrock (Edinger et al. 2002).

1. Maritime post oak forest
2. Maritime beech forest
3. Maritime holly forest
4. Maritime red cedar forest
5. Coastal oak–heath forest
6. Coastal oak–hickory forest
7. Coastal oak–beech forest
8. Coastal oak–laurel forest
9. Coastal oak–holly forest
10. Pitch pine–oak forest
11. Appalachian oak–hickory forest
12. Allegheny oak forest
13. Chestnut oak forest
14. Oak–tulip tree forest

15. Appalachian oak–pine forest
16. Rich mesophytic forest
17. Beech–maple mesic forest
18. Maple-basswood–rich mesic forest
19. Hemlock–northern hardwood forest
20. Pine–northern hardwood forest
21. Spruce flats
22. Balsam flats
23. Spruce–northern hardwood forest
24. Mountain spruce–fir forest
25. Mountain fir forest
26. Successional northern hardwoods
27. Successional southern hardwoods
28. Successional maritime forest

D. Terrestrial Cultural. This subsystem includes communities that either are created and maintained by human activities, or are modified by human influence to such a degree that the physical conformation of the substrate or the biological composition of the resident community is substantially different from the character of the substrate or community as it existed prior to human influence (Edinger et al. 2002).

1. Cropland/row crops
2. Cropland/field crops
3. Pastureland
4. Flower/herb garden
5. Orchard
6. Vineyard
7. Hardwood plantation
8. Pine plantation
9. Spruce/fir plantation
10. Conifer plantation
11. Mowed lawn with trees
12. Mowed lawn
13. Mowed roadside/pathway
14. Herbicide-sprayed roadside/pathway
15. Unpaved road/path
16. Railroad
17. Paved road/path
18. Roadcut cliff/slope
19. Riprap/erosion control roadside
20. Rock quarry
21. Gravel mine

22. Sand mine
23. Brushy cleared land
24. Artificial beach
25. Riprap/artificial lake shore
26. Dredge spoil lake shore
27. Construction/road maintenance spoils
28. Dredge spoils
29. Mine spoils
30. Landfill/dump
31. Junkyard
32. Urban vacant lot
33. Urban structure exterior
34. Rural structure exterior
35. Interior of barn/agricultural building
36. Interior of nonagricultural building

VII. Subterranean System. The subterranean system consists of both aquatic and nonaquatic habitats beneath the Earth's surface, including air-filled cavities with openings to the surface (caves), water-filled cavities and aquifers, and interstitial habitats in small crevices within an inorganic matrix. Different subterranean communities are distinguished by hydrology and substrate characteristics (Edinger et al. 2002).

A. Natural Caves. This subsystem includes caves and cavities in which the structure and hydrology have not been substantially modified by human activities, and the native biota are dominant.

1. Aquatic cave community
2. Terrestrial cave community
3. Talus cave community

B. Subterranean Cultural. This subsystem includes communities that either are created and maintained by human activities, or are modified by human influence to such a degree that the physical conformation of the substrate or the biological composition of the resident community is substantially different from the character of the substrate or community as it existed prior to human influence.

1. Mine/artificial cave community
2. Sewer
3. Tunnel
4. Basement/building foundation

CHAPTER FOUR

Land-Use Changes and Breeding Birds

CHARLES R. SMITH AND PETER L. MARKS

ur understanding of how birds relate to habitats to-day is richer if we know how vegetation has changed in the past and how it continues to change today. A discussion about patterns of land-use change over time and across space is a discussion about habitats. In order to facilitate a better understanding of patterns of land use, some conceptual foundations, along with temporal and spatial contexts, need to be established.

Conceptual Foundations

The distinction between "land use" and "land cover" is an important one. Different land uses can lead to different land covers to which different species of birds respond differently. For example, forestry as a land use can lead to a variety of land covers, including plantation stands of Norway spruce or red pine, even-aged stands of trees resulting from clear-cutting as a forest management practice, and "sugar-bush" stands dominated by sugar maple and managed for production of the sap used to produce maple syrup. Agriculture as a type of land use also can lead to different types of land covers, including row crops (e.g., corn, potatoes), field crops (e.g., alfalfa, mixed hay, wheat), and pasture. Because of their economic importance, state and federal agencies have invested more effort over longer periods of time in monitoring patterns of land-cover change resulting from agricultural and forestry land use in New York State than for any other habitats.

The concept of "habitat" is fundamental to many ecological studies and relevant to bird conservation, because much of modern bird conservation is, of necessity, focused on habitat conservation (Smith 1998d). At its simplest, habitat is where an animal or plant lives. A "suitable" habitat should provide all that a species requires for survival and reproduction, including food, water, nesting sites, and shelter from weather and predators. Habitats, however, are variable in quantity and quality over space and time, and some refinement of the concept helps to apply it more precisely in studies of bird ecology and conservation.

In an important paper elucidating the modern ecological concept of habitat, Whittaker et al. (1973) proposed that habitat be defined as the response of species populations to the range of environmental variables that determined the presence of the species across ecological communities. Based on that approach, evaluation of habitat suitability can be refined by assessing the numbers of a species associated with a particular habitat type, or even by assessing the productivity and population growth rates for species within habitats (Knutson et al. 2006). It is assumed that higher numbers of individuals of a species, often measured as density (numbers per unit area) or relative abundance for counts of birds, are correlated with greater habitat suitability, while lower numbers of individuals of a species suggest less desirable habitats. Studies in the United Kingdom also have demonstrated that bird species will occupy a wider range of habitats, including some types judged to be suboptimal, at higher population densities than at lower densities (O'Connor 1986). The significance of the 1973 paper by Whittaker and his colleagues is that it transforms the concept of habitat from an ambiguous abstraction to a measurable, quantitative reality. For a more detailed discussion of habitat and related concepts, the interested reader should see Smith and Gregory (1998).

Temporal and Spatial Contexts

No comprehensive, statewide or ecoregional comparisons of patterns of land-use change over time have been published for New York. A small number of local studies from New York, however, have compared changes in bird species and their densities or relative abundances over time, usually as a result of ecological succession, and with only two sampling events, widely separated in time. Most of these studies focused on changes in bird species composition associated with forest succession. The work of Bollinger (1995), however, described patterns of succession and bird species associated with hayfield abandonment and subsequent changes. Baird (1990) described changes in the species composition and densities for breeding birds in different ecological communities in the Quaker Run Valley of Allegany State Park, based on a comparison of counts of birds done for the periods 1930–31 and 1983–85. Keller et al. (2003) described changes in bird species assemblages following clear-cutting on the Connecticut Hill State Wildlife Management Area, west of Ithaca, Tompkins County, from 1977 through 1984, comparing forest communities ranging from two years old to more than eighty years old. Webb et al. (1977) described responses of breeding birds to habitat changes related to different forest management practices, similar to the work of Keller et al. (2003) but done at the Huntington Forest, near Newcomb in Essex County. For the Sapsucker Woods Sanctuary, in Tompkins County, Litwin and

Smith (1992) compared changes in both vegetation and breeding bird populations over the period from 1950 until 1980.

Other New York studies provide valuable insights into patterns of change in ecological communities and vegetation over time but without corresponding information about breeding birds. DeGloria (1998) described changes in habitats in Finger Lakes National Forest, located between Seneca and Cayuga lakes, from 1938 through 1988. Kudish (1979, 2000) reported on inferred patterns of landscape change in the Catskills from about 12,000 years ago until the late 20th century. McMartin (1994) reported work, similar to that of Kudish (2000), for the Adirondacks over a shorter time period, from the early 19th century through the late 20th century. Patterns of successional change have been reported for locally occurring ecological communities, such as the abandoned cultivated and pasture lands in Tompkins County (Caslick 1975, Stover and Marks 1998, Flinn and Marks 2004) and the multiple ecological communities in the Edmund Niles Huyck Preserve, near Rensselaerville, Albany County (Odum 1943). Fain et al. (1994) described vegetation change over a 50-year period for an upland forest in south-central New York, and B. E. Smith et al. (1993) described vegetation changes in the Finger Lakes region spanning a period of nearly 200 years.

No published studies from New York have tracked simultaneously and continuously changes in both bird species composition and vegetation, with multiple sampling events, over substantially long periods of time. Unfortunately, long-term datasets covering large land areas of the kind used by O'Connor (1981a, b, 1986) for Britain, containing information on contemporaneous habitat-specific nesting productivity and breeding bird population densities for the same survey areas, presently do not exist for North America. In the early to mid-20th century, projects modeled after the Nest Record Scheme and Common Birds Census of the British Trust for Ornithology were initiated independently by the Cornell Lab of Ornithology (Nest Record Card Program) and the National Audubon Society (Breeding Bird Census). The Nest Record Card Program was essentially discontinued in the 1980s, but it is being revived as the new online NestWatch project at Cornell (www.nestwatch.org) and will include all the older data in its database. The Breeding Bird Censuses were last published in 1996 in the *Journal of Field Ornithology* and are now being revived and published in the journal *Bird Populations* (Gardali and Lowe 2006).

Historical Land-Use Changes in New York

Vegetation change has been the rule in New York over both short and long time spans. All but a small part of southwestern New York was under glacial ice 14,000 years ago; as a result, the plants and animals currently in the state arrived from somewhere south of the ice margin in the several thousands of years since glaciation. Landscapes in New York became increasingly forested during the postglacial period as the climate warmed and

as time allowed for more and more species to arrive from farther south. Although forest cover overwhelmingly dominated New York landscapes 500 years ago (prior to the period of major European influence), open habitats were present, though they were mostly small, scattered, and collectively accounted for a small percentage of landscape area. The nature and commonness of open habitats in the primeval landscape are of interest because of the need to understand where open-habitat species were living in an overwhelmingly forested world (Marks 1983). Prairie communities, for example, were found in western New York (Rush Oak Openings, Schmidt 1938) and on Long Island (Hempstead Plains, see below).

There is a more concrete sense of what the landscapes looked like when Europeans began to settle in New York, from the 1600s in the east to about 1800 in central and western parts of the state, because of the accounts kept by the surveyors who divided the land into parcels for homesteading and farming (Marks et al. 1992). These early surveyors were required to record much information about the species of trees and the nature of the vegetation along their traverses, and this information has survived to the present (B. E. Smith et al. 1993). Forests predominated across the state. However, based on the survey records, more can be said about the nature and causes of open habitats. Beaver meadows were mentioned along with a few "fields" cleared by early European settlers. In addition, there were temporary disturbance openings in the forest from windstorms and fire (presumably caused by either lightning or Native Americans).

Between 1700 and 1900, an average of approximately 75 percent of New York's land was cleared of forest for settlement and agriculture. In some areas, 90 percent or more of the forest was converted to agriculture (Caslick 1975). Most of this conversion occurred in the 19th century.

The 20th century brought additional changes to New York's landscapes that were nearly as dramatic as those of the 19th century. As agriculture declined, farmlands were abandoned, and forest developed on these lands in many parts of the state (Stanton and Bills 1996). In contrast to the figures given for the end of the 19th century, New York at the end of the 20th century was nearly 65 percent forest, about 25 percent open lands (overwhelmingly agricultural but also including old fields and marshes), 5 percent water, and nearly 5 percent cities, including roads and other forms of development (Smith et al. 2001). Thus, like much of the northeastern United States, New York has undergone an enormous shift in the configuration of its landscapes in the past 200–300 years, from being overwhelmingly forested, to being overwhelmingly open and agricultural 100 years ago, to being more of a mixture of open and forest lands today. Today's forests, however, are more fragmented and less continuously distributed than historically, and one needs to remember that 40 ha (100 a) of forest distributed among ten 4-ha (10-a) patches is not the same as one 40-ha (100-a) patch of forest. The changes in habitat types occurring over the last 20 years are a continuation of what has been happening over most of the 20th cen-

Table 4.1 Estimated patterns of long-term changes in different community types in New York*

Community type	Estimated decline in area and time period
Hempstead Plains grassland	More than 99.99% loss
Long Island coastal heathland	More than 90% since mid-1800s
Serpentine barrens, maritime heathland, and pitch pine heath barrens	More than 98% probable loss
Coastal plain Atlantic white cedar swamp, maritime oak-holly forest, maritime red cedar forest, marl fen, marl pond shore, and oak openings	More than 90% probable loss
Alvar grassland, calcareous pavement barrens, coastal plain poor fens, dwarf pine ridges, inland Atlantic white cedar swamp, freshwater tidal swamp, inland salt marsh, mountain spruce-fir forest, patterned peatland, perched bog, pitch pine–blueberry peat swamp, rich graminoid fens, rich sloping fens, and riverside ice meadow	Around 70%–90% probable loss
Long Island pine barrens	60%–68% loss
Wetlands	60% loss between 1780s and 1980s
Coastal plain ponds and pond shores	Around 50%–70% loss
Brackish intertidal mudflats, brackish, intertidal shores, coastal plain streams	Around 50%–70% loss
Allegheny oak forest, alpine krummholz, Great Lakes dunes, ice cave talus communities, perched swamp white oak, swamp, rich shrub fen, and sandstone pavement barrens	Around 50% or less probable loss

* Summarized from information in Appendix A of Noss et al. (1995), based largely on work of Reschke (1990). Unless stated otherwise, estimates are for the past 200 years, approximately. Community types are listed in order from those most affected to those less affected.

tury, and they have produced changes in bird occurrences and abundances.

To gain a critical perspective for understanding the changes in bird species abundances in the last 20 years (or more generally throughout the 20th century), one should know how bird species changed in the 19th century. The large alterations in the landscapes described above should have generated certain expected changes in bird species abundances. For example, populations of birds of open habitats, including grasslands, should have increased substantially by the end of the 19th century, compared to their abundance at the time of settlement. And such birds should be declining in abundance today as the landscape has become so much more forested. On the other hand, populations of interior-forest birds in the most heavily agricultural parts of the state should have declined with forest clearance in the 19th century and rebounded with the regrowth of forest lands more recently. For migratory species, these predictions obviously ignore influences on the wintering grounds.

The post-settlement changes in some distinctive habitat types have generally been poorly documented. Noss et al. (1995), however, made some estimations, based largely on the work of

Reschke (1993). The conclusions by Noss et al. are summarized in Table 4.1. The plant communities most dramatically affected were those that occupied relatively small land areas in the first place, or those occurring in areas with the longest histories of settlement and development, such as Long Island. Although local reductions in the numbers of specialist species, such as grassland birds, probably occurred with the loss of patches of prairie grassland such as the Hempstead Plains on Long Island (Stalter and Lamont 1987, Stalter et al. 1991), only one species, the Passenger Pigeon (Haney and Schaadt 1996), and one subspecies, the Heath Hen, can be associated clearly with the loss of grassland and forested habitats in New York. Statewide reductions in the numbers of many species of forest birds, such as the Pileated Woodpecker, Common Raven, and some raptors, probably occurred, but there most likely also were gains in the numbers of species associated with agricultural open lands and successional shrublands that proliferated following the abandonment of some agricultural lands.

The Significance of Succession

Over time, landscapes change as a result of three processes: conversion, degradation, and succession. Conversion occurs when one type of land use is changed to another, usually as a result of human activities. An abandoned farm sold and subdivided for residential development, followed by clearing and construction of homes, is an example of conversion. Degradation, also typically associated with human activities, is a reduction in habitat quality. The fouling of wetlands and open waters by the salt, oil, and gasoline residues carried by storm water flowing from parking lots and highways is an example of habitat degradation. Succession is a natural ecological process of habitat change over relatively long periods of time, often in landscape settings where human influence is minimal. Clearing of forest and cultivation for agriculture can "reset" successional patterns to earlier stages of development. All three processes are relevant to changes in bird populations and distribution.

The landscape changes in New York over the past 250 years have produced two fundamental kinds of forest today. Primary forests do not have a history of clearing for agriculture. They often show a diverse, "pit-and-mound" microtopography, resulting from trees falling, decaying, and leaving behind the dirt from their root mass (the mound) and a depression in which the trees were rooted (the pit). Primary forests can be composed primarily of beech and maple, oak, or other tree species, but they all share the common history of not being cleared for agriculture. In general, they have been logged, often more than once, and they have been disturbed by people in other ways, but the forest habitat has been maintained continuously on the site for the past several thousand years. Old-growth forest (also called "ancient forest," "old forest," or "virgin forest") is a subset of primary forest in which human disturbance is absent (Rackham 1980). Secondary or post-agricultural forest (Mohler et al. 2006), in contrast, has developed on land that was once farmed and from which the pit-and-mound topography of primary forest has been "erased" by agricultural activities, leaving a smoother, less diverse microtopography than found in primary forest. In more mountainous parts of the state, most of the forest today is primary because little of it was cleared for farming. In other parts of the state where agriculture has been more prevalent and has undergone a "boom-and-bust" cycle, there is much abandoned farmland, and so secondary forest is more common than primary forest. Older stands of secondary forest (say, 100 years after agricultural abandonment) are structurally mature in the sense that they have large trees, trees in the whole range of sizes (though not necessarily ages) from seedlings to big trees, and dead trees, both standing and on the ground (Flinn and Marks 2007). To a casual observer walking through them, these forests are impressive; they look like a mature forest.

Current Patterns of Land-Use Change

For New York State, there is limited, long-term information on the changes in patterns of land use and the habitats associated with those changes. Because of their economic value, agricultural and forestry land uses are assessed periodically in an organized, repeatable manner. Patterns of agricultural land use are reported annually by the New York State Agricultural Statistics Service within the New York State Department of Agriculture and Markets (New York State Agricultural Statistics Service 1986–2005). Through its Forest Inventory and Analysis (FIA) Program, the U.S. Forest Service periodically assesses patterns of forest land cover across New York (U.S. Forest Service 2005). In addition, the New York State Department of Environmental Conservation (NYSDEC) has compared changes in freshwater and tidal wetlands (NYSDEC [2001], [2007a]) from the mid-1980s to the mid-1990s.

Wetlands

The total area of New York's wetlands is estimated to be 971,246 ha (2.4 million a), or about 8.1 percent of the state. Freshwater and tidal wetlands are among the most protected habitats in New York, with the possible exception of some streams and lakes. Of the bird species identified as Species of Greatest Conservation Need (SGCN) in New York (see Chapter 6), 25 (30 percent) are associated with wetlands. Since the 1970s, freshwater wetlands have been protected under provisions of the Freshwater Wetlands Act (Article 24, New York State Environmental Conservation Law) and tidal wetlands have been protected under the Tidal Wetlands Act (Article 25, New York State Environmental Conservation Law).

Freshwater wetlands are distributed throughout the state, with the largest areas of regulated freshwater wetlands within the Great Lakes Plain and Adirondacks ecozones. From the mid-1980s through the mid-1990s, there was a net gain of approximately 6,273 ha (15,500 a) of wetlands (NYSDEC [2007a]), mostly in the Great Lakes Plain. The most common wetland habitat is forested wetland (swamp—mostly dominated by red maple, 70 percent), followed by shrub/scrub wetlands (16 percent), emergent wetlands (marsh, 9 percent), and open-water wetlands (5 percent) (NYSDEC [2007a]). Largely as a result of ecological succession and changes in hydrology, shrub/scrub and emergent wetlands are being lost. The gains in freshwater wetland habitat area resulted largely from ecological succession associated with agricultural reversion and from increased run-off associated with hydrological regimes modified by human activities (NYSDEC [2007a]).

Beaver activities cause landscape changes that lead to the formation of habitats suitable for use by a variety of wetland birds. Based on field studies in south-central New York, Grover and Baldassarre (1995) showed that wetlands occupied by beaver contained significantly more bird species and a greater average number of species than did inactive sites of the same size. In 1993, there were an estimated 17,579 active beaver colonies in New York, representing an increase of 19 percent since 1990 (NYSDEC 2007b). Trapping results for beaver (NYSDEC unpubl. data) show that the numbers of beaver trapped and reported to NYSDEC from the 1983–84 trapping season until the 2005–06 trapping season increased by 133 percent, from 9,789 to 22,492.

Tidal wetlands are found on Long Island and up the Hudson River as far north as the Troy Dam, wherever tidal influences can be found. In the Jamaica Bay area of Queens County, approximately 213 ha (526 a) of marsh island habitat were lost between 1974 and 1994, at an average rate of 11 ha (26 a) per year. From 1994 until 1999, 89 ha (220 a) were lost in Jamaica Bay, at an accelerated average rate of 18 ha (44 a) per year. The losses largely reflect conversion of vegetated intertidal marsh to nonvegetated underwater lands, possibly attributable to rising sea levels (NYSDEC [2001]). Farther eastward on Long Island, between 1974 and 1999, approximately 172 ha (424 a) of tidal wetlands were lost.

Agriculture and Open Lands

Historically, habitats with prairie vegetation existed in New York (Schmidt 1938), with possibly the largest contiguous area of prairie habitat occurring at the Hempstead Plains on Long Island, having an original area estimated at 24,300 ha (60,000 a) circa 1892. Although no remnants of undisturbed Hempstead Plains exist today, a portion of Mitchell Field in Nassau County is thought to be the least disturbed example of original Long Island prairie vegetation (Stalter and Lamont 1987, Stalter et al. 1991).

Today, birds requiring open habitats for nesting depend largely on agricultural activities and the maintenance of grassy areas around airports and on some golf courses. Figures 4.1 and 4.2 show how farm acreages and four types of land cover associated with agriculture and beneficial to breeding birds have changed since the field work for the first Breeding Bird Atlas was concluded in 1985. Of the bird species identified as Species of Greatest Conservation Need in New York, 13 (16 percent) are associated with agriculture and open lands. The declines in acreage for some types of agricultural land cover (Figure 4.2) are more modest over the past 20 years than the statewide decline in agricultural acreage (Figure 4.1).

The declines of the past 20 years for New York continue the pattern of decreasing farmland acreage that began in the early 20th century (Smith and Gregory 1998). The decreases in agricultural land areas are coincident with the widespread and widely publicized declines (Brennan and Kuvlesky 2005) in the populations of birds that breed in the grasslands and open lands of New York and the Northeast, which was first described for the northeastern United States by C. R. Smith et al. (1993). Grassland birds often are associated with agriculture (Smith 1997). Though lumped together as "grassland birds" by C. R. Smith et al. (1993), perhaps incorrectly, this artificial assemblage of bird species traditionally has included species of open lands other than grasslands, such as the Horned Lark, which is largely dependent on agricultural fields with patches of nearly bare ground for its nesting habitats (e.g., fields of row crops, some pastures). It might be better and more informative to consider grassland birds as a sub-assemblage of species within the category of open-land species, or even agricultural bird species. In that context, other species, including the Killdeer, American Kestrel, Eastern Bluebird, and possibly others, could be included in an assemblage of bird

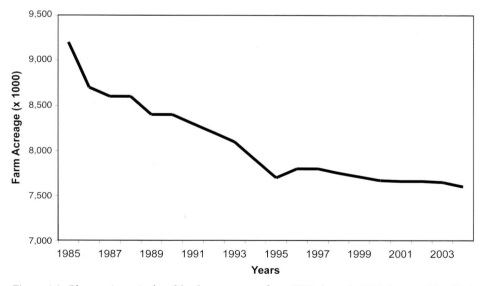

Figure 4.1 Changes in agricultural land-use acreages from 1985 through 2004. Source: New York State Agricultural Statistics Service. 1986–2005. New York Agricultural Statistics. New York State Department of Agriculture and Markets, Division of Statistics. Albany, NY.

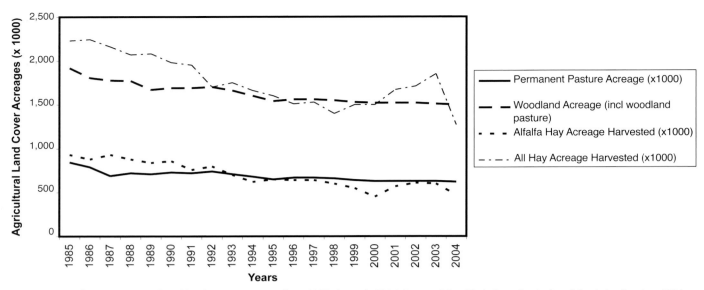

Figure 4.2   Changes in agricultural land-cover acreages from 1985 through 2004. Source: New York State Agricultural Statistics Service. 1986–2005. New York Agricultural Statistics. New York State Department of Agriculture and Markets, Division of Statistics. Albany, NY.

species associated with agricultural habitats. Incentive programs, such as the Conservation Reserve Program (CRP) and Grassland Reserve Program (GRP), managed by the U.S. Department of Agriculture's Natural Resources Conservation Service, encourage farmers to manage some types of agricultural open lands to benefit grassland birds. In the Midwest in particular, studies have shown clear benefits to grassland birds from the CRP (Johnson and Igl 1995), but no comparable studies on the effects of either the CRP or GRP east of the Mississippi River have been published, except for one study of limited scope in Maryland (Gill et al. 2006). A series of reports by Ochterski (2005, 2006a, b) demonstrated the benefits of pastures and hayfields for open-land birds in New York and discussed how those habitats can be managed to enhance nesting opportunities for open-land bird species.

Shrublands

Naturally occurring shrublands in upland habitats in New York are dominated by various combinations of different species of viburnum, shrub dogwood, and hawthorn. Of the bird species identified as Species of Greatest Conservation Need in New York, 12 (14 percent) are associated with shrublands. With reference to the northeastern United States, Dettmers (2003) observed that shrubland bird species contribute a relatively large number of individuals but a relatively small proportion of the region's bird species variety (15 percent). Dettmers (2003) suggested that managing 10–15 percent of the northeastern landscape as shrubland habitats could provide adequate habitat for maintaining minimal populations of shrubland birds, but that larger areas of shrubland will be necessary if population increases are desirable for such bird species. At this time, no program keeps

track of the status and trends for shrublands in New York. While there are a variety of incentives to maintain agricultural and forestry land, no similar incentive programs exist to encourage the maintenance of shrublands by private land owners. Further, it is worth noting that some shrub thickets that develop on abandoned farmland have been shown to be persistent, resisting invasion by trees for many decades (Niering et al. 1986, Putz and Canham 1992).

Forests

Unlike for agriculture, forestry statistics are not reported annually, except for agricultural woodlands (see Figure 4.2). Results from the FIA Program of the U.S. Forest Service are reported at approximately 10-year intervals. FIA information relevant to this discussion was available in reports for 1980, 1993, and 2004 (U.S. Forest Service 2005). Patterns of forested land cover are more complex than those of other land-cover types. Forests of different species compositions and with trees of different age-class structures often support different assemblages of breeding bird species, as described by DeGraaf and Yamasaki (2001) and Keller and Smith (1983). This differentiation of bird species associated with tree species is caused by the responses of breeding birds to spatial patterns created in forests by blowdowns of large canopy-dominant trees and the vertical structure that results from layering of shrubs, saplings, and mature trees in most forests (Roth 1976). Of the bird species identified as Species of Greatest Conservation Need in New York, 25 (30 percent) are associated with forests. Except for declines in agricultural woodland acreage (see Figure 4.2), forest cover changed little from 1980 through 2004 (Figures 4.3, 4.4), with approximately 62 percent of New York defined as forest land by the U.S. Forest

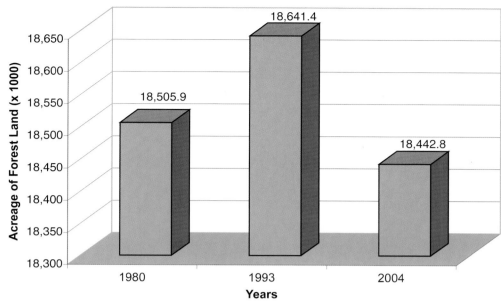

Figure 4.3 Total acreage of forested land in New York State for the years 1980, 1993, and 2004. Over the 25-year period, there has not been a substantial change. Source: U.S. Forest Service. 2007. Northeastern Forest Inventory and Analysis - Statewide Results. http://www.fs.fed.us/ne/fia/states/ny/index.html.

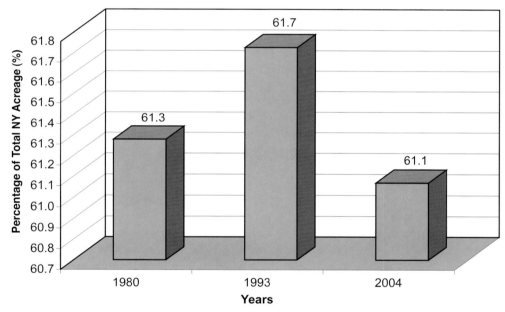

Figure 4.4 Total acreage of forested land as a percentage of the total land area of New York (30.2 million acres) for the years 1980, 1993, and 2004. Source: U.S. Forest Service. 2007. Northeastern Forest Inventory and Analysis - Statewide Results. http://www.fs.fed.us/ne/fia/states/ny/index.html.

Service. As in pre-settlement times, major natural weather events still can have significant effects. The extensive blowdown of July 1995 affected approximately 40,470 ha (100,000 a) in the Adirondacks (Jenkins 1995).

The relatively stable forest area of the past 20 years suggests that the statewide pattern of increasing forested area, which began in the early 20th century with the abandonment of agri-

cultural land, may have ended. From 1980 through 2000, New York's human population grew by 7.5 percent, with only 18 of the 62 counties showing declines. Suburban and rural development associated with human population growth likely is eroding the effects of forest area regained by ecological succession. The next 20 years will probably see a pattern of conversion and degradation of existing forested habitats, characterized by greater forest fragmentation, as a result of increased commercial and residential development, especially outside the Adirondack and Catskill forest preserves. If such a pattern occurs, it underscores the necessity of developing more sophisticated, more frequently applied methods for assessing status and trends and patterns of change in land uses and habitats throughout all of New York, assuming that land use in a landscape dominated by human activities is a significant factor in determining the distributions and abundances of breeding birds and other wildlife. As better tools become available for quantifying habitat patterns at landscape scales, metrics in addition to habitat area can and should be considered, including measures of edge-to-area ratios, juxtaposition, contiguity, and connectivity, among others (Turner and Gardner 1991, McGarigal and McComb 1995, Penhollow and Stauffer 2000, Turner 2005).

Although New York is predominantly a forested state, it contains relatively modest amounts of "old forest." Kershner and Leverett (2004) estimated that the total area of "old-growth" forest in New York was approximately 161,874 ha (400,000 a, or 2.2 percent of New York's forested land), with much of it concentrated in the Adirondacks. At least one recent study concentrated on characterizing the vegetation structure for a stand of old forest contained within the Nelson Swamp State Unique Area, Madison County (Forrester et al. 2005), but it did not include information about breeding birds. The work of Keller et al. (2003) did include counts of birds from forests 70–80 years old. Interestingly, Keller et al. found that in older forests the values for density and species richness for breeding birds were lower than in younger forests. It does not appear that there are any extant species of breeding birds in the northeastern United States that depend on old-growth forest, as is the case for the Pacific Northwest (DeGraaf and Yamasaki 2001).

While the FIA Program provides information about the quantity of forest in New York over time, it tells little about the quality of forested land cover, though program data do show that existing forests are growing older. Information about the landscape patterns of forest, including sizes of forest patches, extent of contiguous forests, degree of fragmentation of forested cover types, distances among forest patches, and amount of forest edge, all of which have been shown to influence the distributions and abundances of forest-breeding bird species (Keller and Smith 1983, Robbins et al. 1989), is not provided. Some sources of information and tools (McGarigal and McComb 1995, Penhollow and Stauffer 2000, Turner 2005) give information related to landscape patterns, but no published studies provide that kind of information for statewide or ecoregional scales for New York.

Responses of Birds to Patterns of Ecological Succession

Different species of birds are found in habitats at different stages of succession, from an abandoned, agricultural field to an older secondary forest (Keller 1980, 1982). In New York, a very general pattern of changes in representative bird species in association with ecological succession might occur as follows: Immediately after agricultural land has been abandoned, especially following cultivation, open-land species that often include bare soil within their territories, such as the Killdeer, Horned Lark, and Vesper Sparrow, might prevail. As grasses and forbs invade, the Red-winged Blackbird and Bobolink can be expected to appear, along with other grassland species (Bollinger 1995). With the establishment of shrubs and tree saplings, the habitat becomes a mosaic of patches of meadow interspersed with woody thickets, and the Field Sparrow, Song Sparrow, and American Goldfinch can be expected. As woody plants begin to prevail and develop a closed canopy, especially shrubby species such as hawthorns and dogwoods, the Brown Thrasher and Eastern Towhee typically are observed. By 40 years out of agriculture, the vegetation has become a closed, young forest perhaps 9 m (30 ft) tall, but the bark of the trees lacks the complex structure of ridges, fissures, and crevices characteristic of older trees. When trees become old enough to develop a species-typical, complex bark structure, they become more attractive to foraging assemblages of bark-gleaning and probing birds such as woodpeckers (Keller at al. 2003). The aging of New York forests, suggested by FIA data, might account for the more widespread distributions of many woodpeckers (especially pileated), nuthatches, and the Brown Creeper revealed in this Atlas in comparison with the first Atlas. Between 40 and 100 years, the trees grow larger in diameter and taller, with a more complex branching structure, and forest-interior bird species become established (Keller et al. 2003). In even-aged forest stands that develop following clear-cutting, Keller et al. (2003) reported that density and species richness values for breeding birds peak when the stands are approximately five to seven years old. It is at that age that leaf areas and stem densities are at their greatest near the ground, with substantial insect biomass and more foraging locations and opportunities.

The Complicating Effects of Invasive Plants, Overabundant Herbivores, and Predators

Many invasive plant species respond to disturbances that result from human activities, often in the contexts of land-use changes, plant succession, habitat fragmentation, and the associated habitat changes at local scales and ecoregional scales. Managing invasive, non-native plants is one of the great conservation challenges of the 21st century. Only a few studies on the effects of invasive, non-native plants on bird populations have been published, and none of them are based on research done in New York. A study in Illinois (Schmidt and Whelan 1999) concluded that nests of American Robin placed in a non-native honeysuckle and in buckthorn experienced greater nest predation than robin nests in native dogwood and viburnum shrubs or native trees. Schmidt and Whelan (1999) believed that the higher predation rate resulted from a combination of lower nest height, an absence of sharp thorns on the non-native species, and a branching structure that facilitated predator movement within the non-native species.

Borgmann and Rodewald (2004), based on their work in Ohio, reported that nests of Northern Cardinal and American Robin placed in exotic shrubs, including honeysuckles and multiflora rose, experienced greater predation than did nests in native plant species. They concluded that the lower height and branching structure of those shrub species make nests especially vulnerable to climbing mammalian predators, such as raccoon, opossum, eastern chipmunk, and possibly even mice and snakes, which can climb such shrubs more easily. Tartarian honeysuckle, buckthorn, and multiflora rose are widespread in New York (Weldy and Werier 2005), largely because state and federal agencies introduced and promoted those species for their "wildlife value" during the mid-20th century. In some New York settings, tartarian honeysuckle and multiflora rose dominate early successional stages following abandonment of pastures and other farmlands, conceivably creating "sinks" where loss of eggs and nestlings to predation exceeds the production of young. Clearly, this phenomenon needs further study in New York and elsewhere, and adds another, complicated dimension to consideration of the effects of land-use changes on breeding birds.

The effects of high population densities of white-tailed deer on the structure, age composition, and species composition of forests have been studied widely (Alverson et al. 1988, McShea and Rappole 2000, Augustine and deCalesta 2003, Horsley et al. 2003). Excessive browsing of woody plants, especially at the seedling and sapling stages, can affect dramatically the future age composition, species composition, and structure of forests, thereby altering the kinds and distributions of birds in forested habitats as forest succession progresses (Roth 1976). In extreme cases, when seedlings and saplings are browsed sufficiently to be killed, the very capacities of forests to regenerate themselves will be diminished (McShea and Rappole 2000) and cover is lost for ground-nesting birds. Linkages of white-tailed deer to the spread of invasive, non-native plants and to decreased productivity of forest songbirds also have been described. Vellend (2002) showed that white-tailed deer contribute to the spread of tartarian honeysuckle and other invasive species by dispersing the seeds of the shrubs in their feces. Working in northwestern Pennsylvania, deCalesta (1994) studied the effects of different simulated densities of white-tailed deer browsing within enclosures over a 10-year period and found that densities of between 7.9 and 14.9 deer per square kilometer (247 a) had measurable negative effects on the abundances of the Eastern Wood-Pewee, Indigo Bunting, Least Flycatcher, Yellow-billed Cuckoo, and Cerulean Warbler. At the highest deer densities, even American Robin abundance declined. In northern Virginia, McShea and Rappole (2000) also reported declines in abundances of breeding birds associated with high deer densities.

In New York State, information about estimated deer densities is not readily available. Numbers and densities of deer taken during the annual hunting season in New York are available, however (NYSDEC 2005b), but not in such a way that one can obtain an overall population index. During the 2005 deer-hunting season in New York, the numbers of deer harvested averaged 1.7 per square kilometer, ranging from one to five deer harvested per square kilometer at the county level. If one assumes conservatively that at least four deer are left on the range for every deer harvested, then 22 of the 56 New York counties in which deer are harvested have densities in excess of 7.9 deer per square kilometer, the threshold at which deCalesta (1994) reported detectable declines in forest songbird abundances. Those 22 counties add up to nearly 32 percent of the land area of New York.

In addition to the effects of invasive plants and overabundant herbivores, diseases and insects can have dramatic effects on the composition and structure of forest tree species, and subsequently on birds. Noteworthy, widespread fungal infestations include those that attacked American chestnut in the early 20th century, American elm in the mid-20th century, and American beech in the latter part of the 20th century (Sinclair et al. 1987). In all cases the fungi were introduced into North America, and none of the affected tree species have been extirpated. American chestnut still sprouts from its roots, but trees rarely reach maturity, succumbing to infection from the fungus, which remains resident in the roots of affected trees. As Dutch elm disease has moved westward and southward in North America, American elms have begun to reappear after the front of the disease has passed. In other areas, American beech continues to regenerate after beech bark disease has killed older trees. In Maine, where beech bark disease has been present since the mid-1900s, there are beech stands in their third wave of regrowth after deaths of larger trees (Mohler et al. 2006). Studies at Sapsucker Woods in Ithaca, Tompkins County (Litwin and Smith 1992), showed that from 1950 until 1980, silver maple and sugar maple largely replaced American elm and American beech lost to Dutch elm disease and beech bark disease, respectively.

In addition to the interacting effects of invasive shrubs, predators, and deer, invasive, non-native insects, such as viburnum leaf beetle, emerald ash borer, and hemlock woolly adelgid, also have the potential to affect habitat structure and composition dramatically. In areas invaded by viburnum leaf beetle, which infests all native species in the genus *Viburnum*, whole stands of arrowwood have been eliminated (C. R. Smith and P. L. Marks pers. obs.). Similar effects of hemlock woolly adelgid on eastern hemlock can be seen in the Palisades along the Hudson River (C. R. Smith pers. obs.). The effects of emerald ash borer on ashes in the Upper Great Lakes states have been pervasive, though it has not yet been recorded from New York (as of the end of 2007). Both these insect pests will affect successional patterns and the species composition and structure of shrub and forest communities for many years to come. The effects of emerald ash borer could be as extensive as those of the fungus that attacked the American chestnut or comparable to the effects of Dutch elm disease on the American elm. So far, no studies on the effects of these insect pests on bird species have been reported. The patterns of shrubland succession following the loss of viburnums and forest succession following the loss of ashes, and the associated patterns of bird species responses will be interesting to document. For example, on Long Island, there is evidence that the Brown Creeper expanded its range in response to the numbers of standing dead elms, which provided nest sites in the wake of Dutch elm disease (Bull 1974).

Recently published work (Morton 2005) also showed that for the Ovenbird, more complex forces, such as predation, require perceptions of a forest-interior species to be contextually qualified. The Ovenbird long has been considered an archetypical area-sensitive, forest-interior bird species (Van Horn and Donovan 1994). Morton's work showed successful use of forest edges for nesting when the Ovenbird is confronted with forest-interior predator pressure from the eastern chipmunk. In settings where chipmunk densities and predation on eggs and nestlings were higher in the forest interior than at the forest edge, Morton (2005) found more Ovenbirds nesting at the forest edges, with greater productivity of young. These studies show clearly that the effects of changing patterns of land-use and patterns of ecological succession have to be evaluated both temporally and spatially in a more complicated landscape. The individual as well as the synergistic effects of invasive plant species, predators, overabundant herbivores, and invasive, non-native insect pests should be taken into consideration when evaluating potential causes for changes in the numbers of breeding birds over large areas and long periods of time.

Summary

The use of standard terminology and definitions is fundamental to unambiguous communication about the associations of breeding birds with habitats and patterns of land-use change. An understanding of the effects of changing land-use practices on breeding birds requires a clear understanding of the differences among human land uses and the resulting land covers and a sound, conceptual understanding of habitat as a fundamental ecological concept.

Freshwater wetlands in New York are increasing in area and shifting in geographic distribution, though little information is available about the quality of those wetlands. Tidal wetlands have shown modest reductions in area on the Coastal Lowlands. Agricultural lands, which include most grassland and open-land habitats, continue to decline in area throughout New York. Shrubland habitats, in spite of their importance to many species of birds whose numbers are declining statewide and regionally, are not monitored at all in New York.

Forest habitats amount to about 62 percent of the land area of New York and have been relatively stable and growing more mature over the past 20 years. The maturation of forests might account for the increases in distribution of many woodpecker species, nuthatches, and the Brown Creeper since the first Atlas survey. More information about the quality of those forests in relation to their use by breeding birds and surrounding landscape patterns would be useful.

Invasive, non-native plant species, introduced insect herbivores, and overabundant mammalian herbivores (e.g., white-tailed deer) complicate the relationships of birds to habitats and can modify the natural patterns of succession and vegetative species composition and structure significantly. Predators on eggs and nestlings also modify typical patterns of habitat use by birds, and some non-native, invasive shrubs actually facilitate nest predation. More research on these factors and their interactions needs to be done in New York.

It is remarkable that greater effort has not been invested in an ongoing, standardized approach to tracking the status and trends of a greater variety of habitat types in New York. With the exception of wetlands, agricultural lands, and forest, bird habitats are not monitored with sufficient frequency or detail to establish meaningful, long-term correlations between patterns of changes in breeding bird distributions and patterns of changes in land use.

CHAPTER FIVE

Ornithology and Birding in New York State

JOHN M. C. PETERSON

s observed in the opening pages of *Bull's Birds of New York State* (Levine 1998), the last major work on birds in this state prior to the present volume, "Any book updating a state's ornithological history will be out of date before it is published." With that caveat, the history of ornithology and birding in New York is still worthy of examination here, with a focus on recent avian projects and field studies.

New York State has been well served for over a century and a half by the publication of a series of six major works on its birds. As compared with Europe, ornithology might have been slow in developing here. Even neighboring Canada benefited from the writings of explorers, missionaries, Hudson's Bay Company traders, and visitors during the 17th and 18th centuries. The first naturalist of note to visit New York appears to have been Pehr (or Peter) Kalm, the Swedish disciple of Carolus Linnaeus, whose travels in northeastern North America from June to October 1749 brought him up the Hudson River and Lake Champlain to Quebec, but his observations of birds were buried in the narrative of his trip and not published in English until 1770. Not until the mid-19th century did the first book devoted specifically to New York ornithology appear, *Part 2, Birds of Zoology of New-York, or the New-York Fauna* (1844) by James E. DeKay (DeKay 1844).

Five more major works followed: *Birds of New York* by Elon Howard Eaton (1910, 1914); *Birds of New York State* by John Bull (1974), with a 1976 supplement; *The Atlas of Breeding Birds in New York State*, edited by Robert F. Andrle and Janet R. Carroll (1988); *Bull's Birds of New York State*, edited by Emanuel Levine (1998); and the current volume, edited by Kevin J. McGowan and Kimberley Corwin. Each of these includes prefatory historical matter. The New York State Ornithological Association (NYSOA) was instrumental in the publication of the four books that followed Eaton's, and the New York State Department of Environmental Conservation (NYSDEC) and Cornell University have played a major role since the publication of the first Atlas.

With that as background, recent developments in ornithology and birding can be examined. A logical starting point is the NYSOA. This group, originally the Federation of New York State Bird Clubs (FNYSBC), was founded in 1948 to fill a desire that birders in the state had to share ideas and experiences and to promote research and conservation of birds in New York (Lincoln 1998b). One of the organization's objectives was to produce a statewide ornithological journal, and publication of *The*

Kingbird commenced in December 1950. This journal, which has appeared quarterly without interruption since that first issue, is devoted to New York ornithology. It includes information on research, rarities, interesting observations, and perhaps most importantly, seasonal reports of bird observations by region. A quarterly newsletter, *New York Birders*, was started in 1972; it provides a means of communication among members and member clubs, disseminating information on activities, meetings, and other issues pertinent to birds and birding in the state (Lincoln 1998b). NYSOA currently includes 48 member clubs, Audubon societies, and nature organizations, as well as individual members.

A vital offshoot of NYSOA was established in 1977 with creation of the New York State Avian Records Committee (NYSARC), charged with maintaining and publishing the official list of species of birds in the state and adjacent ocean, the *Checklist of the Birds of New York State*, most recently updated in 2007. The committee reviews reports of any species new to the state, any addition to the list of species proven to nest here, and rarely documented subspecies. It provides a list of birds to be reported anywhere within New York, in Upstate New York, outside the Adirondacks, or (especially upstate) in spring. At its discretion, the committee can also review extreme out-of-season records. New to NYSOA's web site is a searchable database of all NYSARC reports, which allows one to see how often a rare species has been reported, when, and where (http://www.nybirds.org/NYSARC/RecordsSummary.htm).

NYSOA also holds an annual fall meeting of member clubs, presents awards, and sponsors field trips around the state, among other activities. Three annual awards serve to recognize individuals. The Elon Howard Eaton Memorial Award, sponsored by the Eaton Bird Club of Geneva, recognizes significant contributions to the study of avian biology in New York State. Awarded since 1964, the John J. Elliott Award recognizes the best article in *The Kingbird*; John Jackson Elliott (b. 1896) was president of the FNYSBC from 1962 until his sudden death on 28 June 1963. The Lillian Stoner Award—initiated by a charter member of the FNYSBC—defrays the expenses of secondary-school or college students attending the annual meeting of NYSOA, with nominations submitted by member clubs. NYSOA also awards Certificates of Appreciation and Member Club Grants. Its greatest accomplishment, however, has been the successful conclusion of the two monumental Atlas field projects conducted in 1980–85 and 2000–05. The two resultant publications leave a rich legacy for future generations.

NYSDEC, as mentioned, has also been a major force in the success of the two Atlas projects, employing project coordinators Janet R. Carroll during the first project and Kimberley Corwin during the second to oversee the regional coordinators and volunteers, data collection and entry, and a host of other tasks. All people of the state can take great pride in the professionalism and broad ornithological interests of this department. Ongoing monitoring projects at the NYSDEC include the Niagara Frontier Colonial Waterbird Survey and the St. Lawrence River Common Tern Monitoring and Management Project. The Endangered Species Unit (ESU) oversees the Midwinter Bald Eagle Survey, as well as nest surveys of Bald Eagle, Osprey, and Peregrine Falcon. In 1989, the NYSDEC Bald Eagle restoration program "put itself out of business," according to ESU leader Peter Nye, by achieving its goal of 10 breeding pairs. By 2007, there were 115 breeding pairs of eagles in the state, and 87 of those were successful in raising young, with 153 young fledged. The Peregrine Falcon restoration program has enjoyed similar success. The results of both eagle and falcon recovery efforts are described in the Atlas species accounts.

The NYSDEC also supports many projects relating to birds with funds from the State Wildlife Grants program and the Return a Gift to Wildlife tax check-off. Recent projects supported by grants have included the Boreal Forest Bird Assessment, a Comprehensive Bird Monitoring Plan, Golden-winged Warbler Habitat Restoration, Marshbird Conservation in Upstate New York, and Status Assessment and Delineation of Essential Bald Eagle Habitats in the Upper Delaware River. Without the funding, staffing, and resources provided through NYSDEC, neither Atlas project would have been possible.

Colleges and universities throughout New York offer courses and programs in ornithology, with faculty and students involved in a variety of research projects. Holding a special place among these institutions is Cornell University, home of the Cornell Lab of Ornithology, now located in the new Johnson Center for Birds and Biodiversity in Ithaca. The Lab is deeply involved in research, notably the Bird Population Studies program, currently examining the effects of disease on bird populations, as well as the variation of nesting seasons of birds from north to south in North America. The presence of the Macaulay Library, formerly the Library of Natural Sounds, provides a locus for the Bioacoustics Research Program. Research also extends to BirdSource Projects, developed and managed with the National Audubon Society (Christmas Bird Counts, eBird, the Great Backyard Bird Count, and Project FeederWatch), and the Evolutionary Biology Program.

Perhaps the most important facet of the work being done at the Lab of Ornithology is the increasing focus on Citizen Science projects that strive to employ the talents of birders in a wide variety of ornithological studies. The most recent program made available to birders in New York is eBird, a web-based technology used to track birds and share information on sightings with scientists, conservationists, educators, and other birders (http://ebird.org). In 2006, NYSOA and Audubon New York launched NY eBird, linked to the Cornell Lab continent-wide version. The state-specific project provides a simple way for birders to keep track of their observations in New York, while contributing to the growing database of bird records available to researchers who seek information on the distribution and patterns of movement of birds in New York State and beyond.

Other year-round projects offered to citizen scientists, currently popular in New York, are the House Finch Disease Survey, employed to track the spread of avian eye disease across the continent; the House Finch Nest Survey; PigeonWatch, in which students monitor the different colors of Rock Pigeons in urban flocks; and Urban Bird Studies, which joins city residents with scientists to track birds in urban landscapes.

Spring and summer projects offered by the Lab of Ornithology and of great value in New York State include The Birdhouse Network and Birds in Forested Landscapes. The Birdhouse Network, now evolving into NestWatch, asks volunteers to devote a small amount of time during spring and summer to monitor the cavity-nesting birds in their nest boxes. Birds in Forested Landscapes, formerly Project Tanager, and now conducted with The Nature Conservancy in the Catskills, helps scientists examine the effects of habitat change (e.g., forest fragmentation) on North American birds. Participants in New York choose study sites in forests of various sizes, then survey for target species by broadcasting recordings of the species' vocalizations. Other projects have studied the population status and habitat requirements of Cerulean and Golden-winged warblers.

Three more projects center on fall and winter activities: Classroom FeederWatch, the Great Backyard Bird Count, and the highly popular Project FeederWatch. Students participating in Classroom FeederWatch not only observe and then record counts of birds, but also interact with university scientists, knowing that data gathered in New York is part of a continent-wide effort to learn more about the dynamics of bird populations. The Great Backyard Bird Count, a joint project with the National Audubon Society and promoted by many of its chapters in New York, is a free, online four-day survey of birds conducted in February for the past decade. In 2006, some 60,000 observers reported 7.5 million birds of 623 different species. Results can be tracked online in real time (http://www.birdsource.org/gbbc/). New York birders have been participating in Project FeederWatch since it was launched in 1987 by the Cornell Lab of Ornithology and Canada's Long Point Bird Observatory (now Bird Studies Canada), paying a modest fee for materials and joining more than 16,000 other citizen scientists to count birds that visit feeders from November to April. The resultant online maps can show the movement of a species over the course of a single winter, or over the course of all winters, and provide a fascinating winter supplement to the information on New York State birds presented in this Atlas (http://www.birds.cornell.edu/pfw/).

In addition to these ongoing projects at the Lab of Ornithology, which also serves as the repository of the Nest Record Program, many other departments at Cornell University are engaged in avian research. Several of the institutions within the State University of New York (SUNY) system are similarly recognized for avian research. SUNY Albany was the site of revealing studies on Red and White-winged crossbills. The SUNY College of Environmental Science and Forestry (ESF), when known as the New York State College of Forestry at Syracuse University, published the *Roosevelt Wild Life Bulletin of the Roosevelt Wild Life Forest Experiment Station* between 1821 and 1950, as well as the *Roosevelt Wild Life Annals* between 1926 and 1936, which included now-classic articles on summer birds of the western Adirondacks by Perley M. Silloway (1923) and of the northern Adirondacks by Aretas A. Saunders (1929), as well as a reprint of the annotated 1877 Adirondack list of Franklin County summer birds by Theodore Roosevelt Jr. and Henry D. Minot. More recently, SUNY ESF has also conducted studies of the Spruce Grouse and other boreal birds. SUNY Potsdam has been recently involved in the status and ecology of the Spruce Grouse in the Adirondacks as well, with fieldwork on the distribution and ecology of this New York State Endangered Species being conducted throughout the lowland boreal forest habitat of the northern and central Adirondacks. A number of other colleges and universities in New York are similarly developing reputations for their focus on specific birds, such as current research on "winged warblers" (Blue-winged and Golden-winged warblers, and their hybrids) at Ithaca College, to offer but a single example.

Education is not limited to institutions of higher learning. The Roger Tory Peterson Institute for the Study of Natural History moved into a new facility in Jamestown, New York, in October 1993. The institute continues the legacy of the late Roger Peterson by promoting nature study and striving to create an appreciation of the natural world. The new facility was built, in part, to house the lifetime body of work by the great ornithologist, artist, and writer, and a portion of his personal library is housed there. The Roger Tory Peterson Institute also has education and reference libraries, with strong holdings of bird books for young people, and the facility hosts exhibitions, programs, and special events. Courses are offered, some for credit in cooperation with SUNY Fredonia. The Institute of Ecosystem Studies (IES) in Millbrook, New York, does avian studies as well.

Museums throughout the state also serve as centers of ornithology. Many public and university museums serve as repositories of bird collections; the Buffalo Museum of Science, for example, curates 9,000 avian specimens. Many records of New York birds are supported with voucher specimen numbers deposited at the American Museum of Natural History, the Cornell University Museum of Vertebrates, or the New York State Museum. The American Museum of Natural History in New York City has a Department of Ornithology that was home to John Bull while he wrote *Birds of New York State*. The next generation of that publication, *Bull's Birds of New York State* (Levine 1998), was a project of NYSOA and the Museum of Natural History. The museum's Ornithology Department maintains the world's largest collection of birds, with 99 percent of living species represented by more than a million specimens of skins, skeletons, nests, eggs, and anatomical preparations.

Equally important to the reputation of New York as a center of ornithology is the New York State Museum in Albany, which published Eaton's *Birds of New York* (1910, 1914) almost a century ago. The State Museum, which itself holds over 10,000 bird specimens, conducted a 1990 Survey of Biological Collections at 102 institutions throughout New York State, listing on the museum web site at least 35 that also hold collections of birds, ranging from a handful to many thousands, with the two largest collections held at the American Museum of Natural History and the Cornell University Museum of Vertebrates. The State Museum now plays an increasingly important role in protecting biodiversity. The State Education Law of 1993 mandated the establishment of the New York State Biodiversity Research Institute (BRI) within the State Museum to meet the urgent need to preserve local and global biodiversity. Funded through the Environmental Protection Fund, BRI includes a number of collaborators, including the NYSDEC, New York Natural Heritage Program, and New York State Office of Parks, Recreation and Historic Preservation. Projects focus on biodiversity, stewardship, education, and research to assess environmental quality and change. In addition to its publications, BRI offers an annual Biodiversity Grants Program. Of the 26 projects funded in 2006–07, seven dealt directly with birds. These seven studies examined a wide range of species and topics related to New York birdlife: the birds of Dutchess County, use of birds and citizens to advance the ecological health of New York forests, long-term responses of breeding birds to habitat loss, shrubland bird habitats of the lower Great Lakes Plain in the state, impacts of the Double-crested Cormorant on New York Harbor heronries, Piping Plover predator exclosures, and Cerulean Warbler habitat requirements in New York.

In addition to the NYSDEC at the state level, the U.S. Fish and Wildlife Service (USFWS) maintains a vital federal presence here. At Montezuma National Wildlife Refuge and Iroquois National Wildlife Refuge in western New York, plus eight more National Wildlife Refuges on Long Island, the USFWS provides habitat monitoring and management, with a focus on waterfowl, but benefiting a wide range of wetland species. In 1966 the USFWS initiated the annual Breeding Bird Survey (BBS), with routes throughout the state. The BBS is now run by the U.S. Geological Survey and the Canadian Wildlife Service. BBS volunteers start a 24.5-mile route a half-hour before local sunrise during June, stopping every half-mile for three minutes to look and listen for birds. New York has a BBS density of eight routes for each degree block of latitude and longitude, the highest of any states except Delaware and Maryland, and many of the

BBS trends are cited in this Atlas. The USFWS also published the 351-page *Migratory Nongame Birds of Management Concern in the Northeast* (Schneider and Pence 1992), dealing with 20 species of concern, all native to New York, including the now-extirpated Loggerhead Shrike.

Another important federal monitoring program is bird banding, formerly conducted under the USFWS but now the responsibility of the U.S. Geological Survey, in cooperation with Environment Canada of the Canadian Wildlife Service, with U.S. headquarters at the Bird Banding Laboratory in Laurel, Maryland. The number of private, institutional, and governmental banders active in New York is in constant flux. The following long-term banding stations (with the name of the county provided in parentheses) currently report their spring and fall results to the journal *North American Bird Bander*: Alfred Station (Allegany), Braddock Bay Bird Observatory (Monroe), Crown Point State Historic Site (Essex), Ellenville Station (Ulster), Kestrel Haven Avian Migration Observatory (Schuyler), Lewiston (Niagara), Northview Sanctuary (Tioga), and Powderhouse Road Station (Broome). In recent years, a growing number of specialized banding projects have used radio and satellite technology to supplement the use of traditional metal bands and color markings in order to track bird movements, even on a real-time basis. The NYSDEC can track individual Bald Eagles banded in southeastern New York State, following movements to their Canadian nesting grounds and back. Other technological advances include the study of isotopes in feathers to determine the general place of origin of individual birds, based on their diet, thus offering yet another monitoring method.

Audubon New York, in Albany and Ithaca, is active in the protection of the Great Lakes and Long Island Sound, and Audubon has recently added to its statewide centers and sanctuaries a new interpretive center at the Northern Montezuma Wildlife Management Area. Audubon chapters across the state take part in the annual Christmas Bird Count, established in 1900 by the National Audubon Society. Audubon also initiated in 1937 the Breeding Bird census, 249 censuses having been conducted in the state in 1937–90, and in 1948 the Winter Bird Population study.

The cornerstone of current conservation efforts by Audubon New York is its Important Bird Areas (IBA) program, established in 1996. The simple goals of this program are to identify the most important places for birds in New York and then to conserve them. BirdLife International identified the first IBAs in Europe in the mid-1980s, and the concept swiftly spread, reaching North America a decade later. The National Audubon Society and the newly created American Bird Conservancy adopted the idea in the United States, with the Audubon launching IBA programs in Pennsylvania in 1995 and New York in 1996. During the latter year, programs were also established in Canada and Mexico. When the first edition of *Important Bird Areas in New York State* (1998) by Jeffrey V. Wells appeared, 127 sites in the state had been identified for their importance to birds. By the time

the second edition by Michael F. Burger and Jillian M. Liner (2005) was published, the volume described 136 areas, some of the original areas having been de-listed and several new areas added. The program served as a model for the Bird Conservation Areas Law, passed as legislation in New York in 1997. Approximately 50 Bird Conservation Areas have been identified to date, with all located on state land, and their protection carries the force of law.

Other organizations focus on certain families of birds, or even on a single species. The Hawk Migration Association of North America (HMANA) was founded in 1974 to monitor raptor populations and provide a data bank on migrations through the use of standard reporting forms and procedures. Hawkwatches currently active in the collection of data in New York are located at Braddock Bay, Chestnut Ridge, Derby Hill, Fire Island, Franklin Mountain, Hamburg, Hook Mountain, the I-84 Overlook, Kestrel Haven, Lenoir Wildlife Sanctuary, the Marine Natural Study Area, Mohonk Preserve, Mount Peter, Ripley, and Summitville.

Since 2001, the Adirondack Cooperative Loon Program has conducted an annual census of Adirondack loons. A partnership of Audubon New York, BioDiversity Research Institute, Natural History Museum of the Adirondacks, NYSDEC, and Wildlife Conservation Society, the program follows breeding trends and the effects of mercury contamination. Banding and color banding of Common Loons on Adirondack lakes in summer, as well as the recent use of satellite telemetry, allows the program to track individuals as far as wintering grounds in Florida.

Several projects focus on birds of marshes and beaches. The Marsh Monitoring Program (MMP), initiated in 1994 by Bird Studies Canada and Environment Canada, now includes wetland conservation on both sides of the border. MMP survey routes stretch from the Midwest to lower St. Lawrence River and as far south as Long Island, with many located in western New York. The International Shorebird Survey (ISS) and Program for Regional and International Shorebird Monitoring (PRISM) includes New York sites at Carmans River Marshes, Captree Island, Jamaica Bay, Jones Beach, Moriches Bay and Inlet, and Shinnecock Bay and Inlet. The NYSDEC also cooperates with the International Piping Plover Census.

The Vermont Institute of Natural Science established Mountain Birdwatch as an offshoot of the Vermont Forest Bird Monitoring Program in 2000 to establish a long-term monitoring program for Bicknell's Thrush and other montane forest birds. Volunteers in New York surveyed routes on 39 mountains in the Adirondacks and Catskills during 2005, locating 74 Bicknell's Thrushes (J. Hart pers. comm.) and contributing data not only to Mountain Birdwatch but also to this Atlas. In a more proactive effort to protect montane birds, Partners in Flight, which produces plans by physiographic area, has produced a Bird Conservation Plan for the Adirondacks.

With birding and birding festivals growing in popularity across the continent and in New York, more birders are maintaining personal lists of state, regional, and county bird sightings. New York Bird List Reports have been compiled and published by NYSOA since 1992. This increase in local listing has led to a growing series of county references, including recent editions on birds of Clinton County by Charles W. Mitchell and William E. Krueger (1997); Essex County by Geoffrey Carleton and John M. C. Peterson (1999); Hamilton County by Peterson and Gary N. Lee (2004); a Clinton County supplement by Krueger (2006); Dutchess County by Stan DeOrsey and Barbara Butler (2006); and Franklin County by Peterson (2006). In addition, the Adirondack North Country Association issued a map and guide to 86 birding sites in 2006. Mention should also be made of *Birds of New York State*, a field guide by Robert E. Budliger and Gregory Kennedy (2005), devoted to birds of the state. Field checklists have been published for a number of counties by NYSOA member clubs, and the New York State Office of Parks, Recreation, and Historic Preservation has brought out a series of checklists for State Parks and Crown Point State Historic Site.

With the publication of this second Atlas on the breeding birds of the state, New York continues a rich tradition of bird studies based on fieldwork by volunteers, with McGowan and Corwin and authors of the current work adding to the framework erected by DeKay, Eaton, Bull, Andrle and Carroll, Levine, and a host of others. The current state of ornithology and birding in New York State is vibrant and the future full of promise.

CHAPTER SIX

Conservation of New York's Breeding Birds

KENNETH V. ROSENBERG AND MICHAEL F. BURGER

reeding bird atlases comprehensively assess which species breed in a designated area, and where they breed
within that area, providing information that is valuable to the field of bird conservation in several ways.
Because the distribution of a species is one of the key population characteristics determining how vulnerable it is to local
extirpation or even extinction, atlas data can help evaluate the
conservation status of species. Also, occupancy data provided by
atlases can indicate a species's relative abundance, because the
two population characteristics are often correlated (Gaston et
al. 2000, Zuckerberg 2008). And finally, because atlas data provide relatively detailed knowledge of a species's distribution, the
information can help identify the areas where conservation can
be undertaken most effectively (e.g., see Burger and Liner 2005,
NYSDEC 2005a, M. Morgan pers. comm.). With the collection and analysis of data for this second New York Breeding Bird
Atlas completed, breeding distributions from both Atlas surveys
can be compared and the trends in occupancy can be quantified, providing even greater information about the breeding
status of species than the snapshots given by either Atlas alone.
During the second Atlas survey, some species were detected in
fewer blocks than during the first one, while others were detected in more blocks, and still others were detected in roughly
the same number of blocks. These patterns suggest species with
apparently decreasing, increasing, and stable breeding distributions across the state, respectively (see Chapter 2). The purpose of
this chapter is to interpret the apparent changes in distribution in
the context of bird conservation within and beyond the borders
of New York State. In particular, we address the following five
questions: 1) Do the changes parallel those occurring at broader
scales in species considered of regional or continental concern?
2) Do the changes portend significant implications for a species
with a large proportion of its population in New York? 3) For
species that are at the edge of their range in New York, are the
observed changes likely to have widespread significance beyond
the boundaries of New York? 4) Do the changes represent conservation successes? 5) Do the negative changes represent future
conservation challenges?

A Continental Perspective for Bird Conservation in New York

In the 20 years since the fieldwork for New York's first Breeding Bird Atlas was completed, the populations and ranges of many
bird species have changed dramatically, not just in New York but
throughout the Northeast region and across North America.
Through organized long-term monitoring programs such as the
Breeding Bird Survey (BBS) (Sauer et al. 2007) and Christmas
Bird Count (CBC) (National Audubon Society [2007]), as well
as more casual observations, birders have helped to document
population declines and explosions, range expansions and contractions. These changes have been chronicled in New York on
the pages of *The Kingbird*, and continentally in *American Birds*
and *North American Birds*, and elsewhere in the scientific literature. During this same period, concern for widespread declines
in bird populations and their habitats led to the creation of several broad, partnership-based conservation initiatives, bringing
together federal- and state-agency biologists, academic scientists,
conservation organizations, and the public, all focused on proactive measures to protect habitats and reverse population declines. These national and continental initiatives provide a larger
context for understanding the significance of bird population
changes in New York, and for establishing state-level conservation priorities.

Setting the course for this new age of bird conservation was
the North American Waterfowl Management Plan (NAWMP
Plan Committee 2004), which since 1986 has generated $4.5 bil-
lion for wetlands protection and restoration, primarily through
public-private funding guided by Joint Ventures (USFWS 2006a).
Building on this successful model, an even larger international
consortium, Partners in Flight (PIF), formed in 1990 with the
broad goals of "keeping common birds common" and preventing additional species from becoming threatened or endangered
(Ruth 2006). Focusing initially on declines in Neotropical migrant songbirds, PIF working groups developed bird conservation plans for most physiographic regions across the United
States (Pashley et al. 2000) and later synthesized continental priorities and strategies in the first North American Landbird Conservation Plan (Rich et al. 2004). To address the specific needs of
aquatic bird species, two additional partnerships formed to produce the U.S. Shorebird Conservation Plan (S. Brown et al. 2001)
and the North American Waterbird Conservation Plan (Kushlan
et al. 2002). This proliferation of continental-scale conservation

planning at the turn of the new millennium for the first time focused significant attention and resources toward non–game bird species and their habitats.

As a cornerstone of its conservation planning process, PIF created a quantitative system for assessing the status of all bird species based on ranked scores for vulnerability factors that provide an overall assessment of a species's risk of endangerment (Beissinger et al. 2000, Carter et al. 2000, Panjabi et al. 2001, 2005, Rich et al. 2004). The factors include total population size, range size, population trend, and threats during the breeding and nonbreeding seasons. An additional factor, area importance, is used to determine the regions where each species is a conservation concern or stewardship responsibility. This system has been refined over time, and each of the non–game bird conservation plans uses a variation of this assessment process to identify the highest-priority species in need of conservation action. Based primarily on the priority species lists from these plans, the U.S. Fish and Wildlife Service recognized 158 species as either national or regional Birds of Conservation Concern (USFWS 2002), representing 16 percent of all nonhunted species protected under the Migratory Bird Treaty Act. In addition, both the National Audubon Society (2002) and the American Bird Conservancy ([2007]) have published a "Watch List" identifying the species of highest conservation priority, based on a common set of assessment scores using the PIF system.

Among New York's breeding avifauna, species of highest range-wide conservation concern based on small range and small, declining, or threatened populations include the Black Rail, Piping Plover, Bicknell's Thrush, Golden-winged Warbler, Henslow's Sparrow, and Saltmarsh Sharp-tailed Sparrow. Species of moderate continental concern that consistently appear on northeastern regional concern lists include most beach- and saltmarsh-nesting birds, many species breeding in agricultural grasslands, many species that utilize shrublands and early-successional forests, and a subset of the suite of forest-breeding, long-distance Neotropical migrants including the Wood Thrush, Cerulean Warbler, Kentucky Warbler, and Canada Warbler. Other species appearing on state endangered species lists throughout the Northeast, such as freshwater marsh birds, raptors, and boreal-forest breeders, often are indicative of locally rare populations that are peripheral to larger, widespread populations of otherwise secure species. Nonetheless, these "edge of range" populations are recognized as important components of the native avifauna and can contribute to the overall genetic diversity of species and facilitate adaptation to future challenges such as climate change (e.g., see Davis and Shaw 2001). Bird conservation at the state level should include both a global perspective, to ensure that actions contribute to regional and continental goals, and a more local perspective that considers rare populations, to ensure that the full range of avian diversity is maintained.

Bird Conservation Priorities in New York

During the period of 2002–04, concurrent with the data collection phase of the second New York Breeding Bird Atlas project, the New York State Department of Environmental Conservation (NYSDEC) led an effort to create a comprehensive list of bird species of conservation concern in New York incorporating both the continental and local perspectives. The impetus for the creation of this list was the federally supported State Wildlife Grants program administered by the U.S. Fish and Wildlife Service. To receive these federal conservation dollars, states were required to draft a Comprehensive Wildlife Conservation Strategy (aka State Wildlife Action Plan), which required the creation of a list of Species of Greatest Conservation Need (NYSDEC 2005a) to be included with the plan. Because the list of Species of Greatest Conservation Need addresses more than just birds, an initial list was created from sources that address multiple taxa, including the federal list of endangered and threatened species; the state list of endangered, threatened, and special concern species; status assessments of the New York Natural Heritage Program; and species identified as Wildlife Species of Regional Conservation Concern in the Northeastern United States (Therres 1999).

Recognizing the considerable progress made by continental bird conservation initiatives during the previous decade in assessing the conservation status of birds and the additional knowledge of various experts across the state, NYSDEC led an inclusive process to supplement the initial list of birds categorized as Species of Greatest Conservation Need. The process included meetings with amateur and professional ornithologists and bird conservation experts from government agencies and nongovernmental organizations (NGOs), and consultation of status assessments of the North American Waterfowl Management Plan, the U.S. Shorebird Conservation Plan, Waterbird Conservation for the Americas, "Partners in Flight" land bird plans, the Audubon WatchList 2002, and Birds of Conservation Concern identified by the U.S. Fish and Wildlife Service. The process resulted in a final list that included 118 bird species that met one or more of the criteria for inclusion on the list of Species of Greatest Conservation Need (NYSDEC 2005a).

Patterns of Change among 84 Breeding Species of Greatest Conservation Need in New York

For the purpose of this chapter, we began with those 118 species and eliminated all that do not breed in New York. The remaining 84 species provide a basis on which to evaluate changes between the first and second breeding bird Atlas surveys in the context of conservation. The 84 breeding species identified as Species of Greatest Conservation Need by NYSDEC's State Wildlife Action Plan (SWAP) can be grouped into 10 broad habitat or management categories, following closely the groupings within the SWAP (see Table 6.1; Appendix A1 in NYSDEC

2005a). Within nearly every category, some species stand out as representing continental priorities (i.e., range-wide conservation action is required), others are considered species of regional concern in regions that include New York, and still other species are of concern in New York based on their rarity or local habitat threats and might not necessarily represent broader concerns. Continentally important bird species breed in the full range of habitats in New York, from coastal beaches and salt marshes to high-elevation coniferous forests of the Adirondacks, and all the habitat suites have species that require conservation action.

Below we discuss the conservation status of species in each of the taxon/habitat categories (see Table 6.1) in relation to population and distributional changes evident from the data collected during the second Atlas survey. In addition, we provide a summary of the current state of knowledge regarding the causes of population changes for these species and/or groups of species. For most species, the actual causes of population changes are unknown or only partially known, as the limiting factors and demographic characteristics of populations are difficult to ascertain. Nonetheless, most species have been studied sufficiently to provide a base of knowledge concerning threats and probable causes of population and distribution changes. In this section, the threats and possible causes of population changes are summarized for each of the species groupings, focusing on the situation in New York when possible and drawing from recent summarizations compiled for New York's SWAP (NYSDEC 2005a) as well as other sources.

Breeding Waterfowl

Four species are recognized as needing conservation attention in New York, two of which are peripheral breeders whose numbers appear to have increased over the last 20 years (see Table 6.1). The American Black Duck is a high-priority species under the North American Waterfowl Management Plan (NAWMP), and many habitat improvement projects implemented through the Atlantic Coast Joint Venture have focused on this species. The 34 percent decline in distribution documented by the fieldwork for this Atlas corresponds with a steep decline in population size reported in NAWMP (2004). Although the American Black Duck nests throughout New York, strongholds for the species are the Adirondacks and the coastal marshes of Long Island; habitat requirements and threats faced by this species therefore vary widely across the state. Blue-winged Teal is another species for which a decrease in distribution (–63 percent) corresponds with a significant population decline on the Breeding Bird Survey (BBS) (Sauer et al. 2007) in New York and in the Northeast region. This species is not recognized as a high-priority species under NAWMP, however, as range-wide populations have not shown a decline. According to NAWMP (2004), the Common Goldeneye population shows no long-term trend, and the Ruddy Duck population is increasing. Finally, we note that tremendous increases in Atlas distributions of introduced Mute Swan (+87

percent) and resident Canada Geese (+275 percent) pose a new conservation problem, with potential negative effects on native waterfowl, other marsh birds, and their habitat.

The threats affecting American Black Duck populations most likely result from interactions with the Mallard, including competition, displacement, interbreeding, and hybridization. These factors were and continue to be exacerbated by the rearing and intentional release of Mallards for various reasons. Additionally, marsh loss and degradation on Long Island may be affecting the black duck. The remaining three species in this group have more limited breeding distributions than the black duck, and all may be threatened by habitat loss or degradation of their respective breeding habitats. The Blue-winged Teal population is likely declining from a loss of wetland-associated grasslands and open fields where it breeds.

Freshwater Marsh Birds

The six marsh and lake breeders primarily represent widespread species with small, often peripheral, populations in New York. An exception, perhaps, is the American Bittern, with large, well-distributed populations at least in the Adirondacks and St. Lawrence Valley. A modest 10 percent decline in American Bittern distribution corresponds with a significant decline in numbers over the same 20-year period in New York, according to the BBS. BBS data for this species do not show a significant decrease in the larger Northeast region or range-wide, but a targeted marsh bird monitoring program showed a decline from 1995 through 2003 in the Great Lakes Basin (Crewe et al. 2005). The state-endangered Black Tern, although receiving management attention during the past 20 years (e.g., Mazzocchi and Muller 2000), registered the largest loss in distribution (–40 percent) over this period. In New York, the Black Tern is largely peripheral to the continental population centered on the midwestern Prairie Pothole Region. The King Rail, a species of high continental importance because of shrinking range-wide populations, is barely represented as a breeder in New York. Large marshes at Montezuma, Iroquois, and elsewhere have supported this species, and proper management could potentially increase local populations. Overall, freshwater marsh–breeding species, especially those such as the Pied-billed Grebe and American Coot that use more open marshes, have enjoyed modest increases in distribution and population, probably in response to active management of impoundments and other wetlands over the past 20 years. Finally, the Common Loon, in its own management category under SWAP, has increased its distribution in New York by 43 percent, corresponding with increasing BBS trends in New York, the Northeast region, and range-wide.

Overall, habitat loss, degradation, and fragmentation are considered the leading causes of decreases in freshwater marsh bird distribution. Factors driving these habitat changes include draining of marshes (although perhaps less of a factor recently), development, changes in hydrology, prevention of natural disturbance

Table 6.1 Breeding birds (n = 84) determined to be Species of Greatest Conservation Need in New York State (NYSDEC 2006) and conservation status of each (see bottom of table for summary of criteria included within the three scales of concern)★

Taxon/Habitat Group	Common Name	Change (%)	No. of blocks 1980–85	No. of blocks 2000–05	Continental Concern[†]	Regional Concern[‡]	State Concern[§]
Breeding Waterfowl	Blue-winged Teal	−63	460	170			DEC
	American Black Duck	−34	1,102	728	WL, GL, Waterfowl		
	Common Goldeneye	29	24	31			NHP-S2
	Ruddy Duck	157	7	18			NHP-S1
Freshwater Marsh Birds	Black Tern	−40	73	44		NEC, WB-M	NY-E, NHP-S2
	American Bittern	−10	534	478		NEC, WB-H	NY-SC
	Least Bittern	−9	142	129		WB-H	NY-T
	King Rail	0	5	5	GL	WB-H	NY-T, NHP-S1
	Common Loon	43	369	528		WB-M	NY-SC
	Pied-billed Grebe	47	182	267		NEC, WB-H	NY-T
Colonial Nesting Herons	Cattle Egret	−65	20	7		WB-LL	NHP-S2
	Snowy Egret	−38	94	58		WB-H	
	Yellow-crowned Night-Heron	−28	40	29		WB-M	NHP-S2
	Glossy Ibis	−19	47	38		WB-M	NHP-S2
	Little Blue Heron	−5	19	18	GL	WB-H	NHP-S2
	Black-crowned Night-Heron	1	211	213		WB-M	
	Tricolored Heron	18	11	13		WB-H	NHP-S2
	Great Egret	71	65	111		WB-LL	NHP-S2
Salt Marsh Breeders	Laughing Gull	−81	32	6		WB-LL	NHP-1
	Seaside Sparrow	−25	48	36	WL, GL, PIF		NY-SC
	Saltmarsh Sharp-tailed Sparrow	−15	72	61	WL, GL, PIF	PIF, PIF-S	
	Black Rail	0	1	1	WL, GL	WB-HH	NY-E, NHP-S1
	Gull-billed Tern	67	3	5	GL	WB-H	NHP-S1
	Willet	77	43	76		SB-H	
	Forster's Tern	400	2	10		WB-M	NHP-S1
Beach and Island Nesters	**Roseate Tern**	−37	19	12	GL	WB-H	NY-E★★, NHP-S1
	Black Skimmer	−32	37	25	GL	WB-H	NY-SC, NHP-S2
	Least Tern	-21	87	69	GL	NEC, WB-H	NY-T
	Common Tern	−1	122	121		FWS, NEC, WB-L	NY-T
	Piping Plover	1	75	76	WL, GL	SB-HI	NY-E
	American Oystercatcher	51	45	68	WL, GL	SB-H	
	Caspian Tern	67	3	5		WB-L	NHP-S1
Forest-Breeding and Other Raptors	Long-eared Owl	−41	81	48		NEC	
	Northern Goshawk	−20	445	355			NY-SC
	Golden Eagle	13	8	9		NEC	NY-E, NHP-SH
	Red-shouldered Hawk	23	702	865			NY-SC
	Sharp-shinned Hawk	68	859	1,440			NY-SC
	Cooper's Hawk	146	550	1,355			NY-SC
	Osprey	147	335	826			NY-SC
	Peregrine Falcon	553	17	111		FWS, PIF	NY-E
	Bald Eagle	1,171	35	445			NY-T★★
Grassland Birds	Loggerhead Shrike	−83	24	4		NEC	NY-E, NHP-S1
	Henslow's Sparrow	−80	348	70	WL, GL, PIF	FWS, NEC, PIF	NY-T
	Barn Owl	−78	126	28			NHP-S1S2
	Upland Sandpiper	−65	476	165		FWS, NEC, SB-H	NY-T
	Vesper Sparrow	−49	1,116	564			NY-SC
	Grasshopper Sparrow	−42	822	477		PIF	NY-SC
	Horned Lark	−37	1,105	698			NY-SC
	Short-eared Owl	−33	36	24	WL, GL, PIF	FWS, NEC	NY-E, NHP-S2
	Eastern Meadowlark	−25	3,506	2,635		PIF	
	Bobolink	−8	3,465	3,178		PIF	
	Northern Harrier	−1	930	917		NEC, PIF	NY-T

Taxon/Habitat Group	Common Name	Change (%)	No. of blocks 1980–85	No. of blocks 2000–05	Continental Concern[†]	Regional Concern[‡]	State Concern[§]
	Sedge Wren	21	57	69		FWS, NEC, PIF	NY-T
	Dickcissel	400	1	5	WL, GL		
Early-Successional/ Shrubland Birds	Yellow-breasted Chat	−78	122	27		PIF	NY-SC
	Common Nighthawk	−71	477	138			NY-SC
	Whip-poor-will	−57	564	241		FWS, NEC, PIF	NY-SC
	Golden-winged Warbler	−53	577	270	WL, GL, PIF	FWS, NEC, PIF	NY-SC
	Brown Thrasher	−30	3,341	2,337		PIF	
	Northern Bobwhite	−26	236	175		PIF	
	Ruffed Grouse	−18	3,152	2,579		PIF	
	American Woodcock	4	1,926	2,004	WL, GL	SB-H	
	Black-billed Cuckoo	4	1,963	2,034		FWS, PIF, PIF-S	
	Blue-winged Warbler	17	1,867	2,189	WL, GL, PIF	PIF, PIF-S	
	Prairie Warbler	20	731	875	WL, GL, PIF	FWS, PIF	
	Willow Flycatcher	36	1,932	2,619	WL, GL, PIF		
Deciduous and Mixed Forest Birds	**Red-headed Woodpecker**	−76	691	167	WL, GL, PIF	FWS, NEC, PIF	NY-SC
	Kentucky Warbler	−72	39	11	WL, GL, PIF	FWS, PIF, PIF-S	NHP-S2
	Prothonotary Warbler	−50	22	11	WL, GL, PIF		NHP-S2
	Canada Warbler	−23	1,684	1,299	WL, GL, PIF	FWS, NEC, PIF, PIF-S	
	Louisiana Waterthrush	−21	1,055	838		NEC, PIF, PIF-S	
	Cerulean Warbler	−13	279	244	WL, GL, PIF	FWS, NEC, PIF, PIF-S	NY-SC
	Wood Thrush	−7	4,764	4,428	WL, GL, PIF	FWS, PIF, PIF-S	
	Worm-eating Warbler	−1	225	223	WL, GL, PIF	FWS, PIF, PIF-S	
	Scarlet Tanager	1	4,299	4,338		PIF, PIF-S	
	Black-throated Blue Warbler	10	1,738	1,919		PIF-S	
Coniferous and High-Elevation Forest Breeders	**Bay-breasted Warbler**	−63	32	12	WL, GL, PIF	PIF-S	NHP-S2
	Olive-sided Flycatcher	−34	479	316	WL, GL, PIF	FWS, PIF	
	American Three-toed Woodpecker	−32	22	15			NHP-S2
	Spruce Grouse	−26	27	20			NY-E, NHP-S2
	Rusty Blackbird	−23	151	117	WL, GL, PIF		
	Cape May Warbler	−22	18	14			NHP-S2
	Tennessee Warbler	4	27	28			NHP-S2
	Bicknell's Thrush	46	39	57	WL, GL, PIF	NEC, PIF-S	NY-SC

★ Within each Taxon/Habitat Group, species are listed in order of their percentage change in the Atlas distribution. Species in boldface are those of continental concern.

[†] Continental Concern identifies species on the Audubon WatchList 2002 (WL; National Audubon Society 2002); the American Bird Conservancy Green List 2004 (GL, http://www.abcbirds.org/greenlist.htm); those determined to be of continental concern by Partners in Flight according to the 2005 assessment (PIF, http://www.rmbo.org/pif/pifdb.html); and identified in the North American Waterfowl Management Plan (NAWMP 2004) for which the long-term (1970–2002) trend was indicated as decreasing (Waterfowl).

[‡] Regional Concern identifies the regional conservation plan or priority species listing in which species are identified as regional concerns, where FWS indicates species on the U.S. Fish and Wildlife Service list of Birds of Concern (USFWS 2002); "NEC" indicates species on the Northeast Concern list created by the Northeast Endangered Species and Wildlife Diversity Technical Committee to include species of regional conservation concern (Therres 1999); WB-HH, WB-H, WB-M, WB-L, WB-LL indicate species listed as Highest, High, Moderate, Low, and Lowest Concern, respectively, in Bird Conservation Regions 14 or 30 in the Waterbird Conservation Plan for the Mid-Atlantic/New England/Maritimes Region (MANEM 2006); SB-HI and SB-H indicate Highly Imperiled species and species of High Concern, respectively, according to the Northern Atlantic Regional Shorebird Plan (Clark and Niles 2000); and PIF and PIF-S indicate land bird species considered of regional concern or regional stewardship, respectively, in one or more of the Bird Conservation Regions covering New York State, based on the Partners in Flight 2005 species assessment (PIF 2005, http://www.rmbo.org/pif/pifdb.html).

[§] State Concern identifies species listed in New York State, where NY-E, NY-T, and NY-SC indicate species on the current New York State list of endangered, threatened, or special concern species, respectively; NHP-S1, NHP-S2, and NHP-SH indicate species ranked S1, S2, and SH, respectively, by the New York Natural Heritage Program, based on number and type of occurrences in the state (NY Natural Heritage Program, http://www.dec.state.ny.us/website/dfwmr/heritage); and DEC indicates a species included due to concerns of NYSDEC experts. Federally listed species are also state-listed; ★★ indicates species on the federal endangered or threatened species list.

events that can rejuvenate marshes, and colonization by invasive exotic plants. Human disturbance is a potential threat to these species, potentially causing exposure of chicks or nest destruction. Additionally, siltation and changes in hydrology can affect the structure, diversity, and productivity of marsh habitat, including food webs, with negative implications for marsh birds.

Colonial Nesting Herons

The eight species of colonial nesting herons are distributed widely throughout the Western Hemisphere; therefore, the range-wide conservation status of these species is difficult to assess. Most of the species in this group occur only on Long Island or in the lower part of the Hudson River Valley, and several are at the northern extent of their ranges here in New York. Changes in Atlas distributions of these highly colonial species in New York reflect changes in the number of active breeding sites and not necessarily changes in total population size. The large decrease reported for Cattle Egret (−65 percent), however, corresponds with a recent steep decline for this species throughout the Northeast, following a half-century of continued range expansion. The Black-crowned Night-Heron and Glossy Ibis show significant population declines in the Northeast region according to the BBS, but only the Little Blue Heron shows a decline throughout its U.S. range. The large increase and spread inland noted for the Great Egret corresponds with a significant regional population increase and 20 percent increase in Atlas distribution for Great Blue Heron, with which it often nests. Overall, continued conservation efforts to protect colonial heron rookeries are important for maintaining statewide diversity, but reflect local rather than continental conservation priorities.

While more study is needed to determine the limiting factors for many of these species, loss and degradation of breeding and foraging habitat appear to be the most significant factors affecting their distributions. In particular, shrinking distributions of coastal herons likely reflect a loss of habitat on Long Island. Competition for nesting sites from other water birds also is potentially a factor.

Salt Marsh Breeders

Seven salt marsh breeders are recognized as Species of Greatest Conservation Need in New York, three of which are also species of high continental concern. The poorly known Black Rail is most likely endangered throughout its patchy Atlantic Coast range; this species continues to barely hang on as a breeder, with a single site on the south shore of Long Island. Thorough surveys for this secretive species, as well as management to potentially expand its habitat, should be a high priority. Both Seaside and Saltmarsh Sharp-tailed sparrows are species of high continental concern, with core ranges that include the New York coastline. Although these sparrows are poorly monitored by existing sur-

veys, the Atlas data suggest shrinking distributions in New York. The fourth widespread salt marsh breeder is the Willet, which has nearly doubled its distribution on Long Island as part of its overall expansion northward along the Atlantic Coast. The Gull-billed Tern, while largely peripheral in New York, is considered a species of continental concern; the population has declined in the region by 22 percent (MANEM 2006). The two remaining species in this group are peripheral breeders of lower conservation importance; distribution of the Forster's Tern has increased slightly, while that of the Laughing Gull has declined from 32 Atlas blocks in 1980–85 to only 6 blocks in 2000–05. Change in the Laughing Gull's distribution does not necessarily represent a true decline, however, because records of single birds (reported as Possible breeders) were removed from the second, but not the first, Atlas database.

All the leading threats to this group of species relate to habitat changes. Loss of salt marsh habitat occurs as a result of erosion, development, and, increasingly, sea level rise. Changes in the distributions of some of these species appear to be resulting from continued encroachment into salt marshes from urban development. The sparrows are particularly susceptible to a loss of buffer habitats surrounding the "high marsh" zone, fluctuating water levels from changes in hydrology, and invasion by the exotic common reed. Ditching for mosquito control can also degrade salt marsh habitat. Additionally, some species in this group potentially are threatened by human disturbance.

Beach and Island Nesters

Beach- and island-nesting birds are highly susceptible to human disturbance, and not surprisingly, all seven of New York's breeding species are recognized as Species of Greatest Conservation Need, and most are considered species of continental concern. The species receiving the greatest conservation attention is the federally threatened Piping Plover, which as a result has maintained a stable distribution over the past 20 years. Colonial nesting terns have not fared as well. Distribution of the Black Skimmer has declined by 32 percent, and that of the federally endangered Roseate Tern (breeding primarily on offshore islands) by 37 percent. Least Tern distribution has decreased by 21 percent, while distribution of the Common Tern, which nests inland as well as on coastal beaches, has remained fairly stable statewide but has declined on Long Island. Although the American Oystercatcher is a high-priority shorebird along the Atlantic Coast, it is expanding its distribution northward, and this is reflected in a 51 percent increase in the number of Atlas blocks showing records of this species in New York. Finally, the single nesting colony of Caspian Terns, at Little Galloo Island, Lake Ontario, has expanded in recent years, although a very recent outbreak of type E botulism is cause for concern.

Beach- and island-nesting birds face a host of threats that likely would have caused the distributions of more species to decline or decline further without the intensive monitoring and management efforts of several organizations. Threats during the breeding season include habitat loss from several factors, such as prevention of natural beach maintenance via storm events, development on or adjacent to nesting or foraging habitats, and use of appropriate habitat for recreational activities; disturbance from human activities; and nest predation. Rising sea level and erosion have reduced available nesting areas in some locations and are expected to be of increased importance in the future (NYSDEC 2005a).

Forest-Breeding and Other Raptors

As a group, raptors in New York have enjoyed much conservation attention over the past 20 years, ranging from inclusion on the state endangered species list to intensive management and even reintroduction programs. Most of these species have responded positively, with the federally listed Bald Eagle and Peregrine Falcon among the species with the most dramatically increasing distributions in the state. The Osprey and Cooper's Hawk also have more than doubled their distributions since the first Atlas survey, the latter species adapting strongly enough to human development to become a common backyard breeder in many areas (also evident with the recently expanding distribution of the Merlin). Sharp-shinned and Red-shouldered hawks also show healthy and expanding populations in the state, whereas, according to the Atlas data, the Northern Goshawk and Long-eared Owl were noted as declining in distribution; the Long-eared Owl is among the poorest-known species and its population is notoriously difficult to monitor. Overall, these raptors continue to deserve management attention and positive outreach to the public, but their large ranges and increasing populations make them a low conservation concern from a regional or continental perspective.

Disturbance around nest sites can be problematic for some of these species, although others, including the Cooper's Hawk and Merlin, seem to be adjusting well to humans. Historically, pesticides are believed to have played a role in past population declines in many raptors, which, because of their positions at the top of food chains, would be susceptible to this hazard in the future as well. Populations of several species have increased recently as the pesticide threat has subsided and also as a result of intensive management efforts for some of the species (e.g., Bald Eagle and Peregrine Falcon).

Grassland Birds

With 13 species, this is the largest suite of birds recognized in the New York SWAP (see Table 6.1). The distribution of nearly every species in this group has declined according to the Atlas data, with five species showing a roughly 50 percent or greater decline in the number of blocks occupied. These shrinking distributions correspond with significant declining population trends for most grassland birds in New York and the Northeast region, as measured by the BBS. In particular, Henslow's Sparrow, Vesper Sparrow, Grasshopper Sparrow, and Eastern Meadowlark have lost 85 percent or more of their statewide populations since 1966. Henslow's Sparrow and Short-eared Owl, two species of high continental concern, are rapidly disappearing as breeding birds in New York and other Northeast states. Because of their widespread distributions and locally high densities, however, some grassland birds (e.g., Bobolink) remain relatively abundant and are not in imminent danger of extirpation in New York.

Grassland-breeding birds have experienced widespread declines within and beyond New York State, caused primarily by loss, degradation, and fragmentation of grassland habitat (Askins et al. 2007). Principal factors driving these habitat changes include farmland abandonment and succession to shrub and forest habitats, more intensive management of the remaining agricultural grasslands, conversion of some agricultural grasslands to row crops, and sprawl development. Many grassland-breeding species require large expanses of grassland, as well as relatively specialized field conditions. To provide adequate habitat for these focal species, and to benefit the largest number of grassland birds, a mosaic of field types will be required, consolidated into core landscapes and maintained using a variety of management methods.

Early-Successional / Shrubland Birds

As with grassland birds, birds of early-successional or shrub habitats are among the most steeply declining species in New York and the Northeast region. Populations of all of the 12 species, with the exception of the Willow Flycatcher, have declined significantly in the region over the past 20 years, according to the BBS. Of the seven species showing shrinking Atlas distributions in New York, however, only the Golden-winged Warbler is of high continental concern. The large reduction in distribution of the Golden-winged Warbler (−53 percent) that has occurred since the first Atlas survey coincides with the northward spread of the Blue-winged Warbler and with the overall loss of early-successional habitats throughout most of the state. Three additional species of high continental concern are the American Woodcock, Blue-winged Warbler, and Prairie Warbler. These species show either stable or increasing distributions, but all have declined significantly in abundance in the Northeast region and range-wide (although the Prairie Warbler has been stable in New York since 1980). According to the *American Woodcock Population Status, 2007* report (Kelley et al. 2007), the woodcock population has declined across the eastern region and in New York from 1968 to 2007. Other birds with declining populations in early-successional habitats, such as the Brown Thrasher, Northern Bobwhite, and Whip-poor-will, are high regional priorities for Partners in Flight, but continental concern is lower because of their wide ranges and large overall populations. The Willow

Flycatcher is on the continental Watch List based on threats to western populations and on the wintering grounds, but this species has increased in numbers throughout the East, including in New York.

The species in this group have various specific habitat requirements within the early-successional or "disturbance" habitats. Some, such as the Whip-poor-will, prefer natural disturbance habitats like pine barrens, while others seem to do well in anthropogenic disturbance habitats such as utility rights-of-way and abandoned agricultural lands succeeding to forest. Leading threats include habitat loss and degradation from the suppression of natural disturbance factors like fire and beaver activity, as well as incompatible or reduced anthropogenic disturbance factors, for example, changes in agricultural techniques and forest management. Many natural and anthropogenic disturbance habitats are under great pressure from sprawl development. The Golden-winged Warbler is suffering population declines in most parts of its range and is rapidly disappearing from much of its historic range in the Appalachian region. In New York, it is now dependent on native and managed shrublands in the Hudson Highlands region and on abandoned farmland in the St. Lawrence Plains. The Golden-winged Warbler also is threatened by interbreeding and hybridization with the Blue-winged Warbler.

Deciduous and Mixed Forest Birds

Several forest birds have declined in New York, even as forest cover has increased statewide. Of the ten forest species in this group, seven are of continental concern, and the remaining three are high regional priorities and stewardship responsibilities. Large or moderate decreases in distribution, as indicated by the Atlas data, for the Red-headed Woodpecker, Kentucky Warbler, Canada Warbler, Louisiana Waterthrush, Cerulean Warbler, and Wood Thrush correspond with significant losses in population of 50 percent or greater in New York or in the Northeast region, based on the BBS (however, note that some BBS trends must be interpreted with caution because of small sample sizes and some data deficiencies). The Prothonotary Warbler also showed a large reduction in its small range within New York. The Worm-eating Warbler, Scarlet Tanager, and Black-throated Blue Warbler showed stable or slightly expanded distributions in New York, but all three also have declined significantly in abundance since the first Atlas fieldwork was completed. All of these species, except the Red-headed Woodpecker, are Neotropical migrants that winter in forested habitats in Latin America or the Caribbean; therefore, nonbreeding ground issues as opposed to breeding ground issues could be causing declines.

Many of the forest species with declining distributions in this group require rather specialized forest conditions, such as broken emergent canopy (Cerulean Warbler), clear-flowing streams (Louisiana Waterthrush), or dense understory vegetation created by disturbance. As a result, the specific threats to them may vary, but in spite of that, some common themes emerge. Habitat loss

and degradation affect nearly all of these species. In some parts of the state, forest fragmentation from sprawl development and other factors that convert forest to other land uses is a likely problem, while in other parts of the state, acid rain and other pollutants may be important. In addition, changes in forest structure, caused by overabundant deer populations and maturing of forests to a closed-canopy condition, may negatively affect species dependent on shrubby understory. Many of these species also may be limited by causes that exist in nonbreeding areas, such as in winter habitat in the tropics.

Coniferous and High-Elevation Forest Breeders

The community of birds restricted mostly to coniferous forests and bogs of the Adirondacks represents a small but distinct component of New York's avian diversity. Of the eight species in this group, most are widespread boreal species at or near the edge of their range. By far, the species of greatest continental concern is Bicknell's Thrush. With one of the smallest ranges and total populations of any North American passerine, the contribution of Adirondack and Catskill high peaks populations to the well-being of the entire species is enormous. Relatively little is known about the population status and trend of Bicknell's Thrush, as the BBS does not sample well its high-elevation habitat. Mountain Birdwatch data suggest a declining then recovering regional population trend during the data collection period for New York's second Atlas (Lambert 2006). In 1995, Bicknell's Thrush was determined to be a distinct species rather than a subspecies of the Gray-cheeked Thrush (AOU 1995). This change created considerable interest among birders, and therefore the sizable increase in distribution evident in the second Atlas data compared to the first may be a result of increased effort by volunteers to document this "new" species. The other continentally important species are the Olive-sided Flycatcher, Bay-breasted Warbler, and Rusty Blackbird. For all of these, shrinking distributions within New York parallel significant survey-wide population declines according to the BBS. The Rusty Blackbird in particular appears to be experiencing one of the steepest declines of any North American bird, although it is poorly monitored in much of its range. Of the remaining species recognized in SWAP, the Spruce Grouse, a widely distributed species outside of New York, has received some management attention as a state-endangered species. Nonetheless, its distribution has contracted by 26 percent since the first Atlas survey period, almost the same amount of range reduction seen for the Three-toed Woodpecker. The Cape May, Tennessee, and Bay-breasted warblers have exhibited cyclic population changes associated with spruce-budworm outbreaks, and their current conservation status is difficult to assess.

Threats to this group of species include habitat loss or alteration from the maturation of conifer forests, acid precipitation, mercury pollution, and global climate change (NYSDEC 2005a). Threats to Bicknell's Thrush may be greater on its Caribbean wintering grounds, but considering the small population size, high responsibility, and very restricted breeding range, this species continues to merit close observation and efforts to protect and enhance habitat quantity and quality.

Current Conservation Efforts

Given the large number of bird species of conservation concern and the complex mix of habitat issues and other threats facing them, it is not surprising to see the numerous programs and efforts striving to conserve these species in New York. From a continental perspective, the most important conservation actions are those directed toward species of continental concern for which New York is included as part of their core range; that is, these actions can have the largest measurable effects on the global status of the species. This perspective is complemented by actions that address threats of a more local nature aimed at maintaining avian diversity within the state and sustaining healthy populations of species of stewardship responsibility. Though too numerous to mention in detail, current conservation actions for these species fall into three broad categories: 1) protection of key habitats, 2) targeted management and restoration of public lands, and 3) incentive and educational programs to help private landowners manage their lands. In New York, many federal and state agencies, local municipalities, universities, NGOs, and private individuals and companies are involved in one way or another in efforts to conserve birds and their habitats. Most of these efforts and needs have been identified as priority actions in New York's SWAP. We conclude this chapter with a brief summary of some of the conservation efforts currently underway in New York. It is through these efforts that continued or future declines of species of conservation concern might be averted and restoration commenced.

Habitat Protection

Many of the key sites in New York supporting bird species of conservation concern have been identified (e.g., as Important Bird Areas, Burger and Liner 2005), and where appropriate, public entities and NGOs are taking steps to protect some of those sites through acquisition of fee title or conservation easements. Various mechanisms exist for directing habitat protection funding toward priority sites for these species, including formalized public processes like the Federal Land and Water Conservation Fund, the North American Wetlands Conservation Act, and the New York State Open Space Conservation Plan, as well as local efforts resulting from the focus of individual land trusts. A successful example of this latter type of approach is the Finger Lakes Land Trust's acquisition of several properties that support the Cerulean Warbler and other priority species. In some cases, habitat is protected not through acquisition, but by steering development away from important habitats for species of concern through zoning, local open-space plans, and "smart growth" planning.

Public Lands Management

Although the vast majority of land in New York State is privately owned, numerous public holdings provide significant habitats for species of conservation concern. The U.S. Fish and Wildlife Service is striving to manage the refuges in New York for species such as the Cerulean Warbler and American Bittern, as well as priority waterfowl, grassland-nesting birds, and migrants such as shorebirds. Similarly, New York State, through such programs as the State Bird Conservation Area Program, NYSDEC Unit Management Plans, and State Park Master Plans, continues to identify important state-owned bird habitats and integrate the needs of priority species into the management of those sites. In some areas, like the Montezuma Wetlands Complex, federal, state, private, and NGO partners are collaborating to restore and manage wetlands for the benefit of species such as the American Black Duck, Black Tern, and both bitterns, in addition to many other species. Many of these public land managers are attempting to address the increasing problems caused by invasive plants in aquatic, grassland, shrubland, and forest ecosystems on both private and public lands. In a unique public-private partnership in the Adirondacks, the Olympic Regional Development Authority, Adirondack Park Agency, and NYSDEC are collaborating with NGOs to manage the breeding habitat for Bicknell's Thrush on Whiteface Mountain. The efforts of this group have gone even further: it has established an international conservation fund to help protect the wintering habitat of Bicknell's Thrush on the island of Hispaniola.

Private Land Stewardship

Many efforts are underway to encourage stewardship and proper management of private lands for the benefit of birds of conservation concern. One example is the vigorous protection and management actions by federal, state, and NGO partners for beach-nesting birds, especially measures to increase the productivity of the Piping Plover and tern and skimmer colonies on Long Island. Similarly, several organizations are promoting habitat stewardship for grassland, early-successional, and wetlands species, including the U.S. Department of Agriculture's Natural Resources Conservation Service, which administers conservation provisions of the Federal Farm Bill; NYSDEC (in collaboration with Audubon New York), which administers the Landowner Incentive Program; and the U.S. Fish and Wildlife Service, which runs the Partners for Fish and Wildlife Program. With regard to grassland birds, these programs are coordinated such that they focus their efforts in regions of New York with the greatest likelihood of supporting viable populations of grassland birds. While these programs attempt to protect and restore populations of the most specialized and area-sensitive species (i.e., Henslow's Sparrow, Upland Sandpiper, and Short-eared Owl), they will benefit many other species in this habitat group, as well as wintering raptors that also use grassland habitats. Others, including Cornell

University Forestry Extension, are taking a lead role in assisting private forest owners with management practices to improve habitat conditions required by early-successional forest birds with declining populations, as well as birds that benefit from a more diverse forest structure, including the American Woodcock, Canada Warbler, Wood Thrush, and many other species.

Summary

The data collected for the second Atlas project provide an important window into changes in the status of bird species in New York. Viewed in the context of continental, regional, and state-level conservation priorities, these changes will help guide conservation actions and point to habitats and regions of the state that are most in need of attention. We are optimistic that implementation of the priorities and actions laid out in the SWAP, in collaboration with the many active conservation organizations in the state, will lead to a positive outlook for priority bird species and their habitats. Continued vigilance is necessary, however, on the part of New York birders and ornithologists to help monitor future bird population changes. In particular, annual participation in the Breeding Bird Survey is critical for continuing to track regional population trends, and in new programs such as New York eBird (http://www.ebird.org/NY/) will help us track changes in bird distributions between now and the next statewide Atlas survey.

The Species Accounts

Mute Swan and Mallard on the Hudson River

The Hudson River, which flows 315 miles from the forested slopes of Mount Marcy in the Adirondacks to New York Harbor, provides a breeding ground for countless waterfowl. Recent efforts at pollution reduction have greatly improved the overall quality of this rich and diverse aquatic resource.

Canada Goose

Branta canadensis

KEVIN J. MCGOWAN

One of the most common and familiar waterfowl in North America, the Canada Goose was once a breeder only in northern Canada and the north-central United States. Today, as a result of introductions and translocations, it can be found nesting in every province in Canada and all 49 continental states in the United States (Mowbray et al. 2002). The Canada Goose breeds in a variety of wetland habitats. Marshes with reeds and muskrat houses may be the classic breeding location, but it also breeds successfully in agricultural fields, reservoirs, sewage lagoons, city lakes and parks, golf courses, highway medians, and housing subdivisions (Mowbray et al. 2002). Historically, the Canada Goose did not breed in New York and primarily occurred here as a common migrant (Bull 1974). Introduction programs and unregulated releases from private collections in the 1930s led to successful breeding by the 1950s (Eaton 1988e). The form primarily introduced was the "Giant" Canada Goose, a subspecies from the Midwest that was nearly extirpated in the early 1900s (Mowbray et al. 2002). It is believed that the subsequent increase in nesting in New York and surrounding areas resulted from the dispersal and reproduction by descendants of the introduced individuals, rather than from wild migratory birds remaining to breed (Griffith 1998a, Giroux et al. 2001). By the 1960s and 1970s geese were breeding at a number of wildlife refuges and management areas upstate and along Long Island (Eaton 1988e), as well as up the Hudson River to Dutchess County (DeOrsey and Butler 2006).

During the first Atlas period, the Canada Goose was concentrated as a breeder primarily in the Hudson Valley, Taconic and Hudson highlands, Manhattan Hills, Triassic Lowlands, and Coastal Lowlands. Significant populations were also scattered in the Cattaraugus Highlands, Great Lakes Plain, and St. Lawrence Transition, especially around national wildlife refuges. Many other reports were scattered across the state. The Canada Goose was much more commonly found during the second Atlas period, with Confirmed reports occurring across nearly all of the state.

The number of blocks with nesting geese increased 275 percent. Gaps in its distribution were noticeable only in the Adirondacks, where it is a scattered breeder, and in the Catskill Mountains. A possible gap in central New York may be a coverage problem or the result of a highly cultivated landscape.

The number of breeding pairs of Canada Geese in New York was estimated to be about 5,000 in 1978, increasing to approximately 20,000 by 1990 and to 90,000 in 2005 (NYSDEC unpubl. data). Breeding Bird Survey data also show a dramatic increase in Canada Geese numbers in New York beginning in the 1970s and accelerating dramatically in the 1990s (Sauer et al. 2007). Continent-wide, the same phenomenon is quite apparent (Sauer et al. 2007). A dramatic increase in the number of Canada Geese in the "Atlantic Flyway Resident Population," which includes New York, occurred during the early 1990s, reaching an apparent plateau in 1997 (USFWS 2006c). Most increases in surrounding states are also the result of the successful introduction programs of the "Giant" form of the Canada Goose (e.g., Connecticut: Zeranski and Baptist 1990; Massachusetts: Heusmann 2003; New Jersey: Walsh et al. 1999; Pennsylvania: McWilliams and Brauning 2000; Vermont: Kibbe 1985; Quebec: Giroux et al. 2001).

Canada Geese using open lawn areas near lakes and ponds, such as parks, golf courses, business parks, and airport runways, are often considered pests. The capture of problem geese in one area and their release in another has resulted in the spread of breeding populations (Mowbray et al. 2002). Although a number of techniques are being tested to reduce resident goose populations and decrease their negative impacts, the trend for continued increases indicates that the goose "problem" will remain for the near future.

ATM@2006

2000–05 Distribution Map

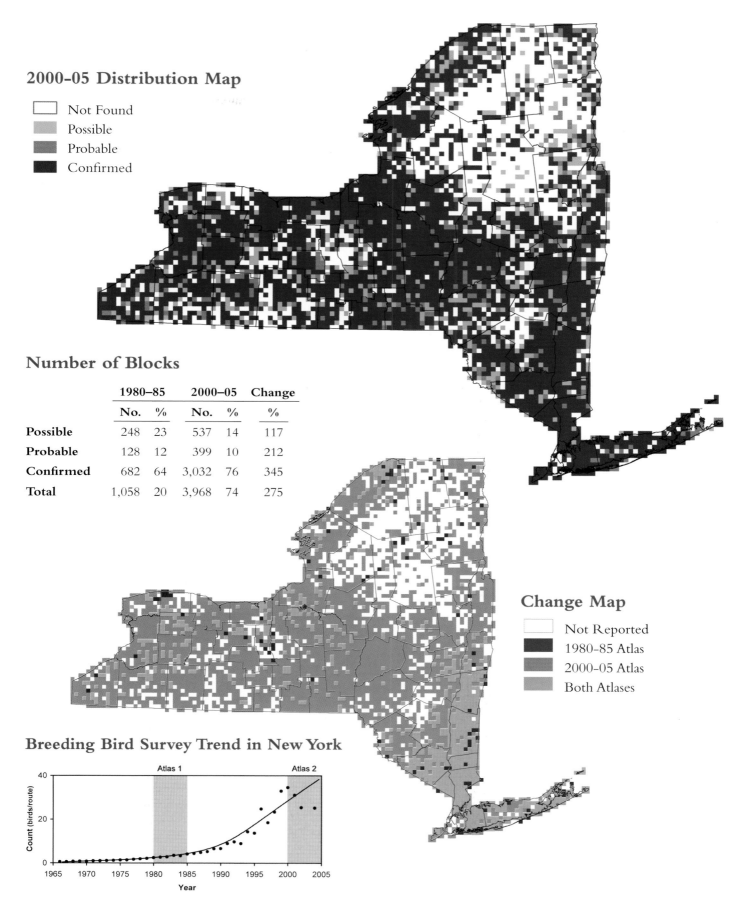

- ☐ Not Found
- Possible
- Probable
- Confirmed

Number of Blocks

	1980–85		2000–05		Change
	No.	%	No.	%	%
Possible	248	23	537	14	117
Probable	128	12	399	10	212
Confirmed	682	64	3,032	76	345
Total	1,058	20	3,968	74	275

Change Map

- ☐ Not Reported
- 1980–85 Atlas
- 2000–05 Atlas
- Both Atlases

Breeding Bird Survey Trend in New York

Mute Swan
Cygnus olor

KEVIN J. McGOWAN

Introduced into North America to adorn the ponds of parks and estates, the Mute Swan is native to northern and central Eurasia. Intentionally released and escaped individuals have established breeding populations along the middle Atlantic Coast from Massachusetts to Virginia, around the Great Lakes, and along portions of the Pacific Coast (Ciaranca et al. 1997). The Mute Swan was introduced into New York in 1910 in the lower Hudson Valley and in 1912 on the south shore of Long Island, and it quickly became established in those areas (Bull 1974). It was most numerous on the east end of Long Island and only became common on the west end in the 1980s (Marcotte 1998b). Individuals and pairs, probably escaped from captivity, were seen scattered throughout the state since the first introductions. The Mute Swan became established along Lake Ontario in the 1990s (Marcotte 1998b), presumably from an expanding population in Ontario, the number reaching 270 birds on the annual state midwinter waterfowl count in 2005 (NYSDEC unpubl. data).

During the first Atlas survey, the Mute Swan was found breeding throughout the Coastal Lowlands and the lower Hudson Valley, northward to Dutchess and Ulster counties. Only one pair was confirmed breeding upstate, at Perch River Wildlife Management Area in Jefferson County, and another individual was seen in Genesee County. During the second Atlas fieldwork, the large, conspicuous Mute Swan was found in nearly twice as many blocks, scattered throughout the state. It is clearly established along the Lake Ontario shore, especially around Rochester, and up the Hudson Valley to Columbia County. It remained numerous in the Coastal Lowlands, with breeding confirmed along the extent of both shores, and was present in 14 more blocks there during the second Atlas period than during the first one. Breeding was also confirmed inland away from the Great Lakes and the Hudson Valley in nearly a dozen counties. The source of these breeding pairs is unknown, but it is reasonable to suspect that they represent dispersal from feral populations as well as escapes from captivity. The New York State Department of Environmental Conservation now prohibits any release of a Mute Swan to the wild.

The Mute Swan began colonizing the lower Great Lakes in the mid-1960s and 1970s. Using data from aerial surveys, ground-based waterfowl surveys, and Christmas Bird Counts, Petrie and Francis (2003) estimated population growth around Lake Erie and Lake Ontario to be 10–18 percent per year, resulting in a doubling of the population every seven to eight years.

ATM©2006

The Atlantic Flyway population in the United States increased by approximately 8 percent per year between 1986 and 1999 and numbered approximately 13,000 swans in 2005 (Perry in Petrie and Francis 2003, Raftovich 2005). Data from the annual New York State winter waterfowl count mirror these trends, with a dramatic appearance and population growth in Region 2 along Lake Ontario since the 1990s, steady increases in the lower Hudson Valley (Region 9) since the 1970s, and a doubling of numbers along Long Island (Region 10) since 1980 (NYSOA 2005). Summer surveys counted nearly 2,500 Mute Swans statewide in 2002. Most were in the lower Hudson Valley or on Long Island, but more than 200 were counted around Lake Ontario (NYSDEC unpubl. data). Because of its destructive foraging behavior on submerged aquatic vegetation and its aggression toward other waterfowl, Petrie and Francis (2003) recommended active management and reduction of Mute Swan populations before they grew too much larger.

2000–05 Distribution Map

- ☐ Not Found
- ☐ Possible
- ☐ Probable
- ■ Confirmed

Number of Blocks

	1980–85		2000–05		Change
	No.	%	No.	%	%
Possible	21	10	72	18	243
Probable	17	8	83	20	388
Confirmed	180	83	252	62	40
Total	218	4	407	8	87

Change Map

- ☐ Not Reported
- ■ 1980-85 Atlas
- ☐ 2000-05 Atlas
- ☐ Both Atlases

Breeding Bird Survey Trend in New York

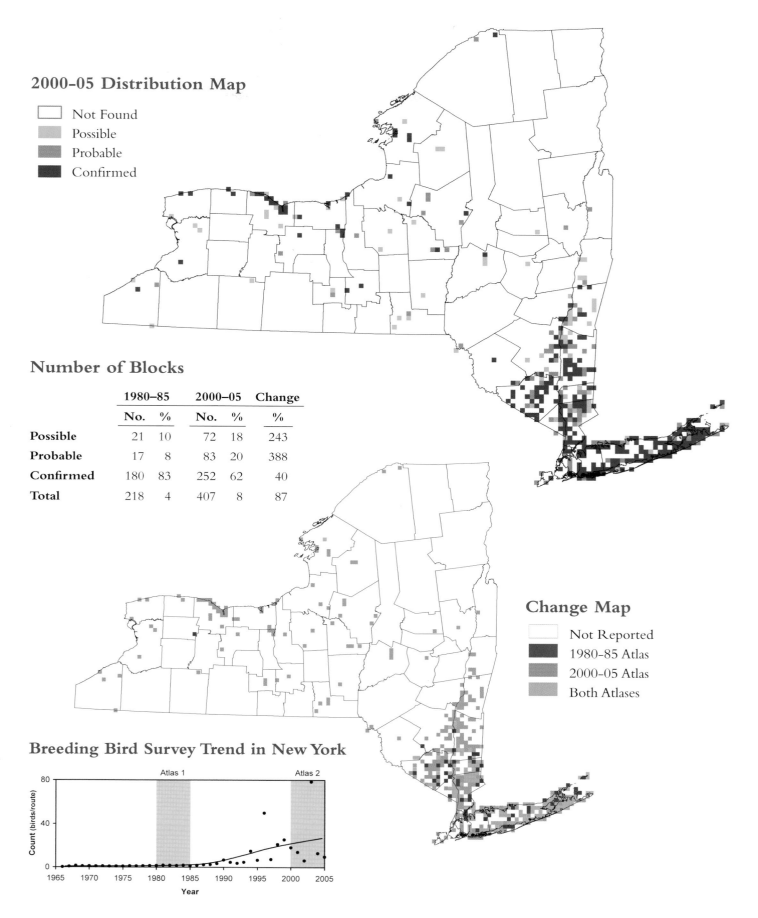

Trumpeter Swan
Cygnus buccinator

KEVIN J. MCGOWAN

The Trumpeter Swan was hunted for its feathers throughout the 1600s to 1800s, causing a tremendous population decline and range contraction (Banko 1960). It now breeds locally from central Alaska to western South Dakota and northern Nebraska and was introduced farther eastward in Minnesota, Iowa, Wisconsin, Michigan, Ohio, and Ontario (Mitchell 1994). Although the Trumpeter Swan is resident in much of its breeding range, some populations migrate southward in winter. The nature of this swan's historic occurrence in New York is unclear. Early reports did not distinguish adequately between Trumpeter and Tundra swans. Some authors believe that the Trumpeter Swan bred throughout eastern North America (Mitchell 1994, Shea 2002), while others suggest that Michigan was the southeastern limit (Whan and Rising 2002). Lumsden (1984) presented evidence that the Trumpeter Swan might have been present in the St. Lawrence area in the 1500s. What is undisputed is that by the 1800s the Trumpeter Swan was no longer extant in any numbers in eastern North America. De-Kay (1844) called it extra-limital to New York. Rathbun (1879) mentioned a single specimen from Cayuga Lake (no date given), and another was possibly taken near Buffalo in 1863 (Beardslee and Mitchell 1965). Neither specimen survived for subsequent examination, however, and the species was considered hypothetical by Eaton (1910), Beardslee and Mitchell (1965), and Bull (1974).

The first modern sighting of Trumpeter Swan in New York was of a pair in Dunkirk Harbor on Lake Erie on 24 December 1988. Wing tags revealed that the swans had been raised in captivity and released in March 1988 at Long Point, Ontario, as part of a reintroduction program (Eaton 1989). An immature was reported in February 1989 at Ft. Erie (Eaton 1989). Another tagged swan from Ontario was observed on a small pond near Seneca Falls from 26 March through 11 May 1990. An adult was discovered in the Savannah Mucklands of Wayne County on 23 April 1993, but its origins were unknown (NYSARC 1995), as was true of another individual seen on a pond near the Russell Power Plant in Greece, Monroe County, in February and March 1994 (NYSARC 1996). The first confirmed nestings in New York occurred in 1996, with one pair being found at the Perch River Wildlife Management Area in Jefferson County, and another pair in a private wetland in Wayne County (Carroll and Swift 2000). These pairs were believed to have been bred and then escaped from a private collection in New York, rather than being from the Ontario release project (Carroll and Swift 2000). In the summer of 1999 the New York State Department of En-

vironmental Conservation (NYSDEC) counted 14 Trumpeter Swans in the state (Carroll and Swift 2000).

During the second Atlas period, a second pair joined the first at Perch River in 2000, and a pair was reported at Lake Como in Cayuga County (Carroll and Swift 2000). Trumpeter Swans were reported from 18 blocks in the Great Lakes Plain, with breeding confirmed in 6. Three pairs were confirmed breeding in Wayne County and another in St. Lawrence County. It is unclear whether these swans were offspring of the original two pairs, came from the private collection that did not control its progeny, or were from the Ontario program. A 2005 survey by NYSDEC found five pairs in the state, only one with cygnets (USFWS 2006b).

All Trumpeter Swan populations are currently increasing, including the introduced interior population (USFWS 2006b). Tagged swans from the Ontario program appear annually in New York, primarily in the winter. The second Ontario Breeding Bird Atlas reported finding the Trumpeter Swan in 109 squares province-wide, with a cluster of reports occurring just across the St. Lawrence River from New York (Bird Studies Canada et al. 2006). A total of 644 swans were counted in Ontario in 2005 (USFWS 2006b). It is possible that Ontario swans eventually will join the few already breeding in New York, and the next Atlas project may find a dramatically larger population.

ATM©2006

2000-05 Distribution Map

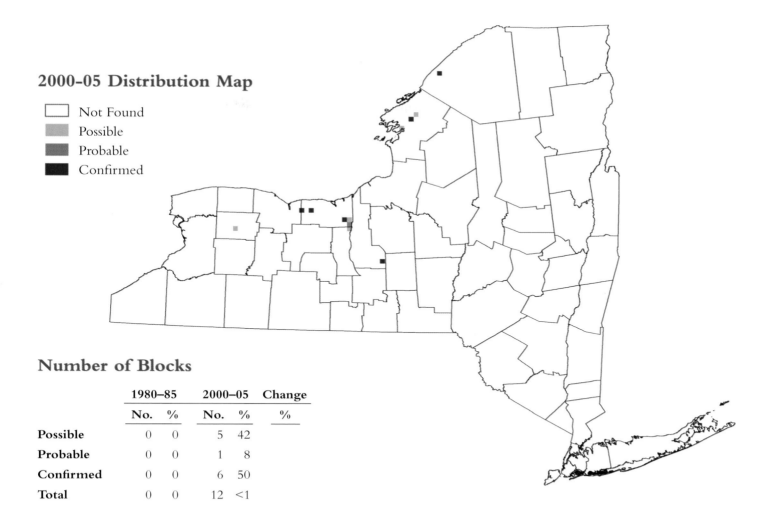

- ☐ Not Found
- ☐ Possible
- ☐ Probable
- ■ Confirmed

Number of Blocks

	1980–85		2000–05		Change
	No.	%	No.	%	%
Possible	0	0	5	42	
Probable	0	0	1	8	
Confirmed	0	0	6	50	
Total	0	0	12	<1	

Wood Duck
Aix sponsa

BRYAN SWIFT

The Wood Duck, one of the most beautiful ducks in the world, is also distinctive in its distribution, being a cavity-nester common to bottomland forests, swamps, beaver flows, and slow-moving streams. It is found only in North America, with its primary range occurring in the eastern half of the United States and southeastern Canada. A separate population extends from British Columbia and the northwestern United States southward along the Pacific Coast to southern California (Hepp and Bellrose 1995). The Wood Duck was thought to be on the verge of extinction in the early 1900s, but the reversion of farmlands to forest, legal protection from harvest, increasing beaver populations, and ambitious nest box programs all contributed to its dramatic resurgence during the 20th century (Hepp and Bellrose 1995). New York populations followed the trends. Eaton (1910) reported that the Wood Duck was "formerly a common resident throughout the State," but by the early 1900s it was "fairly common only in the most favorable localities," such as marshes bordering the Seneca River and eastern Lake Ontario. New York prohibited Wood Duck hunting in 1905, as did many other states around that time (Bellrose and Holm 1994). Recovery was indicated in many states during 1920–45, and in 1942 New York allowed hunters to take one Wood Duck per day. The limit was increased to two per day in 1959. By the early 1970s the Wood Duck was a widespread but local breeder in New York (Bull 1974), and by the mid-1980s waterfowl managers were no longer concerned that it was a species at risk (Serie and Chasko 1990). The Wood Duck is now the second most common duck taken by waterfowl hunters in the Atlantic Flyway, with more than 300,000 harvested annually during the 2001–05 hunting seasons (Serie and Raftovich 2006).

During the first Atlas period, the Wood Duck was the second most common waterfowl species recorded, occurring in 36 percent of all blocks. Concentrations were in central and western New York, the Hudson Valley, and areas to the south. Occurrence was sparser in the Mohawk Valley and Adirondacks, as well as in the Catskill Peaks. During the second Atlas period, the Wood Duck was found in 45 percent more blocks, with the increases rather evenly distributed across most of the state. A major factor favoring Wood Duck populations throughout Upstate New York was the dramatic increase in beaver populations during the 1970s and 1980s; the area in beaver impoundments increased by approximately 80,937 ha (200,000 a) in 1975–90 (NYSDEC Beaver Management Team 1992). There were slightly fewer records in the Coastal Lowlands, perhaps due to habitat loss or fragmentation, although the Wood Duck does nest in urban-suburban areas.

Despite their limitations for this species, Breeding Bird Survey data are the only available source of long-term Wood Duck regional population trends, and they show significant increases over the last 40 years in the eastern United States (Sauer et al. 2005). These data are in accord with the Atlas data and the increases found by the Ontario and Vermont atlas projects (Bird Studies Canada et al. 2006, R. Renfrew pers. comm.). BBS data from New York, however, indicate that Wood Duck populations have not increased significantly since the late 1960s (Sauer et al. 2005). Breeding waterfowl surveys indicate a relatively stable Wood Duck population in New York as well, averaging approximately 42,000 pairs from 1989 to 2006 (NYSDEC unpubl. data). Statewide harvests of Wood Duck have actually declined, from 31,000 per year during 1981–85 to about 23,000 during 2001–05 (Serie and Raftovich 2003, 2006). Future changes in distribution and abundance of the Wood Duck will likely hinge on the status of beaver populations and wetland conservation programs in New York. Artificial nest boxes can enhance local numbers but probably support less than 5 percent of the total Wood Duck population in New York (NYSDEC unpubl. data).

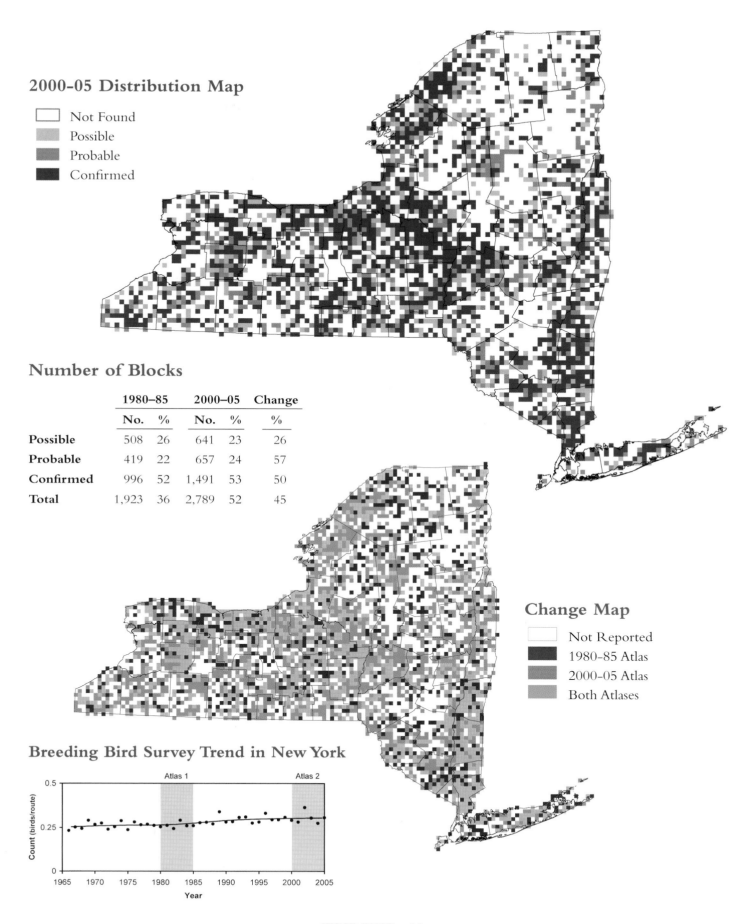

2000-05 Distribution Map

- ☐ Not Found
- Possible
- Probable
- Confirmed

Number of Blocks

	1980–85		2000–05		Change
	No.	%	No.	%	%
Possible	508	26	641	23	26
Probable	419	22	657	24	57
Confirmed	996	52	1,491	53	50
Total	1,923	36	2,789	52	45

Change Map

- ☐ Not Reported
- 1980–85 Atlas
- 2000–05 Atlas
- Both Atlases

Breeding Bird Survey Trend in New York

Gadwall
Anas strepera

KEVIN J. MCGOWAN

A drab duck of lakes and ponds, the Gadwall breeds from southeastern Alaska to the Great Lakes, southward to Texas and California, as well as in central Eurasia. The greatest breeding density is in the prairie states and provinces; New York is far removed from the main breeding range. The Gadwall nests in dense herbaceous vegetation near water, typically in grass on an island or in an upland area. DeKay (1844) listed the Gadwall as a New York breeder but considered it rare. Eaton (1910) could not verify its breeding status and considered it uncommon in any part of the state at any time. During the 20th century the Gadwall changed its breeding range in North America more than any other duck species (LeShack et al. 1997). Before 1939, no confirmed breeding records existed for eastern North America, but the species was locally common in some areas by the 1970s (LeShack et al. 1997). A few summering individuals in western New York in the 1940s and 1950s suggested the possibility that the species nested there (Beardslee and Mitchell 1965), but the first confirmed nesting was in 1947 at the other end of the state, at Tobay Pond, Nassau County (Sedwitz et al. 1948, Bull 1964). The second confirmed nest was at Montezuma National Wildlife Refuge in 1950, and at least 40 broods were produced there in 1971 (Bull 1974). Ducklings from Montezuma were introduced to the Iroquois NWR starting in 1969, and breeding there began in 1971 (Henny and Holgerson 1974). Bull (1974, 1976) listed nesting only in the Montezuma and Oak Orchard/Iroquois areas, along the St. Lawrence at Wilson Hill Wildlife Management Area, and at seven locations on Long Island.

The first Atlas results showed that the Gadwall had further extended its breeding range in New York, but it occurred primarily in the same four breeding areas reported by Bull. Clusters of reporting blocks could be seen in the Oak Orchard Area, at Montezuma NWR, around Wilson Hill WMA, and along the south shore and tip of Long Island. Additional breeding locations were found along the St.

Lawrence, Lake Champlain, lower Hudson River, and Long Island, and in scattered blocks throughout the state. The second Atlas data revealed few changes in breeding distribution in New York. The Gadwall was reported in only one more block for the second Atlas compared with the first. Again, concentrations of reporting blocks were apparent near Oak Orchard, Montezuma, Wilson Hill, and Long Island, although no breeding was confirmed at Oak Orchard or Wilson Hill. One notable difference was the apparent expansion into blocks along the eastern Lake Ontario shore in Jefferson County, an area that is contiguous with the breeding distribution in Canada, directly across the north shore of Lake Ontario (Bird Studies Canada et al. 2006). After the first Atlas was completed, Spahn (1998b) reported three additional breeding localities, in Orleans, Monroe, and Saratoga counties, but of those, only Braddock Bay in Monroe County had reports for the second Atlas, and breeding was not confirmed.

The establishment of water impoundments with emergent vegetation for food on national wildlife refuges and wildlife management areas created nesting habitat for the Gadwall and probably contributed to the expansion of its breeding range in eastern North America (Henny and Holgerson 1974). Continental Gadwall populations have increased substantially over the last 40 years, although their numbers may have peaked in the late 1990s (USFWS 2006c). The main breeding areas of the Gadwall continue to be the prairies of western North America, and the expanded eastern populations are small in comparison. The breeding population in New York remains small as well, showing no signs of increase over the past 25 years. The Gadwall probably will remain an uncommon local breeder in New York.

©SdA 2004

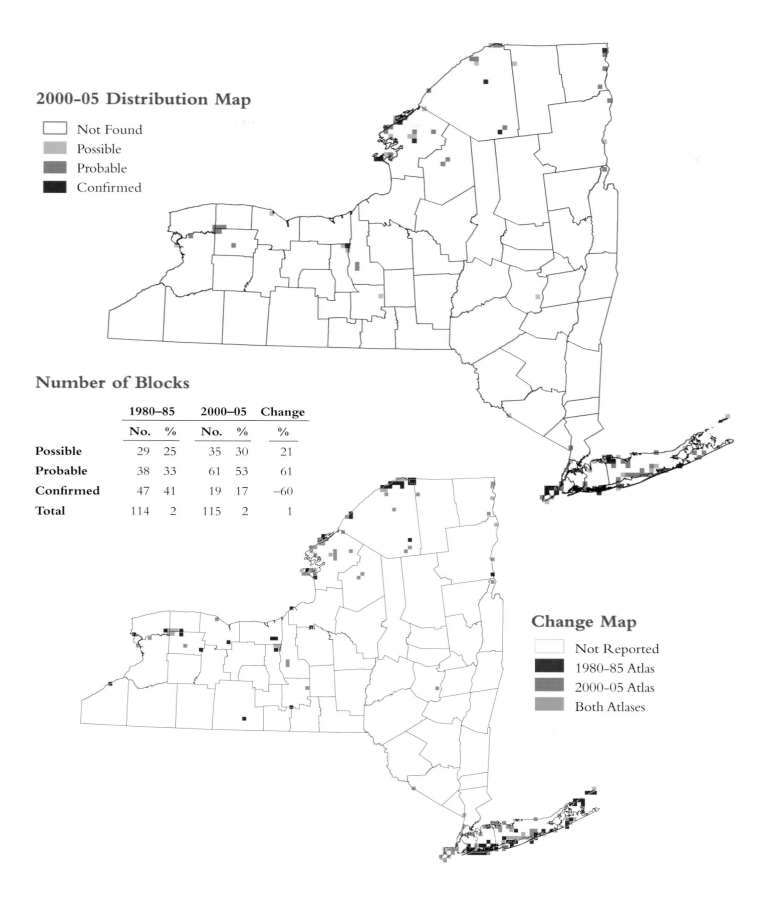

2000-05 Distribution Map

- ☐ Not Found
- Possible
- Probable
- Confirmed

Number of Blocks

	1980–85		2000–05		Change
	No.	%	No.	%	%
Possible	29	25	35	30	21
Probable	38	33	61	53	61
Confirmed	47	41	19	17	−60
Total	114	2	115	2	1

Change Map

- ☐ Not Reported
- 1980-85 Atlas
- 2000-05 Atlas
- Both Atlases

American Wigeon

Anas americana

KEVIN J. MCGOWAN

The American Wigeon breeds across Alaska and Canada, southward to the northern tier of the United States. In the eastern portion of its range it is more localized in breeding. The main portion of its breeding range lies in the northwest of the continent, far from New York. The wigeon prefers shallow freshwater wetlands, including ponds, marshes, and rivers, where it eats primarily plants, plant parts, and seeds (Mowbray 1999a). Its nest is placed in grass or brushy vegetation near water. Early writers mentioned the American Wigeon only as a migrant in New York, and the first breeding record did not occur until 1959 at Montezuma National Wildlife Refuge (Bull 1974). The American Wigeon expanded its breeding range eastward in the 1950s, reaching New England and the Maritime Provinces (Mowbray 1999a). Possible reasons for the expansion include habitat loss and drought conditions in the prairie breeding grounds, as well as the creation of suitable breeding areas in the East, such as farm ponds, sewage lagoons, and water impoundments (Mowbray 1999a). Still, only seven New York breeding locations were documented by the mid-1970s: Oak Orchard Swamp; Montezuma marshes; Howland Island, Cayuga County; Wilson Hill area along the St. Lawrence; Piermont Marsh, Rockland County; Jamaica Bay, Queens County; and Flushing Meadows, Queens County (Bull 1974, 1976).

During the first Atlas survey, the American Wigeon was found in 42 blocks and breeding was confirmed in 10. The only significant cluster of blocks was in the Wilson Hill Wildlife Management Area along the St. Lawrence. Confirmations were also made at Montezuma NWR, Buffalo Harbor on Lake Erie, Perch River WMA, Chazy Landing along Lake Champlain, and at North Sea in the Great Peconic Bay, Suffolk County. Already a rare breeder in the state, the American Wigeon became even rarer by the second Atlas survey period, when it was found in only 22 blocks and confirmed in only 3. Most noticeable was the nearly complete disappearance from along the St. Lawrence, its stronghold during the first Atlas period. It also completely disappeared from the Coastal Lowlands. Breeding was confirmed only at Kings Bay WMA along Lake Champlain, south of Buffalo along Lake Erie at Tifft Nature Preserve, and in Delaware Park in Buffalo. Reports were again received from the Oak Orchard area, Montezuma NWR, and Perch River WMA. As with other duck species, summer sightings might occur in isolated wetlands and might or might not indicate breeding.

Continental populations of the American Wigeon fluctuate in response to prairie habitat conditions. Numbers peaked around 1980 and then declined by approximately 50 percent in the 1980s as a result of extended drought in prairie regions (Mowbray 1999a). Some recovery was made in the next decade, but numbers dropped again after 1997 (USFWS 2006c). The eastward expansion of the breeding range does not seem to be continuing, so the sparse occurrence of this species in New York may simply reflect the overall status of the population. The second Ontario Breeding Bird Atlas reported little change in American Wigeon numbers, and few new reports were made along the New York frontier (Bird Studies Canada et al. 2006). The population to the west across the St. Lawrence River from the Wilson Hill WMA was still present and did not show the decline noted on the New York side. The American Wigeon appears likely to remain a rare breeder in New York, with only isolated nesting attempts at managed wetlands and scattered ponds.

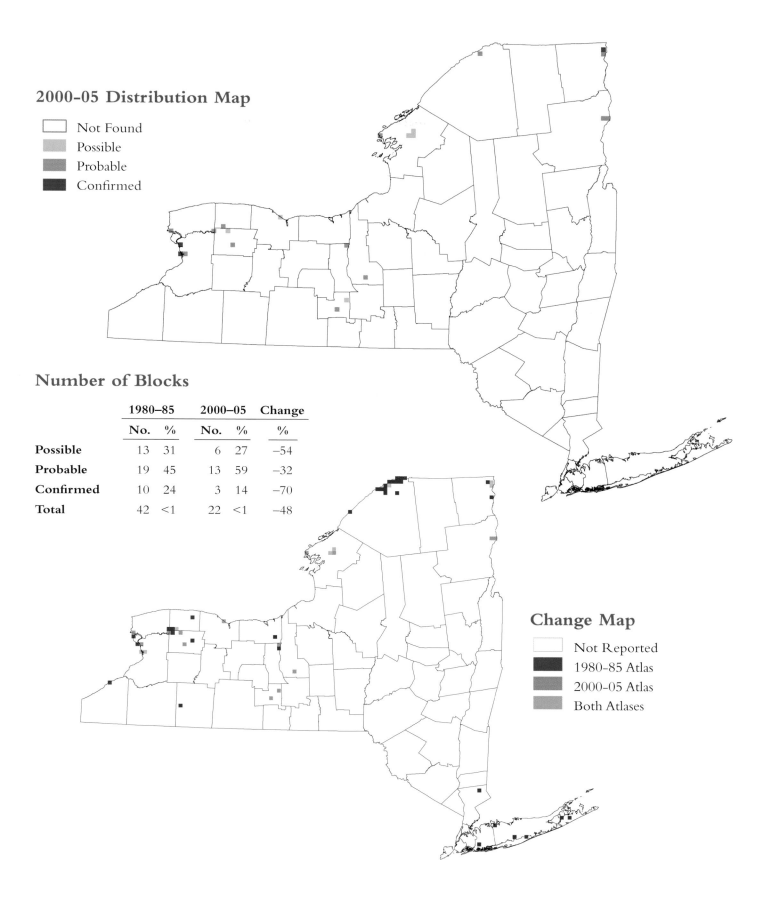

2000-05 Distribution Map

- ☐ Not Found
- Possible
- Probable
- Confirmed

Number of Blocks

	1980–85		2000–05		Change
	No.	%	No.	%	%
Possible	13	31	6	27	−54
Probable	19	45	13	59	−32
Confirmed	10	24	3	14	−70
Total	42	<1	22	<1	−48

Change Map

- ☐ Not Reported
- 1980-85 Atlas
- 2000-05 Atlas
- Both Atlases

American Black Duck

Anas rubripes

Bryan Swift

The American Black Duck occurs only in eastern North America, breeding from eastern Manitoba to the Maritimes, and from Minnesota to North Carolina and northward (Longcore et al. 2000). This species is typically associated with wetlands and bogs in the boreal forest and with tidal salt marshes along the Atlantic Coast, but Bull (1964) described it as adaptable, "nesting in fresh-water marshes, coastal salt marshes, along the shores of lakes, ponds, and streams, and even in scrub fields or open woodland some distance from water."

The American Black Duck was the most common breeding duck in New York in the early 20th century (Eaton 1910, Saunders 1926, Hyde 1939). Foley (1960) reported that it had remained stable over the years. Since the 1950s, however, American Black Duck populations have declined sharply, especially in western and southern parts of the black duck's range, including New York (Sibley 1988a) and southern Ontario (Dennis 1987).

The first Atlas revealed that the American Black Duck had become an uncommon breeder in New York, occurring in only 21 percent of all blocks. Notable breeding areas were in the Coastal Lowlands, the Hudson Valley and areas to the east, the Central Adirondacks and Western Adirondack Foothills, and the Champlain Valley. By the second Atlas period, the black duck occurred in only 14 percent of all blocks, and the number of blocks with Confirmed records decreased by nearly 50 percent. Concentrations were in the Coastal Lowlands, Central Adirondacks, Western Adirondack Foothills and Transition areas, St. Lawrence Valley, and southeastern Appalachian Plateau.

The disappearance of breeding American Black Duck in New York coincides with a long-term decline in winter counts in the Atlantic Flyway, which averaged about 400,000 (36,000 in New York) in the late 1950s to 225,000 (20,000 in New York) in the early 1980s. Since then, black duck winter counts in the flyway have been relatively stable, averaging about 215,000 (17,500 in New York) during 2001–05 (Serie and Raftovich 2006). Winter counts likely reflect the status of black ducks breeding in eastern Canada, where surveys indicate stable or increasing numbers from 1989 to 2006 (Canadian Wildlife Service Waterfowl Committee 2006), although the second Ontario Breeding Bird Atlas reported significant declines across the province (Bird Studies Canada et al. 2006).

Breeding Bird Survey data show no significant range-wide trends, but New York data show a nonsignificant decline from 0.30 bird per route in the late 1960s to 0.12 in the early 1980s, and fewer than 0.08 per route since 2000 (Sauer et al. 2007). New York's black duck breeding population is currently estimated at about 5,000 pairs, about 1 American Black Duck pair for every 20 Mallard pairs (NYSDEC unpubl. data). No estimates were available prior to the late 1980s.

Possible reasons for the long-term decline in continental populations of this species include habitat loss, over-harvest by hunters, human disturbance, and interactions with Mallards (Longcore et al. 2000). Of these, habitat changes seem least likely, since Mallard and Wood Duck populations have been stable or increasing, and with increasing forest acreage and beaver impoundments, habitat for the American Black Duck should have increased. A New York study found no differences in habitats selected for breeding by black duck and Mallard, and nest success rates were similar (Dwyer 1992). High hunter harvest of black duck occurred historically, but this take has been greatly reduced by hunting restrictions throughout the Atlantic Flyway since 1983. Expanding Mallard populations may have affected the black duck through competitive exclusion or hybridization (Heusmann 1974, Brodsky et al. 1988, Kirby et al. 2004, Mank et al. 2004). Environmental contaminants and acid deposition are not believed to be major factors in the decline (Longcore et al. 2000). The future of the American Black Duck as a breeding species in New York seems uncertain at this time.

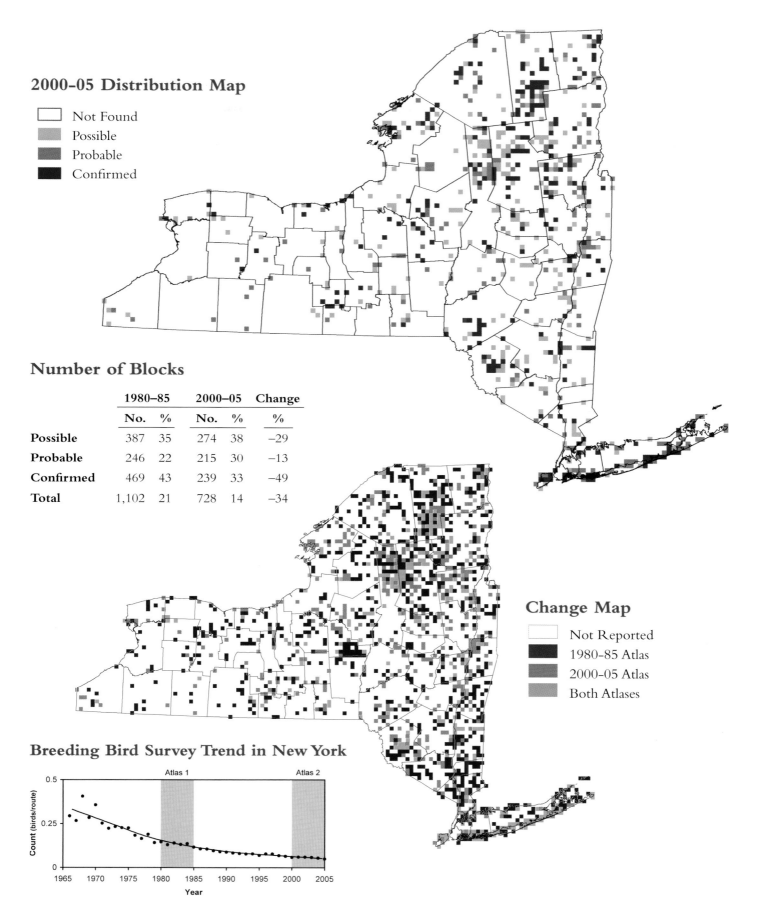

2000–05 Distribution Map

- ☐ Not Found
- Possible
- Probable
- Confirmed

Number of Blocks

	1980–85		2000–05		Change
	No.	%	No.	%	%
Possible	387	35	274	38	−29
Probable	246	22	215	30	−13
Confirmed	469	43	239	33	−49
Total	1,102	21	728	14	−34

Change Map

- ☐ Not Reported
- 1980-85 Atlas
- 2000-05 Atlas
- Both Atlases

Breeding Bird Survey Trend in New York

Mallard
Anas platyrhynchos

BRYAN SWIFT

The Mallard is the most abundant and widely distributed duck in the Northern Hemisphere, ranging from the Arctic to the subtropics in Europe, Asia, and North America (Bellrose 1980). It breeds throughout the United States and Canada, from California to Alaska and across the central plains to the Atlantic Coast southward to South Carolina, nesting in marshes, farmlands, forests, and urban parks (Drilling et al. 2002). Despite its widespread distribution, the Mallard is a relative newcomer as a breeding species in New York State; prior to the 20th century it bred only in western and central North America (Drilling et al. 2002). Early reports suggested breeding around lakes in the interior of New York (DeKay 1844, Foley et al. 1961), but Eaton (1910) reported that the Mallard bred only rarely in central New York. Several decades later, it was clear that a dramatic range expansion was underway in the state. The Mallard may have expanded eastward from the prairies into the more open landscape created by the clearing of forests for agriculture (Foley et al. 1961, Heusmann 1974). The creation and enhancement of many freshwater wetlands by the New York State Conservation Department could have facilitated such a range expansion. Dramatic increases in beaver populations also occurred in New York during the 1970s and 1980s, providing much additional breeding habitat for the Mallard and other waterfowl (NYSDEC Beaver Management Team 1992). However, the Mallard's eastward range expansion is largely attributed to releases of captive-reared birds for hunting (Ankney et al. 1987). Between 1934 and 1954, the Conservation Department released more than 30,000 pen-reared Mallards, and New York's Mallard population is believed to be the product of these stocking efforts (Foley et al. 1961, Browne 1971). Many private groups and individuals also released Mallards, helping to establish feral populations around New York City and Long Island before the 1950s (Cruickshank 1942). Mallard releases continue, mostly by private shooting preserves and other licensed game bird breeders (NYSDEC unpubl. data). The Mallard owes its wide distribution, in part, to its tremendous adaptability (Drilling et al. 2002). It nests in a wide variety of habitats across New York, including emergent marsh, scrub-shrub and forested wetlands, alfalfa fields, grasslands close to water, beaver flows and remote bogs, tidal marshes, suburban gardens, and urban park ponds (Figley and VanDruff 1982, Estel 1989, Dwyer 1992, Houston 1992, Losito 1993).

By the time of the first Atlas, the Mallard was well established across New York, with notable gaps in the Adirondacks, Tug Hill Plateau, and Catskill Peaks. Centers of abundance were the Great Lakes Plain, Hudson Valley, and Coastal Lowlands. This pattern was still evident during the second Atlas survey, but many of the gaps were filled, as the total number of blocks with Mallards increased 27 percent. The Mallard was noticeably absent only in the Adirondack High Peaks, Western Adirondack Foothills, and Catskill Peaks. Atlas data likely reflect a real increase in Mallard distribution and abundance, as this species is easy to find and identify.

Continental Mallard populations show marked fluctuations but no long-term trend since 1955 (USFWS 2006c). Breeding Bird Survey data indicate that the Mallard is now twice as numerous in New York as it was in the early 1980s, and five times more numerous than in the mid-1960s (Sauer et al. 2005). The statewide Mallard breeding population is approximately 100,000 pairs, with no apparent trend from 1989 to 2005 (NYSDEC unpubl. data). Highest densities occur in the Coastal Lowlands, St. Lawrence Valley, and Great Lakes Plain. Thus, it appears that Mallard populations have stabilized, and future changes in distribution and abundance may be on a smaller scale than what occurred during the past 20 years.

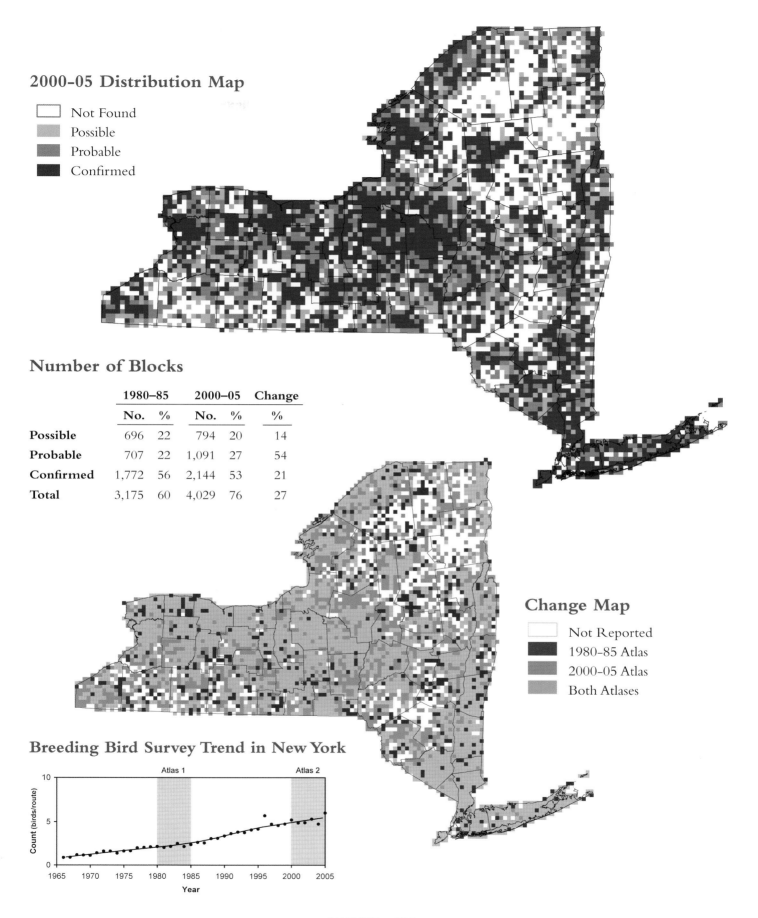

2000-05 Distribution Map

☐ Not Found
▨ Possible
▨ Probable
■ Confirmed

Number of Blocks

	1980–85		2000–05		Change
	No.	%	No.	%	%
Possible	696	22	794	20	14
Probable	707	22	1,091	27	54
Confirmed	1,772	56	2,144	53	21
Total	3,175	60	4,029	76	27

Change Map

☐ Not Reported
■ 1980-85 Atlas
▨ 2000–05 Atlas
▨ Both Atlases

Breeding Bird Survey Trend in New York

Mallard × American Black Duck Hybrid

Anas platyrhynchos × A. rubripes

Bryan Swift

The Mallard × American Black Duck hybrid is the most common waterfowl hybrid in New York State. The Mallard hybridizes with at least 40 other species in captivity, but in the wild it interbreeds most often with the American Black Duck (Johnsgard 1968, Palmer 1976, Drilling et al. 2002). Mallard and black duck are close relatives, and some experts question whether they are distinct species or subspecies (Ankney et al. 1986, Mank et al. 2004). Unlike many hybrids, Mallard × black duck offspring and their backcrosses are usually fertile (Phillips 1915). Mallard × black duck hybrids occur throughout the range of the American Black Duck, without any particular areas of abundance or habitat preference. Consequently, hybrids can be found in a variety of wetland habitats wherever the parent species are found. The first record of a Mallard × black duck hybrid on the New York State Ornithological Association winter waterfowl count was reported in 1960 (Jones 1980), not long after the Mallard became established throughout the state. It seems likely that hybrids would have occurred in New York before then, but records are lacking.

Mallard × American Black Duck hybrids and mixed species pairings were found in 73 blocks during the first Atlas survey, or about 7 percent of the number of blocks with black duck. The greatest concentration of hybrids was in the Coastal Lowlands, where substantial numbers of each species coexist during winter, when pair formation begins (Baldassarre and Bolen 2006). During the second Atlas survey, Mallard × American Black Duck hybrids were found in 86 blocks, or about 12 percent of the number of blocks with black ducks. Thus, while black duck numbers declined, the occurrence of hybrids tended to increase. Mallard × black duck hybrids were again scattered throughout the state, with somewhat greater prevalence in the Coastal Lowlands and in central New York. However, no hybrids were reported from the Central Adirondacks, where the Mallard has recently expanded into the core habitat for breeding black ducks. The sporadic nature of hybrid occurrence was indicated by the fact that only six blocks had evidence of hybrids during both Atlas periods.

The prevalence of Mallard × American Black Duck hybrids has increased also among waterfowl harvested by hunters. During 1981–85 the estimated harvest of this hybrid in the Atlantic Flyway averaged about 6 percent of the estimated harvest of black ducks, whereas during 2001–05 this total increased to 11 percent (Serie and Raftovich 2006). Whether this increase reflects a real change in abundance or a change in procedures used to classify wings submitted by hunters is unknown. One possible explanation for the higher prevalence of hybrids in recent years is the greater abundance of Mallards, resulting in more opportunity for interspecific matings. Where both species occur, Mallard males may outcompete black duck males for mating with female black ducks (Brodsky et al. 1988). While hybridization threatens the genetic integrity of the American Black Duck, and genetic distance between the species appears to be decreasing (Mank et al. 2004), it seems unlikely that a hybrid form will become self-sustaining.

As noted in the first Atlas account (Carroll 1988d), Atlas workers may have under-reported Mallard × American Black Duck hybrids not only because identification is difficult but also because second-generation hybrids resulting from a cross between a hybrid and a typical Mallard or black duck are only slightly different from the pure species (Johnsgard 1968). Also, if only one member of a mixed pair was seen, it would not have been recorded as such. Unfortunately, Atlas data do not distinguish between observations of mixed pairs and observations of individuals with hybrid characteristics. Mallard × American Black Duck hybrids will likely continue to appear on occasion almost anywhere in New York where both species occur.

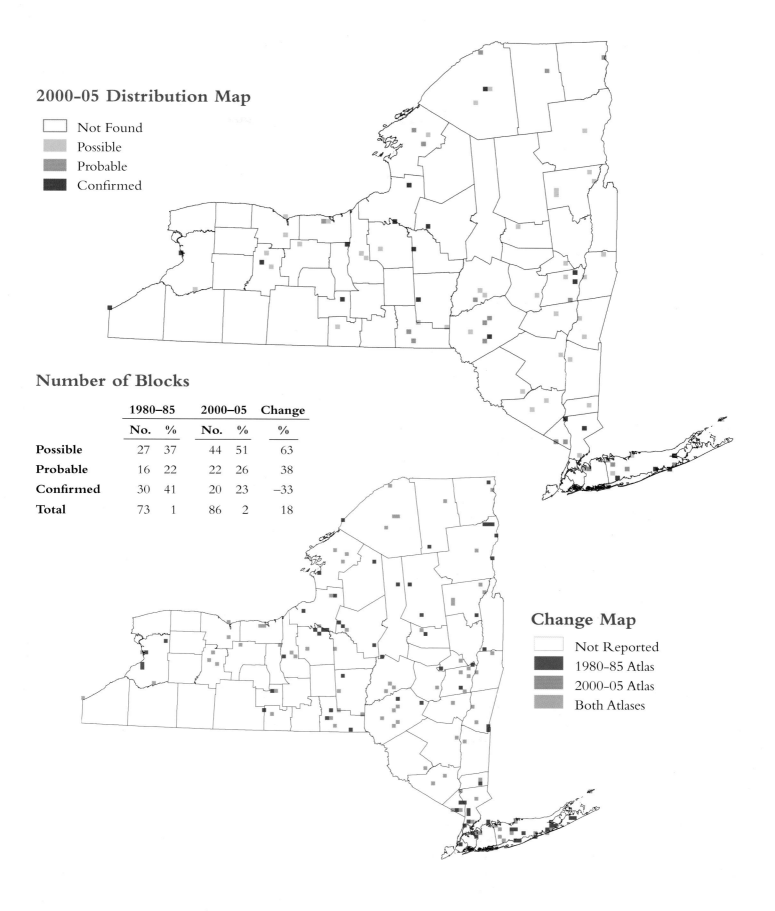

2000-05 Distribution Map

- ☐ Not Found
- Possible
- Probable
- Confirmed

Number of Blocks

	1980–85		2000–05		Change
	No.	%	No.	%	%
Possible	27	37	44	51	63
Probable	16	22	22	26	38
Confirmed	30	41	20	23	−33
Total	73	1	86	2	18

Change Map

- ☐ Not Reported
- 1980-85 Atlas
- 2000-05 Atlas
- Both Atlases

Blue-winged Teal
Anas discors

KEVIN J. MCGOWAN

A small dabbling duck of shallow ponds, the Blue-winged Teal breeds throughout much of North America, from southeastern Alaska to the Atlantic Coast, southward to Pennsylvania and through the Great Plains as far south as the Gulf Coast of Texas and Louisiana (Rohwer et al. 2002). The Blue-winged Teal nests along shallow ponds with abundant invertebrates and will use seasonal ponds and larger wetlands (Rohwer et al. 2002). It places its nest away from the water, in grass or herbaceous vegetation. DeKay (1844) was uncertain whether this duck bred in the state, whereas Giraud (1844) noted that some nested on Long Island. Short (1893) considered it a migrant in western New York, but Rathbun (1879) listed it as an uncommon breeder in the central part of the state. Reed and Wright (1909) called it a common transient in the Cayuga Lake Basin but noted that it formerly bred in large numbers. Eaton (1910) said that it was common in the marshes of Lake Ontario and the greater Finger Lakes, and bred rarely on Long Island. Beardslee and Mitchell (1965) called this the most common breeding duck in some parts of the Niagara Frontier where only 50 years previously it had been considered rare. Bull (1974) termed it common but local across the state, with the largest breeding population in the Montezuma area. He considered breeding to be concentrated in three areas: the Niagara Frontier, the central zone extending from Jefferson County southward to the Pennsylvania border at Tioga and Chemung counties, and the coastal portions of Staten and Long islands.

The first Atlas data showed no discontinuity of Blue-winged Teal distribution across Upstate New York; it was common throughout nearly all of the Great Lakes and St. Lawrence plains. It bred in scattered locations across the northern part of the Appalachian Plateau and the Mohawk Valley, as well as in the Lake Champlain Valley. It was uncommon in the Adirondacks and Hudson Valley. Sibley (1988d) commented on the decline of the Blue-winged Teal population at Montezuma National Wildlife Refuge, and after completion of the first Atlas fieldwork, Sherony (1998a) noted similar declines for unknown reasons in other marshes along Lake Ontario. The second Atlas results revealed a marked decline in Blue-winged Teal numbers all across the state. The overall distribution was essentially unchanged, but the number of blocks reporting teal was greatly reduced across all regions. No reports came from the lower Hudson Valley, and breeding was not confirmed on the Coastal Lowlands. The largest declines came from the western Great Lakes Plain, where it virtually disappeared from the lake shore and was confirmed breeding only at Iroquois NWR and the Tifft Preserve along Lake Erie. It was still widely reported along the St. Lawrence Plains, but even there numbers declined.

Continental populations of the Blue-winged Teal fluctuate greatly depending on the breeding conditions in the main production area of the Prairie Pothole Region (Rohwer et al. 2002) but show no significant long-term trend (USFWS 2006c). A large increase in the early 1990s was followed in a few years by large declines, but current numbers are above the long-term average (USFWS 2006c). Data from the second Ontario Breeding Bird Atlas show significant declines in all parts of the province, as in New York, although teal were still confirmed breeding in most squares on the northern side of Lake Ontario and along the St. Lawrence (Bird Studies Canada et al. 2006).

The decline of the Blue-winged Teal in New York is marked. Several factors may be involved, including loss of agricultural lands and changing agricultural practices. It is possible that factors on the wintering grounds play some role as well. Nearly all winter recoveries of banded young Blue-winged Teal hatched in New York occurred in the Caribbean and South America (Bull 1974), areas of current conservation concern. This species will bear watching over the next 20 years.

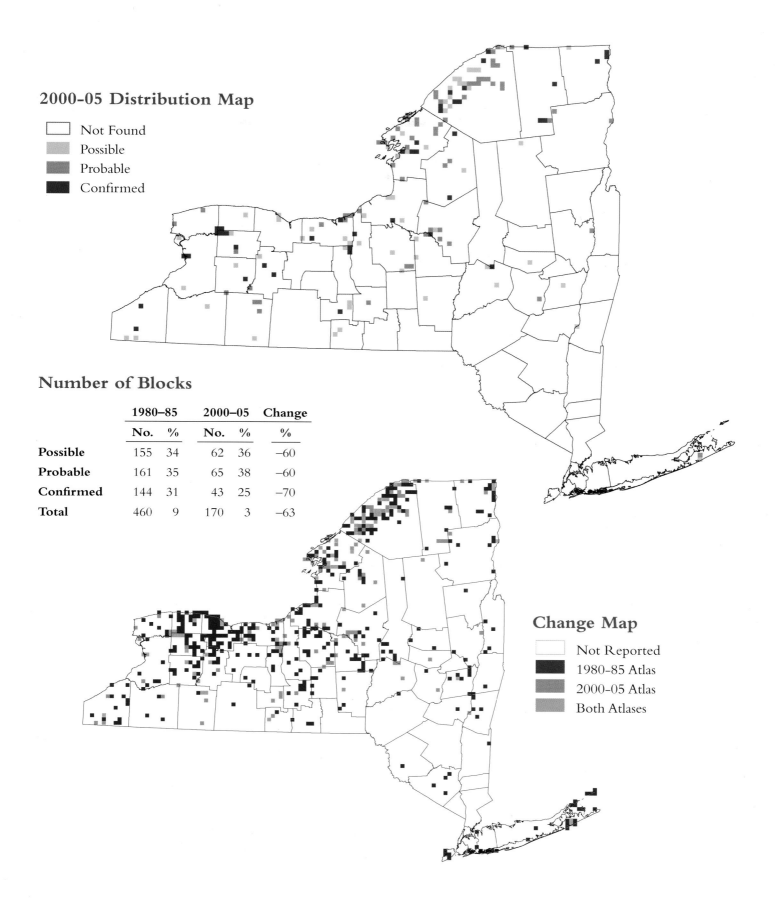

2000-05 Distribution Map

- ☐ Not Found
- Possible
- Probable
- Confirmed

Number of Blocks

	1980–85		2000–05		Change
	No.	%	No.	%	%
Possible	155	34	62	36	−60
Probable	161	35	65	38	−60
Confirmed	144	31	43	25	−70
Total	460	9	170	3	−63

Change Map

- ☐ Not Reported
- 1980-85 Atlas
- 2000-05 Atlas
- Both Atlases

Northern Shoveler
Anas clypeata

KEVIN J. MCGOWAN

The Northern Shoveler is a distinctive, large-billed dabbling duck. It uses its outsized bill to strain small invertebrates and other food particles from the surface of the water. It breeds across most of northern North America from Alaska to New Mexico, and eastward locally to the Great Lakes and the Gulf of St. Lawrence. The bulk of the species breeds in the Prairie Pothole Region of the Great Plains. New York is at the southeastern edge of the range and has only a small population of breeding shovelers. This duck prefers the margins of open, shallow wetlands, usually with submerged vegetation, with nearby grasslands or rangelands for nesting (DuBowy 1996). Such habitat is rare in New York, and the species is found in only a few scattered locations in the state. It has been known nesting in New York since an early-20th-century report at the Montezuma marshes (Eaton 1910), but it has never been common.

During the first Atlas survey, the Northern Shoveler was found in 19 blocks, with Confirmed breeding only at Montezuma National Wildlife Refuge, Jamaica Bay Wildlife Refuge, and at Lawrence Marsh, Nassau County. It was known to have nested at eight other locations before the second Atlas project started: Oak Orchard Wildlife Management Area and Batavia Wastewater Treatment Plant, Genesee County; Wilson Hill WMA, St. Lawrence County; Howland Island WMA, Cayuga County; Tobay Pond, Nassau County; Tifft Nature Preserve, Erie County; Chazy-Little Chazy rivers area, Clinton County; Rockland Lake State Park, Rockland County; (Marcotte 1998c, Miga 1999). During the second Atlas survey, the shoveler was found in 25 blocks with breeding confirmed in 10. Sites where nesting was confirmed include the Batavia Wastewater Treatment Plant in Genesee County, the Akwesasne Mohawk Reserve in Franklin County, and Lake Champlain near Long Point in Clinton County. New locations for reports were in the Oswego Lowlands, Black River Valley, and Tug Hill Transition, with a concentration appearing in the Eastern Ontario Plain. Nesting was not confirmed at Montezuma NWR, a longtime stronghold of this duck in the state, and only one record came from the coastal areas, on Staten Island.

Northern Shoveler populations across North America were steady from the 1950s through the 1980s and then increased significantly in the 1990s (NAWMP 2004, USFWS 2006c). This duck remains a rare breeder in Pennsylvania (McWilliams and Brauning 2000), New Jersey (Walsh et al. 1999), and Massachusetts (Veit and Petersen 1993, Andrews 2003). Populations in Ontario have always been small (Peck and James 1983), but the second Ontario Breeding Bird Atlas reported more pairs, and it confirmed breeding in more than 20 new squares along the Niagara Frontier (Bird Studies Canada et al. 2006). This increase was not evident on the New York side, with reports from single blocks in Erie and Genesee counties being the only new records in the region.

Marcotte (1998c) suggested that a peak in continental breeding numbers in the mid-1990s reported by the U.S. Fish and Wildlife Service might signal a resurgence of Northern Shoveler in New York, but numbers in the state remain low, and New York remains unimportant for the breeding of the species.

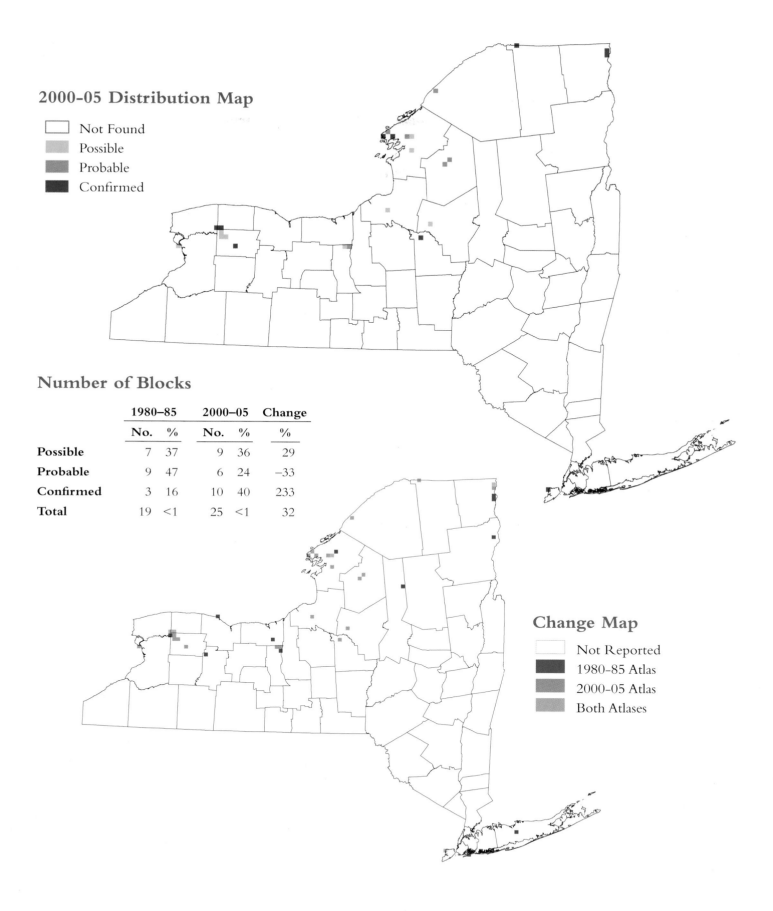

2000-05 Distribution Map

- ☐ Not Found
- Possible
- Probable
- ■ Confirmed

Number of Blocks

	1980–85		2000–05		Change
	No.	%	No.	%	%
Possible	7	37	9	36	29
Probable	9	47	6	24	−33
Confirmed	3	16	10	40	233
Total	19	<1	25	<1	32

Change Map

- ☐ Not Reported
- 1980-85 Atlas
- 2000-05 Atlas
- Both Atlases

Northern Pintail

Anas acuta

Kevin J. McGowan

A long-necked dabbling duck, the Northern Pintail breeds throughout Alaska and Canada, southward to the central Great Plains and along the Great Lakes, as well as in northern Eurasia. New York is at the southeastern edge of the pintail's breeding range, far from the main production areas in the Prairie Pothole Region and Alaska (Austin and Miller 1995). The pintail nests in open country with shallow, seasonal wetlands and low vegetation. The nest is placed in short grasses or other vegetation, usually well away from the water but occasionally along the water's edge (Austin and Miller 1995). The lack of shallow ponds adjacent to open, grassy areas probably meant that pre-colonial New York was not a favorable breeding ground for the Northern Pintail. The first documented breeding in New York occurred on the Perch River flat in Jefferson County in 1945, a year with above-average rainfall that created shallow wetlands with emergent vegetation favorable for waterfowl nesting along the flat (Kutz and Allen 1946). The pintail became a regular, if uncommon breeder across the northeastern corner of Lake Ontario from Perch River in the late 1940s and later (Sandilands 1987b). This minor spread of nesting, combined with releases of pintails by the New York State Department of Environmental Conservation at several refuges, resulted in eight known nesting sites in the state by the 1970s, including at Jamaica Bay on Long Island (Bull 1974, 1976).

During the first Atlas period the Northern Pintail was found in 35 blocks scattered across the state, with breeding confirmed in three (Montezuma National Wildlife Refuge, Chazy Landing on Lake Champlain, and in the St. Regis Lakes area in Franklin County). Additional sightings were made in the Iroquois/Oak Orchard area; along the north shore of Oneida Lake; Rome

Wildlife Management Area, Oneida County; Lake Alice and the shore of Lake Champlain, Clinton County; and at Hempstead Lake, Nassau County. Fewer reports of Northern Pintail were made during the second Atlas period, with only ten records scattered across the northern half of the state, and only two blocks with Confirmed breeding. Breeding was confirmed north of Long Point on Lake Champlain in Clinton County and at a wetland on private property in Westmoreland, Oneida County. No sighting came from the Montezuma area, only two from the Oak Orchard area, and none were made on Long Island.

No large-scale changes have been documented for the Northern Pintail breeding or wintering distributions (Austin and Miller 1995). The exclusion of eastern Canada in early reports may have been the result of a recent range expansion or incomplete early surveys (Austin and Miller 1995). Although the Northern Pintail is one of the most abundant ducks in North America, it is subject to large swings in its total population. Continental breeding waterfowl surveys showed high populations in the 1950s and the 1970s (USFWS 2006c). Numbers reached record lows during the extensive prairie drought in 1988–91, and only a little recovery has been made since then (USFWS 2006c). The pintail was not a common nesting species in southern Ontario, but the second Ontario Breeding Bird Atlas reported a significant decrease in the Simcoe-Rideau region of the province, which borders northern New York and where it had been the most abundant (Bird Studies Canada et al. 2006). The population near Kingston and the eastern edge of Lake Ontario remained but apparently declined. Like the other predominantly tundra and prairie-pothole breeding ducks, the Northern Pintail remains an uncommon and sporadic breeder in New York. The creation of shallow impoundments at wildlife refuges and wildlife management areas, along with other man-made bodies of water, may have been the cause of the periodic breeding attempts far from the main breeding range of the Northern Pintail and other ducks, but New York remains unimportant to their overall population numbers.

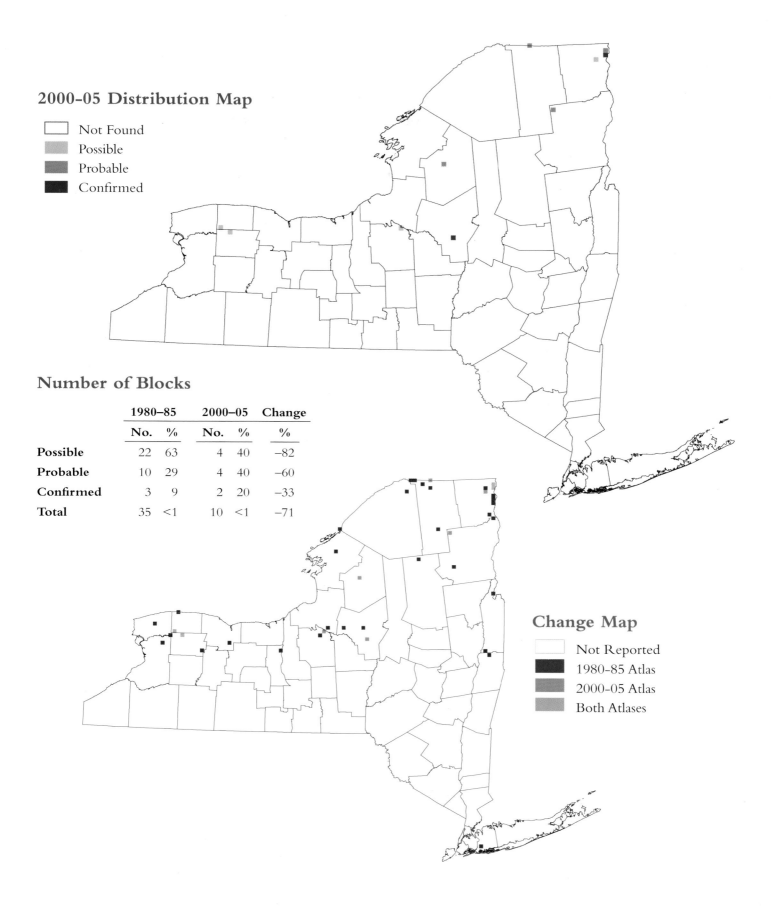

2000-05 Distribution Map

- ☐ Not Found
- ▨ Possible
- ▨ Probable
- ■ Confirmed

Number of Blocks

	1980–85		2000–05		Change
	No.	%	No.	%	%
Possible	22	63	4	40	−82
Probable	10	29	4	40	−60
Confirmed	3	9	2	20	−33
Total	35	<1	10	<1	−71

Change Map

- ☐ Not Reported
- ■ 1980-85 Atlas
- ▨ 2000-05 Atlas
- ▨ Both Atlases

Green-winged Teal

Anas crecca

KEVIN J. McGOWAN

The Green-winged Teal is the smallest dabbling duck in North America. It breeds throughout Alaska and Canada, southward to the northern Great Plains and Great Lakes, as well as in northern Eurasia. New York is at the southeastern edge of its breeding range. It breeds primarily in river deltas and forested wetlands, especially in the boreal forest and deciduous parklands (Johnson 1995). The nest is usually placed in dense vegetation in grasslands, thickets, meadows, or woods away from the water (Johnson 1995). Early accounts included no reports of breeding in New York (DeKay 1844, Giraud 1844, Rathbun 1879, Short 1893, Reed and Wright 1909). Eaton (1910) listed only two known breeding locations, at the Montezuma marshes and on Strawberry Island in the Niagara River, but gave no detailed information on either nesting event. The first known nest was discovered at Oak Orchard Swamp in 1940 (Beardslee and Mitchell 1965). A slight range expansion occurred in the 1950s, with breeding reports extending to Long Island, Massachusetts, Pennsylvania, New Jersey, and Virginia (Bull 1964). Bull (1974) listed 22 known nesting localities in New York, scattered throughout most of the state except in the eastern Appalachian Plateau and the Champlain Valley.

During the first Atlas survey, the Green-winged Teal was found breeding at isolated locations throughout the state. Breeding was confirmed in 32 blocks. Nearly a third of those confirmations came from the marshes and refuges of the Great Lakes and St. Lawrence plains, but several were from the Central Adirondacks and the High Peaks area, and another from along Lake Champlain. The largest cluster of blocks extended across Long Island, with 12 Confirmed records in the Coastal Lowlands. During the second Atlas survey, the Green-winged Teal was found in far fewer blocks, with breeding confirmed in only six: Fishers Island, Suffolk County; Tifft Farm Nature Preserve, Erie County; Upper and Lower Lakes Wildlife Management Area, St. Lawrence County; King's Bay WMA, Clinton County; and Labrador Pond, Onondaga County. No area in the state showed a noticeable concentration of blocks with Green-winged Teal, and the former "stronghold" of the Coastal Lowlands had only eight reports.

Most of the continental population of Green-winged Teal breeds in deciduous parklands and wetlands in the boreal forest instead of the largely agricultural prairie potholes, so it has not suffered from the widespread loss of breeding habitat faced by many other dabbling ducks (Johnson 1995). In fact, breeding populations have been increasing over the last 50 years (USFWS 2006c). The second Ontario Breeding Bird Atlas reported little change in Green-winged Teal reports over the last 20 years, and a modest breeding population is present across the St. Lawrence from New York and along the northeastern shore of Lake Ontario (Bird Studies Canada et al. 2006). That cluster of squares is directly adjacent to Jefferson and St. Lawrence counties in New York, which accounted for nearly one-fourth of all the New York reports.

Reasons for the apparent decline across the state and especially on Long Island are not clear. The Green-winged Teal has always been a local breeder in New York, and it probably will remain as such in the next 20 years, until the next Atlas survey is conducted.

© SdA 2005

2000–05 Distribution Map

- ☐ Not Found
- ▨ Possible
- ▨ Probable
- ■ Confirmed

Number of Blocks

	1980–85		2000–05		Change
	No.	%	No.	%	%
Possible	55	46	34	52	−38
Probable	33	28	26	39	−21
Confirmed	32	27	6	9	−81
Total	120	2	66	1	−45

Change Map

- ☐ Not Reported
- ■ 1980–85 Atlas
- ▨ 2000–05 Atlas
- ▨ Both Atlases

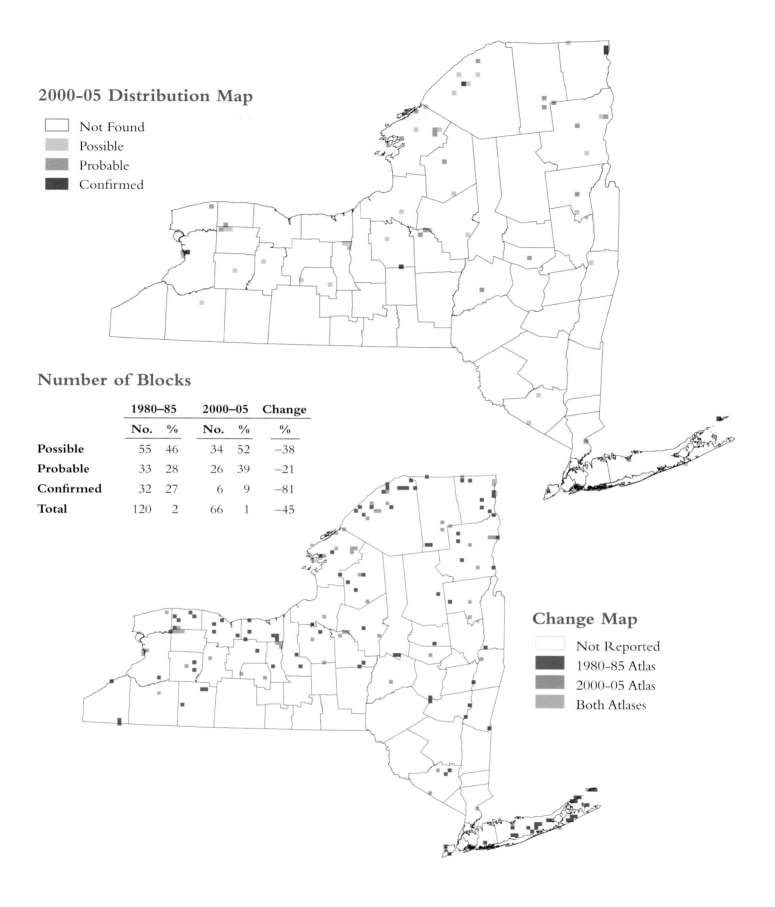

Canvasback

Aythya valisineria

KEVIN J. MCGOWAN

A striking diving duck with a unique sloping profile, the Canvasback breeds from Alaska to the Northwest Territories southward to Nevada and Minnesota. New York is far outside its central breeding range. The Canvasback breeds in small lakes, deepwater marshes, ponds, sloughs, potholes, and shallow river impoundments. It places its nest in emergent vegetation over water, such as in dense cattails, and occasionally on land (Mowbray 2002). Potential nesting sites exist in New York, and summer sightings of single Canvasbacks have been reported since at least 1948 (Beardslee and Mitchell 1965, Bull 1974). A pair and a brood of six young were observed in the Montezuma marshes in 1962 (Hoyt 1962) for the first confirmed breeding record for the state. Although Hoyt (1962) reported that no captive Canvasbacks were kept on the refuge, Bull (1974) believed this and subsequent breeding at Montezuma to be the result of introductions.

In the first Atlas, Canvasback was confirmed as a breeder only at Montezuma National Wildlife Refuge. A single brood of young was seen on the Main Pool of the refuge in July of both 1980 and 1981. After the first Atlas fieldwork was completed, single broods were discovered on the refuge in 1992 and 1993. Those broods could have come from wild stock, but in 1993 through 1995 Canvasbacks were released into the refuge and any subsequent breeding would have been suspect (Brock 1998). The second Atlas data revealed no change in the status of the Canvasback in New York. Again, it was reported in just a single block, at Montezuma NWR. Breeding was not confirmed, however, and only a single observation was made on 31 July 2002. The releases of the 1990s were not sufficient to establish a breeding population of Canvasback at the refuge.

Continental Canvasback populations have fluctuated widely in the last century. Low levels in the 1980s put the Canvasback on lists of special conservation concern (Mowbray 2002), but numbers increased greatly in the 1990s (USFWS 2006c). Weather conditions at the main breeding grounds and hunting pressure have the largest effects on overall Canvasback numbers (Mowbray 2002). Unlike some other ducks, the Canvasback has little history of breeding range expansions into eastern North America. It has been recorded breeding in Ontario but only in a few areas in the far western and southern regions (Sandilands 1987a). The second Ontario Breeding Bird Atlas documented only a few pairs nesting in the same general regions, but three additional blocks had reports of the bird along the western shore of Lake Ontario (Bird Studies Canada et al. 2006). These reports do not indicate a significant range expansion but suggest that periodic isolated breeding events by the Canvasback could still be expected in New York.

2000–05 Distribution Map

- ☐ Not Found
- ☐ Possible
- ☐ Probable
- ■ Confirmed

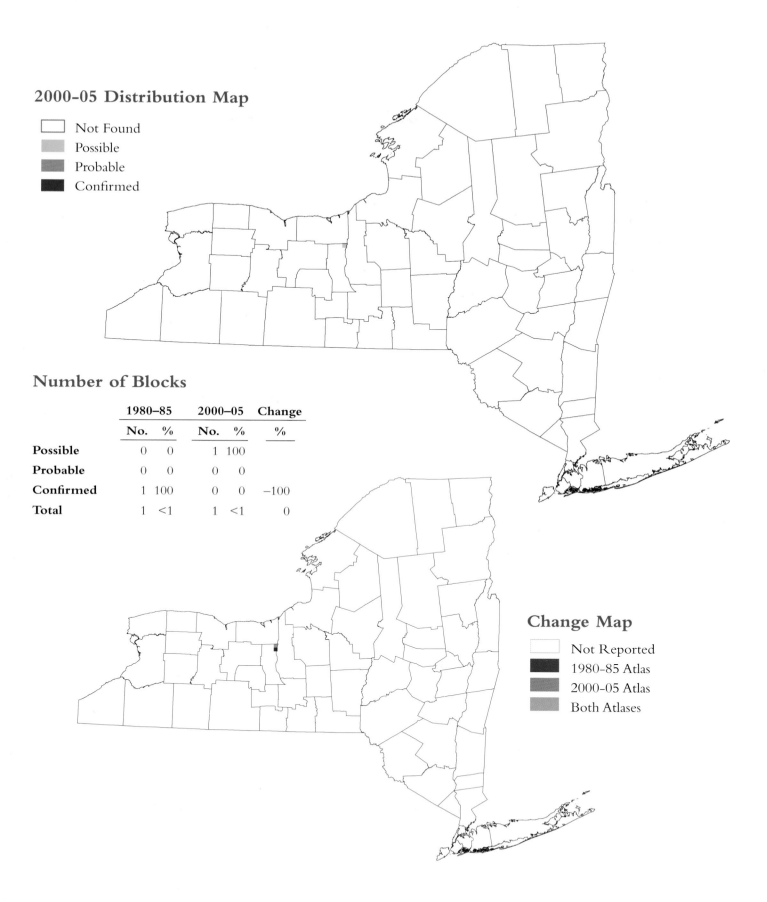

Number of Blocks

	1980–85		2000–05		Change
	No.	%	No.	%	%
Possible	0	0	1	100	
Probable	0	0	0	0	
Confirmed	1	100	0	0	–100
Total	1	<1	1	<1	0

Change Map

- ☐ Not Reported
- ■ 1980–85 Atlas
- ■ 2000–05 Atlas
- ■ Both Atlases

Redhead
Aythya americana

KEVIN J. MCGOWAN

©JPB 2005

A handsome diving duck, the Redhead breeds in central Alaska, on the Great Plains, and locally throughout western North America. It also breeds irregularly and in small numbers in scattered localities around the Great Lakes eastward to Quebec (Woodin and Michot 2002). The prairie potholes of the Great Plains are the main nesting area (Weller 1964). The Redhead typically nests in non-forested habitats with open water sufficiently deep to provide permanent, dense vegetation for nesting cover. The female places her nest in emergent vegetation, such as rushes and cattails, over the surface of the water (Woodin and Michot 2002). New York is well east of the main breeding range. Few records exist to suggest the Redhead bred historically in northeastern North America, beginning with only a small number of documented records before the 1950s (Weller 1964). Droughts on the prairie breeding grounds in the late 1950s and 1960s resulted in some shifts in the Redhead's breeding distribution and led to isolated breeding attempts in the Midwest and Ontario (Weller 1964). Although a report of Redhead breeding in the Montezuma marshes in the late 1930s (Benson and Browne 1972) followed an earlier drought and other scattered reports of breeding in the Midwest and East (Weller 1964), the first documented breeding record in New York did not take place until after stocking programs were carried out by the New York State Department of Environmental Conservation in the 1950s (Bull 1974). Bull (1974) listed ten breeding areas in the state, all the result of releases: King's Bay on northern Lake Champlain; Wilson Hill Wildlife Management Area along the St. Lawrence; Perch Lake and nearby Perch River Refuge in Jefferson County; Three Rivers Refuge in Onondaga County; Beaver Lake, Onondaga County; Howland Island, Cayuga County; Montezuma National Wildlife Refuge; Oak Orchard Refuge, Genesee County; and Jamaica Bay Refuge on Long Island.

During the first Atlas period, the Redhead was found in only six locations, with Confirmed breeding in only four blocks: Montezuma NWR; Upper Chateaugay Lake, Clinton County; along the Saranac River, Franklin County; and at Jamaica Bay. Possible and Probable breeding was also reported near the Wilson Hill WMA in St. Lawrence County and at Ausable Marsh WMA in Clinton County. During the second Atlas period, the Redhead was seen in more blocks, but it still remained a rare breeding bird in the state. Breeding was confirmed in five blocks but only at two locations, the Montezuma and Iroquois/Oak Orchard refuges.

Redhead numbers in North America have fluctuated widely over the last 50 years, with no significant long-term trend (Woodin and Michot 2002). Declines in the late 1950s and early 1960s, and again in the early 1980s, were largely balanced by increases in the 1970s and mid-1990s (USFWS 2006c). Data from the second Ontario Breeding Bird Atlas show a slight increase in the number of records in the province since the first Atlas survey, but the Redhead is still rare there (Bird Studies Canada et al. 2006). Several new sightings were made in Ontario along the northwest shore of Lake Ontario and the St. Lawrence, but no new obvious breeding populations have been established. The introduction programs that attempted to establish Redhead as a breeder in New York do not seem to have worked, and it appears that this duck will remain a rare and localized breeder in the state.

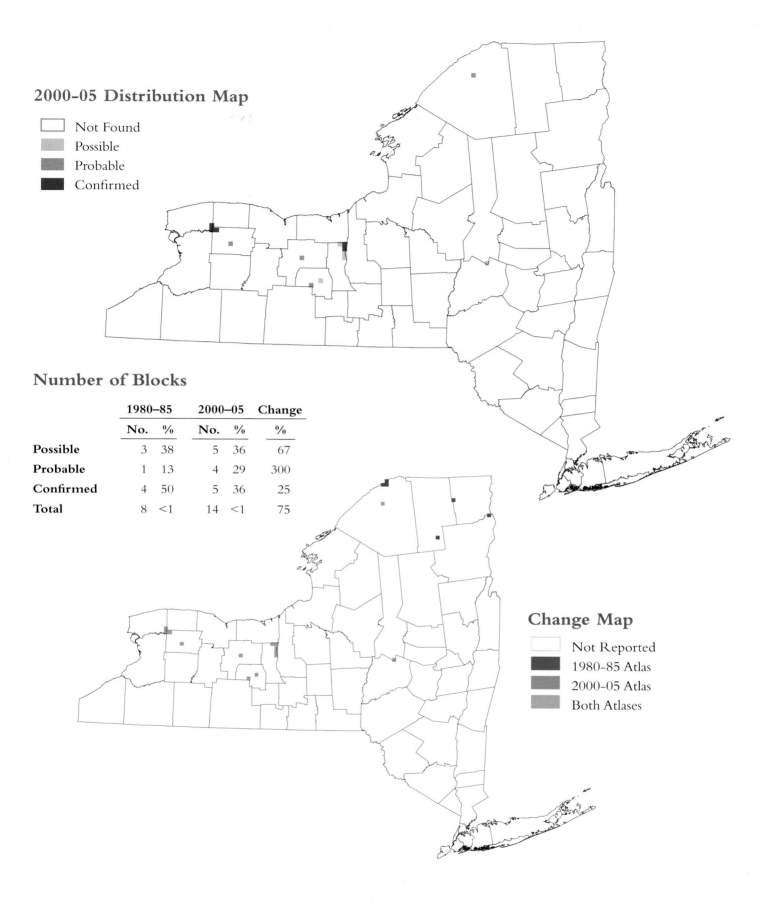

2000–05 Distribution Map

- ☐ Not Found
- ▨ Possible
- ▨ Probable
- ■ Confirmed

Number of Blocks

	1980–85		2000–05		Change
	No.	%	No.	%	%
Possible	3	38	5	36	67
Probable	1	13	4	29	300
Confirmed	4	50	5	36	25
Total	8	<1	14	<1	75

Change Map

- ☐ Not Reported
- ■ 1980-85 Atlas
- ▨ 2000–05 Atlas
- ▨ Both Atlases

Ring-necked Duck

Aythya collaris

KEVIN J. MCGOWAN

The Ring-necked Duck is the diving duck found most commonly on small ponds during migration. It breeds across Canada southward to the northern United States and farther southward to northern California and Colorado. New York is at the southern edge of its breeding range. The Ring-necked Duck breeds in shallow wetlands with emergent or floating vegetation around the edges, such as beaver ponds, marshes, fens, bogs, and, to a lesser extent, prairie potholes (Hohman and Eberhardt 1998). Early authors did not mention it as a breeder in New York (DeKay 1844, Eaton 1910). Prior to 1925 no nesting records for the Ring-necked Duck existed east of southwestern Ontario and eastern Wisconsin, except for mid-1800 reports of it nesting along the Maine/New Brunswick border (Mendall 1938, 1958). Abruptly in the early 1930s it became increasingly common during migration in the Northeast, and it established a significant breeding population in eastern states and provinces shortly thereafter (Mendall 1958). Severinghaus and Benson (1947) mentioned summer records in New York from the Finger Lakes, Lake Champlain, and the western Adirondacks preceding the first confirmed breeding in 1946 at Jones Pond, Franklin County, in the north-central Adirondacks. Within 10 years, over half of all duck broods found in the Adirondacks were Ring-necked Ducks (Mendall 1958). Bull (1974) listed 17 breeding locations in the Adirondacks, two along Lake Champlain, and one at Perch Lake in Jefferson County.

The first Atlas revealed a slight expansion of the breeding range in New York, with confirmation of breeding in the additional three counties of Herkimer, Warren, and Washington in the Central Adirondacks and Western Adirondack Foothills. Breeding was confirmed in 23 blocks, with most being centered around this species's historical stronghold of south-ern Franklin County. The Ring-necked Duck was not recorded in some of the locations where it was previously known to breed, including Perch Lake. J. M. C. Peterson (1988m) suggested that the population in the state had peaked and was undergoing a decline. The second Atlas survey found no evidence of a decline; instead the number of blocks with reports of Ring-necked Duck more than doubled. Breeding was confirmed in 34 blocks, all in the Adirondacks except for one at the Upper and Lower Lakes Wildlife Management Area in St. Lawrence County. It appears that the species expanded southward, as the center of abundance now seems to be northern Herkimer and Hamilton counties. Because the Ring-necked Duck lingers in migration until May or June, some of the sightings outside the Adirondacks may not represent actual breeding attempts. A pair first observed in mid-May 2002 in Orleans County remained there for over a month.

The eastward expansion of the Ring-necked Duck in the 1920s and 1930s was followed in the 1980s by a similar westward expansion reaching into Alaska (Hohman and Eberhardt 1998). Eastern populations of the Ring-necked Duck have been increasing gradually since 1990 (USFWS 2006c). The second Ontario Breeding Bird Atlas reported a significant increase in the number of squares with reports of Ring-necked Duck compared with the first Atlas number (Bird Studies Canada et al. 2006). The species is primarily restricted to the boreal forest on the Canadian Shield in the province, but breeding was reported in many new squares south of there in the Simcoe-Rideau region and along the St. Lawrence.

The Ring-necked Duck appears to be well established as a breeder in the Adirondacks, but whether it will expand to other parts of the state remains to be seen.

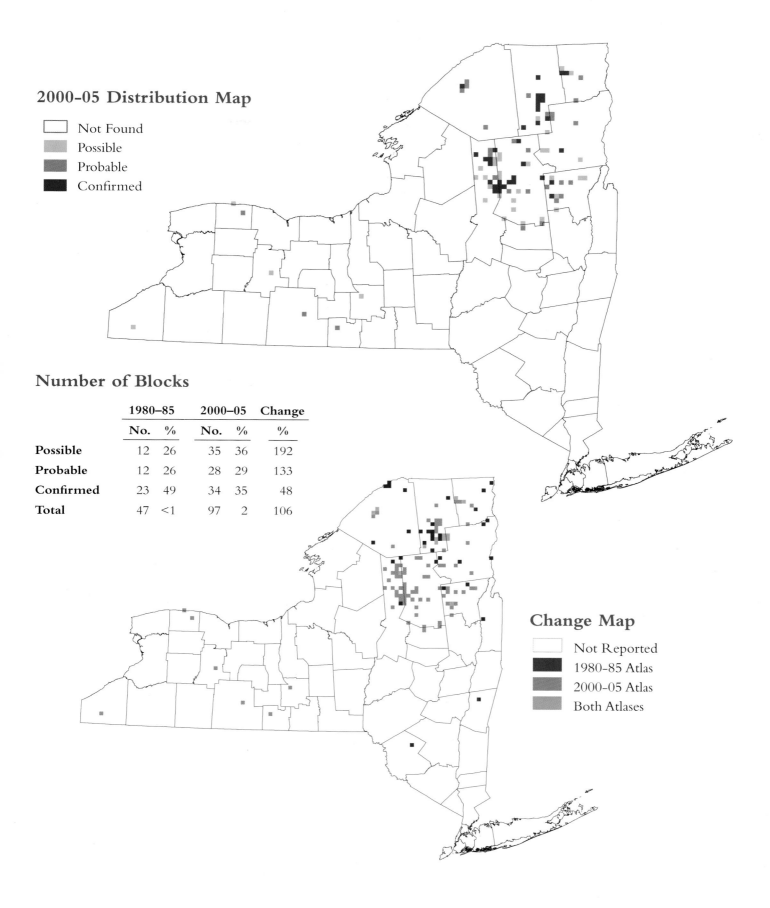

2000-05 Distribution Map

- ☐ Not Found
- Possible
- Probable
- Confirmed

Number of Blocks

| | 1980–85 | | 2000–05 | | Change |
	No.	%	No.	%	%
Possible	12	26	35	36	192
Probable	12	26	28	29	133
Confirmed	23	49	34	35	48
Total	47	<1	97	2	106

Change Map

- ☐ Not Reported
- 1980-85 Atlas
- 2000-05 Atlas
- Both Atlases

Common Eider

Somateria mollissima

Kevin J. McGowan

A large, colorful sea duck, the Common Eider is a new breeding species in New York since the first Atlas fieldwork was completed. It typically breeds in colonies on marine coasts and offshore islands from arctic Alaska and Canada southward to southern Alaska and Massachusetts, along Greenland, and throughout northern Eurasia (Goudie et al. 2000). Eaton (1910) considered it rare in New York waters at any time, but it became a fairly common winter visitor to the Montauk area of eastern Long Island by the mid-20th century. Bull (1964) mentioned a notable increase in New York starting in 1942, which followed a dramatic winter population increase in the 1930s in Massachusetts (David 2003). Four summer records of Common Eider in New York exist for Jamaica Bay Wildlife Refuge and the Montauk-Orient area between 1974 and 1994 (Spahn 1998a), but those were of single individuals with no breeding evidence. Following record high numbers of wintering eiders in 1995–96 and 1996–97, record numbers summered off Montauk Point, with 11–14 present in 1996 and an amazing 200 in 1997 (Schiff and Wollin 1997).

Common Eider was first confirmed breeding in New York when a female with chicks was observed and photographed in August 2000 in the West Harbor of Fishers Island off the northeastern tip of Long Island (Horning and Williamson 2001). An eider and a chick may have been seen there in the previous year, but breeding was not documented (Horning and Williamson 2001). Another sighting was made on 19 May 2004: 30 adults with about ten baby eiders from three broods off the nearby South Dumpling Island, as well as four active nests on the island (G. Williams in Mitra 2004). The same observer had seen about 40 adults in the same area the previous year, but no nests or young (Mitra 2004).

The Common Eider was introduced from Maine to the Elizabeth Islands off the coast of Massachusetts in the 1970s, where it became an established breeder by the 1980s and subsequently expanded (Veit and Petersen 1993, David 2003). At approximately the same time, the species was spreading southward from Maine. It was confirmed breeding on the Isles of Shoals off the coast of New Hampshire in 1977 (Borror 1994) and had established a significant breeding population as far south as Boston Harbor by 2001 (Petersen 2001). The first record of breeding in Rhode Island came in 1999, when two females with chicks were sighted off Sakonnet Point (Petersen 1999), only 20 km (12.4 mi) to the west of the Elizabeth Islands. The first New York breeding record may well have been the result of those introduced Massachusetts eiders or their Rhode Island descendants, as the Elizabeth Islands are only 90 km (56 mi) from Fishers Island and Sakonnet Point is only 70 km (43 mi) away.

Common Eider populations have been heavily influenced by hunting pressure, and they were nearly extirpated from their breeding range in the United States by the beginning of the 20th century (Goudie et al. 2000). Populations rebounded strongly from those low points; the population in Maine increased from one breeding colony in 1907 to over 28,000 breeding pairs by the 1990s (Goudie et al. 2000). The St. Lawrence estuary breeding population in eastern Canada recovered from the lows of the early 20th century but has been declining over the last third of the century (Goudie et al. 2000). Populations are currently declining in the Canadian Arctic, Alaska, and Russia (Goudie et al. 2000) but appear to be increasing in Labrador (Chaulk et al. 2005). Winter numbers off of Long Island increased dramatically in the 1990s, for unknown reasons (Spahn 1998a). Christmas Bird Count numbers in New York have fluctuated more than 100-fold since the high of 16,841 in 1996–97 but still have remained above pre-1990 numbers (National Audubon Society [2007]). Given the regional population growth, additional breeding locations in New York may be expected in the future.

2000-05 Distribution Map

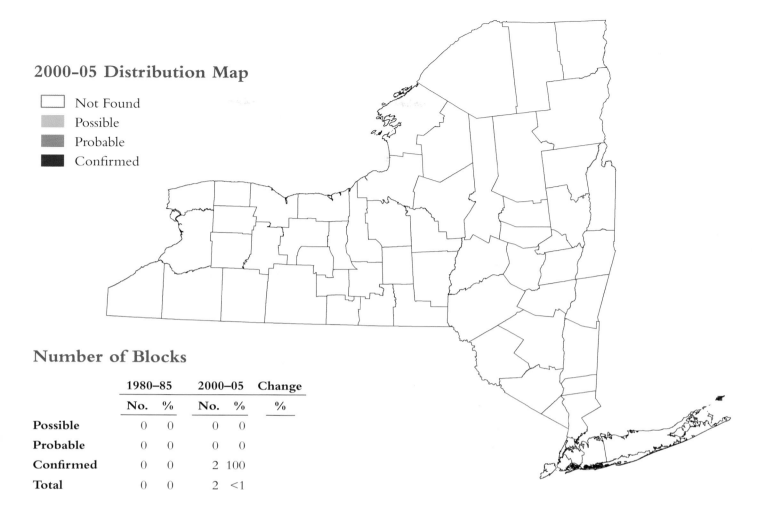

- ☐ Not Found
- Possible
- Probable
- Confirmed

Number of Blocks

	1980–85		2000–05		Change
	No.	%	No.	%	%
Possible	0	0	0	0	
Probable	0	0	0	0	
Confirmed	0	0	2	100	
Total	0	0	2	<1	

Common Goldeneye

Bucephala clangula

JOHN M. C. PETERSON

The Common Goldeneye breeds in boreal forests across North America and Eurasia and appears to be the only waterfowl species to derive short-term benefits from lake acidification (Eadie et al. 1995). In North America, this diving duck nests from Alaska to Newfoundland, southward barely into New York and a handful of other northern states. Eaton (1910) knew the species nested in the Adirondacks, although his sources were vague: Ralph and Bagg stated that the goldeneye "nested" at Deer and Jones lakes, Hamilton County, in 1878–79, and Merriam (1881) called it a summer resident, "breeding in various places." Well away from the boreal forest, the Common Goldeneye was first recorded nesting on Lake Champlain at Milton, Vermont, in 1928 (Gretch 1988). Bull (1974) reported breeding at three Clinton County sites, two on the Champlain shoreline and one at Lake Alice, in addition to five Adirondack locales.

These two distinct populations were mapped in the first Atlas. The boreal cohort nested in Essex, Franklin, Herkimer, and St. Lawrence counties, with the major concentration in southern Franklin County, while the Champlain range extended along the shoreline of eastern Clinton County, southward to Wickham Marsh in northeastern Essex County. The division is no longer that clear or simple. The second Atlas data showed that the Common Goldeneye nesting along Champlain extended their range southward in Essex County to waters near Willsboro. The Franklin County concentration was not detected during the second Atlas fieldwork, but the Adirondack sites are now loosely connected to Lake Champlain along the Ausable River watershed, and breeding was confirmed as far south in Hamilton County as the border with Fulton County. The now-blurred Adirondack range also appears to have pushed slightly westward, with Confirmed records in four northern Herkimer County blocks. Quite unexpected were two records in adjacent blocks on the Appalachian Plateau, one of which is a Confirmed record of a hen with young on the Chemung River, southeastern Chemung County.

The Common Goldeneye is known to avoid waters with fish that compete for its small aquatic invertebrate food, especially yellow perch (Eadie and Keast 1982, Hansen 1987, Gretch 1988), which are abundant in Lake Champlain. Clinton and northern Essex counties, however, have a series of wildlife and game management areas with nest boxes, large islands forested with mature trees for natural cavities, and a lower shoreline than the lake to the south, where high sandy bluffs and shale cliffs predominate. Champlain also provides an abundance of favored food items, such as mollusks and the parr and eggs of Salmonidae (Eadie et al. 1995).

The outward expansion in the Western Adirondack Foothills of southern Franklin County and the Central Adirondacks may be the result of increased lake acidification, which provides clear lakes without fish, but some new records may simply be serendipitous finds. The Common Goldeneye is known to respond quickly to changes in prey resulting from environmental degradation, and populations may even decline as boreal lakes recover from acid rain, providing this species with great potential as a biological indicator of ecological conditions in aquatic habitats (Eadie et al. 1995).

Eastern populations of the Common Goldeneye in North America show no long-term trend, remaining near 300,000 from 1990 through 2006 (USFWS 2006c). The second Ontario Breeding Bird Atlas reported a significant increase in goldeneye records in the province, with three instances of confirmed breeding at the New York border along the St. Lawrence (Bird Studies Canada et al. 2006). Bordage (1996) reported declining populations in Quebec but also indicated confirmed breeding on the St. Lawrence at the New York border. For the present, the species seems stable, even expanding, in New York State.

2000-05 Distribution Map

- ☐ Not Found
- Possible
- Probable
- Confirmed

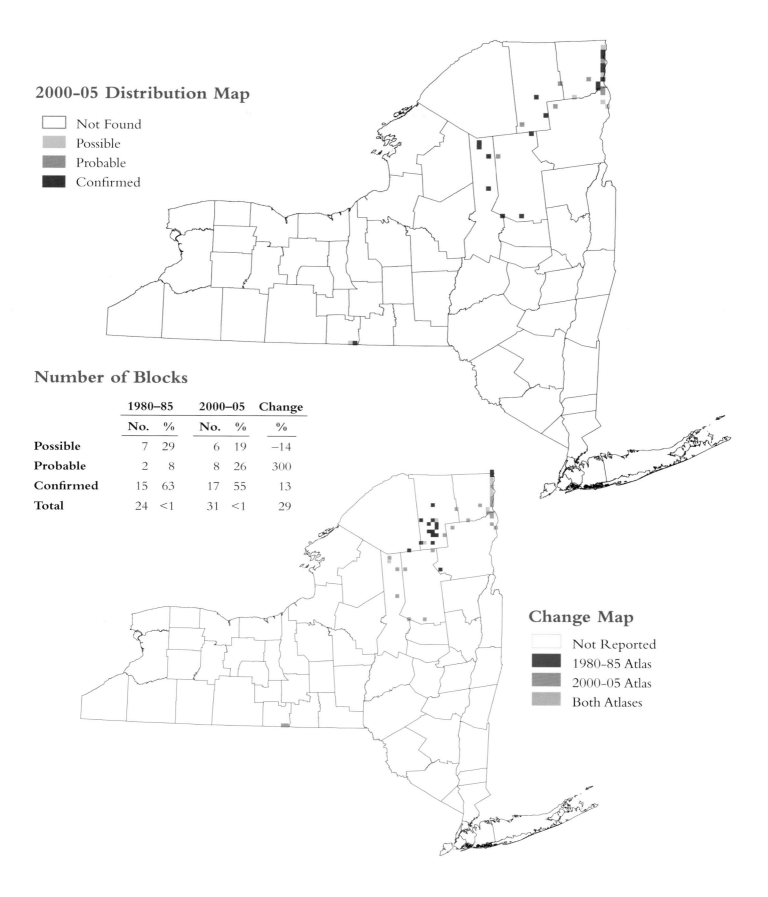

Number of Blocks

	1980–85		2000–05		Change
	No.	%	No.	%	%
Possible	7	29	6	19	−14
Probable	2	8	8	26	300
Confirmed	15	63	17	55	13
Total	24	<1	31	<1	29

Change Map

- ☐ Not Reported
- 1980-85 Atlas
- 2000-05 Atlas
- Both Atlases

Hooded Merganser

Lophodytes cucullatus

KEVIN J. MCGOWAN

A small, tree-nesting diving duck, the Hooded Merganser is typically found breeding in wooded freshwater wetlands. It breeds in the Pacific Northwest and all across eastern North America and is most abundant around the Great Lakes (Dugger et al. 1994). The Hooded Merganser nests in holes in trees near clear, shallow water where its fish and invertebrate prey are easily seen. Areas with exposed rocks and logs provide ample loafing sites and are preferred places to brood its young (Dugger et al. 1994). Such sites are abundant in much of New York State, especially in more remote areas with high forest cover, as found in the Appalachian Plateau and the Adirondacks. It probably was more abundant in New York before the destruction of forests by European settlers. Eaton (1910) listed it as breeding in scattered locations across the state, as well as in the Adirondacks and Catskills, and thought that it could become more common if it was better protected. It did appear to rebound somewhat during the 20th century with the return of the forests and increasing populations of beaver and Pileated Woodpecker, but its stronghold in the state remained the Adirondacks (Levine 1988b, Eaton 1998d).

During the first Atlas survey, the Hooded Merganser was found throughout New York State in small numbers, with a significant concentration in the Adirondacks. The 43 counties with records represented a significant increase over the 26 counties with known nests recorded through the 1970s (Browne 1975, Levine 1988b). Breeding in the Champlain Valley was not re-corded until the first Atlas project (Levine 1988b). The increasing trend continued to the second Atlas survey, with the species being found in 49 counties and more than twice as many blocks as during the first Atlas. A concentration was still apparent in the Adirondacks, but other clusters of blocks were found throughout the state, especially in the eastern Appalachian Plateau. Reports in the Appalachian Plateau increased 265 percent, and this ecozone surpassed the Adirondacks for most records. The few pairs nesting on Long Island in the 1980s were not detected during the second Atlas fieldwork. Levine (1988b) commented that the dearth of the species found in the Catskills for the first Atlas was puzzling, given the presence of much forested area with the clear streams preferred by this duck. The mystery still exists, as the Hooded Merganser records did not increase appreciably in that area for the second Atlas. Its preference for wooded swamps may have resulted in its being missed in some blocks, but the pattern of increase is clear and consistent across most of the state.

Little is known about the long-term continental population trends for the Hooded Merganser, but increases in some states and an increasing hunter harvest throughout the continent suggest populations are currently stable and likely growing over much of the range (Dugger et al. 1994, NAWMP 2004). Numbers appear to be rising in Quebec (Bordage et al. 2003) and Ontario (Bird Studies Canada et al. 2006), as well as in Massachusetts, Maine, New Hampshire, and Vermont (Heusmann et al. 2000). The Hooded Merganser remains uncommon in Connecticut (Zeranski and Baptist 1990), New Jersey (Walsh et al. 1999), and Pennsylvania (McWilliams and Brauning 2000), though its numbers appear to be increasing in Pennsylvania (R. Mulvihill pers. comm.). The deployment of nest boxes may have contributed to some local increases, but reforestation and increased beaver populations are more likely to have made greater contributions to the larger continental trend.

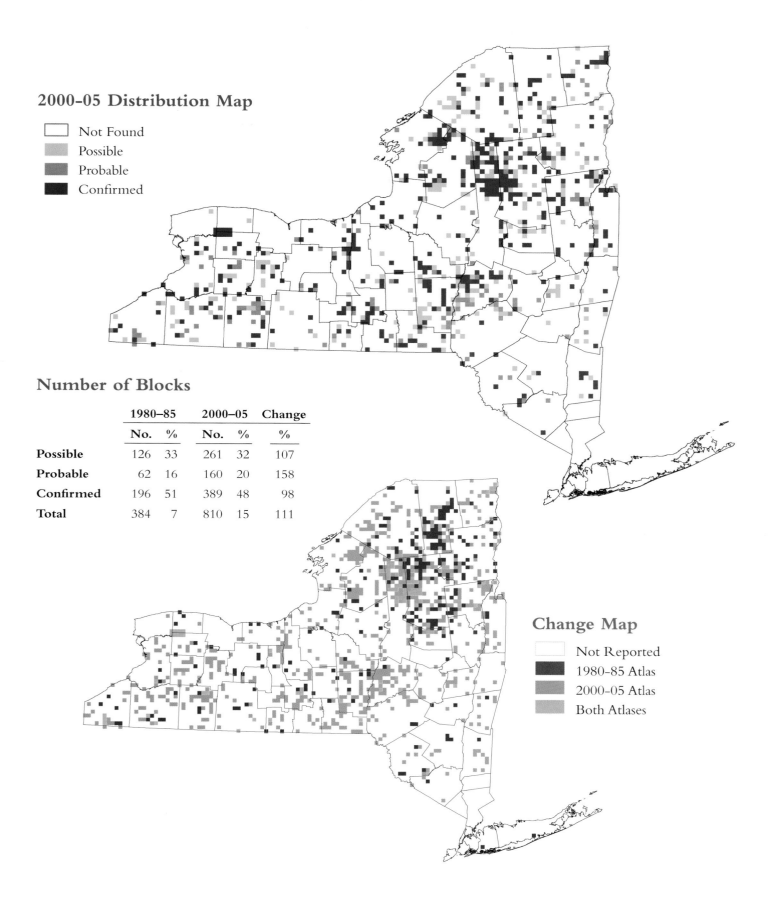

2000-05 Distribution Map

- ☐ Not Found
- Possible
- Probable
- Confirmed

Number of Blocks

	1980–85		2000–05		Change
	No.	%	No.	%	%
Possible	126	33	261	32	107
Probable	62	16	160	20	158
Confirmed	196	51	389	48	98
Total	384	7	810	15	111

Change Map

- ☐ Not Reported
- 1980-85 Atlas
- 2000-05 Atlas
- Both Atlases

Common Merganser
Mergus merganser

KEVIN J. McGOWAN

A large, fish-eating diving duck, the Common Merganser is found across the Northern Hemisphere. It breeds from Alaska to Newfoundland, southward to Pennsylvania, Minnesota, New Mexico, and California, as well as across northern Eurasia (Mallory and Metz 1999). It nests along lakes and rivers bordered by forests. Most often a tree cavity-nester, it will also use a nest box or occasionally a rock crevice, hollow log, or other hole (Mallory and Metz 1999). It was likely common throughout pre-colonial New York and declined in numbers after the destruction of the forests. DeKay (1844) listed the Common Merganser as occurring throughout the state in summer, from Pennsylvania northward, and Merriam (1881) called it common in the Adirondacks. By the late 19th century the population appears to have declined in most of the state, and it was not mentioned as a breeder in the western regions (Rathbun 1879, Short 1893, Reed and Wright 1909). Eaton (1910) called it common but gave breeding locations only near Buffalo, at Montezuma, Little Sodus Bay, and the lakes of the Adirondacks, where he noted that human disturbance was causing a decline. Bull (1974) considered it a rare breeder in New York outside of the Adirondacks. He remarked on the continuing decline of the species there, where it was mostly restricted to the more remote lakes and ponds. He noted an expansion after the early 1950s into the Delaware River drainage, as well as an isolated nesting in southern Allegany County. Its appearance in southeastern New York was followed by appearances in northern Pennsylvania in the 1970s and 1980s (Reid 1992) and the first confirmed nesting in New Jersey along the Delaware River in 1973 (Walsh et al. 1999).

The first Atlas data showed the Common Merganser to be relatively common across the Adirondacks and along Lake Champlain, with additional breeding along the large rivers and tributaries in the Appalachian Plateau and the Catskill region, much as noted by Bull (1974). Breeding also was confirmed in blocks scattered across the Appalachian Plateau, in the Tug Hill Plateau, the Hudson Valley, the Taconic Foothills, and along Lake Erie. The second Atlas results documented noticeable increases in the species. Increases in records were noted in every ecozone, except from the Lower Hudson Valley and southward, where it remained mostly missing and unconfirmed as a breeder. Within its core area of the Adirondacks it was found in 25 percent more blocks. The largest gain was on the Appalachian Plateau, where the number of blocks increased by 533 percent, rivaling the Adirondacks as a population stronghold.

Overall population trends are difficult to assess for the Common Merganser. It is not well covered by the Breeding Bird Survey, and continental monitoring schemes combine all three merganser species when collecting and reporting data (USFWS 2006c). What few BBS data exist show a general increase in the Northeast in the last 25 years (Sauer et al. 2005). Populations of all mergansers in the eastern region of the United States are above the average of the last 25 years (USFWS 2006c). Christmas Bird Count data for the United States show no clear trend since 1980 (National Audubon Society [2007]). Populations in southern Quebec appear to have been stable over the last 25 years (Bordage et al. 2003). The second Ontario Breeding Bird Atlas reported a decline in northern Ontario but an increase south of the Canadian Shield near the New York border (Bird Studies Canada et al. 2006). The merganser was found in many new squares in Ontario, along the northeastern shore of Lake Ontario and the mouth of the St. Lawrence River, adjacent to the newly established breeding population in Jefferson County, New York. The maturation of trees in reforested areas has provided more potential nesting cavities. This, and the improvement of stream quality over the last four decades, could be factors in the Common Merganser's reclamation of its former breeding range.

2000-05 Distribution Map

- ☐ Not Found
- Possible
- Probable
- Confirmed

Number of Blocks

	1980–85		2000–05		Change
	No.	%	No.	%	%
Possible	149	32	391	35	162
Probable	42	9	261	24	521
Confirmed	279	59	452	41	62
Total	470	9	1,104	21	135

Change Map

- ☐ Not Reported
- 1980-85 Atlas
- 2000-05 Atlas
- Both Atlases

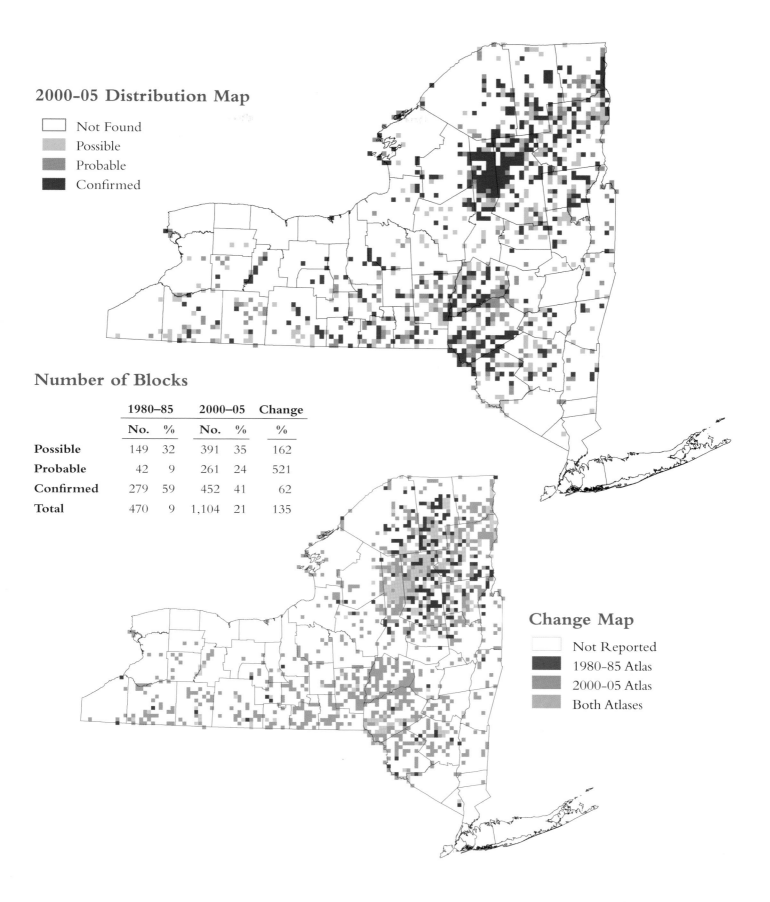

Red-breasted Merganser

Mergus serrator

KEVIN J. MCGOWAN

The fish-eating Red-breasted Merganser breeds across Alaska and northern Canada southward to the very northeastern United States, as well as in Greenland, Iceland, and across northern Eurasia (Titman 1999). It places its nest on the ground in dense cover along wooded shorelines or islands (Titman 1999). It typically breeds along rocky shorelines of larger lakes and rivers, and near the coast in saltwater wetlands with sheltered bays in the boreal forest or tundra zones (Titman 1999). New York may always have had only a sparse breeding population, as it lies outside this merganser's main breeding range. DeKay (1844) listed this duck as breeding in the middle of the state, but other early authors (Rathbun 1879, Short 1893, Reed and Wright 1909) did not list it as a breeder. Eaton (1910) stated that "a few are known to nest in the Adirondacks," although Merriam (1881) mentioned it only as a migrant there. Beardslee and Mitchell (1965) listed a few individuals summering in the Buffalo area, and although they assumed most were nonbreeders, they suggested looking for breeders at the mouths of creeks flowing into Lake Erie. Bull (1974) questioned the accuracy of most written accounts of Red-breasted Merganser in the state, asserting that many people confused the species with Common Merganser. He declared that no records existed for the Adirondacks and that the only two areas of known nesting were in islands in northeastern Lake Ontario (Little Galloo and Gull islands) and in seven locations along the southern shore and eastern tip of Long Island. The problem of identification remains (Eaton 1998f) and might always confound breeding reports of this species.

The first Atlas confirmed breeding in only two blocks. Broods were seen in Shinnecock Bay on the southern shore of Long Island and on Four Brothers Islands in Lake Champlain. Other sightings came from known previous breeding locations on the eastern end of Long Island and in Henderson Bay in eastern Lake Ontario, as well as new sites along rivers in Steuben and St.

Lawrence counties. During the second Atlas project, the Red-breasted Merganser was confirmed breeding in only four blocks, and the species remains rare. Females with broods were seen at two locations on Long Island near Shinnecock Bay, and in Henderson Bay in Lake Ontario. A female was observed going to a possible nest site in St. Lawrence County. A Probable observation was made again at Four Brothers Islands. Scattered reports throughout the state suggest isolated breeding events as have been recorded in the past, but the cluster of sightings in Shinnecock Bay and eastern Lake Ontario in Jefferson County suggests the potential establishment of small breeding populations.

Overall population trends are difficult to assess for the Red-breasted Merganser (Titman 1999). It is not well covered by the Breeding Bird Survey, but existing data indicate declines (Sauer et al. 2005). Continental monitoring schemes combine all three merganser species when collecting and reporting data, and populations of all mergansers in the eastern region of the United States are currently above the average of the last 25 years (USFWS 2006c). Christmas Bird Count data show no clear trends (National Audubon Society [2007]). The Red-breasted Merganser was not common in southern Quebec over the last 25 years, but the population appears to have declined dramatically in the 1990s and has virtually disappeared there (Bordage et al. 2003). The second Ontario Breeding Bird Atlas reported a decline in records in northern Ontario, but in southern Ontario, where it is generally rarer, it was found in ten new squares along the northeastern shore of Lake Ontario and the mouth of the St. Lawrence River (Bird Studies Canada et al. 2006). These sightings are directly adjacent to the locations of several breeding reports in Jefferson County, New York, and support the possible existence of a new small breeding population of mergansers in eastern Lake Ontario.

2000–05 Distribution Map

- [ ] Not Found
- Possible
- Probable
- Confirmed

Number of Blocks

	1980–85		2000–05		Change
	No.	%	No.	%	%
Possible	8	57	6	30	−25
Probable	4	29	10	50	150
Confirmed	2	14	4	20	100
Total	14	<1	20	<1	43

Change Map

- [ ] Not Reported
- 1980–85 Atlas
- 2000–05 Atlas
- Both Atlases

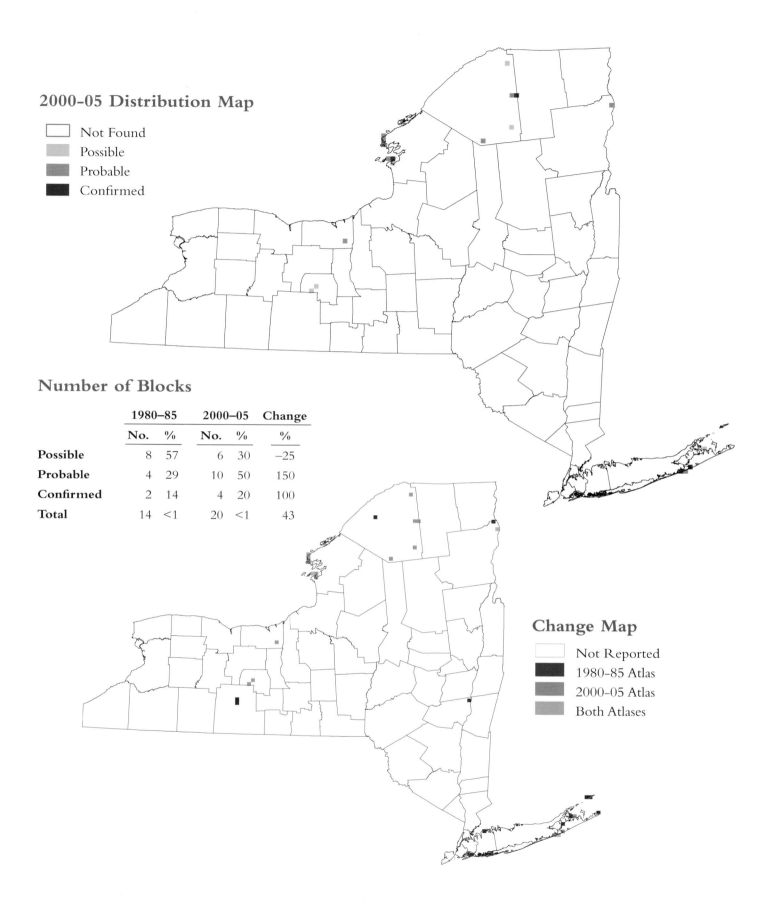

Ruddy Duck

Oxyura jamaicensis

KEVIN J. MCGOWAN

The stiff-tailed Ruddy Duck breeds across the American West from the Northwest Territories southward to Mexico, and in scattered localities in the Midwest and Northeast. It also breeds in the Caribbean and was introduced to Britain (Brua 2001). This duck breeds primarily in the Prairie Pothole Region of the Great Plains, where its nest is woven into dense emergent vegetation in marshes and around the edges of ponds (Brua 2001). New York lies far to the east of its main breeding range. The Ruddy Duck was considered a fairly common to rare migrant throughout the state in the 19th century (DeKay 1844, Giraud 1844, Rathbun 1879, Short 1893). The first report of breeding was of a pair with a brood of young seen in 1891 on Sandy Creek in western Monroe County (Beardslee and Mitchell 1965). Eaton (1910) apparently did not know of this report and mentioned only a brood seen in the Seneca River marshes, near what is now Montezuma National Wildlife Refuge "several years ago." He also reported a suspected case of breeding near Rochester. Beardslee and Mitchell (1965) mentioned another five locations in Ontario and western New York along the Niagara Frontier where breeding was known or suspected between 1947 and 1955. The Oak Orchard Swamp was the site of two breeding attempts in 1961 and 1977 (Bull 1974, Eaton 1988o). Breeding continued in the Montezuma area periodically through the 1960s and 1970s (Bull 1974, Eaton 1988o). Beginning in 1955 the Ruddy Duck nested at Jamaica Bay refuge in Queens County, with a maximum of 40 broods observed there in 1963 (Bull 1974).

During the first Atlas survey, the Ruddy Duck was seen in only seven blocks, and breeding was confirmed in three, at Montezuma NWR, Jamaica Bay refuge,

and Patchogue Bay on the south shore of Long Island. Individuals were seen in summer at Wilson Hill Wildlife Management Area and Tallman Mountain State Park. During the second Atlas survey, the Ruddy Duck was seen in more blocks across the state, but breeding was confirmed only at Montezuma NWR. A male was seen for several summers at the Iroquois NWR, and one or two pairs were present at Jamaica Bay into July 2004, but no additional evidence of breeding was obtained. The Jamaica Bay breeding population, the only "well-established" one in the state (Eaton 1988o), may have disappeared during the 1990s as the West Pond became more brackish (DiCostanzo 1998).

Although the estimates of Ruddy Duck numbers across North America are variable, breeding populations appear to be stable or increasing, especially in the Prairie Pothole Region where 87 percent of the breeding population is located (Brua 2001). Reports of Ruddy Duck in the second Ontario Breeding Bird Atlas were more than double those in the first Atlas, with many new nesting locations found across the southern portion of the province (Bird Studies Canada et al. 2006). No established populations were apparent near the New York border, however.

The Ruddy Duck does not appear to have any established breeding populations in New York, but isolated incidents of breeding can be expected from time to time virtually anywhere in the state where open water and emergent vegetation exist, especially at the wildlife refuges and management areas. If the increase in numbers in southern Ontario continues, New York may see more occurrences of Ruddy Duck breeding in the state in the future.

JPB © 2006

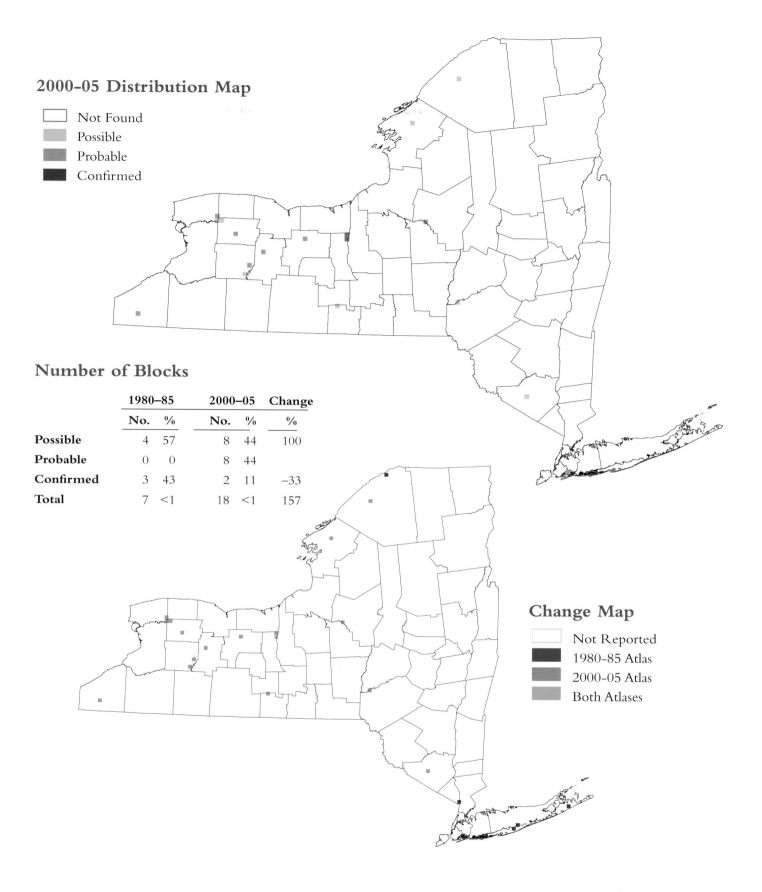

2000-05 Distribution Map

- ☐ Not Found
- Possible
- Probable
- Confirmed

Number of Blocks

| | 1980–85 | | 2000–05 | | Change |
	No.	%	No.	%	%
Possible	4	57	8	44	100
Probable	0	0	8	44	
Confirmed	3	43	2	11	−33
Total	7	<1	18	<1	157

Change Map

- ☐ Not Reported
- 1980-85 Atlas
- 2000-05 Atlas
- Both Atlases

Wild Turkey and Ruffed Grouse along a woodland edge

Thirty-five years ago it was rare to see a Wild Turkey in most of the state. Today, after a very successful reintroduction program by the New York State Department of Environmental Conservation, the Wild Turkey is a common sight from the roadside ditches of the Adirondacks to the backyards of Westchester County.

Gray Partridge

Perdix perdix

TIMOTHY J. POST

The Gray Partridge, or Hungarian Partridge, is a gallinaceous game bird native to central and western Eurasia that was introduced to agricultural areas in North America to provide hunting opportunities. Its primary range on this continent includes much of the northern Great Plains and the Great Basin in the northern United States and south-central Canada (Carroll 1993). Documented efforts to introduce the Gray Partridge to New York began in 1916–21 (Wilson 1959) and continued with an intensive trap-and-transfer program in 1927–32 (Bump 1941, Brown 1954). Efforts to establish populations continued in the late 1960s, 1970s, and early 1980s when birds were transferred within the state (DeGraff et al. 1983). The most successful introductions were in the eastern Lake Ontario Plain and St. Lawrence Valley, particularly Jefferson, St. Lawrence, and Clinton counties. In the 1940s, Gray Partridge populations in the northeastern Lake Ontario Plain and St. Lawrence Valley flourished, but by 1964 populations were steadily declining (DeGraff et al. 1983). Apparently critical for Gray Partridge is the presence of grain fields, in particular those that provide small grains. Habitat quality is greatly improved if such fields are adjacent to grasslands and hedgerows that provide cover (Carroll 1993). Population declines in the early 1960s were probably due to farmland abandonment and conversion to more intensive agricultural practices that greatly reduced the amount and quality of habitat for the Gray Partridge in New York. The effects of habitat loss can be further exacerbated by severe winters and ice storms, which limit access to food and increase vulnerability to predation.

During the first Atlas survey, the Gray Partridge was found scattered through the St. Lawrence Valley and into the upper Champlain Valley, with a small concentration in Jefferson County. The partridge was found in 81 percent fewer blocks during the second Atlas survey. It occurred in only three scattered blocks in Clinton and Franklin counties and four blocks grouped in western Jefferson County in the area of Cape Vincent and Point Peninsula. St. Lawrence County, which accounted for several records in the first Atlas, showed none for the second Atlas. Of particular interest is the decrease in the number of records in the former stronghold of Jefferson County (from 20 to 4). In fact, local ef-

forts suggest the status of Gray Partridge in Jefferson County may be even worse than shown by the Atlas data. G. Smith (pers. comm.) reported that informal efforts failed to find the species in Cape Vincent after 2003; several were found on Pillar Point in 2004, but no reports have been made since then. Reports from Chaumont, Jefferson County, however, indicate that the Gray Partridge was still breeding there in 2006 (J. Bolsinger pers. comm.). The very small size and isolated distribution of populations in New York probably resulted in poor detection during the second Atlas project.

Nationwide and range-wide trends, as measured by Breeding Bird Survey data, for the Gray Partridge indicate stable to slightly declining populations, but the data have some deficiencies and may not be reliable (Sauer et al. 2005). BBS data for New York and the northeastern region do not detect sufficient numbers to provide trend information. Data from the second Ontario Breeding Bird Atlas also indicate significant declines (Bird Studies Canada et al. 2006). Partners in Flight and the North American Bird Conservation Initiative show very low rankings for the Gray Partridge in the Northeast (Panjabi et al. 2005), reflecting its status in New York as an introduced species at the edge of its range with a stable population at the core of its range. The future of the Gray Partridge in New York is questionable. Remaining small and isolated populations may continue to disappear, and the species could be extirpated from New York in the foreseeable future. Changes in habitat and farm practices probably make restoration infeasible.

2000-05 Distribution Map

- ☐ Not Found
- Possible
- Probable
- Confirmed

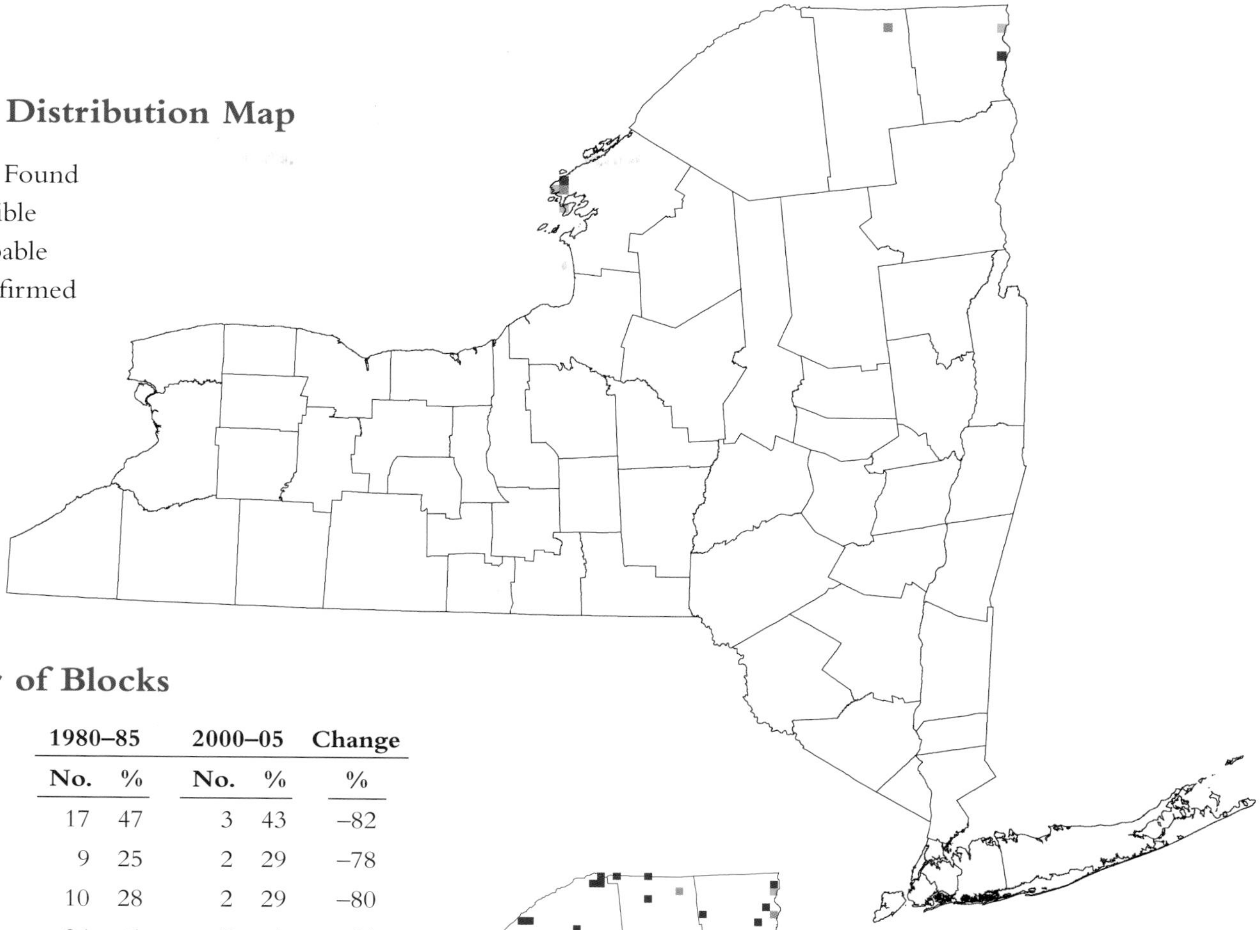

Number of Blocks

	1980–85		2000–05		Change
	No.	%	No.	%	%
Possible	17	47	3	43	−82
Probable	9	25	2	29	−78
Confirmed	10	28	2	29	−80
Total	36	<1	7	<1	−81

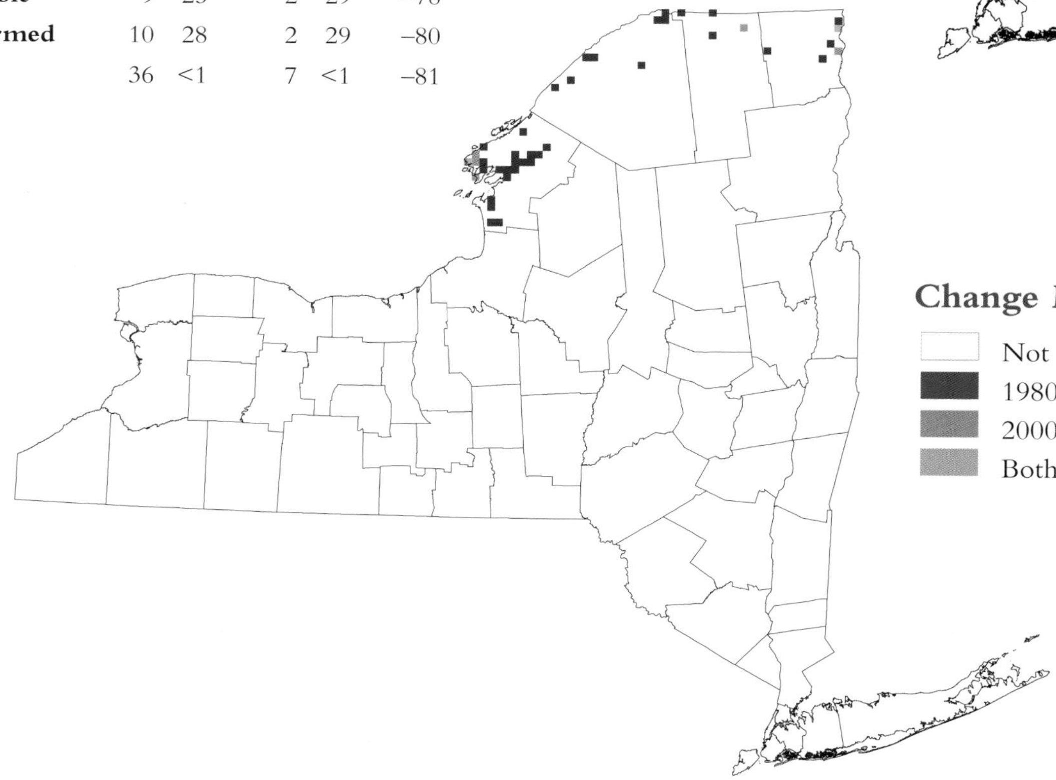

Change Map

- ☐ Not Reported
- 1980-85 Atlas
- 2000-05 Atlas
- Both Atlases

Ring-necked Pheasant

Phasianus colchicus

MIKE MURPHY

The Ring-necked Pheasant is one of the most popular game birds in North America. The male's beautiful plumage, territorial crowing, and distinctive cackle when flushed make it a favorite among hunters and rural landowners. The pheasant inhabits southern portions of Canada and much of the United States, with the exception of the Southeast. It occurs in greatest abundance in the Midwest states, while New York and the Northeast are at the periphery of its range (Johnsgard 1975). The Ring-necked Pheasant prefers fertile agricultural lands associated with grain farming. In New York this habitat predominantly occurs in the Great Lakes Plain. Preferred areas usually contain brush and cattails for winter cover, grain crops such as corn, wheat, and oats for food, and fallow grasslands for nesting and brood rearing. Penrod et al. (1986) found fallow grasslands to be the most important cover type in western New York. Native to Asia, the Ring-necked Pheasant was successfully introduced in New York on Gardiners Island in 1892 and on the Wadsworth estate in the Genesee Valley in 1903 (Brown and Robeson 1959). Eaton (1910) noted pheasants in the lower Hudson Valley, Long Island, Genesee Valley, lowlands south of Lake Ontario, and "about the Central Lakes." By the 1920s most suitable habitats in New York were occupied by pheasants (Brown and Robeson 1959). The population declined during the 1940s before slowly rising to an all-time high in the 1960s. In the early 1970s the population plummeted and remains at all-time lows (Murphy 2005).

During the first Atlas survey, the Ring-necked Pheasant was found throughout the Great Lakes Plain, the Finger Lakes Highlands, Taconic Highlands, Manhattan Hills, Hudson Valley, and Coastal Lowlands. Eaton (1988n) believed that populations outside the Great Lakes Plain were primarily released birds. In the second Atlas data, the total number of pheasant records significantly decreased, and the number of Confirmed records decreased 77 percent. Major declines were noted in the Great Lakes Plain, Hudson Valley, Taconic Highlands, Manhattan Hills, and Coastal Lowlands. The only notable increase was in the Eastern Ontario Plain, likely the result of released stock, mild winters, and corn production coupled with good grassland cover. It should be noted that the New York State Department of Environmental Conservation and its cooperators release approximately 75,000 pheasants annually for hunters (R. S. Rathman pers. comm.). Some Breeding Bird Survey and Atlas records may be the result of these releases, especially those outside of the Great Lakes Plain.

The decline in Atlas records echoes results found in the NYSDEC Farmer Pheasant Inventory, where the number of pheasant broods observed per observer index decreased 76 percent between 1985 and 2004 (Murphy 2005). Breeding Bird Survey data for the period 1980–2005 (Sauer et al. 2005) indicate declines of 4.3 percent per year in New York and 6.5 percent per year in Pennsylvania, continuing a downward trend that began in the 1970s. Continental populations also have been decreasing significantly over the last 25 years (Sauer et al. 2005). Pheasant abundance is linked to federal agricultural programs that retire large amounts of farmland in fallow grasses and legumes for multiple years (Berner 1988). In New York no such program has benefited pheasants since the Soil Bank program retired 333,000 acres of land in the Great Lakes Plain in 1968 (NYSDEC 1979). Burger (1988) attributed the pheasant population decline to the establishment of large farms with monotypic crops, and the loss of fence rows, odd-shaped field corners, hedgerows, woodlots, ditchbanks, and wetlands. Combine these changes with the loss of fallow grasslands, increased urbanization, and a reversion to a forested landscape, and a decline in population is fully understandable. Future land-use changes in New York will pose serious challenges to sustaining wild populations of this popular game bird.

2000–05 Distribution Map

- ☐ Not Found
- ▨ Possible
- ▨ Probable
- ■ Confirmed

Number of Blocks

	1980–85 No.	1980–85 %	2000–05 No.	2000–05 %	Change %
Possible	554	33	579	54	5
Probable	513	30	344	32	−33
Confirmed	632	37	146	14	−77
Total	1,699	32	1,069	20	−37

Change Map

- ☐ Not Reported
- ■ 1980–85 Atlas
- ▨ 2000–05 Atlas
- ▨ Both Atlases

Breeding Bird Survey Trend in New York

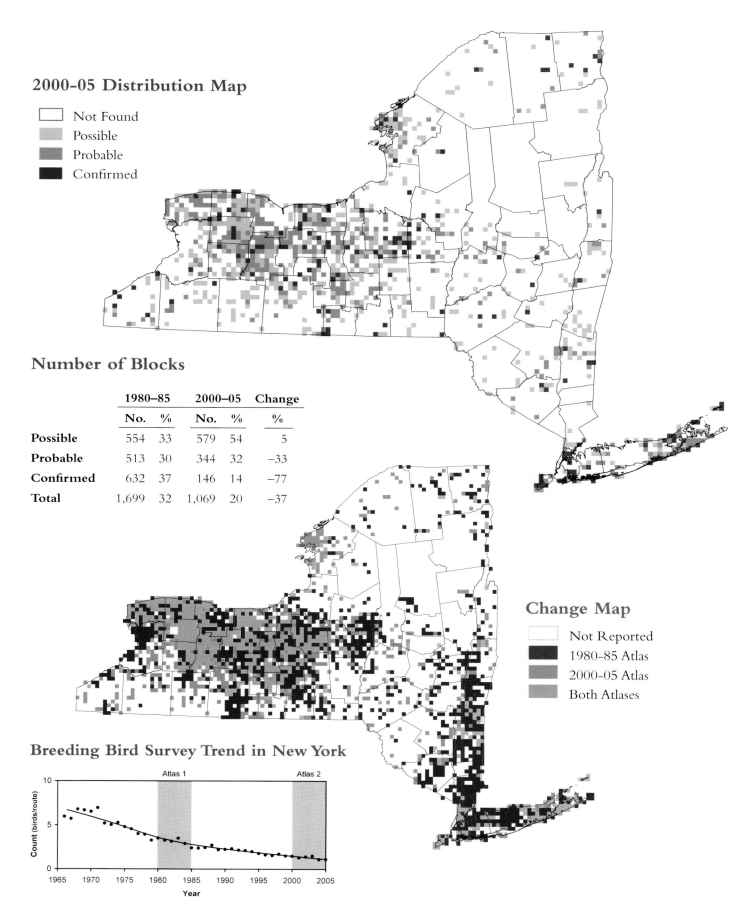

Ruffed Grouse

Bonasa umbellus

Timothy J. Post

The Ruffed Grouse, commonly known as "partridge," is a year-round resident in New York. Its range stretches across much of Canada, extending northward into Alaska with southward extensions into Washington, Oregon, and northern California, the Midwest, and the Northeast and mid-Atlantic states (Rusch et al. 2000). The Ruffed Grouse is a bird of forested landscapes and prefers a mix of habitats, with regenerating hardwood forest or shrub habitat important to its survival (Edminster 1947). The Ruffed Grouse occurred historically throughout much of New York, though populations have fluctuated as land cover changed (Bump et al. 1947). Natural disturbance events and Native American activities created early-successional habitat and increased populations (Dessecker et al. 2006), while forest maturation caused declines. The 1950s to 1970s may have represented the peak of populations as extensive farmland abandonment and active silviculture resulted in expanded areas of appropriate habitat (Askins 2001, R. Chambers pers. comm.).

The Ruffed Grouse was found throughout most of the forested areas of New York during the first Atlas project. Substantially fewer grouse were recorded during the second Atlas survey, and gaps are apparent. The species was found in only one Long Island block and virtually disappeared from most of the Hudson Valley and the surrounding highlands. Declines also occurred on the Appalachian Plateau and in portions of the Great Lakes Plain. Grouse are still found throughout much of the more heavily forested portions of the state, with concentrations of Confirmed blocks occurring in the western Adirondacks and the Tug Hill Plateau, although even in the Adirondacks the number of reports declined 6 percent. The only areas of increase were the Tug Hill and the Champlain transitions.

Although the Ruffed Grouse occurs only at low frequency on Breeding Bird Survey routes, and conclusions based on these data must be treated with caution, nationwide, regional, and New York trends show significant declines in 1966–2005 (Sauer et al.

2005). Partners in Flight and the North American Bird Conservation Initiative listed the grouse as a species of conservation concern in New York, and consider it a high priority for conservation in portions of the state (PIF [n.d.], NABCI 2007).

From the early 1970s until 2004, the amount of early-successional habitat decreased by 52 percent in New York's portion of the St. Lawrence Valley and upper Great Lakes Plain (Kelley 2006). Early-successional habitat and Ruffed Grouse populations declined as abandoned farms grew into mature forests, silvicultural activities dwindled, intensive agricultural practices removed shrub habitats, and development destroyed forest habitats (R. Chambers pers. comm.). Decreases in the lower Hudson Valley and Long Island are likely due to increases in development and to forest maturation. Early-successional habitats preferred by grouse require disturbance that opens the forest canopy and allows sunlight to reach the ground, promoting vigorous new growth. The reluctance of many to cut forests, along with the suppression of fires, has greatly reduced the amount of early-successional forest habitat being created (Whitney 1994, Lorimer 2001). Reluctance to cut trees can be based on the misconception that it is bad for birds and other wildlife. In fact, properly planned forest harvest can greatly increase the abundance and diversity of birds and many other wildlife species in a forest (Webb et al. 1977, Hartley et al. 2003, Keller et al. 2003) including many species that are in long-term decline. Ruffed Grouse populations can be readily restored through proper forest harvest and management, which involves clearing 2–4-ha (5–10-a) patches through the forest in rotation, creating a mosaic of diverse forest structures (Gullion 1984). The implementation of such practices could ensure the continued health of Ruffed Grouse populations in New York for years to come.

2000-05 Distribution Map

- ☐ Not Found
- Possible
- Probable
- Confirmed

Number of Blocks

	1980–85		2000–05		Change
	No.	%	No.	%	%
Possible	957	30	994	39	4
Probable	442	14	501	19	13
Confirmed	1,753	56	1,084	42	−38
Total	3,152	59	2,579	48	−18

Change Map

- ☐ Not Reported
- 1980-85 Atlas
- 2000-05 Atlas
- Both Atlases

Breeding Bird Survey Trend in New York

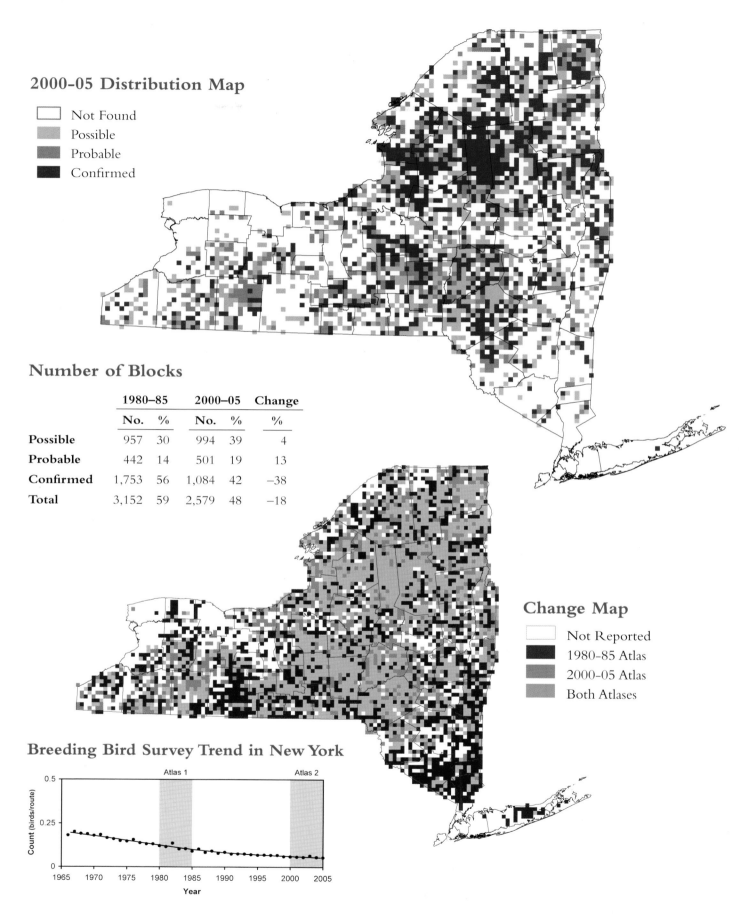

Spruce Grouse
Falcipennis canadensis

GLENN JOHNSON AND

ANGELENA ROSS

The Spruce Grouse is distributed in a transcontinental band across the northern third of North America that generally conforms to the boreal forest biome (Boag and Schroeder 1992). Over much of this range it is common; in New York, however, the species is limited to small, isolated populations in the northwest quadrant of the Adirondack Park, making it one of the rarest resident birds in the state. In peripheral parts of its range, such as New York and Vermont, the Spruce Grouse is restricted to lowland coniferous forests dominated by spruce, tamarack, and balsam fir (Bouta and Chambers 1990, Pence et al. 1990). Areas of young trees with a shrubby understory interspersed with closed-canopy older stands with an open understory are preferred, while mature stands (> 70 years old) are avoided (Bouta 1991). The Spruce Grouse population has undergone a dramatic decline in New York since the earliest published accounts of Adirondack bird life. DeKay (1844) described the species as common in Hamilton County. Burroughs (1895), Roosevelt and Minot (1877), and Merriam (1881) also described it as a relatively common bird in some Adirondack regions. By the early 1900s, however, declines were already being noted (Eaton 1910, Silloway 1923, Saunders 1929). Bull (1974) listed the Spruce Grouse as rare to uncommon, with no records of nests or eggs reported from New York. By 1976, populations at many sites were extirpated and the species had become quite rare (Fritz 1977). Bouta and Chambers (1990) suggested that this historical population decline resulted from the loss and fragmentation of habitat resulting from widespread softwood logging and increasing development that began in earnest around 1880 (McMartin 1994). Dams installed to create large reservoirs, such as those at Lows Lake and Stillwater Reservoir, caused the flooding and fragmentation of large tracts of lowland coniferous habitat (Jenkins 2004). In addition, spruce budworm outbreaks that occurred from 1870 to 1885 killed one-third to one-half of Adirondack spruces (Fox 1895).

The first Atlas reported the Spruce Grouse in 27 blocks, with Confirmed breeding in 12. Most records occurred in a core region in the Western Adirondack Foothills; there were also several Confirmed records in the Central Adirondacks and Adirondack High Peaks. Spruce Grouse was recorded in 20 blocks during the second Atlas project, with Confirmed breeding in only 6 blocks, a reduction of nearly 50 percent in breeding records since 1986. All Confirmed records for the second Atlas were confined to the core region in the Western Adirondack Foothills. Intensive surveys conducted between 2000 and 2006 suggest that viable populations may remain only within this core region (Johnson and Ross 2003 and unpubl. data), although anecdotal reports suggest that populations may persist in the Central Adirondacks of Hamilton County.

Within the majority of its range, Spruce Grouse populations are considered secure, but along the southern boundary, loss or fragmentation of coniferous forests has resulted in local extirpations (Boag and Schroeder 1992). Vermont populations are apparently in decline (Oatman 1985) and are possibly limited to only one location (C. E. Alexander pers. comm.).

Bouta (1991) estimated the New York population to be 175–315 individuals in the late 1980s. Surveys by Johnson and Ross (2003) indicated that populations at several of Bouta's study sites have become extirpated, suggesting a continued Adirondack population decline. This more recent decrease may be a reflection of the combined effects of reduced dispersal between populations in isolated habitats and the maturation of coniferous forests to older-aged stands. Because of the evident decline, Spruce Grouse was listed as Endangered in New York in December 1999 (NYSDEC 1999). Management at population, habitat, and landscape levels may be required for this species to persist and be recorded in future Atlas efforts.

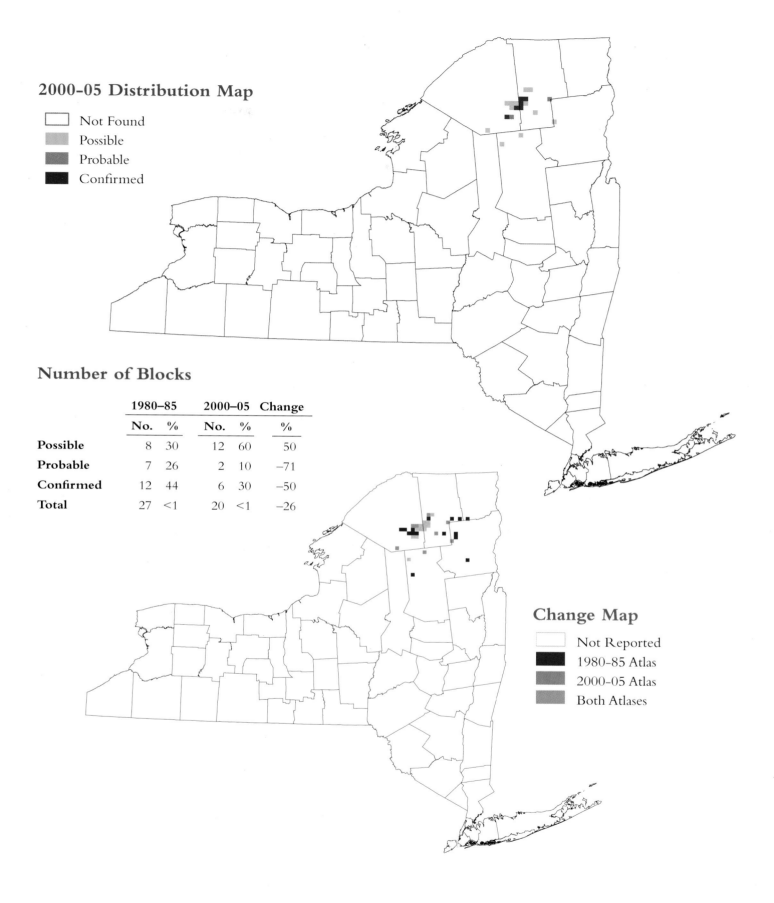

2000-05 Distribution Map

- ☐ Not Found
- Possible
- Probable
- Confirmed

Number of Blocks

	1980–85		2000–05		Change
	No.	**%**	**No.**	**%**	**%**
Possible	8	30	12	60	50
Probable	7	26	2	10	−71
Confirmed	12	44	6	30	−50
Total	27	<1	20	<1	−26

Change Map

- ☐ Not Reported
- 1980-85 Atlas
- 2000-05 Atlas
- Both Atlases

Wild Turkey

Meleagris gallopavo

KEVIN J. MCGOWAN

A large bird of open, mature forest, the Wild Turkey is found across much of the United States from very southern Canada southward to Florida and Mexico. In pre-colonial times the turkey was found in large numbers throughout most of New York south of the Adirondacks. As the result of hunting, domestic poultry diseases, and especially habitat destruction, Wild Turkey numbers declined catastrophically after European settlement (Eaton 1992). By the early 1800s it was restricted to only a handful of southern counties in New York (DeKay 1844), and by the start of the 20th century it was gone from the state entirely, as well as from New England (Eaton 1910). Attempts to reintroduce the turkey to the state in the 1930s failed (Bump 1941). A small population that had remained in central Pennsylvania expanded into the Allegany Hills of New York during the 1940s (Eaton 1988q). A New York population was well established by the 1950s. A Conservation Department attempt to boost turkey numbers by releasing farm-reared birds into the wild had little effect and was discontinued in 1959 (NYSDEC unpubl. report). At that time free-ranging turkeys were trapped in Allegany State Park and introduced into other areas of the state (NYSDEC unpubl. data). These translocations helped establish the Wild Turkey across the southern half of the state. Nearly 1,700 turkeys were transferred to 42 New York counties and other states, with the last in-state transfer being to Long Island in 1992 and 1993 (NYSDEC unpubl. data). New York turkeys released in Vermont were so successful there that the population expanded back into New York, in Washington County, by the 1970s (DeGraff 1973).

During the first Atlas survey, the Wild Turkey was reported breeding throughout the state. Concentrations were highest across the Appalachian Plateau and the Taconic Highlands, but some turkeys were found all the way to the northern boundaries, into the Adirondacks, and on Long Island. During the second Atlas survey, the Wild Turkey was found in more than twice as many blocks as during the first Atlas. It was clearly established in all regions of the state, even in those areas considered to have "no potential" for future establishment by DeGraff (1973), such as the Central Adirondacks and the heavily populated areas of the Great Lakes Plain and downstate. The turkey was found in nearly all blocks in Rockland and Westchester counties, and even on Staten Island. New York, Kings, and Queens counties were the only ones in the state that did not report turkeys.

The Wild Turkey has gone from having its populations at critically low levels at the beginning of the 20th century to becoming one of the most numerous game animals in North America 100 years later. Management programs across the United States have succeeded in re-establishing this species throughout its range and introducing it into areas where it never occurred (Eaton 1992). Breeding Bird Survey data show tremendous increases survey-wide since the 1980s, with no sign of a downturn (Sauer et al. 2005). BBS data from New York show a more gradual increase, with a possible leveling off in the late 1990s (Sauer et al. 2005).

Optimal turkey habitats are landscapes with a mix of mature hardwoods and agriculture (Roberts et al. 1995, Fleming and Porter 2003). Eaton (1988q) stated that the Central Adirondacks and Tug Hill Plateau probably would never have sustainable turkey populations because of the lack of mast and the presence of deep winter snow. The presence of turkey in 45 percent of blocks in the Adirondacks, 77 percent of blocks in the Great Lakes Plain, and its extension into the Manhattan Hills and Coastal Lowlands show that it is more adaptable than previously thought, and that it can flourish in a number of areas of "suboptimal" habitat. Much of the turkey's capability to successfully colonize new habitats is related to its ability to use human-created habitats such as agricultural fields, parkland, and backyards.

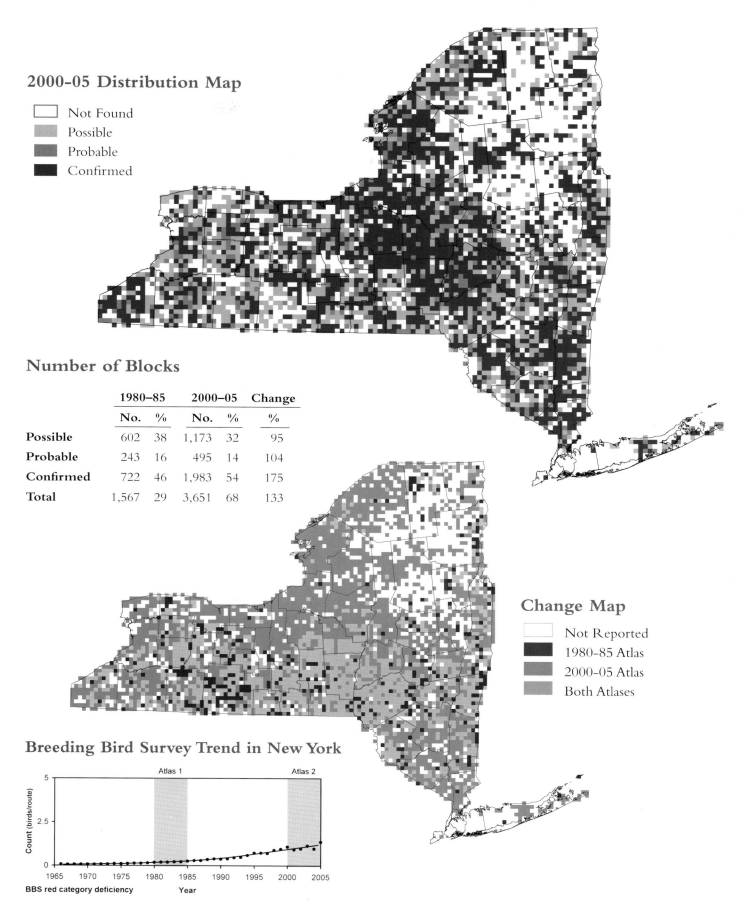

2000-05 Distribution Map

- ☐ Not Found
- Possible
- Probable
- Confirmed

Number of Blocks

	1980–85		2000–05		Change
	No.	%	No.	%	%
Possible	602	38	1,173	32	95
Probable	243	16	495	14	104
Confirmed	722	46	1,983	54	175
Total	1,567	29	3,651	68	133

Change Map

- ☐ Not Reported
- 1980–85 Atlas
- 2000–05 Atlas
- Both Atlases

Breeding Bird Survey Trend in New York

BBS red category deficiency

Northern Bobwhite

Colinus virginianus

KEVIN J. McGOWAN

The Northern Bobwhite is a bird of open, early-successional habitats and farmland. Found across the eastern United States into Mexico, its range barely reaches New York. The bobwhite was probably restricted to the coastal grasslands before European settlement but became common throughout the state by the early 1800s, present as far northward as Jefferson, Oneida, Saratoga, and Washington counties (DeKay 1844, Eaton 1910). It was likely always absent from the Adirondacks and the Catskills (Bull 1974). By the end of the 19th century the Northern Bobwhite was rare everywhere in the state except Long Island, the Delaware Valley, and the lower Hudson Valley (Eaton 1910). Birds were released into western New York by the Conservation Department in the 1930s and 1950s (Beardslee and Mitchell 1965), but those restoration attempts were mostly unsuccessful. Bull (1974) considered it an uncommon to rare resident of lower elevations and listed reasons for its decline: the decrease in agriculture, development of open country, excessive hunting, severe winters, and introduction of southern and western birds that "reduced the vitality" of the original stock. The influence of introductions, if any, is unclear, although the idea of vitality reduction is often repeated. Though 750 bobwhite released early on Long Island were from Mexico, birds subsequently released were from Long Island, Virginia, Ohio, and Wisconsin (Bump 1941, Beardslee and Mitchell 1965).

The first Atlas showed the Northern Bobwhite to be common only on Long Island. Scattered reports occurred up the lower Hudson Valley, across the central Appalachian Plateau, and onto the Great Lakes Plain. Levine (1988c) explained upstate reports as the result of releases of captive quail for hunting or dog training and considered only the Long Island populations as established. The second Atlas work revealed a similar distribution, with most records occurring on eastern Long Island and a number of reports evenly distributed across the lower two-thirds of the state. The scattered nature of the upstate reports, with few clusters of contiguous blocks, suggests that releases of captive-raised quail still account for most bobwhite found outside of eastern Long Island. On Long Island it was observed in 35 percent fewer blocks, and confirmations there went from 105 during the first Atlas period to 17 in the second. The species was nearly gone from Nassau County, and only one report was made from Kings County.

The Northern Bobwhite population is declining in most areas across its range (Brennan 1999) and may be extirpated in some states within a decade (Dimmick et al. 2002). Breeding Bird Survey data show a steady, steep decrease nationwide for the duration of the survey (Sauer et al. 2005). BBS data for New York show a precipitous decline in the late 1960s and 1970s, approaching zero near 2000 (Sauer et al. 2005). Christmas Bird Count data and records from state game agencies corroborate the nationwide decline (Brennan 1999). CBC data from New York show a nearly complete loss of bobwhite in the state, with only 44 individuals seen on four Long Island counts during the 2005–06 season (McGowan 2006).

The major limiting factor over much of this bird's range might be a lack of nesting and brood-rearing cover, resulting from the long-term practice of replacing native warm-season grasses with exotic grasses, and of completely eliminating nesting habitat in intensive cropland and dense pine forests (Dimmick et al. 2002). Such factors probably are not responsible for the loss of bobwhite on Long Island but could account for the lack of recovery across the rest of the state. Loss of woodland, old field, and hedgerows on Long Island may have been an important factor causing the declines there (Salzman and Parkes 1998). It is unlikely that the Northern Bobwhite will recover in New York to any significant levels, and the Northern Bobwhite Conservation Initiative (Dimmick et al. 2002) did not even list the state in its recovery plans.

2000–05 Distribution Map

- ☐ Not Found
- ▨ Possible
- ▨ Probable
- ■ Confirmed

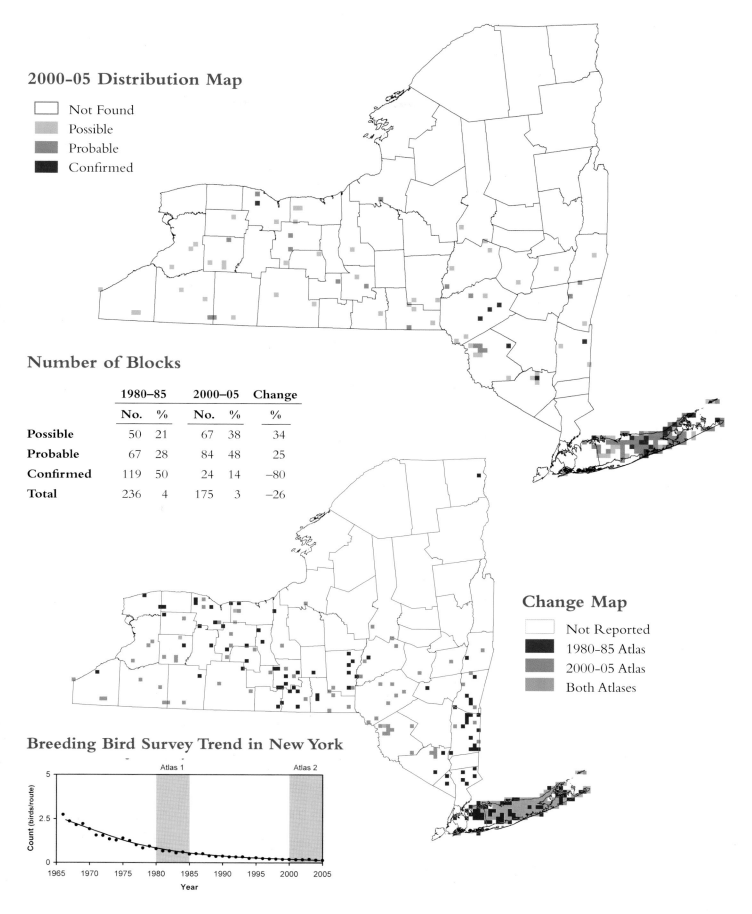

Number of Blocks

	1980–85		2000–05		Change
	No.	%	No.	%	%
Possible	50	21	67	38	34
Probable	67	28	84	48	25
Confirmed	119	50	24	14	−80
Total	236	4	175	3	−26

Change Map

- ☐ Not Reported
- ■ 1980-85 Atlas
- ▨ 2000-05 Atlas
- ▨ Both Atlases

Breeding Bird Survey Trend in New York

Common Loon and Pied-billed Grebe on an Adirondack lake

Although the Common Loon and Pied-billed Grebe are treasured residents of the Adirondack lakes, they were once considered pests. Frederic Remington is said to have delighted in the challenge of shooting "hell–divers" from the porch of his lakeside camp, though he rarely, if ever, hit one.

Common Loon

Gavia immer

NINA SCHOCH

The charismatic Common Loon breeds in freshwater habitats throughout northern North America, from Washington to Maine and in Canada and Alaska to the taiga shield (Evers 2007). It nests on bog mats, logs, large rocks, and the shoreline of islands. New York is at the southern extent of the breeding range. Prior to the 1970s the status of New York's loon population was poorly known. Roosevelt and Minot (1877) found loons to be rare in the St. Regis area of Franklin County in 1874–75, where Roosevelt had observed them commonly in 1870. Eaton (1910) reported a few loons in the Adirondacks in Franklin, Hamilton, Herkimer, and St. Lawrence counties but none in Essex County. He noted that Audubon had observed loons breeding on Cayuga Lake in 1824. Arbib (1963) reported loons breeding regularly at more than 90 locations on the St. Lawrence River and in the Adirondacks, with occasional reports of breeding in the Finger Lakes. He estimated New York's breeding loon population at approximately 240 pairs (Arbib 1963). In 1977–78, the New York State Department of Environmental Conservation surveyed 301 Adirondack lakes and found 105 territorial pairs on 83 lakes, estimating the total Adirondack population at fewer than 200 pairs (Trivelpiece et al. 1979). Comparing Arbib's 1963 data with their own from the same 51 lakes, Trivelpiece et al. (1979) estimated a 47 percent decrease in the number of pairs. Parker et al. (1986) reported that a NYSDEC survey of 557 Adirondack lakes in the 1980s

found 157 breeding loon pairs on 128 lakes; they estimated the northern New York loon population at 804–1,036 adults, including 216–270 breeding pairs. Based on the increase between the 1970s and 1980s surveys, Parker and Miller (1988) concluded that the Adirondack loon population was stable and probably expanding.

In the first Atlas, the Common Loon was reported primarily in the Central Adirondacks, Western Adirondack Foothills, and Adirondack High Peaks. A small number of reports came from the Eastern Ontario Plain, St. Lawrence Plain, and Indian River Lakes, with several Possible and Probable records from Lake Champlain, and scattered Possible records from Central Tug Hill, Oneida Lake, and Cayuga Lake. The second Atlas results showed a significant increase and a range expansion. The population spread in all directions, with an increase in the number of Probable and Confirmed reports in Lake Champlain, the St. Lawrence River area, and the eastern and southern Adirondacks, extending into the Eastern Adirondack Foothills. Especially noteworthy are the Confirmed records in central and western New York, on Chautauqua, Keuka, and Skaneateles lakes.

The Northeastern loon population appears to have increased in the last half-century (Rimmer 1992). The second Ontario Breeding Bird Atlas reported a slight but not significant increase, with new breeding locations found along the St. Lawrence River (Bird Studies Canada et al. 2006). Breeding populations have also increased in Vermont (Hanson et al. 2006) and Massachusetts (R. Miconi pers. comm.). In New Hampshire and Maine, however, loon populations may have reached a plateau (Loon Preservation Committee 2005, Northeast Loon Study Workgroup unpubl. data). Pennsylvania's Atlases have recorded the Common Loon in a small number of blocks, but breeding has not yet been confirmed (Brauning 1992, R. Mulvihill pers. comm.).

The banning of DDT, improved population management efforts in some states, adaptability of the birds to human activity, and more habitat availability from the creation of reservoirs may explain the recent increase in the breeding loon population in New York and throughout northeastern North America. Still, the Common Loon is a Species of Special Concern in New York, and continued monitoring of New York's loon population is recommended to document changes and to examine the effects of environmental pollutants on aquatic ecosystems.

2000–05 Distribution Map

- ☐ Not Found
- ▨ Possible
- ▨ Probable
- ■ Confirmed

Number of Blocks

	1980–85		2000–05		Change
	No.	%	No.	%	%
Possible	143	39	131	25	–8
Probable	74	20	145	27	96
Confirmed	152	41	252	48	66
Total	369	7	528	10	43

Change Map

- ☐ Not Reported
- ■ 1980-85 Atlas
- ▨ 2000-05 Atlas
- ▨ Both Atlases

Breeding Bird Survey Trend in New York

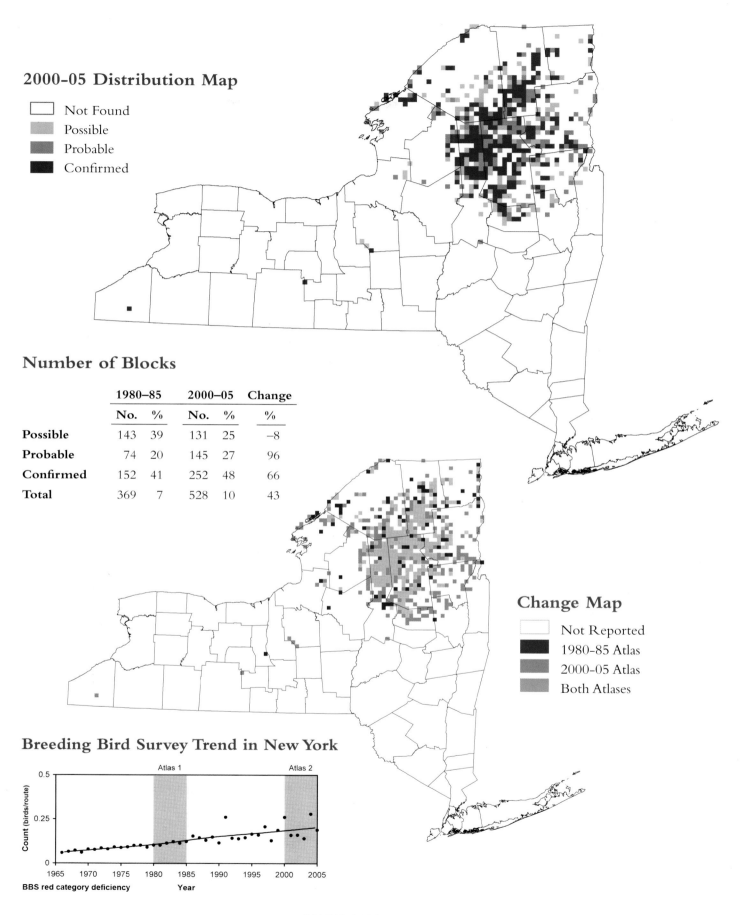

BBS red category deficiency

COMMON LOON 149

Pied-billed Grebe

Podilymbus podiceps

KEVIN J. McGOWAN

A small diving bird, the Pied-billed Grebe breeds from central and southern Canada southward across the United States into Central America, the Caribbean, and South America (Muller and Storer 1999). It breeds on seasonal or permanent ponds and other slow-moving or still-water bodies, where it puts its floating nest in dense stands of emergent vegetation. It was likely a locally common breeder in New York during pre-colonial times, and its population probably declined with the subsequent removal of beaver and the draining of wetlands. DeKay (1844) listed it as common in the ponds and lakes of the state, although he also ascribed it to breeding in high northern latitudes. Eaton (1910) said it was to be found throughout New York, wherever appropriate habitat still existed. He noted that the drainage of ponds and streams had led to the retreat of the species; undoubtedly the widespread loss of small wetlands and marshes throughout the United States in the 19th and 20th centuries led to loss of suitable breeding habitat and declines in populations. Bull (1974) called it a common breeder throughout the state and noted that its absence as a breeder from the Catskills and parts of the Adirondacks could be because the deep lakes there lacked shallow areas with emergent vegetation. Connor (1988e) commented on a decline in the late 1970s and early 1980s, perhaps part of a larger trend across the eastern United States (Muller and Storer 1999), although few data exist to support these claims.

During the first Atlas survey, the Pied-billed Grebe was found breeding across the state, scattered widely, but with 30 percent in the Great Lakes Plain. The species was missing entirely from the Catskill Peaks, Allegany Hills, Adirondack High Peaks, and Sable Highlands and was only sparsely recorded in most upland areas. During the second Atlas survey, the grebe was found in 47 percent more blocks, again scattered across the state and with 31 percent in the Great Lakes Plain. Blocks with reports were slightly more numerous in most regions and ecozones, with the largest increases occurring in the Adirondacks, St. Lawrence Plains, and Great Lakes Plain. Particularly noticeable was the development of a cluster of blocks in Jefferson and St. Lawrence counties. Only the Coastal Lowlands and parts of the lower Hudson Valley showed declines in reporting blocks, and those were modest. The species was still missing from the highland areas across the state, and wildlife refuges and wildlife management areas accounted for perhaps even a larger percentage of breeding records than what was reported in the first Atlas.

As a water bird, the Pied-billed Grebe is not well monitored by the Breeding Bird Survey, but BBS data show no trends in the continental population. Monitoring data from the Great Lakes Basin show a decline in summer numbers of 11 percent per year from 1995 to 2003 (Crewe et al. 2005). Data from the second Ontario Breeding Bird Atlas show a significant increase in Pied-billed Grebe numbers in the province, with new breeding locations found across southern Ontario (Bird Studies Canada et al. 2006). Especially notable is an increase in reports along the northeastern portion of Lake Ontario and northward along the St. Lawrence River. This dense cluster of records is mirrored by increased reports in Jefferson and St. Lawrence counties, across the border in New York.

The Pied-billed Grebe is listed as Threatened in New York. This bird of marshy areas can be expected to remain only locally common in the state, with its continued existence tied to the protection of wetlands. The preservation of habitat in preserves and refuges undoubtedly benefits the Pied-billed Grebe. Many bird species that depend on these areas are difficult to monitor, but because the grebe is vocal during the day throughout its breeding season and spends some time foraging in open water, it is easier to detect than most. Still, targeted monitoring efforts are needed to obtain dependable measures of Pied-billed Grebe population trends.

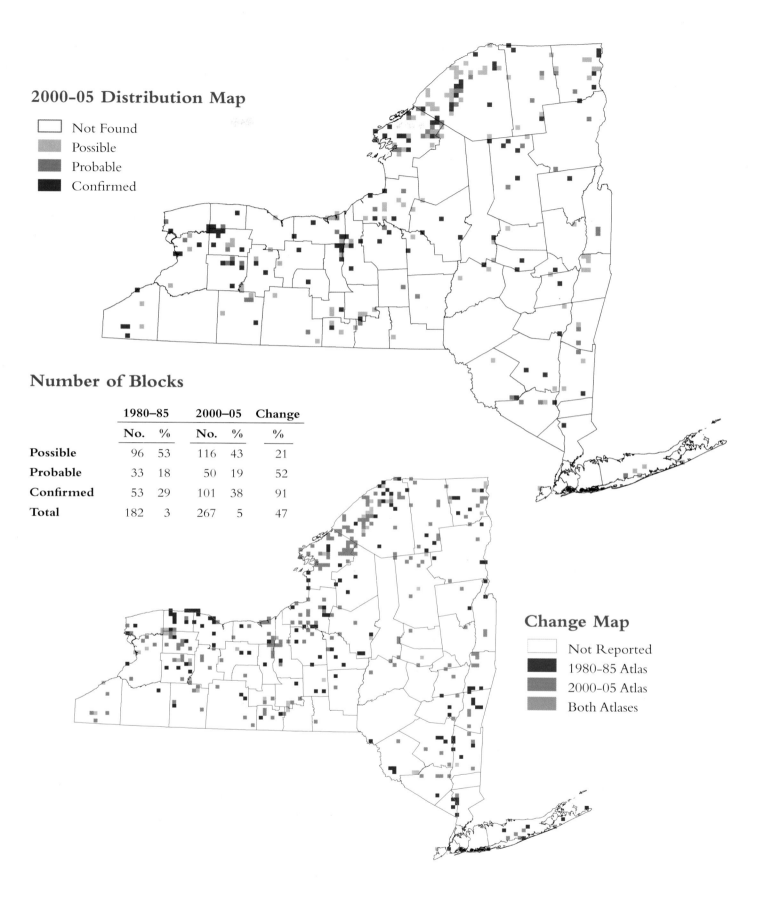

2000-05 Distribution Map

- ☐ Not Found
- Possible
- Probable
- Confirmed

Number of Blocks

	1980–85		2000–05		Change
	No.	%	No.	%	%
Possible	96	53	116	43	21
Probable	33	18	50	19	52
Confirmed	53	29	101	38	91
Total	182	3	267	5	47

Change Map

- ☐ Not Reported
- 1980-85 Atlas
- 2000-05 Atlas
- Both Atlases

Double-crested Cormorant

Phalacrocorax auritus

JEREMY T. H. COLEMAN

The Double-crested Cormorant has been exceedingly prolific since 1972, after DDT was banned and the species gained federal protection under the Migratory Bird Treaty Act. It has gone from being a rarity to being a common sight along lakes and waterways throughout much of North America. Nesting in trees or on the ground, the cormorant generally establishes colonies on small islands or in wetland areas that offer protection from mammalian predation. This is the most populous of the six cormorant species native to North America, breeding from Alaska and Newfoundland in the north to the Baja and Yucatan peninsulas in the south. The subspecies *P. auritus auritus* has the largest distribution of five described subspecies and accounts for the two largest populations, the Atlantic and the Interior (Hatch and Weseloh 1999), both of which breed in New York.

Accounts of the historical breeding range of the Double-crested Cormorant correspond with current distributions, suggesting that recent population increases may be recolonization events and not range expansion (see review in Wires and Cuthbert 2006). This assertion cannot be verified for Great Lakes and inland sites in New York, as breeding records are lacking prior to 1945 (Kutz and Allen 1947). Eaton (1910) documented the presence of the cormorant in central and western New York; however, he characterized it as an uncommon migrant at inland sites based on autumnal reports dating back to 1865. In contrast, the cormorant has been more prevalent along the coast historically (Giraud 1844), and Eaton (1910) described it as a common visitant to Long Island.

During the first Atlas period, the Double-crested Cormorant established breeding colonies at Oneida Lake (Claypoole 1988) and at Four Brothers Islands in Lake Champlain (Peterson 1984b). The already existing colony at Little Galloo Island in eastern Lake Ontario was on its way to becoming the largest in the United States, reaching 8,410 nesting pairs in 1996. On Long Island, cormorants first nested on Fishers Island in 1977 (Bull 1981), then spread to nearby Gardiners Island and to South Brother Island in the Bronx. The second Atlas data revealed considerable geographic expansion throughout New York, most notably along the Niagara Frontier, St. Lawrence River, central New York, Hudson Valley, central Long Island, and New York Harbor. The number of blocks with Confirmed breeding increased over sevenfold, mirroring the population growth statewide, from approximately 2,100 pairs in 1985 (Miller 1998) to approximately 10,500 pairs in 2003 (NYSDEC 2004). This rapid population growth has made the cormorant a conspicuous visitor to waterways throughout New York, as evidenced by the many new Possible breeding blocks, particularly in the Hudson Valley and adjoining counties.

The growing continental cormorant population has been a cause of concern and controversy for aquaculturists, anglers, and resource managers in both the breeding and the wintering ranges of the species (Wires et al. 2001, Herbert et al. 2005). In response to these concerns, a public resource depredation order was finalized in 2003 as part of a new national management plan (USDI/FWS 2003). Under this order, New York is one of 24 states in which cormorants can be managed to control impacts to public resources. While there currently are no plans to manage coastal cormorant colonies, control programs are in place at or near all the major upstate breeding sites (NYSDEC 2004). These efforts have succeeded in reducing locally the reproductive success and size of select breeding populations, but might also be instrumental in displacing birds to new sites. Additional factors that might also affect future cormorant population growth are declining numbers of alewife in the Great Lakes and increasing numbers of the invasive round goby, which is a vector for type E botulism infection in cormorants and other fish-eating birds.

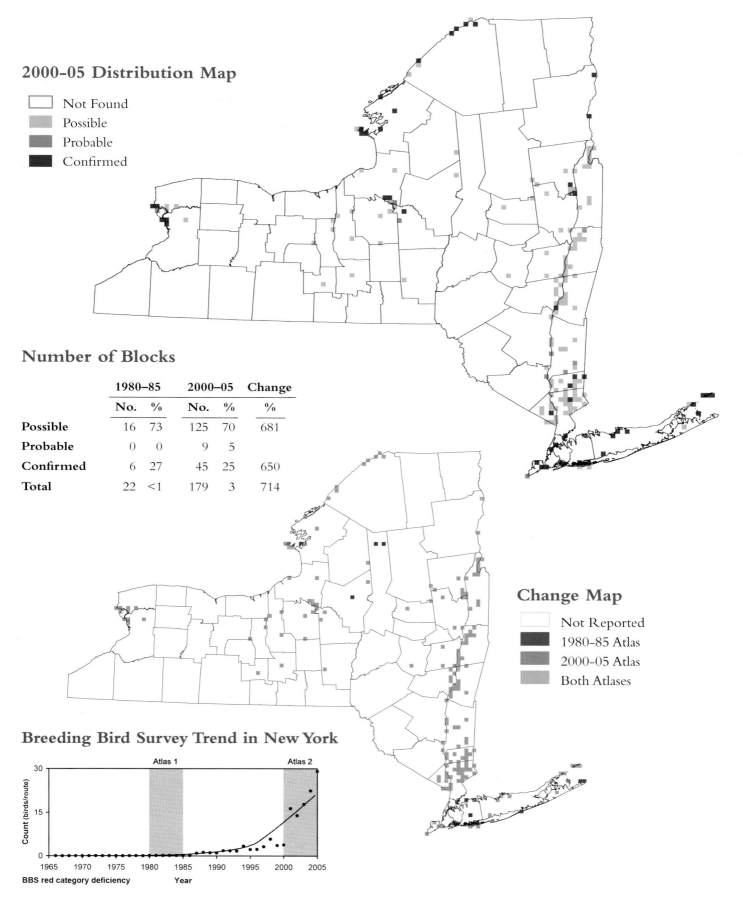

2000–05 Distribution Map

- ☐ Not Found
- Possible
- Probable
- Confirmed

Number of Blocks

| | 1980–85 | | 2000–05 | | Change |
	No.	%	No.	%	%
Possible	16	73	125	70	681
Probable	0	0	9	5	
Confirmed	6	27	45	25	650
Total	22	<1	179	3	714

Change Map

- ☐ Not Reported
- 1980-85 Atlas
- 2000-05 Atlas
- Both Atlases

Breeding Bird Survey Trend in New York

Atlas 1

Atlas 2

Count (birds/route)

30

15

0

1965 1970 1975 1980 1985 1990 1995 2000 2005

BBS red category deficiency   Year

Great Blue Heron along the St. Lawrence River

A Great Blue Heron flies through the early-morning mist of the St. Lawrence River, searching out a shallow pool at river's edge where it might find breakfast. Wading birds can be found throughout the state wherever there is shallow water harboring suitable prey.

154

American Bittern
Botaurus lentiginosus

Kevin J. McGowan

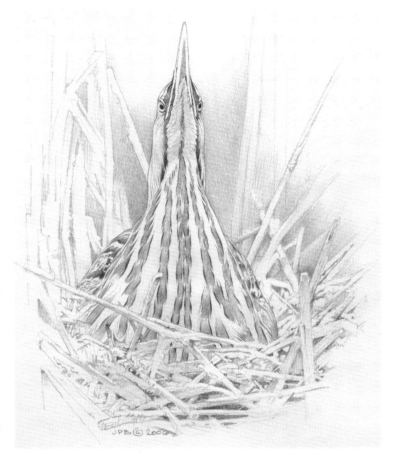

A secretive heron of dense reed beds, the American Bittern breeds across most of Canada and the northern United States, from the Northwest Territories and Newfoundland southward to California, New Mexico, Kentucky, and Virginia (Gibbs et al. 1992a). It breeds in freshwater wetlands with tall emergent vegetation, especially larger wetlands with abundant amphibian populations, and rarely in tidal marshes (Gibbs et al. 1992a). It was probably common in wetlands across New York in pre-colonial times, but the decline of the beaver and the draining of wetlands after European settlement undoubtedly led to population decreases. DeKay (1844) listed it as a breeder in the state, and Giraud (1844) indicated that it was rather uncommon on Long Island, but the exact status of such a secretive species is hard to gauge from their accounts. Later authors considered it common, breeding in any suitable marsh (Rathbun 1879, Short 1893, Reed and Wright 1909). Eaton (1910) also called it fairly common throughout the state, breeding on eastern Long Island, in all of the marshes of the interior, and throughout the Adirondacks. Bull (1974) noted no change in distribution or abundance since Eaton's comments. Beardslee and Mitchell (1965), however, noted a marked decline in bittern numbers in western New York in the 1950s and 1960s. Temple and Temple (1976) noted a similar decline in the central part of the state and suggested that the cause was the loss of appropriate wetland habitat, an explanation that is still offered as the main reason for decline (Gibbs et al. 1992a).

During the first Atlas survey, the American Bittern was found in marshes throughout the state. It was most numerous in the central Adirondacks, along the Lake Ontario Plain, and in the St. Lawrence Plains and Transition. It was least numerous on the Appalachian Plateau, especially the eastern portions, where suitable wetlands are scarce. During the second Atlas survey, the American Bittern was found in 10 percent fewer blocks throughout the state, with declines noted in most regions. Modest increases were found only in the Champlain Valley, the Tug Hill Plateau, the Mohawk Valley, and the Taconic Highlands. The current center of abundance appears to be in Jefferson and St. Lawrence counties and in the scattered wetlands of the Adirondacks. Atlas methods may not adequately detect such a secretive bird as the American Bittern, and more targeted monitoring may be necessary. Bitterns are relatively rarely seen, and although the pumping calls are distinctive and carry far, they are given predominantly early in the breeding season, and many nesting bitterns undoubtedly go undetected.

Breeding Bird Survey techniques do not cover this marsh-nesting bird well either, and the existing data must be viewed with caution. Routes reporting bitterns in New York are few, but the data from those show a nonsignificant population decline in the last 25 years (Sauer et al. 2007). Across all of North America, a 1.5 percent decline per year since 1966 approaches significance (Sauer et al. 2007). A targeted marshbird monitoring program extending through the Great Lakes Basin showed an 8.8 percent yearly decline from 1995 through 2003 (Crewe et al. 2005). The second Ontario Breeding Bird Atlas reported a slight decline in American Bittern populations in the province, with a significant decline in the southern-most region (Bird Studies Canada et al. 2006). The American Bittern is a Species of Special Concern in New York and is considered Endangered in a number of other Northeastern states. Obligate marsh-nesting birds such as the American Bittern are sensitive not only to loss of wetlands but also to their degradation. The invasion of non-native plants, such as purple loosestrife and common reed, could have significant effects. The preservation of wetlands in refuges and management areas will be an important part of preserving the American Bittern in New York, but more information is needed about the causes of the apparent population decline if the species is to remain common.

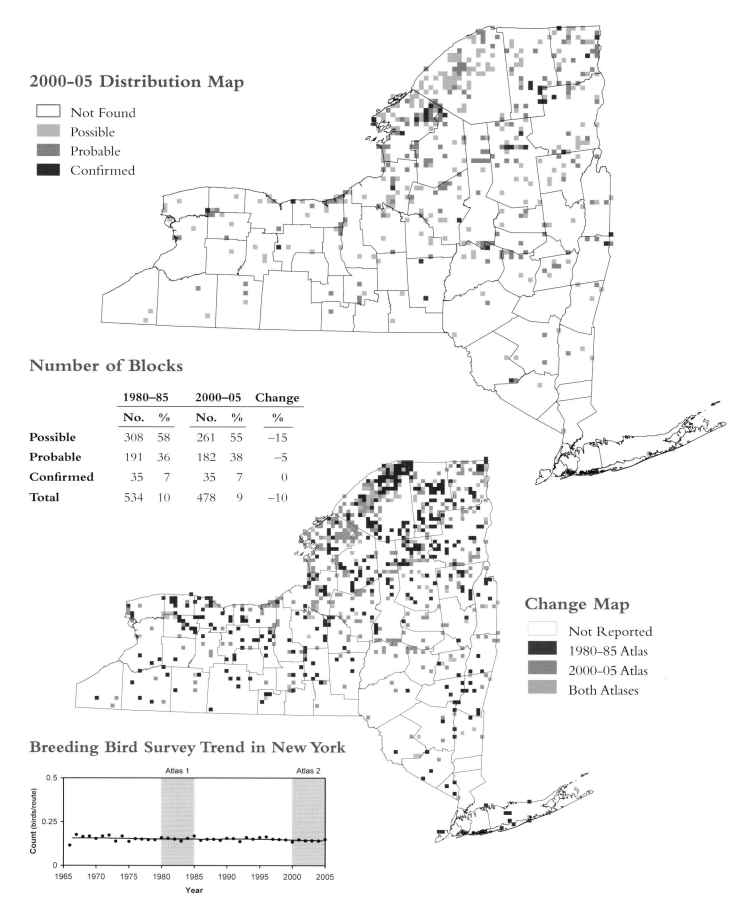

2000-05 Distribution Map

- ☐ Not Found
- ▨ Possible
- ▨ Probable
- ■ Confirmed

Number of Blocks

	1980–85		2000–05		Change
	No.	%	No.	%	%
Possible	308	58	261	55	−15
Probable	191	36	182	38	−5
Confirmed	35	7	35	7	0
Total	534	10	478	9	−10

Change Map

- ☐ Not Reported
- ■ 1980-85 Atlas
- ▨ 2000-05 Atlas
- ▨ Both Atlases

Breeding Bird Survey Trend in New York

Least Bittern
Ixobrychus exilis

HEIDI BOGNER KENNEDY

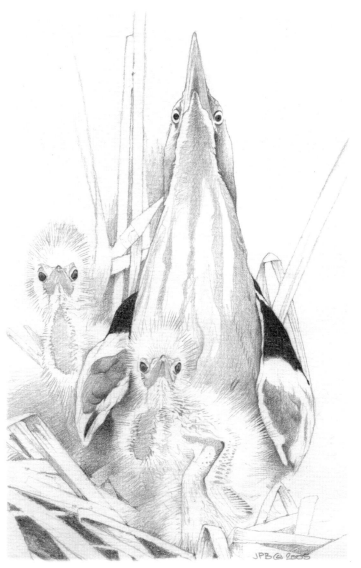

The Least Bittern is an inconspicuous marsh bird whose secretive nature and dense breeding habitat make it difficult to detect and monitor. Its breeding range includes most of the United States east of the Great Plains, as well as scattered locations in west-central and western United States, and areas southward to Costa Rica. New York is near the northern periphery of the range, with populations extending northward into southeastern Canada and Maine (Gibbs et al. 1992b). Its preferred breeding habitat in New York is freshwater marsh with tall emergent vegetation, such as cattail, interspersed with open water. Recent breeding reports on Long Island have been from freshwater and brackish marshes, which appear to be favored over salt marsh habitat (K. Feustel pers. comm.). Eaton (1910) described the Least Bittern as locally common in marshes of the Great Lakes Plain, Coastal Lowlands, and Hudson Valley, and a possible breeder in the Champlain Valley. Bull (1974) considered it uncommon and local in the southern and western portions of the state and rare or absent in higher elevations and in the most northern portions.

The first Atlas showed the Least Bittern to have a spotty distribution in New York, with Confirmed and Probable blocks concentrated in the Great Lakes Plain and along the Hudson Valley. Other records came from the St. Lawrence Plains and Transition, Coastal Lowlands, and Champlain Valley. The Least Bittern was reported in only slightly fewer blocks during the second Atlas period and had a similar distribution with some visible differences. Noticeably fewer reports came from the lower Hudson Valley, the Coastal Lowlands, and the Champlain Valley. Several blocks in Niagara County reported the bittern where it was not recorded during the first Atlas survey. A shift was also noticeable from more blocks in northern St. Lawrence County to more blocks in northern Jefferson and southern St. Lawrence counties. Concentrations were apparent near the Iroquois and Montezuma wetland complexes. Possible threats to the Least Bittern include loss, degradation, and fragmentation of habitat from development, agriculture, invasive species, and Lake Ontario water-level management (DesGranges et al. 2005). Some of these threats may be particularly relevant in portions of the Hudson Valley and the Coastal Lowlands (D. Adams pers. comm.). Differences between the two Atlas findings, however, may also result from this species being overlooked, especially when only passive surveys are made from marsh edges.

The scattered distribution of the Least Bittern in the state is due to the limited remaining appropriate wetland habitat (Stoner 1998). In addition, the Least Bittern may be area dependent, pre-ferring marshes greater than 5 ha (12.3 a) (Brown and Dinsmore 1986). Bull (1974) and both Atlas results indicate that large emergent marshes and marsh complexes such as the Iroquois and Montezuma wetland complexes and the larger marshes along the Lake Ontario shoreline are important to this species in New York. Recent marsh bird research at the Iroquois wetland complex has shown that the Least Bittern can be locally very abundant in large marsh areas with appropriate habitat (Lor 2000, Bogner and Baldassarre 2002).

The Least Bittern is listed as a Threatened species in New York, Connecticut, and Pennsylvania and as Endangered in Massachusetts, but little is known about its continental population levels and trends. The Breeding Bird Survey does not gather sufficient data on this species to generate reliable trends (Sauer et al. 2005), but the Marsh Monitoring Program found a significant decline of 8.5 percent per year in the Great Lakes Basin between 1995 and 2003 (Crewe et al. 2005). Implementation of a large-scale targeted monitoring program is necessary to adequately track population trends of this and other secretive marsh birds.

2000–05 Distribution Map

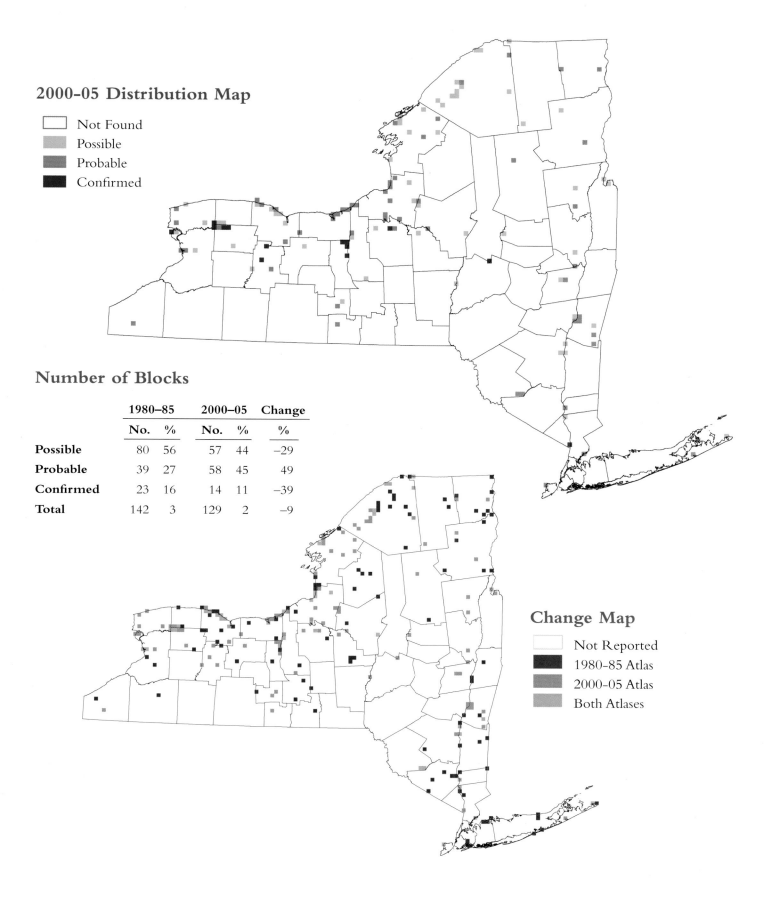

Not Found
Possible
Probable
Confirmed

Number of Blocks

	1980–85		2000–05		Change
	No.	%	No.	%	%
Possible	80	56	57	44	−29
Probable	39	27	58	45	49
Confirmed	23	16	14	11	−39
Total	142	3	129	2	−9

Change Map

Not Reported
1980–85 Atlas
2000–05 Atlas
Both Atlases

Great Blue Heron

Ardea herodias

Donald A. McCrimmon Jr.

The Great Blue Heron is a widespread species, breeding throughout the United States and Canada. The largest heron in North America, it is familiar to many persons with only a casual interest in birds. It is found from Nova Scotia to British Columbia and southward into Central America, absent primarily only from high mountains and very arid regions. Its diet consists mostly of fish, but it will also take amphibians, invertebrates, reptiles, mammals, and even other birds (Butler 1992). The Great Blue Heron forages in both fresh and brackish water and will occasionally feed in open fields. It typically nests in tall trees, generally near water (Butler 1992). In New York, islands or swamps are frequent colony sites, but the crown canopies of deciduous woods on hillsides are also used (McCrimmon 1982). In the 19th century, DeKay (1844) noted nesting in the Coastal Lowlands of New York, and Giraud (1844) described foraging activity in Long Island salt marshes. Eaton (1910) discussed the severe decline of breeding colonies state-wide, as a result of both forestry practices and plume hunting on Long Island (see review by Griffith 1998b). Significant population growth has occurred since the 1960s (McCrimmon 1982, Griffith 1998b).

The total number of blocks with Great Blue Heron records increased by 20 percent between Atlas periods. Increases were seen in all ecozones except the Catskill Highlands. The number of blocks with Confirmed records more than doubled. Both Atlas results showed a population that is widely distributed throughout Upstate New York, with abundant Confirmed breeding in blocks along the Hudson Valley, Great Lakes, Eastern Ontario, and St. Lawrence plains, and the Appalachian Plateau. Confirmed breeding was not reported for the species in the Coastal Lowlands during either Atlas period, and none has been documented there for more than 100 years.

Populations in New York have recovered from the feather hunting of the early 20th century. Reforestation and an increase in beaver populations impounding stream flowages have likely provided more areas of foraging and breeding habitat. Colonies range in size from just one or two nesting pairs to several hundred, and colony sites may be used for decades. During the 1988 winter, 785 nests were counted at a colony at the Iroquois National Wildlife Refuge (P. Hess pers. comm.). In 2001 the largest colony reported in the state, with 552 active nests, was at Valcour Island in Lake Champlain (D. Adams pers. comm.).

The North American Waterbird Conservation Plan (Kushlan et al. 2002) assessed the Great Blue Heron continent-wide population as increasing and not currently at risk. It is not listed as of conservation concern in New York or other nearby northeastern states or the province of Ontario, although the second Ontario Breeding Bird Atlas shows significant declines all across the province since the first Atlas survey in Ontario was completed (Bird Studies Canada et al. 2006). The Great Blue Heron is reasonably tolerant of human activity. Some colonies, such as the one at Ironside Island in the St. Lawrence River, are immediately adjacent to human dwellings. The availability of colony sites is likely not limiting. The number of breeding pairs in colonies, however, is positively correlated to the size of nearby wetlands (Gibbs et al. 1987), suggesting that food supply is a critical limiting factor to local or regional population sizes.

Systematic aerial statewide census of the Great Blue Heron last occurred in the early 1980s (McCrimmon 1982). Repeating the census after a lapse of more than two decades to secure colony-specific population and habitat information is warranted. Atlases provide excellent distributional data, but not at the level of detail that allows trend analysis of population size or that provides information about the size and success of individual colonies or groups of colonies.

JPB © 2005

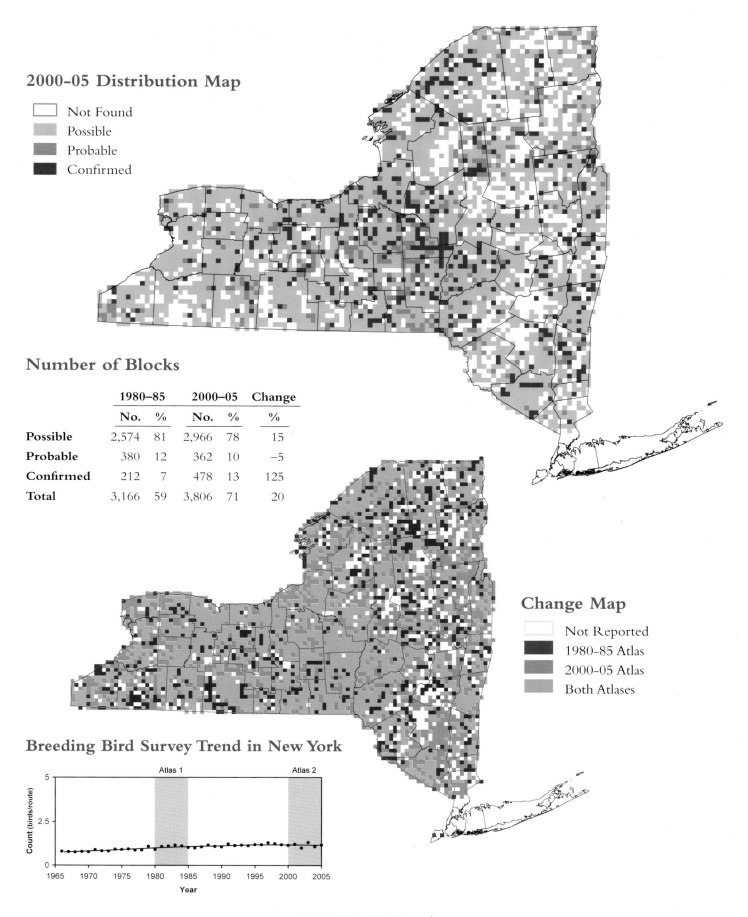

2000–05 Distribution Map

- ☐ Not Found
- Possible
- Probable
- Confirmed

Number of Blocks

	1980–85		2000–05		Change
	No.	%	No.	%	%
Possible	2,574	81	2,966	78	15
Probable	380	12	362	10	−5
Confirmed	212	7	478	13	125
Total	3,166	59	3,806	71	20

Change Map

- ☐ Not Reported
- 1980-85 Atlas
- 2000-05 Atlas
- Both Atlases

Breeding Bird Survey Trend in New York

Great Egret

Ardea alba

Donald A. McCrimmon Jr.

Intermediate in size among wading birds, the white-plumaged Great Egret is widely recognized in North America. The slaughter of the Great Egret and other wading birds during the early 20th century helped spark the formation of conservation organizations, especially the National Audubon Society, as well as the enactment of laws protecting these birds (McCrimmon et al. 2001). The Great Egret breeds in the eastern United States from extreme southern Maine southward along the Atlantic Coast and throughout the southern states. It also breeds at scattered sites along the Pacific Coast and inland, as well as in South America, Eurasia, Africa, and Australia (McCrimmon et al. 2001). It nests locally and sporadically in New York and in southern Ontario and Quebec, mostly in woody vegetation, shrubs, and trees, either over water or on islands in both freshwater wetlands and marine-estuarine habitats. In New York it nests most frequently in maritime scrub thickets on Long Island (Bull 1964), but it also breeds on islands in Lake Champlain and the Niagara River Basin (McCrimmon et al. 2001). It forages in a wide variety of wetland and occasionally upland habitats (see McCrimmon et al. 2001 for details). A summer "visitant" in the 19th and early 20th centuries (Giraud 1844, Eaton 1910), the species was first recorded nesting in New York on Fishers Island, Suffolk County, in 1953 (Bull 1964). Over more than 50 years, the number of breeding sites on Long Island slowly increased.

During the first Atlas survey, Great Egret breeding was restricted to the Coastal Lowlands and the southern Manhattan Hills. During the second Atlas survey, breeding was confirmed at three additional locations: Motor Island in the Niagara River (where the population seems to be increasing; M. Kandel pers. comm.), Erie County; the Four Brothers Islands in Lake Champlain; and in the Triassic Lowlands. The number of blocks with Great Egret records increased by 71 percent, and the number of blocks in which nesting was confirmed increased by 59 percent. When the data from the second Atlas is combined with that of the Long Island Colonial Waterbird Survey and the Harbor Her-

ons Program of the New York City Audubon Society (Sommers et al. 2001, Kerlinger 2004, D. Adams pers. comm.), one notices the overwhelming prevalence of nesting in the Coastal Lowlands of the New York Harbor area and Long Island, including at the Isle of Meadows, Richmond County; South Brother Island and Goose Island, Bronx County; Canarsie Pol in Jamaica Bay, Queens County; Huckleberry Island, Westchester County; sites in Middle, East, and South Oyster bays, Nassau County; and sites in Great South Bay, Moriches Bay, Youngs Island, Warner Islands West Island, Gardiners Island, Plum Island, and around Fishers Island, Suffolk County.

The combined breeding population of Long Island and the New York Harbor region increased substantially from 296 pairs in 1985 to a peak of 875 in 2001 (Sommers et al. 2001, Kerlinger 2004, D. Adams pers. comm.). Although the number of birds nesting on individual islands changed dramatically in 2001–04, the New York Harbor population of Great Egrets seems to be stable overall (Kerlinger 2004).

The North American Waterbird Conservation Plan (Kushlan et al. 2002) assessed the breeding population of Great Egret continent-wide as increasing and not currently at risk. Great Egret is not listed as a species of conservation concern in New York, but it is listed as Threatened in Connecticut and Pennsylvania. Protection of wetlands is critical to the maintenance of healthy populations of this species (Parnell et al. 1986). Many nesting areas are protected, but often associated foraging grounds are not. The Harbor Herons Wildlife Refuge in the Arthur Kill was created in response to severe pollution incidents that afflicted the waterway and disrupted the recovery of heron populations in the New York Harbor area, which had begun in the 1980s.

2000-05 Distribution Map

- ☐ Not Found
- Possible
- Probable
- Confirmed

Number of Blocks

	1980–85		2000–05		Change
	No.	%	No.	%	%
Possible	44	68	69	62	57
Probable	4	6	15	14	275
Confirmed	17	26	27	24	59
Total	65	1	111	2	71

Change Map

- ☐ Not Reported
- 1980-85 Atlas
- 2000-05 Atlas
- Both Atlases

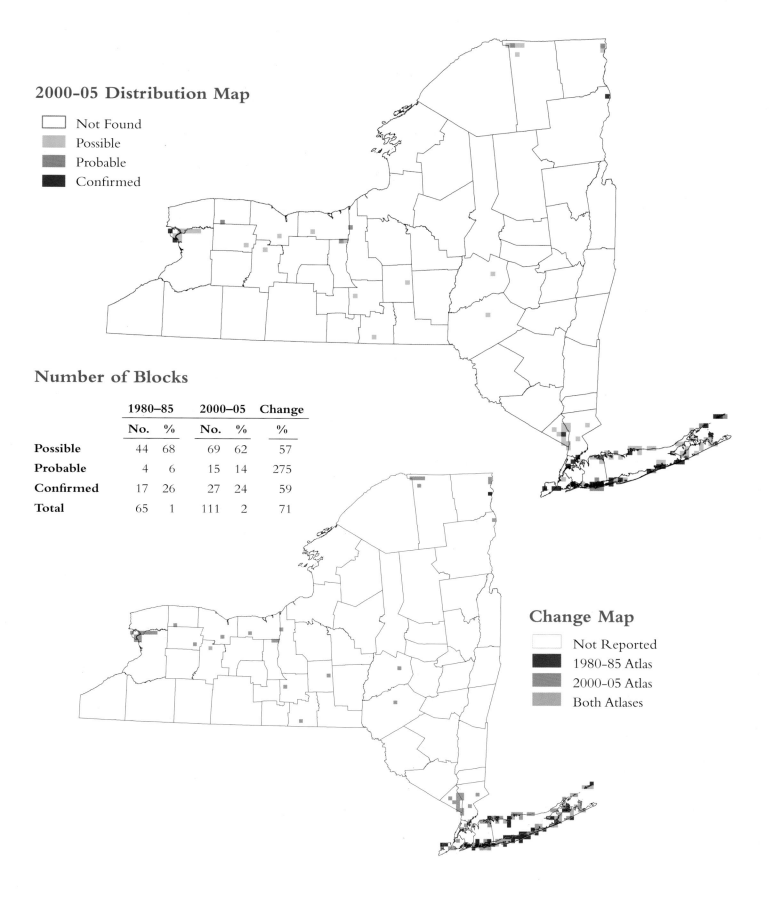

Snowy Egret
Egretta thula

DONALD A. McCRIMMON JR.

The Snowy Egret is a bird of the estuary, breeding in mixed-species sites and preferring shallow estuarine areas for feeding (Parsons and Master 2000). Its *aigrette* plumes were among the most sought after during the period of market hunting between 1880 and 1910 (Parsons and Master 2000). Following protection efforts, Snowy Egret populations rebounded, even extending beyond the historical records (Parsons and Master 2000). Breeding occurs along the coasts of the United States and at scattered locations in the interior, as well as throughout Central America, northern South America, and the Caribbean. Its breeding range extends eastward continuously along the Gulf Coast to include southern Alabama, southern Georgia, and all of Florida. Nesting is more local along the immediate Atlantic Coast from midcoastal Georgia to southern Maine. Limited numbers of egrets appear to have bred locally on the coastal islands of Long Island in the mid-1880s; Giraud (1844) reported them as "not abundant but by no means uncommon." Dutcher (1886) wrote of apparent nest building by two pairs near Great South Beach, Suffolk County, in 1885. Eaton (1910) regarded the Snowy Egret as rare or visiting only occasionally. No breeding was recorded in New York again until 1949, when two nests were found at Oak Beach, Suffolk County (Bull 1964). The population grew through the mid-1970s and peaked at 21 active colonies (1978) and 1,401 nesting pairs (1977) (Buckley and Buckley 1980, D. M. Peterson 1988e). Since then, the population has undergone cycles of growth and decline, averaging 780 pairs per season. In 2004, the population stood at 664 breeding pairs at 13 sites, both on Long Island and in the New York Harbor (Sommers et al. 2001, Kerlinger 2004, D. Adams and M. Gibbons pers. comm.).

In both Atlas surveys, Snowy Egret breeding was restricted to the Coastal Lowlands and adjacent Manhattan Hills. The first Atlas showed a cluster of 10 adjacent blocks with Confirmed breeding in the southwestern shore at Middle, East, South Oyster, and Great South bays. Also on the south shore, breeding was confirmed in Kings County at Canarsie Pol in Jamaica Bay and in Suffolk County at West Inlet Island in Moriches Bay and at Warner Islands West Island in Shinnecock Bay. Three Confirmed records came from Gardiners and Plum islands. Breeding colonies were also reported in Jamaica Bay, Kings County; Staten Island, Richmond County; South Brother Island, Bronx County; and Huckleberry Island, Westchester County.

The second Atlas findings revealed little change in the number of blocks with Confirmed records. Data from the second Atlas can be combined with those from Harbor Herons and Long Island Colonial Waterbird Surveys (Sommers et al. 2001, Kerlinger 2004, D. Adams pers. comm.). Breeding was newly confirmed in 2000 and 2001 at Isle of Meadows in the Arthur Kill, off Staten Island, but that site was subsequently abandoned (Kerlinger 2002). Breeding was also newly confirmed at Hoffman Island, Richmond County, and at Goose Island, Bronx County. In eastern Suffolk County, breeding continued at Gardiners Island but was not confirmed at Plum Island. On the north shore, Confirmed breeding was reported at Youngs Island, Suffolk County. A pair was observed in 2000 in the Great Egret colony at Motor Island in the Niagara River, but the first nesting in New York away from the coast could not be confirmed (Watson 2001).

The North American Waterbird Conservation Plan (Kushlan et al. 2002) estimated Snowy Egret populations as declining nationwide, primarily because the species nests colonially in limited and threatened habitats. This assessment is congruent with one by Parsons and Master (2000) indicating general population declines along the Atlantic Coast. The Snowy Egret is listed as Threatened in Connecticut but is not listed in other northeastern states or provinces. Successful protection of the Snowy Egret will depend on regular monitoring of its distribution and abundance.

2000-05 Distribution Map

- ☐ Not Found
- Possible
- Probable
- Confirmed

Number of Blocks

	1980–85		2000–05		Change
	No.	%	No.	%	%
Possible	60	64	29	50	−52
Probable	14	15	10	17	−29
Confirmed	20	21	19	33	−5
Total	94	2	58	1	−38

Change Map

- ☐ Not Reported
- 1980-85 Atlas
- 2000-05 Atlas
- Both Atlases

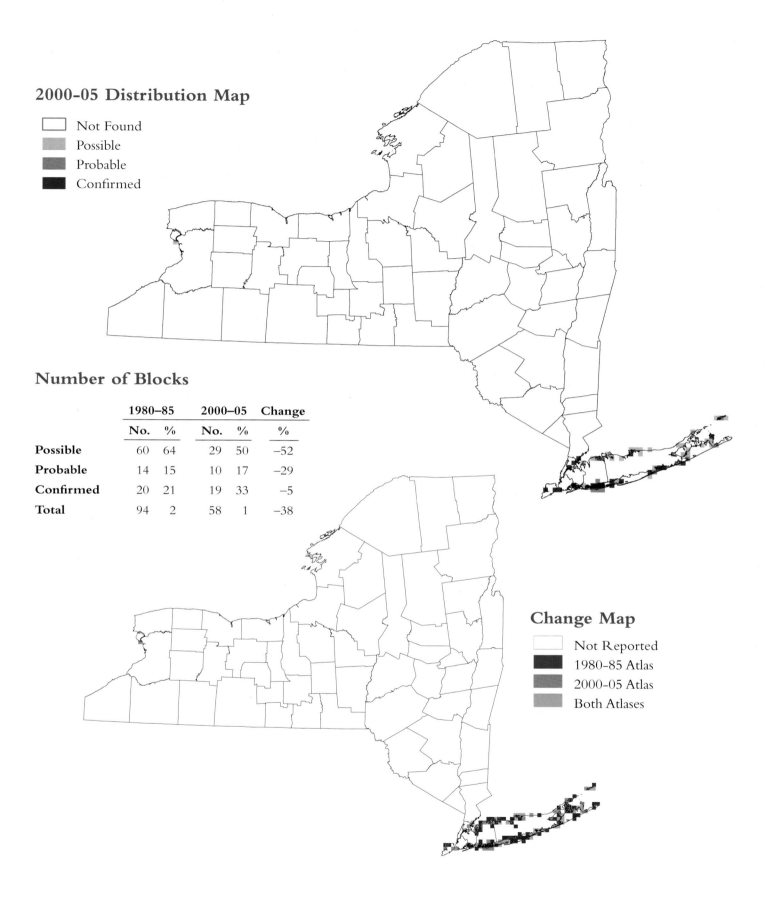

Little Blue Heron

Egretta caerulea

Donald A. McCrimmon Jr.

In the United States, the majority of the Little Blue Heron population breeds in the Southeast. As one moves northward along the Atlantic Coast, the species nests with steadily declining abundance to southern Maine. Outside the United States, it breeds in the West Indies, the east and west coasts of Mexico and occasionally inland, and in South America (Rodgers and Smith 1995). The Little Blue Heron nests colonially in shrubs and small trees over standing fresh or salt water or on islands. Foraging in a variety of freshwater, estuarine, or marine habitats, the opportunistic diet of the Little Blue Heron includes small fish, amphibians, and invertebrates, including crustaceans (Rodgers and Smith 1995). Giraud (1844) described it as a rare summer visitor, and Eaton (1910) reported only one spring and two summer records from 1847 to 1885. Bull (1964) reported the first instance of Little Blue Heron breeding in New York State, at Tobay Pond in Nassau County in 1958. Peterson et al. (1985) reported 68 pairs in 8 colonies on Long Island. Between 1985 and 1995, a mean of 51 herons nested among some 20 colonies on Long Island (Sommers et al. 1996, Lauro 1998b). Combined records for 1998, 2001, and 2004 yielded averages of 21 nesting pairs at between 4 and 10 sites (Sommers et al. 2001, Kerlinger 2004, D. Adams pers. comm.).

The first Atlas reported Confirmed breeding in only nine blocks in the Coastal Lowlands, with most along the southwestern shore of Long Island and one each on Plum and Gardiners islands. The second Atlas survey showed little change, with Confirmed breeding in 11 blocks, again with none upstate but with 2 new blocks in Long Island Sound in Bronx County. Breeding was confirmed in 2000–01 at Isle of Meadows in the Arthur Kill off Staten Island, Richmond County, but that site was subsequently abandoned (Kerlinger 2001, 2004). Breeding was also confirmed at Hoffman Island, Richmond County; at Goose Island, Bronx County; on the southwestern Long Island shore at colonies in the Middle and East Bay areas; at sites in Moriches Bay; and at Warner Islands West Island in the Shinnecock Bay area. In easternmost Suffolk County, breeding was confirmed for the second Atlas only at Plum Island.

Though the Breeding Bird Survey was not designed to monitor populations of wading birds and the data must be viewed with caution, they show a significant nationwide decline in Little Blue Heron numbers since 1966 (Sauer et al. 2005). The North American Waterbird Conservation Plan (Kushlan et al. 2002) noted the lack of sufficient data for estimating the Little Blue Heron population continent-wide, but considered the species at high risk, primarily because it nests colonially in vulnerable habitats. The species is not listed in New York but is identified as a Species of Special Concern in Connecticut. Because the Little Blue Heron is nesting in New York near the northern limit of its breeding range and it can be difficult to detect, close monitoring of this species is very important. Foot surveys are necessary since the dark-plumaged adults nest under the canopy.

2000-05 Distribution Map

- ☐ Not Found
- ▨ Possible
- ▩ Probable
- ■ Confirmed

Number of Blocks

	1980–85		2000–05		Change
	No.	%	No.	%	%
Possible	10	53	7	39	−30
Probable	0	0	0	0	
Confirmed	9	47	11	61	22
Total	19	<1	18	<1	−5

Change Map

- ☐ Not Reported
- ■ 1980-85 Atlas
- ▩ 2000-05 Atlas
- ▨ Both Atlases

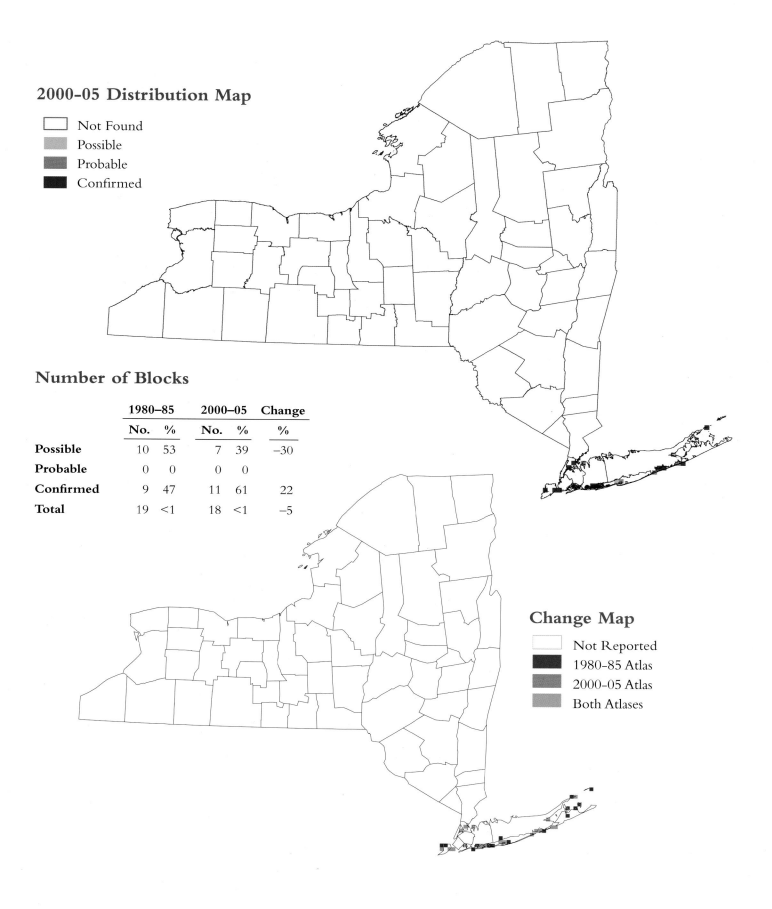

Tricolored Heron

Egretta tricolor

Donald A. McCrimmon Jr.

Though the lovely dark feathers of the Tricolored Heron were probably not important to the plume trade, its habit of nesting with more commercially important species left this coastal wading bird at risk (Frederick 1997). The species breeds in coastal areas throughout the Western Hemisphere, including South and Central America and the Caribbean. In the United States, the Tricolored Heron breeds primarily along the Atlantic and Gulf coasts northward to southern Maine (Frederick 1997); New York is approaching the northern limit of the range. The species generally nests on islands in areas of higher ground that support small trees or shrubs, with open water or wetlands nearby. It forages in wetlands, and small fishes make up almost all of its diet, with insects, crustaceans, and frogs taken only infrequently (Frederick 1997). The Tricolored Heron was first recorded breeding in New York in 1955 at Jamaica Bay Refuge (Meyerriecks 1957). Prior to that, the only sightings had been reported on Long Island (Cruickshank 1942), and only one specimen had been collected since 1836 (Giraud 1844, affirmed by Eaton 1910). By 1989, 52 pairs bred on Long Island (Sommers et al. 2001). Since 1985, and with the exception of the relatively large population of 1989, populations have averaged slightly over 17 breeding pairs (Sommers et al. 2001, Kerlinger 2004, D. Adams pers. comm.).

During the first Atlas period, Tricolored Heron breeding was restricted to a small region of southwestern Long Island. During the second Atlas period, it was still confined to the Coastal Lowlands, but reports extended from islands off Staten Island, along the southern shore of Long Island, to Shinnecock Bay. The second Atlas results can be combined with those from Harbor Herons and Long Island Colonial Waterbird Surveys (Sommers et al. 2001, Kerlinger 2004, D. Adams pers. comm.). Confirmed nesting occurred in 2001 at Canarsie Pol in Jamaica Bay, Kings County. Confirmed nesting was also reported in 2000–01 on the southern Long Island shore at colonies in the Middle, East, and South Oyster Bay areas, and in 2004 in the Moriches Bay area. Nesting may have occurred at Hoffman Island, Richmond County, in 2001 (Kerlinger 2001).

Lauro (1998c) suggested that Tricolored Heron populations may have increased slightly and stabilized. However, an analysis of trends based on data from Sommers et al. (2001), Kerlinger (2004), and D. Adams (pers. comm.) points to a declining population. The Tricolored Heron appears to be decreasing in number throughout much of the United States (Frederick 1997). The North American Waterbird Conservation Plan (Kushlan et al. 2002) considered the species at high risk primarily because it nests colonially in limited and threatened habitats. The Tricolored Heron is not listed as of conservation concern in New York or most other northeastern states, but clearly, continued close monitoring of populations in New York is warranted.

2000–05 Distribution Map

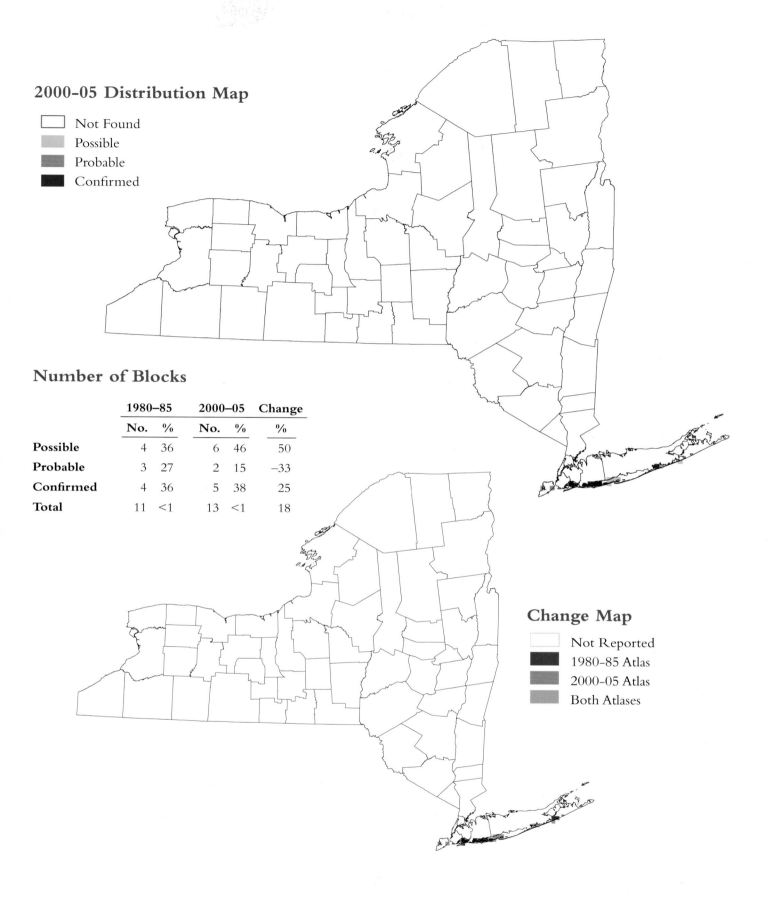

- ☐ Not Found
- Possible
- Probable
- Confirmed

Number of Blocks

	1980–85		2000–05		Change
	No.	%	No.	%	%
Possible	4	36	6	46	50
Probable	3	27	2	15	−33
Confirmed	4	36	5	38	25
Total	11	<1	13	<1	18

Change Map

- ☐ Not Reported
- 1980–85 Atlas
- 2000–05 Atlas
- Both Atlases

Cattle Egret
Bubulcus ibis

Donald A. McCrimmon Jr.

The Cattle Egret is an insectivorous bird that feeds in grassy habitats, and in the southern United States it is often seen in pastures in association with livestock. It is found globally, occurring on all continents with the exception of Antarctica, and is continuing to extend its range. The North American expansion of the Cattle Egret's range has been complex and dynamic since the species was first found breeding in 1953 in Florida (Telfair 2006). In North America, it is now found throughout the continent, although the bulk of its breeding population is within the southeastern United States. Telfair (2006) described the Cattle Egret as the most terrestrial heron, but it is also regularly found in aquatic areas. It is adapted to disturbed habitats where the insects on which it feeds are abundant. It typically nests in mixed-species colonies in a wide variety of locations, and in vegetation ranging from structurally relatively simple, uniform associations of one or a few species of plants, to more complex stands of multiple shrubs or trees (Burger 1978, McCrimmon 1978, Wiese 1978). The Cattle Egret first nested in New York at Gardiners Island, Suffolk County, in 1970 (Puleston 1970). Bull (1974) reported a second Long Island nesting site at Jones Beach, Nassau County, in 1973. In 1974, nesting was confirmed upstate at Four Brothers Islands, Essex County, and Braddock's Bay, Monroe County (Bull 1976).

The first Atlas reported only two upstate colonies but documented expansion into four new blocks with confirmed nesting colonies in the western Long Island/Staten Island region. The second Atlas survey showed that the number of blocks recording Confirmed breeding declined by 38 percent, from eight to five. Nesting continued upstate only at the Four Brothers Islands, Essex County. The Cattle Egret no longer nested at Gardiners Island, Suffolk County. In the western Long Island/New York City region, the number of blocks showing Confirmed breeding declined to four, affirming Kerlinger's (2004) assessment that the peak of 100 nesting pairs in the mid and early 1990s in this area had declined to "almost nothing" in the early 2000s. In 2004, surveys in the New York Harbor area showed breeding of Cattle Egret only at South Brother Island in Bronx County and Hoffman Island in Richmond County (Kerlinger 2004), and in 2005 only at South Brother Island (Bernick 2005).

The North American Waterbird Conservation Plan (Kushlan et al. 2002) assessed breeding Cattle Egret populations as increasing and not at risk. Breeding Bird Survey data, although not particularly good for monitoring colonial wading bird species, show a continental trend of significant increase for 1966–79 but significant decline for 1980–2005 (Sauer et al. 2007). The species is not listed as of conservation concern in any northeastern state or province. The New York population of the Cattle Egret demonstrates the complex and variable dynamics of a species at the northern limit of its range. While the species is not threatened, local breeding populations such as those that exist in New York are also inherently unstable. Continued monitoring is warranted.

2000-05 Distribution Map

- ☐ Not Found
- ▨ Possible
- ▨ Probable
- ■ Confirmed

Number of Blocks

	1980–85		2000–05		Change
	No.	%	No.	%	%
Possible	7	35	2	29	−71
Probable	5	25	0	0	−100
Confirmed	8	40	5	71	−38
Total	20	<1	7	<1	−65

Change Map

- ☐ Not Reported
- ■ 1980-85 Atlas
- ▨ 2000-05 Atlas
- ▨ Both Atlases

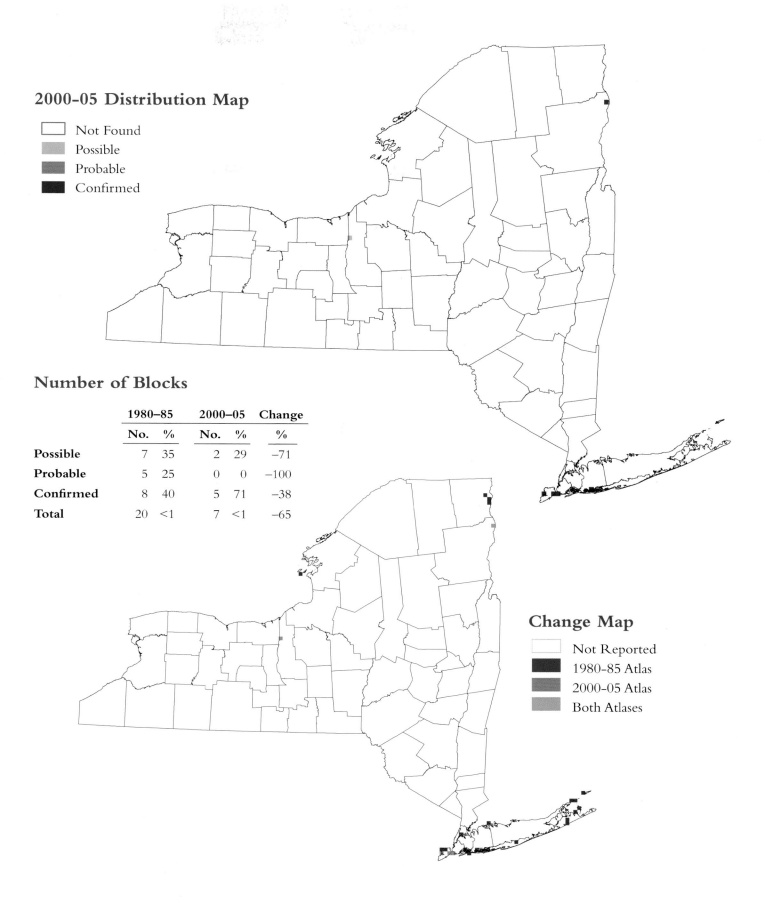

Green Heron

Butorides virescens

DONALD A. McCRIMMON JR.

The Green Heron is common yet easily overlooked in wetlands throughout much of New York. It is found throughout eastern North America from southeastern Canada southward to Florida and westward to eastern North Dakota and Texas, Arizona, and New Mexico (Davis and Kushlan 1994). It is also found along the Pacific Coast of the United States and southward through Central America and the Caribbean into South America (Davis and Kushlan 1994). New York is near the northern edge of its breeding range. It is considered semi-colonial, nesting either solitarily or in loose aggregations in suitable habitat. Often found in swampy thickets, the species actually is rather flexible in its use of habitats. Typically, it nests in forest and swamp patches, or to a lesser degree drier sites that are at least near water. DeKay (1844) reported the species as a common breeder throughout the lower elevations of New York, but Giraud (1844) regarded it as relatively less abundant, although still common on Long Island. Eaton (1910) regarded it as the most familiar heron in most of the state.

The first Atlas survey found the Green Heron present in all ecozones and counties, with Confirmed breeding in all counties but Herkimer, Hamilton, Schoharie, and Greene. These absences were attributed to low atlasing effort in those areas (Sibley 1988j). It was largely missing from most of the Adirondacks, the Central Tug Hill, much of the eastern end of the Appalachian Plateau, and the Catskill region, all areas of continuous forest. In the second Atlas survey, the total number of blocks for which the species was reported declined by 13 percent, with declines noted in all ecozones except the Mohawk Valley and Tug Hill Plateau. The ecozone with the greatest decline at all breeding levels was the Adirondacks (52 percent). Nonetheless, the fact that the Green Heron was detected in more than 41 percent of all blocks during the second Atlas period is testament to its widespread occurrence throughout the state. With regard to Confirmed breeding, the most notable changes occurred in northwestern New York counties, along the Hudson Valley, and in the Coastal Lowlands of Long Island. Although the species is still commonly found on Long Island and in the Hudson Valley, these changes may reflect the growth of human populations in those areas, and associated modifications of the landscape, or they may be the result of decreased effort during the second Atlas fieldwork.

The Green Heron's retiring, semi-colonial nature makes population estimates difficult. For example, on the Long Island Colonial Waterbird Surveys, nest counts are not reported for the

Green Heron (Sommers et al. 2001), although they are for seven other species of herons and egrets. For the New York Harbor area, Kerlinger (2004) reported that although the Green Heron seemed to be a relatively common nester in the metropolitan area, it had not been found nesting on the harbor islands for several years. A. J. Bernick (pers. comm.), however, reported Confirmed breeding in three blocks in the Staten Island area during the second Atlas period, one of these on the perimeter of Isle of Meadows in 2001 and the other two at mainland sites in 2002.

The North American Waterbird Conservation Plan (Kushlan et al. 2002) made no estimate of continental populations of the Green Heron, citing insufficient data. Breeding Bird Survey data suggest a slightly, but significantly, declining continental population since 1966, with most of the decline occurring since the 1980s (Sauer et al. 2005). No trend is apparent in the sparse New York BBS data. The second Ontario Breeding Bird Atlas reported slight but significant declines in Green Heron numbers across that province (Bird Studies Canada et al. 2006), much as found in New York. Though not listed as a species of conservation concern in New York or adjacent states, it bears watching in the future.

2000–05 Distribution Map

- ☐ Not Found
- Possible
- Probable
- Confirmed

Number of Blocks

	1980–85		2000–05		Change
	No.	%	No.	%	%
Possible	1,485	58	1,237	56	−17
Probable	615	24	599	27	−3
Confirmed	444	17	377	17	−15
Total	2,544	48	2,213	41	−13

Change Map

- ☐ Not Reported
- 1980-85 Atlas
- 2000-05 Atlas
- Both Atlases

Breeding Bird Survey Trend in New York

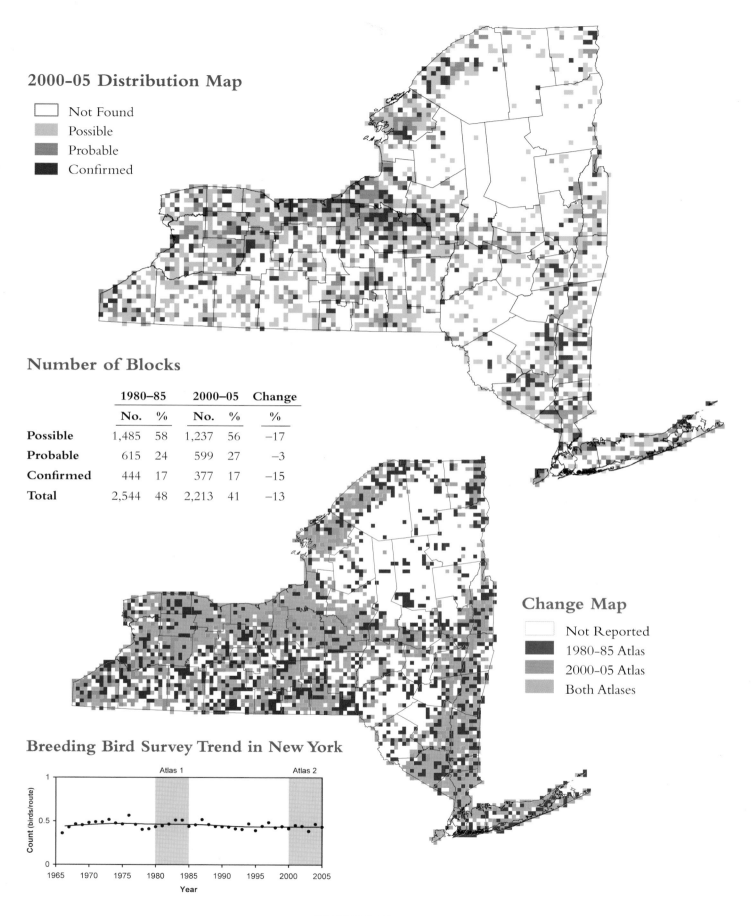

Black-crowned Night-Heron

Nycticorax nycticorax

DONALD A. McCRIMMON JR.

Named for its nocturnal feeding habits, the Black-crowned Night-Heron breeds worldwide, throughout the Americas as well as in Europe, India, Asia, and Africa (Davis 1993). In eastern North America, it nests colonially as far north as Labrador. This heron's general habitat preferences are varied. It is found in coastal, estuarine, and freshwater locations including swamps, streams and rivers, the edges of ponds, lakes, lagoons, tidal mudflats, salt marsh, canals, and reservoirs, as well as in wet farming fields (Davis 1993). The species was common on Long Island in the 19th century but apparently less so upstate (Giraud 1844, Eaton 1910). For coastal locations in the 20th century, substantial population declines occurred from the 1940s through the 1970s, as well documented by Marcotte (1998a). Marcotte reported even more dramatic declines upstate during the 1970s and 1980s, with the loss of colonies totaling 600 nests at Grand Island in Erie County and the disappearance of about 10 nesting sites along the Hudson River.

During the first Atlas survey, most Confirmed breeding was recorded in blocks of the Coastal Lowlands on the north and south shores of Long Island. Upstate, the Black-crowned Night-Heron nested at Lake Champlain, along the eastern shore of Lake Ontario and the St. Lawrence River, and at locations in two blocks bordering Lake Ontario in Monroe County, west of Rochester. Breeding was also confirmed in five adjacent blocks at Montezuma National Wildlife Refuge. The second Atlas survey revealed a modest increase statewide in the number of blocks with Confirmed breeding, but 12 percent fewer blocks with Confirmed breeding in the Coastal Lowlands. On the other hand, an almost doubling of the number of blocks upstate from 16 to 30 is dramatic, with particularly notable increases along the Triassic Lowlands of Rockland County and the Niagara River. Two Confirmed records also came from the Appalachian Plateau (Tompkins and Schuyler counties), where the species was not confirmed during the first Atlas survey.

For the New York City/Long Island area, Atlas results are supported by data from other studies (Sommers et al. 2001, Ker-

linger 2004, Bernick 2005, D. Adams pers. comm.). From 1984 to 1995, an average of 1,500 nesting pairs of Black-crowned Night-Heron nested on Long Island. This average declined to slightly over 1,000 nesting pairs from 1995 to 2004. At the same time, declines in the number of nesting pairs in the New York Harbor area were reported (Kerlinger 2004), as well as substantial variability in the numbers and turnover rates of nesting colonies. Unfortunately, little systematically collected data are available for upstate Black-crowned Night-Heron populations.

The North American Waterbird Conservation Plan (Kushlan et al. 2002) assessed continental Black-crowned Night-Heron populations as declining. Populations in the northeastern United States have declined by approximately 50 percent since 1970 (K. Parsons pers. comm.). The species is not listed as of conservation concern in New York, Ontario, Pennsylvania, Massachusetts, Vermont, or Connecticut, but it is listed as Threatened in New Jersey. Although the Atlas data do not indicate significant declines in New York, the Black-crowned Night-Heron will bear watching in the future.

2000-05 Distribution Map

- ☐ Not Found
- Possible
- Probable
- ■ Confirmed

Number of Blocks

	1980–85		2000–05		Change
	No.	%	No.	%	%
Possible	129	61	106	50	−18
Probable	29	14	44	21	52
Confirmed	53	25	63	30	19
Total	211	4	213	4	1

Change Map

- ☐ Not Reported
- ■ 1980-85 Atlas
- 2000-05 Atlas
- Both Atlases

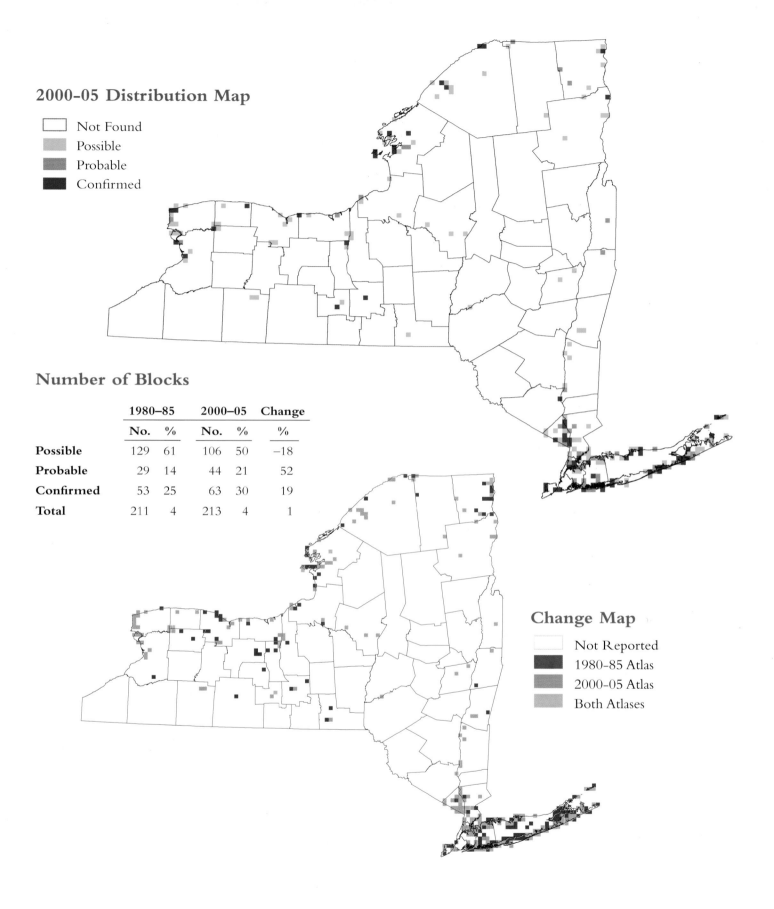

Yellow-crowned Night-Heron

Nyctanassa violacea

DONALD A. MCCRIMMON JR.

rincipally a bird of southerly latitudes through-out the Western Hemisphere, the Yellow-crowned Night-Heron breeds along the Atlantic Coast from New York and Connecticut southward to South America, and up the large river systems in the center of the United States to Kansas and Indiana. It nests in shrubby vegetation on islands and in forested wetlands and forested uplands near bodies of water (Watts 1995). It is quite tolerant of human habitation and has recently nested in densely populated residential areas in Staten Island, Far Rockaway, and various locations in Nassau County (A. Bernick pers. comm.). The species forages in coastal areas having high concentrations of crustaceans (Watts 1995). Reported as rarely being sighted in New York by Giraud (1844) and Eaton (1910), the Yellow-crowned Night-Heron was first recorded nesting in New York in 1938 at Massapequa, Nassau County (Cruickshank 1942). The Long Island breeding population increased through the 1940s and 1950s until 13 nesting sites were known in the 1960s (Bull 1964). In the early to mid-1990s, populations appeared to decline on Long Island (Lauro 1998e), but since the species can breed in isolation from colonies (D. M. Peterson 1988f), detectability might bias survey results. Since 1995 the number of breeding pairs on Long Island and the New York Harbor area has averaged about 18 annually (Sommers et al. 2001, Kerlinger 2004, M. Gibbons pers. comm.).

In the first Atlas, Confirmed records of Yellow-crowned Night-Heron were restricted to the Coastal Lowlands and the Manhattan Hills along Long Island Sound. Results of the second Atlas can be combined with those from Harbor Herons and Long Island Colonial Waterbird Surveys (Sommers et al. 2001, Kerlinger 2004, M. Gibbons pers. comm.). Confirmed nesting occurred at islands in the Arthur Kill, Richmond County; Hoffman Island, Rockland County; the Hempstead Lake area, Nassau County; and at sites in the Middle and East bays, Nassau County. During the second Atlas survey, new nesting sites were identified in Moriches and Shinnecock bays, Suffolk County, but there were no records from previously Confirmed blocks at Southold and around western Great Peconic Bay. On the northern Long Island shore, Confirmed breeding continued to be recorded at sites around Stony Brook and Smithtown, Suffolk County, and Oyster Bay, Nassau County. Confirmed nesting was not reported in the most northwestern blocks of Long Island Sound in Bronx

and Westchester counties this time. However, Bernick (2005) and the Long Island Colonial Waterbird Survey (M. Gibbons pers. comm.) recorded breeding at South Brother Island and Goose Island, Bronx County. The single record of Confirmed breeding away from the coast occurred in a block in the Triassic Lowlands of Rockland County.

The North American Waterbird Conservation Plan (Kushlan et al. 2002) assessed the continent-wide Yellow-crowned Night-Heron population as apparently stable, though data are extremely limited; the population is viewed as at moderate risk. Yellow-crowned Night-Heron is not listed as of conservation concern in New York but is listed as Threatened in Pennsylvania and as Special Concern in Connecticut. Though Yellow-crowned Night-Heron populations are small, with relatively few and scattered breeding locations, and its habitat continues to be threatened, the conservation and protection of wetlands appear to have had some beneficial effect. Targeted monitoring efforts such as those conducted by the New York City Audubon Society and the Long Island Colonial Waterbird Survey are warranted and should continue into the future.

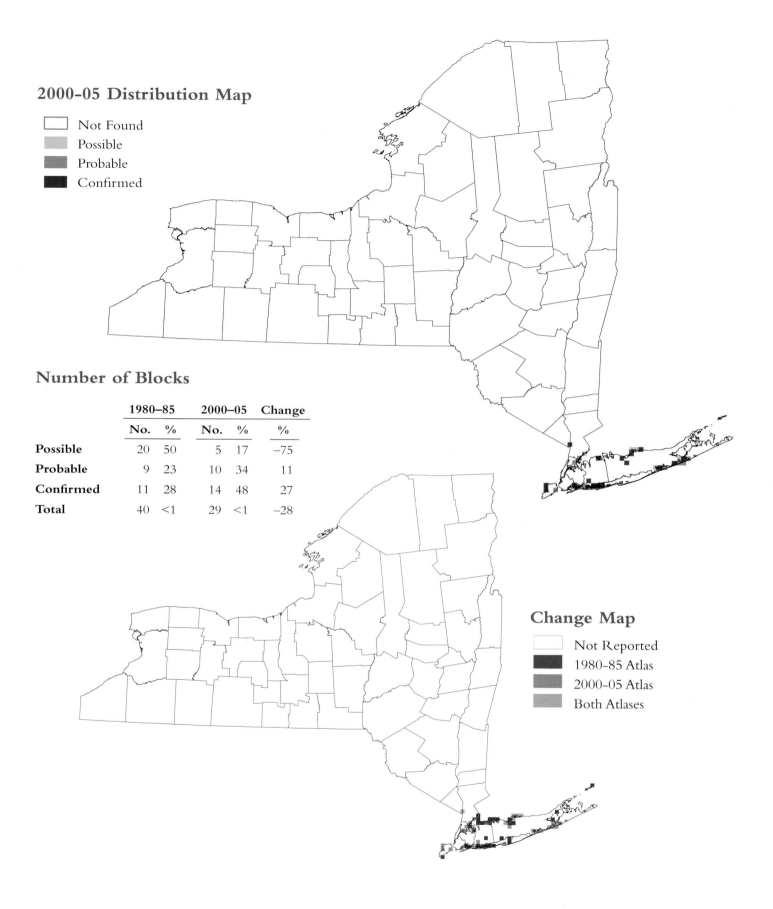

2000-05 Distribution Map

- Not Found
- Possible
- Probable
- Confirmed

Number of Blocks

	1980–85		2000–05		Change
	No.	%	No.	%	%
Possible	20	50	5	17	−75
Probable	9	23	10	34	11
Confirmed	11	28	14	48	27
Total	40	<1	29	<1	−28

Change Map

- Not Reported
- 1980-85 Atlas
- 2000-05 Atlas
- Both Atlases

Glossy Ibis
Plegadis falcinellus

Matthew D. Medler

One of the most widespread birds in the world, the Glossy Ibis is found on every continent but Antarctica. In North America this ibis underwent a dramatic range expansion in the 1900s, increasing from a rare, local breeder in Florida to a species that now nests along the Atlantic Coast from Maine to Florida and along much of Louisiana's Gulf Coast (Davis and Kricher 2000). During the breeding season the Glossy Ibis occurs in a variety of wetland habitats, including freshwater, brackish, and saltwater marshes (Davis and Kricher 2000). In New York it has nested in mixed-heron colonies, usually on sandy islands with dense vegetation (Bull 1974). The first state record was a specimen collected at Great South Bay, Long Island, in 1840 (Bull 1964). Two other specimens were collected from Long Island in the 1840s, but then the species went unrecorded in the New York City area until 1935 (Cruickshank 1942). Eaton (1910) considered this ibis to be an occasional summer visitant to the state, on the basis of Long Island specimens and six records from central and western New York. Cruickshank (1942) still considered the Glossy Ibis to be accidental in the New York City area, but it soon became nearly annual along the coast (Bull 1974). The state's first confirmed breeding came in 1961, with the discovery of three nests with eggs at Jamaica Bay (Post 1962), and by 1970, breeding was confirmed as far eastward as Gardiners Island (Bull 1974).

The first Atlas results showed Glossy Ibis breeding to be concentrated on the south shore of Long Island between Jamaica Bay and the western end of Fire Island. Breeding was also confirmed on Staten Island and along eastern Long Island. The number of Confirmed records (19) was close to the number of ibis colonies (15) reported from a 1985 survey of colonial water birds on Long Island and Staten Island (D. M. Peterson 1988a); some discrepancy is expected because of the species's tendency to use different sites from year to year. The numerous Possible and Probable records likely represented sightings of foraging birds, as the Glossy Ibis often flies several miles between breeding sites and foraging grounds

(Bull 1974). This bird's distribution in the state remained similar during the second Atlas survey, with the notable exception of a Confirmed record from Lake Champlain's Four Brothers Islands, where the species first nested in 1999 (Peterson 1999). In the New York City area, the Atlas data again documented breeding from Staten Island to eastern Long Island, as well as new nesting in the Bronx. However, the second Atlas results show a substantial decrease in the number of Confirmed records from the 1980s stronghold. Throughout the Long Island–New York City area, both the number of blocks with Confirmed breeding (14) and the number of ibis colonies (12) reported from regional colonial waterbird surveys have decreased since the first Atlas survey was completed.

From a maximum of 892 pairs in 1979 (Peterson et al. 1985), the breeding population of Glossy Ibis in the New York City area has declined, with region-wide survey totals of 450 and 541 pairs in 2001 and 2004, respectively (NYSDEC unpubl. data). A similar decline was noted in New Jersey, with numbers there decreasing 63 percent between surveys in 1978 and 1995 (Walsh et al. 1999). Population regulation is poorly understood in this species, but storms, drought, habitat alteration, pesticides, food availability (Davis and Kricher 2000), and predation (Post 1990) can all affect local populations. On Staten Island, the Glossy Ibis population decreased 42 percent in 1991 after the 1990 Arthur Kill oil spill (Parsons 1994), but the entire regional population decreased only 20 percent that same year, and in 1995 it actually exceeded 1990 numbers (Sommers et al. 1996). Lower numbers during the past three triennial surveys, though, highlight the importance of continued population monitoring of this and other colonial waterbirds.

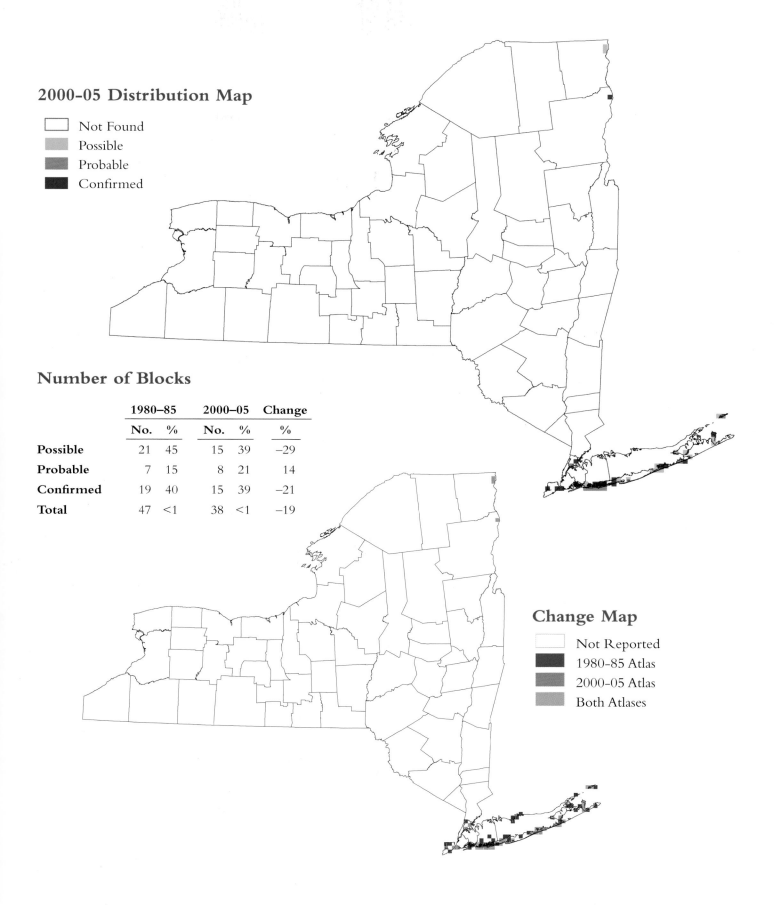

2000-05 Distribution Map

- ☐ Not Found
- Possible
- Probable
- Confirmed

Number of Blocks

	1980–85		2000–05		Change
	No.	%	No.	%	%
Possible	21	45	15	39	−29
Probable	7	15	8	21	14
Confirmed	19	40	15	39	−21
Total	47	<1	38	<1	−19

Change Map

- ☐ Not Reported
- 1980-85 Atlas
- 2000-05 Atlas
- Both Atlases

Raptors in the Susquehanna Valley

A Red-tailed Hawk and a Northern Harrier hunt small mammals in the Susquehanna Valley. Since the banning of DDT, such sights have become increasingly common throughout the state.

Black Vulture

Coragyps atratus

KEVIN J. MCGOWAN

The Black Vulture is resident from southern New York and southern Ohio, throughout the southeastern United States, and southward to southern South America. It forages in open country but breeds and roosts in forests (Buckley 1999). It does not build a nest; instead it places its two eggs under cover in thickets, hollow trees, caves, abandoned buildings, and crevices, as well as among rocks, brush piles, and beside or under trees and logs in undisturbed areas (Buckley 1999). The Black Vulture was probably always no more than a rare species in New York, and Bull (1974) mentioned only slightly more than 35 records. Most reports were from Long Island, but others came from as far northward as Franklin and Cayuga counties. In the 1980s sightings became more frequent, with most occurring in the Hudson Valley, Hudson Highlands, and Shawangunk Hills (Andrle 1998). The first winter sightings occurred when three individuals were seen during the East Orange County Christmas Bird Count in December 1990 (Manson 1991). Because this vulture is resident throughout its range (Buckley 1999), these winter sightings might indicate breeding residence. Black Vulture became annual on the New York CBCs after that time, but totals remained small until 1999–2000, when 52 individuals were seen on five different New York counts (National Audubon Society [2007]). Numbers increased to 290 in 2001–02, but the latest total was 179 in 2005–06 (National Audubon Society [2007]). The first confirmed nesting occurred in 1997 on the Mohonk Preserve in Ulster County (Bridges 1998). An incubating vulture was discovered on 27 April in a tunnel-like rock enclosure near the base of a 36 m (118 ft) high cliff overlooking the Wallkill Valley (Bridges 1998). A possible nest was discovered the same summer in a similar location, 19 km (11.8 mi) to the southeast in Ulster County (Bridges 1998).

Black Vulture was not observed during the first Atlas period but was reported from 100 blocks during the second Atlas period. Breeding was confirmed in five blocks, with nests located in the Shawangunk Hills and Taconic Highlands, and a brood of fledged young observed in the Hudson Highlands. A cluster of Probable

records in the Central Hudson suggests breeding there. Because vultures range widely to forage and are not conspicuous in their breeding behavior, it is difficult to assess if the many Possible records represent sightings of known breeders foraging away from nest sites or additional breeders.

The Black Vulture has been expanding its breeding range northward along the Atlantic Coast since the 1940s (Buckley 1999). Breeding Bird Survey data show a significant 3.1 percent per year increase in Black Vulture numbers across the range in the United States since 1966, with an even greater increase throughout the Northeast (Sauer et al. 2007). All significant trends in the BBS data are positive (Sauer et al. 2007). These data indicate that the range is expanding along with population increases inside the historic breeding range. The first confirmed New Jersey nesting was in 1981; rapid expansion across that state followed (Walsh et al. 1999). The causes of the range expansion into the Northeast are not well understood, but explanations put forth include increased food. Significant food source changes include an increase in poultry farming in parts of the range and, most important, the explosion in white-tailed deer populations (Coleman and Fraser 1989). Although the Black Vulture may be using primarily cliff and rock nests in New York, it is not restricted to such sites in other parts of its range, and it might continue its expansion into other portions of New York. Little range expansion is being found during the second Pennsylvania Atlas survey, however. Most reports are still restricted to the southeastern portion of that state (R. Mulvihill pers. comm.), so it is possible that the Black Vulture will always be restricted to the southeastern portion of New York.

2000-05 Distribution Map

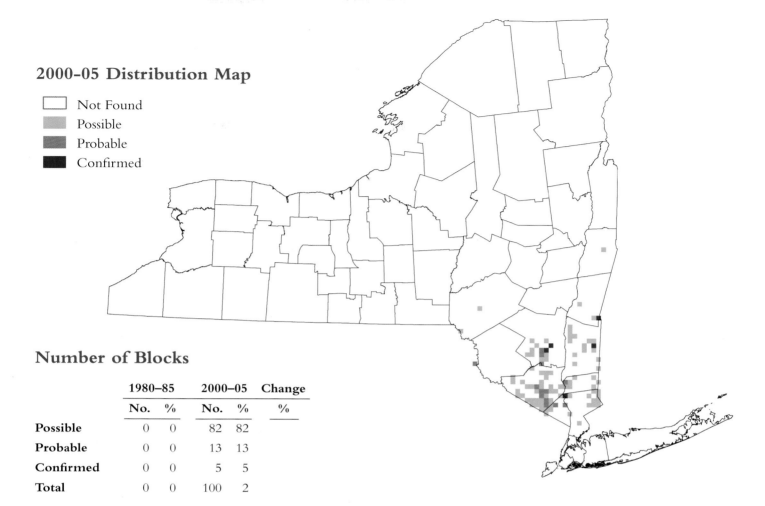

- ☐ Not Found
- Possible
- Probable
- ■ Confirmed

Number of Blocks

	1980–85		2000–05		Change
	No.	%	No.	%	%
Possible	0	0	82	82	
Probable	0	0	13	13	
Confirmed	0	0	5	5	
Total	0	0	100	2	

Turkey Vulture

Cathartes aura

KEVIN J. McGOWAN

The Turkey Vulture is the most widespread of the American vultures, breeding from southern Canada throughout the United States and southward through southern South America and the Caribbean. It prefers rangeland and areas of mixed farmland and forest. It builds no nest structure, putting its eggs directly on the ground in caves, crevices, mammal burrows, hollow logs, under fallen trees, or in abandoned buildings (Kirk and Mossman 1998). This large bird was rare in New York in the 19th century, found primarily farther southward and in the West, with southern New Jersey the closest breeding locality (DeKay 1844, Giraud 1844). Eaton (1914) listed the vulture as a summer visitor, more common on Long Island, in the Hudson Valley, and the warmer areas of western New York, with only scattered reports in most of upstate. The first confirmed nesting in New York was in a cave in Westchester County in 1925 (Howes 1926), and the second, in a hollow log in Orleans County in 1927 (G. M. Smith in Tyler 1937). Numbers subsequently increased in New York (Eaton 1953). Vultures occurred in most of the state by the middle of the century, although remained rare in the Adirondacks (Bull 1974).

During the first Atlas period the Turkey Vulture was found throughout most of the state but with few Confirmed breeding records. Few observations were made within an area stretching from the central Adirondacks to the Central Appalachians that does not correspond with any obvious elevation or landscape feature. It was also absent from the Coastal Lowlands and most of Saratoga County. During the second Atlas period the Turkey Vulture was found in 71 percent more blocks than during the first Atlas, with increases noted in nearly every region. It was reported across most of the state, with gaps remaining in the Central Adirondacks, Central Tug Hill, Coastal Lowlands, most of Saratoga County, and most of northern Jefferson County. Because this vulture conspicuously forages miles away from its nest, breed-

ing was easily recorded as Possible but was difficult to confirm. Still, Confirmed records increased by 330 percent. A fledged young on Staten Island was unexpected. It should be noted that up to 70 percent of any Turkey Vulture population in an area might not actually be breeding (Kirk and Mossman 1998). Consequently, unlike most other species covered in this Atlas, many of the blocks with Possible and Probable records might not have had breeding vultures. Many of the codes that result in a Probable ranking are not strictly applicable for this species, and should probably have been downgraded to Possible.

The Turkey Vulture began extending its breeding range northward some time between 1920 and 1940, continuing at least into the 1990s (Kirk and Mossman 1998). Data from seven eastern hawkwatches show significant increases in Turkey Vulture sightings between 1990 and 2000 (Raptor Population Index Project 2006). Breeding Bird Survey data, not particularly well suited to monitoring vultures, show a significant increase in numbers since 1966, with the largest increase occurring in the last 25 years (Sauer et al. 2005). New York BBS data, although sparse, show a significant increase of 6.4 percent per year, with most of that increase occurring since 1980 (Sauer et al. 2005). Most of the states surrounding New York show similar increases, and in states and provinces to the northeast, numbers increased markedly after the late 1980s.

The movement of the Turkey Vulture into the Northeast in the early 1900s might have been the result of more roads and more road kill, as well as a burgeoning deer population that produced more carcasses to scavenge (Sutton 1928, Bagg and Parker 1951). The continental population of this bird remained relatively stable during 1940–70, then shifted northward in the East as northern deer populations exploded, persecution from accidental and intentional trapping and shooting declined, and pesticide contamination decreased (Kirk and Mossman 1998).

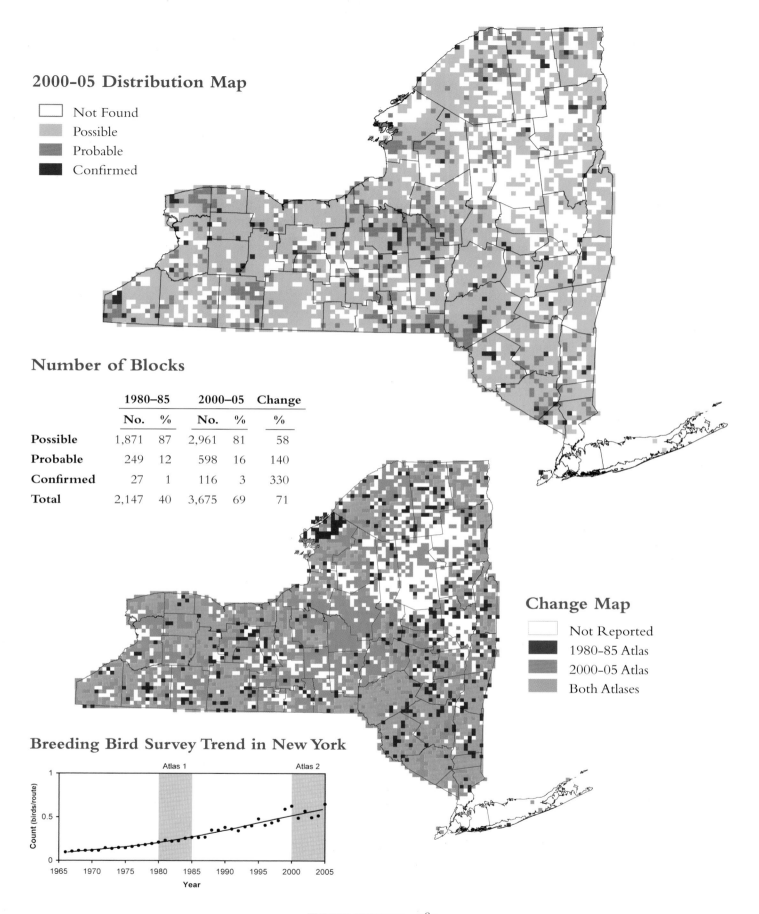

2000–05 Distribution Map

- ☐ Not Found
- Possible
- Probable
- ■ Confirmed

Number of Blocks

	1980–85		2000–05		Change
	No.	%	No.	%	%
Possible	1,871	87	2,961	81	58
Probable	249	12	598	16	140
Confirmed	27	1	116	3	330
Total	2,147	40	3,675	69	71

Change Map

- ☐ Not Reported
- ■ 1980-85 Atlas
- 2000-05 Atlas
- Both Atlases

Breeding Bird Survey Trend in New York

Osprey
Pandion haliaetus

PETER E. NYE

One of North America's best-studied raptors, and a species of worldwide distribution, the "fish hawk" is the only American bird of prey that relies virtually exclusively on live fish. As such, the Osprey is found along coastal and inland waterways with abundant fish populations. An adaptable breeder, it readily uses a variety of man-made structures for nesting, including buildings, buoys, towers, and poles, and will also nest on rocks on the ground. Mostly, however, the Osprey chooses to place its nest in trees, usually dead snags. Although reported to breed in "considerable numbers" in eastern Long Island (especially Plum and then Gardiners islands), by the early 1900s the Osprey no longer bred in interior counties of New York except in parts of the Adirondacks, "where it continues to breed but yearly becomes rarer and rarer on account of the relentless persecution of thoughtless tourists and campers" (Eaton 1914). Chapman (1908) reported 150–200 nesting pairs on Gardiners Island and suggested it might be the largest known colony in the world. Bull's (1974) distribution map of 45 breeding locations mirrored Eaton's earlier account, citing two main breeding areas, the "southeastern section" (mostly eastern Long Island) and the "Adirondack–St. Lawrence valley section." Bull (1974) reported the nadir for Osprey on Gardiners Island occurred in 1962, when only 21 nests there were "active."

The first Atlas described Osprey as "a common breeding species on eastern Long Island" but "still uncommon in the Adirondacks and St. Lawrence River Valley, and rare elsewhere in the state" (Carroll 1988e). The status of Osprey in New York has improved significantly since then. During the second Atlas survey it was reported in 147 percent more blocks; the number of blocks with Confirmed records increased by 163 percent. Outside of the Adirondacks and Coastal Lowlands, three additional clusters of blocks with Confirmed breeding are now apparent. The St. Lawrence River Osprey population has grown over the past three decades and now contains 36 breeding pairs (B. Town pers. comm.). While no nesting was reported in southwestern New York during the first Atlas period, 15 breeding pairs were present in the area in 2006 (NYSDEC unpubl. data). In 1980–87 the Department of Environmental Conservation hacked out 36 Long Island nestlings into the Allegheny Reservoir area. At least 40 pairs of Osprey were present in central-western New York by 2006 (NYSDEC unpubl. data). Osprey also appears to be establishing itself in south-central and southeastern New York, although curiously, Confirmed breeding records there were few. An Osprey rarely establishes a nest site more than 50 km (31 mi) from its natal area, and the species is thus slow to colonize new areas (Poole et al. 2002). Interestingly, the Adirondack Osprey population appears to have remained relatively stable over the past 30 years, with 20–40 breeding pairs identified annually (NYSDEC unpubl. data). On Long Island, Osprey numbers climbed back from below 100 pairs in the late 1960s to nearly 300 pairs since 2000, mirroring the overall statewide increase (NYSDEC unpubl. data). Similar increases have been reported in much of the United States (Poole et al. 2002).

Despite the overall healthy increases in the number of Osprey breeding pairs statewide, problems may be looming on Long Island and particularly on Gardiners Island. Increased nestling predation by the Great Horned Owl, limited nesting sites, and limited food resources are thought to be a concern on Long Island (M. Scheibel pers. comm.). On Gardiners Island, the number of active nesting pairs and young fledged has dropped annually since 1996, believed to be the result of prey limitations, perhaps exacerbated by an increasing population of the Double-crested Cormorant (P. Spitzer pers. comm.). Statewide, electrocution, entanglement with monofilament fishing line, mercury contamination of prey, and a potentially limited food supply will be of continuing concern to Osprey.

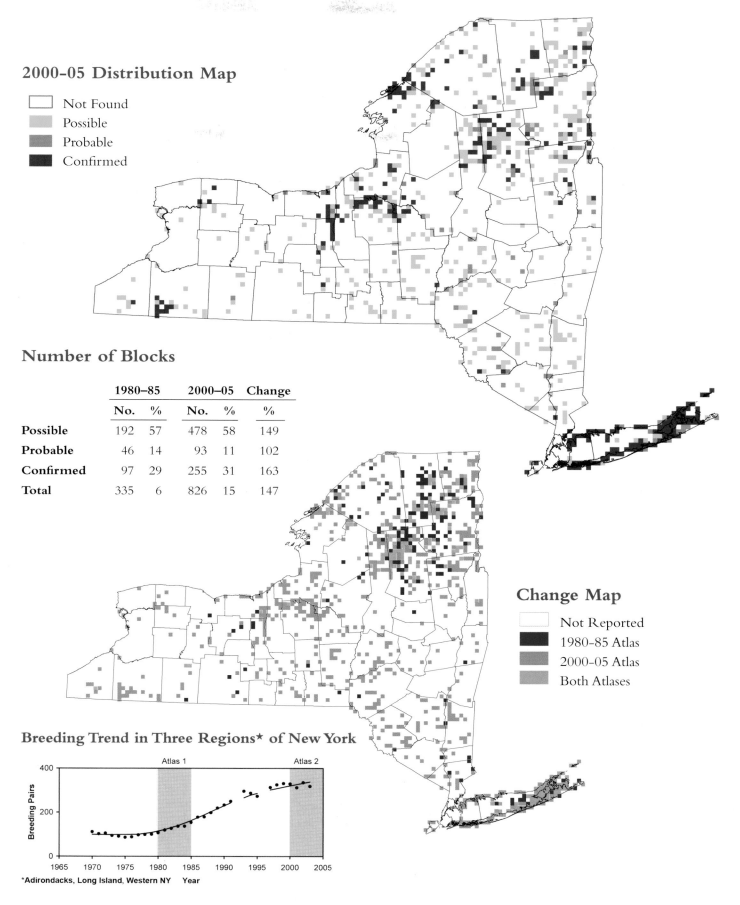

2000–05 Distribution Map

- ☐ Not Found
- Possible
- Probable
- Confirmed

Number of Blocks

	1980–85		2000–05		Change
	No.	%	No.	%	%
Possible	192	57	478	58	149
Probable	46	14	93	11	102
Confirmed	97	29	255	31	163
Total	335	6	826	15	147

Change Map

- ☐ Not Reported
- 1980-85 Atlas
- 2000-05 Atlas
- Both Atlases

Breeding Trend in Three Regions★ of New York

*Adirondacks, Long Island, Western NY   Year

Bald Eagle

Haliaeetus leucocephalus

PETER E. NYE

primarily piscivorous raptor at the top of the food chain, the unmistakable national symbol of the United States has undergone a dramatic change in its breeding population since the first Atlas survey period, both in New York and throughout its range. Found only in North America, the Bald Eagle prefers undisturbed, forested habitat near lakes, rivers, or wetlands, especially complex forested habitats with variable structure containing super-canopy trees. The species is widespread throughout Canada and the United States (with the exception of Hawaii). Rarely reported to nest on the ground or on cliffs (Sherrod et al. 1976, M. Shieldcastle pers. comm.), the Bald Eagle prefers to nest in white pines in New York. Where that tree species is not available, the eagle chooses a variety of deciduous trees, often according to availability and dominance.

Although reported as numerous during the 19th century (Giraud 1844, Mearns 1879), little information is available on the status of the Bald Eagle prior to European settlement. However, the vast forested areas of New York and associated aquatic habitats at this time made the presence of a substantial breeding population likely. Eaton (1914) stated that eagles "formerly nested in many places along the shores of Long Island, along the Hudson, the Great Lakes, the central lakes, the Adirondack lakes and Lake

Champlain," but noted that persecution caused abandonment of many nesting localities. By the mid-20th century this species had almost disappeared from the state, including from the five remaining nesting locations reported by Eaton in 1914 (Lake Ontario, Oneida Lake, Indian Lake, Taylor Pond, and Whelby Pond in Dutchess County), even before the use and effects of DDT drove the species nearly to extirpation. Bull (1974), citing Spofford (1960), reported no nesting success at Montezuma or at Selkirk Shores in Oswego County after 1955.

Because the Bald Eagle was a functionally extirpated species with only one, unproductive breeding pair remaining in 1974, an aggressive restoration program was mounted as part of the New York State Department of Environmental Conservation's early Endangered Species Program. This program included fostering of young (8) and hacking/release of nestlings (198), beginning in 1976 (Nye 1998a). During the first Atlas period, the Bald Eagle was found in fewer than 1 percent of the blocks, with breeding confirmed in only two blocks, in the Appalachian Plateau and the Eastern Ontario Plain. During the second Atlas period, the Bald Eagle was reported in 445 blocks (8 percent), with breeding confirmed in 124, and was distributed throughout the state with the exception of New York City and Long Island. In 2005, NYSDEC confirmed 92 breeding pairs, fledging a total of 112 young (Nye 2005). Remote, undisturbed, protected areas were the first breeding habitats to be reoccupied, including most of New York State's wildlife management areas and national wildlife refuges. Subsequent nests have occurred in other, mostly undisturbed areas with suitable nest trees and fish prey. In contrast to Bull's (1974) distribution map, which showed earlier nesting primarily in northern and western New York, the reestablished population has shown the greatest increases in southeastern New York, with 55 percent of the 2005 pairs found in this region. Interestingly, of the five areas Eaton cites as harboring nesting eagles in the early 1900s, none are currently reoccupied. Although still listed as Threatened in New York and surrounding states, the Bald Eagle was completely delisted federally in 2007 (USFWS 2007).

While eagles still die from shooting, lead poisoning, collisions, and other anthropogenic factors, direct human disturbance and, most importantly, habitat alteration and loss remain the most significant issues for this sensitive species. The status of the Bald Eagle in New York in 2020 will be predicated on how well the habitats the species is currently using are protected.

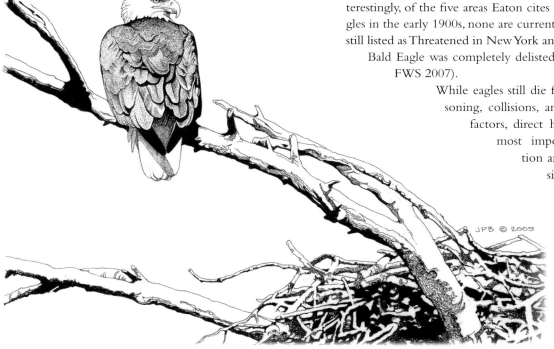

JPB © 2005

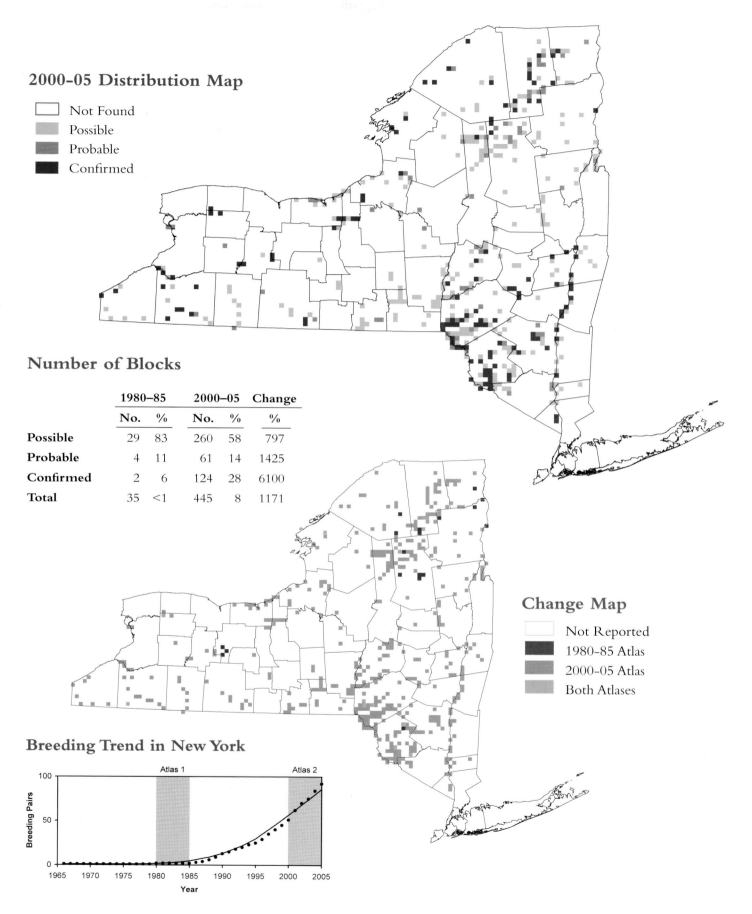

2000-05 Distribution Map

- ☐ Not Found
- Possible
- Probable
- Confirmed

Number of Blocks

	1980–85		2000–05		Change
	No.	%	No.	%	%
Possible	29	83	260	58	797
Probable	4	11	61	14	1425
Confirmed	2	6	124	28	6100
Total	35	<1	445	8	1171

Change Map

- ☐ Not Reported
- 1980-85 Atlas
- 2000-05 Atlas
- Both Atlases

Breeding Trend in New York

Northern Harrier

Circus cyaneus

TIMOTHY J. POST

The Northern Harrier is a hawk of open grasslands, shrublands, and marshes, where it can be seen flying, gliding, or hovering low over the ground while foraging. It breeds across Alaska and Canada, southward to California, Oklahoma, Wisconsin, and Maryland, as well as across Eurasia (MacWhirter and Bildstein 1996). New York is near the southeastern edge of the primary breeding range. The Northern Harrier likely increased its range in New York as forests were cleared by European settlers and converted to agriculture. When these farms were abandoned over the last century, the habitat declined as grass and shrub eventually gave way to young forest (Whitney 1994, Askins 2001). Eaton (1914) considered the Northern Harrier common throughout all parts of the state, from high in the Adirondacks to the lower Hudson Valley and Long Island. Bull (1974) called it common and widespread but declining in numbers. Marsi and Kirch (1998) stated that the harrier was considered a fairly common breeder in New York until the mid-1950s, when the population declined drastically in the state, probably owing in part to the intensive use of pesticides. In New York, the harrier breeds in agricultural, grassland, old field, marsh, and wet meadow habitats.

The first Atlas data showed strong concentrations of the Northern Harrier in the Coastal Lowlands, the St. Lawrence River Valley and extending onto the Eastern Ontario Plain, and across western New York. The second Atlas results showed a similar distribution, although a shift in some of the areas where harriers were found was apparent. Overall, the number of blocks with harriers was similar, with only a 1 percent decrease. Reports declined in the Adirondacks, Coastal Lowlands, St. Lawrence Plains, and Tug Hill Plateau. Increases occurred in the Champlain Valley southward into the northern Hudson Valley, in the Mohawk Valley, and across the Appalachian Plateau. This species needs a relatively large home range in which to forage, and is typically quite easy to detect and identify. Nests, however, are difficult to locate, which resulted in a low number of Confirmed records and a high number of Probable records. The Northern Harrier's large home range means many individuals use more than one Atlas block and might be reported twice, possibly leading to overestimation of distribution. The Atlas results suggest that the Northern Harrier population in New York is relatively stable.

Breeding Bird Survey trends in New York and the Northeast are not statistically meaningful because of deficiencies in the data, but survey-wide the harrier population has declined 1.7 percent per year since 1966 (Sauer et al. 2005). The second Ontario Breeding Bird Atlas reported no significant change in harrier distribution (Bird Studies Canada et al. 2006). Partners in Flight did not include the Northern Harrier as a Watch List or Stewardship species, in part because of its wide distribution (Rich et al. 2004). The Northern Harrier is listed as Threatened in New York, but no bordering states or provinces list it as Endangered or Threatened.

Threats to the Northern Harrier include loss, degradation, and fragmentation of grassland and wetland habitat resulting from succession, intensive agricultural practices, and development. Wetland loss has been slowed by state regulations protecting wetlands and projects to enhance wetlands. However, the suitability of these regulated habitats is reduced as the surrounding upland landscape is converted to inhospitable uses. The timing of mowing of fields where harriers nest is a critical concern; early mowing can result in nest destruction and the death of chicks. Delaying mowing until after chicks have fledged would be highly beneficial. Serrentino (1987) recommended active maintenance of old fields and shrubby habitats through prescribed burning and grazing to prevent reforestation and to maintain harrier breeding populations.

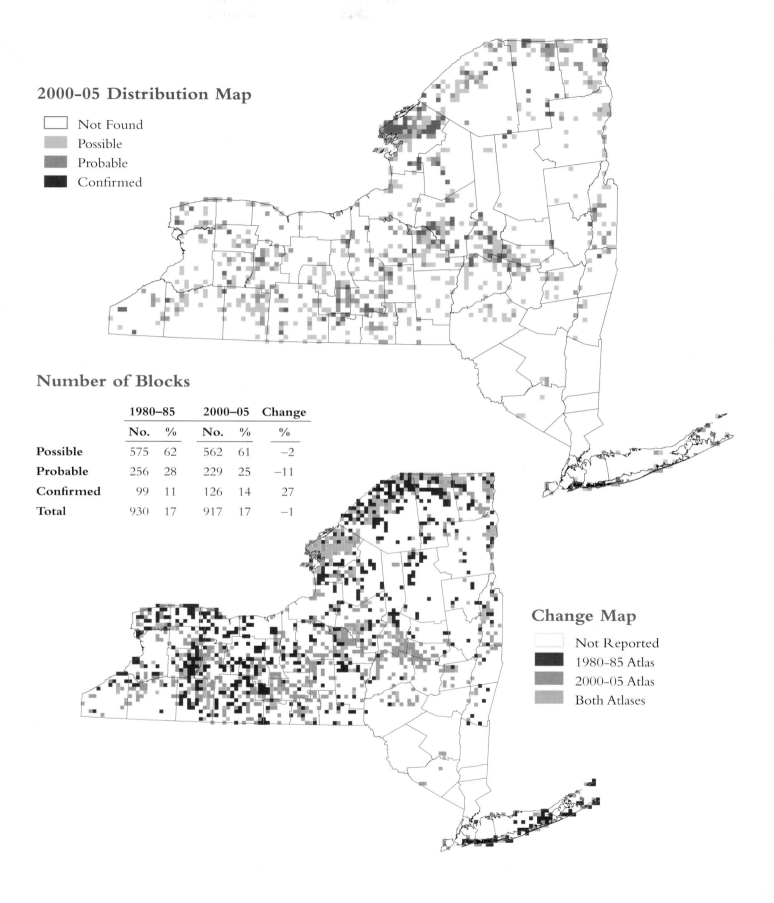

2000-05 Distribution Map

- ☐ Not Found
- Possible
- Probable
- Confirmed

Number of Blocks

	1980–85		2000–05		Change
	No.	%	No.	%	%
Possible	575	62	562	61	−2
Probable	256	28	229	25	−11
Confirmed	99	11	126	14	27
Total	930	17	917	17	−1

Change Map

- ☐ Not Reported
- 1980-85 Atlas
- 2000-05 Atlas
- Both Atlases

Sharp-shinned Hawk
Accipiter striatus

Ralph S. Hames and James D. Lowe

The Sharp-shinned Hawk uses its short rounded wings for active flight and its long tail like a rudder to make lightning-fast surprise attacks (Bildstein and Meyer 2000) on small groups of birds, such as birds at a feeder (Dunn and Tessaglia 1994). This hawk is the smallest of the three North American accipiter species and takes small songbirds almost exclusively (Storer 1966). The Sharp-shinned Hawk breeds along the Appalachians, through the Allegany Plateau, northward to Quebec, Labrador, and Newfoundland, westward to Alaska, southward through the Rockies, along the Pacific Coast, and down the mountainous spine of Mexico. New York is squarely within the eastern range of the species. Although the species is a partial migrant (Bildstein and Meyer 2000), it is found across most of New York throughout the winter (National Audubon Society [2007]). It nests in mixed, coniferous (G. A. Smith 1988b), and deciduous forests (Windsor 1998b, Bildstein and Meyer 2000), but nest sites are most frequently in wooded areas with a dense canopy cover, small-diameter trees, and high number of trees per hectare (Bildstein and Meyer 2000). As a forest bird, the Sharp-shinned Hawk probably was common in New York before European settlement. It managed to persist wherever forest remained, and Eaton (1914) stated that it nested throughout New York. Bull (1974) also suggested that this species nested in wooded habitat throughout the state.

During the first Atlas period, the Sharp-shinned Hawk was distributed across the state. It was present in a large number of blocks in the Adirondacks (193 blocks), the Appalachian Plateau (326), and the Great Lakes Plain (136). The second Atlas survey revealed a statewide increase of 68 percent, although no reports came from the Coastal Lowlands this time. The number of blocks in the Appalachian Plateau increased by 70 percent; the Catskill Highlands, by 114 percent; the Great Lakes Plain, by 120 percent; the Hudson Valley, by 189 percent; the Champlain Valley, by 107 percent; and finally, the Tug Hill Plateau increased by 113 percent. This remarkable increase may be the result of the curtailment of widespread shooting of hawks after legislation was enacted to protect them in 1972, and of the ban on the sale and use of DDT in the United States and Canada, also in 1972 (Bednarz et al. 1990).

Many susceptible raptor species suffered population declines (Bednarz et al. 1990), based on data derived from migration watches, beginning in the late 1940s and continuing through the 1970s (Snyder et al. 1973). The numbers of Sharp-shinned Hawks counted at Hawk Mountain, Pennsylvania, for example, decreased significantly in the period 1950–64 (Snyder et al. 1973) and then increased significantly over the years 1965–86 (Bednarz et al. 1990), although populations were still slowly recovering from the effects of DDT. Elliott and Martin (1994) and Wood et al. (1996) showed DDT and DDE contamination in Sharp-shinned Hawks breeding in Ontario and in migrating hawks in Pennsylvania, although the degree to which this contamination compromised breeding success is not known. In fact, the Sharp-shinned Hawk population experienced strong increases across North America, based on Breeding Bird Survey data, with a significant survey-wide increase of 3.7 percent over the period 1980–2005 (Sauer et al. 2005). BBS data from New York showed a significant 6.3 percent increase from 1966 to 2005 and a nonsignificant 2.2 percent increase from 1980 to 2005 (Sauer et al. 2005). The Christmas Bird Count revealed a 1.7 percent increase per year from 1959 to 1988 (National Audubon Society [2007]). Nevertheless, the Sharp-shinned Hawk remains sensitive to contaminants, such as mercury, which may be magnified in its songbird prey (Hames and Lowe unpubl. data), and it remains a Species of Special Concern in New York.

2000-05 Distribution Map

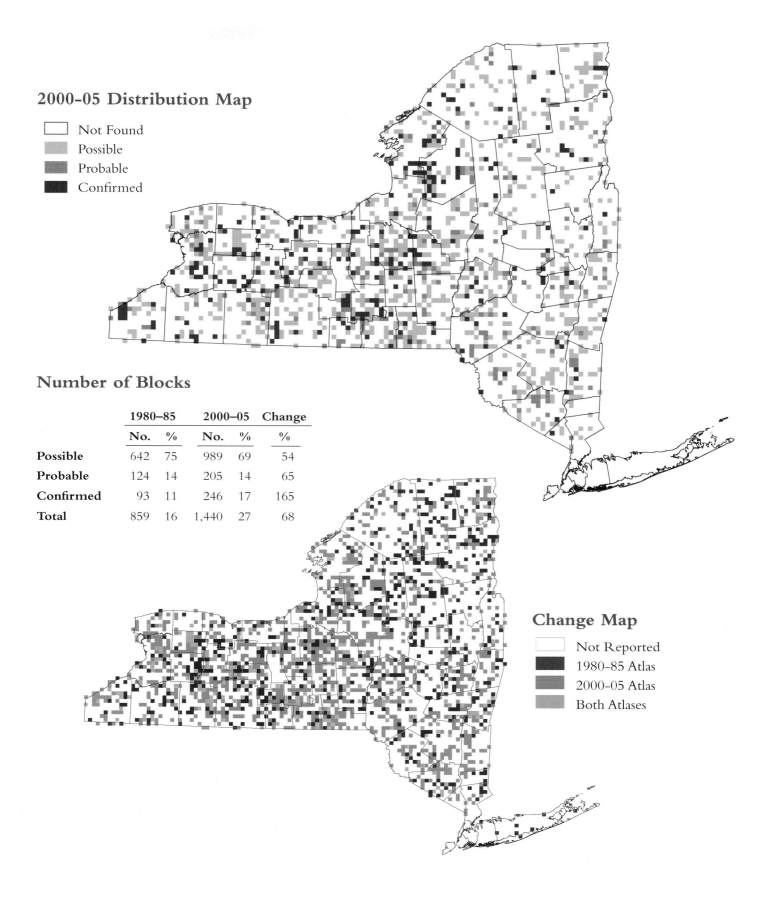

- ☐ Not Found
- Possible
- Probable
- Confirmed

Number of Blocks

	1980–85		2000–05		Change
	No.	%	No.	%	%
Possible	642	75	989	69	54
Probable	124	14	205	14	65
Confirmed	93	11	246	17	165
Total	859	16	1,440	27	68

Change Map

- ☐ Not Reported
- 1980-85 Atlas
- 2000-05 Atlas
- Both Atlases

Cooper's Hawk

Accipiter cooperii

Ralph S. Hames and James D. Lowe

The Cooper's Hawk is a secretive woodland raptor that breeds across North America from southern Canada to Mexico (Curtis et al. 2006). A powerful and agile flyer, it specializes in avian prey (Meng 1959, Bosakowski et al. 1992, but see Bielefeldt et al. 1992), which it takes by stealth, using rapid low-level attacks or by ambush of birds flying near a forest edge (Meng 1951, Curtis et al. 2006). The Cooper's Hawk uses its short, rounded wings for powerful active flight and long tail as a rudder (Curtis et al. 2006), making this hawk capable of full-speed flight through all but the densest forest (R. S. Hames pers. obs.).

The Cooper's Hawk was reviled as the "chicken hawk" for its reputed propensity to raid farmyards (Meng 1959). This reputation resulted in widespread shooting in the East (Curtis et al. 2006). In the late 1940s, Cooper's Hawk populations in New York began a steep decline that was later linked to use of the pesticide DDT (Eaton 1988g, Curtis et al. 2006). Similar declines in migrating hawk numbers were noted at the Hawk Mountain watch in Pennsylvania (Snyder et al. 1973, Bednarz et al. 1990). While prohibitions on the use of DDT in the United States in 1972 allowed this species to rebound, the Cooper's Hawk's main prey includes Neotropical migrants that might be exposed to pesticides on their wintering grounds. Likewise, some of these raptors winter in northern Mexico, where they might be exposed to pesticides that are no longer used in the United States (Curtis et al. 2006). Low-level DDE contamination of Cooper's Hawk tissue samples has been noted as recently as 1989 (Elliott and Martin 1994, Wood et al. 1996), although the effects of such low levels of contaminants are unknown (but see Wood et al. 1996).

In the first Atlas, Cooper's Hawk was reported as widely distributed, occurring in all ecozones but the Coastal and Triassic lowlands. It was especially numerous in the Appalachian Plateau, Adirondacks, and Great Lakes Plain. The second Atlas survey found that the population of this bird had exploded, with an increase in oc-cupied blocks of 146 percent, perhaps to historic levels, after a long period when populations were artificially low as the result of human activities (Curtis et al. 2006). No ecozone showed a decrease in reports, and all but two showed increases greater than 100 percent. The largest increases in the number of occupied blocks were in the Great Lakes Plain (268 percent), Tug Hill Plateau (270 percent), and Hudson Valley (338 percent). A substantial increase was also seen in the Coastal Lowlands, from 0 to 45 blocks. The Adirondack ecozones showed little change.

Breeding Bird Survey data show a significant survey-wide increase of 4 percent per year from 1980 to 2005, and an 8.1 percent increase per year in the Eastern BBS Region, but no significant trend in New York (Sauer et al. 2005). The Christmas Bird Count data show a significant increase of 1.1 percent per year in New York, and an approximate threefold increase in the number of this species seen per party-hour nationwide since 1980 (National Audubon Society [2007]). The Cooper's Hawk remains a Species of Special Concern in New York and a State Endangered Species in New Jersey.

Despite some evidence to the contrary (Bosakowski et al. 1993), the Cooper's Hawk tolerates human activities extremely well, reaching the highest known nesting density in a small town in Wisconsin (Rosenfield et al. 1995) and similar densities in New York (R. S. Hames unpubl. data). The increased feeding of wild birds may well be providing a concentrated food source for this accipiter (Dunn and Tessaglia 1994), including during winter. In fact, analysis of the movement of one radio-tagged female in Tompkins County, New York, suggested she was "trap-lining" feeders in suburban backyards (R. S. Hames unpubl. data). Such behavior bodes well for the future of the Cooper's Hawk in New York.

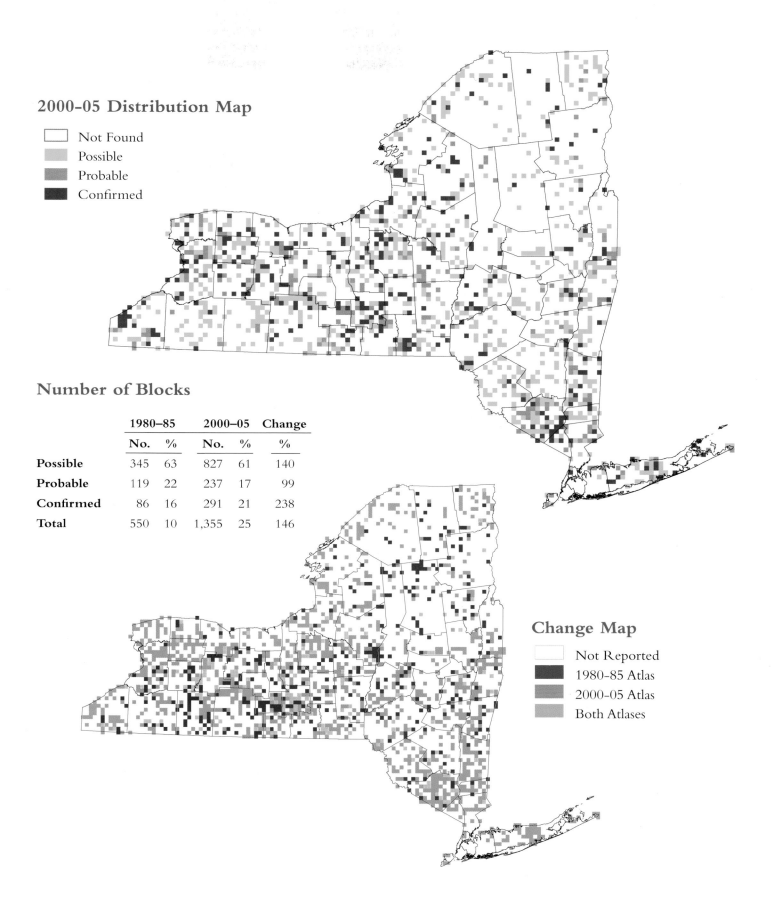

2000–05 Distribution Map

- ☐ Not Found
- Possible
- Probable
- Confirmed

Number of Blocks

	1980–85		2000–05		Change
	No.	%	No.	%	%
Possible	345	63	827	61	140
Probable	119	22	237	17	99
Confirmed	86	16	291	21	238
Total	550	10	1,355	25	146

Change Map

- ☐ Not Reported
- 1980–85 Atlas
- 2000–05 Atlas
- Both Atlases

Northern Goshawk
Accipiter gentilis

SCOTT CROCOLL

The Northern Goshawk is found in boreal and temperate forests across northern North America and Eurasia (Squires and Reynolds 1997). It breeds throughout the boreal forests of Canada and Alaska southward through the western United States to Mexico, and eastward through the forests of the northern United States as far south as West Virginia (Squires and Reynolds 1997). New York is near the southeastern edge of its breeding range. The goshawk nests in mature deciduous, coniferous, and mixed deciduous-coniferous forests with a relatively open understory. In New York it is also found nesting in mature conifer plantations. As a bird of mature forests, it probably was common in New York before European settlement, but its population must have declined precipitously as the forests were cut down. Audubon (1835) mentioned finding a nest along the Niagara River, for the earliest report of breeding in the state. Merriam (1881) and Eaton (1914) noted that the goshawk bred in the Adirondacks, but it was rare even there. Beardslee and Mitchell (1965) cited eggs collected in Erie County in 1908, but then there were no other breeding records in the Niagara region until 1955. Bull (1974) documented a dramatic increase in the number of breeding reports starting in 1952, from four known breeding localities over 117 years to at least 52 in the next 19 years. He stated that the goshawk was found primarily at higher elevations in the Adirondacks, Tug Hill Plateau, Catskills, Taconic Mountains, Finger Lakes Highlands, and Appalachian Plateau.

The first Atlas revealed continued expansion and a widely scattered distribution of the Northern Goshawk across the state. It was absent only along the Lake Erie and Lake Ontario shores and in the New York City and Long Island regions, where suitable extensive forest habitat did not exist. The distribution of records made during the second Atlas period was approximately the same as for the first, although the goshawk was found in 20 percent fewer blocks. Blocks with records decreased in all ecozones where it had been most numerous, and increased only in the Tug Hill Plateau. The number of Confirmed breeding records remained remarkably similar. The reasons for the apparent decline are not clear. Although the goshawk is vocal around its nest, it was undoubtedly under-reported during both Atlas surveys. Concentrations of blocks with records in the first Atlas were the result of a targeted research effort (Eaton 1988l), and many of the local changes seen may well represent differences in coverage rather than changes in goshawk populations.

The continent-wide trend for the Northern Goshawk population is difficult to interpret (Anderson et al. 2005, DeStefano 2005). Breeding Bird Survey data show serious deficiencies in all regions (Sauer et al. 2005). BBS data show a declining trend from 1966 to 2005 in New York, but only six survey routes were used to derive this information, and the detection of this species is very difficult (Sauer et al. 2005). Biologists interviewed in the New England states believed that the Northern Goshawk was distributed widely, although uncommonly, in forested habitat there, but its actual population status is unknown (DeStefano 2005). A petition made to the U.S. Fish and Wildlife Service in 1997 to list the species as Threatened west of the 100th meridian was rejected (Anderson et al. 2005). In New York, the Northern Goshawk is listed as a Species of Special Concern because not enough information exists on its population status, and there is concern for its population stability. The major threats facing this species may be loss of extensive forest habitat in local areas and loss of habitat for major prey species, such as the Ruffed Grouse, whose population has declined 18 percent since the first Atlas survey. Long-term monitoring of nest territories where the Northern Goshawk currently exists and where it has disappeared is warranted, as well as the development of land management regimes that will favor the species and its prey.

© JPB 2004

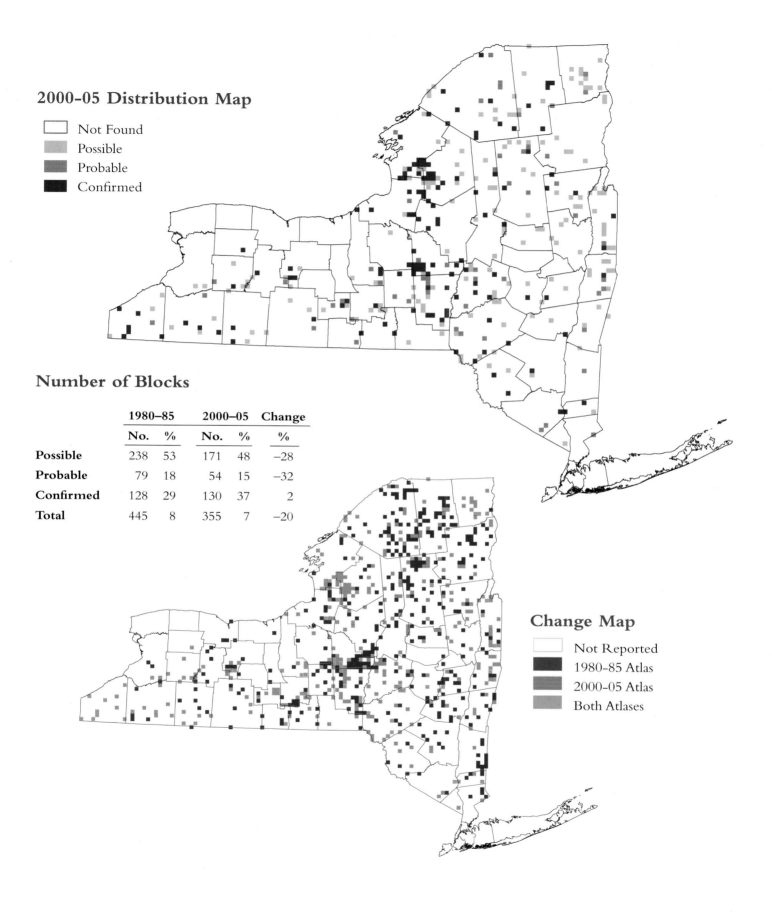

2000-05 Distribution Map

- ☐ Not Found
- ▨ Possible
- ▨ Probable
- ■ Confirmed

Number of Blocks

	1980–85		2000–05		Change
	No.	%	No.	%	%
Possible	238	53	171	48	−28
Probable	79	18	54	15	−32
Confirmed	128	29	130	37	2
Total	445	8	355	7	−20

Change Map

- ☐ Not Reported
- ■ 1980-85 Atlas
- ▨ 2000-05 Atlas
- ▨ Both Atlases

Red-shouldered Hawk

Buteo lineatus

Scott Crocoll

The Red-shouldered Hawk is a bird of extensive, mature mixed forests throughout much of its eastern North American range, and especially likes bottomland hardwood forests, riparian areas, and flooded swamps (Crocoll 1994). It breeds from Minnesota to New Brunswick, southward to eastern Texas and Florida, and in a disjunct population on the Pacific Coast (Crocoll 1994). New York is near the northeastern edge of its breeding range. This bird of mature forests might be expected to have been common in New York before colonization, declining with deforestation in the 19th century and then increasing with the decline in agriculture, but the literature does not support this scenario. The earliest authors called this species rare in the state (DeKay 1844, Giraud 1844, Langille 1884), but in the late 1800s, when deforestation was at its maximum, it was considered a common bird throughout central and western New York (Rathbun 1879, Short 1893, Reed and Wright 1909). Eaton (1914) called it a common breeder throughout New York outside of the Adirondacks, found in patches of woodland remaining along streams and in swampy areas. Its numbers appeared to decline in the mid-1900s, possibly because of pesticides, and it was considered only fairly common by Bull (1974). Red-shouldered Hawk populations were reported to have declined in seven states and in Ontario by the mid-1980s (Crocoll 1994), but those fortunes may have changed. G. A. Smith (1988a) described a change in its distribution and habitat use in New York, with its abandonment of wooded swamps and riparian areas and increased use of extensive forests. Crocoll (1998) also noted increases in heavily wooded upland regions.

The first Atlas showed the Red-shouldered Hawk sparsely distributed over most of the state, with a few reports on the Great Lakes Plain and Coastal Lowlands. It was concentrated primarily in the Appalachian Plateau and Tug Hill Transition. The second Atlas survey revealed a similar distribution but with a 23 percent increase in the number of blocks. As with the first Atlas, this species is scarce to nearly absent on the Great Lakes Plain. It was not reported in the Coastal Lowlands, and the number of reports declined in the Manhattan Hills, Adirondacks, and Champlain Valley. The Coastal Lowlands may have supported a marginal population that was not able to survive human development pressures. The Hudson Valley, along with the former areas of concentration, Catskill Peaks, western Appalachian Plateau, Oswego Lowlands, and Tug Hill Transition, had even more reports in the second Atlas than the first, possibly because of better coverage or more forest habitat maturing to appropriate age.

Survey-wide, Breeding Bird Survey data show a significant 2.7 percent yearly increase over the last 40 years (Sauer et al. 2005). BBS data for New York are sparse, but they show no significant trend. Fall migration data gathered at hawkwatch locations show stable numbers or a slight increasing trend over the last 30 years (C. Farmer pers. comm.). In Ontario, the population has been stable during the last 10 years, although much below historic levels (Crewe and Badzinski 2006). The second Ontario Breeding Bird Atlas reported a slight increase, significant in the Southern Shield region (Bird Studies Canada et al. 2006). The Red-shouldered Hawk is not federally listed, but as of 1994 it was listed as Endangered, Threatened, of Special Concern, or Rare by 12 states (Crocoll 1994). Partners in Flight listed it as a Stewardship Species for the Eastern Avifaunal Biome, but gave it a low combined score, indicating no imminent threat (Rich et al. 2004). In New York, the Red-shouldered Hawk was downlisted from Threatened to Special Concern because its population in the mid-1990s was thought to be stable or increasing statewide. The Red-shouldered Hawk's distribution has not changed dramatically since the mid-1980s, and in fact, the population appears to be increasing.

2000-05 Distribution Map

- ☐ Not Found
- Possible
- Probable
- Confirmed

Number of Blocks

	1980–85		2000–05		Change
	No.	%	No.	%	%
Possible	418	60	440	51	5
Probable	182	26	232	27	27
Confirmed	102	15	193	22	89
Total	702	13	865	16	23

Change Map

- ☐ Not Reported
- 1980-85 Atlas
- 2000-05 Atlas
- Both Atlases

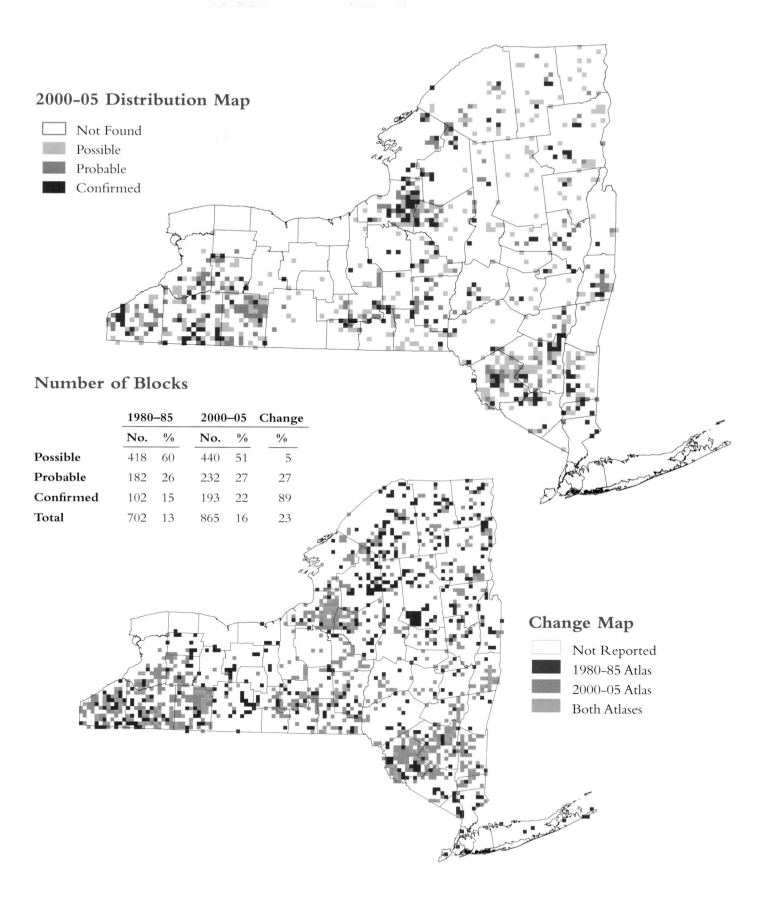

Broad-winged Hawk

Buteo platypterus

SCOTT CROCOLL

The Broad-winged Hawk is a common breeder throughout its range, which includes most of eastern North America from Alberta to Nova Scotia, southward to eastern Texas and northern Florida (Goodrich et al. 1996); it winters in Central and South America. The Broad-winged Hawk nests in extensive mature deciduous or mixed deciduous-coniferous forests (Crocoll and Parker 1989, Goodrich et al. 1996), where it is often seen perched along forested roads or small openings. It can be located when flushed from its perch or by the sounds of begging young. The nest is usually near a small forest opening and a wetland or stream (Crocoll and Parker 1989), but it is seldom found because the hawk tends to be quiet near the nest. As a bird of mature forests, the Broad-winged Hawk was undoubtedly common in New York before European colonization, and its numbers must have declined as the forests were cut down. DeKay (1844) and Giraud (1844) both called it rare. Although Merriam (1881) called it rather common in the Adirondacks, other late-19th-century writers called it uncommon to rare in the central and western parts of the state (Rathbun 1879, Short 1893, Reed and Wright 1909). Eaton (1914) stated that the Broad-winged Hawk was fairly common in the wooded districts, common in the Adirondacks, irregular on Long Island and eastern New York, but nearly unknown in the central and western regions. Beardslee and Mitchell (1965) called the species uncommon in western New York, suggesting an increase there, and Bull (1974) gave its status as a statewide breeder, but local in western New York.

The first Atlas data showed the Broad-winged Hawk distributed across the state in the more forested regions. It was common throughout the Adirondacks, Tug Hill Plateau, Catskills, Taconic Highlands, Hudson Highlands, and Manhattan Hills. It was more thinly distributed across the Appalachian Plateau, Coastal Lowlands, St. Lawrence Plains, and Champlain Valley but was mostly absent from the Great Lakes Plain and Mohawk Valley. The distribution of the Broad-winged Hawk changed little between the Atlas periods. Statewide, the number of blocks with reports increased less than 1 percent. Occurrences declined in the Coastal Lowlands, Manhattan Hills, Hudson Highlands, and St. Lawrence Plains but increased in the Appalachian Plateau, Great Lakes Plain, Tug Hill Plateau, and Mohawk Valley. These changes might be the result of the increasing maturation of forests on the Appalachian Plateau and increasing urban and suburban development in southeastern New York.

The Broad-winged Hawk's population status range-wide is considered to be stable, although recent migration counts (1990–2000) suggest a decline in the eastern portion of its range, where forest fragmentation from clear-cut logging in boreal forests and pesticide misuse have been suggested as possible threats (Farmer 2006). Breeding Bird Surveys typically detect low numbers of Broad-winged Hawk, making the data "deficient" in nearly all regions, but BBS data show a significant increase in hawk numbers continent-wide since 1966; the positive trend in New York is not statistically significant (Sauer et al. 2007). Though forests in New York have matured between Atlas periods and thus provided more potential habitat for the Broad-winged Hawk, a corresponding population increase has not occurred; it is possible that some unknown factor in its wintering grounds is preventing a population increase here.

The Broad-winged Hawk has no current listing, but there is serious concern for the survival of the Caribbean subspecies. Basic research still needs to be collected on its home-range size and the minimum forest size necessary for population stability (Goodrich et al. 1996). Additional research is needed to develop accurate survey methods for this and other woodland raptors (Titus et al. 1989).

200

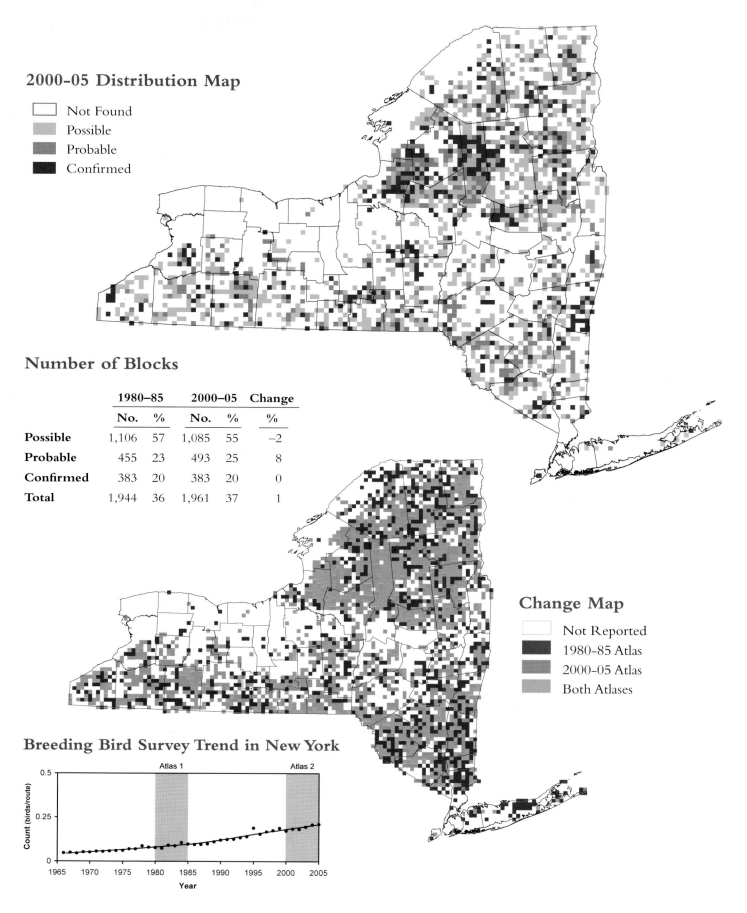

2000–05 Distribution Map

- ☐ Not Found
- Possible
- Probable
- Confirmed

Number of Blocks

	1980–85		2000–05		Change
	No.	%	No.	%	%
Possible	1,106	57	1,085	55	−2
Probable	455	23	493	25	8
Confirmed	383	20	383	20	0
Total	1,944	36	1,961	37	1

Change Map

- ☐ Not Reported
- 1980-85 Atlas
- 2000-05 Atlas
- Both Atlases

Breeding Bird Survey Trend in New York

Red-tailed Hawk

Buteo jamaicensis

Scott Crocoll

The Red-tailed Hawk is likely the most conspicuous raptor in New York and one of the most commonly observed in North America. Adult birds are confidently identified by their rufous-colored tail feathers by birders of all skill levels. This hawk breeds over almost all of North America north of Mexico, southward into the Caribbean and through Central America (Preston and Beane 1993). It generally uses open habitats interspersed with forest of varying sizes, or where other structures useful for nesting are found, including power poles and cactus (Preston and Beane 1993, Preston 2000). Commonly seen perched on trees, power poles, and fences along roadways, this species appears to be tolerant of human modification of its habitat, nesting equally successfully in rural, suburban, and urban settings (Preston 2000). This bird of open areas was probably less common before European settlement of New York. As the forests were removed, the resulting open agricultural land became more favorable for this hawk, and populations probably increased. Early authors considered it a common resident in most parts of the state by the late 19th century (Rathbun 1879, Merriam 1881, Short 1893, Reed and Wright 1909). Eaton (1914) said it was common throughout the state, nesting more in the hills than in the swamps. Bull (1974) listed it as a widespread breeder, nesting mostly in open country, but also in the Adirondacks and Long Island pine-oak barrens if forest openings were present.

The first Atlas data showed the Red-tailed Hawk to be widespread across the state, missing only from the heavily urbanized areas around New York City and the heavily forested areas of the Adirondacks, Catskills, and Tug Hill Plateau. The second Atlas results revealed a 6 percent increase in the number of blocks with records of this hawk. Again, it was found across the state, with gaps still apparent in the Adirondacks and Tug Hill Plateau, but it was found in more blocks in the New

York City metropolitan area and the Catskills. The Adirondacks was the only ecozone showing a decline, a 15 percent drop. The Red-tailed Hawk's current distribution is not surprising, given its affinity for forest land associated with extensive areas of open habitat. Because of its preference for open areas for feeding, it is also not surprising that it is much less common in the continuously forested regions of New York. It is, however, surprising that the hawk expanded its range into the New York City area. The reasons for this change are not apparent.

Continentally, the Red-tailed Hawk has expanded its range during the last century as a result of deforestation and fire suppression in the West (Preston and Beane 1993, Preston 2000). This expansion has resulted in the Red-tailed Hawk replacing the Red-shouldered Hawk in portions of eastern North America, and Swainson's and Ferruginous hawks in portions of the Great Plains. Breeding Bird Survey data for the Red-tailed Hawk show significant increases since 1966 across the survey area and in the north Atlantic states (USFWS Region 5), but no significant trend in New York (Sauer et al. 2005). BBS trend maps indicate increases in the eastern portion of New York and declines from the Finger Lakes westward for the period 1996–2003. Most of the surrounding states showed an increasing trend for the same period. The second Ontario Breeding Bird Atlas reported no significant change in Red-tailed Hawk numbers (Bird Studies Canada et al. 2006).

The Red-tailed Hawk is not listed either at the federal level or at the state level, and Partners in Flight gave it the lowest combined score of any North American hawk (Rich et al. 2004). Its population in New York is probably secure, although as the forests in the state continue to mature and agricultural land continues to disappear (see Chapter 4), suitable habitat for this species will decline, possibly bringing some reductions in Red-tailed Hawk numbers as well.

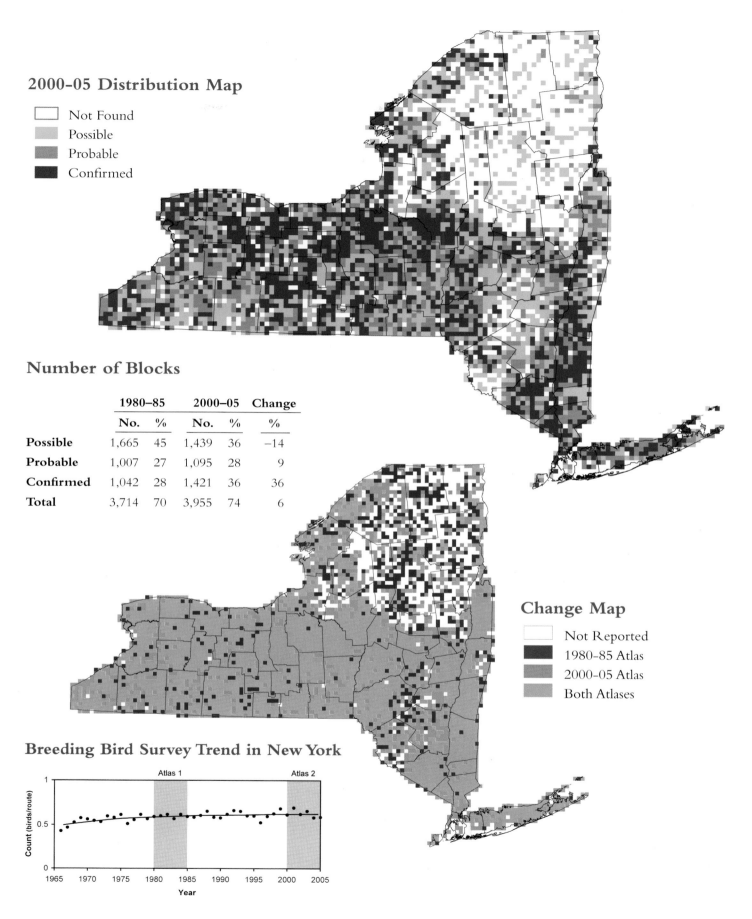

2000-05 Distribution Map

- ☐ Not Found
- Possible
- Probable
- Confirmed

Number of Blocks

	1980–85		2000–05		Change
	No.	%	No.	%	%
Possible	1,665	45	1,439	36	−14
Probable	1,007	27	1,095	28	9
Confirmed	1,042	28	1,421	36	36
Total	3,714	70	3,955	74	6

Change Map

- ☐ Not Reported
- 1980-85 Atlas
- 2000-05 Atlas
- Both Atlases

Breeding Bird Survey Trend in New York

Golden Eagle
Aquila chrysaetos

PETER E. NYE

Largely a bird of open country where it can hunt small mammals, and one of only two North American breeding eagles, this holarctic species breeds primarily in northern Canada and in the western United States. It is an uncommon breeder in eastern Canada and is now extirpated as a breeder in the eastern United States (Nye 1998b). Never common in the eastern United States, the Golden Eagle did breed occasionally at probably fewer than two-dozen sites in New York and New England during the 20th century (NYSDEC unpubl. data), although productivity was extremely sporadic (Spofford 1971a). Historical nesting has been confirmed in Maine, New Hampshire, New York, and Vermont (Todd 1989). The Golden Eagle appears to prefer cliff nesting sites overlooking water. Spofford (1971b) remarked that "the only nest of the golden eagle reported in New York State prior to 1900 was one noted by Audubon in 1833," active for eight successive years and believed to have been on Storm King Mountain near West Point. Eaton (1914) listed the Golden Eagle as "never common in New York" and "as an accidental, rare transient visitant" even though at that time, considerable, suitable open-country habitat existed after extensive logging of the 19th century. Eaton also asserted, without supporting evidence or locations, that the Golden Eagle "undoubtedly nested in the Highlands, Catskills and Adirondacks in early colonial days, but at the present time there seems to be no evidence of its nesting within our borders." Bull (1974) reiterated these probable former breeding locations, but stated of them, "in all instances without certain proof." Information concerning recent nesting of the Golden Eagle in New York comes from Greenleaf Chase (pers. comm. and NYSDEC unpubl. data) and from Walter Spofford (1971a and pers. comm.), who indicated that at least one nest site was known dating back to 1915.

In New York, six nesting sites are known from the 20th century, all within the Adirondack region. Four of these nest sites were on cliff ledges, most often overlooking mountain lakes, while two were in trees, both in a white pine (NYSDEC unpubl. data). The last confirmed successful nesting in New York occurred in Hamilton County in 1970. A more recent nesting attempt (eggs laid) was made at the same site by a pair in 1979, although no young were hatched (Nye and Loucks 1996). This was the last nesting attempt known for the Golden Eagle in New York.

The first Atlas reported only six Possible and two Probable breeding records for the Golden Eagle. Seven of these records came from the Central Adirondacks in the vicinity of the last confirmed nesting site (Carroll 1988b). The second Atlas survey tallied nine Possible records, mostly from the Central Adirondacks and Appalachian Plateau. Despite intensive searches by New York State Department of Environmental Conservation staff and others, breeding-season sightings of an adult Golden Eagle are extremely rare. In February 1993 a pair that annually wintered in Dutchess County built a nest in a white pine in early March but abandoned it and migrated north as usual in late March, as occasionally happens with wintering eagles. Migrant and wintering eagles have become more numerous, and the population appears to be continuing to increase. It is believed that all eagles of this species currently observed in New York hail from eastern Canada.

With ever-declining open habitats, prospects for future Golden Eagle breeding in New York, or elsewhere in the Northeast, are bleak. Twenty eagles, mostly immatures, have been recovered in New York since 1969, with 13 found dead and 7 found alive (NYSDEC unpubl. data). Most recoveries are made in spring (7) and fall (10). Traps and lead poisoning are the leading causes of morbidity/mortality, followed by shooting, vehicle collisions, and electrocution. Lead poisoning, believed from eating unrecovered upland game shot with toxic lead, will continue to be an issue for this species and others that scavenge on upland game.

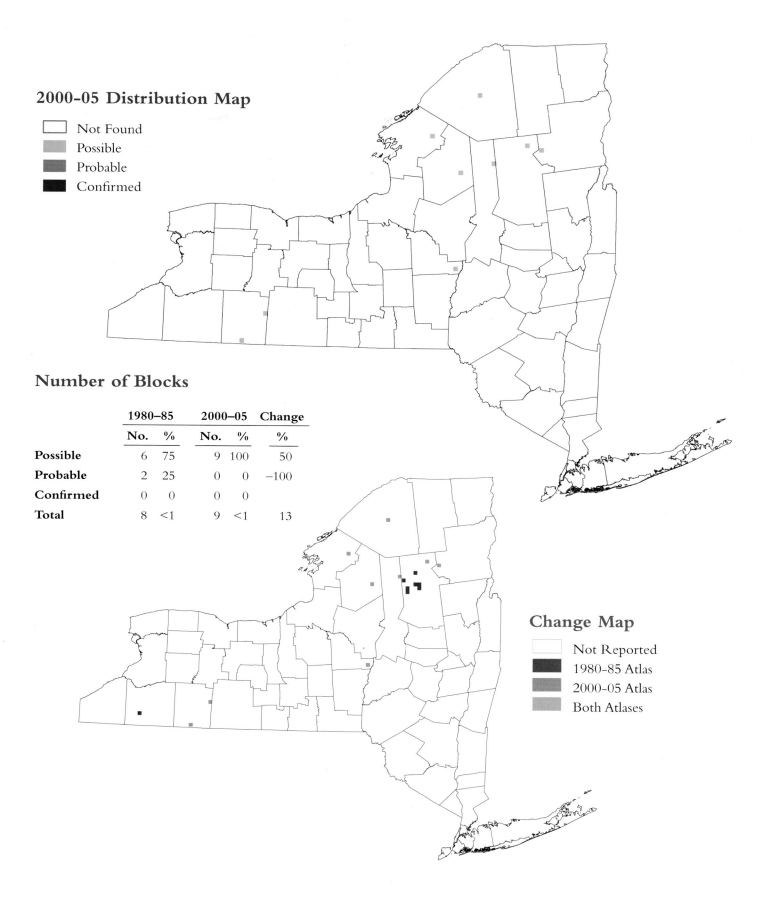

2000–05 Distribution Map

- ☐ Not Found
- Possible
- Probable
- Confirmed

Number of Blocks

| | 1980–85 | | 2000–05 | | Change |
	No.	%	No.	%	%
Possible	6	75	9	100	50
Probable	2	25	0	0	−100
Confirmed	0	0	0	0	
Total	8	<1	9	<1	13

Change Map

- ☐ Not Reported
- 1980-85 Atlas
- 2000-05 Atlas
- Both Atlases

American Kestrel
Falco sparverius

PETER E. NYE

The smallest falcon in North America, the American Kestrel is one of the most obvious diurnal raptors, readily recognized as it hovers over fields in search of prey. Previously known as the Sparrow Hawk, it is the most numerous and widespread falcon in North America. It is a breeder and winter resident from coast to coast and from Alaska to Central America (Smallwood and Bird 2002). Although the kestrel is often seen hovering, it more often hunts from a perch; dead trees fill this need while also providing nesting cavities. As an obligate secondary-cavity nester, the kestrel requires woodpecker holes or other natural cavities for its nest sites, but it also uses artificial nest boxes or nooks and crannies in buildings (Smallwood and Bird 2002). A raptor of open country, the kestrel prefers pastures, fallowed fields, and open patches with short vegetation for foraging, to pursue its prey, terrestrial arthropods and small vertebrates. Although the kestrel may have been scarce in New York before European settlers cut the extensive forests, it has long been widespread in the state in the summer (Eaton 1914). Bull (1974) indicated that the kestrel was common in all open country, including airports, golf courses, and parks, as well as other urban-suburban areas.

The first Atlas reported observations of the American Kestrel statewide except in the heavily forested areas, including the high peaks of the Catskills, Allegany Hills, Central Tug Hill, and Adirondacks. Changes between the first and second Atlas periods are minor but reflect a 14 percent decline in the number of occupied blocks, with fewer records in all three breeding categories. There appears to have been a loss in the Coastal Lowlands, lower Hudson Valley, Manhattan Hills, Hudson Highlands, and Triassic Lowlands. This falcon also appears to have retreated from the periphery of the Adirondacks. Otherwise, the statewide distribution appears similar between the two Atlas surveys.

That a decline may be underway in New York is not surprising, as more of the kestrel's favored habitat disappears from the landscape each year. While the 18th and 19th centuries saw major increases in this species because of deforestation and agriculture (Smallwood and Bird 2002), the trend in New York and elsewhere in the Northeast has recently been just the opposite, owing to a loss of open lands, extensive reforestation, urbanization, and residential development. Together, these factors have resulted in significantly less suitable habitat for kestrels. Further, the availability of nesting cavities appears to limit American Kestrel populations in many parts of its breeding range (Balgooyen 1976), a problem partially ameliorated by the placement of artificial nesting boxes, which are readily used when in a suitable habitat (Smallwood and Collopy 1993). While the Breeding Bird Survey detected significant increases in kestrel numbers from 1966 to 2005 in much of the Midwest and central United States, significant declines were noted in southern New England and the Northeast, including New York, and the continental trend is negative (Sauer et al. 2007). Also, although Partners in Flight ranks the American Kestrel as essentially "stable" on a continental basis, concern is expressed within all four of the Bird Conservation Regions in New York (Panjabi et al. 2005).

For now, the American Kestrel remains fairly numerous, widespread, and secure in New York. However, habitat alteration and loss trends are expected to continue. A key to a secure future for this species may be in a concerted effort to place nest boxes in remaining suitable habitats. As the miles of highways and numbers of vehicles continue to climb, mortality from vehicle collisions will take an increasing toll. Additionally, habitat management efforts designed to hold vegetative succession at bay, such as is now being done for the Karner blue butterfly, bog turtle, and grassland birds, will not only help the kestrel but also be critical to its future in New York.

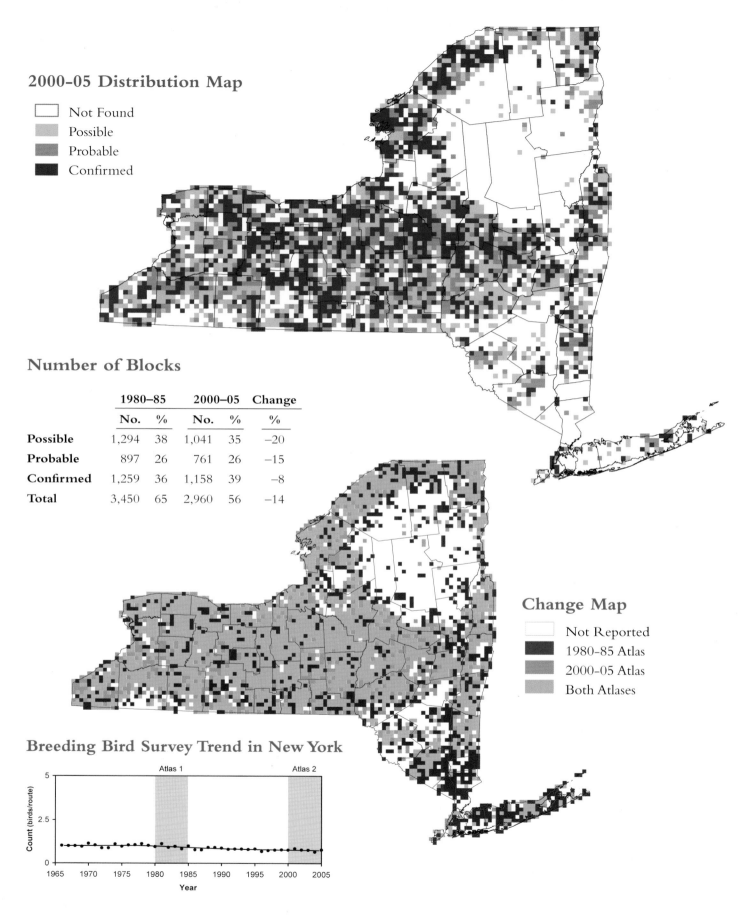

2000–05 Distribution Map

- ☐ Not Found
- Possible
- Probable
- Confirmed

Number of Blocks

	1980–85		2000–05		Change
	No.	%	No.	%	%
Possible	1,294	38	1,041	35	−20
Probable	897	26	761	26	−15
Confirmed	1,259	36	1,158	39	−8
Total	3,450	65	2,960	56	−14

Change Map

- ☐ Not Reported
- 1980–85 Atlas
- 2000–05 Atlas
- Both Atlases

Breeding Bird Survey Trend in New York

Merlin

Falco columbarius

KEVIN J. MCGOWAN

A small, bird-eating falcon of northern forests and prairies, the Merlin is found across the northern reaches of North America and Eurasia, southward to the northern United States. New York is at the very southern edge of its current eastern breeding range. The Merlin breeds in open areas with scattered trees, in woodlots, in forests near openings, and in open boreal forest, often near water (Warkentin et al. 2005). Although it is known to nest on the ground, it typically nests in trees, using the old nests of other birds. DeKay (1844) did not know the Merlin as a breeder in New York. Merriam (1881) called it rare in the Adirondacks but thought it must breed there. Eaton (1914) also believed the species bred in New York but indicated that the evidence was inconclusive. Bull (1974) discounted all reports of breeding for lack of concrete evidence. He noted that the report accepted by Beardslee and Mitchell (1965) from Monroe County (not Genesee County, as stated by Bull) sounded more like an American Kestrel than a Merlin. The two nesting reports from Ontario County mentioned by Eaton (1914) also seem unlikely, but the one from Herkimer County, and especially the sighting of a young fledgling in eastern Hamilton County, might have been accurate (Spahn 1998c).

Merlin was not found during the first Atlas survey. Some sightings in the Adirondacks during 1980–85, including recently fledged young seen on Cascade Mountain in Essex County in 1985, unfortunately were not reported to Atlas personnel (Spahn 1998c). The first verified nesting in New York occurred near Saranac Lake in 1992 (Montgomery 1992). Nesting has been confirmed in the Adirondacks each year since the first discovery (Spahn 1998c).

The extent of the breeding range in New York outlined by the second Atlas survey was surprisingly large. Merlin was found throughout the Adirondacks, Champlain Valley, and onto the St. Lawrence Plains. Breeding was not restricted to the Adirondacks, though, with sightings recorded in 28 blocks outside of that area, primarily in urban areas. Nesting was confirmed for the first time outside the Adirondacks in 2003, in a cemetery in Binghamton (Petuh 2003), but probably occurred in that area at least the year before, as a fledgling Merlin was taken to a local wildlife rehabilitator and photographed. Breeding was also confirmed in urban settings in Cortland, Ithaca, Rochester, Buffalo, and Salamanca. Fortunately, the species is not shy, is not deterred by people, and is noisy when feeding at the nest, so detection was not difficult.

Merlin populations declined across North America through the middle of the 20th century as a result of the use of pesticides (Warkentin et al. 2005). Populations began increasing in the 1960s, and at the same time the breeding range expanded into the northern Great Plains (Warkentin et al. 2005). During this expansion the Merlin began moving into urban areas to breed. It expanded its breeding range into northern New York and northern New England during 1992–2004, and now it is breeding virtually statewide in Maine (Warkentin et al. 2005). Merlin was found in small numbers across Ontario in the 1980s (Peck and James 1983), but the second Ontario Breeding Bird Atlas reported significant increases all across the province (Bird Studies Canada et al. 2006). Merlin was found across southern Ontario from the New York border of Jefferson and St. Lawrence counties westward to the Upper Peninsula of Michigan, in roughly a band connecting to the Adirondack population. Warkentin et al. (2005) suggested that urban nesting was a key factor in the expansion of Merlin into New England, but the appearance and establishment of the Adirondack Merlin population clearly was not assisted by urban nesting. The Merlin does appear well on its way to being a common urban nester in the rest of New York, however, and the results of the next Atlas project should prove very interesting.

2000-05 Distribution Map

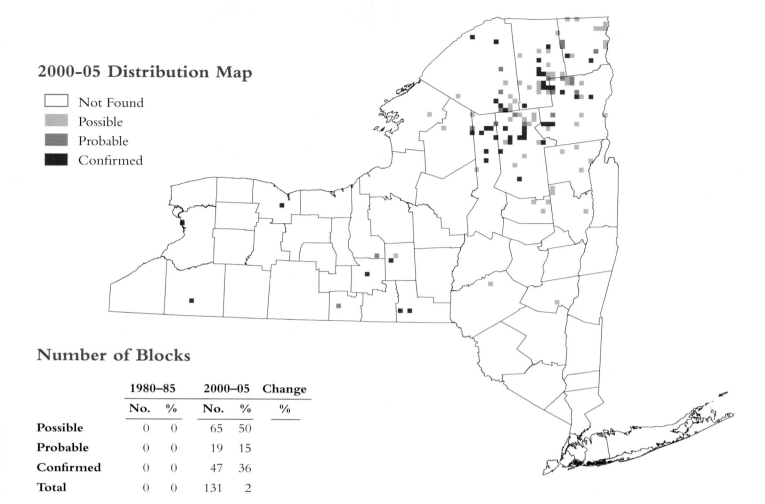

- ☐ Not Found
- Possible
- Probable
- Confirmed

Number of Blocks

	1980–85		2000–05		Change
	No.	%	No.	%	%
Possible	0	0	65	50	
Probable	0	0	19	15	
Confirmed	0	0	47	36	
Total	0	0	131	2	

Peregrine Falcon
Falco peregrinus

Barbara Allen Loucks

The Peregrine Falcon is one of the most widely distributed bird species in the world, occurring and breeding on all continents but Antarctica. In North America it is patchily distributed across the continent, breeding from Alaska, northern Canada, and Greenland southward to Georgia in the East and Mexico in the West (White et al. 2002). It once occupied roughly 400 cliffs in eastern North America (Hickey 1942). Before the 1950s, about 50 pairs were thought to be present in New York State, mainly at cliffs but also at a few buildings and bridges (Bull 1974, NYSDEC unpubl. data). The peregrine's largely avian diet led to trouble with pesticide poisoning, and by the early 1960s it disappeared as a breeder from its eastern haunts. Bull (1974) described this bird as an extirpated local breeder with 42 former nest sites, mainly in the Adirondacks and Hudson Valley. Thanks to an intensive widespread restoration program started by The Peregrine Fund, and carried out with state agencies and the U.S. Fish and Wildlife Service, the Peregrine Falcon has made a remarkable range-wide recovery (Cade et al. 1988, Loucks 1998, Cade and Burnham 2003). The peregrine returned to New York State as a nesting species in 1983.

During the first Atlas survey, the Peregrine Falcon was confirmed breeding in just four blocks: two in New York City and two in the Adirondack High Peaks. The population has undergone remarkable growth since then, with breeding confirmed in 68 blocks during the second Atlas survey. The Adirondack High Peaks population increased and expanded into the Eastern Adirondack Foothills and Champlain Valley. The New York City population also increased and expanded northward into the Shawangunk Hills, Catskill Peaks, and Hudson Valley, where the species has nested on every major Hudson River bridge north to Albany. Urban peregrines were also found breeding in Niagara Falls, Buffalo, Rochester, Syracuse, and Binghamton. In 2006 the New York State Department of Environmental Conservation reported 62 territorial pairs, 52 breeding pairs, and 96 young produced. More remote, cliff-nesting pairs may have gone undetected. In 2006, new pairs were reported in the St. Lawrence Plains and Schoharie Hills, further expanding the distribution in the state. Although Peregrine Falcon populations have increased in all neighboring states and provinces, New York has the largest population in the East.

About half of New York's nests are on cliffs and half on artificial structures, usually buildings or bridges. More recently, tower platforms designed specifically for peregrines, power-plant stacks, and Osprey nesting platforms have all been used successfully. Many of the urban sites, especially those on bridges, are vulnerable to disturbance. The New York City Department of Environmental Protection cooperates with NYSDEC, and together with bridge authorities and building management they ensure that necessary maintenance and other work takes place in a manner that avoids disturbing the falcons during the nesting season (Loucks and Nadareski 2005).

Although some pairs exhibit remarkable tolerance for nearby human activity—one pair nested successfully for two consecutive years on a cliff in an active quarry—others appear to need a buffer. Cooperation and assistance from recreational and professional rock climbers in respecting seasonal cliff closures at a handful of particularly popular areas have been instrumental in helping to protect nesting falcons in the Adirondack High Peaks and Shawangunk Hills areas.

The Peregrine Falcon was removed from the federal endangered species list in 1999 and will likely be reclassified from Endangered to Threatened in New York in the next revision of the state list. Suitable habitat still exists for further range expansion. Where and when the population might reach a plateau in New York is unknown. Continued protection and management are warranted to promote the Peregrine Falcon's successful recovery.

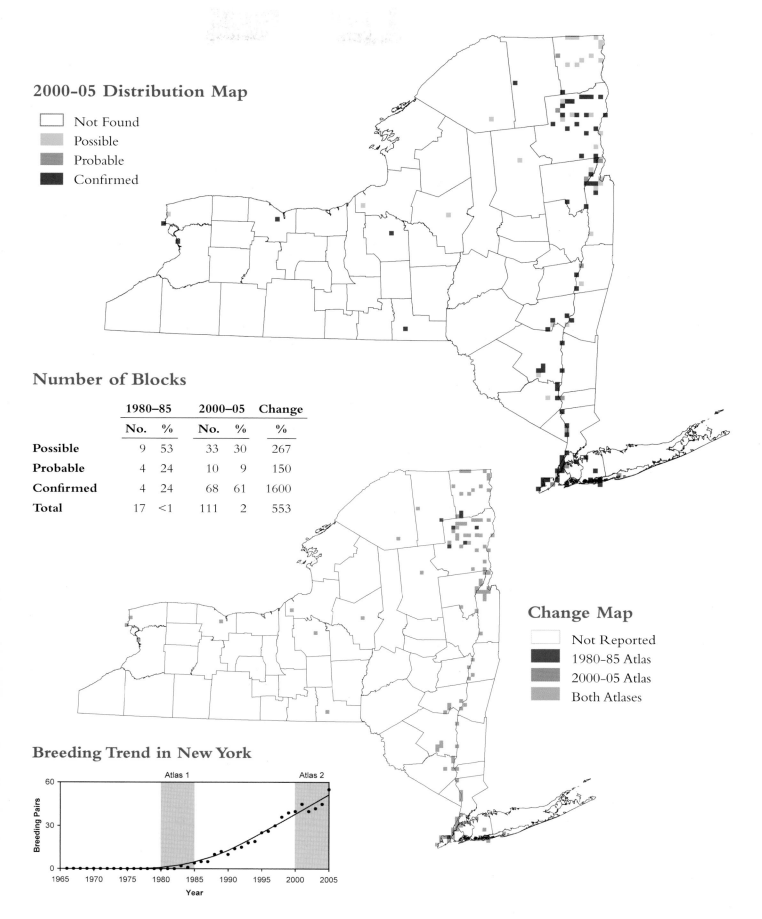

2000-05 Distribution Map

- ☐ Not Found
- Possible
- Probable
- Confirmed

Number of Blocks

	1980–85		2000–05		Change
	No.	%	No.	%	%
Possible	9	53	33	30	267
Probable	4	24	10	9	150
Confirmed	4	24	68	61	1600
Total	17	<1	111	2	553

Change Map

- ☐ Not Reported
- 1980-85 Atlas
- 2000-05 Atlas
- Both Atlases

Breeding Trend in New York

Rails at Montezuma National Wildlife Refuge

Every April numerous Virginia Rails, American Coots, and Common Moorhens return to the Montezuma National Wildlife Refuge to breed and raise young. Moorhens are commonly seen throughout the marsh; however, spotting a Virginia Rail requires great patience and good luck.

212

Black Rail

Laterallus jamaicensis

MATTHEW D. MEDLER

The Black Rail is the smallest rail in North America and one of New York's rarest breeding birds. Patchily distributed throughout the Americas, in North America it breeds irregularly along sections of the Atlantic Coast, Gulf Coast, and Pacific Coast, along part of the lower Colorado River, and at isolated inland sites from Kansas to Ohio (AOU 1998). New York represents the northern limit of the Atlantic Coast population, which stretches southward to Florida (AOU 1998). This species nests in salt marshes, shallow freshwater marshes, wet meadows, and flooded grassy areas (Eddleman et al. 1994). It favors the high portions of marshes and, compared to other North American rails, breeds in sites with shallower water (Eddleman et al. 1988). In New York, the Black Rail occurs in coastal salt marshes, where it has been confirmed breeding in saltmeadow cordgrass (Bull 1964) and suspected of breeding in saltwater cordgrass (Post and Enders 1969). DeKay (1844) listed the Black Rail as an extralimital species, occurring as far north as New Jersey. Eaton (1910) was aware of only five specimens from New York, but based on breeding records from New Jersey and Connecticut, he had little doubt that it bred on Long Island and perhaps in the Hudson Valley and western New York. Despite suspected breeding reported by Eaton (1910) and Griscom (1923), it was not until 1937 that Carleton confirmed Black Rail breeding in New York State with the discovery of a nest with eggs at Oak Beach, Suffolk County (Bull 1964). With only two other records of confirmed nesting in the state, both from southern Nassau County and the last in 1940, Bull (1974) described the Black Rail as rare to uncommon and restricted to the south shore of Long Island.

During the first Atlas survey, the Black Rail was found only at Oak Beach. In subsequent years, summer reports came from several Long Island sites (Able 1998), but during the second Atlas survey, the Black Rail was again reported only from Oak Beach. In addition to the Long Island records between the two Atlas periods, there were two other notable records of this species: the state's first summer record away from Long Island, at the Marshlands Conservancy, Westchester County, in June 1986 (NYSARC 1987); and the state's first inland summer record, at Perch River Wildlife Management Area, Jefferson County, in June 1996 (NYSARC 1999). This latter, unexpected record demonstrates some degree of conspicuousness in this species. But, as with all secretive marsh birds, it is possible that the diminutive Black Rail was overlooked by Atlas observers.

The Black Rail is listed as Endangered in New York and Threatened in New Jersey. Although it is more common in New Jersey, its population has declined there, especially in its southern New Jersey stronghold (Walsh et al. 1999). Post and Enders (1969), who studied this species at an unditched salt marsh at Oak Beach, suggested that the lack of any records of summering Black Rail in New York between 1940 and 1968 might have been related to the ditching of salt marshes for mosquito control. They postulated that this species might have been attracted to Oak Beach by a superior food supply resulting from a lack of marsh ditching (Post and Enders 1969). The spread of common reed into the higher portions of salt marshes can also degrade Black Rail habitat (Eddleman et al. 1994), but at least at Oak Beach, where the reed has been common since the 1950s, the rail can apparently tolerate this invasive plant (Post and Enders 1969). Even there, though, Black Rail is not reported every year, and with no confirmed breeding records in the state in more than 65 years, this bird's status as a breeding bird in New York seems tenuous at best.

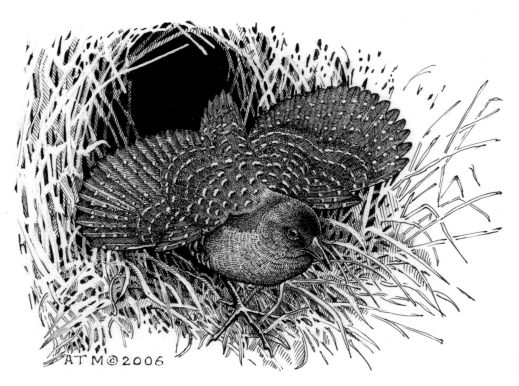

2000-05 Distribution Map

- ☐ Not Found
- Possible
- Probable
- Confirmed

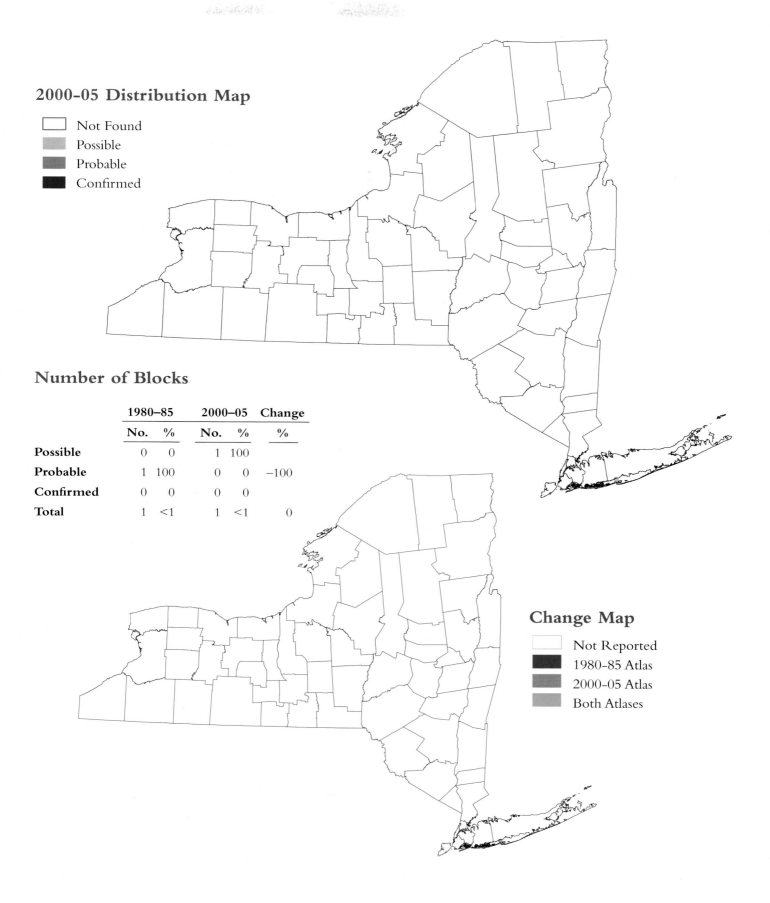

Number of Blocks

	1980–85		2000–05		Change
	No.	%	No.	%	%
Possible	0	0	1	100	
Probable	1	100	0	0	−100
Confirmed	0	0	0	0	
Total	1	<1	1	<1	0

Change Map

- ☐ Not Reported
- 1980-85 Atlas
- 2000-05 Atlas
- Both Atlases

Clapper Rail

Rallus longirostris

Matthew D. Medler

The Clapper Rail is a common species in the salt marshes of the eastern United States, breeding along the Atlantic and Gulf coasts from Massachusetts to southern Texas (Eddleman and Conway 1998). It also breeds in coastal areas of California, Central America, the Caribbean, and northern South America; one subspecies breeds in freshwater marshes in the southwestern United States (Eddleman and Conway 1998). In New York, this species currently breeds only in coastal salt marshes, although historical nesting records exist from the tidal marshes of the Harlem and Hudson rivers (Bull 1964). MacNamara and Udell (1970) documented Clapper Rail nesting most commonly in high marsh saltmeadow cordgrass in Long Island's Hempstead marshes, but suggested that this apparent preference might have been a one-year aberration due to climatic conditions, as this rail has been shown to prefer low marsh saltwater cordgrass in New Jersey (Kozicky and Schmidt 1949). DeKay (1844) described the "Saltwater Meadow-Hen" as very abundant along New York's shores during breeding season. Giraud (1844) also found the Clapper Rail to be very abundant in the salt marshes along the south shore of Long Island, but noted that it was not common on the eastern part of the island. Eaton (1910) echoed Giraud's assessment of this rail's status on Long Island and added that the species was uncommon on Staten Island. Griscom (1923) deemed the Clapper Rail common on western Long Island but rare on the eastern end and felt that it probably still bred on Staten Island. Griscom also noted that the species was unrecorded from the Long Island Sound salt marshes of Bronx and Westchester counties. Cruickshank (1942) cited single breeding records from each of these counties but noted a general decline throughout the New York City area as the result of salt marsh destruction. Bull (1974) still considered the species to be a common to locally abundant breeder, especially on the south shore of Long Island west of Great South Bay, but he also noted its rarity on Staten Island, extreme eastern Long Island, and in Bronx and Westchester counties.

During the first Atlas period, the Clapper Rail was reported from both shores of Long Island, along the Westchester County shore of Long Island Sound, and in the Bronx. The species was less common on eastern Long Island and went unreported on Staten Island. The Clapper Rail's distribution remained similar during the second Atlas period, except on Staten Island, where it was reported from seven blocks. On Long Island, both the number of total records (55 to 46) and Confirmed records (21 to 14) decreased. Unlike the first Atlas period, when Confirmed records on Long Island were heavily concentrated in the Jamaica Bay–Oak Beach area, during the second Atlas period such records were evenly split between there and the Moriches Bay–Shinnecock Bay area.

The Breeding Bird Survey is not well suited for monitoring this species, but available data show no significant state, regional, or continental trends from 1966 to 2006 (Sauer et al. 2007). There has been no Clapper Rail monitoring on Long Island since the 1980s (J. Zarudsky pers. comm.), but the population at Jamaica Bay has likely been affected by the drastic loss of breeding habitat there, with approximately 304 of 799 ha (751 of 1,974 a) of vegetated salt marsh lost from 1974 to 1999 (Hartig et al. 2002). On average, Jamaica Bay salt marsh islands have lost 38 percent of their low marsh vegetation since 1974 (Hartig et al. 2002). If the current rates of loss continue, most of the bay's saltwater cordgrass could disappear in the next few decades, even before the predicted sea-level rise associated with global warming takes effect (Hartig et al. 2002). Future sea-level rises could significantly affect Clapper Rail populations in many parts of New York City and western Long Island, where urban development will limit the ability of salt marshes to migrate inland.

ATM © 2006

2000–05 Distribution Map

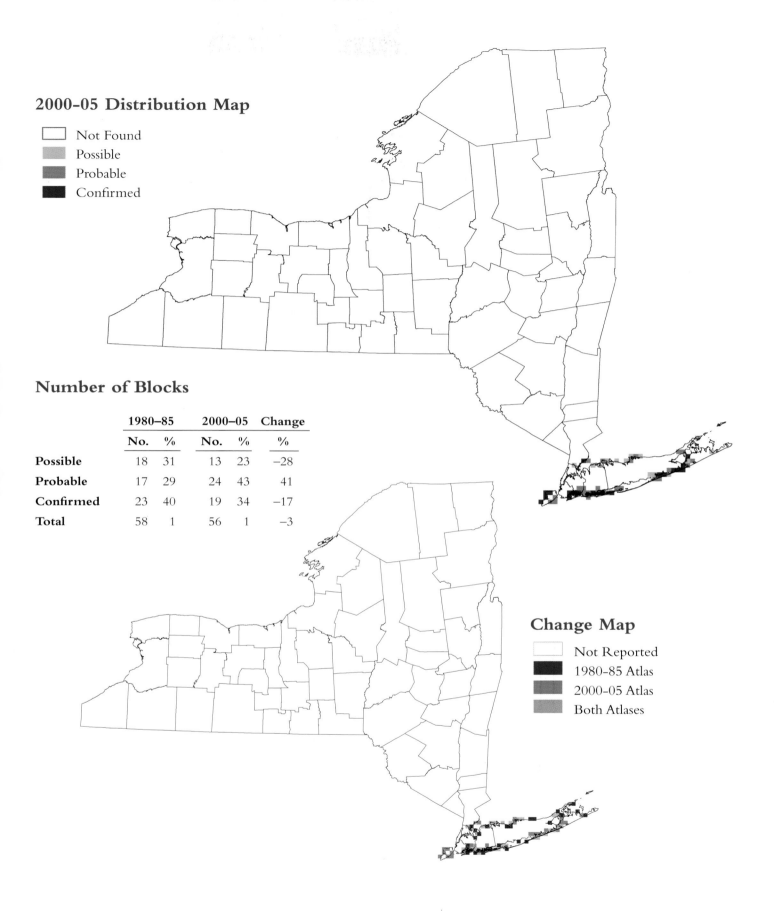

- ☐ Not Found
- Possible
- Probable
- ■ Confirmed

Number of Blocks

	1980–85		2000–05		Change
	No.	%	No.	%	%
Possible	18	31	13	23	−28
Probable	17	29	24	43	41
Confirmed	23	40	19	34	−17
Total	58	1	56	1	−3

Change Map

- ☐ Not Reported
- ■ 1980–85 Atlas
- 2000–05 Atlas
- Both Atlases

King Rail

Rallus elegans

MATTHEW D. MEDLER

ATM©2006

Known to early authors as the "Great Red-breasted Rail," the King Rail is one of the state's rarest breeding birds. New York is near the northeastern limit of its range, which stretches from the Gulf Coast to southern Ontario and from the Atlantic Coast to the Great Plains; the species also breeds in Mexico and Cuba (Poole et al. 2005). This rail is most common along the Gulf Coast and is a rare breeder across much of the rest of its range (Poole et al. 2005). Often described as the freshwater counterpart of the closely related (or conspecific) Clapper Rail, the King Rail breeds in tidal freshwater and brackish marshes, nontidal freshwater marshes, and marsh-shrub swamps (Poole et al. 2005). DeKay (1844) described the "Fresh-water Meadow-Hen" as very rare in New York, but then added, "or at least has not often been observed in this State." DeKay's King Rail account and the existence of several 19th-century specimens (see Giraud 1844, Eaton 1910, Beardslee and Mitchell 1965) contradict Carroll's (1988c) assertion that the species was not observed in the state until the early 1900s. Eaton (1910) thought it was an uncommon summer resident and highlighted the marshes of central and western New York as the areas of greatest abundance. Bull (1974) considered the King Rail a rare and local breeder and identified two breeding populations: a coastal population with known localities in Suffolk, Nassau, Queens, and Bronx counties; and an inland population with known localities stretching from Cattaraugus to Onondaga counties. Despite a long history of occurrence on Long Island (Giraud 1844), the King Rail has always been described as rare there (Griscom 1923, Cruickshank 1942, Bull 1964). On the Great Lakes Plain, Reed and Wright (1909) considered it not uncommon in the marshes at the north end of the Cayuga Lake Basin, but by the 1960s Beardslee and Mitchell (1965) called this rail a rare breeder in the Niagara Frontier region.

During the first Atlas period, King Rail was reported from five blocks but breeding was confirmed in none. Two records came from the Hudson Valley, an area not mentioned for this species by earlier authors, and two came from the Appalachian Plateau, site of two historical records (Bull 1974). Only one record came from the Great Lakes Plain marshes, a former stronghold, and the species went unrecorded in the Coastal Lowlands of Long Island. During the second Atlas survey, the King Rail was also found in five blocks, but again, breeding was not confirmed. Four reports came from the Great Lakes Plain marshes, and the fifth record was from a salt-brackish-freshwater marsh

along Long Island Sound in Westchester County. This last locality, the Marshlands Conservancy in Rye, was the site of confirmed King Rail breeding in 1997, but the species has not been observed there since a common reed control project began in 2003 (T. Burke pers. comm.). As is the case with all rails, it is possible that Atlas observers overlooked the King Rail. However, the depiction of this rail in the Atlases as a very rare species is supported by the results of extensive secretive marsh bird surveys at state-owned freshwater marshes between 2004 and 2006, in which the King Rail was not detected despite the use of taped recordings to elicit responses (NYSDEC unpubl. data).

While the Breeding Bird Survey is poorly suited for monitoring King Rail populations, available data suggest significant population declines between 1980 and 2005 (Sauer et al. 2005), and this species is considered the most threatened rail in North America (Poole et al. 2005). It is listed as Threatened in New York, Pennsylvania, and Massachusetts and is considered Endangered in Ontario and Ohio, where it was once the most common rail in some of that state's marshes (Peterjohn and Rice 1991). With a scarcity of recent records from New York, and a similar status in neighboring states and provinces, the King Rail faces an uncertain future in our state.

2000-05 Distribution Map

- ☐ Not Found
- ☐ Possible
- ☐ Probable
- ■ Confirmed

Number of Blocks

| | 1980–85 | | 2000–05 | | Change |
	No.	%	No.	%	%
Possible	3	60	1	20	−67
Probable	2	40	4	80	100
Confirmed	0	0	0	0	
Total	5	<1	5	<1	0

Change Map

- ☐ Not Reported
- ■ 1980-85 Atlas
- ■ 2000-05 Atlas
- ■ Both Atlases

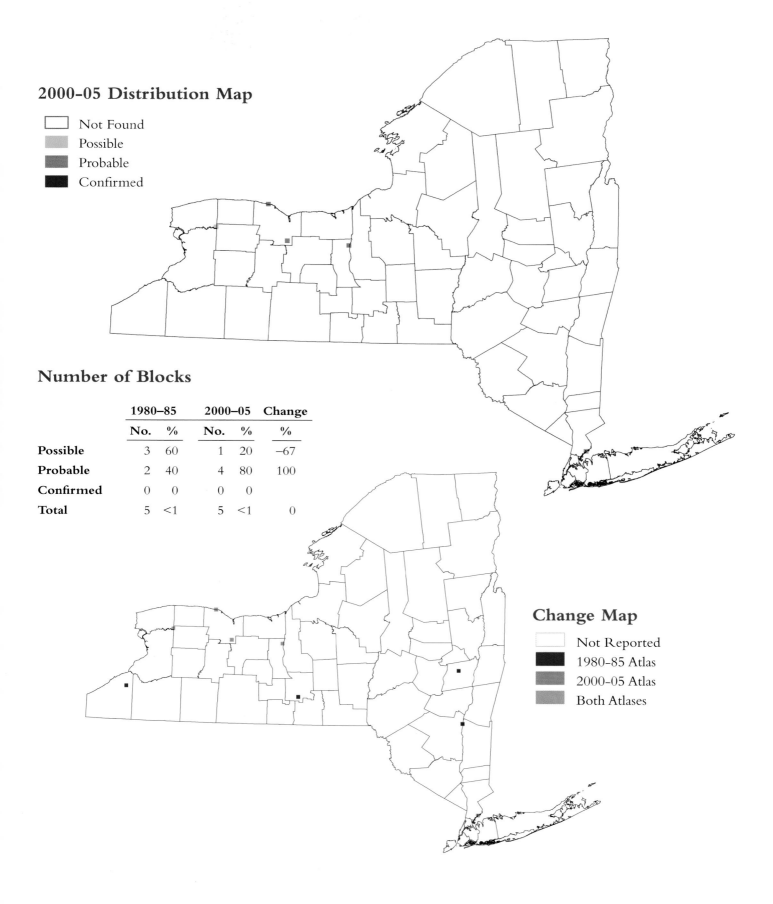

Virginia Rail
Rallus limicola

MATTHEW D. MEDLER

ATM © 2006

The most common species of rail in New York, the Virginia Rail has a breeding range that extends primarily across the middle latitudes of North America. This rail breeds from Quebec's Gaspé Peninsula to coastal North Carolina in eastern North America, with western breeding limits ranging from central Alberta to northern Baja California; isolated populations also occur in southern Mexico and Guatemala (Conway 1995). The Virginia Rail typically breeds in freshwater marshes, preferring those with shallow water and emergent vegetation, such as cattail or bulrush (Conway 1995). It also nests in salt marshes and has been documented breeding in saltwater cordgrass at Oak Beach, Suffolk County (Post and Enders 1970). DeKay (1844) described the "Virginian Rail" as occurring throughout the state, while noting both its preference for freshwater and its occurrence along the coast. Eaton (1910) believed that this species was under-reported, and asserted that it bred in every county of the state except for those in the Adirondacks. He described it as being fairly common in the marshes of Long Island and central and western New York. Bull (1974) depicted the Virginia Rail as breeding widely across the lower elevations of the state, and identified the Montezuma marshes and Oak Orchard Swamp as areas where it was particularly common.

During the first Atlas period, the Virginia Rail was widely but rather sparsely distributed across the state except for two major concentrations: one in the St. Lawrence Plains and Transition, and the other in the western Erie-Ontario Plain. Few records came from high-elevation areas such as the Adirondacks, Catskill Peaks, or Tug Hill Plateau. The Virginia Rail's overall distribution did not change markedly between Atlas periods, but the second Atlas results revealed slightly different areas of abundance. The St. Lawrence Plains and neighboring ecozones, which had the highest concentration of records during the first Atlas survey, showed a 58 percent decrease. The number of records from Mohawk Valley and Champlain Valley and Transition, meanwhile, more than doubled. These two areas contained the greatest concentrations of rail records, followed by the Great Lakes Plain, which had the most records for both Atlas periods. The Atlas map undoubtedly under-represents the actual status of this rail in the state, however, due to its secretive nature and the special effort required to detect it.

The Marsh Monitoring Program reported a significant decline in Virginia Rail numbers over the entire Great Lakes Basin from 1995 to 2003, with a significant decrease in the Lake Erie Basin and no change in the Lake Ontario Basin (Crewe et al. 2005). The second Ontario Breeding Bird Atlas noted a significant increase province-wide, based on significant increases in the Southern Shield and Simcoe-Rideau regions (Bird Studies Canada et al. 2006). This latter region showed an increase in the number of records near the St. Lawrence River, suggesting that the sizable decrease seen directly across the river in New York might be largely the result of observer coverage. The effect that rail-specific searches can have on Atlas results is dramatically illustrated in the Mohawk Valley, where one observer reported the Virginia Rail from 25 blocks, single-handedly exceeding the ecozone's total (16) from the first Atlas. The decrease in the number of records from the St. Lawrence Plains area might also be partly the result of a decrease in available habitat, as the amount of emergent wetland declined 9.5 percent (approximately 2,630 ha or 6,500 a) in the combined Great Lakes Plain–St. Lawrence Plains region between the mid-1980s and mid-1990s (Huffman & Associates, Inc. 1999). Targeted monitoring efforts should be continued and implemented statewide to assess the population status of the Virginia Rail and other secretive marsh birds.

2000-05 Distribution Map

- ☐ Not Found
- Possible
- Probable
- Confirmed

Number of Blocks

	1980–85		2000–05		Change
	No.	%	No.	%	%
Possible	170	37	172	31	1
Probable	201	44	292	53	45
Confirmed	87	19	89	16	2
Total	458	9	553	10	21

Change Map

- ☐ Not Reported
- 1980-85 Atlas
- 2000-05 Atlas
- Both Atlases

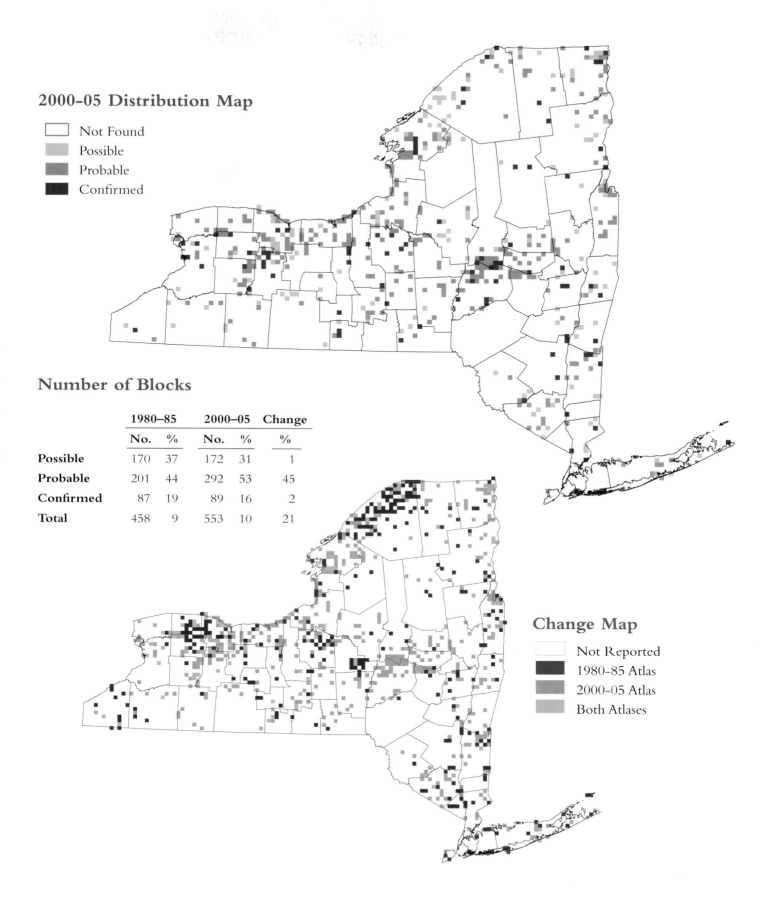

Sora

Porzana carolina

MATTHEW D. MEDLER

The most widespread rail in North America, the Sora breeds across most of the northern United States and southern Canada. New York is near the southeastern limit of its breeding range, which extends to the Northwest Territories and New Mexico (Melvin and Gibbs 1996). Sora breeds primarily in freshwater marshes where emergent vegetation such as cattails, sedges, burreeds, or bulrushes predominates (Melvin and Gibbs 1996). Along the Atlantic Coast, however, this rail can sometimes be found in salt marshes, where it nests in saltwater cordgrass; such nesting has been documented in New York at Oak Beach, Suffolk County (Greenlaw and Miller 1982). DeKay (1844) stated that the Sora occurred "sparingly" in New York, but considered it a breeder and noted its occurrence in both freshwater marsh and salt marsh. Eaton (1910), in contrast, wrote, "It is our most abundant species of Rail, being common in the marshes of central New York and the Great Lake region and probably breeding in nearly every county in the State, but is uncommon as a summer resident in our coastal district." Bull (1974) considered the Sora to be a local breeder in New York and felt that it was "nowhere really common," except possibly in the extensive Montezuma and Oak Orchard marshes. He noted considerable declines in New York and throughout the northeastern United States after 1900 (Bull 1974). While including six Long Island records, Bull (1974) pointed out that the Sora had not bred there in more than 35 years, and considered it to be confined to freshwater marshes.

During the first Atlas survey, the Sora records were sparsely scattered across most of the state. Only the St. Lawrence Plains and Transition and the Erie-Ontario Plain contained sizable concentrations of records. The species was almost completely absent from all Adirondack ecozones, as well as the Catskill Peaks and neighboring subzones. However, several Confirmed breeding reports came from above 305 m (1,000 ft) elsewhere on the Appalachian Plateau. The one Confirmed report from the Coastal Lowlands represented Long Island's first confirmed breeding since 1935 (Greenlaw and Miller 1982). Though

the statewide distribution remained largely unchanged based on the second Atlas results, the number of records increased by 15 percent. Both the Erie-Ontario Plain and the St. Lawrence Plains and Transition remained areas of abundance, although records in the latter area decreased by 39 percent. The number of records in both the Mohawk Valley and Champlain Valley and Transition more than doubled. Because of the special effort needed to find it, the Sora was unquestionably underdetected by Atlas efforts.

The Marsh Monitoring Program reported a significant decline in Sora numbers for the entire Great Lakes Basin from 1995 to 2003 but no significant changes in the Lake Erie and Lake Ontario basins (Crewe et al. 2005). The second Ontario Breeding Bird Atlas reported no significant change in the province's two southernmost regions but significant increases in the Canadian Shield (Bird Studies Canada et al. 2006). In New York, the statewide increase and the localized St. Lawrence Plains decrease might simply reflect different levels of rail-specific effort between the two Atlas projects. Thirty-seven percent of all Sora records came from just 12 of the 129 atlasers who reported the bird, highlighting the effect that a single dedicated rail-searcher (or lack thereof) could have on results for an area. The combined Great Lakes Plain–St. Lawrence Plains region of New York did experience a 9.5 percent decrease in emergent wetlands between the mid-1980s and mid-1990s (Huffman & Associates, Inc. 1999), but even if this loss was entirely in the St. Lawrence region, it does not seem sufficient to explain the 39 percent decrease in the number of Sora records there. Marsh bird monitoring efforts should be expanded statewide to develop more comprehensive population information for this and other species.

ATM©2006

2000-05 Distribution Map

- ☐ Not Found
- ▨ Possible
- ▨ Probable
- ■ Confirmed

Number of Blocks

	1980–85		2000–05		Change
	No.	%	No.	%	%
Possible	108	45	124	45	15
Probable	97	40	133	48	37
Confirmed	36	15	21	8	−42
Total	241	5	278	5	15

Change Map

- ☐ Not Reported
- ■ 1980-85 Atlas
- ▨ 2000-05 Atlas
- ▨ Both Atlases

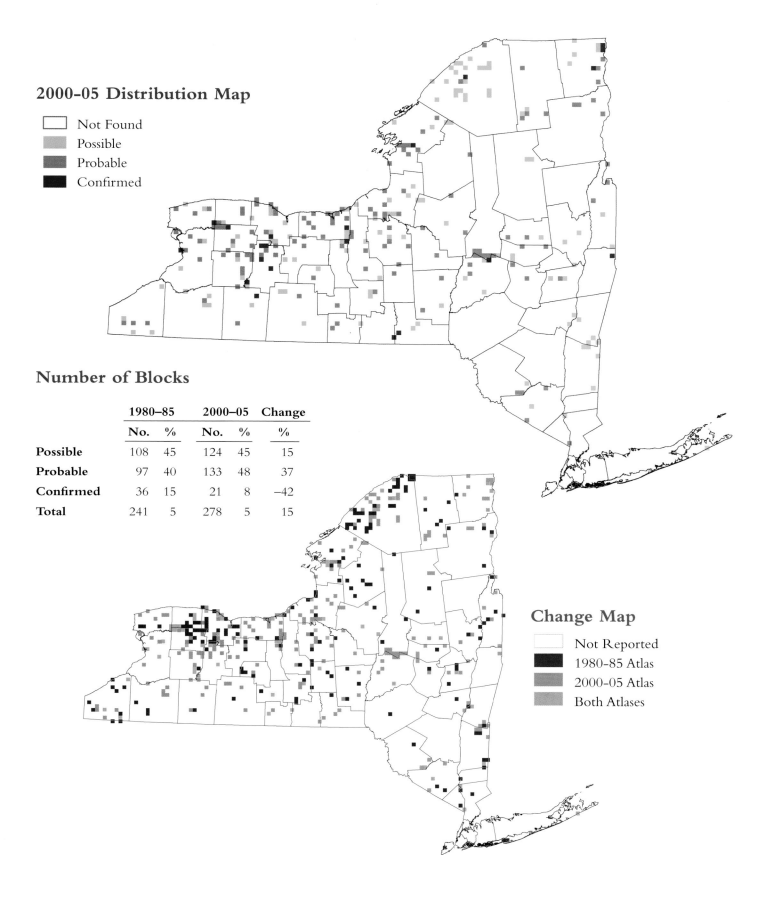

Common Moorhen

Gallinula chloropus

MATTHEW D. MEDLER

Found on all continents but Australia and Antarctica, the Common Moorhen is near the northeastern limit of its North American range in New York. Migratory breeding populations extend from Nova Scotia and southern Quebec to Oklahoma and Texas, while the species occurs year round along the Atlantic and Gulf coasts, in scattered sites in the western United States, and throughout much of Mexico (Bannor and Kiviat 2002). In New York this bird nests primarily in marshes with open water for swimming and abundant cattail, pickerel weed, burreed, arum, and buttonbush (Bull 1974). DeKay (1844) considered the "Florida Gallinule" to be a rare visitor to the shores of New York, while Giraud (1844) was aware of a few records from the south shore of Long Island and a specimen from Staten Island. Rathbun (1879) and Short (1893) listed the species as a breeding bird in central and western New York, respectively, and Eaton (1910) described it as a fairly common summer resident in these regions and in the Ontario–St. Lawrence valley. Eaton (1910) specifically noted its abundance at the Montezuma marshes, where he said "hundreds of broods" were raised each year. Bull (1974) described the "Common Gallinule" as a local but occasionally numerous breeder at lower elevations in the state, including the Hudson-Mohawk valleys and Lake Champlain and St. Lawrence River lowlands. He also highlighted its abundance at Montezuma, including the refuge manager's 1970 estimate of 100 pairs and 400 young produced (Bull 1974).

During the first Atlas period, the greatest concentrations of Common Moorhen records were found in the Great Lakes Plain, St. Lawrence Plains and Transition, and Champlain Valley. The species was completely absent from the Catskill Peaks and four neighboring subzones and was nearly absent from all Adirondack ecozones. However, despite the characterization of moorhen as a lowland species by Bull (1974) and Sibley (1988g), 49 records from the first Atlas survey came from an elevation of at least 305 m (1,000 ft). During the second Atlas survey, the Common Moorhen's overall distribution changed little, but the number of records decreased 33 percent.

Declines were especially large in the Coastal Lowlands, from which the species nearly disappeared; St. Lawrence Plains and Transition; and Appalachian Plateau. Only the Hudson Valley and Mohawk Valley showed increases of more than one block. More visually conspicuous than rails, the Common Moorhen required less special effort by observers, meaning that Atlas results for this species should be more representative of its true status than those for secretive rails.

Marsh Monitoring Program results from 1995 to 2003 showed no change in Common Moorhen numbers in the Lake Ontario Basin, but a significant decline in the Lake Erie Basin and the larger Great Lakes Basin (Crewe et al. 2005). The second Ontario Breeding Bird Atlas reported significant declines for this bird in all three regions of southern Ontario (Bird Studies Canada et al. 2006). The marked decrease in New York Atlas records for the moorhen is not easily explained by habitat availability, as the amount of emergent wetlands in the state declined only slightly between the mid-1980s and mid-1990s (Huffman & Associates, Inc. 1999). Citing refuge staff, Sibley (1988g) reported only two nesting moorhen pairs at Montezuma National Wildlife Refuge in 1985 and suggested the invasion of purple loosestrife as a contributing factor in the species's decline there. Biological control of purple loosestrife began at Montezuma in 1996, and breeding moorhens averaged nearly 15 broods per year from 2000 to 2004, up from one or two broods per year in the early 1990s (MNWR unpubl. data). However, substantial annual variability in brood counts from 1993 to 2004, including a total of 20 in 1995, suggests that other factors are also affecting Common Moorhen populations. This species and its wetland habitat should be closely monitored in the future.

ATM©2005

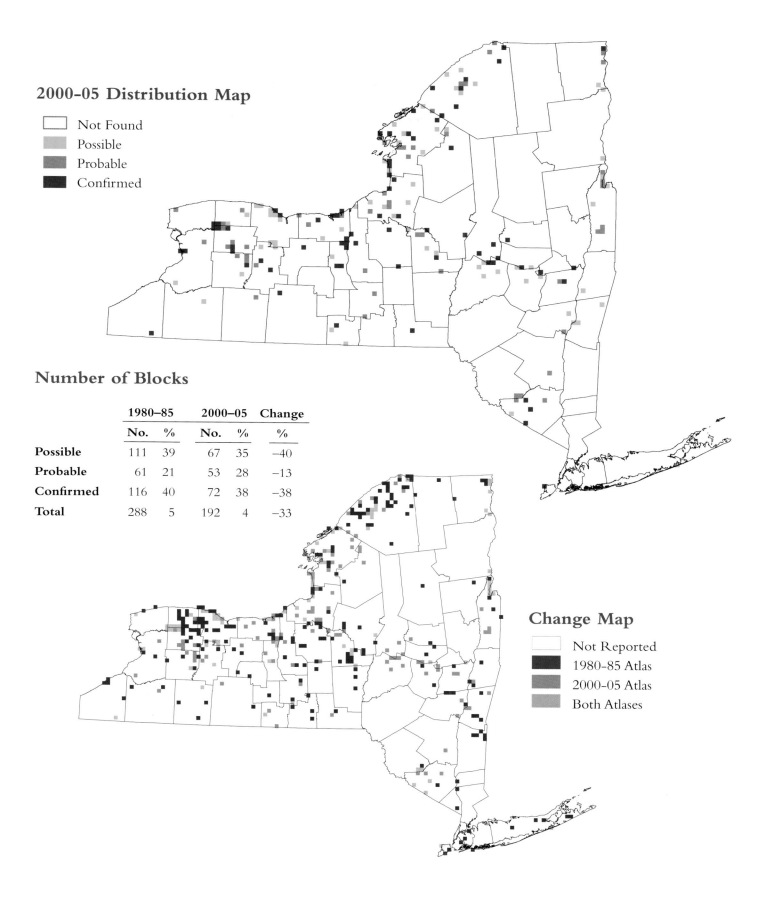

2000-05 Distribution Map

- ☐ Not Found
- Possible
- Probable
- Confirmed

Number of Blocks

	1980–85		2000–05		Change
	No.	%	No.	%	%
Possible	111	39	67	35	−40
Probable	61	21	53	28	−13
Confirmed	116	40	72	38	−38
Total	288	5	192	4	−33

Change Map

- ☐ Not Reported
- 1980-85 Atlas
- 2000-05 Atlas
- Both Atlases

American Coot

Fulica americana

MATTHEW D. MEDLER

Although frequently seen in New York as a migrant or winter visitor, the American Coot is an uncommon breeder in the state, which is near the northeastern limit of the coot's breeding range (Brisbin et al. 2002). The species nests in highest densities in the Prairie Pothole Region of North America, although it also breeds throughout much of the western United States, eastward through the Great Lakes region to the St. Lawrence Valley, and in Florida, Texas, Mexico, and the Caribbean (Brisbin et al. 2002). The American Coot nests in a host of freshwater wetlands, but breeding densities are greatest in well-flooded semipermanent wetlands in which open water and emergent vegetation are highly interspersed (Brisbin et al. 2002).

Eaton (1910) described the American Coot primarily as a transient visitant to New York but also noted breeding at the Montezuma marshes and along the eastern shore of Lake Ontario. By 1932 the species was nesting in the western Great Lakes Plain, at Oak Orchard Swamp (Beardslee and Mitchell 1965). Bull (1974) provided a breeding map showing 26 known sites, with most coming from central and western New York and Long Island. Overall, he considered the coot to be a rare and local breeder, except at Montezuma, where he noted the production of at least 200 broods in 1968, and at Jamaica Bay, where he included an estimate of 50 breeding pairs in 1961 (Bull 1974).

During the first Atlas survey, the highest concentrations of American Coot records were found in the Coastal Lowlands, St. Lawrence Plains and Transition, and Great Lakes Plain. Breeding was confirmed primarily in the Great Lakes Plain, specifically at Montezuma National Wildlife Refuge and at the Oak Orchard Wildlife Management Area–Iroquois NWR–Tonawanda WMA complex. Two breeding records from the Champlain Valley, including one Probable, suggested expansion into northeastern New York. Based on second Atlas data, the number of American Coot records increased slightly, and the species's statewide range remained similar. Within this range, however, the number of reports from the Coastal Lowlands and St. Lawrence Plains and Transition declined, while the number of Great Lakes Plain records increased substantially. Sixty percent of all records came from the Great Lakes Plain, compared to 40 percent in the first Atlas. Notable records elsewhere included Confirmed breeding in the Mohawk Valley and Champlain Valley. While the American Coot could potentially be overlooked in the dense cattail stands that it uses, or confused vocally for the more widespread Common Moorhen, it is New York's most conspicuous member of the rail family, often seen swimming in areas of open water. As such, Atlas maps likely provide a fairly accurate depiction of this species's statewide distribution.

No meaningful Breeding Bird Survey data exist for the American Coot in New York, but survey-wide data showed a nonsignificant decline of 1 percent per year from 1980 to 2006 (Sauer et al. 2007). Similarly, Marsh Monitoring Program results from 1995 to 2003 indicated a nonsignificant decline in the Great Lakes Basin (Crewe et al. 2005). The second Ontario Breeding Bird Atlas reported no significant province-wide trend, despite a significant decline in the Simcoe-Rideau region (Bird Studies Canada et al. 2006). In New York, American Coot production at the Montezuma NWR increased markedly between the Atlas periods, perhaps providing dispersers that bred elsewhere in the Great Lakes Plain. Eaton (1988b) reported an average annual production of 33 young at Montezuma from 1980 to 1985; the average was 81 from 2000 to 2004 (MNWR unpubl. data). Declines in the Coastal Lowlands are not easily explained by continued development there, as the amount of emergent wetlands in this ecozone remained essentially unchanged between the mid-1980s and mid-1990s (Huffman & Associates, Inc. 1999). In general, the species is affected by seasonal precipitation levels, with drought conditions resulting in decreases in reproductive success and abundance (Brisbin et al. 2002). Since 1994 thousands of American Coot in the southeastern United States have died from avian vacuolar myelinopathy, a poorly understood disease that may further affect wintering populations (Wilde et al. 2005).

ATM©2006

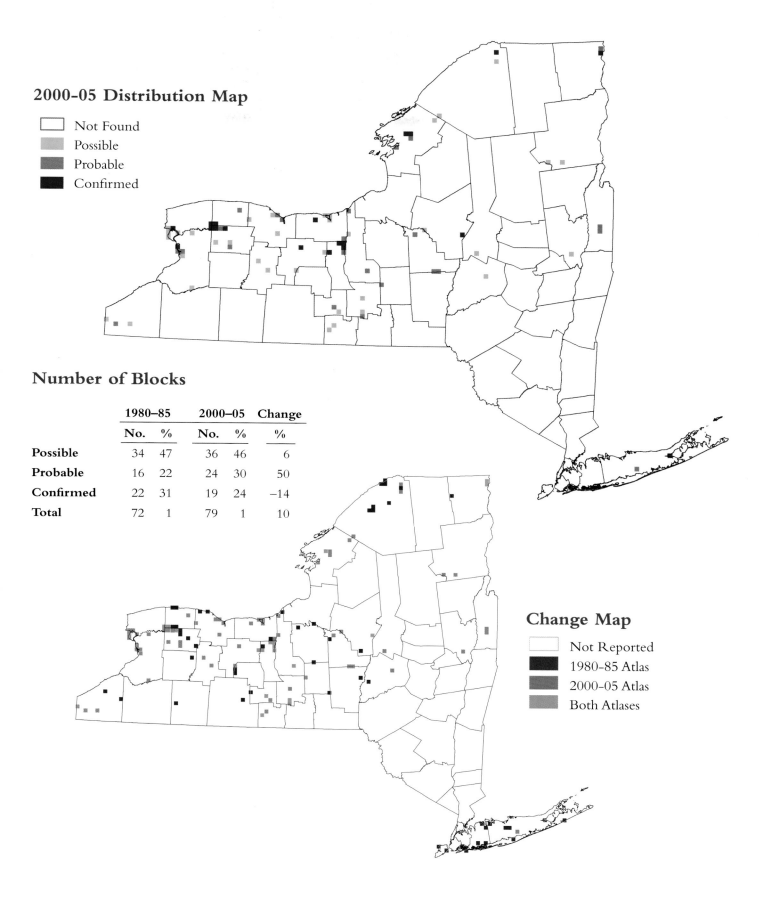

2000-05 Distribution Map

- ☐ Not Found
- Possible
- Probable
- Confirmed

Number of Blocks

	1980–85		2000–05		Change
	No.	%	No.	%	%
Possible	34	47	36	46	6
Probable	16	22	24	30	50
Confirmed	22	31	19	24	−14
Total	72	1	79	1	10

Change Map

- ☐ Not Reported
- 1980-85 Atlas
- 2000-05 Atlas
- Both Atlases

Sandhill Crane
Grus canadensis

KEVIN J. MCGOWAN

A tall gray bird of open grasslands, meadows, and wetlands, the Sandhill Crane breeds from Alaska eastward to western Quebec, southward to the northern United States, and in scattered localities across the western and southeastern United States, as well as in Cuba. Eaton (1910) stated that the crane occurred in New York in colonial times, although probably just as a migrant. Archaeological remains from Fulton County (Steadman 1988) and Barton's (1799) report of large flocks of cranes passing over Pennsylvania, New York, and New Jersey going to more northern nesting grounds support this idea. After that time, however, the species virtually disappeared from the state. The 19th-century authors did not mention it (DeKay 1844, Giraud 1844, Rathbun 1879, Short 1893), and Eaton (1910) listed only three specimens. Bull (1974) cited only 15 records, with 11 occurring after 1965. Sightings increased through the 1990s (Chamberlaine 1998c), and the New York State Avian Records Committee accepted 39 records between 1980 and 2000, at which point it was removed from the review list (NYSARC 2000a, 2007). Most records came from spring or late fall, but in 1990 one individual spent a summer in Chemung County (Clements 1990), and in 1993 another summered in Lewis County, courting an escaped Common Crane (Long 1993). More summer reports followed, and by 1999 summer sightings in the Great Lakes Plain were becoming regular (Griffith 1999). A pair seen near Richmond, Ontario County, in June of 1997 suggested possible breeding (Griffith 1997).

The Sandhill Crane was not found during the first Atlas survey, but it was seen in nine blocks during the second Atlas effort, with breeding confirmed in two. The first breeding record for the state was established when John Foust and John Van Niel spotted a chick with a pair of cranes on 5 June 2003 in the North Montezuma Wildlife Management Area, northeast of Savannah, Wayne County. A pair of cranes had been present in the area for several years, and breeding had been suspected. The Savannah pair produced chicks each year through 2007 (the time of this writing). A pair with a nest in central Yates County in 2004 was the only other confirmation. That pair possibly bred in 2003 but was not seen after 2004.

Unlike nearly all other species of cranes in the world, most Sandhill Crane populations are now stable or increasing (Tacha et al. 1992). Breeding Bird Survey data show a significant increase in crane numbers over the last 20 years across the range, with especially large increases in the last 10 years in Michigan and Ontario, the most likely source of cranes in New York (Sauer et al. 2005). The second Ontario Breeding Bird Atlas reported significant increases in squares reporting the Sandhill Crane throughout the province, including breeding in several squares just to the west of the Niagara Frontier (Bird Studies Canada et al. 2006). Pennsylvania had few crane records in the 19th and early 20th centuries, but sightings increased after 1960 (McWilliams and Brauning 2000). Nesting was first confirmed there in 1993 and has been documented in several counties in the extreme northwest of that state (McWilliams and Brauning 2000).

The Sandhill Crane breeds in open marshes or bogs surrounded by shrubs and forests, typically far from people (Tacha et al. 1992). Cranes nesting in New York and Pennsylvania are using agricultural land, especially harvested fields and cornfields, for foraging and the feeding of chicks. Standing water with emergent aquatic vegetation has been found to be important for the nest site, and the nest is a mound of vegetation, often floating on the water (Tacha et al. 1992). The Yates County nest was in an old beaver meadow that was dredged to form ponds and runs. It is unlikely that the Sandhill Crane will ever be a numerous breeder in New York because of the limited amount of suitable breeding habitat, but it may well become established in small numbers.

2000–05 Distribution Map

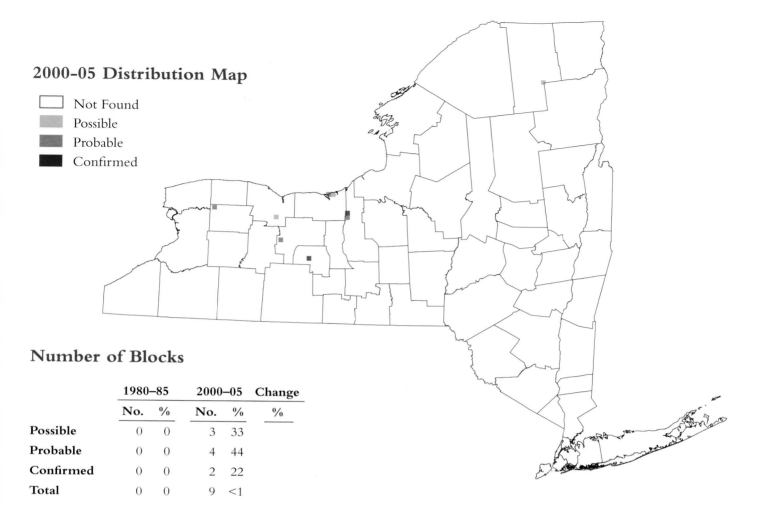

- ☐ Not Found
- ◻ Possible
- ◼ Probable
- ◼ Confirmed

Number of Blocks

	1980–85		2000–05		Change
	No.	%	No.	%	%
Possible	0	0	3	33	
Probable	0	0	4	44	
Confirmed	0	0	2	22	
Total	0	0	9	<1	

Piping Plover, Willet, and Black Skimmer on Long Island beach

Long Island has numerous and extensive beaches where shorebirds can nest and feed. As a result of conservation efforts, portions of them have been fenced and designated as protected breeding areas for Piping Plover and other shorebird species.

Piping Plover
Charadrius melodus

MICHAEL R. WASILCO

The Piping Plover, a small sand-colored bird of open beach habitat, is found in three populations in North America (USFWS 1996) with two subspecies: *C. m. melodus* (Atlantic Coast) and *C. m. circumcinctus* (both Northern Great Plains and Great Lakes) (Haig and Elliot-Smith 2004). New York is in the core of the Atlantic Coast population, which nests on coastal beaches from Newfoundland to South Carolina (USFWS 1996). Historically, New York supported breeding by both the Great Lakes and Atlantic Coast populations, both of which have gone up and down over the past 150 years (USFWS 1996, 2003). Both populations hit their modern peaks in New York in the 1930s (Wilcox 1939, Bull 1974). Since then, their fates have followed very different paths. There has been only one record of Piping Plover nesting along the New York shoreline of the Great Lakes since 1955, that being a brood found at Sandy Pond, Oswego County, in 1984 during the first Atlas survey (Spahn 1984, D. M. Peterson 1988c, Paxton 1998d). Only occasional reports of transient birds seen during migration have been made in the years since then.

During the first Atlas survey, the Piping Plover was found in 75 blocks, with all but the Sandy Pond record coming from Long Island. During the second Atlas survey, the Piping Plover was recorded in 76 blocks, with none found upstate. On Long Island the distribution shifted subtly from southern bayside beaches to the Atlantic Ocean and Long Island Sound beaches. Most of the new blocks were along Long Island Sound and Peconic Bay, and likely represented plovers expanding into new areas, as well as better coverage during the annual surveys of all suitable Piping Plover habitat on Long Island coordinated by the New York State Department of Environmental Conservation. Many blocks where Piping Plover formerly bred no longer provide suitable habitat because of increased vegetation at the nesting areas, especially on former dredge spoil sites.

The total Great Lakes population of Piping Plover declined from a historic level of several hundred pairs to its all-time low of 12 pairs in 1990, then increased to 51 pairs by 2002, mostly in Michigan (USFWS 2003).

The Atlantic Coast population has fared a bit better, steadily increasing from 790 pairs in 1986 (USFWS 1996) to its recent estimated high of 1,632 pairs in 2005 (Hecht 2005). The entire global breeding population was estimated at 2,747 pairs in 2001 (Haig et al. 2005). The Atlantic Coast and Northern Great Plains populations are federally listed as Threatened, while the Great Lakes population is listed as Endangered. The Piping Plover is listed as Endangered in New York. On the coast of Long Island, it is locally common in stretches of suitable habitat. While still below the 500 pairs estimated by Wilcox in 1939, the Long Island population has increased from an estimated 166 individuals (likely 88 pairs) at 41 sites when first listed by the state in 1983 (Peterson and Litwin 1983) to a recent high of 386 pairs at 80 sites in 2003 (NYSDEC unpubl. data).

The Piping Plover's dependence on open or sparsely vegetated beach habitat for nesting and brood rearing has led to direct competition with human development and recreation. The birds also face threats from increased predator numbers in association with beachfront development, as well as shoreline hardening and dune stabilization, which are reducing the amount of habitat that is created and maintained by annual storms through overwashes, breaches, and blowouts. Sea-level rise might further reduce the available habitat. Much of the success in raising plover numbers to their current levels is the result of continual management efforts by the NYSDEC, the U.S. Fish and Wildlife Service, and a dedicated cadre of stewards to protect the birds and their nesting areas from disturbance, development, and predation. The future of the Piping Plover in New York depends on continued protection and management of the remaining shorelines to provide and maintain suitable nesting areas.

2000-05 Distribution Map

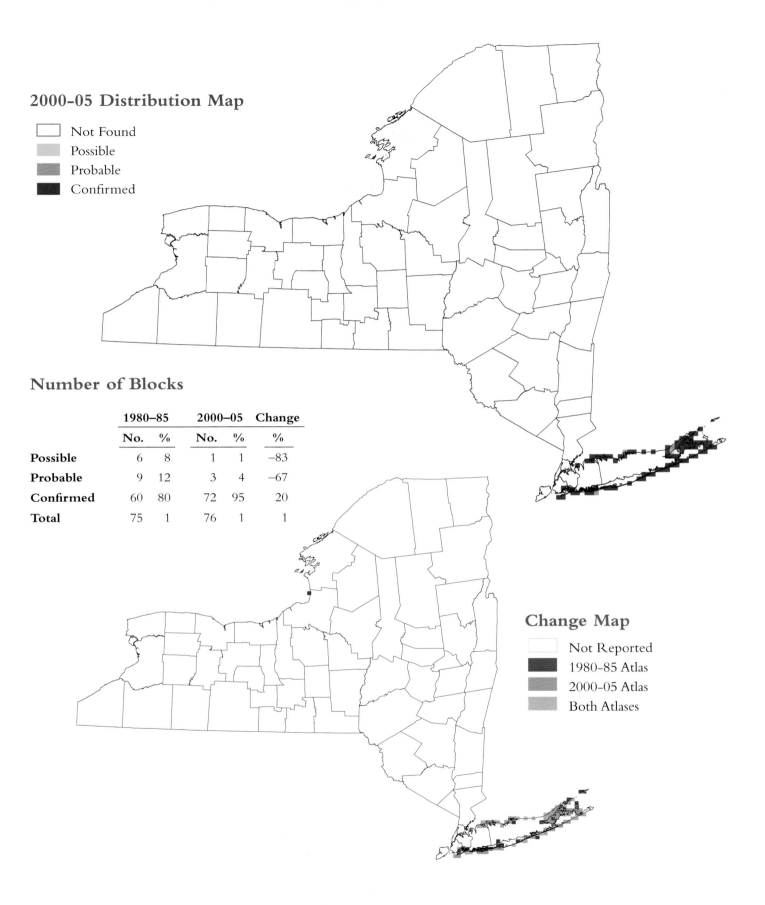

- ☐ Not Found
- ▨ Possible
- ▨ Probable
- ■ Confirmed

Number of Blocks

	1980–85		2000–05		Change
	No.	%	No.	%	%
Possible	6	8	1	1	−83
Probable	9	12	3	4	−67
Confirmed	60	80	72	95	20
Total	75	1	76	1	1

Change Map

- ☐ Not Reported
- ■ 1980–85 Atlas
- ▨ 2000–05 Atlas
- ▨ Both Atlases

Killdeer
Charadrius vociferus

KEVIN J. MCGOWAN

The most widespread and familiar of the American plovers, the Killdeer is a common bird in farmyards, fields, and parking lots. It breeds from east-central Alaska across most of Canada, southward to southern Mexico and the Caribbean, and in disconnected populations in Costa Rica, coastal Peru, and northwestern Chile (Jackson and Jackson 2000). The Killdeer breeds in open areas, especially sandbars, mudflats, pastures, cultivated fields, athletic fields, airports, golf courses, gravel parking lots, and graveled rooftops. It probably was not especially common in pre-colonial New York. The removal of forests and the creation of open farmland should have resulted in increased breeding opportunities. DeKay (1844) merely mentioned the Killdeer as a resident of the state. Giraud (1844) noted that it was common on the north side of Long Island, less so on the southern; that it preferred open, dry ground in the summer; and that it was found at the shore in winter. Rathbun (1879) and Short (1893) called it a common summer breeder in central and western New York, but Reed and Wright (1909) indicated that it was less common as a breeder than a migrant in the Cayuga Lake Basin. Merriam (1881) listed it as only a migrant in the Adirondacks. Eaton (1910) called the Killdeer a common breeder in central and western New York but mostly lacking from the southern Hudson Valley and Long Island; he did not discuss its status in the Adirondacks. The status provided by Eaton was likely the result of opposing forces: hunting pressure and destruction of beach and gravel bar habitat on Long Island, and the creation of new habitat inland as the result of land clearing (Jackson and Jackson 2000). The enactment of the federal Migratory Bird Treaty Act in 1918 afforded protection to shorebirds and undoubtedly led to increased populations of many species. Eaton (1953) described a great increase in Killdeer numbers in the interior of New York by 1930. Griscom (1923) called the species rare in the New York City area, but Cruickshank (1942) termed it a local and increasing summer resident in the area and fairly common on Long Island. Bull (1964) called it a local breeder in the New York City area. Bull (1974) gave its range only as "widespread breeder, but rare in the Adirondack region."

During the first Atlas the Killdeer was found breeding across most of the state, including the lower Hudson Valley, much of the greater New York City area, and across most of Long Island. It was missing only from the most urban areas and the heavily forested regions of the state. The second Atlas survey revealed little change in distribution, with only a slight decline in the number of blocks with reports. Again, it was absent only from most of the Adirondacks, the Central Tug Hill, and portions of the southeastern highlands. The only ecozones with notable losses were the Hudson Highlands (−35 percent) and the Adirondacks (−33 percent), where it already was not very common.

The Killdeer breeding range expanded in the early 20th century, extending both northward and southward in North America and to the coasts from inland areas (Jackson and Jackson 2000). During the late 20th century, however, it experienced a population decline, with Breeding Bird Survey data showing a significant annual decrease of 1.1 percent survey-wide from 1980 to 2005 (Sauer et al. 2005). BBS data for New York show the same trend of increase then decline (Sauer et al. 2005). Data from the second Ontario Breeding Bird Atlas show a significant decline in Killdeer numbers across the province (Bird Studies Canada et al. 2006). The U.S. Shorebird Conservation Plan (USFWS 2004) lists the Killdeer in its category of Moderate Concern, based primarily on its population trend. Despite these declines the Killdeer is still a common species in New York and should remain so.

2000-05 Distribution Map

- ☐ Not Found
- Possible
- Probable
- Confirmed

Number of Blocks

	1980–85		2000–05		Change
	No.	%	No.	%	%
Possible	1,014	26	916	24	−10
Probable	748	19	840	22	12
Confirmed	2,177	55	2,024	54	−7
Total	3,939	74	3,780	71	−4

Change Map

- ☐ Not Reported
- 1980-85 Atlas
- 2000-05 Atlas
- Both Atlases

Breeding Bird Survey Trend in New York

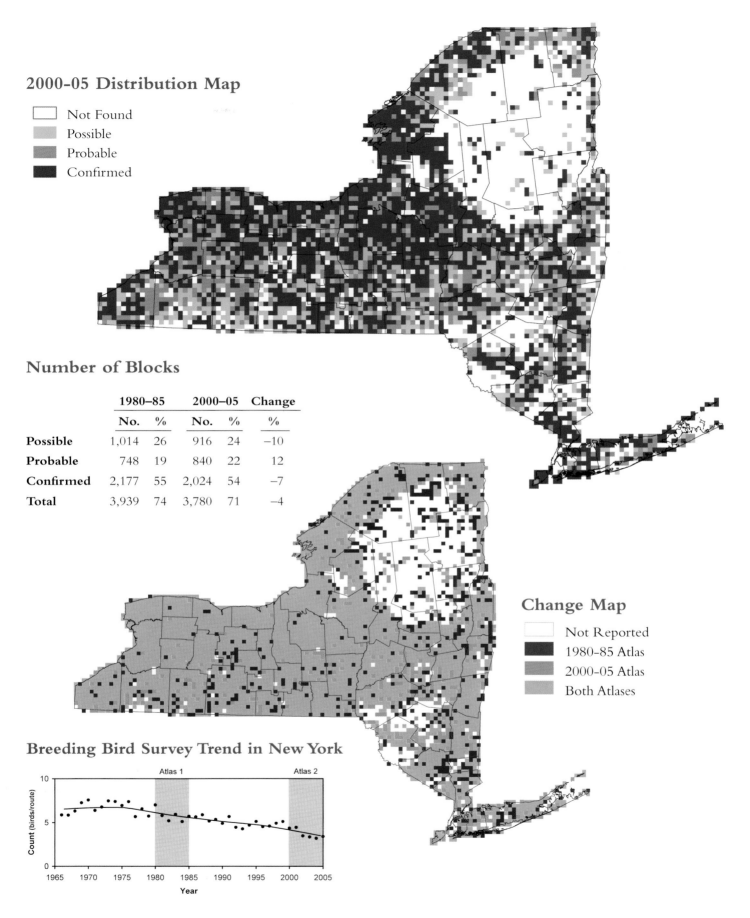

American Oystercatcher
Haematopus palliatus

Michael R. Wasilco

The American Oystercatcher is easily the most strikingly colored shorebird to regularly breed in New York. From its heavy red bill and black head to the crisp lines dividing the white and brown of the body, it is a bird of contrast. The oystercatcher once bred on the Atlantic Coast as far northward as Labrador, but its range was greatly reduced by the late 1800s (Mawhinney et al. 1999), and it was extirpated from New York by 1896 (Griscom 1923). Eaton (1910) considered it to be only a casual visitor to New York coastal areas at a time when Virginia was considered the northern limit of its breeding range. Since the 1930s the species has steadily returned to its former breeding range in the Northeast (Post 1961, Post and Raynor 1964, Nol and Humphrey 1994), reaching Nova Scotia in 1997 (Mawhinney et al. 1999).

The first Atlas survey found the American Oystercatcher to be limited mainly to the south shore of Long Island, from Jamaica Bay to Southampton and the outer Peconic Bay area of Gardiners Island to Fishers Island. The second Atlas results documented both an increase in the number of records and an expansion of the bird's breeding range. Only four blocks with records of oystercatchers during the first Atlas period were not occupied during the second Atlas period, and 27 new blocks were added. The American Oystercatcher is now breeding at several sites along the western Long Island Sound area, both on the north shore of Long Island and in Westchester County, where nesting was first confirmed in 1994 (Askildsen 1994). The species was also confirmed breeding on Staten Island during the second Atlas survey, where it was reported summering as early as 1991 (Paxton 1998a). The oystercatcher has an expanded presence in Peconic Bay as far west as the Flanders area and Robins Island. It has also expanded along the South Shore from the Rockaways to Montauk, filling in most of the gaps shown in the first Atlas.

Zarudsky (1985) estimated the American Oystercatcher breeding population for Long Island to be well in excess of 100 pairs, with most of the birds located along the south shore and Peconic Bay, from Jamaica Bay to Gardiners Island. The population trend from 1986 through 2004 was upward, but some significant swings occurred. Most notable was a decline from a high of an estimated 213 pairs at 52 sites in 1993 (Sommers et al. 1994) to a low of 122 pairs at 43 sites in 1998 (Sommers et al. 2001). The most recent estimate based on the 2004 Long Island Colonial Waterbird Survey is a minimum of 200 pairs at 52 sites (NYSDEC unpubl. data), although not all active sites, including several historic sites, were surveyed.

Over the past 20 years, the number of breeding American Oystercatchers in the species's former Atlantic stronghold (Virginia to Florida) has declined, while the population and range to the north have increased (Davis et al. 2001). Much of this seeming conflict between an expanding range and shrinking population size has been attributed to an increased flexibility in nest-site choice by the more northerly birds (Lauro and Burger 1989). Traditionally, American Oystercatcher nested mainly in sand dunes along barrier islands (Nol and Humphrey 1994), but more recently it has begun to nest on salt marsh islands (Zarudsky 1985, Lauro and Burger 1989). Lauro and Burger (1989) found that while all nests in North Carolina were in dune habitats, nests in New York were almost always in salt marshes. This adaptation to nesting in the more remote and predator-free marsh islands may be critical to the expansion of the population into the Northeast. Increased management efforts to reduce human disturbance of the nesting Piping Plover and Least Tern have allowed many oystercatchers to nest in more traditional habitat in recent years (M. Wasilco pers. obs.).

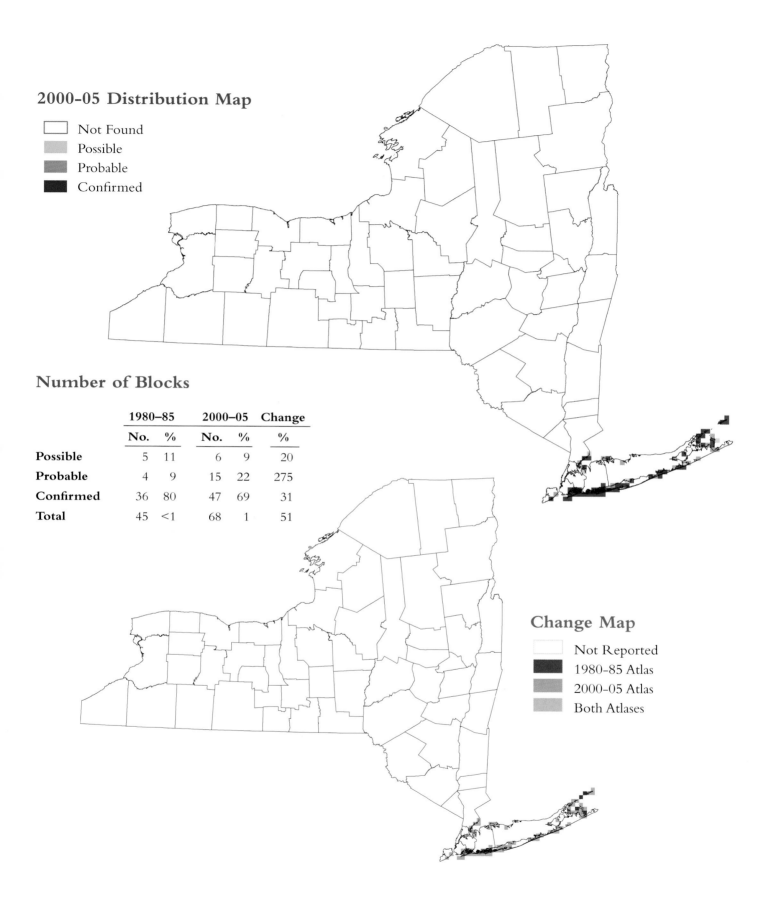

2000–05 Distribution Map

- ☐ Not Found
- Possible
- Probable
- ■ Confirmed

Number of Blocks

	1980–85		2000–05		Change
	No.	%	No.	%	%
Possible	5	11	6	9	20
Probable	4	9	15	22	275
Confirmed	36	80	47	69	31
Total	45	<1	68	1	51

Change Map

- ☐ Not Reported
- ■ 1980-85 Atlas
- 2000-05 Atlas
- Both Atlases

Spotted Sandpiper

Actitis macularius

KEVIN J. McGOWAN

The Spotted Sandpiper is one of the relatively few bird species with reversed sex roles. The male performs nearly all parental care while the more aggressive female defends the territory, and she may even mate with more than one male at a time (Oring et al. 1997). This sandpiper breeds across most of northern North America, from Alaska to Newfoundland, southward to central California, southern Nebraska, and northern North Carolina (Oring et al. 1997). It nests along the edges of nearly any water source, at home around urban ponds as well as tundra pools. It breeds in a variety of habitats, such as sagebrush, grassland, forest, lawn, and park, but its territories must include some shoreline of a stream, lake, or pond (Oring et al. 1997). In pre-colonial New York the Spotted Sandpiper was probably relatively common, breeding along stream and lake shores and the edges of beaver ponds. DeKay (1844) called it common along every stream, lake, and pond in the country. Giraud (1844) deemed it very common along streams and ponds on Long Island. Merriam (1881) noted it as common in the Adirondacks, and most early authors gave the same assessment in their region of the state (Rathbun 1879, Short 1893, Judd 1907, Reed and Wright 1909). Eaton (1910) called it common in every county in the state, nesting along every stream, pond, and lake except those with woods to the water's edge. Its status in the state changed little over the next half-century, and Bull (1974) termed it a widespread breeder.

The results of the first Atlas survey supported the earlier accounts of a widespread distribution in the state. The Spotted Sandpiper was scattered across all regions but sparsely so in areas with extensive forest and few lakes or ponds, such as the western Appalachian Plateau, Catskill Highlands, and much of the Adirondacks. It was recorded in the most blocks across the Great Lakes Plain, from Buffalo due eastward into the Mohawk Valley. The second Atlas survey found the Spotted Sandpiper in roughly the same distribution as the first, but with an overall 12 percent decline in the number of blocks with records. An 18 percent decline was noted in the Great Lakes Plain, its former stronghold. The number of blocks with Spotted Sandpiper declined 43 percent in the Coastal Lowlands, the largest decline of any ecozone. Increases were noted only in the Adirondacks (up only 3 percent) and the Tug Hill Plateau (up 29 percent). It was still largely missing from much of the Western Adirondack Foothills but showed a new area of concentration in the western half of the Central Adirondacks. It was a relatively easy bird to find, as its nesting habitat is rather obvious and its ringing call is given when it is disturbed.

Breeding Bird Survey data show little trend in continental Spotted Sandpiper populations since 1966 (Sauer et al. 2005). BBS data for New York show a continuous decline in numbers since 1966, and the species is barely detected on routes anymore (Sauer et al. 2005). BBS data are not completely adequate for the Spotted Sandpiper, and the results must be treated cautiously. Still, the declining trend for New York and the rest of the Northeast is disquieting. Data from the second Ontario Breeding Bird Atlas show significant declines in Spotted Sandpiper numbers in all areas of the province (Bird Studies Canada et al. 2006). Despite these apparent declines, the U.S. Shorebird Conservation Plan (USFWS 2004) listed the Spotted Sandpiper in its lowest concern category. It will be well worth keeping an eye on future population trends of Spotted Sandpiper in New York.

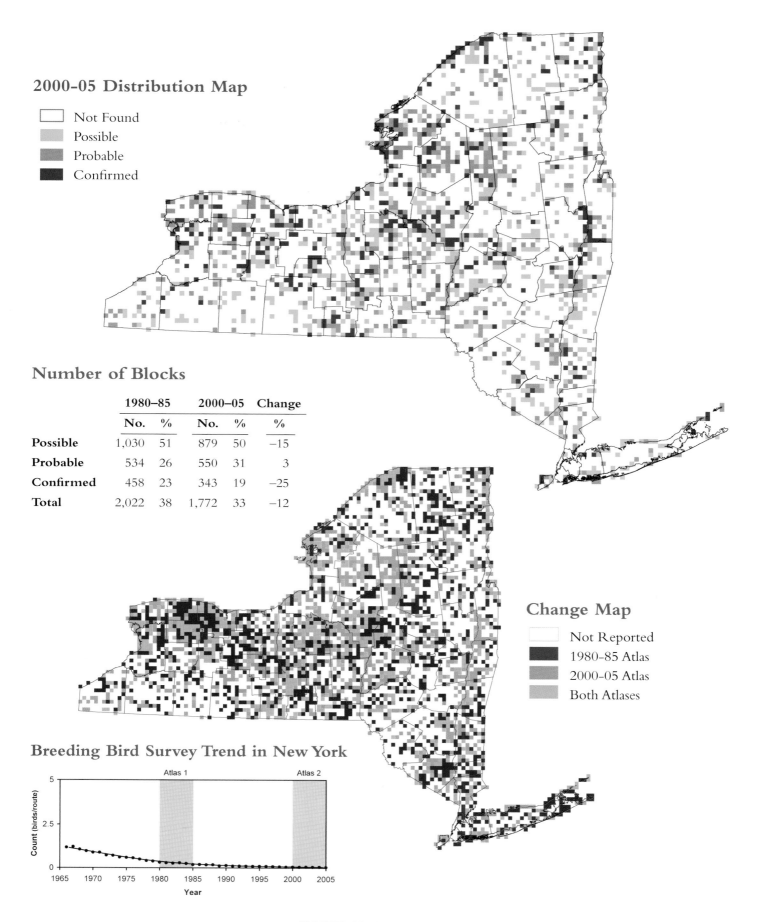

2000-05 Distribution Map

- ☐ Not Found
- Possible
- Probable
- Confirmed

Number of Blocks

	1980–85		2000–05		Change
	No.	%	No.	%	%
Possible	1,030	51	879	50	−15
Probable	534	26	550	31	3
Confirmed	458	23	343	19	−25
Total	2,022	38	1,772	33	−12

Change Map

- ☐ Not Reported
- 1980-85 Atlas
- 2000-05 Atlas
- Both Atlases

Breeding Bird Survey Trend in New York

Willet
Tringa semipalmata

MICHAEL R. WASILCO

The Willet's ringing *pill-will-willet* call resounds across the extensive salt marshes of the Atlantic Coast during the breeding season, announcing the presence of this large, drab shorebird with flashy, white wing patches. Although both "Eastern" (*T. s. semipalmata*) and "Western" (*T. s. inornata*) Willet subspecies occur in New York during migration and especially in late summer, only the eastern subspecies breeds here (Paxton 1998e). It is limited to the Atlantic and Gulf coasts, while the western subspecies breeds in the freshwater wetlands of the western states and provinces (Lowther et al. 2001). Willets often nest closely together in preferred habitats (Burger and Shisler 1978, Howe 1982), such as salt marshes, often just above the high tide line (Wilcox 1980). They will also nest in beach areas, dunes, marsh edges (Burger and Shisler 1978), and sparsely vegetated dredge spoil islands (Zarudsky 1980). By the 1890s, the Willet had been extirpated from most of its former Atlantic Coast breeding range north of South Carolina, with the exception of a small population in Nova Scotia. The species has since reclaimed much of that range, where suitable habitat still exists, and it can be found all along the coast from Newfoundland to Mexico (Lowther et al. 2001). While Giraud (1844) and DeKay (1844) indicated that the Willet likely bred in New York prior to the mid-1800s, no nesting was documented until 1966, when three nests were found in Hempstead, Nassau County (Davis 1968). Once established, the population grew steadily and slowly spread eastward.

During the first Atlas the Willet was found to be fairly well established in the salt marshes of southwestern Long Island and in Moriches and Shinnecock bays, but more scattered eastward of Shinnecock Bay. The second Atlas survey documented the continued expansion of the population. Only six blocks (one with Confirmed breeding) where the Willet was reported during the first Atlas period did not have recorded sightings during the second Atlas period, while the overall number of blocks with reports nearly doubled. The Willet now occupies most of the salt marsh habitat along the southern bays and through the Peconic Bay area, as seen by the nearly continuous coverage of the blocks in southern Queens, Nassau, and Suffolk counties in the current distribution map. Also notable are the three blocks on Staten Island and the single block in northern Nassau County.

Despite the appearance of possibly prospecting birds in the salt marshes of the Rye Marshlands Conservancy, Westchester County, in the 1990s (Manson 1991, Askildsen 1994), the Willet has yet to fulfill Paxton's (1998e) prediction of expanding into all remaining coastal salt marshes. In fact, only one Possible breeding record was noted along Long Island Sound during the second survey. This gap is rather odd, as the Willet has been increasing in numbers and expanding its range in Connecticut since the 1990s and is found at several sites there along the northern coast of Long Island Sound (CTDEP 1999). The difference in the abundance of Willets breeding along the Connecticut and New York shores of the Sound is likely the result of available habitat. Most of the breeding sites in Connecticut are near the mouths of rivers, which often support fairly large areas of salt marsh. New York's Sound shoreline has relatively little salt marsh available for nesting, much of which is inside harbors or otherwise disjunct from adjacent habitat and may be susceptible to flooding during storm tides.

Continental Willet populations appear to be relatively stable (Morrison et al. 2001), although Breeding Bird Survey data show a significant long-term decline survey-wide (Sauer et al. 2005). The U.S. Shorebird Conservation Plan lists the Willet as a species of Moderate Concern (USFWS 2004). The Willet's seemingly ubiquitous presence in the salt marshes along Long Island's south shore and the increases found during the second Atlas survey suggest that this species is currently secure and will remain so.

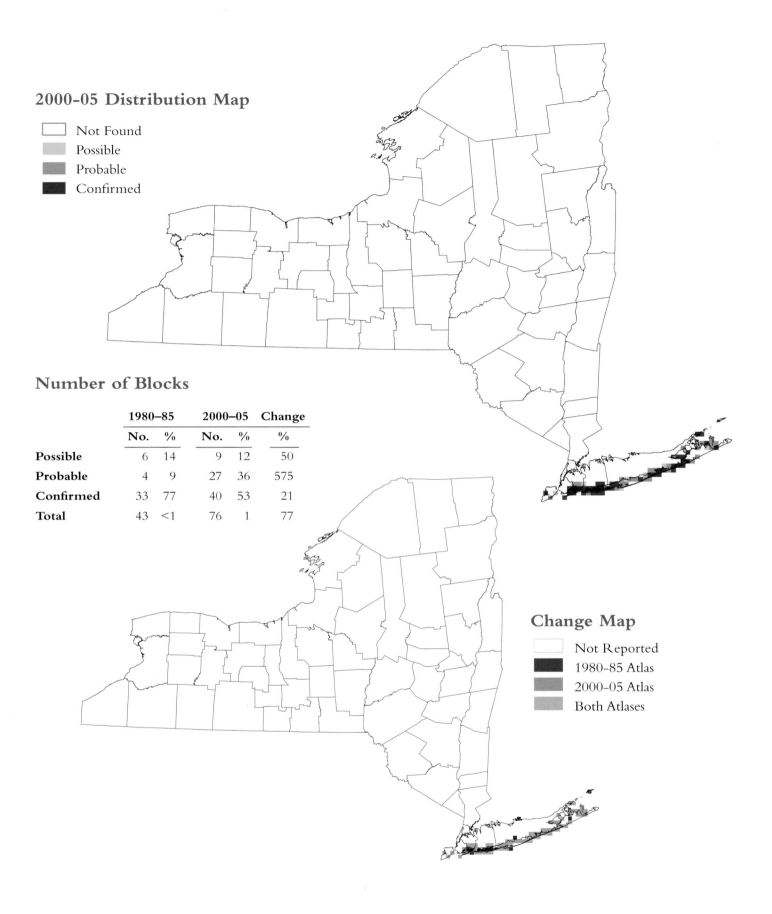

2000-05 Distribution Map

- ☐ Not Found
- Possible
- Probable
- Confirmed

Number of Blocks

	1980–85		2000–05		Change
	No.	%	No.	%	%
Possible	6	14	9	12	50
Probable	4	9	27	36	575
Confirmed	33	77	40	53	21
Total	43	<1	76	1	77

Change Map

- ☐ Not Reported
- 1980-85 Atlas
- 2000-05 Atlas
- Both Atlases

Upland Sandpiper
Bartramia longicauda

KEVIN J. MCGOWAN

The Upland Sandpiper is a shorebird of prairies and open grasslands, breeding from Alaska to New Jersey but primarily in the Great Plains. As a grassland bird, it was probably rare and restricted in New York before the 1800s, present perhaps only on the Long Island prairies, but the conversion of forests to agriculture would have created new breeding habitat across much of the state. In the 19th century the Upland Sandpiper was common on the eastern tip of Long Island (Giraud 1844) and uncommon to rare in central and western New York (Rathbun 1879, Short 1893). Eaton (1910) showed it breeding across the Great Lakes Plain, into the Mohawk Valley to the Hudson Valley, and on the eastern portion of Long Island. He reported the Long Island population as declining but the interior one as increasing. Bull (1974) listed it as nearly gone from Long Island, lost with the destruction of the former prairie, but still locally common, though declining, in the mid-Hudson-Mohawk valley region and in the agricultural districts of central and western New York.

During the first Atlas survey, the Upland Sandpiper was found to be uncommon, occurring across western New York, up the Great Lakes Plain, across the St. Lawrence-Champlain lowlands, and across the Mohawk Valley to the upper Hudson Valley. It was present in smaller numbers in the Central Hudson and on the southern shore of Long Island and scattered across the Appalachian Plateau. During the second Atlas survey it was found in most of the same areas, but the number of blocks with records was down by 65 percent overall, and it had virtually disappeared from a former stronghold extending from the St. Lawrence Plains to the Champlain Transition. The only significant concentrations remaining were in the Eastern Ontario Plain, in the Black River Valley, and to a lesser extent, in the Mohawk Valley. Smaller concentrations were in the upper Hudson Valley, Central Hudson, and Cattaraugus Highlands. A few records remained in eastern Long Island.

Breeding Bird Survey data show a significant negative trend for continental Upland Sandpiper populations since 1980 (Sauer et al. 2005). The U.S. Shorebird Conservation Plan (USFWS 2004) listed the species as a high conservation concern, and it is listed as Threatened in New York. The second Ontario Breeding Bird Atlas reported a significant decline in reports, but the range was comparable in the two Atlases (Bird Studies Canada et al. 2006).

Hunting probably accounted for much of the Upland Sandpiper's decline starting 100 years ago, and it remains a concern in the West Indies (Houston and Bowen 2001). Conversion of native grasslands to croplands in both North and South Amer-

ica likely contributed even more (Houston and Bowen 2001). In New York, the Upland Sandpiper breeds primarily in old pastures, hayfields, airports, and other similarly mowed areas. The loss of agricultural land and the increased planting of corn rather than other grains may have contributed to the decline there (Eaton 1988p). Smith (1998f) suggested that populations of Upland Sandpiper might have stabilized in the 1990s, but the losses occurring between the two Atlas periods suggest otherwise. Habitat management will be necessary to retain this species as a breeder in the state but may not be sufficient. Smith (1998f) detailed such procedures and indicated that they were in place in the Finger Lakes National Forest, but no Upland Sandpipers were observed there during the second Atlas effort. Houston and Bowen (2001) reported that three different habitats in close proximity are required: perches and low vegetation for visibility during courting; higher vegetation to hide the nest; and lower vegetation during supervision of young. Such areas may be difficult to provide on a large scale. Airports now supply half or more of this species's nesting sites in several northeastern states, where adequate grasslands are otherwise in short supply (Houston and Bowen 2001), and may provide some of the last refuges of the Upland Sandpiper in New York.

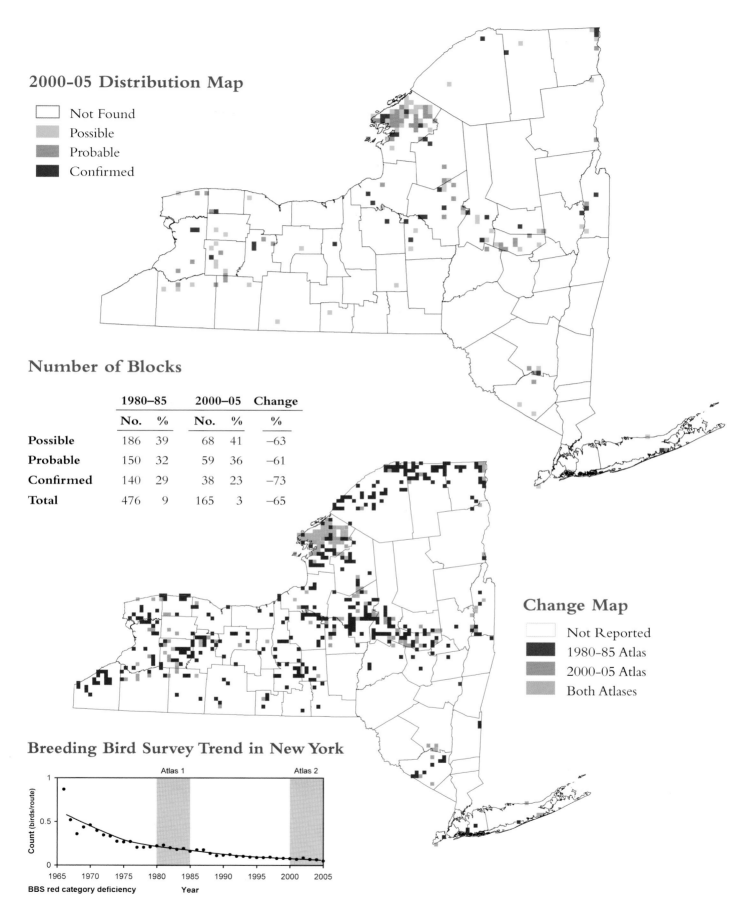

2000-05 Distribution Map

- ☐ Not Found
- Possible
- Probable
- Confirmed

Number of Blocks

	1980–85		2000–05		Change
	No.	%	No.	%	%
Possible	186	39	68	41	−63
Probable	150	32	59	36	−61
Confirmed	140	29	38	23	−73
Total	476	9	165	3	−65

Change Map

- ☐ Not Reported
- 1980-85 Atlas
- 2000–05 Atlas
- Both Atlases

Breeding Bird Survey Trend in New York

BBS red category deficiency

Wilson's Snipe
Gallinago delicata

KEVIN J. MCGOWAN

A common shorebird of wet, grassy spots, Wilson's Snipe breeds across Alaska and Canada, southward to the northern United States (Mueller 2005), with New York at the southeastern edge of its breeding range. It breeds in bogs, fens, swamps, and along the edges of rivers and ponds but avoids areas with tall, dense vegetation, such as cattails (Tuck 1972), although in New York, Eaton (1988f) noted it is found "in and around the margins of the large cat-tail-bulrush marshes" and "in smaller sedge meadows." DeKay (1844) noted that the "Drowned Lands" of Orange County were a particularly good snipe breeding locality. Several early authors listed it as a migrant (Giraud 1844, Rathbun 1879, Short 1893), and Reed and Wright (1909) called it a rare breeder at the north end of Cayuga Lake. Eaton (1910) considered the snipe an uncommon breeder, irregular in its occurrence at any given site; he listed known breeding events across the Great Lakes and St. Lawrence plains and noted that it might become more common along the shores of Lake Ontario and in central New York with a reduction in spring hunting and disturbance on the breeding grounds. Bull (1974) called the snipe a fairly common breeder in the central and western parts of the state, most common around the large marshes, local in the Adirondacks, rare in the Mohawk and Hudson valleys, and missing from the Catskills.

In the first Atlas, Wilson's Snipe was reported as widely scattered, especially from the Eastern Ontario and St. Lawrence plains to the Champlain Valley. Higher densities were also found in the Black River Valley and western Mohawk Valley, and from the Great Lakes Plain to the northern section of the Appalachian Plateau, with a cluster in the Cattaraugus Highlands. Occurrence in the Adirondacks was spotty, and it was missing from the Catskills and most of the eastern Appalachian Plateau uplands. A concentration was noted in the lowlands of Orange County, much as described by DeKay (1844). During the second Atlas survey, the snipe was found in slightly more blocks, with a similar distribution. A concentration remained from the Champlain Valley westward across the northern perimeter of the state along the St. Lawrence Plains, down the Black River Valley and the Tug Hill Plateau into the western section of the Mohawk Valley. Apparent declines occurred along the Erie-Ontario Plain and in the Cattaraugus Highlands, although some of this change may be the result of observer effects. Possible breeding was recorded again in Orange County, but the species remains uncommon across the southern portion of New York. Although the snipe's courtship display is loud and distinctive, it performs primarily at night, and it ceases calling after eggs are laid (Mueller 2005). This well-camouflaged snipe then becomes difficult to detect, and the atlasers may well have missed some breeding locations.

Wilson's Snipe is relatively common across its range and is hunted widely, with over 200,000 taken annually (Mueller 2005). Though the Breeding Bird Survey may not treat this species adequately (Mueller 2005), data show no significant trends since 1966 across the continent, in the northeastern region, or in New York (Sauer et al. 2005). The U.S. Shorebird Conservation Plan (USFWS 2004) put Wilson's Snipe in the Moderate Risk category, noting a declining population trend. However, a recent analysis of migrant shorebirds in central and eastern North America found no significant trend for snipe numbers between 1974 and 1998 (Bart et al. 2007). The second Ontario Breeding Bird Atlas reported a significant increase in snipe numbers in northern sections of the province but significant declines in the southern regions (Bird Studies Canada et al. 2006). As with other secretive wetland-nesting birds, a targeted survey effort may be necessary to accurately track population changes for Wilson's Snipe. Still, the data provided by the two Atlas projects are encouraging for its prospects in New York.

2000-05 Distribution Map

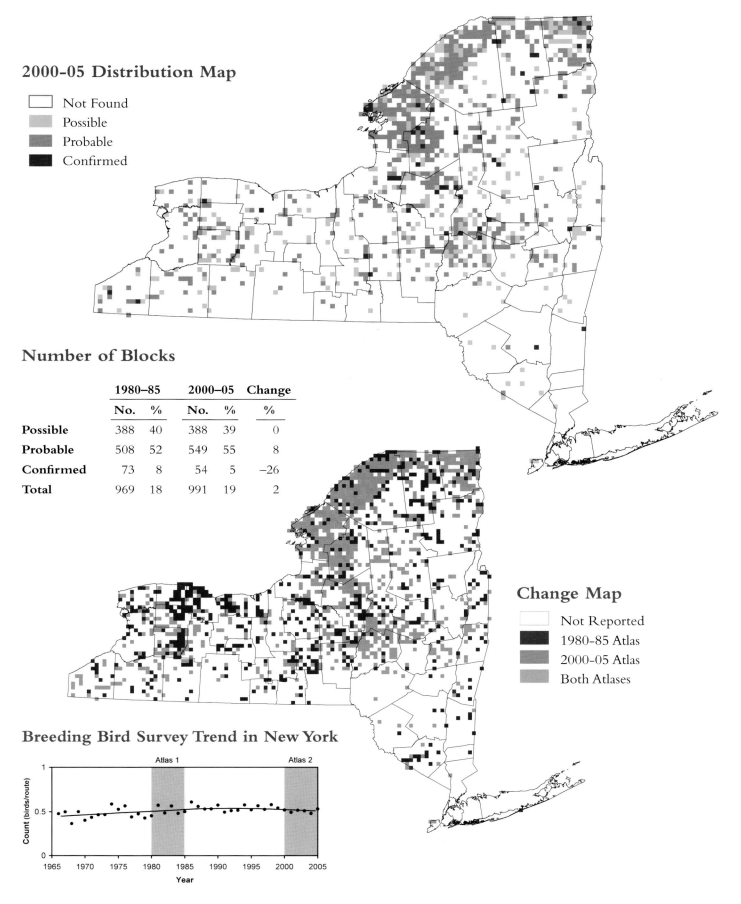

	Not Found
	Possible
	Probable
	Confirmed

Number of Blocks

	1980–85		2000–05		Change
	No.	%	No.	%	%
Possible	388	40	388	39	0
Probable	508	52	549	55	8
Confirmed	73	8	54	5	−26
Total	969	18	991	19	2

Change Map

	Not Reported
	1980-85 Atlas
	2000-05 Atlas
	Both Atlases

Breeding Bird Survey Trend in New York

American Woodcock

Scolopax minor

Timothy J. Post

The American Woodcock is a shorebird that has moved inland and taken up residence in forest thickets. It has a long bill specially adapted for probing into moist soil for its preferred meal of earthworms (Sheldon 1967). The American Woodcock breeds in the eastern half of North America, from southeastern Manitoba to Nova Scotia, southward to eastern Texas and northern Florida (Kelley et al. 2007). With New York falling within its primary breeding range, the woodcock breeds in suitable habitat throughout much of the state. Woodcock require a mix of habitats, in relatively close proximity. The most critical habitat contains early-successional forests or shrublands with canopy cover, moist soils, and abundant worm populations for feeding (Mendall and Aldous 1943). Riparian shrublands and forests, which possess many of these characteristics, can be a particularly important habitat type (Sheldon 1971). The American Woodcock was probably common in pre-colonial New York, breeding around beaver meadows and other forest openings, and numbers might even have increased with the beginning of forest clearing. DeKay (1844) said it bred in all parts of the state. Eaton (1910) stated that the woodcock was formerly common throughout the state, but that its numbers were declining in the face of hunting pressure, development, and habitat alteration and destruction. Bull (1974) noted that woodcock populations had increased again with protection, but that they had not reached their former levels.

During the first Atlas survey, the American Woodcock was found to be rather evenly, if spottily, distributed across the state, with clusters and gaps perhaps attributable in part to Atlas coverage. The woodcock was detected in a similar number of blocks during the second Atlas survey, with minimal changes in distribution occurring between the two Atlas periods. Areas that had been subject to heavy development, such as the lower Hudson Valley and urban portions of the upper Great Lakes Plain, showed fewer records. The St. Lawrence Valley and Eastern Ontario Plain showed increases in the number of blocks with detections, although this finding may be the result of increased Atlas effort. Because of its secretive nature, the early mating period (April–mid-May), and the narrow window when the male is active and detectable at dusk, the woodcock is not likely to be detected unless it is specifically sought. Consequently, patterns of distribution change for the American Woodcock are difficult to assess, and interpretations must be treated with caution.

The trend results of the U.S. Fish and Wildlife Service Singing Ground Survey for the American Woodcock in the eastern flyway, including New York, show a 1.9 percent decline per year since the 1960s (Kelley 2006). Since 1995, the rate of decline has slowed. Declines in American Woodcock abundance in New York can be attributed to a loss of upland and wetland habitat to development, succession, and maturation of forests (Kelley 2006). Wetland filling and alteration have greatly reduced the amount of woodcock habitat in some areas. Reductions in the amount of silviculture, and decreases in even-aged forest management have been significant contributors to the loss of habitat. Range-wide, changes and losses in migration habitats and wintering areas may also be affecting populations (Kelley 2006).

The American Woodcock is considered a shorebird species of high conservation concern (USFWS 2004). Woodcock is recognized by the New York State Comprehensive Wildlife Conservation Strategy as a Species of Greatest Conservation Need (NYSDEC 2005a). The American Woodcock Conservation Plan (Kelley 2006) provides habitat goals and guidance on conservation. The greatest need in New York is to increase the amount of even-aged forest management, including riparian areas, and to manage and protect existing shrub habitats.

2000–05 Distribution Map

- ☐ Not Found
- Possible
- Probable
- Confirmed

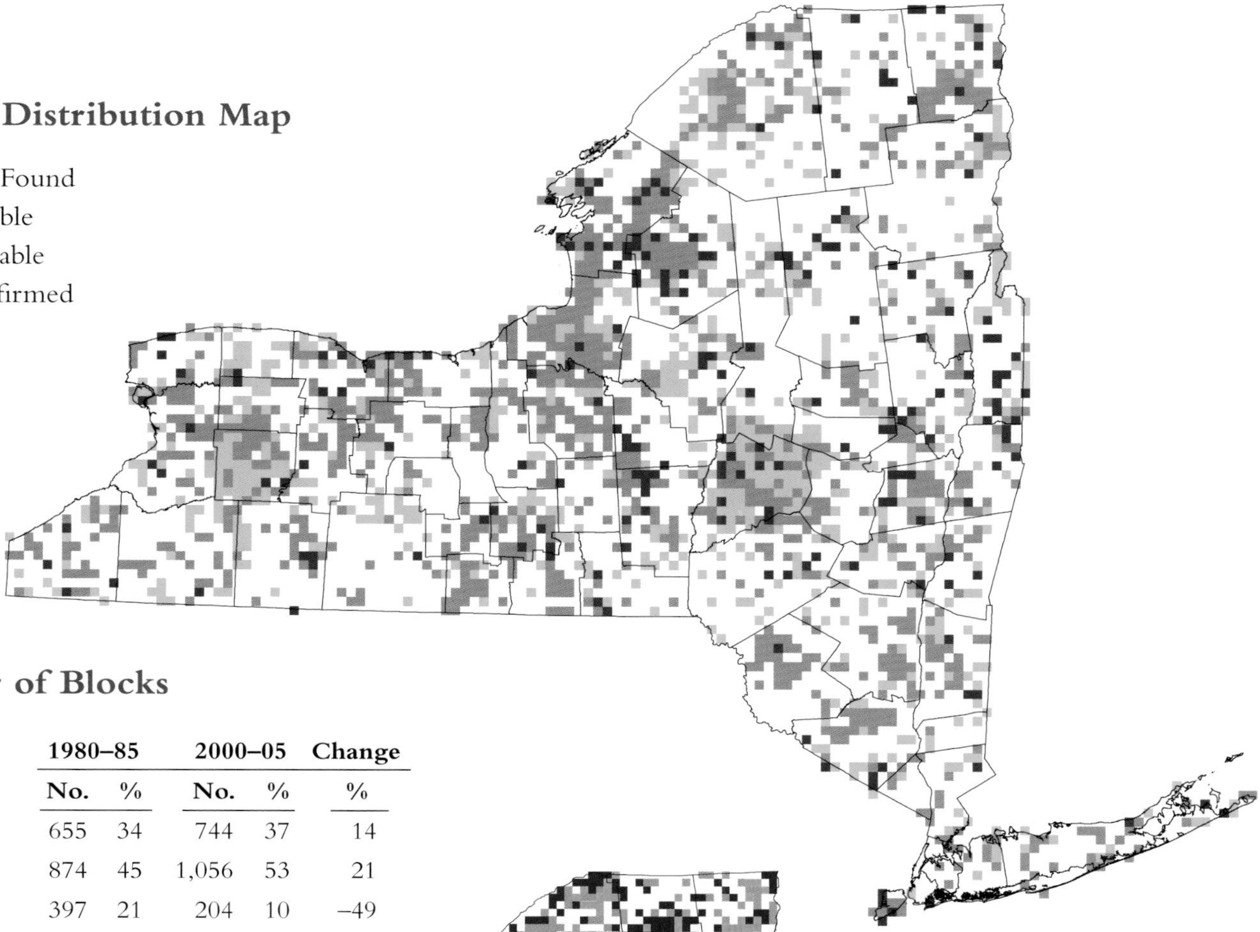

Number of Blocks

	1980–85		2000–05		Change
	No.	%	No.	%	%
Possible	655	34	744	37	14
Probable	874	45	1,056	53	21
Confirmed	397	21	204	10	−49
Total	1,926	36	2,004	38	4

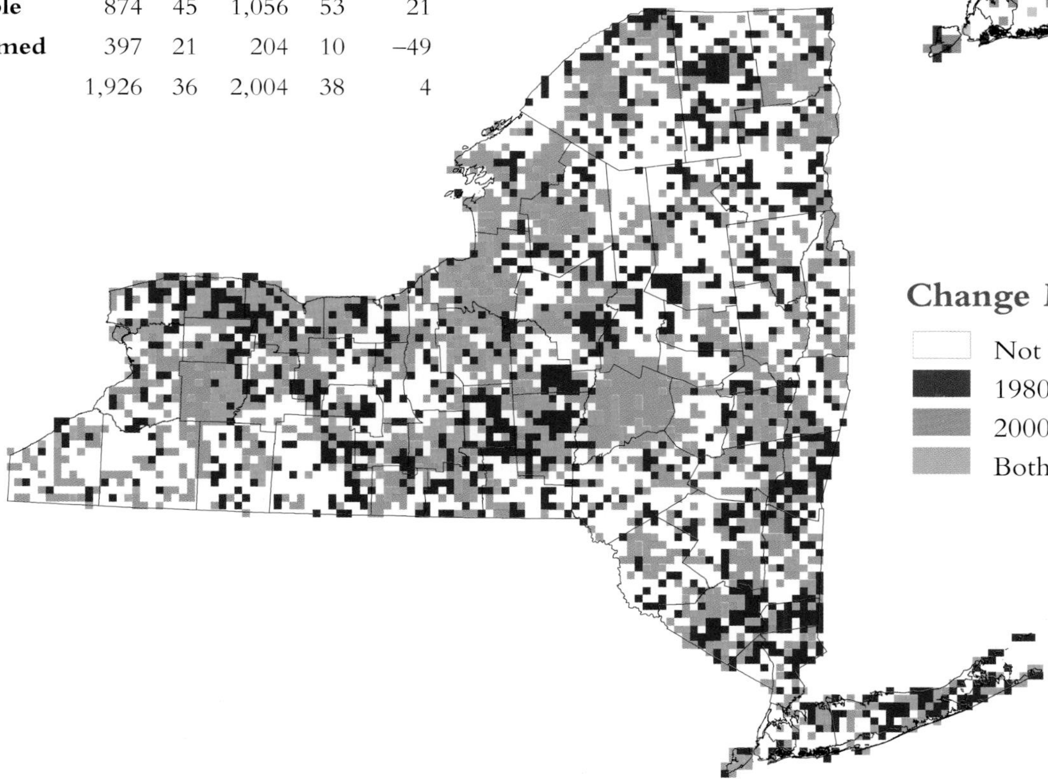

Change Map

- ☐ Not Reported
- 1980-85 Atlas
- 2000-05 Atlas
- Both Atlases

Wilson's Phalarope
Phalaropus tricolor

MATTHEW D. MEDLER

Wilson's Phalarope is one of six new confirmed breeders in New York since the first Atlas survey was completed. Traditionally found breeding in the wetlands of central and western North America, this species began expanding eastward in the second half of the 19th century into Michigan (Adams 1991) and Ontario (Baillie and Harrington 1936). More recently, Wilson's Phalarope has bred in widely isolated areas, including Alaska, Massachusetts, New Brunswick, and Texas (Colwell and Jehl 1994). In its prairie breeding range, this species nests in areas with ponds and lakes near wet meadow vegetation (Johnsgard 1981). Most nesting in southern Ontario has occurred in marshes or near sewage lagoons with lush vegetation nearby (Cadman 1987). The few confirmed New York breeding records have come from pastures along the shore of Lake Champlain (W. Krueger pers. comm.). DeKay (1844) described Wilson's Phalarope as being very rare in New York, and Eaton (1910) described it as an "occasional transient." Bull (1974) listed the species as a regular fall migrant, and he also considered it to be a rare, but probably regular, spring migrant. While not specifically suggesting breeding by Wilson's Phalarope in New York, Bull did note a breeding record in southeastern Ontario, 40 km (25 mi) west of Buffalo (Beardslee and Mitchell 1965).

Wilson's Phalarope was not documented as a breeding species during the first Atlas project, although a pair was observed in suitable habitat near Lake Champlain from 21 to 27 May 1981 (Krueger 1993). The state's first confirmed breeding record came on 18 June 1993, with the sighting of an adult male with three chicks in the town of Champlain, Clinton County, just a few hundred yards from the 1981 site (Krueger 1993). Breeding was confirmed in the same area in 1994 and 1997, but the next observed nesting, and first Confirmed Atlas record, did not occur until July 2002, when a juvenile was found with one male and two females (W. Krueger pers. comm.). Breeding was also confirmed in a neighboring block 11 days later (W. Krueger pers. comm.). In addition to these two Confirmed re-

cords, the species was reported from two blocks on the Erie-Ontario Plain.

Wilson's Phalarope is not detected in large numbers by the Breeding Bird Survey, but the species experienced a significant annual increase of 1.8 percent in the Western BBS Region between 1966 and 2005; there was no significant survey-wide trend during this time period (Sauer et al. 2005). The second Ontario Breeding Bird Atlas reported a significant decline in the Simcoe-Rideau region, home to a majority of phalarope records according to both Ontario Atlases (Bird Studies Canada et al. 2006). Despite this recent decline in Ontario, New York's breeding records are likely the result of a century-long expansion of Wilson's Phalarope through Ontario and into the St. Lawrence Valley of Quebec. Ontario's first documented nesting, from the southwestern part of the province, came in 1879 (Baillie and Harrington 1936). Quebec's first nest was discovered near Montreal in 1974 (Steeves and Holohan 1975), and confirmed nesting during the Quebec Atlas included several sites northeast of Quebec City (Jauvin and Lafontaine 1996). New York's Clinton County breeding sites are about 17 km (10 mi) from the Quebec border and are linked with the St. Lawrence by the Richelieu River, which drains Lake Champlain. The main Wilson's Phalarope population faces two major threats: the loss and degradation of prairie wetland habitat, which might be the cause of recent nesting in disjunct locations (Colwell and Jehl 1994); and changes in hydrology at large saline lakes in western North America that serve as important migratory staging areas (Wells 2007). It is unclear how these threats might affect the species's status in New York, but additional Wilson's Phalarope breeding should be looked for, especially in the Great Lakes Plain and St. Lawrence Plains.

2000-05 Distribution Map

- ☐ Not Found
- Possible
- Probable
- ■ Confirmed

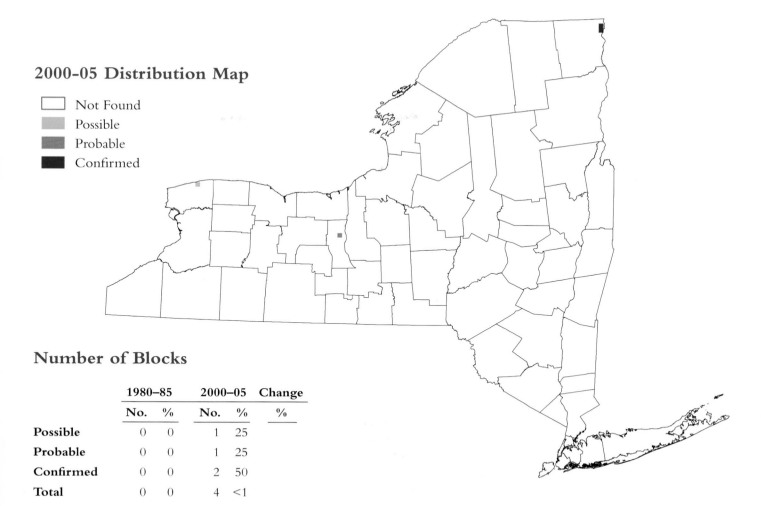

Number of Blocks

	1980–85		2000–05		Change
	No.	%	No.	%	%
Possible	0	0	1	25	
Probable	0	0	1	25	
Confirmed	0	0	2	50	
Total	0	0	4	<1	

Laughing Gull and Common Tern at Kennedy Airport

The marshes adjacent to the John F. Kennedy International Airport seem an unlikely spot for a colony of breeding birds, yet the Laughing Gull nests there in great numbers. Its raucous, intensely social behavior seems to fit right in with the noise and confusion of this important transportation hub.

Laughing Gull
Larus atricilla

MICHAEL R. WASILCO

The Laughing Gull is the only hooded gull to nest in New York and also has the most restricted breeding distribution within the state. This gull nests only in coastal areas of eastern North America (Burger 1996). Along the Atlantic Coast, Laughing Gull colonies are most numerous from New Jersey southward through the mid-Atlantic states (Belant and Dolbeer 1993). Northward of New Jersey, the gull is a very local breeder, found in few, yet relatively large colonies as far northward as Maine. Historically much more numerous in the northern part of its range, this species was decimated by the millinery trade and commercial egg collecting in the late 19th century (Buckley et al. 1978). In much of its range, it has recovered from these losses, but in the northern regions, competition from larger gull species expanding southward prevented the Laughing Gull from reclaiming many colony sites (Burger 1996). In New York, the Laughing

ATM©2006

Gull was eliminated as a breeder by 1900 (Lent 1988). Despite being an increasingly common migrant and summer visitor to New York Harbor and Long Island through the mid-1900s, it was not found nesting in the state again until 1978, when three nests were discovered on the Line Islands in Nassau County (Buckley et al. 1978). Since then, it has formed and maintained several large colonies in Jamaica Bay but has failed to expand out from that area to form any other lasting colonies (Paxton 1998c).

Direct comparison of the results of the two Atlas surveys is problematic, as the criteria for reporting Possible and Probable breeding records for colonial nesting species were restricted slightly for the second Atlas; only birds exhibiting an attachment to a colony site were reported. The Laughing Gulls recorded as Possible breeders were associated with the gull and heron colony at Youngs Island in Stony Brook Harbor. However, the seemingly ubiquitous groups of breeding plumaged and immature Laughing Gulls that show up all along the coastal areas in June were not included in the Atlas records, as they were known to not be breeding in those areas. Similar failed breeders or nonbreeding birds are likely the source of many of the Possible breeding records reported in the first Atlas.

The first Atlas reported the species in 32 blocks around the state's marine coast. Most of those records were Possible, with only two Probable and one Confirmed. The single Confirmed record was at Jamaica Bay. The second Atlas findings, six blocks with records, still probably over-represented the true nesting distribution. The Laughing Gull fledges in mid-July, and young are fed by the parents for 2 to 3 weeks after fledging. Thus, the blocks showing Confirmed breeding in Nassau County are questionable and may have included birds that dispersed from Jamaica Bay, as they all represent FL or FY breeding codes recorded after mid-July. Notable is the Confirmed record (FY in 2001) in the Moriches Bay area, where extensive areas of habitat and several gull and tern colonies exist, but no Laughing Gull nests are known.

The main Laughing Gull colonies in New York are in a particularly troubling and vulnerable location, at the end of the main runways at John F. Kennedy International Airport (Brown et al. 2001). These colonies caused an average of 157 airplane-bird strikes per year in the late 1980s (Dolbeer et al. 2003) and could be devastated by a plane crash. This situation led to the development of a gull-control program at the airport. This program, which continues today, removed 63,838 Laughing Gulls (mostly either failed breeders or nonbreeders) from the air over the airport in the period 1991–2003 (Dolbeer et al. 2003). During this same period the number of Laughing Gulls nesting in Jamaica Bay dropped by about 60 percent (Washburn et al. 2005). This drop in the New York population comes at the same time that the northern Atlantic Coast population has held steady or increased (Dolbeer et al. 2003, GOMSWG 2005).

2000–05 Distribution Map

- ☐ Not Found
- Possible
- Probable
- ■ Confirmed

Number of Blocks

	1980–85		2000–05		Change
	No.	%	No.	%	%
Possible	29	91	1	17	−97
Probable	2	6	0	0	−100
Confirmed	1	3	5	83	400
Total	32	<1	6	<1	−81

Change Map

- ☐ Not Reported
- ■ 1980-85 Atlas
- 2000–05 Atlas
- Both Atlases

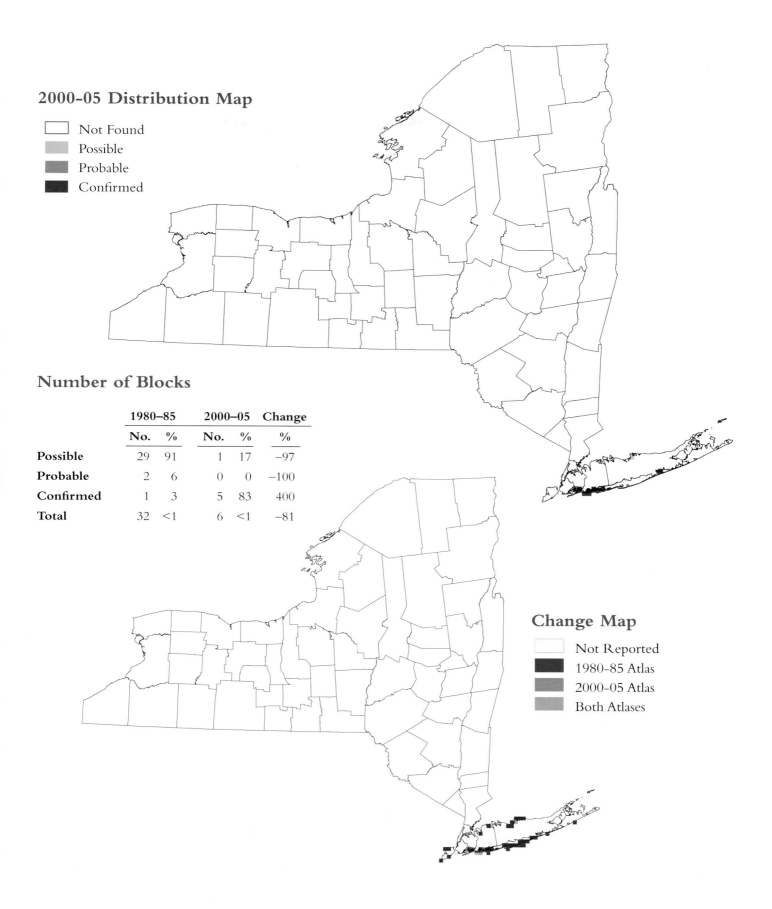

Ring-billed Gull
Larus delawarensis

MILO E. RICHMOND

The Ring-billed Gull is the most common of the gulls regularly seen in New York. However, early writers (Giraud 1844, Eaton 1910) considered this species as present but not nesting in the state. Its proliferation in the latter half of the 20th century may be tied to its foraging habits, which include consuming a range of invertebrates and grain from agricultural fields (Ryder 1993), as well as opportunistic scavenging at waste disposal sites and parking lots (Vermeer 1970). The core of the Ring-billed Gull range is central Canada's boreal region and southward to northern California, Wyoming, Minnesota, and the Great Lakes region (Ryder 1993). New York lies on the southeastern edge of the overall breeding range. The first report of nesting in the state was in 1936 on Gull Island in eastern Lake Ontario (Hyde 1939). By 1938 nesting expanded to nearby Little Galloo Island, where its population grew rapidly. The breeding population on this 17-ha (42-a) island reached 19,000 pairs by 1950 and 75,000–80,000 pairs by 1965 (Bull 1976). Currently more than 53,000 pairs nest on this rocky, grass-covered island, down from 84,230 pairs in 1990 (Scharf et al. 1998), but still possibly the largest nesting colony in existence. Five other notable colonies developed during the same period, the largest of which is in excess of 2,500 pairs on Four Brothers Islands in Lake Champlain (Cuthbert et al. 2002). While all the expansion colonies in the 1950s and 1960s were found on islands (Bull 1976), recent nesting has occurred in a variety of habitats, including breakwaters, dredge spoils, concrete dikes, gravel piles, and other open areas near water (Blokpoel and Tessier 1986). Although Ring-billed Gull totals of 56,977 in 1984 and 58,178 in 1985 were reported from the lower Hudson River and Long Island in winter, the species is not yet nesting there (Brock 1998).

Ring-billed Gull numbers continued to increase during the 1970s and 1980s throughout New York's eastern basin. There was an average of over 1,200 nests each year on Oneida Lake from 1983 through 1994; nesting peaked there in 1985, with 2,269 pairs (Coleman and Richmond 2004). A decline in the Oneida Lake population began in about 1996, due to planned removal of nests and increasing numbers of nesting Double-crested Cormorant and Herring Gull. Since 2000, between 50 and 150 nests have occurred annually at this managed site (Coleman and Richmond 2005).

Atlas results indicate a continuing expansion of Ring-billed Gull nesting across acceptable habitat in New York. In the first Atlas, breeding was confirmed in 13 blocks in five areas: Lake Erie, the eastern end of Lake Ontario, the St. Lawrence River, Oneida Lake, and Lake Champlain. The number of blocks with Confirmed breeding more than doubled in the second Atlas survey, with 28 blocks in the same five locations noted in the first Atlas, plus new areas in northern St. Lawrence, Fulton, and Delaware counties. Notable are observations from the west-central part of the state, which showed no evidence of nesting during the first Atlas period but now has eight new sites with Confirmed records. Ring-billed Gulls displaced by management actions on Little Galloo Island and Oneida Lake may be the source of gulls at these new nesting locations. This nesting expansion is in concert with reports from surrounding regions in the eastern Great Lakes Basin (Lock 1988, Coleman and Richmond 2005).

Conservation implications include the caution that the increase in the number of nesting locations does not certify population growth but does indicate expansion of this species into areas where its nesting and foraging may present problems. Monitoring should be continued to identify possible threats to human health and aircraft safety. At this time additional federal or state protection is not warranted. However, there may be local need to reduce populations in critical areas through management action.

ATM ©2006

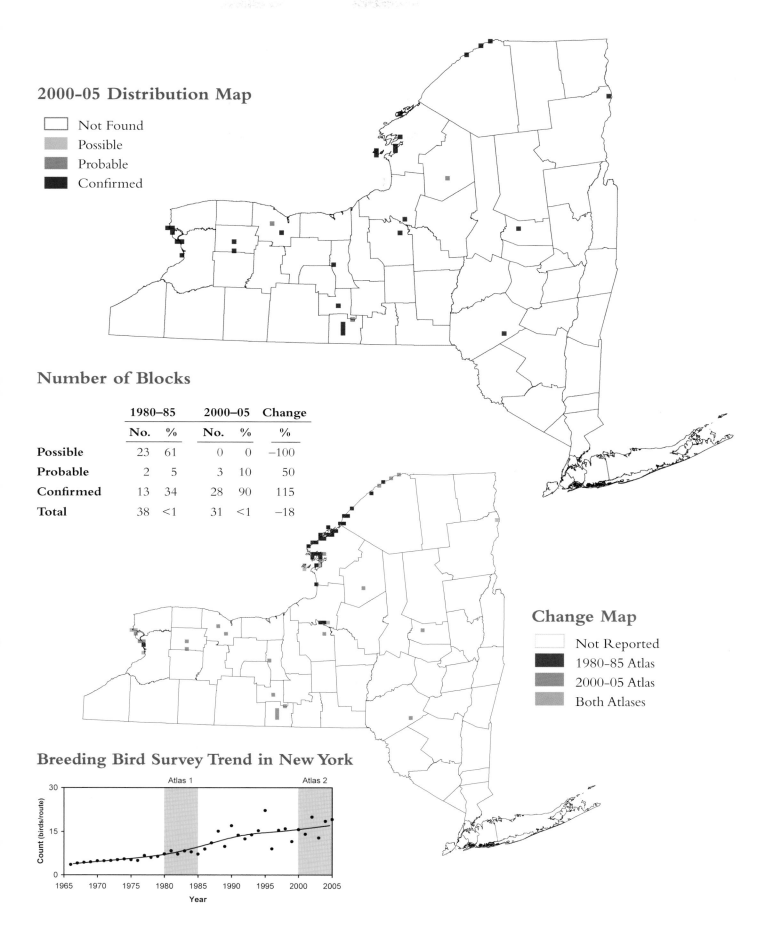

2000–05 Distribution Map

- ☐ Not Found
- ☐ Possible
- ☐ Probable
- ■ Confirmed

Number of Blocks

	1980–85		2000–05		Change
	No.	%	No.	%	%
Possible	23	61	0	0	−100
Probable	2	5	3	10	50
Confirmed	13	34	28	90	115
Total	38	<1	31	<1	−18

Change Map

- ☐ Not Reported
- ■ 1980-85 Atlas
- ☐ 2000-05 Atlas
- ☐ Both Atlases

Breeding Bird Survey Trend in New York

Herring Gull
Larus argentatus

Milo E. Richmond

The Herring Gull breeds across Alaska and Canada and the northeastern United States from North Carolina to Newfoundland, and throughout the Great Lakes (Harrison 1983). Nesting is often in large, mixed colonies, but single pairs are common, especially in the Adirondacks. Successful nesting is usually near water and safe from ground predators (Pierotti and Good 1994). Records indicate that persecution by gunners and egg collectors in the 1800s drove this large gull to near extirpation in New York, and only a few pairs may have continued nesting in the Adirondacks (J. M. C. Peterson 1988h). Neither Giraud (1844) nor DeKay (1844) indicated nesting anywhere in New York, but Merriam (1881) called this gull a common breeder in certain Adirondack Lakes. Jordan (1888) confirmed nesting at Four Brothers Islands, Lake Champlain, where 50 pairs remained from a larger colony first reported by Thompson (1853). Eaton (1910) confirmed continuation of nesting in the Adirondacks but not elsewhere in the state. Collectively, these reports suggest that the Adirondacks provided a refugium from gunners of that era. Federal protection in 1918 coupled with vigilant protection of nesting gulls in New York in the first quarter of the 20th century marked the beginning of the recovery of the Herring Gull and other persecuted species of the time (Bull 1976, Pierotti and Good 1994). Previously nesting only as far south as central Maine (Bent 1921), this gull expanded southward along the coast to several sites during 1930–70 (Drury 1973). By 1931 it had reached Long Island, where it established nesting on the eastern and southern shores (Bull 1976). On Oneida Lake, where the Herring Gull first nested in 1940 (Bull 1976), the population grew to 60 pairs by 1985 (Claypoole 1986). Despite the fact that, or possibly because, it shared the small islands in Oneida Lake with several other species, the Herring Gull population continued to expand, reaching 91 pairs by 1995. Its obvious predatory tendencies prompted a managed reduction at that time, and over the past decade numbers have been limited to under 70 pairs, allowing better nesting opportunities for terns (Coleman and Richmond 2004). Other nesting has occurred inland along eastern Lake Erie and Lake Ontario and in smaller colonies in the Adirondacks and along Lake Champlain (Brinkley 1998).

The first Atlas reported the Herring Gull as breeding primarily in the known locations described above. The second Atlas data showed a similar distribution but revealed a slight decline on the Coastal Lowlands. The number of blocks with records in the Adirondacks was remarkably similar in the two surveys: 160 blocks (22 percent Confirmed) in the first Atlas and 165 blocks (21 percent Confirmed) for the second Atlas. The number of blocks in the eastern basin of Lake Ontario and far western counties near Buffalo were nearly the same as well. New blocks with Confirmed breeding records on Seneca Lake and the Chemung River, plus continued nesting presence at Oneida Lake, suggest further inland expansion of the species.

The Herring Gull population has shown great resilience in its recovery from historical persecution. Growth from 8,000 pairs located entirely in Maine in 1900 to 100,000 pairs nesting from Maine to Virginia in the mid-1980s, to an estimated 116,100 pairs from this same group of coastal states (Andrews 1990), shows that the species has recovered nicely. The New York population, estimated at 25,000 in 1990 (Andrews 1990), appears stable or slightly expanding. Significant numbers are produced in Long Island coastal nesting colonies, while several other sites, especially in the Adirondacks, accommodate numerous but dispersed, successfully nesting pairs. Local needs may occasionally dictate removal of certain birds, particularly during restoration of smaller species. With nesting known from three designated Important Bird Areas (Burger and Liner 2005), no additional protection of this species is currently warranted.

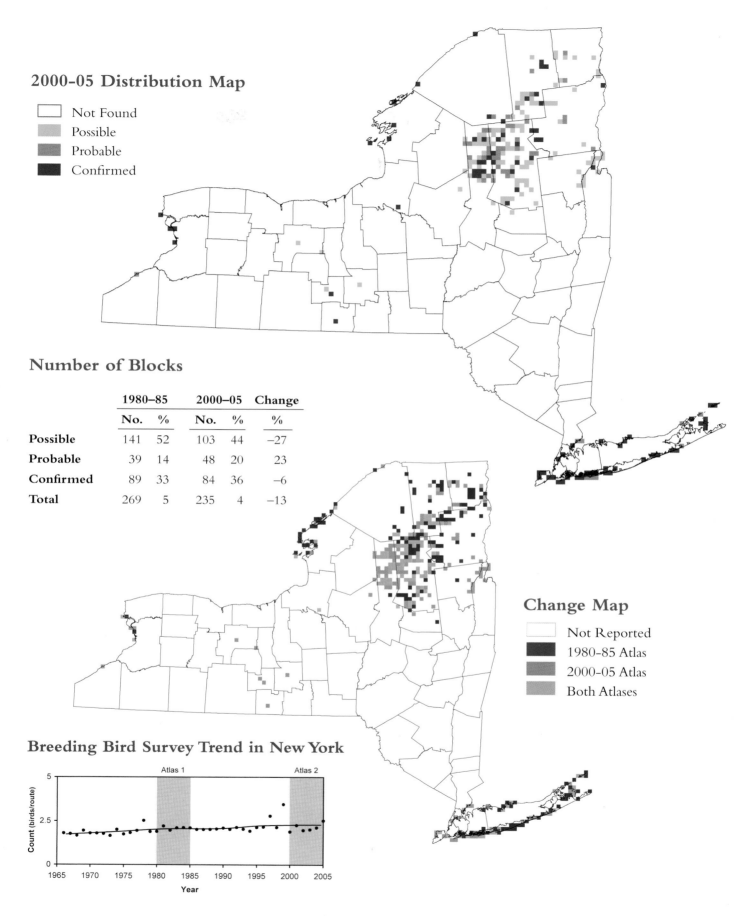

2000-05 Distribution Map

- ☐ Not Found
- Possible
- Probable
- Confirmed

Number of Blocks

	1980–85		2000–05		Change
	No.	%	No.	%	%
Possible	141	52	103	44	−27
Probable	39	14	48	20	23
Confirmed	89	33	84	36	−6
Total	269	5	235	4	−13

Change Map

- ☐ Not Reported
- 1980–85 Atlas
- 2000–05 Atlas
- Both Atlases

Breeding Bird Survey Trend in New York

Great Black-backed Gull

Larus marinus

MILO E. RICHMOND

The Great Black-backed Gull is the largest of the gulls, and the adult is easily recognized by its size and its black back and wings. The breeding distribution includes Greenland, northern Europe, eastern Canada, northeastern United States, and Great Lakes (Cramp and Simmons 1983). It occurs year round on the east coast of North America, breeding from North Carolina to Labrador and inland to the Great Lakes (Good 1998). Other nesting locations are spread across the eastern Canadian provinces and northward to arctic Canada (Godfrey 1986, Erskine 1992). While the breeding range is large, this gull is patchy in distribution and selective of large islands for breeding colony establishment. The largest colonies, exceeding several hundred pairs, include Smuttynose Island, Maine; Monomoy Island, Massachusetts; and Gardiners Island, New York (Buckley and Buckley 1984).

The Great Black-backed Gull, like so many colonial nesting coastal birds, suffered through the 1800s when egg and feather harvesting were rampant (Bent 1921). Recovery of the U.S. populations became possible only after the Lacey Act of 1900 and the Migratory Bird Treaty Act of 1918. Before 1925 only wintering birds were known along the East Coast, southward to New Jersey (Bent 1921). In 1928 breeding was first recorded at the Isles of Shoals, Maine (Jackson and Allen 1932), but by 1931 nesting had expanded to ten different islands along the Maine coast (Norton and Allen 1931). The first New York nest was found in 1942 (Bull 1974). By 1965, a total of 12,400 pairs nested across 180 islands from Maine to Long Island, New York (Nisbet 1978). Great Lakes populations began a comeback in 1954, with regular nesting on Lake Huron in the 1960s and 1970s (Angehrn et al. 1979, Peck and James 1983). In New York, the first inland breeding occurred on Four Brothers Islands in Lake Champlain in 1975 (Meade 1988b).

During the first Atlas survey, breeding was confirmed on the Coastal Lowlands and at the state's larger water bodies, including Oneida Lake, Lake Champlain, Lake Ontario, and the St. Lawrence River. Little change was detected during the second Atlas survey, with the Coastal Lowlands remaining this gull's primary nesting location. Nesting efforts along the northwestern shoreline of Long Island and in lower Westchester County are all near dense human populations. Confirmed nesting was reported for Four Brothers Islands, Lake Champlain, in the 1980s, but a steady decline in numbers beginning in 1994 is noted from annual surveys (Audubon Vermont 2003). Absence of nesting on Lake Champlain is likely accurate because the species is easily recognized and Atlas coverage of the area was complete. The potential inland nesting sites along the Lake Erie and Lake Ontario shorelines may be sustainable and suggest at least that foraging and safe roosting options exist. In Oneida Lake, an unsuccessful first nesting attempt was recorded in 1983 on Long Island (DeBenedictis 1983), but a successful nest was not observed until 1993 (Richmond 1993). Nesting there has continued since 1995, increasing from one to four pairs by 2003. Three pairs nested at Oneida Lake in 2004 and 2005, on Long and Wantry islands (Coleman and Richmond 2005). Confirmed nesting still occurs on Little Galloo Island in Lake Ontario and on the St. Lawrence River along the northern edge of St. Lawrence County.

The trend of continental populations of the Great Black-backed Gull is unclear (Good 1998). The second Ontario Breeding Bird Atlas reported the Great Black-backed Gull breeding in several new areas along the New York border, on the northeastern shore of Lake Ontario and along the St. Lawrence River (Bird Studies Canada et al. 2006). Because of this gull's proclivity for consuming the young of other species within reach at a colony, it requires monitoring and occasional management where a mixed species aggregate is deemed desirable.

ATM©2006

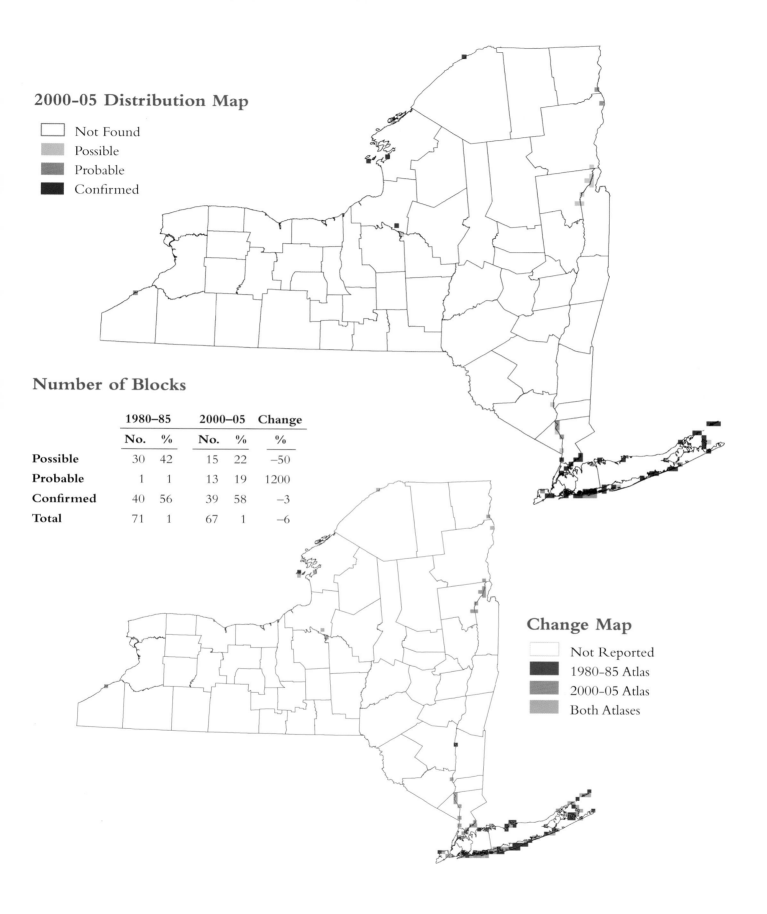

2000-05 Distribution Map

- ☐ Not Found
- Possible
- Probable
- Confirmed

Number of Blocks

	1980–85		2000–05		Change
	No.	%	No.	%	%
Possible	30	42	15	22	−50
Probable	1	1	13	19	1200
Confirmed	40	56	39	58	−3
Total	71	1	67	1	−6

Change Map

- ☐ Not Reported
- 1980-85 Atlas
- 2000-05 Atlas
- Both Atlases

Least Tern
Sternula antillarum

MICHAEL R. WASILCO

The Least Tern, as its name implies, is the smallest of the terns breeding in North America. It nests across the continent, on open sandy beaches, sand bars, dredge spoil, and similar shoreline habitats at sites along both coasts, as well as along some major river and reservoir systems in the interior (Thompson et al. 1997). Least Tern nests are normally no more than a shallow depression scraped into the sand, sometimes lined with bits of shell, and are often found in the same habitats as nesting Piping Plover. Along the coast, the Least Tern can be found nesting from southern Maine to Florida and Texas (Thompson et al. 1997). In New York, it is locally common in coastal areas with suitable habitat of sandy substrates relatively free of vegetation, but is rare away from the salt water (Skelly 1998b). Historically, the Least Tern was common on Long Island in the mid-1800s (Giraud 1844), but overhunting for plumes caused it to become extirpated as a nesting species from 1882 until it re-established a small colony in 1926 (Cruickshank 1942). By the 1970s, colonies could be found around much of coastal New York, from Staten Island, along the south shore of Long Island, to the Peconic Bay and Fishers Island, and as far westward along the north shore as Eatons Neck, where 851 pairs nested in 1976 (D. M. Peterson 1988b).

The first Atlas survey recorded the Least Tern in nearly continuous blocks along the shores of Queens, Nassau, and Suffolk counties, with the exception of some areas along Long Island Sound. The species was noticeably absent from Staten Island and all the mainland counties. The current Atlas fieldwork documented a shift in distribution from the first Atlas. The Least Tern is no longer found at many of the sites within Long Island's south shore bays, especially the Great South Bay and Fire Island, where a large gap exists in the current distribution map. The tern has, however, expanded its presence on the north shore of Nassau and Suffolk counties, filling in some of the gaps seen in the original Atlas. Much of this increased expansion likely coincides with the expansion of the Piping Plover population in the same areas, and the accompanying management and protection efforts.

Surveys in the mid-1970s documented 1,719–2,628 pairs nesting at 29–47 colonies around Long Island (Peterson 1988b). Results of the first Atlas surveys showed that the population was relatively stable at 2,536–3,114 pairs using 39–59 sites along the coast each year (Peterson et al. 1985). In 1983 the Least Tern was listed as Endangered in New York. Through the 1990s the population averaged 2,500–3,000 pairs nesting at 40–60 sites each year, with most colonies comprising fewer than 100 pairs (Sommers et al. 2001). Because the populations appeared stable, New York reclassified the Least Tern as Threatened in 1999. During the second Atlas period, the annual surveys found 2,069–3,267 pairs nesting at 48–62 sites each year (NYSDEC unpubl. data). Surrounding coastal states (New Jersey, Massachusetts, and Connecticut) have also experienced relatively stable or even increasing populations in recent years (NJDEP [n.d.], Mostello 2002, Victoria 2005).

Large and rapid changes in colony size can occur from year to year and within years because of disturbance at colony sites and changes in vegetation. Heavily vegetated sites are no longer suitable for nesting until they become disturbed in some way to re-create the open sandy conditions needed by the Least Tern. This vegetative succession and lack of new dredge spoil are likely the reasons behind the loss of many of the Least Tern colonies on the islands within the south shore bays of Long Island. Disturbance by human recreation is likely why most of the new colonies have shown up in the same areas as Piping Plover, where they are protected from disturbance by people, pets, and beach driving.

ATM© 2006

2000-05 Distribution Map

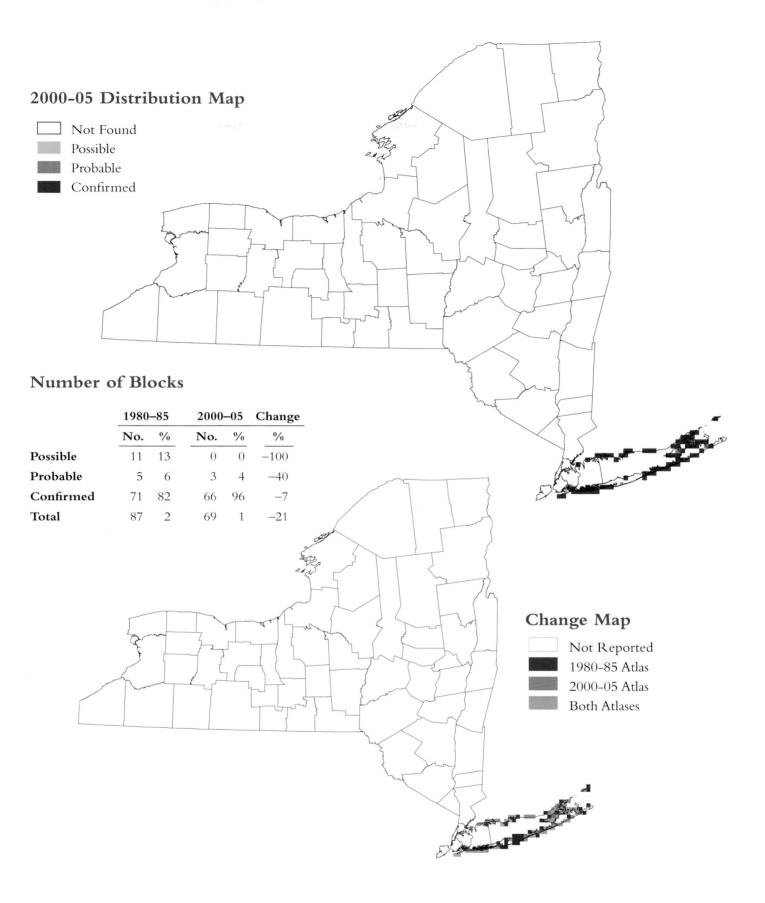

- ▢ Not Found
- ▨ Possible
- ▨ Probable
- ■ Confirmed

Number of Blocks

	1980–85		2000–05		Change
	No.	%	No.	%	%
Possible	11	13	0	0	−100
Probable	5	6	3	4	−40
Confirmed	71	82	66	96	−7
Total	87	2	69	1	−21

Change Map

- ▢ Not Reported
- ■ 1980–85 Atlas
- ▨ 2000–05 Atlas
- ▨ Both Atlases

Gull-billed Tern

Gelochelidon nilotica

SHAIBAL S. MITRA

This cosmopolitan but locally distributed species is found in North America along the coasts of Mexico, inland in extreme southern California, and along the Atlantic Coast northward to Long Island (Parnell et al. 1995). Although the Gull-billed Tern occurs in inland areas in some parts of its far-flung range, definite records in New York have always been strictly coastal (Skelly 1998a). Vague statements by DeKay (1844) concerning "Marsh Terns" in inland New York are puzzling and unconvincing, especially given Giraud's (1844) explicit statement that he had never encountered the species on Long Island. The earliest definite records are specimens taken in the 1880s, involving at least one (Bull 1964) and probably two (Griscom 1923) pairs, plus two additional individuals, all taken during June and July at sites where breeding is presently known or suspected. Although these records are suggestive of breeding, the species was almost certainly extirpated from New York soon thereafter, as Griscom (1923) knew of no records after these specimens were collected. The next series of records commenced in 1934 and consisted of fall sightings, most in association with hurricanes (Cruickshank 1942), and this basic pattern continued until the discovery of breeding on a spoil island in southern Nassau County (Buckley et al. 1975). Thus began a period of regular, if highly localized, occurrence that has continued to the present. But even today, this species remains rare at any appreciable distance from its actual breeding sites, even elsewhere on Long Island.

The first Atlas reported the Gull-billed Tern as breeding at several sites on southwestern Long Island, in two distinct settings: dredge spoil islands within bays and marshes, and the barrier beach itself. The species continues to breed in small numbers in Nassau County and probably also near Jamaica Bay, Queens County (Mitra and Lindsay 2005a, b), and Fire Island Inlet, Suffolk County (Schiff and Wollin 2001a, b). At present, all known or suspected breeding sites are on bay islands. During early May, returning birds are briefly conspicuous at specific sites, notably Jamaica Bay, Jones Beach West End, and Fire Island Inlet. By June the birds withdraw to the bays and marshes, where they are difficult to detect. Later in the summer they reappear, sometimes with young, at the sites mentioned above. This pattern is so strikingly different from the sporadic, storm-driven, late-season records characteristic of other sites along the New York coast that it must be regarded as strongly indicative of breeding. Thus, the consistent occurrence at Jamaica Bay of adults in spring and adults with juveniles in summer suggests that pre- and post-breeding field observations might be superior to nest searches as a means of detecting this species's breeding activity in the New York area.

The appearance of nesting Gull-billed Terns on Long Island in 1975 fit into a pattern of near-simultaneous northward expansion by several southeastern species. During the spring and summer of 2006, the Gull-billed Tern was observed repeatedly between Moriches and Shinnecock inlets (Lindsay and Mitra 2006a, b), considerably farther eastward than breeding had been suspected previously. Seemingly suitable nesting sites are present in this area, and additional fieldwork may prove that the Gull-billed Tern, like the American Oystercatcher, Willet, and Boat-tailed Grackle before it, has expanded eastward to Moriches and Shinnecock bays. Even farther east, Veit and Petersen (1993) described a series of recent spring records from plausible breeding sites in Massachusetts and discussed the possibility of future breeding there. Although these records suggest the possibility of an ongoing population expansion, it must be remembered that the total number of pairs involved is small, and that the persistence even of these few pairs depends on the continued protection of beaches and salt marshes.

ATM© 2006

2000-05 Distribution Map

- ☐ Not Found
- ▨ Possible
- ▧ Probable
- ■ Confirmed

Number of Blocks

	1980–85		2000–05		Change
	No.	%	No.	%	%
Possible	0	0	1	20	
Probable	0	0	1	20	
Confirmed	3	100	3	60	0
Total	3	<1	5	<1	67

Change Map

- ☐ Not Reported
- ■ 1980-85 Atlas
- ▨ 2000-05 Atlas
- ▧ Both Atlases

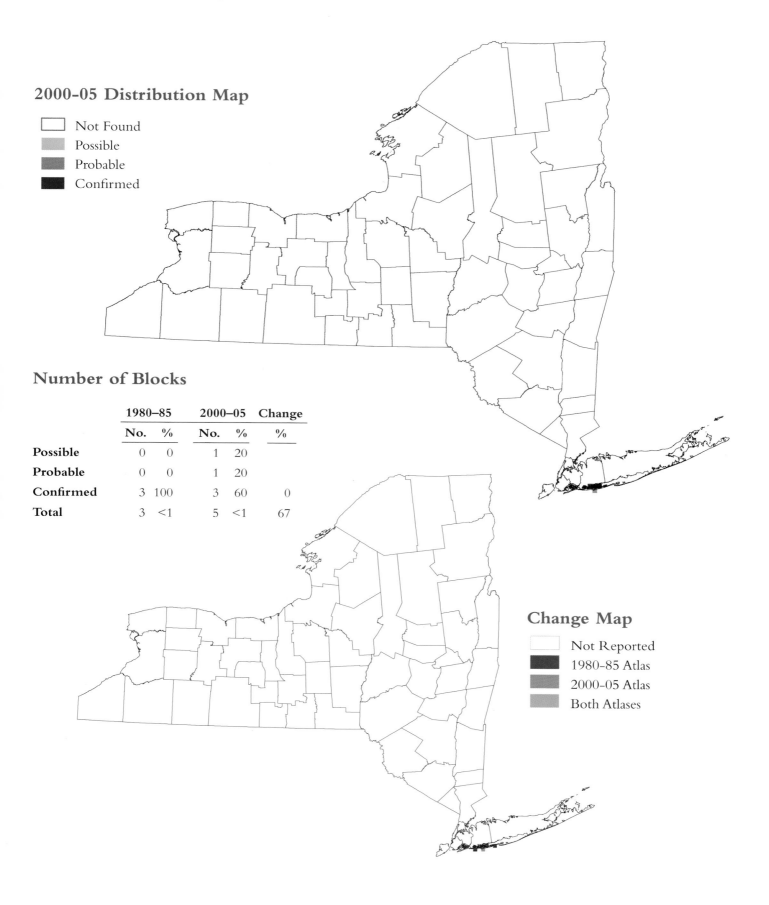

Caspian Tern
Hydroprogne caspia

GERRY SMITH

The Caspian Tern breeds in many widely separated populations worldwide, on all continents except Antarctica. In North America, six distinct populations exist: in the Pacific Northwest to Alaska; central Canada; the west-central interior United States; the Gulf Coast; the northeastern Atlantic Coast; and the Great Lakes region (Cuthbert and Wires 1999). This species was recorded only as a migrant in New York until 1986, the year of its first breeding record in the state. It is likely that New York nesting is a result of an eastward expansion of the Great Lakes population that was concentrated in Lakes Huron and Michigan in the 1960s. Kress et al. (1983) documented the first 20 years of expansion.

The first Atlas reported the Caspian Tern only as a Probable breeder in New York. Confirmed breeding was documented in 1986, after completion of Atlas fieldwork, when 112 nests were found on Little Galloo Island in Jefferson County (J. M. C. Peterson 1988e). Since that year, the colony at Little Galloo stabilized at around 1,400 nests, and breeding was confirmed there again during the second Atlas survey. Birds from this and the nearby colony at Pigeon Island, Ontario, are present throughout eastern Lake Ontario and the western St. Lawrence River from mid-April to mid-September. These terns range widely while searching for food, and their presence may obscure other small breeding sites on islands in the western St. Lawrence River, where a high probability of future breeding exists. Confirmation of such breeding will require extensive searches, as the area is large and suitable islands are widely scattered. The other Confirmed breeding site documented during the second Atlas fieldwork was at Four Brothers Islands in Lake Champlain. Small numbers of nests were reported for four years at Four Brothers, as expected for a fledgling colony (Peterson 2004). By 2006, a total of 56 terns were found on the Four Brothers Islands in late May (D. Capen pers. comm.). The Four Brothers colony is likely a result of continued expansion of the Great Lakes population. The other Atlas records illustrate the difficulty of assessing breeding status for a colonial waterbird that ranges widely away from its colonies to feed. In addition, some individuals may be southbound by July and some may be floating nonbreeders. Assessing records that lack confirmation is problematic at best. The Probable record near Dunkirk, Chautauqua County, could involve breeding, as the Dunkirk Harbor breakwalls might be suitable for a few pairs and the location along the Lake Erie shore seems reasonable. The remaining records are likely of migrants or wandering birds.

Continental Caspian Tern populations appear to be continuing a decades-long increase (Cuthbert and Wires 1999). The Great Lakes population is expanding (Cuthbert and Wires 1999), as it has since a decline in 1925–60 (Ludwig 1965). Little is known about the occurrence of population cycles of the Caspian Tern and the potential impacts of human activities on these fluctuations. This species is not listed as Threatened or Endangered in New York, but its limited breeding distribution makes it a candidate for careful monitoring. Although the large colony at Little Galloo Island seemed secure in 2005, in the late summer of 2006 a total of 672 Caspian Terns, 80 percent adults, were found dead on the island from type E botulism (W. Stone pers. comm.). It is obvious that a few more years of such losses could devastate this once-thriving colony. Loss of breeding adults in long-lived seabird species such as the Caspian Tern is far more of a threat to population stability than occasional disruptions of reproduction. The future of this magnificent seabird in New York will benefit from careful monitoring of existing colonies by resource managers and early detection and documentation of new colonies by birders.

ATM©2006

264

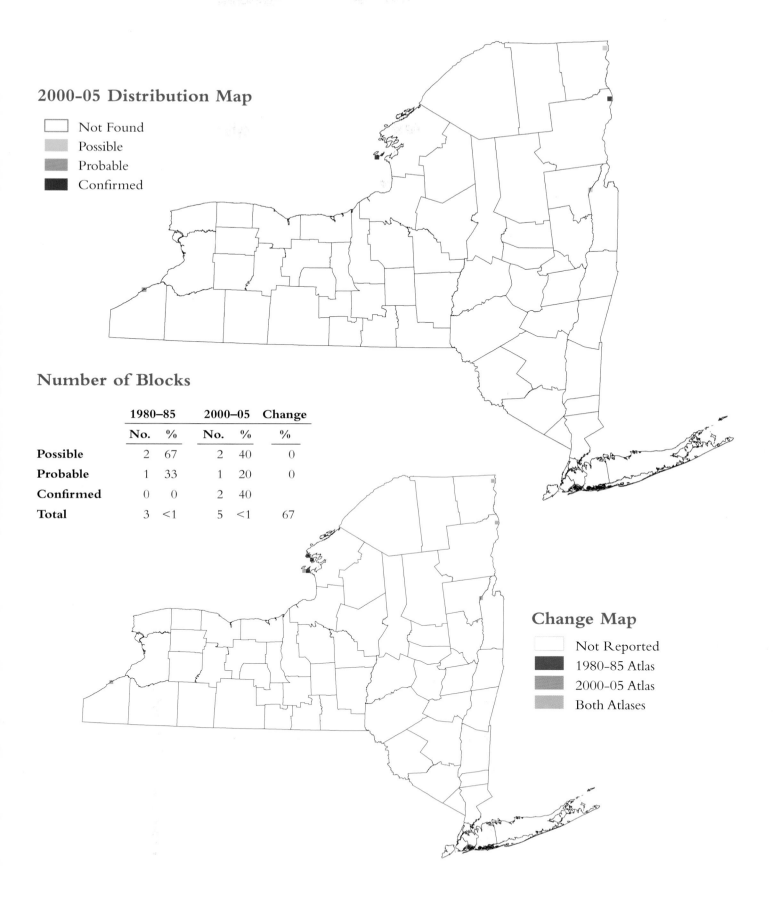

2000–05 Distribution Map

- ☐ Not Found
- Possible
- Probable
- Confirmed

Number of Blocks

	1980–85		2000–05		Change
	No.	%	No.	%	%
Possible	2	67	2	40	0
Probable	1	33	1	20	0
Confirmed	0	0	2	40	
Total	3	<1	5	<1	67

Change Map

- ☐ Not Reported
- 1980-85 Atlas
- 2000-05 Atlas
- Both Atlases

Black Tern

Chlidonias niger

IRENE MAZZOCCHI AND SANDY MULLER

The Black Tern is a semi-colonial bird that has been referred to as the "jewel of the marsh" (McDonald 1991). This handsome and graceful bird nests in semi-secluded, freshwater emergent marshes and can often be seen foraging over nearby bodies of open water. Its preferred breeding habitat consists of an approximately 1:1 ratio of emergent vegetation interspersed with small pools of open water (Chapman Mosher 1986, Hickey 1997). Found across the Northern Hemisphere, its breeding range in North America extends throughout Canada and roughly the northern half of the United States. New York is at the southeastern edge of the range. This species has nested in the state since at least the early 1900s (Eaton 1910), and its population increased throughout the first half of the 20th century (Spahn 1988a). Colonies often included 50 pairs or more (Bull 1974). Black Tern numbers declined steadily during the past half-century, and now fewer breeding colonies exist, with fewer birds per colony (Mazzocchi and Muller 2000).

During the first Atlas period, the Black Tern was found primarily in several of the lakeshore marshes from Orleans County to St. Lawrence County, and in the marshes at the Oak Orchard Wildlife Management Area–Iroquois National Wildlife Refuge complex and adjacent to Montezuma NWR. The second Atlas results showed the Black Tern in 40 percent fewer blocks. It disappeared from the lakeshore of Monroe and Wayne counties, possibly because of habitat changes at the lakeshore marshes. Water level management on the St. Lawrence Seaway has curtailed dramatic annual fluctuations in water levels. Consequently, the marsh vegetation has undergone compositional changes and has increased in density, gradually diminishing the Black Tern's preferred breeding habitat. Inland marshes including Perch River WMA (Jefferson County), Upper and Lower Lakes WMA (St. Lawrence County), and the Tonawanda marsh complex (Niagara, Orleans, and Genesee counties) supported from 20 to 53 percent of the Black Tern population in the state between 1989 and 2004 (Mazzocchi and Muller 2000, NYSDEC unpubl. data). These areas have the capability of water level management and are not directly affected by the St. Lawrence Seaway's water regulations.

It is evident that the Black Tern population in New York State is declining. Historical records document 56 colonies in the state prior to 1980 (Carroll 1988g), with 4 reported to have more than 100 pairs each (Bull 1974). During 1989, the statewide population was estimated at 235 pairs at 28 nesting sites (Mazzocchi and Muller 2000). During the last statewide count in 2004, the population estimate was 178 pairs at 14 sites (NYSDEC unpubl. data). Similar trends are apparent in neighboring states and in Ontario, although continental population levels show no significant change since 1980, as measured by Breeding Bird Survey data (Sauer et al. 2007). In Vermont, the Black Tern was listed as Endangered in 2005, and the population has diminished to a single colony (N. Shambaugh pers. comm.). The second Ontario Breeding Bird Atlas reported a 25 percent decline in the number of squares with Black Tern (Bird Studies Canada et al. 2006). In New York it has been listed as Endangered since 1999. Continuing loss of wetlands threatens its future in the state. Invasive plant species including purple loosestrife pose a threat by disrupting the preferred vegetation structure at breeding marshes. The disturbance caused by increasing use of recreational watercraft, particularly in lakeshore marshes, can also interfere with nesting success. Changes in water level management in Lake Ontario and the St. Lawrence River greatly affect habitat quality. The shift of breeding activity to inland marshes shows that habitat manipulation through water level control can be an effective tool for maintaining quality breeding sites. It is important that the populations of Black Tern continue to be monitored closely in the state, and that this species and its habitat remain protected.

2000–05 Distribution Map

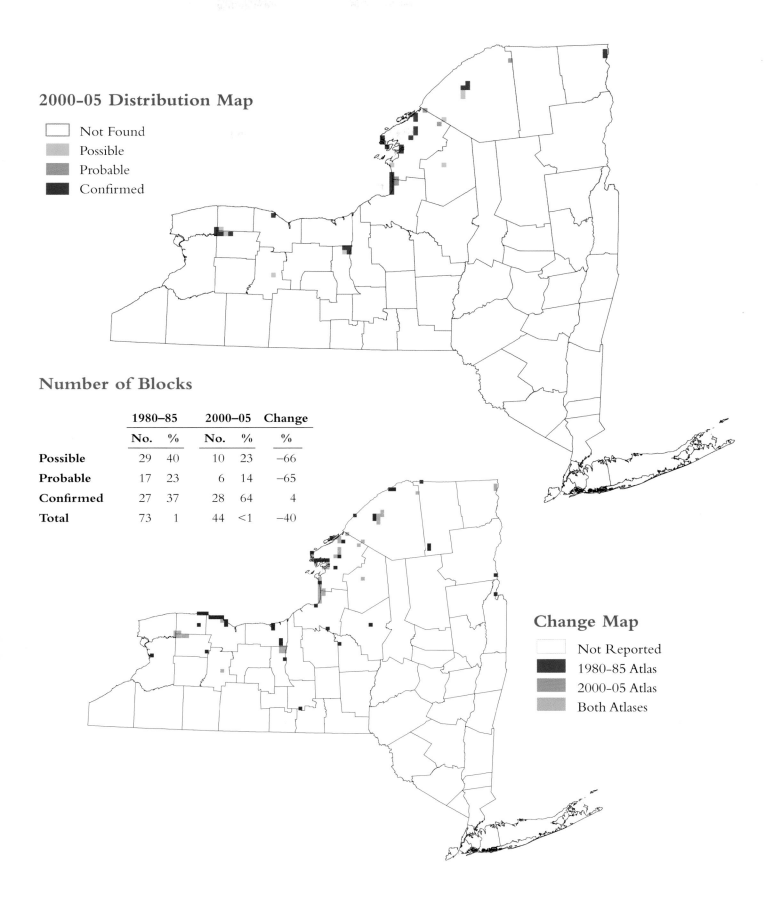

- ☐ Not Found
- ▨ Possible
- ▨ Probable
- ■ Confirmed

Number of Blocks

	1980–85		2000–05		Change
	No.	%	No.	%	%
Possible	29	40	10	23	−66
Probable	17	23	6	14	−65
Confirmed	27	37	28	64	4
Total	73	1	44	<1	−40

Change Map

- ☐ Not Reported
- ■ 1980-85 Atlas
- ▨ 2000-05 Atlas
- ▨ Both Atlases

Roseate Tern
Sterna dougallii

Shaibal S. Mitra

The Roseate Tern occurs widely around the world, but major breeding colonies are few and highly localized. In North America this tern breeds only around the Caribbean Sea, including the Florida Keys, and from Long Island, New York, to Nova Scotia (AOU 1998). New York's large colony on Great Gull Island, Suffolk County, is a regionally and globally significant station for this endangered species (Cooper et al. 1970, Gochfeld 1983). On Long Island the Roseate Tern generally nests in colonies with the Common Tern, where the former prefers settings more thickly vegetated than those preferred by the latter (Bull 1964, Gochfeld et al. 1998).

At the height of the era of persecution, Eaton (1910) could cite only "a few nests" known to Long Island's most active field ornithologists. Considerable recovery during the mid-20th century (Bull 1974) was followed by a period of diminishing numbers during the 1970s and 1980s (Buckley and Buckley 1981) and federal listing of the Roseate Tern as an Endangered Species in 1987 (USFWS 1987a). Since this designation and the completion of the first Atlas, the number of successful colonies on Long Island has diminished somewhat, but the general distribution has remained relatively stable. The breeding population has been dominated by the colony at Great Gull Island, home to 1,200 pairs in 1988, 1,500 pairs in 1996, and 1,273 pairs in 2005 (Gochfeld et al. 1998, Paxton et al. 2005), consistently accounting for 90 percent or more of the state-wide population. Long Island's other colonies have tended to be much smaller (frequently just one or two pairs), variable in location from year to year, and generally concentrated in the eastern area. Recent positive developments include the resumption of breeding at Stony Brook Harbor, on Long Island's North Shore; increased nesting on salt marsh islands (e.g., 11 pairs at Goose Flat, Great South Bay, in 2004 and 2005; M. Gibbons pers. comm.); and increases at Cartwright Point, Gardiners Island (322 pairs in 2004 vs. 36 in 2001, but only 80 in 2005; M. Gibbons pers. comm.).

Despite a great deal of research on the species's foraging ecology and nest-site preferences (reviewed by D. M. Peterson 1988d and Gochfeld et al. 1998), the ecological basis of its extremely localized distribution is still not completely understood. Although somewhat more specialized than the Common Tern in terms of foraging habitat, prey selection, and, especially, nesting substrate, the Roseate Tern can scarcely be regarded as an extreme habitat specialist given its ability to nest on a variety of substrates, including open sand and salt marsh islands, and in settings as diverse as the ocean coast, Peconic Bay, and Long Island Sound. Regardless of its causes, the consistent concentration of a large proportion of the regional population in just a handful of major colonies is a continuing source of conservation concern. Even under the best of circumstances, individual waterbird colonies tend to be ephemeral, or at least subject to considerable fluctuations, as documented in nearby Rhode Island, not only for terns but also for cormorants, herons, ibises, and gulls (Ferren and Myers 1998). The stochastic nature of Long Island's Roseate Tern colonies, even under intense protection, is illustrated by the losses of the large Cedar Beach (1995–96) and smaller Warner Islands (2001) colonies and by the dramatic fluctuations at Cartwright Point, mentioned above. The causes of these changes, including human disturbance, human-commensal predators, rising sea levels, and the natural physical and ecological dynamism of coastal islands, can be managed only within limits. The long-term survival of this especially localized species would be served best by continued protection of a large number of potentially suitable sites, even through periods when some are unoccupied by this and other listed species.

ATM© 2006

2000-05 Distribution Map

- ☐ Not Found
- Possible
- Probable
- Confirmed

Number of Blocks

	1980–85		2000–05		Change
	No.	%	No.	%	%
Possible	4	21	1	8	−75
Probable	2	11	4	33	100
Confirmed	13	68	7	58	−46
Total	19	<1	12	<1	−37

Change Map

- ☐ Not Reported
- 1980-85 Atlas
- 2000-05 Atlas
- Both Atlases

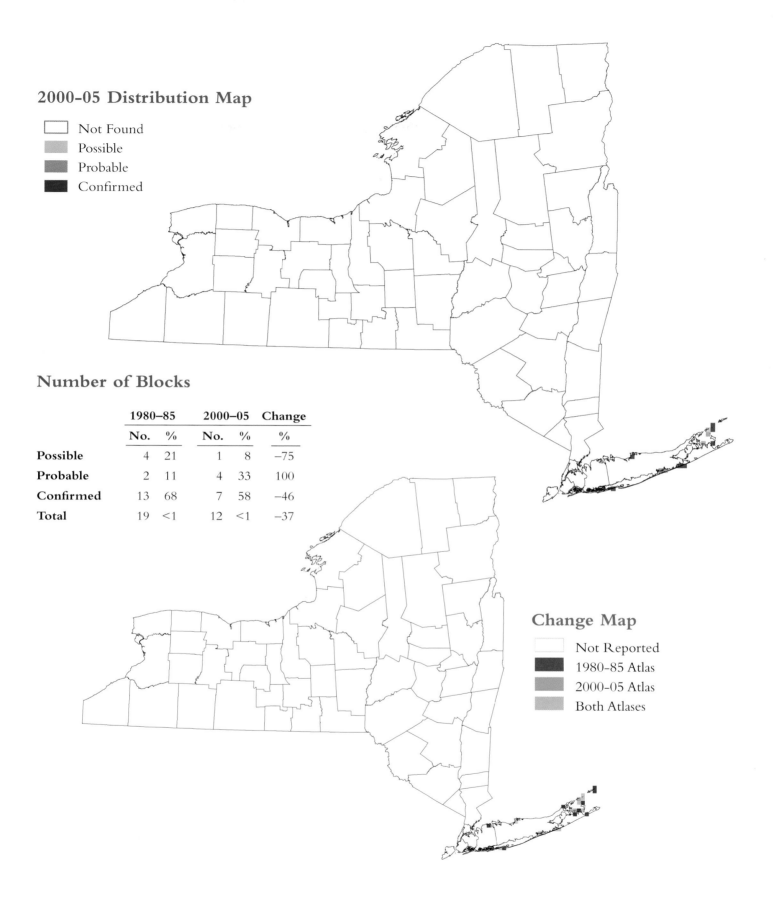

Common Tern

Sterna hirundo

Milo E. Richmond

The Common Tern can be seen from April through September in New York, primarily in coastal areas, where the species nests and is most abundant. Holarctic in range, in North America it breeds from central Canada southward to the northern United States, and along the Atlantic Coast from Labrador to North Carolina (Hays 1998, Nisbet 2002). Currently, breeding in New York occurs inland along the coastlines of Lake Erie and Lake Ontario, extending up the St. Lawrence River, where small islands and a variety of man-made navigation structures are often used. The largest nesting colonies are along the sandy beach, dune, and salt marsh habitats of the north and south shores of Long Island, including a few islands off the eastern tip. This coastal nesting population reached 27,270 pairs in 1987 (Hays 1998) but declined to a low of 17,442 pairs by 1995 (Sommers et al. 1994, Hays 1998). Historically, both Giraud (1844) and DeKay (1844) reported "large numbers of Common Tern" on Long Island in the mid-1800s despite its being persecuted by gunners and plume hunters. DeKay even suggested the possibility of inland breeding at these early dates. Eaton (1910), however, reported the species as rare and only a transient visitor inland. Eaton did confirm it to be "still a common resident" on Gardiners and Fishers islands, where wardens worked to protect nesting areas. Full protection in 1918 allowed for a notable return of nesting colonies over the next two decades and into the 1960s, when nesting numbers peaked (Courtney and Blokpoel 1983, Peterson et al. 1985). This same recovery period also revealed first breeding records for inland nesting colonies at Thousand Islands in 1917 (Merwin 1918); in Constantia on Oneida Lake in 1929 (Stoner 1932); and Buffalo in 1944 (Beardslee and Mitchell 1965). In contrast, the 1970s saw a decline in upstate populations in the eastern Ontario basin, St. Lawrence River, and Oneida Lake, where the number of nesting pairs dropped from 2,500 to 1,000 (Burtch 1941, Smith et al. 1984). A similar decline was noted for the Lake Erie region (Hotopp 1986). At the same time, Long Island populations were expanding, with colonies of 1,000 to 6,000 pairs becoming established at four major inlets (Bull 1964, Hays 1998).

Statewide, the numbers of Confirmed and Probable breeding records are quite similar for the two Atlas projects. The Coastal Lowlands show little change, with 47 Confirmed and 8 Probable in 1980 and 48 Confirmed and 9 Probable for 2000. Inland nesting data from upstate freshwater sites suggest expansion of Common Tern nesting, with 21 Confirmed and 4 Probable reported in the first Atlas versus 29 Confirmed and 13 Probable recorded during the second Atlas survey. Noteworthy are three new blocks with Confirmed records on the Hudson River, Westchester County, and the continued efforts by inland terns to make use of man-made nesting structures. The detectability and recognition of the Common Tern is high; therefore, assessment accuracy is likely reliable. Presence or absence revealed in this Atlas is in concert with numbers reported in other local and regional surveys.

The Common Tern is not federally listed but is considered Endangered, Threatened, or a Species of Special Concern in most states around the Great Lakes (Nisbet 2002). Its status is Threatened in New York and it is on Audubon's Watch List (National Audubon Society 2002). Four Important Bird Areas (IBAs) in Upstate New York have more than 300 nesting pairs; Buffalo Harbor is the largest, with 1,100 pairs. Seven IBAs on Long Island have more than 500 pairs, Great Gull Island being the largest, with about 10,000 pairs (Hays 1998). The continental population is widespread and productive. Nevertheless, threats are numerous, including prey contamination, mismanagement on wintering grounds, violent weather, displacement by gulls, beach traffic, and vandalism (Nisbet 2002).

ATM © 2006

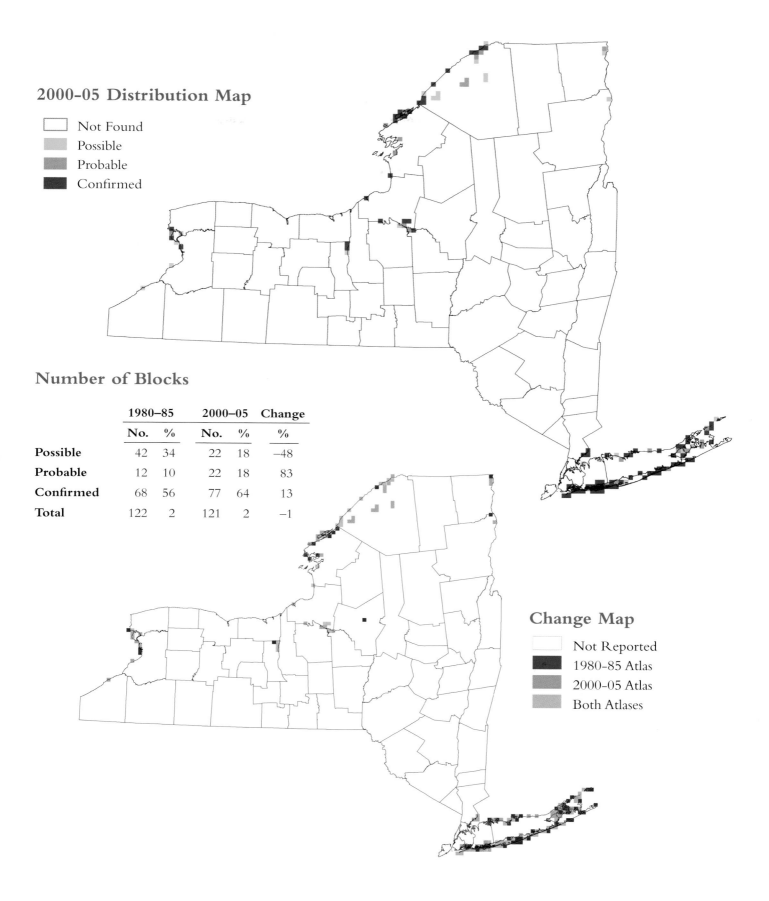

2000-05 Distribution Map

Not Found
Possible
Probable
Confirmed

Number of Blocks

	1980–85		2000–05		Change
	No.	%	No.	%	%
Possible	42	34	22	18	−48
Probable	12	10	22	18	83
Confirmed	68	56	77	64	13
Total	122	2	121	2	−1

Change Map

Not Reported
1980-85 Atlas
2000-05 Atlas
Both Atlases

Forster's Tern
Sterna forsteri

MICHAEL R. WASILCO

ATM© 2006

orster's Tern closely resembles the more widespread and numerous Common Tern, with which it often shares colony sites. In the field, only its pale, silvery primaries and nasal, raspy call notes separate Forster's Tern from the Common Tern. This identification difficulty could lead to Forster's Tern being overlooked by surveyors where the two species nest together. The breeding range of Forster's Tern is limited to North America, where it is found along the Gulf of Mexico, the mid-Atlantic Coast, and the mid-continental area, which includes portions of the Great Lakes, Great Plains, and Intermountain West (Martin and Zwank 1987, McNicholl et al. 2001). It has been known to breed in New York only since 1981 (Zarudsky 1981), nesting mainly on marsh islands within the bays on the south side of Long Island (Connor 1988b, Sommers et al. 2001), which, with the exception of a single pair in Massachusetts, represents the northernmost edge of the Atlantic Coast range (McNicholl et al. 2001, Kress and Hall 2002). In this habitat, it often nests on top of the storm-deposited wrack material that accumulates within stands of cordgrass during winter storms and high-tide events. The presence of these mats of vegetative debris within the taller marsh vegetation heavily influences the use of a site by nesting terns (Martin and Zwank 1987). The additional elevation provided by the mats of wrack protects the nests, eggs, and chicks from flooding by waves and most storm tides, especially when the mats are able to float in place while the surrounding marsh floods. At inland sites, nests are often found on structurally similar floating mats of cattails (Hyde 2001, Graham et al. 2002).

Forster's Tern was slow to become established as a regular breeder in New York. Following sighting of the initial pair in 1981 at Hewlett Hassock, Nassau County (Zarudsky 1981), no confirmed breeding was reported until 1984, when a single pair was found at nearby North Green Sedge Island (Peterson et al. 1985). No nesting birds were found in 1985. The first Atlas documented the initial expansion of this species into New York, showing only two blocks with records of breeding (one Confirmed). The second Atlas, with breeding recorded in ten blocks (eight Confirmed), seems to demonstrate a more established population. The only block recording Forster's Tern in the first Atlas and not the second contains Jo Co Marsh, which has not been surveyed since 1998 (NYSDEC unpubl. data).

The New York Forster's Tern population became firmly established by 1989, and birds have been found annually since then (Sommers et al. 2001). Tern numbers slowly increased to 5 pairs in 1991 and exploded to 78 pairs in 1992, mostly at Jo Co Marsh in Jamaica Bay (Sommers et al. 1994). Since then, the recorded

numbers ranged from 27 to 77 pairs in the late 1990s, excluding the two years (2 and 8 pairs) when Jo Co Marsh was not surveyed (Sommers et al. 2001). Recently, numbers have been much higher, ranging from 158 pairs in 2001 to 263 pairs in 2005, with a record high of 333 pairs in 2004 (NYSDEC unpubl. data). This increase in New York also correlates with the increase and fluctuation seen in New Jersey's tern population for the same time period (C. Kisiel pers. comm.).

After the first modern documented breeding in Ontario in the 1970s (McNicholl 1987), Forster's Tern in Ontario went through rapid increases in population in the1980s and early 1990s. However, numbers of breeding pairs in many outlying sites declined just as quickly by 2001 (Graham et al. 2002). The range expansion seems to have continued along the Great Lakes, with four new colony sites observed along the north shore of Lake Ontario near Toronto (Graham et al. 2002) but apparently missed during the second Ontario Breeding Bird Atlas (Bird Studies Canada et al. 2006). Thus far, the expansion seems to be limited to the Canadian side of the lakes, as Forster's Tern has not yet been found nesting on the New York side.

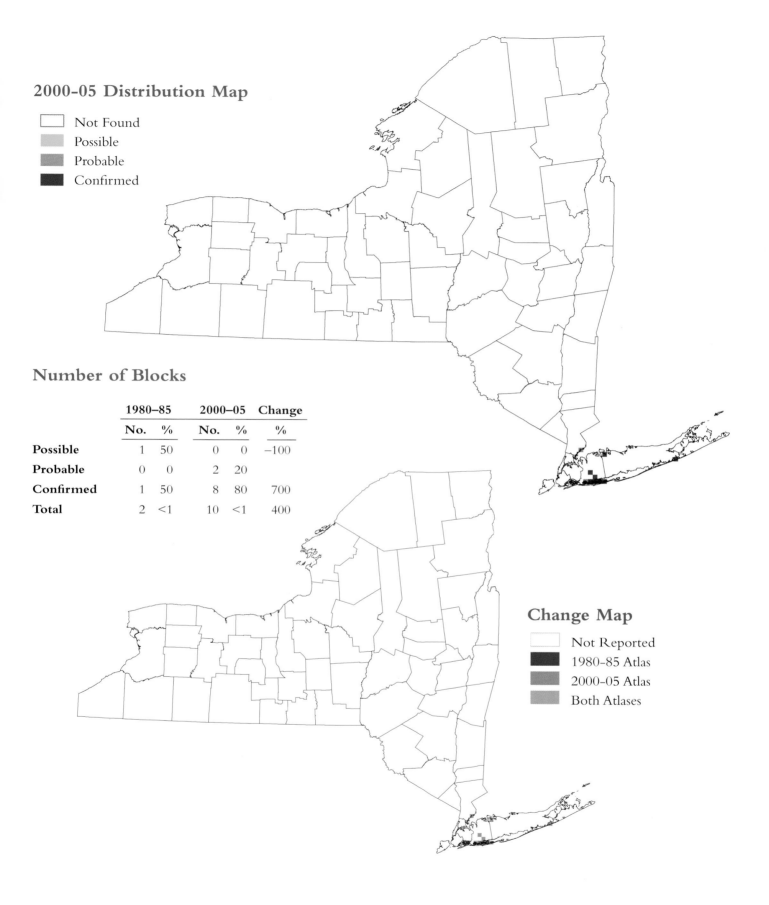

2000-05 Distribution Map

- ☐ Not Found
- Possible
- Probable
- Confirmed

Number of Blocks

	1980–85		2000–05		Change
	No.	%	No.	%	%
Possible	1	50	0	0	−100
Probable	0	0	2	20	
Confirmed	1	50	8	80	700
Total	2	<1	10	<1	400

Change Map

- ☐ Not Reported
- 1980–85 Atlas
- 2000–05 Atlas
- Both Atlases

Black Skimmer
Rynchops niger

MATTHEW D. MEDLER

One of three skimmer species worldwide, the Black Skimmer is one of New York's most distinctive breeding birds. New York is near the northern limit of the species's breeding range, which stretches along the Atlantic Coast from Massachusetts to Florida and along the Gulf Coast from Florida to northeastern Mexico (Gochfeld and Burger 1994). Isolated breeding populations occur in southern California and western Mexico, and the species also breeds in South America (Gochfeld and Burger 1994). In eastern North America, the Black Skimmer occurs almost exclusively along the coast, where it nests on sparsely vegetated sandy beaches, dredge spoil islands, and in salt marshes (Gochfeld and Burger 1994). In New York, the species has recently begun using salt marshes more, because of development and recreation pressures on Long Island's sandy beaches (Gochfeld and Burger 1994), but Long Island Colonial Waterbird Survey (LICWS) data from 2000 to 2005 showed the vast majority of nesting pairs occurring at sandy beach sites (NYSDEC unpubl. data). While no definitive historical breeding record exists for New York, available evidence at least suggests that the Black Skimmer nested in New York and New England until about the mid-1800s (Gochfeld and Burger 1994). DeKay (1844) noted that the Black Skimmer returned to New York's coast in May, and described it as "common enough with us," but could not determine if the species bred in the state. Giraud (1844), however, wrote that the species was "not very common with us." Eaton (1910) considered the skimmer to be an occasional summer visitor to Long Island's shores, but said it did not breed north of New Jersey. New York's first nesting record occurred in 1934 at Gilgo Beach, Suffolk County (Cruickshank 1942), and within 40 years Bull (1974) described it as a locally common to abundant breeder on Long Island's south shore.

In the first Atlas, the Black Skimmer was confirmed breeding in 23 blocks, with most records occurring along the south shore of Long Island from Jamaica Bay to Shinnecock Bay. Several Confirmed records also came from the eastern end of Long Island. During the sec-

ond Atlas survey, skimmer breeding was confirmed in 18 blocks. Almost all of these records were from the south shore of Long Island, as nesting at the eastern end of Long Island was noticeably reduced. The north shore of Long Island was also home to one Confirmed record. Black Skimmer is a conspicuous colonial breeder, meaning that its true breeding status is best represented by Confirmed records, with Possible and Probable records likely reflecting foraging birds away from nest sites.

Previously considered Threatened in New York (Gochfeld and Burger 1994), the Black Skimmer is now listed as a Species of Special Concern. LICWS counts of nesting pairs from 1985 to 2005 ranged from a high of 599 in 1995 to a low of 265 in 2004 but showed no obvious population trend (Sommers et al. 2001, NYSDEC unpubl. data). During the second Atlas period, LICWS totals included a low of 265 in 2004 and a high of 511 in 2001, with an average of 399 pairs. By comparison, counts from 1984 to 1989 varied from 359 to 562 pairs, with an average of 450 (Downer and Liebelt 1990). It is important to note, though, that LICWS totals may under-represent the actual number of Black Skimmer nesting pairs in some years, as individuals often nest much later than the June survey period. In 2005, approximately 750 pairs of skimmers nested extremely late in the season at two Long Island sites, with very small young found at both sites in late August (Mitra and Lindsay 2005b). Major factors affecting skimmer breeding success include flooding, storms, predation, and human disturbance (Gochfeld and Burger 1994). Thus, the species has likely benefited from Piping Plover and Least Tern conservation efforts on Long Island, but sea level rises predicted as a result of global warming may pose a serious new threat to the Black Skimmer and other coastal beach-nesting species.

ATM© 2006

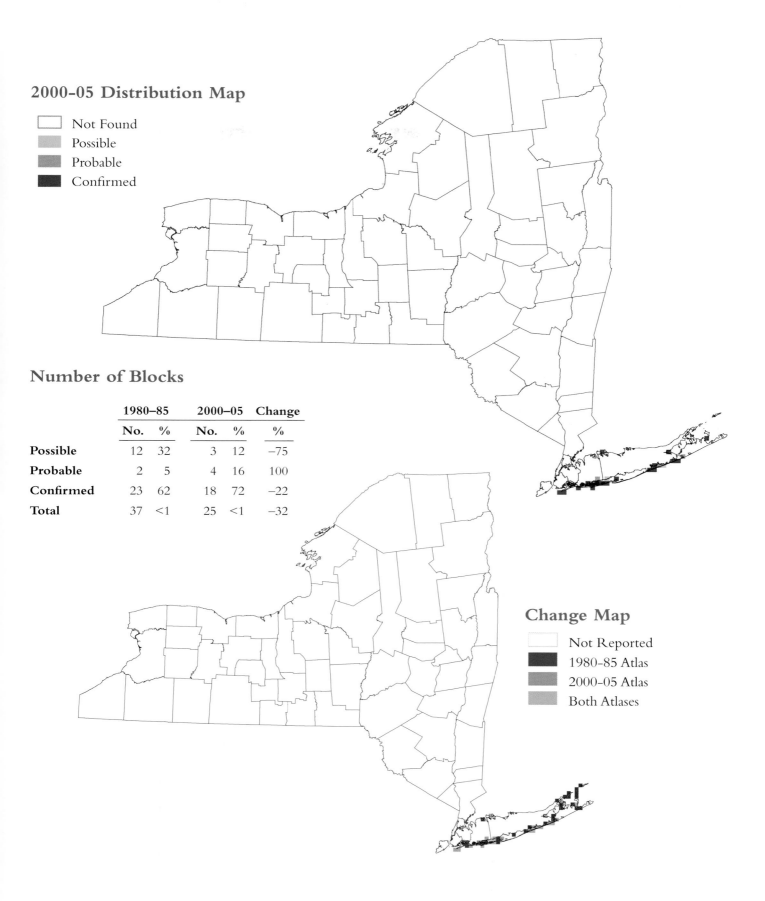

2000–05 Distribution Map

- ☐ Not Found
- ☐ Possible
- ☐ Probable
- ■ Confirmed

Number of Blocks

	1980–85		2000–05		Change
	No.	%	No.	%	%
Possible	12	32	3	12	−75
Probable	2	5	4	16	100
Confirmed	23	62	18	72	−22
Total	37	<1	25	<1	−32

Change Map

- ☐ Not Reported
- ■ 1980–85 Atlas
- ■ 2000–05 Atlas
- ☐ Both Atlases

**Monk Parakeet and
Yellow-billed Cuckoo
in Green-Wood
Cemetery**

Brooklyn's Green-Wood
Cemetery, a National
Historic Landmark, is considered one of the most
beautiful cemeteries in the
world. A final resting place
for some 600,000 people,
its 480 acres also provide
habitat for more than 200
bird species. Among them
is the Monk Parakeet,
which nests in the impressive gothic entrance gate
off 25th Street.

Rock Pigeon
Columba livia

KEVIN J. McGOWAN

Domesticated over 5,000 years ago and kept for food and entertainment, the Rock Pigeon has been introduced throughout the world where it is a common sight in urban areas (Johnston 1992). It was first introduced into North America in the early 1600s (Schorger 1952). Unlike the other established European introductions, the European Starling and the House Sparrow, the pigeon was introduced as a domestic "working" animal, brought for food, not for aesthetic reasons. It became feral soon after its introduction (Johnston 1992) and is now resident from southern Alaska and southern Canada southward throughout the Americas. Buildings and other man-made structures mimic the rocky cliffs preferred by wild pigeons and therefore are widely used for roosting and nesting. The feral pigeon is also found around natural cliffs and in agricultural areas, but rarely far from people. Because the introduction of the Rock Pigeon into North America happened so early, and was repeated frequently for several hundred years, the exact history of the species in New York is difficult to trace. Probably because of its domesticated status, the Rock Pigeon was not treated by early authors, and the American Ornithologists' Union did not even include it in its check-list of birds of North America until the fourth edition (AOU 1931). Even then, the AOU did not attempt to describe its range in North America. Bull (1974) called it an "abundant resident, except forested portions."

True to Bull's terse description, the first Atlas reported the Rock Pigeon as breeding throughout most of the state except in part of the Allegany Hills, the Central Tug Hill, much of the Catskill Peaks, Delaware and Mongaup hills, and most of the Adirondacks.

All of these regions are characterized by high elevation and extensive regions of continuous forest. The second Atlas survey revealed very little change in the distribution of the Rock Pigeon, with breeding records from only 30 fewer blocks. No substantial change was noted in any geographic region or ecozone. Its range did not extend farther into the Adirondacks, and although it was found in nearly twice as many blocks in the Catskill Peaks than in the first Atlas, that still accounts for only 19 of 65 blocks in that region, and a gap in the distribution still exists there.

Periodic trapping and poisoning efforts are made to reduce pigeon populations in some areas (see, e.g., Beardslee and Mitchell 1965), but they seem to have little effect. Long-term changes in pigeon populations are difficult to measure because formal censuses ignored the species until 1966 (Johnston 1992). Breeding Bird Survey data show no long-term trends in Rock Pigeon population numbers survey-wide or in New York since 1966, but they show a significant annual increase in both areas from 1966 through 1979, and then a slight but significant decline from 1980 to 2005 (Sauer et al. 2005). Christmas Bird Count data started including Rock Pigeon only in 1974, but those data for both New York and the United States show an increase until the 1990s, after which numbers appeared to remain more or less steady (National Audubon Society [2007]). The Rock Pigeon is not protected by the federal Migratory Bird Treaty Act or any other wildlife law. But such protections are not needed, and the pigeon will likely remain a part of the New York State avifauna for a long time to come.

ATM©2006

2000–05 Distribution Map

- ☐ Not Found
- Possible
- Probable
- Confirmed

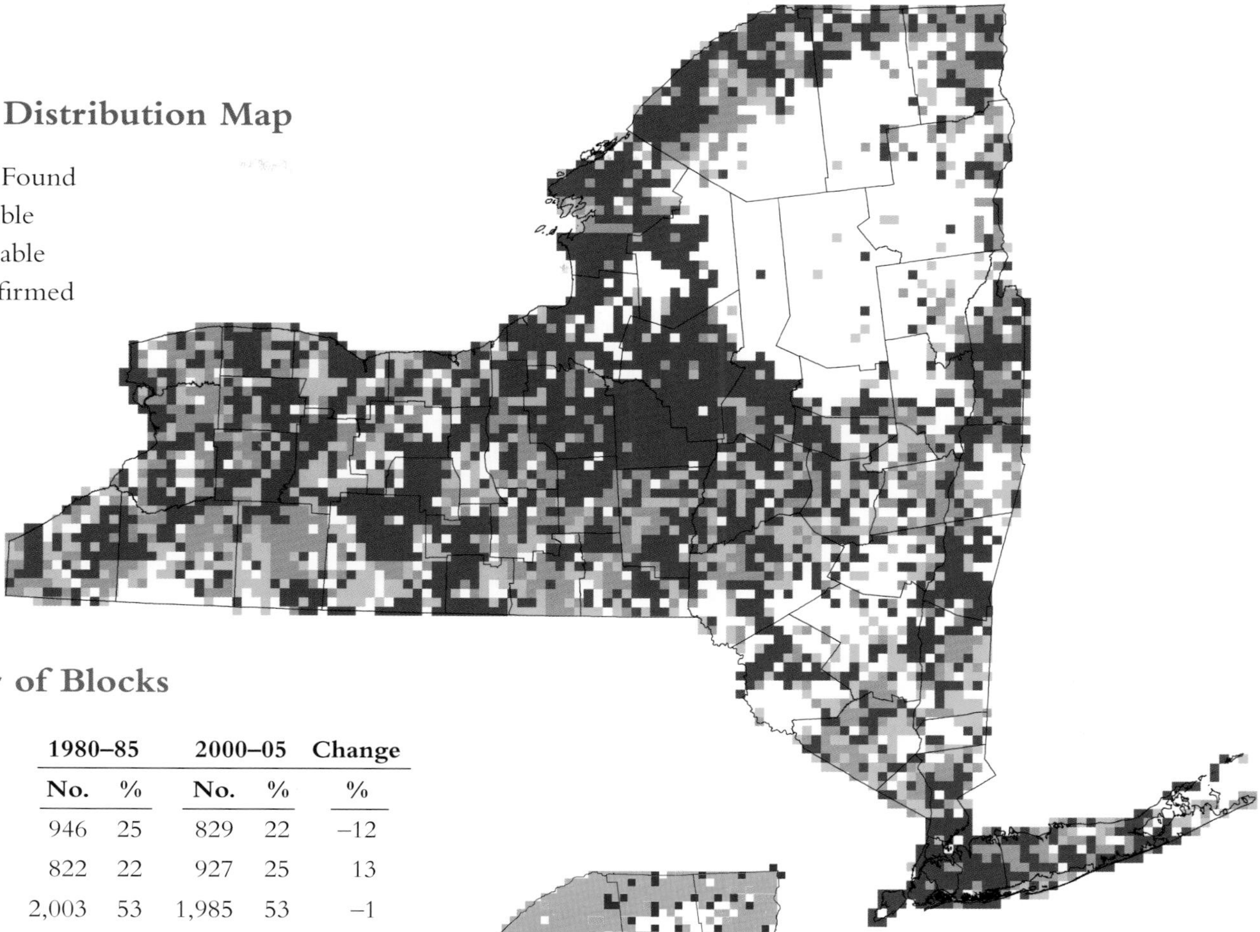

Number of Blocks

	1980–85		2000–05		Change
	No.	%	No.	%	%
Possible	946	25	829	22	−12
Probable	822	22	927	25	13
Confirmed	2,003	53	1,985	53	−1
Total	3,771	71	3,741	70	−1

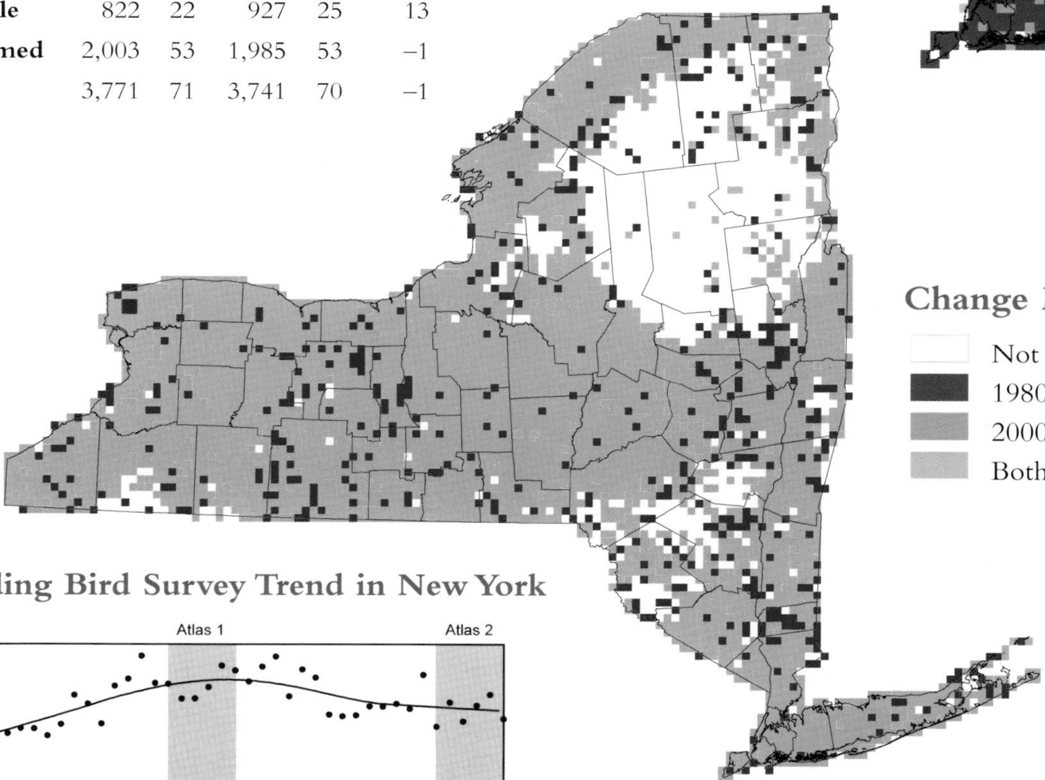

Change Map

- Not Reported
- 1980-85 Atlas
- 2000-05 Atlas
- Both Atlases

Breeding Bird Survey Trend in New York

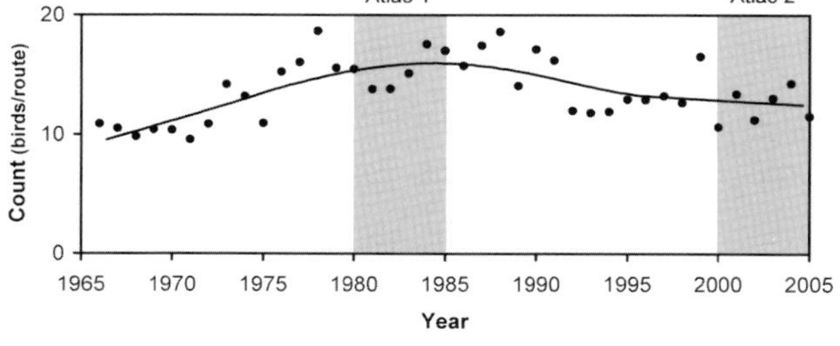

Mourning Dove
Zenaida macroura

KEVIN J. MCGOWAN

One of the most widespread and abundant birds in North America, the Mourning Dove breeds from southern Canada throughout the United States to Central America and the Caribbean. It breeds in a variety of open habitats, including agricultural areas, open woods, deserts, forest edges, cities, and suburbs (Mirarchi and Baskett 1994). As a species of open areas, the Mourning Dove likely was relatively uncommon in New York before European settlement, when the forest-dwelling Passenger Pigeon was the predominant columbid. With the clearing of the forests and the planting of grasses and agricultural grains, Mourning Dove populations undoubtedly increased in post-colonial New York. DeKay (1844) listed this dove as a breeder in New York but indicated that it did not winter here and was resident only from Pennsylvania southward. Other authors reported it as a common summer resident throughout the southern, central, and western portions of the state (Giraud 1844, Rathbun 1879, Short 1893, Reed and Wright 1909). Merriam (1881) did not know the Mourning Dove from the Adirondacks and mentioned only that it was known to breed in Warren County at the southern end of Lake George. Eaton (1910) listed it as a common summer breeder in all areas except "the northern portions and the Highlands ...above 305 m (1,000 ft) in elevation, where it is rather uncommon." Bull (1974) gave a similar breeding distribution but noted that it had become a common winter resident as well.

The first Atlas reported the Mourning Dove as breeding across most of the state, with obvious gaps in the Central Tug Hill, western Allegany Hills, Catskill Peaks, and most of the Adirondacks (especially the Central Adirondacks and Western Adirondack Foothills). The Mourning Dove remained common during the second Atlas survey period and was found in slightly more blocks overall. It essentially saturated the state outside of the above-mentioned areas, so nearly all of the change represents movement of the dove into the large gaps. Blocks with sightings increased 52 percent in the Adirondacks and 48 percent in the Catskill Peaks. Increases also took place in the Tug Hill Plateau and Allegany Hills, but gaps are still apparent in those two areas. The Central Adirondacks remains the largest blank spot on the Atlas map, but the dove is moving into those areas along the highways. The pattern of distribution in the first Atlas was suggestive, but from the second Atlas data it is clear that the Mourning Dove occurs along the roads and in the towns. The delineation of state Route 28 from west of Old Forge eastward to Chestertown is striking. The current distribution shows that the Mourning Dove can be found above 305 m (1,000 ft) wherever people and open habitats exist. It is likely that the remaining gaps in New York are predominantly the result of heavily forested and mostly roadless areas, not elevation per se.

The Mourning Dove expanded its breeding range northward into southern Canada in the 1950s through the 1980s (Mirarchi and Baskett 1994). Although the population appears to be declining somewhat in the western portion of its range, overall its numbers are stable and the species remains one of the most abundant birds on the continent (Mirarchi and Baskett 1994). Breeding Bird Survey data show a stable trend across the survey area, with significant declines in the western and central regions, but a significant increase in the East (Sauer et al. 2005). BBS data from New York show a significant increase of 2.6 percent per year since 1960. Data from the U.S. Fish and Wildlife Service call-counts also show a significant increase in New York over the last 41 years (Dolton and Rau 2006). Both the second Ontario Breeding Bird Atlas and the Vermont Atlas reported slight increases as well (Bird Studies Canada et al. 2006, R. Renfrew pers. comm.). Because of its tolerance of human-modified habitats, the Mourning Dove may very well be at or near an all-time population high in New York State.

280

2000–05 Distribution Map

- ☐ Not Found
- Possible
- Probable
- ■ Confirmed

Number of Blocks

	1980–85		2000–05		Change
	No.	%	No.	%	%
Possible	1,085	25	712	15	−34
Probable	1,202	27	1,773	37	48
Confirmed	2,115	48	2,318	48	10
Total	4,402	83	4,803	90	9

Change Map

- ☐ Not Reported
- 1980–85 Atlas
- 2000–05 Atlas
- Both Atlases

Breeding Bird Survey Trend in New York

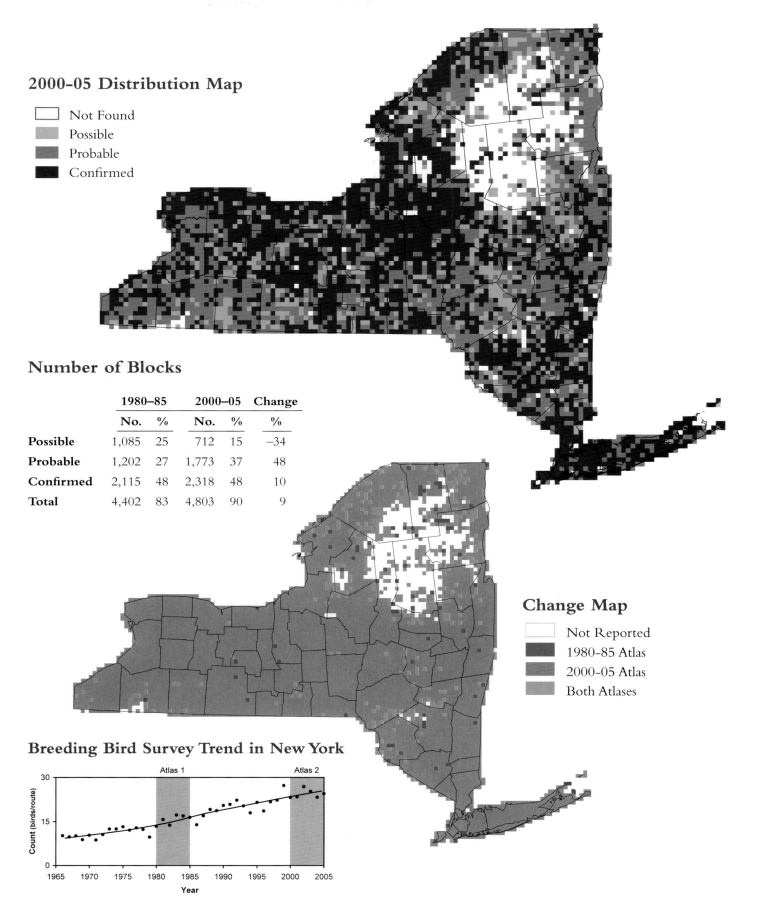

Monk Parakeet
Myiopsitta monachus

Shaibal S. Mitra

Native to temperate southern South America, the Monk Parakeet is an established resident in parts of North America, including portions of Alabama, Connecticut, Delaware, Florida, Illinois, Louisiana, New Jersey, New York, Oregon, Rhode Island, and Texas (Spreyer and Bucher 1998). The number of independent events involved in the establishment of these populations is unknown but probably includes many instances in which birds escaped from captivity or were deliberately released. In North America the Monk Parakeet is an urban and suburban bird, often building its unique stick nest on or near man-made structures (Hyman and Pruett-Jones 1995, Pranty and Garrett 2003). In colder areas, such as New York and Illinois, it may depend on feeding stations for winter survival (Bull 1974, South and Pruett-Jones 2000). Monk Parakeets were present in the wild in New York by 1968 (Bull 1974), after which the number of observations rapidly increased near New York City. Local breeding was documented in 1971 in Nassau and Richmond counties (Bull 1974), and parakeets were recorded almost statewide by 1973 (Sibley 1988l). Efforts to eradicate the Monk Parakeet from New York in the mid-1970s (see Roscoe et al. 1973) were perceived as generally successful by some authors (e.g., Neidermyer and Hickey 1977, Sibley 1988l), and were even used to justify the removal of the species from the official New York State Checklist in 1982 (NYSARC 1982). However, not only did these efforts fail to eliminate local populations, but also they helped obscure the bird's actual status for decades. Some people were reluctant to reveal breeding localities for fear of putting the birds at risk of removal; others simply did not consider the birds "countable," and therefore not worthy of mention. Although the number of reports declined in the 1970s, they did not stop completely, and the parakeet continued to be recorded on New York Christmas Bird Counts (National Audubon Society [2007]).

During the first Atlas survey, the Monk Parakeet was recorded from only three blocks, on Staten Island and along Long Island's North Shore in Nassau and Suffolk coun-

ties. Breeding was not confirmed, and one of the nests was reported to have been removed (Sibley 1988l). Reports of the parakeet increased after the first Atlas was completed (e.g., National Audubon Society [2007]), but the species continued to be grossly under-reported for reasons of protection or neglect (Salzman 1998f, pers. obs.). During the second Atlas fieldwork, the Monk Parakeet was found in 15 blocks, with breeding confirmed in 10, representing Suffolk, Nassau, Kings, Bronx, Westchester, and Albany counties. Numbers were higher in the Coastal Lowlands and Manhattan Hills, and two reports came from the central Hudson Valley, but given the problems afflicting the historical record, the true extent of this species's increase since the first Atlas period remains unclear.

Monk Parakeet populations are thriving today in several parts of New York City and Long Island, and the species is being reported from upstate areas once again. This status is consistent with growing populations in North America as a whole (Van Bael and Pruett-Jones 1996, Pranty 2002). These increases continue in spite of, or perhaps more accurately because of, the Monk Parakeet's preferences for urban habitats and artificial food sources. Indeed, local populations of parakeets are often protected by public sentiment, and this factor has sometimes proved strong enough to discourage attempts at local eradication (Spreyer 1994). As North American populations grow, it is reasonable to expect them to expand geographically, especially as their urban and suburban foci sprawl outward themselves. Even so, it is important to note that early fears that the Monk Parakeets would develop into agricultural pests have not been realized during almost four decades of naturalization in North America (Spreyer and Bucher 1998).

ATM©2006

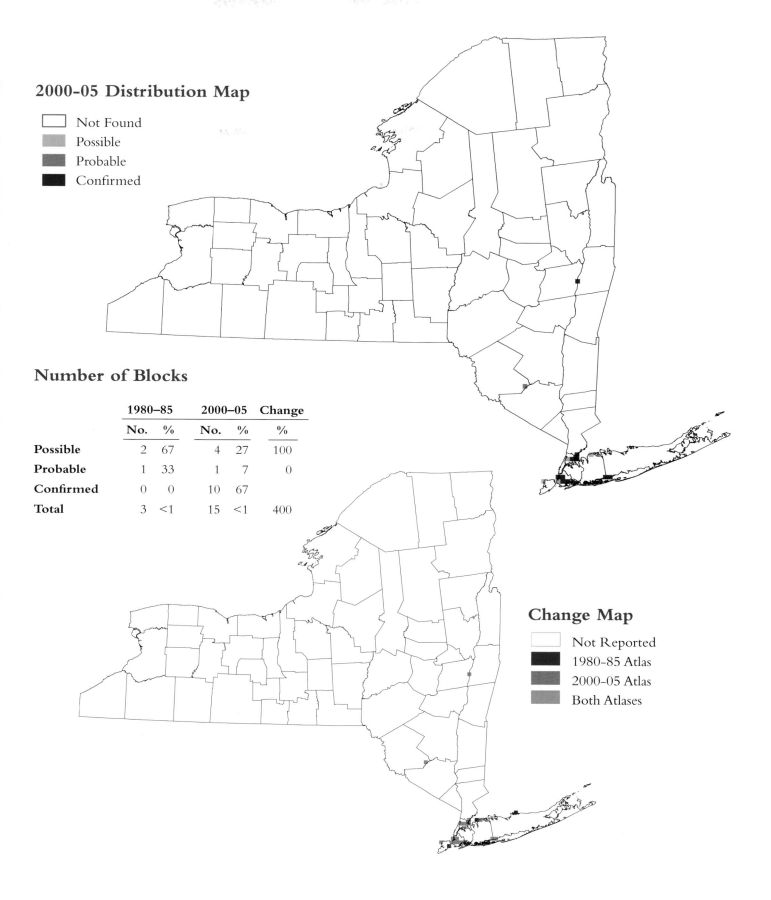

2000-05 Distribution Map

- ☐ Not Found
- Possible
- Probable
- Confirmed

Number of Blocks

	1980–85		2000–05		Change
	No.	%	No.	%	%
Possible	2	67	4	27	100
Probable	1	33	1	7	0
Confirmed	0	0	10	67	
Total	3	<1	15	<1	400

Change Map

- ☐ Not Reported
- 1980-85 Atlas
- 2000-05 Atlas
- Both Atlases

Yellow-billed Cuckoo
Coccyzus americanus

KEVIN J. McGOWAN

The Yellow-billed Cuckoo breeds from southeastern Canada southward to Mexico and the Caribbean, westward to the Great Plains, and in scattered localities across the western United States. It nests in open woodlands with clearings and dense scrubby vegetation, often along water (Hughes 1999). As a bird of open canopies and secondary growth, it was probably not particularly common before European settlement. DeKay (1844) thought it bred throughout New York but noted that it was not particularly common. Giraud (1844) considered it rather common on Long Island. Rathbun (1879) and Short (1893) considered both it and the Black-billed Cuckoo to be relatively common breeders in central and western New York. Eaton (1914) noted the Yellow-billed Cuckoo was fairly common throughout most of southern New York but was completely absent from all but the edges and valleys of the Adirondacks and the Catskills. Beardslee and Mitchell (1965) listed the Yellow-billed Cuckoo as nesting primarily at lower elevations and in the vicinity of streams and lakes in the Niagara region. Bull (1974) considered it a local breeder at low elevations, rare farther northward in the state, and absent from the mountains.

The first Atlas data showed the Yellow-billed Cuckoo to be widely distributed across New York southward of the Adirondacks. Highest concentrations were found in the Coastal Lowlands, Manhattan Hills, Triassic Lowlands, and Hudson Highlands, with other clusters of records in the lower Hudson Valley, Central Appalachians, Finger Lakes Highlands, and western Erie-Ontario Plain. It was also found in the St. Lawrence Plains and Transition. The species was present in both the Catskill Peaks and Adirondack High Peaks in limited numbers but was largely absent from most of the Adirondacks. The second Atlas survey found this cuckoo in slightly more blocks across the state. Increases in the number of blocks with reports were most striking in the Mohawk Valley and Cattaraugus Highlands, but the number of Adirondack blocks with records more than doubled, and the Great Lakes Plain showed an increase of nearly 25 percent. A large forest tent caterpillar outbreak in St. Lawrence County in 2002–05 (Kraus 2006) might account for the increase in cuckoos seen there. Yellow-billed Cuckoo reports declined substantially from the Coastal Lowlands to the Hudson Highlands, but this area still supported the highest concentrations in the state. Whereas Eaton (1988r) suggested that the Yellow-billed Cuckoo was found most commonly below 305 m (1,000 ft), and Marcotte (1998e) implied that it occurred only below that elevation, there are numerous records from both Atlas projects of the cuckoo above 305 m on the Appalachian Plateau and several records of it above 610 m (2,000 ft) in the same region. The secretive nature of all cuckoos makes them difficult to census, and their short nesting and fledgling feeding period makes breeding confirmation difficult.

The Yellow-billed Cuckoo is common in the southeastern United States, but populations are declining throughout much of its range (Hughes 1999). Large movements of cuckoos into an area can follow caterpillar outbreaks (Hughes 1999), making continental and local population levels difficult to track. Breeding Bird Survey data show a significant survey-wide decline in numbers from 1980 to 2005, but a significant annual increase for the period 1966–79 (Sauer et al. 2005). BBS data from New York are sparse and show no significant trends, but the Northeast region data show the same pattern of significant increase followed by a significant decrease (Sauer et al. 2005). Data from the second Ontario Breeding Bird Atlas show a significant decrease in the Simcoe-Rideau region of southern Ontario but a significant increase in the Southern Shield, near the northern limit of the cuckoo's range (Bird Studies Canada et al. 2006). The succession of abandoned farmlands and orchards into more mature forest might be responsible for the slight decline seen in BBS data in the northeastern United States.

ATM©2006

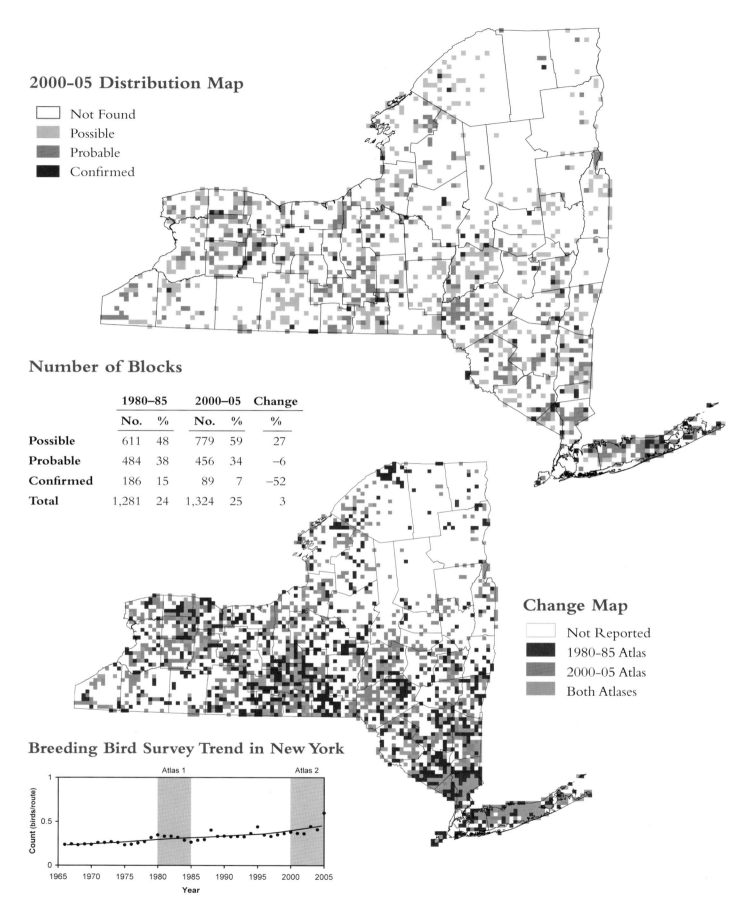

2000–05 Distribution Map

- ☐ Not Found
- Possible
- Probable
- ■ Confirmed

Number of Blocks

	1980–85		2000–05		Change
	No.	%	No.	%	%
Possible	611	48	779	59	27
Probable	484	38	456	34	–6
Confirmed	186	15	89	7	–52
Total	1,281	24	1,324	25	3

Change Map

- ☐ Not Reported
- ■ 1980-85 Atlas
- 2000-05 Atlas
- Both Atlases

Breeding Bird Survey Trend in New York

Black-billed Cuckoo
Coccyzus erythropthalmus

KEVIN J. MCGOWAN

ATM©2006

The Black-billed Cuckoo has the slightly more northern distribution of the two cuckoos in New York, breeding from southern Canada east of the Rockies, southward to Oklahoma and Virginia. It nests in thickets, orchards, abandoned farmland, brushy hillsides, and along forest edges, often near water (Hughes 2001). As a bird of forest edges, the Black-billed Cuckoo population may have increased in New York with deforestation during European settlement. DeKay (1844) knew it as a breeder but said little else. Giraud (1844) considered it as common on Long Island as the Yellow-billed Cuckoo. Rathbun (1879) and Short (1893) considered both cuckoos to be relatively common breeders in central and western New York, with the Black-billed slightly more common. Eaton (1914) noted that the Black-billed Cuckoo was fairly common throughout the state, slightly more common than the Yellow-billed Cuckoo in the western part, but they were about equally common in the southern regions. The Black-billed Cuckoo penetrated farther into the Adirondacks via valleys than the Yellow-billed, but it was missing from the "Canadian zone." Bull (1974) considered both species to be nearly equally common throughout the southern half of the state, but the Black-billed was more common in the highlands and was the only species to penetrate the valleys of the Catskills and the Adirondacks.

During the first Atlas survey, the Black-billed Cuckoo was found breeding throughout most of the state. It was less common in the Central Tug Hill, Mohawk Valley, most of the Adirondacks, and greater New York City area. It was most abundant in the central Appalachian Plateau, western Erie-Ontario Plain, and lower Hudson Valley. During the second Atlas survey, this cuckoo was found in a similar distribution, still widely scattered across the state and still missing from most of the Adirondacks and the higher portions of the Appalachian Plateau and Catskill regions. It was reported in slightly more blocks during the second Atlas period, and, as might be expected with a slightly irruptive species, the losses and gains were scattered throughout the state. Centers of abundance seemed to shift from the western Erie-Ontario Plain and the central Appalachian Plateau to the eastern Great Lakes Plain and the Mohawk Valley. A 20 percent increase was found in the Adirondacks, but a general decline was noticeable in the Hudson Valley southward to the Coastal Lowlands. This cuckoo is a secretive species and can be easily overlooked. Although it calls at night through the summer, it stops calling during the day once eggs are laid (Hughes 2001). Conse-

quently, any conclusions about changes in distribution must be treated cautiously.

Substantial movements of cuckoos into an area can occur with caterpillar outbreaks (Hughes 2001), making population levels difficult to track. A notable forest tent caterpillar outbreak occurred in St. Lawrence County in 2002–05 (Kraus 2006). That area showed an increase in cuckoo reports in the second Atlas data, although the pattern of defoliation did not correspond very closely to the Atlas map. The Black-billed Cuckoo population has declined across its range throughout the 20th century, possibly because of the use of pesticides and the subsequent reduction of caterpillar outbreaks (Hughes 2001). Breeding Bird Survey data show a significant decline survey-wide since 1966, even though the trend for the period of 1966–79 was significantly positive (Sauer et al. 2007). BBS data from New York show no significant long-term trend (Sauer et al. 2007). Nearly all significant trends in recent BBS data are negative (Sauer et al. 2007), but the species is not currently listed as a Watch List or Stewardship Species by Partners in Flight (Rich et al. 2004). Hypotheses to explain the recent declines in the Northeast include the loss of farmland and the maturation of forests, modification of habitat on the wintering grounds, hazards during migration, and pesticide use (Hughes 2001).

2000-05 Distribution Map

- ☐ Not Found
- Possible
- Probable
- Confirmed

Number of Blocks

	1980–85		2000–05		Change
	No.	%	No.	%	%
Possible	972	50	1,097	54	13
Probable	724	37	733	36	1
Confirmed	267	14	204	10	−24
Total	1,963	37	2,034	38	4

Change Map

- ☐ Not Reported
- 1980-85 Atlas
- 2000-05 Atlas
- Both Atlases

Breeding Bird Survey Trend in New York

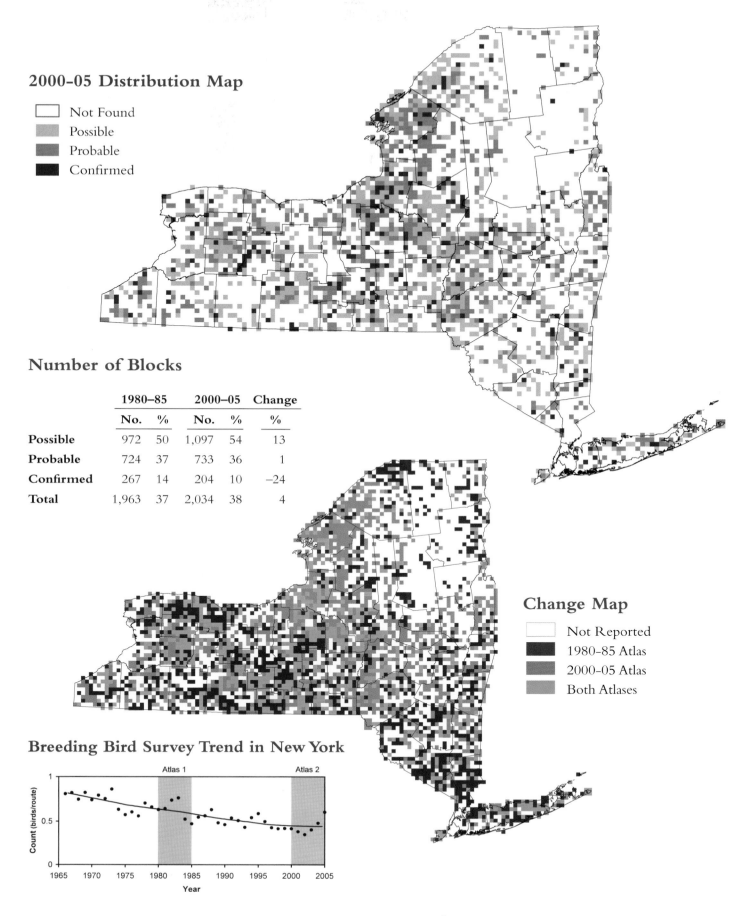

Great Horned Owl and Eastern Screech-Owl in mixed woodland

Even a small patch of mixed hardwoods, such as this community park in western New York, can provide tree cavity–nesting sights for owls. For this reason, it is important to leave suitable dead or dying trees standing when managing private or public woodlots.

Barn Owl
Tyto alba

KEVIN J. MCGOWAN

The Barn Owl is one of the most widely distributed birds in the world, being resident from the northern United States and southern British Columbia southward through Central and South America and the Caribbean, as well as in Africa, Europe, southeastern Asia, Australia, and some oceanic islands (Marti et al. 2005). New York is at the northeastern edge of its North American range. The Barn Owl breeds in open habitats, such as grasslands, marshes, and agricultural areas. It nests in cavities in trees, cliffs, buildings, or nest boxes and forages in nearby open areas (Marti et al. 2005). As a bird of open areas, the Barn Owl probably was rare in New York before European settlement, and even though the clearing of forests created appropriate open habitat, it apparently never became common in most of the state. DeKay (1844) assumed it was a rare resident in New York, but Giraud (1844) did not mention it. Short (1879) did not list it in western New York, and Rathbun (1879) recorded only a single specimen from central New York. Reed and Wright (1909) mentioned seven records of Barn Owl in the Cayuga Lake Basin, the first one in 1880, and noted that the population was increasing. Eaton (1914) called it a rare bird in New York, with known breeding locations only from the Genesee Valley, Staten Island, and Long Island. Beardslee and Mitchell (1965) noted it as rare but increasing in numbers along the Niagara Frontier. Bull (1974) considered the Barn Owl uncommon and local throughout the state, being most common along the coast. He indicated that it was missing from the mountainous areas and the more northern reaches of the state. He showed it breeding along Long Island and up the Hudson Valley, along the western Great Lakes Plain to the Finger Lakes region, and southward from there through the Appalachian Plateau to the Pennsylvania border.

The first Atlas survey found the Barn Owl in few blocks, with about half concentrated in the lower Hudson Valley and the Coastal Lowlands. The distribution map closely resembled that shown by Bull (1974), with the exception of fewer reports along the Great Lakes Plain and new reports from the Western Adirondack Transition and Eastern Adirondack Foothills. The owl was missing from the Central Adirondacks and the higher elevations in the state. The second Atlas data showed that the Barn Owl population has declined drastically, practically disappearing from most of the state. Only 11 records came from north of Long Island. Breeding was confirmed only in the Coastal Lowlands and Hudson Valley. Even on the Coastal Lowlands blocks with reports fell by 66 percent. The Orange and Livingston county concentrations were essentially gone, although sightings were made in two blocks in Livingston County. Because the Barn Owl is strictly nocturnal and does not advertise its territory as other owls do, some breeding individuals undoubtedly were missed.

The Barn Owl population has been declining in the United States and Europe (Marti et al. 2005). The reasons are uncertain, but possible factors include pesticide use, changes in agriculture from hay to row crops, and the decrease in available nest sites (Marti et al. 2005). The species is not included on the New York endangered species list, although it is recognized as a Species of Greatest Conservation Need (see Chapter 6). Nest box programs have helped increase populations in some areas (Marti et al. 2005), but the release of captive-raised owls has been ineffective (Solymár and McCracken 2002, Marti et al. 2005). Hawk Creek Wildlife, Inc., in Erie County has released over 170 Barn Owls in western New York since 1994 (Hawk Creek Wildlife Inc. 2006). Although the program has apparently been unsuccessful in creating a breeding population in western New York, it may be responsible for scattered sightings in the area. It remains to be seen if the Barn Owl will ever recover substantially in Upstate New York.

2000–05 Distribution Map

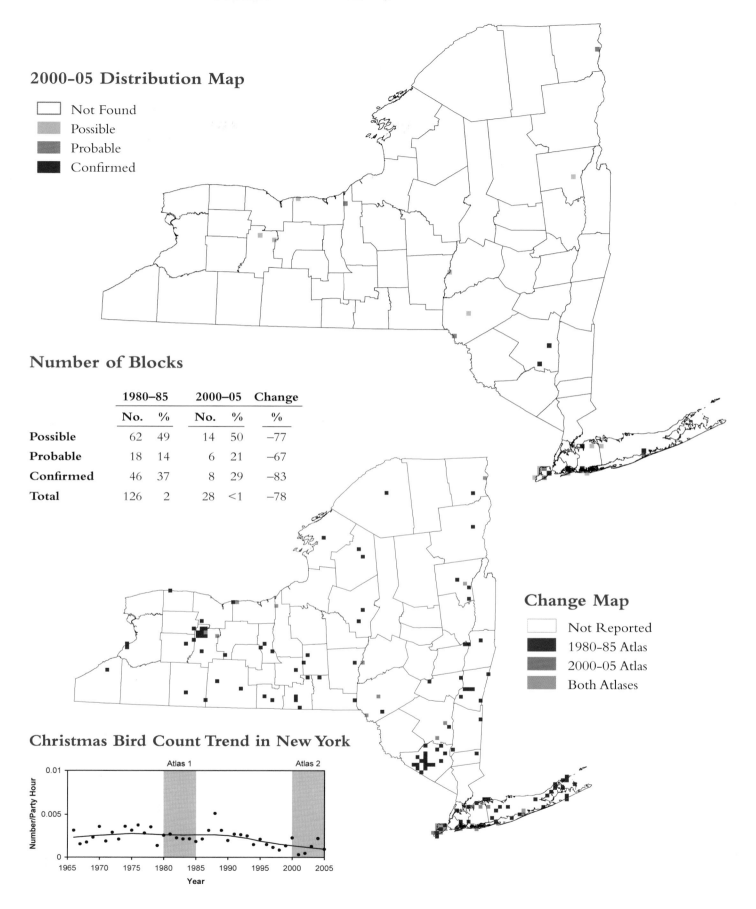

Not Found
Possible
Probable
Confirmed

Number of Blocks

	1980–85		2000–05		Change
	No.	%	No.	%	%
Possible	62	49	14	50	−77
Probable	18	14	6	21	−67
Confirmed	46	37	8	29	−83
Total	126	2	28	<1	−78

Change Map

Not Reported
1980-85 Atlas
2000-05 Atlas
Both Atlases

Christmas Bird Count Trend in New York

Eastern Screech-Owl

Megascops asio

CHARLES R. SMITH

The Eastern Screech-Owl is the only breeding bird species in New York to show two, conspicuously distinctive color forms: one reddish brown, the other gray. Mosher and Henny (1976) suggested that reddish brown owls are less able to survive cold temperatures than gray-plumaged ones. Panko and Battaly (1998) reported that the gray form is more common in the western part of New York and the red form more common in the warmer, coastal areas and on Long Island, lending support to this idea. The Eastern Screech-Owl occurs throughout the United States east of the Rocky Mountains and mostly south of Canada, though its range extends into southern Ontario and northern Mexico (Gehlbach 1995). New York is at the northeastern limit of the range. The species uses a variety of wooded habitats in all types of terrain, primarily deciduous and mixed forests from early-successional to mature stages, as well as urban and suburban areas (Gehlbach 1995). Panko and Battaly (1998) noted that this owl is not common in the more forested areas of New York and that it prefers "fragmented" habitats, though a thorough study of its use of forest fragments in New York has not been conducted. Beardslee and Mitchell (1965), Bull (1974), and Eaton (1988i) all believed the screech-owl population to be declining in the state. Panko and Battaly (1998) suggested it had undergone local declines and increases, but the species was more numerous than before forest cutting by European settlement.

The first Atlas data showed the Eastern Screech-Owl to be widespread across New York, with concentrations on Long Island, the Hudson River Valley, and across the Erie-Ontario Plain and Appalachian Plateau. It was mostly absent from higher elevations of the Adirondack, Catskill, and Allegheny mountains. The second Atlas survey found little change in its distribution and only a 1 percent increase in the number of blocks with records compared to the first Atlas. Local decreases, such as in the Hudson Highlands, and increases, such as in the Mohawk Valley and Cattaraugus Highlands, are likely the result of different coverage and not true distribution changes. Though its song is distinctive, an absence of fieldwork during the evening hours could account for the apparent absence of the screech-owl in some areas. It is probably more widespread than the map suggests.

As a nocturnal species, the Eastern Screech-Owl is not censused well by the Breeding Bird Survey. BBS data show no significant trends for New York, the Northeast, or the entire survey area (Sauer et al. 2005). No significant change in distribution was observed for screech-owl across Ontario between the first and second Ontario Breeding Bird Atlases either, but increases were recorded in the two most southern regions (Bird Studies Canada et al. 2006).

DeCandido (2005) concluded that the Eastern Screech-Owl population declined throughout the New York City area after about 1950, even in places that were protected as parklands. He identified a number of factors that could have contributed to the decline, including increased use of insecticides and anticoagulant rodenticides; removal of dead trees and snags; more frequent collisions with vehicles; increased competition for tree cavities from the eastern gray squirrel, raccoon, and European Starling; increased predation by the American Crow; predation and disturbance by nocturnal mammals; and increased disturbance by people near nest sites.

Partners in Flight has not identified any specific management needs for the Eastern Screech-Owl (Rich et al. 2004), and it is not considered in need of conservation attention in New York or any surrounding state. It is likely that Eastern Screech-Owl populations in New York are effectively stable. Still, better, more consistently applied, statistically valid methods are needed for monitoring the distribution and abundance of this and other nocturnal species.

2000-05 Distribution Map

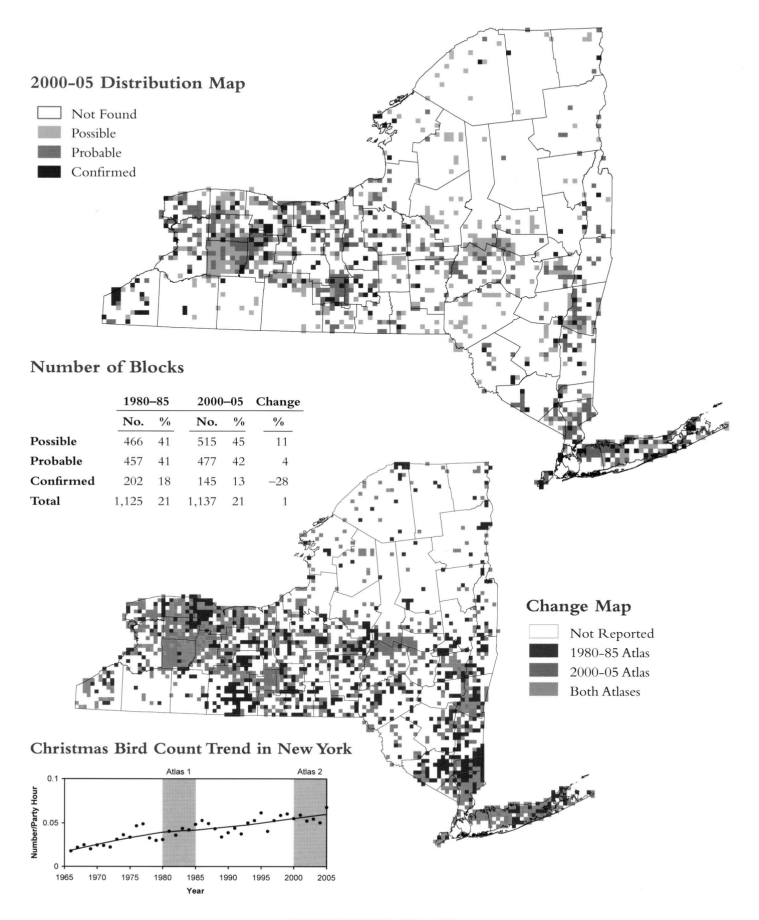

- ☐ Not Found
- Possible
- Probable
- Confirmed

Number of Blocks

	1980–85		2000–05		Change
	No.	%	No.	%	%
Possible	466	41	515	45	11
Probable	457	41	477	42	4
Confirmed	202	18	145	13	−28
Total	1,125	21	1,137	21	1

Change Map

- ☐ Not Reported
- 1980-85 Atlas
- 2000-05 Atlas
- Both Atlases

Christmas Bird Count Trend in New York

Great Horned Owl
Bubo virginianus

KEVIN J. McGOWAN

One of the largest owls in North America, the Great Horned Owl is also one of the most widespread. It is resident across virtually all of North America except northern Alaska and Canada, as well as across parts of Central and South America (Houston et al. 1998). It is found in a wide variety of habitats, including old-growth forests, deserts, and even urban areas, but it prefers open and second-growth woodlands, swamps, and agricultural areas (Houston et al. 1998). The Great Horned Owl was probably relatively uncommon throughout thickly forested New York during pre-colonial time, and the opening of the forests may have increased the habitat for it. Persecution by the European settlers, though, may well have decreased its populations. DeKay (1844) listed it only as breeding in the state, and Giraud (1844) said it was not common on Long Island. It was considered common to uncommon throughout the state in the late 1800s (Rathbun 1879, Short 1893, Reed and Wright 1909), including in the Adirondacks (Merriam 1881). Eaton (1914) listed the Great Horned Owl as a resident throughout the state but noted that it was no longer common outside of the wooded districts. He cited a decrease in the number of hollow nesting trees, along with persecution from people, as causes of its decline. Beardslee and Mitchell (1965) noted that it had formerly been abundant (at least in the late 1800s), but that it had declined throughout the 20th century such that it was found only in more secluded woodlands. Bull (1974) called it uncommon to fairly common throughout the state. As Salzman (1998d) noted, the apparent preference for remote areas described by many authors was most likely the result of persecution by people, not a true habitat preference. Changing attitudes, as well as legal protection starting in 1972, may have resulted in an increased Great Horned Owl population during the late 20th century.

During the first Atlas survey, the Great Horned Owl was found nesting throughout the state, present in all ecozones, but most abundant on the Great Lakes Plain and central Appalachian Plateau. It was noticeably scarcer (or less frequently detected) in all Adirondack ecozones, Tug Hill Plateau, western Appalachian Plateau, sections of the Catskill region, and southwestern Long Island. During the second Atlas survey, this owl had essentially the same distribution, but it was reported from 18 percent fewer blocks. Declines were noted in all ecozones except for the Tug Hill Plateau, St. Lawrence Plains and Transition, and Coastal Lowlands. This owl's nocturnal nature and early breeding season, beginning in January, make its detection highly dependent on the amount of special effort expended to document it. Despite its great size, the adults' loud territorial calls, and juveniles' persistent begging, this species is undoubtedly under-represented on Atlas maps, although perhaps more accurately represented than some owl species.

As a nocturnal bird, the Great Horned Owl is not well sampled by the Breeding Bird Survey. Existing BBS data show a significant decline in detections survey-wide since 1980, following a period of no change in 1966–79 (Sauer et al. 2005). BBS data from New York are too sparse to analyze. Christmas Bird Count data for New York show an increase in Great Horned Owl numbers from 1960 through about 1990, and then an apparent decline through 2006 (National Audubon Society [2007]). The second Ontario Breeding Bird Atlas also reported a significant decline in Great Horned Owl numbers across the province (Bird Studies Canada et al. 2006). The maturing forests of New York could be less favorable to this owl than second growth, as the species appears to prefer a fragmented habitat (Morrell and Yahner 1994). Such landscape change might be responsible for some of the population declines seen in the state. Nocturnal birds require special efforts for adequate monitoring, and Great Horned Owl populations should be watched for continuing declines.

2000-05 Distribution Map

- ☐ Not Found
- Possible
- Probable
- Confirmed

Number of Blocks

	1980–85		2000–05		Change
	No.	%	No.	%	%
Possible	810	41	673	41	−17
Probable	605	31	531	33	−12
Confirmed	553	28	418	26	−24
Total	1,968	37	1,622	30	−18

Change Map

- ☐ Not Reported
- 1980-85 Atlas
- 2000-05 Atlas
- Both Atlases

Christmas Bird Count Trend in New York

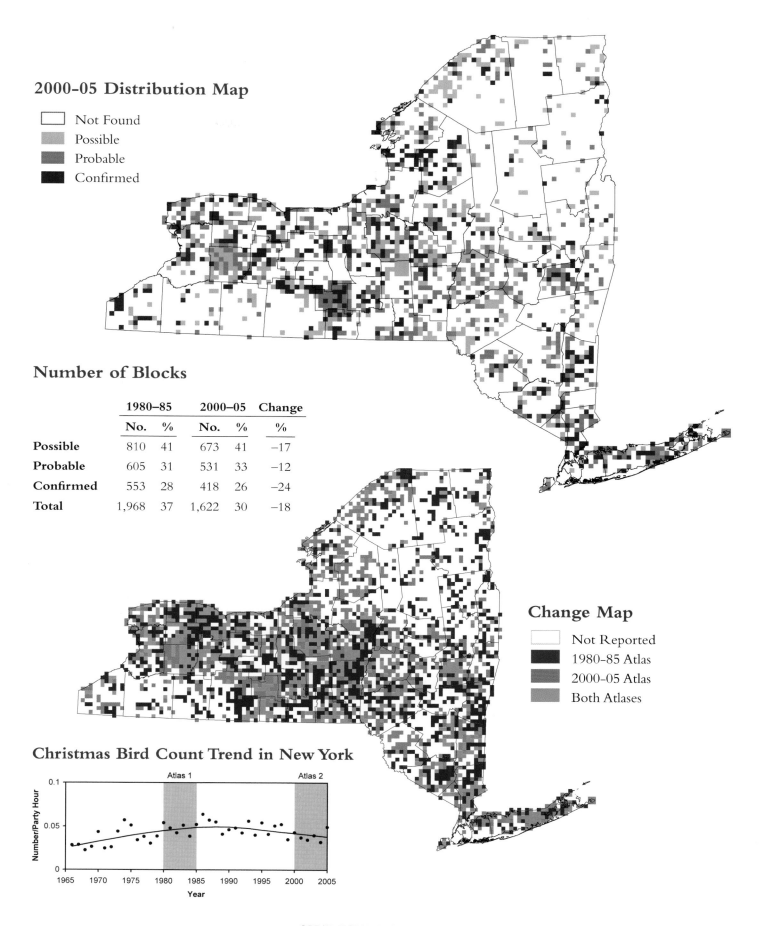

Barred Owl
Strix varia

KEVIN J. MCGOWAN

The Barred Owl is a widespread resident of forests east of the Great Plains from southern Canada to the Gulf Coast and Florida. It also occurs across central Canada to southeastern Alaska and southward to northern California and Idaho, with disjunct populations in southern Mexico (Mazur and James 2000). It lives in wooded areas and swamps and favors large blocks of forest (Mazur and James 2000). As a species that prefers old-growth forest, the Barred Owl was undoubtedly common in New York before European settlement, and its numbers declined with the destruction of the forests. DeKay (1844) described it as common in the state, and Giraud (1844) suggested it bred on Long Island but gave no specifics. Merriam (1881) called it common in the Adirondacks. Although Rathbun (1879) considered it a common resident in central New York, and Reed and Wright (1909) listed it as uncommon in the Cayuga Lake Basin, Short (1893) considered it a rare visitor to western New York. Eaton (1914) called it the most common owl in the Adirondacks and described it as present throughout the state wherever swampy woods or forests were extensive enough to keep the owl secure from people. Griscom (1923) described it as rare or extirpated near New York City and rare and local on Long Island. Beardslee and Mitchell (1965) considered the Barred Owl relatively common in western New York, although less common than the Great Horned Owl, except in the southern counties and around the Oak Orchard Swamp area. Bull (1974) called the Barred Owl locally uncommon to fairly common throughout the state but noted that it was very rare on Long Island.

During the first Atlas period, the Barred Owl was widely distributed across the state, except for in the Coastal Lowlands, where it was found only on Fishers Island. It was most common in the more heavily forested regions, especially the Adirondacks and the Tug Hill Plateau. The second Atlas data also showed the Barred Owl to be present across the state but absent from most of the Coastal Lowlands. Again it was confirmed nesting on Fishers Island and also detected in one block on the north shore of Long Island. Overall, the Barred Owl was recorded in 43 percent more blocks. The Adirondacks, Appalachian Plateau, and Tug Hill Plateau remain the stronghold of the species in the state. The owl's distribution shows a general correspondence to that of extensive forest, with lower densities along the Great Lakes Plain, St. Lawrence Plains, and Mohawk and upper Hudson valleys, although the gaps in the southern tier are perhaps surprising. The distribution of the Barred Owl is generally the reverse of that of the Great Horned Owl in the state, suggesting either avoidance or some degree of habitat segregation. The loss and gain of contiguous areas of occurrence across the Appalachian Plateau may well represent the differences in owling effort in those blocks between the two Atlas periods. As a nocturnal species, Barred Owl records depend on the effort made to census it specifically.

The Barred Owl has been extending its range westward through Canada over the last century (Mazur and James 2000), but population trends in the East are harder to track. Because it is nocturnal, the Barred Owl is not well sampled with Breeding Bird Survey protocols, but the existing data show a significant increase continent-wide since 1966 (Sauer et al. 2007). The increase from 1980 to 2005 is not significant, however, and BBS data from New York are too sparse to analyze. Christmas Bird Count data show an increasing trend of this resident species since about 1970 in both national and New York data (National Audubon Society [2007]). The second Ontario Breeding Bird Atlas also reported a significant increase in Barred Owl numbers across the province (Bird Studies Canada et al. 2006). The continuing maturation of forests in New York favors this forest-dwelling owl, and its population may continue to increase into the future.

2000–05 Distribution Map

- ☐ Not Found
- Possible
- Probable
- Confirmed

Number of Blocks

| | 1980–85 | | 2000–05 | | Change |
	No.	%	No.	%	%
Possible	519	48	759	49	46
Probable	433	40	619	40	43
Confirmed	123	11	156	10	27
Total	1,075	20	1,534	29	43

Change Map

- ☐ Not Reported
- 1980-85 Atlas
- 2000-05 Atlas
- Both Atlases

Christmas Bird Count Trend in New York

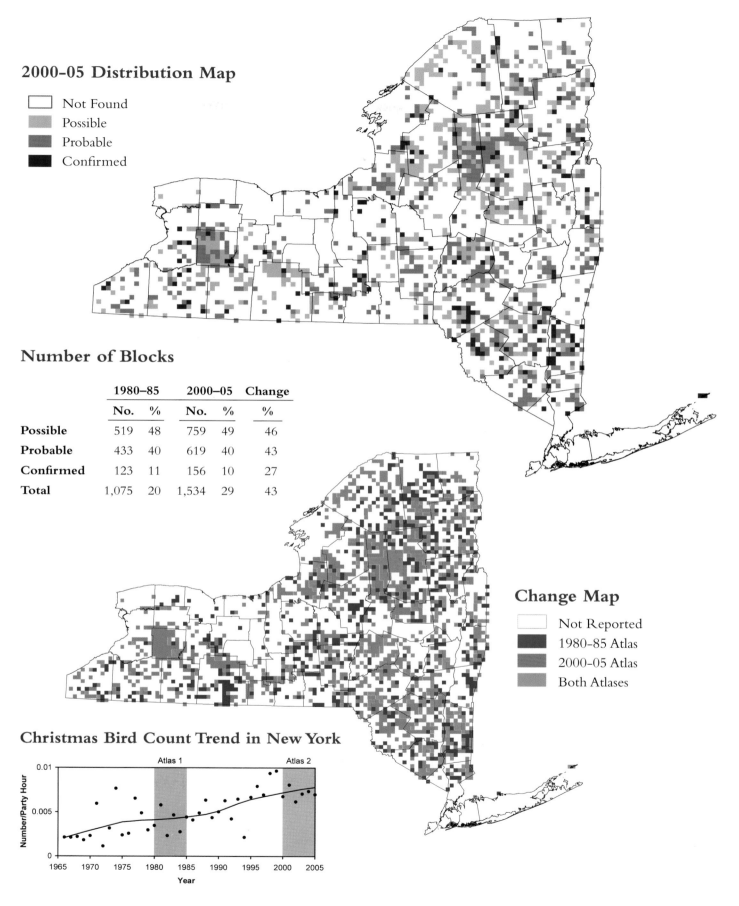

Long-eared Owl
Asio otus

Matthew D. Medler

One of the world's most widespread owls, the Long-eared Owl occurs across large portions of North America and Eurasia and also breeds in northwestern Africa (AOU 1998). In North America, its main breeding range extends from the Northwest Territories to Nova Scotia, southward to Pennsylvania, Minnesota, and New Mexico; isolated breeding populations are found as far south as Baja California (AOU 1998). Although sometimes depicted as strictly a forest species, the Long-eared Owl breeds in open forests and where dense woods occur adjacent to grasslands, shrublands, and other open areas (Marks et al. 1994). DeKay (1844) made no clear statement about the Long-eared Owl's breeding status in New York, whereas Eaton (1914) provided this cryptic assessment: "It is one of our strictly resident species, and is not very uncommon about dense wooded swamps and hillsides in most parts of the State, but is apparently uncommon in the Adirondack forests." Bull (1974) considered the Long-eared Owl to be a rare to uncommon breeder, fairly widely distributed in central and western New York, and locally distributed in southeastern New York and Long Island. He described it as little known in the Catskills and throughout northern New York, including the Adirondacks.

During the first Atlas survey, the Long-eared Owl was sparsely distributed across much of the state, with no significant concentration in any ecozone. Although reported from five blocks in the Coastal Lowlands, it went undetected throughout the rest of southeastern New York. More than 30 records from northern New York, including Confirmed records from the Champlain Transition, Western Adirondack Foothills, and St. Lawrence Plains, helped clarify the owl's status in this part of the state. During the second Atlas survey, the Long-eared Owl was reported from 41 percent fewer blocks, with all ecozones experiencing declines except for the Hudson Valley and Taconic Highlands. The number of Adirondack records decreased from 23 to 5. The only notable concentration of records came from the Livingston County area, where there was considerable owling effort in select blocks (J. Kimball pers. comm.). The Atlas maps for the Long-eared Owl are influenced by both the inclusion of records that might represent migrants and the difficulty in detecting nocturnal species. Eleven of the 48 records from the second Atlas period were Possible records reported between 1 March and 14 April. These could represent wintering or migrant individuals, as Slack et al. (1987) documented spring migration of the Long-eared Owl in Oswego County as occurring between 21 March and 14 April. As a nocturnal species, this owl was undoubtedly overlooked in some blocks that had little or no nighttime effort. However, the combined Atlas results for the Great Horned Owl, Barred Owl, and Eastern Screech-Owl strongly suggest that nocturnal coverage was adequate in a variety of habitats across the state during the Long-eared Owl's breeding season. In Wyoming County, where there was owling effort in most of the county's 63 Atlas blocks, the number of blocks with Long-eared Owl (4) was substantially lower than the totals for the Eastern Screech-Owl (58), Barred Owl (51), Great Horned Owl (51), and Northern Saw-whet Owl (19). While the Long-eared Owl is likely more difficult to detect than these other species, these totals suggest that the Long-eared Owl truly is a rare to uncommon breeder in New York.

Breeding Bird Survey trend data do not exist for the Long-eared Owl, nor does any other quantitative trend information for breeding populations of this species. The second Ontario Atlas revealed no significant change province-wide (Bird Studies Canada et al. 2006). Although not listed in New York, it is listed as Endangered in Connecticut, Threatened in New Jersey, and of Special Concern in Massachusetts. Intensive study and monitoring of the Long-eared Owl is needed in New York to more clearly define its breeding status in the state.

2000-05 Distribution Map

- ☐ Not Found
- ▨ Possible
- ▨ Probable
- ■ Confirmed

Number of Blocks

	1980–85		2000–05		Change
	No.	%	No.	%	%
Possible	44	54	30	63	−32
Probable	22	27	11	23	−50
Confirmed	15	19	7	15	−53
Total	81	2	48	<1	−41

Change Map

- ☐ Not Reported
- ■ 1980–85 Atlas
- ▨ 2000–05 Atlas
- ▨ Both Atlases

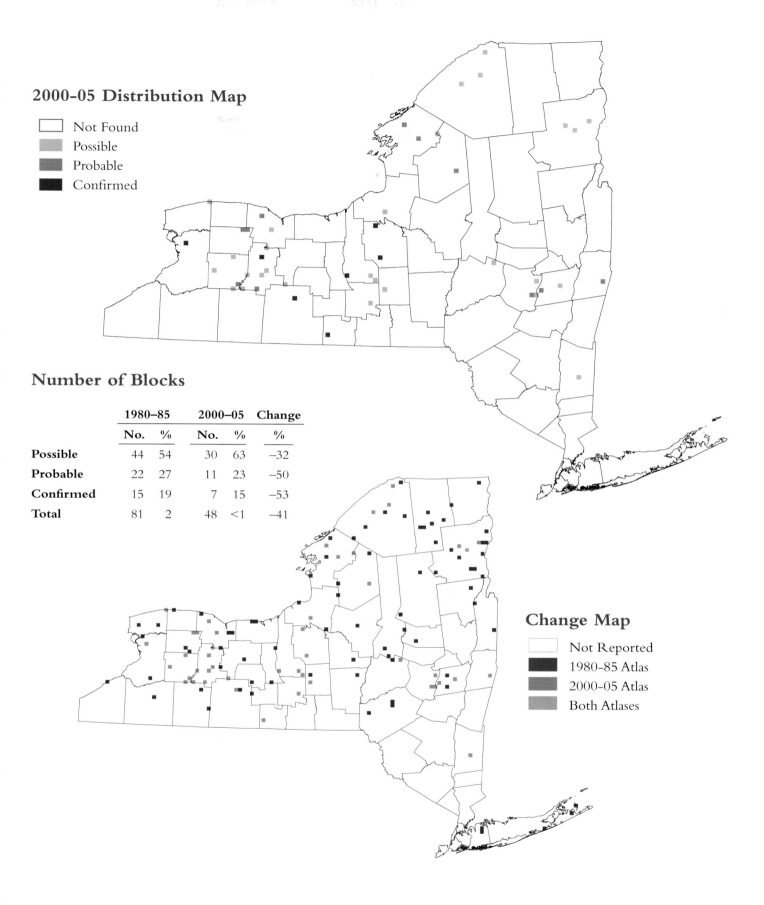

Short-eared Owl
Asio flammeus

KATHRYN J. SCHNEIDER

The most diurnal of all New York's owls, the Short-eared Owl is usually observed in the late afternoon and at dawn or dusk flying low over grasslands, marshes, and other open country. Its extensive global range includes every continent except Australia and Antarctica, but the breeding range of the nominate subspecies found in North America and Eurasia reaches its southern limit in New York. Migratory northern populations typically arrive here in November, where they winter and roost communally until late March or early April (Clark 1975). Territorial behavior and courtship displays occur during the breakup of winter roosts, a fact that makes unconfirmed probable breeding records from March and April especially suspect (Clark 1975, Holt and Leasure 1993). However, the few Short-eared Owls that breed in New York are often found at or near wintering areas (Eaton 1914, Reilly and Parkes 1959, Bull 1974, Schneider 2003).

Eaton (1914) compiled data from published local lists and personal communications that documented breeding in 16 New York counties. Sixty years later Bull (1974) noted a change in status, calling the bird a "local breeder, greatly decreased in recent years," and by 1965 Beardslee and Mitchell considered it an irregular summer resident in western New York. Historical records show nesting on Long Island, in western New York, and south and east of Lake Ontario, with the most common breeding sites in the marshes above and below Montezuma and east of Lake Ontario (Schneider 2003).

During the first Atlas survey, the Short-eared Owl was recorded in 36 blocks but confirmed in only 5, including 1 in St. Lawrence County and 4 on Long Island. Upstate breeding was scattered over western and central New York, particularly in the St. Lawrence watershed and the Erie-Ontario Plain. A few Probable records were also reported in the Champlain Valley

and in the Brandon Burn, a large, formerly forested burn site in Franklin County. During the second Atlas survey, the Short-eared Owl was found in only 24 blocks, one-third fewer than previously reported. The most marked changes occurred on Long Island, where the Short-eared Owl was recorded from only one block, compared to nine in the first Atlas. All the blocks with Confirmed breeding records were north of Long Island, on the Great Lakes Plain in Jefferson and Onondaga counties, and in the Champlain Valley of Clinton County. Aside from the near disappearance of nesting on Long Island, the statewide distribution appeared largely unchanged.

This declining trend is not unique to New York. Downward population trends are documented throughout much of the Short-eared Owl's North American range. In Canada, Kirk and Hyslop (1998) reported a highly significant decline based on Breeding Bird Survey data from 1966–94, particularly in the Prairies and Boreal Plains ecozones, regions that represent the core of the species's range in Canada (Cadman 1993). While BBS data are deficient for the United States (Sauer et al. 2005), Christmas Bird Count data for both Canada and the entire survey area show highly significant declines from 1959 to 1988 (Sauer et al. 1996). Within the contiguous United States approximately half the states in its breeding range identify this owl as a bird of conservation concern. In the Northeast it is listed or proposed for listing as endangered or threatened in eight states, including New York, where it is listed as Endangered (NYSDEC 1999).

Loss, degradation, and fragmentation of grassland and wetland habitats are the primary factors linked to the declining populations in North America (Holt 1986, Holt and Leasure 1993, Cadman and Page 1994, Wiggins 2004). South of the arctic tundra the Short-eared Owl prefers extensive areas of contiguous dense grassland that support large numbers of small mammals. The loss of breeding owls on Long Island, where marshes and coastal grasslands were the primary breeding habitats, can probably be attributed to residential and recreational development.

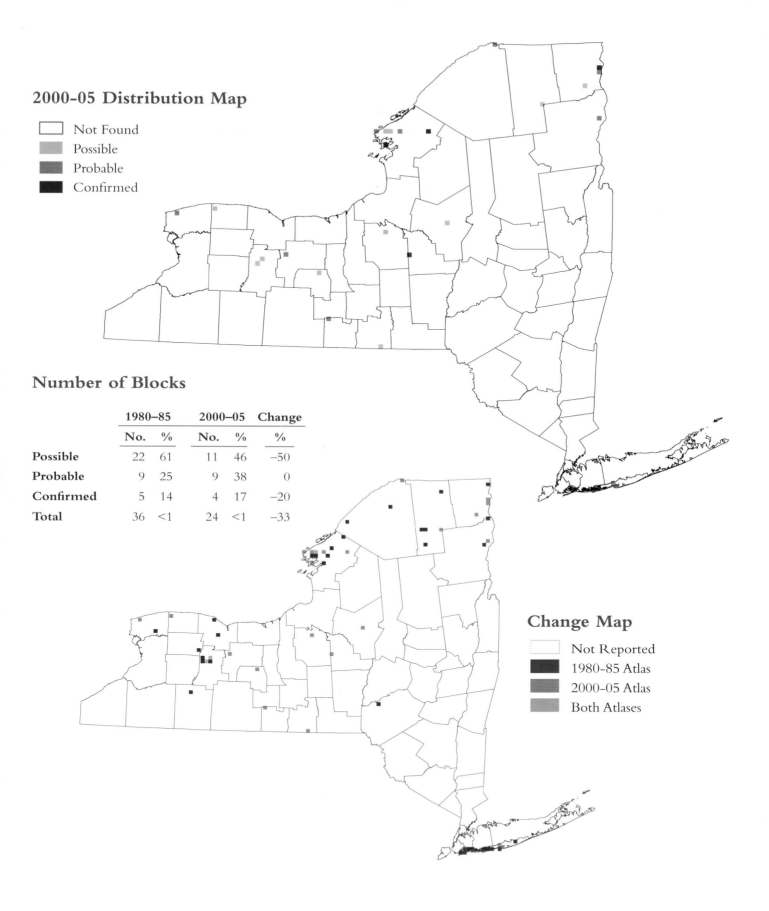

2000-05 Distribution Map

- ☐ Not Found
- ☐ Possible
- ☐ Probable
- ☐ Confirmed

Number of Blocks

	1980–85		2000–05		Change
	No.	%	No.	%	%
Possible	22	61	11	46	−50
Probable	9	25	9	38	0
Confirmed	5	14	4	17	−20
Total	36	<1	24	<1	−33

Change Map

- ☐ Not Reported
- ☐ 1980-85 Atlas
- ☐ 2000-05 Atlas
- ☐ Both Atlases

Northern Saw-whet Owl
Aegolius acadicus

KEVIN J. MCGOWAN

The smallest of New York's owls, the Northern Saw-whet Owl breeds from southern Alaska eastward to Nova Scotia, southward to the northern United States, and farther southward in mountains to North Carolina and southern Mexico (Cannings 1993). It breeds in many types of forests, with the highest densities in coniferous woods (Cannings 1993). It is not as restricted to dense forests for nesting and foraging as it seems to be for roosting (Cannings 1993). The Northern Saw-whet Owl was probably always moderately common in New York, but its secretive nature has made it easy to miss, and even now its exact range is a bit of a mystery. Adding further confusion is the fact that the breeding season overlaps the migration period (Cannings 1993). In New York, breeding begins in March and April (Bull 1974), which is also the peak of spring migration (Slack et al. 1987), and assigning breeder or migrant status to April reports is problematic. DeKay (1844) mentioned only that the owl bred in the state. Giraud (1844) called it rare on Long Island, more common in the coastal swamps in New Jersey and Maryland. It was considered a rare, but likely breeding, bird in western and central New York in the late 19th century (Rathbun 1873, Short 1893, Reed and Wright 1909). Merriam (1881) considered it a moderately common resident in the Adirondacks. Eaton (1914) knew of only a few breeding records in New York but thought it might be fairly common in some parts of the state. Bull (1974) called it a rare and local breeder. He listed 29 known breeding locations across the state (only 5 in the Adirondacks) and noted that it was certainly overlooked and could be present elsewhere. Most of the known nest sites were from wooded swamps, but nests were also found in a spruce-sphagnum bog, an old apple orchard, and an open sand dune near a salt marsh (Bull 1974).

During the first Atlas survey, the Northern Saw-whet Owl was concentrated in the Adirondacks but scattered across the rest of the state. The owl was reported from nearly all ecozones, with Confirmed breeding in the Coastal Lowlands, Hudson Highlands, western Appalachian Plateau, Great Lakes Plain, and St. Lawrence Transition. The second Atlas survey revealed an increase in blocks with reports across the state. The Appalachian Plateau nearly equaled the Adirondacks for the most records. The number of records within the Adirondacks declined slightly. Breeding was confirmed across the Adirondacks, on the Appalachian Plateau, in the Helderberg Highlands, and on the Great Lakes Plain. No reports were made in the lower Hudson Valley or the

Coastal Lowlands. Whether changes indicated by the second Atlas data are real or related to differences in effort on the part of the atlasers is difficult to assess. The appearance of a large block of reports across Wyoming County probably reflects the increased owling effort in that area rather than a new colonization.

As a secretive nocturnal bird, the Northern Saw-whet Owl is difficult to monitor. Cannings (1993) stated that no population data exist for it, and no Breeding Bird Survey data are available. The second Ontario Breeding Bird Atlas reported some local declines and increases in squares with records but no significant change over the entire province (Bird Studies Canada et al. 2006). A recently recorded extension of the owl's breeding range northward in Quebec might have represented a true range expansion or discovery of an existing population (Buidin et al. 2006). Because of the combination of the owl's secretive habits and the confused timing of breeding and migration, the current information from the Atlas projects does not allow confidence in making conclusions about the current status of the Northern Saw-whet Owl in New York. It may be necessary to develop targeted monitoring efforts to accurately assess population changes of this small owl.

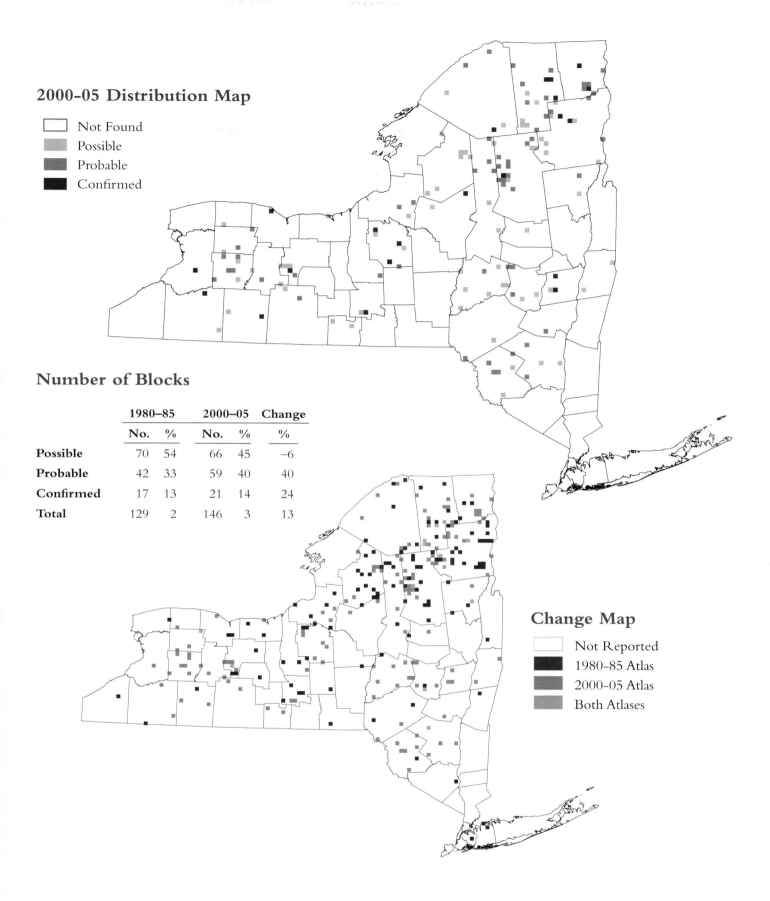

2000-05 Distribution Map

- ☐ Not Found
- Possible
- Probable
- ■ Confirmed

Number of Blocks

| | 1980–85 | | 2000–05 | | Change |
	No.	%	No.	%	%
Possible	70	54	66	45	−6
Probable	42	33	59	40	40
Confirmed	17	13	21	14	24
Total	129	2	146	3	13

Change Map

- ☐ Not Reported
- ■ 1980-85 Atlas
- 2000-05 Atlas
- Both Atlases

Small-footed birds on an Albany evening

Although on the surface it may seem an inhospitable environment, the Chimney Swift and Common Nighthawk prefer to breed in the city with its plentiful nesting sites and healthy insect population.

Common Nighthawk

Chordeiles minor

MATTHEW D. MEDLER

nce a common summertime sight in New York's cities, the Common Nighthawk is now a rare breeder throughout the state. It breeds across most of North America, ranging from Yukon to Labrador, southward through the contiguous United States, and into Mexico; isolated breeding populations also exist as far south as Panama (Poulin et al. 1996). Nighthawks nest in a variety of habitats, and in New York alone this species historically was found nesting in pine barrens, fields, pastures, sand dunes, gravel beaches, rocky outcrops, forest burns, and on gravel rooftops in cities and villages (Bull 1974, Sibley 1988h). Eaton (1914) described the Common Nighthawk as a widespread but local breeder, occurring in every county and nesting in both natural and urban settings. Both Rathbun (1879) and Reed and Wright (1909) considered it to be a common summer resident in central New York. Beardslee and Mitchell (1965) depicted the species as a common breeder in the cities and larger towns of western New York. In the New York City area, rooftop nesting was first documented by Zerega (1882), and Griscom (1923) called this nighthawk a common summer resident on Long Island. Cruickshank (1942) noted a marked population decline in the entire New York City area, and Bull (1964) considered the nighthawk a rare nester within city limits. Statewide, Bull (1974) portrayed the species as a familiar, frequently encountered bird on summer evenings in cities and some villages, mentioning Albany, Buffalo, Rochester, and Syracuse among the cities with nesting nighthawks in the early 1970s. Bull (1974) also noted that the species was formerly a common and widespread ground nester but that its numbers had declined markedly in natural habitats.

During the first Atlas period, Common Nighthawk records were distributed across the state, but most concentrations were found around cities. The species was reported from 71 percent fewer blocks during the second Atlas period, and it had disappeared from most of the state's cities, including Albany, Syracuse, and Rochester. There were no Confirmed breeding records from urban areas, and only a few Probable records from cities such as New York City, Binghamton, and Buffalo. The state's largest concentrations of nesting nighthawks are ground-nesting populations found at the Fort Drum Military Reservation and in the Champlain Transition. The species is common at Fort Drum in a variety of habitats where sandy soils predominate (J. Bolsinger pers. comm.) and in at least two jack pine barrens in the Champlain Transition: Altona Flat Rock and the Gadway Sandstone Pavement Barrens. The second Atlas data might actually over-represent the extent of nighthawk breeding in New York, as 20 percent of all records came from May, when the species is still migrating through the state. Actual breeders could have been overlooked in some remote areas, however, as special evening effort is often required to detect this crepuscular species.

The Breeding Bird Survey is not especially well suited for monitoring Common Nighthawk populations, but surveywide data show a significant annual decline of 1.8 percent from 1966 to 2005; the species essentially disappeared from New York routes by the 1980s (Sauer et al. 2005). The second Ontario Breeding Bird Atlas reported a significant decline in nighthawk numbers all across the province (Bird Studies Canada et al. 2006). The Common Nighthawk is currently a Species of Special Concern in New York, as it was during the first Atlas period, and is considered Endangered in Connecticut and Threatened in New Hampshire. Reasons for population declines are not well known, but suggested explanations include changes in roofing practices, from gravel to rubberized roofs (Marzilli 1989, Wedgwood 1992); pesticide spraying (Wedgwood 1992); and urban predation by gulls and crows. Current trends, combined with their unexplained causes, do not bode well for the Common Nighthawk's future in New York.

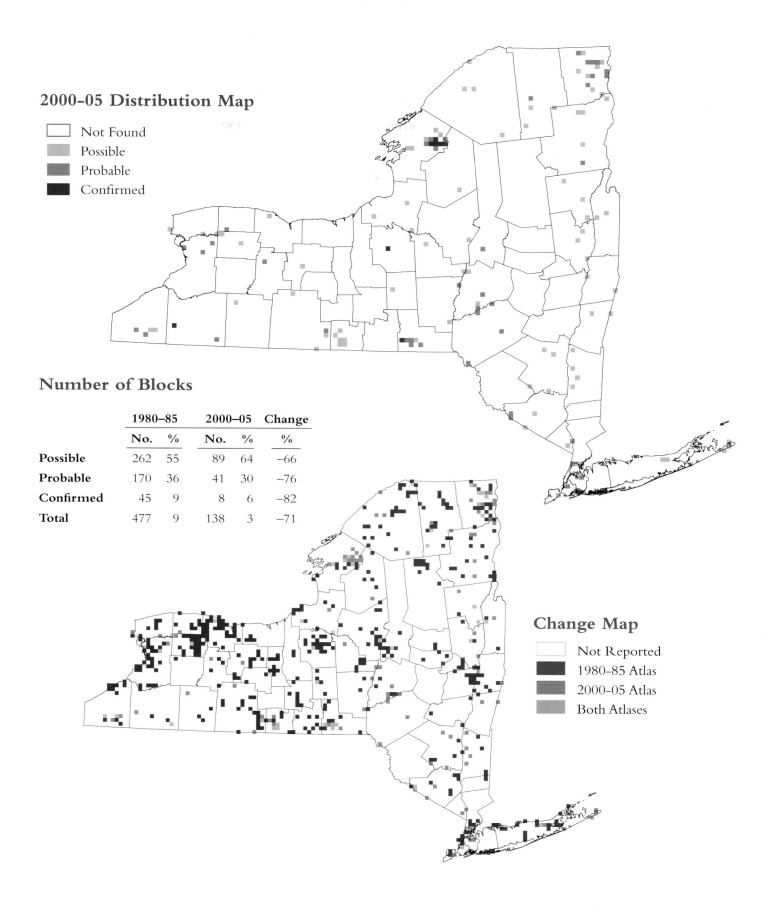

2000–05 Distribution Map

- ☐ Not Found
- Possible
- Probable
- Confirmed

Number of Blocks

	1980–85		2000–05		Change
	No.	%	No.	%	%
Possible	262	55	89	64	−66
Probable	170	36	41	30	−76
Confirmed	45	9	8	6	−82
Total	477	9	138	3	−71

Change Map

- ☐ Not Reported
- 1980–85 Atlas
- 2000–05 Atlas
- Both Atlases

Chuck-will's-widow
Caprimulgus carolinensis

Shaibal S. Mitra

A nocturnal summer resident of the United States' southeastern coastal plain and lower Mississippi River valley, Chuck-will's-widow reaches its northeastern limits in coastal New York (Straight and Cooper 2000). This species breeds in a variety of open pine and oak woodlands, and in New York it is present not only in extensive pine and oak barrens but also in barrier beach settings from which the Whip-poor-will is typically absent. New York's first breeding record came in 1975, in a grove of Japanese black pines at Oak Beach, near Fire Island Inlet, Suffolk County, after a period of rapidly increasing occurrence: just three records statewide prior to 1969, six records in 1969–72, and ten records in 1973–75, including some duplication involving birds returning from year to year (Davis 1975). Colonization of New York came roughly two decades after southern New Jersey was occupied (Bull 1964).

During the first Atlas survey, Chuck-will's-widow was found in two blocks on Staten Island and 19 blocks in Suffolk County, but breeding was confirmed only at Oak Beach. The Suffolk County blocks can be divided into three categories: extensive pitch pine barrens in Brookhaven and Riverhead; coastal sites near or on the outer beach, such as Oak Beach, Fire Island, and Napeague; and South Fork sites away from the ocean coast, including Gardiners Island. During the second Atlas survey, the species was found in one block on Staten Island but just six in Suffolk County. Again, breeding was confirmed only at Oak Beach, possibly the only place where breeding has ever been proved in the state. One of only three blocks occupied during both Atlas periods, this site has not been occupied since 2002 (pers. obs.). Abandonment coincided with the demise of the Japanese black pine groves there. The widespread loss of these exotic pines along the Long Island coast has probably reduced the prospects for the Chuck-will's-widow in outer beach settings. Even more striking is the species's almost complete withdrawal from central-eastern Long Island's pitch pine barrens. The precise reasons for this withdrawal are not known but are likely related to forest fragmentation (Andren and Angelstam 1988, Keyser et al. 1998), an ongoing process also suspected of affecting the Whip-poor-will and other ground-nesting birds in Long Island's increasingly urbanized landscape.

The disappearance of Chuck-will's-widow from all but 3 of the 21 blocks occupied during the first Atlas period and the overall reduction in the number of occupied blocks are consistent with the significant range-wide decline shown by Breeding Bird Survey data (Sauer et al. 2007), and justify concern for the species in the state. The local trends, however, should be interpreted in a regional context and in view of special factors relating to the detection of this nocturnal species. Since the first Atlas project was completed, Chuck-will's-widow has been recorded on New York's Ontario Plain (NYSARC 1995, 2006), regularly in coastal Massachusetts (Veit and Petersen 1993), increasingly often in Connecticut (Mantlik et al. 1998), and at least eight times in Rhode Island (R. Ferren pers. comm.). These patterns of occurrence closely resemble those observed in New Jersey and on Long Island prior to the first proven instances of breeding there, and given how rarely breeding is ever proved, it seems unreasonable to dismiss the many recent records throughout the Northeast as mere vagrants. Instead, these records suggest that the species's geographic expansion in the region, well documented over more than half a century, might be continuing. Viewed in this light, the species's appearance in four new blocks during the second Atlas period suggests that birds are still taking advantage of suitable sites where and when they become available, even as local conditions deteriorate at many traditional breeding sites. If so, the species might be expected to persist as a breeder in New York if enough appropriate habitat can be protected.

2000–05 Distribution Map

- ☐ Not Found
- ▨ Possible
- ▨ Probable
- ■ Confirmed

Number of Blocks

	1980–85		2000–05		Change
	No.	%	No.	%	%
Possible	8	38	1	13	−88
Probable	12	57	6	75	−50
Confirmed	1	5	1	13	0
Total	21	<1	8	<1	−62

Change Map

- ☐ Not Reported
- ■ 1980-85 Atlas
- ▨ 2000-05 Atlas
- ▨ Both Atlases

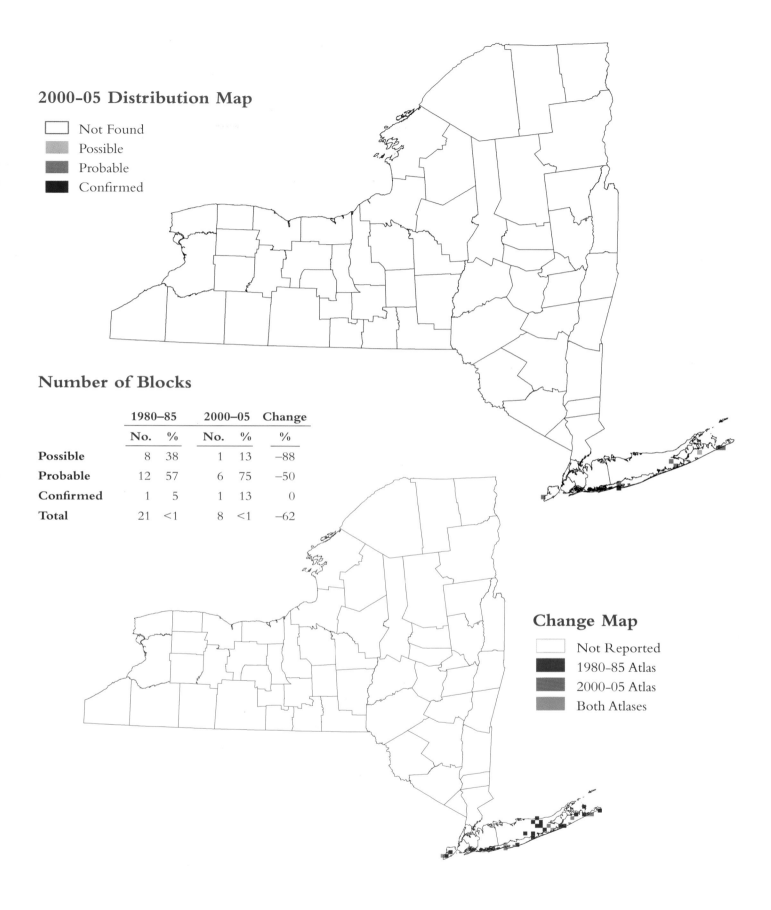

Whip-poor-will

Caprimulgus vociferus

MATTHEW D. MEDLER

Well known because of its namesake song, the Whip-poor-will is nonetheless one of New York's least understood breeding birds. Two distinct groups of this species occur in North America: the Eastern Whip-poor-will, which breeds from southern Canada to Oklahoma and Georgia, and the Western Whip-poor-will, which ranges from Arizona to Honduras (Cink 2002). The Eastern Whip-poor-will breeds in several different habitats, all of which provide open areas for aerial foraging and shaded areas for nesting and roosting. Although described as a forest species, this bird is generally absent from large undisturbed forested areas (Cink 2002) and areas with an extensive closed forest canopy (James and Neal 1986). In New York, the Whip-poor-will is most abundant in barrens communities and Fort Drum's barrens-like areas and occurs in lower densities where forest is interrupted by fields, quarries, power-line cuts, and other openings. DeKay (1844) listed the Whip-poor-will as a breeder in the state and cited the Dutch name "Quok-korr-ee" for the species, implying its presence in eastern New York in the early 1600s. Eaton (1914) and Bull (1974) portrayed this nightjar as a locally distributed summer resident across New York but largely absent from the Adirondack wilderness. Bull (1974) also noted its abundance on Long Island's coastal plain, where it has long been common in pine barrens (Giraud 1844, Griscom 1923, Cruickshank 1942, Bull 1964).

The Whip-poor-will was found in all of New York's major ecozones during the first Atlas survey but went unreported from most of the Appalachian Plateau, Great Lakes Plain, Mohawk Valley, and Central Adirondacks. The greatest concentrations of records were in the Champlain Valley and Transition, Coastal Lowlands, Adirondack foothill and transition ecozones, and hills and highlands bordering the Hudson Valley. The second Atlas data revealed that the number of blocks with Whip-poor-will records decreased 57 percent, with all major ecozones showing declines. The concentration on the edge of the Adirondacks largely disappeared, and the species went virtually undetected in central and western New York. Concentrations of records remained only in the Champlain Valley and Transition, Coastal Lowlands,

Shawangunk Hills, and Fort Drum area. This species was undoubtedly overlooked in some blocks during both Atlas surveys because of insufficient nocturnal fieldwork and a Whip-poor-will detection probability of less than 50 percent even under ideal moonlit conditions (Wilson and Watts 2006).

The Breeding Bird Survey is not designed to monitor nocturnal species, but available data suggest a survey-wide Whip-poor-will decline in numbers between 1966 and 2005 (Sauer et al. 2005). The second Ontario Breeding Bird Atlas reported a significant decline province-wide (Bird Studies Canada et al. 2006). Whip-poor-will is listed as a Species of Special Concern in New York and is a conservation priority in all neighboring states; such concern has led to the creation of a coordinated monitoring program in the northeastern United States (Hunt 2005). Forest maturation (Mills 1987), increases in industrial pollution and pesticide use (Eastman 1991), and declines in Saturniid moth numbers (Robbins et al. 1986) are all suggested but untested explanations for population declines. The maturation of, and resultant structural changes in, the northern hardwood forests that cover much of New York could explain Whip-poor-will's disappearance from much of the state, while still allowing for the species's abundance in Jefferson County's alvar communities, Clinton County's jack pine barrens, and Suffolk County's pitch pine barrens. These areas differ in geography, geology, and dominant vegetation types, yet all host high densities of Whip-poor-will, suggesting that habitat structure might play an important role in its abundance. Regional monitoring and associated research should begin to answer the many questions surrounding this nightjar.

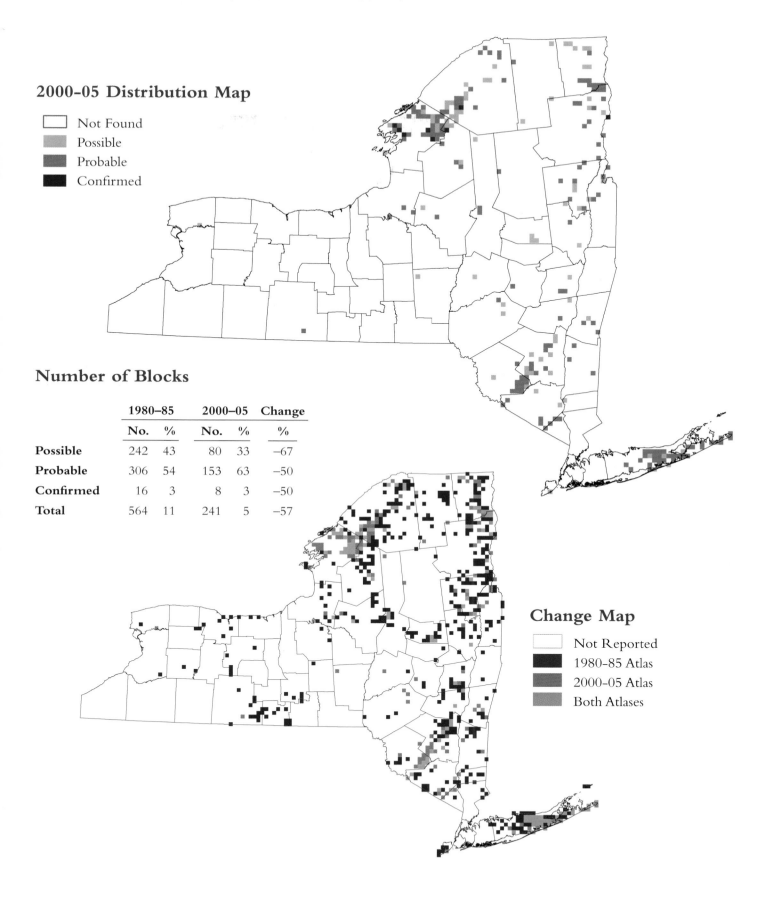

2000-05 Distribution Map

- Not Found
- Possible
- Probable
- Confirmed

Number of Blocks

| | 1980–85 | | 2000–05 | | Change |
	No.	%	No.	%	%
Possible	242	43	80	33	−67
Probable	306	54	153	63	−50
Confirmed	16	3	8	3	−50
Total	564	11	241	5	−57

Change Map

- Not Reported
- 1980-85 Atlas
- 2000-05 Atlas
- Both Atlases

Chimney Swift
Chaetura pelagica

KEVIN J. MCGOWAN

The Chimney Swift is a small, insect-eating bird that catches all of its food in flight. It breeds east of the Rocky Mountains from southeastern Canada southward to the Gulf Coast. Although it originally nested in hollow trees and perhaps caves, it readily took to building nests in chimneys and other artificial sites when Europeans settled North America. It may have been thinly distributed throughout most of its range, nesting in scattered hollow trees in old-growth forests (Cink and Collins 2002), and it is likely that its population increased with the settlement of North America and the subsequent creation of abundant nesting sites. By the early 1800s it was reported as nesting only in chimneys in New York (DeKay 1844), although it probably was still nesting in natural sites in the Adirondacks and other remote portions of the state. Bull (1974) gave a number of examples of nesting sites other than chimneys, including inside hollow trees and interior building walls. It was considered abundant in most of the state by the end of the 19th century (Rathbun 1879, Short 1893, Reed and Wright 1909, Eaton 1914). Eaton (1914) called it common in all portions of the state and stated that even in the Adirondacks it preferred to nest in buildings. Little change in its population was noticeable during most of the 20th century until a slight decreasing trend in the last half (D'Anna 1998b).

The first Atlas map showed the Chimney Swift to be well distributed across the state, with most sightings confined to cities, towns, and villages. Confirmation of breeding was difficult, occurring in only 16 percent of blocks. The species was more widely distributed in the Adirondacks than was expected, and much less widely distributed than expected in other parts of the state (Sibley 1988f). Concentrations appeared to be in the Great Lakes Plain, Central Adirondacks, and Hudson Valley and southward. The range found during the second Atlas survey was approximately the same, but the number of blocks with swifts declined by 15 percent. Decreases were spread rather evenly across the state, with only the St. Lawrence Plains showing a slight increase. The same areas of concentration in the Great Lakes Plain, Central Adirondacks, Hudson Valley, and southward were still in evidence, and breeding was confirmed in 17 percent of blocks. Because the Chimney Swift can forage several kilometers from its nest site (Cink and Collins 2002), some reports may refer to birds nesting in other blocks.

Over the past 20 years, Chimney Swift populations have been decreasing, as newly constructed chimneys are less suitable for nest sites (Cink and Collins 2002). Eaton (1914) related that the Chimney Swift's habit of early rising, combined with the noise of the wings in a communal roost, made people dislike them and try to cover chimneys to keep them out. Breeding Bird Survey data indicate a significant 1.7 percent yearly decline across the range over the last 40 years, with decreases in all regions (Sauer et al. 2007). BBS data for New York show a similar decline of 1.6 percent per year (Sauer et al. 2007). The same data show the Adirondack population decreasing at 5 percent a year, dwindling to fewer than one bird per route. This decline corresponds to the marked losses seen between the two Atlas periods, although the Chimney Swift was still reported in 49 percent of Adirondack blocks. Loss of nesting habitat, especially in urban areas, is considered an important factor in its decline (Cink and Collins 2002). Some people are suggesting the construction of artificial towers to provide nesting habitat as a management tool. Such management might be necessary in New York in the future if populations continue to decline.

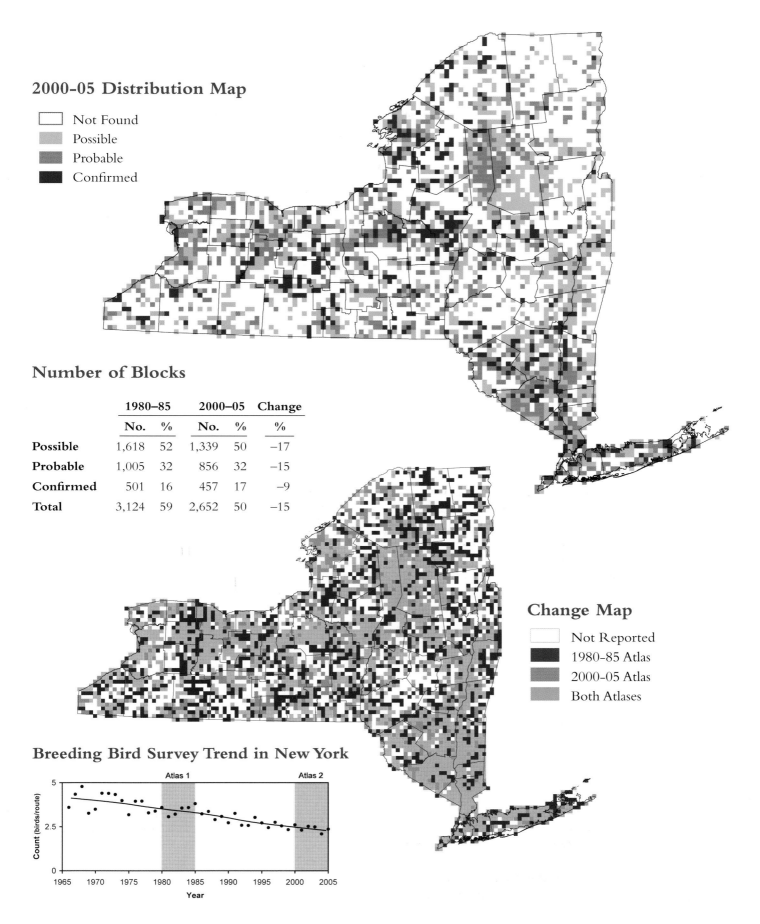

2000-05 Distribution Map

- ☐ Not Found
- Possible
- Probable
- Confirmed

Number of Blocks

	1980–85		2000–05		Change
	No.	%	No.	%	%
Possible	1,618	52	1,339	50	−17
Probable	1,005	32	856	32	−15
Confirmed	501	16	457	17	−9
Total	3,124	59	2,652	50	−15

Change Map

- ☐ Not Reported
- 1980-85 Atlas
- 2000-05 Atlas
- Both Atlases

Breeding Bird Survey Trend in New York

Ruby-throated Hummingbird
Archilochus colubris

KEVIN J. McGOWAN

The Ruby-throated Hummingbird can be found breeding across nearly all of eastern North America, from central Canada eastward to Nova Scotia, southward to eastern Texas and Florida, and it is the only breeding hummingbird in its range. It breeds in deciduous forests and mixed woodlands, including gardens and orchards. Although considered primarily a woodland breeder (Robinson et al. 1996), the extensive deforestation of New York in the 19th century appeared to have little effect on its populations or distribution in the state. DeKay (1844) called it an abundant breeder in New York, and it was considered common throughout Upstate New York in the second half of the 19th century (Rathbun 1879, Short 1893, Judd 1907, Reed and Wright 1909). Eaton (1914) described it as a common breeder in all parts of the state, including the higher elevations of the Adirondacks. Bull (1974) described no change in its distribution and noted that it bred in a variety of predominantly rural habitats, especially in forests near streams.

During the first Atlas survey, the Ruby-throated Hummingbird was reported breeding across the entire state, except in the New York City and western Long Island area. It was present in smaller numbers in other urban areas, the Eastern Ontario and St. Lawrence plains, Mohawk Valley, and parts of the Hudson Valley. During the second Atlas survey, the Ruby-throated Hummingbird was found in 21 percent more blocks throughout the state. It was still essentially missing from New York City and western Long Island. It showed increases across the rest of the state, however, and was no longer scarce along the Eastern Ontario and St. Lawrence plains, Mohawk Valley, or, indeed, any other region. The only ecozone to show a decrease (25 percent) was the Coastal Lowlands, where the hummingbird was already at its lowest density.

Breeding Bird Survey data show a slight but steady and significant increase in Ruby-throated Hummingbird populations across its range and throughout the length of the survey (Sauer et al. 2005). The same trends were apparent in the New York data (Sauer et al. 2005). All eastern Fish and Wildlife Service regions showed significant increases (Sauer et al. 2005). The Ontario Breeding Bird Atlas reported a significant increase in the number of squares with hummingbirds across the province (Bird Studies Canada et al. 2006).

The ability of the Ruby-throated Hummingbird to adapt to modified forests and to use gardens and orchards probably kept its populations from declining with the cutting of New York's forests in the 19th century. Subsequent to that time, little evidence exists of any population changes until the advent of the Breeding Bird Survey in the 1960s. BBS data and the increase documented during the second Atlas project indicate a significant change has taken place. One possible factor in the increase in Ruby-throated Hummingbird records between the two Atlas periods could be the spread of the Yellow-bellied Sapsucker in the state. The sapsucker increased its distribution markedly between the Atlas periods, and its habit of establishing sap wells on trees is heavily exploited by hummingbirds (Robinson et al. 1996). This explanation is not entirely sufficient to explain hummingbird increases, however, as hummingbirds were found in more blocks in ecozones without sapsuckers too.

2000-05 Distribution Map

- ☐ Not Found
- Possible
- Probable
- Confirmed

Number of Blocks

	1980–85		2000–05		Change
	No.	%	No.	%	%
Possible	1,941	55	1,945	46	0
Probable	1,209	34	1,675	39	39
Confirmed	368	10	634	15	72
Total	3,518	66	4,254	80	21

Change Map

- ☐ Not Reported
- 1980-85 Atlas
- 2000-05 Atlas
- Both Atlases

Breeding Bird Survey Trend in New York

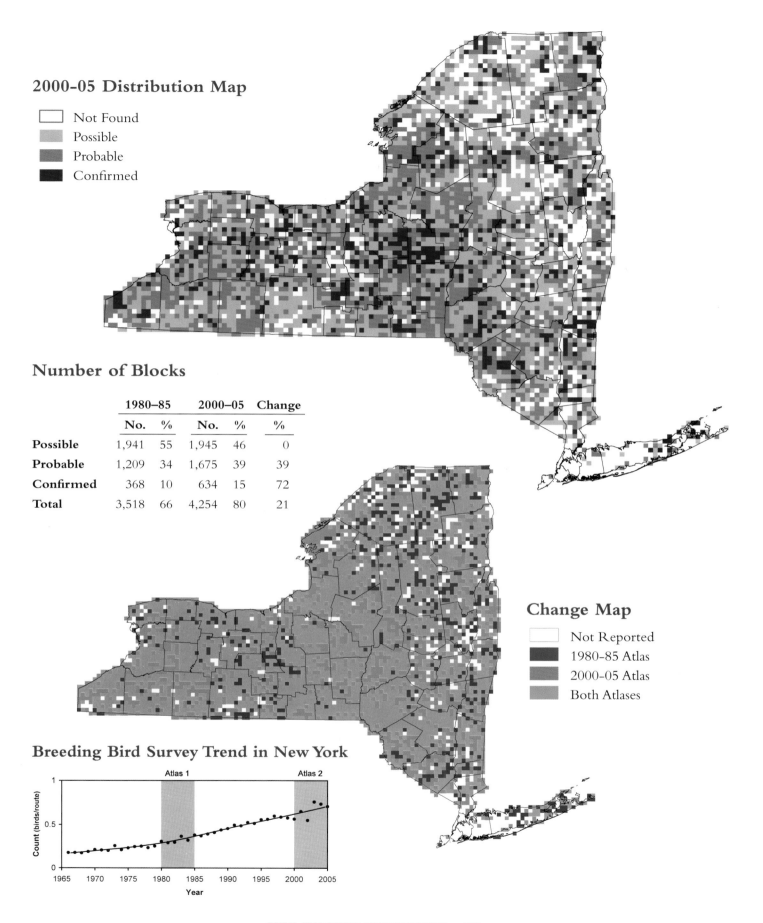

Belted Kingfisher

Megaceryle alcyon

KEVIN J. McGOWAN

The Belted Kingfisher breeds wherever streams and banks can be found across most of Canada and the United States, from Alaska and Labrador southward to California, northern Texas, and northern Florida (Hamas 1994). The bird prefers streams, lakes, and calm marine waters in which it can easily see its fish and aquatic invertebrate prey. It nests in burrows dug in earthen banks. Although the Belted Kingfisher prefers to nest near its foraging territory, it can make a burrow up to 2 km (1.2 mi) away from water and travel up to 8 km (5 mi) away from the nest to forage (Hamas 1994). Because its breeding success depends nearly exclusively on the availability of open water for feeding and banks for nesting, it is possible that this species was little affected by the widespread habitat changes of the 19th and early 20th centuries. In fact, little change has been noted in its distribution in New York at all. Early authors called it common throughout the state (Giraud 1844, Rathbun 1879, Merriam 1881, Short 1893, Reed and Wright 1909). Eaton (1914) reported the kingfisher as a common breeder in all counties in the state, and Bull (1974) agreed.

The first Atlas map showed little change in the breeding distribution of the Belted Kingfisher from Eaton's report, with breeding confirmed in all regions of the state. It was found in 71 percent of blocks, but no pattern of absence was obvious, except for regions of New York City and western Long Island. The second Atlas data supported essentially the same pattern, with breeding confirmed in all regions of the state. Overall, the number of blocks with reports of kingfishers was down slightly, compared with the first Atlas number. Though the Belted Kingfisher can forage outside the block in which it is nesting, the Atlas map is probably representative of the true distribution.

The breeding distribution of the Belted Kingfisher is limited in some areas of North America by the availability of suitable nesting sites. Human activity, such as building roads and digging gravel pits, has created banks where kingfishers can nest, and allowed the expansion of the breeding range (Hamas 1994). The Breeding Bird Survey does not census the Belted Kingfisher particularly well and the findings must be treated with some caution, but the data that do exist suggest a continual and significant decline since 1966 across most of its range, including New York (Sauer et al. 2007). The second Ontario Breeding Bird Atlas reported a significant decline in Belted Kingfisher occurrence across that province (Bird Studies Canada et al. 2006). Although the population trend as indicated by BBS data is downward, because of its large range and the lack of significant threats to its breeding or wintering populations, Partners in Flight gave the Belted Kingfisher a relatively modest combined threat score (PIF 2005). It was, however, listed as a species of regional concern in the Appalachian, Northern Atlantic Forest, and Great Lakes Bird Conservation regions (PIF 2005). If these declines continue, the next Atlas map may look rather different, but for now the position of this species in the state seems secure.

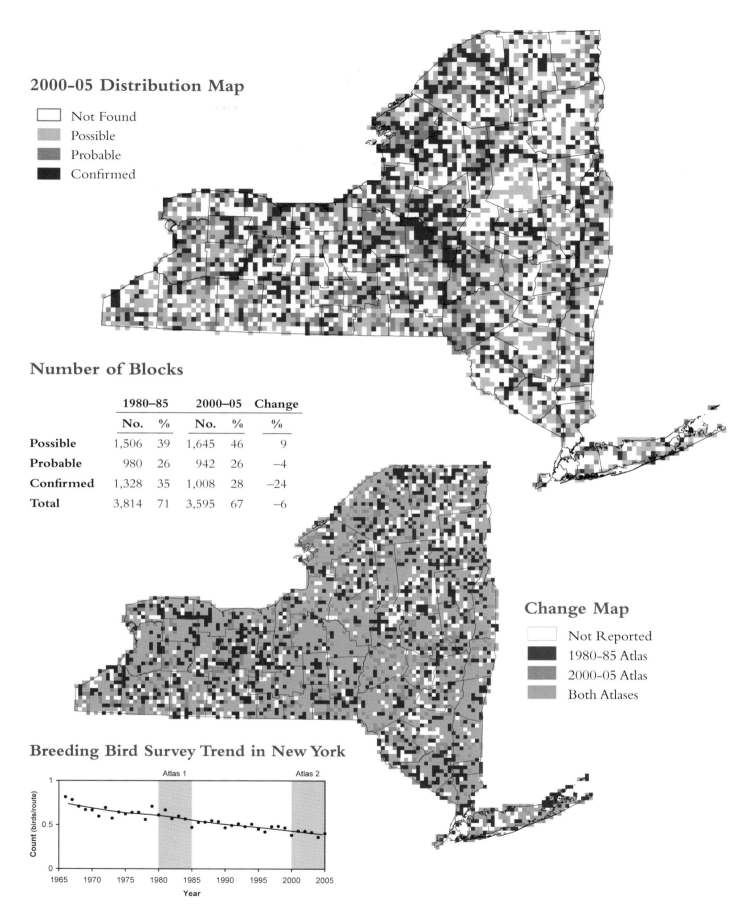

2000–05 Distribution Map

- ☐ Not Found
- Possible
- Probable
- Confirmed

Number of Blocks

	1980–85		2000–05		Change
	No.	%	No.	%	%
Possible	1,506	39	1,645	46	9
Probable	980	26	942	26	−4
Confirmed	1,328	35	1,008	28	−24
Total	3,814	71	3,595	67	−6

Change Map

- ☐ Not Reported
- 1980-85 Atlas
- 2000–05 Atlas
- Both Atlases

Breeding Bird Survey Trend in New York

Pileated and Hairy woodpeckers in a Finger Lakes gorge

The densely wooded, yet impossible to log, gorges of the Finger Lakes contain much dead, insect-infested timber that says "banquet" to all woodpecker species. Their preference for insects benefits the forest, helping to keep destructive pests in check.

318

Red-headed Woodpecker
Melanerpes erythrocephalus

KEVIN J. MCGOWAN

The Red-headed Woodpecker is found throughout the eastern and central United States and into very southern Canada (Smith et al. 2000). New York is near the northeastern edge of its range. The woodpecker breeds in open deciduous woodlands, especially beech or oak, groves of dead and dying trees, orchards, parks, open country with scattered trees, forest edges, and open wooded swamps with dead trees and stumps (Smith et al. 2000). In New York it breeds in two distinct habitats (Bull 1964): open, park-like upland woods, including golf courses and along roadsides with large scattered trees; and open wooded swamps and river bottoms with dead trees standing in water, such as beaver ponds. It was common and widespread during the late 1700s and 1800s throughout the northeastern and northern United States but has undergone a long, slow decline since (Smith et al. 2000). Giraud (1844) mentioned it as declining on Long Island from its status as one of the most common woodpeckers, but it remained common in central and western New York through the 19th century (Rathbun 1879, Short 1893, Reed and Wright 1909). Formerly common in New England and eastern New York, the Red-headed Woodpecker was rare there by the beginning of the 20th century (Eaton 1914). Beardslee and Mitchell (1965) called it fairly common in western New York but less so than formerly. Bull (1974) considered it rare in the southeastern portions of the state and fairly common but local in much of the rest, being most plentiful around the Oneida Lake region.

The first Atlas map showed the Red-headed Woodpecker to be moderately common in the Great Lakes Plain, the adjacent Cattaraugus and Finger Lakes highlands, the Mohawk Valley, and to a lesser extent in the southern Hudson Valley. Additional reports were scattered across the state. It was mostly absent from the central Adirondacks, Catskills, and urban regions downstate. During the second Atlas fieldwork, the Red-headed Woodpecker was found in far fewer blocks, and it did not appear to be common anywhere. It declined in every ecozone except the Coastal Lowlands, and it was found in few contiguous blocks, making it even more locally distributed than before. Although this species still occurred in roughly the same pattern as that shown in the first Atlas, most often in the lower elevations of upstate, no region could be considered its "stronghold."

Breeding Bird Survey data show the Red-headed Woodpecker population is declining over most of its breeding range, with nearly no significant positive trends in any region (Sauer et al. 2005). BBS data are too sparse in New York to show reliable

trends, with detections dropping to near zero in the mid-1990s (Sauer et al. 2005). The second Ontario Breeding Bird Atlas reported the Red-headed Woodpecker in half as many squares as the first, with significant declines across the province (Bird Studies Canada et al. 2006). Partners in Flight put the Red-headed Woodpecker on its Watch List because of declining population trends (Rich et al. 2004). The decrease in Red-headed Woodpecker numbers in the 19th century has been attributed to the increasing use of automobiles and the resulting roadkill, and competition from the introduced European Starling (Bull 1964). Just how important traffic was or is as a source of mortality is open to debate, however, and recent evidence indicates that the Red-headed Woodpecker competes successfully with starlings (Smith et al. 2000). Smith et al. (2000) reported that the woodpecker numbers are improving in areas where increasing beaver populations create more flooded meadows with dead snags, but that situation does not seem to have helped in New York. Much suitable habitat remains for the Red-headed Woodpecker, but its future in the state looks dim. It is listed as a Species of Special Concern in New York, though its status should probably be changed to Threatened or Endangered.

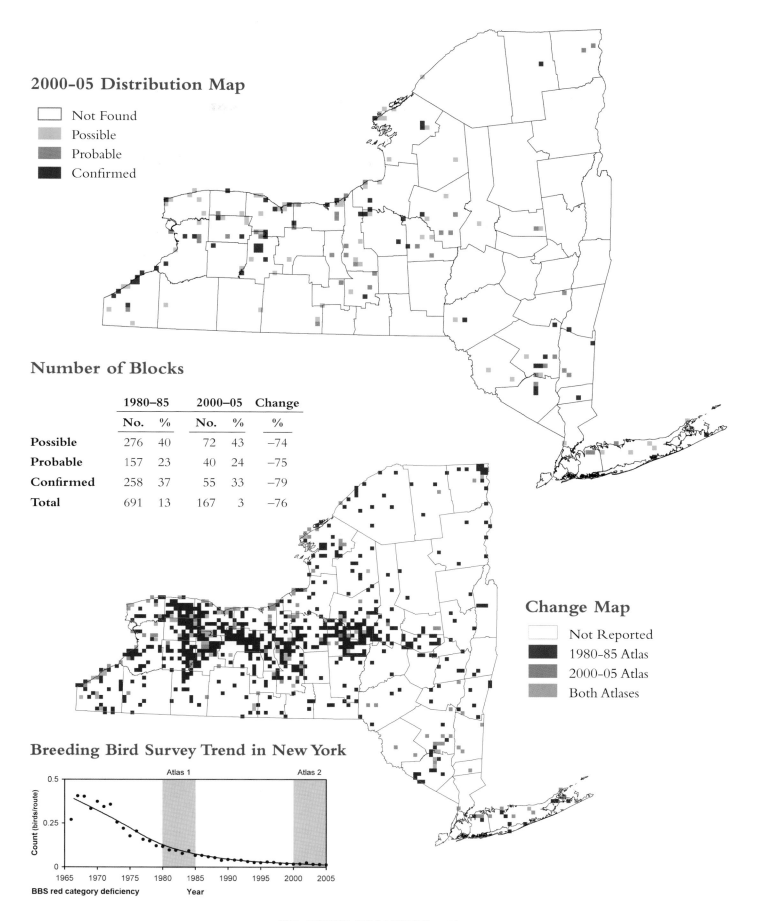

2000–05 Distribution Map

- [ ] Not Found
- Possible
- Probable
- Confirmed

Number of Blocks

| | 1980–85 | | 2000–05 | | Change |
	No.	%	No.	%	%
Possible	276	40	72	43	−74
Probable	157	23	40	24	−75
Confirmed	258	37	55	33	−79
Total	691	13	167	3	−76

Change Map

- [ ] Not Reported
- 1980-85 Atlas
- 2000-05 Atlas
- Both Atlases

Breeding Bird Survey Trend in New York

Atlas 1   Atlas 2

BBS red category deficiency

Red-bellied Woodpecker

Melanerpes carolinus

KEVIN J. McGOWAN

A bird of mixed deciduous-coniferous forests and suburbs, the Red-bellied Woodpecker is found throughout the eastern United States into southern Canada (Shackelford et al. 2000). New York is at the northeastern edge of the range. DeKay (1844) suggested that the Red-bellied Woodpecker bred in New York but gradually had become less abundant here and in adjacent states. The woodpecker was known in central and western New York primarily as a winter visitor in the 19th century but also as an occasional breeder (Rathbun 1879, Short 1893, Eaton 1914). Giraud's (1844) description of it being "not very abundant . . . prefers . . . the lonely part of the woods" suggests a breeding presence on Long Island, but Bull (1964) rejected that report and concluded that prior to 1955 it was primarily a rare vagrant to the New York City area. Jackson and Davis (1998) suggested that European colonization caused an initial reduction in Red-bellied Woodpecker numbers and fragmentation of populations, with a loss from large parts of its range in the Northeast by 1900. Subsequently, conditions improved with reforestation, and populations began to climb. While that explanation is somewhat unsatisfying, undisputed is that in the 1950s and 1960s the Red-bellied Woodpecker expanded its range both northward and westward (Shackelford et al. 2000). Before that, the species was not even common in northern Pennsylvania (McWilliams and Brauning 2000) or northern New Jersey (Walsh et al. 1999). After that point it was common in the Genesee Valley and Finger Lakes regions of New York but rare and local in the southeastern portion of the state (Bull 1974). The origin of the oddly disjunct western New York population is open to dispute (Chamberlaine 1998b), but increasing numbers along the Atlantic Coast undoubtedly came from an expanding New Jersey population.

During the first Atlas survey, the Red-bellied Woodpecker was found in the same two distinct regions mentioned by Bull (1974). Most were found in the Finger Lakes Region and the Genesee Valley in the Great Lakes Plain, with scattered records reaching into the Appalachian Plateau. It was also well established in the lower Hudson Valley and associated highlands and along the northern shore of Long Island. By the second Atlas period, the Red-bellied Woodpecker had expanded its range dramatically, with increases in blocks with reports in all ecozones. It was recorded in nearly the entire Hudson Valley, with scattered reports through the Champlain Valley to Clinton County. The western population extended to the Pennsylvania border and along the Great Lakes Plain southwestward to Lake Erie and northward to the St. Lawrence Plains. The two previously separate populations joined across the Mohawk Valley and to a lesser extent across the southern Appalachian Plateau. The current distribution follows a rough correspondence to areas under 600 m (2,000 ft) in elevation and with a mean July temperature under 70 degrees Fahrenheit. It is possible that winter, not summer, temperatures are the limiting factor for this resident species.

Breeding Bird Survey data show a very slight but continuous increase in Red-bellied Woodpecker numbers throughout its range since 1966, with most of the increase occurring after 1980 (Sauer et al. 2005). Data for the north Atlantic states (U.S. Fish and Wildlife Service Region 5) and New York are similar, with the New York increase an amazing 10.7 percent per year since 1980. The second Ontario Breeding Bird Atlas reported the woodpecker expanding northward into the province and becoming more numerous in the southern region (Bird Studies Canada et al. 2006). The first Vermont Breeding Bird Atlas did not document the presence of the Red-bellied Woodpecker, but the second Vermont Atlas confirmed it breeding in multiple blocks (R. Renfrew pers. comm.). The expansion of the Red-bellied Woodpecker's range is clearly continuing, and it will be interesting to see the distribution map of this species in the next Atlas.

2000-05 Distribution Map

- [ ] Not Found
- Possible
- Probable
- Confirmed

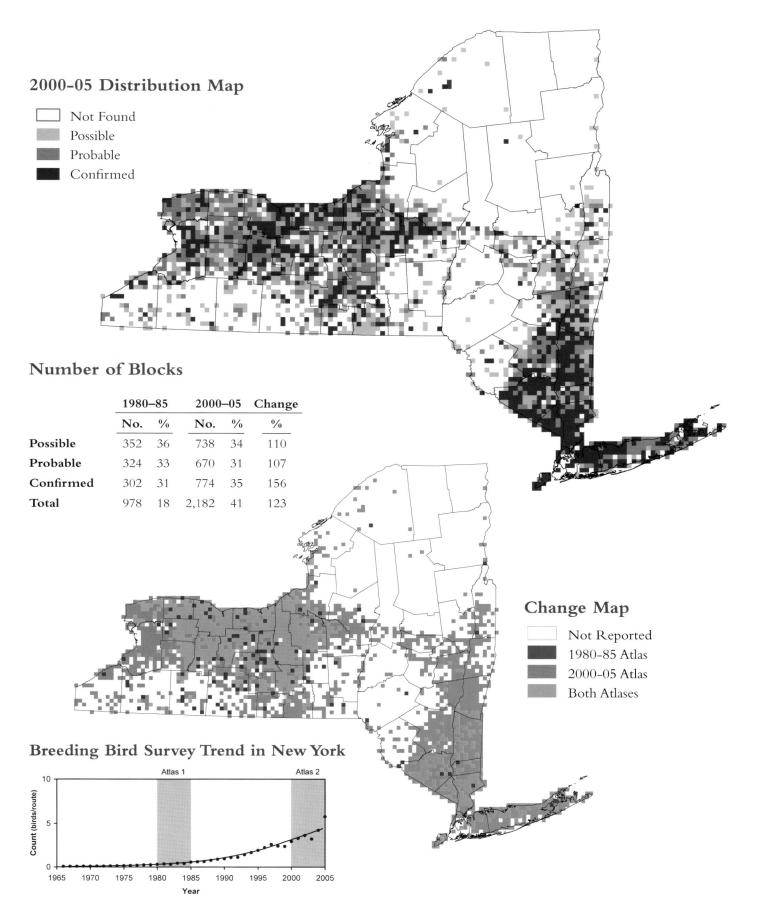

Number of Blocks

	1980–85		2000–05		Change
	No.	%	No.	%	%
Possible	352	36	738	34	110
Probable	324	33	670	31	107
Confirmed	302	31	774	35	156
Total	978	18	2,182	41	123

Change Map

- [ ] Not Reported
- 1980-85 Atlas
- 2000-05 Atlas
- Both Atlases

Breeding Bird Survey Trend in New York

Yellow-bellied Sapsucker
Sphyrapicus varius

KEVIN J. McGOWAN

The Yellow-bellied Sapsucker breeds from central Alaska to Newfoundland, southward to southern Alberta, northern Iowa, and Pennsylvania, and locally in the Appalachian Mountains to North Carolina. Primarily a northern species, its range in New York has often been given as "higher elevations." Eaton (1914) described its breeding range as essentially confined to the Adirondacks and the Catskills, with birds scattered in central and western New York and along the Pennsylvania border. Sixty years later Bull (1974) gave nearly the same description, noting perhaps more sapsuckers in the center of the state, a population on the edge of the Taconic and Berkshire mountains, and a small population on the Great Lakes Plain east of Niagara.

The first Atlas map showed the Yellow-bellied Sapsucker's range to be similar to that described by Bull (1974), but with more records from the Catskills across the Appalachian Plateau, especially eastward of the Finger Lakes. Only scattered observations were made on the Great Lakes Plain. The species was noticeably scarcer, but present, across the St. Lawrence Plains, Mohawk Valley, and northern Hudson Valley. It was absent from the central Hudson Valley and southward of the Taconic Highlands and Mongaup Hills. The second Atlas survey found the Yellow-bellied Sapsucker to be much more common throughout the state. Most striking was the filling in of the Mohawk Valley and the western portion of the Appalachian Plateau. Although it was still not common on the Great Lakes Plain, it was present in 14 percent more blocks there. The sapsucker also expanded its range in the Taconic Highlands, reaching southward to the Hudson Highlands into northern Rockland County. It was still absent from most of the Hudson Valley, the Manhattan Hills, and the Coastal Lowlands. Its affinities with the Adirondacks and Catskills are no longer apparent, although it still is scarce or absent in the lowest-elevation areas in the state.

Breeding Bird Survey data show a significant increase for Yellow-bellied Sapsucker numbers in the eastern region since 1966, but the significant positive trend since 1980 follows a significant negative trend from 1966 to 1979 (Sauer et al. 2005). BBS data for New York show the same pattern, with little apparent change but a statistically significant decline from 1966 to 1979, and then a significant increase over the next 25 years (Sauer et al. 2005). The second Ontario Breeding Bird Atlas reported a significant increase in sapsucker records across most of the province (Bird Studies Canada et al. 2006).

Sapsucker populations may be higher now than in presettlement times, before the clearing of the old-growth forests of northeastern North America. European settlement created forest gaps and edge, which allowed for growth of the young forests preferred by sapsuckers and therefore supported higher densities of sapsuckers than climax forests supported (Walters et al. 2002). The succession of farmland to forest should have favored increases in sapsucker numbers in New York throughout the 20th century, but the largest increases have occurred in the last 20 years, when little new forest land has been gained, only matured. In fact, the maturation of forests should be causing a decline in some areas, not the existing increases. Just why a "northern" species should be spreading out of its ancestral habitat is not readily apparent. Perhaps it was originally more widespread within the state than has been previously suggested, declined with the deforestation of the 19th century, and is now reclaiming some of that range, as is the case for the Common Raven. Although Walters et al. (2002) stated that the Yellow-bellied Sapsucker prefers young forests with small trees, Paradis (1996) gave its preference in Quebec as mature deciduous or mixed forest. It is possible that the sapsucker prefers mature deciduous forest with smaller trees than what existed in the original forests in New York, and that the structure of the currently maturing forests is more to its liking, with a closed canopy and trees of intermediate size.

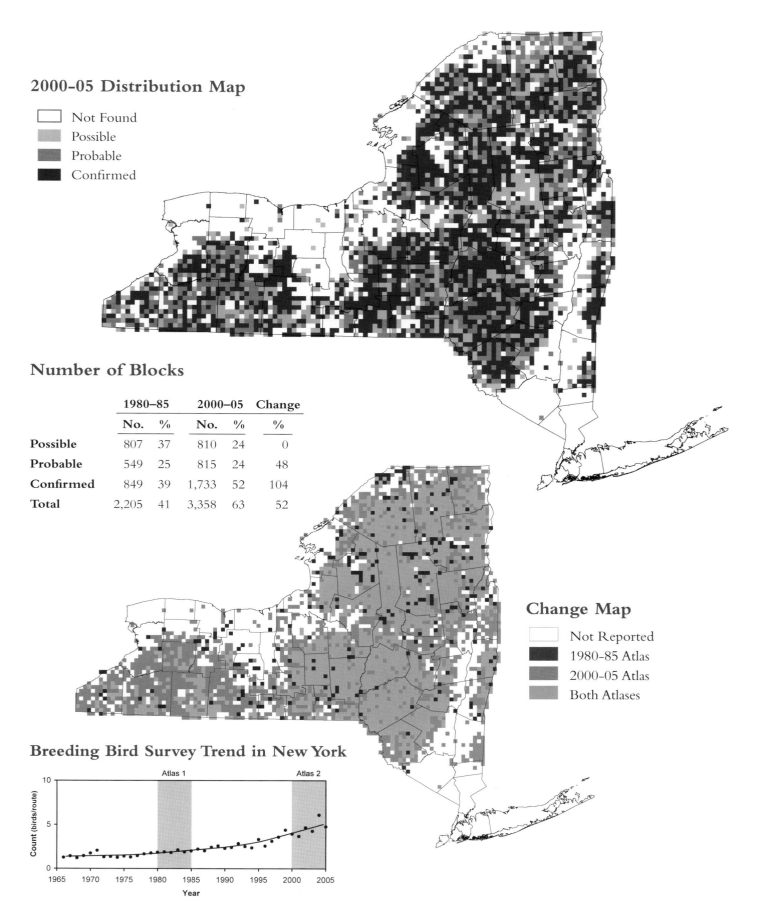

2000-05 Distribution Map

- ☐ Not Found
- Possible
- Probable
- Confirmed

Number of Blocks

	1980–85		2000–05		Change
	No.	%	No.	%	%
Possible	807	37	810	24	0
Probable	549	25	815	24	48
Confirmed	849	39	1,733	52	104
Total	2,205	41	3,358	63	52

Change Map

- ☐ Not Reported
- 1980–85 Atlas
- 2000–05 Atlas
- Both Atlases

Breeding Bird Survey Trend in New York

Downy Woodpecker

Picoides pubescens

KEVIN J. MCGOWAN

The Downy Woodpecker is one of the most widespread and abundant woodpeckers in North America, found from Alaska and Canada southward to Florida and the edge of southwestern deserts. It uses a variety of hardwood forests, including mature, young, fragmented, and suburbanized ones. It prefers open woodlands and is less common in dense forests or in conifers (Jackson and Ouellet 2002). It also can be found nesting in abandoned orchards, parks, and pastures. It reaches its highest nesting densities in deciduous woodlands that include small trees with low canopy heights (Jackson and Ouellet 2002). The Downy Woodpecker probably has always been common in New York. It was at home in the native forests, although its preference for younger, more open woodlands suggests it was present at lower densities than now. It adapted better to the clearing of the forests than many woodland species, using orchards and woodlots and breeding in close proximity to people. Nineteenth-century authors listed it as common in all parts of the state (DeKay 1844, Giraud 1844, Rathbun 1879, Merriam 1881, Short 1893), as did later 20th-century authors Eaton (1914) and Bull (1974). It is likely that the abandonment of farms and the recovery of forests in the early and mid-20th century increased nesting habitat for this woodpecker, and its populations might have peaked at that time (Confer 1988b).

The first Atlas map showed the Downy Woodpecker to be widespread across the state, present in 86 percent of blocks. It was missing only from the highest elevations and least accessible blocks, mostly in the western Appalachian Plateau and the Adirondacks. Except for the mountain spruce-fir forests of the Adirondacks and areas with little forest cover, its absence in many places might reflect a lack of intense Atlas coverage. The second Atlas survey revealed a similar distribution. Again, the Downy Woodpecker was widespread, found in 88 percent of blocks, with most of the empty blocks in the Adirondacks and the Allegany Hills. Minor changes in distribution may well be the result of differing observer effort in blocks between the two Atlas periods.

Partners in Flight estimated the Downy Woodpecker to be the second most numerous woodpecker on the continent, trailing only the Northern Flicker (Rich et al. 2004). Breeding Bird Survey data show no survey-wide change in Downy Woodpecker populations over the entire period (Sauer et al. 2005). The BBS data for New York show no significant trend either, although a significant decline was evident in the Allegheny Plateau and in the north Atlantic states (U.S. Fish and Wildlife Service Region 5) (Sauer et al. 2005). Those declines were primarily in the years before 1979, and no significant trends existed for the subsequent years. The reforestation of the Northeast and the subsequent maturation of those forests do not seem to have affected populations of the Downy Woodpecker, perhaps because it adapted well to fragmented landscapes and urbanizing areas and the additional forest cover does not provide additional nesting areas.

2000-05 Distribution Map

- ☐ Not Found
- Possible
- Probable
- Confirmed

Number of Blocks

	1980–85		2000–05		Change
	No.	%	No.	%	%
Possible	1,489	33	1,400	30	−6
Probable	1,046	23	1,110	24	6
Confirmed	2,027	44	2,173	46	7
Total	4,562	86	4,683	88	3

Change Map

- ☐ Not Reported
- 1980-85 Atlas
- 2000-05 Atlas
- Both Atlases

Breeding Bird Survey Trend in New York

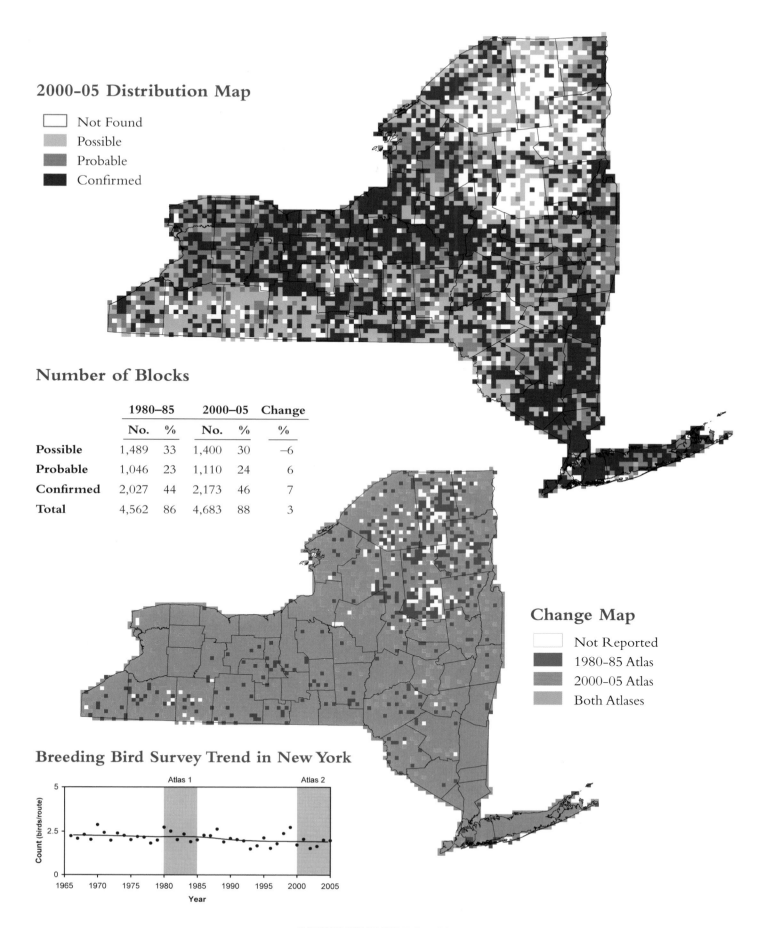

Hairy Woodpecker
Picoides villosus

KEVIN J. MCGOWAN

The Hairy Woodpecker is the most widespread woodpecker in North America, found from central Alaska to Newfoundland, southward to Florida, the Bahamas, and Central America. It breeds at a range of elevations and in a wide variety of habitats, including mature woods, small woodlots, wooded parks, and residential areas with large trees (Jackson et al. 2002). Although this woodpecker is primarily a bird of mature forests, it occurs in other, more broken wooded areas as well, albeit usually at lower densities (Jackson et al. 2002). It has apparently always been common throughout New York, even after the widespread deforestation during the 19th century (DeKay 1844, Giraud 1844, Rathbun 1879, Merriam 1881, Short 1893, Reed and Wright 1909). The Hairy Woodpecker was able to use orchards and small woodlots, although it was less common in settled areas than in areas of undisturbed woodland (Eaton 1914), a pattern that remained true throughout the next century (Bull 1974).

During the first Atlas survey, the Hairy Woodpecker was found throughout the state except in the New York City area, the south shore of western Long Island, parts of the western Appalachian Plateau, parts of the western Erie-Ontario Plain, and the heavily agricultural sections of the Eastern Ontario and St. Lawrence plains where few woodlands existed. Its distribution was more scattered in the western portion of the state. The spotty nature of its occurrence in the western Appalachian Plateau was suggested as potentially a reflection of the coverage of the area rather than a true absence (Sibley 1988k), although coverage in that region was not unusually light. During the second Atlas survey, a similar distribution of the Hairy Woodpecker was found, with a possible increase in the western portion of the state. Overall it was found in 77 percent of blocks, up slightly from the 71 percent reported in the first Atlas. It was still missing from the south shore of western Long Island, most of New York City, portions of the eastern St. Lawrence Plains, and portions of the western Appalachian Plateau. A gap appeared in the western Finger Lakes region. A 14 percent increase was detected on the Appalachian Plateau, with most of that increase in the western region. A 13 percent increase also was noted on the Great Lakes Plain, and a 25 percent increase on the Tug Hill Plateau. The 18 percent decline in the Hudson Highlands may reflect continuing development there, or may be a factor of decreased observer effort this time.

The Hairy Woodpecker was included on the Blue List of the National Audubon Society from 1975 to 1982 and was considered a Species of Special Concern by Audubon in 1986, because populations were reported to be down in several regions of the country (Jackson et al. 2002). Breeding Bird Survey data, however, show a significant positive continent-wide trend from 1966 to 2005 (Sauer et al. 2005). BBS data for New York show a just-nonsignificant increase over the last 25 years, with no trend before that (Sauer et al. 2005). The second Ontario Breeding Bird Atlas reported a small but significant increase in occurrence in the province (Bird Studies Canada et al. 2006). Partners in Flight gave the Hairy Woodpecker the lowest combined assessment score (i.e., least endangered) of any North American woodpecker (Rich et al. 2004).

The continuing maturation of woodland in New York should benefit the Hairy Woodpecker and could account for the slight increase noted between the two Atlas periods. These trends should continue through the foreseeable future, and the Hairy Woodpecker should continue to be a common member of the New York avifauna.

2000-05 Distribution Map

- ☐ Not Found
- Possible
- Probable
- Confirmed

Number of Blocks

	1980–85		2000–05		Change
	No.	%	No.	%	%
Possible	1,422	38	1,577	39	11
Probable	1,006	27	1,013	25	1
Confirmed	1,340	36	1,505	37	12
Total	3,768	71	4,095	77	9

Change Map

- ☐ Not Reported
- 1980-85 Atlas
- 2000-05 Atlas
- Both Atlases

Breeding Bird Survey Trend in New York

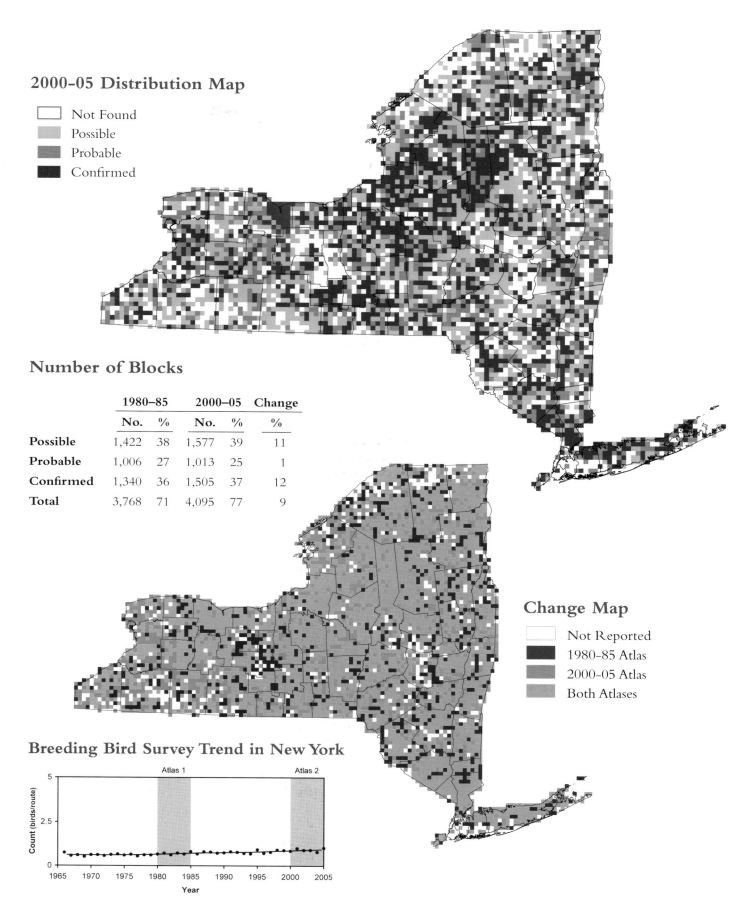

American Three-toed Woodpecker

Picoides dorsalis

John M. C. Peterson

At the time of the first Atlas project, this elusive woodpecker was believed to be a member of the Holarctic species *Picoides tridactylus*, found in northern spruce forests of both the Old and New Worlds, and was known as the Three-toed Woodpecker. Based on molecular and vocal differences between the Palearctic and Nearctic birds, the North American representative is now recognized as a separate species, American Three-toed Woodpecker (Banks et al. 2003). This woodpecker's range extends across the continent from Alaska to Newfoundland, reaching as far southward as Arizona and New Mexico in the West (Leonard 2001). Individuals nesting in New York are at the southern edge of the range in the East and are isolated from the contiguous population to the north in Ontario and Quebec, as well as the neighboring isolate populations of Vermont and New Hampshire. Range and habitat are shared with the Black-backed Woodpecker, mainly black spruce bogs and mountain spruce-fir forests. The two species differ in food preferences: this smaller, lighter-billed species feeds mainly on bark beetles, while the larger, heavier-billed Black-backed Woodpecker specializes on wood-boring beetles and their larvae (Leonard 2001). Both birds depend on disturbances within the boreal forest created by fire, wind, tree diseases, and insects (Leonard 2001). DeKay (1844) suspected the American Three-toed Woodpecker lived in the northern parts of New York, and Roosevelt and Minot (1873) and Merriam (1881) knew it as a resident in the Adirondacks. Eaton (1914) said it was confined to the Adirondacks, where it was uniformly, if sparsely, distributed through the spruce and balsam forests. Bull (1974) listed nine breeding localities in the Adirondack High Peaks, Central Adirondacks, and Western Adirondack Foothills, and noted apparent declines.

During the first Atlas survey, records of the American Three-toed Woodpecker were limited to the Adirondack High Peaks, Central Adirondacks, and Western Adirondack Foothills, with a peripheral record on the Central Tug Hill. During the second Atlas fieldwork, the woodpecker was found in the same ecozones in a similar though not identical distribution. Again, it was found in a single block in the Central Tug Hill, adjacent to the block noted in the first Atlas. Observers were less successful in locating the woodpecker this time, recording it in a third fewer blocks. Bull (1974) reported the presence of the Black-backed and the American Three-toed Woodpecker in 18 and 9 localities, respectively, or a ratio of 2:1; the first Atlas reported them in 114 and 22 blocks, for a ratio of about 5:1. The second Atlas survey located the Black-backed Woodpecker in more blocks (127) and this species in fewer, for a ratio of just 8:1, supporting earlier indications that the American Three-toed Woodpecker had become scarcer (cited in J. M. C. Peterson 1988s). Given the difficulties of finding this inconspicuous woodpecker and the paucity of records from across the difficult and vast habitat, this conclusion is still uncertain.

The American Three-toed Woodpecker lives at low densities across immense stretches of boreal forest, and consequently its populations are difficult to monitor (Leonard 2001). Breeding Bird Survey data are few, and the positive survey-wide trend from 1966 to 2005 must be treated with caution. The second Ontario Atlas data show no significant change in three-toed woodpecker populations there in the last 20 years (Bird Studies Canada et al. 2006). Threats include fire suppression and salvage logging. Degradation of habitat by timber harvesting and forest fragmentation should be monitored. In black spruce forests, habitat loss to logging may be permanent, as this woodpecker is restricted to mature forests that may be older than what typical cutting rotations allow (Imbeau et al. 1999). Efforts to monitor the species in the Adirondacks could focus on areas disturbed by recent fires or blowdowns, but tracking a population so thinly distributed, yet relatively widespread, is difficult.

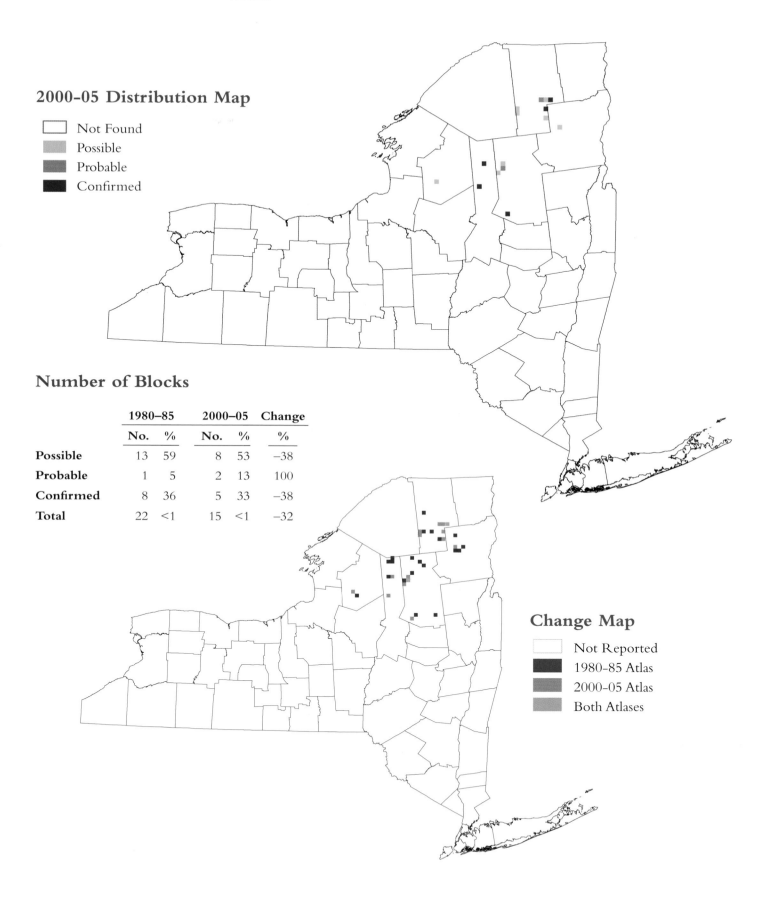

2000-05 Distribution Map

- ☐ Not Found
- Possible
- Probable
- ■ Confirmed

Number of Blocks

	1980–85		2000–05		Change
	No.	%	No.	%	%
Possible	13	59	8	53	−38
Probable	1	5	2	13	100
Confirmed	8	36	5	33	−38
Total	22	<1	15	<1	−32

Change Map

- ☐ Not Reported
- 1980-85 Atlas
- 2000-05 Atlas
- Both Atlases

Black-backed Woodpecker
Picoides arcticus

John M. C. Peterson

Although restricted in New York to the coniferous forests of the Adirondacks and Tug Hill, the glossy Black-backed Woodpecker may outnumber the Hairy Woodpecker in some boreal areas within the limited breeding range (Peterson and Lee 2004, Peterson 2006), and the fortunate observer may encounter a half-dozen or more during the course of a single day. The Black-backed Woodpecker nests in northern forests across North America from Alaska to Newfoundland, extending southward to New York and northern New England, the upper Great Lakes states, and into the mountains of northern California (Dixon and Saab 2000). In the Northeast, the New York population resembles an island at the southernmost edge of the range. Favored habitats in this state are mountain spruce–balsam fir or spruce–fir–northern hardwoods, especially disturbed areas where fire, blowdowns, or disease provide an abundance of wood-boring larvae and bark-borers for food. Wet areas are especially favored, such as beaver ponds, lakes, rivers, streams, and swampy openings in the forest (J. M. C. Peterson 1988b). Wildfires in the Adirondacks result annually from lightning strikes and careless campers. Since 1995, significant fires have burned Mount Discovery and Raven Hill, Noonmark Mountain, and Sunrise Mountain. In 2002, a total of 70 Adirondack wildfires burned during July–August, creating potential Black-backed Woodpecker habitat. A major windstorm flattened forests across Franklin and Hamilton counties on 15 July 1995, and smaller microbursts continue to down trees, providing new sources of borers. Since the first New York Black-backed Woodpecker nest was found by C. H. Merriam near Inlet, Hamilton County, in May 1883 (Bendire 1895), there have undoubtedly been shifts within the range, but the outline of the population in the early 21st century seems much as it was during the latter part of the 19th and the intervening years.

During the first Atlas survey, the Black-backed Woodpecker was located primarily in the Central Adirondacks, Adirondack High Peaks, Western Adirondack Foothills, and Sable Highlands. One Possible breeding record came from the Champlain Valley, and two Possible records were made in the Central Tug Hill. The woodpecker was found in more blocks during the second Atlas fieldwork, but with fewer Confirmed records. The nearly contiguous main range again was confined to the northeastern counties, largely circumscribed by the Blue Line of the Adirondack Park, with a satellite population on the Central Tug Hill. The range does not extend into the more deciduous Eastern Adirondack Foothills or even southern parts of the Central Adirondacks, where hardwoods also prevail. As a result of the bird's quiet habits, the original Atlas map was considered incomplete, though generally correct in outline (Peterson 1988b). That assessment is true of the latest map, as well, but the two provide an increasingly accurate geographic picture. Apparent changes may represent moves of the woodpecker to track shifting resources, but they may well be artifacts of differing coverage, and the map of collective coverage probably presents the truest image of the Black-backed Woodpecker's range in the state.

Because its range extends across vast inaccessible boreal areas, continental population levels of the Black-backed Woodpecker are difficult to monitor. The Breeding Bird Survey does not track the species well, and all available BBS data for this species have important deficiencies (Sauer et al. 2007). The New York population appears to face few threats. Fire suppression and salvage logging may be detrimental, but fires continue to break out, and little salvage logging is done within the Adirondack Park, beyond some cleanup following the blowdown in 1995 and Hurricane Floyd in 1999. The sight of a Black-backed Woodpecker hitching around a spruce trunk should continue to thrill Adirondack visitors for the foreseeable future.

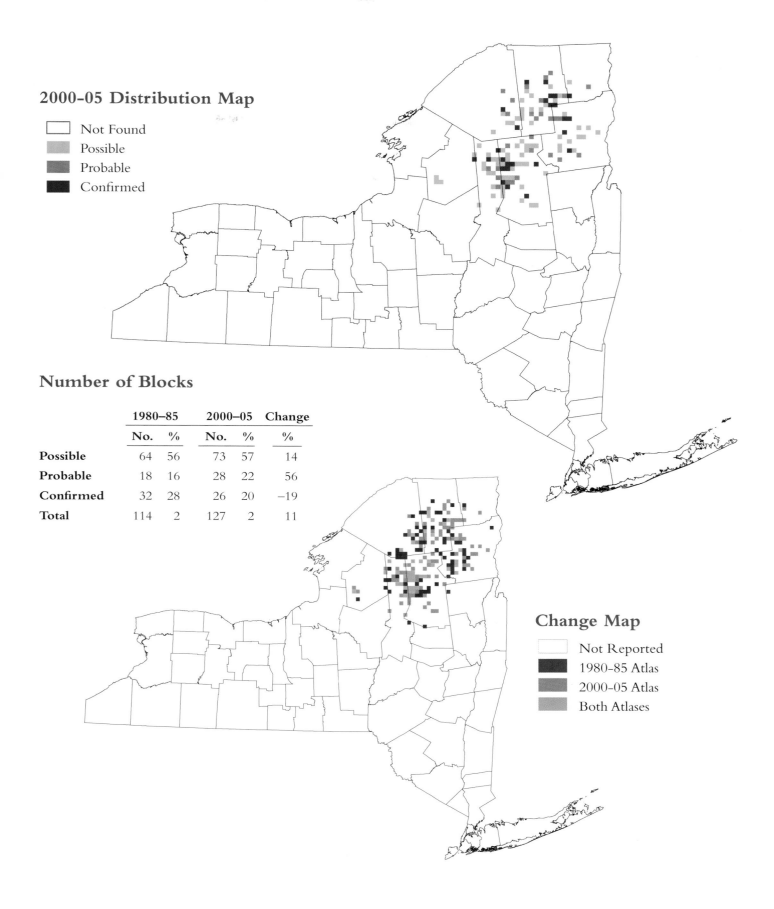

2000–05 Distribution Map

- ☐ Not Found
- Possible
- Probable
- Confirmed

Number of Blocks

	1980–85		2000–05		Change
	No.	%	No.	%	%
Possible	64	56	73	57	14
Probable	18	16	28	22	56
Confirmed	32	28	26	20	−19
Total	114	2	127	2	11

Change Map

- ☐ Not Reported
- 1980–85 Atlas
- 2000–05 Atlas
- Both Atlases

Northern Flicker
Colaptes auratus

KEVIN J. MCGOWAN

The Northern Flicker is a common ant-eating woodpecker of open areas and savannah. It breeds across North America, from Alaska and northern Canada southward to Cuba and Central America (Moore 1995). It is found in open woodlands and along forest edges, including in cities and suburbs. As a species that prefers open areas, it is likely that the flicker was less common in New York before the widespread deforestation of the 19th century. By early in that century, however, it was abundant throughout most of the state, and by the middle to the end of the century it was considered the most common woodpecker in many areas (e.g., Rathbun 1879). Eaton (1914) considered it to be uniformly distributed across the state and one of the most dominant bird species. Bull (1974) considered it the most numerous woodpecker in New York.

The first Atlas survey showed the Northern Flicker to be one of the most common birds in the state, present in 92 percent of all blocks. It was missing only from portions of the Central Adirondacks, the Adirondack High Peaks, and the Allegany Hills, primarily in forested areas above 610 m (2,000 ft) in elevation, and especially in the spruce–fir–northern hardwood forest areas of the Adirondacks. The second Atlas survey detected the Northern Flicker in nearly the same number of blocks. Any gaps in the western portion were less noticeable this time. Once again portions of the Adirondacks contained the largest areas lacking flickers. Within the Adirondacks, the flicker was detected in a similar number of blocks, but the gaps appeared to include portions of the Western Adirondack Foothills in addition to the Central Adirondacks and High Peaks. Such small local changes could easily be the result of differing coverage during the Atlas projects.

The Northern Flicker has been undergoing an alarming population decline since at least 1966 (Moore 1995). Breeding Bird Survey data show a significant continent-wide decline of an estimated 2 percent per year, with a drop to half of 1966 levels, and declining trends throughout its range (Sauer et al. 2005). BBS data for New York show a pronounced decline of 4.1 percent each year, with current levels at approximately one-fifth of 1966 levels (Sauer et al. 2005). Most of the decline in New York took place before the 1980s, and the negative BBS trend from 1980 to 2005 was not significant (Sauer et al. 2005). The continuing decline throughout the north Atlantic states (U.S. Fish and Wildlife Service Region 5), however, did remain significant (Sauer et al. 2005). Although Northern Flicker numbers have been declining, Partners in Flight (PIF 2005) estimated the species to be the most numerous woodpecker in North America (Rich et al. 2004) and did not list it as a species of Continental Concern (PIF 2005). PIF, however, listed it as a species of Regional Concern in the Appalachian (Bird Conservation Region 28), Lower Great Lakes and St. Lawrence (BCR 13), and New England/Mid-Atlantic Coast (BCR 30) regions (PIF 2005). The causes of declining flicker numbers are unknown, but two hypotheses have been advanced to explain them: competition for nest cavities from the European Starling and loss of nesting snags (Moore 1995). Fewer nesting snags might be available as more forests are managed and people remove the standing dead trees from their woodlots, but no data exist on this possibility. Although the starling often evicts the flicker from nest holes, a recent study on the effects of starlings on native cavity-nesting bird populations found surprisingly little effect (Koenig 2003). Forest maturation may be playing a role in flicker population declines in some areas. The Northern Flicker is a species whose population changes may not be adequately tracked by repeated atlas efforts, at least in the short term, because atlas protocols are not designed to detect changes in common and widespread species. The Northern Flicker is a bird to watch during the third Atlas project.

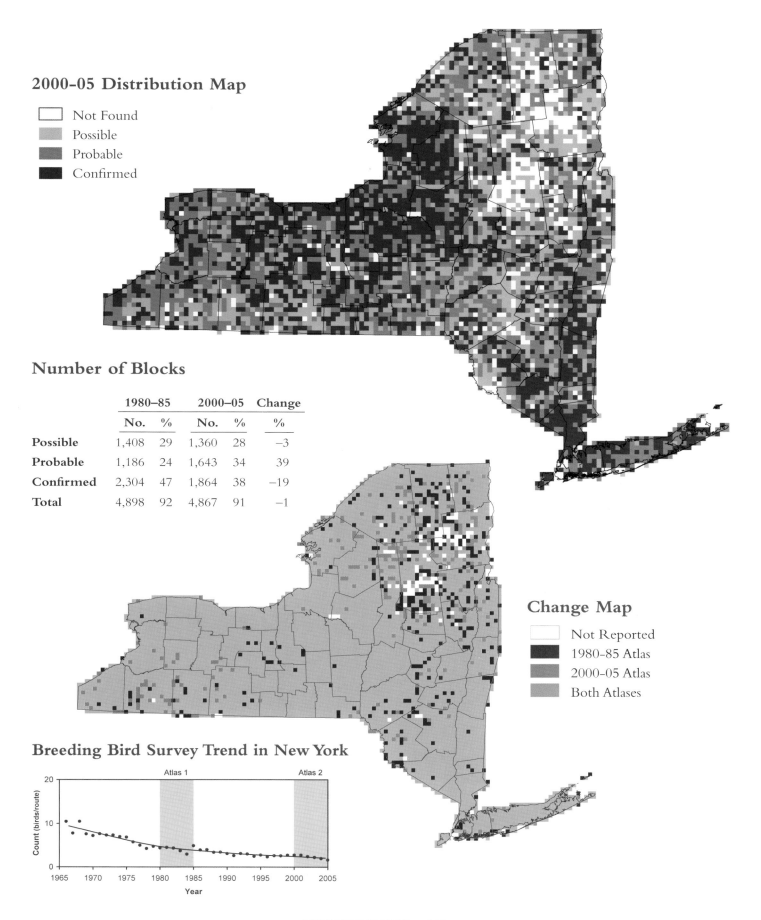

2000-05 Distribution Map

- ☐ Not Found
- Possible
- Probable
- Confirmed

Number of Blocks

	1980–85		2000–05		Change
	No.	%	No.	%	%
Possible	1,408	29	1,360	28	−3
Probable	1,186	24	1,643	34	39
Confirmed	2,304	47	1,864	38	−19
Total	4,898	92	4,867	91	−1

Change Map

- ☐ Not Reported
- 1980-85 Atlas
- 2000-05 Atlas
- Both Atlases

Breeding Bird Survey Trend in New York

Pileated Woodpecker
Dryocopus pileatus

KEVIN J. McGOWAN

The largest woodpecker in New York, the Pileated Woodpecker is resident throughout southern Canada, the Midwest, and the East, westward to eastern North Dakota and eastern Texas, as well as along the Pacific Coast and the northern Rockies of the United States (Bull and Jackson 1995). It lives in mature deciduous or coniferous forests, or younger forests with scattered large, dead trees (Bull and Jackson 1995). The Pileated Woodpecker was probably abundant throughout New York State before European colonization but might have been missing from the coastal areas (DeKay 1844). As the forests were removed in the 19th century, the Pileated Woodpecker disappeared. By the start of the 20th century it was found only in the remaining large tracts of coniferous forest in the Adirondacks and Catskills and in a few remaining areas of forest in central and western New York (Eaton 1914). Eaton (1914) wrote, "More than any of our native species, with the possible exception of the Spruce grouse and some of the larger hawks, this bird disappears with the destruction of the forests, and it probably will never be reestablished in the State except in the larger evergreen forest of the Canadian zone." The Pileated Woodpecker, however, staged a remarkable comeback through the 20th century. It began to use smaller trees and second growth and started to inhabit scattered woodlots (Hoyt 1957). Bull (1974) reported it as being present in all heavily forested parts of the state, as well as moving into suburban and urban areas, although Beardslee and Mitchell (1965) still considered it rare in the Niagara Frontier region. It began visiting bird feeders in the 1950s and 1960s (Hoyt 1957, Bull 1974) and demonstrated that it could exist with civilization.

During the first Atlas survey, the Pileated Woodpecker was recorded in every region of the state; however, only one Probable breeding record came from the Coastal Lowlands. Although common in the heavily forested and mountainous regions of the state, it was not restricted to those areas. Fewer records were from the Great Lakes and St. Lawrence plains and much of the western Appalachian Plateau. The second Atlas survey revealed 29 percent more blocks with records statewide, with increases in all ecozones except the Hudson Highlands and Manhattan Hills. The woodpecker was still missing from the Coastal Lowlands, with no reports south of Westchester County. The resulting distribution covers nearly the entire state, with only a few obvious gaps in the Western Adirondack Foothills and Sable Highlands, the western portions of the Appalachian Plateau and the Great Lakes Plain, and the heavily agricultural region around the Finger Lakes. Many small local changes could be the result of coverage issues.

Breeding Bird Survey data show a continent-wide increase in Pileated Woodpecker numbers since the survey began in 1966, with the largest increases occurring in the Midwest and Northeast (Sauer et al. 2005). The significant increase of 3.6 percent per year shown in the New York BBS data is typical for the region (Sauer et al. 2005). The second Ontario Breeding Bird Atlas also reported a significant increase in Pileated Woodpecker numbers across that province (Bird Studies Canada et al. 2006). Protection from hunting, changes in its tolerance of people, and especially the reappearance of forest in the East in the early 20th century allowed the Pileated Woodpecker to recover from severe population declines that followed European colonization of North America. The current maturation of forests in New York should continue to favor the Pileated Woodpecker, and populations should continue to increase into the next Atlas survey period.

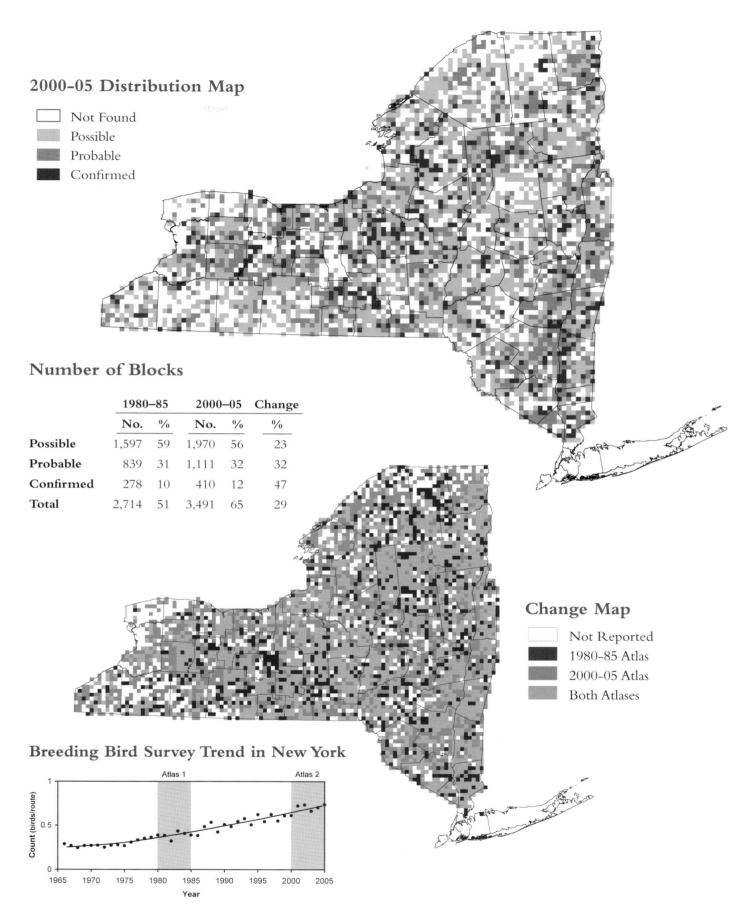

2000–05 Distribution Map

- ☐ Not Found
- Possible
- Probable
- Confirmed

Number of Blocks

	1980–85		2000–05		Change
	No.	%	No.	%	%
Possible	1,597	59	1,970	56	23
Probable	839	31	1,111	32	32
Confirmed	278	10	410	12	47
Total	2,714	51	3,491	65	29

Change Map

- ☐ Not Reported
- 1980–85 Atlas
- 2000–05 Atlas
- Both Atlases

Breeding Bird Survey Trend in New York

Eastern Kingbird and Eastern Phoebe in the Albany Pine Bush

One of the best examples of an inland pine barrens ecosystem in the world, the Albany Pine Bush hosts a uniquely diverse population of rare as well as common species of plants and animals, including the lovely but federally endangered Karner blue butterfly.

Olive-sided Flycatcher

Contopus cooperi

JOHN M. C. PETERSON

Long a favorite of visitors to New York's mountains, the Olive-sided Flycatcher is a large boreal flycatcher noted for its loud, ringing, whistled call. It nests across North America from Alaska to Baja California in the West, and from Labrador and Newfoundland as far southward as the mountains of North Carolina and Tennessee in the East (Altman and Sallabanks 2000). New York is at the southeastern limit of the core range, with only scattered breeding to the south. This flycatcher favors edges and openings in coniferous or mixed woods, along ponds and rivers, and in burned-over forests (Altman and Sallabanks 2000). In New York it favors small mountain tarns and quaking bogs, swampy lake shores, marshy streams, river backwaters, and beaver meadows. The surrounding forest is often black or red spruce, mixed with balsam fir, tamarack, or eastern hemlock. Dead standing trees provide perches for sallying food flights and singing. DeKay (1844) did not know the species in New York, but Merriam (1881) called it a common summer bird of the Adirondacks. Eaton (1914) found it in the Adirondacks and Catskills where burned lands, timber slashings, and flooded lands, along with swamps, were the major habitats. By the mid-20th century such human disturbance was far less frequent, but beavers had recovered from near extirpation in the 19th century and were creating many new nesting areas for this flycatcher (J. M. C. Peterson 1988j). Bull (1974) showed the Olive-sided Flycatcher to be common across much of the Adirondacks, fairly common in the Tug Hill Plateau, and less common and more local in the Catskills.

The first Atlas map was strikingly similar to that presented by Bull (1974), except for additional records in Fulton and Rensselaer counties. The Adirondack population, which extended north to The Gulf State Unique Area in Clinton County, was the largest in the state, with a peripheral portion on the Tug Hill Plateau. To the south, in addition to a few records from the Rensselaer Hills, the Catskill population stretched across Greene, Ulster, and Sullivan counties. The second Atlas survey revealed generally the same distribution but with several significant changes. Overall, the number of blocks with Olive-sided Flycatcher reports declined by a third. The Adirondack population still stretched northward to The Gulf on the Canadian border, but the number of blocks with records declined by 34 percent. In the Rensselaer Hills, the flycatcher was found in only one block, at an upland beaver pond west of the Hoosic River. Losses in the Catskill Peaks were severe, with the species now absent from Greene County and the Delaware Hills of Sullivan County. Isolated records came from new areas on the edge of the Appalachian Plateau in Otsego County, and in the Shawangunk Hills of southern Ulster County.

Breeding Bird Survey data show that the continental population of Olive-sided Flycatcher has declined steadily since 1966, and the bird has nearly disappeared from New York routes (Sauer et al. 2005). Partners in Flight put the Olive-sided Flycatcher on its Watch List and indicated that threats were greatest on its wintering grounds (Rich et al. 2004). Deforestation in its South American winter range is considered to be a prime threat (Altman and Sallabanks 2000). Habitat alteration on the breeding grounds is a possible but less likely factor (Altman and Sallabanks 2000). Within the Adirondacks, the amount of available habitat has not changed greatly since the first Atlas survey period; if anything, there are more beavers today providing more potential breeding habitat. The Olive-sided Flycatcher has a special fondness for wild bees and other *Hymenoptera* species (Peterson and Fichtel 1992, Altman and Sallabanks 2000), and the current decline in domestic bee populations from introduced diseases and parasites, and potentially in wild bees as well (Committee on the Status of Pollinators in North America 2007), might be playing a quiet role in this flycatcher's decline.

2000–05 Distribution Map

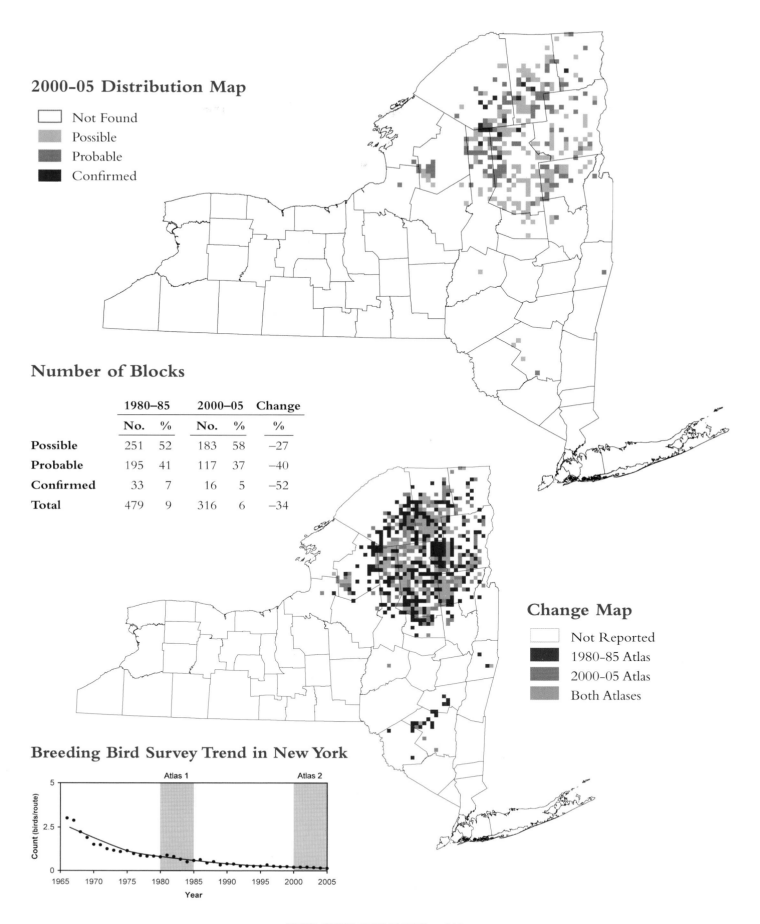

- ☐ Not Found
- Possible
- Probable
- Confirmed

Number of Blocks

	1980–85		2000–05		Change
	No.	%	No.	%	%
Possible	251	52	183	58	−27
Probable	195	41	117	37	−40
Confirmed	33	7	16	5	−52
Total	479	9	316	6	−34

Change Map

- ☐ Not Reported
- 1980-85 Atlas
- 2000-05 Atlas
- Both Atlases

Breeding Bird Survey Trend in New York

Eastern Wood-Pewee

Contopus virens

KEVIN J. MCGOWAN

The Eastern Wood-Pewee is one of the characteristic birds of the eastern deciduous forest. It breeds from southeastern Saskatchewan eastward to Nova Scotia and southward to central Texas and northern Florida. It breeds in all types of woodlands, deciduous as well as coniferous. It prefers rather open forests but can be found in areas of closed canopy (McCarty 1996). It forages primarily in the middle part of the understory up to the lower canopy, higher in the trees than the Least and Acadian flycatchers but lower down than the Great Crested Flycatcher (McCarty 1996). The pewee does not appear to be affected by forest fragmentation and can be found along forest edges, in clearings, and in suburban areas (McCarty 1996). As a bird of open forests the Eastern Wood-Pewee population may have declined somewhat with the clearing of the forests in New York in the early 19th century, but would have benefited by the subsequent regrowth. This species was able to adapt to the changes in landscape brought about in the 19th century, and it remained common throughout all parts of the state (Rathbun 1879, Short 1893, Reed and Wright 1909, Eaton 1914, Bull 1974). Its numbers decreased around New York City with the increasing spread of urbanization (Cruickshank 1942), but some pairs still remained (Bull 1964).

The first Atlas results showed the Eastern Wood-Pewee common throughout New York State, missing only from the most urban areas of New York City. It was more sparsely distributed in the Central Adirondacks, Adirondack High Peaks, and western Appalachian Plateau. Contra Sibley (1988i), no effect of agriculture was obvious, and gaps in western New York may have reflected coverage, as many empty blocks contained apparently appropriate woodlands. The second Atlas survey revealed only a few differences in distribution. Again the species was found throughout most of the state, but significant declines in the Adirondacks were apparent. Overall the number of blocks with records of the pewee decreased only slightly, but in the Adirondacks the number of occupied blocks declined by 22 percent. Changes in other parts of the state were small, although an 11 percent decline on Long Island could be real. No gaps were apparent in the western Appalachian Plateau.

According to Breeding Bird Survey data, Eastern Wood-Pewee numbers have been decreasing steadily and significantly at 1.8 percent each year since at least the 1960s (Sauer et al. 2005). BBS data for New York show a significant decline of 2.1 percent per year, with a decline of 3.7 percent per year in the Adirondacks (Sauer et al. 2005). Populations are decreasing throughout the pewee's range, but it is not listed as of special concern anywhere. The maturation of forests in New York and the Northeast may be negatively affecting pewee populations, as the canopies close and create less desirable habitat. Another potential cause of decline is the overpopulation of white-tailed deer in the eastern forests, although this explanation would not apply to the Adirondacks. In areas with high deer density, the intermediate canopy is disturbed by browsing, affecting the foraging space of the flycatcher (McCarty 1996). The widespread decline of the pewee across its entire range raises the possibility that the causes are not on the breeding grounds but rather on the wintering grounds in northern South America, much as for other species wintering in the same area, such as the Canada Warbler. The Eastern Wood-Pewee is still a common and widespread bird, and Atlas methods are not well designed to detect changes in the population of such species. Nevertheless, declines are apparent in the area of previously lowest concentration, the Adirondacks, and it is in these areas of perhaps marginal habitat that one might expect to detect changes first. It will be interesting to see how the distribution changes in the next Atlas project.

2000-05 Distribution Map

- ☐ Not Found
- Possible
- Probable
- Confirmed

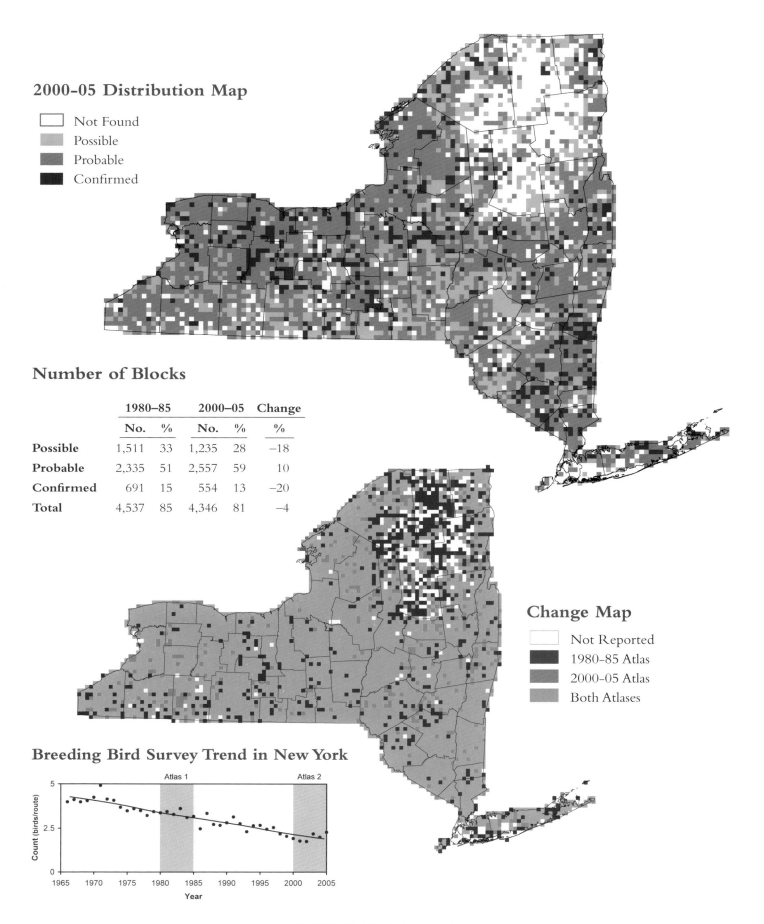

Number of Blocks

	1980–85		2000–05		Change
	No.	%	No.	%	%
Possible	1,511	33	1,235	28	−18
Probable	2,335	51	2,557	59	10
Confirmed	691	15	554	13	−20
Total	4,537	85	4,346	81	−4

Change Map

- ☐ Not Reported
- 1980-85 Atlas
- 2000-05 Atlas
- Both Atlases

Breeding Bird Survey Trend in New York

Yellow-bellied Flycatcher
Empidonax flaviventris

JOHN M. C. PETERSON

A diminutive resident of shady, mossy boreal forests, the Yellow-bellied Flycatcher may spend only a few months on its breeding grounds each year. This flycatcher breeds from Alaska eastward across boreal Canada to Newfoundland, extending southward to the upper Midwest, northern New England, New York, and isolated highlands of northern Pennsylvania, West Virginia, sometimes Virginia, and perhaps North Carolina (Gross and Lowther 2001). The three populations in New York are separated from the contiguous main range in Canada by the Ottawa Valley and St. Lawrence Plains, with the Adirondack core population constituting an island, neighbored by the smaller islets of the Catskill Peaks and Central Tug Hill. Short (1893) called the Yellow-bellied Flycatcher a rare breeder in western New York, while Merriam (1881) gave it the same designation in the Adirondacks. Eaton (1914) noted a few western reports but mentioned it primarily in the Adirondacks. Eaton's (1910) earlier range map showed the flycatcher throughout the higher elevations of the Adirondacks and Catskills and in the Tug Hill Plateau, with indications of occurrence in Madison, Onondaga, Monroe, and Erie counties. Bull (1974) discounted the early western reports and those cited in Beardslee and Mitchell (1965). He stated that no proven breeding existed outside the Adirondacks or Catskills, discounting even the Tug Hill reports for lack of solid evidence, although he acknowledged the possibility of breeding there.

The first Atlas data showed the distribution of the Yellow-bellied Flycatcher to closely resemble that depicted in the map provided by Eaton (1910). The flycatcher was widely distributed throughout the Adirondacks, with smaller numbers in the Catskill Peaks and Central Tug Hill. A Probable breeding record came from central Madison County where Eaton had marked it earlier, but no records came from farther west. The second Atlas project revealed a similar distribution, with this species again found breeding throughout the Adirondacks, in the Catskill Peaks, and in the Tug Hill Plateau. The total number of blocks with reports of the flycatcher increased 42 percent, and increases were seen in both the Adirondacks and Tug Hill, but the number of blocks with reports declined in the Catskills by 26 percent. No observations were made in Madison County this time, but new sightings, including a Confirmed report of birds feeding young, were made on the St. Lawrence Plains. Additional reports along the northern Clinton-Franklin county lines near Quebec in the St. Lawrence and Champlain transitions put the new map in agreement with the northern extent shown by Bull's (1974) shaded map.

The late migration period of the Yellow-bellied Flycatcher presents the possibility of mistaking late migrants for summering breeders. This species arrives in New York during May, sometimes not until early June, and departs by August or early September (Bull 1974, Carleton and Peterson 1999); the summer stay of this Neotropical migrant often lasts fewer than 70 days (Gross and Lowther 2001). To add more possible confusion, the songs and calls resemble those of other species: the *killink* song is similar to that of a Least Flycatcher, and the *tu-wee* call reminiscent of the Eastern Wood-Pewee. Add in the difficulties of access to the bird's habitat, and observers for both Atlas projects are to be commended.

Although the survey-wide increase in Yellow-bellied Flycatcher numbers since 1966 shown by the Breeding Bird Survey is not quite significant, the 6 percent per year increase in the north Atlantic states (U.S. Fish and Wildlife Service Region 5) is (Sauer et al. 2005). The BBS data from New York are too sparse to show a statistically significant trend. The second Ontario Breeding Bird Atlas reported a significant increase in Yellow-bellied Flycatcher numbers in that province (Bird Studies Canada et al. 2006). With these indications of population increases, the Yellow-bellied Flycatcher now appears secure, perhaps with its population even expanding, in New York.

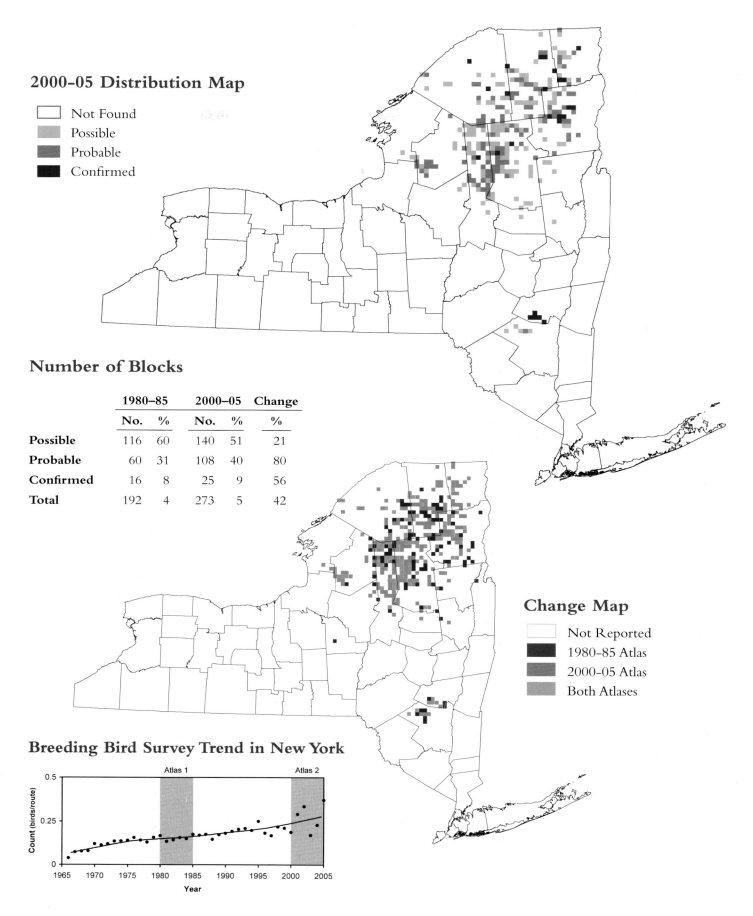

2000-05 Distribution Map

- ☐ Not Found
- Possible
- Probable
- Confirmed

Number of Blocks

	1980–85		2000–05		Change
	No.	%	No.	%	%
Possible	116	60	140	51	21
Probable	60	31	108	40	80
Confirmed	16	8	25	9	56
Total	192	4	273	5	42

Change Map

- ☐ Not Reported
- 1980-85 Atlas
- 2000-05 Atlas
- Both Atlases

Breeding Bird Survey Trend in New York

Acadian Flycatcher

Empidonax virescens

CHARLES R. SMITH

Over the past 100 years or so, the Acadian Flycatcher has undergone a breeding range contraction, followed by a recovery, in New York (Eaton 1988a). Its current range extends from extreme southeastern Minnesota eastward to Massachusetts, southward to eastern Texas and northern Florida (Whitehead and Taylor 2002). New York is at the northeastern limit of its range. While breeding, it generally is associated with mature forest and forested swamps (Whitehead and Taylor 2002). In New York, the Acadian Flycatcher often is associated with mature eastern hemlock growing in forested areas along streams (Eaton 1988a). Historically, this species appears to have had two distinct population centers in New York; a breeding population on the Great Lakes Plain of western New York is widely separated from the breeding birds along the lower Hudson Valley and on Long Island (Bull 1974). A decline in numbers after 1900 led to its nearly complete disappearance from the state by the mid-20th century (Bull 1974), but it began to reappear in the late 1950s to the 1970s (Eaton 1998a).

The first Atlas results showed the Acadian Flycatcher to be uncommon, but it was sighted across much of southern New York. Concentrations were present in the Allegany State Park, Cattaraugus Highlands, Hudson Highlands, and Manhattan Hills. Additionally this flycatcher was found in scattered localities across Long Island, on the Erie-Ontario Plain, and across the Appalachian Plateau, although a significant gap was still evident between the western and eastern populations. The second Atlas survey revealed that the Acadian Flycatcher had increased its breeding distribution in New York by 48 percent. Concentrations again were apparent in the Allegany Hills and Cattaraugus Highlands, extending now into the adjacent Great Lakes Plain, as well as in the Catskills southeastward to eastern Long Island. The gap between eastern and western occurrences appeared to be disappearing as a result of range expansion across the High Allegheny Plateau. Remarkably, the Acadian Flycatcher held its own on Long Island, even expanding its range slightly. It is probable that this small flycatcher is responding to patterns of forest expansion and maturation in New York that have been ongoing, at varying rates, since the early 20th century (Smith and Gregory 1998). Because its distinctive song still could be overlooked by

an inexperienced observer, or not be audible from the hemlocks along a rushing stream, this species may well be more widespread in New York than indicated by the current map.

Breeding Bird Survey data show no significant trend for Acadian Flycatcher numbers survey-wide since 1966 (Sauer et al. 2007). New York BBS data are too sparse to provide a meaningful trend. A national map of Acadian Flycatcher population trends for the period 1966–2003 shows decreases across much of the range, with modest increases at the northeastern and southwestern margins (Sauer et al. 2007). The second Ontario Breeding Bird Atlas reported that the Acadian Flycatcher population increased in southern Ontario, but it still is relatively uncommon there (Bird Studies Canada et al. 2006). Partners in Flight identified the Acadian Flycatcher as a species of continental conservation importance for the United States and Canada (Rich et al. 2004). It is not listed at the state level in the adjoining states of Massachusetts, Connecticut, and New Jersey, and it does not have special conservation status in New York.

Because of its relatively recent increase and range expansion in New York, the Acadian Flycatcher would be worthy of further study, especially on Long Island, where it may use habitats different from those used in other parts of New York. At this time, there are no substantive, published field studies detailing its ecology, reproductive behavior, specific habitat requirements, or sensitivity to habitat fragmentation in New York. It is encouraging to see the Acadian Flycatcher, a Neotropical migrant songbird, actually expanding its breeding range in New York.

2000-05 Distribution Map

- ☐ Not Found
- Possible
- Probable
- ■ Confirmed

Number of Blocks

	1980–85		2000–05		Change
	No.	%	No.	%	%
Possible	75	46	90	38	20
Probable	59	36	120	50	103
Confirmed	28	17	29	12	4
Total	162	3	239	4	48

Change Map

- ☐ Not Reported
- ■ 1980-85 Atlas
- 2000-05 Atlas
- Both Atlases

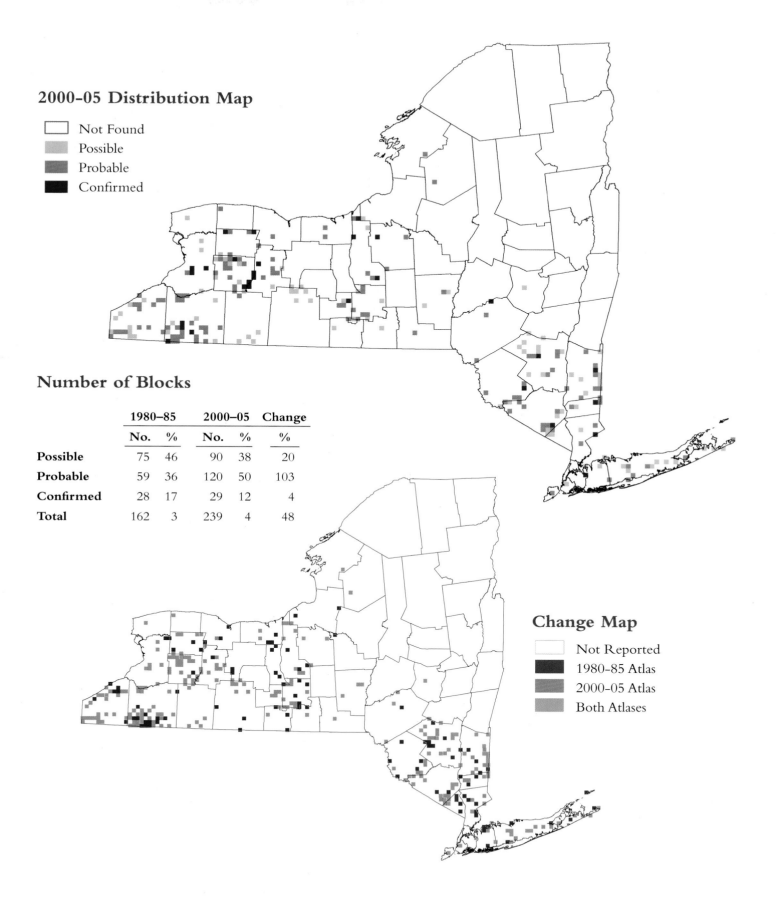

Alder Flycatcher

Empidonax alnorum

TIMOTHY J. POST

The Alder Flycatcher can be identified by its buzzy *fee-bee-o* song, which is the most reliable field method of differentiating it from the Willow Flycatcher (Lowther 1999). Until 1973, Alder and Willow flycatchers were considered a single species, the Traill's Flycatcher (AOU 1973). The breeding range of the Alder Flycatcher includes Alaska, most of Canada, and the northern portions of the eastern United States, southward to Pennsylvania. Historical information on the status of this species in New York is confused by the species identity problem. It was probably always present in New York, breeding in the beaver meadows and shrubby wetlands of the higher elevations. DeKay (1844) did not know of Traill's Flycatcher in New York, but Merriam (1881) considered it an uncommon breeding species in the Adirondacks. Eaton (1914) considered Traill's (what he called "Alder") Flycatcher to be breeding in the colder districts and into the transition zones. He described it as common in mountainous areas and particularly in the Adirondacks and Catskills, but uncommon in southern and western New York, present there in the colder swamps. Based on Eaton's descriptions of the species and its habits, Parkes (1954) stated that Eaton was referring to the Alder Flycatcher. The Willow Flycatcher spread into the western portion of the state during the early 1900s (see account, this volume), further confusing the status of the Alder Flycatcher. Stein (1958) noted that the Alder Flycatcher was predominant across New England, the Adirondacks, and the northern portions of the Appalachian Plateau, but noted that both it and the Willow Flycatcher occurred together in parts of western New York. Bull (1974) listed the Alder Flycatcher as occurring primarily in the bogs, swamps, and streamsides at the higher elevations and northward, while the Willow Flycatcher bred more in the brushy grassland areas at lower elevations, such as the lake plains, Hudson Valley, and on Long Island.

During the first Atlas survey, the Alder Flycatcher had a widespread, if scattered, distribution in the state, but with low numbers of blocks with records in the southeastern region. It was also less widely distributed in urban areas, the Mohawk Valley, the Catskills, and in areas of heavy agricul-

tural production in the Great Lakes Plain, and was nearly absent from Long Island. The number of records in the second Atlas far exceeded those for the first Atlas, in almost all of the ecozones, especially in the Mohawk Valley and Taconic Highlands. The exception is in the southeastern portion of the state, in the Coastal Lowlands, Manhattan Hills, and Triassic Lowlands, all of which had very low numbers of records in both Atlas databases. The Alder Flycatcher was a relatively new species in the first Atlas survey, and atlasers may have become more familiar with its song by the time of the second Atlas fieldwork, perhaps lending to an increase in the number of blocks with records in the second Atlas data, though records of both flycatcher species increased.

Breeding Bird Survey records combine Willow and Alder flycatchers into one trend estimate, so species-specific trend data are not available, although the combined estimate shows significantly increasing numbers in New York and the north Atlantic states (U.S. Fish and Wildlife Service Region 5) (Sauer et al. 2007). Alder Flycatcher populations have increased substantially in the Appalachian Mountains (Bird Conservation Region 28), shown modest increases in the Lower Great Lakes/St. Lawrence Plain (BCR 13) and the Atlantic Northern Forest (BCR 14), and are stable or have shown no significant trend in New England/Mid Atlantic Coast (BCR 30) (PIF 2005). Alder Flycatcher is one of the few bird species that relies on early-successional habitats whose population is stable or increasing in New York or the Northeast, although why this should be true is unknown.

2000-05 Distribution Map

- ☐ Not Found
- ☐ Possible
- ☐ Probable
- ■ Confirmed

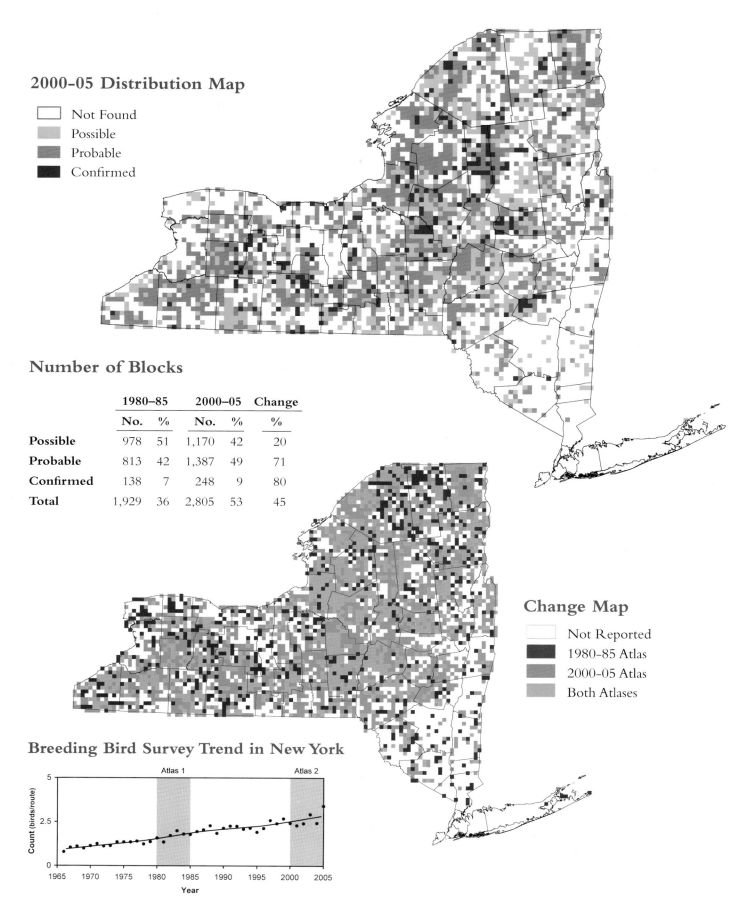

Number of Blocks

| | 1980–85 | | 2000–05 | | Change |
	No.	%	No.	%	%
Possible	978	51	1,170	42	20
Probable	813	42	1,387	49	71
Confirmed	138	7	248	9	80
Total	1,929	36	2,805	53	45

Change Map

- ☐ Not Reported
- ■ 1980-85 Atlas
- ☐ 2000-05 Atlas
- ☐ Both Atlases

Breeding Bird Survey Trend in New York

Willow Flycatcher

Empidonax traillii

TIMOTHY J. POST

ield identification of the Willow Flycatcher relies on its sneezy, *fitz-bew* song, which is the only reliable method to differentiate it from the Alder Flycatcher (Sedgwick 2000). The Alder and Willow flycatchers were considered a single species, known as Traill's Flycatcher, until 1973 (AOU 1973). The Willow Flycatcher is found in a variety of brush and shrubby habitats, such as uplands thickly overgrown with shrubs, shrubs along stream and pond edges, and wet thickets of alder, buttonbush, viburnum, and willow. It favors drier sites than the Alder Flycatcher does (Sedgwick 2000) and occurs at lower elevations within New York. The breeding range of the Willow Flycatcher encompasses most of the northern United States and portions of southern Canada, southward to Arizona, Missouri, and Virginia (Sedgwick 2000). Subsequent to European settlement, much of the mature forest vegetation covering most of New York was replaced by shrub and early-successional forest habitats that should have been favorable to the Willow Flycatcher, allowing it to expand its range into New York. Eaton (1914) indicated that Traill's Flycatcher (what he called "Alder") was largely unknown in a large portion of western and southern New York in 1860–85 but was breeding in those areas in the early 1900s, although Reed and Wright (1909) considered it rare. The Willow Flycatcher expanded its range northward and eastward into and through New York by the early to mid-1900s (Stoner 1932, Parkes 1954, Stein 1963). In some areas, as the Willow Flycatcher expanded its range, it may have displaced the Alder Flycatcher (Stein 1963).

During the first Atlas survey, the Willow Flycatcher was found across most of New York outside of the more mountainous areas. It was noticeably absent from most of the Adirondacks, Tug Hill Plateau, Catskills, and much of the Appalachian Plateau. The number of records collected during the second Atlas survey far exceeded those reported in the first Atlas. Most of the increases occurred in areas where the Willow Flycatcher was present during the first Atlas, although the species spread across the St. Lawrence and Champlain transitions into the northeastern corner of the state, and into the Central Adirondacks in small numbers. The Willow Flycatcher song can be somewhat difficult to differentiate from that of the Alder Flycatcher, which may lead to misidentification of the species. Willow Flycatcher was a rela-

tively new species for the first Atlas project, and atlasers may have become more familiar with its song during the second Atlas fieldwork. Increasing familiarity might perhaps have caused an increase in the number of reports, although the number for both species increased for the second Atlas.

The North American Bird Conservation Initiative does not consider the Willow Flycatcher to be a Species of Conservation Concern in New York. The Partners in Flight Bird Conservation Plan (Robertson and Rosenberg 2003) considered the Willow Flycatcher to be a priority species of conservation concern in the Allegheny Plateau, Lower Great Lakes Plain, and Northern Ridge and Valley physiographic areas. These listings are based on continental concerns for range-wide population declines, and because those geographic areas have a high regional responsibility for the species since they sustain substantial portions of the its population. Because Breeding Bird Survey data combine the Willow and Alder flycatcher data, no trend can be elucidated for each species, although the combined data indicate increasing numbers in New York and the north Atlantic states (U.S. Fish and Wildlife Service Region 5) (Sauer et al. 2005). The Partners in Flight Species Assessment indicates that the Willow Flycatcher population is increasing in the Appalachian Mountains (Bird Conservation Region 28), the Atlantic Northern Forest (BCR 14), and in New England/Mid Atlantic Coast (BCR 30), with a stable or nonsignificant trend in the Lower Great Lakes/ St. Lawrence Plain (BCR 13) (PIF 2005). Why this bird of early-successional habitats is increasing in population and distribution while the amount of habitat declines is unknown.

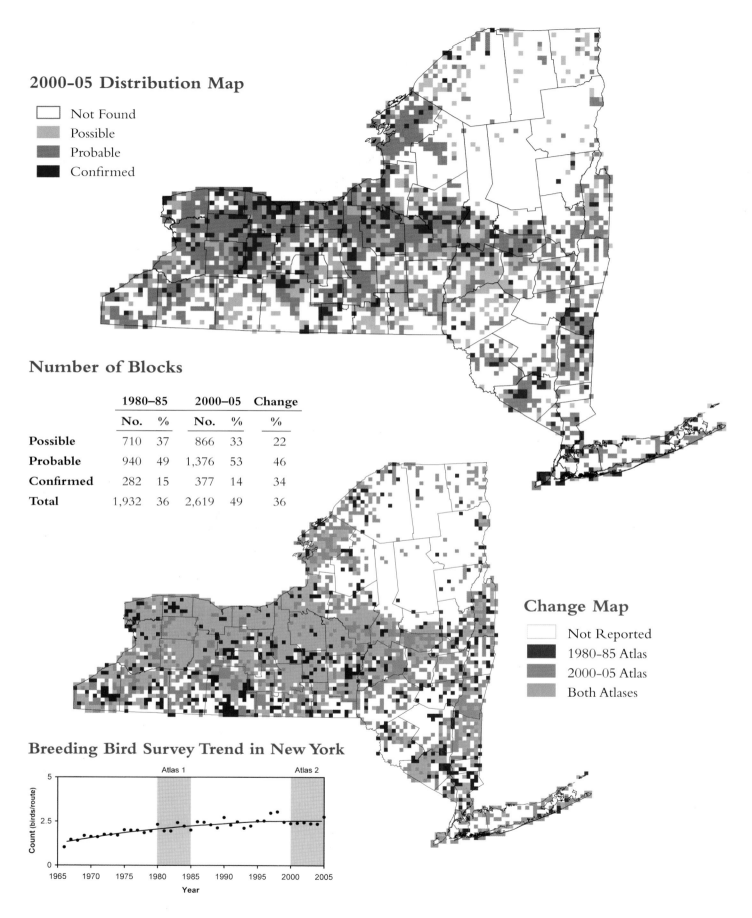

2000-05 Distribution Map

- ☐ Not Found
- Possible
- Probable
- Confirmed

Number of Blocks

	1980–85		2000–05		Change
	No.	%	No.	%	%
Possible	710	37	866	33	22
Probable	940	49	1,376	53	46
Confirmed	282	15	377	14	34
Total	1,932	36	2,619	49	36

Change Map

- ☐ Not Reported
- 1980-85 Atlas
- 2000-05 Atlas
- Both Atlases

Breeding Bird Survey Trend in New York

Least Flycatcher
Empidonax minimus

KEVIN J. MCGOWAN

The Least Flycatcher is a small, drab bird of open forests. It breeds from southern Yukon to Newfoundland, southward to northern Wyoming, Nebraska, northern Ohio, and New Jersey, and farther southward in the Appalachians (Briskie 1994). New York is near the southeastern edge of its main range and represents its southern extent along the Atlantic Coast. It breeds in semi-open woodlands, including second-growth and mature deciduous and mixed woods, orchards, burns, swamp and bog edges, and shrubby fields (Briskie 1994). Before European settlement the Least Flycatcher probably was common and widespread where it likely associated with the frequent gaps in the mature forest resulting from tree falls, stream edges, and beaver meadows. Perhaps because of the difficulty in identifying Empidonax flycatchers, its early presence in the state is unclear. Although it should have been a common species, DeKay (1844) and Giraud (1844) did not mention it; however, Giraud's description of "Least Pewee, *Muscicapa pusilla*" sounds more like the Least Flycatcher than the Alder or Willow Flycatcher to which the scientific name seems to refer (AOU 1886). Giraud mentioned this bird as uncommon in the woods of Long Island. Rathbun (1879) called the Least Flycatcher common in central New York, and Reed and Wright (1909) termed it abundant in the Cayuga Lake Basin, but Short (1893) thought it rare in western New York. Eaton (1914) called it common in all portions of the state. Griscom (1923) noted that its population had been declining for 25 years in the New York City area and was nearly gone, although the species was still common in rural areas. He called it rare on Long Island and a local breeder on the north shore. Bull (1974) wrote, "Widespread breeder, but on Long Island restricted to the north shore where it is local."

During the first Atlas period, the Least Flycatcher was well distributed across the state north of the southern Manhattan Hills. It was missing from the greater New York City area and was reported in only eight blocks on Long Island, where breeding was not confirmed. It was less densely distributed in the heavily farmed portions of the state, although many of the scattered gaps in its distribution are not easily explained. During the second Atlas survey, the Least Flycatcher was again found across most of the state but with slightly fewer blocks with records. The species disappeared from the Coastal Lowlands and experienced substantial declines in reports in the Manhattan Hills, Hudson Highlands, and southern Hudson Valley. A noticeable gap also formed in the Capital District area of the Hudson Valley, and the species was more patchily distributed on the Great Lakes Plain.

Breeding Bird Survey data show a steady and significant decline in Least Flycatcher numbers survey-wide since the inception of the survey in 1966 (Sauer et al. 2005). In New York, the decline was significant at 1.9 percent per year from 1966 to 2005, and 2.5 percent per year from 1980 to 2005 (Sauer et al. 2005). Significant declines are apparent all across its range, except in the southwestern portion (Sauer et al. 2005). Data from the second Ontario Breeding Bird Atlas show a slight decline in squares with reports in the southern portions of the province but a significant increase in the Northern Shield region and no significant change overall (Bird Studies Canada et al. 2006). The maturation of the eastern forests may be the cause of some of the declines in the population of this species (Briskie 1994), although the increase in forest cover over the last century should have been to its liking. The Least Flycatcher remains a common and widespread bird in New York but is a species to watch in the next Atlas project.

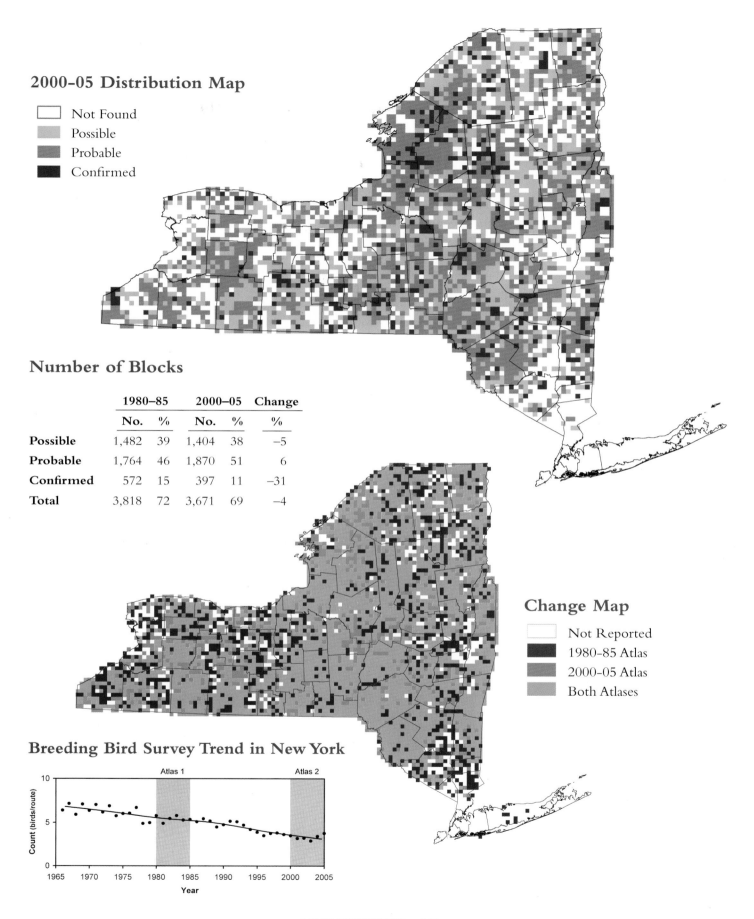

2000-05 Distribution Map

- ☐ Not Found
- Possible
- Probable
- Confirmed

Number of Blocks

	1980–85		2000–05		Change
	No.	%	No.	%	%
Possible	1,482	39	1,404	38	–5
Probable	1,764	46	1,870	51	6
Confirmed	572	15	397	11	–31
Total	3,818	72	3,671	69	–4

Change Map

- ☐ Not Reported
- 1980-85 Atlas
- 2000-05 Atlas
- Both Atlases

Breeding Bird Survey Trend in New York

Eastern Phoebe

Sayornis phoebe

KEVIN J. McGOWAN

The tail-wagging Eastern Phoebe is perhaps the most common and recognizable member of the flycatcher family in eastern North America. It breeds from southeastern Yukon and northeastern British Columbia eastward to Nova Scotia and southern Quebec, southward to central Texas, northern Mississippi, and central Georgia (Weeks 1994). It breeds in woodlands and along forest edges, often near water, and makes extensive use of human-created structures to nest, including under the eaves of houses, porches, barns, and garages. The phoebe also nests under bridges, a habit that helped it expand its range into the Great Plains and the southeastern United States (Weeks 1994). It will still use natural rock outcroppings and upturned tree roots for nesting when they are available. The phoebe is more limited by suitable nesting sites than by foraging habitat (Weeks 1994). It has probably always been fairly common in New York. It was able to adapt well to the changes wrought by European settlement in the 1800s, and it remained abundant. DeKay (1844) said it bred in every part of the state. E. H. Eaton (1914) called it the most common flycatcher in New York, found everywhere except in the spruce and balsam forests of the Catskills and Adirondacks. S. W. Eaton (1998c) reported that blizzards and bad winters in the 1970s had large negative effects on phoebe populations in the state by killing many in the northern part of the wintering range, but that numbers had returned to normal by the mid-1980s. Breeding Bird Survey data agree with this idea, showing cyclical fluctuations in numbers in New York (Sauer et al. 2005).

During the first Atlas survey, the Eastern Phoebe was found throughout most of the state, missing only from much of the Central Adirondacks, Adirondack High Peaks, Western Adirondack Foothills, and the New York City area. It appeared more locally on Long Island and the western Great Lakes Plain. The second Atlas survey revealed little change in distribution. The phoebe was found in a slightly higher percentage of blocks overall, with the largest increases occurring in the western Appalachian Plateau, the Great Lakes Plain, Central Adirondacks, and Champlain Valley and Transition. It was found in 11 percent more blocks in the Adirondacks and may have made a significant inroad into the southern part of the Central Adirondacks. The species was still missing from much of the Adirondacks and New York City area and was still local on Long Island. The Eastern Phoebe is a relatively easy bird to detect and confirm, and the map should be a good representation of its actual range in the state.

Breeding Bird Survey data show a slight but significant long-term increase in Eastern Phoebe populations across its range, with most of the gain occurring in the last 25 years (Sauer et al. 2005). The New York data show no significant long-term change, but considerable fluctuations have occurred over shorter periods. Analyses of data from 1966 to 1979 show a significant decline, while those from 1980 to 2005 show a significant increase (Sauer et al. 2005). Region-wide data show a similar pattern but with a significant long-term decline in Massachusetts (Sauer et al. 2005). The second Ontario Breeding Bird Atlas reported a significant increase in phoebe populations across that province (Bird Studies Canada et al. 2006). The Eastern Phoebe is a common species in New York that appears to undergo periodic population fluctuations, perhaps as the result of bad weather conditions on its wintering grounds. It is able, however, to recover quickly from such downturns, and it appears to be in little danger of serious population declines.

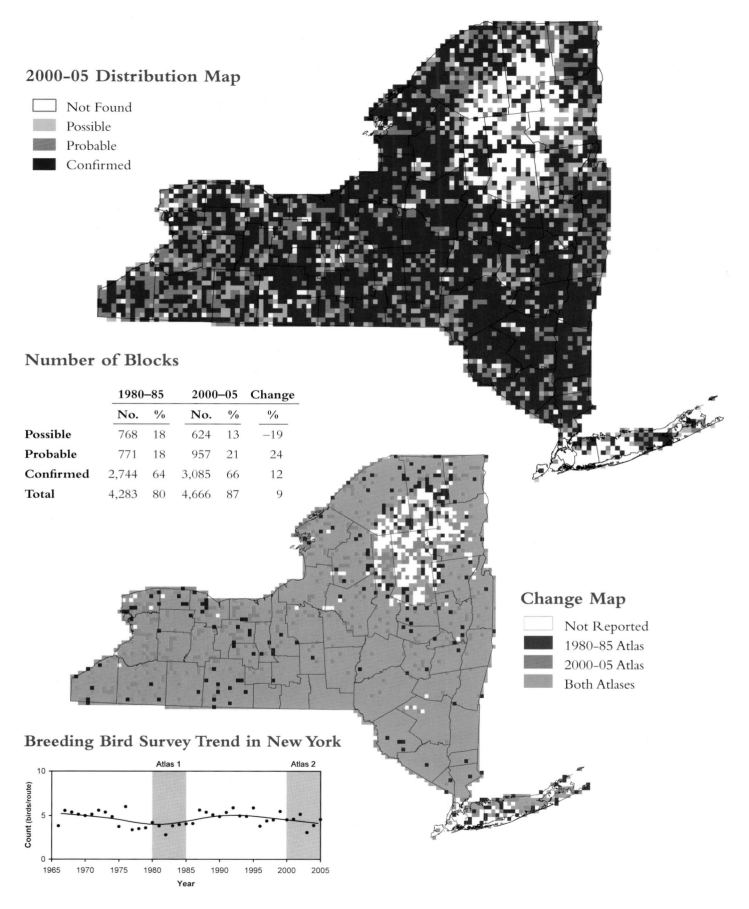

2000-05 Distribution Map

- ☐ Not Found
- Possible
- Probable
- Confirmed

Number of Blocks

	1980–85		2000–05		Change
	No.	%	No.	%	%
Possible	768	18	624	13	−19
Probable	771	18	957	21	24
Confirmed	2,744	64	3,085	66	12
Total	4,283	80	4,666	87	9

Change Map

- ☐ Not Reported
- 1980-85 Atlas
- 2000-05 Atlas
- Both Atlases

Breeding Bird Survey Trend in New York

Great Crested Flycatcher

Myiarchus crinitus

KEVIN J. MCGOWAN

A bird of the treetops, the Great Crested Flycatcher is the only cavity-nesting flycatcher in eastern North America. Its breeding range extends from eastern Alberta through southern Canada to Nova Scotia, and southward to central Texas and Florida. It breeds in open deciduous woodlands, old orchards, riparian corridors, wooded swamps, parks, cemeteries, and urban areas with large shade trees (Lanyon 1997). Although it will use closed-canopy forests, it prefers isolated woodlots, second-growth woodlands, or other open forests and avoids boreal forest (Lanyon 1997). The Great Crested Flycatcher may have benefited from the opening of the primary forests and the subsequent regrowth in New York, although no clear evidence exists to support or refute that assertion. DeKay (1844) called it rare in New York, and Giraud (1844) deemed it not common on Long Island. By the late 19th century it was considered common, at least in the central and western regions (Rathbun 1879, Reed and Wright 1909). Eaton (1914) described it as common to fairly common throughout most of the state but nearly absent from the interior of the Adirondacks and Catskills. Bull (1974) considered it a widespread breeder, more common in the southern portion of the state and in the lowlands.

During the first Atlas survey, the Great Crested Flycatcher was found across most of the state, missing primarily from the interior of the Adirondacks, Catskill Peaks, Delaware Hills, Schoharie Hills, portions of the western Appalachian Plateau, and much of New York City and western Coastal Lowlands. Fewer records were collected at higher elevations, and though it was found in blocks throughout the Central Adirondacks, it was missing from the spruce-fir forests there. The second Atlas survey revealed a similar distribution, but the gaps at the higher elevations were even more pronounced. It was missing from large portions of the Central Adirondacks, Adirondack High Peaks, Western Adirondack Foothills, Sable Highlands, Catskill Peaks, Schoharie Hills, Allegany Hills, and portions of the Appalachian Plateau. Overall the Great Crested Flycatcher was found in slightly fewer blocks during the second Atlas fieldwork. The decline was 22 percent in the Catskill Peaks and 14 percent within the Adirondacks. Increases were seen on the Great Lakes Plain and in the Champlain Valley.

Breeding Bird Survey data show no trends for Great Crested Flycatcher numbers survey-wide (Sauer et al. 2005). BBS data for New York show no significant long-term trend, although the decline of 1.3 percent per year after 1980 is significant (Sauer et al. 2005) and parallels the slight decline seen in the Atlas data. In the Adirondacks, BBS data indicate a significant annual decrease of 4.2 percent from 1980 to 2005 (Sauer et al. 2005), mirroring the more dramatic decrease documented by the Atlas project. BBS data also show significant declines in the surrounding areas of Ontario, Massachusetts, Pennsylvania, and Ohio. The Ontario Breeding Bird Atlas data indicate a slight but significant decrease too (Bird Studies Canada et al. 2006). Reasons for the modest declines noted are unclear. The maturation of forests may be responsible, as this flycatcher prefers open and fragmented woods. Competition for nesting cavities might be a factor, but the presence of holes is probably increasing with the spread of beech blight, as is evidenced by increasing woodpecker numbers (McGowan 2005). The Atlas protocols are not well constructed to detect changes in common and widespread breeders such as the Great Crested Flycatcher, but like other species, such as the Eastern Wood-Pewee, changes may be detected in regions of less preferred habitat such as the Adirondacks. The Great Crested Flycatcher is another species to watch during the next Atlas project.

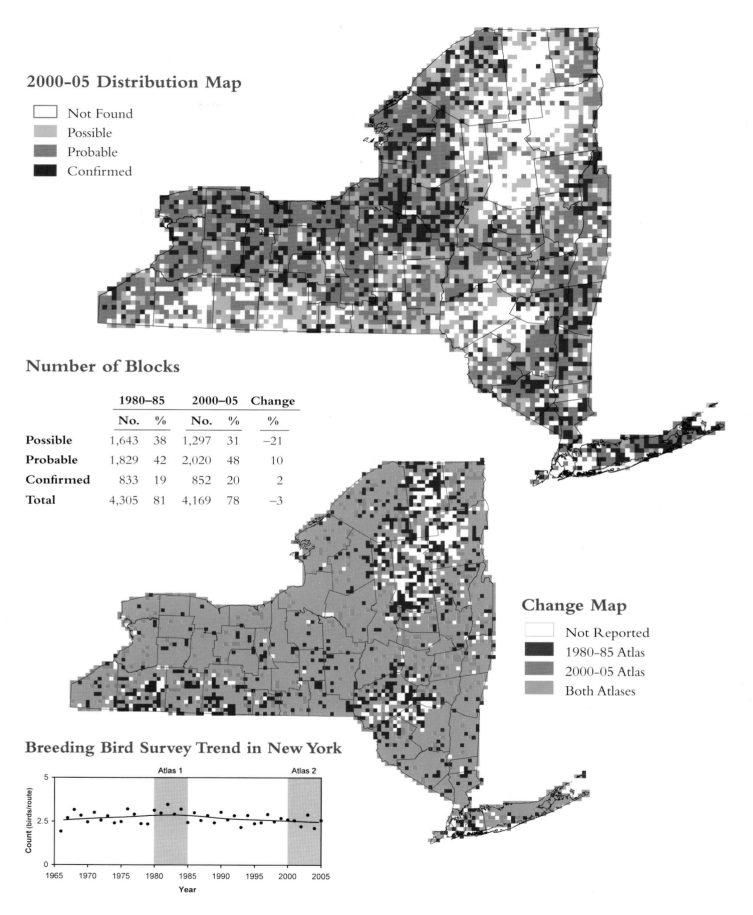

2000–05 Distribution Map

- ☐ Not Found
- Possible
- Probable
- Confirmed

Number of Blocks

	1980–85		2000–05		Change
	No.	%	No.	%	%
Possible	1,643	38	1,297	31	−21
Probable	1,829	42	2,020	48	10
Confirmed	833	19	852	20	2
Total	4,305	81	4,169	78	−3

Change Map

- ☐ Not Reported
- 1980–85 Atlas
- 2000–05 Atlas
- Both Atlases

Breeding Bird Survey Trend in New York

Eastern Kingbird

Tyrannus tyrannus

KEVIN J. MCGOWAN

The Eastern Kingbird is a large, aggressive flycatcher of open areas. It breeds from western Northwest Territories and eastern and southern British Columbia eastward across Canada, across all of the eastern United States, and southward in the western states to eastern Oregon, northern Nevada, northern New Mexico, and southern Texas (Murphy 1996). It breeds in open environments with scattered perches, such as fields, orchards, shelterbelts, forest edges, urban parks, and golf courses (Murphy 1996). As a savannah-loving bird, the Eastern Kingbird was probably not common in precolonial New York. It may have been limited to beaver meadows, swamps, marshes, edges of lakes and rivers, and open areas created by forest fires or storms. It adapted well to the destruction of the forests by European colonists, and by the early 1800s it was common, breeding in all parts of the state (DeKay 1844). Eaton (1914) listed it as one of the most common birds of open areas in New York. He said it was present everywhere except in the most densely forested areas, even reaching into the Adirondacks and the Catskills up to the edge of the spruce-fir forests via clearings and river valleys. Little change in its distribution has been noted since.

The first Atlas reported the Eastern Kingbird to be the 16th most common species, found across the state in all regions. It was missing only from parts of New York City, the Central Adirondacks, Adirondack High Peaks, Western Adirondack Foothills, Central Tug Hill, and Allegany Hills. During the second Atlas survey, the Eastern Kingbird was found in 7 percent fewer blocks, but it was still present across most of the state. The number of blocks with records declined in all regions, but the 33 percent decline in the Catskill Peaks and the 31 percent decline in the Adirondacks were the most striking. Gaps in its distribution are noticeable in the Central Adirondacks, Adirondack High Peaks, Western Adirondack Foothills, Central Tug Hill, Allegany Hills, and Catskill Peaks, all areas of extensive forest and higher elevation. As a conspicuous bird of open areas, often found near people and roads, the kingbird was easy to detect within an Atlas block, and breeding was confirmed in more than half the blocks where it was found.

Breeding Bird Survey data show a significant decline in Eastern Kingbird numbers across the survey area (Sauer et al. 2005). BBS data from New York also indicate a significant decrease over the last 40 years, with a significant 2.5 percent yearly decrease since 1980 (Sauer et al. 2005), and BBS numbers from all parts of the species's range except the Great Plains document declines. Data from the second Atlas efforts in Ontario show significant declines in kingbird populations there too (Bird Studies Canada et al. 2006). The Eastern Kingbird remains a common and widespread bird, and as such, significant changes are difficult to detect with Atlas methods. Still, the decreases noted by the Atlas data and other studies in New York (e.g., Murphy 2001a) suggest that serious decreases in kingbird populations are taking place. The continuing abandonment of farmlands and the maturation of the replacing forests may be responsible in some part for the observed population declines (Murphy 1996), with loss of farmland especially important for New York (Murphy 2001b). Declines in the East, however, may be balanced to some degree by increases in abundance in the central and western parts of the bird's range (Murphy 1996). The Eastern Kingbird will remain common in New York for the near future, and its declining populations may stabilize at a lower level than before, still much higher than it probably was 300 years ago.

2000-05 Distribution Map

- ☐ Not Found
- Possible
- Probable
- ■ Confirmed

Number of Blocks

	1980–85		2000–05		Change
	No.	%	No.	%	%
Possible	841	18	681	15	−19
Probable	1,337	28	1,418	32	6
Confirmed	2,627	55	2,361	53	−10
Total	4,805	90	4,460	84	−7

Change Map

- ☐ Not Reported
- 1980-85 Atlas
- 2000-05 Atlas
- Both Atlases

Breeding Bird Survey Trend in New York

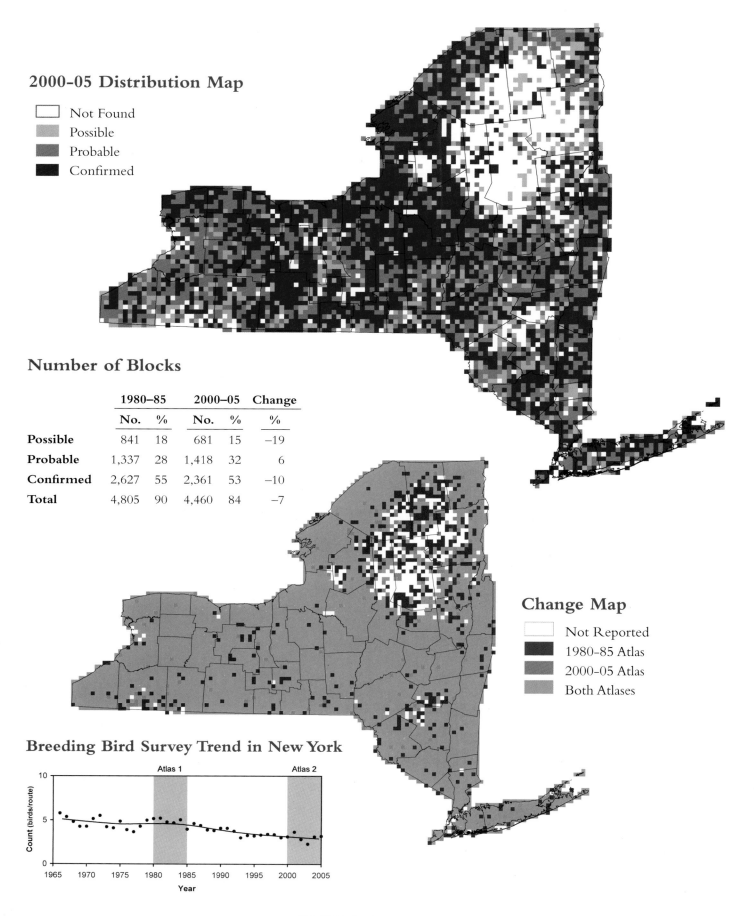

Loggerhead Shrike
Lanius ludovicianus

PAUL NOVAK

The Loggerhead Shrike is well known for its peculiar habit of impaling prey on sharp objects such as thorns and barbed-wire fence. The breeding range stretches from coast to coast across the southern United States and into the interior of the continent to the Great Plains of Canada; this range is much reduced from what it was in the early 1900s, particularly in the northeastern states and provinces, where the species is largely extirpated. It is a bird of open landscapes including pastures, other agricultural lands, roadsides, golf courses, riparian areas, steppes, deserts, savannahs, prairies, and in some regions, suburban areas. The Loggerhead Shrike expanded its range into eastern North America with the widespread clearing of forests and settlement of the region (Palmer 1898, Forbush 1939, Bull 1974). Although the first documented breeding in New York was from Buffalo in 1869 (Allen 1869), at least some of DeKay's (1844) earlier observations of breeding Northern Shrike were undoubtedly loggerheads and the species likely moved into New York through the Niagara Frontier region during the 1840s (Spahn 1988b, Novak 1989). By the 1890s it was well established in western and central New York, particularly in the lake plains counties and in the counties surrounding Oneida Lake (Novak 1989). Eaton (1914) described the Loggerhead Shrike as a "fairly common breeder in western and central New York, in the Black River Valley, Mohawk Valley, and around the outskirts of the Adirondacks." By 1930, however, he noted it was "decidedly less common than formerly" (Eaton 1953). Bull (1974) noted further declines.

The Loggerhead Shrike was one of the least frequently encountered species during the first Atlas period. All 13 Confirmed or Probable breeding records came from former strongholds, including the Great Lakes and St. Lawrence plains and Champlain Valley (Spahn 1988b). It was recorded in just four blocks during the second Atlas period, all Possible breeding records and none after 2001. This change over 20 years continues the decline that began in the early 1900s, proceeding inexorably toward the extirpation of the Loggerhead Shrike in New York.

Nationwide, the Loggerhead Shrike is one of the few species to exhibit significant population declines in most parts of the continent (Robbins et al. 1986). For decades, Breeding Bird Survey data for Region 5 have not recorded the Loggerhead Shrike with enough frequency for statistical analysis. Only Ontario and Virginia support regular breeding populations into the 21st century, though these are much reduced from their former numbers. Breeding Loggerhead Shrikes were distributed across southern Ontario according to data in the first Ontario Breeding Bird Atlas, but by 1990 the population was largely confined to three population centers associated with the southern edge of the Precambrian Shield (Cadman et al. 1987). The second Ontario Atlas reported shrike populations hanging on in these same areas (Bird Studies Canada et al. 2006), where a captive breeding program is underway. In the United States the Loggerhead Shrike is listed at the federal level as a Migratory Nongame Species of Management Concern (USFWS 1987b). It was listed as Threatened in Canada in 1986, with the eastern population (*L. l. migrans*) classified as Endangered (Cadman 1985). Virtually every northeastern and north-central state, including New York, lists the species as Endangered or Threatened (Pruitt 2000).

The timing and nature of the Loggerhead Shrike population decline coincides with dramatic changes in land use, including major reductions in the amount of optimal breeding and wintering habitat. Collisions with vehicles and, possibly, accumulation of contaminants are also implicated (Novak 1989, Yosef 1996). Timely follow-up on breeding season sightings in New York could reveal that an occasional pair still nests in the state, but for all intents and purposes New York appears to have joined the ranks of northeastern states where the Loggerhead Shrike is extirpated as a breeder.

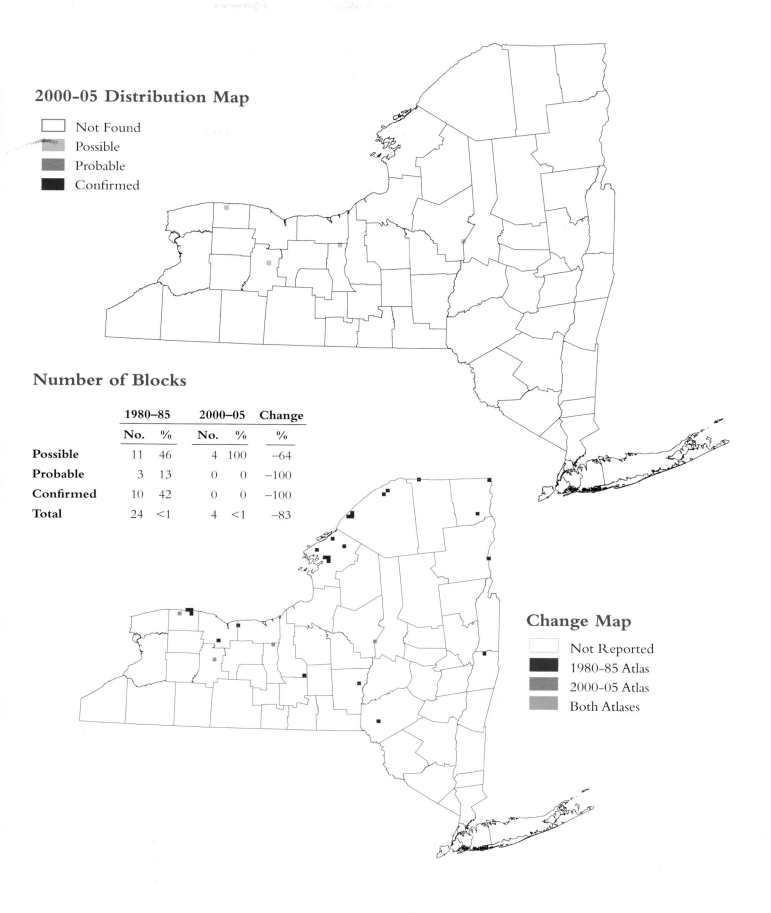

2000-05 Distribution Map

- ☐ Not Found
- ☐ Possible
- ☐ Probable
- ■ Confirmed

Number of Blocks

	1980–85		2000–05		Change
	No.	%	No.	%	%
Possible	11	46	4	100	−64
Probable	3	13	0	0	−100
Confirmed	10	42	0	0	−100
Total	24	<1	4	<1	−83

Change Map

- ☐ Not Reported
- ■ 1980-85 Atlas
- ☐ 2000-05 Atlas
- ☐ Both Atlases

Red-eyed and Warbling vireos in Central Park

New York City's Central Park supports a surprisingly large, diverse population of both year-round and migratory birds, and a dedicated population of both year-round and migratory birders who watch and enjoy them.

White-eyed Vireo

Vireo griseus

KEVIN J. McGOWAN

The White-eyed Vireo is a small secretive bird of shrubby areas in the eastern and southern United States. Breeding occurs from Iowa to very southern Ontario and Massachusetts, southward to Florida and Mexico. New York is near the northeastern limit of this range. This vireo breeds in dense deciduous scrub, overgrown pastures, old fields, wood margins, streamside thickets, and mangroves (Hopp et al. 1995). It was probably rare and restricted to coastal areas in New York before European settlement. DeKay (1844) called it common in the state, with no indication of any local restrictions. Giraud (1844) called it only a bird of the hedges, which perhaps indicates that it was common on Long Island. Rathbun (1879) called it "not common" in central New York, and Short (1893) and Reed and Wright (1909) did not even mention it for western New York and the Cayuga Lake Basin. Eaton (1914) called it common to abundant in the lower Hudson Valley, on Staten Island, and on Long Island, but uncommon in the western regions of the state. Bull (1974) gave essentially the same range, noting that its numbers had declined in the lower Hudson Valley and on western Long Island.

During the first Atlas period the White-eyed Vireo was found primarily in its longtime stronghold of the greater New York City area and Long Island. In addition, the data indicated a possible minor range expansion up the Hudson Valley northward to Hamilton and Warren counties, although the birds sighted could have been migrants overshooting their breeding grounds. Despite a growing number of records across western New York before the Atlas fieldwork commenced (Meade 1988d), five widely scattered reports were the only other sightings. During the second Atlas period the White-eyed Vireo had essentially the same range, again being most common in the lower Hudson Valley and on Long Island, with a few scattered reports in central and western New York. Any advance up the Hudson retreated, with no sightings north of Columbia County. Although new sightings were made away from the vicinity of the Hudson River in Ulster and Dutchess counties, the number of sightings declined in Westchester County. Despite a number of breeding reports in western New York made between the two Atlas periods (Salzman 1998i), little evidence was found of an increasing breeding population outside of the southeastern region, although breeding was confirmed in Chautauqua County.

No consistent population trend is apparent in White-eyed Vireo numbers in North America. Breeding Bird Survey data show no change in numbers across the survey (Sauer et al. 2005). BBS data from New York are too sparse for statistical analysis or to glean meaningful trends. Data from New Jersey show a significant decline, the sparse Pennsylvania data show no trend, while those from Ohio show a significant increase (Sauer et al. 2005). The second Ontario Breeding Bird Atlas reported no change in numbers of White-eyed Vireos, but the bird is not common there (Bird Studies Canada et al. 2006). The history of the vireo in Massachusetts has been one of change, with the species being common and widespread in the 1800s, nearly disappearing by 1930, then gradually increasing in numbers on the coastal plain to become relatively common in that restricted region (Veit and Petersen 1993). The White-eyed Vireo expanded its range substantially in Ohio in the second half of the 20th century (Peterjohn and Rice 1991), and some expansion of that population into western New York might be expected. Preliminary results of the second Pennsylvania Breeding Bird Atlas already show more reports of the White-eyed Vireo in the northwestern counties than the number recorded in the first Atlas (R. Mulvihill pers. comm.). Perhaps rather than another example of an isolated upstate occurrence, the confirmed nesting in Chautauqua might be a harbinger of that future expansion. However, the decline of shrubby habitats in the state could provide an obstacle to expansion.

2000-05 Distribution Map

- ☐ Not Found
- ☐ Possible
- ☐ Probable
- ■ Confirmed

Number of Blocks

	1980–85		2000–05		Change
	No.	%	No.	%	%
Possible	42	24	47	29	12
Probable	65	37	79	49	22
Confirmed	67	39	36	22	−46
Total	174	3	162	3	−7

Change Map

- ☐ Not Reported
- ■ 1980-85 Atlas
- ☐ 2000-05 Atlas
- ☐ Both Atlases

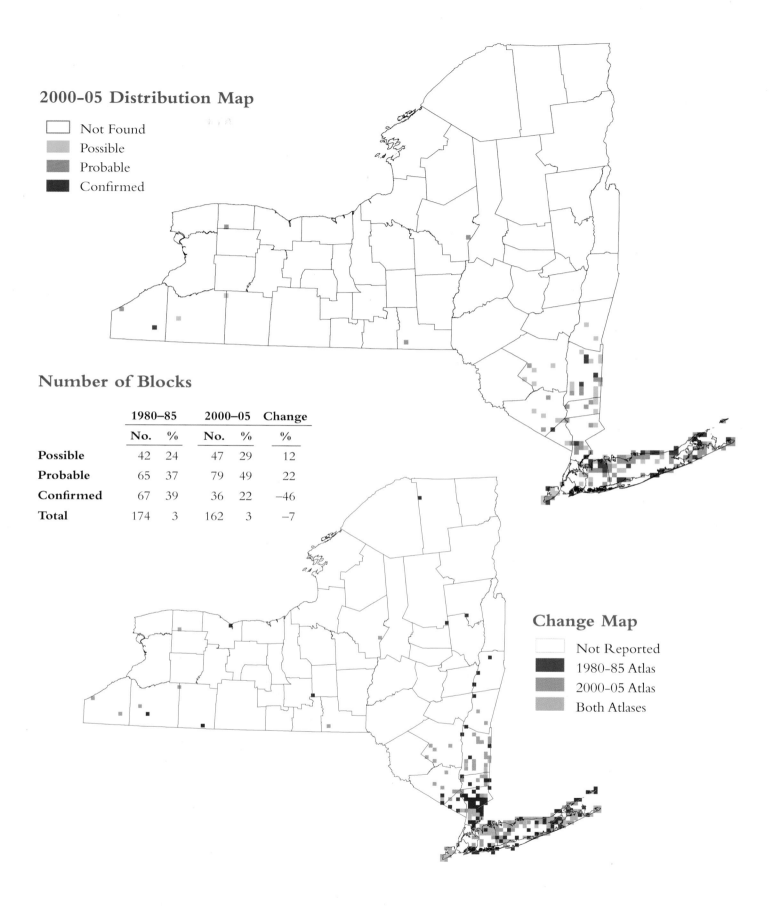

Yellow-throated Vireo
Vireo flavifrons

KEVIN J. MCGOWAN

*A*colorful bird of open deciduous forests, the Yellow-throated Vireo breeds from very southern Canada southward to eastern Texas and northern Florida. New York is near the northeastern edge of the range. It breeds in forest-edge habitats and in open wooded habitats with tall deciduous trees, and can be found along forested streams, rivers, swamps, and roads, as well as in parks, orchards, and small towns (Rodewald and James 1996). It generally does not breed in the forest interior, except near openings created by fallen trees or roads (Rodewald and James 1996). While the Yellow-throated Vireo prefers forest-edge habitat, it actually requires large blocks of forest to breed successfully; numbers decrease sharply in forests smaller than 100 ha (250 a) in the northeastern states (Rodewald and James 1996). Despite the comment by Salzman (1998j) that it spread into New York at the end of the 19th century, DeKay (1844) and Giraud (1844) considered this vireo common, although less so than the White-eyed Vireo. Rathbun (1879) and Reed and Wright (1909) also considered it common, but Short (1893) termed it uncommon in western New York. Eaton's (1914) description of its range as widespread in the "Alleghanian" and "Carolinian" zones, but missing from the Catskills and Adirondacks, applied consistently over the next century, although Temple and Temple (1976) did note a significant decline in central New York in the 1950s. Griscom (1923) stated that it was once common in the New York City area but that its numbers declined rapidly starting in 1917. Cruickshank (1942) mentioned that it had recovered somewhat, but that it was still mostly missing from Long Island. Bull (1974) still considered this species rare to uncommon in the coastal region.

The first Atlas reported the Yellow-throated Vireo as being widespread, occurring in most of the state's ecozones. Areas of abundance included the Drumlin; Finger Lakes Highlands; eastern Appalachian Plateau; eastern Tug Hill Transition; Central Tug Hill; and the Hudson Highlands and adjacent areas of the Manhattan Hills, Taconic Highlands, and lower Hudson Valley. It was largely, or completely, absent from the Adirondack High Peaks, Central Adirondacks, Black River Valley, western Appalachian Plateau, and Coastal Lowlands. The second Atlas data showed no clear pattern of change. The total number of blocks with breeding records declined slightly, but half of the ecozones showed an increase or no change; declines were not centered in any particular area. Salzman (1998j) stated that the vireo population was increasing along the edges of the Long Island moraine, but the Atlas data did not show such a pattern, as the number of blocks with records decreased across Long Island. The overall distribution in New York remained the same, with centers of abundance in the southeastern part of the state (Hudson Highlands and neighboring areas) and in the area stretching from the Drumlin on the Great Lakes Plain into the Tug Hill Plateau.

The Yellow-throated Vireo has not changed its distribution in North America much over the last century, although its breeding range has decreased locally in areas where extensive clearing of forests has resulted in the loss and fragmentation of habitat (Rodewald and James 1996). In the early 20th century, localized disappearances in northeastern towns may have been the result of insecticide spraying of shade trees (Rodewald and James 1996). Breeding Bird Survey data show a slight but significant increase in Yellow-throated Vireo numbers across the survey area, especially in the last 20 years (Sauer et al. 2005). New York BBS data, however, show a slight but nonsignificant negative trend. Data from the second Ontario Breeding Bird Atlas show a slight decline in the southernmost region (Bird Studies Canada et al. 2006). Reasons for these changes are unclear, but the maturation of forests with loss of edge habitat in New York could be causing some local population declines.

2000–05 Distribution Map

- ☐ Not Found
- Possible
- Probable
- Confirmed

Number of Blocks

| | 1980–85 | | 2000–05 | | Change |
	No.	%	No.	%	%
Possible	733	44	713	46	−3
Probable	693	41	673	43	−3
Confirmed	253	15	175	11	−31
Total	1,679	31	1,561	29	−7

Change Map

- ☐ Not Reported
- 1980-85 Atlas
- 2000-05 Atlas
- Both Atlases

Breeding Bird Survey Trend in New York

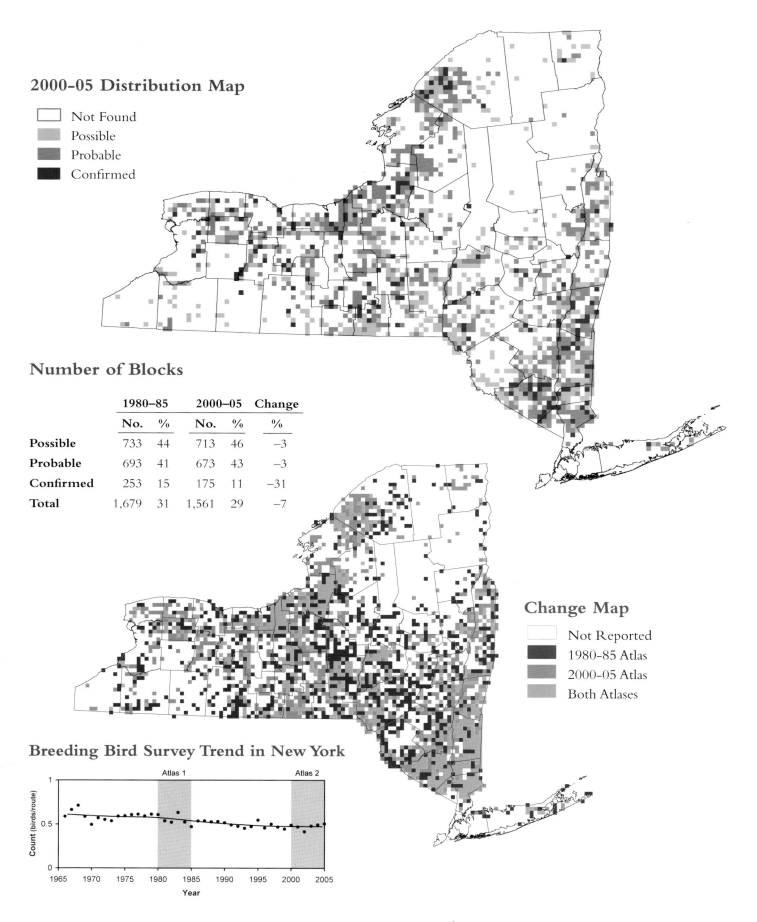

Blue-headed Vireo

Vireo solitarius

KEVIN J. MCGOWAN

The Blue-headed Vireo is a common and vocal bird of northern forests. It breeds from the southern part of the Northwest Territories eastward across Canada to Newfoundland, and from northern Minnesota to Connecticut, and southward in the Appalachians (James 1998). New York is near the southeastern limits of its main range. As a bird that prefers relatively large, mature forests with an understory of shrubs and small trees (James 1998), the Blue-headed Vireo was probably common in New York before the clearing by European settlers. It likely reached its lowest population levels at the peak of land clearing in the late 19th century. DeKay (1844) considered it the rarest of the vireos in the state (but he did not mention the Philadelphia Vireo). Rathbun (1879) and Short (1893) called it only a migrant in central and western New York. Reed and Wright (1909) considered it a common migrant and rare breeder in the Cayuga Lake Basin. Eaton (1914) reported the Blue-headed Vireo as nesting in the Adirondacks but mostly absent from other areas. He mentioned breeding records from the Catskills and near Ithaca but reported that he failed to find it himself in western New York, even where he found other cool-forest birds breeding (e.g., Hermit Thrush, Blackburnian Warbler, Dark-eyed Junco). The population may have increased in the western portion after that time; Saunders (1923) called the species well distributed in the Allegany State Park in the 1920s, though not common anywhere, but by 1938 he described it as common (Saunders 1938). Bull (1974) reported this vireo as local in the highlands of southern and southeastern New York.

During the first Atlas survey, the Blue-headed Vireo was found in approximately one-third of all blocks in the state, primarily at higher elevations. Its distribution was densest in the Adirondacks and Tug Hill, and it was found in slightly lower proportions throughout the Appalachian Plateau, with concentrations in the Allegany Hills and the highland subzones in the east. Additional sightings came from the Rensselaer Hills and southeastern highlands and were scattered across the Great Lakes Plain, St. Lawrence Plains and Transition, and Mohawk Valley. According to the second Atlas data, the Blue-headed Vireo's range expanded dramatically. The species was found in nearly half of all blocks, and the number of blocks with reports of breeding increased 39 percent overall. Records increased in all ecozones where the species occurred, except the Hudson Highlands, but it was still absent from the Coastal Lowlands. The statewide distribution changed little, with gaps still apparent in the Great Lakes Plain, Mohawk Valley, and Hudson Valley. There were fewer empty blocks, however, in every region, and the distribution across the Appalachian Plateau was nearly continuous. A potentially significant expansion may have occurred in the Champlain Transition of northern Clinton County. The Manhattan Hills of Westchester County remained the southernmost outpost in the state.

Breeding Bird Survey data show a strong positive trend in Blue-headed Vireo numbers across the survey area since 1966, and all significant trends for the various regions are positive (Sauer et al. 2007). The BBS trend in New York also is significantly positive, showing an average increase of 2.7 percent each year since 1966, and a 1.8 percent increase since 1980 (Sauer et al. 2007). The second Ontario Breeding Bird Atlas reported a similar and significant increase in numbers (Bird Studies Canada et al. 2006). The increasing number of Blue-headed Vireos breeding in New York probably reflects the maturation of forests in the state. It appears that the species is returning to population levels potentially present before the extensive logging by European settlers. Currently, the expansion is limited to higher elevations, and it may remain that way, but the next Atlas survey may well show expansion into the Great Lakes Plain and Mohawk Valley.

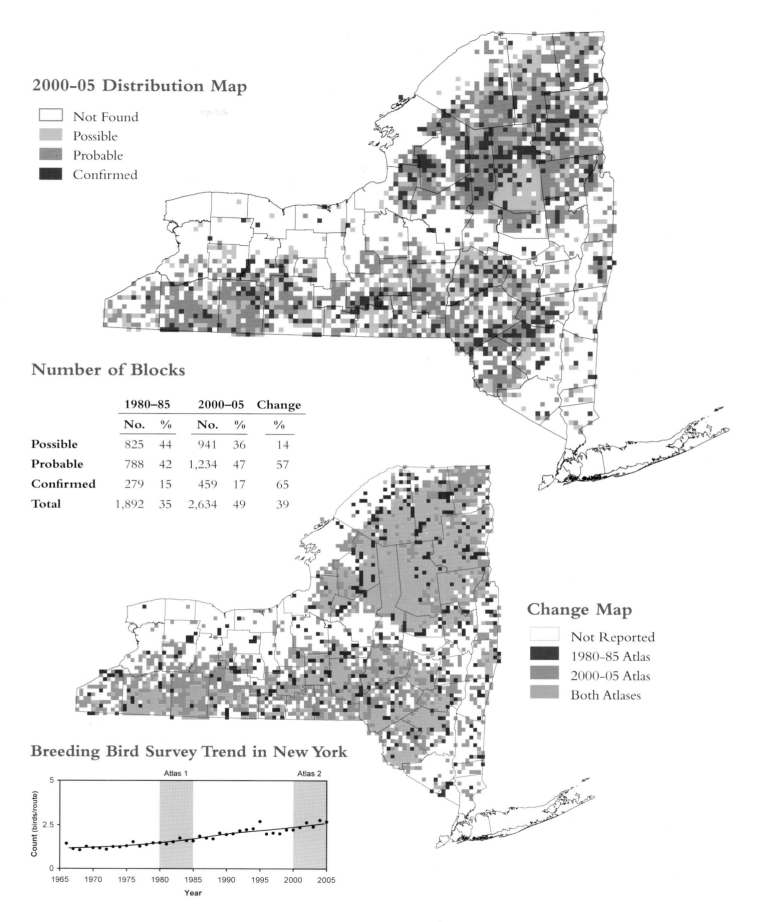

2000–05 Distribution Map

- ☐ Not Found
- Possible
- Probable
- Confirmed

Number of Blocks

| | 1980–85 | | 2000–05 | | Change |
	No.	%	No.	%	%
Possible	825	44	941	36	14
Probable	788	42	1,234	47	57
Confirmed	279	15	459	17	65
Total	1,892	35	2,634	49	39

Change Map

- ☐ Not Reported
- 1980–85 Atlas
- 2000–05 Atlas
- Both Atlases

Breeding Bird Survey Trend in New York

Warbling Vireo
Vireo gilvus

KEVIN J. McGOWAN

A drab woodland bird, the Warbling Vireo is more easily heard than seen. It breeds from the Yukon to Nova Scotia, southward to central Mexico, Mississippi, and northern Virginia (Gardali and Ballard 2000). It breeds in mature deciduous woodlands, often near water. Throughout its range it is frequently associated with riparian forests dominated by cottonwoods and poplars (Gardali and Ballard 2000). It requires large trees with a semi-open canopy, but the understory does not seem to matter. It can be found in urban parks and gardens, orchards, deciduous patches in pine forests, and mixed hardwood-coniferous forests, and rarely in pure coniferous forests (Gardali and Ballard 2000). In pre-colonial times it was probably a localized species of riparian woodlands in New York, and it most likely expanded its range within the state as the forests were felled. DeKay (1844) listed it as breeding in various locations across the state, and other early authors called it common in the central and western regions (Rathbun 1879, Short 1893, Reed and Wright 1909). Eaton (1914) called it a common bird of orchards and shade trees, found in nearly every village and park across the state but missing from the interior of the Catskills and Adirondacks. Bull (1974) described a similar range in New York but noted that it was rare on the coastal plain and that its population was declining in many areas because of the spraying of diseased elms. Cruickshank (1942) and Bull (1964) asserted that the Warbling Vireo was formerly common around New York City but its numbers had decreased in the early part of the 20th century. However, little evidence exists that it was ever common there. Giraud (1844) indicated that the Warbling Vireo was rare on Long Island and that although it was found in trees in the city, it was nowhere common. Griscom (1922) indicated that it had been common only as close to New York City as Ossining in Westchester County. He stated that it had been a regular summer resident in Central Park and the Bronx, but gave only a few records after 1902 and stated that it disappeared from there by around 1918. Siebenheller (1981) listed a first record of this vireo breeding on Staten Island in 1887 and indicated that it must have been gone from there by 1905. It remained rare and localized in the Coastal Lowlands for most of the 20th century (Bull 1974).

During the first Atlas period the Warbling Vireo was widely distributed across the state, missing primarily from the Central Adirondacks, Adirondack High Peaks, Western Adirondack Foothills, Central Tug Hill, and most of the Coastal Lowlands. It was more scattered in portions of the Appalachian Plateau and Catskills. The second Atlas data revealed a modest increase in the number of blocks with records of the Warbling Vireo. A dramatic expansion occurred across the Coastal Lowlands and the New York City area, where the number of occupied blocks increased 390 percent. The species was found across Staten Island and confirmed in all the New York City counties. The Warbling Vireo was still mostly absent from the Adirondack High Peaks, Central Adirondacks, Western Adirondack Foothills, and Central Tug Hill. Gaps were still apparent in portions of the Appalachian Plateau, especially in the Catskill Peaks, Mongaup Hills, and Allegany Hills.

Breeding Bird Survey data show a continuous and significant increase in Warbling Vireo numbers across the survey area since 1966, with only a few areas of significant decline (Sauer et al. 2005). BBS data for New York and the north Atlantic states (U.S. Fish and Wildlife Service Region 5) indicate significant increases of 1.7 percent each year (Sauer et al. 2005). The second Ontario Atlas reported significant declines in Warbling Vireo numbers in parts of the province, but no significant trend overall (Bird Studies Canada et al. 2006). Land-use changes in New York are apparently favorable for the Warbling Vireo, and it appears to be using human-modified landscapes to its advantage.

2000–05 Distribution Map

- ☐ Not Found
- Possible
- Probable
- ■ Confirmed

Number of Blocks

	1980–85		2000–05		Change
	No.	%	No.	%	%
Possible	1,098	35	953	27	−13
Probable	1,487	47	1,911	54	29
Confirmed	548	17	673	19	23
Total	3,133	59	3,537	66	13

Change Map

- ☐ Not Reported
- 1980–85 Atlas
- 2000–05 Atlas
- Both Atlases

Breeding Bird Survey Trend in New York

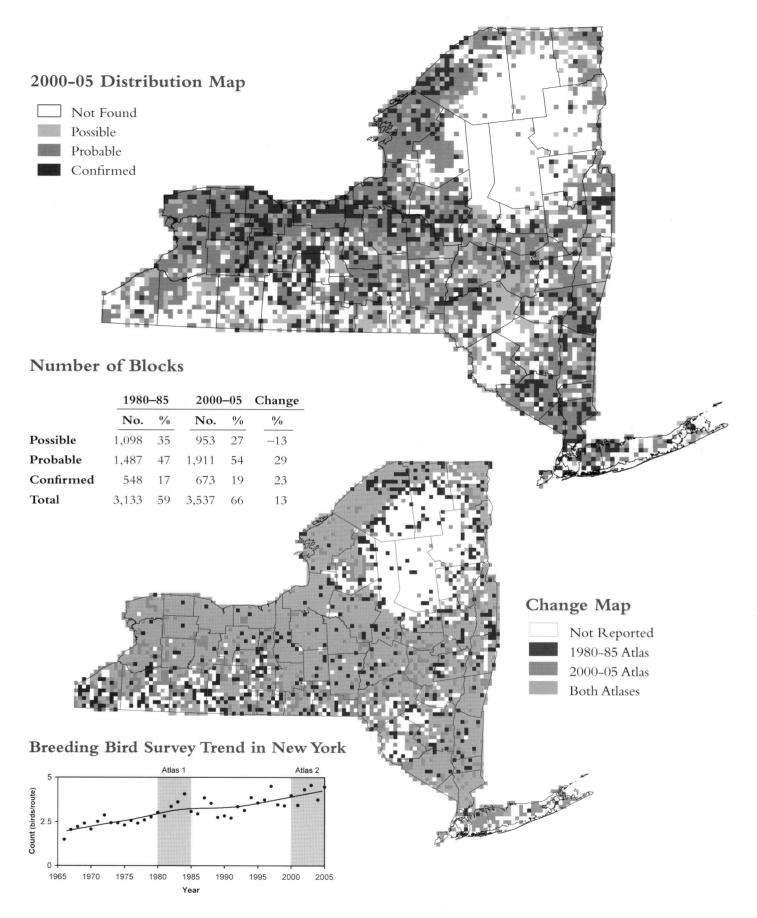

Philadelphia Vireo

Vireo philadelphicus

KEVIN J. MCGOWAN

A bird of the northern forests, Philadelphia Vireo breeds from northeastern British Columbia across Canada to New Brunswick, and in the very northern tier of the United States from North Dakota to Maine (Moskoff and Robinson 1996). Its breeding in New York represents a slightly disjunct population south of the main range. The Philadelphia Vireo breeds in early- and mid-successional deciduous woods and parklands, especially among aspens, birches, alders, and ashes (Moskoff and Robinson 1996). Eaton (1914) did not list the Philadelphia Vireo as a breeding bird in the state. He suggested that it possibly bred somewhere in the Adirondacks, but he had purposefully looked for it and failed to find it. The first summer records of the species in the state were in 1926 (Saunders 1929) and in 1933 (Carleton 1935) in Essex County, in an area recovering from a forest fire in 1903 (J. M. C. Peterson 1988k). The first "confirmed" record of breeding in the state was not until 1963 in Essex County, when two birds were observed nest-building (Sheffield and Sheffield 1963); this record would be categorized as only Probable in Atlas terms. About a dozen documented summer records were made from then until 1980 in Essex, Franklin, and Hamilton counties (Peterson 1988k).

During the first Atlas survey, the Philadelphia Vireo was found in 46 blocks scattered throughout the Adirondack High Peaks, Central Adirondacks, Eastern Adirondack Foothills, Sable Highlands, Western Adirondack Foothills, and Central Tug Hill. Peterson (1988k) noted that much suitable successional habitat was available in the Adirondacks and in other areas of the state where the vireo could potentially breed, and suggested that it would eventually move out of the first breeding areas as they matured into unsuitable habitat. During the second Atlas survey, the Philadelphia Vireo was found in 72 blocks, 13 outside of the Adirondacks. It was confirmed breeding on the St. Lawrence Plains in northern St. Lawrence and Franklin counties, and re-ported as Possible in the Champlain Valley. It disappeared from southern Hamilton County, an area of concentration during the first Atlas period, and spread to northern Franklin County. The number of blocks with records in the Tug Hill region increased from two to ten. Overall, it was reported in only seven blocks during the second Atlas period where it had been present during the first Atlas period. Because of its dull coloring and the similarity of its song to that of the much more common Red-eyed Vireo, the Philadelphia Vireo could be easily overlooked by observers.

Much of the breeding range of the Philadelphia Vireo is outside the area covered by Breeding Bird Survey routes, but the data that exist show a significant positive trend in numbers across the survey area since 1966, and especially since 1980 (Sauer et al. 2006). The BBS data from New York are too sparse to provide trustworthy patterns. In the northern sections of Ontario, the population increased significantly from the first Breeding Bird Atlas study period to the second (Bird Studies Canada et al. 2006). The maturation of abandoned farmland, burned forests, and clear-cuts back to forest has provided much new potential breeding habitat for the Philadelphia Vireo. As the forests mature, these areas will become unsuitable, but at the moment a great deal of habitat is available for this species in New York.

2000-05 Distribution Map

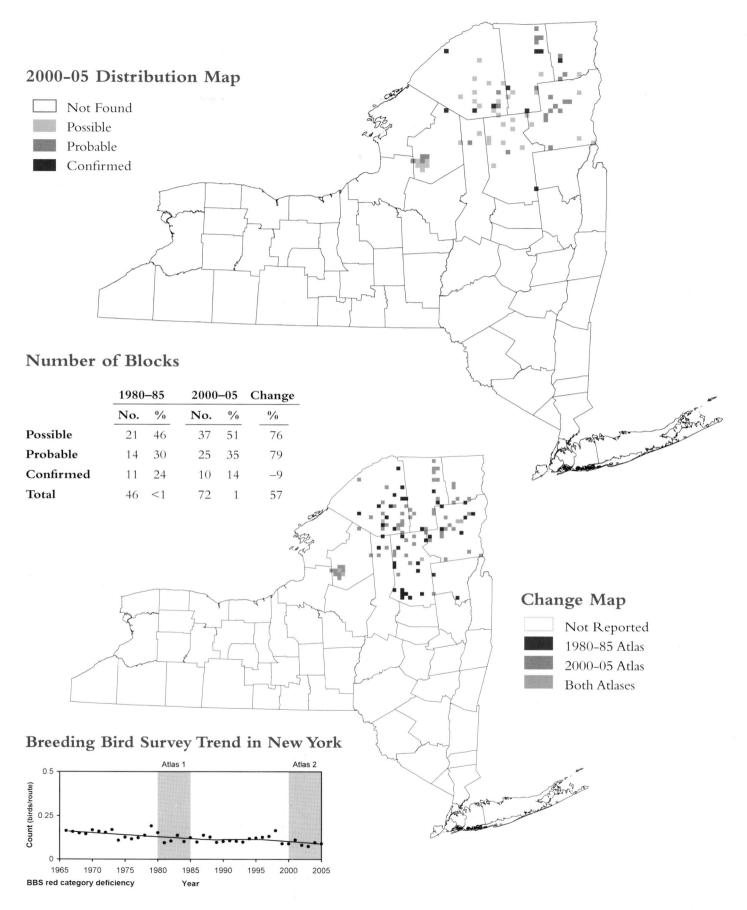

- ☐ Not Found
- Possible
- Probable
- Confirmed

Number of Blocks

	1980–85		2000–05		Change
	No.	%	No.	%	%
Possible	21	46	37	51	76
Probable	14	30	25	35	79
Confirmed	11	24	10	14	–9
Total	46	<1	72	1	57

Change Map

- ☐ Not Reported
- 1980-85 Atlas
- 2000-05 Atlas
- Both Atlases

Breeding Bird Survey Trend in New York

BBS red category deficiency

Red-eyed Vireo

Vireo olivaceus

KEVIN J. MCGOWAN

The Red-eyed Vireo is one of the most common and vocally conspicuous birds of the eastern forests. It breeds from southeastern Alaska eastward to Newfoundland, and from Canada southward to Oregon, Idaho, South Dakota, eastern Texas, and Florida. It breeds in deciduous and mixed deciduous–coniferous forests and is most abundant in the forest interior (Cimprich et al. 2000). It does not require mature forests but can be found in alder thickets, aspen groves, and urban areas and parks with large trees. As an interior-forest bird, it was probably abundant before European settlement in New York, decreased in numbers with the loss of forests in the 19th and early 20th centuries, and increased again along with the regrowth of forests across the state. DeKay (1844) listed it as common throughout the state, and almost no author has disagreed with that assessment since. Cruickshank (1942) thought that its population was declining in heavily settled areas around New York City, but Bull (1964) considered it very common in the same region.

The first Atlas reported the Red-eyed Vireo as breeding across the entire state, in all ecozones. It was the eighth most common species reported. It was missing only from scattered blocks and the heavily urban areas of New York City. The second Atlas survey revealed little change for the Red-eyed Vireo, with a slight increase in the total number of blocks with records, moving it up to the sixth most reported species. Again, the Red-eyed Vireo was found in all ecozones. Small gaps in its distribution occurred in the heavily agricultural area where the Great Lakes Plain dips into the Finger Lakes region (mostly Yates County), the most urban areas of New York City, and central Suffolk County.

Breeding Bird Survey data show that Red-eyed Vireo numbers have been increasing survey-wide since 1966 at a rate of 1.2 percent per year (Sauer et al. 2005). Only in the Western BBS Region, where the species is least common, does a nonpositive trend exist. BBS data for New York show an even stronger positive trend, with a yearly increase of 2.3 percent (Sauer et al. 2005). Because the Red-eyed Vireo is already a common and widespread species, Atlas methods cannot detect much change. Found in 96 percent of all blocks, it has little room for an increase. The continuing maturation of forests and the loss of farmland in New York favor the Red-eyed Vireo. Although urbanization should negatively affect it, the vireo seems tolerant of some urbanization and is able to survive in a wide variety of habitats.

2000-05 Distribution Map

- ☐ Not Found
- Possible
- Probable
- Confirmed

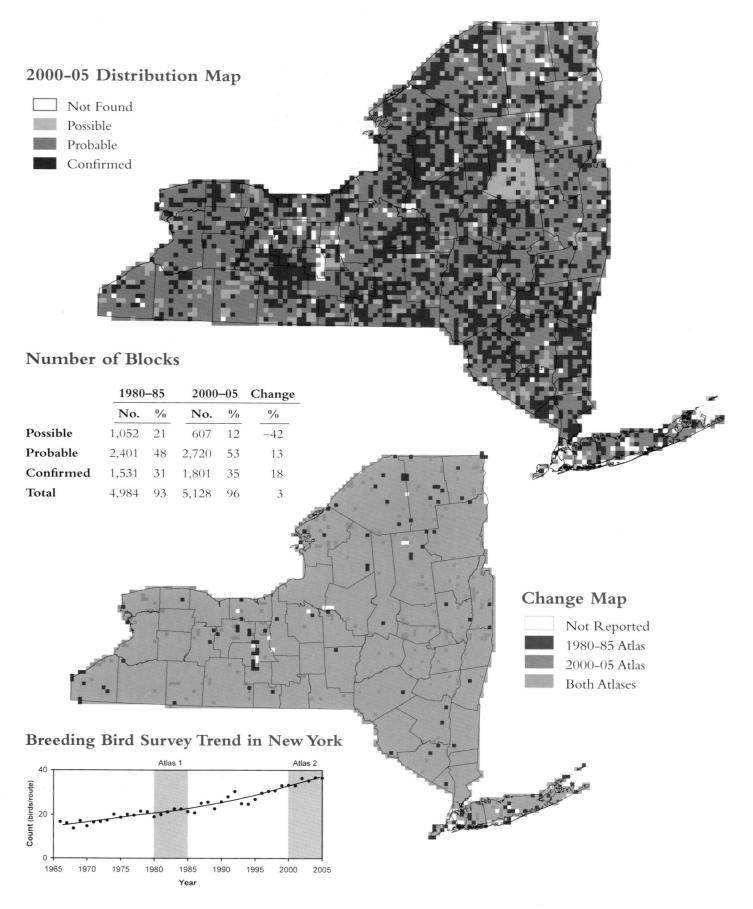

Number of Blocks

	1980–85		2000–05		Change
	No.	%	No.	%	%
Possible	1,052	21	607	12	−42
Probable	2,401	48	2,720	53	13
Confirmed	1,531	31	1,801	35	18
Total	4,984	93	5,128	96	3

Change Map

- ☐ Not Reported
- 1980-85 Atlas
- 2000-05 Atlas
- Both Atlases

Breeding Bird Survey Trend in New York

**Common Raven
and Gray Jay in the
Adirondacks**

The quiet of deep Adirondack forests is broken with the gurgles and croaks of the Common Raven and awakened by the mischief of the Gray Jay. About 40 percent of the park's almost six million acres is classified as wilderness or wild forest. In this winter scene an unfortunate moose blends into the intricate ecosystem.

Gray Jay
Perisoreus canadensis

KEVIN J. McGOWAN

The Gray Jay is a denizen of the boreal and sub-alpine forests of North America, reaching from Alaska to Newfoundland, southward to New England and New York, and in the mountains to Arizona. Historical changes in its distribution across its range have been minor (Strickland and Ouellet 1993). Within New York it has been restricted to the Adirondacks throughout recorded history, where changes are more difficult to track. The Gray Jay prefers medium to mature boreal forest, especially where spruces are present (Strickland and Ouellet 1993). In New York the bird is most commonly found in black spruce at lower elevations, but it does occur in white and red spruce on higher ground (J. M. C. Peterson 1988g). The logging of spruce for timber and pulp and its replacement with red pine, Scotch pine, and Norway spruce, especially after extensive fires, may have made large areas of the Adirondacks unsuitable to the Gray Jay and resulted in the splintering of some populations (Peterson 1988g). It was once reported to be a fairly common resident of Clinton County (Eaton 1914) but was considered a rare to accidental winter visitor there by the 1970s, with the last report occurring in 1974 (Mitchell and Krueger 1997).

The first Atlas results showed the Gray Jay breeding in only 95 blocks, all within the Adirondacks. Only two were in the High Peaks region, with the others in the Central Adirondacks and the Western Adirondack Foothills. Peterson (1988g) suggested that the discontinuity between the two High Peaks blocks and the other observations might represent a real separation. The second Atlas data revealed roughly the same distribution but with many minor shifts. Again, most observations were within the Central Adirondacks and Western Adirondack Foothills, with three in the High Peaks. The Gray Jay was seen in slightly more blocks during the second Atlas survey, and the Essex County blocks did not appear as disjunct as in the first Atlas. It is difficult to know whether the minor changes in distribution between the two Atlas periods represent true local movements or just different coverage, but the latter could well account for the differences. The Gray Jay was found in 50 of the same blocks it was sighted in during the first survey, was "lost" from 45 blocks, and appeared in 64 new blocks. Although the record from southwestern Hamilton County extended the range southward to the latitude of the Black Creek Lake, Herkimer County, locality reported by Bull (1974), and additional observations were made to the northeast of those reported in the first Atlas, this species did not reclaim Clinton County.

The Gray Jay is not well covered by the Breeding Bird Survey in much of its range, but what data do exist show no continent-wide trends (Sauer et al. 2005). New York data are particularly sparse, with no Gray Jays appearing on BBS routes since 1971. BBS data for U.S. Fish and Wildlife Service Region 5, based primarily on data from Maine, show an increasing but insignificant trend (Sauer et al. 2005). Although the population in Algonquin Park in southern Ontario appears to be declining (Strickland and Ouellet 1993), the second Ontario Breeding Bird Atlas reported little change in Gray Jay populations in the province and found a significant increase on the Northern Shield (Bird Studies Canada et al. 2006). In New York, the Gray Jay should remain a moderately common Adirondack specialty for years to come.

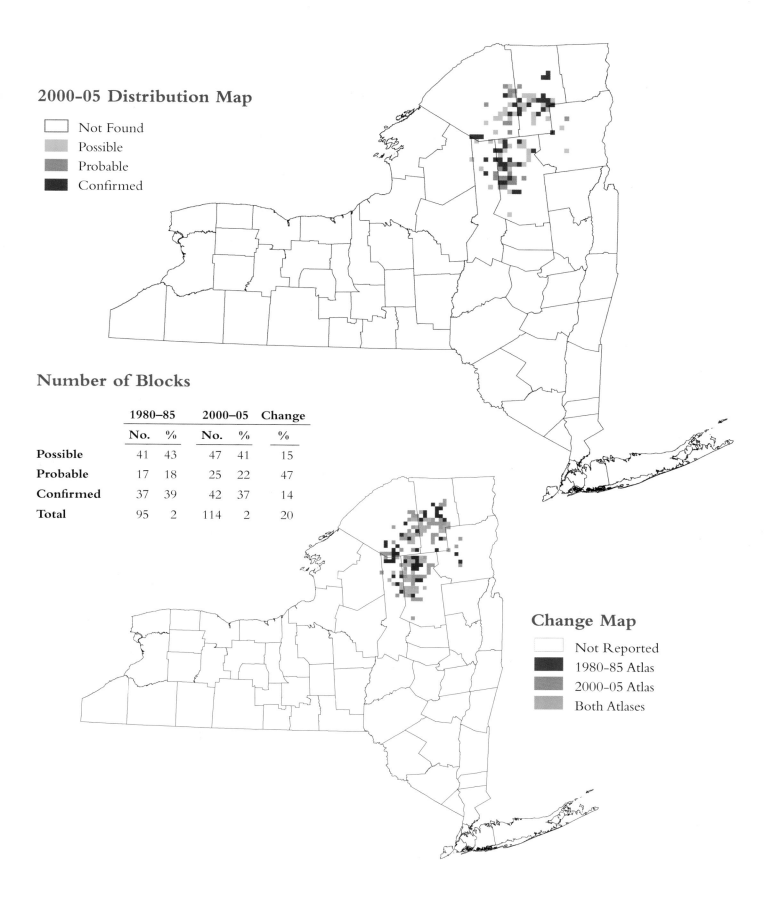

2000-05 Distribution Map

- Not Found
- Possible
- Probable
- Confirmed

Number of Blocks

| | 1980–85 | | 2000–05 | | Change |
	No.	%	No.	%	%
Possible	41	43	47	41	15
Probable	17	18	25	22	47
Confirmed	37	39	42	37	14
Total	95	2	114	2	20

Change Map

- Not Reported
- 1980-85 Atlas
- 2000-05 Atlas
- Both Atlases

Blue Jay
Cyanocitta cristata

KEVIN J. McGOWAN

The Blue Jay is a common forest bird of North America east of the Rocky Mountains, ranging from southern Canada to the Gulf Coast. The Blue Jay was probably always common in New York. Although now it is abundant in parks and suburbs, it is primarily a bird of forests and forest edges. It subsists in large part on mast. Acorns, beechnuts, chestnuts (formerly), hickory nuts, and hazelnuts are known to be important in its diet (Tarvin and Woolfenden 1999) and would have been present in abundance across much of the state in pre-colonial times. The destruction of the forests in the early 1800s may have moved the Blue Jay to remnant forest patches. Rathbun (1879) called it an uncommon resident of central New York. Short (1893) described it as local in distribution in western New York, where Eaton (1914) said that it was confined mostly to the larger forests, swamps, and ravines. Eaton (1914) considered it a resident in all portions of the state but common only in less settled areas, preferring evergreen or mixed woodlands. By the 1950s the Blue Jay was considered common in western New York, and it then occasionally began to be found in cities (Beardslee and Mitchell 1965). Griscom (1932) listed the Blue Jay as common and present in all wooded sections around New York City and Long Island, absent only from the outer beaches, Gardiners Island, and Orient. This situation held true into the 1940s (Cruickshank 1942), but subsequently the species became common even in those latter areas (Sibley 1988c). Bull (1974) listed the species as widely distributed throughout the state although relatively scarce in the more heavily forested portions at higher elevations.

The Blue Jay was one of the most common birds reported in the first Atlas, ranking fourth in occurrence. It was found throughout the state in all regions and habitats, and no pattern could be seen in the few blocks without records. The second Atlas data revealed little change, with the Blue Jay being the third most reported species. Again it was found throughout the state with little pattern to the areas where it was absent. Breeding was confirmed in roughly half the blocks in which the bird was seen. The Blue Jay is surprisingly quiet around its nest, and nests were discovered in only 7 percent of blocks. Most confirmations (56 percent) were observations of recently fledged young, as was true for the first Atlas.

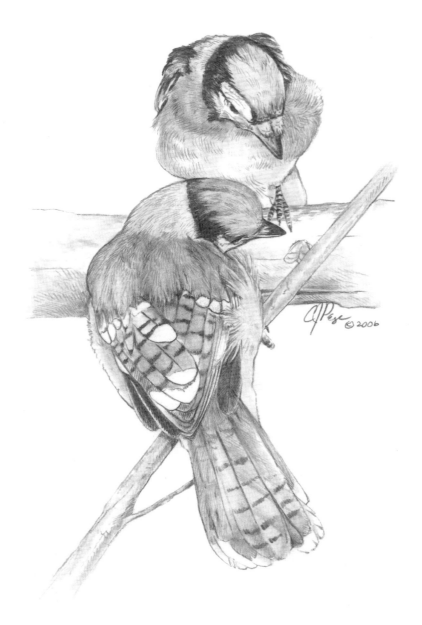

Breeding Bird Survey data show a slight but significant decline in Blue Jay numbers across the continent over the last 40 years (Sauer et al. 2007). The New York BBS data do not show the same trend, although the data for the north Atlantic states (U.S. Fish and Wildlife Service Region 5) do indicate a significant decline (Sauer et al. 2007). The Blue Jay spread westward in the 1940s, with dramatic increases in the 1970s (Tarvin and Woolfenden 1999). The spread was aided by the planting of shelterbelts and wooded residential areas across the Great Plains, as well as by the development of urban areas (Tarvin and Woolfenden 1999). This jay is susceptible to the West Nile virus (WNV) (Komar et al. 2003), and the disease could have a potentially significant negative impact on jay populations. BBS data show some local declines after the outbreak of WNV but none as dramatic as in the American Crow. In New York some recovery from an initial decline is indicated by the BBS data (Sauer et al. 2007).

2000-05 Distribution Map

- ☐ Not Found
- Possible
- Probable
- Confirmed

Number of Blocks

| | 1980–85 | | 2000–05 | | Change |
	No.	%	No.	%	%
Possible	1,358	26	1,124	22	−17
Probable	1,235	24	1,496	29	21
Confirmed	2,561	50	2,557	49	0
Total	5,154	97	5,177	97	0

Change Map

- ☐ Not Reported
- 1980-85 Atlas
- 2000-05 Atlas
- Both Atlases

Breeding Bird Survey Trend in New York

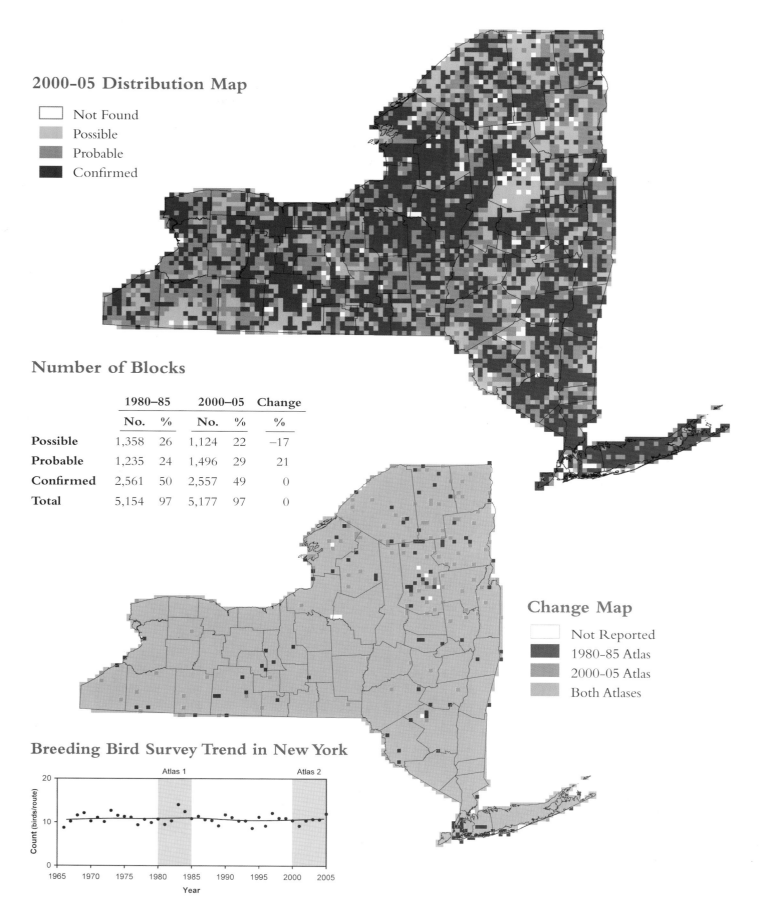

American Crow
Corvus brachyrhynchos

KEVIN J. MCGOWAN

The American Crow is a common and familiar bird throughout its range. It breeds across most of North America, being absent only from the high mountains, deserts, arctic tundra, and northwest coast. The crow prefers park-like settings where it can find trees for nesting and open ground for foraging. This rather general preference allows it to nest in a great variety of habitats. It probably evolved as a bird of river courses, beaver meadows, and fire-maintained open areas, rather than deep forests, and likely was not especially common in New York in pre-colonial times. As the forests were felled and land opened to agriculture, the American Crow undoubtedly prospered. In 1810 the crow was apparently absent from the Geneva area, where the Common Raven was common, but the situation reversed itself within 50 years as the area was developed for agriculture (Eaton 1914, Smith 1998a). DeKay (1844) considered the crow present across the state but in lower numbers in the northern and western parts where the raven was found. By 1900 the crow was breeding in every county, entering the center of the Adirondacks and Catskills along the river valleys and corridors of cleared land, while the raven was nearly exterminated (Eaton 1914). Bull (1974) considered the American Crow a thriving and widespread breeder in the state, most numerous in agricultural districts.

During the first Atlas survey, the American Crow was found throughout the state, absent only from parts of the Central Adirondacks, High Peaks, and Catskill Peaks. Present in 93 percent of all blocks, it was the ninth most prevalent species. The second Atlas data revealed little change in distribution. Still the ninth most prevalent species in the Atlas database, it was reported in only slightly more blocks. It was unreported, once again, from blocks in the center of the Catskill Peaks, Central Adirondacks, Adirondack High Peaks, and portions of the Western Adirondack Foothills, where it may well be missing.

American Crow populations across the continent experienced a slow, but steady

and significant increase over the last 40 years (Sauer et al. 2007). Breeding Bird Survey data in New York show a similar long-term trend, which appeared to accelerate in the 1980s. Crows moved into urban areas to roost and nest starting in the second half of the 20th century (Verbeek and Caffrey 2002). This change in habitat use might, or might not, have contributed to the simultaneous population increases, but it certainly led to the incorrect public perception of exploding populations (McGowan 2001a). The appearance of West Nile virus (WNV) in North America in 1999 (Lanciotti et al. 1999) changed the fortunes of crow populations on the continent. The American Crow appears to be uniquely susceptible to the disease (Komar et al. 2003), as WNV has had devastating effects on local populations (Yaremych et al. 2004; Caffrey et al. 2003, 2005). Although WNV outbreaks often are local in nature and may be more prevalent in urban areas (Ringia et al. 2004), the virus's effect on larger populations is beginning to become apparent. BBS data for Illinois, Indiana, and Ohio show that the WNV outbreak in 2002 caused huge drops in crow populations, plunging in just one year from record or near record high levels to the lowest in 40 years (Sauer et al. 2007). Survey-wide data showed a 20 percent drop across the continent after the 2003 season, despite the fact that the disease had not yet reached the West Coast (Sauer et al. 2007). New York BBS data do not show decreases as dramatic as in the Midwest, but numbers have declined since the arrival of WNV (Sauer et al. 2007). The long-term effects of this disease on crow populations in New York will not be known for some time, but local effects have been just as devastating as in the Midwest (Clark et al. 2006), and WNV probably will cause significant declines.

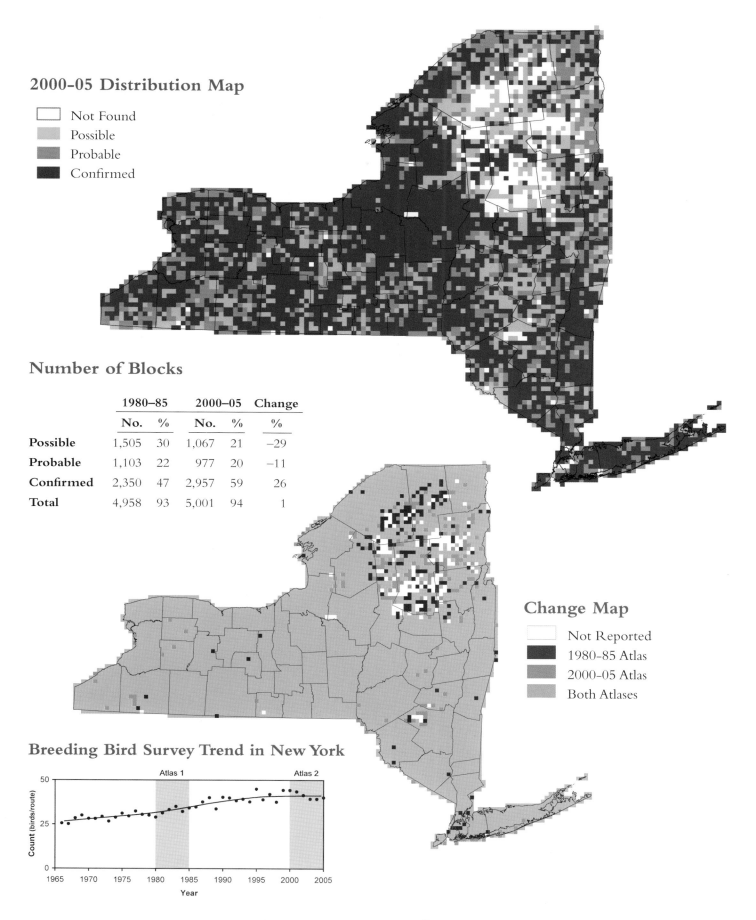

2000–05 Distribution Map

- ☐ Not Found
- Possible
- Probable
- Confirmed

Number of Blocks

	1980–85		2000–05		Change
	No.	%	No.	%	%
Possible	1,505	30	1,067	21	−29
Probable	1,103	22	977	20	−11
Confirmed	2,350	47	2,957	59	26
Total	4,958	93	5,001	94	1

Change Map

- ☐ Not Reported
- 1980-85 Atlas
- 2000-05 Atlas
- Both Atlases

Breeding Bird Survey Trend in New York

Atlas 1   Atlas 2

Count (birds/route)

50

25

0

1965 1970 1975 1980 1985 1990 1995 2000 2005

Year

Fish Crow
Corvus ossifragus

KEVIN J. MCGOWAN

The Fish Crow is a small crow species restricted to the southeastern United States, where it is found primarily along the coast and up large river valleys from eastern Texas to Illinois, Florida, and southern Maine. It may breed in urban areas and farmland away from the coast or other large bodies of water (McGowan 2001b). A relative newcomer to New York, the Fish Crow was not included by Giraud (1844) and was considered rare by DeKay (1844), who mentioned it as being seen occasionally along the shores of Long Island and breeding along the shore of New Jersey. By 1880 it was breeding sparingly but regularly on Staten Island (Siebenheller 1981). At the beginning of the 20th century it was found up the Hudson River as far as West Point, and on the western portion of Long Island (Eaton 1914). It subsequently spread to eastern Long Island by the 1940s (Cruickshank 1942) and up the Hudson to Ulster County by the 1970s (Bull 1974). In the 1970s a small population was discovered in Ithaca, Tompkins County, 200 km (125 mi) from the nearest known breeding site (Comar 1974, Kibbe 1975, Wells and McGowan 1991). Further movements of the Fish Crow were noted in the 1980s and 1990s up the Susquehanna River to Broome County, to Syracuse, and up the Hudson River to Saratoga Springs (Salzman 1998c).

During the first Atlas survey, the Fish Crow was found breeding throughout Long Island, Staten Island, and up the Hudson River to Albany and Rensselaer counties. Away from the coast or the Hudson, breeding was confirmed only in Ithaca but was suspected in another Ithaca block and in Vestal, Broome County. The second Atlas data showed a continuation of range expansion, with the Fish Crow reported in half-again as many blocks. Contrary to Bonney's (1988b) prediction that it would not extend up the Hudson past the end of tidal influence, it was confirmed breeding as far northward as Glens Falls and Lake George. The Fish Crow appeared to have effectively colonized the central Appalachian Plateau along the Chemung and Susquehanna rivers. It was also found along the Dela-

ware River into Sullivan County and up the Mohawk River to Schenectady and Utica. It moved away from the lower Hudson Valley into the Mongaup Hills and Neversink Highlands, and onto the Great Lakes Plain from Jefferson County to Monroe County. Although the Fish Crow appeared to follow major river systems as it spread through New York, its presence in Ithaca, Syracuse, Watertown, and near Rochester show that it can disperse to other areas as well. Confirmation of nesting is more difficult with this species than for the American Crow, as it nests later, does not frequent lawns and open fields with its fledglings, and moves it fledglings away from the nesting area relatively quickly.

The Fish Crow has been expanding its range throughout the United States through the last third of the 20th century (McGowan 2001b). It expanded up major river systems as well as moved inland from coastal areas. Populations in the heart of the range have been increasing at the same time, perhaps fueling the range expansion (McGowan 2001b). Breeding Bird Survey data show a constant increase since 1966 (Sauer et al. 2005). Too few BBS routes in New York record the species to assess changes accurately, but BBS data do show an increase in New York in the late 1970s and another in the 1990s. The West Nile virus (WNV) killed large numbers of Fish Crows when it first appeared in New York City in 1999 (Lanciotti et al. 1999), but the Fish Crow is not as susceptible to the disease as the American Crow (Komar et al. 2003). The impact of WNV on Fish Crow populations remains to be seen, but it is possible that the disease may help the Fish Crow take over areas by reducing the numbers of the American Crow, a potential competitor.

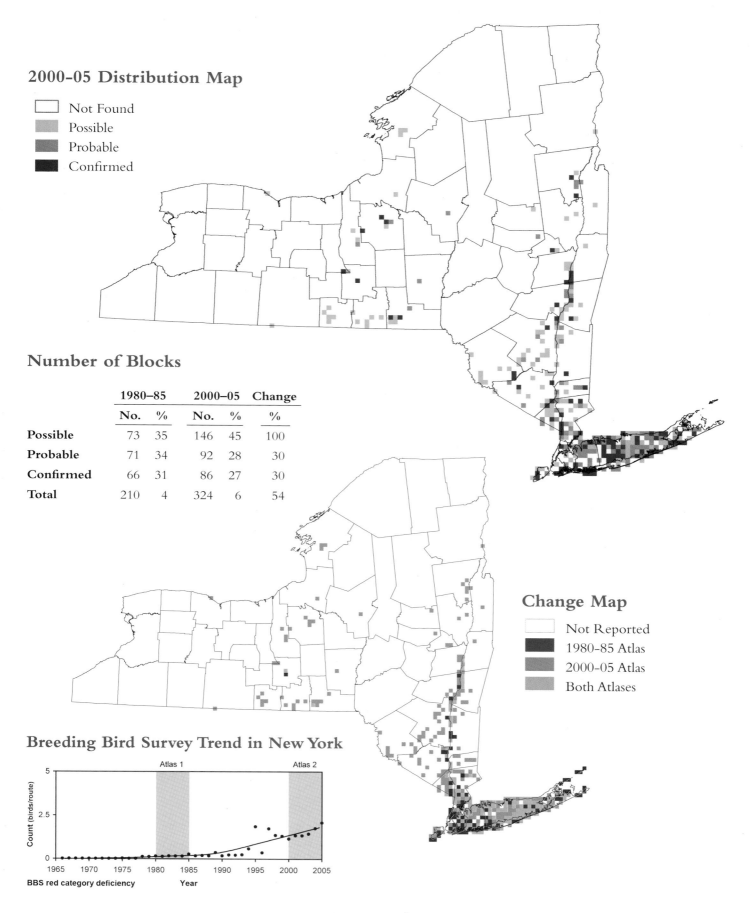

2000–05 Distribution Map

- ☐ Not Found
- Possible
- Probable
- Confirmed

Number of Blocks

	1980–85		2000–05		Change
	No.	%	No.	%	%
Possible	73	35	146	45	100
Probable	71	34	92	28	30
Confirmed	66	31	86	27	30
Total	210	4	324	6	54

Change Map

- ☐ Not Reported
- 1980–85 Atlas
- 2000–05 Atlas
- Both Atlases

Breeding Bird Survey Trend in New York

Atlas 1   Atlas 2

Count (birds/route)

5

2.5

0

1965 1970 1975 1980 1985 1990 1995 2000 2005

BBS red category deficiency   Year

Common Raven

Corvus corax

KEVIN J. McGOWAN

The Common Raven is the largest of the songbirds, and one of the most widely distributed in the world, found across North America and Eurasia. It was nearly exterminated from eastern North America by 1900, from forest destruction and persecution, and retreated to the wilderness areas of higher mountains and northern forests. In the 1600s it was probably common throughout New York, but by 1900 only a few breeding pairs remained in the Adirondacks (Eaton 1914). The population began to recover by the 1970s (Chamberlaine 1998a).

The first Atlas reported the Common Raven to be common throughout the Adirondacks, with only a few pairs found in the Tug Hill Transition, Catskill Peaks, Taconic Highlands, and Champlain Valley. A few sightings in the western portion of the Appalachian Plateau suggested an impending colonization from Pennsylvania. The second Atlas data revealed quite a different story, with confirmed nesting in the same areas and, in addition, all across the southern portion of the state, reaching the Manhattan Hills of Westchester County. Breeding activity was noted in the eastern Great Lakes Plain and even in the Mohawk Valley. Only the Coastal Lowlands and the western Great Lakes Plain were without ravens, and individual sightings have been made there outside of the breeding season (e.g., Griffith 2004, Morgante 2004). Within the Adirondacks the raven appeared to be increasing as well, with blocks with records up 175 percent.

Continued forest maturation could be partly responsible for the recovery of the Common Raven in New York, as in the East the species prefers mature forest (unlike its broad habitat preferences in many other parts of its range). Clearly, however, other explanations are necessary for its rapid movement into the many areas reported here, as the forest composition has changed little in comparison to the explosion of raven reports. Although the raven's preference for nesting on cliff ledges could be a factor, the species is not restricted to those sites and will nest in trees in the forest interior (Boarman and Heinrich 1999). Chamberlaine (1998a) suggested that suitable nesting sites would be a limiting factor in the spread of this species throughout New York, but the current wide distribution suggests that not to be the case, and the use of trees for nesting seems widespread.

Common Raven populations are increasing across the country. The first modern nesting in Massachusetts occurred in 1982 (Veit and Petersen 1993), and subsequently the population has been increasing (Petersen and Meservey 2003). Connecticut had its first modern nesting record in 1987 (Zeranski and Baptist 1990), and New Jersey in 1991 (Walsh et al. 1999). In Ontario, it has been expanding its breeding range southward (Peck 2005). Breeding Bird Survey data show increasing raven numbers continent-wide beginning in the late 1970s (Sauer et al. 2005). BBS data for New York show comparable timing, with a change to nearly geometric increases in the 1990s. Only in the southernmost eastern portion of the raven's range in the Blue Ridge Mountains of North Carolina and Virginia does the population appear to be declining (Sauer et al. 2005). Decreasing persecution and changes in its tolerance to people are probably the primary reasons for the return of the raven in many areas, including New York. The Common Raven was previously listed as a Species of Special Concern in New York but was removed from the list in 1999.

Increasing populations of these opportunistic predators in the desert southwest have presented conservation concerns because they threaten some prey species already at risk by human development (Boarman and Heinrich 1999). Ravens in New York do not appear to present the same concerns, as they are not moving into threatened habitats and appear to be occurring at such low densities that their impact on other species should be minimal.

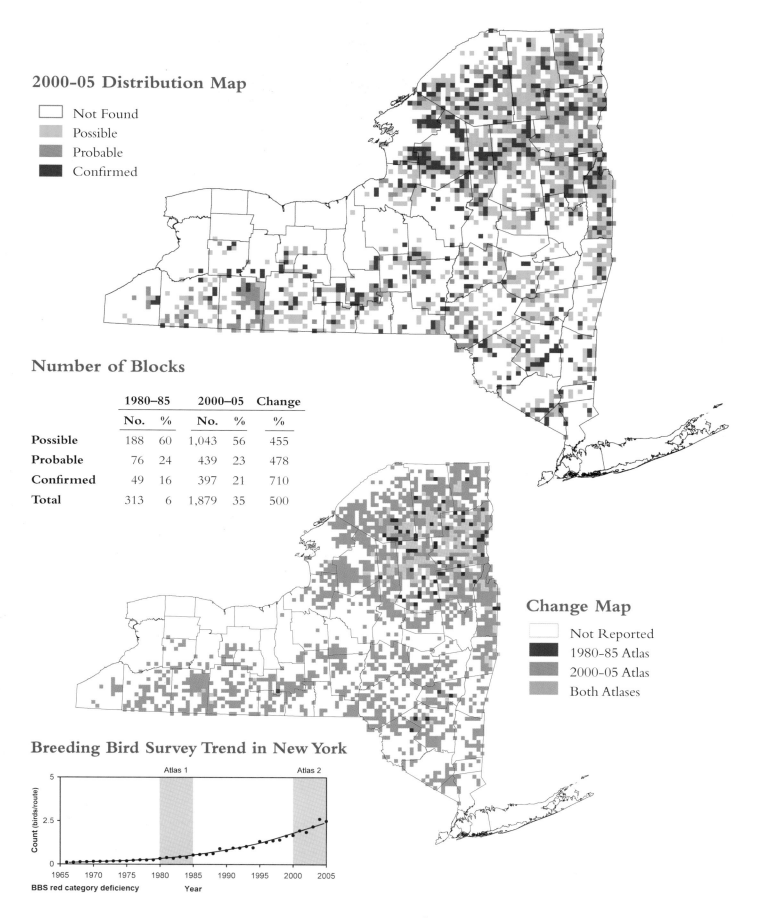

2000-05 Distribution Map

- ☐ Not Found
- Possible
- Probable
- Confirmed

Number of Blocks

	1980–85		2000–05		Change
	No.	%	No.	%	%
Possible	188	60	1,043	56	455
Probable	76	24	439	23	478
Confirmed	49	16	397	21	710
Total	313	6	1,879	35	500

Change Map

- ☐ Not Reported
- 1980-85 Atlas
- 2000-05 Atlas
- Both Atlases

Breeding Bird Survey Trend in New York

BBS red category deficiency

Barn and Tree swallows on a dairy farm

Dairy barns and other farm buildings provide ready-made sites for nesting swallows and a wealth of insect prey items. This arrangement benefits both the farmer and the birds.

Horned Lark
Eremophila alpestris

CHARLES R. SMITH

The Horned Lark nests earlier than any other native New York songbird; Bull (1974) reported a nest for 28 February with snow on the ground. Ranging across North America and Eurasia, the lark is distributed as a permanent resident throughout the lower 48 states, north of Florida, and as a breeding species throughout much of Canada, except for the interior boreal forest regions (Beason 1995). A bird of open, barren country, the Horned Lark reaches its greatest abundance in the short-grass prairie regions west of the Mississippi River (Sauer et al. 2005). It became established as a breeding species in the northeastern states in the wake of settlement and clearing of land for agriculture (Eaton 1914, Bent 1942, Bull 1974). DeKay (1844) and Giraud (1844) mentioned the lark only as a migrant along the coast, and the first definite breeding record occurred in 1875 near Buffalo (Bull 1974). The species quickly spread across the agricultural areas of the state, and Eaton (1914) commented on the dramatic increase in the numbers of the lark in New York and surrounding states. Bull (1974) said it bred in every county in the state. The species has adapted well to modern agriculture, often nesting and fledging young before plowed fields are planted in spring. It continues to occupy active pastures and fields planted with corn, beans, and potatoes well into mid-summer. Pickwell (1931) described Horned Lark habitats in New York to include old meadows, plowed fields, pastures, potato and cabbage fields, racetrack grounds, golf courses, sheep pastures, and sandy barrens. Along with the Vesper Sparrow, the Horned Lark prefers the least vegetated of the areas frequented by birds of open lands and grasslands (Wiens 1969).

During the first Atlas survey, the Horned Lark was found across the lowlands of New York, especially in the Great Lakes Plain, central Appalachian Plateau, Mohawk Valley, and Coastal Lowlands. The second Atlas data showed a similar distribution across the state, but it became more patchy, especially on the Appala-

chian Plateau. The Horned Lark showed a 37 percent decrease in the number of blocks with records and declines in every ecozone, with a notable 62 percent decrease in the Coastal Lowlands. Because it nests early, the Horned Lark may not be detected well by atlasers, and its breeding range in New York may be greater than that reported for either Atlas.

Breeding Bird Survey data for the Horned Lark show a population decline throughout most of its continental range since 1966 (Sauer et al. 2005). In New York the Horned Lark's pattern of change in relative abundance is one of a 4.7 percent decline per year over the period 1966–2005, and 1 percent per year over the period 1980–2005; both rates of change are statistically significant (Sauer et al. 2005). Because of its early nesting and the later timing of Breeding Bird Surveys (typically during June in New York), the BBS data may not represent accurately the relative abundance for the Horned Lark, but there is no reason to believe that BBS trends are inaccurate. As for many other breeding bird species of grasslands and open lands, the gradual decline in the population of the Horned Lark in New York and the Northeast coincides with the patterns of declining agriculture, regrowth of forests, and suburban and urban development described by other researchers (Caslick 1975, Nicholson 1985, Smith et al. 1993, Smith and Marks this volume). Partners in Flight does not identify any specific North American conservation needs for the Horned Lark, in part because of its extensive worldwide range (Rich et al. 2004), but it is identified as a Species of Special Concern in New York. The Horned Lark is considered a Threatened species in Connecticut, where forest, woodlands, and suburban and urban areas are the prevalent landcover types (Mitchell et al. 2000). This species is likely to benefit from efforts to manage habitats for other open-land and grassland nesting birds.

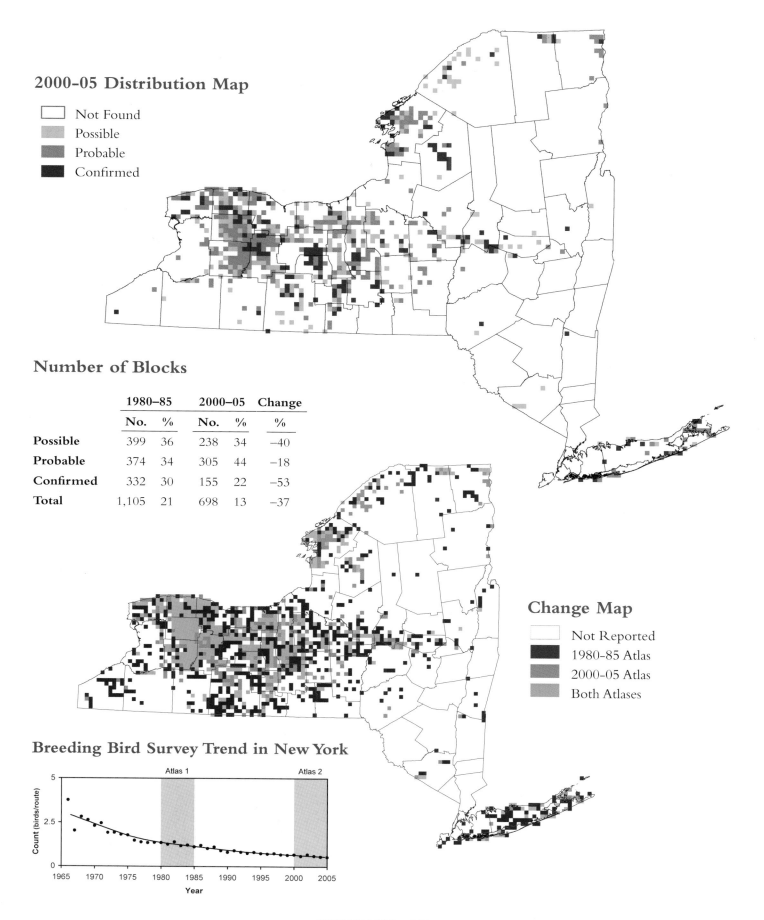

2000–05 Distribution Map

- [ ] Not Found
- Possible
- Probable
- Confirmed

Number of Blocks

	1980–85		2000–05		Change
	No.	%	No.	%	%
Possible	399	36	238	34	−40
Probable	374	34	305	44	−18
Confirmed	332	30	155	22	−53
Total	1,105	21	698	13	−37

Change Map

- [ ] Not Reported
- 1980–85 Atlas
- 2000–05 Atlas
- Both Atlases

Breeding Bird Survey Trend in New York

Atlas 1   Atlas 2

Count (birds/route)

Year

Purple Martin

Progne subis

MATTHEW D. MEDLER

New York's largest swallow species, the Purple Martin breeds across much of eastern North America, ranging from the Great Plains to the Atlantic Coast; several disjunct western populations occur from the Pacific Northwest to central Mexico (Brown 1997). New York is near the northeastern limit of the species's range, which extends into Quebec, New England, and the Maritime Provinces (Brown 1997). Eastern martins are almost entirely dependent on birdhouses and are thus found only near human habitation, but western birds still nest largely in natural cavities (Brown 1997). While Sibley (1988m) asserted that "the habitat of the Purple Martin must be near water," Brown (1997) did not note any current preference among eastern martins for water or any other general habitat feature. Eaton (1914) described the Purple Martin as a widespread but very local breeder, largely restricted to populated areas of Long Island and eastern, northern, and western New York. Because of the effects of nest-site competition from the House Sparrow, he estimated that "only one-half or one-third of the villages and cities which were summer homes of this species fifty years ago" were still inhabited by martins (Eaton 1914). In the New York City area, Bull (1964) also noted a rapid decline in martin numbers following the introduction of the House Sparrow and European Starling. In the Niagara Frontier, however, Beardslee and Mitchell (1965) commented that the martin had "held its own remarkably well" against these two nest competitors, and considered it to be a very common summer resident. Bull (1974) described this species as a local but widespread breeder in the lower elevations of the state.

During the first Atlas survey, the Purple Martin was seen largely, but not entirely, in low-lying areas near major bodies of water. It was found in largest concentrations in the Great Lakes Plain, Champlain Valley, St. Lawrence Plains, and Coastal Lowlands and along the Finger Lakes. The species was nearly absent, though, from the Mohawk Valley and was only sparsely distributed in the Hudson Valley.

While not found in most higher-elevation areas, it did occur above 305 m (1,000 ft) in many blocks in the Cattaraugus Highlands. The Purple Martin's distribution during the second Atlas survey was largely unchanged, but it was reported from nearly 40 percent fewer blocks. Major declines were evident almost everywhere, including the Great Lakes Plain, Champlain Valley, and St. Lawrence Valley. The Coastal Lowlands was the only area of abundance to show an increase. The Atlas likely provides an accurate picture of the Purple Martin's current statewide distribution because of the species's reliance on artificial nesting sites in human-inhabited areas.

Breeding Bird Survey data for this species show a significant annual increase of 2.4 percent for the Northeast (U.S. Fish and Wildlife Service Region 5) from 1966 to 2005, but no significant statewide or survey-wide trend for this period (Sauer et al. 2005). In Ontario, the Purple Martin experienced a significant annual decrease of 4 percent from 1980 to 2005 (Sauer et al. 2005), and the second Ontario Atlas reported a significant decline in all three southern regions of the province (Bird Studies Canada et al. 2006). Causes of large-scale Purple Martin population changes are not well understood but may include usurpation of nest sites by sparrows and starlings and, in the northern part of this insectivore's range, prolonged adverse weather conditions (Brown 1997). On a local scale, active management efforts, especially the erection of birdhouses and the exclusion of nest competitors, can be highly effective in increasing martin numbers (Brown 1997). Management and monitoring efforts should be pursued in New York to help determine the reason for the dramatic decline seen in the second Atlas data and possibly to augment the state's Purple Martin population.

2000–05 Distribution Map

- ☐ Not Found
- Possible
- Probable
- Confirmed

Number of Blocks

| | 1980–85 | | 2000–05 | | Change |
	No.	%	No.	%	%
Possible	251	26	169	29	−33
Probable	94	10	76	13	−19
Confirmed	618	64	338	58	−45
Total	963	18	583	11	−39

Change Map

- ☐ Not Reported
- 1980-85 Atlas
- 2000-05 Atlas
- Both Atlases

Breeding Bird Survey Trend in New York

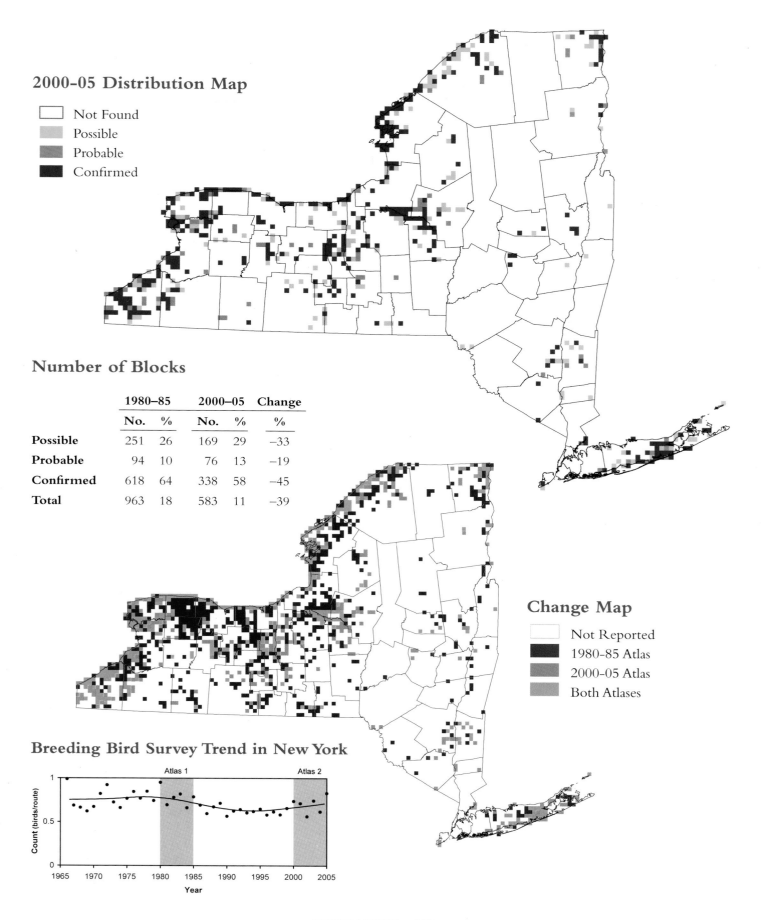

Tree Swallow

Tachycineta bicolor

MATTHEW D. MEDLER

Once known as the White-bellied Swallow, the Tree Swallow nests from tree line in Alaska and Canada through the northern United States, and breeds as far south as southern California, northern New Mexico, and northern Georgia (Robertson et al. 1992). The Tree Swallow is found in a variety of open habitats, including fields, meadows, marshes, and wooded swamps, requiring only a cavity for nesting and some open area for foraging. Eaton (1914) described the Tree Swallow as a widespread breeder, occurring in all parts of the state, but noted that it was much less common and more locally distributed in "the southern counties." This status as a scarce local breeder in southeastern New York was first suggested by Giraud (1844) and later echoed by Griscom (1923), Cruickshank (1942), and Bull (1964, 1974). This swallow was also historically uncommon in western New York, with Short (1893) noting that it was "not as common as most of our swallows." Beardslee and Mitchell (1965) considered the Tree Swallow to be a common but local breeder in the Niagara Frontier. In central New York, Rathbun (1879) depicted the species as an abundant breeder, and Reed and Wright (1909) described it as a "common summer resident." In the Adirondack High Peaks and adjacent Western Adirondack Foothills, Saunders (1929) considered the Tree Swallow to be very common during early summer.

During the first Atlas survey, the Tree Swallow was found across New York, breeding in all ecozones. The Catskill Peaks, western Erie-Ontario Plain, southern Manhattan Hills, and western Coastal Lowlands were the only areas with sizable gaps in the bird's distribution. During the second Atlas period, the Tree Swallow was again absent from some blocks in the western Coastal Lowlands, but the species largely filled the distributional gaps noted in the first Atlas, and was recorded in more blocks than any other swallow. However, the second Atlas data showed a decrease in the number of occupied blocks in the Adirondack High Peaks, Western Adirondack Foothills, and Central Adirondacks. Overall, the number of Adirondack blocks with this swallow decreased nearly 11 percent, while the number of records statewide increased 4 percent. Because this species occurs conspicuously in open areas, it is likely that the Atlas map provides an accurate picture of the Tree Swallow's distribution in New York.

The Atlas results, showing a decline in the Adirondacks and an increase throughout the rest of the state, match Breeding Bird Survey trends from 1980 to 2005. During that time, the Tree Swallow experienced a significant annual decline of 4.4 percent in the Adirondacks but a significant annual increase of 2.5 percent in New York as a whole (Sauer et al. 2005). BBS trends for this same period show significant increases in Pennsylvania, New Jersey, Connecticut, and most of the rest of the United States but significant declines in northern New England, Ontario, and Quebec (Sauer et al. 2005). The second Ontario Atlas reported significant declines in the Canadian Shield but not in the southernmost portions of the province (Bird Studies Canada et al. 2006). Atlas results from the Adirondacks and Canadian Shield, both calcium-poor granitic regions, raise the question of whether calcium availability might be affecting populations in such areas (M. Wasson pers. comm.). Forest maturation on Adirondack Forest Preserve land might explain some losses in the Adirondacks, but much of the Adirondack decline occurred in parts of Franklin and St. Lawrence counties that are not in the forest preserve, and blocks recording the species increased substantially in the Catskill Peaks, which also contains forest preserve land. Local Tree Swallow increases might be due to an increased number of nest boxes in some areas, as boxes make better nest sites than natural cavities, but nest boxes are unlikely to have had an effect on the statewide population (D. Winkler pers. comm.).

2000–05 Distribution Map

- ☐ Not Found
- Possible
- Probable
- Confirmed

Number of Blocks

	1980–85		2000–05		Change
	No.	%	No.	%	%
Possible	1,063	23	716	15	−33
Probable	524	11	608	13	16
Confirmed	3,063	66	3,528	73	15
Total	4,650	87	4,852	91	4

Change Map

- Not Reported
- 1980-85 Atlas
- 2000-05 Atlas
- Both Atlases

Breeding Bird Survey Trend in New York

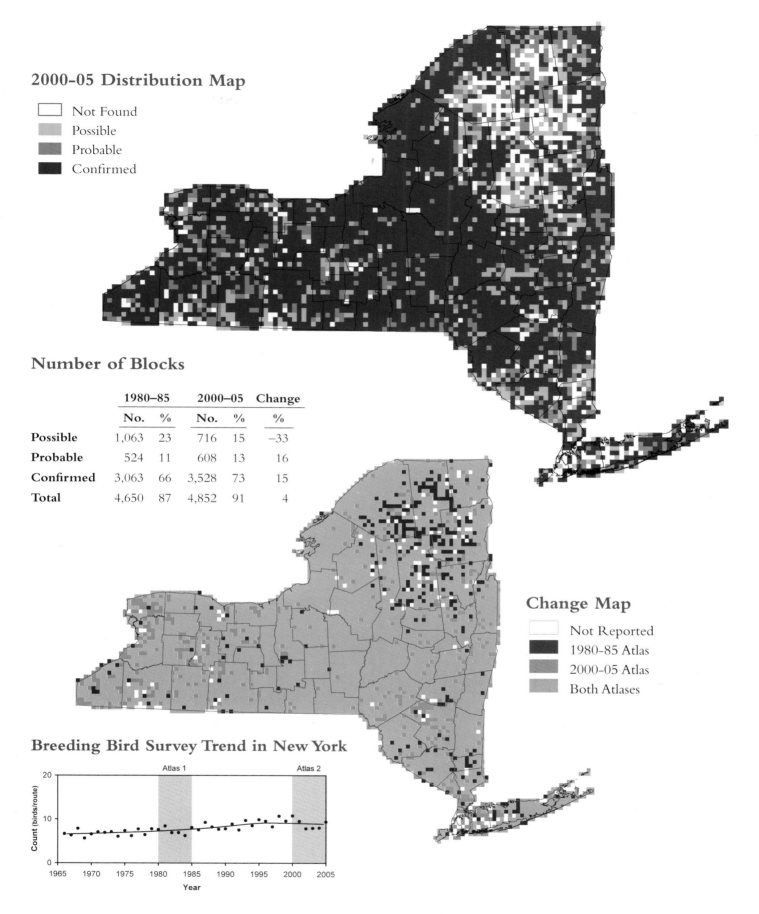

Northern Rough-winged Swallow

Stelgidopteryx serripennis

KEVIN J. MCGOWAN

The dull brown Northern Rough-winged Swallow breeds from southern Canada to southern Central America, including all of the contiguous United States. New York is near the northeastern edge of the range. It breeds in a wide variety of open habitats from sea level to elevations over 2,000 m (6,500 ft), but its local distribution depends more on nest site availability than habitat (De Jong 1996). It nests in holes in various vertical surfaces, including banks, gorges, and human structures. Unlike other hole-nesting swallows, the Northern Rough-winged Swallow usually nests alone or in small groups, although some may be associated with Bank Swallow colonies (De Jong 1996). As a species that prefers open habitats, it may have been relatively uncommon in New York in pre-colonial times. The clearing of the forests and the construction of road banks and artificial structures probably made New York more hospitable. DeKay (1844) did not count this swallow as occurring in New York, calling it instead "extralimital," found in the southern states. Rathbun (1879) listed only a single specimen from central New York. The first known nesting records were in the lower Hudson Valley and Long Island in 1872 (Bull 1974). Short (1893) listed it as breeding in western New York, where it appeared to be confined to localities where stone work provided crevices in which to breed. By the early part of the 20th century it was more common in the state. Reed and Wright (1909) called it a common summer resident in the Cayuga Lake Basin. Eaton (1914) documented it expanding its range across the southern and western parts of the state and was confident that the increase in the number of records after 1870 reflected a true expansion into the state. Eaton (1910) showed the swallow breeding all across the Great Lakes Plain, Mohawk Valley, Coastal Lowlands, and most of the Hudson Valley, with several other scattered locations. His distribution was confined mostly to the lowest elevations of the state. Bull (1974) listed it as breeding in nearly all of the river valleys and lake shores, up to the edges of the Adirondacks and Catskills.

During the first Atlas survey, the Northern Rough-winged Swallow was seen widely across the state, although it was rather localized. It was most common across the Great Lakes Plain, the northern edge of the Appalachian Plateau, and southern Hudson Valley and Manhattan Hills. It was sparsely distributed in the Adirondacks, the Catskill region, along the St. Lawrence Plains, and in the New York City area. During the second Atlas survey, this species was found in 21 percent more blocks, although the distribution in the state looked roughly the same. Increases were greatest in the Taconic Highlands, Manhattan Hills, Triassic Lowlands, Hudson Highlands, St. Lawrence Plains, and Great Lakes Plain. Gaps in the distribution were still apparent in the Central Adirondacks, Central Tug Hill, Catskill Peaks and nearby eastern Appalachian Plateau, Allegany Hills, and Cattaraugus Highlands.

The Northern Rough-winged Swallow has been expanding its range northward in the Northeast and Midwest for over 100 years (De Jong 1996). Although the increase in continent-wide populations as measured by the Breeding Bird Survey was significant between 1966 and 1979, the trend from 1966 to 2005 was not (Sauer et al. 2005). The New York BBS data show a slight but statistically significant increase since 1966. BBS data for Ontario show a significant decline, especially in the last 25 years (Sauer et al. 2005), which corresponds with the significant decline found between the two Ontario Breeding Bird Atlas survey periods (Bird Studies Canada et al. 2006). The availability of suitable nesting sites may well limit populations in specific areas, but the ability of the Northern Rough-winged Swallow to use a variety of nest sites and not just sand banks has allowed it to increase its numbers in New York while the more restricted Bank Swallow has declined.

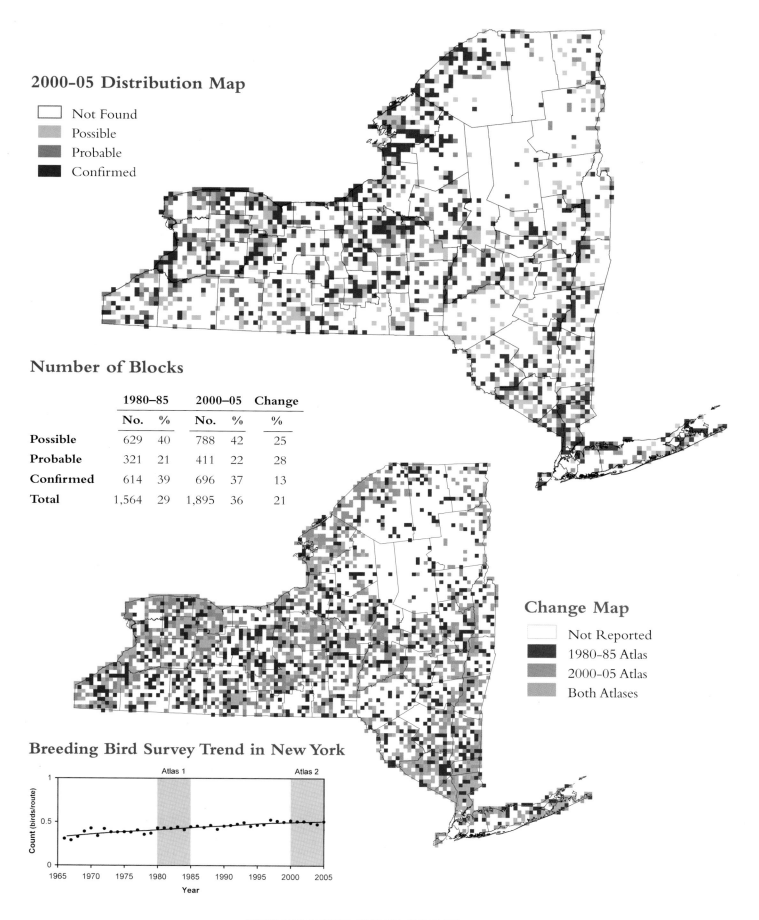

2000–05 Distribution Map

- ☐ Not Found
- Possible
- Probable
- Confirmed

Number of Blocks

	1980–85		2000–05		Change
	No.	%	No.	%	%
Possible	629	40	788	42	25
Probable	321	21	411	22	28
Confirmed	614	39	696	37	13
Total	1,564	29	1,895	36	21

Change Map

- Not Reported
- 1980–85 Atlas
- 2000–05 Atlas
- Both Atlases

Breeding Bird Survey Trend in New York

Count (birds/route) vs Year (1965–2005), with Atlas 1 and Atlas 2 shaded regions.

Bank Swallow

Riparia riparia

VALERIE M. FREER

The Bank Swallow, New York's smallest swallow, is a colonial breeder that nests in burrows it digs in vertical surfaces of sand banks, cliffs, and bluffs. One of the most widely distributed swallows in the world (Garrison 1999), it breeds in much of Eurasia and North America, including most of Alaska, non-arctic Canada, and across the United States from northeastern California to southern Pennsylvania and New Jersey. Colony sites are ephemeral and can be renewed by erosion of stream banks or new excavation of sand. Historically, all Bank Swallow colonies in North America were found in natural sites in banks along rivers, streams, lakes, and coasts. DeKay (1844) commented on this swallow digging holes in high sandy bluffs. Eaton (1914) noted it was especially abundant on the shores of Lake Ontario, in the Genesee and Hudson valleys, and on Long Island. In his studies of Oneida Lake colonies, Stoner (1936) found the largest numbers concentrated along the steep sandy banks of creeks and streams. Bull (1974) gave early recognition of the Bank Swallow's acceptance of human-made sites in noting that it nested in gravel pits and road cuts and, rarely, in sawdust or coal piles. Today, many colonies are in human-made sites, especially in eastern North America (Garrison 1999). In New York some colonies occur in natural sites, including the lakeside cliffs and dunes of Lake Ontario and the shores of Long Island. In the southern Catskill foothills and eastern portions of the Great Lakes Plain, however, almost all colonies are in artificial sites, most frequently quarries or large sand piles. In Oswego and Oneida counties, for example, colonies occur in sand piles left over from winter road care at most highway department facilities (W. Purcell pers. comm.).

During the first Atlas survey, the Bank Swallow was found in 37 percent of all blocks. It was missing only from the Catskill Peaks but was uncommon in the Central Adirondacks, Allegany Hills, and central and southern Coastal Lowlands. Concentrations were found in Orleans, Genesee, and Wayne counties within the Great Lakes Plain. In the second Atlas survey, the Bank Swallow showed the second-largest decline (after Purple Martin) of the swallows, occurring in 28 percent fewer blocks. While losses occurred in most regions of the state, they were especially apparent in portions of the Great Lakes Plain, the St. Lawrence regions, both Western and Eastern Adirondack Foothills, and the Hudson Valley. Modest concentrations appeared in Oneida, Oswego, and Madison counties, with a new cluster in northern Steuben County.

Breeding Bird Survey results show a significant decline in New York since the 1960s, and a continental decline over the last 25 years that is significant (Sauer et al. 2007). Because of the ephemeral nature of colony sites, the BBS may not represent the best long-term population-monitoring technique, whereas atlasing allows colonies to be sought out and documented more readily (Garrison 1999). The second Ontario Atlas reported a strong decline in the Southern Shield area, with less pronounced decreases south of the shield (Bird Studies Canada et al. 2006).

One factor in the decline of the Bank Swallow in New York may be the loss of nesting habitat from flood and erosion control projects. The species was locally extirpated in California as a result of river channelization and the placement of large rocks along the full bank height (Moffatt et al. 2005). Other factors include declines in sand and gravel excavation, regulation of water flow from reservoirs, and shoreline development (Garrison 1999). In addition, New York State law now requires the grading of banks following excavation, leaving slopes unsuitable for nesting. The adaptability of the Bank Swallow as exemplified by its recent use of highway department sand piles for nest sites bodes well for its future, however, in areas of the state where such piles are available.

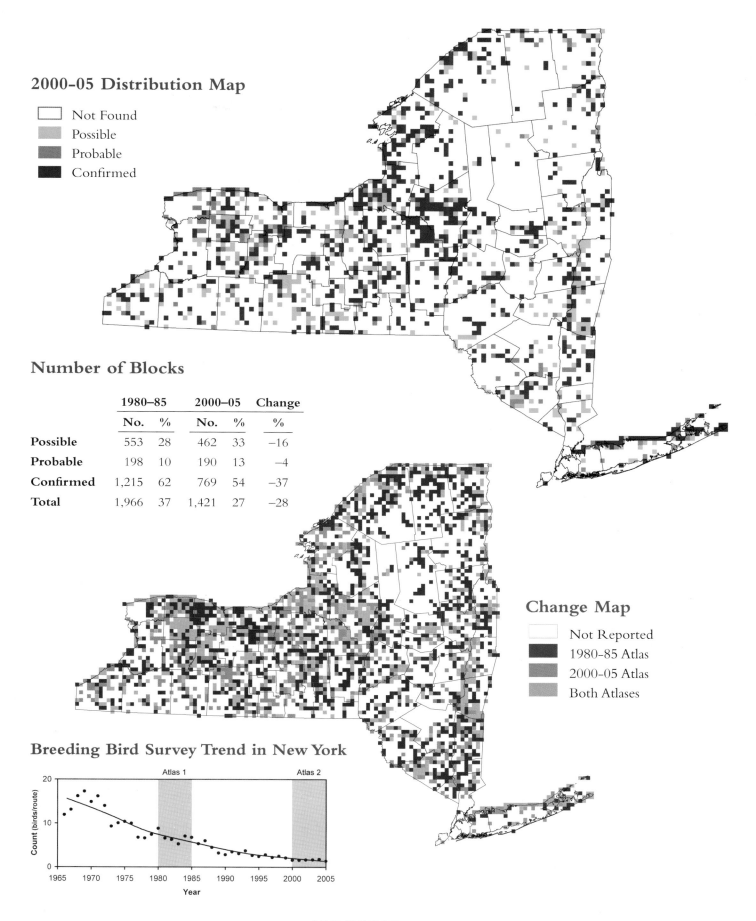

2000–05 Distribution Map

- ☐ Not Found
- Possible
- Probable
- Confirmed

Number of Blocks

	1980–85		2000–05		Change
	No.	%	No.	%	%
Possible	553	28	462	33	−16
Probable	198	10	190	13	−4
Confirmed	1,215	62	769	54	−37
Total	1,966	37	1,421	27	−28

Change Map

- ☐ Not Reported
- 1980-85 Atlas
- 2000-05 Atlas
- Both Atlases

Breeding Bird Survey Trend in New York

Cliff Swallow

Petrochelidon pyrrhonota

MATTHEW D. MEDLER

Historically found in the mountains of western North America, the Cliff Swallow expanded its range eastward during the 1800s, utilizing newly constructed bridges, buildings, and highway culverts as nesting sites (Brown and Brown 1995). The Cliff Swallow now breeds across most of North America, ranging from western Alaska to Nova Scotia and southward to central Mexico (Brown and Brown 1995). In western North America, the species still commonly nests under rock ledges, but in New York it is dependent on artificial nest sites, with cliff-nesting last documented in 1932 (Bull 1964). This swallow typically breeds in the vicinity of fields and pastures with sources of water and mud nearby (Brown and Brown 1995). New York's first Cliff Swallow record came from the southern end of Lake Champlain at Whitehall, Washington County, in 1817 (Baird et al. 1874). DeKay (1844) noted a subsequent increase, coupled with westward and southward expansion through the state. Eaton (1914) wrote that this species was found locally throughout New York and identified the Adirondacks and Catskills as areas of abundance. Eaton (1914) also noted that it had largely disappeared from many areas where it was previously very common. Evidence for local declines or disappearances exists for the Cayuga Lake Basin (Reed and Wright 1909), Niagara Frontier (Beardslee and Mitchell 1965), and Long Island (Bull 1964). Statewide, Bull (1974) considered the Cliff Swallow to be less numerous and widespread than previously, although he still described it as a locally common breeder "upstate," especially at higher elevations.

During the first Atlas period, Cliff Swallow records were concentrated in four areas of the state, with scattered records in all other ecozones except the Triassic and Coastal lowlands. The areas of abundance were the southeastern Appalachian Plateau, especially the hills and highlands bordering the Catskill Peaks; the St. Lawrence Plains and Transition; the Oswego Lowlands, Tug Hill Transition, and Black River Valley; and the Champlain Valley and Transition. The Adirondack High Peaks and Western Adirondack Foothills also contained clusters of records, but the species was otherwise scarce in the Adirondacks. This swallow's overall distribution remained similar in the second Atlas findings, but it experienced numerous small-scale, local changes, as expected with a colonial nester prone to erratically abandoning and colonizing sites. Overall, the number of blocks with Cliff Swallow records declined 12 percent, with especially large declines reported from the Adirondacks and the St. Lawrence Plains and Transition. The Manhattan Hills, Great Lakes Plain, and Appalachian Plateau all had notable increases in reports of this swallow, which is both easily detected and confirmed because of its use of artificial structures for nesting sites.

Because many Cliff Swallow colonies are not consistently occupied from year to year, trends seen in Breeding Bird Survey data must be treated with caution (Brown and Brown 1995). Survey-wide data show a significant increase from 1966 to 2005, while the sparse New York data suggest no change during the same period (Sauer et al. 2005). The second Ontario Breeding Bird Atlas reported a significant decline for this swallow for all of Ontario, but a significant increase in the province's southernmost region (Bird Studies Canada et al. 2006). At a colony level, weather-related starvation, ectoparasitism, and nesting failure caused by the House Sparrow can be important sources of mortality for the Cliff Swallow (Brown and Brown 1995). House Sparrow eradication can result in significant growth of a local colony, but the effect of such control on regional populations is unclear, as is the impact of painted barn surfaces, which were implicated for some northeastern U.S. population declines because of their purported tendency to cause more nests to fall (Brown and Brown 1995).

2000-05 Distribution Map

- ☐ Not Found
- ▨ Possible
- ▨ Probable
- ■ Confirmed

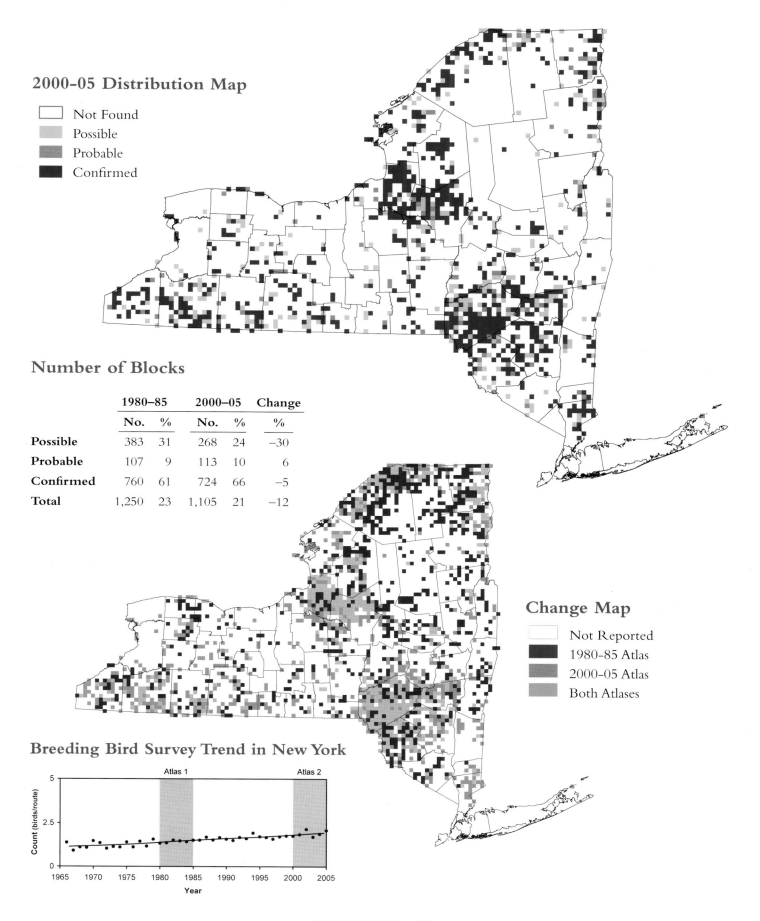

Number of Blocks

| | 1980–85 | | 2000–05 | | Change |
	No.	%	No.	%	%
Possible	383	31	268	24	−30
Probable	107	9	113	10	6
Confirmed	760	61	724	66	−5
Total	1,250	23	1,105	21	−12

Change Map

- ☐ Not Reported
- ■ 1980-85 Atlas
- ▨ 2000-05 Atlas
- ▨ Both Atlases

Breeding Bird Survey Trend in New York

Atlas 1   Atlas 2

y-axis: Count (birds/route) 0, 2.5, 5
x-axis: Year 1965 1970 1975 1980 1985 1990 1995 2000 2005

Barn Swallow

Hirundo rustica

Matthew D. Medler

The Barn Swallow is the most common and widespread swallow in the world, breeding across most of North America, Europe, and Asia (Brown and Brown 1999). The species's extensive North American range stretches from the Atlantic to the Pacific and from southern Alaska and southern Newfoundland to central Mexico (Brown and Brown 1999). Historically a cliff- and cave-nesting species, the Barn Swallow now breeds almost exclusively on buildings, bridges, and other human-made structures (Brown and Brown 1999). It is typically found where such nesting sites are near open areas, such as fields and meadows, and a source of water. This species has long been a common member of the New York State avifauna, with DeKay (1844), Rathbun (1879), Short (1893), Reed and Wright (1909), Eaton (1914), Saunders (1929), and Beardslee and Mitchell (1965) all describing the Barn Swallow as either a common, very common, or abundant summer resident. Both Eaton (1914) and Bull (1974) considered the species to be a widespread breeder, with Eaton calling it "the most generally distributed swallow" in the state.

This swallow was one of the most common species found in New York during the first Atlas survey, breeding in all of the state's ecozones and counties. The only major gaps in its distribution were in the Adirondack High Peaks, Central Adirondacks, Western Adirondack Foothills, and Central Tug Hill. The Barn Swallow continued to be widely distributed during the second Atlas survey period, again breeding in all ecozones and counties, but gaps noted in the first Atlas became more pronounced. Major declines were evident in the same ecozones where this swallow was already patchily distributed, and the species largely disappeared from the Sable Highlands. Overall, the number of Adirondack blocks with Barn Swallow decreased by nearly 28 percent. Because this bird is conspicuous and closely tied to human habitation, the Atlas map likely provides an accurate representation of this swallow's distribution in the state.

The localized Barn Swallow decline seen in the Atlas results is supported by Breeding Bird Survey data. BBS results from 1980 to 2005 show a significant annual decline of 6 percent in the Adirondacks region (Sauer et al. 2005). During the same time period, the BBS data indicate a significant annual decline of 2 percent in New York (Sauer et al. 2005), but this decline is not reflected in the Atlas results because the species is still common to abundant across much of the state. In Ontario, where BBS results for 1980 to 2005 showed a significant annual

decrease of 3.5 percent (Sauer et al. 2005), the second Ontario Atlas reported significant declines for the Barn Swallow in two of the three southern regions of the province, with the decline in the Southern Shield being especially drastic (Bird Studies Canada et al. 2006).

With its reliance on human-made structures for nesting and open spaces for foraging, the Barn Swallow has undoubtedly been negatively affected by forest maturation in the Adirondack Forest Preserve and some private lands in the Adirondack Park. The remaining major clusters of Barn Swallow records within the Adirondacks are associated with large villages such as Lake Placid, Saranac Lake, and Tupper Lake and with major roads such as Route 28. Because suitable nesting sites are limited within the Adirondacks, this species is more likely to nest colonially there (Shields and Crook 1987). In Cranberry Lake, Shields and Crook (1987) found that colonially nesting Barn Swallows experienced increased pressure from a blowfly ectoparasite that contributed to nestling mortality and nest failure. This, in turn, could reduce local breeding populations and contribute to a local decline (W. M. Shields pers. comm.). If current statewide population declines for this species continue, the next Atlas findings could show additional localized losses in other heavily forested areas.

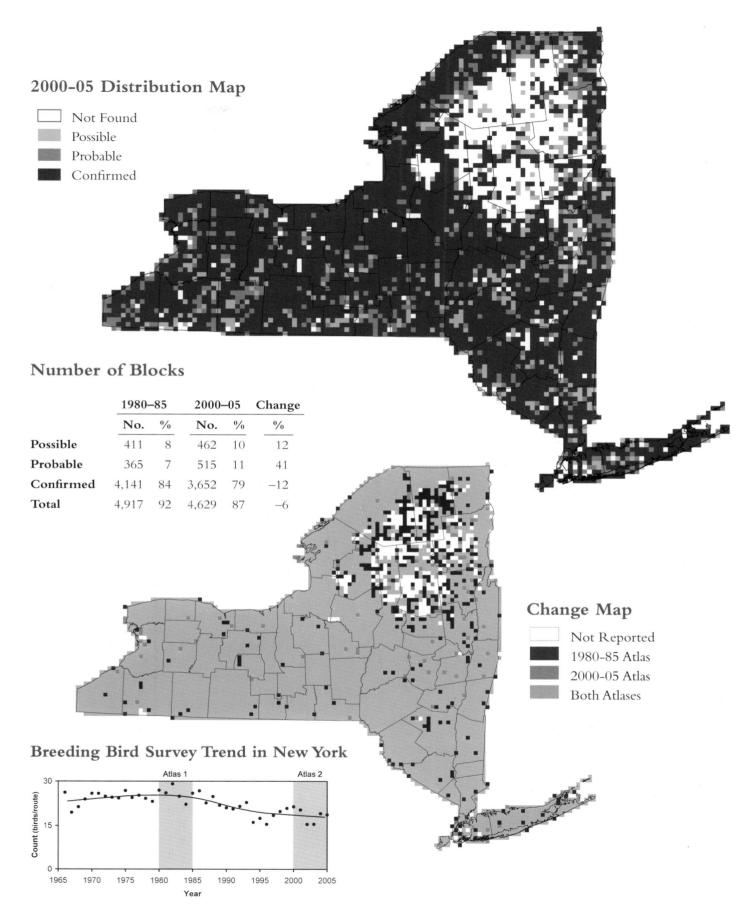

2000-05 Distribution Map

- ☐ Not Found
- Possible
- Probable
- Confirmed

Number of Blocks

	1980–85		2000–05		Change
	No.	%	No.	%	%
Possible	411	8	462	10	12
Probable	365	7	515	11	41
Confirmed	4,141	84	3,652	79	–12
Total	4,917	92	4,629	87	–6

Change Map

- Not Reported
- 1980-85 Atlas
- 2000-05 Atlas
- Both Atlases

Breeding Bird Survey Trend in New York

**Black-capped
Chickadee and Red-
breasted Nuthatch on
an Adirondack peak**

While the Red-breasted
Nuthatch is principally
a resident of New York's
northern forests, the
Black-capped Chickadee
is far less habitat specific.
These adaptable little birds
can be found most every-
where, from the timber-
lines of the Adirondacks to
New York City's Central
Park.

Black-capped Chickadee
Poecile atricapillus

KEVIN J. MCGOWAN

The Black-capped Chickadee is a familiar and conspicuous resident of the northern third of the United States and the southern two-thirds of Canada. It is found in deciduous or mixed forests, open woods, second-growth woods, old fields, parks, and suburban areas, where it is a frequent and welcomed visitor to bird feeders. This bird is seen throughout New York State and southward into Pennsylvania and New Jersey. In the 1800s, however, it was abundant in the central and western parts of the state (Rathbun 1879, Short 1893) but was considered rare in the southern parts (DeKay 1844), although Giraud (1844) ranked it as common throughout Long Island. DeKay (1844) suggested that the Carolina Chickadee might even be the resident chickadee in parts of the state, and described a specimen taken in Rockland County. No specimen currently exists, however, and this southern species is not on the official New York State list (NYSOA [2006]). By the 20th century the Black-capped Chickadee was found in all counties and was common in forests, groves, and near human habitation (Eaton 1914). It is not, however, a bird of truly urban areas, and its occurrence around New York City has varied. The first nest of the Black-capped Chickadee on Staten Island was discovered in 1885 (Siebenheller 1981). Griscom (1923) considered it common throughout the area but not breeding in Central Park or along the southern shore of Long Island. Cruickshank (1942) stated that it no longer bred in Central Park (implying that it once did) and that its population was declining throughout the city and in the more thickly settled sections of the suburbs. It was considered a rare nester on Staten Island at that point (Siebenheller 1981) and was not found breeding again in Central Park until 1954 (Carleton 1958). Subsequent to that time it became more common (Sibley 1988b), perhaps because of the increasing popularity of feeding birds.

The Black-capped Chickadee was the fifth most reported species in the first Atlas. It was found throughout the state, except for parts of New York City and some areas along the southern shore of Long Island. Absences from the Eastern Ontario Plain and the St. Lawrence Transition were likely the result of poor coverage. The second Atlas survey revealed no discernable change from the first Atlas findings. Again the chickadee was one of the most common breeding birds, sighted throughout nearly all of the state. It still was missing from some New York City and southern Long Island blocks.

Black-capped Chickadee numbers are known to fluctuate widely, and periodic winter irruptions can be caused in part by high reproduction years (Smith 1993). Breeding Bird Survey data show a significant long-term increase in numbers across the continent, with an even stronger increase in New York (Sauer et al. 2007). Some concern was expressed about a dramatic decline in chickadee populations following the West Nile Virus (WNV) outbreak of the summer of 2002 (Bonter and Hochachka 2003), but numbers returned to normal in the next year (D. N. Bonter pers. comm.). With nearly total saturation of the blocks with chickadees, the next Breeding Bird Atlas will be able to detect only losses and not increases.

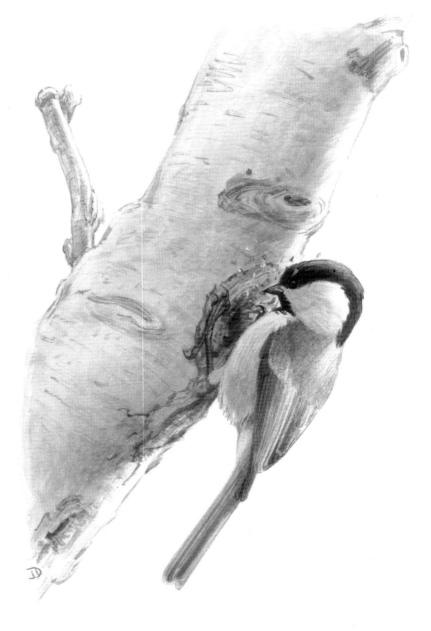

2000-05 Distribution Map

- ☐ Not Found
- Possible
- Probable
- Confirmed

Number of Blocks

	1980–85		2000–05		Change
	No.	%	No.	%	%
Possible	886	17	513	10	–42
Probable	1,003	19	1,128	22	12
Confirmed	3,260	63	3,564	68	9
Total	5,149	97	5,205	98	1

Change Map

- ☐ Not Reported
- 1980-85 Atlas
- 2000-05 Atlas
- Both Atlases

Breeding Bird Survey Trend in New York

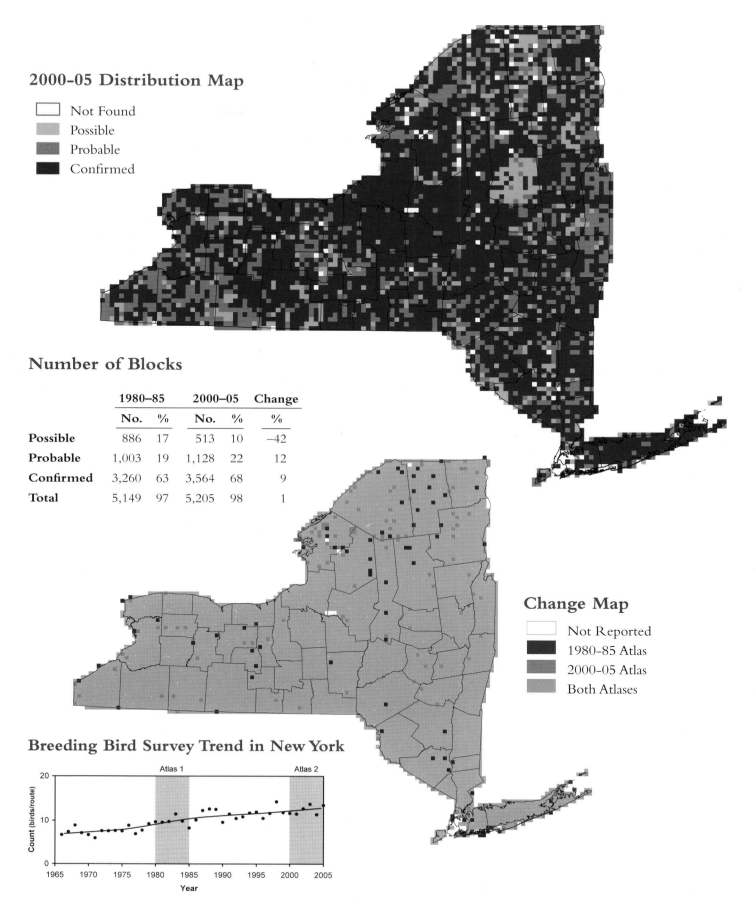

Boreal Chickadee

Poecile hudsonica

John M. C. Peterson

Far more restricted in range than the ubiquitous Black-capped Chickadee, the Boreal Chickadee is a bird of spruce-fir forests and is largely limited to the Adirondacks within New York State. The Boreal Chickadee nests to the tree line of North America across Alaska to Newfoundland and southward into spruce-fir forests of the northern United States (Ficken et al. 1996). The Adirondack population is isolated from the main range to the north. Considered rather rare in the Adirondacks by Merriam (1881), this bird was found to be as abundant as the Black-capped Chickadee in Herkimer County in 1882 by F. H. Headly (in Eaton 1914). Eaton (1914) listed 10 known breeding locations in the Adirondacks, and 60 years later Bull (1974) had increased that number to only 21. Bull (1974) noted that the chickadee was found at the edges of spruce-tamarack swamps and in high-elevation fir forests. Yunick (1984) showed evidence of an increase in Boreal Chickadee populations in the Adirondacks beginning in the 1960s, with an invasion of lower-altitude habitats for breeding.

The first Atlas results showed the Boreal Chickadee confined to the Adirondack High Peaks, Central Adirondacks, Western Adirondack Foothills, and Sable Highlands. The distribution was similar to that shown by Bull (1974), including an obvious gap along the Essex-Hamilton-Warren county boundaries where heavy logging for pulpwood in the past may have resulted in overharvesting of native spruce-balsam (J. M. C. Peterson 1988c). The main range was much the same in the second Atlas survey, but the Boreal Chickadee was found in 12 percent more blocks. Perhaps the most interesting change was a slight outward expansion. Most notable were the first records from Central Tug Hill: one in western Lewis County, 11 July 2005; a second on the Lewis-Oswego county line, 16 July 2005. This chickadee was also recorded from Warren County for the first time, found in thick spruce-fir at the 991-m (3,254-ft) summit of Crane Mountain, Johnsburg, on 20 June 2004. Birds were also found farther southeast in the Adirondack High Peaks of Essex County and farther north in Franklin County. A sin-gle sighting was made at The Gulf State Unique Area, Clinton County, on 11 July 2002, in mixed forest in an extensive flat rock area. The bird was not seen again on subsequent searches and was judged to be not breeding (J. Heintz pers. comm.), although there was some boreal habitat nearby. Apparent increases might be the result of continued reforestation of the Adirondack Park (and perhaps now the Central Tug Hill), which has provided more boreal habitat (Yunick 1984), or might reflect data from Mountain Birdwatch, a project begun during the early years of the Atlas project by the Vermont Institute of Natural Science, designed to monitor high-elevation boreal bird species (Lambert 2006). Adirondack coverage presents differing challenges of access to each generation, and imperfections in the resulting maps are bound to occur. In addition, this chickadee can be rather quiet and secretive during the breeding season (Ficken et al. 1996), and the remoteness of habitat makes actual numbers difficult to survey.

As is true for most other boreal birds, few data exist to track continental trends in Boreal Chickadee populations. The Breeding Bird Survey does not cover most of this bird's breeding range, but available data show a significant decline survey-wide, even though the trend for the last 25 years was not quite significant (Sauer et al. 2007). The second Ontario Breeding Bird Atlas reported no significant change in Boreal Chickadee numbers across the province, but it did find a significant increase in the Northern Shield region (Bird Studies Canada et al. 2006). Perhaps the Mountain Birdwatch program will provide additional data that will help better track the species's fortunes in this state, but at present this brown-capped favorite appears to remain secure within New York.

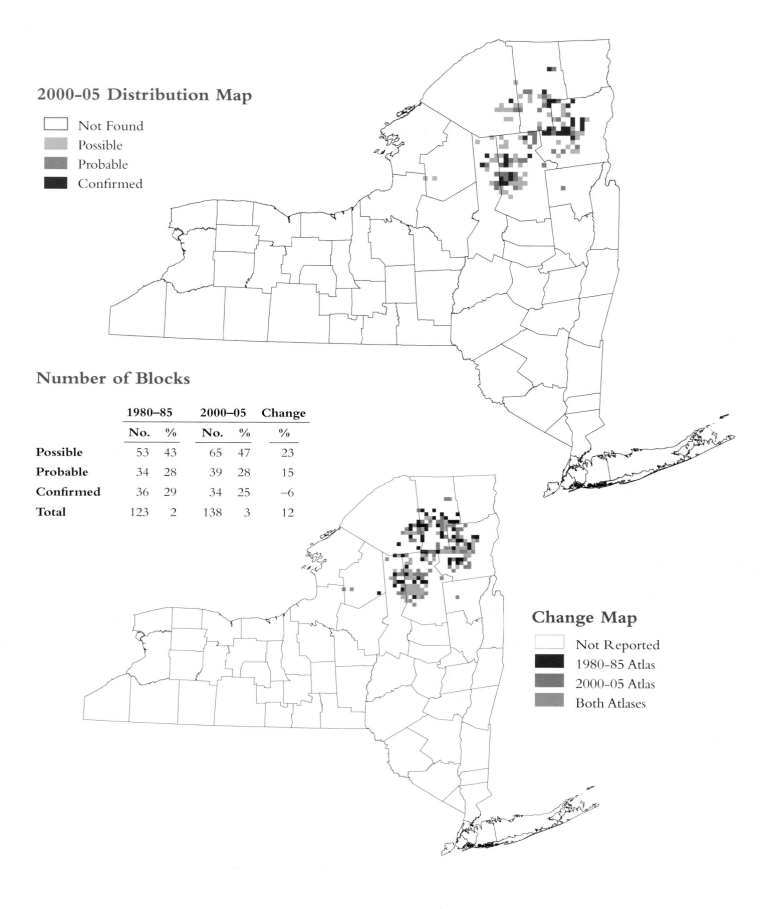

2000–05 Distribution Map

- Not Found
- Possible
- Probable
- Confirmed

Number of Blocks

	1980–85		2000–05		Change
	No.	%	No.	%	%
Possible	53	43	65	47	23
Probable	34	28	39	28	15
Confirmed	36	29	34	25	−6
Total	123	2	138	3	12

Change Map

- Not Reported
- 1980-85 Atlas
- 2000-05 Atlas
- Both Atlases

Tufted Titmouse

Baeolophus bicolor

KEVIN J. MCGOWAN

A common bird of deciduous woods and suburban areas, the Tufted Titmouse is resident in eastern North America from southern Minnesota, northern Michigan, southern Ontario, and southern Vermont, southward to northeastern Texas and the Gulf Coast. New York is at the northern edge of its range. The Tufted Titmouse expanded into much of New York in the last half of the 20th century. Before that time it was a rare breeder in the Hudson River area (Bull 1974). Only one nest was known at the beginning of the 20th century, on Staten Island, although isolated records occurred across the state as far north as Rochester (Eaton 1914). Griscom (1923) called it a permanent resident on Staten Island but accidental elsewhere in New York, including Long Island, where it had been common previously (Giraud 1844). It was established in the New York City area in limited numbers by 1942 (Cruickshank 1942). Eaton (1959) documented the spread of the titmouse through the center of the state in the 1950s. He found that the principal invasion appeared to be occurring up the Susquehanna River and from areas in northwestern Pennsylvania, and saw no spread up the Hudson River or the Mohawk Valley. Although he collected a titmouse at the elevation of 610 m (2,000 ft) near Vandalia, Cattaraugus County, Eaton (1959) believed that the higher plateaus and the mountains were constricting the invasion to the larger river valleys.

During the first Atlas period, the Tufted Titmouse was well established through the entire Hudson Valley, the New York City area, and the Coastal Lowlands. It was also common through the central Appalachian Plateau, the Finger Lakes region, and northward to the central Lake Ontario shore. The distribution reported in the first Atlas remained similar to that described by Eaton (1959) and by Bull (1974) but extended northward to the Champlain Valley. The second Atlas survey found the titmouse to be more common across the entire southern portion of the state. The distribution filled in across the Mohawk Valley and into the western quarter of the state. It was always more common at lower elevations, and gaps were still obvious in the Catskill Peaks and the higher portions of the Ap-

palachian Plateau. Interestingly, the Confirmed blocks recorded during the second Atlas survey closely mirror the overall distribution reported in the first Atlas. Scattered sightings extended northward to the Canadian border during the first Atlas survey, but the species is now firmly established in the Champlain Valley. It still is rare and local in the Adirondacks and the St. Lawrence Plains, although it did extend into the Tug Hill Plateau. It expanded away from the main valleys in Warren and Clinton counties and extended into the Central Adirondacks.

The breeding range of the Tufted Titmouse expanded northward in the 1940s to include Wisconsin, Connecticut, and eastern Massachusetts (Grubb and Pravosudov 1994). The explanations offered for the northward extension include a general warming climate, the maturation of forest on abandoned farmlands, and an increase in winter bird feeding (Grubb and Pravosudov 1994). Breeding Bird Survey data show a slow and steady increase in Tufted Titmouse numbers across its range since the 1960s, but the noticeable increase in New York (9.8 percent) only appears after 1980 (Sauer et al. 2005). The second Ontario and Vermont Breeding Bird atlases showed changes similar to those in New York, with significant increases in the number of reports but little expansion northward (Bird Studies Canada et al. 2006, R. Renfrew pers. comm.). Appropriate titmouse habitat is abundant across New York, and the spread of the species into the state appears not to have been constrained by habitat. It is perhaps surprising that the colonization of the western portion of the state and the Great Lakes Plain took as long as it did. It will be interesting to see if the Tufted Titmouse population fills in the rest of the state by the time of the next Atlas project.

2000–05 Distribution Map

- ☐ Not Found
- Possible
- Probable
- Confirmed

Number of Blocks

	1980–85		2000–05		Change
	No.	%	No.	%	%
Possible	488	31	777	25	59
Probable	383	25	1,082	35	183
Confirmed	686	44	1,262	40	84
Total	1,557	29	3,121	59	100

Change Map

- ☐ Not Reported
- 1980-85 Atlas
- 2000-05 Atlas
- Both Atlases

Breeding Bird Survey Trend in New York

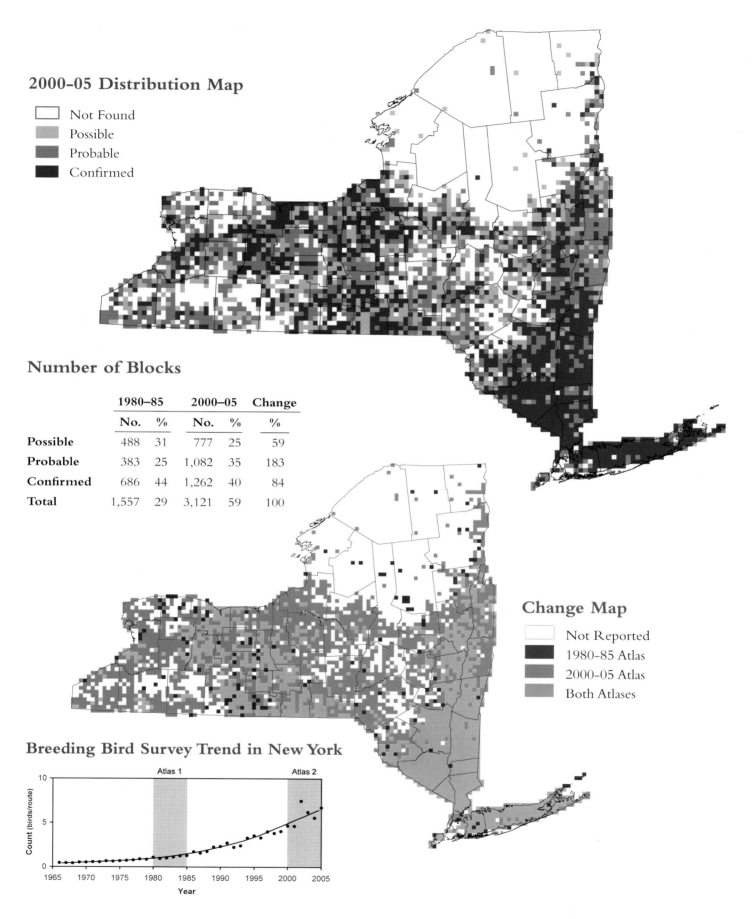

Red-breasted Nuthatch
Sitta canadensis

KEVIN J. MCGOWAN

The Red-breasted Nuthatch is a characteristic bird of spruce-fir forests in Canada and the northern United States, found southward in mountains to Georgia and New Mexico (Ghalambor and Martin 1999). New York is near the southeastern edge of its main range. The nuthatch occurs in mature coniferous forests, especially spruce, fir, larch, and cedar, and in mixed deciduous-coniferous forests with a high number of conifers, as well as in suburban habitat (Ghalambor and Martin 1999). DeKay (1844) considered the Red-breasted Nuthatch to be only a migrant through the state. Merriam (1881) described it as breeding abundantly in the Adirondacks, but accounts from other parts of the state did not list it as a breeder (Giraud 1844, Rathbun 1879, Short 1893, Reed and Wright 1909). Eaton (1914) called it a common breeder in the Adirondacks and Catskills above 600 m (2,000 ft), but gave only a few scattered breeding localities in the rest of the state, in Oneida, Madison, Yates, and Erie counties. Bull (1974) described it as breeding widely in the Adirondacks and Catskill regions and commented on its spread to lower elevations. He gave 40 other locations outside of those regions where it was a local breeder, stretching from the Great Lakes Plain, across the Appalachian Plateau to Ulster County, and in the Taconic Highlands. It was absent as a breeder southward of the southern Hudson Valley (Bull 1974).

The first Atlas reported the Red-breasted Nuthatch as breeding primarily throughout the Adirondacks and Tug Hill Plateau, but it was present in smaller numbers in all ecozones of the state except the Triassic Lowlands. It was confirmed breeding in four blocks in the Coastal Lowlands. The second Atlas results demonstrated a notable increase in Red-breasted Nuthatch numbers. It was found in more blocks in all regions of the state, except the Coastal Lowlands, Hudson Highlands, and St. Lawrence Plains. Increases were marked in the western Appalachian Plateau, especially the Cattaraugus Highlands, where the number of blocks with records of nuthatches nearly doubled, and the Great Lakes Plain. The number of occupied blocks on Long Island declined, and breeding was not confirmed there. The center of abundance for the

Red-breasted Nuthatch still seemed to be the Adirondacks and Tug Hill, but the bird was rather evenly distributed across the Appalachian Plateau and the northern Taconic Highlands.

Breeding Bird Survey data show that Red-breasted Nuthatch numbers have been increasing survey-wide, especially in the last 20 years (Sauer et al. 2005). BBS data from New York show the same trend, with a significant increase since 1980 (Sauer et al. 2005). Although the Red-breasted Nuthatch is resident across its breeding range, varying numbers move southward each winter. Consequently, winter populations change dramatically from year to year, making accurate estimates difficult (Ghalambor and Martin 1999). Christmas Bird Count data, however, show an approximately sixfold increase in the number of counts per party-hour across the range over the last 40 years, with an approximately threefold increase in New York (National Audubon Society [2007]). The second Ontario Breeding Bird Atlas reported significant increases in the nuthatch population across the province (Bird Studies Canada et al. 2006). The Red-breasted Nuthatch has been expanding its breeding populations southward (Ghalambor and Martin 1999), and in the southeastern part of its range it is breeding at lower elevations (Renfrow 2005), much as has occurred on a larger scale in New York.

The reforestation of New York, and especially the widespread planting of conifer plantations in the 1930s, provided much new breeding habitat for the Red-breasted Nuthatch throughout the 20th century. The maturation of those plantings and the rest of the forests in New York has been favorable to the nuthatch as well. Whether these factors alone can explain a change of the magnitude found over the 20 years since the last Atlas survey remains to be seen.

2000–05 Distribution Map

- ☐ Not Found
- Possible
- Probable
- Confirmed

Number of Blocks

	1980–85		2000–05		Change
	No.	%	No.	%	%
Possible	826	49	966	42	17
Probable	505	30	731	32	45
Confirmed	359	21	609	26	70
Total	1,690	32	2,306	43	36

Change Map

- ☐ Not Reported
- 1980–85 Atlas
- 2000–05 Atlas
- Both Atlases

Breeding Bird Survey Trend in New York

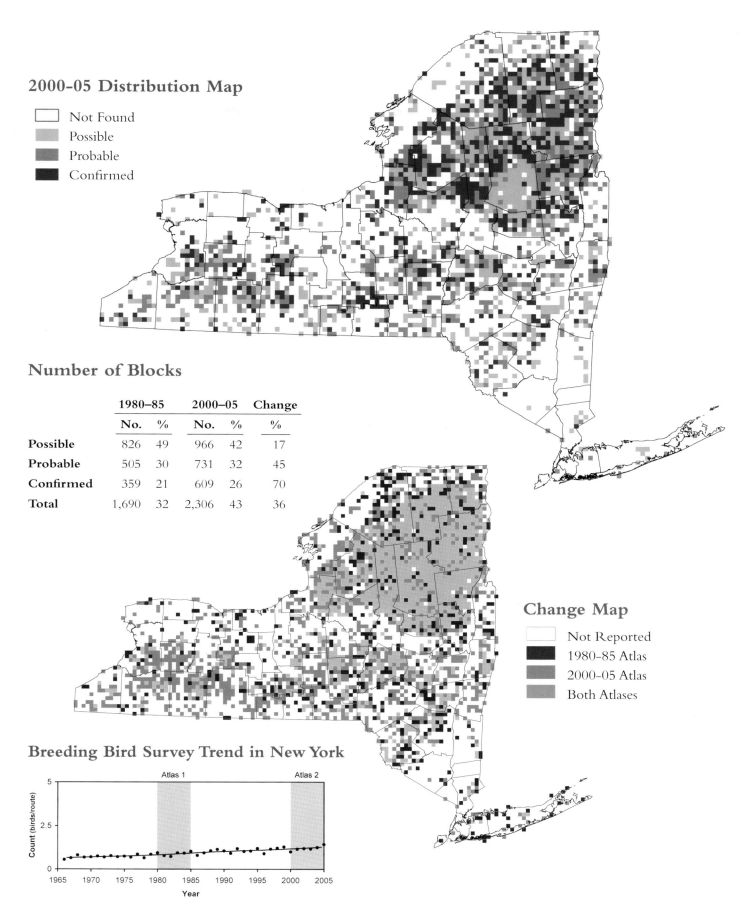

White-breasted Nuthatch

Sitta carolinensis

Kevin J. McGowan

A common bird of deciduous forests and wooded suburbs, the White-breasted Nuthatch can be seen hopping headfirst down the trunks of trees in search of insect food. It is resident from southern Canada southward to northern Florida and southern Mexico (Pravosudov and Grubb 1993). The nuthatch breeds in mature deciduous forests, especially near openings and edges, as well as in parks and suburbs with large trees (Pravosudov and Grubb 1993). The species probably always has been common in New York, almost certainly abundant in the pre-colonial forests. It managed to adapt to the dramatic landscape changes wrought by the European settlers. DeKay (1844) and Giraud (1844) were familiar with it, and most early authors called it common to abundant across the various parts of the state (Rathbun 1879, Short 1893, Reed and Wright 1909), although Merriam said it was a rather uncommon breeder in the Adirondacks. Eaton (1914) listed it as common throughout most of the state but less so in the northern parts and in the balsam belt and the Canadian zone of the Catskills and Adirondacks. It was considered uncommon in the New York City area and on Long Island (Griscom 1923, Cruickshank 1942). Bull (1974) called it a local but widespread breeder, rare on the coastal plain and in the higher mountains.

The first Atlas reported the White-breasted Nuthatch as breeding across nearly all of the state. It was found on most of Long Island except the western end, representing a possible expansion since the 1970s (Bonney 1988g). Gaps in the distribution were found in much of the Adirondacks and St. Lawrence Plains and Transition, the western Appalachian Plateau, and the New York City area. It was missing from the areas of highest elevation and mountain spruce-fir forests. The distribution found during the second Atlas survey was similar to that reported in the first, with a few differences. Again, the species was common and widespread, found across most of the state, but with a slight increase in the number of blocks with records. Again the blocks without White-breasted Nuthatch sightings were most numerous in the Adirondacks and New York City region. In the western Appalachian Plateau, however, the bird was found in most blocks, including many where it was not detected during the first Atlas period. Declines were apparent in the Coastal Lowlands, Taconic Highlands, Adirondacks, and St. Lawrence Plains. Bonney (1988g) suggested that the distribution of the White-breasted Nuthatch reflected the intensity of coverage to some extent, and

the same thing might be true for apparent local changes and range shifts seen in the second Atlas data. The White-breasted Nuthatch calls conspicuously at the end of winter and in the beginning of the breeding season in April, but is quiet from then on (Pravosudov and Grubb 1993). Quiet nuthatches might have been overlooked in blocks covered only later in the Atlas period, and the timing of coverage might be the cause of many apparently unoccupied blocks.

Breeding Bird Survey data show a continent-wide increase in White-breasted Nuthatch numbers over the last 40 years, with increases in most regions (Sauer et al. 2005). Data from New York show a less pronounced trend over the life of the survey, but still a slight significant increase over the last 25 years (Sauer et al. 2005). Christmas Bird Count data show only a slight increase in White-breasted Nuthatch numbers since the 1940s, with fluctuations in the New York data too large to confidently interpret (National Audubon Society [2007]). The second Breeding Bird Atlas in Ontario reported no significant change in White-breasted Nuthatch numbers over the entire province but did reveal significant increases in the Simcoe-Rideau and Southern Shield regions (Bird Studies Canada et al. 2006). The increased and maturing forest cover in New York continues to favor the White-breasted Nuthatch, and the species has little to fear from habitat changes in the near future.

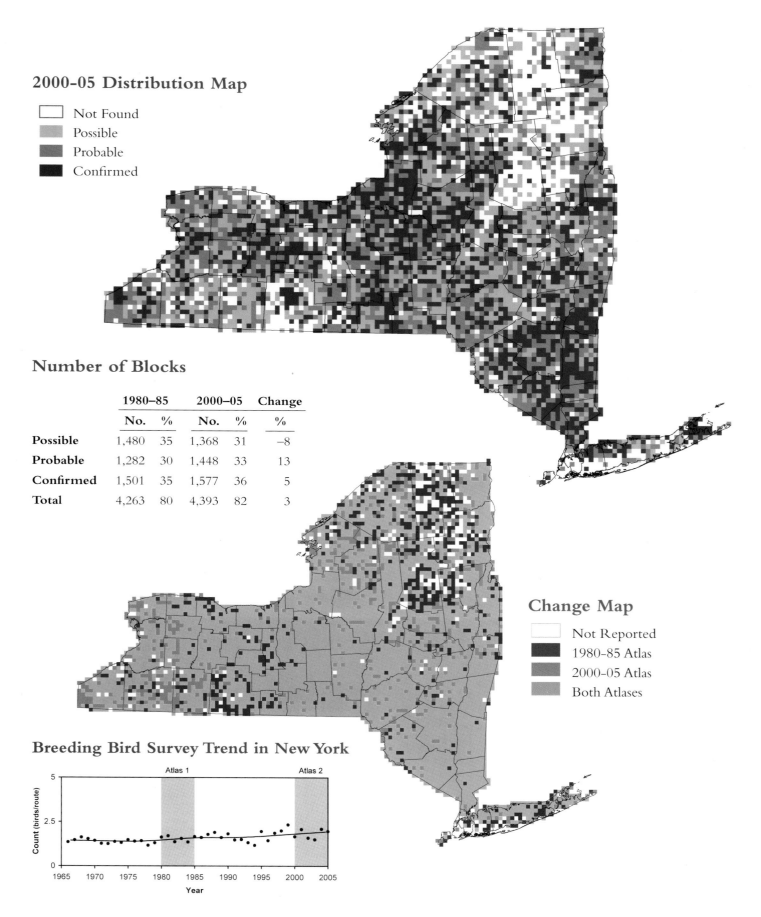

2000-05 Distribution Map

- ☐ Not Found
- Possible
- Probable
- Confirmed

Number of Blocks

	1980–85		2000–05		Change
	No.	%	No.	%	%
Possible	1,480	35	1,368	31	−8
Probable	1,282	30	1,448	33	13
Confirmed	1,501	35	1,577	36	5
Total	4,263	80	4,393	82	3

Change Map

- ☐ Not Reported
- 1980-85 Atlas
- 2000-05 Atlas
- Both Atlases

Breeding Bird Survey Trend in New York

Brown Creeper
Certhia americana

KEVIN J. MCGOWAN

The Brown Creeper is a small, well-camouflaged forest bird that breeds in the northeastern United States and eastern Canada, from Newfoundland to northern Virginia, and westward across much of central Canada. It also breeds throughout the mountains and coastal regions of the western United States and Canada, from southern Alaska to Mexico and Central America (Hejl et al. 2002). It nests in coniferous and mixed coniferous-deciduous forests and is especially common in old-growth stands (Hejl et al. 2002). This bird was probably much more numerous in New York before European settlement and the widespread destruction of the forests. Rathbun (1879) called the Brown Creeper resident in central New York, whereas Short (1893) and Reed and Wright (1909) listed it as only a migrant and winter visitor in central and western New York. Merriam (1881) said it was a tolerably common breeder in the Adirondacks, absent in winter. Eaton (1914) called it an abundant breeder in the Adirondacks and Catskills but only a local one in the rest of the state, albeit common in some areas. Bull (1974) considered it common in the mountains but a very local breeder in the Great Lakes Plain, and rare and local southward and on Long Island. The Brown Creeper expanded southward as a breeder into the New York City area and onto Long Island, where it was first found breeding in 1947 (Bull 1964) and then with increasing incidence through the 1970s (Salzman 1998b).

During the first Atlas survey, the Brown Creeper was found throughout the state. Areas of concentration included most of the Adirondacks, Tug Hill Plateau, western Mohawk Valley, and eastern Appalachian Plateau, including the Catskill region, the highlands along the lower Hudson Valley, the Rensselaer Hills, and the eastern Cattaraugus Highlands. It was detected in slightly more blocks during the second Atlas survey. Some significant changes were noted, with increases in the Adirondacks and Appalachian Plateau and decreases in the Great Lakes Plain, St. Lawrence Plains, Mohawk Valley, and central Hudson Valley southward. The distribution reflected in the second Atlas data corresponds more closely to elevation differences than does the distribution reported in the first Atlas. Apparent are gaps in the Great Lakes Plain, extending southward in the central Finger Lakes region, the St. Lawrence Valley, the Mohawk Valley, and the lower Hudson Valley. The distribution is now continuous across the Appalachian Plateau. None of these features were apparent in the first Atlas map. The blocks recording the creeper declined 72 percent in the Coastal Lowlands, with no confirmed breeding. It appears that gains made there in the 1960s are being lost.

Because the Brown Creeper is not common on many Breeding Bird Surveys, confidence in population trends is low, but no significant trend is seen either survey-wide or in New York (Sauer et al. 2007). The second Ontario Breeding Bird Atlas reported a significant increase in Brown Creeper numbers across that province (Bird Studies Canada et al. 2006). Increased creeper numbers in New England in the 1960s and 1970s were possibly the result of American elm mortality from Dutch elm disease, tree mortality from gypsy moths, and reforestation (Hejl et al. 2002). Davis (1978) suggested that the spread of Dutch elm disease provided breeding sites for the creeper and could be responsible for a range expansion, but the expansion would be temporary as the bark would eventually fall off dead trees. Salzman (1998b) noted that this explanation could not account for the spread onto Long Island, where elms were not the main breeding sites, and instead favored reforestation and forest maturation. The loss of Brown Creeper from much of Long Island, the lower Hudson Valley, western Mohawk Valley, and the Great Lakes Plain suggests that a previous range expansion might indeed have been temporary and that reforestation alone appears insufficient to explain the expansion that occurred during the mid-1900s.

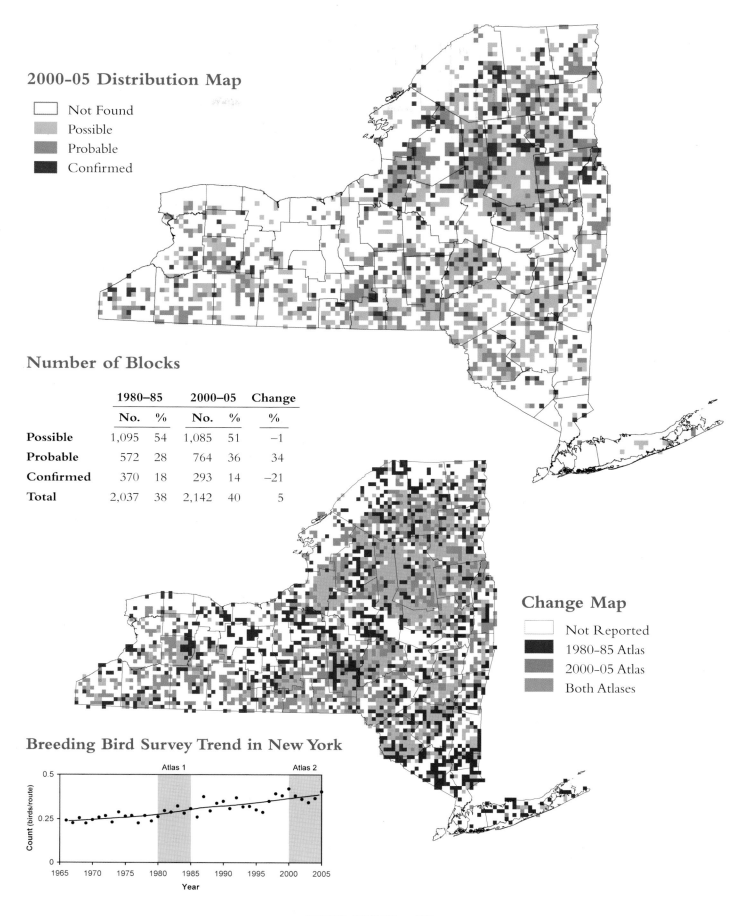

2000–05 Distribution Map

- ☐ Not Found
- Possible
- Probable
- Confirmed

Number of Blocks

	1980–85		2000–05		Change
	No.	%	No.	%	%
Possible	1,095	54	1,085	51	−1
Probable	572	28	764	36	34
Confirmed	370	18	293	14	−21
Total	2,037	38	2,142	40	5

Change Map

- ☐ Not Reported
- 1980–85 Atlas
- 2000–05 Atlas
- Both Atlases

Breeding Bird Survey Trend in New York

Wrens in a suburban backyard

Both Carolina and House wrens have adapted to suburban living; neither species seems to fear humans. The Carolina Wren is happy to nest in an upturned flowerpot or berry basket in the tool shed, while the simplest nest box seems to please the House Wren.

Carolina Wren
Thryothorus ludovicianus

CHARLES R. SMITH

The Carolina Wren is a characteristic bird of the southeastern United States that reaches the northeastern limits of its distribution in New York. Its range extends from southwestern Texas and the southern tip of Florida, northward to the southern tip of Lake Michigan and eastward to southern New York and Massachusetts (Haggerty and Morton 1995). The wren's northern distribution is limited by severe winter weather, with population declines following particularly bad winters (see summary in Melin 1998a), though actual data from Christmas Bird Counts and the Breeding Bird Survey show that it can recover quickly after severe winters (Robbins et al. 1986). This wren uses a wide range of habitats, including suburban settings, usually requiring moderate to dense shrub or brushy cover and often favoring ravines and gorges (Haggerty and Morton 1995). Forest fragmentation and the presence of shrublands may have benefited the Carolina Wren in some parts of its range (Haggerty and Morton 1995). DeKay (1844) and Giraud (1844) considered the wren a rare visitor to New York, although DeKay suspected it bred in Westchester and Rockland counties. Reed and Wright (1909) reported two observations of breeding pairs 13 years apart around Ithaca, and a nest was known from Genesee County in 1894 (Beardslee and Mitchell 1965). Eaton (1914) called the wren a regular breeder only in the lower Hudson Valley but probably an occasional breeder in other warm parts of the state, and he noted that the species appeared to be extending its breeding range northward. Beardslee and Mitchell (1965) and Bull (1974) described increases in the species upstate starting in the 1950s. Bull (1974) noted increases especially in the mid-Hudson and Mohawk valleys, the western Finger Lakes, the Great Lakes Plain near Syracuse and Rochester, and across the central Appalachian Plateau.

The first Atlas showed the Carolina Wren's distribution to be very similar to that represented in Bull's (1974) map: it was most common in the Coastal Lowlands and the lower Hudson Valley, with scattered reports up the Hudson and across the Appalachian Plateau and Erie-Ontario Plain, and concentrations around the Finger Lakes. A single Confirmed breeding record was made in the Champlain

Valley. Between the first and second Atlas survey periods, the Carolina Wren expanded its distribution by more than three-fold. Its greatest areas of increase were in western New York, west of the Finger Lakes region, in the lowlands and highlands along the lower Hudson Valley, and on Long Island. It appears to have followed major rivers as it expanded southward from the Great Lakes Plain along the Genesee River and northward along the Susquehanna and Hudson river drainages. It remained absent from much of the Adirondack, Catskill, and Allegheny mountain regions, while expanding into the northernmost counties along the St. Lawrence Plains and the Champlain Valley and Transition. The expansion of the wren was possibly in partial response to patterns of global climate change (Haggerty and Morton 1995), although the widespread growth of winter bird feeding also might contribute to its winter survival (Bull 1974, Haggerty and Morton 1995).

Breeding Bird Survey data show that the Carolina Wren has significantly increased in abundance across its range since 1980 (Sauer et al. 2007). New York BBS data are sparse, but they show a statistically significant increasing trend since 1980 as well (Sauer et al. 2007). BBS data for the north Atlantic states (U.S. Fish and Wildlife Service Region 5) show clearly significant increasing trends since 1966 (Sauer et al. 2007). The second Ontario Breeding Bird Atlas also reported a range expansion across southern Ontario (Bird Studies Canada et al. 2006). The Carolina Wren's high reproductive potential, adaptability, and capacity to recover from dramatic population declines in the wake of severe winter weather suggest a potentially secure future in New York.

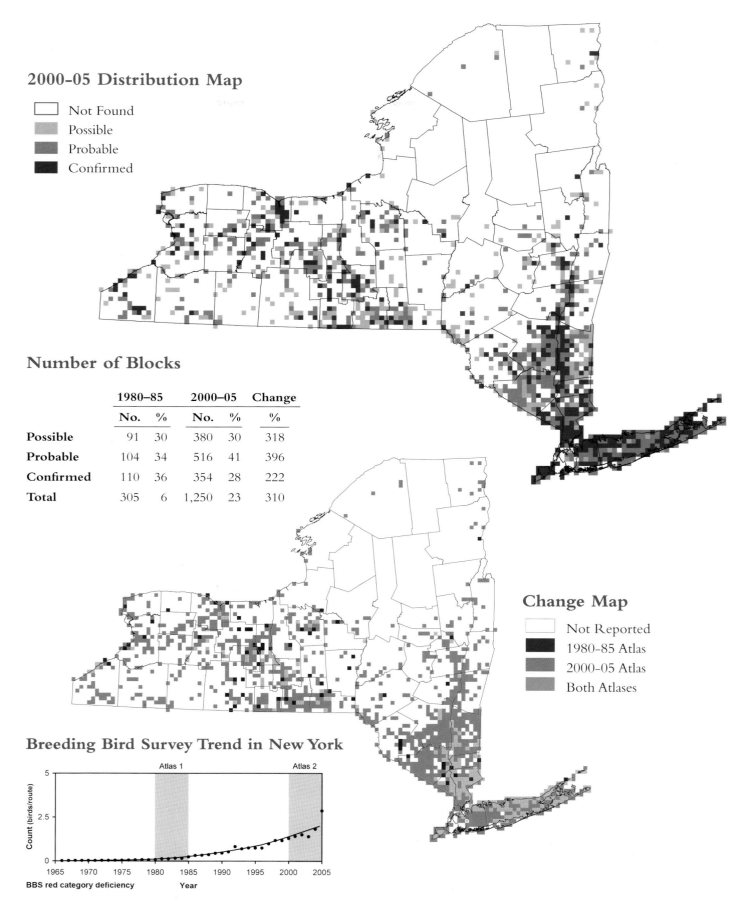

2000-05 Distribution Map

- ☐ Not Found
- Possible
- Probable
- Confirmed

Number of Blocks

	1980–85		2000–05		Change
	No.	%	No.	%	%
Possible	91	30	380	30	318
Probable	104	34	516	41	396
Confirmed	110	36	354	28	222
Total	305	6	1,250	23	310

Change Map

- ☐ Not Reported
- 1980-85 Atlas
- 2000-05 Atlas
- Both Atlases

Breeding Bird Survey Trend in New York

Atlas 1   Atlas 2

Count (birds/route)

5

2.5

0

1965 1970 1975 1980 1985 1990 1995 2000 2005

BBS red category deficiency   Year

House Wren

Troglodytes aedon

KEVIN J. MCGOWAN

The House Wren is a familiar and noisy inhabitant of forest edges and open, shrubby woodlands, as well as city parks and residential areas with trees. The House Wren breeds from southern Canada southward to central California, central New Mexico, northern Arkansas, and northern Georgia (Johnson 1998). New York is near the northeastern edge of the range. The opening of the forests by European colonization and the creation of farms and woodlots undoubtedly benefited the House Wren. It was already common around towns in New York by the early 1800s (Giraud 1844) and was common across most of the state by the end of the century (Rathbun 1879, Short 1893, Reed and Wright 1909). Merriam (1881) said that it was confined to the edges of the Adirondack wilderness. Eaton (1914) listed the House Wren as common throughout New York except in the "Canadian zone." Its breeding range was essentially the same 60 years later (Bull 1974). Population declines were described across the state in the late 1890s (Eaton 1914) and around New York City in the early 1900s (Griscom 1923). These changes were attributed to competition with the increasing House Sparrow (Eaton 1914, Griscom 1923), although Eaton (1914) thought severe weather on the wintering grounds was a more likely cause. The increasing urbanization of the New York City area probably played a role in its decline there (Cruickshank 1942), although some recovery occurred subsequently (Bonney 1988d).

During the first Atlas survey, the House Wren was widely distributed across New York, including most of the Coastal Lowlands. It was noticeably absent only from parts of the Adirondacks, with other small gaps in the Central Tug Hill and the Catskill Peaks. Ellison (1985b) stated that this species did not breed above 641 m (2,102 ft). Despite this assertion, and repetition of the citation in Bonney (1988d) and in Quinlan and Fritz (1998), breeding was in fact confirmed in many blocks with elevations above 610 m (2,000 ft) and Possible reports came from some blocks with elevations over 914 m (3,000 ft). It is not clear whether these reports actually indicate breeding at the higher elevations or breeding in some part of each block that was at a lower altitude. The distribution of the House Wren recorded during the second Atlas fieldwork was much the same as that reported in the first Atlas. The bird was found in only slightly fewer blocks across the state, and it was missing primarily from most of the Adirondacks and a section of the Catskill Peaks. Declines in the number of blocks with records occurred mostly in the higher-elevation ecozones, with a 22 percent decline in the Catskill Peaks and a 17 percent decline across the Adirondacks. New gaps appeared in the Allegany Hills, again an area of higher elevation and therefore of marginal breeding quality.

The House Wren has been expanding its breeding range southward since the 1800s, and this expansion continued at least through the late 20th century (Johnson 1998). Across its North American range the House Wren has been increasing slightly in numbers according to Breeding Bird Survey data (Sauer et al. 2005). In the Northeast, however, populations have been declining significantly, if only modestly (Sauer et al. 2005). New York BBS data show a nonsignificant decline of less than 1 percent per year in the last 25 years, following a slight but significant increase (Sauer et al. 2005). The second Breeding Bird Atlas in Ontario reported no significant change in House Wren numbers in the province overall but a significant increase in the Southern Shield region (Bird Studies Canada et al. 2006). Atlas methods are not well suited to detect a slight decrease in populations of such a common and easily detected bird. Declines would only be detectable in areas where the species was already present in low numbers, such as the Adirondacks. Whether these declines in marginal areas presage declines in other areas is a question that might be answered by future Atlas surveys.

2000-05 Distribution Map

- ☐ Not Found
- Possible
- Probable
- Confirmed

Number of Blocks

	1980–85 No.	1980–85 %	2000–05 No.	2000–05 %	Change %
Possible	721	16	576	14	−20
Probable	929	21	1,255	29	35
Confirmed	2,746	62	2,428	57	−12
Total	4,396	82	4,259	80	−3

Change Map

- ☐ Not Reported
- 1980-85 Atlas
- 2000-05 Atlas
- Both Atlases

Breeding Bird Survey Trend in New York

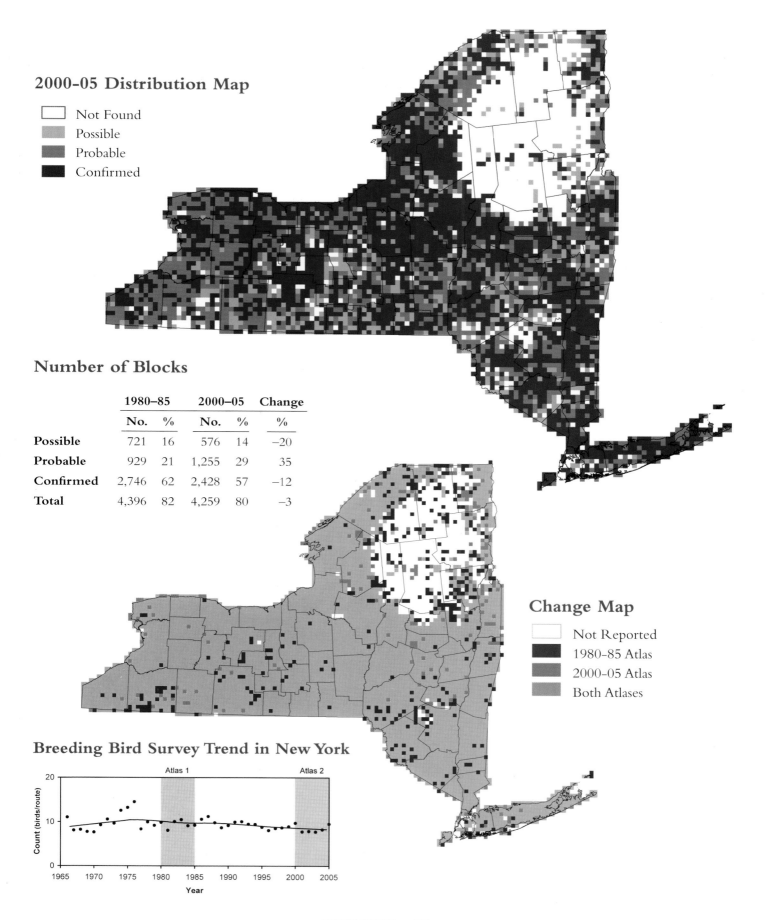

Winter Wren

Troglodytes troglodytes

KEVIN J. MCGOWAN

The Winter Wren breeds from coastal Alaska southward to northern California, Idaho, and Montana, across Canada to the Great Lakes, Maritime Provinces, and eastern United States, and as far southward as the mountains in northern Georgia (Hejl et al. 2002). It is the only wren species to have left the New World, as it also breeds throughout Europe, Asia, and into North Africa. New York is near the southeastern edge of its main range. The Winter Wren breeds in many different habitat types, from cliff faces to riparian areas to various forests. It occurs in greatest densities in coniferous forests and prefers areas with fallen logs and other dead wood (Hejl et al. 2002). In New York it breeds in montane coniferous forests, primarily spruce and balsam fir, and in lowland bogs and swamps, especially hemlock–white cedar bogs (Bull 1974). As a species that uses old-growth forests (Hejl et al. 2002), the Winter Wren was probably more numerous in New York before European colonization. By the late 19th century it was confined primarily to the Adirondacks and Catskills, with a few found in other locations in central and western New York (Eaton 1910, 1914). Eaton (1914) considered it a boreal bird, but much like the Brown Creeper its existence in isolated pockets of remaining forest suggests that its distribution in New York was related more to its preference for mature forest than for boreal habitats. Bull (1974) called it a common breeder in the mountains but local at high elevations elsewhere.

During the first Atlas survey, the Winter Wren was found primarily in the higher elevations in the state, with most records coming from above 305 m (1,000 ft). It was found in all parts of the Adirondacks, the Tug Hill Plateau, the Catskills, and across the Appalachian Plateau. Scattered records occurred throughout nearly every region of the state at lower elevations too, southward to the Triassic Lowlands and the Manhattan Hills. No Winter Wrens were recorded in the Coastal Lowlands. The pattern of distribution found during the second Atlas survey was roughly similar, but the Winter Wren was seen in 49 percent more blocks. It was found in more blocks in every ecozone, with the greatest increases occurring across the Appalachian Plateau, Great Lakes Plain, Champlain Valley, and Mohawk Valley. The Adirondacks, Tug Hill, and Catskills still appeared to be the strongholds of the species in the state, but the eastern and western ends of the Appalachian Plateau were regions of abundance too. The Winter Wren was still not found in the Coastal Lowlands, but breeding was confirmed just north, in the Manhattan Hills of southern Westchester County. The single Long Island breeding record from Connetquot River State Park, Suffolk County, in 1976 (Davis 1976) remains an anomaly.

Breeding Bird Survey data show that Winter Wren numbers survey-wide have been increasing over 2.2 percent per year since 1963, with most of the gain occurring in the last 25 years (Sauer et al. 2005). BBS data from New York show a nonsignificant increase of 2.7 percent over the same time, with a statistically significant 4.9 percent increase per year over the last 25 years. The second Breeding Bird Atlas in Ontario reported significant increases in Winter Wren detections across most of that province (Bird Studies Canada et al. 2006). Although positive trends are seen across much of its range, concern exists about some populations, notably in the Northwest and the southern Blue Ridge and Allegheny Mountains, owing to the negative effects of logging and forest fragmentation, and its association with complex forest floors and rare community types (Hejl et al. 2002). The expansion of the Winter Wren's range in New York is probably a function of reforestation and the maturation of forests in the state, and it may finally be recovering most of its original New York range.

2000-05 Distribution Map

- ☐ Not Found
- Possible
- Probable
- Confirmed

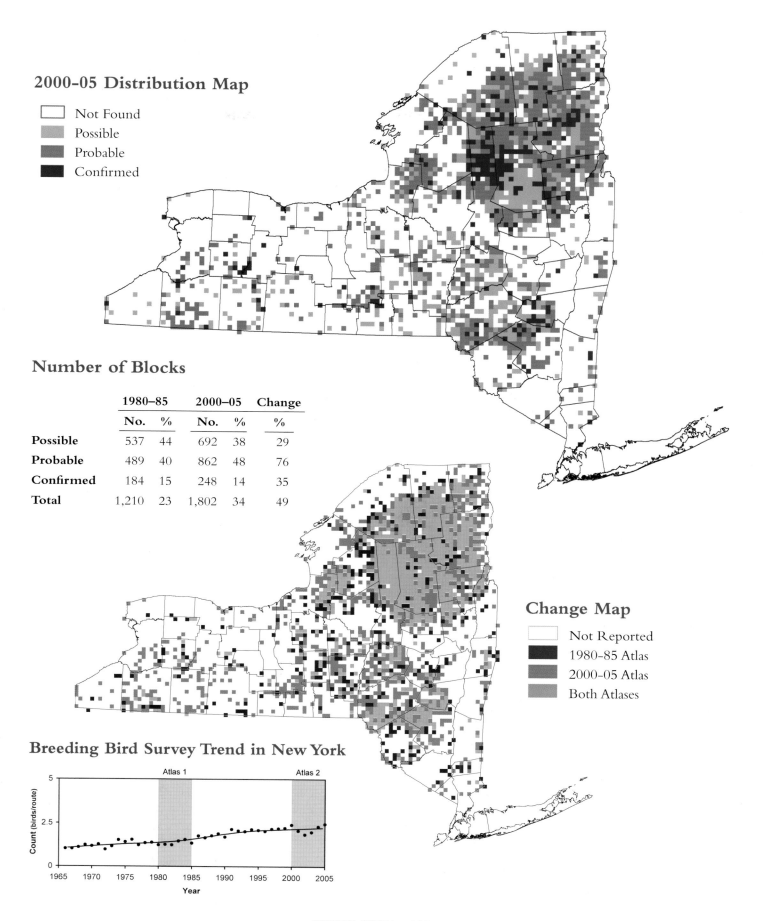

Number of Blocks

	1980–85		2000–05		Change
	No.	%	No.	%	%
Possible	537	44	692	38	29
Probable	489	40	862	48	76
Confirmed	184	15	248	14	35
Total	1,210	23	1,802	34	49

Change Map

- ☐ Not Reported
- 1980-85 Atlas
- 2000-05 Atlas
- Both Atlases

Breeding Bird Survey Trend in New York

Sedge Wren
Cistothorus platensis

KEVIN J. McGOWAN

The secretive Sedge Wren nests in dense tall sedges and grasses in wet meadows, hayfields, and marshes, avoiding cattails and standing water (Herkert et al. 2001). It breeds in the central Prairie Provinces and the upper midwestern states eastward to Quebec and New Hampshire (Herkert et al. 2001). New York is at the southeastern edge of its breeding range. This wren has an unusual breeding pattern, breeding in late May and June primarily in the upper midwestern United States and adjacent Canada, and then expanding out into the southern and northeastern portions of the breeding range to nest again in July to September (Herkert et al. 2001). The widespread clearing of the forests by European settlement created extensive grassland that would have been available to the wren, although little evidence exists that it used it to its fullest extent. DeKay (1844) listed the Sedge Wren as "not numerous" in the state. Giraud (1844) had not encountered it on Long Island although he knew of a Rockland County record. Rathbun (1879) and Short (1893) called it a breeder in central and western New York, but Reed and Wright (1909) listed only a single specimen for the Cayuga Lake Basin. Eaton (1914) called the Sedge Wren local and uncommon in all parts of the state except for a few colonies in the lower Hudson Valley and in parts of central and western New York. Bull (1974) indicated that it was still as local and uncommon as in Eaton's day. He noted that former breeding colonies on Long Island had disappeared, and that breeding localities along the east side of the Hudson River up to Dutchess County had been largely destroyed.

During the first Atlas survey, the Sedge Wren was found in only 57 blocks scattered across the state, with over half of the reporting blocks in the Great Lakes and St. Lawrence plains. Only one Probable sighting was listed for southeastern New York, in Westchester County. The second Atlas found only slightly more blocks with Sedge Wren reports than the first, and the species was still rare. Nearly half of all reports were concentrated in three counties in the Eastern Ontario Plain and the St. Lawrence Plains. Differences between the Atlas findings in this region could well be the result of lower coverage during the first Atlas period. Again, few reports came from southeastern New York and none from Long Island. Fittingly for this nomadic species, only seven blocks had Sedge Wren sightings during both

Atlas surveys. Breeding reports of Sedge Wren came from both early and late in the season, suggesting that New York may have both first and second broods (*sensu* Herkert et al. 2001), with different patterns in different years (J. Bolsinger pers. comm.). The combination of late nesting and its secretive nature may have caused this species to be overlooked by Atlas workers.

Because of its odd breeding behavior, the Sedge Wren might not be sampled effectively by the Breeding Bird Survey. BBS data show a significant increase in Sedge Wren numbers across the survey since 1966, but the data from New York and the northeastern states are too sparse to evaluate (Sauer et al. 2005). Data from the heart of the breeding range in the Great Plains indicate an increasing population (Sauer et al. 2005). No significant changes in Sedge Wren numbers were detected by the two Ontario Breeding Bird Atlas surveys (Bird Studies Canada et al. 2006). The Sedge Wren is listed as Threatened in a number of northeastern states, including New York. Because populations in the heart of its range seem secure, Partners in Flight gave it a rather low combined score, suggesting that the continental population is in no eminent danger (Rich et al. 2004). Although a consistently breeding population may be establishing itself in Jefferson and St. Lawrence counties, New York appears to be outside the main breeding range of the Sedge Wren, and continued irregular and local reports of the species can be expected throughout the state in the future.

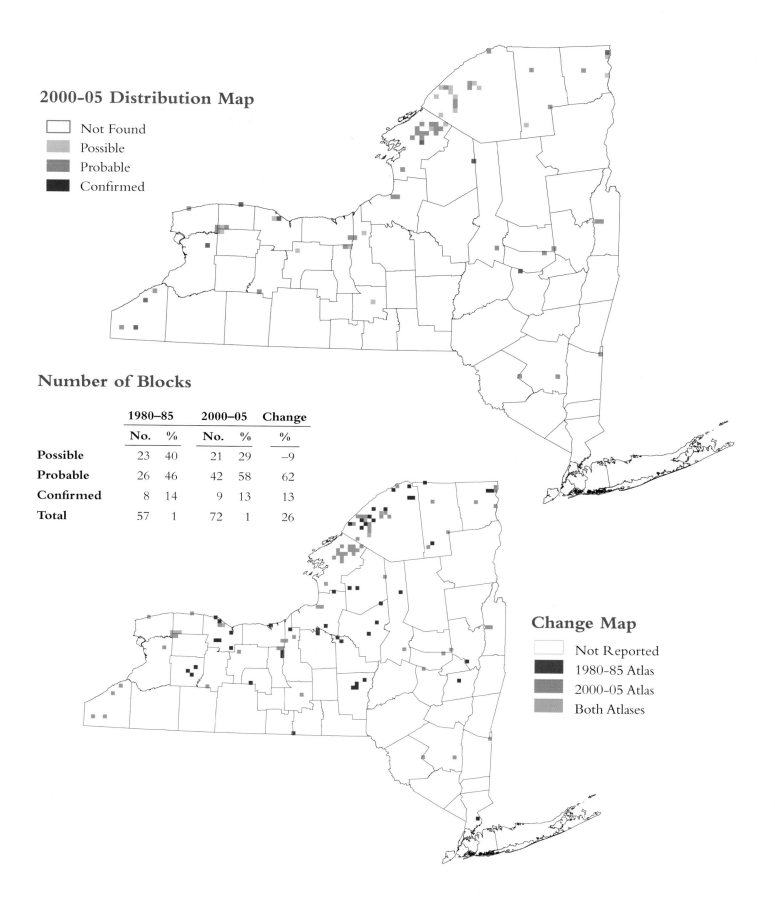

2000-05 Distribution Map

- Not Found
- Possible
- Probable
- Confirmed

Number of Blocks

| | 1980–85 | | 2000–05 | | Change |
	No.	%	No.	%	%
Possible	23	40	21	29	−9
Probable	26	46	42	58	62
Confirmed	8	14	9	13	13
Total	57	1	72	1	26

Change Map

- Not Reported
- 1980-85 Atlas
- 2000-05 Atlas
- Both Atlases

Marsh Wren
Cistothorus palustris

KEVIN J. McGOWAN

The Marsh Wren is a loud, if nearly invisible, denizen of reedy marshes. It breeds from British Columbia to Maine, southward to Kansas, southern Indiana, and northern Virginia, as well as throughout the intermountain West and along all the coasts southward to Mexico. It nests in a variety of marshes in both fresh and salt water, especially those with dense reeds (Kroodsma and Verner 1997). Little evidence exists for much change in the status of the Marsh Wren in New York, where it has probably always been common in the appropriate marsh habitat. DeKay (1844) assumed the Marsh Wren nested in New York although he had no evidence of it. Giraud (1844) called it plentiful on Long Island. Rathbun (1879), Short (1893), and Reed and Wright (1909) called it common to abundant in western and central New York in the appropriate habitat. Eaton (1914) listed it as a common summer resident in all extensive marshes along the coast, the Hudson River, the Niagara River, both Great Lakes, and the central lakes. Beardslee and Mitchell (1965) stated that all extensive marshes in western New York had their breeding colony, and Bull (1974) indicated little change from Eaton's account. Although the extent and abundance of the Marsh Wren in existing marshes did not change much, the widespread draining of wetlands in the 19th and 20th centuries must have caused the loss of many local populations (Connor 1988c).

The first Atlas reported the Marsh Wren to be widely distributed on the coast, along the Hudson River, on the Great Lakes and St. Lawrence plains, and near both ends of Lake Champlain. Elsewhere it was local. As an indication of a notable population decline from the time of Eaton (1914), few were found in areas of former abundance at the outlets and heads of Canandaigua, Seneca, and Cayuga lakes and along the Niagara River (Connor 1988c). Those historic marshes are largely gone, and with them went the Marsh Wren. It was still found in abundance along the south shore of Long Island and in the Tonawanda and Oak Orchard wildlife management areas and the Iroquois National Wildlife Refuge. Only a few reports came from the Appalachian Plateau, Mohawk Valley, or Adirondacks. The second Atlas survey data showed the Marsh Wren in a similar distribution across the state, but in a slightly larger number of blocks. It remained most common on the Great Lakes Plain and in the Coastal Lowlands. Perhaps the most notable changes were apparent declines in blocks with breeding records in regions of the lower Hudson Valley and at the junction of Monroe, Orleans, and Genesee

counties. In both cases, however, it is difficult to separate changes in status from local changes in Atlas coverage. It was still uncommon and local in the Adirondacks and Appalachian Plateau and practically missing from the eastern end of the Appalachian Plateau.

As a species with a restricted wetland breeding habitat, the Marsh Wren is not well suited to monitoring by Breeding Bird Survey methods. BBS data that exist show a significant increasing trend in Marsh Wren numbers across the survey area, but all the eastern U.S. Fish and Wildlife Service regions show declining trends (Sauer et al. 2005). BBS data from New York are too sparse to analyze statistically, but the species essentially disappeared from state surveys in the mid-1980s. Data from the second Ontario Breeding Bird Atlas show no significant change province-wide in Marsh Wren numbers (Bird Studies Canada et al. 2006).

The specific habitat requirements of the Marsh Wren make it a rather easy bird to predict and protect. Wherever marshes have been destroyed, restored, or created throughout its range, Marsh Wren populations have decreased or increased accordingly (Kroodsma and Verner 1997). With the current level of wetland protection and management in place, the Marsh Wren should remain a common, if local, breeding bird in New York.

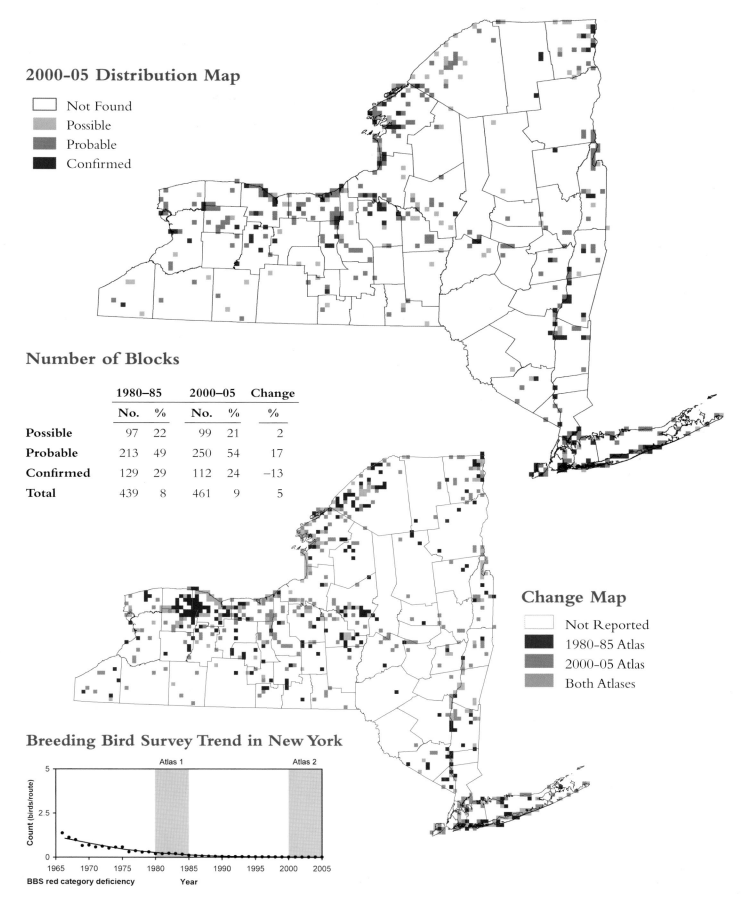

2000-05 Distribution Map

- ☐ Not Found
- Possible
- Probable
- Confirmed

Number of Blocks

	1980–85		2000–05		Change
	No.	%	No.	%	%
Possible	97	22	99	21	2
Probable	213	49	250	54	17
Confirmed	129	29	112	24	−13
Total	439	8	461	9	5

Change Map

- ☐ Not Reported
- 1980-85 Atlas
- 2000-05 Atlas
- Both Atlases

Breeding Bird Survey Trend in New York

BBS red category deficiency

Golden-crowned Kinglet

Regulus satrapa

KEVIN J. MCGOWAN

The Golden-crowned Kinglet, a tiny bird of northern coniferous forests, breeds from southern Alaska eastward to Newfoundland and southward to the northern United States, extending farther southward in the mountains to North Carolina and Arizona (Ingold and Galati 1997). New York is near the southeastern edge of its main range. This kinglet breeds in spruce and fir, mixed pine and spruce, balsam fir, and hemlock forests, as well as in some mixed coniferous-deciduous forests (Ingold and Galati 1997). DeKay (1844) described the Golden-crowned Kinglet as rare in New York, not known to breed, but he admitted "its history is incomplete." Early authors described it as only a migrant through most parts of the state (Giraud 1844, Rathbun 1879, Short 1893, Reed and Wright 1909), but Merriam (1881) thought it bred in the Adirondacks. Eaton (1914) gave its breeding range as restricted to the Adirondacks and Catskills, where it was common at higher elevations. Only a scattering of other reports were known from near the southern edge of the Adirondacks in the first half of the 20th century (Bull 1974). Starting in the early 1950s the Golden-crowned Kinglet was found breeding outside of these areas (Beardslee and Mitchell 1965, Andrle 1971). Andrle (1971) found the Golden-crowned Kinglet breeding primarily in maturing stands of introduced spruces, especially in dense, closed stands that had not been thinned. These stands were planted mostly in the 1930s across the Appalachian Plateau, but they could be found virtually anywhere in the state (Andrle 1971).

The first Atlas reported that the Golden-crowned Kinglet bred across much of the state. It was found in native spruces and other conifers in the Adirondacks, Catskills, Tug Hill Plateau, and in small numbers in the Taconic Highlands. It was also found wherever spruce stands were planted across the state. It was largely missing from the Great Lakes Plain, St. Lawrence Plains, and Mohawk and Hudson valleys, and was completely missing from the Coastal Lowlands. The second Atlas data revealed a similar distribution, with the Golden-crowned Kinglet breeding across much of the state.

The largest concentrations were in the Adirondacks, the Tug Hill Plateau, and across the Appalachian Plateau. Overall, the kinglet was found in 13 percent more blocks in the state. An increase in the number of blocks with records was noted in the Catskill Peaks (up 42 percent), but otherwise a slight decline occurred in the eastern Appalachian Plateau. The number of blocks with breeding records of the kinglet nearly doubled in the western portion of the Appalachian Plateau. Within the Adirondacks, the number of blocks increased 14 percent. A fledgling kinglet was discovered on Long Island near Muttontown Preserve, Nassau County, on 16 July 2005, the first breeding record on Long Island since 1963 (Mitra and Lindsay 2005b).

Breeding Bird Survey data show a continuous and significant, albeit slight, decline in Golden-crowned Kinglet numbers survey-wide since 1966, but all regions reporting declines are in the western part of the range; eastern regions show nonsignificant positive trends (Sauer et al. 2005). BBS data from New York are sparse but also show a nonsignificant positive trend. The second Ontario Breeding Bird Atlas reported a significant increase in kinglet numbers across that province (Bird Studies Canada et al. 2006). Expansion of the breeding range of the Golden-crowned Kinglet by the use of spruce plantations has been documented in Ontario, Pennsylvania, Maryland, Illinois, Indiana, and Ohio (Ingold and Galati 1997). Despite its declining continental population, Partners in Flight gave it a relatively low overall conservation score (Rich et al. 2004). Andrle's (1971) conclusion about kinglets nesting in plantations in New York still reads true after 35 years: "If forest practices and commercial use permit enough spruce plantations suitable for kinglets to remain, the range extension outlined here will probably persist indefinitely."

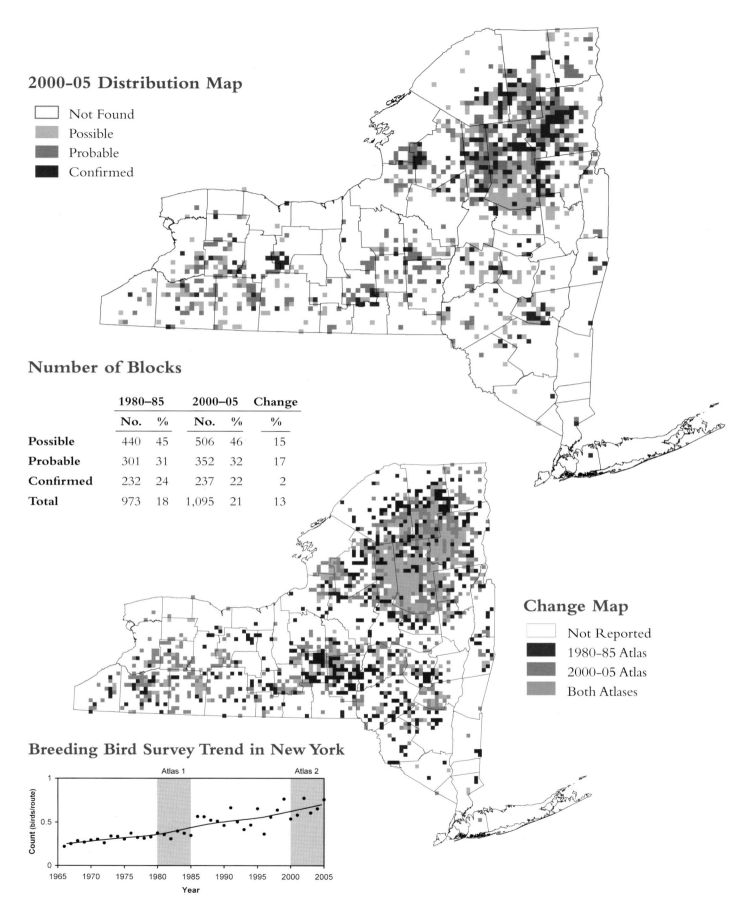

2000-05 Distribution Map

- ☐ Not Found
- Possible
- Probable
- Confirmed

Number of Blocks

	1980–85		2000–05		Change
	No.	%	No.	%	%
Possible	440	45	506	46	15
Probable	301	31	352	32	17
Confirmed	232	24	237	22	2
Total	973	18	1,095	21	13

Change Map

- ☐ Not Reported
- 1980-85 Atlas
- 2000-05 Atlas
- Both Atlases

Breeding Bird Survey Trend in New York

Ruby-crowned Kinglet

Regulus calendula

KEVIN J. MCGOWAN

One of the smallest birds in North America, the Ruby-crowned Kinglet breeds from Alaska to Newfoundland, southward to New Hampshire, northern Wisconsin, and central Alberta, and farther southward in the western mountains to southern California, Arizona, and New Mexico (Ingold and Wallace 1994). The New York breeding population is at the southeastern edge of, and slightly removed from, the main breeding range. The kinglet nests near water in open black spruce forests, black spruce and tamarack bogs, and mixed coniferous–northern hardwood forests, particularly in white spruce, black spruce, and paper birch (Ingold and Wallace 1994). The Ruby-crowned Kinglet was unknown as a breeder in New York until 1942, when a nest with young was discovered at Bay Pond, Franklin County (Parkes 1952). Eaton (1914) had earlier reported seeing a Ruby-crowned Kinglet carrying food for its young (which would be coded as Confirmed according to Atlas definitions) on the slopes of Mt. Marcy in the Adirondack High Peaks. By the 1970s this kinglet was still considered a rare breeder in the Adirondacks, with 16 known or suspected breeding locations in Franklin, Essex, Herkimer, and Hamilton counties (Bull 1974). Bull (1974) predicted that more records would be produced by more fieldwork, especially in St. Lawrence and Hamilton counties. The first nesting outside of the Adirondacks was documented in Allegany State Park, Cattaraugus County, in 1977 (Andrle 1978).

The first Atlas data proved Bull's prediction correct, with many Ruby-crowned Kinglet breeding records coming from the Adirondack High Peaks, Central Adirondacks, Western Adirondack Foothills, and Sable Highlands. Coverage may have been affected by the remoteness of some blocks, but gaps in distribution were apparent even in well-covered blocks (J. M. C. Peterson 1988n). No breeding was confirmed outside the Adirondacks, but the Ruby-crowned Kinglet was seen in coniferous habitat in Erie County; Letchworth State Park, Wyoming County; in the Central Tug Hill; and in the Champlain Transition. The distribution of the Ruby-crowned Kinglet found for the second Atlas looked somewhat different from that reported in the first. Again, most records were in the Adirondacks, but reports outside that area increased. A number of records were scattered throughout the central and eastern Appalachian Plateau, with Confirmed breeding in the Schoharie Hills and Catskill Peaks. One report came from the Rensselaer Hills, and several from the Great Lakes Plain. None of the blocks outside the Adirondacks that had records of kinglets during the first Atlas period had records during the second one. Within the Adirondacks, the number of blocks reporting kinglets declined 21 percent. Apparent was a cluster of blocks in St. Lawrence, Herkimer, and Hamilton counties where kinglets were not found during the second Atlas survey. Local changes in species occurrence between the two Atlas periods, especially in difficult terrain like the Adirondacks, is always potentially the result of coverage changes, not bird distribution.

Breeding Bird Survey data show a significant decline in Ruby-crowned Kinglet numbers survey-wide since 1966, although the negative trend in the last 25 years is not significant (Sauer et al. 2005). BBS data in New York are sparse and so statistical significance is suspect, but they do show a significant decline, with the largest effect in the last 25 years (Sauer et al. 2005). Data from Ontario indicate no change in Ruby-crowned Kinglet numbers between the two Ontario Breeding Bird Atlas projects (Bird Studies Canada et al. 2006), and it still remains an uncommon bird near the New York border. It appears that the Ruby-crowned Kinglet is expanding out of the Adirondacks, where its numbers are declining. In the future, this northern species may be looked for in any region of the state where suitable habitat is available, although one hopes that the declines in the main portion of the range do not continue and that it remains a fixture in the Adirondacks.

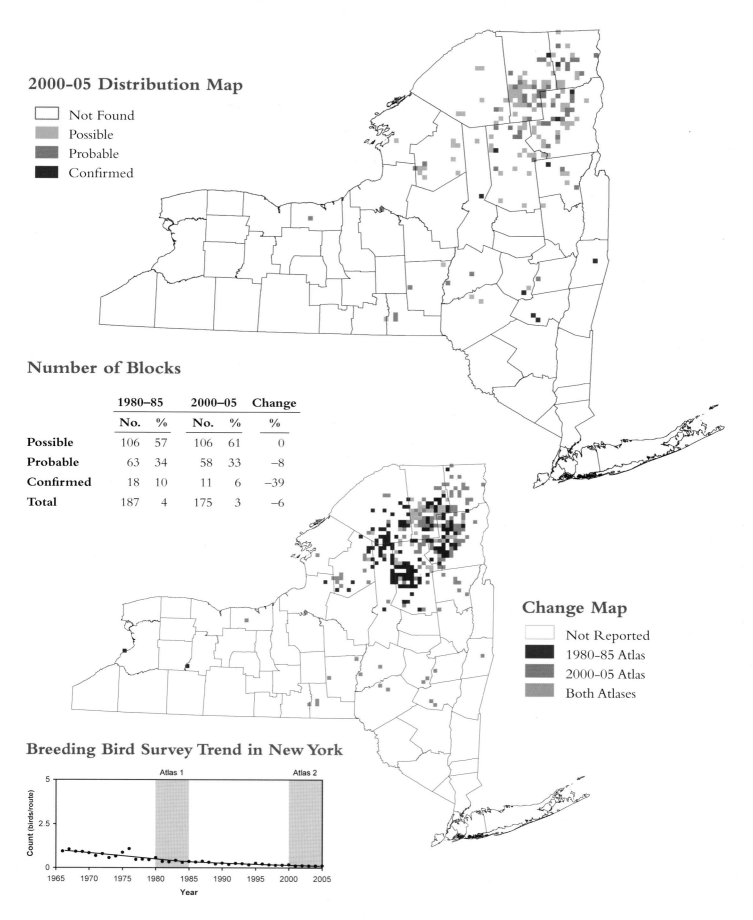

2000-05 Distribution Map

- ☐ Not Found
- Possible
- Probable
- ■ Confirmed

Number of Blocks

	1980–85		2000–05		Change
	No.	%	No.	%	%
Possible	106	57	106	61	0
Probable	63	34	58	33	–8
Confirmed	18	10	11	6	–39
Total	187	4	175	3	–6

Change Map

- ☐ Not Reported
- ■ 1980-85 Atlas
- 2000-05 Atlas
- Both Atlases

Breeding Bird Survey Trend in New York

Blue-gray Gnatcatcher
Polioptila caerulea

KEVIN J. MCGOWAN

The Blue-gray Gnatcatcher is a tiny, long-tailed bird of deciduous forests. It breeds from northern California, southwestern Wyoming, southern Minnesota, southern Ontario, and southern Maine southward to southern Mexico and El Salvador (Ellison 1992). New York is near the northeastern limits of its breeding range. It breeds in a variety of deciduous wooded habitats from shrubland to mature forest, especially near water. In northeastern North America it is generally confined to lowlands, especially near rivers and lakes, and shows a fondness for oaks (Ellison 1992). DeKay (1844) listed the Blue-gray Gnatcatcher as a possible breeder in the western counties of New York. Rathbun (1879) considered it rare in central New York, and Short (1893) listed one breeding record, in Monroe County in 1890. Eaton (1914), also reporting the Monroe County record, stated that like the Tufted Titmouse and the Carolina Wren, the gnatcatcher was a species that occurred frequently in the interior of the state but had not established a breeding population. The gnatcatcher expanded its breeding range northward during the 20th century (Ellison 1992), and it nested along Lake Erie in Chautauqua County in 1943 (Bull 1974). Bull (1974) reported three large flight years (1947, 1954, 1963) that resulted in both sightings and breeding, and he listed breeding localities along the lower Hudson River, a few on eastern Long Island, in the center of the state from Rochester to Syracuse and southward to the Pennsylvania border, and scattered locations along the western frontier. Further expansion as a breeder into New England occurred in the 1970s (Ellison 1993).

The first Atlas map showed the Blue-gray Gnatcatcher in roughly the same areas of the state as reported by Bull (1974), but more common and more widespread in small numbers. Its population was concentrated primarily in the lower Hudson Valley and a broad interior region running southward from Lake Ontario through the Finger Lakes to the Susquehanna River Valley. It had extended its range into the Mohawk and Lake Champlain valleys and up to the St. Lawrence Plains. The second Atlas survey found the Blue-gray Gnatcatcher in roughly the same distribution, but the number of blocks with records increased 19 percent. The increase was most notable along the western Great Lakes Plain. The gnatcatcher's chief stronghold remained the southern Hudson Valley, with substantial increases there and in the Taconic Highlands. It remained absent from nearly all of the Adirondacks. The Blue-gray Gnatcatcher is primarily a lower-elevation bird in New York, with few being found above 610 m (2,000 ft).

Breeding Bird Survey data show little trend in continent-wide gnatcatcher numbers (Sauer et al. 2007). New York data are too sparse for much analysis but no significant trend exists. The second breeding bird atlases from Ontario and Vermont also reported increases in gnatcatcher numbers (Bird Studies Canada et al. 2006, R. Renfrew pers. comm.). The explanation for the mid-20th-century expansion of the Blue-gray Gnatcatcher into New York and other parts of the Northeast remains elusive. Increasing forest cover and the abandonment of farmland could have played some role. The dramatic increase in the numbers of vagrant Blue-gray Gnatcatchers in the 1940s and 1950s implied a corresponding increase in the total gnatcatcher population (Ellison 1993). Ellison (1993) hypothesized that larger populations led to increased spring vagrancy, helped along by favorable weather conditions in certain years. These invasions led to the establishment of breeding populations. Unlike other more southern species that expanded northward in the 20th century (e.g., Tufted Titmouse, Carolina Wren, Northern Cardinal), the gnatcatcher would not have benefited from bird feeders and other such obvious anthropogenic assistance.

2000–05 Distribution Map

- ☐ Not Found
- Possible
- Probable
- Confirmed

Number of Blocks

	1980–85		2000–05		Change
	No.	%	No.	%	%
Possible	318	36	387	37	22
Probable	248	28	349	34	41
Confirmed	310	35	303	29	–2
Total	876	16	1,039	19	19

Change Map

- ☐ Not Reported
- 1980–85 Atlas
- 2000–05 Atlas
- Both Atlases

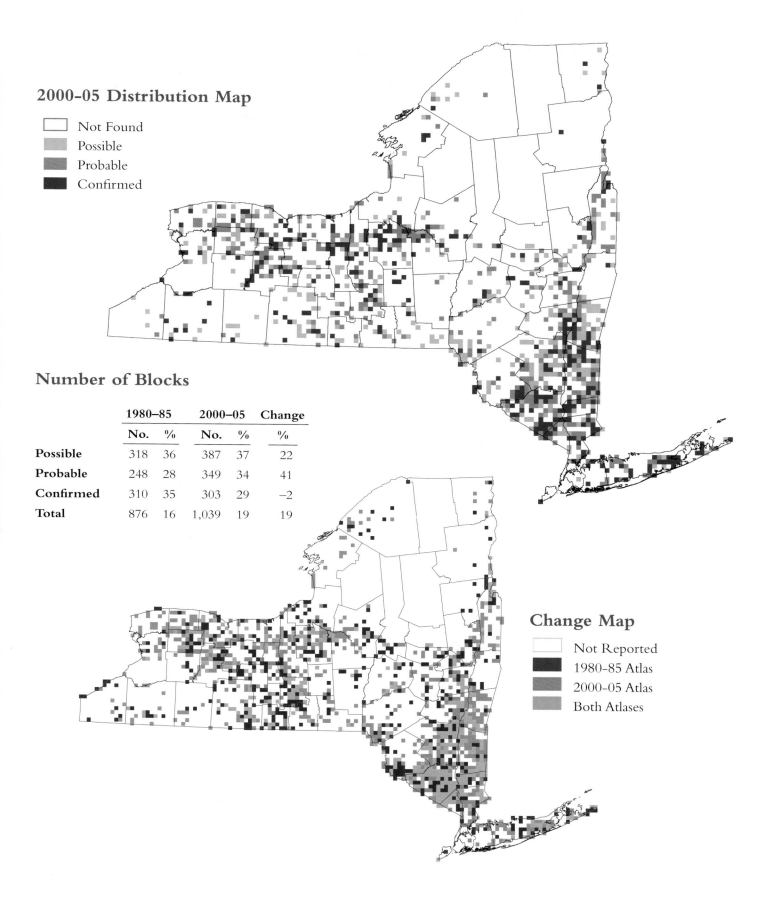

Thrushes along a Catskill stream

Whether fishing the evening rise on the Willowemoc Creek or relaxing on the porch at the Mohonk Mountain House, a Catskill evening would not be the same without the flute-like calls of Hermit and Wood thrushes.

Eastern Bluebird
Sialia sialis

KEVIN L. BERNER

The Eastern Bluebird, declared the New York state bird in 1970 (Kinkead 1973), occurs across most of North America east of the Rocky Mountains, breeding from southern Saskatchewan to Texas and from the Maritime Provinces to Florida; resident populations also stretch from southeastern Arizona to northern Nicaragua (Gowaty and Plissner 1998). A bird of open habitats, this species probably increased its range and population with land clearing in the 1800s (Burrill and Bonney 1988). Eaton (1914) considered the bluebird a common breeding bird throughout New York, and Bull (1974) found it to be a widespread breeder upstate. However, Bull (1974) also noted population declines in urban, suburban, and rural areas, resulting from the decrease in the number of nesting cavities available, as well as nest-site competition with the European Starling and House Sparrow.

The first Atlas map showed the Eastern Bluebird to be widely distributed throughout the state, breeding in nearly every ecozone. The Appalachian Plateau contained the highest percentage of blocks with Confirmed breeding, while the bluebird was missing from significant portions of the Great Lakes Plain, Coastal Lowlands, and Adirondacks. The second Atlas survey showed that the number of blocks with Eastern Bluebird increased by more than 50 percent. The gap seen on the Great Lakes Plain in the first Atlas was almost completely filled, as were most other smaller gaps across the state. Major gaps were again apparent in the Coastal Lowlands, Central Tug Hill, Central Adirondacks, and Western Adirondack Foothills. The Eastern Bluebird is not secretive and its visible nesting sites are readily detected; the Atlas maps should accurately represent bluebird distribution in the state.

The Breeding Bird Survey showed an increase of 3.2 percent per year in Eastern Bluebird numbers in New York in 1980–2005, similar to the increase of 2.6 percent per year found across the range of the species (Sauer et al. 2005). The increase for the north Atlantic states (U.S. Fish and Wildlife Service Region 5) in 1985–2005 was 1.5 percent per year. The second Ontario Breeding Bird Atlas reported significant increases across the province (Bird Studies Canada et al. 2006).

The Eastern Bluebird was listed as a Species of Special Concern in New York during the last Atlas period but was removed from that list in 1997. Most bluebirds now nest in nest boxes (Davis and Roca 1995), and their success is strongly tied to the availability of these boxes. The New York State Bluebird Society (NYSBS) and other bird clubs have promoted the placement of nest boxes in appropriate habitat to increase bluebird populations. In 1993 the NYSBS created a nest box trail along U.S.

Route 20, crossing east to west through the center of New York, where many blocks lacked bluebirds during the first Atlas period. Annual counts by the NYSBS showed an increase in fledging numbers during the second Atlas period: 3,530 young birds fledged from 3,462 nest boxes in 2000, and 5,007 young birds fledged from 3,965 nest boxes in 2006 (R. Briggs pers. comm.). In 1997 NYSBS developed a north-south nest box trail through the center of the state along U.S. Route 11. These boxes produced 127 bluebirds in 2000 and 519 bluebirds in 2006 (Heidenreich 2006). The availability of nesting cavities in suitable habitat has affected the distribution and abundance of all three bluebird species in North America (Berger et al. 2001). Many states and provinces now have bluebird organizations dedicated to increasing bluebird numbers through placement and active monitoring of nest boxes. Future threats to bluebirds in New York may come from the loss of farmland and other open spaces to natural succession and development. Suburban development and sprawl also negatively affect bluebirds because the House Sparrow follows high densities of people. The tending of nest boxes should continue to encourage healthy populations of the Eastern Bluebird in New York.

2000–05 Distribution Map

- ☐ Not Found
- Possible
- Probable
- Confirmed

Number of Blocks

	1980–85		2000–05		Change
	No.	**%**	**No.**	**%**	**%**
Possible	517	21	506	13	−2
Probable	424	17	620	16	46
Confirmed	1,519	62	2,670	70	76
Total	2,460	46	3,796	71	54

Change Map

- ☐ Not Reported
- 1980–85 Atlas
- 2000–05 Atlas
- Both Atlases

Breeding Bird Survey Trend in New York

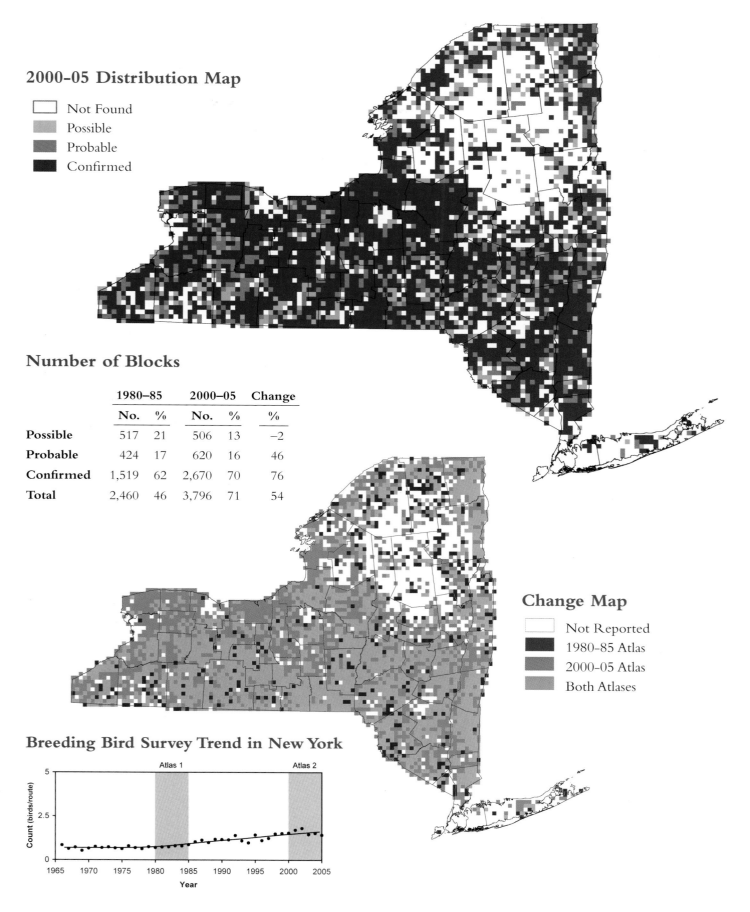

Veery
Catharus fuscescens

James D. Lowe and Ralph S. Hames

Like most woodland thrushes, the Veery is heard more often than it is seen. Its descending flutelike song is easy to identify and is often heard in the morning and evening. The breeding range of the Veery extends along the border of the United States and Canada, southward in the Rocky Mountains and Appalachians. Most of New York has a medium to high population density as compared with the rest of the breeding range, although lower densities occur in the Great Lakes Plain (Sauer et al. 2005). The Veery generally nests in damp, deciduous forests with dense undergrowth. Preferred habitats include disturbed forest, probably because of its denser understory, and late shrub or early-successional trees (Bevier et al. 2004). In some areas the Veery uses coniferous and mixed forests as well (Bevier et al. 2004). It is area sensitive, meaning it is more likely to be present in larger forest patches (Robbins et al. 1989, Rosenberg et al. 2003, Bevier et al. 2004), but Birds in Forested Landscapes data (Rosenberg et al. 2003) suggest that it is less area sensitive in the Northern Forest Region, which includes the Adirondacks, Adirondack Foothills, and Tug Hill. The Veery is currently considered a widespread and generally common breeder in New York (Ellison 1998c). This situation was also true nearly a century ago when Eaton (1914) said, "It is a common summer resident of a large portion of the state," although he also commented that it was uncommon on Long Island and "practically absent from the spruce and balsam forests of the Catskills and Adirondacks."

The first Atlas documented the Veery breeding throughout the state, with slightly fewer blocks with records in parts of the Adirondacks, in some areas of the Great Lakes Plain, and the western Coastal Lowlands. Overall, results from the second Atlas survey were almost identical, except that 19 percent fewer blocks with breeding records were reported both in the Adirondacks and in the Coastal Lowlands. These decreases were somewhat offset by modest increases in the Taconic Highlands, where 10 percent more blocks were reported, and in the western Great Lakes Plain,

specifically in Atlas Region 1, where 17 percent more blocks were reported. The first Atlas noted high elevations in the Adirondacks and the lack of suitable forest cover in the Great Lakes Plain as the primary reasons for the gaps it described (Bonney 1988f). Those ideas still explain the current gaps in distribution, but they do not necessarily explain the apparent changes since the first Atlas survey period. These changes may be related to large-scale declines in Veery numbers. Because it is area sensitive, habitat fragmentation may be a factor in the declines.

Breeding Bird Survey data from 1966 to 2005 show that Veery populations have declined range-wide at a significant rate of −1.5 percent per year. A significant decline of −1.5 percent per year was found in New York as well (Sauer et al. 2005). For the years 1980–2005, the declines are even greater and still significant, with a range-wide decline of −2.0 percent per year and a decline in New York of −2.1 percent per year (Sauer et al. 2005). The BBS data also show that the highest decreases are in the northern part of the state, including the Adirondacks, Adirondack Foothills, St. Lawrence Plains, and Champlain Valley.

The Veery is not a state-listed species, but because of widespread and steady population declines, it warrants conservation concern. The Partners in Flight North American Landbird Conservation Plan (Rich et al. 2004) suggested that threats during the nonbreeding season are also a reason for concern. Because the population declines are widespread, other large-scale environmental issues such as atmospheric deposition of pollutants and climate change might also be contributing to the problem. At this time, monitoring efforts across the breeding range are generally considered adequate (Rich et al. 2004), but more research into the causes of the declines is certainly needed.

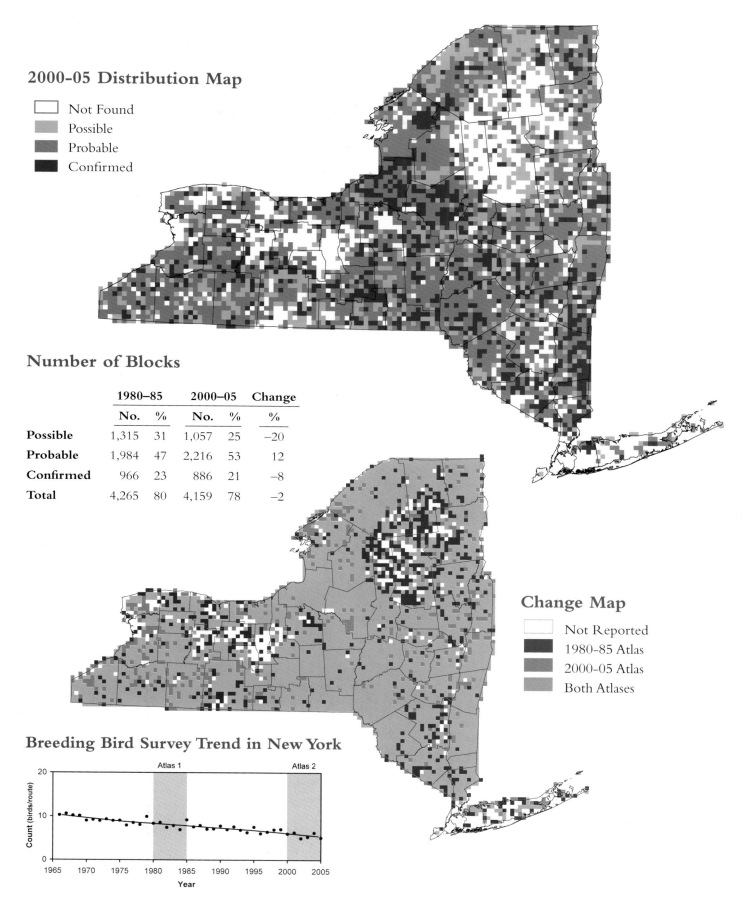

2000–05 Distribution Map

- ☐ Not Found
- Possible
- Probable
- Confirmed

Number of Blocks

	1980–85		2000–05		Change
	No.	%	No.	%	%
Possible	1,315	31	1,057	25	−20
Probable	1,984	47	2,216	53	12
Confirmed	966	23	886	21	−8
Total	4,265	80	4,159	78	−2

Change Map

- ☐ Not Reported
- 1980-85 Atlas
- 2000-05 Atlas
- Both Atlases

Breeding Bird Survey Trend in New York

Bicknell's Thrush

Catharus bicknelli

CHRISTOPHER C. RIMMER

Bicknell's Thrush, classified as a species distinct from the Gray-cheeked Thrush in 1995 (AOU 1995), was first discovered in 1881 on Slide Mountain in the Catskills by amateur ornithologist Eugene Bicknell. This habitat specialist occupies a naturally fragmented breeding range extending from the Catskills and Adirondacks of New York, through the mountains of northern New England, to the Gulf of St. Lawrence and Cape Breton Island, Nova Scotia (Atwood et al. 1996, Rimmer et al. 2001). Within this range, it inhabits dense montane forests dominated by balsam fir, with lesser amounts of red and black spruce, white birch, and mountain-ash. Lambert et al. (2005) estimated that 23.5 percent of this species's habitat in the United States is in New York. Bull (1974) noted that the species was "generally distributed" in the Adirondacks at elevations of 914–1,523 m (3,000–5,000 ft), but his map depicted only six Catskills peaks with known occurrences. A coordinated, statewide distributional survey in 1992–94 revealed the presence of Bicknell's Thrush on 75 percent of the peaks surveyed, with detections on all 10 Catskills peaks and 23 of the 34 Adirondack peaks surveyed (Atwood et al. 1996). The lowest elevation for a New York peak with a Bicknell's Thrush record was 1,152 m (3,780 ft). It was found on all 16 peaks surveyed that had historic (pre-1992) records, suggesting that no pronounced distributional changes had occurred (Atwood et al. 1996).

During the first Atlas survey, Bicknell's Thrush was found in 14 blocks in the Catskills and 25 in the Adirondacks. During the second Atlas survey, it was documented in 17 blocks in the Catskills and 39 in the Adirondacks. More survey effort was directed in high-elevation habitats during the second Atlas period, primarily because of the launching of Mountain Birdwatch (MBW) in 2000 (Lambert 2006). MBW observers contributed Bicknell's Thrush data from 27 blocks to the second Atlas results. Thus, while it is not possible to directly compare observer effort for this species between the two Atlas projects, the apparent difference complicates any assessment of changes in distribution between the two periods. Local extinctions and colonizations may have occurred, as have been documented throughout the species's breeding range (Rimmer et al. 2001, Lambert et al. 2005), but there is no evidence of a statewide expansion or contraction between 1980–85 and 2000–05.

Bicknell's Thrush is inadequately monitored by traditional sampling methods such as the Breeding Bird Survey (Rimmer et al. 1996). Range-wide data collected during 2001–05 by targeted high-elevation bird monitoring through MBW show no significant population trend (J. D. Lambert unpubl. data), but additional years of data collection will be necessary to generate robust trend estimates. Meaningful state-specific trend data exist only for New Hampshire's White Mountain National Forest, where Bicknell's Thrush showed a statistically significant annual decline of 7 percent on 39 survey routes from 1993 to 2000 (J. D. Lambert unpubl. data). Partners in Flight (Pashley et al. 2000, Rich et al. 2004) ranks Bicknell's Thrush as one of the top conservation priority species among Neotropical migrants continent-wide, owing to its rarity, limited distribution, and documented threats on its breeding and wintering ranges. In New York, this thrush is listed as a Species of Special Concern, as it is in Vermont, New Hampshire, and Maine. Its global population is believed to number fewer than 50,000 individuals (Rimmer et al. 2001, Rich et al. 2004), with some recent estimates suggesting a range-wide population of fewer than 20,000 birds (Lambert et al. 2005, Hale 2006). Although evidence for population declines remains inconclusive, winter habitat loss, acid deposition and mercury accumulation in mountain ecosystems, climatic warming, and human development of breeding habitat are threats. The future of this rare, geographically restricted species is far from secure.

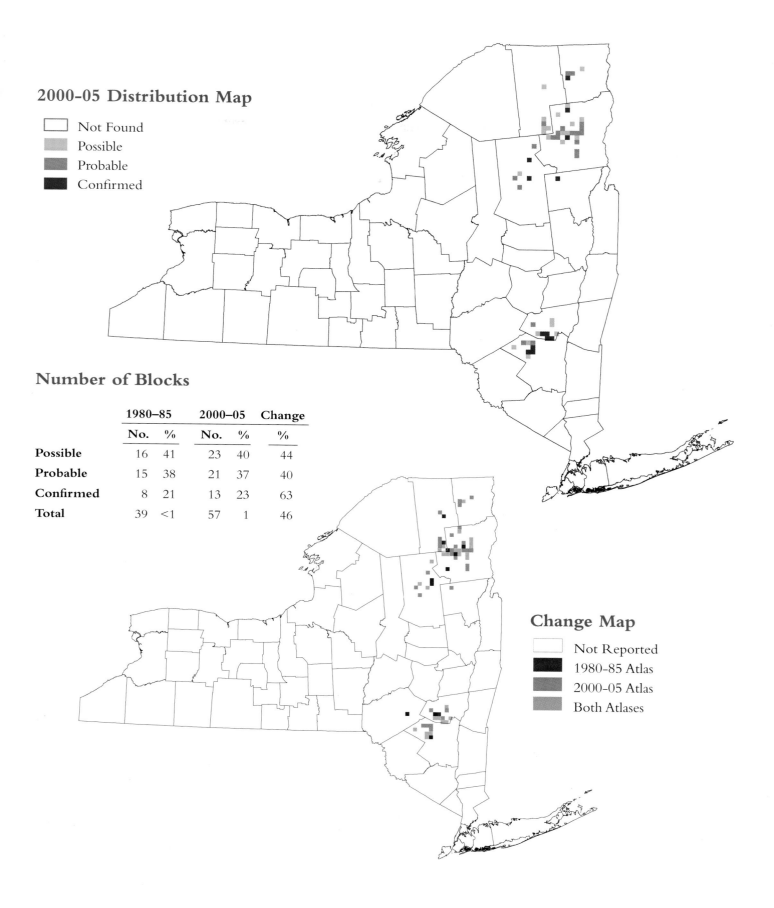

2000-05 Distribution Map

- ☐ Not Found
- Possible
- Probable
- Confirmed

Number of Blocks

	1980–85		2000–05		Change
	No.	%	No.	%	%
Possible	16	41	23	40	44
Probable	15	38	21	37	40
Confirmed	8	21	13	23	63
Total	39	<1	57	1	46

Change Map

- ☐ Not Reported
- 1980-85 Atlas
- 2000-05 Atlas
- Both Atlases

Swainson's Thrush
Catharus ustulatus

James D. Lowe and Ralph S. Hames

Although common in the vast boreal forests to the north, Swainson's Thrush is New York's second-rarest breeding thrush, ranking behind only Bicknell's Thrush. New York is situated on the southern edge of a large breeding range that extends from Alaska to Labrador and Newfoundland and southward into New England, the Appalachians, the Rocky Mountains, and along the Pacific Coast of California (Evans Mack and Yong 2000). Swainson's Thrush can be found breeding in many types of forest, but throughout most of its range it is seen most frequently in coniferous habitats (Evans Mack and Yong 2000). This is true in New York, where it occurs in Adirondack and Catskill red spruce–balsam fir forests (Dilger 1956, Hough 1964). At lower elevations in the mountains, and elsewhere in the state, it can be found in northern hardwoods mixed with red spruce or hemlock (Dilger 1956), or along black spruce–tamarack bogs (Ellison 1998b). Some New York populations (in Chenango County, for example) can be found in reforestation areas planted in Norway and white spruce (J. M. C. Peterson 1988q). Eaton (1914) described Swainson's Thrush as a common summer resident of the higher forests of the Catskills and Adirondacks, with some also breeding in the highest mountains near the Pennsylvania border. Bull (1974) simply stated it was a common breeder in the mountains, with sparse breeding records outside the Catskill, Adirondack, and Tug Hill regions.

The first Atlas map showed Swainson's Thrush to be widespread in the Adirondacks (including the Eastern and Western Adirondack foothills) with restricted populations in the Central Tug Hill, Taconic Highlands, Helderberg Highlands, Schoharie Hills, Catskill Peaks, Delaware Hills, Allegany Hills, Cattaraugus Highlands, and Appalachian Plateau (especially in Chenango County). At first glance, the second Atlas map looks almost identical to the first one, but the total number of blocks in which Swainson's Thrush was recorded dropped 16 percent. The Change Map, however, shows an interesting pattern. The majority of de-

clines occurred in the Western Adirondack Foothills, Tug Hill Transition, and Delaware Hills. Each of these areas is located on the western side of a main population center.

Breeding Bird Survey trends show an interesting mosaic of increases and decreases in different areas, but overall, populations have significantly declined survey-wide at a rate of 0.9 percent per year from 1980 to 2005 (Sauer et al. 2005). A similar, but nonsignificant, decline of 2 percent per year was found in New York over the same period (Sauer et al. 2005). BBS results for Swainson's Thrush should be interpreted with caution because of low numbers, small sample sizes, and conflicting trends in different areas or from different time periods. Various explanations for these declines have been presented, such as forest management practices in the boreal zone, forest destruction on the wintering grounds, and collisions with man-made structures during migration (Evans Mack and Yong 2000). The pattern of change seen in New York, however, hints at another possible cause. The declines in areas facing the prevailing west winds suggest that large-scale factors relating to atmospheric conditions, such as air pollution and acid deposition, may play a role in New York.

The Partners in Flight North American Landbird Conservation Plan (Rich et al. 2004) indicated that breeding range-wide monitoring of the Swainson's Thrush had inadequate northern coverage because much of the species's breeding range is located north of the area that is well covered by BBS routes. In New York and New England, however, Swainson's Thrush is now being monitored by Mountain Birdwatch, a project of the Vermont Institute of Natural Science (Lambert 2006). Better monitoring elsewhere combined with some detailed studies might help illuminate the actual causes of the population declines.

2000-05 Distribution Map

- ☐ Not Found
- Possible
- Probable
- Confirmed

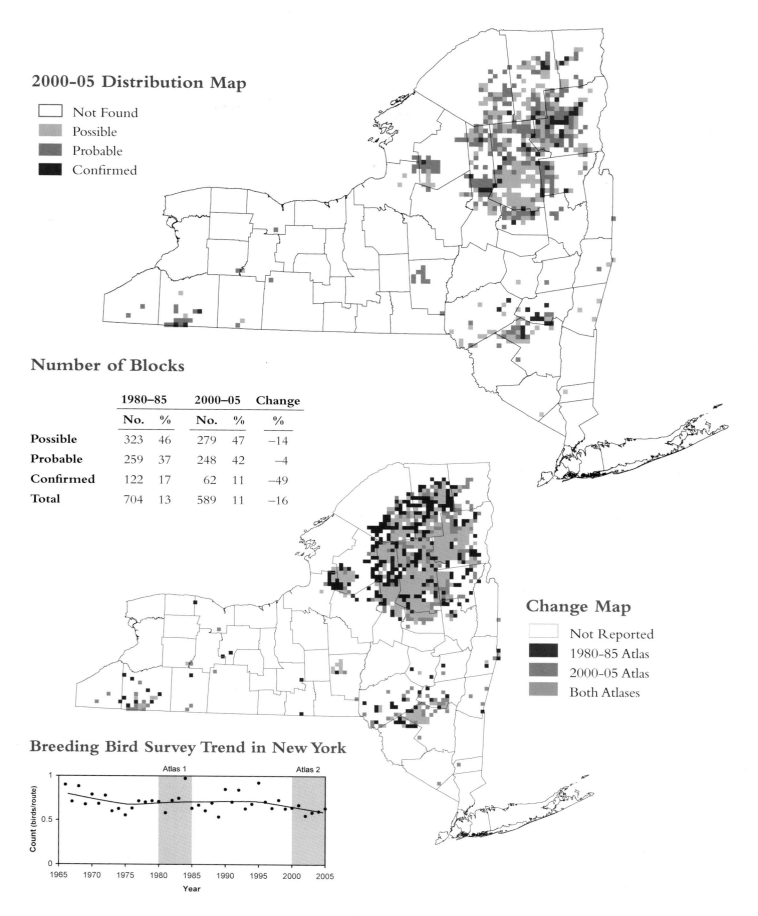

Number of Blocks

	1980–85		2000–05		Change
	No.	%	No.	%	%
Possible	323	46	279	47	−14
Probable	259	37	248	42	−4
Confirmed	122	17	62	11	−49
Total	704	13	589	11	−16

Change Map

- ☐ Not Reported
- 1980-85 Atlas
- 2000-05 Atlas
- Both Atlases

Breeding Bird Survey Trend in New York

Hermit Thrush
Catharus guttatus

RALPH S. HAMES AND JAMES D. LOWE

The drab, unobtrusive Hermit Thrush forages in the lower branches of saplings in coniferous and mixed forests, where it nests (Jones and Donovan 1996). While inconspicuous, this thrush produces perhaps the most beautiful song of any North American species. This splendid singer breeds from Alaska southward to Baja California and the Mexican border, across much of Canada to Labrador and Newfoundland, and then southward through New England, New York, and the Appalachians as far as West Virginia (Jones and Donovan 1996). Bull (1974) noted that the Hermit Thrush was common at higher elevations in coniferous and mixed woodlands across the state, as well as in the pine barrens on Long Island, but was local and spotty in occurrence at lower elevations in other regions.

During the first Atlas period, the centers of abundance for the Hermit Thrush were the Adirondacks, Tug Hill Plateau, and Catskills, with many also scattered across the Appalachian Plateau and Taconic Highlands. Smaller numbers were found in other ecozones. Interestingly, 3 percent of the blocks occupied during the first Atlas period were at relatively low elevations in the Champlain Valley and the Coastal Lowlands. The number of occupied blocks increased 31 percent according to the second Atlas findings. The largest increases were in the Great Lakes Plain, Mohawk Valley, and Champlain Valley. Especially notable were gap-filling increases in occupied blocks in the Appalachian Plateau and St. Lawrence Plains. The only decline was in the Coastal Lowlands, where effort also was down, but the thrush is still present on the eastern end of Long Island. The distribution of the Hermit Thrush in the state still shows large gaps in the areas of lowest elevation, across the Great Lakes Plain, through the Mohawk Valley, and in the Hudson Valley.

Survey-wide, Breeding Bird Survey data show the Hermit Thrush increasing significantly in abundance by an average of 0.8 percent per year between 1980 and 2000 (Sauer et al. 2005). In New York, the increase was 4.4 percent per year over the same period (Sauer et al. 2005). The causes of these increases may perhaps be found in changes to the environment, including acid rain (Hames et al. 2002a, Hames et al. 2006), and declines in the distribution of other thrush species.

While the Hermit Thrush is perhaps seen most frequently in coniferous or mixed woodlands (Dilger 1956, Jones and Donovan 1996, Ellison 1998a), it is also found in a "broad spectrum" (Jones and Donovan 1996) of habitat types. Of the thrushes breeding in North America that occur together, the Hermit Thrush uses the widest variety of habitats (Noon 1981). Morse (1971) postulated that while nesting in the presence of the Wood Thrush, both the Hermit Thrush and the Veery chose nest sites that would have otherwise been avoided, because the Wood Thrush was dominant and took the better sites.

Noon (1981) showed that the Wood Thrush did not use any habitats not used by the Veery or the Hermit Thrush, and pointed out that when these species were not found together, the two smaller thrushes used a larger variety of habitats. Thus, the declining trends in the other thrush species (Sauer et al. 2005) may allow the Hermit Thrush to exploit habitats that were precluded in the presence of other thrushes. Further, although others have suggested that the Hermit Thrush prefers high-elevation sites (Bull 1974, Bonney 1988c, Jones and Donovan 1996, Hames et al. 2002b), it is equally possible that this species is adapted to coniferous forests and their acidic soils, which occur more often at higher elevations. This adaptation would explain the presence of this species at low-elevation pine barren sites and in areas receiving heavy acid deposition where other thrush species are in decline.

2000-05 Distribution Map

- ☐ Not Found
- Possible
- Probable
- Confirmed

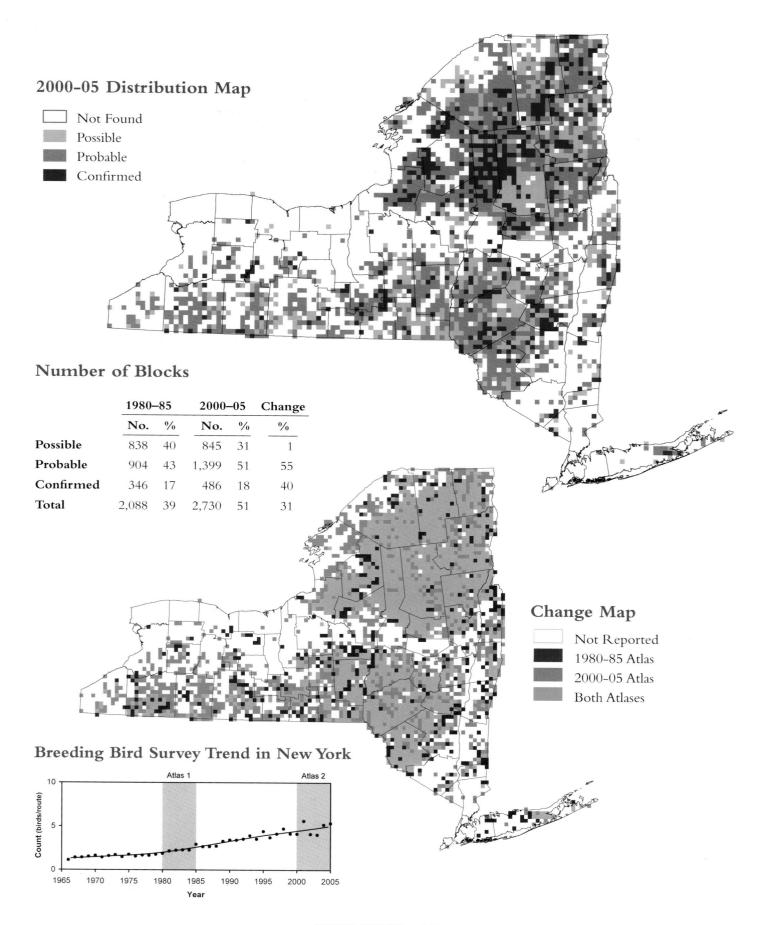

Number of Blocks

	1980–85		2000–05		Change
	No.	%	No.	%	%
Possible	838	40	845	31	1
Probable	904	43	1,399	51	55
Confirmed	346	17	486	18	40
Total	2,088	39	2,730	51	31

Change Map

- ☐ Not Reported
- 1980-85 Atlas
- 2000-05 Atlas
- Both Atlases

Breeding Bird Survey Trend in New York

Wood Thrush

Hylocichla mustelina

RALPH S. HAMES AND JAMES D. LOWE

The haunting, flute-like tones of the Wood Thrush are familiar sounds in New York's eastern hardwood forests. The Wood Thrush is found throughout North America east of the Great Plains, from Minnesota and Quebec to eastern Texas and northern Florida. It breeds in deciduous forests with a high canopy, a well-developed understory and leaf litter layer, and some moisture (Roth et al. 1996). Historically, the Wood Thrush was nearly ubiquitous in New York, only "absent in higher mountains" (Bull 1974).

The first Atlas map showed the Wood Thrush distributed widely across the state, missing only from scattered areas in the Adirondacks and much of the New York City area. The second Atlas results revealed a similar distribution but an overall decrease of 7 percent in the number of blocks with breeding records. Most of the decrease occurred in the Adirondacks, where the number of occupied blocks declined 34 percent. Losses in the Central Adirondacks and Western Adirondack Foothills were especially prominent.

Populations of the Wood Thrush are declining in most regions across its range (Sauer et al. 2005). It is a Species of Greatest Conservation Need (NYSDEC 2005a), and Partners in Flight listed it as a Bird of Conservation Concern (Rich et al. 2004). From 1966 to 2004, Wood Thrush populations declined 1.8 percent per year range-wide, based on Breeding Bird Survey data (Sauer et al. 2005). In New York the species has declined at 3.1 percent per year (Sauer et al. 2005) since 1980. This statewide average masks even larger regional declines, including a shocking 5.7 percent annual decline in the Adirondacks (Sauer et al. 2005). Several studies have postulated mechanisms behind these population declines (Donovan et al. 1995, Hoover et al. 1995, Holmes and Sherry 2001, Donovan and Flather 2002, Driscoll et al. 2005), including loss of habitat on the wintering ground (Rappole and McDonald 1994), over-winter mortality (Rappole et al. 1989), acid rain (Hames et al. 2002a, Hames et al. 2006), and mercury deposition (Hames et al. unpubl. data). These postulated mechanisms, however, are unlikely to have caused patterns such as the loss of occupied blocks concentrated in the Adirondacks.

Hames et al. (2002a) showed that acid rain was related to the declining probability of nesting by the Wood Thrush across its range. At 45 sites in four regions of New York (including 15 in the Adirondacks), Hames et al. (2006) also showed that Wood Thrush breeding attempts were negatively correlated with acid rain–caused leaching of calcium from the soil and declines in the numbers of calcium-rich invertebrates needed during breeding. The thin, low pH soils of the Adirondacks may be particularly sensitive to the effects of acid rain (Schoch 2002, NYSDEC 2005a). Certainly the patterns of high acid rain (Ollinger et al. 1993) and mercury deposition (Miller et al. 2005) in the western and central Adirondacks appear to correspond with loss of occupied blocks. It is likely, however, that these declines are the result of multiple influences on this thrush (Hames et al. 2006), rather than one cause alone.

Because the observation of only one singing individual is necessary for a block to be counted as Possible breeding for a species, the Atlas methodology, while good for addressing distribution, is not good for assessing abundance. If the number of any abundant bird in a block is decreased by half, there still are many individuals in the block, and the probability of detecting one would be high. This means that local population sizes have to decrease by a very large proportion until the species is rare enough to miss with a high probability. Then the block is no longer marked as Possible breeding, because a singing individual cannot be found. Because the declines in the Adirondacks were severe and concentrated in a small area, the Atlas methodology could detect them while missing smaller trends statewide. The next Atlas project, however, may find many fewer blocks occupied by the Wood Thrush across the state.

2000-05 Distribution Map

- ☐ Not Found
- Possible
- Probable
- Confirmed

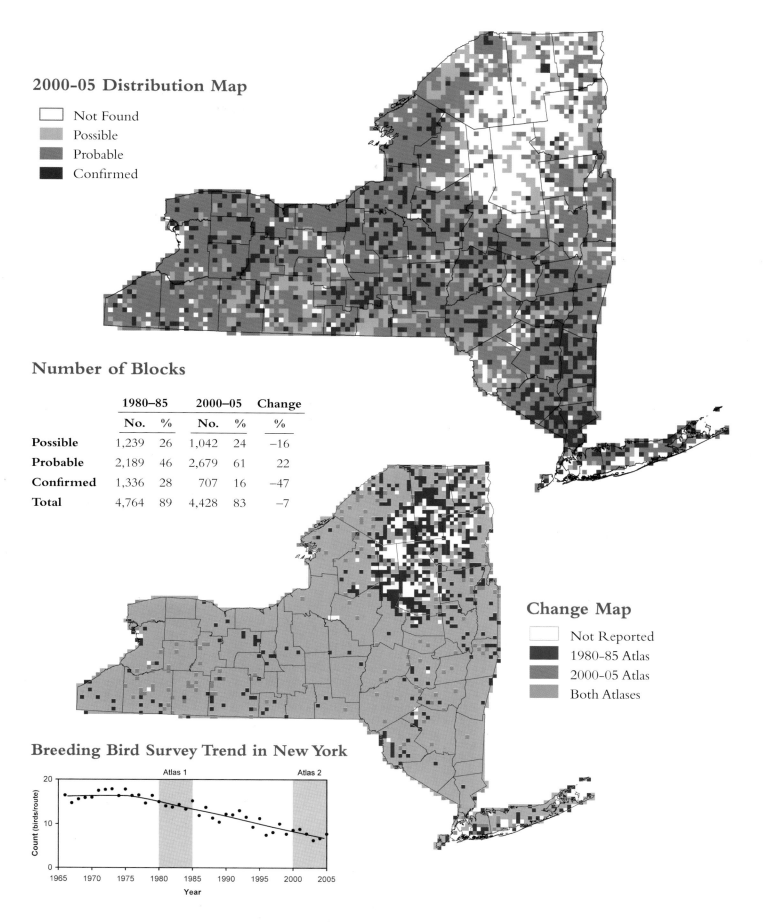

Number of Blocks

	1980–85		2000–05		Change
	No.	%	No.	%	%
Possible	1,239	26	1,042	24	−16
Probable	2,189	46	2,679	61	22
Confirmed	1,336	28	707	16	−47
Total	4,764	89	4,428	83	−7

Change Map

- ☐ Not Reported
- 1980–85 Atlas
- 2000–05 Atlas
- Both Atlases

Breeding Bird Survey Trend in New York

American Robin

Turdus migratorius

KEVIN J. McGOWAN

The American Robin is one of the most familiar birds in North America, as it breeds in a variety of habitats from Alaska and northern Canada to northern Florida and Mexico. It uses forests, woodlands, and gardens, especially short-grass areas interspersed with shrubs and trees. Although originally primarily a bird of mature forests and clearings, it is tolerant of people and quickly adapted to the opening of the primeval forests by European settlers. It has been one of the most common birds in New York State from pre-colonial times to the present. The species is seen throughout the state, breeding in the Adirondack wilderness as well as in urban and suburban landscapes. Considered abundant upstate since the early 1800s (De-Kay 1844, Rathbun 1879), the American Robin began breeding on Long Island only in the early 1900s (Griscom 1923) but was abundant there by the 1940s (Cruickshank 1942).

The first Atlas reported the American Robin breeding in all corners of the state. It was found in 97 percent of all blocks, a prevalence second only to the Song Sparrow. It was confirmed breeding in 90 percent of the blocks where it was found, and in 87 percent of all Atlas blocks, more than any other species. Its absence in some blocks in the Adirondack High Peaks, Central Adirondacks, Western Adirondack Foothills, and Western Adirondack Transition may have reflected coverage limitations instead of true absences. The second Atlas survey found essentially the same distribution. This time the robin was found in 98 percent of blocks, with absences again suggesting lack of coverage not lack of robins. It replaced the Song Sparrow as the most reported species in the Atlas. Obvious gaps were present only in the Central Tug Hill, Central Adirondacks, and Western Adirondack Foothills.

With a few exceptions, robin populations appear to be increasing or stable throughout North America (Sallabanks and James 1999). Partners in Flight gave it one of the lowest assessment scores of any North American bird because of its wide breeding range, its high breeding density, and its stable or positive population trends (Rich et al. 2004). Breeding Bird Survey data show a significant continuous increase across the continent throughout the life of the survey (Sauer et al. 2007). In New York, however, BBS data show a slight but significant decline between 1966 and 1979. Since that time no significant trend has been apparent in the state, and breeding populations remain at 1970 levels (Sauer et al. 2007).

Although the American Robin is vulnerable to pesticide poisoning because of its heavy use of human-modified environments, poisoning is rare and the robin will undoubtedly remain a conspicuous part of New York's avifauna long into the future.

2000-05 Distribution Map

- ☐ Not Found
- Possible
- Probable
- Confirmed

Number of Blocks

	1980–85		2000–05		Change
	No.	%	No.	%	%
Possible	283	5	259	5	−8
Probable	261	5	441	8	69
Confirmed	4,645	90	4,539	87	−2
Total	5,189	97	5,239	98	1

Change Map

- ☐ Not Reported
- 1980-85 Atlas
- 2000-05 Atlas
- Both Atlases

Breeding Bird Survey Trend in New York

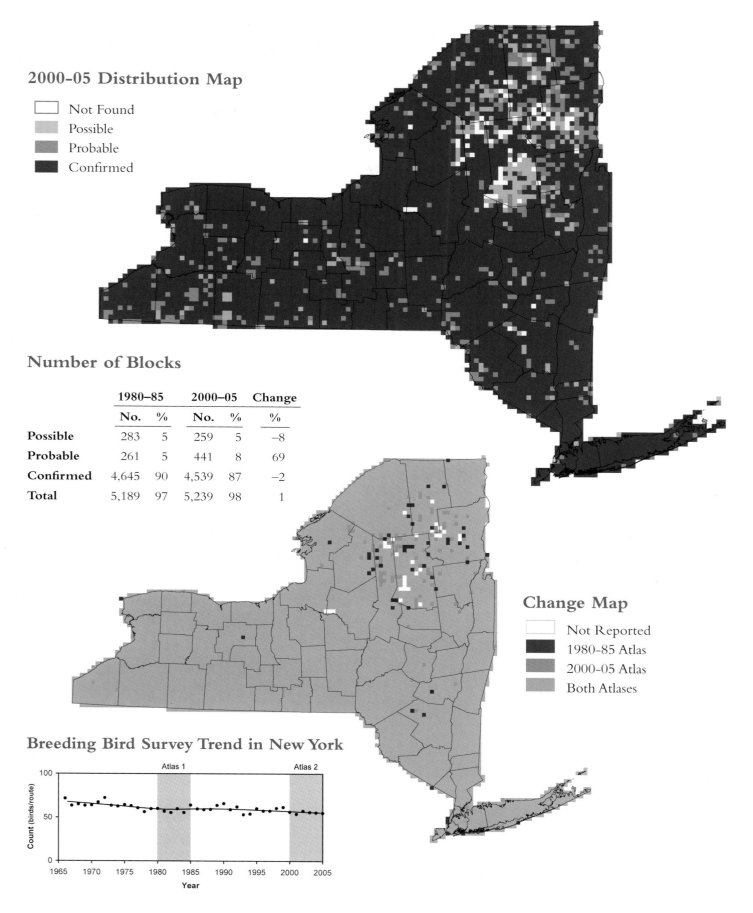

Cedar Waxwing, Northern Mockingbird, and European Starling in a Finger Lakes vineyard

Air temperatures on the slopes above Central New York's Finger Lakes region are several degrees warmer during winter than in the surrounding area. This circumstance creates an ideal situation for viniculture, as well as for more southern bird species such as the Northern Mockingbird.

Gray Catbird
Dumetella carolinensis

Kevin J. McGowan

The Gray Catbird is a noisy, if secretive, inhabitant of dense shrubs and vine tangles. It breeds coast-to-coast across southern Canada, southward to northeastern Arizona, eastern Texas, and northern Florida (Cimprich and Moore 1995). It is found in dense, shrubby habitats, such as abandoned farmland, fencerows, roadsides, streamsides, forest edges and clearings, as well as residential areas (Cimprich and Moore 1995). As a bird of second-growth and mid-successional stages, it was probably uncommon in New York before the clearing of the forests during European colonization and might have been restricted to river edges, beaver meadows, and areas of forest damaged by fire and storms. The clearing of the forests and the creation of shrubby habitats was to its liking, and it was common to abundant across most of the state by the mid-1800s (DeKay 1844, Giraud 1844, Rathbun 1879, Short 1893). Merriam (1881) said it bred along the borders of the mountains but that it rarely penetrated the wilderness of the Adirondacks to any extent. Eaton (1914) gave its range as extending across the whole state except the spruce-fir forests of the Adirondacks and Catskills. He listed it as one of the most abundant species in the settled regions of the state. The abandonment of farmland in the early 20th century created even more habitat for the catbird, and it is likely that it reached an all-time high population in New York in the middle of that century. Bull (1974) called it a widespread breeder common throughout the state but rare to absent in the mountains or at high elevations.

The Gray Catbird was the 10th most frequently reported species in the first Atlas, absent only from some areas of the Central Adirondacks, Adirondack High Peaks, and the northern part of the Western Adirondack Foothills, all areas of high elevation and deep forest with little shrubby habitat. It remained one of the most common birds found during the second Atlas survey, but it dropped to being the 16th most common species, and it was found in 4 percent fewer blocks. Blocks recording the catbird declined a significant 24 percent within the Adirondacks. It was mostly absent from the Central Adirondacks, Adirondack High Peaks, Sable Highlands, much of the Western Adirondack Foothills, and portions of the Eastern Adirondack Foothills. Although the catbird likes to skulk in dense vegetation, it is a vigorous singer with an easily recognizable song, and its presence was easily detected by atlasers.

Breeding Bird Survey data show no change in Gray Catbird populations survey-wide since 1966 (Sauer et al. 2005). BBS data from New York also show no change (Sauer et al. 2005). BBS data from the Adirondacks and farther north show significant declines, however, and the numbers from Northern New England indicate a precipitous decrease since 1980 (Sauer et al. 2005). The second Ontario Breeding Bird Atlas also reported a significant decrease in squares with catbird detections across that province, with the largest declines occurring in the more northern regions (Bird Studies Canada et al. 2006). The numbers from the Adirondacks and from farther northward in the catbird's range suggest a real decline in part of the catbird's population. As a bird that prefers mid-successional stages, the spread and especially the maturation of forests in these regions must result in some decreases. Just how significant and widespread these will be remains to be seen. The Gray Catbird readily uses human-modified habitats and will nest in close proximity to people, however, so its prospects could be good in the long run.

2000-05 Distribution Map

- [ ] Not Found
- Possible
- Probable
- Confirmed

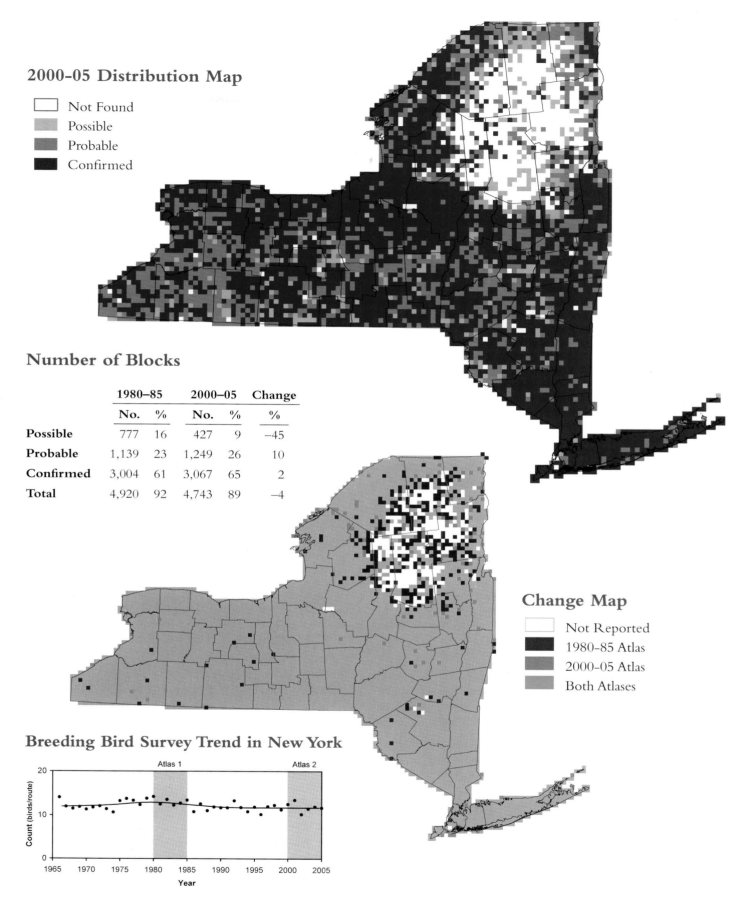

Number of Blocks

	1980–85		2000–05		Change
	No.	%	No.	%	%
Possible	777	16	427	9	−45
Probable	1,139	23	1,249	26	10
Confirmed	3,004	61	3,067	65	2
Total	4,920	92	4,743	89	−4

Change Map

- [ ] Not Reported
- 1980-85 Atlas
- 2000-05 Atlas
- Both Atlases

Breeding Bird Survey Trend in New York

Northern Mockingbird

Mimus polyglottos

KEVIN J. MCGOWAN

The Northern Mockingbird is resident from southern Canada southward to southern Mexico and the Caribbean. It is found in areas with open ground and shrubby vegetation, such as parkland, cultivated land, and suburbs. It eats fruit and insects and commonly forages for prey on mowed lawns (Derrickson and Breitwisch 1992). Primarily a southern species, the Northern Mockingbird was rare and coastal in New York in the mid-1800s (DeKay 1844, Giraud 1844) and may have been missing entirely from the state before European settlement. Rathbun (1879) and Reed and Wright (1909) did not mention it as a bird of central New York, and Short (1893) called it rare but a possible breeder in western New York. Eaton (1914) reported it as occurring, and possibly breeding, on Long Island and southeastern New York, but it was apparently not common there. The first confirmed nesting in the state was in 1925 in Erie County (Beardslee and Mitchell 1965). In the 1950s through the 1970s the mockingbird population increased throughout the state, with more than 100 breeding localities recorded within 20 years (Bull 1974). Bull's (1974) map showed it breeding across the Coastal Lowlands, up the Hudson Valley to Saratoga County, in the southern Finger Lakes region southward, and along the Great Lakes Plain. He noted that it was missing from the Mohawk Valley but suggested the gap was the result of few observers. Reasons for the expansion are unclear.

The first Atlas map showed the Northern Mockingbird to be common across the Coastal Lowlands and the lower Hudson Valley, extending northward to the Champlain Valley. In western New York it was most numerous in the central Lake Ontario Plain, through the Finger Lakes region, into the Central Appalachians. Scattered reports were made in all counties and even into the Central Adirondacks. Although the second Atlas survey showed the mockingbird's distribution to have increased, as predicted by Meade (1988c), the expansion was perhaps less than expected. Statewide, the number of blocks with breeding records increased only 10 percent and actually declined in half of the Atlas regions. Increases occurred in the central and western portions of the state where it was already reasonably common, filling gaps more than expanding farther outward. It remains uncommon and sparsely distributed in much of the western and eastern Appalachian Plateau and north of the Mohawk Valley. In the southeastern portion the Northern Mockingbird is still common, but it appears to have declined somewhat at the edge of the range, especially where it had extended up onto the Appalachian Plateau. The overall range still looks much as it did in the first Atlas and in the outline of the range given by Bull (1974) after the major expansion in the mid-20th century. That period was unique, apparently, as the expansion has either slowed or come to a stop. Despite Melin's (1998b) statement that the mockingbird used the Mohawk Valley as a dispersal route into the center of the state, that valley remains mostly without mockingbirds, as it has since Bull's (1974) report.

Breeding Bird Survey data show a significant but slight decline in Northern Mockingbird numbers across the survey area (Sauer et al. 2005). Previous analyses have noted this decline but stated that it was in the southern portion of the range and that the species was still expanding its range northward (Derrickson and Breitwisch 1992). The long-term trend in the Northeastern Region, however, is significantly negative (Sauer et al. 2005). BBS data from New York show a significant increase, but the trend for the last 25 years is negative (Sauer et al. 2005). These data agree with the Atlas data and suggest that the population of the Northern Mockingbird in New York may have reached a stable plateau. The expansion may be continuing in Ontario; the second Ontario Breeding Bird Atlas reported mockingbirds in more than double the number of blocks as in the first Atlas (Bird Studies Canada et al. 2006).

2000-05 Distribution Map

Not Found
Possible
Probable
Confirmed

Number of Blocks

| | 1980–85 | | 2000–05 | | Change |
	No.	%	No.	%	%
Possible	398	27	456	28	15
Probable	403	27	519	32	29
Confirmed	689	46	660	40	−4
Total	1,490	28	1,635	31	10

Change Map

Not Reported
1980-85 Atlas
2000-05 Atlas
Both Atlases

Breeding Bird Survey Trend in New York

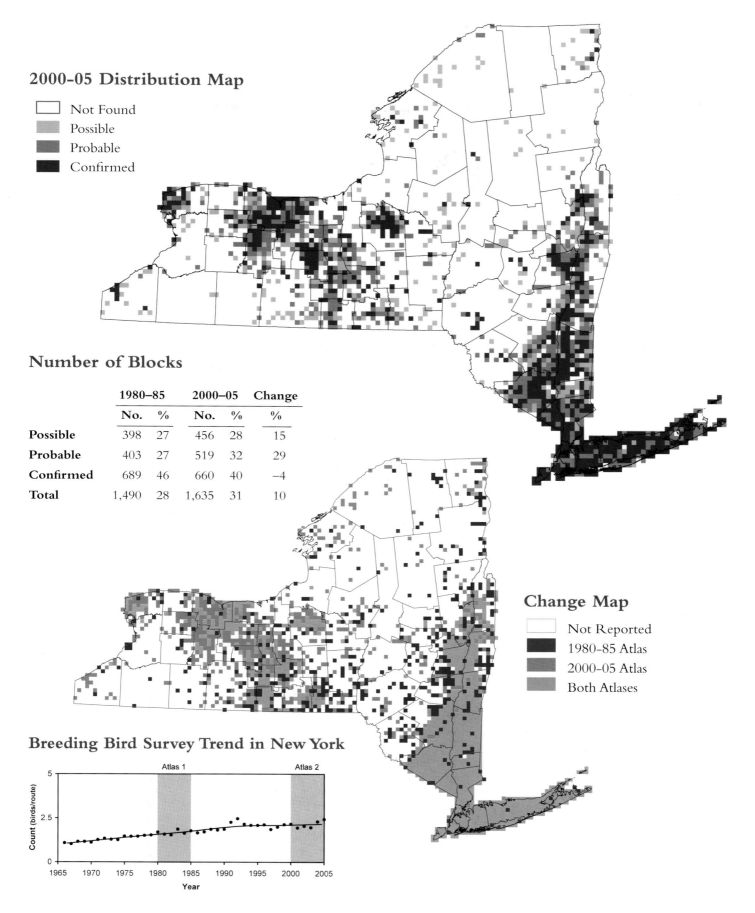

Brown Thrasher

Toxostoma rufum

KEVIN J. MCGOWAN

A large, long-tailed songbird of thickets, hedgerows, and forest clearings, the Brown Thrasher is found across the eastern United States and southern Canada, from Alberta to New Brunswick, and from eastern Texas to Florida (Cavitt and Haas 2000). It breeds in brushy open country, thickets, shelter belts, riparian areas, and suburbs. As a bird of early-successional habitats, the Brown Thrasher was probably not common in the mostly forested landscape preceding European settlement in New York. The resulting creation of open agricultural areas would have created much potential thrasher habitat, and DeKay (1844) said the bird bred in all parts of the state. Other authors, however, considered the thrasher uncommon or irregular in central and western New York (Rathbun 1879, Short 1893, Reed and Wright 1909). Eaton (1914) attributed part of its scarcity to its lack of tolerance of people, in contrast to the more common and less wary Gray Catbird. Bull (1974) called the thrasher a widespread breeder, most numerous in the Coastal Lowlands, but rare to absent in the mountains and northeastern sections of the state.

The first Atlas map showed the Brown Thrasher distributed throughout New York, occurring in all ecozones. The southeastern part of the state (Hudson Highlands, Triassic Lowlands, Manhattan Hills, and Coastal Lowlands) contained a high concentration of occupied blocks and Confirmed breeding records. Notable gaps in its distribution occurred in the Central Adirondacks, Western Adirondack Foothills, Central Tug Hill, Catskill Peaks, and Allegany Hills, presumably because of the higher elevations and more extensive forests in these areas. The Brown Thrasher experienced the greatest absolute decrease in records of any species in New York State between the two Atlas periods, having been found in 1,004 fewer blocks during the second Atlas period and declining in all ecozones. While never common in the Adirondacks, the number of blocks with records decreased by 61 percent (by 200 blocks) in all Adirondack ecozones. The only areas where this bird did not experience a decline of greater than 20 percent were the Mohawk Valley, Champlain Valley / Champlain Transition, and the St. Lawrence Plains and associated ecozones. The Brown Thrasher is a relatively easy bird to detect because it is a vigorous singer and its song is easy to recognize; it was unlikely to have been missed in many blocks.

The Brown Thrasher population has been declining significantly continent-wide at least since the beginning of the Breeding Bird Survey in 1966, at an average rate of 1.2 percent each year (Sauer et al. 2007). New York BBS data show a precipitous decline starting around 1970 and continuing through the most recent years, at a rate of 5 percent each year (Sauer et al. 2007). Declines were apparent in regional spring and fall counts along the Niagara Frontier as well (Rising 1998a). The second Ontario Breeding Bird Atlas also reported significant declines across that province (Bird Studies Canada et al. 2006). Partners in Flight lists the Brown Thrasher as a Continental Stewardship Species (Rich et al. 2004), but it is not yet listed as a species of conservation concern in New York. Explanations put forth for continental declines include the maturation and loss of shrublands in the East and the loss of fencerows and shelter belts in the Great Plains (Cavitt and Haas 2000). The same trends in habitat loss in New York might account for the population decline of the thrasher in the state, but such widespread losses across all regions suggest some other, as yet unknown, root cause. Other shrubland species declined between the two Atlas projects, but none showed the same scale of losses as the thrasher.

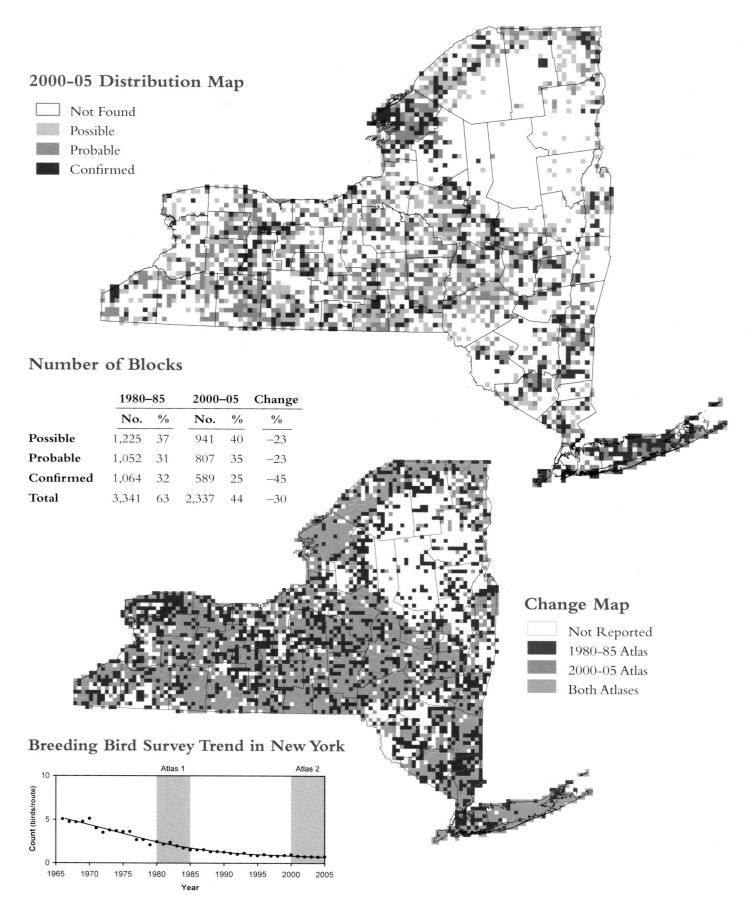

2000–05 Distribution Map

- ☐ Not Found
- Possible
- Probable
- Confirmed

Number of Blocks

	1980–85		2000–05		Change
	No.	%	No.	%	%
Possible	1,225	37	941	40	−23
Probable	1,052	31	807	35	−23
Confirmed	1,064	32	589	25	−45
Total	3,341	63	2,337	44	−30

Change Map

- ☐ Not Reported
- 1980-85 Atlas
- 2000-05 Atlas
- Both Atlases

Breeding Bird Survey Trend in New York

European Starling
Sturnus vulgaris

Daniel R. Ardia

The European Starling, a ubiquitous resident of human-dominated landscapes, was introduced to the United States in releases from 1850 to 1890 (Kessel 1951). While the putative successful release occurred in 1890 in New York City, sightings of starlings hundreds of miles from release sites prior to 1890 suggest that the North American population may have arisen from multiple releases (Kessel 1951). The lack of genetic structure of starlings in Europe precludes determination of whether multiple or single founding attempts are responsible for North America's birds (Cabe 1998). Once introduced, the starling spread steadily across New York State, being reported in the lower Hudson Valley in 1905, Erie County by 1914, and Lake Champlain by 1917 (Bull 1974). As it is the origin of North American starlings, New York is in the heart of the range. The spread of starlings to every state shows a slow methodical wave of colonization, ending in western North America in 1960 (Cabe 1993).

The first Atlas reported the European Starling to be abundant everywhere in New York except portions of the Central Adirondacks, Adirondack High Peaks, and Eastern and Western Adirondack foothills. It was also absent from parts of other relatively high-elevation forested areas, such as the Central Tug Hill, Allegany Hills, Catskill Peaks, and Delaware Hills. Breeding is likely limited in these locations by lack of suitable habitat, as it prefers short vegetation for foraging. The second Atlas survey found similar results, with the starling confirmed as breeding in a vast majority of blocks across the state. Gaps were present in the same high-elevation areas. In the Adirondacks, starling occurrence decreased by 7 percent. Where reported within the Adirondacks, the starling was found in blocks crossed by major roads, perhaps because of a combination of increased detectability and higher habitat suitability. In addition, the slight decline in reports of starlings in the Adirondacks could be due to changes in habitat cover or changes in environmental conditions. The lower occurrence of starlings in higher-elevation areas is due in part to climatic limitation.

The population of starlings in New York as estimated from Breeding Bird Survey data declined by 1.2 percent per year since 1980; similar values were found for the Eastern BBS Region (–0.4 percent) and the BBS survey area overall (–0.2 percent) (Sauer et al. 2005). The second Ontario Breeding Bird Atlas revealed a slight, nonsignificant decline in southern Ontario, which contains similar habitat to New York. However, province-wide, Ontario has experienced a slight but significant decline in starling occurrence (Bird Studies Canada et al. 2006). Interestingly, the European Starling has declined considerably across its native range, primarily by a reduction in foraging habitat (Crick et al. 2002).

Atlas methods are not sensitive to detecting population changes in widespread and common species. The changes reported here are likely real, as the starling possesses a range of characteristics that facilitate breeding confirmation: nests are near human habitation and nestlings are loud, juveniles have distinct plumage and congregate in large numbers, and breeding adults forage in conspicuous locations. Although the slight declines noted in the second Atlas data are supported by the declining BBS numbers, the European Starling is sure to remain among New York's most abundant birds owing to its aggressive nature, prolific breeding, and plentiful nesting sites.

The European Starling is presumed to have negative effects on other hole-nesting species because of its aggressive competition for nesting holes. A thorough analysis of the influence of starlings on other species confirmed negative effects only on the Yellow-bellied Sapsucker, suggesting that the overall impact of starlings on native avifauna may be less than thought (Koenig 2003).

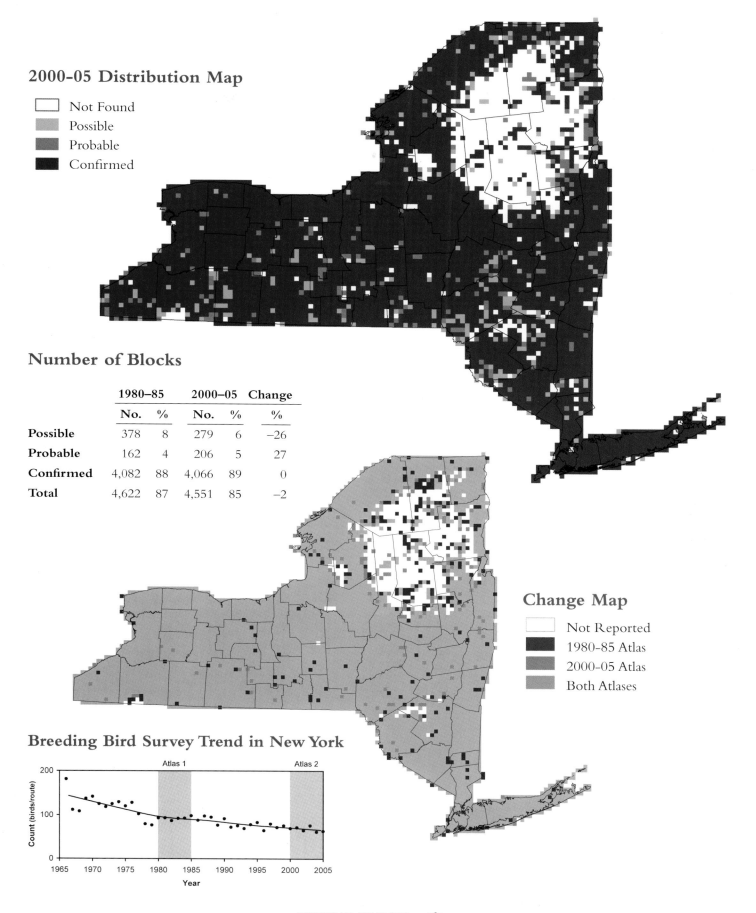

2000-05 Distribution Map

- ☐ Not Found
- ☐ Possible
- ☐ Probable
- ■ Confirmed

Number of Blocks

	1980–85		2000–05		Change
	No.	%	No.	%	%
Possible	378	8	279	6	−26
Probable	162	4	206	5	27
Confirmed	4,082	88	4,066	89	0
Total	4,622	87	4,551	85	−2

Change Map

- ☐ Not Reported
- ■ 1980-85 Atlas
- ☐ 2000-05 Atlas
- ☐ Both Atlases

Breeding Bird Survey Trend in New York

Cedar Waxwing
Bombycilla cedrorum

Mark Witmer

pecialization on sugary fruits by the Cedar Waxwing is associated with distinctive aspects of its breeding biology (Sibley 1988e, Witmer et al. 1997). It is among the latest nesting passerines in New York State, initiating breeding from early June until early August, with active nests occurring as late as September and early October (Mearns 1879, Hamilton 1933). Late breeding is likely cued to ripening of fruits. Also, the Cedar Waxwing may nest semi-colonially, probably a result of patchy fruit crops that permit flock foraging even during the nesting season. It breeds across North America, from mid-latitudes of Canada to mid-latitudes of the United States. The species is most abundant in the northeastern United States and southeastern Canada, with the highest breeding densities of the continent reported from Breeding Bird Survey routes in the Adirondacks (Robbins et al. 1986, Feustel 1998). The Cedar Waxwing has historically been a common breeder throughout the state, shunning only dense forests (DeKay 1844, Mearns 1879, Reed and Wright 1909, Eaton 1914); it prefers wetlands and open woodland habitats that offer fruit and insect foods (Lea 1942, DeGraaf et al. 1980, Feustel 1998). The Cedar Waxwing sallies from exposed perches near water bodies for emergent insects, such as mayflies, but it also gleans insects from vegetation (Witmer et al. 1997). This species no doubt benefited as eastern forests became fragmented with human settlement, generating more habitat with fruiting shrubs. The Cedar Waxwing is among the most common breeding birds in New York State (Mearns 1879, Sibley 1988e).

The first Atlas project found the Cedar Waxwing throughout the state, with noticeable gaps only in the Central Adirondacks (Adirondack High Peaks and Sable Highlands), Manhattan Hills, and southwestern Coastal Lowlands (Sibley 1988e). The second Atlas results confirmed breeding in these small gaps, including the first Confirmed breeding on Staten Island since 1967. The number of blocks reporting any evidence of breeding and number of blocks with Confirmed breeding were very similar to the data reported for the first Atlas project, with only a minor total increase. Confirmed breeding was documented throughout state, and as noted by Sibley (1988e), the small gaps in Upstate New York are likely the result of lack of detection, rather than absence.

Breeding populations of the Cedar Waxwing in eastern North America have steadily increased over the past 40 years (Sauer et al. 2007). From 1965 to 1989 the numbers of birds counted on Breeding Bird Survey routes more than doubled in the eastern United States (Robbins et al. 1986, Droege and Sauer 1990). Subsequently, analysis showed that Cedar Waxwing numbers in New York declined slightly in the 1980s, followed by stabilization in the past 15 years (Sauer et al. 2007). The second Ontario Breeding Bird Atlas also reported little change between Atlases, although the trend there was negative (Bird Studies Canada et al. 2006). The numbers of breeding Cedar Waxwings in Pennsylvania tripled from 1965 to 1990, with most of the increase occurring between 1975 and 1980 (Gross 1992). Similarly, the number of breeding Cedar Waxwings in British Columbia increased steadily from 1973 to 1990 (Witmer et al. 1997). It is plausible that this widespread population increase was a rebound after the outlawing of DDT in 1972, because the surge in the breeding population closely followed this date. The propensity of the Cedar Waxwing to feed on abundant fruit crops and concentrate its feeding on insect outbreaks would make it especially vulnerable to pesticides (Ellison 1985a, Witmer et al. 1997). The Cedar Waxwing is tolerant of human activities, often nesting close to human habitation and benefiting from creation of early-successional shrublands by humans. Population sizes are robust and stable so that there is no current conservation concern for this species.

2000-05 Distribution Map

- ☐ Not Found
- Possible
- Probable
- Confirmed

Number of Blocks

	1980–85		2000–05		Change
	No.	%	No.	%	%
Possible	1,466	30	1,149	23	–22
Probable	1,930	39	2,366	47	23
Confirmed	1,519	31	1,510	30	–1
Total	4,915	92	5,025	94	2

Change Map

- ☐ Not Reported
- 1980-85 Atlas
- 2000-05 Atlas
- Both Atlases

Breeding Bird Survey Trend in New York

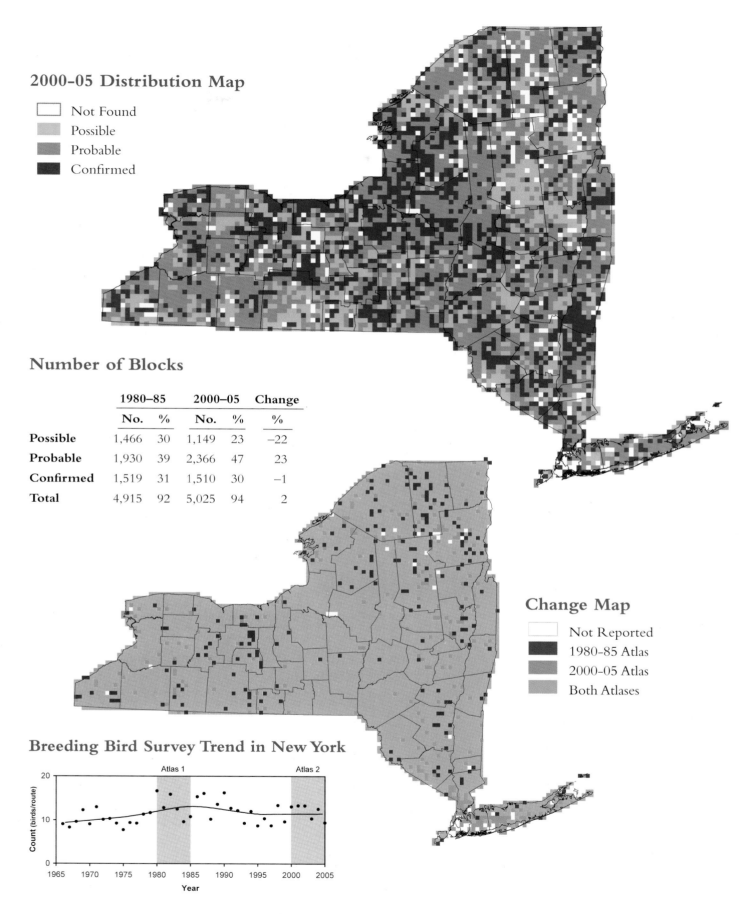

Warblers in Letchworth State Park

Letchworth State Park, the "Grand Canyon of the East," is one of New York State's natural wonders. A magnificent gorge channeling the Genesee River, it is surrounded by a lush woodland that serves as a summer home to the Chestnut-sided, Hooded, and many other breeding warbler species.

Blue-winged Warbler
Vermivora pinus

JOHN CONFER

The Blue-winged Warbler is primarily yellow with gray wings and white wingbars but no blue. Further, it eats caterpillars, not worms, and it does not particularly like pine trees. This species probably originated in the Ozark Mountains and the southwestern Appalachians (Gill et al. 2001); it now is found from the Midwest to southern New England. It breeds in dry, early- to middle-successional habitat and in swamps with a high density of shrubs (Gill et al. 2001). More than a century ago, the Blue-winged Warbler began expanding into the footprint of the original eastern deciduous forest by using abandoned farmland (Gill et al. 2001). It continues to expand northward, now often using clear-cuts and abandoned pastureland. This species was once rare in New York with fewer than a dozen cited records from 1844 to 1909 (DeKay 1844, Giraud 1844, Rathbun 1879, Short 1893, Reed and Wright 1909). Eaton (1914) called it common only on Long Island and the lower Hudson Valley. It reached central New York by the 1940s and was established there by 1960 (Confer 1988a).

In the first Atlas map, the Blue-winged Warbler was shown to be common across the state from the Mohawk Valley southward. It was scarce in the highlands of the eastern Appalachian Plateau and parts of the Great Lakes Plain and missing from the greater New York City area. In the 20 years between the two Atlas periods, the Blue-winged Warbler continued its northward expansion. The second Atlas survey found it occurring statewide, even reaching the northeastern portion, albeit in low density. Although there might have been some decline in the southern portions of the state, the number of blocks overall with Blue-winged Warbler increased 17 percent. It remains absent from a few regions with a scarcity of disturbance habitat, notably areas with intensive agriculture, extensive forest cover, or high human density. Throughout the last century, the Blue-winged Warbler followed the Golden-winged Warbler northward, but lagged behind by about 40–56 km (25–35 mi) and 15–25 years. This situation continues today, with expansion of the Blue-winged Warbler into parts of the Great Lakes Plain, Indian River Lakes, and St. Lawrence Plains since the 1980s, following movement into the same area by the Golden-winged Warbler between the 1970s (Bull 1974) and the 1980s (Confer 1988c). Though both species nest in successional habitat, the Blue-winged Warbler prefers habitat with more trees (Confer and Knapp 1981, Gill et al. 2001, Confer et al. 2003). It is possible that the Blue-winged Warbler expands into an area later because it prefers later stages of succession.

The second Ontario Breeding Bird Atlas also found a slight increase in Blue-winged Warbler numbers (Bird Studies Canada et al. 2006). Breeding Bird Survey data show the Blue-winged Warbler population declining in the northern Atlantic states (U.S. Fish and Wildlife Service Region 5), although no significant trend exists in New York (Sauer et al. 2007). The Blue-winged Warbler population declines in much of its range correlate with the loss of habitat from reforestation and forest maturation (Brooks 2003). Partners in Flight put the species on its Watch List (Rich et al. 2004).

Where their ranges overlap, intrusion of the Blue-winged Warbler into the Golden-winged Warbler's range is followed by the decline and sometimes the extirpation of the latter species (Gill et al. 2001). In New York, as noted, the Blue-winged Warbler was generally absent from the Great Lakes Plain in the early 1970s (Bull 1974) and 1980s (Confer 1988a). The Golden-winged Warbler was widely distributed in this area during that time (Bull 1974, Confer 1988c). However, as the Blue-winged Warbler expanded into this area between the first and second Atlas periods, the Golden-winged Warbler numbers declined precipitously. Perhaps the Blue-winged Warbler causes this decline by competition and hybridization (Confer et al. 2003, Confer 2006).

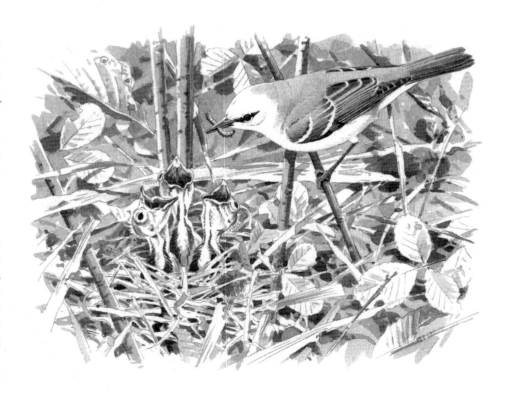

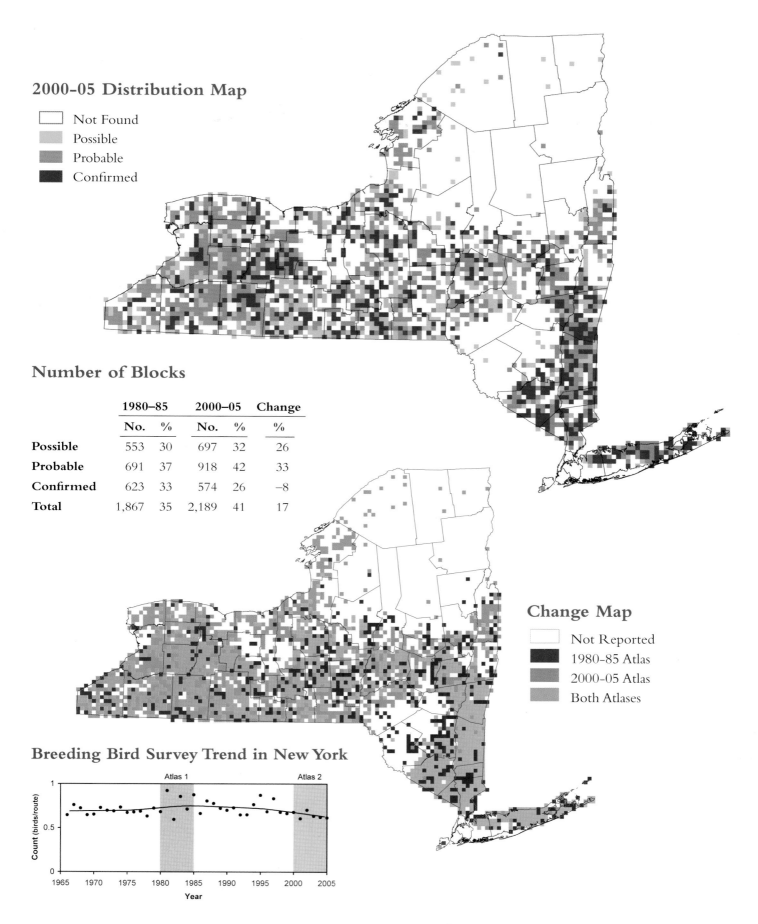

2000–05 Distribution Map

- ☐ Not Found
- Possible
- Probable
- Confirmed

Number of Blocks

	1980–85		2000–05		Change
	No.	%	No.	%	%
Possible	553	30	697	32	26
Probable	691	37	918	42	33
Confirmed	623	33	574	26	−8
Total	1,867	35	2,189	41	17

Change Map

- ☐ Not Reported
- 1980–85 Atlas
- 2000–05 Atlas
- Both Atlases

Breeding Bird Survey Trend in New York

Golden-winged Warbler
Vermivora chrysoptera

JOHN CONFER

The Golden-winged Warbler, stunning in appearance with its white, gray, black, and bright yellow plumage, winters in Central America and breeds in the northeastern and north-central United States and southern Ontario and Quebec (Confer 1992). A bird of patchy shrublands with a forest edge (Confer 1992), the Golden-winged Warbler expanded from the southeastern Appalachians into abandoned farmland in coastal New England in the late 1800s (Gill 1980). It occurred at scattered locations throughout southern and central New York in the mid to late 1800s (DeKay 1844, Giraud 1844, Rathbun 1879, Short 1893) and was moderately abundant in southern New York by the early 1900s (Eaton 1914). During the 20th century, it expanded northward in the state (Bull 1974, Confer 1988c), as well as throughout the northeastern and north-central states into southern Canada (Confer 1992). It reached the northeastern limits of New York by the 1990s (Confer 1998c), a northward movement of about 483 km (300 mi) or approximately 6.4 km (4 mi) a year. This expanding population nested in the extensive disturbed habitat created as agricultural lands in New York were abandoned. Now, most of these sites are maturing forests (Brooks 2003). The Golden-winged Warbler has higher nesting success in earlier stages of old field succession and rarely uses forests (Confer et al. 2003).

The first Atlas documented the northward movement of the Golden-winged Warbler in New York (Confer 1988c) and found it breeding in localized clusters throughout most of the state, absent only from the Central Adirondacks, Western Adirondack Foothills, and Coastal Lowlands. Although the second Atlas survey detected this warbler in small numbers in each ecozone where it was found during the first Atlas work, the number of blocks decreased 53 percent, with declines occurring throughout the central and southern portions of the state. In contrast, numbers of blocks with the species increased in the Eastern Ontario Plain, Indian River Lakes, and St. Lawrence Plains. This increase may be real, continuing a trend of movement into this area, perhaps aided by the appearance of early-successional habitat on recently abandoned pastureland, but it might

also be an artifact of increased effort (J. Bolsinger pers. comm.). The expanded distribution is nearly unique in the entire golden-wing range, except the northern fringe (Sauer et al 2005). This Atlas documented another unusual population in the western portion of the Hudson Highlands, where a sustained and moderately dense population has co-occurred with the Blue-winged Warbler for over a century (Confer 1988c, 1998).

Although the Golden-winged Warbler continues to expand at the northern fringe of its range, population trends are now generally downward. Breeding Bird Survey data show an annual decline of 5.6 percent in New York and 8.6 percent in the northeastern states from Virginia to Maine (U.S. Fish and Wildlife Service Region 5) (Sauer et al. 2005). It is one of the most endangered species in this region and is on the Partners in Flight Watch List (Rich et al. 2004). It is a Species of Special Concern in New York. Much suitable habitat is available on utility rights-of-way in regions where the Golden-winged Warbler once occurred but is now extirpated (Confer and Pascoe 2003). The most severe declines and even extirpation correlate with the intrusion of the Blue-winged Warbler. Nesting success of the Golden-winged Warbler declines as proximity to the Blue-winged Warbler increases (Confer at al. 2003). Hybridization between these two species is common (Gill et al. 2001), and DNA analyses show that blue-wing genes generally replace golden-wing genes (Confer 2006). Perhaps for these reasons, the co-occurrence of these two species is extremely rare. In the Hudson Highlands, only the Golden-winged Warbler nests in locally abundant swamp forests. Further studies of distribution may establish that habitat segregation allows coexistence in other regions as well.

2000-05 Distribution Map

- ☐ Not Found
- Possible
- Probable
- Confirmed

Number of Blocks

| | 1980–85 | | 2000–05 | | Change |
	No.	%	No.	%	%
Possible	236	41	106	39	−55
Probable	231	40	113	42	−51
Confirmed	110	19	51	19	−54
Total	577	11	270	5	−53

Change Map

- ☐ Not Reported
- 1980-85 Atlas
- 2000-05 Atlas
- Both Atlases

Breeding Bird Survey Trend in New York

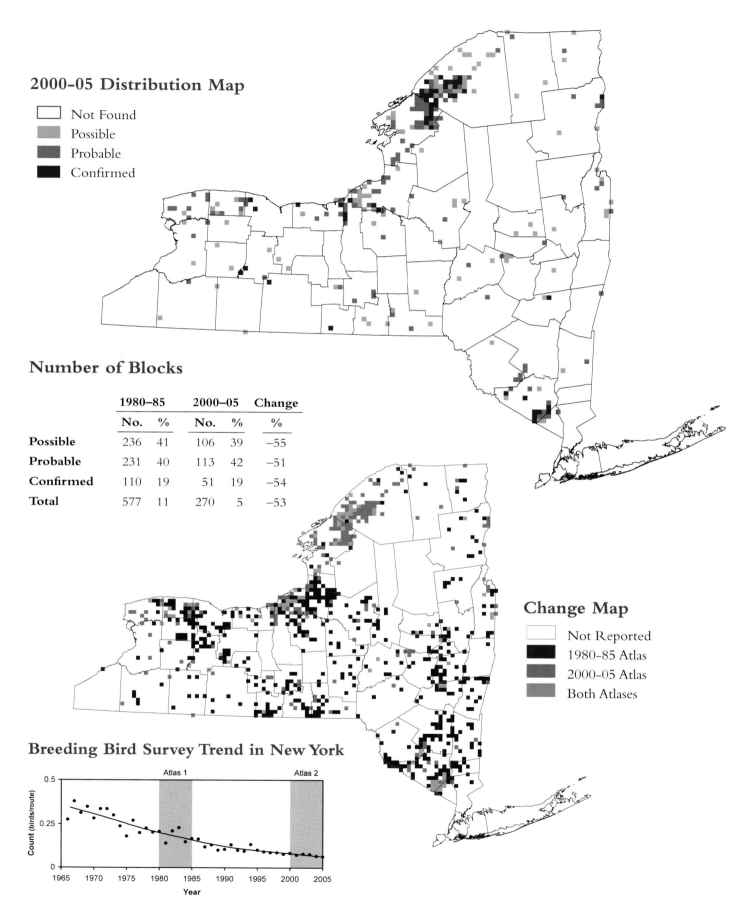

GOLDEN-WINGED WARBLER 469

Blue-winged x Golden-winged Warbler hybrids

Vermivora pinus x Vermivora chrysoptera complex

JOHN L. CONFER

Brewster's ("*Vermivora leucobronchialis*") and Lawrence's ("*V. lawrencei*") warblers were originally described as full species but are now known to be hybrid progeny of Golden-winged and Blue-winged warblers. The frequency of hybrid phenotypes varies among study areas, but hybrids make up, on average, about 5 percent of singing males (Gill et al. 2001). Both parent species and their hybrids nest in early-successional habitat, usually with patches of herbs and shrubs and a few trees along the edge of the territory. They often create overlapping territories. In uplands, the nest site and nest structure are similar for all. The Golden-winged Warbler sometimes uses wetlands not utilized by the others (J. L. Confer pers. obs.). Before European colonization, the distribution of the two parental species probably did not overlap, and they came together only after both species expanded into disturbed habitat created by settlement. Long known to occur in New York, Brewster's and Lawrence's warbler specimens from Ossining and Highland Falls along the Hudson River contributed to early understanding that the two forms were hybrids and not full species or color phases (Brewster 1881). Eaton (1914) knew of multiple specimens of both named types collected in the lower Hudson Valley, Staten Island, and on Long Island, including a Brewster's Warbler taken in Rockland in 1832, 42 years before its formal description. The expansion of both Blue-winged and Golden-winged warblers northward in the state in the 20th century provided opportunities for the occurrence of hybrids, and Bull (1974) showed Brewster's Warbler occurring across the width of the state south of the Mohawk Valley. He showed Lawrence's Warbler occurring primarily in the southeastern part of the state east of the Hudson River, from Dutchess County south to eastern Long Island.

Hybrids are found only where at least one of the parental species occurs. The hybrids are, consequently, absent from the Adirondacks, Catskills, and extreme northeastern portion of the state where neither the Blue-winged Warbler nor the Golden-winged Warbler is common. During the first Atlas survey, Brewster's Warbler was found in blocks scattered across the state south of the Adirondacks and north of the Coastal Lowlands. Lawrence's Warbler had a similar range but was found on the north shore of Long Island. During the second Atlas survey, Brewster's Warbler was found in a distribution similar to that mapped in the first Atlas, but with a few more records at the northern edge of the range, in the Champlain Valley and the Eastern Ontario Plains. Although a single Possible breeding record came from Nassau County, the hybrid disappeared from the Manhattan Hills, where it was reported from seven blocks in the first Atlas. Lawrence's Warbler showed a similar distribution in both Atlases, although more records came from the western counties in the second Atlas, and two came from the St. Lawrence Plains to the north. From the first to the second Atlas period, the distribution of the hybrids increased in the Erie-Ontario Plain as the distribution of the Blue-winged Warbler increased in this region, and increased in the Eastern Ontario Plain as the distribution of both the Golden-winged and the Blue-winged warblers increased there. Overall, the number of blocks with reports for either hybrid declined 8 percent, perhaps because of the general decline in the range of the Golden-winged Warbler. Because hybrids sing a song that matches that of the parental species (Confer 1992), many hybrid individuals may have been overlooked during Atlas fieldwork. In addition, recent genetic research has shown that in areas of active hybridization, a proportion of individuals that look like the Golden-winged

470

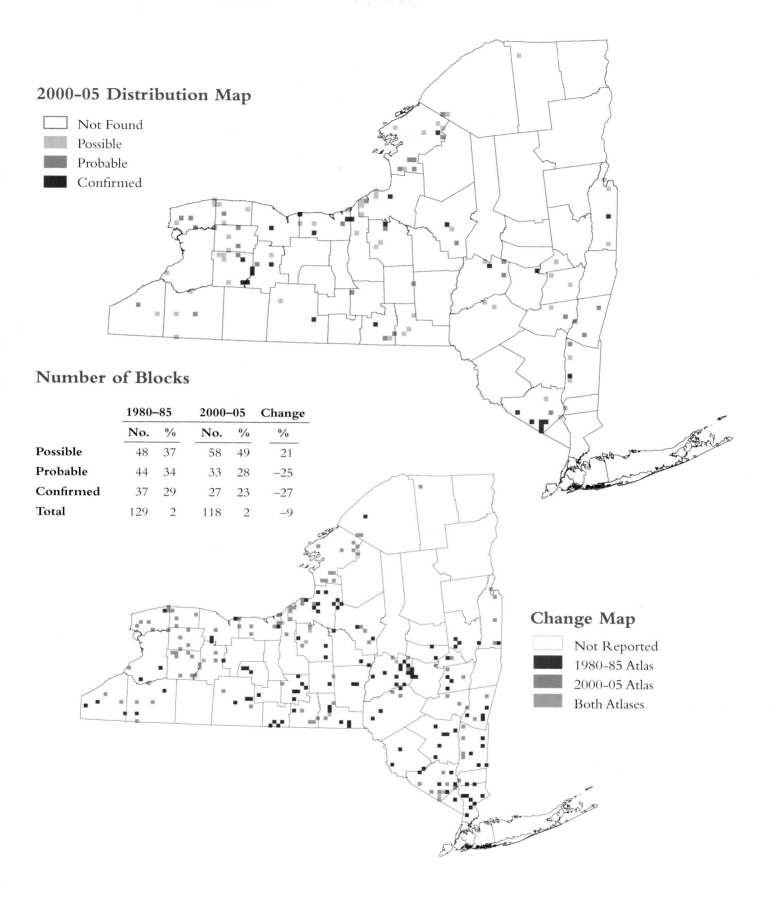

2000-05 Distribution Map

- ☐ Not Found
- Possible
- Probable
- ■ Confirmed

Number of Blocks

	1980–85		2000–05		Change
	No.	%	No.	%	%
Possible	48	37	58	49	21
Probable	44	34	33	28	−25
Confirmed	37	29	27	23	−27
Total	129	2	118	2	−9

Change Map

- ☐ Not Reported
- ■ 1980-85 Atlas
- 2000-05 Atlas
- Both Atlases

Parkes (1951) noted that other plumage patterns can occur, suggesting that a full explanation of color inheritance involves more than two pairs of genes. He speculated that a Brewster's Warbler with a yellow wash on the underside was heterozygous with one golden-wing allele for white and one blue-winged allele for yellow. If true, then most first-generation hybrids should have this yellow wash because the heterozygous condition should be more common. Yet most of over 100 Brewster's phenotypes throughout New York had almost totally white undersides (J. L. Confer pers. obs.), and the genetic nature of hybrids with a partially yellow underside is still speculative.

Molecular DNA analyses of this *Vermivora* complex have provided new insights. The mitochondrial DNA of Golden-winged and Blue-winged warblers differ by about a 4.5 percent in the sequence of nucleotides (reviewed by Confer 2006). This genetic divergence could be acquired over about two million years of separation (Dabrowski et al. 2005). The timing matches the start of the last, major glacial advance, which might have separated the range of the two precursor species. This extent of divergence suggests the two are truly different species, as this level of divergence is on par with differences between other wood warbler species (Johnson and Cicero 2004).

Hybridization might be the major force that leads to extirpation of the Golden-winged Warbler, which generally occurs after intrusion by the Blue-winged Warbler (Gill et al. 2001, Confer et al. 2003). In some areas, genetic flow between these two species might be dominated by movement of blue-wing genes into birds with golden-wing phenotype (Gill 1997), which would contribute to species replacement (Confer 2006). In addition, it has been shown that Golden-winged Warblers pair with hybrids more often and produce more hybrid young than Blue-winged Warblers (Confer et al. 2003). Moreover, in some populations it appears as though hybrid males often fail to obtain mates (Ficken and Ficken 1968, Confer and Tupper 2000, Leichty and Grier 2006), which would also reduce the passage of golden-wing genes to the next generation. How important these mechanisms are for the decline of the Golden-winged Warbler remains to be seen, but these hybrid forms can be expected to occur in New York for as long as both species remain there.

Warbler may in fact be genetic hybrids (Vallender et al. 2007), and the maps may not represent the full extent of hybrids in the state.

Plumage patterns in these warblers generally are determined by two pairs of genes: dominant alleles for white undersides and gray back from the Golden-winged Warbler, and dominant alleles for white wing bars and a black eyestripe from the Blue-winged Warbler. The black throat and eye patch and the yellow wing patch of the Golden-winged Warbler and the yellow body color of the Blue-winged Warbler appear to be due to recessive alleles. In this model, Lawrence's Warbler has four recessive alleles, and this phenotype should appear in about 1 of every 16 progeny of a pair of hybrids. Surprisingly, the number of blocks with records of the Lawrence's phenotype in both Atlases is one-fourth the number with the Brewster's phenotype. Perhaps this departure from the expected ratio is partly the result of observer bias, with the striking Lawrence's Warbler easier to identify and more exciting to report.

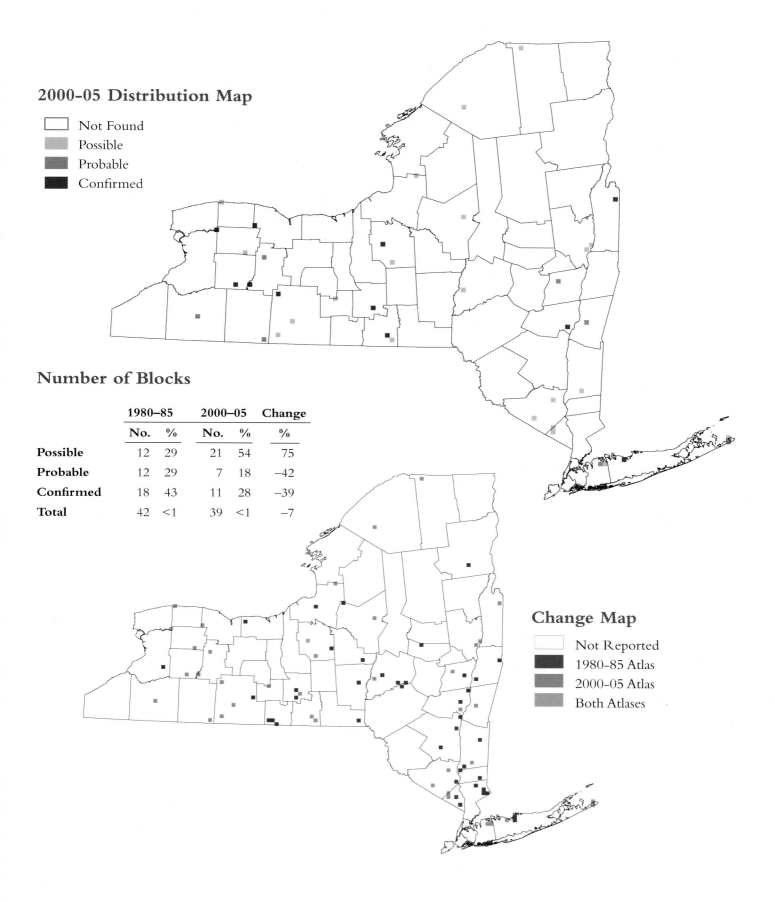

2000-05 Distribution Map

- ☐ Not Found
- ▨ Possible
- ▧ Probable
- ■ Confirmed

Number of Blocks

	1980–85		2000–05		Change
	No.	%	No.	%	%
Possible	12	29	21	54	75
Probable	12	29	7	18	−42
Confirmed	18	43	11	28	−39
Total	42	<1	39	<1	−7

Change Map

- ☐ Not Reported
- ■ 1980-85 Atlas
- ▧ 2000-05 Atlas
- ▨ Both Atlases

Tennessee Warbler

Vermivora peregrina

JOHN M. C. PETERSON

amed by Alexander Wilson, who collected a migrant along the Cumberland River in 1832, the Tennessee Warbler nests across boreal Canada and southward into northern Minnesota, Wisconsin, Michigan, New York, Vermont, New Hampshire, and Maine (Rimmer and McFarland 1998). In the summer of 1926, Aretas Saunders (1929) found an adult male Tennessee Warbler feeding recently fledged young among aspens and willows along Alcohol Brook, now North Meadow Brook, near Heart Lake Road in North Elba, Essex County. This sighting was the first confirmed record of breeding in New York State and ended years of uncertainty about the status of this warbler in the Adirondacks (Eaton 1914, J. M. C. Peterson 1988r). Since the 1926 discovery by Saunders, breeding has been confirmed only six more times, five times during the first Atlas period and just once during the second period. A nest has still not been found in New York.

The first Atlas map showed the Tennessee Warbler confined to the Adirondack High Peaks, Central Adirondacks, Sable Highlands, and Western Adirondack Foothills and located within the six northeastern counties of Clinton, Essex, Franklin, Hamilton, St. Lawrence, and Warren. The second Atlas data revealed a similar, though slightly different distribution. Improved coverage of western Clinton County during the second Atlas period may be responsible for the expansion of the known range into the Champlain, St. Lawrence, and Western Adirondack transitions, northward to the border with Quebec. North of the Canadian border, this species is uncommon in the Central St. Lawrence Lowland (Limoges and Gauthier 1996), and the populations are separated by the St. Lawrence Plains. Some birds seen in southern Quebec are believed to be unpaired males (Limoges and Gauthier 1996), and that may be the case with birds in northern Clinton County as well. The only Confirmed breeding record for the second Atlas was of a bird feeding young in northern Herkimer County, where the species was recorded for the first time. Although recorded in nearly the same number of blocks during each Atlas period, all were in different blocks, with no duplication between the two efforts. The first Atlas showed a concentration in western Franklin County that included the Boreal Heritage Preserve, but this population was missed entirely during the second Atlas survey; this omission is believed to be the result of differences in coverage.

Tennessee, Cape May, Bay-breasted, and sometimes Blackpoll warblers are often called "spruce budworm warblers," experiencing population explosions in response to periodic budworm outbreaks (Bolgiano 2004). The eastern spruce budworm irrupted in 1910–20, 1945–55, and 1968–85, each infestation larger than the last, and defoliated approximately 55 million hectares (136 million acres) of boreal forest during the 1970s, in a swath stretching from Lake Superior to the Atlantic Provinces and Newfoundland (Blais et al. 1981, Hardy et al. 1983). Breeding Bird Survey data for the entire survey area and especially for Quebec showed a sharp spike in Tennessee Warbler populations in the late 1980s, and then a subsequent collapse (Sauer et al. 2005). Lepidopteran larvae are a major food source of this sharp-billed gleaner, and the larvae and pupae of budworms constitute the main, sometimes exclusive, prey item during these outbreaks (Rimmer and McFarland 1998). As foresters replant with black spruce and jack pine, which are less preferred by budworms, this change could have a negative impact on the balsam fir forest, and in turn on the Tennessee Warbler, which depends on balsam-loving budworms. Aerial spraying of insecticides for budworm control, carried out annually in Canada, can affect foraging behavior and perhaps clutch size and hatching rates (Rimmer and McFarland 1998). Although the population is seemingly stable now, the Tennessee Warbler still faces threats outside its Neotropical wintering grounds.

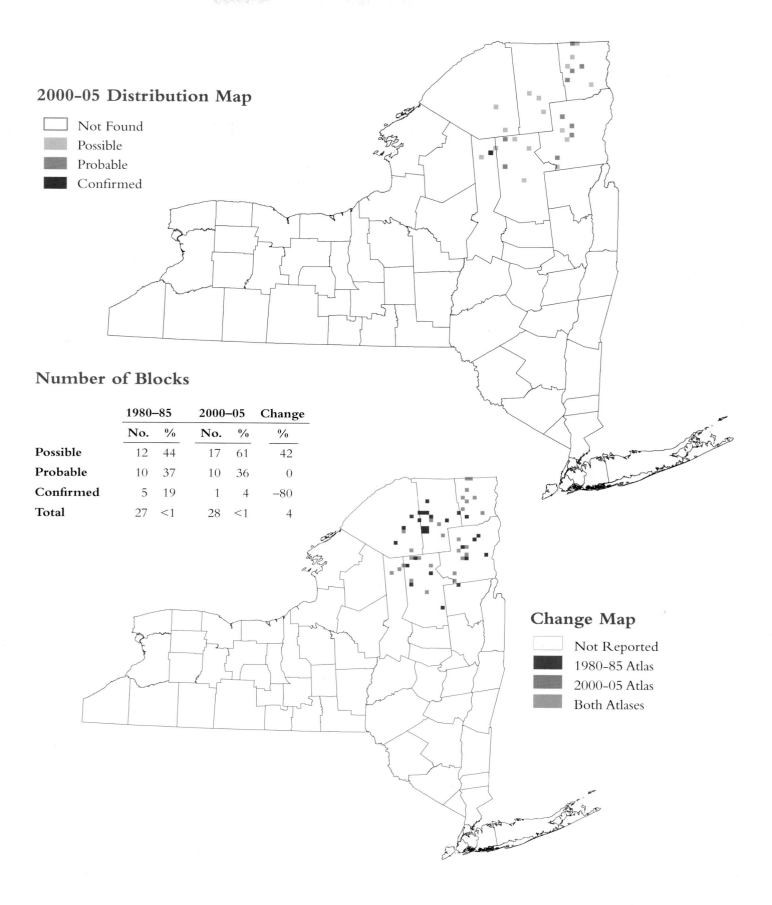

2000-05 Distribution Map

- ☐ Not Found
- Possible
- Probable
- Confirmed

Number of Blocks

	1980–85		2000–05		Change
	No.	%	No.	%	%
Possible	12	44	17	61	42
Probable	10	37	10	36	0
Confirmed	5	19	1	4	−80
Total	27	<1	28	<1	4

Change Map

- ☐ Not Reported
- 1980-85 Atlas
- 2000-05 Atlas
- Both Atlases

Nashville Warbler

Vermivora ruficapilla

JOAN E. COLLINS

The distinctive two-part song of the colorful Nashville Warbler is a familiar sound arising from the edges of innumerable wetlands within the Adirondacks. In eastern North America, this species breeds from central Saskatchewan to Nova Scotia, and from northern Minnesota to New England southward to Pennsylvania and into the Appalachian Mountains as far south as northeastern West Virginia (Williams 1996). A disjunct western population occurs from southern British Columbia and Alberta as far south as central California (Williams 1996). The Nashville Warbler occurs in highest densities at the edges of wet areas such as swamps, bogs, marshes, and beaver wetlands, in tamarack, spruce, and alders (Dunn and Garrett 1997, pers. obs.). Although much of this habitat is found in lowland areas of the Adirondacks, the species also occurs in lower densities at higher-elevation forest openings on mountains, but well below the tree line (pers. obs.). It also breeds at the edges of dry, successional open deciduous or mixed forest areas with shrubby undergrowth, including the edges of fields. Eaton (1914) found the species common in the north, local from Albany to Orange County, and "extremely rare" in central and western New York. Bull (1974) called the species locally numerous in both the mountains and the central part of the state but uncommon in the western part and rare in the southeast.

During the first Atlas survey, the Nashville Warbler was concentrated in the Adirondacks and Appalachian Plateau but it was present in all ecozones north of the Hudson Highlands. As a result of forest maturation, much of the successional habitat used by the species in the central and western parts of the state proved temporary. The second Atlas fieldwork found 7 percent fewer blocks with breeding records of the Nashville Warbler. Although the overall distribution of the species did not change, declines primarily occurred in central and western sections of the state, while the northern regions showed increases. The Appalachian Plateau had a 23 percent decline in the number of blocks with records, and the Catskill Highlands, Catskill Peaks, Great Lakes Plain, Hudson Valley, Mohawk Valley, Taconic Highlands, and St. Lawrence

Plains also showed declines. The Adirondacks had the largest increase in the number of occupied blocks, and the Champlain Transition and Tug Hill Plateau also had increases. The wetland areas of the north are relatively stable habitats. The beaver population in the northern part of the state continued to increase since the first Atlas period, creating new wetland edges and increasing the breeding habitat for the Nashville Warbler. Ongoing logging activity, on over two million acres of actively managed forest in the Adirondack Park, continues to open up potential successional breeding habitat for the species.

Although Breeding Bird Survey data for New York show no significant Nashville Warbler population trends, the data for the Northern New England, Pennsylvania, and Alleghany Plateau BBS regions showed significant yearly declines from 1966 to 2005, and counts in the Vermont BBS region declined significantly from 1980 to 2005 (Sauer et al. 2005). The Quebec BBS data show a significant yearly increase for the species from 1966 to 2005 (Sauer et al. 2005). The second Breeding Bird Atlas in Ontario reported no significant changes for the species in southern Ontario but significant increases in the northern sections of the province (Bird Studies Canada et al. 2006).

As a species that adapts well to second-growth and cut-over areas, the Nashville Warbler is less vulnerable to habitat changes than many other Neotropical warbler species (Williams 1996). It may continue to show some decline in New York in areas where the forest is maturing, mainly within the central and western portions of the state, but it should remain common in the north where its preferred wetland edge habitat is abundant and continued logging creates successional forest.

476

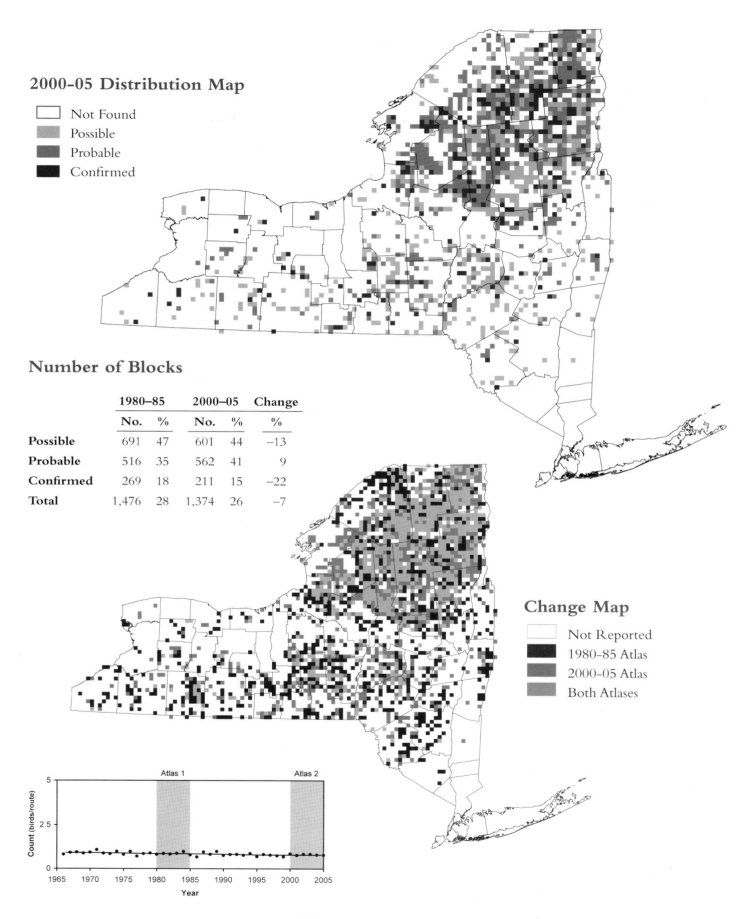

2000-05 Distribution Map

- ☐ Not Found
- Possible
- Probable
- Confirmed

Number of Blocks

	1980–85		2000–05		Change
	No.	%	No.	%	%
Possible	691	47	601	44	−13
Probable	516	35	562	41	9
Confirmed	269	18	211	15	−22
Total	1,476	28	1,374	26	−7

Change Map

- ☐ Not Reported
- 1980-85 Atlas
- 2000-05 Atlas
- Both Atlases

Northern Parula

Parula americana

KEVIN J. McGOWAN

The Northern Parula is a small, creeping warbler of the treetops. It breeds in two rather distinct populations, with an odd break in the middle separating a northern region from a more southern one (Moldenhauer and Regelski 1996). It ranges from southern Ontario to Nova Scotia, southward to northern Minnesota, northern New York, and southern New Hampshire. It also breeds from southern Iowa to southern New York southward to eastern Texas and Florida. New York straddles the two breeding areas. The southern population nests primarily in hanging Spanish moss, while the northern population uses the similar-looking old man's beard lichen (*Usnea*) (Moldenhauer and Regelski 1996). In the southern portion of its range it nests in bottomland swamp forests, while in the northern portion it uses primarily mature coniferous forests in moist bog and swamp habitats where beard lichen is abundant. It was probably common throughout much of New York before European colonization and remained so into the late 19th century (Rathbun 1879, Merriam 1881, Short 1893). Eaton (1914) stated that it bred throughout the state, probably most commonly in the Adirondacks, Catskills, and on Long Island. He described it as nearly restricted to damp areas like swamps and bogs, especially where *Usnea* lichen was common, and in hemlocks along gorges in the Finger Lakes region. Bull (1974) reported a decline in parula populations in the state, with no certain breeding records outside of the Adirondacks and the Tug Hill Plateau after 1955, although he suspected it still could be found in the Catskills. The warbler also disappeared from much of the northeastern portion of its range, perhaps as the result of loss of forest habitat or the loss of *Usnea* lichen from air pollution (Moldenhauer and Regelski 1996).

The first Atlas map showed the Northern Parula to be common within the Adirondacks, especially the Central Adirondacks, but rare elsewhere. Only three confirmations were made outside of the Adirondacks: one in the Catskill Peaks/Helderberg Highlands, one in the Schoharie Hills, and one in the Cattaraugus Highlands. Other reports were scattered primarily across the Appalachian Plateau and Tug Hill, with another five from Long Island. The second Atlas survey documented a noticeable increase in Northern Parula reports. The Adirondacks remained the stronghold of the species in the state, showing a 32 percent increase in the number of blocks with records. Increasing reports from the Tug Hill Plateau made that area a secondary stronghold. Notable gains were made across the Appalachian Plateau and the Coastal Lowlands. Breeding was confirmed in one block in the Central Tug Hill, five blocks in the Appalachian Plateau, one block in the Great Lakes Plain south of Buffalo, one in the Taconic Highlands, and one on Long Island.

Breeding Bird Survey data show no significant trend in Northern Parula numbers survey-wide since 1966 (Sauer et al. 2005). Data from New York are sparse, and nearly all are from the Adirondacks, but they show a significant increase of 5.9 percent per year since 1980 (Sauer et al. 2005). BBS data from the north Atlantic states (U.S. Fish and Wildlife Service Region 5) show a significant 1.4 percent yearly increase since 1966 (Sauer et al. 2005). The second Ontario Breeding Bird Atlas reported a significant increase in Northern Parula records across the province except in the northernmost and southernmost regions, where it was rare (Bird Studies Canada et al. 2006). Preliminary results for the second Vermont and Pennsylvania Atlases show more records of the parula as well (R. Renfrew pers. comm., R. Mulvihill pers. comm.). Reasons for these increases are unclear, but forest maturation might be playing a role. The increased number of Atlas reports across the southern portion of New York, and especially the Confirmed one on Long Island and the cluster in Cattaraugus County, suggest a return of the Northern Parula to much of its former breeding range after an absence of nearly a half-century.

2000-05 Distribution Map

- ☐ Not Found
- ░ Possible
- ▒ Probable
- ■ Confirmed

Number of Blocks

	1980–85		2000–05		Change
	No.	%	No.	%	%
Possible	198	58	223	43	13
Probable	117	34	250	49	114
Confirmed	27	8	42	8	56
Total	342	6	515	10	51

Change Map

- ☐ Not Reported
- ■ 1980–85 Atlas
- ▒ 2000–05 Atlas
- ░ Both Atlases

Breeding Bird Survey Trend in New York

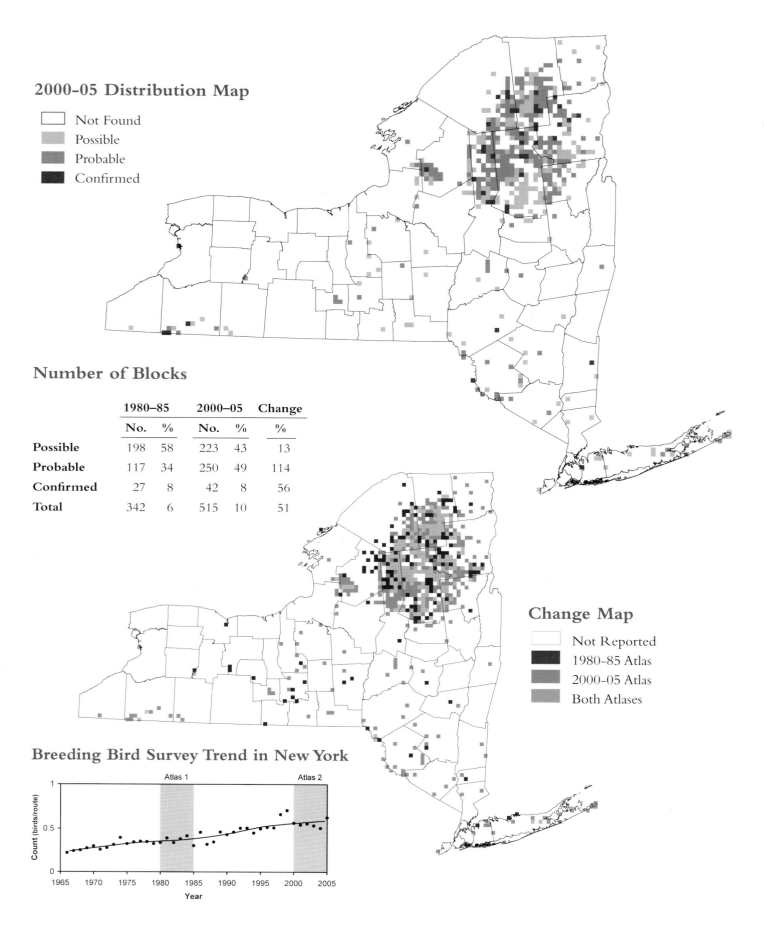

Yellow Warbler

Dendroica petechia

Shaibal S. Mitra

The Yellow Warbler breeds from Alaska and Newfoundland southward through the northern two-thirds of the United States, locally in the arid Southwest, and throughout Mexico's central plateau, with additional populations in the Caribbean and along the Atlantic and Pacific coasts of northern South America (AOU 1998). Although this warbler thrives in disturbed and early-successional habitats and probably benefited from European settlement, the early accounts of DeKay (1844) and Giraud (1844) imply that this species has long been among the most familiar birds in the state. Eaton (1914) called it common throughout, except in parts of the Adirondacks and Catskills, and Bull (1974) noted it only as a widespread and adaptable breeder. The Yellow Warbler uses a wide variety of breeding habitats, ranging from maritime shrub-thickets to the margins of marshes, swamps, ponds, and streams, to upland gardens, orchards, and old fields (Bonney 1988h, McKinney and Parkes 1998). Sites near water are almost always occupied when adequate shrubby vegetation is present, whereas occupancy of upland sites is more localized, with many unoccupied sites at least superficially similar to occupied ones.

During the first Atlas survey, the Yellow Warbler was found statewide, absent only from the highest elevations and most heavily forested portions of the Adirondacks, the Catskill Peaks, and the most densely urbanized portions of New York City. The second Atlas survey results showed that little had changed; in fact, the number of occupied blocks was nearly the same for each Atlas period, although many blocks were occupied during one period but not the other. Both gains and losses appear concentrated in the same high-elevation, heavily forested regions where consistently unoccupied blocks were most prevalent. It seems likely that the unusually dynamic pattern of block occupancy in these regions is an artifact of sampling associated with low breeding densities, rather than some unique pattern of disturbance and reforestation. Indeed, Enser (1992) attributed unoccupied Atlas blocks in Rhode Island's forested interior to low breeding densities documented by independent surveys. In most of New York, a 5 × 5 km survey block is more likely to remain occupied, even as the distribution of local breeding sites changes with the appearance and disappearance of appropriate habitat through localized disturbance and succession (Lowther et al. 1999, Mitra 1999).

Breeding Bird Survey data show no change in Yellow Warbler populations across the continent or in New York from 1966 to 2005, even within the dynamic Adirondacks region, although a decline in the last 25 years is statistically significant for the whole state and the north Atlantic states (U.S. Fish and Wildlife Service Region 5) (Sauer et al. 2005). Abundant and widespread, the Yellow Warbler is rarely mentioned as a species of conservation concern. Comments by Griscom (1923), Cruickshank (1942), and Siebenheller (1981) concerning population reductions as formerly rural areas became urbanized near New York City stand out against more numerous statements emphasizing the species's ubiquity and familiarity. Time will tell how tolerable the expanding urban and suburban environments of the future will prove, even for this relatively adaptable species. Additionally, as is true for all Neotropical migrants, the future of New York's breeding Yellow Warblers depends not only on land-use patterns here but also on conditions thousands of miles away. Boulet et al.'s (2006) continent-wide study of migratory connectivity in the Yellow Warbler, which included analyses of feather samples collected from birds banded in Monroe and Suffolk counties, affirmed that the Yellow Warbler breeds in northeastern North America but winters primarily in South America.

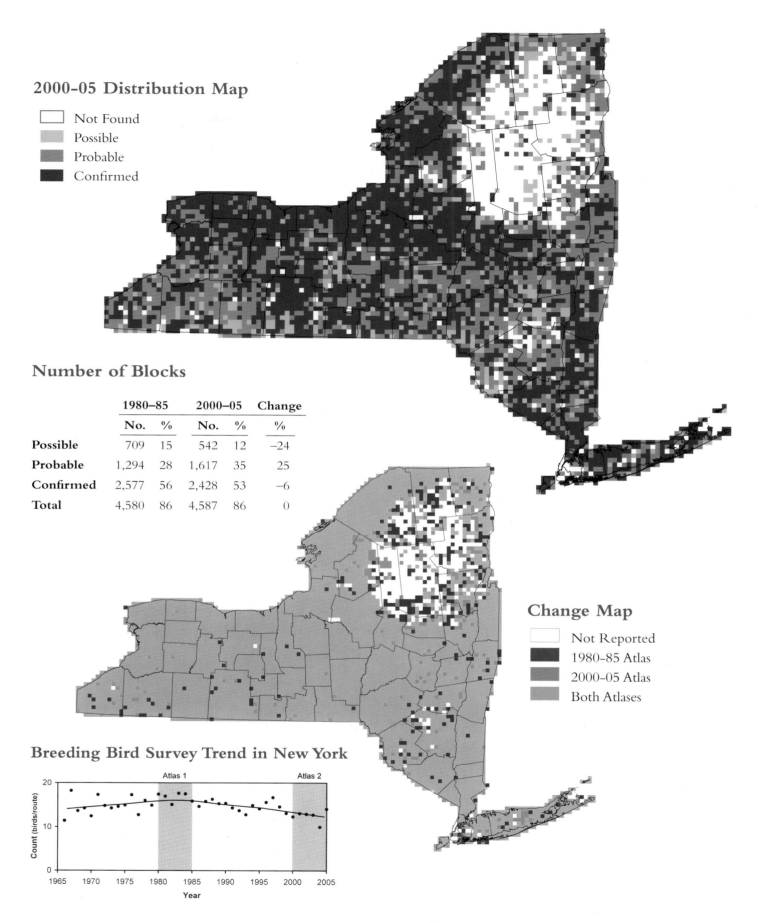

2000-05 Distribution Map

- ☐ Not Found
- Possible
- Probable
- Confirmed

Number of Blocks

	1980–85		2000–05		Change
	No.	%	No.	%	%
Possible	709	15	542	12	−24
Probable	1,294	28	1,617	35	25
Confirmed	2,577	56	2,428	53	−6
Total	4,580	86	4,587	86	0

Change Map

- ☐ Not Reported
- 1980-85 Atlas
- 2000-05 Atlas
- Both Atlases

Breeding Bird Survey Trend in New York

Chestnut-sided Warbler
Dendroica pensylvanica

TIMOTHY J. POST

The Chestnut-sided Warbler is a bird of forest edges and early-successional deciduous forest habitats, such as abandoned farmlands and regenerating clear-cuts. It prefers small trees or saplings to perch on while singing but spends much of its time near the ground in shrubs and thickets (Richardson and Brauning 1995). New York is within the core of the breeding range for the Chestnut-sided Warbler, which extends from central Saskatchewan eastward to Nova Scotia, southward to northern Minnesota, southern Pennsylvania, and in the Appalachians to northern Georgia (Richardson and Brauning 1995). Prior to European settlement, the Chestnut-sided Warbler was probably less common in New York. Large-scale clearing of forests followed European settlement and continued into the early 1900s (Lorimer 2001). As cleared areas regenerated to early-successional forest, Chestnut-sided Warbler populations probably increased. Eaton (1914) called the species common throughout the state where its brushy breeding habitat was found, around the outskirts of the Adirondacks, but only locally in the southeastern portion of the state. Extensive habitat was also created in the early to mid-1900s, as farmlands across New York were abandoned and allowed to succeed into old fields, shrublands, and young forests (see Chapter 4). Bull (1974) considered the Chestnut-sided Warbler common and widespread in appropriate habitat across the state but rare and local on the Coastal Plain. Habitat trends since the 1960s show declines in the amount of shrubland and early-successional habitat and increases in more mature forest. In the St. Lawrence Valley and upper Great Lakes Plain, the amount of early-successional habitats declined 52 percent from the early 1970s until 2004 (T. Post unpubl. data).

In the first Atlas period, the Chestnut-sided Warbler was distributed across much of the state, but the species was uncommon on the Great Lakes Plain and other areas with intensive agriculture. It was also uncommon in much of the Mohawk Valley, on Long Island, and in the lower Hudson Valley, and it was missing from the greater New York City area. Areas in the Adirondacks with mature forests, such as State Forest Preserve portions where logging is prohibited, showed somewhat scattered populations. The distribution of the Chestnut-sided Warbler showed modest changes between the first and second Atlas periods, and the number of blocks with detections increased statewide by 10 percent. The largest increases occurred in the Great Lakes Plain and the Mohawk Valley. Decreases were noticeable in the lower Hudson Valley and Coastal Lowlands and are probably the result of increased development and maturing forests. Gaps still exist in the heavily agricultural parts of the Great Lakes Plain and in the densely forested regions of the Adirondack High Peaks and Central Adirondacks.

Breeding Bird Survey trend data for the Chestnut-sided Warbler indicate significant declines of 0.8, 0.6, and 0.6 percent per year for New York, the north Atlantic states (U.S. Fish and Wildlife Service Region 5), and survey-wide, respectively, since 1966 (Sauer et al. 2007). While a 0.8 percent decline per year appears low, it equates to a population decline of 27 percent during the survey period (1966–2005). The overall declines shown by BBS data are probably caused by the statewide maturation of forests, loss of early-successional habitat, and development in populated areas. So while the Atlas data show that the distribution of the Chestnut-sided Warbler is expanding in New York, its population may be declining. The Chestnut-sided Warbler is considered a Species of Conservation Concern by Partners in Flight (Rich et al. 2004). It is not considered a high priority because it is still widespread and common in much of its breeding range, but it bears watching as early-successional habitats continue to decline.

2000-05 Distribution Map

- ☐ Not Found
- Possible
- Probable
- ■ Confirmed

Number of Blocks

	1980–85		2000–05		Change
	No.	%	No.	%	%
Possible	1,093	30	989	25	−10
Probable	1,377	38	1,748	44	27
Confirmed	1,164	32	1,256	31	8
Total	3,634	68	3,993	75	10

Change Map

- ☐ Not Reported
- ■ 1980-85 Atlas
- 2000-05 Atlas
- Both Atlases

Breeding Bird Survey Trend in New York

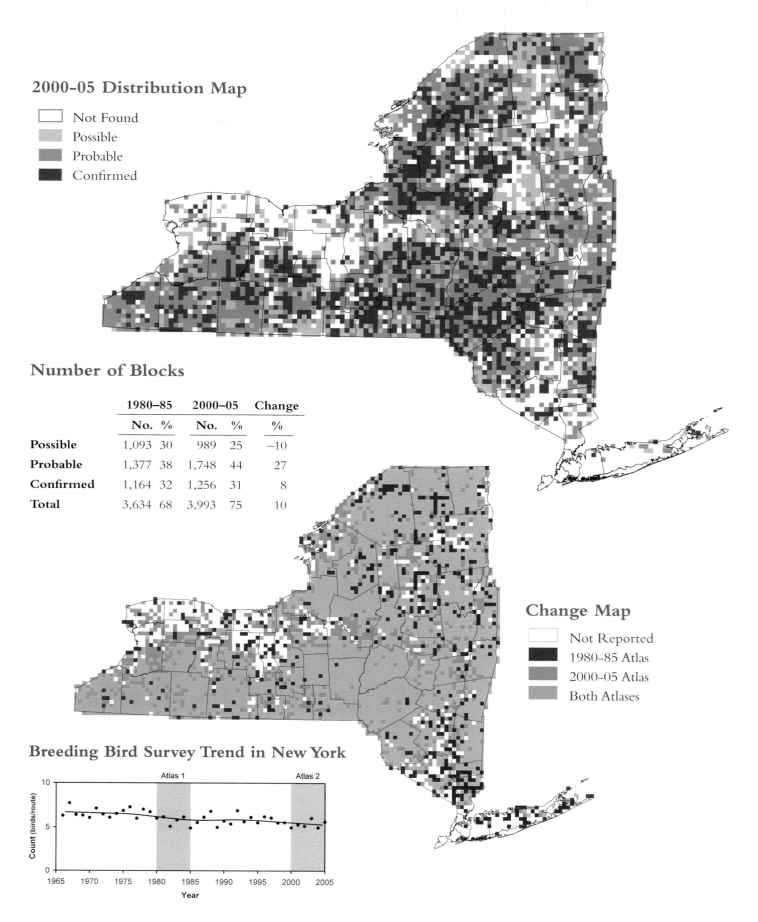

Magnolia Warbler

Dendroica magnolia

KEVIN J. McGOWAN

The Magnolia Warbler is a common bird of the eastern boreal forest. It breeds from the Northwest Territories to Newfoundland, southward to central Alberta, Wisconsin, and Pennsylvania, and farther southward in the mountains to Tennessee (Hall 1994). New York is near the southeastern edge of its range. It breeds in small, dense conifers, especially young spruces, in purely coniferous stands or in mixed forest. It is densest in young second-growth spruces but can also be found in mature forest if a dense understory is present (Hall 1994). DeKay (1844) considered it to be rare in New York, although he quoted Audubon as having documented it breeding in Pennsylvania. Rathbun (1879) considered it only a migrant in central New York, but Short (1893) termed it a rare breeder in western New York, a designation that fits the description by Reed and Wright (1909) for the Cayuga Lake Basin. Eaton (1914) considered the Magnolia Warbler a common breeder in the Catskills and Adirondacks but local in appropriate habitat in central and western New York. Bull's (1974) range description was little changed: a common breeder in mixed forests at higher elevations, especially in the Adirondacks, Tug Hill, and Catskills; breeding in suitable habitats across central New York; but virtually absent from the Great Lakes Plain and the southeastern portion of the state. This warbler began using plantations of pine and spruce at least by the 1960s (Rosche 1967).

During the first Atlas survey, the Magnolia Warbler was common in most of the Adirondacks at elevations below 1,219 m (4,000 ft) (Eaton 1988k) and in the Tug Hill Plateau. It was well distributed across the western and eastern portions of the Appalachian Plateau at elevations above 305 m (1,000 ft) and in the Rensselaer Hills. A few reports were made in hemlock ravines in the Great Lakes Plain (Eaton 1988k), but the only

Confirmed breeding there was in the Indian River Lakes region. Only scattered reports were made in the Finger Lakes region, central Appalachian Plateau, and Mohawk Valley. The second Atlas survey documented a 26 percent increase in the number of blocks with records of the Magnolia Warbler and increases in every ecozone in which it occurred. The overall distribution was essentially the same, with the species present in most blocks in the Adirondacks and Tug Hill Plateau and in significant concentrations in the eastern and western portions of the Appalachian Plateau. Little change was apparent in the Adirondacks, with only a 4 percent increase, but substantial increases were noticeable in the Appalachian Plateau, where the number of blocks increased 47 percent, and especially in the western portion. Blocks with reports from the Great Lakes Plain increased, but confirmations still were scarce there. More reports were made in the Hudson Valley and to the east of the Hudson River, but confirmations there were still restricted to the Rensselaer Hills. The Magnolia Warbler remained less common in the central Appalachian Plateau, mostly absent from the Finger Lakes, Great Lakes Plain, Mohawk Valley, and Hudson Valley, and completely absent from the Coastal Lowlands.

Breeding Bird Survey data show a significant increase of 1.3 percent a year in Magnolia Warbler numbers continent-wide since 1966 (Sauer et al. 2005). BBS data from New York show a significant 2.1 percent increase over the same time period, although the increase of 0.3 percent per year since 1980 was not statistically significant (Sauer et al. 2005). The second Ontario Breeding Bird Atlas also reported a significant increase in Magnolia Warbler records province-wide (Bird Studies Canada et al. 2006). Partners in Flight listed the warbler as a Continental Stewardship Species, although with a relatively low risk score (Rich et al. 2004). As a bird that prefers young second-growth trees, the Magnolia Warbler should benefit by reforestation, but its numbers should decline in areas where forest is maturing. No sign of such declines were noticeable in the New York Atlas data.

484

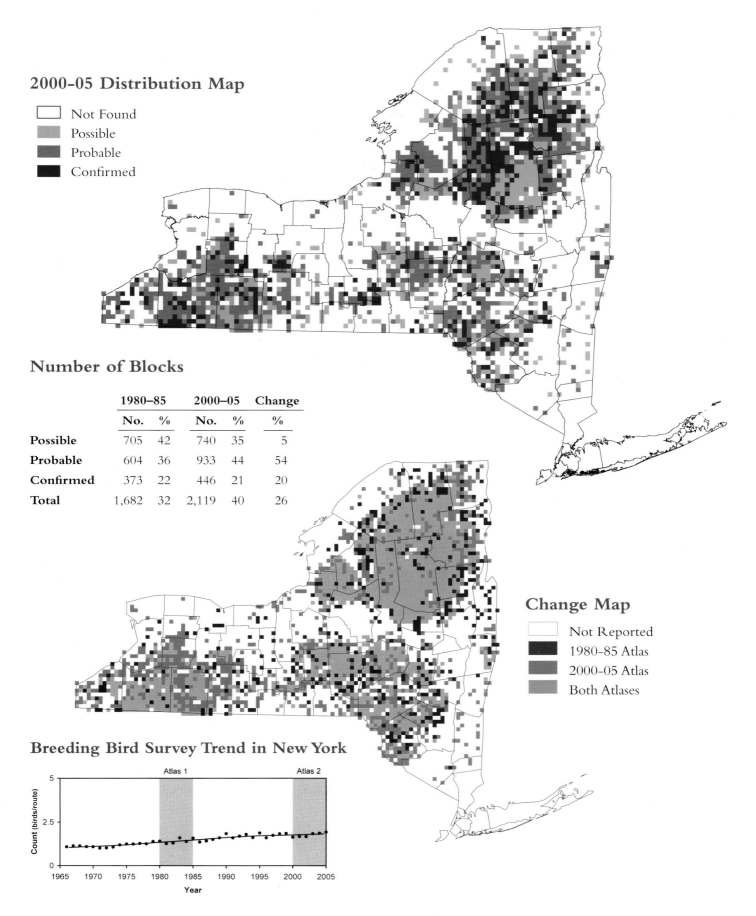

2000-05 Distribution Map

- ☐ Not Found
- Possible
- Probable
- Confirmed

Number of Blocks

	1980–85		2000–05		Change
	No.	%	No.	%	%
Possible	705	42	740	35	5
Probable	604	36	933	44	54
Confirmed	373	22	446	21	20
Total	1,682	32	2,119	40	26

Change Map

- ☐ Not Reported
- 1980-85 Atlas
- 2000-05 Atlas
- Both Atlases

Breeding Bird Survey Trend in New York

Cape May Warbler
Dendroica tigrina

John M. C. Peterson

The Cape May Warbler remains something of an enigma in New York State, even after two Atlas surveys. This spruce budworm specialist nests in boreal spruce forests from the Northwest Territories and eastern British Columbia to Newfoundland, and southward into the United States to northern Minnesota and Michigan, the Adirondacks of New York, and northern New England (Baltz and Latta 1998). From the Eastern Townships of southern Quebec, the range extends south to the vicinity of Lake Memphremagog and across the border into the Northeast Highlands of Vermont (Lanoue and Morrier 1996). Cape May Warblers in New York are separated from those nesting in neighboring Canada and Vermont by the Champlain Valley; the Champlain, St. Lawrence, and Western Adirondack transitions; and the Malone and St. Lawrence plains. Adirondack birds are isolated from the main breeding population and represent the southern limits of this warbler's range. In New York State, the Cape May Warbler was first confirmed nesting at North Meadow, Essex County, on 4 July 1947, where a female was feeding two recently fledged young (Carleton et al. 1948). A second confirmation was obtained on 23 June 1964, with another female seen feeding young near Madawaska, Franklin County, by Rusk and Scheider (Bull 1974).

During the first Atlas period, the Cape May Warbler was confined to the Adirondack High Peaks, Sable Highlands, and Western Adirondack Foothills, with scattered locations in the Central Adirondacks and a concentration on the 30,300-ha (75,000-a) Boreal Heritage Preserve then being formed by The Nature Conservancy in western Franklin County. The second Atlas results showed a continued Adirondack presence in a similar number of blocks but at quite different locations. Only two locations were the same on both surveys: Bloomingdale Bog on the Essex-Franklin county line, and Chubb River, Essex County. No records were obtained from Hamilton County, where the Cape May Warbler was previously found in four blocks. Nor did any records in the second Atlas survey come from the vicinity of the now-established Boreal Heritage Preserve. Franklin County sightings came from farther to the north in the town of Santa Clara, near Madawaska, and along the East Branch St. Regis River. Records were obtained for the first time from the Eastern Adirondack Foothills, with one near Elizabethtown in eastern Essex County. None of the 18 records documented in the first Atlas were of Confirmed breeding; a female with two young along Potter Brook, St. Lawrence County, remained a frustrating Possible record (J. M. C. Peterson 1988d). The only Confirmed record of either Atlas project finally came on 18 June 2000 when Hagar and O'Brien observed adult birds carrying food to young along the West Branch Ausable River, North Elba, Essex County. Singing males and pairs were found in that month along the length of River Road, which traverses three Atlas blocks (L. L. Master pers. comm.). The possibility is strong that the Cape May Warbler might have been breeding in the two neighboring blocks as well. A nest of Cape May Warbler, a bulky cup usually well concealed and placed against the trunk high in a conifer (Baltz and Latta 1998), has not yet been found in New York State.

Cape May Warbler populations fluctuate with the availability of large larvae and pupae of the eastern spruce budworm to feed its young (Baltz and Latta 1998). Although much of the Cape May Warbler's breeding range lies outside the area covered by the Breeding Bird Survey, BBS data in the closed boreal forest show increases and decreases roughly corresponding to spruce budworm outbreaks but no significant long-term trends (Sauer et al. 2007). The lack of any major spruce budworm outbreaks in the Adirondacks in recent years may be a limiting factor for this species in New York, in spite of increasingly superb spruce habitat.

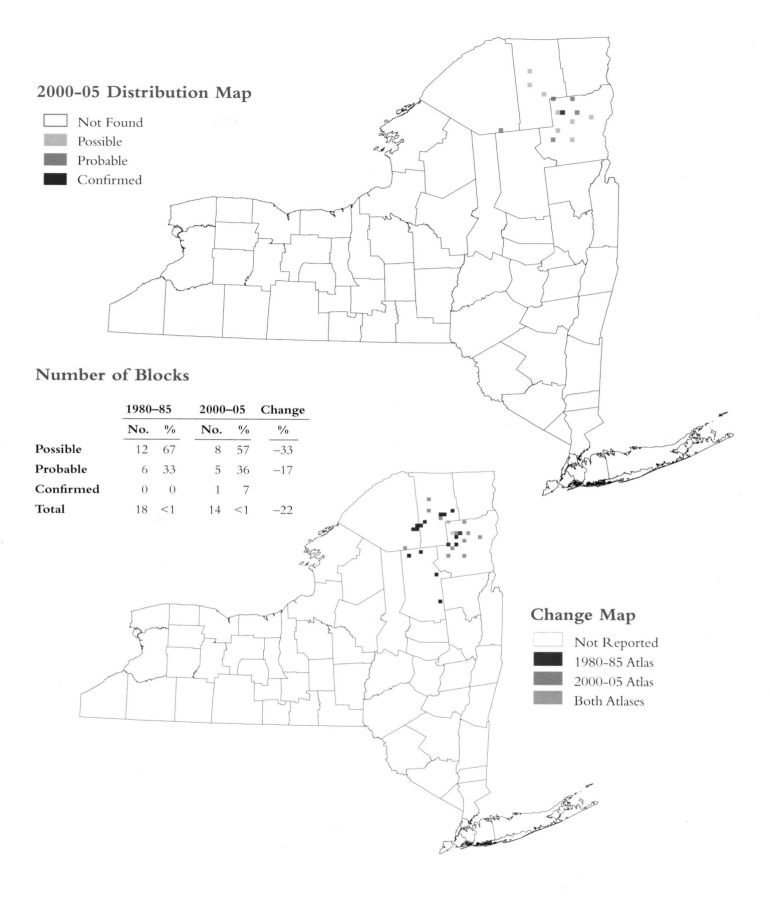

2000-05 Distribution Map

- ☐ Not Found
- Possible
- Probable
- Confirmed

Number of Blocks

	1980–85		2000–05		Change
	No.	%	No.	%	%
Possible	12	67	8	57	−33
Probable	6	33	5	36	−17
Confirmed	0	0	1	7	
Total	18	<1	14	<1	−22

Change Map

- ☐ Not Reported
- 1980-85 Atlas
- 2000-05 Atlas
- Both Atlases

Black-throated Blue Warbler

Dendroica caerulescens

JOAN E. COLLINS

On hot, lazy, summer afternoons, after many other species become quiet, the slow, buzzy voice of the Black-throated Blue Warbler can still occasionally be heard emanating from a low perch near a patch of bushy vegetation in the cool, shaded, mature woodlands of the Adirondacks. It breeds from southwestern Ontario eastward to Nova Scotia, southward to Pennsylvania and along the higher elevations of the Appalachian Mountains to northern Georgia. The preferred breeding habitat for the Black-throated Blue Warbler includes large tracts of relatively undisturbed hardwood and mixed forest, with a closed tree canopy and dense undergrowth that often contains hobblebush (Holmes et al. 2005, pers. obs.). DeKay (1844) found the species to be more common in the western and northern regions of the state. With more land cleared for agriculture, Eaton (1914) described the species as scarce in central and western New York but a common summer resident of the Adirondack and Catskill regions, where Bull (1974) also found it "one of the more numerous" warblers.

The first Atlas map showed the Black-throated Blue Warbler in areas mainly above 305 m (1,000 ft), concentrated in the Adirondacks, eastern Appalachian Plateau, Tug Hill Plateau, greater Catskills area, Rensselaer Hills, and Allegany Hills. While the second Atlas results did not show a change in the overall distribution of the Black-throated Blue, the number of blocks with breeding records increased 10 percent, probably as a result of continued forest maturation within the state. The Appalachian Plateau had a 16 percent increase in the number of blocks with records, which represented over 40 percent of the total increase. The Adirondacks, already largely saturated with the species based on the first Atlas data, showed a smaller increase of 3 percent, representing over 15 percent of the total increase.

Breeding Bird Survey data show stable or increasing population trends for the Black-throated Blue Warbler across most of its breeding range, including a significant survey-wide increase of 1.6 percent per year from 1980 to 2006 (Sauer et al. 2007). However, the Adirondack Mountains is the only BBS region to show a significant yearly decline from 1966 to 2006 (of 2.1 percent) (Sauer et al. 2007). In addition, the New York BBS region shows a significant decline for the species of 2.3 percent per year from 1980 to 2006 (Sauer et al. 2007). The second Atlas results are consistent with the generally stable or increasing overall population trends shown for the species, but are contrary to the significant declines for the New York and Adirondack Mountains BBS regions, which are more difficult to explain. In the Adirondacks, some of the BBS decline for the species may be attributed to roadside habitat degradation as a result of human activities such as clear-cut logging, increased development (Bauer 2001), and wide edge-clearing along roadways. The second Breeding Bird Atlas in Ontario reported a significant increase in the number of squares reporting the Black-throated Blue Warbler across the province (Bird Studies Canada et al. 2006).

Partners in Flight identified the Black-throated Blue Warbler as a "priority species" of the "northern hardwood and mixed forest" habitat in the Adirondacks because the region contains 5 percent of the world population for this species (PIF 2000). Clear-cut logging on its breeding grounds negatively affects abundance of the species (Holmes 1990, Hartley et al. 2003). However, it is just as common in both managed and unmanaged northern hardwood forests (Welsh and Healy 1993, Buford and Capen 1999) as long as there is a relatively complete canopy cover (Jobes et al. 2004). The stable to increasing population trends for the species could be reversed in the future by loss of forests on its Caribbean winter grounds (Holmes et al. 2005). Despite the apparent increase in distribution shown in the Atlas data, the significant population declines in the state shown in the BBS data make this a species that warrants close monitoring in the future.

488

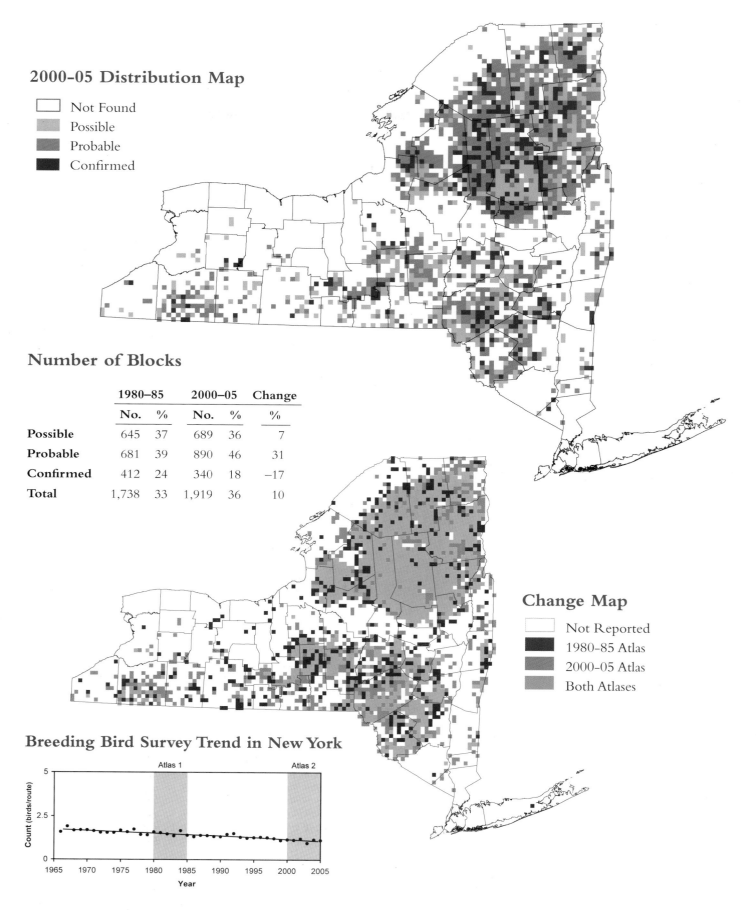

2000–05 Distribution Map

- ☐ Not Found
- Possible
- Probable
- Confirmed

Number of Blocks

	1980–85		2000–05		Change
	No.	%	No.	%	%
Possible	645	37	689	36	7
Probable	681	39	890	46	31
Confirmed	412	24	340	18	−17
Total	1,738	33	1,919	36	10

Change Map

- ☐ Not Reported
- 1980–85 Atlas
- 2000–05 Atlas
- Both Atlases

Breeding Bird Survey Trend in New York

BLACK–THROATED BLUE WARBLER 489

Yellow-rumped Warbler

Dendroica coronata

KEVIN J. MCGOWAN

One of the most abundant warblers in North America, the Yellow-rumped Warbler breeds from Alaska and Canada southward to the northern United States, and southward in the western mountains through Mexico to Guatemala (Hunt and Flaspohler 1998). The "Myrtle" form breeds from Alaska to Newfoundland, southward to Minnesota, Pennsylvania, and West Virginia. New York is near the southern edge of the breeding range. The warbler breeds in mature coniferous and mixed coniferous-deciduous woodlands, using a broad range of these habitats, and may be present in lower numbers in early-successional stages as well (Hunt and Flaspohler 1998). As a bird of mature forests, the Yellow-rumped Warbler probably was most abundant before European settlement and declined with the loss of the forests. DeKay (1844) listed it as common in the state but thought it traveled farther northward to breed. Eaton (1914) called it a common breeder restricted to the spruce belt of the Adirondacks and the Catskills. He mentioned breeding reports at Utica and Buffalo but considered those unconfirmed, or at most casual breeding records. Bull (1974) listed 25 breeding locations outside of the Adirondacks or Catskills (six in the Tug Hill Transition) and reported that only since the 1950s did the bird breed at lower elevations, nesting in spruce and red pine plantations, and to a lesser extent in white pine and hemlock.

The first Atlas documented a significant breeding range expansion of Yellow-rumped Warbler. The warbler was found throughout the Tug Hill and the Adirondacks to the Champlain Valley, including areas of low elevation. It was less continuous, but still widespread, across the Appalachian Plateau, especially in the eastern region into the Catskills and surrounding highlands. It was well represented in the Taconic Highlands to their southern limit, and especially in the Rensselaer Hills. Scattered reports came from across the Great Lakes Plain. A single Confirmed breeding record came from the Coastal Lowlands in Suffolk County. The second Atlas survey documented a contin-

ued expansion of this warbler in New York, although the distribution map looks little different from that in the first Atlas, with the warbler restricted primarily to areas of higher elevation. All ecozones reported increases, except the Coastal Lowlands where the bird was not reported this time. The most noticeable change between the two Atlas periods was the expansion in the western Appalachian Plateau. With the exception of parts of the Finger Lakes Highlands and a large section of the Allegany Hills, the breeding distribution of the Yellow-rumped Warbler was nearly continuous across the Appalachian Plateau. It did not spread southward in the Taconic Highlands or into the Hudson Valley. Its presence in the Mohawk Valley and the Great Lakes Plain remains limited and scattered, but with a new cluster of blocks in the St. Lawrence Plains.

Reforestation and the establishment of large pine and spruce plantations resulted in a southward expansion of the Yellow-rumped Warbler during the 1970s in New York, Pennsylvania, and West Virginia (Hunt and Flaspohler 1998) and into northern New Jersey (Walsh et al. 1999). Although Breeding Bird Survey data show no significant continent-wide trend, Yellow-rumped Warbler numbers have been significantly increasing in the north Atlantic states (U.S. Fish and Wildlife Service Region 5) since 1966, with a significant 2.5 percent yearly increase in New York since 1966 and a significant 1.5 percent annual increase since 1980 (Sauer et al. 2006). The second Ontario Breeding Bird Atlas also reported a significant increase (Bird Studies Canada et al. 2006). It is likely that the establishment and spread of the Yellow-rumped Warbler throughout the Appalachian Plateau and the St. Lawrence Valley are the result of the restoration of forest and its maturation, and may be expected to continue.

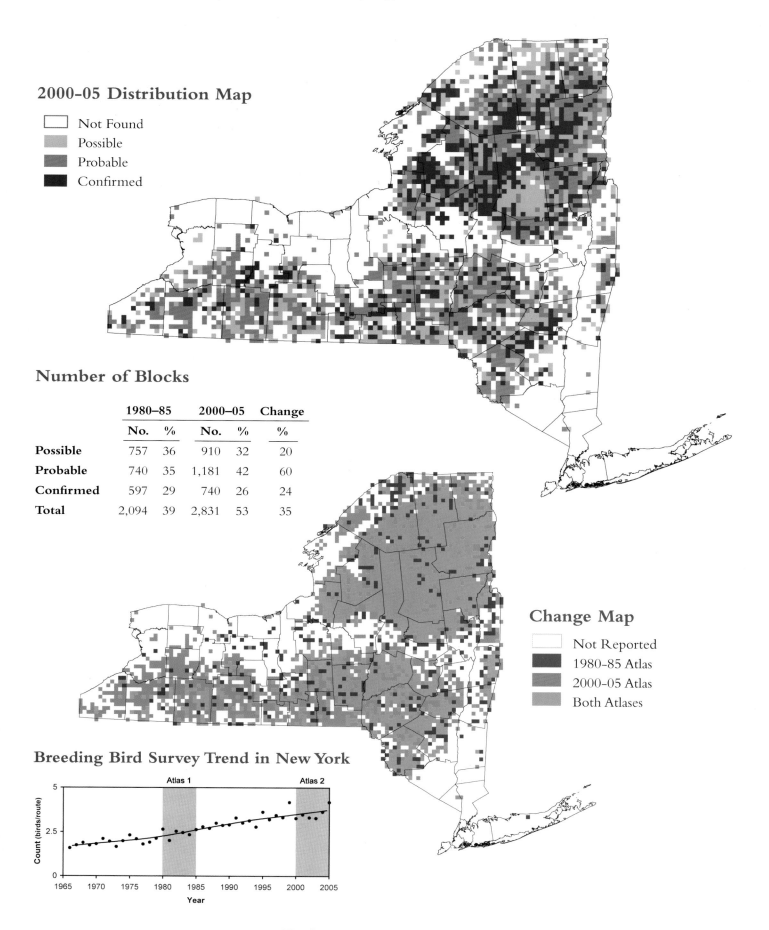

2000–05 Distribution Map

- ☐ Not Found
- Possible
- Probable
- Confirmed

Number of Blocks

	1980–85		2000–05		Change
	No.	%	No.	%	%
Possible	757	36	910	32	20
Probable	740	35	1,181	42	60
Confirmed	597	29	740	26	24
Total	2,094	39	2,831	53	35

Change Map

- ☐ Not Reported
- 1980–85 Atlas
- 2000–05 Atlas
- Both Atlases

Breeding Bird Survey Trend in New York

Black-throated Green Warbler

Dendroica virens

TIMOTHY J. POST

The Black-throated Green Warbler is one of the most common breeding species of the northeastern coniferous forests (Morse and Poole 2005). It is also found in mixed forests but generally in or near conifers. It typically avoids small, fragmented forest patches (Askins and Philbrick 1987). The Black-throated Green Warbler breeds from the northeastern United States across southern Canada to northeastern British Columbia, and southward through the Appalachian Mountains to northern Alabama (Morse and Poole 2005). New York is within the core breeding range. This warbler is found throughout the more heavily forested portions of New York, preferring larger forest patches and especially hemlocks. It was probably common before European settlement, and even after the destruction of the forests in the 19th century it remained common wherever suitable habitat remained. Eaton (1914) called it abundant in the Adirondacks, Catskills, and in appropriate habitat across all portions of the state, even on Long Island. Bull (1974) gave a similar description of the warbler's distribution, and Eaton (1988d) declared that the status of the Black-throated Green Warbler had changed little in the 100 years prior to the first Atlas survey, except that conifer plantations had likely benefited the species by providing more suitable habitat.

During the first Atlas period the Black-throated Green Warbler was found across the Appalachian Plateau, in the Adirondacks, Tug Hill Plateau, Taconic Mountains, Hudson Highlands, and Manhattan Hills. It was noticeably infrequent or absent from the Coastal Lowlands, Hudson Valley, St. Lawrence Plains, Great Lakes Plain, and Mohawk Valley. No breeding was confirmed on Long Island. The second Atlas data showed a substantial increase in the number of blocks with breeding records of the Black-throated Green Warbler. Increases occurred in every region where the warbler was found commonly during the first Atlas period, but it was also found in more blocks on the St. Lawrence Plains, Eastern Ontario Plain, and in the Mohawk and Hudson valleys, where it had been sparsely distributed. It remained largely absent from the Coastal Lowlands, Hudson and Mohawk valleys, and Great Lakes Plain; again no breeding was confirmed on Long Island. The Black-throated Green Warbler has a distinctive, persistent song, which makes detection easy, and it should be well represented by the Atlas results.

Breeding Bird Survey data show a nonsignificant declining trend for the Black-throated Green Warbler in New York since 1966 but a significant increase in the north Atlantic states (U.S. Fish and Wildlife Service Region 5) (Sauer et al. 2007). Range-wide, the trend since 1966 is negative, though not significant, but data for the last 25 years show a significant population increase of 1.2 percent per year (Sauer et al. 2005). The second Ontario Breeding Bird Atlas also reported significant increases across that province in the last 20 years (Bird Studies Canada et al. 2006).

Range-wide, Black-throated Green Warbler numbers are thought to have decreased during periods of heavy use of persistent pesticides such as DDT and again when fenitrothion was used to control the spruce budworm (Pearce et al. 1979). Invasive pests, such as the hemlock woolly adelgid, which destroys untreated hemlock populations, could have a substantial effect on Black-throated Green Warbler populations if it continues to expand northward through New York. In areas where the adelgids have killed hemlocks, the population of this warbler has declined or disappeared (Benzinger 1994, Tingley et al. 2002). In parts of New York, hemlock stands within mixed forests can be an important habitat for the Black-throated Green Warbler, and the loss of this habitat would negatively affect distribution and probably statewide populations.

2000–05 Distribution Map

- ☐ Not Found
- Possible
- Probable
- Confirmed

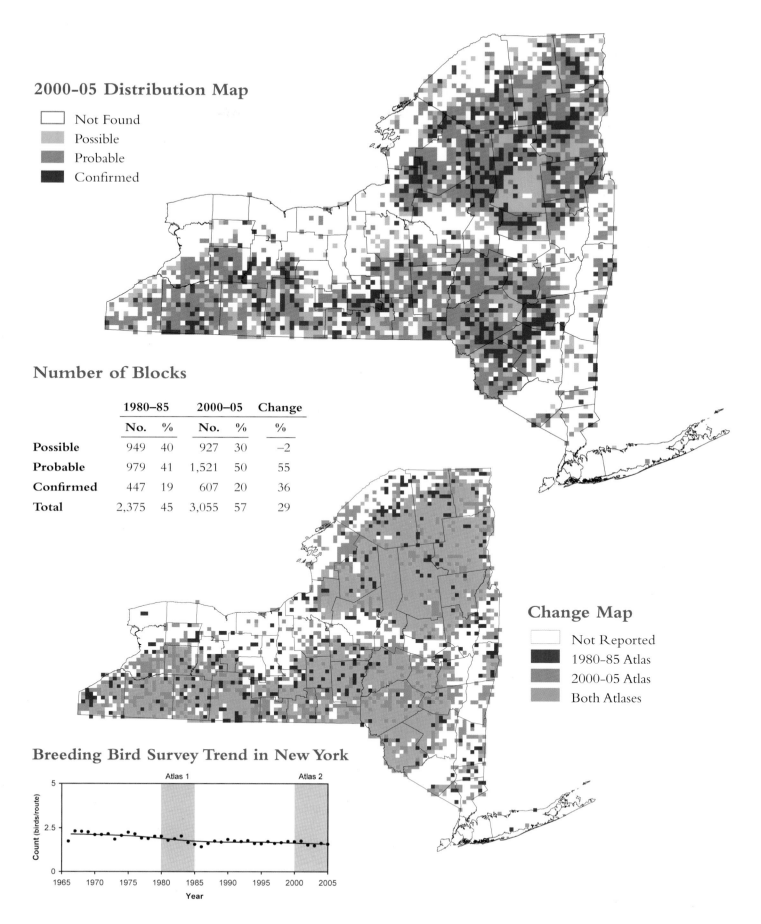

Number of Blocks

| | 1980–85 | | 2000–05 | | Change |
	No.	%	No.	%	%
Possible	949	40	927	30	−2
Probable	979	41	1,521	50	55
Confirmed	447	19	607	20	36
Total	2,375	45	3,055	57	29

Change Map

- ☐ Not Reported
- 1980–85 Atlas
- 2000–05 Atlas
- Both Atlases

Breeding Bird Survey Trend in New York

Blackburnian Warbler
Dendroica fusca

JOAN E. COLLINS

One of the characteristic birds of the Adirondacks, the flame-throated Blackburnian Warbler is often encountered singing from high atop a conifer. It breeds from eastern Alberta to southwestern Newfoundland and from northern Minnesota to the Northeast, southward to Pennsylvania and along the higher elevations of the Appalachian Mountains to northern Georgia (Morse 2004). The treetop-dwelling Blackburnian Warbler breeds in tall, mature coniferous forest and mixed woodlands where it shows a preference for hemlock (Dunn and Garrett 1997, Morse 2004). Eaton (1914) described the species as a common summer resident of the Catskill and Adirondack regions and as a local breeder "throughout the cooler swamps, gullies and highlands of central and western New York." Bull (1974) called it widespread at higher elevations and "plentiful enough at much lower elevations in central and western New York."

The first Atlas map showed the Blackburnian Warbler concentrated in heavily forested areas at elevations over 305 m (1,000 ft) in the Adirondacks, Catskills, Tug Hill Plateau, eastern Appalachian Plateau, and Allegany Hills (Levine 1988a), and present in lower-elevation areas, including the Champlain Valley. While the second Atlas findings did not show any change in the overall distribution of this species, the number of blocks with breeding records increased 19 percent. More than two-thirds of this increase occurred in the Appalachian Plateau, where an area representing a 44 percent increase stretched across the entire ecozone, including a large increase in the Cattaraugus Highlands of the western section. Significant increases in the number of blocks with records also occurred in the Catskill Highlands, Hudson Highlands, Hudson Valley, Champlain Valley, Taconic Highlands, and Tug Hill Plateau, and only slight increases in the Adirondacks and Catskill Peaks, which were already largely saturated with the species. Reforested areas of the state have continued to mature, providing additional nesting habitat for this species.

Blackburnian Warbler population trends appear to be stable or increasing across most of the breeding range. Morse (2004) suggested that as a forest-interior breeding species, the Blackburnian Warbler is probably under-represented on roadside Breeding Bird Surveys, but that sample sizes should be adequate enough to identify trends. The BBS data for the Blackburnian Warbler show a nearly significant increase of 1.1 percent per year across the survey areas from 1980 to 2006, as well as a nearly significant increase of 1.2 percent per year for the Eastern BBS Region during the same time period, but the trends for New York were not significant (Sauer et al. 2005). The second Breeding Bird Atlas in Ontario reported significant increases in the Canadian Shield regions of that province (Bird Studies Canada et al. 2006).

Partners in Flight has identified the Blackburnian Warbler as a "priority species" representing the "mature conifer forest" habitat of the Adirondacks, due to its abundance and current stable population trends (PIF 2000). However, there are several conservation concerns for the Blackburnian Warbler. The species is sensitive to forest fragmentation (Hagen et al. 1996, Hobson and Bayne 2000), and removal of large conifers also results in population declines (Webb et al. 1977). In addition, Hartley et al. (2003) have shown that the abundance of this species in mature forest drops off significantly as logging intensity increases. Two introduced insects, the balsam woolly adelgid and the hemlock woolly adelgid, are moving northward as a result of a warming climate, and destroying fir and hemlock trees, respectively, which may negatively affect the Blackburnian Warbler's breeding habitat (Morse 2004). Rapid deforestation occurring on its limited tropical wintering range in southern Central America and northern South America is also cause for serious concern (Morse 2004). For now, however, populations in New York appear healthy.

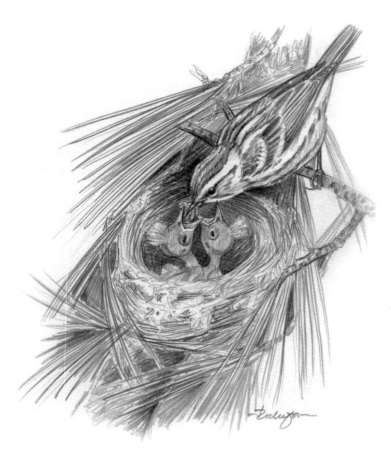

2000–05 Distribution Map

- ☐ Not Found
- Possible
- Probable
- Confirmed

Number of Blocks

	1980–85		2000–05		Change
	No.	%	No.	%	%
Possible	716	42	737	36	3
Probable	625	37	946	46	51
Confirmed	371	22	357	18	−4
Total	1,712	32	2,040	38	19

Change Map

- ☐ Not Reported
- 1980-85 Atlas
- 2000-05 Atlas
- Both Atlases

Breeding Bird Survey Trend in New York

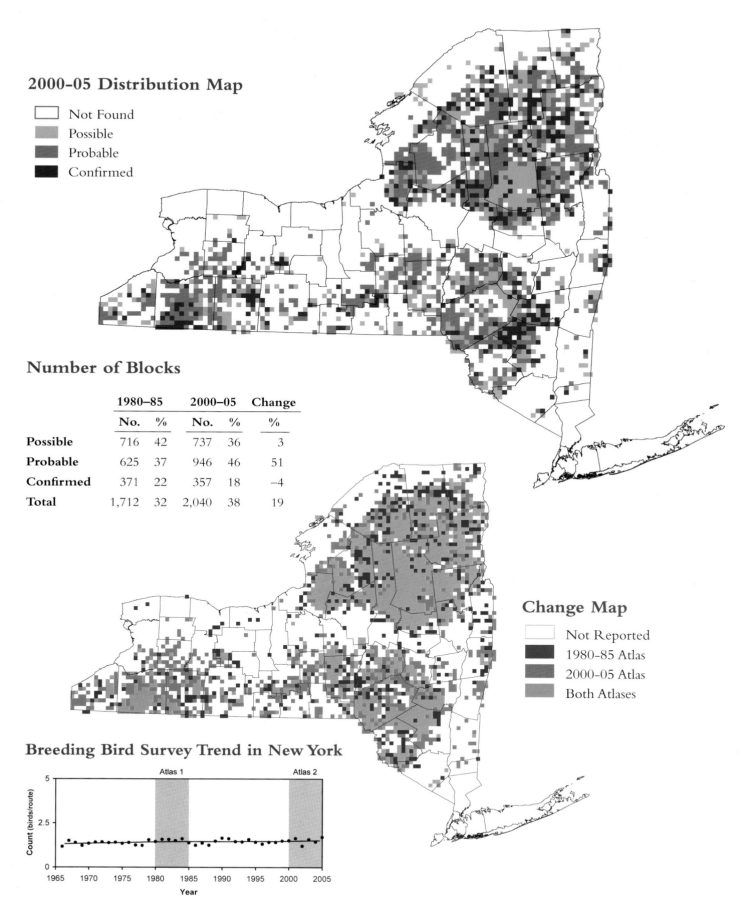

BLACKBURNIAN WARBLER 495

Yellow-throated Warbler

Dendroica dominica

KEVIN J. MCGOWAN

The Yellow-throated Warbler is a bird of tall trees found primarily in the southeastern United States, breeding from Iowa to Pennsylvania and New Jersey, southward to eastern Texas and Florida. It uses two distinct habitats: mature bottomland woodlands and swamps, and dry upland pine–oak forests (Hall 1996). It is a relatively rare visitor to New York, which is just north of its normal breeding range. It has long been a casual visitor here, primarily individuals that overshoot the breeding grounds during spring migration. Eaton (1914) knew of only two specimens from Long Island, but its occurrence increased in the 1950s (Bull 1974). It is now nearly annual as a migrant in the New York City area (Sherony 1998b).

The first confirmed nesting of the Yellow-throated Warbler in New York occurred during the first Atlas period. Nests were discovered in 1984 along Catskill Creek in Greene County (Carroll 1988h) and along Science Lake in Allegany State Park, Cattaraugus County (Baird 1984). A sighting in Hamilton County in May 1980 was likely to have been a spring overshoot. After the first Atlas survey was completed, breeding was detected at Science Lake again in 1987 and 1988 (NYSARC 1990). No further confirmation of breeding was made in the state again until the second Atlas period. Sightings in 1994 (Kelling 1994) and 1997 (Sherony 1998b) might indicate breeding, but no evidence of breeding was found. During the second Atlas survey, the Yellow-throated Warbler was detected in five blocks. A nest with adults feeding young was observed 21–27 June 2004, in Cattaraugus County, approximately 4.5 km (3.2 mi) from the nesting locality found during the first Atlas period. The birds nested in a location similar to where the species nested in 1984: high up in a red pine at the edge of a mature pine plantation, near a road and open areas. Repeated observations of singing males were made in scattered blocks in Chautauqua, Erie, Broome, and Orange counties in areas of tall pines or sycamores. Up to four individuals were seen in June 2001 near the Delaware River on the Sullivan/Orange county border (Bochnik 2001), in a location where multiple males had been present since 1997 (Sherony 1998b). This area seems a likely location for breeding, but no such activity was detected. The presence of a singing male in a maple swamp on Long Island suggests the possibility of a breeding expansion to the Coastal Lowlands.

Breeding Bird Survey data show a positive increase in Yellow-throated Warbler numbers across its range and in the mid to north Atlantic region (U.S. Fish and Wildlife Service Region 5) (Sauer et al. 2005). In the 19th century the Yellow-throated Warbler nested as far northward as southern Michigan and the Lake Erie shore of Ohio, but it retreated to southern Ohio in the late 19th and early 20th centuries (Hall 1996). After 1940, populations at the northern edge of the range increased, and the breeding range expanded northward again (Hall 1996). It first nested in New Jersey in 1922, and by 1981 it had established populations in the southern part of the state and along the Delaware River to the northern counties (Walsh et al. 1999). In Pennsylvania, the Yellow-throated Warbler is found primarily in the southwestern corner, with populations scattered throughout the state (Brauning 1992). Preliminary results from the second Pennsylvania Breeding Bird Atlas show an increase in the number of records from the northwestern part of the state (R. Mulvihill pers. comm.), just to the south of the Cattaraugus County breeding site in New York. A single report was also made across the Delaware River from where the Sullivan/Orange county sightings occurred.

Although little appears changed in the New York distribution of the Yellow-throated Warbler between the two Atlas periods, and the species does not appear to have established much of a foothold in the state, the presence of populations in western Pennsylvania and northwestern New Jersey suggest that such a foothold may soon be established, with increases to be expected in the near future.

2000-05 Distribution Map

- ☐ Not Found
- ☐ Possible
- ☐ Probable
- ■ Confirmed

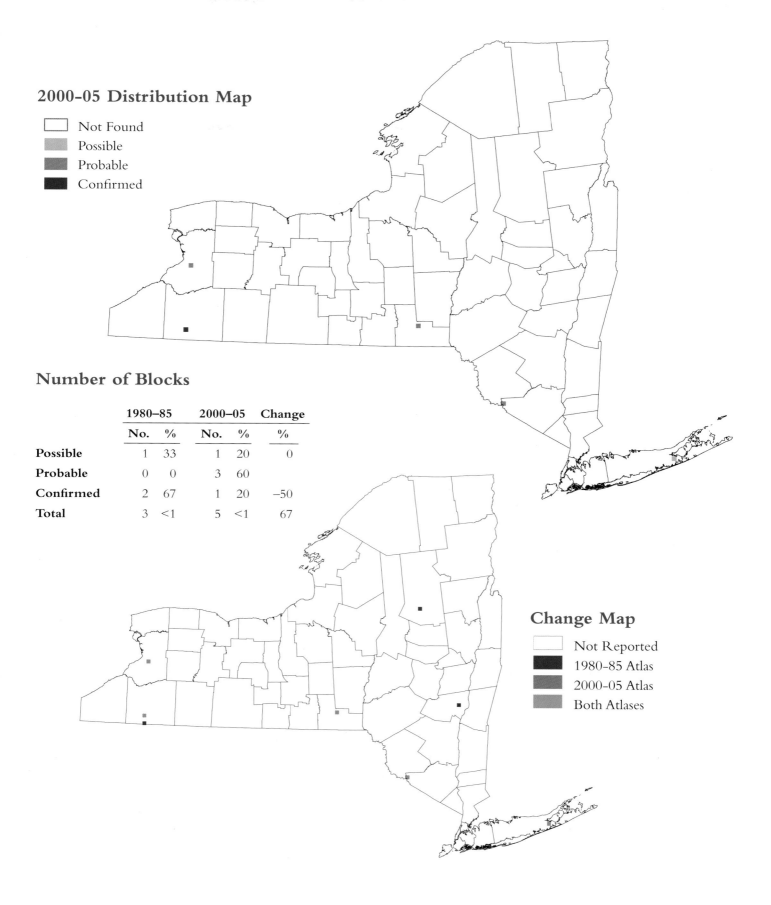

Number of Blocks

	1980–85		2000–05		Change
	No.	%	No.	%	%
Possible	1	33	1	20	0
Probable	0	0	3	60	
Confirmed	2	67	1	20	−50
Total	3	<1	5	<1	67

Change Map

- ☐ Not Reported
- ■ 1980-85 Atlas
- ☐ 2000-05 Atlas
- ☐ Both Atlases

Pine Warbler

Dendroica pinus

KEVIN J. McGOWAN

The Pine Warbler breeds from southern Canada to the southeastern United States and the Caribbean. New York is in the middle of the range, where, oddly enough, the species is least common and most scattered. True to its name, the Pine Warbler is found in forests of many species of pines but not in other coniferous forest types, such as spruces hemlock, or larch (Rodewald et al. 1999). It probably was common in pine woodlands across New York before European settlement. Both DeKay (1844) and Giraud (1844) called it common. The largest populations in New York may always have been in the pine barrens of eastern Long Island. The loss of pineland on Long Island caused some decline in its numbers there (Bull 1974), but preservation of the forests and decrease in logging resulted in a spread of the population (Salzman 1998h). Upstate, the Pine Warbler has long been found in small numbers locally (Reed and Wright 1909, Eaton 1914). Bull (1974) outlined four separate populations in New York: eastern Long Island, along the Hudson and Champlain valleys, the Finger Lakes region, and the Great Lakes and St. Lawrence plains.

J. M. C. Peterson (1988l) stated that the first Atlas map did not show the same distribution pattern that Bull (1974) described, with records from the Adirondacks, Catskills, and other areas scattered throughout the state. In fact, the first Atlas map did show the same strongholds in the same general regions as reported by Bull (1974), with only the significant cluster of blocks in Sullivan, Ulster, and Orange counties and the scattering of blocks in the Adirondacks differing from his general outline. The pattern did indicate, however, that the state did not have four isolated populations but rather four or five areas of abundance, loosely connected by scattered breeding localities. The Atlas results might represent some range expansion, but they also might be the consequence of the large field effort put forth in detecting many new locations for this highly localized breeder. The second Atlas survey revealed a substantial increase in the number of blocks with breeding records and a significant expansion of range within the state to all counties outside of New York City. Although the same regional strongholds were apparent, the species was continuously distributed across the state. The Pine Warbler was virtually absent from the very western counties during the first Atlas period, where it had been historically a rare breeder (Beardslee and Mitchell 1965), but it was found throughout the region in small numbers during the second Atlas period. Expansion of range occurred on Long Island as well; the number of blocks with records of the Pine Warbler increased 47 percent in the Coastal Lowlands.

Nationwide the Pine Warbler has shown a slow but significant and continued increase in numbers since 1966, based on Breeding Bird Survey data (Sauer et al. 2005). BBS data from New York show few birds detected until the late 1980s, after which time the population increased dramatically (Sauer et al. 2005). Similar patterns can be seen in BBS data for most other states in the mid-Atlantic region into New England (Sauer et al. 2005).

Salzman (1998h) suggested that protection of pine stands, decreased logging, and fire suppression were responsible for the slight increase in Pine Warbler numbers on Long Island. Similar habitat changes are unlikely to be responsible for the expansion in the rest of the state. The Pine Warbler prefers mature stands of pines, with a closed canopy that lacks a deciduous understory (Rodewald et al. 1999). The acreage of pine plantings or forests has not changed appreciably since the first Atlas fieldwork was completed (see Chapter 4), and most of the large plantings from the early 20th century have long since reached maturity. Perhaps the maturation of secondary forests with scattered native white pine is responsible for the spread of the Pine Warbler in New York and the Northeast.

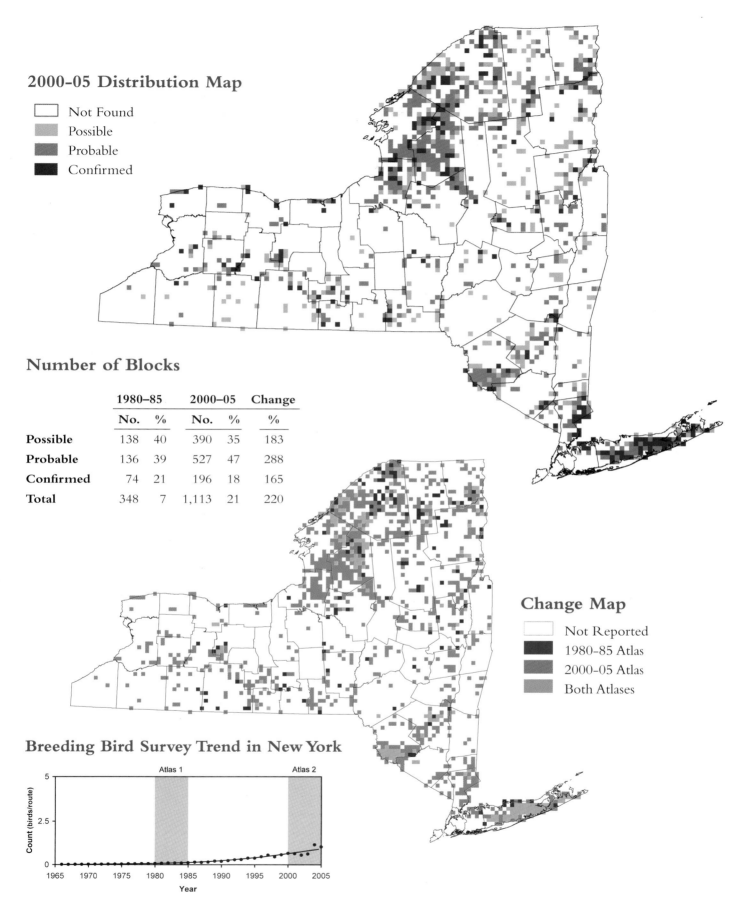

2000–05 Distribution Map

- ☐ Not Found
- Possible
- Probable
- Confirmed

Number of Blocks

	1980–85		2000–05		Change
	No.	%	No.	%	%
Possible	138	40	390	35	183
Probable	136	39	527	47	288
Confirmed	74	21	196	18	165
Total	348	7	1,113	21	220

Change Map

- ☐ Not Reported
- 1980-85 Atlas
- 2000-05 Atlas
- Both Atlases

Breeding Bird Survey Trend in New York

Prairie Warbler

Dendroica discolor

CHARLES R. SMITH

The relatively open nature of its preferred breeding habitat and its distinctive, buzzy song make the Prairie Warbler difficult to overlook. This warbler breeds from southern Maine and southeastern Ontario to the southern half of Missouri and southward to northern Florida and eastern Texas (Nolan et al. 1999). New York is near the northeastern limit of its breeding range. The Prairie Warbler is a species of ephemeral, successional habitats, as well as more permanent plant communities, often dominated by pitch pine or scrub oaks, like those found in the pine barrens of Long Island and Albany. Its habitats often have a savannah-like appearance, with widely spaced woody plants of low stature, interspersed with grasses and forbs (Nolan et al. 1999). Edinger et al. (2002) identified the Prairie Warbler as among the characteristic bird species from the following ecological communities in New York: alvar pavement grasslands, dwarf pine plains (Long Island only), pitch pine–scrub oak barrens, pitch pine–oak–heath woodland (Long Island only), successional red cedar woodland, and pitch pine–oak forest (Long Island and Hudson Valley only). DeKay (1844) said the Prairie Warbler was relatively common on Long Island and occurred in great numbers along Lake Erie. Eaton (1914) thought that reports from western New York may well have been in error, and he listed only four upstate nesting records. Bull (1974) considered the Prairie Warbler an "erratic" breeding species in New York and more common on Long Island and the lower Hudson Valley than in any other regions of the state, and largely absent from the western part of the state.

During the first Atlas survey, the Prairie Warbler was found breeding extensively in the Coastal Lowlands and in the lowlands and highlands of the Hudson Valley northward to the Mohawk Valley, with scattered reports up to Lake George. It was also present in numbers across the southern portion of the Appalachian Plateau, with isolated reports on the Great Lakes Plain and parts of the Adirondacks, northward to the Adirondack High Peaks. From the first to the second Atlas survey period, the breeding range of the Prairie Warbler expanded, with the number of blocks with records increasing 20 percent. The greatest increase occurred in the region west of the Catskills on the Appalachian Plateau. Distribution was largely unchanged in the Coastal Lowlands, with a modest decline in the Hudson Valley and associated highlands. This species also was present in modest but increased numbers of blocks on the Eastern Ontario Plain and reached to the northern boundary of the state in the St. Lawrence Plains.

Prairie Warbler populations have been declining steadily and significantly across the entire Breeding Bird Survey area and in the north Atlantic states (U.S. Fish and Wildlife Service Region 5) since 1966 (Sauer et al. 2005). For New York, BBS data show a statistically significant increase of 4 percent per year over the 1966–2005 period, although the data are marked as having deficiencies because few birds were present on relatively few routes (Sauer et al. 2005). The second Ontario Breeding Bird Atlas reported no substantial change in breeding distribution of this warbler since the first Ontario Atlas (Bird Studies Canada et al. 2006). The Prairie Warbler is identified as a species of conservation concern and placed on the Watch List of Partners in Flight (Rich et al. 2004). Why the Prairie Warbler population is increasing in New York but declining throughout most of its range is unclear. While little can be done to ensure cost-effective conservation of the less persistent, successional plant communities where the Prairie Warbler breeds, increased protection and management of native pine barrens and related habitats will be important for the persistence of this species in New York. An opportunity exists for gaining a better understanding of the ecology, habitat associations, and breeding biology of the Prairie Warbler, and its responses to suburban development, especially on Long Island.

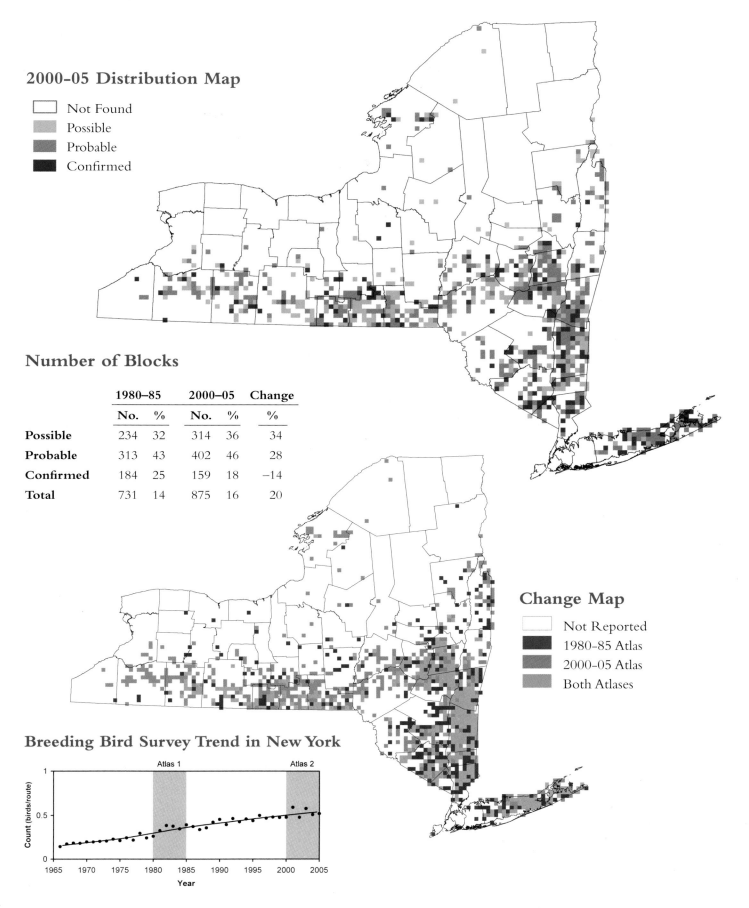

2000-05 Distribution Map

- ☐ Not Found
- Possible
- Probable
- Confirmed

Number of Blocks

	1980–85		2000–05		Change
	No.	%	No.	%	%
Possible	234	32	314	36	34
Probable	313	43	402	46	28
Confirmed	184	25	159	18	−14
Total	731	14	875	16	20

Change Map

- ☐ Not Reported
- 1980-85 Atlas
- 2000-05 Atlas
- Both Atlases

Breeding Bird Survey Trend in New York

Palm Warbler

Dendroica palmarum

KEVIN J. McGOWAN

A mostly terrestrial, tail-wagging warbler, the Palm Warbler is relatively common in New York during migration but an uncommon breeder. A bird of the boreal forest, this warbler breeds across Canada from the Northwest Territories to Newfoundland, southward to Minnesota, Wisconsin, Michigan, central Ontario, southern Quebec, and Maine (Wilson 1996). New York lies well southward of the main breeding range. The Palm Warbler breeds in bogs, open boreal coniferous forest, and partly open areas with scattered trees and heavy undergrowth, usually near water (Wilson 1996). The species has long been a common migrant through New York, but Bull (1974) made no suggestion of it breeding in the state. The closest breeding populations of Palm Warbler at that time were in Quebec (Ibarzabal and Morrier 1996), central Maine (Palmer 1949), and northeastern New Hampshire (Richards 1994), although the later New Hampshire Breeding Bird Atlas did not confirm any breeding in that state (Richards 1994).

The first known nesting of the Palm Warbler in New York—in fact the first record of the species in the state in June or July—was discovered during work for the first Atlas. A nest being built (later with one egg) was found in the Adirondacks in June 1983 at Bay Pond Bog in Waverly, Franklin County (Peterson 1984a). After the first Atlas fieldwork was completed, a pair of Palm Warblers was seen in the nearby Spring Pond Bog, in 1986 (Carroll 1988f). In 1994 a singing Palm Warbler was found in Massawepie Mire in St. Lawrence County, the largest bog in the state (Long 1994). The next year a more intensive effort to survey the area resulted in the discovery of 20 pairs in Massawepie Mire and 2 more in the nearby Hitchins Bog (Long 1995). Because these areas were closed to the first Atlas efforts, it is unclear if the discoveries represented a sudden influx of birds into the area or a gradual increase over time (Rising 1998b). At the same time additional Palm Warblers were being discovered in other bogs in Franklin and Hamilton counties, with nine present in 1997 on two bogs in Franklin, where a nest with young was photographed (Peterson 1997).

The expansion of Palm Warbler breeding in New York continued into the second Atlas period, with reports from 43 blocks, including 15 Confirmed records. Reports came from six counties and every year of fieldwork. The warbler was seen in the Central Adirondacks, Western Adirondack Foothills, Adirondack High Peaks, and the Champlain Transition of northern Clinton County along the Quebec border.

The Palm Warbler breeding range is not well covered by Breeding Bird Surveys, but the data that exist show a significant increasing trend survey-wide since 1966, and especially since 1980 (Sauer et al. 2005). BBS data from Maine, while too sparse for statistical confidence, show a clear increase after the mid-1980s (Sauer et al. 2005). Christmas Bird Count data covering the primary wintering grounds in the southeastern United States show a decline in numbers from 1960 until about 1980, but then an increase until the end of the dataset in 2006 (National Audubon Society [2007]). The first Vermont Atlas survey failed to find Palm Warbler breeding in the state, but the second Atlas effort found it breeding in several blocks during the first years of fieldwork (R. Renfrew pers. comm.). The second Ontario Breeding Bird Atlas reported that Palm Warbler numbers significantly increased in the two northernmost regions of the province, although the mapped range changed very little, with essentially no expansion into southern Ontario (Bird Studies Canada et al. 2006). Just what fueled the dramatic increase in Palm Warbler breeding in New York is not obvious, but it is possible that the expanding population in Maine is the source of the New York birds. Wherever the birds came from, it appears that the Palm Warbler is now a well-established member of the bog-dwelling avifauna of the Adirondacks.

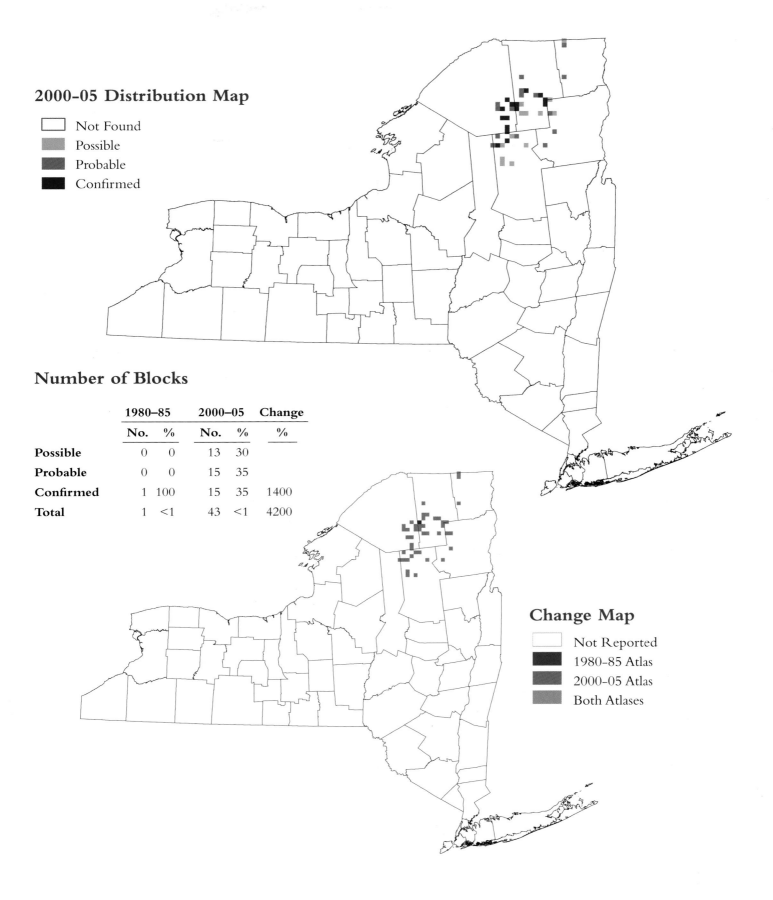

2000-05 Distribution Map

- ☐ Not Found
- ▥ Possible
- ▨ Probable
- ■ Confirmed

Number of Blocks

	1980–85		2000–05		Change
	No.	%	No.	%	%
Possible	0	0	13	30	
Probable	0	0	15	35	
Confirmed	1	100	15	35	1400
Total	1	<1	43	<1	4200

Change Map

- ☐ Not Reported
- ■ 1980-85 Atlas
- ▨ 2000-05 Atlas
- ▥ Both Atlases

Bay-breasted Warbler

Dendroica castanea

John M. C. Peterson

The fortunes of the Bay-breasted Warbler are closely tied to the activities of the eastern spruce budworm (Bolgiano 2004), as with other spruce budworm specialists, the Tennessee, Cape May, and Blackpoll warblers. The main population nests across boreal Canada from the Northwest Territories and northeastern British Columbia to the Maritime Provinces and southwestern Newfoundland, and into the United States in extreme northern Minnesota and Michigan, the Adirondacks, and northern New England (Williams 1996). This boreal warbler is at the extreme southern end of its range in New York and largely cut off from the main population. Early authors knew it only as a migrant in New York, and although Eaton (1914) suspected the Bay-breasted Warbler bred in the Adirondacks, he was unable to find the species there in summer. The first summer record occurred in Hamilton County in 1924, and breeding was finally confirmed in Essex County in 1926 (Bull 1974). Bull (1974) listed 11 breeding localities in the Adirondacks and suggested intensive fieldwork would find more. This warbler favors the midlevel of mature conifer forests, especially spruce-fir, with only a scattering of deciduous trees, and in New York most sightings occur below 853 m (2,800 ft) (J. M. C. Peterson 1988a).

During the first Atlas survey, the Bay-breasted Warbler was distributed sparsely, but fairly evenly, over the Adirondack High Peaks, Central Adirondacks, Sable Highlands, and Western Adirondack Foothills and Transition. Two blocks in the Central Tug Hill extended the range known by Bull (1974) slightly to the south and west, fulfilling his prediction. There were only two Confirmed breeding records, however, each of adults carrying food for young (Peterson 1988a). During the second Atlas period, the Bay-breasted Warbler was reported from just 12 blocks, a decline of 63 percent. No birds were found in the Western Adirondack Transition or on Central Tug Hill, and they disappeared from Lewis and Oneida counties. The single Confirmed record came from Flowed Land, Essex County, on 10 August 2000, where recently fledged young were accompanied by an adult. No blocks had records from both Atlas surveys, so the species has now

been recorded in 44 different blocks. Virtually all of the former southwestern range is now vacant, and the current map closely resembles that shown by Bull (1974). The slight range expansion represented in the first Atlas might have been a temporary result of a major spruce budworm outbreak across eastern Canada that ended in 1985 (Bolgiano 2004), and the population might have contracted into a tighter core range afterward.

Bay-breasted Warbler populations can explode with outbreaks of spruce budworm, then subsequently decline (Morse 1980). Breeding Bird Survey data show no significant long-term trend across the breeding range, but a decline is apparent after the 1980s (Sauer et al. 2007). A spruce budworm infestation from 1968 to 1985 defoliated 55 million hectares (135,907,960 a) in eastern Canada and had a significant influence on Bay-breasted Warbler numbers, which began a steep decline on BBS routes in eastern Quebec in 1987 (Bolgiano 2004). This warbler also feeds on other caterpillars, including the black-headed budworm (Morse 1979) and forest tent caterpillar (Sealy 1979), and although there was an outbreak of the latter in the Adirondacks in 2005 (Peterson 2005), no change in Bay-breasted Warbler numbers was detected, perhaps because the caterpillars appeared to defoliate mainly hardwoods (pers. obs.). The Forever Wild provision of the New York State constitution, together with stringent control of forest fires, should allow spruces to reach maturity, which makes the trees more vulnerable to budworm attack. The Bay-breasted Warbler's preference for mature forests on both its breeding and wintering grounds makes the species potentially vulnerable to deforestation, and this boreal warbler has been placed on the Partners in Flight Watch List (Rich et al. 2004).

2000–05 Distribution Map

- ☐ Not Found
- Possible
- Probable
- Confirmed

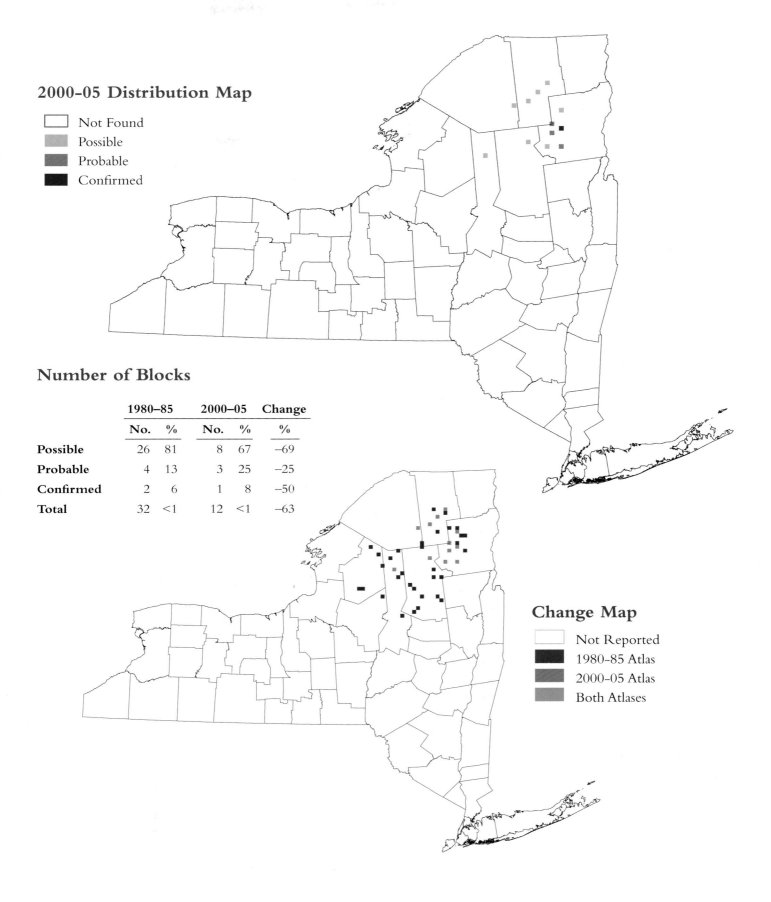

Number of Blocks

| | 1980–85 | | 2000–05 | | Change |
	No.	%	No.	%	%
Possible	26	81	8	67	−69
Probable	4	13	3	25	−25
Confirmed	2	6	1	8	−50
Total	32	<1	12	<1	−63

Change Map

- ☐ Not Reported
- 1980-85 Atlas
- 2000-05 Atlas
- Both Atlases

Blackpoll Warbler
Dendroica striata

KENT MCFARLAND AND
CHRISTOPHER C. RIMMER

The Blackpoll Warbler is a characteristic songbird of New York's high-elevation conifer forests. It occupies an extensive range from the northern coniferous forests of Alaska eastward through the transition zone between taiga and tundra, to montane and coastal spruce-fir forests of eastern North America (Hunt and Eliason 1999). Its distribution in the northeastern United States is local and patchy, with most birds limited to mountainous areas of New England, New York, and as far south as northeast Pennsylvania. New York breeding populations are confined to the mountains of the Adirondacks and the Catskills. Historically, the Blackpoll Warbler was thought to breed only in montane forests of New York, generally above elevations of 760–915 m (2,500–3,000 ft) (Eaton 1914). Bull (1974) refined this distribution, noting that the species is restricted in the Adirondacks to elevations mostly above 1,067 m (3,500 ft) and in the Catskills above 1,128 m (3,700 ft). Although his map depicted only six Catskills peaks with known occurrences of Blackpoll Warbler, he considered it to be the most common warbler on the summits of the highest peaks.

The first Atlas findings extended the Blackpoll Warbler's known New York distribution, particularly into the Western Adirondack Foothills of Franklin, Hamilton, Herkimer, Lewis, and St. Lawrence counties. Although no breeding records were confirmed, Atlas observers found numerous singing males in suitable habitat at elevations of 455–490 m (1,500–1,600 ft) and rarely as low as 305 m (1,000 ft). Whether these records reflected an actual breeding range expansion, an extralimital movement of nonbreeding males, or increased sampling because of atlasing efforts is unknown. The number of blocks with reports from the Western Adirondack Foothills in Herkimer, Lewis, and St. Lawrence counties declined from 13 during the first Atlas survey to 1 during the second. This difference is difficult to explain and may or may not have represented an actual range contraction. Observer bias (e.g., sampling effort or detectability of songs), early signs of climatic warming, spruce budworm cycles, changes in forest structure, or other variables might have accounted individually or collectively for the observed range shift between the two Atlas periods. The distribution delineated by the second Atlas data conforms more closely to that depicted by Bull (1974), suggesting that the records obtained during the first Atlas project, while valid, may have been anomalous and not representative of a true range extension. The first Atlas reported the Blackpoll Warbler in 125 blocks, 21 in the Catskills and 103 in the Adirondacks. During the second Atlas fieldwork the species was documented in 115 blocks, 24 in the Catskills and 90 in the Adirondacks. It was found during both Atlas periods in 16 Catskill blocks but only 38 Adirondack blocks.

The Blackpoll Warbler is inadequately monitored throughout most of the northeastern United States by the Breeding Bird Survey. A range-wide analysis from 1966 to 1979 showed a statistically significant annual increase of 15.4 percent, but from 1980 to 2006 Blackpoll Warbler populations significantly decreased at an annual rate of 9.6 percent (Sauer et al. 2007). Preliminary analysis of Mountain Birdwatch data from 2001 to 2004, using the mean number of Blackpoll Warblers recorded per survey point, revealed a significant 8.7 percent annual decline in the northeastern United States. Census data from montane fir forests in the White Mountains of New Hampshire (1993, 1995–2000) and the Green Mountains of Vermont (1992, 1994–2000), however, showed stable populations.

Although evidence for population declines of the Blackpoll Warbler remains inconclusive for New York and elsewhere, there are several potential or existing threats. These include acidic precipitation and mercury accumulation in mountain ecosystems (Rimmer et al. 2005), climatic warming (Rodenhouse et al. 2008), and development or forestry management of breeding habitat.

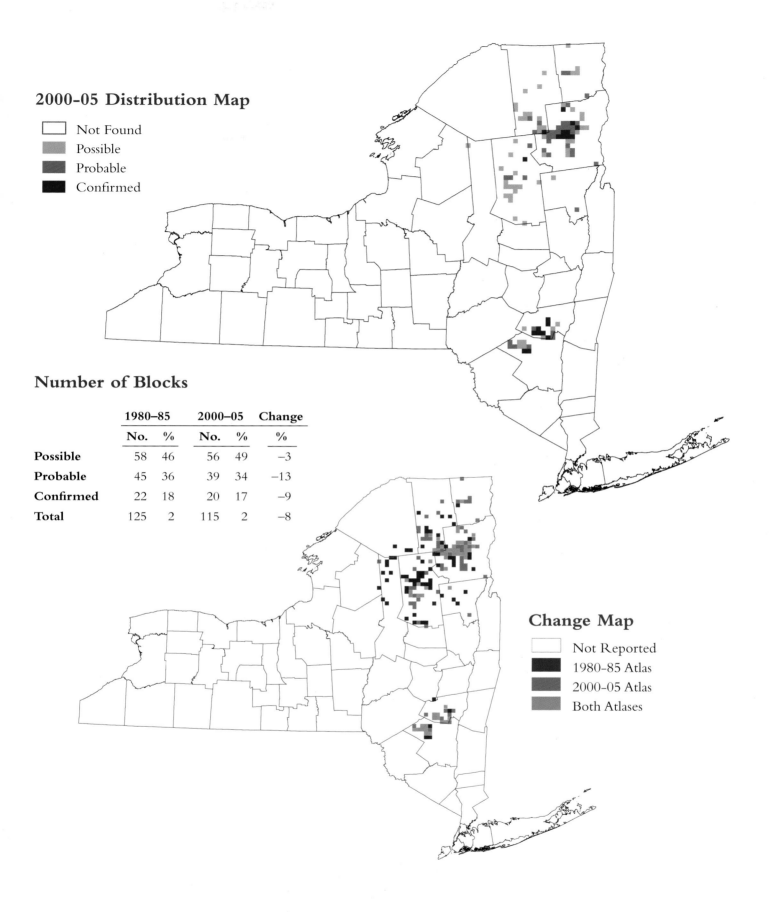

2000-05 Distribution Map

- ☐ Not Found
- Possible
- Probable
- Confirmed

Number of Blocks

| | 1980–85 | | 2000–05 | | Change |
	No.	%	No.	%	%
Possible	58	46	56	49	−3
Probable	45	36	39	34	−13
Confirmed	22	18	20	17	−9
Total	125	2	115	2	−8

Change Map

- ☐ Not Reported
- 1980-85 Atlas
- 2000-05 Atlas
- Both Atlases

Cerulean Warbler

Dendroica cerulea

KENNETH V. ROSENBERG

The Cerulean Warbler's patchy breeding distribution extends from southern New England, southern Ontario, and the Great Lakes states southward through the Appalachian Mountains and the Mississippi River drainage to northern Georgia, Tennessee, and Arkansas (Hamel 2000). This warbler was historically present in western New York (Eaton 1914) and in the mid-20th century expanded its range from multiple sources (Lindsay 1998), including the spread of western populations into the Appalachian Plateau, colonization of the Hudson Highlands from northern New Jersey, and establishment of a small population in Jefferson and St. Lawrence counties, perhaps from southeastern Ontario (Bull 1974). Uncommon and rather inconspicuous, the Cerulean Warbler's persistent and distinctive song is the best clue to its presence in the tallest treetops of mature deciduous forests. Two distinct habitat types are used: forested wetlands and riparian corridors dominated by sycamore, cottonwood, silver and red maples, and green ash; and dry ridgetops and hillsides dominated by mature oak-hickory and mixed mesophytic forests (Rosenberg et al. 2000).

The first Atlas documented a widespread but patchy distribution of Cerulean Warbler through the Great Lakes Plain, with scattered concentrations in the Allegany Hills, Hudson Highlands, and Hudson and Mohawk valleys. A few outlying birds were found in the Coastal Lowlands (subsequently documented as breeding by Lindsay and Vezo [1994]), the Indian River Lakes region, and along Lake Champlain. During 1996–99, the Cerulean Warbler Atlas Project (Rosenberg et al. 2000) located roughly 1,100 singing males throughout New York, primarily concentrated in the vicinity of the Montezuma Wetlands complex including Galen Wildlife Management Area (420 males), Iroquois–Oak Orchard–Tonawanda complex (138 males), Allegany State Park and vicinity (166 males), and Hudson Highlands (53 males). The second Atlas data showed the species in roughly the same distribution as in the first Atlas, but the number of blocks with records declined by 13 percent. The largest declines were noted in the Appalachian Plateau (−17 percent) and Great Lakes Plain (−13 percent), both strong-

holds for the species in the state. The Cerulean Warbler appears to have disappeared from Long Island, southern Westchester and Rockland counties, and many sites along the Hudson and Mohawk valleys. Consolidation of breeding sites in the St. Lawrence Plains and the presence of new sites along the Delaware River and in Ulster County are encouraging. Whether these additions represent newly occupied breeding sites or better Atlas coverage is unclear.

The Cerulean Warbler is listed as a Species of Special Concern in New York. It is on the Partners in Flight Watch List (Rich et al. 2004) because the relatively small global population (probably under 300,000 pairs) has declined range-wide by 4 percent annually since 1966 according to the Breeding Bird Survey; BBS data from New York are too sparse to analyze (Sauer et al. 2007). The second Ontario Atlas reported a significant decline in southern Ontario (Bird Studies Canada et al. 2006), and it is clear that the northeastward expansion of the Cerulean Warbler has not continued. As threats in other parts of its range increase, such as from mountaintop-removal coal mining in the central Appalachians and habitat destruction in South American wintering areas, healthy breeding populations in New York are becoming increasingly important. Fortunately, a majority of the state's population breeds on protected lands. Threats here include continued loss of mature deciduous forest on private lands, and subtle changes in forest structure through loss of dominant canopy trees on managed lands. A targeted, site-based monitoring program is necessary to track population changes between Atlas periods. Additional research on habitat requirements and response to management practices will aid in future conservation efforts.

2000-05 Distribution Map

- ☐ Not Found
- ▨ Possible
- ▩ Probable
- ■ Confirmed

Number of Blocks

	1980–85		2000–05		Change
	No.	%	No.	%	%
Possible	100	36	94	39	−6
Probable	130	47	116	48	−11
Confirmed	49	18	34	14	−31
Total	279	5	244	5	−13

Change Map

- ☐ Not Reported
- ■ 1980–85 Atlas
- ▨ 2000–05 Atlas
- ▩ Both Atlases

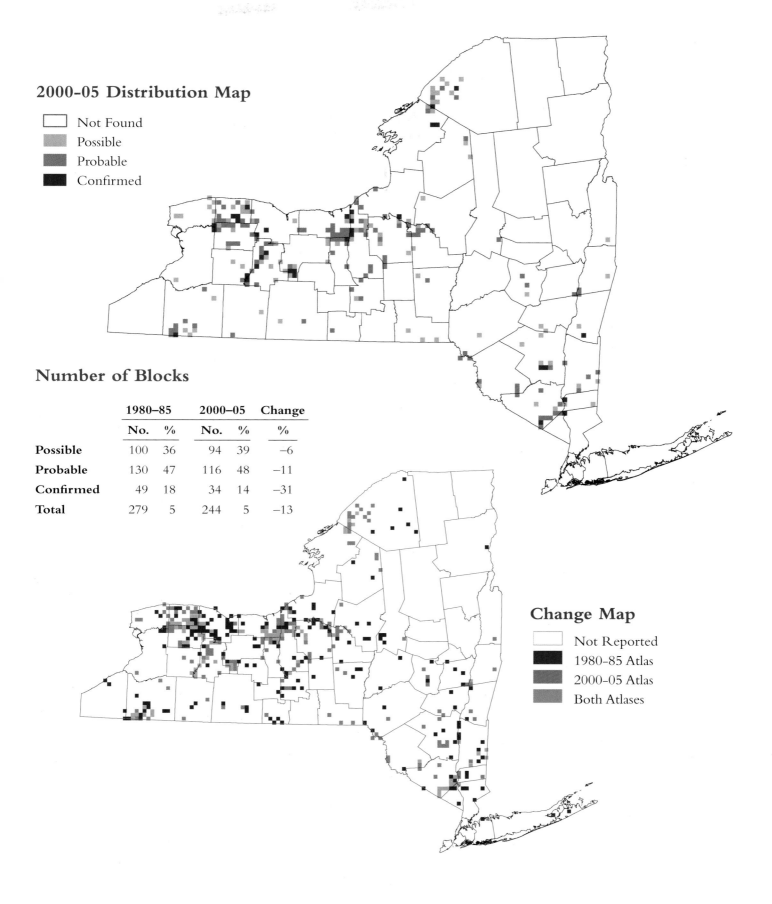

Black-and-white Warbler

Mniotilta varia

TIMOTHY J. POST

The Black-and-white Warbler forages methodically along tree trunks, much like a nuthatch, but it will also catch insects on the wing, like most other wood warblers (Kricher 1995). This adaptability in foraging helps explain why the Black-and-white Warbler can occupy a diversity of forest habitats. Breeding habitats include alpine krummholz (Eaton 1914), early- to mid-successional forests, mature and second-growth deciduous and mixed forests (DeGraaf et al. 1980), and forested wetlands (Kricher 1995). It appears to prefer areas of extensive forest. Kricher (1995) referenced several studies that indicated a preference of the Black-and-white Warbler for mature forest in portions of its range, and other studies that showed a preference for early-successional forest conditions. Hartley et al. (2003) found that in New York and the Northeast, the Black-and-white Warbler was most abundant in early-successional forests. This warbler's breeding range includes most of the southern half of Canada (with the exception of the westernmost portions), the northern tier of the Midwest, and from the Northeast through the Appalachian Mountains and extending into the lower Midwest and western Gulf Coast states (Kricher 1995). The Black-and-white Warbler has probably always been found throughout New York, although its range within the state is somewhat odd. Eaton (1914) called it a common breeder in the eastern part of the state from Long Island and the southern Hudson Valley to the Catskills and Adirondacks but rare in the western regions. This east–west distribution is not readily explained by habitat or geographic features, but it has persisted for at least a century.

The first Atlas map showed the Black-and-white Warbler to be a common and widespread breeder throughout most of the eastern half of the state but largely absent in the western portion of the state. It was missing from most of the Great Lakes Plain, the western portion of the Appalachian Plateau, most of the Mohawk Valley, and the greater New York City area. The Black-and-white Warbler was found in nearly the same number of blocks during the first and second Atlas periods. The second Atlas distribution was similar as well, the species being widespread in the eastern half of the state but scarce in the western half. Moderate declines in blocks with reports occurred in the Coastal Lowlands, Manhattan Hills, and Hudson Highlands. These areas are subject to intense development pressure that destroys and fragments forests. Deer overbrowsing further reduces the amount of suitable habitat by removing much of the desirable understory. The Adirondacks also had slightly fewer blocks with records, although the Black-and-white Warbler is still widespread there. Increases were seen in the Champlain Valley, Tug Hill Plateau, and Eastern Ontario Plain. Jefferson County in particular showed dramatic increases in the number of blocks with records. These increases may be partly attributable to increases in forest acreage as farmlands have reverted to more forested habitats.

Breeding Bird Survey data show significant declining trends in Black-and-white Warbler populations since 1966 in New York, the north Atlantic states (U.S. Fish and Wildlife Service Region 5), and across the survey area (Sauer et al. 2007). Partners in Flight lists the Black-and-white Warbler as a species of conservation concern in several Bird Conservation Regions that include New York (PIF 2005, Panjabi et al. 2005). It is not considered a high priority because it is still fairly common and widespread. Populations of the Black-and-white Warbler are declining throughout the Northeast, possibly as a result of forest fragmentation and reductions in shrub and sapling cover in forested areas. However, because it will use a variety of habitats, it is likely to have a better long-term outlook than species that are reliant on more specialized habitat conditions.

2000–05 Distribution Map

- ☐ Not Found
- Possible
- Probable
- Confirmed

Number of Blocks

	1980–85		2000–05		Change
	No.	%	No.	%	%
Possible	1,186	43	1,093	40	−8
Probable	929	33	1,082	39	16
Confirmed	660	24	581	21	−12
Total	2,775	52	2,756	52	−1

Change Map

- ☐ Not Reported
- 1980–85 Atlas
- 2000–05 Atlas
- Both Atlases

Breeding Bird Survey Trend in New York

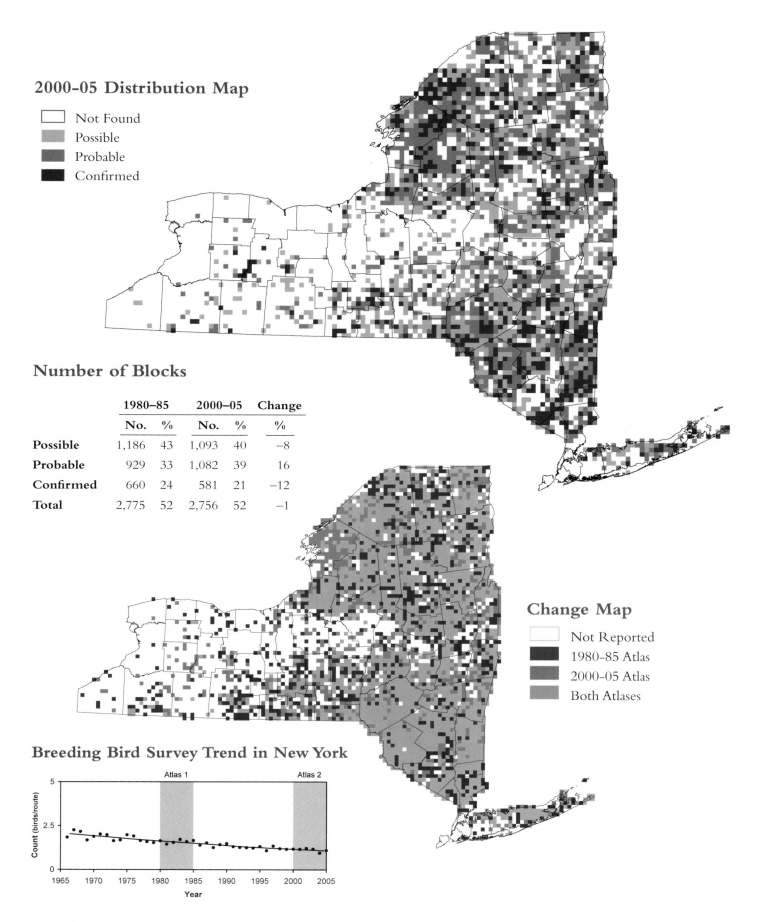

American Redstart

Setophaga ruticilla

KEVIN J. McGOWAN

The American Redstart is an active, fly-catching warbler. It breeds from southeastern Alaska eastward to Newfoundland, and southward to Utah, Louisiana, and Georgia primarily in moist second-growth deciduous forests with abundant shrubs in the understory (Sherry and Holmes 1997). Before European settlement, the American Redstart probably was less common in New York than currently, being primarily a bird of tree-fall gaps, edges of old beaver meadows, old burned areas, and other areas where the primary forest had been disturbed and was growing back. With the opening of the forests much additional habitat was created, and the redstart was considered common to abundant by the end of the 19th century (Rathbun 1879, Short 1893, Reed and Wright 1909). Although DeKay (1844) noted an avoidance of people, Eaton (1914) called the redstart common throughout all parts of the state, even breeding in Central Park. Eaton (1914) found it in all the deciduous woodlands examined, even in "slashings" up the slopes of Mt. Marcy. Bull (1974) called it a widespread breeder but rare and local on the Coastal Plain.

The first Atlas reported the American Redstart to be widespread with localized gaps, especially in the western quarter of the state. Eaton (1988c) described these gaps as occurring mainly in areas where cropland and orchards replaced deciduous forest, such as near the Finger Lakes. Additional, less easily explained gaps occurred in the western Appalachian Plateau. The redstart was largely missing from the most heavily developed areas around New York City and western Long Island. The second Atlas survey data revealed little change in this warbler's distribution, with only a 2 percent increase in the number of blocks with breeding records. Again it was widely distributed, with localized gaps. These gaps were still in evidence around the Finger Lakes region and large urban areas, but the gaps in the western Appalachian Plateau were gone. The number of reporting blocks increased 13 percent across the entire Appalachian Plateau with the strongest increase notable in the western section in Atlas Region 1 where blocks with records increased 33 percent. Blocks with reports increased 11 percent on the Great Lakes Plain. Declines in the number of blocks with records were apparent primarily in the Coastal Lowlands (–19 percent) and the Adirondacks (–13 percent), especially in parts of the Adirondack High Peaks, Western Adirondack Foothills, and Eastern Adirondack Foothills. These declines might be the result of continued urban development and forest maturation.

Breeding Bird Survey data show a significant continent-wide decline in American Redstart numbers of 0.9 percent per year in the last 26 years (Sauer et al. 2007). BBS data from New York show an even more pronounced decline, 2 percent per year since 1980 (Sauer et al. 2007). Data from states and provinces to the northeast of New York show a similar trend, with the annual drop in the Northern New England region at 1.2 percent since 1980 (Sauer et al. 2007). The redstart population appears to have declined over the last 60 years across its breeding range in a patchy fashion, largely because of loss of habitat (Sherry and Holmes 1997). As a bird of second-growth forests, the maturation of forests in New York and the Northeast, as well as the spread of urbanization, could be responsible for the declines (Sherry and Holmes 1997). The population is increasing or stable in some areas, especially following extensive logging, such as in Quebec (Sherry and Holmes 1997). Although the American Redstart population seems to be declining significantly in a major portion of its range, the declines are not extensive enough to warrant management concern. It is still locally abundant in many areas, is still widely distributed, and is tolerant of a range of habitat conditions (Sherry and Holmes 1997). Although an apparent decline in the Adirondacks may presage a more widespread trend across New York, the redstart remains an abundant bird and should remain so until the next Atlas project.

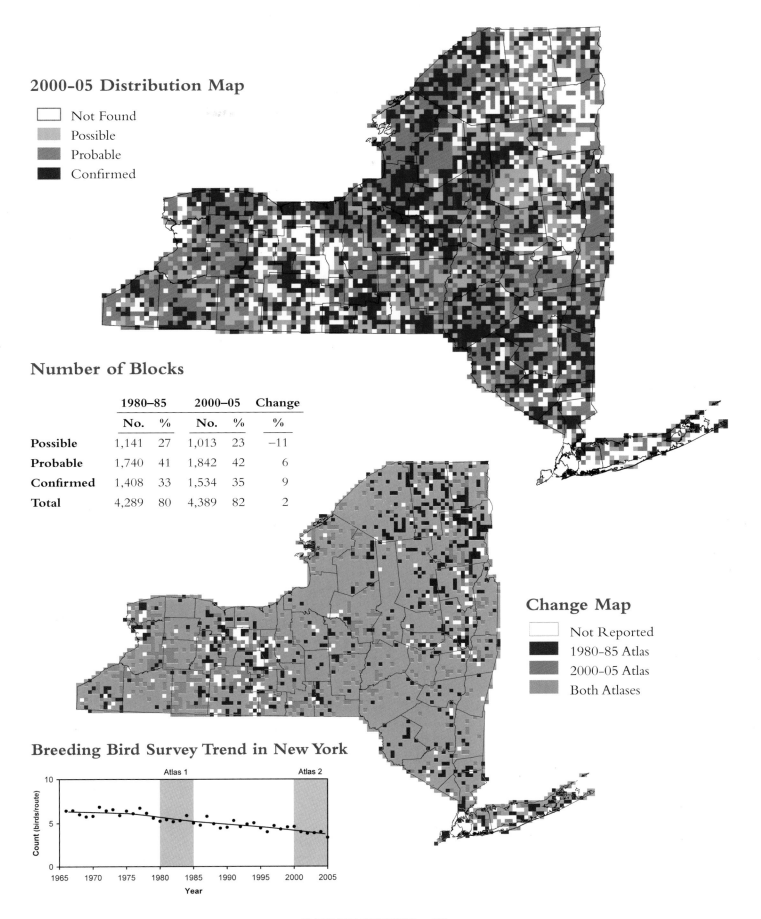

2000-05 Distribution Map

- ☐ Not Found
- Possible
- Probable
- Confirmed

Number of Blocks

	1980–85		2000–05		Change
	No.	%	No.	%	%
Possible	1,141	27	1,013	23	−11
Probable	1,740	41	1,842	42	6
Confirmed	1,408	33	1,534	35	9
Total	4,289	80	4,389	82	2

Change Map

- ☐ Not Reported
- 1980–85 Atlas
- 2000–05 Atlas
- Both Atlases

Breeding Bird Survey Trend in New York

Prothonotary Warbler
Protonotaria citrea

Kevin J. McGowan

The Prothonotary Warbler is a brilliant yellow-orange bird of southeastern wooded swamps. It breeds from southern Minnesota and southern Ontario southward to eastern Texas and Florida and is an uncommon and local breeder at the edges of its range (Petit 1999). New York is well to the north of this warbler's main breeding range. It breeds in wooded areas near water, especially flooded bottom-land hardwood forests, cypress swamps, and along large lakes and rivers, where it nests in tree cavities (Petit 1999). Eaton (1914) listed the Prothonotary Warbler as a rare visitor to New York and mentioned a nest-building male at Ithaca in 1910 as the only example of possible breeding. Records of spring visitors increased in the 1920s and 1930s (Bull 1974). The first confirmed nesting of the species in the state was recorded in 1931 when at least eight singing males and five nests were found in Oak Orchard Swamp in Genesee County (Beardslee 1932). The species remained breeding in that area through the rest of the 20th century. It was found breeding in a red maple swamp in the Montezuma marshes in 1948 and continued as a breeder there for many years (Bull 1974). Bull (1974) identified six breeding localities in the state but listed only Oak Orchard, Monte-zuma, and Oneida Lake as "permanent colonies." Breeding in the southeastern portion of the state was not suspected until the 1970s when a nest site was discovered in Suffolk County after several years of sightings in the area (Wheat 1979).

During the first Atlas survey, the Prothonotary Warbler was found in only 22 blocks and was confirmed breeding in only seven. It was confirmed at the traditional breeding areas of Oak Orchard Wildlife Management Area and Montezuma National Wildlife Refuge, as well as at Delta Lake north of Rome, Oneida County. It was reported as a Possible breeder at the east end of Oneida Lake. On Long Island this warbler was confirmed in the two blocks where it was previously known to nest, as well as in an additional block, and was sighted in three other blocks on Long Island. The Prothonotary Warbler was found in only half as many blocks during the second Atlas period, with Confirmed breeding in just four. Two confirmations were located on the shore of Oneida Lake, where the species has nested since the 1940s (Bull 1974) but where it went unconfirmed in the first Atlas. Breeding was again confirmed in the Oak Orchard region at Tonawanda Wildlife Management Area, but no individuals were detected around Montezuma NWR, where it was last recorded in 1998 (Ostrander 1998). The other breeding confirmation was an adult feeding fledglings at the edge of a small pond in Orange County. The Prothonotary Warbler was found in only two blocks on Long Island, one at the historical nesting area of

Carl's River near Belmont Lake State Park, and the other near the eastern end of Suffolk County.

Breeding Bird Survey data show a slight but significant decline in Prothonotary Warbler numbers across its range since 1966 (Sauer et al. 2005), but the species remains abundant in appropriate habitat throughout the southeastern states (Petit 1999). Breeding populations are highly localized because of the bird's extreme habitat specificity (Petit 1999), and as a result, it is vulnerable to habitat destruction. This warbler appears on the Partners in Flight Watch List (Rich et al. 2004) as a species of high conservation priority throughout the breeding range, primarily because of threats to its habitat. It is considered Endangered in Canada, mostly because it is at the extreme edge of its range there and populations are small. The Prothonotary Warbler remains a rare and local breeder in New York, and whether the slight decline in breeding distribution noted between the two Atlas periods is significant is an open question. New York remains beyond the main breeding range of the species, and only scattered breeding individuals and small colonies are to be expected in the future.

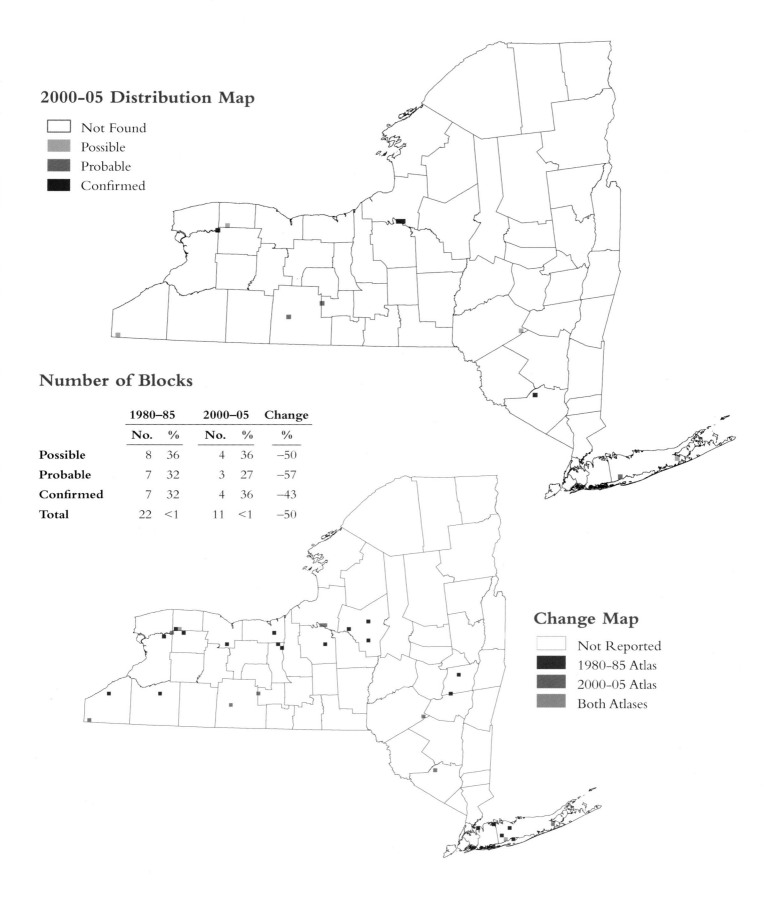

2000–05 Distribution Map

- ☐ Not Found
- ▨ Possible
- ▨ Probable
- ■ Confirmed

Number of Blocks

	1980–85		2000–05		Change
	No.	%	No.	%	%
Possible	8	36	4	36	−50
Probable	7	32	3	27	−57
Confirmed	7	32	4	36	−43
Total	22	<1	11	<1	−50

Change Map

- ☐ Not Reported
- ■ 1980-85 Atlas
- ▨ 2000-05 Atlas
- ▨ Both Atlases

Worm-eating Warbler
Helmitheros vermivorum

CHARLES R. SMITH

The Worm-eating Warbler takes its name from its genus, which is Greek for "worm-hunter" (Holloway 2003), referring to the bird's use of caterpillars in its diet. The summer range of the Worm-eating Warbler extends eastward from Louisiana, Arkansas, and Missouri to northern Georgia and western South Carolina, then northeastward from just south of the Great Lakes to New York and southern Massachusetts (Hanners and Patton 1998). It reaches its greatest abundance along the Appalachian Mountains from West Virginia to Georgia (Sauer et al. 2005). This elusive, somber-colored warbler is near the northern limit of its breeding distribution in New York. It typically breeds in mature deciduous or mixed deciduous-coniferous forest with patches of dense understory, usually on a moderate to steep slope, although flatter areas, including dry islands in "nontidal wetland forests," may be used where the bird occurs on the eastern coastal plain (Hanners and Patton 1998). DeKay (1844) said little about this warbler in New York, except that it was more common in New Jersey. Giraud (1844) described the bird on Long Island as "generally confined to the wet, miry part of the woods." It is possible that this association with wet habitats on Long Island was accurate for the first half of the 19th century, when much of Long Island had been cleared for agriculture. At that time, the only habitats remaining for many species were swampy areas, unsuitable for agriculture, but this warbler actually prefers dry hillsides or areas with some slope, even a slight one (Hanners and Patton 1998). Short (1893) thought the Worm-eating Warbler might occasionally breed in western New York. Eaton (1914) noted the Worm-eating Warbler was common in the lower Hudson Valley, with scattered reports across the central portion of the state but little evidence of it breeding there. Bull (1974) similarly described it as most common in the lower Hudson Valley but noted its presence in the Susquehanna-Chemung river watershed from Binghamton to Elmira.

During the first Atlas survey, the Worm-eating Warbler was found mostly in the southeastern part of the state, es-pecially in the Hudson Highlands and Manhattan Hills, with scattered reports on Long Island and the central Appalachian Plateau. During the second Atlas survey, the Worm-eating Warbler showed little change in the numbers of blocks in which it was detected or in its range, although its distribution in the southern Hudson Valley and adjacent ecozones appeared to become more patchy. Its detection as a Probable breeder in Cattaraugus County occurred substantially farther west than where it was detected during the first Atlas period. The Worm-eating Warbler song resembles that of the Chipping Sparrow, Dark-eyed Junco, and Pine Warbler. Where it occurs together with those species, it could be misidentified based solely on song, even by experienced observers.

Breeding Bird Survey data show no significant trends for the Worm-eating Warbler survey-wide since 1966 (Sauer et al. 2005). BBS data for New York show a declining population tendency for both the 1966–2005 and 1980–2005 periods; however, detections are too few to determine if these patterns are statistically significant. Similar tendencies for the same periods exist for the north Atlantic states (U.S. Fish and Wildlife Service Region 5), but the trends are not statistically significant and the data have deficiencies. Partners in Flight identified the Worm-eating Warbler as a Continental Stewardship Species for the United States and Canada and included the bird on its Watch List (Rich et al. 2004). No particular conservation needs have been identified for the species in New York, and it is not listed there or in any of the surrounding states. Detailed habitat studies, comparable to those of Gale et al. (1997) from Connecticut, are needed to determine the specific, current habitat requirements and ecology of the Worm-eating Warbler in New York.

2000-05 Distribution Map

- ☐ Not Found
- ▨ Possible
- ▦ Probable
- ■ Confirmed

Number of Blocks

	1980–85		2000–05		Change
	No.	%	No.	%	%
Possible	64	28	69	31	8
Probable	64	28	63	28	–2
Confirmed	97	43	91	41	–6
Total	225	4	223	4	–1

Change Map

- ☐ Not Reported
- ■ 1980-85 Atlas
- ▨ 2000-05 Atlas
- ▨ Both Atlases

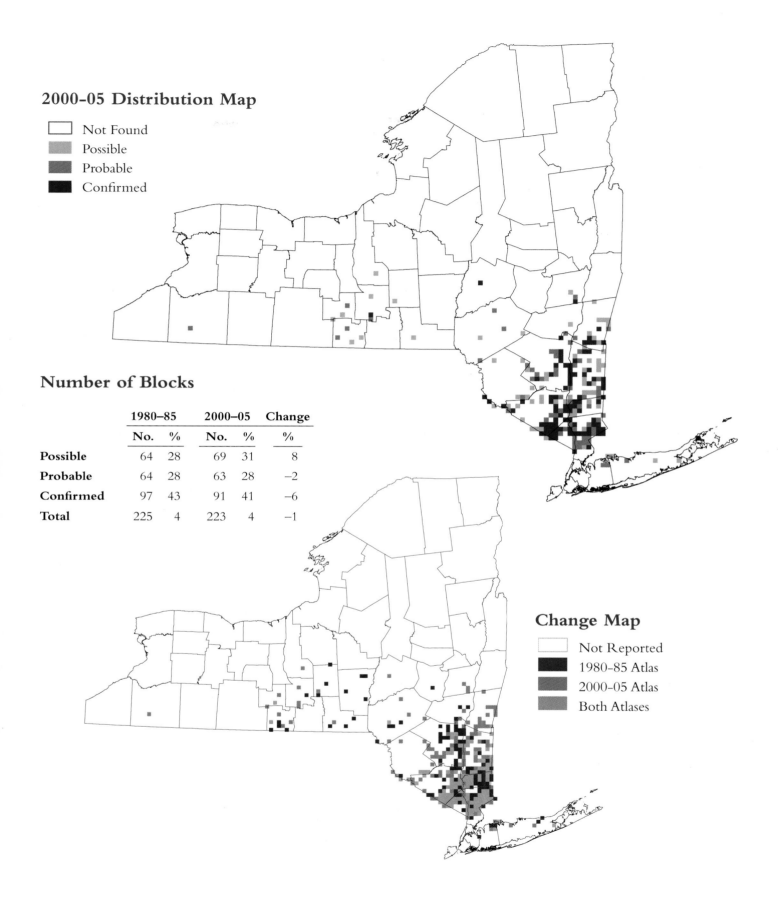

Ovenbird

Seiurus aurocapilla

KEVIN J. MCGOWAN

A small, inconspicuous, but noisy bird of the forest floor, the Ovenbird is one of the most characteristic birds of the eastern forests. It breeds from extreme southeastern Yukon eastward to Newfoundland, and southward to Wyoming, Nebraska, Arkansas, and Georgia (Van Horn and Donovan 1994). This warbler nests in mature deciduous and mixed deciduous-coniferous forests. It prefers climax forests, usually with a canopy height of 16–22 m (52–72 ft) and a canopy closure of 60–90 percent, and requires 100–885 ha (247–2,187 acres) of continuous habitat to breed successfully (Van Horn and Donovan 1994). The Ovenbird was undoubtedly common and widespread in New York before European colonization. Reduction in the amount of forest land probably led to restrictions in its range, although early authors considered it common wherever forest was remaining (DeKay 1844, Giraud 1844, Rathbun 1879, Eaton 1914). Beardslee and Mitchell (1965) listed it as a common migrant through the Niagara Frontier but found it nesting only in the more heavily wooded tracts of this region. Bull (1974) noted that it was common across the state in deciduous and evergreen forests.

The first Atlas map showed the Ovenbird to be common and widespread throughout the state. The only significant gaps in its distribution were in the heavily agricultural Great Lakes Plain, the Mohawk Valley, and the heavily urbanized areas of New York City and western Long Island. The Ovenbird was gone from Bronx, New York, Kings, and Queens counties, but some were still found on Staten Island. The second Atlas data showed the Ovenbird again as widely distributed across New York State, with a 9 percent increase in the number of blocks with breeding records. This increase resulted in the filling of gaps in the Mohawk Valley, Eastern Ontario Plain, and eastern Drumlin. Despite some increases, the Erie-Ontario Plain remained the largest gap in the Ovenbird's distribution. Decreases in the number of occupied blocks were noted in the Hudson Highlands, Manhattan Hills, Triassic Lowlands, and Coastal Lowlands, perhaps suggesting the extent to which the New York urban area has expanded since the first Atlas period, but perhaps resulting from a decrease in Atlas coverage in the area this time.

Although the Ovenbird population showed a slight significant increase across the entire range of the Breeding Bird Survey since 1966, the trend for the last 25 years is flat (Sauer et al. 2005). BBS data for New York show significant increases, especially in the last 25 years, at a rate of 1.5 percent per year (Sauer et al. 2005). The second Ontario Breeding Bird Atlas reported no change in Ovenbird numbers in the province overall, but an increase on the Northern Canadian Shield region and a decline in the southernmost region (Bird Studies Canada et al. 2006), where BBS data also show a slight but significant decline in numbers over the last 25 years (Sauer et al. 2005). With a robust population and a continuing maturation of the state's forests, the Ovenbird should remain a common bird in New York State through the next Atlas survey period.

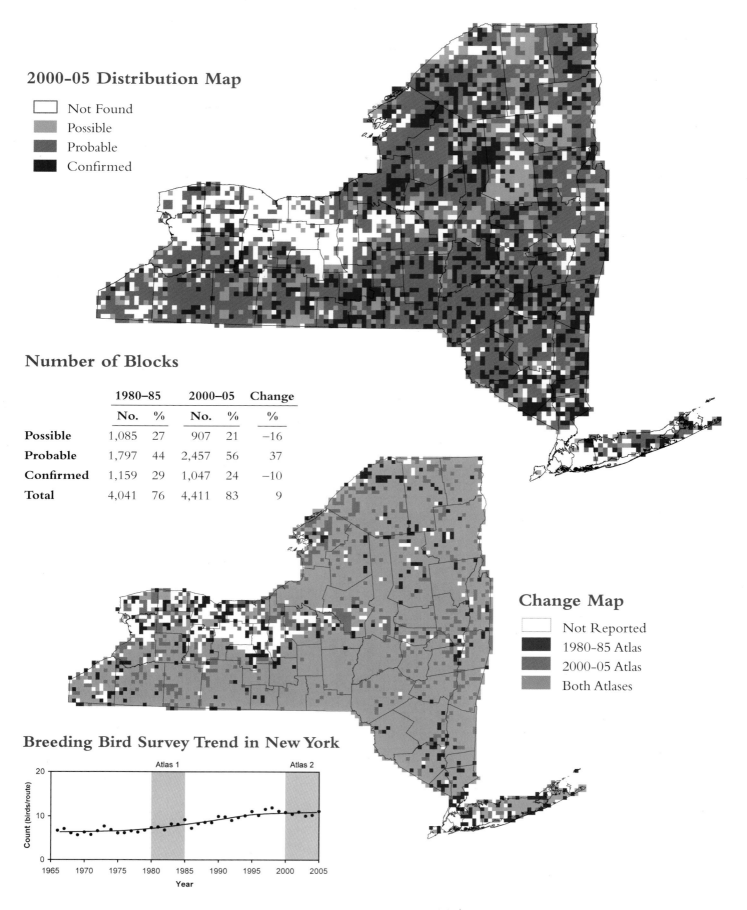

2000-05 Distribution Map

- ☐ Not Found
- Possible
- Probable
- Confirmed

Number of Blocks

	1980–85		2000–05		Change
	No.	%	No.	%	%
Possible	1,085	27	907	21	−16
Probable	1,797	44	2,457	56	37
Confirmed	1,159	29	1,047	24	−10
Total	4,041	76	4,411	83	9

Change Map

- ☐ Not Reported
- 1980-85 Atlas
- 2000-05 Atlas
- Both Atlases

Breeding Bird Survey Trend in New York

Northern Waterthrush

Seiurus noveboracensis

KEVIN J. MCGOWAN

A large, tail-bobbing warbler of wet areas, the Northern Waterthrush breeds from Alaska to Newfoundland southward to the northern United States, extending farther southward in the Appalachians to Virginia (Eaton 1995). It nests in thick vegetation near slow-moving streams, ponds, swamps, beaver ponds, and bogs. In New York the Northern Waterthrush inhabits primarily red maple–hardwood swamps on the Great Lakes Plain; hemlock–northern hardwood swamps on the Appalachian Plateau; and black spruce–tamarack swamps, spruce–balsam swamps, northern white cedar swamps, and alder thicket swamps in the Adirondacks and Tug Hill Plateau (Eaton 1988m). It was probably a common inhabitant of pre-colonial New York and likely suffered from the deforestation and drainage of wetlands that ensued. DeKay (1844) recognized only one species of waterthrush in the state and was uncertain if it bred here. Rathbun (1879) and Short (1893) also did not distinguish the two species but noted that the "Water Thrush" was a rare breeder in central and western New York. Reed and Wright (1909) did distinguish the two species and noted that the Northern Waterthrush bred in small numbers in the Cayuga Lake Basin but that the Louisiana Waterthrush was common. Eaton (1914) considered the Northern Waterthrush a common breeder throughout the Adirondacks and Catskills and the swamps of central and western New York. Bull (1974) gave essentially the same range and noted that although it was found primarily in higher elevations, it also extended into lower elevations on the Lake Ontario Plain. Bull (1974) gave its southernmost extent in the state in Orange and Westchester counties.

The first Atlas map showed the Northern Waterthrush widely scattered throughout most of the state, absent only from Niagara County, the New York City area, and Long Island. It appeared most dense in the Tug Hill Plateau, as well as the Finger Lakes Highlands and eastward across the northeastern section of the Appalachian Plateau. Its distribution was spotty across most other regions, reflecting the dispersed nature of its swampy breeding habitat. The second Atlas data showed little change, with only a slight increase in the number of blocks with breeding records. Its stronghold remained the Tug Hill and surrounding ecozones, from the Drumlin region of the Great Lakes Plain to the St. Lawrence Transition and into the Western Adirondack Foothills. The number of blocks with records declined 14 percent on the Appalachian Plateau but increased 35 percent along the Great Lakes Plain. The species was still missing from the Coastal Lowlands. The waterthrush may have been under-reported in some areas, as it stops singing by mid-June, making detection difficult (Eaton 1988m).

Breeding Bird Survey data show little significant change in Northern Waterthrush populations anywhere in the survey area over the last 40 years (Sauer et al. 2005). New York data show no significant trend, but the species is found only in low numbers in the state. The second Ontario Breeding Bird Atlas reported no province-wide change in Northern Waterthrush numbers since the first Atlas period, but reported a significant increase in squares with reports in the Simcoe-Rideau area south of the Canadian Shield (Bird Studies Canada et al. 2006). Partners in Flight gave the Northern Waterthrush a low combined score, indicating that it was in no immediate danger (Rich et al. 2004), probably because of its widespread breeding and wintering grounds. Mangrove areas important for wintering waterthrushes are under development pressures in the Neotropics (Eaton 1995), but the species uses a wide range of habitats throughout its extensive winter range.

The distribution of the Northern Waterthrush in New York depends on the continued existence of suitable breeding habitat. Laws protecting wetlands and the resurgence in beaver populations in the state have undoubtedly favored this warbler in recent years, and little change might be expected in the next Atlas data unless other factors come into play.

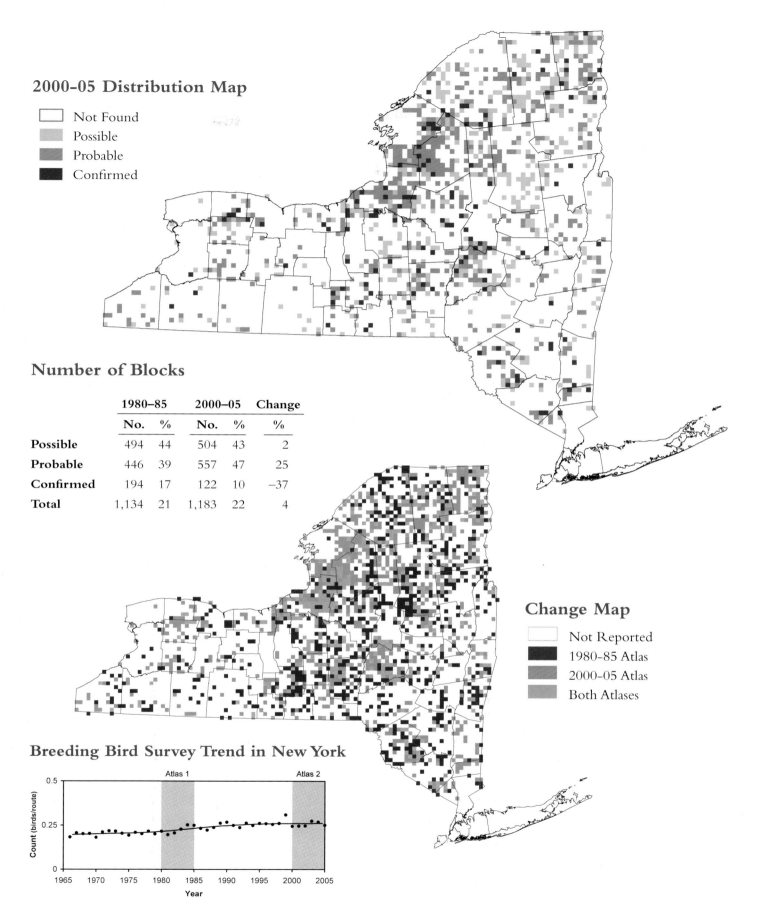

2000-05 Distribution Map

- ☐ Not Found
- Possible
- Probable
- Confirmed

Number of Blocks

	1980–85		2000–05		Change
	No.	%	No.	%	%
Possible	494	44	504	43	2
Probable	446	39	557	47	25
Confirmed	194	17	122	10	−37
Total	1,134	21	1,183	22	4

Change Map

- ☐ Not Reported
- 1980–85 Atlas
- 2000–05 Atlas
- Both Atlases

Breeding Bird Survey Trend in New York

Louisiana Waterthrush

Seiurus motacilla

KENNETH V. ROSENBERG

The Louisiana Waterthrush is among a suite of southeastern species near the northern limit of their distributions in New York. The breeding range extends from extreme southern Ontario southward to the Gulf Coast states and westward to the eastern Great Plains (Robinson 1995). It is a bird of clear, fast-flowing forest streams, where it seeks the shade of hemlocks or other dense riparian vegetation and feeds on aquatic invertebrates. In the Coastal Lowlands this species occurs in wooded swamps and along slow-moving streams (Bull 1974). Early New York authors did not distinguish the two waterthrush species. Eaton (1914) noted the Louisiana Waterthrush breeding up the length of the Hudson River Valley and called it common in the southern portion. He listed it as breeding throughout the ravines of the Finger Lakes Highlands, as well as in the Genesee and Chemung valleys. Bull (1974) reported a similar distribution, common in the streams of central and western New York but lacking from the Lake Ontario Plain, most of the Catskill Mountains, and most of the Coastal Plain.

During the first Atlas survey, the Louisiana Waterthrush was widely distributed across the southern half of New York, including the north shore of Long Island, with concentrations in the southeastern part of the state, encompassing parts of the Manhattan Hills, Hudson and Taconic highlands, Hudson Valley, and eastern Appalachian Plateau. Clusters of Confirmed breeding records also came from the Mohawk Valley, Allegany Hills, and the Genesee Valley of the western Appalachian Plateau. The species was almost completely absent from the Great Lakes Plain and was scarce north of the Mohawk Valley. A continued northward expansion was documented, however, in the Champlain Valley, along with a smaller invasion into the Central Adirondacks.

This waterthrush's statewide range remained largely the same during the second Atlas period, but observers reported it from 21 percent fewer blocks. The most alarming decreases came from the southeastern edge of the Appalachian Plateau, where collectively, the Mongaup Hills, Neversink Highlands, Delaware Hills, Schoharie Hills, and Helderberg Highlands experienced a nearly 55 percent decline. The neighboring Catskill Peaks had 24 percent fewer blocks with records, and the remainder of the Appalachian Plateau also showed a 24 percent decrease. Large gaps appeared in Delaware and Sullivan counties, and the species was more sparsely distributed eastward and southward of the Finger Lakes. In addition, it disappeared from recently colonized Adirondack and Champlain Valley sites, and it was found in only two blocks on the north shore of Long Island. In western New York, change was less dramatic, with a range contraction in the Allegany Hills seemingly offset by an expansion in the Cattaraugus Highlands.

Breeding Bird Survey data indicate a stable range-wide population trend for the Louisiana Waterthrush (Sauer et al. 2005), although low detection rates and high variability make detection of trends for this species difficult. Significant declines in numbers since 1980 are apparent in New York. Recent declines in areas of formerly high abundance in New York are troubling and may warn of more widespread threats to the species. Potential causes include reduction of aquatic prey from acidification of high-elevation streams (Mulvihill 1999) and the loss of streamside hemlocks from infestations of the exotic hemlock woolly adelgid (Evans 2002). The Louisiana Waterthrush also exhibits alarming concentrations of mercury in areas of high acid deposition (Evers and Duron 2006). It is included as a Species of Greatest Conservation Need in New York's Comprehensive Wildlife Action Plan and is listed by Partners in Flight as a Species of Regional Concern in the Appalachian Bird Conservation Region (PIF 2005). Closer monitoring of this species is warranted, and further research into the causes of declines is needed.

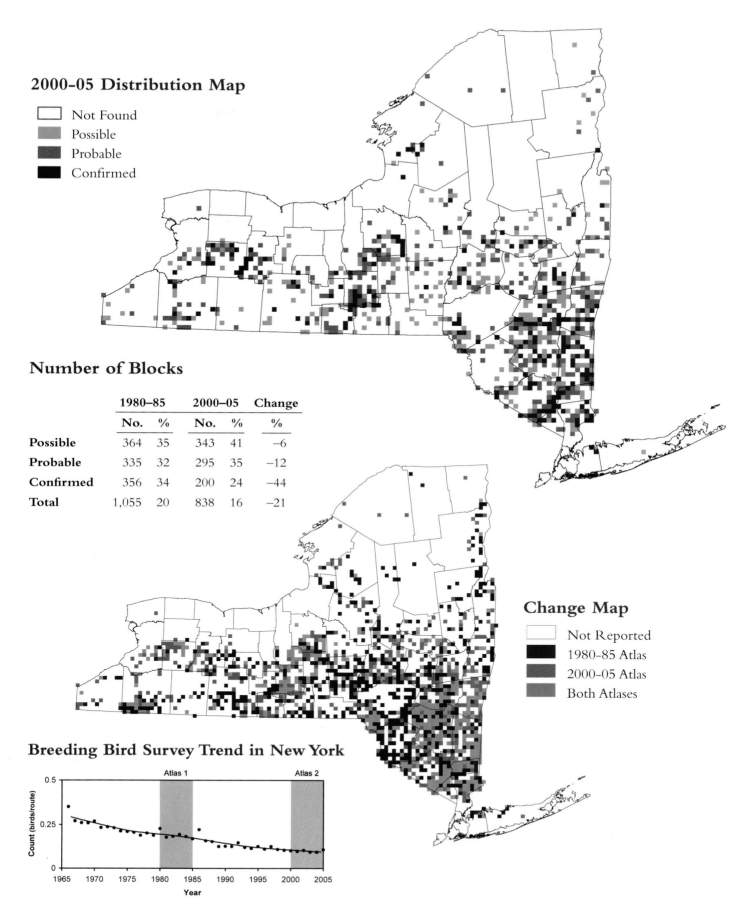

2000-05 Distribution Map

- ☐ Not Found
- ▨ Possible
- ▨ Probable
- ■ Confirmed

Number of Blocks

	1980–85		2000–05		Change
	No.	%	No.	%	%
Possible	364	35	343	41	−6
Probable	335	32	295	35	−12
Confirmed	356	34	200	24	−44
Total	1,055	20	838	16	−21

Change Map

- ☐ Not Reported
- ■ 1980–85 Atlas
- ▨ 2000–05 Atlas
- ▨ Both Atlases

Breeding Bird Survey Trend in New York

Kentucky Warbler
Oporornis formosus

KENNETH V. ROSENBERG

A rather secretive bird of moist deciduous forests, the Kentucky Warbler reaches the northeastern limit of its distribution in southern New York. It is fairly common throughout the southeastern and south-central United States, northward to Ohio, extreme southern Michigan and Wisconsin, westward to Iowa, eastern Kansas, Oklahoma, and Texas (McDonald 1998). Although never an abundant bird in the state, it was present historically in the lower Hudson Valley and on Long Island, with several records farther westward along the Pennsylvania border and in Cortland County (Eaton 1914, Griscom 1923). Bull (1964) outlined a population decline in the state after 1900, with virtual disappearance after 1942. The Kentucky Warbler was again documented as a breeder on Long Island in 1973 (Bull 1974, Ewert 1974) and was noted possibly breeding in the southern Appalachian Plateau at about the same time (Salzman 1998e). In New York, this species prefers hilly woodlands with stream-bearing ravines and a dense shrubby understory (NYNHP 2006).

The first Atlas documented a continued occupation of the historic distribution, with breeding concentrated along the lower Hudson River in the Manhattan Hills. Breeding was also confirmed on the north shore of Long Island, in the Hudson Highlands, and in the Taconic Highlands along the Dutchess County border with Connecticut. Several Probable and Possible records were scattered across the Appalachian Plateau, most in southern-flowing drainages near the Pennsylvania border. Unlike some other expanding southern species, breeding distribution of the Kentucky Warbler experienced a precipitous decline in New York since the first Atlas period, with 72 percent fewer blocks having records. Declines were especially dramatic in its two former strongholds, the Manhattan Hills and Coastal Lowlands, although breeding was still confirmed in these two ecozones despite reduced atlasing effort. Perhaps a glimmer of optimism comes from the four Probable breeding records at new locations in Delaware, Ulster, Orange, and Dutchess counties.

Declines in the breeding distribution of the Kentucky Warbler in New York correspond with a small but significant decline in the numbers of the species range-wide since 1980, according to the Breeding Bird Survey (Sauer et al. 2005), and a steeper decline of 3.8 percent per year throughout the Northeast region (U.S. Fish and Wildlife Service Region 5). Populations in the Southeast and Midwest regions have not declined during this period, suggesting that threats are most severe in the northern portions of the range. Threats include loss and fragmentation of mature, moist deciduous forests, primarily from development, as well as loss of dense shrubby understory in remaining forests, the result of overbrowsing by white-tailed deer and lack of disturbance in closed-canopy forests. The Kentucky Warbler also may be threatened on its wintering grounds from southern Mexico to Panama, where it is among the few warblers seemingly dependent on mature lowland forests in this region of high tropical deforestation (McDonald 1998).

Despite its tenuous status in New York, the Kentucky Warbler is not on the state's Endangered Species List, nor is it a Species of Greatest Conservation Need in the state's Comprehensive Wildlife Action Plan. It is on the Partners in Flight Continental Watch List, however, and it is a priority species in the Appalachian and the New England–Mid-Atlantic bird conservation regions (Rich et al. 2004), which include portions of southeastern New York. At least two known breeding sites, Rockefeller State Park and Fahnstock/Hudson Highlands State Park, are designated as Important Bird Areas (Burger and Liner 2005), and conservation plans at these sites are being developed. Conservation of this species will depend on a regional initiative to protect remaining forest tracts from development and reduce damage to forest understory by deer. Without such aggressive actions the Kentucky Warbler will probably not survive in New York until the next Atlas.

2000–05 Distribution Map

- ☐ Not Found
- ▨ Possible
- ▨ Probable
- ■ Confirmed

Number of Blocks

	1980–85		2000–05		Change
	No.	%	No.	%	%
Possible	12	31	5	45	−58
Probable	20	51	4	36	−80
Confirmed	7	18	2	18	−71
Total	39	<1	11	<1	−72

Change Map

- ☐ Not Reported
- ■ 1980-85 Atlas
- ▨ 2000-05 Atlas
- ▨ Both Atlases

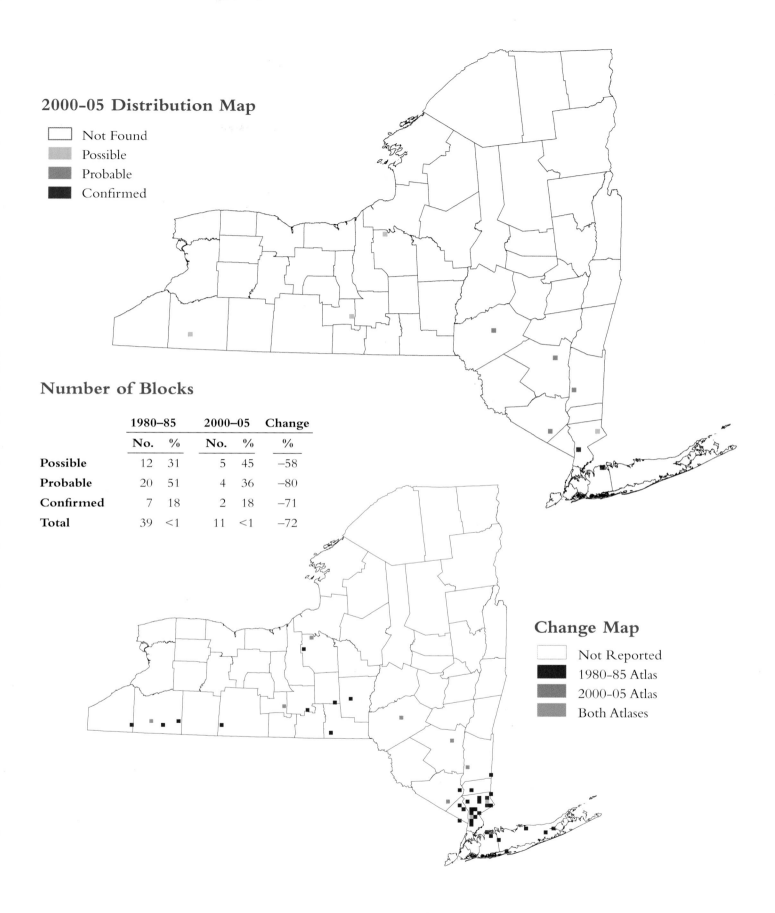

Mourning Warbler
Oporornis philadelphia

JOAN E. COLLINS

The elegant Mourning Warbler can be heard singing from a high exposed perch overlooking a relatively open area of dense vegetation. It breeds from northeastern British Columbia eastward to Newfoundland, and from northern North Dakota eastward to northern New England and into northern Pennsylvania, with an isolated population in the Appalachian Mountains of West Virginia (Pitocchelli 1993). Breeding occurs in dense second-growth vegetation that thrives after fires, forest clearings, beaver openings, windfalls, and road construction, within deciduous, mixed, and coniferous forests (Dunn and Garrett 1997, pers. obs.). The second-growth vegetation it favors includes dense tangles of blackberry and raspberry bushes, and young saplings, with a moderately open canopy of mature trees. It also breeds in wet bottomland woods with a dense growth of ferns, skunk-cabbage, and marsh marigold (Bull 1974, Dunn and Garrett 1997). Pitocchelli (1993) noted that the Mourning Warbler, favoring disturbed areas, may be one of the few Neotropical migrants in North America to have benefited from human settlement. DeKay (1844) described the species as "rare" but noted that "its history is imperfect." Eaton (1914) found the species to be a common summer resident in the Catskills and Adirondacks, as well as in the "highlands and colder swamps of central and western New York," and also lower, in sections of the Great Lakes Plain. Bull (1974) called the species fairly to locally common in the mountains and higher regions of the state, rare to local in the southern tier, and "absent south and east of the Catskills."

The first Atlas map showed the Mourning Warbler concentrated in the Western Adirondack Foothills, eastern Appalachian Plateau, Allegany Hills, Cattaraugus Highlands, Great Lakes Plain, and Tug Hill Plateau. Pitocchelli (1993) commented that local distributions of this species frequently change within its breeding range. Such was the case shown by the second Atlas findings: the overall distribution of the Mourning Warbler did not change much but areas of concentration shifted a bit. Overall, the number of blocks reporting the species increased 4 percent. The 14.5 percent increase in the Appalachian Plateau occurred primarily in the far eastern section and in the Cattaraugus Highlands and east of the Allegany Hills in the western section. Increases also were found in the Catskill Highlands, Champlain Transition, Mohawk Valley, and Tug Hill Plateau. Decreases occurred in the Great Lakes Plain and St. Lawrence Plains. A slight decrease occurred in the Adirondacks ecozone, which, more specifically, showed a decline in the Central Adirondacks but solid concentrations and increases along the Western Adirondack Foothills and Western Adirondack Transition and a slight increase in the northern section of the Eastern Adirondack Foothills. Although the Mourning Warbler male sings a loud, distinctive song, its early-season singing subsides during active nesting and may resume again in August (Pitocchelli 1993). When silent, this secretive bird of dense second-growth vegetation could easily be missed by observers.

Breeding Bird Survey data show no significant population trends for the Mourning Warbler in New York but do show a significant survey-wide decline for the species of 1.2 percent per year from 1966 to 2005 and significant yearly declines for the Ontario and Eastern BBS regions during the same period (Sauer et al. 2005). Conversely, the Vermont BBS data show a significant increase of 6.3 percent per year from 1966 to 2005 (Sauer et al. 2005).

The transitional nature of the breeding habitat of the Mourning Warbler leads to frequent local changes within its breeding range, but the species should continue to remain stable in New York as long as both natural and human-induced forest disturbances continue to occur.

2000–05 Distribution Map

- ☐ Not Found
- Possible
- Probable
- Confirmed

Number of Blocks

	1980–85		2000–05		Change
	No.	%	No.	%	%
Possible	525	38	557	38	6
Probable	547	39	640	44	17
Confirmed	326	23	263	18	−19
Total	1,398	26	1,460	27	4

Change Map

- ☐ Not Reported
- 1980-85 Atlas
- 2000-05 Atlas
- Both Atlases

Breeding Bird Survey Trend in New York

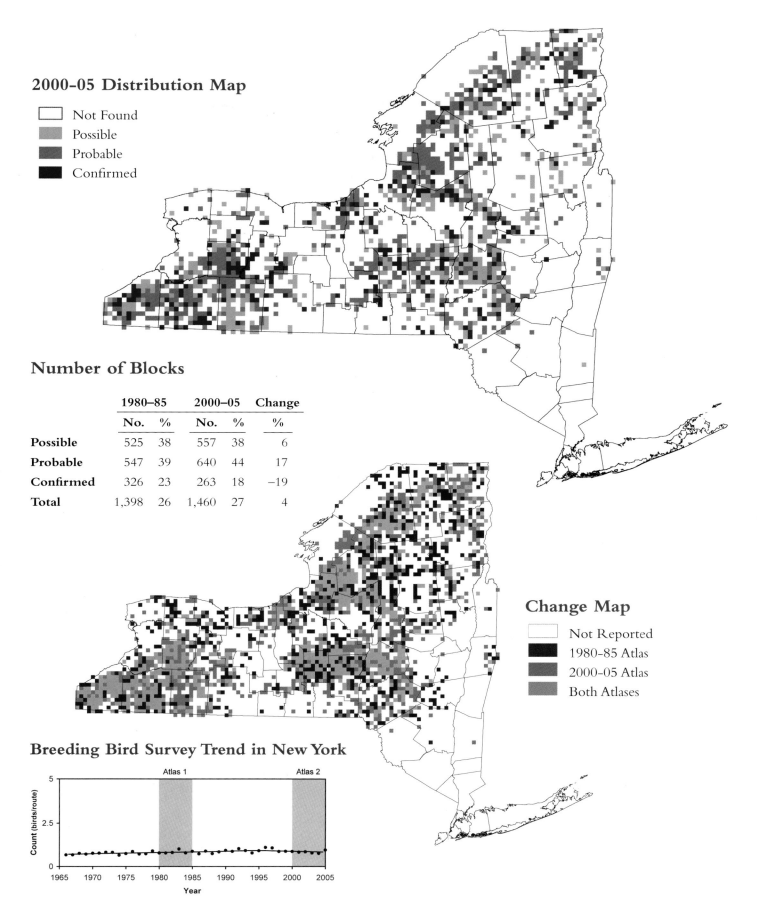

Common Yellowthroat
Geothlypis trichas

KEVIN J. MCGOWAN

One of the most widespread warblers in North America, the Common Yellowthroat breeds from extreme southeastern Alaska and Yukon, across most of Canada to Newfoundland, southward along both coasts to southern Florida and California, to the Gulf Coast and eastern Texas (Guzy and Ritchison 1999). It is also found in scattered and local breeding populations throughout western states and in central to southern Mexico. It is common in thick, tangled vegetation and is most frequently found not only near water but also in prairies and dry, shrubby hillsides (Guzy and Ritchison 1999). Although it is a specialist in shrubby vegetation, such habitats are and always have been scattered throughout New York. But as a bird of marshes and thickets, the Common Yellowthroat likely was less common before European settlement and the opening of the forests. It was probably primarily a bird of marshes, beaver ponds and meadows, tree-fall gaps, and other such openings. The reduction in the amount of forests and the creation of more open habitats were undoubtedly to the yellowthroat's liking, and by the early 19th century it was already described as common and widespread (DeKay 1844, Giraud 1844).

The Common Yellowthroat was the third most commonly reported species in the first Atlas, following the Song Sparrow and American Robin, and was observed in 97 percent of all blocks. It was found across the state at all elevations. Blocks without breeding records may have had little coverage, or some may have been of extensive forest without any shrubby habitat. Little change was noted in the second Atlas data. The species was the fourth most reported bird, again being found in 97 percent of blocks and this time following the American Robin, Black-capped Chickadee, and Blue Jay. No patterns of change are obvious from the Change Map, and empty blocks again may well speak more about coverage than habitat. The Common Yellowthroat is easy to detect, singing loudly and responding well not only to *pishing* but also to a variety of other noises. One atlaser reported a greatly disturbed male rushing out of vegetation and tumbling across the road in a distraction display as she rode slowly by on a bicycle.

Breeding Bird Survey data show a significant, if slight, decrease of 0.5 percent per year in Common Yellowthroat numbers across the continent, with most of the decline occurring in the last 25 years and in the eastern regions (Sauer et al. 2005). BBS data from New York show a significant increase from 1966 to 1979 and a slight but significant decline from then on (Sauer et al. 2005). Data from surrounding states and provinces are similar. Despite the downward BBS trends, the species is still common and widespread and is consequently not listed as threatened or endangered, although some western and southern nonmigratory populations face potential extirpation from habitat loss and disturbance (Guzy and Ritchison 1999). Arbib (1988b) noted that although no data existed to support it, conventional wisdom suggested that Common Yellowthroat populations increased with the settlement of New York. He further suggested that if this speculation was true, then the abandonment of farmland and the maturation of the subsequent successional forests, along with increased urbanization, highway construction, and marsh drainage, should have an opposite effect. Such a negative trend was not apparent in any data set in 1988, but this theory corresponds well with the current BBS data. Atlas methods are not designed to detect slight decreases in populations of common and widespread species, and no such trend was apparent between the two Atlas periods. Any detection of declines in New York awaits the work of future Atlas projects.

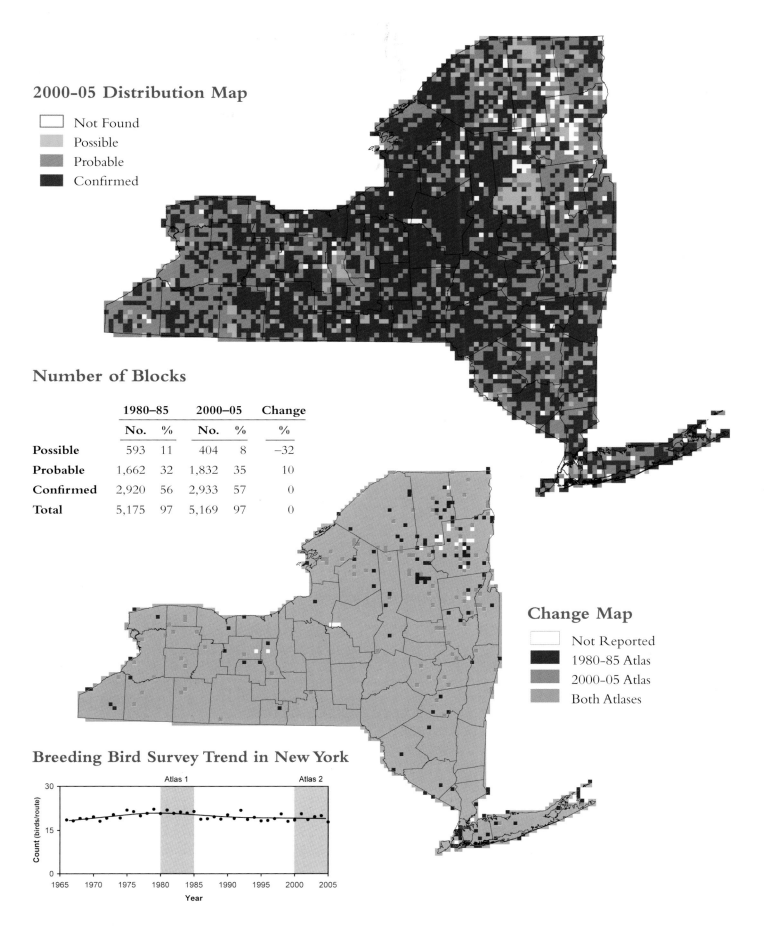

2000–05 Distribution Map

- ☐ Not Found
- Possible
- Probable
- Confirmed

Number of Blocks

| | 1980–85 | | 2000–05 | | Change |
	No.	%	No.	%	%
Possible	593	11	404	8	−32
Probable	1,662	32	1,832	35	10
Confirmed	2,920	56	2,933	57	0
Total	5,175	97	5,169	97	0

Change Map

- ☐ Not Reported
- 1980-85 Atlas
- 2000-05 Atlas
- Both Atlases

Breeding Bird Survey Trend in New York

Hooded Warbler

Wilsonia citrina

KEVIN J. MCGOWAN

The Hooded Warbler is a southern warbler of hardwood forests and swamps. It breeds from southern Wisconsin and southern Ontario eastward to New York, and southward to eastern Texas and northern Florida. It is considered a forest-interior species and is found primarily in larger woodlots (Evans Ogden and Stutchbury 1994). The Hooded Warbler requires a shrub understory and can be found in thickets of mountain laurel or maple saplings (Eaton 1998e). It is common in selectively logged deciduous forests, appearing one to five years after harvesting and remaining as long as suitable understory shrubs exist (Evans Ogden and Stutchbury 1994). Considered rare in the state by DeKay (1844) and Giraud (1844), it was listed as common in central New York by Rathbun (1879). E. H. Eaton (1910) showed it breeding along the Great Lakes Plain, east of the Finger Lakes Highlands on the Appalachian Plateau, and in the Hudson Highlands. Bull (1974) reported the species in three general areas: western New York from Rochester southwestward to the Pennsylvania border, central New York from Wayne and Oswego counties southward to Chenango County, and along the Hudson River from Rensselaer County to the Bronx.

The first Atlas data showed the Hooded Warbler in essentially the same areas that Bull (1974) described. Most records came from the Cattaraugus Highlands and Allegany Hills in the far western corner of the state and the Hudson Highlands and Manhattan Hills in the southeast. Reports also came from the Great Lakes Plain, scattered across the Appalachian Plateau, and on the Tug Hill Plateau. Breeding was confirmed on Long Island for the first time. The second Atlas results documented the Hooded Warbler in many more blocks, up 146 percent overall. The largest increases were in the western portion of the Appalachian Plateau, the Great Lakes Plain, and the Taconic Highlands. The southwestern corner remained the stronghold in the state, and the Hooded Warbler was present in nearly every block in the western Appalachian Plateau and the adjacent regions of the Great Lakes Plain. Declines in the number of blocks with breeding records were apparent only in the Manhattan Hills and Coastal Lowlands, but those areas also received less atlasing effort this time. S. W. Eaton (1988j) stated that the Hooded Warbler avoided the large block of oak–northern hardwood forest south of the Finger Lakes, but the northern half of that area was completely populated with Hooded Warblers during the second Atlas period. Most breeding locations described as "lost" by Eaton (1988j, 1998e) were repopulated by the time of the second Atlas survey.

The Hooded Warbler has been undergoing a slight but significant population increase of 0.8 percent per year throughout its range over the last 25 years (Sauer et al. 2005). The increase since 1980 in the Allegany Plateau region was significant, at 2.7 percent per year (Sauer et al. 2005). The species was not present on enough routes to have much confidence in the data, but its numbers appeared to increase on BBS routes in New York during the same time (Sauer et al. 2005). The second Ontario Breeding Bird Atlas reported significant increases across the southern portion of that province, including just west of the Niagara Frontier (Bird Studies Canada et al. 2006). Just what has been the most significant factor affecting Hooded Warbler populations is difficult to determine. The continuing maturation of forests from shrublands to a closed canopy could account for some increases in populations. The warbler's requirement for understory shrubs, however, could predict a decline in areas of older forest, and increased deer browsing should be a negative factor. Selective logging, though, can increase breeding habitat by creating gaps and increased understory within a forest. It will be interesting to see if the next Atlas reports a continued increase in Hooded Warbler numbers across New York, following the pattern of other expanding southern species.

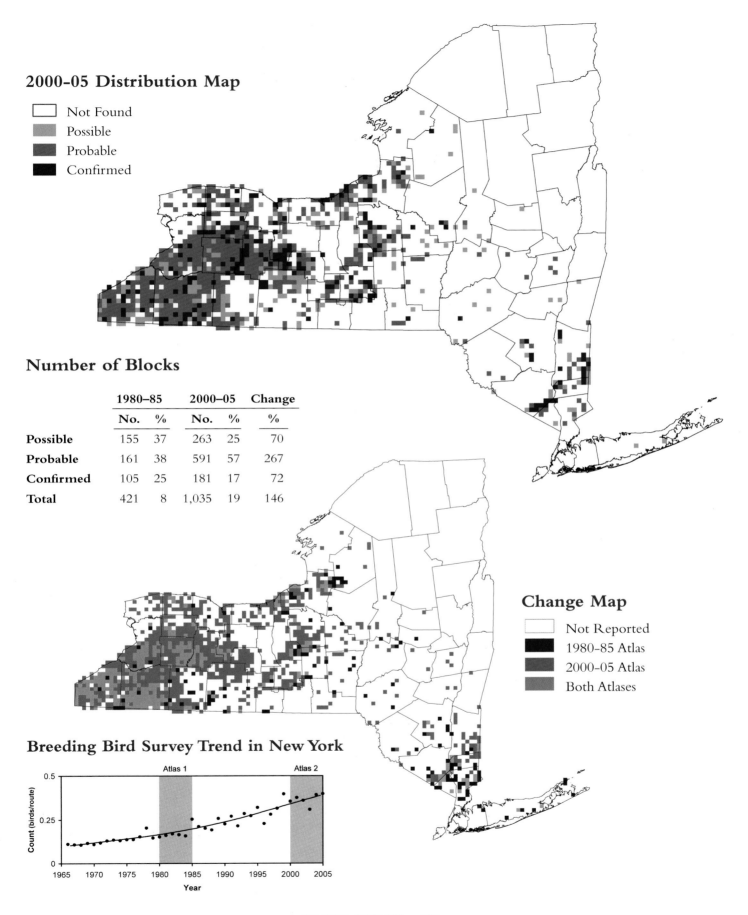

2000–05 Distribution Map

- ☐ Not Found
- Possible
- Probable
- Confirmed

Number of Blocks

	1980–85		2000–05		Change
	No.	%	No.	%	%
Possible	155	37	263	25	70
Probable	161	38	591	57	267
Confirmed	105	25	181	17	72
Total	421	8	1,035	19	146

Change Map

- ☐ Not Reported
- 1980-85 Atlas
- 2000-05 Atlas
- Both Atlases

Breeding Bird Survey Trend in New York

Wilson's Warbler
Wilsonia pusilla

KEVIN J. MCGOWAN

A distinctive bright yellow warbler with a black cap, Wilson's Warbler is most common as a migrant in New York. It breeds across Alaska and Canada, southward to southern California, New Mexico, northern Minnesota, and central Maine (Ammon and Gilbert 1999). New York is south of the main breeding range. Wilson's Warbler breeds in shrub thickets of riparian habitats, along the edges of beaver ponds, lakes, bogs, and in the successional aftermath of clear-cuts in the western mountains and the boreal forest (Ammon and Gilbert 1999). Although this bog-loving warbler breeds in central Maine, central Ontario, and Quebec, and plenty of apparently appropriate habitat is available in the Adirondacks, it is not a regular part of the Adirondack breeding avifauna. Merriam (1881) called it a rare migrant. Eaton (1914) suspected the bird as potentially breeding in New York, but he reported that careful searches had failed to find it. Bull (1974) also intimated that this warbler could nest in the state, but no records yet existed. The first confirmed nesting of the species in New York was in North Meadow in the town of Elba, Essex County, in 1978 (Nickerson 1978), and a few summer sightings have been made since.

The first Atlas fieldwork failed to confirm Wilson's Warbler as a breeder, but the bird was reported in three blocks. Single males were observed in Franklin and Hamilton counties, and a pair was seen in Essex County in North Meadow, the site of the 1978 nesting. During the second Atlas period, only two reports were made in the Central Adirondacks; these were sightings of single birds in Essex and Franklin counties. Although it is easy enough to recognize when one is expecting the species, the trilling song of Wilson's Warbler is not particularly distinctive, and it is possible that the bird has been overlooked in some places. Nickerson (1978) speculated that Wilson's Warbler, along with several other northern species, might be extending its breeding range southward. Although other northern species have indeed expanded into the Adirondacks (notably the Palm Warbler), the Wilson's Warbler does not seem to have become any more common in New York over the last 20 years.

Large-scale destruction of riparian habitat seems to be causing population declines in the western portions of this species's breeding range (Ammon and Gilbert 1999). In eastern North America Wilson's Warbler is uncommon south of the boreal forest, and good data on population trends are scarce. Breeding Bird Survey data show that numbers of this species have increased significantly in Newfoundland and decreased significantly in New Brunswick, but all of the data from states and provinces in the East have serious deficiencies (Sauer et al. 2005). The first Vermont Breeding Bird Atlas reported only a single confirmed nesting in the very northeastern corner of the state, with one other singing male observed (Laughlin and Kibbe 1985), and preliminary results from the second Vermont Atlas indicate the species is still very rare (R. Renfrew pers. comm.). The New Hampshire Atlas reported only 2 blocks with confirmed breeding in the very northern portion of the state and 11 other blocks with possible nesting (Foss 1994). Peck and James (1987) reported the Wilson's Warbler to be a common breeder throughout northern Ontario but absent from the southern region of the province. Data from the second Ontario Breeding Bird Atlas show little change in that distribution but a significant increase in numbers in the northernmost regions (Bird Studies Canada et al. 2006). With no close sources of dispersers and no clear increasing population trends in the East, it appears that Wilson's Warbler will remain a rare breeder in New York State for the near future.

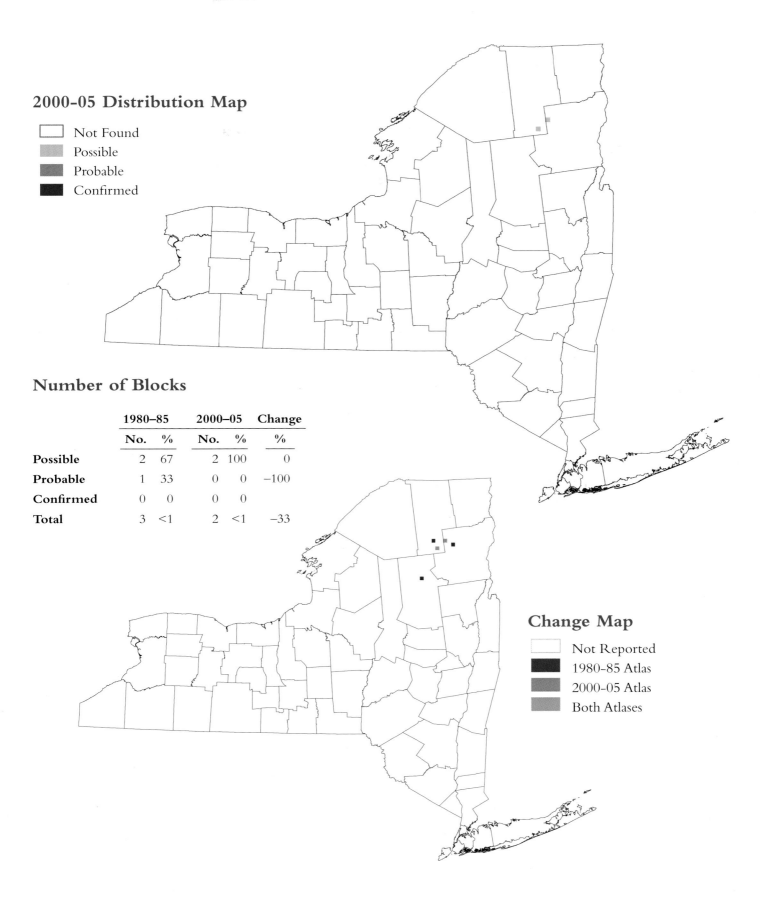

2000-05 Distribution Map

- ☐ Not Found
- Possible
- Probable
- Confirmed

Number of Blocks

	1980–85		2000–05		Change
	No.	%	No.	%	%
Possible	2	67	2	100	0
Probable	1	33	0	0	–100
Confirmed	0	0	0	0	
Total	3	<1	2	<1	–33

Change Map

- ☐ Not Reported
- 1980-85 Atlas
- 2000-05 Atlas
- Both Atlases

Canada Warbler

Wilsonia canadensis

KEVIN J. MCGOWAN

The Canada Warbler is an active bird of the forest understory. It breeds across southern Canada and the northeastern United States southward to northern Pennsylvania, and in the Appalachian Mountains to northern Georgia. It can be found in a variety of deciduous and coniferous forests but prefers moist mixed deciduous-coniferous forests with a well-developed understory (Conway 1999). In the southern part of the range, such as in New York, it is more common at higher elevations in hills and mountains, especially in tangled thickets and streamside vegetation (Conway 1999), but it can also be found at lower elevations in wooded swamps and bogs (Bull 1974). It is frequently found in areas of forest disturbed by natural events or by logging (Lambert and Faccio 2005). DeKay (1844) considered the Canada Warbler rare in southern New York, but Merriam (1881) considered it an abundant breeder in the Adirondacks. Eaton (1910, 1914) called it common in the second-growth areas of the Adirondacks and Catskills, as well as in scattered localities of central and western New York. He showed it to be present in the Allegany and Cattaraugus highlands and swampy localities on the Great Lakes Plain, although Rathbun (1879) did not know of it breeding in central New York, and Short (1893) had listed it only as a possible breeder in the western region. Bull (1974) considered the Canada Warbler to be the most widely distributed of the "northern warblers" in the state, found in a diversity of habitats southward to Westchester County, with one breeding record from Long Island. Bonney (1988a) suggested that the Canada Warbler was extending its range to the southeast in New York, although Baird (1990) found significant declines in western New York at that time.

The first Atlas map showed the Canada Warbler to be widely distributed across the state in the higher elevations, especially in the Adirondacks, Tug Hill Plateau, and Catskills and surrounding highlands. It was more scattered, but still common, across the Appalachian Plateau and in the Taconic Highlands, Hudson Highlands, and Manhattan Hills. Small numbers were found at lower elevations across the state, and even on Long Island, although breeding was not confirmed there. The second Atlas results showed the Canada Warbler in much the same distribution, but the number of occupied blocks was down 23 percent. It was found in fewer blocks in all ecozones across the state, except the Tug Hill, where the number of occupied blocks was unchanged. An apparent increase in the number of blocks with records in northeastern Jefferson County is the result of improved coverage and access to Fort Drum Military Reservation during the second Atlas period.

The Canada Warbler population has been declining throughout its range since at least the 1960s, with the largest declines seen in the northeastern United States (Conway 1999). Breeding Bird Survey data show a 2.4 percent annual decline range-wide since 1966, with New York showing a significant decline of 5 percent per year (Sauer et al. 2007). Although not listed by the New York State Department of Environmental Conservation, the Canada Warbler was listed as a Species of Regional Conservation Concern by the Northeast Endangered Species and Wildlife Diversity Technical Committee (Therres 1999), and was placed on the Watch List of Partners in Flight (Rich et al. 2004). On a local scale, the Canada Warbler responds to changes in forest understory, its numbers increasing in areas with increasing understory after disturbance, but decreasing with forest maturation and increased deer browsing (Conway 1999). Forest maturation and deer browse might explain much of the decline in New York (Eaton 1998b). The widespread decline in all regions of the state, however, even where the populations of other understory species such as the Hooded Warbler and Mourning Warbler are increasing, suggests that at least part of the problem lies outside the state, perhaps on the wintering grounds in northern South America.

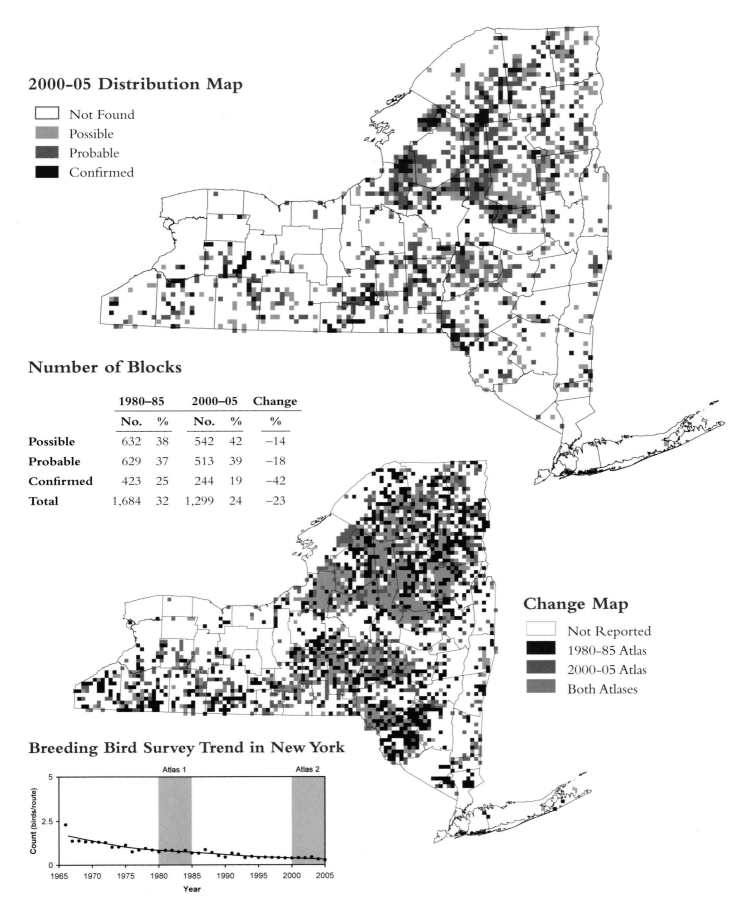

2000-05 Distribution Map

- ☐ Not Found
- Possible
- Probable
- Confirmed

Number of Blocks

	1980–85		2000–05		Change
	No.	%	No.	%	%
Possible	632	38	542	42	−14
Probable	629	37	513	39	−18
Confirmed	423	25	244	19	−42
Total	1,684	32	1,299	24	−23

Change Map

- ☐ Not Reported
- 1980-85 Atlas
- 2000-05 Atlas
- Both Atlases

Breeding Bird Survey Trend in New York

Yellow-breasted Chat

Icteria virens

KEVIN J. MCGOWAN

The Yellow-breasted Chat is a colorful songbird of low, dense scrubby vegetation. It breeds across the eastern United States and southern Canada from Iowa to New York, southward to Texas and northern Florida. It also is found in scattered regions across the West from southern Canada to very northern Mexico (Eckerle and Thompson 2001). The chat breeds in dense second growth, thickets, and brush, including shrubby habitat along streams and ponds, forest edges, regenerating burned-over and logged forest, fencerows, and recently abandoned farmland (Eckerle and Thompson 2001). Before European settlement in New York and the destruction of the forests, the Yellow-breasted Chat was likely very uncommon, if present at all, although it may have bred on Long Island. De-Kay (1844) was uncertain whether it occurred in the state, but Giraud (1844) considered it common on Long Island. Rathbun (1879) and Short (1893) listed the chat as rare in central and western New York. Reed and Wright (1909) called it fairly common in the Cayuga Lake Basin, noting that it formerly was rare but its numbers had increased considerably early in the 20th century. Eaton (1914) listed the Yellow-breasted Chat as common in the lower Hudson Valley and on Long Island, with local occurrence in the central, southern, and western parts of the state. Although the abandonment of farmland in the middle of the 20th century should have provided more habitat for chats, Bull (1974) gave the range in New York as essentially unchanged from Eaton's (1914) account, and his description of it as a local breeder on Long Island suggests a decline in that area.

During the first Atlas survey, the Yellow-breasted Chat was found in 122 blocks. It was scattered across the Appalachian Plateau and Great Lakes Plain from Lake Erie eastward to Madison County, but nowhere was it common. A cluster of reports came from the Coastal Lowlands and the southern Hudson Valley and associated highlands. A few isolated non-Confirmed breeding reports also were made farther north. The overall outline of the distribution mapped in the first Atlas was similar to that depicted by Eaton (1910), but the many gaps and scattered reports suggested a significant decline in

populations. Data from the second Atlas indicate that this decline continued; 78 percent fewer blocks had records. Most of the records were in the western Great Lakes Plain and the southeastern highlands and Coastal Lowlands. The single confirmation was in the Shawangunk Hills.

Yellow-breasted Chat populations appear to be declining in the northeastern part of the breeding range but increasing in the western part (Eckerle and Thompson 2001). The chat's range was fairly stable through much of the 20th century, but local populations and those at the edge of the range have shown large fluctuations, including declines and extirpations (Eckerle and Thompson 2001). Breeding Bird Survey data show no significant trend nationwide since 1966 but a very slight significant increase since 1980 (Sauer et al. 2005). Increases occurred in the South and West, but the Northeast and Midwest had significant declines (Sauer et al. 2005). The second Ontario Breeding Bird Atlas reported a significant decline in the small population there (Bird Studies Canada et al. 2006). Because of the ephemeral nature of its preferred habitat, the decline of Yellow-breasted Chat populations at the edges of its range may not be surprising, and forest maturation and loss of shrublands in the Northeast may be largely responsible for the decreases there (Eckerle and Thompson 2001). Shrubland habitat is declining in New York (see Chapter 4), but whether this loss can explain a decline of this magnitude is debatable; much potential habitat still exists in the state. As a southern species, the chat has had perhaps a tenuous hold on a breeding range in New York for the last 200 years, and it may well disappear completely in the near future.

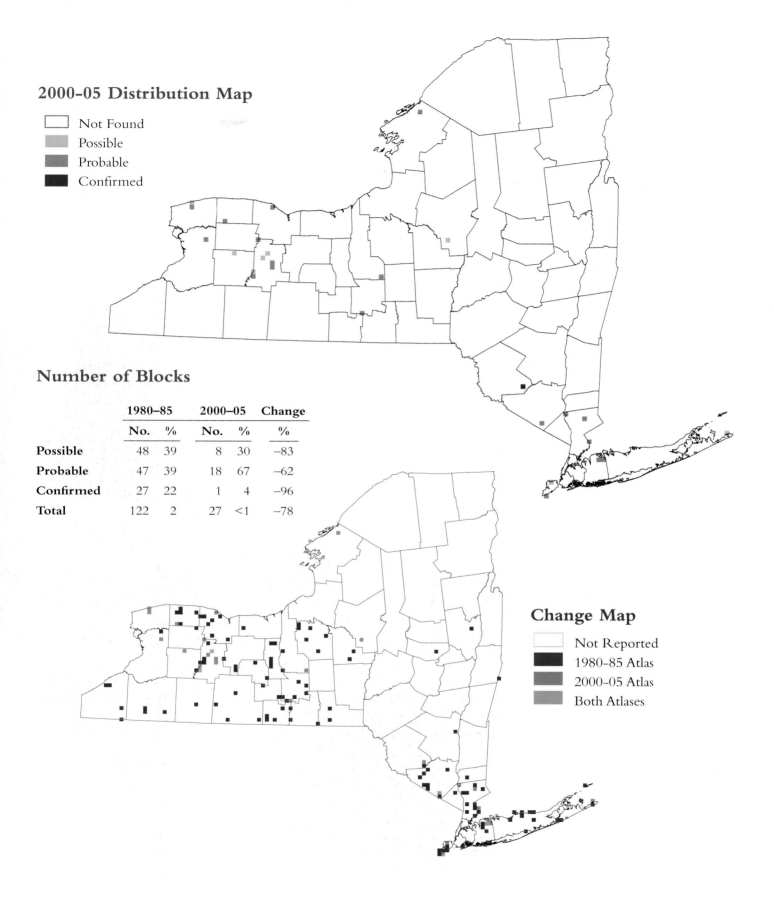

2000-05 Distribution Map

- Not Found
- Possible
- Probable
- Confirmed

Number of Blocks

	1980–85		2000–05		Change
	No.	%	No.	%	%
Possible	48	39	8	30	−83
Probable	47	39	18	67	−62
Confirmed	27	22	1	4	−96
Total	122	2	27	<1	−78

Change Map

- Not Reported
- 1980-85 Atlas
- 2000-05 Atlas
- Both Atlases

Summer Tanager

Piranga rubra

KEVIN J. MCGOWAN

The Summer Tanager is an all-red, bee-eating bird of southern forests. It breeds in the southern United States and northern Mexico, northward to southern Utah, Iowa, and New Jersey. It nests in deciduous forests in the eastern part of its range, especially in open woods and near gaps, and is common in pine-oak forests of the Southeast (Robinson 1996). New York is north of the extent of its normal breeding range in southern Pennsylvania and southern New Jersey, but several individuals are reported from the New York City area and Long Island nearly every year. Eaton (1914) listed 13 specimens of Summer Tanager, all taken on Long Island in April and May, and he considered the species an accidental spring visitor. The first nesting of the species in the state was reported on the grounds of the Brookhaven National Laboratory in the pine barrens of Suffolk County in the summer of 1990 (Schiff and Wollin 1990). That report was initially rejected by the New York State Avian Records Committee because of insufficient information (NYSARC 1992), but it was later accepted after additional information was provided (NYSARC 2006). The listing of the species as a breeding and uncommon summer resident in Albany County in the early 1900s (Judd 1907) has been discounted as not credible (Eaton 1914), although the Albany Pine Bush might conceivably provide suitable habitat.

The Summer Tanager was not a Confirmed breeder in New York during the first Atlas period, but it was listed as a Possible breeder in one block on Staten Island, one in northern Nassau County, and one in central Suffolk County. Little change in its status was noted during the second Atlas fieldwork, with reports in three blocks in Suffolk County, but breeding was confirmed in one block this time. A nest with young was found and photographed in 2002, again at the Brookhaven National Laboratory in Suffolk County, providing the second Confirmed breeding record for the state.

The range of the Summer Tanager appears to be expanding in some areas and contracting in others (Robinson 1996). Breeding Bird Survey data show no significant long-term trends at the national or Fish and Wildlife Service regional level, but they do reveal modest, significant increases in the Southwest and Midwest in the last 25 years (Sauer et al. 2005). The Summer Tanager disappeared from southern New Jersey as a breeder in the early 20th century but recolonized the state at the end of the century (Walsh et al. 1999). The New Jersey Breeding Bird Atlas project reported it to be breeding primarily across the southern portion of the state in the outer coastal plain and the pine barrens, but it was also confirmed breeding in Essex County, to the northwest of New York City (Walsh et al. 1999). Given the expansion of the species in New Jersey, the occurrence of the Summer Tanager in New York seems reasonable. Whether it remains a member of the New York breeding fauna remains to be seen.

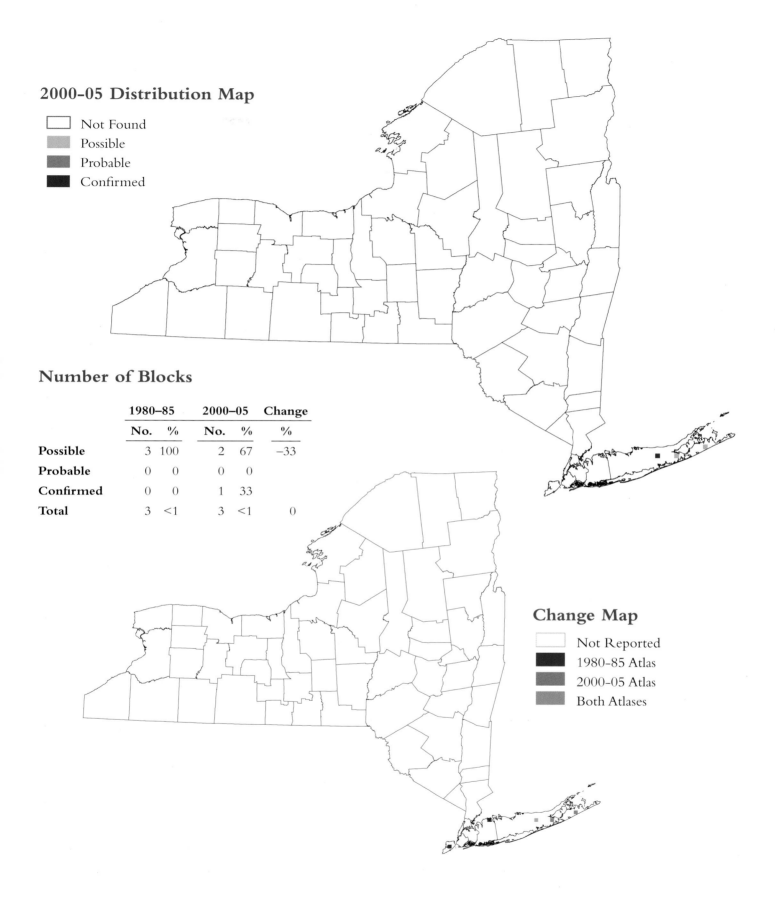

2000-05 Distribution Map

- ☐ Not Found
- Possible
- Probable
- ■ Confirmed

Number of Blocks

	1980–85		2000–05		Change
	No.	%	No.	%	%
Possible	3	100	2	67	−33
Probable	0	0	0	0	
Confirmed	0	0	1	33	
Total	3	<1	3	<1	0

Change Map

- ☐ Not Reported
- ■ 1980-85 Atlas
- 2000-05 Atlas
- Both Atlases

Scarlet Tanager
Piranga olivacea

JAMES D. LOWE AND RALPH S. HAMES

One of New York's most striking breeding birds, the Scarlet Tanager brings a touch of the tropics to the state's northern forests. Though often hard to see, the distinctive hoarse-sounding song and *chip-burr* call are easy to detect. The Scarlet Tanager breeds in a variety of deciduous and mixed forests from the southern edge of Manitoba to the Maritime Provinces, southward to Arkansas and the northern portions of Alabama and Georgia (Mowbray 1999b). It prefers mature forests, especially those with oaks, but can be found in most types of New York's forests (C. R. Smith 1988b, Mowbray 1999b). It was probably always a common bird in New York forests. Eaton (1914) called the Scarlet Tanager a fairly common summer resident of forested areas (found in every county), and Bull (1974) called it a widespread breeder but rare in the Coastal Lowlands.

Like these earlier accounts, field observers for the first Atlas project found the Scarlet Tanager throughout the state. Small gaps in its distribution occurred in areas where forest cover was relatively low, such as the agricultural areas in the Great Lakes Plain and the urban areas of the Coastal Lowlands (Smith 1988b). Other noticeable gaps were present in the Central Adirondacks and Adirondack High Peaks. The Scarlet Tanager was also widely distributed during the second Atlas period, present in the same percentage of blocks. The number of blocks with records from the Great Lakes Plain increased by nearly 16 percent, resulting in the filling of gaps in both the Eastern Ontario Plains and the western part of the Erie-Ontario Plain. The gap in the Adirondack High Peaks, however, widened somewhat, and the number of overall Adirondack blocks with records declined by 5 percent.

Analyses of the Breeding Bird Survey data for New York show a significant declining trend of −1.4 percent per year from 1966 through 2005, with an even steeper decline of −2.4 percent per year since 1980. Range-wide, BBS data indicate that Scarlet Tanager populations are relatively stable with a non-significant ($P = 0.53$) trend of −0.1 percent per year over the period 1966–2005 (Sauer et al. 2005). Regions suffering the highest declines in tanager populations are the Adirondacks and the eastern part of the Appalachian Plateau (Sauer et al. 2005). The Adi-

rondack trend is −3.9 percent per year from 1980 through 2005. BBS data from the Great Lakes Plain (which includes some areas outside of New York) show a trend of +1.9 percent per year from 1980 to 2005.

The Scarlet Tanager is an area-sensitive species, meaning it is more likely to be found in larger forest patches (Robbins et al. 1989, Mowbray 1999b), but Project Tanager data suggest that this is less true in most of New York than in other parts of its breeding range (Rosenberg et al. 1999). It seems to be less area sensitive in regions with more heavily forested landscapes, such as the Appalachian and Northern Forest regions, while it is more area sensitive in the less forested Midwest and Atlantic Coast regions (Rosenberg et al. 1999). Roberts and Norment (1999) found that in western New York pairing success was high in all forest patches greater than 10 ha (25 a), but fledging success increased significantly with forest size. Their study sites were generally in the Midwest region studied by Rosenberg et al. (1999). The Scarlet Tanager is not a state-listed species, but it is identified as a Species of Greatest Conservation Need in New York's Comprehensive Wildlife Conservation Strategy (NYSDEC 2005a). In addition, the Partners in Flight North American Landbird Conservation Plan suggests that it may be vulnerable because of its relatively restricted winter range (Rich et al. 2004). The entire breeding range of the species is well covered by BBS routes, so monitoring efforts are generally considered adequate (Rich et al. 2004), but because of its area sensitivity and declining population trend in the state, continued conservation concern is warranted.

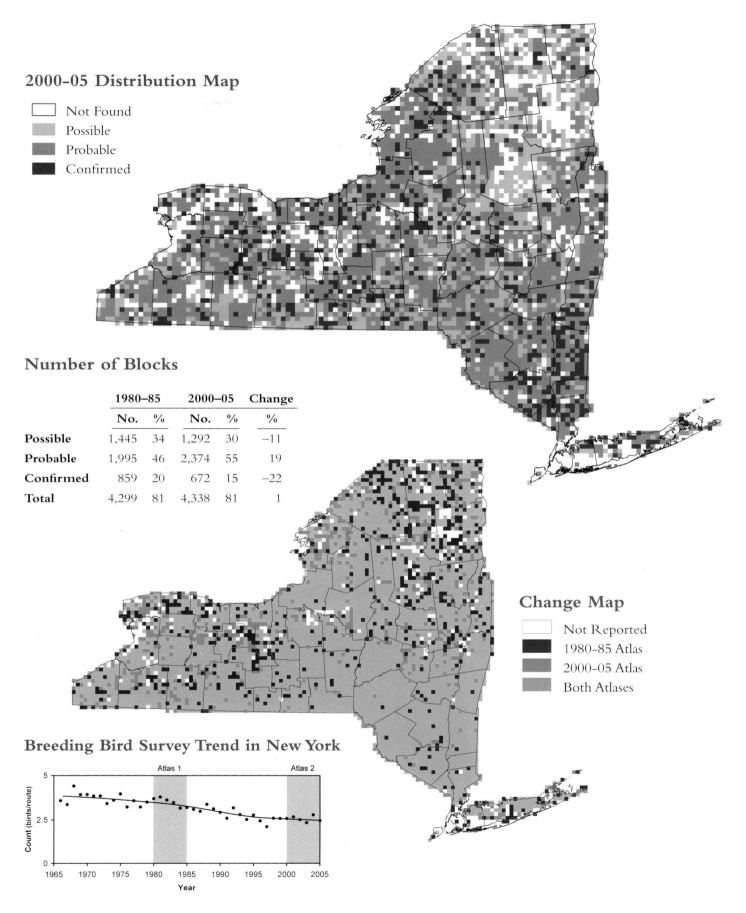

2000–05 Distribution Map

- ☐ Not Found
- Possible
- Probable
- Confirmed

Number of Blocks

	1980–85		2000–05		Change
	No.	%	No.	%	%
Possible	1,445	34	1,292	30	−11
Probable	1,995	46	2,374	55	19
Confirmed	859	20	672	15	−22
Total	4,299	81	4,338	81	1

Change Map

- ☐ Not Reported
- 1980-85 Atlas
- 2000-05 Atlas
- Both Atlases

Breeding Bird Survey Trend in New York

Chipping and Song sparrows at Saratoga Battlefield

Large grasslands are becoming increasingly rare across the state. Those at the Saratoga Battlefield in eastern New York provide breeding habitat for many common field-nesting species, as well as rare species, including breeding Henslow's Sparrows and wintering Short-eared Owls.

©SdA 2006

Eastern Towhee
Pipilo erythrophthalmus

KEVIN J. MCGOWAN

A large, long-tailed sparrow of shrubby habitats, the Eastern Towhee is found across the eastern United States into southern Canada. It breeds in habitats with low, dense cover, often in dry environments with open ground, and can be found in old fields, forest edges, dune scrub, oak scrub, pine barrens, and riparian thickets (Greenlaw 1996). New York is near the northern edge of its range. As a bird of early-successional habitats, the Eastern Towhee was probably less common before European settlement, when it might have been found primarily in pine barrens and areas of forest disturbance. The creation of open areas after settlement provided much potential towhee habitat. Giraud (1844) called the towhee common on Long Island, and Rathbun (1879) termed it "not uncommon" in central New York, but Short (1893) considered it a rare breeder in western New York. Merriam (1881) called it rare and confined to the borders of the Adirondacks. Eaton (1914) said the towhee was generally distributed as a breeder throughout the state, being most common in the southeastern portion and not common in the Catskills, Adirondacks, or the northern counties. Bull (1974) indicated that it moved northward in the state over the last half of the 20th century. It has probably always been most common on Long Island, as pine barrens are areas of concentration across the range (Greenlaw 1996).

The first Atlas map showed the Eastern Towhee distributed throughout the state, missing only from urban areas, the Adirondacks, Central Tug Hill, Catskill Peaks, Champlain Valley and Transition, parts of the Mohawk Valley, and the Erie-Ontario Plain. Arbib (1988g) attributed its absence in the lower-elevation areas to intensive agriculture that left no brushy borders, although he mentioned areas of suitable habitat without towhees. Data from the second Atlas indicated a decline in the distribution of the Eastern Towhee across the state. It was found in fewer blocks in each ecozone, with the exception of the Champlain Valley, Great Lakes Plain, and Tug Hill Plateau. The overall distribution of the towhee in the state was comparable to that reported in the first Atlas, being widespread but absent from the Adirondacks, Catskill Peaks, and much of the western Great Lakes Plain.

Breeding Bird Survey data show that Eastern Towhee populations have been declining since the survey started in 1966, both survey-wide and in the north Atlantic states (U.S. Fish and Wildlife Service Region 5) (Sauer et al. 2005). BBS data show a significant decline in New York since the early 1970s, with the steepest decline occurring between 1970 and 1980, and a continuing 3.9 percent per year drop since 1980 (Sauer et al. 2005). The second Ontario Breeding Bird Atlas reported a significant decline in the southernmost region of the province but no significant change province-wide (Bird Studies Canada et al. 2006). Declines in the amount of shrubland, resulting primarily from the maturation of forests and the spread of urbanization, are causing problems for the Eastern Towhee across its range (Greenlaw 1996), and Partners in Flight considers it a Continental Stewardship Species (Rich et al. 2004).

Baird (1990) found dramatic declines in Eastern Towhee numbers in Allegany State Park between 1930 and 1985, with the number of estimated pairs dropping from 311 to 54. The pasture and early-successional stages that contained all of the towhees in 1930 and 1931 (Saunders 1936) had disappeared in the next 50 years. Baird found the towhee to be the most common bird in his "thicket" habitat, but only 178 ha (440 a) of that existed, in contrast to the 1,147 ha (2,834 a) of towhee-containing pasture, sprout oak-hickory, and aspen-cherry in 1930. The 83 percent decline in towhees at Allegany corresponded to an 84 percent decline in suitable habitat there, indicating that habitat loss is indeed the most serious issue facing towhees in New York.

2000-05 Distribution Map

- ☐ Not Found
- ▨ Possible
- ▨ Probable
- ■ Confirmed

Number of Blocks

	1980–85		2000–05		Change
	No.	%	No.	%	%
Possible	1,112	30	867	26	−22
Probable	1,636	44	1,683	51	3
Confirmed	1,010	27	763	23	−24
Total	3,758	70	3,313	62	−12

Change Map

- ☐ Not Reported
- ■ 1980–85 Atlas
- ▨ 2000–05 Atlas
- ▨ Both Atlases

Breeding Bird Survey Trend in New York

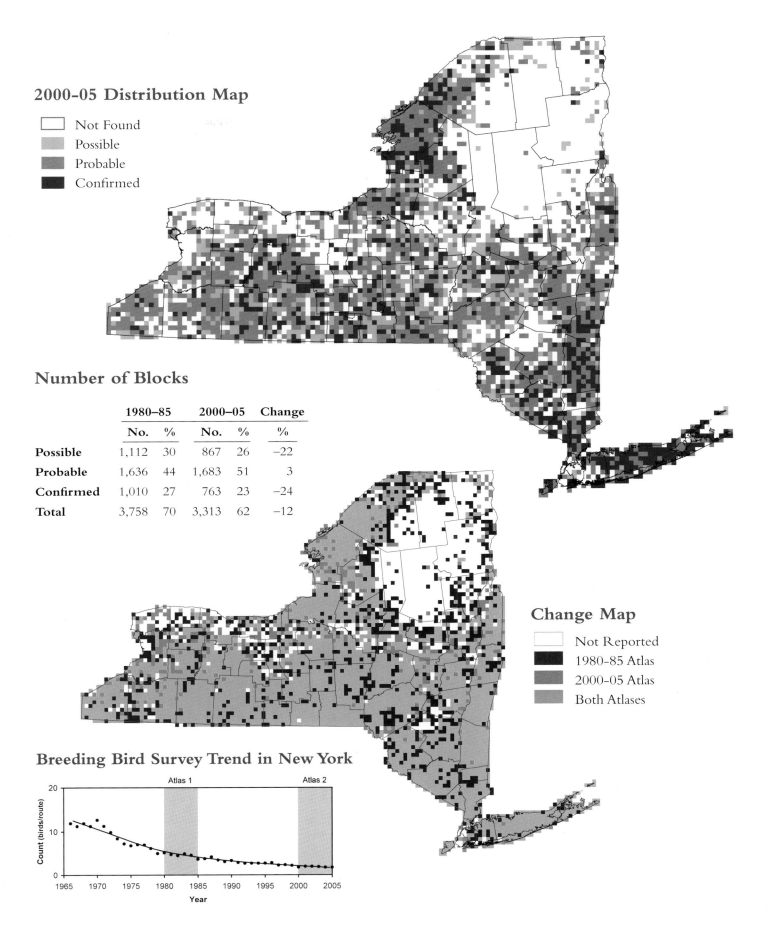

Chipping Sparrow
Spizella passerina

KEVIN J. McGOWAN

A small bird of open areas, the Chipping Sparrow is often found breeding near people. It breeds from very eastern Alaska through Canada, southward to the southern United States and into Mexico and Central America, absent only from the southern Great Plains and Florida. It breeds in open woodlands with grass, along river and lake shorelines, and in orchards, farms, urban and suburban parks, and residential neighborhoods. It often puts its nest in a small coniferous tree surrounded by grass or an open area (Middleton 1998). Because of its habitat preference it probably was less common in New York before European settlement. By the mid-1800s it was common, breeding in gardens, fields, and roadsides across most of the state (Giraud 1844, Rathbun 1879, Short 1893).

During the first Atlas survey, the Chipping Sparrow was found in 91 percent of blocks, being sparsely distributed only in parts of the Adirondacks, the Tug Hill Plateau, most of New York City, and western Long Island. The second Atlas survey did not reveal much change in the bird's distribution. It was found in 92 percent of blocks and still missing from parts of the Adirondacks, the Tug Hill Plateau, most of New York City, and western Long Island. Because of its conspicuous singing and its propensity to nest near humans, the Chipping Sparrow was an easy bird for atlasers to detect and confirm. It was the ninth most commonly confirmed species, with most confirmations resulting from an observation of adults feeding young.

Both Arbib (1988a) and Cook (1998) speculated that the blank blocks in the Adirondacks might fill in over the years with increased forest cutting and recreation, but that has not happened. The distribution of the Chipping Sparrow declined very slightly in the Adirondacks, present in 865 Adirondack blocks during the first Atlas period and 846 during the second.

Breeding Bird Survey data show no changes in population status across the entire survey, but data from New York show a significant decline of 0.8 percent per year since 1966 (Sauer et al. 2007). Such a small decline in such an abundant species would be difficult to detect with Atlas methods. Loss of farmland and the maturation of forests could be causing the slight decline noted. The second Ontario Breeding Bird Atlas reported no significant change in Chipping Sparrow numbers across the province but did detect a significant increase on the Northern Shield and a significant decline on the Southern Shield (Bird Studies Canada et al. 2006). Because of the Chipping Sparrow's fondness for the open grassy spaces with scattered trees created by people, it is unlikely that dramatic changes in its population status will occur any time soon.

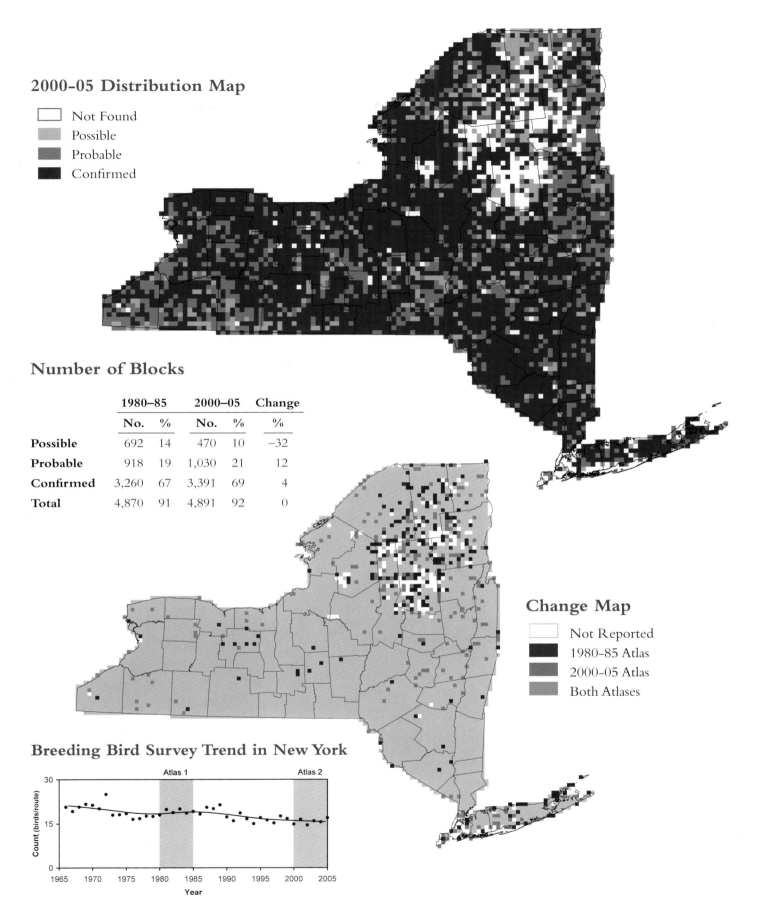

2000–05 Distribution Map

- ☐ Not Found
- Possible
- Probable
- Confirmed

Number of Blocks

	1980–85		2000–05		Change
	No.	%	No.	%	%
Possible	692	14	470	10	–32
Probable	918	19	1,030	21	12
Confirmed	3,260	67	3,391	69	4
Total	4,870	91	4,891	92	0

Change Map

- ☐ Not Reported
- 1980–85 Atlas
- 2000–05 Atlas
- Both Atlases

Breeding Bird Survey Trend in New York

CHIPPING SPARROW   547

Clay-colored Sparrow
Spizella pallida

CHARLES R. SMITH

The Clay-colored Sparrow, a characteristic bird of the northern prairies of North America, is an uncommon breeder in New York. Its North American breeding range extends in a relatively narrow band from eastern British Columbia and eastern Washington, eastward across the northern Great Plains to northern Michigan, central and southern Ontario, and southern Quebec (Knapton 1994). New York is at the southeastern extent of the breeding range. A bird of open shrublands, this sparrow's breeding habitats include abandoned pastures and hayfields that have been invaded by shrubs and saplings, regenerating clear-cuts, and young conifer plantations. It often shares those habitats with the Chipping Sparrow, with which it is known to hybridize—at least two mixed-species breeding pairs have been reported from New York (Novak 1998a). The first New York specimen of Clay-colored Sparrow was taken in 1935 in Ithaca (Bull 1974), and the first breeding record occurred there in 1960 (paired with a Chipping Sparrow) (McIlroy 1961). Although sightings of migrants became nearly annual along the coast in the 1950s (Bull 1974), the second confirmed breeding did not occur until 1971, in Allegany County (Brooks 1971).

During the first Atlas survey, the Clay-colored Sparrow was found in only 23 blocks scattered across the state. The greatest concentration was in east-central Allegany County, with a second concentration in eastern Jefferson County. The single Confirmed breeding report came from Columbia County. The second Atlas survey revealed that the number of blocks with reports of the Clay-colored Sparrow tripled. Breeding was confirmed from 12 counties but not from Columbia County, where the bird was not detected at all. The species was widely distributed in most ecozones north of the Hudson Highlands. The largest concentration of records was on the Fort Drum Military Installation in eastern Jefferson County. Because the Clay-colored Sparrow's buzzy, insect-like song does not carry far and might be overlooked by an inexperienced observer, it is possible that this species is more widespread as a breeder in New York than suggested by current Atlas information.

On a continental level, Clay-colored Sparrow numbers declined significantly across the Breeding Bird Survey area since 1980, with decreases greatest in the prairie provinces where the species is most abundant (Sauer et al. 2007). BBS data for New York and the Northeast are too sparse to determine either a population trend or relative abundance (Sauer et al. 2007). As in New York, results reported in the Ontario and Pennsylvania Breeding Bird atlases show expansions of breeding ranges for this sparrow. With only three field seasons completed, the second Pennsylvania Atlas data already documented the Clay-colored Sparrow in 21 blocks, compared with only 3 blocks during the first Pennsylvania Atlas survey (D. A. Brauning pers. comm.). In Ontario, the range expansion occurred throughout the province, and a significant population now exists across the border from northern New York (Bird Studies Canada et al. 2006). These patterns are consistent with an eastward range expansion for this species that has been documented over the past 100 years and appears to be continuing (Knapton 1994), though reasons for the expansion are not clear. Abandonment of farmland in the eastern part of the range, followed by ecological succession (see Chapter 4), might be creating more habitats suitable for this species and facilitating its range expansion. The Clay-colored Sparrow is not identified as a Species of Conservation Concern by Partners in Flight (Rich et al. 2004). Given its widespread occurrence at Fort Drum, an opportunity exists there for gaining a better understanding of the ecology, habitat associations, and breeding biology at the eastern extent of this bird's breeding range.

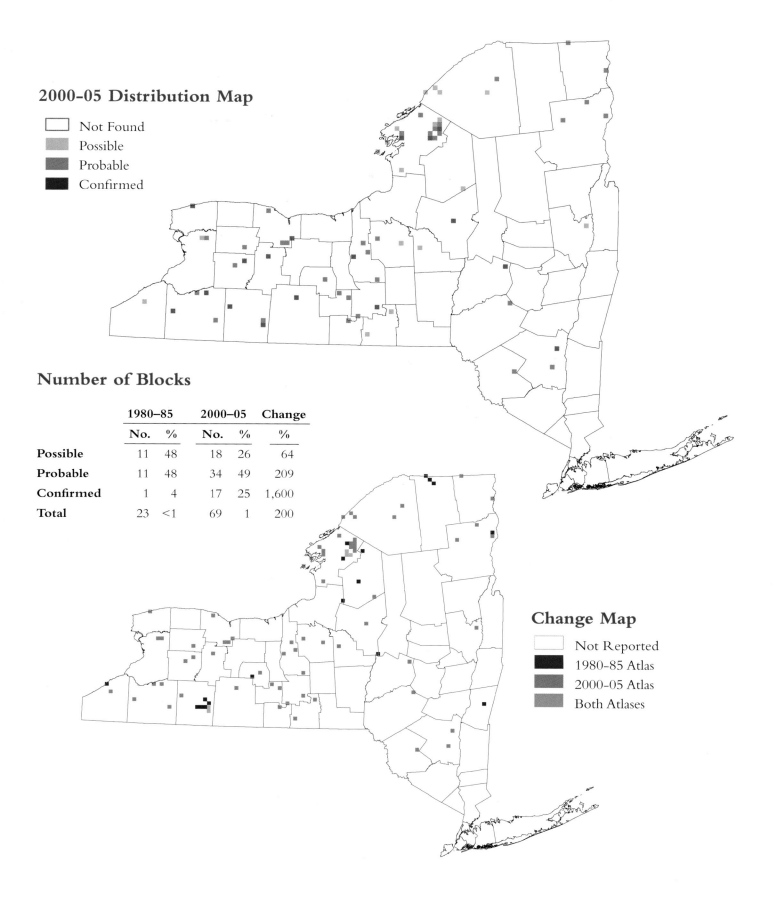

2000-05 Distribution Map

- Not Found
- Possible
- Probable
- Confirmed

Number of Blocks

| | 1980–85 | | 2000–05 | | Change |
	No.	%	No.	%	%
Possible	11	48	18	26	64
Probable	11	48	34	49	209
Confirmed	1	4	17	25	1,600
Total	23	<1	69	1	200

Change Map

- Not Reported
- 1980-85 Atlas
- 2000-05 Atlas
- Both Atlases

Field Sparrow

Spizella pusilla

Timothy J. Post

The Field Sparrow has a distinctive song of almost lyrical notes, ascending the scale and then ending in a trill. It is a common songbird in New York that breeds in old fields, brushy pastures, second-growth shrublands, woodland openings and edges, roadsides, and railroads near open fields (Carey et al. 1994). It will nest in old fields directly after a burn or within a year of cultivation, but only if scattered woody vegetation with elevated perches are present (Carey et al. 1994). As succession changes old fields into a more forested state, Field Sparrow numbers decline. Peterjohn and Rice (1991) noted that it does not breed close to human habitation. The Field Sparrow breeds throughout the eastern two-thirds of the United States, from eastern Montana to southern Ontario and southern Maine, southward to central Texas and northern Florida (Carey et al. 1994). New York is near the northeastern limit of the breeding range. Prior to European settlement the Field Sparrow was probably found only in habitats created by natural disturbance in New York. The clearing of forests for agriculture and for timber must have dramatically increased Field Sparrow populations in many portions of New York (Arbib 1988c). Early authors reported that it was common to abundant in New York by the mid-1800s (DeKay 1844, Giraud 1844, Rathbun 1879), and it continued to be abundant throughout much of New York through the early 1900s (Eaton 1914, Griscom 1923). Beginning in the early to mid-1900s and continuing through much of the 20th century, many farmlands were abandoned and substantial portions of the state reverted to forest (Stanton and Bills 1996). Further, those areas still in agriculture became more intensively managed. These changes in land use resulted in reduced acreage of old-field habitat in New York, and correspondingly the amount of suitable Field Sparrow habitat across the state decreased. Bull (1974) reported that the Field Sparrow was found throughout much of New York but was rare in the northern portions and absent from the mountains.

During the first Atlas period the Field Sparrow was found throughout the state, with gaps seen only in higher, more forested regions, such as most of the Adirondacks, Central Tug Hill, Catskill Peaks, and Allegany Hills, as well as in the St. Lawrence Plains, Champlain Valley, and the predominantly urban Buffalo and greater New York City areas. The second Atlas findings showed the same general distribution but an overall decline of 16 percent in the number of blocks with records. Areas of the state with the largest losses included the Adirondacks, Champlain Valley, Mohawk Valley, Catskill Peaks, Hudson Valley, Hudson Highlands, Manhattan Hills, Triassic Lowlands, and Coastal Lowlands. Although the male's singing diminishes after he finds a mate (Carey et al. 1994), the Field Sparrow is a relatively easily detected species because of its distinctive and persistent song.

The Breeding Bird Survey data indicate that Field Sparrow numbers have declined at a rate of 3.9 percent per year since 1966 in New York, 3.8 percent in the north Atlantic states (U.S. Fish and Wildlife Service Region 5), and 3 percent survey-wide (Sauer et al. 2005). A 4 percent decline per year over the last 40 years equates to a loss of 80 percent of the Field Sparrow population in New York. Despite these declines, the Field Sparrow does not appear as a species of high conservation concern on any national bird conservation lists. This situation is primarily because the Field Sparrow is still common and widespread throughout much of New York and its range. Threats to Field Sparrow habitat include forest succession, more intensive agricultural practices, and development. With these habitat changes, the scrubby old fields that support species like the Field Sparrow are lost. Like other birds of early-successional habitats, it is likely that the Field Sparrow populations will continue to decline in New York for the foreseeable future.

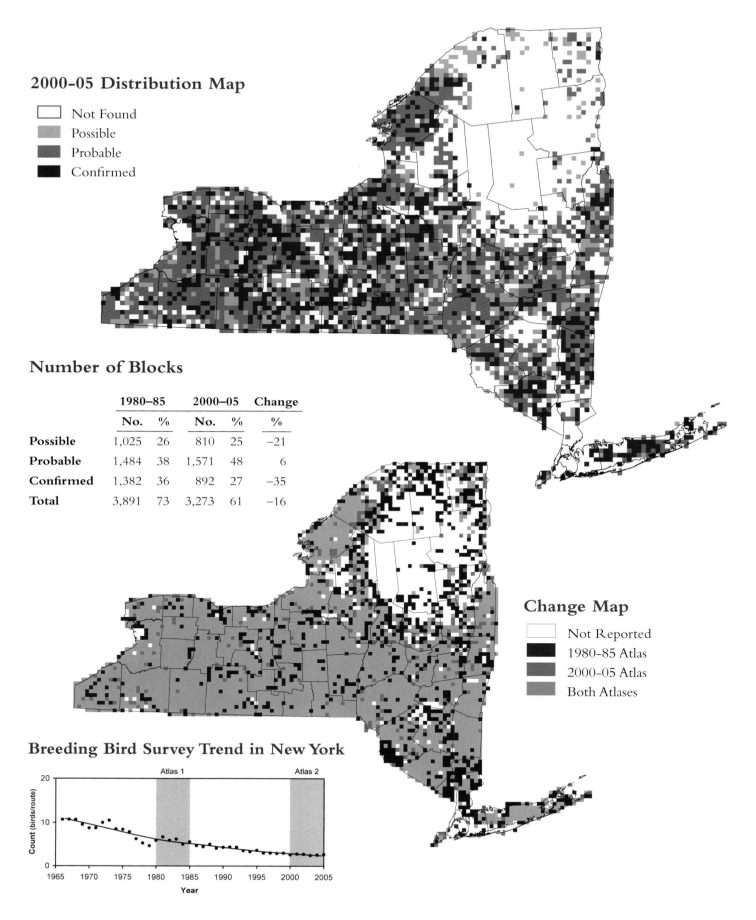

2000-05 Distribution Map

- ☐ Not Found
- Possible
- Probable
- Confirmed

Number of Blocks

	1980–85		2000–05		Change
	No.	%	No.	%	%
Possible	1,025	26	810	25	−21
Probable	1,484	38	1,571	48	6
Confirmed	1,382	36	892	27	−35
Total	3,891	73	3,273	61	−16

Change Map

- ☐ Not Reported
- 1980-85 Atlas
- 2000-05 Atlas
- Both Atlases

Breeding Bird Survey Trend in New York

Vesper Sparrow
Pooecetes gramineus

CHARLES R. SMITH

Named for its habit of singing just before dusk, the Vesper Sparrow breeds from coast to coast across southern Canada and the northern half of the United States (Jones and Cornely 2002). It reaches its greatest abundance in central Montana and southeastern Manitoba, gradually becoming less abundant eastward (Sauer et al. 2005). As a bird of open habitats, the Vesper Sparrow probably was not common in New York before European settlement, but it was abundant in grassy areas throughout the state by the mid to late 19th century (Giraud 1844, Rathbun 1879, Merriam 1881, Short 1893, Reed and Wright 1909). It may have been most numerous shortly after 1900 where sheep were common as grazing animals (Nicholson 1985). The sheep's habit of closely cropping vegetation and a tendency toward overgrazing probably created much optimal habitat for the Vesper Sparrow in the early 20th century; Eaton (1914) called the sparrow common in all parts of the state. Bull (1974) described it as a widespread breeder but rare and local on Long Island and declining inland as well. Baird (1990) reported the complete disappearance of this species from Allegany State Park between 1930 and 1985, coincident with a loss of open, grassy areas within the park. The Vesper Sparrow prefers open-land habitats with short grass and a substantial amount of bare ground (Wiens 1969), rather than hayfields or grassy meadows. The preference of the sparrow for agricultural fields most likely is a reflection of its requirement for bare ground somewhere in its breeding territory. It has been found in potato fields, cornfields, and over-grazed pastures (pers. obs.).

During the first Atlas survey, the Vesper Sparrow was found throughout the state, most numerous in the central regions of the Erie-Ontario Plain and the Central Appalachians. It was mostly absent from the higher elevations of the Adirondack, Allegheny, and Catskill mountains, the southern portions of the Hudson Valley, and western Coastal Lowlands. The second Atlas results showed a similar distribution but with a 49 percent decline in the number of blocks with records. Declines occurred in all ecozones, with its breeding distribution becoming more patchy throughout most of its former range. Some consolidation and expansion of its range might have occurred in the western Great Lakes Plain and northwestern Appalachian Plateau (Genesee, Wyoming, and Livingston counties), but such local changes could also be the result of differences in coverage.

Breeding Bird Survey data show significant and consistent declines throughout the Vesper Sparrow's range since 1966 (Sauer et al. 2005). In New York, Vesper Sparrow numbers declined at a statistically significant annual rate of 7.9 percent over the period 1966–2005, nearly disappearing from the survey. Comparable rates of decline for the north Atlantic states (U.S. Fish and Wildlife Service Region 5) are statistically significant for both the longer time period and since 1980 (Sauer et al. 2005). The second Ontario Breeding Bird Atlas reported significant decreases across that province (Bird Studies Canada et al. 2006). Partners in Flight does not identify any specific conservation needs for the Vesper Sparrow (Rich et al. 2004) despite the declining population trend. The bird is listed as Threatened or Endangered at the state level in the adjoining states of Massachusetts, Connecticut, and New Jersey. Because of the documented decline of its breeding population in New York, the Vesper Sparrow is listed as a Species of Special Concern in New York. With continued loss of early-successional habitats, further declines in the distribution and abundance of the Vesper Sparrow in New York and the Northeast can be expected. This species could benefit from an increase in attention being given to the conservation needs of grassland birds, although its requirement for bare ground and shorter grass sets it apart from most other species of grassland birds.

2000–05 Distribution Map

- ☐ Not Found
- ▨ Possible
- ▨ Probable
- ■ Confirmed

Number of Blocks

	1980–85		2000–05		Change
	No.	%	No.	%	%
Possible	480	43	208	37	−57
Probable	456	41	272	48	−40
Confirmed	180	16	84	15	−53
Total	1,116	21	564	11	−49

Change Map

- ☐ Not Reported
- ■ 1980–85 Atlas
- ▨ 2000–05 Atlas
- ▨ Both Atlases

Breeding Bird Survey Trend in New York

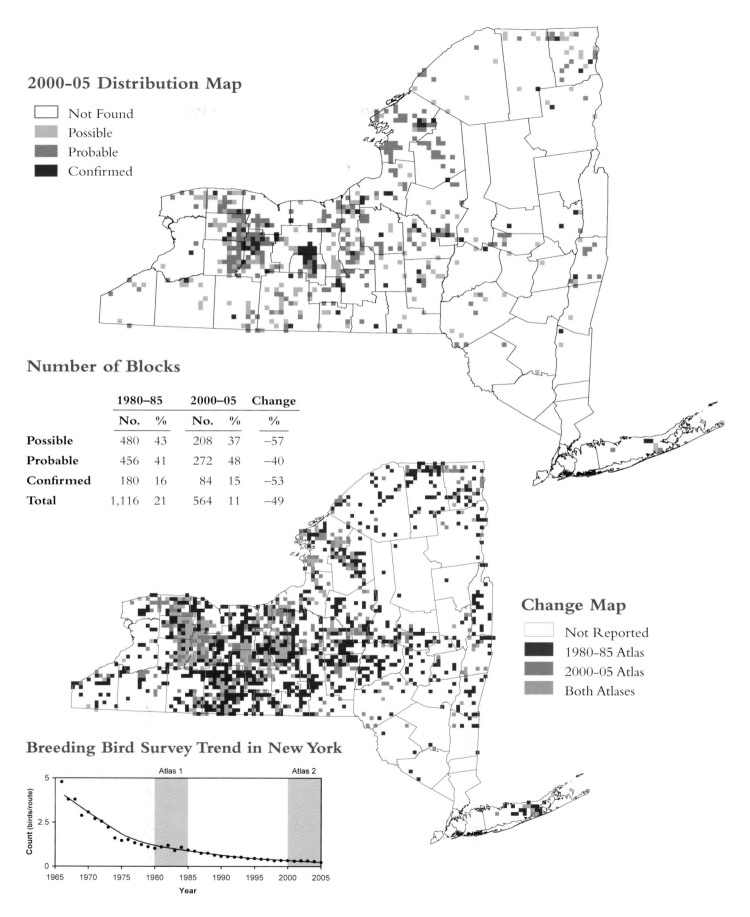

Savannah Sparrow

Passerculus sandwichensis

KEVIN J. McGOWAN

A common bird of open country, the Savannah Sparrow breeds all across Canada and the northern United States, southward to Mexico and in the mountains to Georgia (Wheelwright and Rising 1993). It breeds in a variety of open habitats, including meadows, agricultural fields, pastures, salt marshes, and tundra (Wheelwright and Rising 1993). The Savannah Sparrow accepts a wider range of open and early-successional habitats than other grassland sparrows (Smith 1998e), and in New York it uses grassy fields with scattered forbs; fields of alfalfa, clover, and trefoil; maritime dunes and sand fill covered with beach grass or weeds; and sphagnum bogs (J. M. C. Peterson 1988p). Probably rare before European settlement, this sparrow undoubtedly benefited from the opening of the forests in colonial New York, and populations may have peaked there in the early 20th century. Giraud (1844) noted that it was common on Long Island, and especially numerous on the Hempstead Plains. Most 19th-century authors called it common across the state (DeKay 1844, Rathbun 1879, Short 1893), although Merriam (1881) noted that it was rare in the Adirondacks but breeding in appropriate spots. Eaton (1914) called the Savannah Sparrow a common breeder throughout most of the state, less common in the Coastal Lowlands. Bull (1974) considered the species to be most numerous on Long Island, especially on the southern shore, and common but local upstate, present wherever suitable fields occurred. Bull (1976) noted that the sparrow was disappearing precipitously from the southern shore.

The first Atlas map showed the Savannah Sparrow to be widespread throughout the state, missing only from areas of high elevation and heavy forest cover, and high urban development. Its presence on Long Island appeared much reduced from what Bull (1974) reported. Little change in distribution was seen between the two Atlas periods. The Savannah Sparrow was still found in suitable habitat across the state, in just 2 percent more blocks. Gaps in its distribution were seen in the Allegany Hills, Central Adirondacks, Adirondack High Peaks, Sable Highlands, much of the Western Adirondack Foothills, Central Tug Hill, Catskill Peaks, Delaware Hills, Mongaup Hills, Rensselaer Hills, Hudson Highlands, and Coastal Lowlands. The largest increase was in the Catskill Highlands. It declined most in the Coastal Lowlands, with the number of blocks with records decreasing 37 percent. The appearance and loss of this species from individual blocks across the state could well be the result of differences in coverage for the Atlas projects.

Despite declining populations, the Savannah Sparrow received a relatively low Partners in Flight assessment score because of its wide breeding range and large population size (Rich et al. 2004). Breeding Bird Survey data survey-wide show the species undergoing a slight, though significant, decrease in numbers since 1980 (Sauer et al. 2005). BBS data from New York show a more pronounced decline of 2.6 percent a year since 1966 and a significant decline of 2 percent per year since 1980 (Sauer et al. 2005). As in New York, BBS data for Ontario showed significant population declines, but the second Breeding Bird Atlas survey there failed to find significant changes in Savannah Sparrow populations (Bird Studies Canada et al. 2006). Increasing forest cover over the last 50 years, as well as the continuing loss of agricultural land, and increasing development all should lead to a decline in Savannah Sparrow populations in New York (Smith 1998e), as for many other grassland birds. Despite these factors, no change over the last 20 years is apparent in Atlas data. Because of its wide habitat tolerances, the Savannah Sparrow is able to take advantage of the scattered open areas that appear or are maintained. It is possible that populations in New York are declining, but enough blocks have at least some pairs remaining that the decline is not yet apparent. Perhaps the next Atlas project will reveal a more gloomy result.

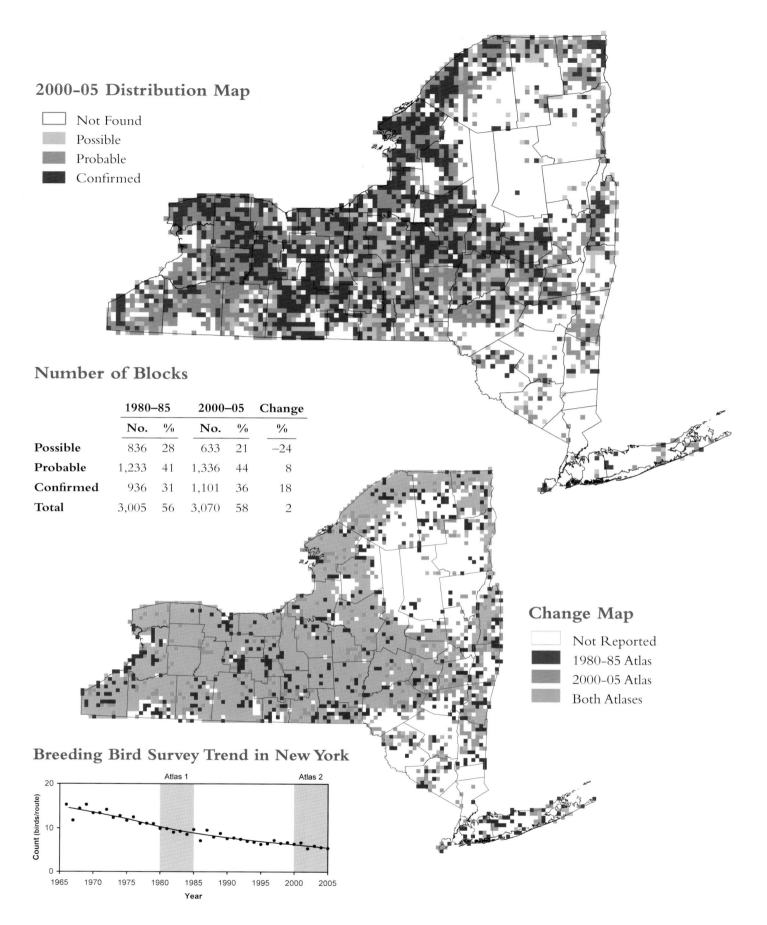

2000-05 Distribution Map

- ☐ Not Found
- Possible
- Probable
- Confirmed

Number of Blocks

| | 1980–85 | | 2000–05 | | Change |
	No.	%	No.	%	%
Possible	836	28	633	21	−24
Probable	1,233	41	1,336	44	8
Confirmed	936	31	1,101	36	18
Total	3,005	56	3,070	58	2

Change Map

- ☐ Not Reported
- 1980-85 Atlas
- 2000-05 Atlas
- Both Atlases

Breeding Bird Survey Trend in New York

Grasshopper Sparrow

Ammodramus savannarum

CHARLES R. SMITH

A bird of open grasslands and prairies, the Grasshopper Sparrow breeds throughout most of the United States east of the Rocky Mountains and south and west of northern Vermont, with disjunct breeding populations in Georgia, Florida, coastal California, the Pacific Northwest, Mexico, the Caribbean, and Central and South America (Vickery 1996). New York lies near the northeastern extent of its breeding range. The Grasshopper Sparrow reaches its greatest abundance in the Great Plains, east of the Rocky Mountains and west of the Mississippi River (Sauer et al. 2005). Although Vickery (1996) reported that this sparrow uses open grasslands with patches of bare ground, and usually avoids areas with an extensive shrub cover, that is not always the case in New York (Smith 1997, Mitchell et al. 2000). Arbib (1988d) suggested that the Grasshopper Sparrow most likely was a rare and local breeding bird in a forested, pre-colonial landscape. Removal of the forest for agriculture allowed the species to spread through the state. Eaton's (1910) map showed the species as widespread across the lowlands of the southern half of New York, from Long Island through western New York, including portions of the Coastal Lowlands, Hudson Valley, central Appalachian Plateau, and Great Lakes Plain. Bull (1974) described the species as "numerous" only on Long Island before 1950, but said it was much reduced there, occurred at lower numbers across the lowlands of the state, and was rare in the St. Lawrence and Champlain valleys. Studies in western New York showed that Grasshopper Sparrow populations are not likely to persist in suitable habitats smaller than 8 ha (20 a) (Balent and Norment 2003).

The first Atlas map showed the species to be widespread on Long Island and in the central and southern Appalachian Plateau northward to the Great Lakes Plain, with scattered reports at lower elevations across the state. The second Atlas survey revealed a 42 percent decline in Grasshopper Sparrow distribution. The greatest decline was in the Appalachian Plateau. The species was not detected from the western half of Long Island, and its statewide distribution became much patchier. It held its own in the northeastern Great Lakes Plain (Jefferson County). Though its buzzy, insect-like song is distinctive, this sparrow could be overlooked by inexperienced observers.

In New York, Breeding Bird Survey data for the Grasshopper Sparrow show a statistically significant annual rate of decline of 9.4 percent over the period 1966–2005 (Sauer et al. 2005). The population is declining in nearly all parts of its range (Sauer et al. 2005). Distribution of the species showed little change in Ontario between the first and second Atlas surveys conducted there, although it declined significantly in the southernmost region (Bird Studies Canada et al. 2006). Partners in Flight considers the Grasshopper Sparrow a Species of Continental Importance for the United States and Canada (Rich et al. 2004). It is listed as either Threatened or Endangered at the state level in the adjoining states of Massachusetts, Connecticut, and New Jersey. The gradual disappearance of the Grasshopper Sparrow from New York coincides with the patterns of declining agriculture, suburban development, and regrowth of forests described by other researchers (see Chapter 4). Because of its specialized habitat requirements, declining breeding population, and limited breeding distribution in New York, the Grasshopper Sparrow has been identified as a Species of Special Concern in New York since 1985. With continued loss of early-successional habitats, further declines in the distribution and abundance of the Grasshopper Sparrow in New York and in the Northeast can be expected. The increased attention being given to the conservation needs of grassland birds could benefit this species.

2000-05 Distribution Map

- ☐ Not Found
- Possible
- Probable
- Confirmed

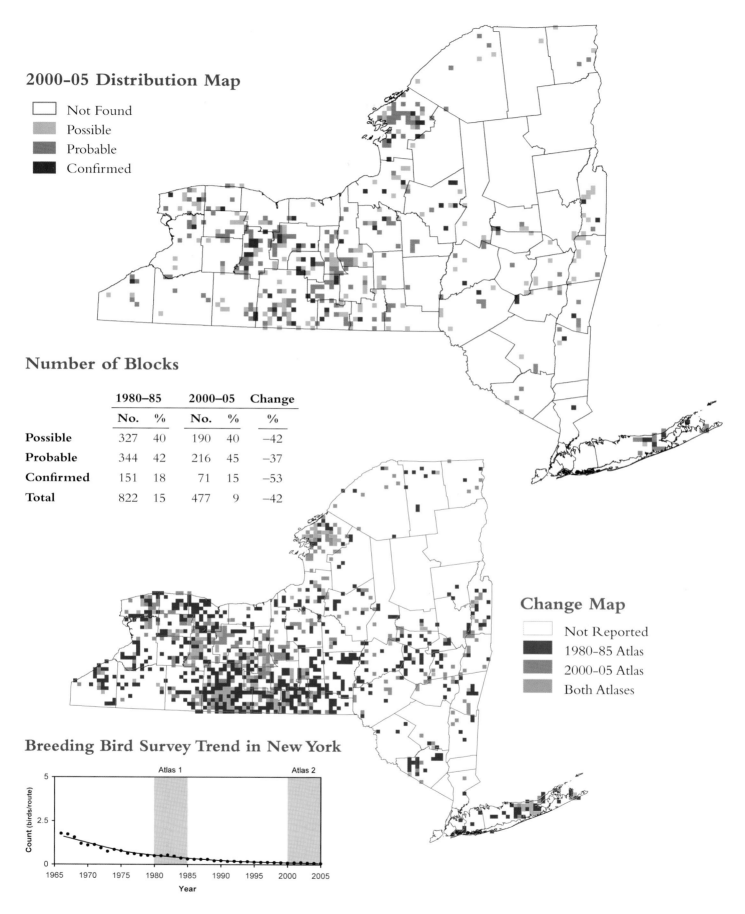

Number of Blocks

	1980–85		2000–05		Change
	No.	%	No.	%	%
Possible	327	40	190	40	−42
Probable	344	42	216	45	−37
Confirmed	151	18	71	15	−53
Total	822	15	477	9	−42

Change Map

- ☐ Not Reported
- 1980-85 Atlas
- 2000-05 Atlas
- Both Atlases

Breeding Bird Survey Trend in New York

Atlas 1   Atlas 2

Count (birds/route)

Year

Henslow's Sparrow
Ammodramus henslowii

KEVIN J. McGOWAN

Henslow's Sparrow is a bird of prairie and wet grasslands. Formerly present from New Hampshire to Kansas, it is now found primarily across the Midwestern states (Herkert et al. 2002). New York represents the eastern boundary of its current range. This sparrow prefers tall, dense grassy fields with no woody plants, some standing dead vegetation, and a thick litter layer (Herkert et al. 2002). It is found largely in pastures, both active and inactive (C. R. Smith 1998b). The Henslow's Sparrow undoubtedly was uncommon in New York before European settlement, although it may well have nested in the native coastal grasslands on Long Island. Giraud (1844) said it occurred on Long Island, and he cited records from Rockland County. Eaton (1914) noted the sparrow as uncommon or rare in all parts of the state, but he did not call it common anywhere. Griscom (1923) called it locally common on Long Island, but it disappeared from there by the 1950s (Bull 1974). Beardslee and Mitchell (1965) indicated the species increased during the early 20th century, peaking in abundance in 1947–52, and then declining to the status of "uncommon . . . in some years." Bull (1974) gave its range as locally common in the northern Hudson Valley, present in the St. Lawrence Valley, locally "not rare" across the Appalachian Plateau, and reaching its most general distribution along the southeast shore of Lake Ontario.

Although considered an uncommon and local breeder during the first Atlas survey, the Henslow's Sparrow was found across much of the state. It was most common in the central and western Appalachian Plateau and the Great Lakes Plain. During the second Atlas period a few birds were present throughout most of the former range, but Henslow's Sparrow underwent an 80 percent decline in the number of blocks with records, the largest proportional decline for any formerly common species reported in the Atlas. The largest concentration remaining in the state is in Jefferson County. This area was not well covered during the first Atlas period, and the apparent increase there is undoubtedly the result of better coverage during the second one. Even there, this sparrow's population declined during the second Atlas period (J. Bolsinger pers. comm.).

The Breeding Bird Survey does not census Henslow's Sparrow well, but existing data show that populations have declined dramatically since 1966 (Sauer et al. 2005). The sparrow was considered for listing as a federally Endangered species in 1998, but the petition was rejected, based on significant increases in the population in the southern Midwest (Herkert et al. 2002). Still, Partners in Flight ranked the sparrow among the most threatened bird species on its Watch List for Landbirds (Rich et al. 2004), and

it is listed as Threatened in New York. Although Henslow's Sparrow formerly bred from Vermont southward to North Carolina, it was virtually gone from New Jersey by the 1970s (Walsh et al. 1999) and now breeds in Massachusetts only occasionally as isolated pairs (Petersen and Meservey 2003). Pennsylvania is the only state that has a significant positive BBS trend for Henslow's Sparrow in the last 20 years (Sauer et al. 2005). There it breeds, to a large extent, on reclaimed strip mines (McWilliams and Brauning 2000).

Loss of farmland, the conversion from pasture to row crops, the regrowth of forests, and the spread of suburbs may account for much of the Henslow's Sparrow decline in New York, but the bird is no longer found in many areas where apparent suitable habitat remains. This fact suggests that other factors are at play, including habitat changes at the landscape level (Lazazzero 2006). Recent increases in Henslow's Sparrow populations in other areas of the country appear to be associated with the creation of managed grassland habitat by the Conservation Reserve Program (Herkert et al. 2002), and the incorporation of similar programs involving private land may help the species recover in New York.

2000-05 Distribution Map

- ☐ Not Found
- ☐ Possible
- ☐ Probable
- ■ Confirmed

Number of Blocks

	1980–85		2000–05		Change
	No.	%	No.	%	%
Possible	135	39	13	19	−90
Probable	152	44	47	67	−69
Confirmed	61	18	10	14	−84
Total	348	7	70	1	−80

Change Map

- ☐ Not Reported
- ■ 1980–85 Atlas
- ☐ 2000–05 Atlas
- ☐ Both Atlases

Breeding Bird Survey Trend in New York

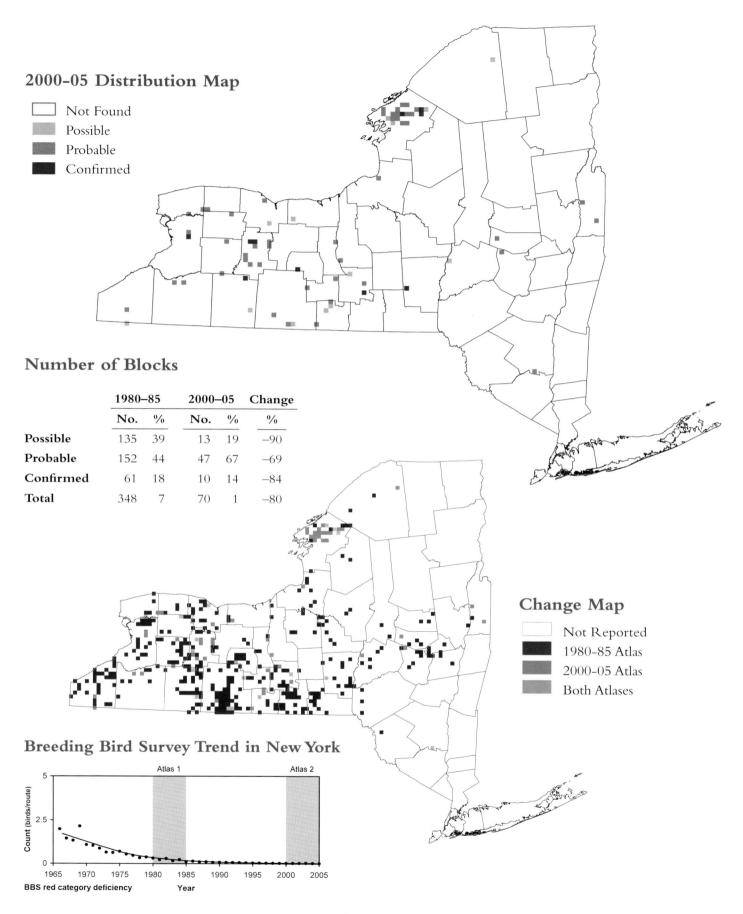

BBS red category deficiency

HENSLOW'S SPARROW 559

Saltmarsh Sharp-tailed Sparrow

Ammodramus caudacutus

Jon S. Greenlaw

The Saltmarsh Sharp-tailed Sparrow is one of the few passerine species in North America that is restricted in all seasons to coastal salt and brackish marshes. It is a regional endemic in the northeastern United States, as it summers in suitable maritime habitat from south-central Maine to northern Virginia (Montagna 1942, Greenlaw and Rising 1994, Hodgman et al. 2002). It favors cordgrass-dominated wet grassland in the upper intertidal and drier saltmeadow habitat (cordgrass, saltgrass) in the supratidal zones, where it can be an abundant breeder locally (Post 1970a, 1970b; J. S. Greenlaw pers. obs.). Only broad outlines of the historic distribution of the Saltmarsh Sharp-tailed Sparrow in New York were provided by early authors (DeKay 1844, Giraud 1844, Eaton 1914). Even then, as now, its headquarters in New York was primarily on Long Island and secondarily in adjoining areas. It must have occurred widely along the coasts of Long Island in summer, as it still does today. This sparrow was found on Staten Island, by inference in Bronx and Westchester counties, and inland on the Hudson River in an isolated tidal marsh at Piermont, Rockland County (Eaton 1914), at least until 1908 (Bull 1964). Until the early 1880s, it also occupied estuarine marshes along the Harlem River (Bull 1964). By the mid-20th century, even with loss of local populations and peripheral shrinkage of its New York range, the species still occurred from Staten Island eastward to Gardiners and Napeague bays on Long Island, and in Bronx and Westchester counties in small numbers (Elliott 1953, 1962; Bull 1964, 1974). Its continued presence on Staten Island after publication of Bull's regional account in 1964 was in doubt. Bull (1974) later included Staten Island within the species's local range, but he provided no supportive evidence.

The first Atlas provided the first comprehensive evaluation of the Saltmarsh Sharp-tailed Sparrow's breeding distribution in New York. Apart from Staten Island and the Piermont Marsh inland on the Hudson River, the sparrow was present in remaining suitable habitat throughout the previously known range in the Coastal Lowlands. The results supported earlier information that summering sharp-tailed sparrows were most widespread in the south shore bays of Long Island. They were less widespread and very local along the north shore, with a gap between the Wading River area and Gardiners Bay where salt marshes were degraded or absent. The second Atlas data showed the Saltmarsh Sharp-tailed Sparrow still occupying all of its modern range on Long Island and in Bronx and Westchester counties, although it was found in 15 percent fewer blocks. Moreover, the study con-firmed its presence on Staten Island, following a report of breeding in 1992 after an apparent 30-year absence (Schiff and Wollin 1992). Once again, the species was most prevalent in the south shore bays. Relative to the first Atlas findings, only one breeding population remained along the Long Island Sound shore in Suffolk County west of Gardiners Bay, producing an even larger geographic gap along this coast. Populations peripheral to the southwestern bays on Long Island are mostly localized and small.

Historically, the Saltmarsh Sharp-tailed Sparrow has suffered from habitat restriction in New York and adjoining regions arising from coastal marsh drainage and shoreline development (e.g., Elliott 1962, Zeranski and Baptist 1990, Walsh et al. 1999). Regional decline remains an issue, and the species is on the Partners in Flight Watch List (Rich et al. 2004). Beyond habitat loss and degradation, reasons for the continued decline are unclear. Breeding Bird Survey data shed little light on long-term population trends in this species, as the survey procedure poorly samples this species's linear, interrupted range (Greenlaw and Rising 1994). Small, localized populations always risk chance extinction. The Saltmarsh Sharp-tailed Sparrow should remain a conservation concern in the state.

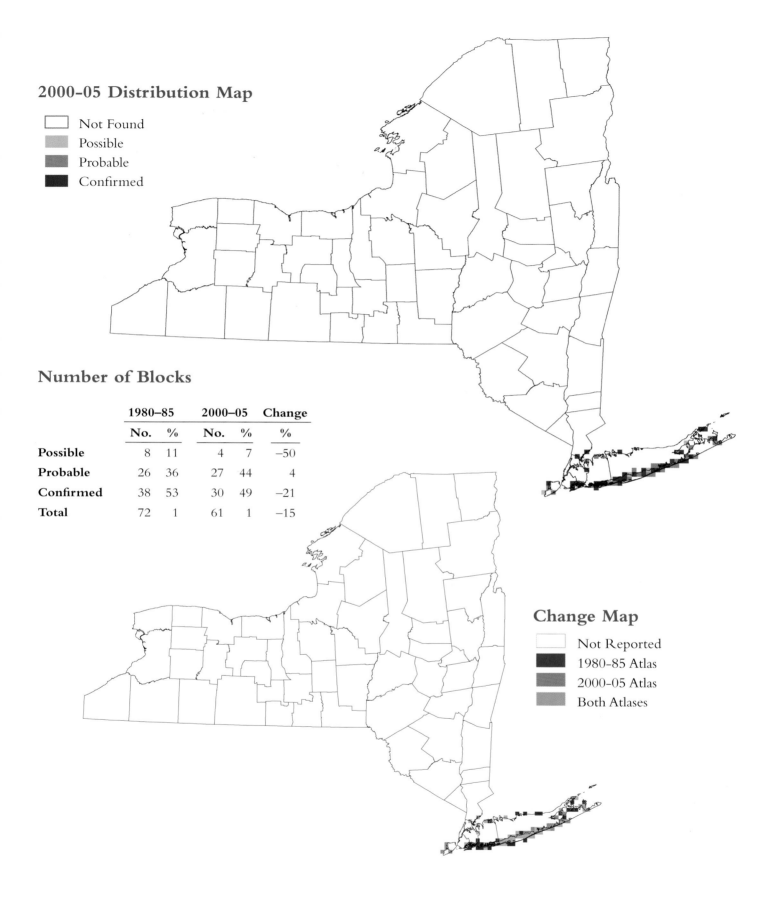

2000–05 Distribution Map

- ☐ Not Found
- Possible
- Probable
- Confirmed

Number of Blocks

	1980–85		2000–05		Change
	No.	%	No.	%	%
Possible	8	11	4	7	−50
Probable	26	36	27	44	4
Confirmed	38	53	30	49	−21
Total	72	1	61	1	−15

Change Map

- ☐ Not Reported
- 1980-85 Atlas
- 2000-05 Atlas
- Both Atlases

Seaside Sparrow
Ammodramus maritimus

JON S. GREENLAW

A tidal marsh specialist, the Seaside Sparrow is a sentinel species whose welfare reflects the health of the coastal wetlands it inhabits. It occurs from Maine to Texas in a broken chain of relatively small populations. In New York, it favors the upper intertidal zone of unaltered marshes (Greenlaw 1983) but also nests at low densities in ditched marshes on grassy marsh elder-dominated spoil deposits (Post 1970, 1974; Greenlaw 1983). Giraud (1844) described it as common to abundant in the south shore bays and on the north shore necks of land on Long Island. Eaton (1914) mentioned it as breeding on Staten Island and inland along the lower Hudson River at Piermont, Rockland County. It has not bred for certain at Piermont Marsh since the late 1800s (Bull 1964), and only a few individuals have been reported there over the last half-century (Treacy 1973). It was formerly present at Orient, Suffolk County, but disappeared early in the 20th century when burning of dry marsh grasses became prevalent (Latham, in Elliott 1962). It bred on Staten Island at least into the 1940s (Cruickshank 1942) but may have become rare or extirpated there by the 1960s (Elliott 1962, Bull 1964). Thus, by mid-century the Seaside Sparrow was still common and widespread in the bays of southwestern Long Island (Cruickshank 1942, Bull 1964), occurred locally in southeastern Long Island (Elliott 1962) and in Bronx and Westchester counties (Griscom 1923, Cruickshank 1942, Bull 1964) and was mostly absent along Long Island Sound (Bull 1964). Bull's (1974) distribution map is over-generalized for that time and best represents the maximal historic distribution in New York.

During the first Atlas period Seaside Sparrow populations were concentrated along the south shore of Long Island from Jamaica Bay, Kings County, to Shinnecock Bay, Suffolk County. In addition, breeding was confirmed along Long Island Sound in Westchester County, and Probable breeding was reported from Gardiners Island and two western locations on the north shore of Long Island. Overall, the distribution of the Seaside Sparrow during the second Atlas period was similar, although the total number of blocks with records declined 25 percent. A concentration of populations was associated with the sheltered bays along the south shore of Long Island eastward to the Southampton area. Scattered peripheral populations still exist, all evidently quite small, such as on Long Island Sound in Rye, Westchester County, and on the east end of Long Island. The sparrow was not recorded in the historically occupied Baychester, Bronx County, site during the first Atlas survey, but was found there again during the second one. It is difficult to determine whether apparently new small, local populations were missed on an earlier survey or represent extirpation and recolonization. Previously, two occupied sites were recorded in the north shores of Queens and Nassau counties, but the recent results suggest that the species may now be gone from the entire north shore of Long Island west of the North Fork. The confirmation of continued breeding on Staten Island, first recorded in 1992 (Schiff and Wollin 1992), is notable.

Breeding Bird Survey data for all eastern populations of the Seaside Sparrow combined show a significant downward trend during 1985–2005, but only a small number of routes are included (Sauer et al. 2005). The historic issue has been local loss and degradation of salt marshes (Elliott 1962, Dahl 1990), and habitat destruction and changes in habitat quality remain problems for tidal wetlands in New York (NYSDEC [2001], Hartig et al. 2002). Climate change may be an emerging factor that can influence the extent and quality of tidal marshes (Hartig et al. 2002). The Seaside Sparrow's current status in New York as a Species of Special Concern is clearly deserved. Outlying, peripheral populations around its core range on Long Island may be ephemeral, but population losses within its core area are more serious and need to be monitored.

2000–05 Distribution Map

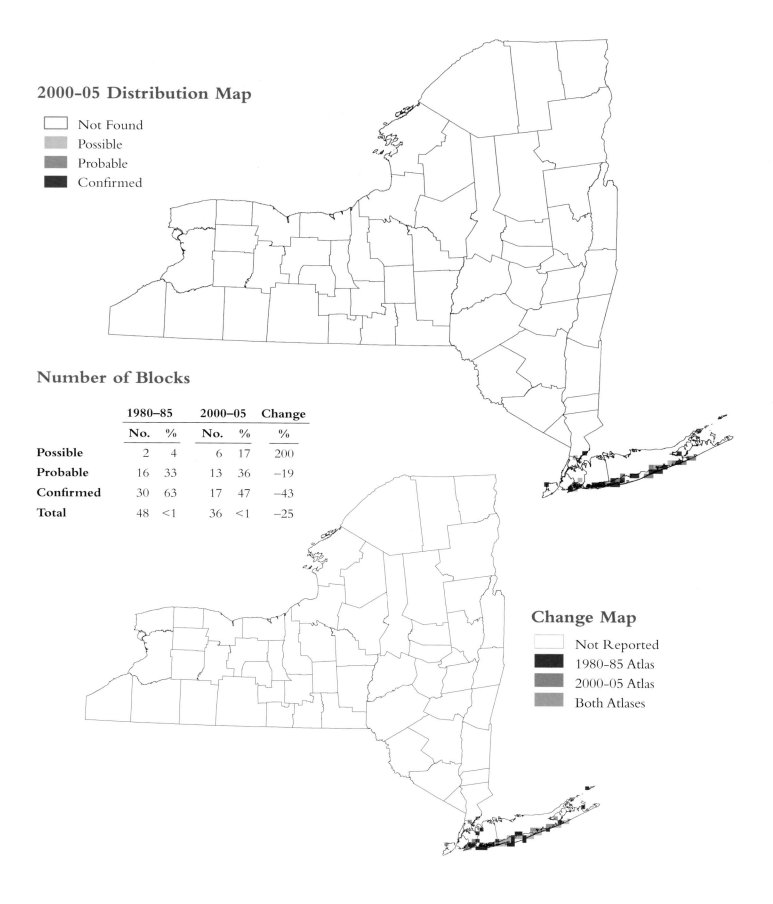

- ☐ Not Found
- Possible
- Probable
- Confirmed

Number of Blocks

	1980–85		2000–05		Change
	No.	%	No.	%	%
Possible	2	4	6	17	200
Probable	16	33	13	36	−19
Confirmed	30	63	17	47	−43
Total	48	<1	36	<1	−25

Change Map

- ☐ Not Reported
- 1980-85 Atlas
- 2000-05 Atlas
- Both Atlases

Song Sparrow
Melospiza melodia

KEVIN J. MCGOWAN

The Song Sparrow is a common and well-known bird that lives in a variety of habitats across most of North America. It breeds from southwestern Alaska across Canada to Newfoundland, and southward to northern Mexico and northern Georgia, as well as in central Mexico, but is missing from much of the Great Plains and the southeastern United States (Arcese et al. 2002). It is found in a wide range of forest, shrub, and riparian habitats, as well as in salt marshes, agricultural areas, suburban parks, and residential areas (Arcese et al. 2002). In New York it is found in all habitats except deep forest, open fields, and marshes devoid of shrubs (Bull 1974). As a species that prefers shrubs, it is likely that the Song Sparrow was less common before the European settlement of New York, but the first accounts in the 19th century called it common to abundant. DeKay (1844) listed it as common but less numerous inland. Giraud (1844) called it one of the most numerous sparrows on Long Island. It was abundant in central and western New York at least by the end of the 19th century (Rathbun 1879, Short 1893, Reed and Wright 1909). Eaton (1914) considered it the most abundant and generally distributed sparrow in the state, common even into the Adirondack wilderness, except in the depths of the forest. Bull (1974) called it a widespread breeder.

During the first Atlas survey, the Song Sparrow was found over nearly the entire state, with gaps only apparent in the Adi-rondack High Peaks, the Central Adirondacks, and in other, scattered blocks where coverage could be an issue. It was the most widespread species reported in the Atlas, found in 97 percent of blocks, in all ecozones. The distribution of the Song Sparrow did not change appreciably in the period between the two Atlas projects. During the second Atlas survey, it was still found in 97 percent of blocks, but its ranking in the list of most common species slipped to fifth. It was still missing from scattered blocks in the Adirondacks, especially in the Adirondack High Peaks and adjacent area of the Central Adirondacks and farther southward in the Central Adirondacks. The Song Sparrow is a persistent singer, and it was an easy species for atlasers to find.

Breeding Bird Survey data indicate that the Song Sparrow has been undergoing a slight (0.6 percent per year) but significant population decline across the continent over the last 40 years (Sauer et al. 2005). New York data show a similar pattern, with a 1 percent yearly decline statewide and an even steeper decline in the Adirondacks (2.1 percent per year) (Sauer et al. 2005). The declines in these areas over the last 25 years are not quite significant. Similar trends can be seen in all of the northeastern states, with the 2.9 percent yearly decline in New Jersey being the steepest. The second Ontario Breeding Bird Atlas reported only slight declines in Song Sparrow numbers across the province, but the declines were significant in the two central regions (Bird Studies Canada et al. 2006). Although the population declines appear real, the populations remain robust for the moment, and no one has yet called for conservation measures to be implemented for the Song Sparrow. The Song Sparrow is another abundant bird that shows declining population trends that are not yet detectable with Atlas methods. Perhaps future Atlases will show different pictures for this species.

2000–05 Distribution Map

- ☐ Not Found
- Possible
- Probable
- Confirmed

Number of Blocks

	1980–85		2000–05		Change
	No.	%	No.	%	%
Possible	536	10	356	7	−34
Probable	1,040	20	1,136	22	9
Confirmed	3,619	70	3,676	71	2
Total	5,195	97	5,168	97	−1

Change Map

- ☐ Not Reported
- 1980-85 Atlas
- 2000-05 Atlas
- Both Atlases

Breeding Bird Survey Trend in New York

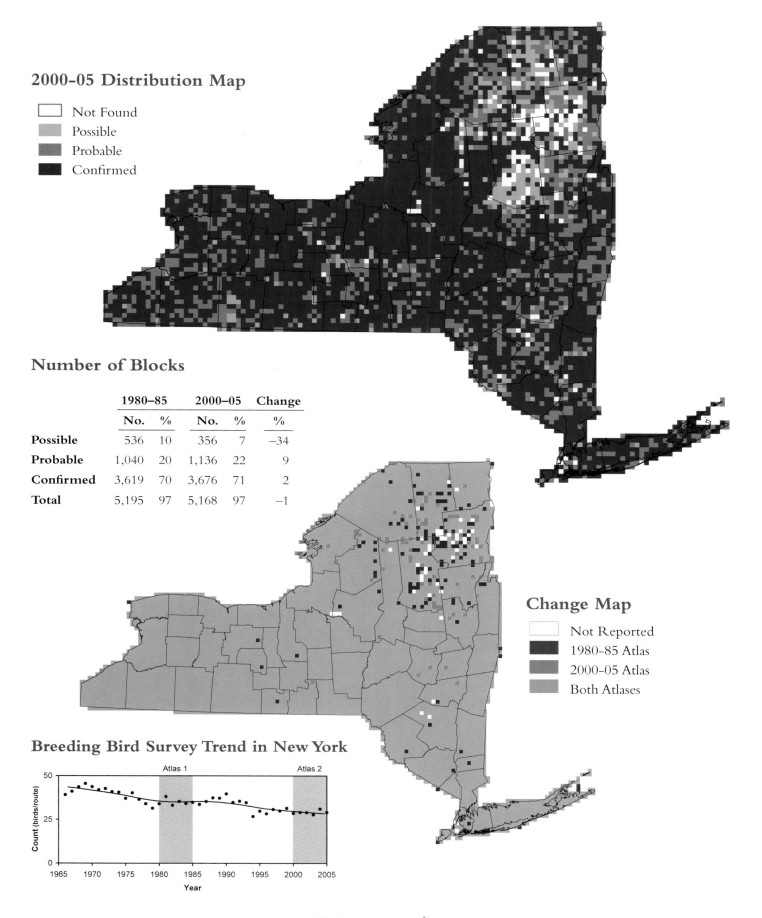

Lincoln's Sparrow

Melospiza lincolnii

JOHN M. C. PETERSON

Many consider this bird of boreal forests and bogs the most attractive of New York's breeding sparrows, the buff breast and finely streaked flanks rather subtle, yet aesthetically pleasing. The Lincoln's Sparrow breeds across Alaska and Canada, southward to the northern United States, and in the mountainous West to southern California, Arizona, and New Mexico (Ammon 1995). In the East, it nears the southern limits of its range in the Adirondacks. Its New York breeding habitat has a northern flavor of balsam fir and spruces, usually wet, but sometimes dry. Merriam (1881) knew this species as a regular, if uncommon breeder in the Adirondacks, as did Eaton (1914). Bull (1974) considered it a rare breeder in the Adirondacks, known from 19 breeding locations in five counties.

The first Atlas map showed the Lincoln's Sparrow as a breeder throughout the Central Adirondacks, Adirondack High Peaks, and Western Adirondack Foothills. It also showed records outside of the Adirondacks: two Possible breeding reports came from the Central Tug Hill, and several records reached into the Champlain Transition and Malone Plain, close to Quebec and the main part of the breeding range. The records that constituted "a thin neck from Quebec" (J. M. C. Peterson 1988i) two decades ago stretched northward along the Clinton-Franklin county line to the Canadian border. The second Atlas data revealed that this population expanded somewhat across the northern reaches of these counties from Lake Champlain westward to Brasher, St. Lawrence County. Records were again obtained as far north as what is now The Gulf State Unique Area on the border with Quebec, with a noticeable spread outward into the Champlain and St. Lawrence transitions. Although still not confirmed, the sparrow was found breeding in four blocks in the Central Tug Hill. Elsewhere, the main contiguous range retained a similar outline as in the first Atlas, encompassing the Adirondack High Peaks, Central Adirondacks, and Eastern and Western Adirondack foothills. Despite the limited expansions outside of the Adiron-

dacks, within the main range the number of blocks with records declined 16 percent, for a 13 percent overall decline. Eaton (1914) stated, "In the Adirondacks I found this bird very difficult to observe due to its shy, retiring habits." Its rich song is loud and easy to locate, but the bird stops singing when incubation begins (Ammon 1995). Consequently, one must use caution when interpreting small changes in its distribution in New York because observer effort, skill, and timing could have significant effects.

Breeding Bird Survey data show no significant continental trend in Lincoln's Sparrow numbers in 1966–2005, although an increase in the shorter period of 1966–79 was significant (Sauer et al. 2005). The trend in New York has been negative since 1966, though it is not statistically significant (Sauer et al. 2005). This sparrow is not found on many BBS routes in the state, however, and the data are flagged as deficient. The second Ontario Breeding Bird Atlas reported increases in Lincoln's Sparrow numbers in the northern sections of the province, but no change was noted overall (Bird Studies Canada et al. 2006). Some of the apparent expansion between the Central Adirondacks and Canadian border can be explained by improved coverage of Clinton County and northern Franklin County during the second Atlas fieldwork, but part of the spread may be quite real. Beavers continue to create new wetlands across northern New York, and relict pockets of boreal habitat continue to seed themselves and recover from the harvesting of previous centuries. Although in neighboring Quebec the Lincoln's Sparrow is most abundant in and near the boreal forest, it was found in two blocks just north of Franklin County, New York (Langevin 1996). At present, this boreal sparrow seems secure in northern New York.

2000–05 Distribution Map

- ☐ Not Found
- ▨ Possible
- ▨ Probable
- ■ Confirmed

Number of Blocks

	1980–85		2000–05		Change
	No.	%	No.	%	%
Possible	84	30	96	40	14
Probable	85	31	74	31	−13
Confirmed	108	39	70	29	−35
Total	277	5	240	5	−13

Change Map

- ☐ Not Reported
- ■ 1980–85 Atlas
- ▨ 2000–05 Atlas
- ▨ Both Atlases

Breeding Bird Survey Trend in New York

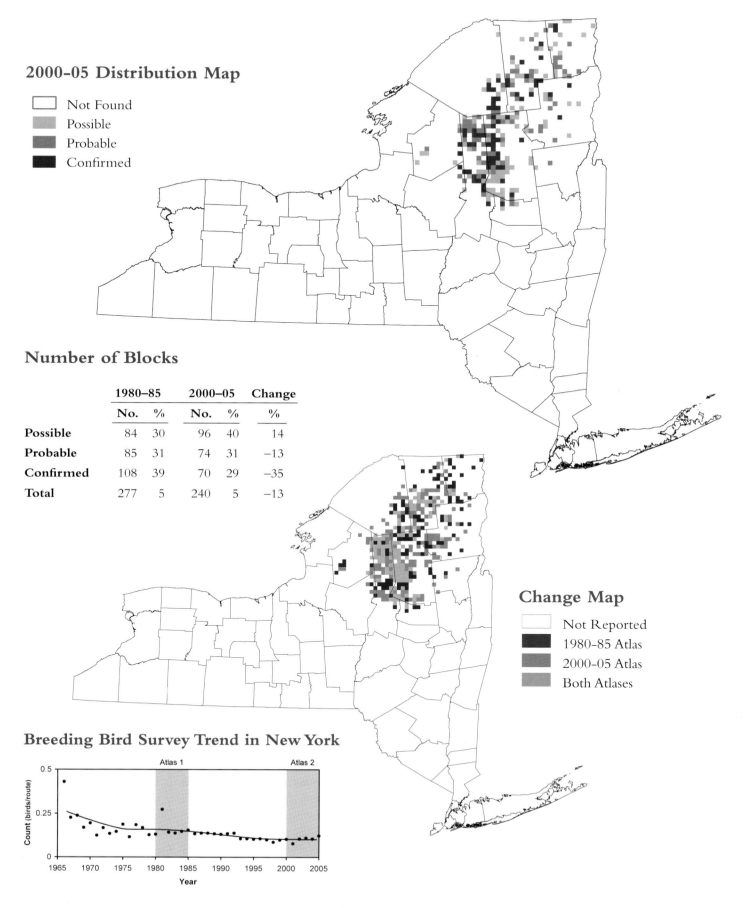

Swamp Sparrow
Melospiza georgiana

Carrie Osborne

The Swamp Sparrow is a common inhabitant of New York's emergent and shrub wetlands, where its musical, one-noted trill can be heard day or night during the breeding season. The breeding range extends across much of boreal Canada, southward to Iowa, the Great Lakes states, West Virginia, and Maryland (Mowbray 1997). New York is near the southeastern edge of the range. In addition to its preferred shrub wetlands, the Swamp Sparrow nests in brackish marshes and beaver ponds (Mowbray 1997). DeKay (1844) noted the abundant breeding of this sparrow in New York, saying that it was most common in the western part of the state. Giraud (1844) noted its presence on Long Island without regard to abundance. The draining of wetlands in New York in the 19th and 20th centuries undoubtedly caused a population decline, but the Swamp Sparrow remained common wherever habitat remained, and Bull (1974) called it a widespread breeder. By the middle of the 1900s the Swamp Sparrow was considered "astonishingly rare" on Long Island, given the amount of suitable habitat, although it occurred commonly in all other areas around New York City (Cruickshank 1942). Bull (1974) noted it was less common and more local in the brackish meadows along the south shore of Long Island.

The first Atlas showed the Swamp Sparrow occurring in every ecozone in the state, although only locally in many areas. The largest gaps were found in the Adirondack High Peaks, Catskill Peaks, and much of the Coastal Lowlands. The second Atlas fieldwork showed the Swamp Sparrow in nearly the same distribution through the state, although statewide it was documented in 6 percent more blocks. Occurrence was still rather spotty in many regions, as are the wetlands this bird uses to breed. Gaps were still apparent in the Adirondack High Peaks, Catskill Peaks, and Coastal Lowlands. Declines occurred primarily in areas where the sparrow was already not common, mostly in the southeastern portion of the state. The Swamp Sparrow has been disappearing from the Coastal Lowlands for quite some time (Cruickshank 1942, Arbib 1988h), and it continues this trend, occurring in 34 percent fewer blocks there than 20 years ago. Despite the secretive nature of this marsh bird, the rusty-crowned male is conspicuous while guarding his breeding territory. Thus, the Atlas map is likely an accurate representation of the range in New York.

Breeding Bird Survey data show a significant increase in numbers in the north Atlantic states (U.S. Fish and Wildlife Service Region 5) and survey-wide since 1966, with most of the increase occurring in the last 25 years (Sauer et al. 2005). The BBS data for New York show no significant trend (Sauer et al.

2005). The second Ontario Breeding Bird Atlas also reported a slight but significant increase in Swamp Sparrow numbers in that province (Bird Studies Canada et al. 2006).

In New York during the period between the mid-1980s and mid-1990s, the acreage of all wetlands increased, but the amount of shrub wetlands decreased as they turned into forested wetlands (NYSDEC [2007a]). In the Lower Hudson and along Long Island, where distribution of this sparrow declined, more than 600 ha (1,500 a) of shrub wetlands were lost (NYSDEC 2006). Many remaining Long Island wetlands have been degraded by grid-ditching for mosquito control, draining, and impounding (Long Island Sound Study 2003). The Swamp Sparrow does not appear to be adversely affected by invasive phragmites and purple loosestrife; in fact, studies have shown a positive correlation between Swamp Sparrow populations and the two exotics (Benoit and Askins 1999, Whitt et al. 1999).

Despite the loss of wetland habitat, the Swamp Sparrow continues to thrive in most of the state. The future of this and other marsh-dwelling birds depends on the preservation of existing marsh habitat and the restoration of altered wetlands in areas heavily affected by human activity.

2000–05 Distribution Map

- ☐ Not Found
- Possible
- Probable
- Confirmed

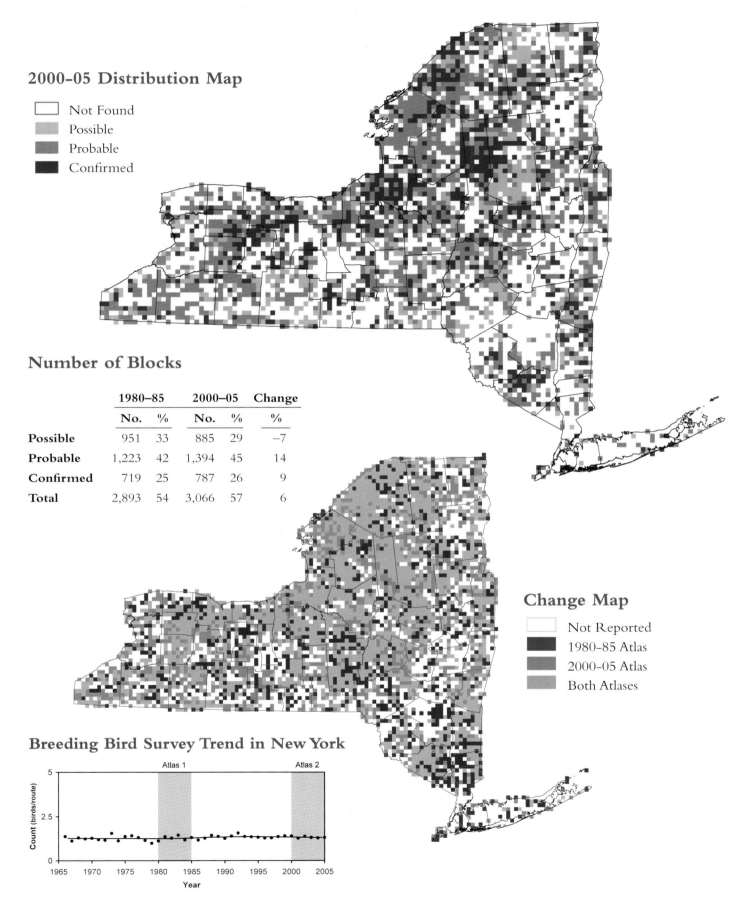

Number of Blocks

	1980–85		2000–05		Change
	No.	%	No.	%	%
Possible	951	33	885	29	−7
Probable	1,223	42	1,394	45	14
Confirmed	719	25	787	26	9
Total	2,893	54	3,066	57	6

Change Map

- ☐ Not Reported
- 1980–85 Atlas
- 2000–05 Atlas
- Both Atlases

Breeding Bird Survey Trend in New York

White-throated Sparrow
Zonotrichia albicollis

John M. C. Peterson

The plaintive, piping notes of the White-throated Sparrow are familiar to hikers in the Adirondacks and other forested regions of the state. This sparrow can be found nesting from western Canada eastward to Newfoundland and southward into the northern states, with isolated populations in the Appalachian Mountains as far south as West Virginia (Falls and Kopachena 1994). New York is near the southeastern limit of the core range. This woodland sparrow favors mixed or coniferous forests with low, dense vegetation, usually second-growth forests that have been disturbed by logging or windstorms. The openings created in forests by clearing in colonial days may have initially benefited the White-throated Sparrow, but as agriculture increased there was undoubtedly a subsequent decline in its fortune. DeKay (1844) suspected it bred in the northern part of the state, and Merriam (1881) confirmed that suspicion, calling it abundant in the Adirondacks. Eaton (1914) listed the sparrow as a common breeder only in the "Canadian zone" of the Adirondacks and Catskills but noted a few other breeding records in the far southwest of the state and in a few other parts of the Appalachian Plateau. Beardslee and Mitchell (1965) listed only a few breeding records for the Niagara Frontier, despite active searching. Bull (1974) called it common only in the Adirondacks and Catskills but noted an expansion in the 20th century to areas of lower elevation across the eastern portion of the Appalachian Plateau.

Distribution of the White-throated Sparrow during the first Atlas period extended more widely than previously documented, from the Champlain Valley across the Adirondacks to the Tug Hill Transition, south from the Canadian border to the Mohawk Valley. East of the Hudson River the sparrow was found in the Rensselaer Hills and northern Taconic Mountains. West of the Hudson Valley a concentration was apparent in the Catskills and the eastern portion of the Appalachian Plateau. The range continued westward, thinning out across the Appalachian Plateau and Finger Lakes Highlands to the western corner of the state, and with scattered records across the Great Lakes Plain. Although previously absent in the southeastern portion of the state, the sparrow was recorded in two blocks in the Hudson Highlands, one in the Manhattan Hills, and eight blocks on the Coastal Lowlands, albeit none confirmed. The second Atlas survey revealed a similar distribution but with a 14 percent decline in the number of occupied blocks statewide and declines in nearly all ecozones. No records were obtained in the Coastal Lowlands, although two Confirmed reports were made in the Triassic Lowlands. North of the Mohawk Valley the range was relatively unchanged, with some declines in Lewis and St. Lawrence counties but apparent gains in Jefferson County and only a 3 percent decline in the Adirondacks. The largest declines occurred in the Catskills and across the Appalachian Plateau, where records decreased by about one-third to one-fourth. Local disappearances and appearances could well be the result of different coverage during the two Atlas projects, but given its loud and familiar song, this sparrow was unlikely to be overlooked by most observers.

The Breeding Bird Survey has documented a gradual decrease in White-throated Sparrow numbers across the survey area since 1966 (Sauer et al. 2005). Declines are apparent in most regions, but the decline in New York is not statistically significant (Sauer et al. 2005). No single cause can be singled out for this decline. The fact that there is now less of the early-successional forest habitat favored by this sparrow in New York, and much more mature forest, certainly must play a part. The White-throated Sparrow is still abundant in northern parts of the state, but its decline is a matter of concern that deserves further study.

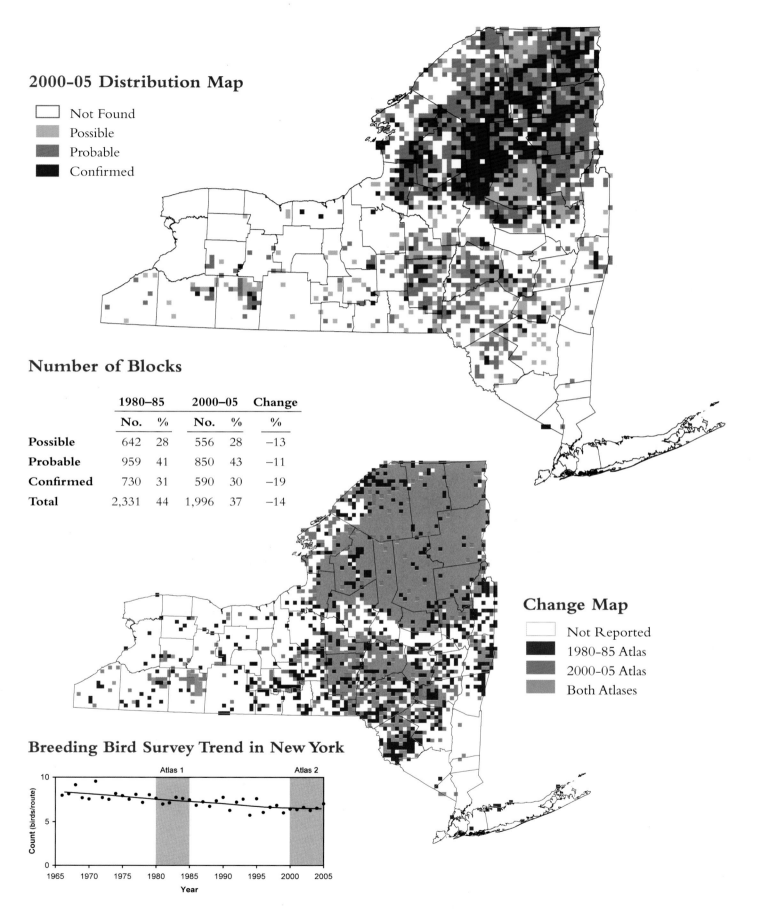

2000-05 Distribution Map

- ☐ Not Found
- ☐ Possible
- ☐ Probable
- ■ Confirmed

Number of Blocks

	1980–85		2000–05		Change
	No.	%	No.	%	%
Possible	642	28	556	28	−13
Probable	959	41	850	43	−11
Confirmed	730	31	590	30	−19
Total	2,331	44	1,996	37	−14

Change Map

- ☐ Not Reported
- ■ 1980-85 Atlas
- ☐ 2000-05 Atlas
- ☐ Both Atlases

Breeding Bird Survey Trend in New York

Dark-eyed Junco
Junco hyemalis

CHARLES R. SMITH

A common bird of the northern forests, the Dark-eyed Junco breeds from the west coast of Alaska throughout most of Canada, with populations from the Rocky Mountains to the West Coast and from the northern Great Lakes region throughout the northeastern states, southward in the Appalachian Mountains to northern Georgia (Nolan et al. 2002). New York is near the southeastern edge of the main, non-mountain breeding range. The Dark-eyed Junco reaches its greatest abundance in the Pacific Northwest and southern British Columbia, with the "Slate-colored" form most abundant in Nova Scotia (Sauer et al. 2005). In the New England states, DeGraaf and Yamasaki (2001) described its typical habitat as edges and small openings in coniferous and mixed forests. Eaton (1988h) reported that the Dark-eyed Junco typically occurs in New York at elevations greater than 305 m (1,000 ft), although it sometimes can be found in suitable habitats at lower elevations. As a bird of forests, the junco likely was common before European settlement, but its population probably declined with the removal of the forests. The Dark-eyed Junco was considered a "rare summer resident" (Reed and Wright 1909) in the Cayuga Lake Basin, where it now is common (Smith and Byrne 1999). Eaton (1910, 1914) showed the junco occurring throughout the Adirondacks and Tug Hill Plateau, in the Taconic Mountains, Catskills, Allegany Hills, and other portions of the Appalachian Plateau above 366 m (1,200 ft), with some records from the "colder swamps and gulleys" of the Great Lakes Plain. Bull (1974) gave a similar distribution but pointed out that the junco was virtually lacking on the lowlands of the Great Lakes Plain. He noted the southernmost breeding records as in the Taconic Highlands of Dutchess County.

During the first Atlas period the Dark-eyed Junco was concentrated across the Appalachian Plateau, in the Tug Hill Plateau, Adirondacks, Catskill Mountains, Shawangunk Hills, and Taconic Highlands. Scattered records also came from the Great Lakes Plain, St. Lawrence Plains, and Champlain Valley. Breeding was confirmed in the southeast in the Hudson Highlands. A similar distribution was found during the second Atlas period, with the same areas of concentration but with expansion into the St. Lawrence and Mohawk valleys. The number of blocks with records was up by 23 percent statewide, increasing in most ecozones, and with large gains across the Appalachian Plateau and Great Lakes Plain. The junco continued its minor southward expansion down the Hudson Valley, being detected in the Triassic Lowlands of Rockland County. The Confirmed report from the far northwestern corner of the state in Niagara County was quite separate from the rest of the records. The current distribution closely resembles that shown by Eaton (1910, p. 23), though Eaton's map suggests a more patchy distribution. Such a small change is not surprising given that the landscape of Eaton's day was largely devoid of forests, compared with today (see Chapter 4).

For the period 1966–2005, Dark-eyed Junco numbers declined throughout much of its continental range, which is covered by Breeding Bird Surveys (Sauer et al. 2005). In New York, however, the Dark-eyed Junco showed no statistically significant change in relative abundance over the periods of 1966–2005 and 1980–2005. Likewise, there were no statistically significant changes in relative abundance for both time periods for the north Atlantic states (U.S. Fish and Wildlife Service Region 5) (Sauer et al. 2005). The second Ontario Breeding Bird Atlas reported no significant change in the last 20 years across that province (Bird Studies Canada et al. 2006). Partners in Flight does not indicate any conservation needs for this junco (Rich et al. 2004). With the continued maturation of forests in New York, and its ability to nest in close association with people (e.g., Smith 2006), the Dark-eyed Junco should continue to be a common bird in New York.

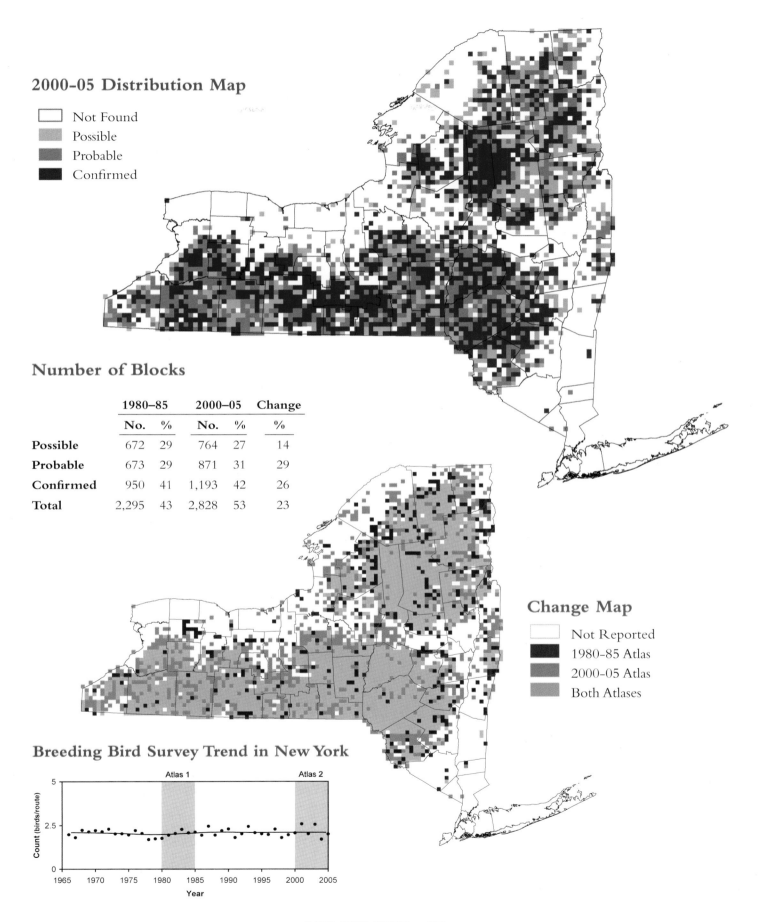

2000–05 Distribution Map

- ☐ Not Found
- Possible
- Probable
- Confirmed

Number of Blocks

	1980–85		2000–05		Change
	No.	%	No.	%	%
Possible	672	29	764	27	14
Probable	673	29	871	31	29
Confirmed	950	41	1,193	42	26
Total	2,295	43	2,828	53	23

Change Map

- ☐ Not Reported
- 1980-85 Atlas
- 2000-05 Atlas
- Both Atlases

Breeding Bird Survey Trend in New York

Northern Cardinal and Indigo Bunting in an old field

Old-field habitat, a vestige of an agrarian past, exists throughout the state from the northern Adirondacks to eastern Long Island, and wherever it remains, one is likely to find an exciting diversity of flora and fauna uniquely adapted to such transitional environments.

574

Northern Cardinal
Cardinalis cardinalis

KEVIN J. MCGOWAN

The brightly colored Northern Cardinal is resident from southeastern Canada, Minnesota, South Dakota, and Maine southward through the eastern United States to Central America. It also occurs locally in Arizona, California, and New Mexico and was introduced to Hawaii and Bermuda (Halkin and Linville 1999). New York lies near the northern end of its range. The cardinal inhabits areas with shrubs and small trees, including forest edges, hedgerows, and suburbs. This bird's breeding range has expanded northward since the mid-1800s (Halkin and Linville 1999). DeKay (1844) considered the cardinal a summer visitor to the Coastal Lowlands extending to Delaware and Chenango counties and suspected that it bred in the state. Eaton (1914) listed it as a local resident on the west side of the lower Hudson Valley, with scattered reports across the western portion of the state. He thought that the conspicuous nature of a singing male cardinal made it too attractive a target for gunners and such persecution resulted in low numbers in the state. He suggested that if people would protect it, it would become more common in the southern part of the state and succeed in colonizing other areas in which it was appearing. Eaton's prophecy came true after the passage of the federal Migratory Bird Treaty Act with Canada in 1918, which gave all songbirds protected status. The cardinal indeed became common in the southern part of the state and established itself in upstate New York. It bred in significant numbers in western and southern central New York by the 1930s (Beardslee and Mitchell 1965, Bull 1974), and its population continued to increase in the state through the rest of the 20th century, perhaps accelerating in the 1950s and 1960s (Bull 1974). By the 1970s the Northern Cardinal had bred in all counties in the state except St. Lawrence, Hamilton, and Clinton (Bull 1974).

During the first Atlas period, the Northern Cardinal was common across most of southern New York. It was absent from much of the Adirondacks and other areas north of the Mohawk Valley, except along Lake Champlain and at the eastern end of Lake Ontario. Gaps were also apparent at higher elevations of the Appalachian Plateau. The Northern Cardinal's distribution continued to increase in the state into the second Atlas period. It was found in 9 percent more blocks across the state, with the largest increases occurring in the Eastern Ontario Plain, the St. Lawrence Plains, and around the periphery of the Tug Hill Plateau. Increases also were noted across the Appalachian Plateau where it had been sparse before, and into the Champlain Transition. The cardinal did not spread into the Adirondacks or onto the Central Tug Hill, and gaps remained in the Catskill Peaks and nearby highlands.

The spread of the Northern Cardinal northward in the 1800s and early 1900s has been attributed to a warming climate that provided less snow and greater winter foraging opportunities, to a reduction in the amount of forests and the creation of suitable edge habitat, and to the establishment of winter feeding stations (Halkin and Linville 1999). Breeding Bird Survey data show a slight but significant increase survey-wide since the 1960s, with most of that increase occurring in the last 25 years (Sauer et al. 2005). BBS data from New York show an even stronger increase of 1.9 percent per year (Sauer et al. 2005). Data for Ontario reveal a similar trend and a higher rate of growth, but a much lower average number of birds seen per census (Sauer et al. 2005). The second Ontario Breeding Bird Atlas also reported a significant increase in Northern Cardinal numbers over the first Atlas, with similar increases found along the St. Lawrence but little penetration onto the Canadian Shield (Bird Studies Canada et al. 2006). It will be interesting to see if the cardinal continues to expand over the next 20 years and moves into the Adirondacks, although the winter snow cover there may prove too great an obstacle.

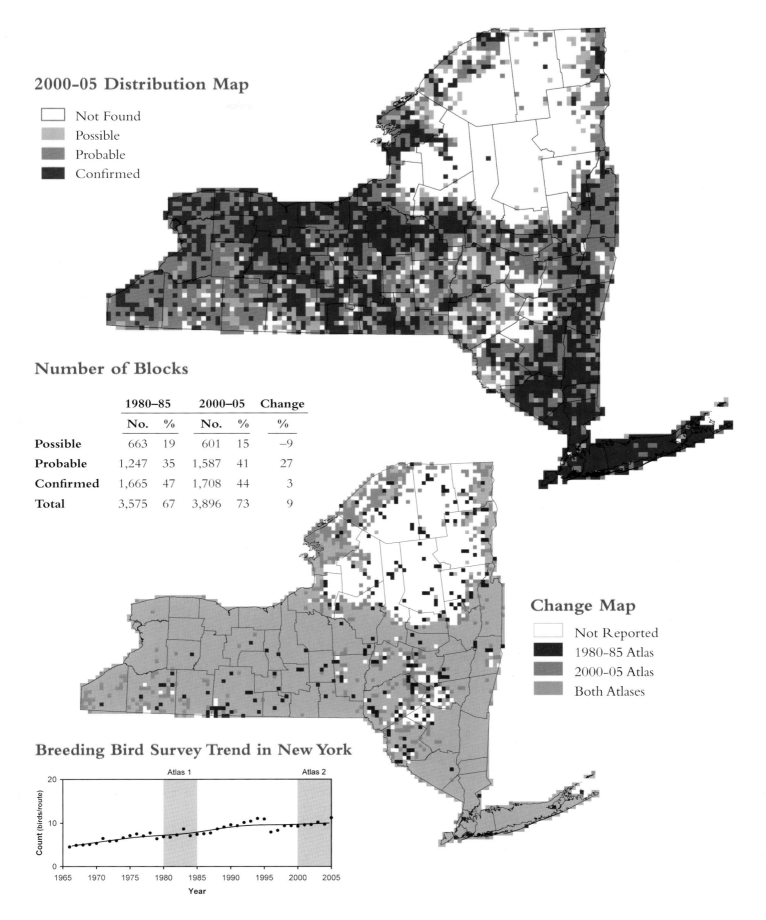

2000-05 Distribution Map

☐ Not Found
▨ Possible
▨ Probable
■ Confirmed

Number of Blocks

| | 1980–85 | | 2000–05 | | Change |
	No.	%	No.	%	%
Possible	663	19	601	15	−9
Probable	1,247	35	1,587	41	27
Confirmed	1,665	47	1,708	44	3
Total	3,575	67	3,896	73	9

Change Map

☐ Not Reported
■ 1980–85 Atlas
▨ 2000–05 Atlas
▨ Both Atlases

Breeding Bird Survey Trend in New York

Rose-breasted Grosbeak
Pheucticus ludovicianus

KEVIN J. MCGOWAN

The Rose-breasted Grosbeak is a colorful, vibrant songster of forests. It breeds from southern Yukon southeastward to northern North Dakota, eastward to Newfoundland, and southward to Nebraska, New Jersey, and in the mountains to northern Georgia (Wyatt and Francis 2002). It prefers deciduous and mixed deciduous-coniferous woodlands, second-growth woodlands, orchards, suburban parks, and gardens (Wyatt and Francis 2002). It is especially fond of the shrubby boundary of woods at streams, ponds, marshes, roads, or pastures (Wyatt and Francis 2002). As a bird of forests, the Rose-breasted Grosbeak was probably common throughout most of New York before European settlement, although its preference for younger woods and edges might have kept its numbers modest. With the removal of the forests, its population likely declined, only to rebound with the decrease in agricultural land and increase in reforestation. DeKay (1844) mentioned it as breeding in the western and Atlantic regions, intimating that it was not common. Giraud (1844) considered it not very common on Long Island, where it was confined to the woods. Most subsequent authors deemed it common around the state (Rathbun 1879, Merriam 1881, Short 1893, Reed and Wright 1909). Eaton (1914) called it widespread and common through most of the state, except for the lower Hudson Valley and the Coastal Lowlands. Griscom (1923) said it was confined on Long Island primarily to the northern shore. Bull (1974) continued to call it widespread but rare on Long Island.

The Rose-breasted Grosbeak was found distributed across nearly all regions of the state during the first Atlas survey. The distribution was somewhat sparser in the Adirondacks and on Long Island. It was missing from most of the southwestern part of Long Island. Bonney (1988e) noted that its presence on Staten Island, the lower Hudson Valley, and much of Long Island represented a slight range expansion and perhaps indicated increased abundance. Any expansion was not continued into the second Atlas period, and overall the number of blocks with records declined slightly. Although the grosbeak remained common across nearly all of the state, occurrence declined at least slightly in most ecozones. The largest declines were in the Coastal Lowlands, Manhattan Hills, and Adirondacks. The grosbeak was not seen on Staten Island and was much less common on Long Island's southern shore, although it was still present. Blocks reporting grosbeaks declined by 19 percent in the Adirondacks, and larger gaps were apparent there this time. Relatively small

and local changes in distribution between the two Atlas periods could easily result from differences in coverage rather than real changes in occurrence, especially in the remote and difficult areas of the Adirondacks, but several of the new gaps there were quite striking.

Breeding Bird Survey data show a slight declining trend in Rose-breasted Grosbeak numbers survey-wide since 1966, and especially since 1980 (Sauer et al. 2005). Trend graphs show a significant increase in counts extending into the early 1980s followed by a significant decline. BBS data for New York show roughly the same pattern of a general, but nonsignificant, increase followed by a significant decline (Sauer et al. 2005). The second Ontario Breeding Bird Atlas reported a significant decrease in Rose-breasted Grosbeak populations across the province but a significant increase in the southernmost region (Bird Studies Canada et al. 2006). A decline in Vermont based on census plots in mature forest was attributed to maturation of the forest (Holmes and Sherry 2001); this explanation might be applicable to the New York trends as well. The first Atlas results could represent an all-time peak of Rose-breasted Grosbeak numbers in the state, with a large presence of second-growth forest. As the state's forests continue to mature, the grosbeak may well stay common but at lower levels than before.

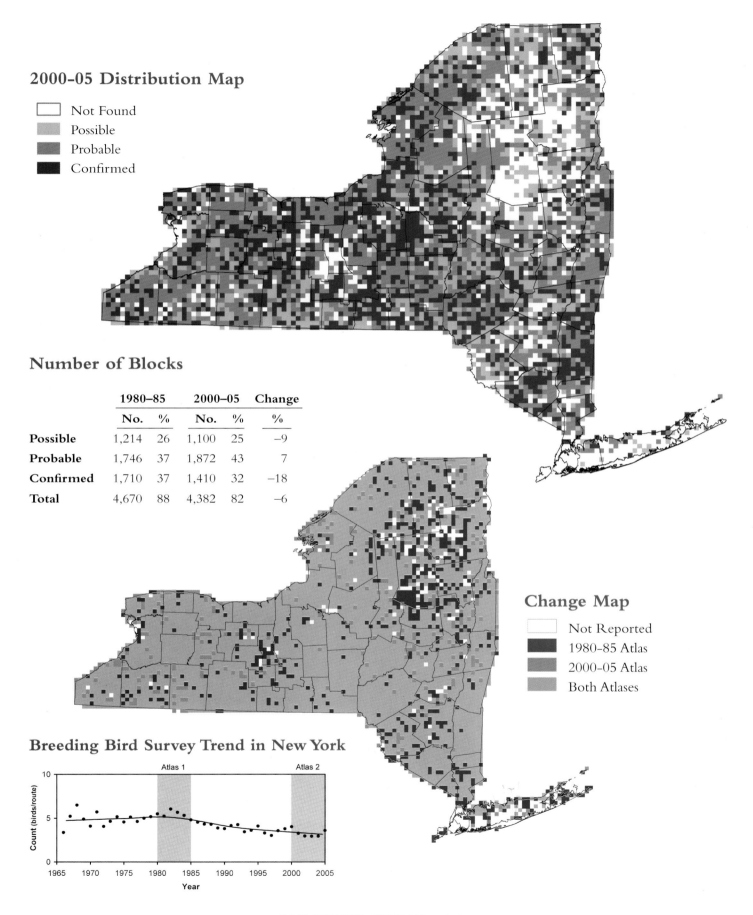

2000–05 Distribution Map

- ☐ Not Found
- Possible
- Probable
- Confirmed

Number of Blocks

	1980–85		2000–05		Change
	No.	%	No.	%	%
Possible	1,214	26	1,100	25	−9
Probable	1,746	37	1,872	43	7
Confirmed	1,710	37	1,410	32	−18
Total	4,670	88	4,382	82	−6

Change Map

- ☐ Not Reported
- 1980–85 Atlas
- 2000–05 Atlas
- Both Atlases

Breeding Bird Survey Trend in New York

Blue Grosbeak
Passerina caerulea

Kevin J. McGowan

The male a striking blue with chestnut wingbars, the Blue Grosbeak is a relatively common bird in rural shrubby areas of the southern United States. It breeds from central California across the central United States, as far north as southern North Dakota and eastward to northern New Jersey (Ingold 1993). Although it generally does not breed along the Gulf Coast, this grosbeak can be found breeding throughout the southern states into Mexico and Central America (Ingold 1993). Coastal New York is at the extreme northeastern limit of its breeding range. Its preferred breeding habitat is forest edge, fields, power-line cuts, riparian areas, hedgerows, and other areas with medium-sized trees and scattered shrubs (Ingold 1993). The first New York specimen was taken on Manhattan Island in 1838 (DeKay 1844), but the Blue Grosbeak was not discovered breeding in the state until 1982, on Staten Island (Siebenheller and Siebenheller 1982), with the second confirmed attempt occurring in 1999 near Riverhead, Suffolk County (Schiff and Wollin 1999). Considered extremely rare anywhere in the state before 1940 (Bull 1974), it has become an uncommon but regular spring and fall migrant on the south shore of Long Island and in the New York City parks, although it is still deemed rare north of Westchester and Orange counties (Paxton 1998b). Stray individuals are seen occasionally upstate, with 11 accepted records between 1982 and 2003 (NYSARC 2007).

The first Atlas confirmed nesting on Staten Island in 1982 and at Merritts Island, Orange County, in 1984. Two other blocks in the Hudson Valley, one in Orange County and the other in Westchester County, had Possible breeding grosbeaks. During the second Atlas period the number of records increased to nine, with seven of the observations from the Coastal Lowlands of Suffolk County, but with only one Confirmed breeding record. In Suffolk County, observations were concentrated in the town of Riverhead and the eastern portion of the town of Brookhaven. Once again, it was seen on Staten Island, and a sighting in the Triassic Lowlands of southern Rock-

land County completed the reports. In central Suffolk County this species was observed in habitats as diverse as a commercial tree and shrub nursery, a vegetated border of a farm field, an abandoned farm field with scattered trees and shrubs, and the forested border of an active landfill (K. Feustel pers. comm.).

Breeding Bird Survey data show a continuous and significant increase, albeit small, in Blue Grosbeak numbers across its range since 1966, although the data from the north Atlantic states (U.S. Fish and Wildlife Service Region 5) at the northeastern portion of its range show a flat or slightly declining trend (Sauer et al. 2007). A northward range expansion has occurred in the last century, but the exact timing is uncertain (Ingold 1993). In New Jersey, the probable source of the birds seen in New York, the first modern breeding record of Blue Grosbeak was in 1952, and by the 1960s it was considered a rare breeder in the southern part of the state (Walsh et al. 1999). The grosbeak population continued to increase, and by the 1980s this species was established across the southern half of the state, where the bulk of its population continues to be found (Walsh et al. 1999). Although the Blue Grosbeak has a long documented history in Pennsylvania, it also increased in population and distribution in the 1960s (McWilliams and Brauning 2000). Such expansions were undoubtedly responsible for the grosbeak breeding in New York. Whether the species has become truly established in the state and whether it will expand or disappear remains to be seen.

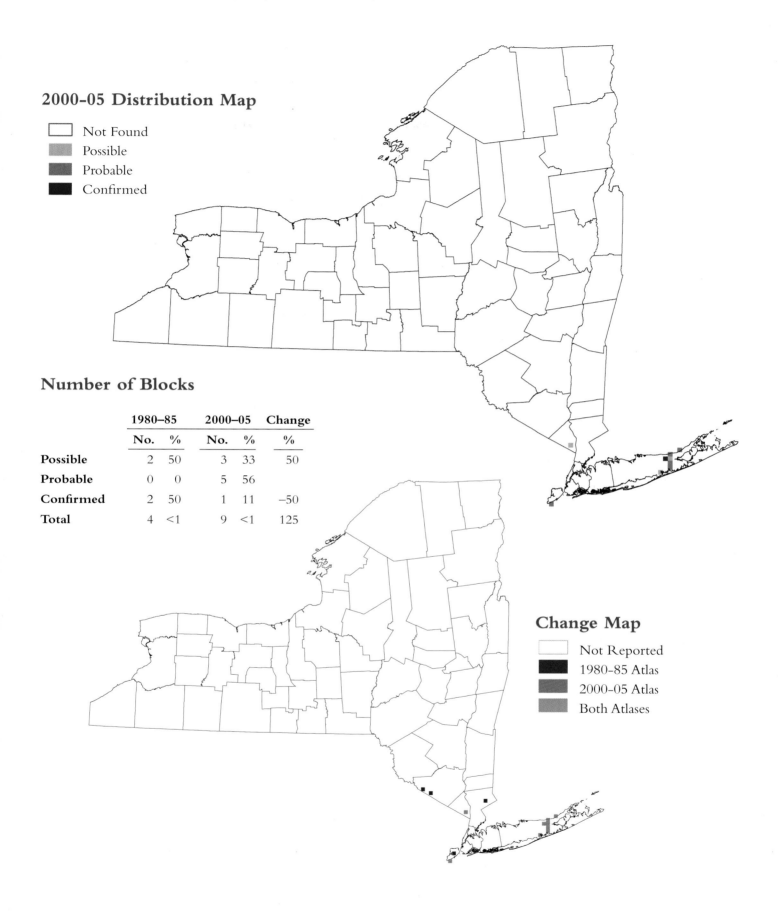

2000-05 Distribution Map

☐ Not Found
▨ Possible
▨ Probable
■ Confirmed

Number of Blocks

	1980–85		2000–05		Change
	No.	%	No.	%	%
Possible	2	50	3	33	50
Probable	0	0	5	56	
Confirmed	2	50	1	11	−50
Total	4	<1	9	<1	125

Change Map

☐ Not Reported
■ 1980-85 Atlas
▨ 2000-05 Atlas
▨ Both Atlases

Indigo Bunting

Passerina cyanea

KEVIN J. MCGOWAN

The Indigo Bunting is a brilliantly colored bird of scrubby old fields. It breeds from southern Manitoba to Maine, southward to northern Florida and eastern Texas, with some isolated populations occurring farther west (Payne 2006). It breeds in brushy and weedy areas along edges of cultivated land, woods, roads, power-line rights-of-way, and in open deciduous woods and old fields (Payne 2006). As a bird of primarily open areas, the Indigo Bunting was undoubtedly much less common in New York before the opening of the forests during European colonization. It became common by the end of the 19th century (Short 1893), when it bred in most of the state, skirting the Catskills and Adirondacks (Eaton 1914). Bull (1974) called it widely distributed but local on Long Island and rare in the higher mountains. Parkes (1952) stated that the Indigo Bunting moved into the Adirondacks in the late 1940s or early 1950s. Although it was once a common bird on Long Island, it was declining in numbers by the 1940s (Cruickshank 1942) and was local by the 1970s (Bull 1974).

During the first Atlas period the Indigo Bunting was common throughout the state, found in 80 percent of all blocks. It was mainly absent from the larger urban areas, parts of Long Island, and at the higher elevations of the Catskill Peaks, Central Tug Hill, and Adirondacks, especially the Adirondack High Peaks and Central Adirondacks. The breeding distribution of the Indigo Bunting was similar during the second Atlas period, with the species shown to be common across most of the state and less so in the Adirondacks. The total number of blocks differed very little, but some changes were apparent. The species was no longer missing from the Central Tug Hill, but its distribution declined in the Adirondacks. Across the state it was found in only 1 percent fewer blocks, but in the Adirondacks it was found in 15 percent fewer. Its distribution declined even more sharply in the Coastal Lowlands, the number of blocks decreasing 32 percent in that region. A gap still exists in the Catskill Peaks, although the distribution increased 11 percent there, and a new gap is

apparent in the St. Lawrence Plains and St. Lawrence Transition where St. Lawrence and Franklin counties meet. Increases in the Tug Hill and the Catskill Peaks were unexpected because the areas of extensive forest there should be maturing, not giving way to the second growth preferred by the bunting.

Breeding Bird Survey data show a significant decline in Indigo Bunting numbers across the survey area, especially in the last 25 years (Sauer et al. 2005). BBS data for New York and U.S. Fish and Wildlife Service Region 5 (the north Atlantic states) show similar trends of significant increases from 1966 to 1979 followed by significant declines from 1980 to 2005, with a decline of 1.2 percent per year in New York, but no significant trends in the Adirondacks (Sauer et al. 2005). The New York data in particular show a large decline between 1984 and 1985 and then distinct cyclical fluctuations that were not apparent before. Populations throughout North America generally increased through the 20th century up until 1979, with some local decreases occurring in areas of increasing forest cover (Payne 2006). Although increasing forest cover in the Northeast could explain declines in Indigo Bunting populations in that region, no such landscape change is occurring in the Midwest, where similar trends in populations are apparent from the BBS data. This fact suggests that wintering ground or migratory route factors might be seriously affecting Indigo Bunting populations. Although numbers from the two New York Atlas projects show little change, their methods are not designed to detect declines in the distribution of abundant species. If the trend continues, however, the next Atlas survey may reveal a different picture for the Indigo Bunting.

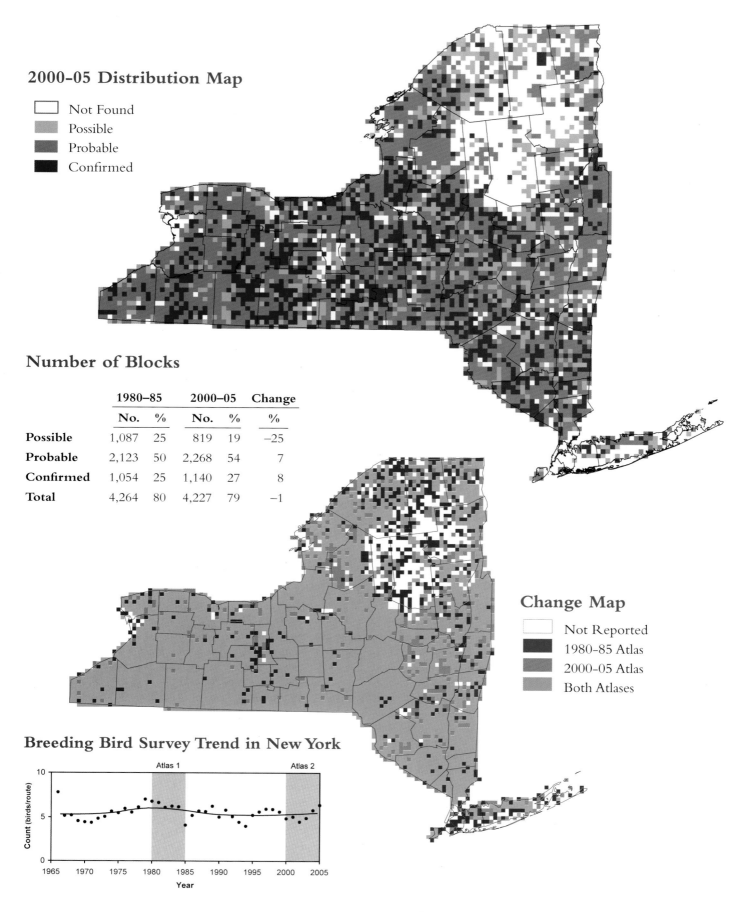

2000–05 Distribution Map

- ☐ Not Found
- Possible
- Probable
- Confirmed

Number of Blocks

	1980–85		2000–05		Change
	No.	%	No.	%	%
Possible	1,087	25	819	19	−25
Probable	2,123	50	2,268	54	7
Confirmed	1,054	25	1,140	27	8
Total	4,264	80	4,227	79	−1

Change Map

- ☐ Not Reported
- 1980-85 Atlas
- 2000-05 Atlas
- Both Atlases

Breeding Bird Survey Trend in New York

Dickcissel
Spiza americana

Kevin J. McGowan

The Dickcissel is a sparrow-like bird of the central North American prairie grasslands. New York lies well outside its current breeding range, but the species is known for its irregular movements to far-flung grasslands to breed (Temple 2002). During the 19th century, the Dickcissel bred commonly in agricultural grasslands in eastern North America from New England to South Carolina (Temple 2002). DeKay (1844) described it as breeding in every part of the "Atlantic and Western Districts" of the state, but by 1875 it had become rare and was essentially gone as a breeder by 1896 (Eaton 1914). The species was simultaneously disappearing from its eastern range (Temple 2002). It is doubtful the Dickcissel was abundant, and perhaps it was not even present in the Northeast before the conversion of forests to agricultural grasslands. The contraction of its range back to the prairies is explained as the result of the abandonment of farmland and regrowth of forests (Temple 2002), although the timing of land-use changes and Dickcissel disappearance is not a perfect match. The Dickcissel breeds in a variety of open grassland habitats (Temple 2002), and suitable areas exist in parts of New York. After its disappearance as a regular breeder, the Dickcissel has made infrequent forays back to New York to breed, with only three documented nests and two other possible attempts recorded between 1914 and 2000 (Novak 1998b), although winter visitors and migrants have become annual.

The only observation of the Dickcissel during the first Atlas survey was a single male seen defending a territory in eastern Wyoming County in 1980. Afterward, a nest with eggs was found in 1988 in Allegany County (Brooks 1988). A nesting attempt was documented in Tompkins County in 1992 when four males and at least one female were observed, but no nesting was confirmed (Novak 1998b). Only a few reports were made during the second Atlas survey, but breeding was confirmed in two blocks. A pair was seen feeding young in 2000 in the town of Pomfret, Chautauqua County, on the same road where a small colony was observed (but not confirmed breeding) in 1976. Several individuals were observed singing in hayfields in Schoharie County in the summer of 2005, and four fledglings were seen (Yandik 2005). A single second-year male was observed singing for several weeks in Tompkins County in June 2004. It was seen courting a Song Sparrow, but no evidence of nesting was discovered. At least five male and one female Dickcissels were seen in June 2005 in Somerset, Niagara County, but breeding was not confirmed (Morgante 2005). Four birds and a nest with eggs were found in Porter, Niagara County in 2006, just after the end of Atlas data collection (Morgante 2006).

The Dickcissel breeds sporadically and in low numbers in disjunct and often temporary locations outside of its core and peripheral breeding areas in the Midwest. Many of these areas, however, are occupied only by unpaired males and no breeding occurs (Temple 2002), despite fitting the Probable category of Atlas protocol. The Dickcissel appears to breed in Pennsylvania more frequently than in New York, though not annually, with numerous summer sightings and several nesting attempts documented in the 1980s through 2000 (McWilliams and Brauning 2000).

Breeding Bird Survey data indicate that Dickcissel populations have fluctuated significantly continent-wide since 1966, declining and then stabilizing at about two-thirds of the 1966 level (Sauer et al. 2005). The greatest threats to Dickcissel populations appear to be on the wintering grounds where their dense aggregations present problems for local agriculture and where they are extensively killed (Temple 2002). Partners in Flight placed the Dickcissel on its Watch List, with a management goal of increasing its population by 50 percent (Rich et al. 2004). Little help will come from New York, as the Dickcissel remains a rare part of the state's breeding fauna.

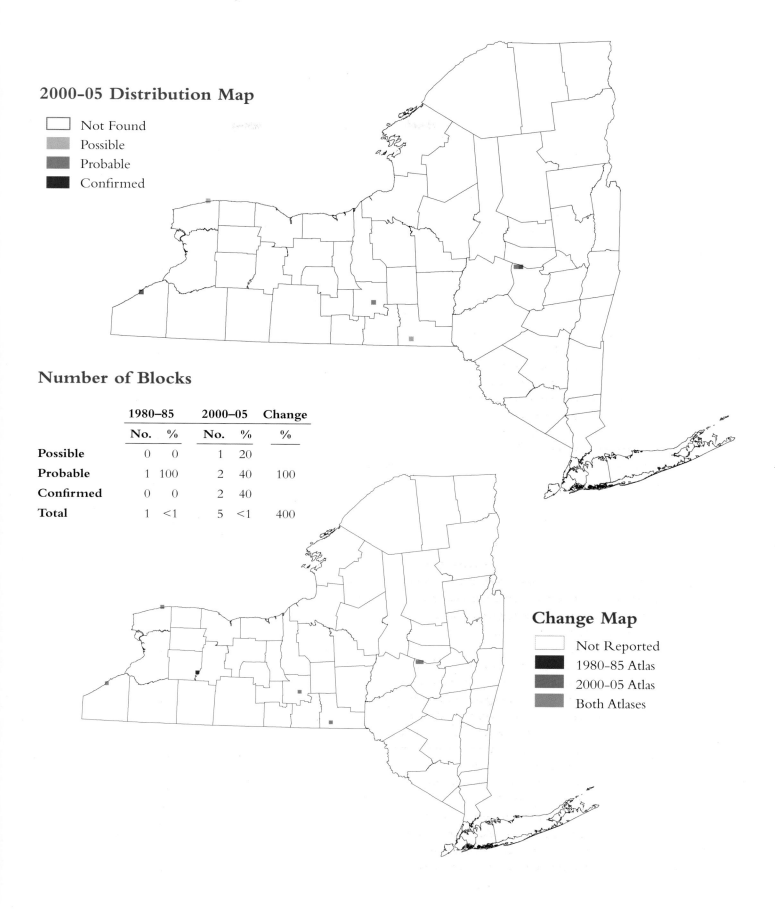

2000-05 Distribution Map

- Not Found
- Possible
- Probable
- Confirmed

Number of Blocks

| | 1980–85 | | 2000–05 | | Change |
	No.	%	No.	%	%
Possible	0	0	1	20	
Probable	1	100	2	40	100
Confirmed	0	0	2	40	
Total	1	<1	5	<1	400

Change Map

- Not Reported
- 1980-85 Atlas
- 2000-05 Atlas
- Both Atlases

Red-winged Blackbird and Bobolink in central New York farmlands

A trend toward more intensive farming practices and an overall reduction in the amount of land in agriculture have led to fewer fields being left fallow long enough for these birds to complete a breeding cycle.

Bobolink
Dolichonyx oryzivorus

CHARLES R. SMITH

Bobolink is a trans-equatorial migrant, with some birds traveling all the way to Argentina to spend the winter. The Bobolink's core breeding range includes parts of the northern United States and southern Canada, from British Columbia and Oregon to western Newfoundland and northern New Jersey (Martin and Gavin 1995). New York lies near the eastern center of the Bobolink's breeding range. In New York, the Bobolink is a species of agricultural landscapes, where it requires hay meadows or grassy pastures for nesting. Larger grazed pastures and larger, older hayfields that contain the least alfalfa support the most Bobolinks (Bollinger and Gavin 1992, Smith 1997). Prior to landscape changes resulting from settlement by western Europeans, it is probable that the Bobolink was relatively rare in New York and used naturally occurring grasslands, including the Hempstead Plains on Long Island, or meadows resulting from sedimentation and ecological succession, which ultimately are natural consequences of impoundment of streams by beaver. European settlement changed much of the state from forest to agriculture, greatly benefiting the Bobolink. By the late 19th century it was abundant across most of the state (Giraud 1844, Rathbun 1879, Merriam 1881, Short 1893, Reed and Wright 1909). Eaton (1914) said it bred in every county in the state, although it was restricted to the settled areas of the Adirondacks and Catskills and was not common on Staten Island or Long Island. Bull (1974) said the Bobolink was widespread and locally common across the state, but noted that it was declining and becoming rare on Long Island and other areas downstate.

The first Atlas map showed the Bobolink widespread across the state, missing only from most of the Adirondacks and Catskills, the Central Tug Hill, parts of the Allegany Hills, the highlands of the southern Hudson Valley, and most of the Coastal Lowlands. The second Atlas data revealed a similar distribution but with a modest decline of 8 percent. Absences were most striking from Long Island and the lower Hudson River Valley, which are areas of increasing urban and suburban development with concomitant declines in agriculture. It is difficult to determine whether the apparent disappearance of the Bobolink from Long Island is real or the result of reduced coverage in that region. The distribution of this species in the Great Lakes Plain and northern Appalachian Plateau, where Bull (1974) believed it to be most numerous, also was more patchy during the second Atlas period. Declines occurred in all ecozones except the Catskill Highlands, Champlain Valley, and Mohawk Valley.

This pattern of a modest decline in breeding distribution correlates with long-term Breeding Bird Survey information, which shows significant decreases across much of the Bobolink's range, especially in the last 25 years (Sauer et al. 2007). In New York, however, BBS data show no statistically significant change in relative abundance of the Bobolink over the period 1966–2005 (Sauer et al. 2007). Partners in Flight does not identify the Bobolink as a species of continental importance for the United States and Canada (Rich et al. 2004). The species is listed as either Threatened or Endangered in the adjoining states of Massachusetts, Connecticut, and New Jersey, though it does not have any special conservation status in New York. Conservation needs for the Bobolink include maintaining hayfields and pastures and deferring mowing of hayfields until late summer or early fall (Bollinger and Gavin 1992). It is noteworthy that the Bobolink has not shown the pattern of gradual disappearance from New York typical of some other bird species of open lands and early-successional habitats, but its falling numbers and the decline in agriculture in the state are not encouraging signs for its future.

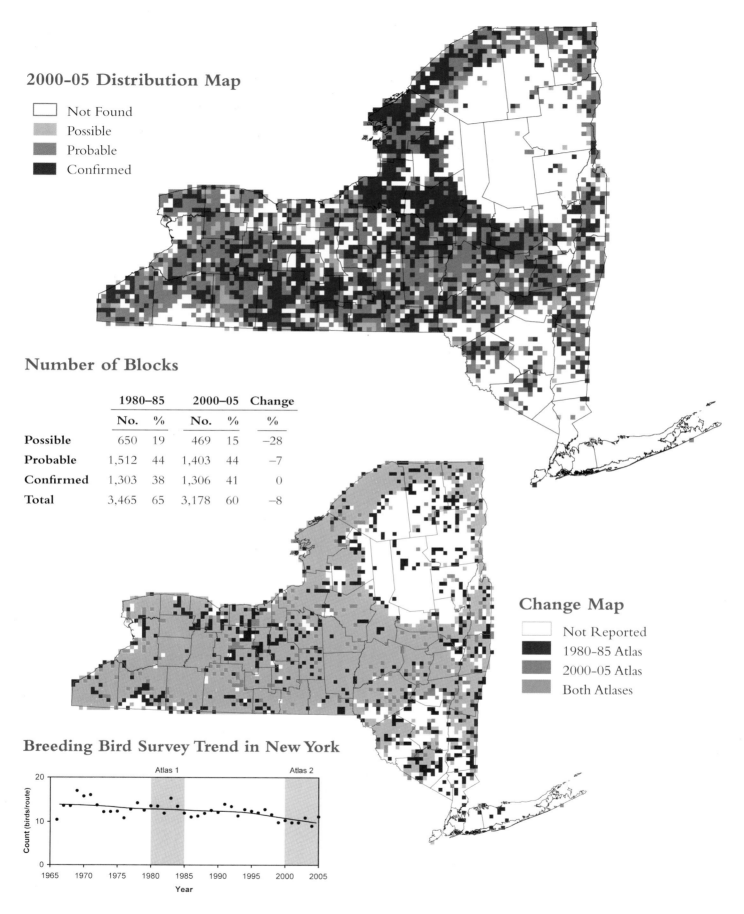

2000–05 Distribution Map

- ☐ Not Found
- Possible
- Probable
- Confirmed

Number of Blocks

	1980–85		2000–05		Change
	No.	%	No.	%	%
Possible	650	19	469	15	−28
Probable	1,512	44	1,403	44	−7
Confirmed	1,303	38	1,306	41	0
Total	3,465	65	3,178	60	−8

Change Map

- ☐ Not Reported
- 1980–85 Atlas
- 2000–05 Atlas
- Both Atlases

Breeding Bird Survey Trend in New York

Red-winged Blackbird

Agelaius phoeniceus

ANNE B. CLARK

The Red-winged Blackbird is a conspicuous, common inhabitant of marshes, swamps, river edges, moist meadows, agricultural fields, and grassy uplands throughout New York. Its extensive breeding range stretches from central Canada and Alaska southward across the United States into Central America and the Caribbean (Yasukawa and Searcy 1995). Historically, as now, it was one of New York's most abundant and widespread birds (Giraud 1844, Eaton 1914, Bull 1974). Through the early 1900s it nested primarily in wet habitats (Forbush 1907, Eaton 1914), but by the 1930s it was also using upland agricultural fields and grasslands in the midwestern and eastern United States, including New York (Bent 1958, Case and Hewett 1963, Ellison 1985c). This species may have been predisposed to this shift; even when nesting in wetlands, it habitually foraged off its territory into surrounding drier areas, including forest edges (Forbush 1907, Orians 1961). It is also adaptable in its nest placement (Yasukawa and Searcy 1995), and in New York it readily nests in the widespread invasive purple loosestrife.

The Red-winged Blackbird was the sixth most commonly reported species in the first Atlas. It was found in every ecozone, and breeding was confirmed in 74 percent of all blocks. It was absent from only 5 percent of all blocks, primarily in forested areas of the Adirondack High Peaks, Central Adirondacks, Western Adirondack Foothills, and Catskill Peaks. The blackbird was still widely distributed during the second Atlas period but dropped to the 10th most frequently reported species. There was little change in the number of occupied blocks, but some that were previously occupied had no records of the blackbird this time. Most of these areas contributed to the enlargement of pre-existing gaps in the Adirondack regions, but, notably, a gap in the Central Tug Hill appeared for the first time. Decreased occupation of blocks in these areas presumably reflects shifts in local land use and forest regrowth. Blackbirds are vocal and easily detected, particularly in colonies. Thus, the Atlas map is likely an accurate representation of breeding in the state.

These changes mirror a larger continental trend of decreasing Red-winged Blackbird populations since the 1960s (Yasukawa and Searcy 1995, Weatherhead 2005).

Breeding Bird Survey data show a steady decrease in breeding populations from 1980 to 2005 in New York (−1.6 percent per year) and survey-wide (−0.8 percent per year) (Sauer et al. 2005). Habitat changes, lower nesting success, winter mortality, and lethal pest control policies may all be factors. In New York, loss of wetlands (Stedman and Hansen [n.d.]) and reforestation over the last decades have reduced nesting areas (Smith 1998c). Population sizes fluctuate with availability of breeding habitat (Yasukawa and Searcy 1995), and historically, population increases were noted in some places with increased upland habitat (Case and Hewitt 1963, Weatherhead and Bider 1979). Nesting success is, however, lower in uplands and hayfields than in marshes (Case and Hewett 1963, Vierling 1999). Changing agricultural practices may explain a 60 percent population decline in Ohio from 1966 to 1996 (Blackwell and Dolbeer 2001), whereas declines in Ontario between 1974 and 1995 are better explained by winter mortality, possibly related to the North Atlantic Oscillation (Weatherhead 2005). Insufficiently evaluated are controls used on this species as a crop pest, including habitat alteration and mass poisoning, sterilization, or feather wetting surfactant applications (Yasukawa and Searcy 1995). Lethal control of flocks overwintering in the southern and western United States may reduce populations of northern breeders. Ironically, the blackbird's impact on crops is often local and exaggerated (Yasukawa and Searcy 1995). The possible decline in Red-winged Blackbird populations in New York needs further study, especially as the species is considered a pest and potential health hazard, subject to both nonlethal and lethal controls in large fall flocks and roosts.

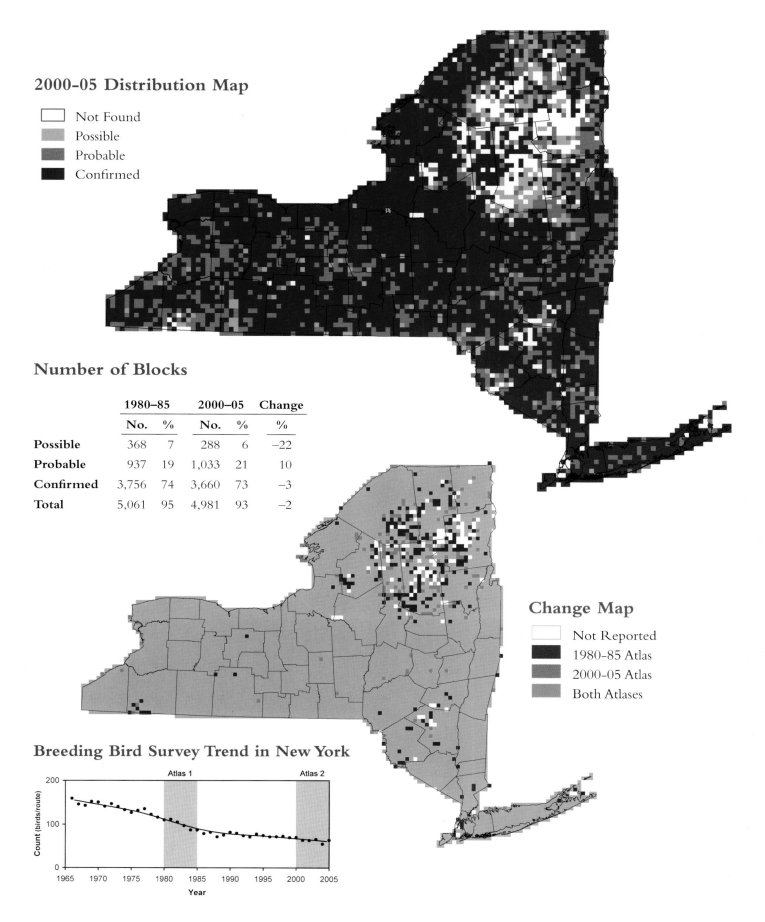

2000-05 Distribution Map

- ☐ Not Found
- Possible
- Probable
- Confirmed

Number of Blocks

	1980–85		2000–05		Change
	No.	%	No.	%	%
Possible	368	7	288	6	−22
Probable	937	19	1,033	21	10
Confirmed	3,756	74	3,660	73	−3
Total	5,061	95	4,981	93	−2

Change Map

- ☐ Not Reported
- 1980–85 Atlas
- 2000–05 Atlas
- Both Atlases

Breeding Bird Survey Trend in New York

Eastern Meadowlark

Sturnella magna

CHARLES R. SMITH

The Eastern Meadowlark is becoming increasingly uncommon throughout New York and most of its North American breeding range. Its core summer range extends from eastern Minnesota and extreme southwestern Ontario eastward to eastern Quebec and southwestern Nova Scotia, southward to Central America, the Caribbean, and northern South America (Lanyon 1995). In New York the Eastern Meadowlark is a species of agricultural and some developed landscapes, where it uses hay meadows, grassy pastures, or the grassy areas of airports and golf courses for nesting. The meadowlark prefers larger, contiguous areas of actively grazed pastures (Smith 1997). As a grassland bird, it was probably uncommon in New York before European settlement. Lanyon (1998a) reported that the population had declined throughout the Northeast with the disappearance of suitable nesting habitat resulting from the succession of open lands to forest and suburban development.

During the first Atlas period the Eastern Meadowlark was widespread throughout New York, though absent from the higher, more forested elevations of the Tug Hill, Allegany Hills, Adirondacks, and Catskills. Results from the second Atlas survey show that its breeding distribution declined by 25 percent. The species remained absent from higher elevations, and detections declined throughout the state, creating a more patchy distribution than reported in the first Atlas, with fewer confirmations of breeding. The reduced distribution of the Eastern Meadowlark is coincident with a widespread decline in agricultural land uses and with urban and suburban development, especially in the southeastern part of New York and on Long Island.

Eastern Meadowlark population trends from the Breeding Bird Survey for the period 1966–2005 show a decline of more than 2.9 percent per year throughout its continental range (Sauer et al. 2005). In New York and the northeastern United States, BBS data show a statistically significant decline over the period 1966–2005, though the decline during the 1980–2005 period is less than during 1966–79 (Sauer et al. 2005). The Second Ontario Breeding Bird Atlas also reported a decrease in Eastern Meadowlark breeding range (Bird Studies Canada et al. 2006). Partners in

Flight does not identify the Eastern Meadowlark as a species of continental conservation importance for the United States and Canada (Rich et al. 2004), and it is not included on the Audubon Watch List (National Audubon Society 2002). It is not listed as Threatened or Endangered in any adjoining states, or in New York.

The conservation needs for the Eastern Meadowlark are summarized well by Lanyon (1995) and include conservation of open lands and early-successional habitats, resulting from both human activities and ecological change. The gradual disappearance of open lands and early-successional habitats in New York (Smith and Gregory 1998; see Chapter 4) does not bode well for the Eastern Meadowlark. Habitats favorable to this bird are typically associated with agricultural land use, which is declining in New York. Where possible, later harvest of hay, ideally not before early August, would benefit the Eastern Meadowlark and other obligate grassland bird species by reducing losses of nests and fledglings. Such timing of hay cutting is not practical, however, for farmers whose livelihood depends on harvesting hay in June and July, when its nutritional value is best for livestock food (Ochterski 2005, 2006a, 2006b). On privately owned agricultural lands, the Conservation Reserve and Grassland Reserve Programs of the Natural Resources Conservation Service show promise for conserving habitats that could benefit the Eastern Meadowlark and other grassland birds, as has been reported for other states (Johnson and Igl 1995).

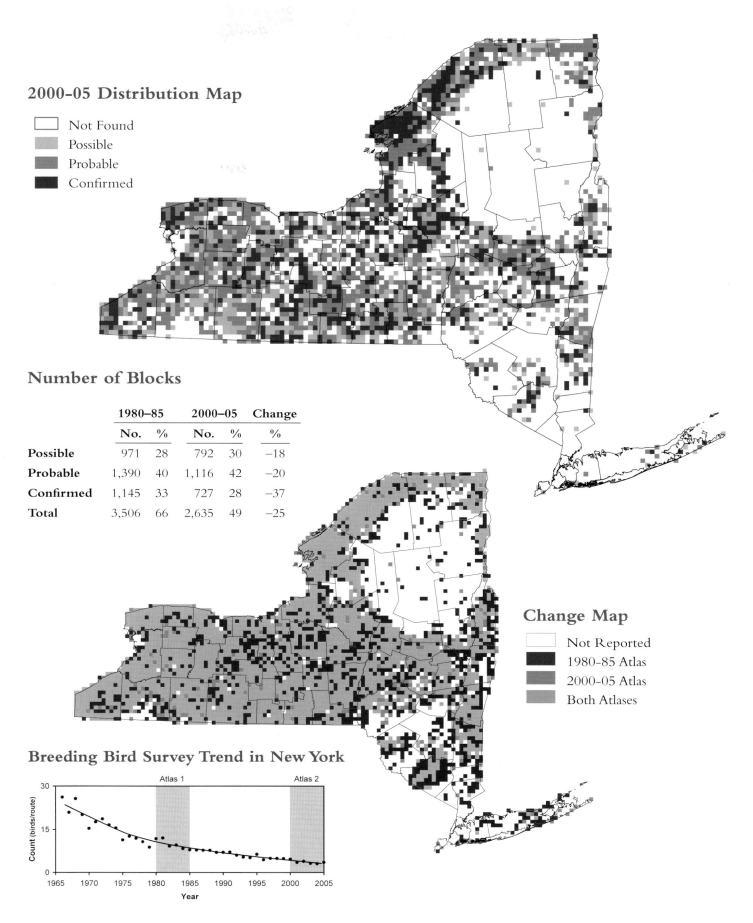

2000-05 Distribution Map

- ☐ Not Found
- Possible
- Probable
- Confirmed

Number of Blocks

| | 1980–85 | | 2000–05 | | Change |
	No.	%	No.	%	%
Possible	971	28	792	30	−18
Probable	1,390	40	1,116	42	−20
Confirmed	1,145	33	727	28	−37
Total	3,506	66	2,635	49	−25

Change Map

- ☐ Not Reported
- 1980-85 Atlas
- 2000-05 Atlas
- Both Atlases

Breeding Bird Survey Trend in New York

Rusty Blackbird

Euphagus carolinus

JOHN M. C. PETERSON

The Rusty Blackbird nests in wetlands associated with coniferous forests across northern North America from Alaska to Newfoundland, northward to the tree line in Canada and southward to the northern United States from eastern Minnesota to southern Vermont and the highlands of northwestern Massachusetts (Avery 1995). The population in New York represents an isolated island. The Rusty Blackbird has a clear affinity for water, favoring fens, alder-willow bogs, muskeg, beaver ponds, and other forest openings such as the swampy shores of lakes and streams (Avery 1995). In New York, typical habitats are similarly boreal bogs, ponds, and swamps, often with standing dead snags, surrounded by forest (J. M. C. Peterson 1988o). Early ornithologists sometimes failed to locate this species in their Adirondack explorations (see Peterson 1988o), but DeKay (1844) suspected it bred there and Merriam (1881) called it a common summer resident. Bull (1974) mapped just 20 known breeding sites.

The first Atlas survey located the Rusty Blackbird in 148 blocks in the Adirondacks, with a probable peripheral population on the Central Tug Hill. Confirmed nesting was confined to the Western Adirondack Foothills, Central Adirondacks, and Adirondack High Peaks. Any apparent expansion of the range noted in the first Atlas was attributed in part to the more dedicated search, but the resurgence of beaver in the state was also a suspected factor (Peterson 1988o). The second Atlas data showed 23 percent fewer blocks with Rusty Blackbird records. The number of Confirmed records fell by about a third. None were detected on the Central Tug Hill. The main range was still confined to the Central Adirondacks, Adirondack High Peaks, and Eastern and Western Adirondack foothills, and breeding was confirmed only in the Central Adirondacks and Western Adirondack Foothills. The Rusty Blackbird was found in a few more outlying areas, however, with the first Possible breeding records coming from Clinton and Fulton counties, and short extensions to the southeast in Warren County, to the east in Essex County, and northward in Franklin County. The apparent disappearances in western Essex and southern Franklin counties, and even those on the Central Tug Hill, may reflect the difficulty in detecting this rather secretive species, a blackbird often confused with the somewhat similar Common Grackle.

The apparent decline in breeding distribution in New York is mirrored in data sets from other areas as well. The Rusty Blackbird does not lend itself well to roadside Breeding Bird Surveys, and caution is advised in reading too much into seeming declines, but its numbers have decreased precipitously (12.5 percent per year), nearly disappearing from BBS routes in the 1990s (Sauer et al. 2005). Christmas Bird Counts show a marked decline (National Audubon Society [2007]) as well. Lethal control of mixed blackbird flocks in winter may play a part (Avery 1995). In Vermont the distribution of blackbirds in Caledonia and Essex counties did not decline appreciably between 1981 and 1990 (Ellison 1990), but subsequent efforts by the second Vermont Atlas found a huge decline in the state, including the loss from Caledonia County (Renfrew 2005). The second Breeding Bird Atlas in Ontario reported a small decline across the whole province (Bird Studies Canada et al. 2006). Because of the alarming trends over the last 20 years, the Rusty Blackbird has been listed on a Watch List by Partners In Flight (Rich et al. 2004).

This species should receive high priority in any studies of boreal birds in the Adirondacks. Given the ease of confusion with the Common Grackle, the relatively inaccessible breeding habitat of the Rusty Blackbird, its confusing songs and calls, and its apparent continent-wide population decline, this enigmatic species provides a future challenge to those who appreciate the complexity of the boreal forest.

2000-05 Distribution Map

- ☐ Not Found
- ▨ Possible
- ▨ Probable
- ■ Confirmed

Number of Blocks

	1980–85		2000–05		Change
	No.	%	No.	%	%
Possible	64	42	63	54	−2
Probable	36	24	22	19	−39
Confirmed	51	34	32	27	−37
Total	151	3	117	2	−23

Change Map

- ☐ Not Reported
- ■ 1980-85 Atlas
- ▨ 2000-05 Atlas
- ▨ Both Atlases

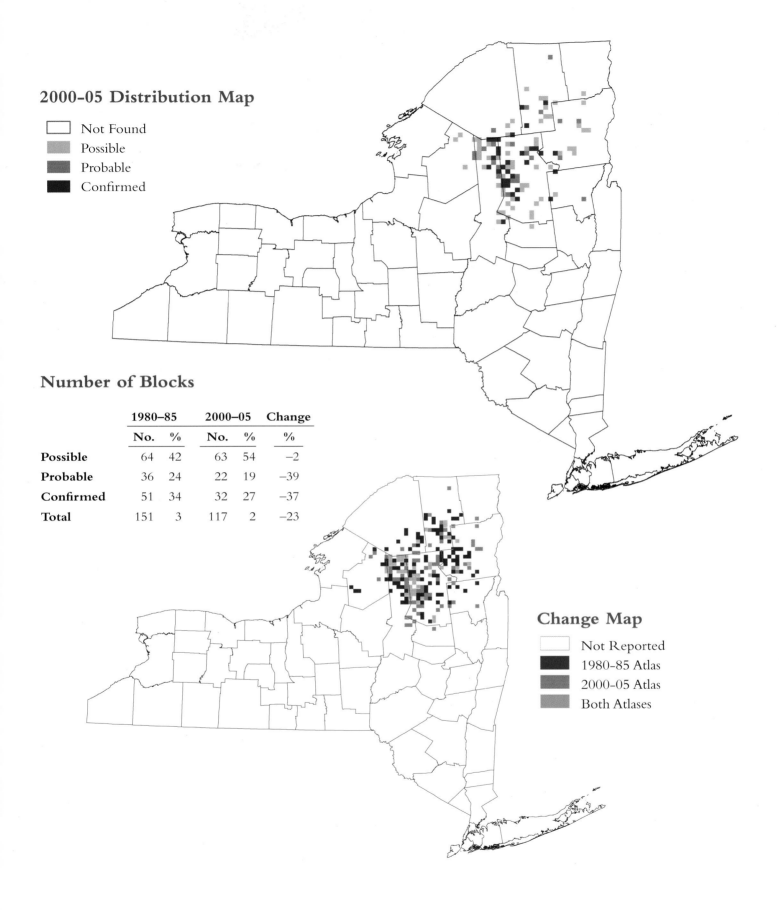

Common Grackle
Quiscalus quiscula

Kevin J. McGowan

A familiar bird across most of eastern North America, the Common Grackle is opportunistic and omnivorous. It is found in a variety of open areas with scattered trees, including open woodland, boreal forest, swamps, marshes, agricultural areas, urban residential areas, and parks (Peer and Bollinger 1997). It breeds from northeastern British Columbia, eastern Idaho, and eastern New Mexico eastward to the Atlantic Coast from Newfoundland to Florida. As a bird of open woodland, the Common Grackle was likely less numerous before European settlement. DeKay (1844) listed the "Common Crow Blackbird" as common and breeding in all parts of the state, but he also thought that its numbers had declined in the coastal and southeastern parts of the state, where he considered them "far less numerous than they were fifteen or twenty years ago." By the end of the 19th century the Common Grackle was common to abundant in most regions of the state (Rathbun 1879, Merriam 1881, Short 1893, Reed and Wright 1909). Eaton (1914) described it as being common to abundant throughout the state, most numerous in cleared lands. He noted that it was found into the Adirondacks and especially along river valleys and lake shores of the western highlands. Beardslee and Mitchell (1965) commented that it was common and that its numbers increased considerably along the Niagara Frontier "in recent years." Bull (1974) considered it common to abundant throughout the state but rare at higher elevations.

The Common Grackle was one of the most common birds recorded during the first Atlas period, reported in 94 percent of all blocks. It was found throughout the state but was missing from the higher elevations of the Adirondacks and Catskills and was less frequent in the more forested areas, where coverage could be a factor. The second Atlas results detected little change in distribution from the first Atlas. The grackle was found in 92 percent of all blocks, with few differences evident between the two Atlas results for any region. An 8 percent decline was noted in the Adirondacks, however. The species was detected even less frequently there where gaps existed during the first Atlas period, areas where elevation, forest cover, and difficulty of access might all play a role. The Common Grackle is a conspicuous bird that does not avoid people, and it was easy to detect in most blocks. Breeding was confirmed in 74 percent of the blocks where it was detected. The grackle brings large items to feed its young, and it is not particularly shy about approaching its nest; the "Feeding Young" code accounted for 58 percent of confirmations. Grackle fledglings are conspicuous after hatching, and seeing recently fledged young (FL code) accounted for 32.5 percent of the confirmations.

The Common Grackle is abundant and widespread and is extending its range westward (Peer and Bollinger 1997). Eastern populations, however, are declining from an all-time high that occurred around 1970 (Peer and Bollinger 1997). Breeding Bird Survey data show a significant survey-wide decrease of 1 percent per year since 1980 (Sauer et al. 2005). The decline in New York is even more pronounced, at 2.7 percent per year in the same time period (Sauer et al. 2005). Data from BBS routes in the Adirondacks, though, have shown no significant change (Sauer et al. 2005). The discrepancy between the Atlas and BBS data in the Adirondacks perhaps can be explained by the roadside BBS protocol, which might disproportionately sample the disturbed habitats favored by the grackle. The dramatic changes apparent in the BBS data throughout the rest of the state demonstrate the limitations of Atlas methods in detecting changes in abundant species. Although the BBS data show nearly a halving of the New York population between 1980 and 2000, no change was apparent in the Atlas data. If the current population declines continue over the next 20 years, signs of this change might be apparent in the third Atlas project.

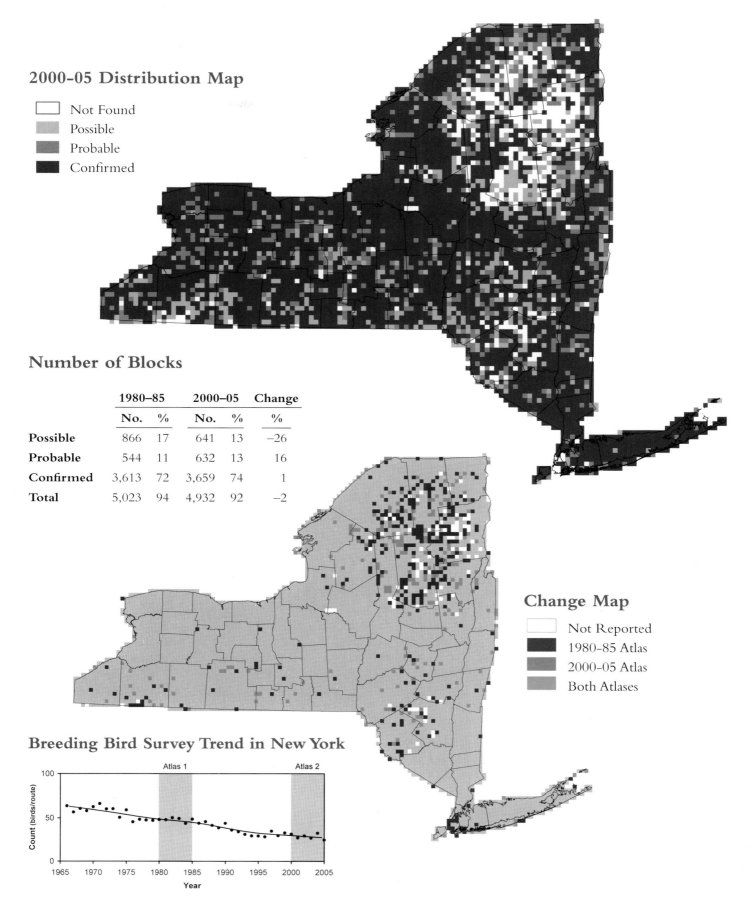

2000–05 Distribution Map

- ☐ Not Found
- Possible
- Probable
- Confirmed

Number of Blocks

	1980–85		2000–05		Change
	No.	%	No.	%	%
Possible	866	17	641	13	−26
Probable	544	11	632	13	16
Confirmed	3,613	72	3,659	74	1
Total	5,023	94	4,932	92	−2

Change Map

- ☐ Not Reported
- 1980–85 Atlas
- 2000–05 Atlas
- Both Atlases

Breeding Bird Survey Trend in New York

Boat-tailed Grackle
Quiscalus major

KEVIN J. MCGOWAN

A noisy and striking long-tailed black bird, the Boat-tailed Grackle is primarily found in marshy areas along the coasts of the eastern United States. It breeds along the Atlantic Coast from New York to Florida, and westward along the Gulf Coast to eastern Texas (Post et al. 1996). New York is at the extreme northern end of its breeding range. This grackle is found in freshwater and salt marshes, open upland habitats, cities, and agricultural fields, usually near the coast (Post et al. 1996). It nests in marshes where the males noisily display and attempt to keep other males away from the clustered nests of the females. The Boat-tailed Grackle was not reported in New York by any early author (DeKay 1844, Eaton 1914), and at the end of the 19th century it probably only bred as far north as North Carolina (Post et al. 1996). It spread gradually northward, reaching Delaware in 1933 and New Jersey in 1952 (Post et al. 1996). The first sighting of the species in New York was a hurricane waif at Brookhaven, Suffolk County, in September 1954, and the first documented bird was photographed in April 1967 coming to a feeder in Queens County (Bull 1974). By the mid-1970s the Boat-tailed Grackle was being seen regularly in several locations in Nassau County, and nesting was suspected when fully grown young were observed near Hewlett Bay, Nassau County, in 1979 (Connor 1988a).

During the first Atlas period, multiple nesting attempts by the Boat-tailed Grackle were seen in the Hewlett Bay area, with fledglings observed in 1981 (Davis 1981, Gochfeld and Burger 1981), and the first nests in the state were found in 1982 on Pearsall's Hassock, Nassau County (Zarudsky and Miller 1983). Breeding was also confirmed at Jamaica Bay, Queens County, where a female was seen carrying food. Two other blocks had Possible and Probable records, both adjacent to the blocks with Confirmed records. After the Atlas fieldwork was completed, the species continued to spread. It began breeding on Staten Island by 1990 and reached Shinnecock Inlet, Suffolk County, by 1994 (Salzman 1998a). During the second Atlas period, the Boat-tailed Grackle was detected in 38 blocks, with Confirmed breeding in 16. It was distributed along the south shore of Long Island wherever marsh habitat existed, eastward to Shinnecock Bay. It was also confirmed breeding on Staten Island, where it was found in five blocks. Observations of the grackle were also made in northern Queens County and along Peconic Bay, suggesting future nesting in those areas as well.

Breeding Bird Survey data indicate that Boat-tailed Grackle numbers have been increasing, but not significantly, over the last 40 years (Sauer et al. 2007). In addition to expanding its range northward, the Boat-tailed Grackle is also breeding in increasing numbers along lakes away from the coast in the southern portion of its range (Post et al. 1996). The first confirmed sighting of this species in Massachusetts occurred in 1986 (Veit and Petersen 1993), a few years after New York's first confirmed nesting record, and continuing reports from Connecticut suggest it is breeding there (Salzman 1998a). New York remains at the northern edge of the breeding range of this species at the moment, but the grackle may move even farther northward in the future.

598

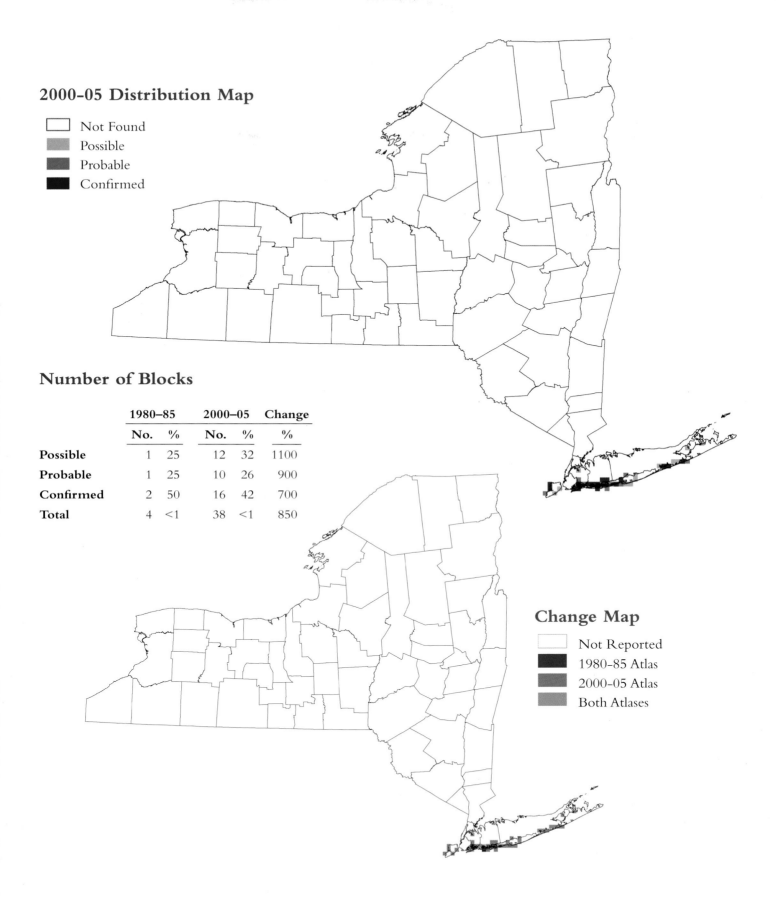

2000-05 Distribution Map

- ☐ Not Found
- Possible
- Probable
- Confirmed

Number of Blocks

	1980–85		2000–05		Change
	No.	%	No.	%	%
Possible	1	25	12	32	1100
Probable	1	25	10	26	900
Confirmed	2	50	16	42	700
Total	4	<1	38	<1	850

Change Map

- ☐ Not Reported
- 1980-85 Atlas
- 2000-05 Atlas
- Both Atlases

Brown-headed Cowbird

Molothrus ater

KEVIN J. MCGOWAN

Originally a bison-following bird of the Great Plains, the Brown-headed Cowbird is the most common brood parasite in North America, laying its eggs in the nests of over 200 other species of birds (Lowther 1993). It breeds from central British Columbia, southeastern Yukon, and Newfoundland southward to central Mexico and northern Florida. The preferred habitat of the cowbird is grassland with low or scattered trees, such as woodland edges, brushy thickets, prairies, fields, pastures, orchards, and residential areas (Lowther 1993). Forest-field edges are preferred breeding sites, based on the location of parasitized nests (Lowther 1993). Before European settlement, the Brown-headed Cowbird was limited to the open grasslands of central North America, and it spread eastward as the clearing of forests created new open habitats (Lowther 1993). Although much of the expansion in the Midwest took place in the early 1800s, it had already established itself in Pennsylvania and New York by the 1790s (Mayfield 1965). Its population continued to increase as more forest was cleared, and it was considered abundant in central and western New York by the late 19th century (Rathbun 1879, Short 1893, Reed and Wright 1909). Even in the Adirondacks, Merriam (1881) deemed it "not rare." Eaton (1914) stated that it was common across most of the state except at higher elevations where the "Canadian zone" began, occurring in the Adirondacks in the valleys and cleared areas. Little changed over the next century, and Bull (1974) called it a "widespread breeder" in the state.

During the first Atlas period the Brown-headed Cowbird was present across the length of the state, missing from the most heavily urbanized areas of New York City and parts of the Adirondack High Peaks, Eastern and Western Adirondack foothills, and Central Adirondacks. Within the Central Adirondacks it seemed to be present primarily along the major road corridors. It was a common species, present in 85 percent of blocks. During the second Atlas survey, the Brown-headed Cowbird was again found in a high percentage of blocks throughout the state, except for in the Adirondacks, with a 7 percent decline overall. The number of Adirondack blocks with cowbird breeding records decreased 40 percent, and the species was almost entirely missing from the Adirondack High Peaks, Central Adirondacks, and much of the Eastern and Western Adirondack foothills. Even

more now, the species seemed linked to major road corridors through the park. Apparent declines also appeared in the Central Tug Hill, the Catskill Peaks and surrounding hills, and to a lesser extent in the Allegany Hills. These are some of the most heavily forested sections of the state, and a decline of this primarily open-country bird there is not unexpected. The Brown-headed Cowbird is a relatively easy bird to detect, as its whistled song is loud and its courtship displays and chases are conspicuous. The fledglings are loud and persistent beggars and readily draw attention to themselves.

The Brown-headed Cowbird is a common bird across most of North America, but its numbers are declining in most areas. Breeding Bird Survey data show a significant decrease of 1.1 percent per year across the survey area since the mid to late 1970s (Sauer et al. 2007). BBS data for New York show an even stronger decline (2.5 percent per year) since the 1960s, and the decline in the Adirondacks is still steeper (5.2 percent per year). This pattern is seen across all of U.S. Fish and Wildlife Service Region 5 (the north Atlantic states). The second Ontario Breeding Bird Atlas also reported decreases across that province (Bird Studies Canada et al. 2006). The reasons for the widespread decline in cowbird numbers are not known, but maturation of forest habitats and the killing of blackbirds in winter flocks may be two factors. The next New York Atlas may very well present a different picture for this species.

2000–05 Distribution Map

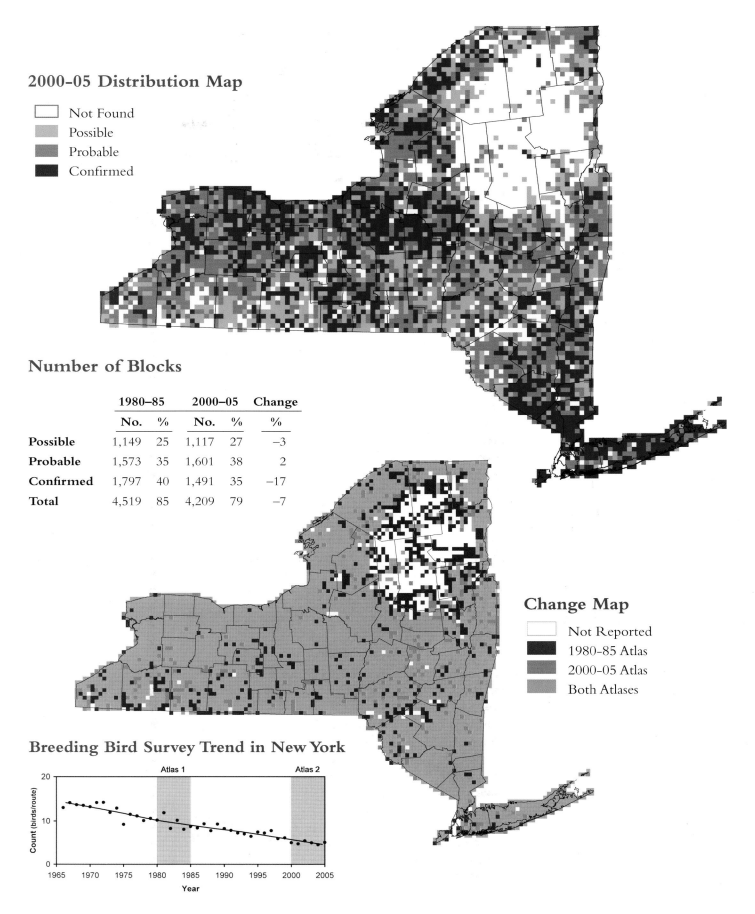

- ☐ Not Found
- Possible
- Probable
- ■ Confirmed

Number of Blocks

	1980–85		2000–05		Change
	No.	%	No.	%	%
Possible	1,149	25	1,117	27	−3
Probable	1,573	35	1,601	38	2
Confirmed	1,797	40	1,491	35	−17
Total	4,519	85	4,209	79	−7

Change Map

- ☐ Not Reported
- ■ 1980-85 Atlas
- 2000-05 Atlas
- Both Atlases

Breeding Bird Survey Trend in New York

Orchard Oriole

Icterus spurius

KEVIN J. MCGOWAN

The Orchard Oriole is a small, dark oriole of eastern North America. It breeds from extreme southern Saskatchewan eastward to southern Ontario and southern New Hampshire, southward to western Texas, central Mexico, and northern Florida (Scharf and Kren 1996). This oriole nests in gardens, orchards, suburban areas, along streams and lakes, and in large planted trees near houses. As a slightly southern species of open wooded areas and streamsides, the Orchard Oriole has never been particularly common in New York outside of the Coastal Lowlands. It was probably absent upstate before the deforestation of the early 1800s, and even after the opening of the forests it remained uncommon to rare there (Rathbun 1879, Short 1893, Reed and Wright 1909). After European settlement the Orchard Oriole was common in the southern parts of the state, including the lower Hudson Valley and Long Island, where it was said to outnumber the Baltimore Oriole (DeKay 1844, Giraud 1844). It remained common around the New York City area and the lower Hudson Valley into the beginning of the 20th century and was also relatively common as far northward as Albany, in the Delaware Valley, and western Long Island (Eaton 1914). Griscom (1923) considered it common in the New York City area, although with a local and erratic distribution. Cruickshank (1942) called it uncommon to rare in the same area, suggesting that its population was declining, although it was still common in the New Jersey lowlands to the west. The decline in the New York City area lasted 50 years (Bull 1964). The Orchard Oriole's distribution up the Hudson Valley in small numbers as far northward as Washington County along Lake Champlain did not change in 60 years (Eaton 1914, Bull 1974). After its period of decline, the Orchard Oriole population appeared to increase again in New York and the Northeast (Connor 1988d).

The first Atlas reported a modest number of Orchard Orioles, mostly in the southeastern part of the state, in the lower Hudson Valley and on Long Island. Few were found in the Triassic Lowlands and New York City, and none were found on Staten Island. It was found locally northward up the Hudson Valley and along Lake Champlain up to the northern boundary of Essex County, and to the southern shore of Lake Ontario and the Mohawk Valley. During the second Atlas period the Orchard Oriole was found in 74 percent more blocks across the state, but its distribution was still mainly concentrated in the same areas of the lower Hudson Valley and Long Island. Although the number of blocks with breeding records was up over most of the state, the largest increase was in the species's stronghold of Long Island, where numbers were up 140 percent. The oriole was found breeding in the Eastern Ontario Plain for the first time, and it reestablished itself across Staten Island. Because of its relative rarity in the state and its rather inconspicuous nature, many observers may not have been familiar with its calls and it might be underreported. Clusters of blocks may reflect observer familiarity in some instances.

Across the country, Breeding Bird Survey data show no change in Orchard Oriole populations over the last 40 years (Sauer et al. 2005). Although a significant, slight negative trend did exist from 1966 to 1979, the trend was flat afterward. BBS data for New York show a significant increase over the 40 years, but the data are sparse, with the species turning up on so few routes that the trend analysis is suspect. Data for the north Atlantic states (U.S. Fish and Wildlife Service Region 5) show a significant and continuing increase of 1.9 percent per year since 1966 (Sauer et al. 2005). These apparent increasing populations have been accompanied by slight range expansions northward, southward, and westward (Scharf and Kren 1996). The second Ontario and Vermont atlases also reported slight increases in Orchard Oriole numbers (Bird Studies Canada et al. 2006, R. Renfrew pers. comm.).

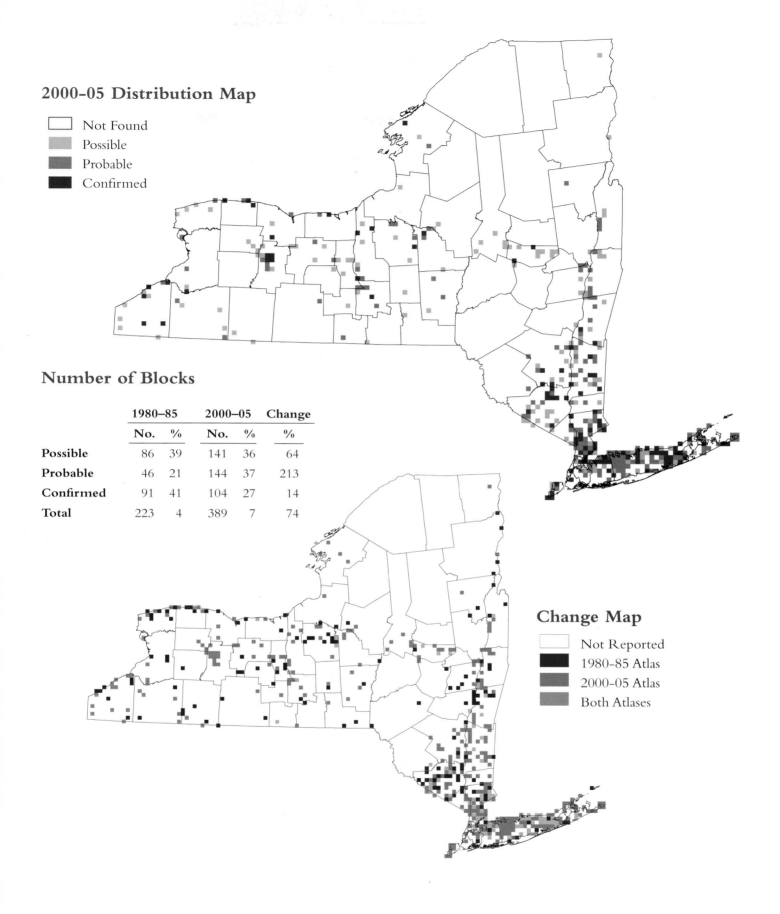

2000-05 Distribution Map

- ☐ Not Found
- Possible
- Probable
- Confirmed

Number of Blocks

	1980–85		2000–05		Change
	No.	%	No.	%	%
Possible	86	39	141	36	64
Probable	46	21	144	37	213
Confirmed	91	41	104	27	14
Total	223	4	389	7	74

Change Map

- ☐ Not Reported
- 1980-85 Atlas
- 2000-05 Atlas
- Both Atlases

Baltimore Oriole

Icterus galbula

KEVIN J. MCGOWAN

The Baltimore Oriole is a bird of tall trees. It breeds across North America east of the Rocky Mountains, from Alberta to Newfoundland and southward to eastern Texas, Louisiana, and Georgia. It nests along woodland edges and open areas with scattered trees, especially deciduous trees, and in parks and wooded urban areas. It frequently hangs its pendulous nest in trees over roads and streams and had a particular fondness for elms before Dutch elm disease devastated this species (Rising and Flood 1998). As a bird of open woodlands, the Baltimore Oriole likely was less common before European colonization of New York and may have been primarily a bird of riverine forests, edges, and beaver meadows. With the opening of the forests it must have spread rapidly; DeKay (1844) considered it common throughout the state. No apparent changes in its distribution in the state have been described since then, although Eaton (1914) mentioned that its populations increased dramatically in the 19th century. He listed it as common throughout New York but missing from most of the Adirondacks. He said that it was most common in the warmer regions and as common in cities and towns as in rural areas. Bull (1974) gave it the same distribution: widespread but absent from the higher mountains.

The first Atlas map showed the Baltimore Oriole to be widespread and common across the state, missing only from most of the Central Adirondacks, Adirondack High Peaks, Western Adirondack Foothills, Central Tug Hill, and the most urban areas of New York City. The second Atlas survey revealed a similar distribution, with the oriole common across most of the state. It was still missing from most of the Adirondacks and heavily urban New York City, but gaps were also apparent in the Catskill Peaks and Allegany Hills. It was found in most of the blocks in the Central Tug Hill this time, a 13 percent increase, which may reflect better coverage during the second Atlas fieldwork. Statewide, the Baltimore Oriole was found in only 3 percent fewer blocks during the second Atlas period than during the first, but it was found in 22 percent fewer blocks in the Adirondacks.

Breeding Bird Survey data show a significant decline in Baltimore Oriole numbers across its range (Sauer et al. 2007). Populations increased from 1966 through 1979 but then began to decline significantly. BBS data for New York showed no trend through 1979 but a significant decline of 1.2 percent per year from 1980 onward (Sauer et al. 2007). BBS data for the north Atlantic and midwestern regions showed a large drop between 1984 and 1985, and the same decline is noticeable in the New York data as well. Just what event triggered this drop and subsequent decline is not known. The American elm was a preferred nesting tree (Rising and Flood 1998), and its decline may have contributed to decreasing Baltimore Oriole populations, but many other suitable tree species exist in the state for the oriole to turn to. BBS data show no declines in the 1960s and 1970s when the disease hit New York. The second Ontario Breeding Bird Atlas also reported a slight, but significant, decrease in oriole numbers (Bird Studies Canada et al. 2006). Because the Baltimore Oriole is a common, widespread species, Atlas methods might not be good at detecting population changes. Its decline from the Adirondacks, Catskills, and Alleghenies represents changes at the periphery of its range, out of marginal habitat where densities are lowest and where changes would be most obvious with Atlas methods. The Baltimore Oriole is a species to watch in the future.

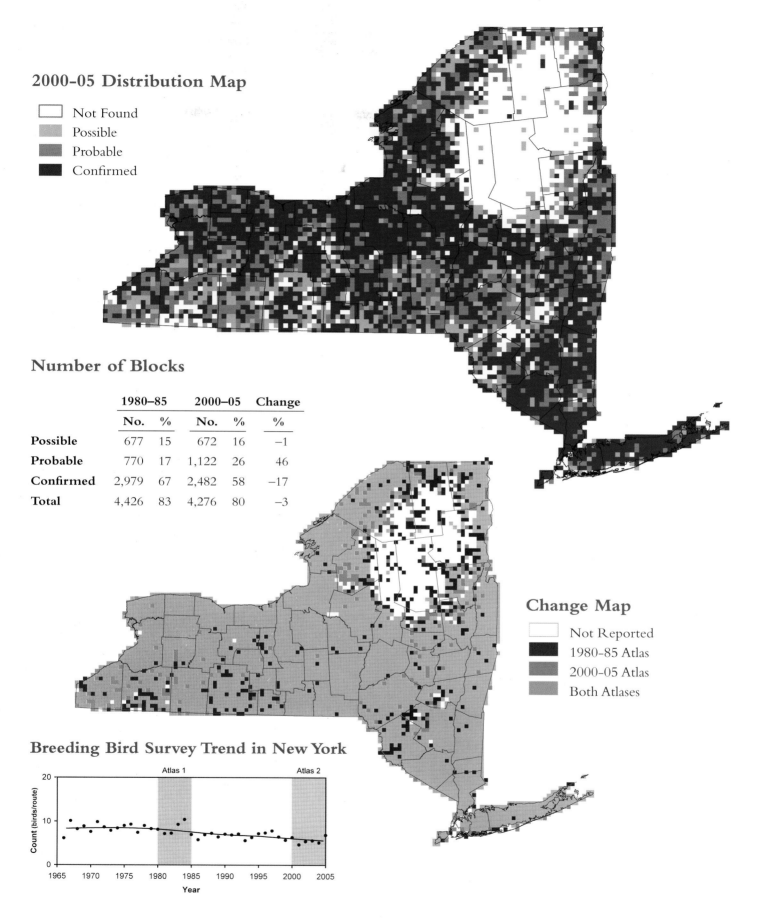

2000–05 Distribution Map

- ☐ Not Found
- Possible
- Probable
- Confirmed

Number of Blocks

	1980–85		2000–05		Change
	No.	%	No.	%	%
Possible	677	15	672	16	−1
Probable	770	17	1,122	26	46
Confirmed	2,979	67	2,482	58	−17
Total	4,426	83	4,276	80	−3

Change Map

- ☐ Not Reported
- 1980–85 Atlas
- 2000–05 Atlas
- Both Atlases

Breeding Bird Survey Trend in New York

**Red Crossbill and
Pine Siskin in a spruce
plantation**

The Red Crossbill and
Pine Siskin are seed eaters.
The Civilian Conservation
Corps (CCC) plantations
of spruce, hemlock, and
larch, planted in mid-20th
century on the worn-out
farmlands of central New
York, provide valuable
food and nesting sites
for these two northern
species.

Purple Finch
Carpodacus purpureus

MATTHEW A. YOUNG

The handsome, raspberry-tinged Purple Finch, with its lovely warbling and sometimes mimicking song, is a favorite among birders, backyard bird-feeding enthusiasts, and ornithologists alike. The Purple Finch is a fairly common bird across much of its range. It breeds across central and southern Canada, along the West Coast, in the north-central and northeastern states, and southward in the Appalachians to Virginia (Wootton 1996). DeKay (1844) listed it as common only in the northern part of New York and uncommon or rare in the rest of the state. Other early authors described it as common to abundant in the central and western regions (Rathbun 1879, Short 1893, Reed and Wright 1909) and in the Adirondacks (Merriam 1881). Eaton (1914) listed it as "common and characteristic" of the open mixed coniferous-deciduous forests of western and northern New York. Beardslee and Mitchell (1965) noted a decline from abundant to uncommon in the Niagara Frontier, although it appeared to become more common in other parts of the state (Arbib 1988f). Bull (1974) called it a common and widespread breeder but less common and more local in the southeastern regions and rare on Long Island. The Purple Finch is found at the edges of coniferous forests and plantations, open mixed deciduous-coniferous forests, conifer plantations, conifer-dominated park-like habitat, and scattered backyard ornamental conifer plantings. In New York it has shown an affinity for spruce of various species (Bull 1974).

The first Atlas map showed the Purple Finch generally distributed across much of the state, most common in forested areas at elevations above 305 m (1,000 ft). It was found in smaller numbers at lower elevations, such as along the Great Lakes and St. Lawrence plains, and was especially sparse in the Hudson Valley and in the Coastal Lowlands. The second Atlas data revealed little change in the number of blocks with records or in distribution, with only slight increases noted in the St. Lawrence Plains, Mohawk Valley, and Catskills; decreases evident in the Great Lakes Plain, Taconic Highlands, and Hudson Valley; and its nearly complete disappearance documented from the Coastal Lowlands. Some changes may well be related to differences in effort between the two Atlas projects. Nesting events at low elevations away from forested areas often occur in fairly open fields with scattered conifers or backyard ornamental conifer plantings, such as Norway spruce and white pine. The Purple Finch is commonly found at elevations below 153 m (500 ft) in the Champlain Valley, where white pine is common.

Purple Finch populations declined by 50 percent in the northeastern states and eastern Canada in 1966–94 (Wootton 1996), although Breeding Bird Survey data do not show a significant pattern from 1980 to 2005 (Sauer et al. 2005). BBS trend data for New York have been largely stable over the past 40 years (Sauer et al. 2005). During the 20th century, conifer plantations that were planted throughout the state during the 1930s and 1940s have matured, providing Purple Finch habitat. One must wonder if these conifer plantings of nearly 141,640 ha (350,000 a) across the eastern Appalachian Plateau of New York (Messineo 1985) helped offset the significant declines noted throughout much of the rest of the Northeast. Some attribute the northeastern decline to the expansion of the House Finch (Wootton 1996), while more recent research suggests that the decline of major outbreaks of spruce budworm infestations might play a role (Bolgiano 2004). House Finch numbers, however, have declined in the Northeast over the past ten years (see the House Finch account, this volume), and during this time Purple Finch numbers seem to have increased or stabilized. The future of this attractive bird breeding in New York appears good, but the Purple Finch could benefit from the protection of northern forests, the replanting of conifer plantations, and the continued use of Norway spruce and white pine in residential areas.

2000–05 Distribution Map

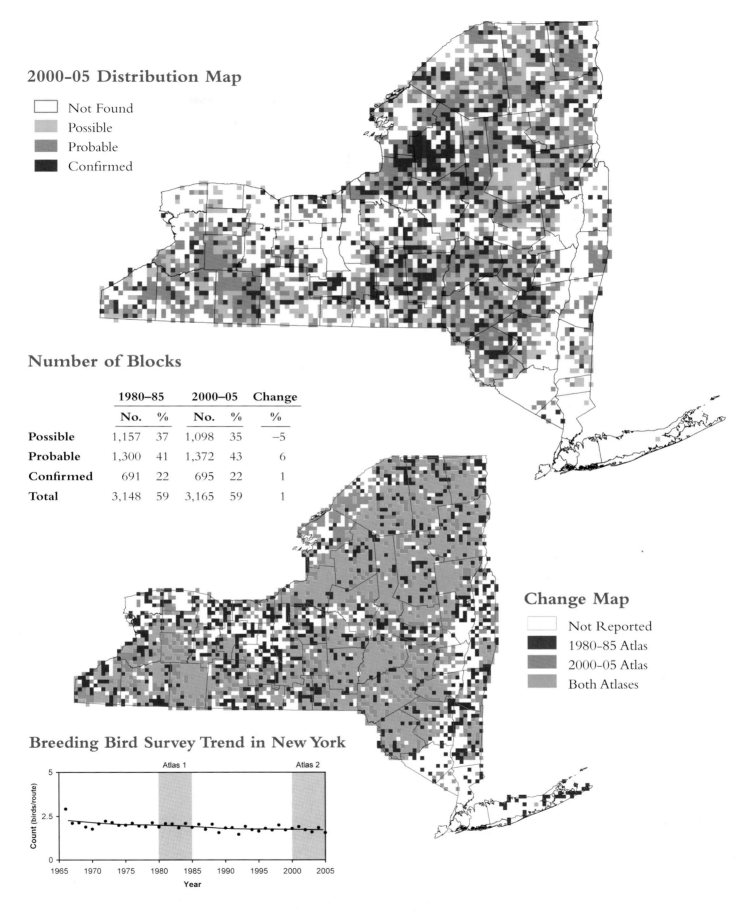

- ☐ Not Found
- Possible
- Probable
- Confirmed

Number of Blocks

	1980–85		2000–05		Change
	No.	%	No.	%	%
Possible	1,157	37	1,098	35	−5
Probable	1,300	41	1,372	43	6
Confirmed	691	22	695	22	1
Total	3,148	59	3,165	59	1

Change Map

- ☐ Not Reported
- 1980-85 Atlas
- 2000-05 Atlas
- Both Atlases

Breeding Bird Survey Trend in New York

House Finch
Carpodacus mexicanus

Melanie J. L. Driscoll

Today, the House Finch is often recognized as the bird that develops "pink eye" or House Finch eye disease. Historically a western species, a few "Hollywood finches" were released from pet stores in 1940 on Long Island (Elliott and Arbib 1953) and began a rapid population increase and range expansion throughout the eastern United States, ultimately joining with the native western population. The species can now be found breeding throughout the United States, with the exception of northern Maine, southern Florida, and parts of Texas, Louisiana, Montana, Wyoming, Minnesota, and the Dakotas. The House Finch feeds primarily on seeds, flower buds, and some fruits; regularly visits feeding stations in winter; and in the East is closely associated with human-dominated habitats (Bull 1974).

During the first Atlas period, the House Finch was widely distributed throughout the southern part of the state, with lower densities found in the Catskill Highlands and the western counties. It was largely absent, except in some villages, from the northern part of the state, especially the Tug Hill Plateau, St. Lawrence Plains, and Adirondacks. During the second Atlas period the House Finch was detected in 19 percent more blocks overall, although the number of Confirmed records decreased 7 percent. The House Finch colonized more of the Appalachian Plateau, Great Lakes Plain, Cattaraugus Highlands, Allegany Hills, Champlain Valley, Champlain Transition, Eastern Ontario Plain, St. Lawrence Plains, and highlands bordering the Hudson Valley. The species is still largely absent from most of the Adirondacks and Tug Hill Plateau, although the number of blocks with records increased 12 percent in the Adirondacks and 139 percent in the Tug Hill. As this species sings frequently from conspicuous perches, the Atlas map likely accurately represents its current range in New York. While the House Finch avoids continuous expanses of forest (Clark 1994), it seems to be present even in blocks with extensive forest cover, presumably near cultivated areas. It remains absent in some areas in New York where the mean July temperature is below 68 degrees Fahrenheit (20 degrees Celsius).

While the House Finch population now occupies most suitable habitat in New York, Breeding Bird Survey data show a decrease in numbers in the state and in the northeastern region since 1995 (Sauer et al. 2005). This situation represents a dramatic change from the population trend found during the previous Atlas period, when the eastern House Finch population was increasing on average 21 percent per year (Robbins et al. 1986). The earlier exponential growth of House Finch populations was stopped in the mid-1990s by an epidemic of House Finch eye disease, caused by the bacterium *Mycoplasma gallisepticum* (MG). This disease was first observed in House Finches in the winter of 1993–94 in Washington, D.C., and rapidly spread throughout the eastern range of the House Finch (Ley et al. 1996, Fischer et al. 1997, Ley et al. 1997). Within 2.5 years of the arrival of MG, House Finch abundance decreased by 60 percent of that expected based on the preceding growth trend (Hochachka and Dhondt 2000). This eye disease reduces apparent survival (Faustino et al. 2004) but is not always fatal; individuals that survive retain temporary, partial immunity. House Finch populations in the eastern United States and in New York have stabilized at lower levels (Sauer et al. 2005). The spread of MG is density dependent (Hochachka and Dhondt 2000), and adults that were previously exposed are less susceptible to re-infection, recover faster if re-infected, and may act as a reservoir for the disease (Sydenstricker et al. 2005). Thus, group sizes at feeders in the Northeast have remained low and relatively stable following establishment of the disease (Hochachka and Dhondt 2006). This pattern, a decline followed by stability in the host population after the emergence of a disease, though unusual, seems likely to continue in the future.

2000–05 Distribution Map

- ☐ Not Found
- Possible
- Probable
- Confirmed

Number of Blocks

	1980–85		2000–05		Change
	No.	%	No.	%	%
Possible	518	18	717	21	38
Probable	724	25	1,197	35	65
Confirmed	1,629	57	1,507	44	−7
Total	2,871	54	3,421	64	19

Change Map

- ☐ Not Reported
- 1980–85 Atlas
- 2000–05 Atlas
- Both Atlases

Breeding Bird Survey Trend in New York

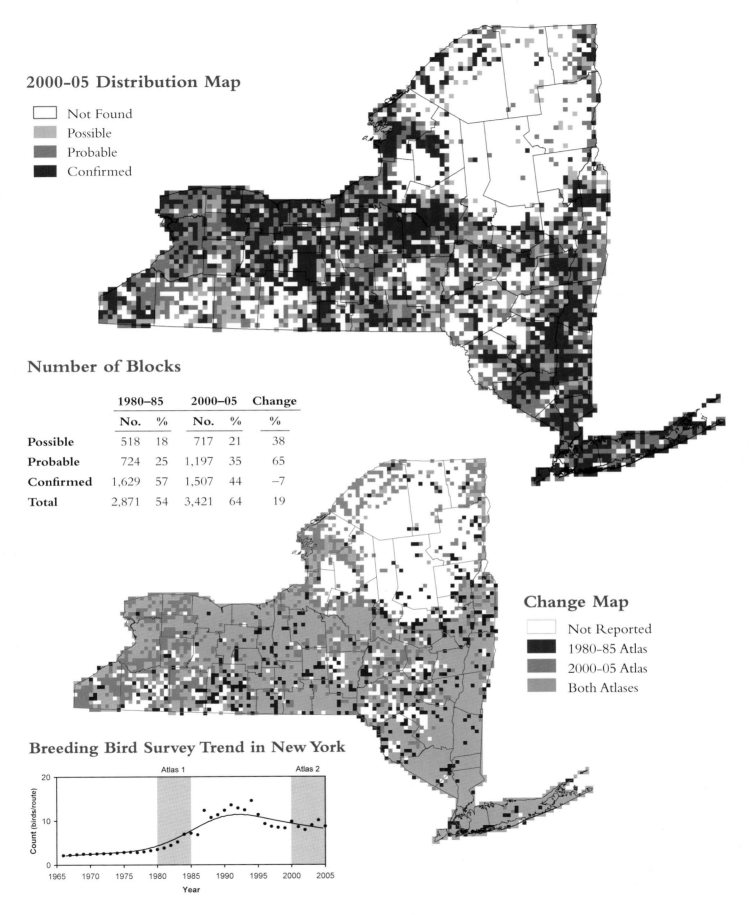

Red Crossbill
Loxia curvirostra

Matthew A. Young

The Red Crossbill is a bird of coniferous forests, found across northern Eurasia and from southern Alaska to Newfoundland, southward to the northern United States, and in mountains to North Carolina and Central America (Adkisson 1996). It is a nomadic and irruptive breeder that in most years is rare in New York. Dickerman (1987) suggested that the species may have been common in the state before the extensive cutting of white pines in the 19th century. Merriam (1881) called it an abundant resident in the Adirondacks. Eaton (1914) considered it to be a common breeder in the Adirondacks and occasional in other parts of the state. Bull (1974) listed 23 known nesting localities in New York, including the Great Lakes Plain, Finger Lakes Highlands, Mohawk Valley, Hudson Highlands, Manhattan Hills, and eastern Long Island. As many as nine call types of the Red Crossbill can be found across North America (Groth 1993, Benkman 1999); each may represent a different species, or, more likely, an evolving species (Parchman et al. 2006). Four types are known to occur in New York: the large-billed hard pine (i.e., red pine) specialist type 2; the small-billed hemlock and spruce specialist type 3; the medium-billed soft-coned conifer (i.e., white pine, spruces, and tamarack) specialist type 1; and the medium-billed soft-coned conifer specialist type 4 (Groth 1998). Nesting can occur at nearly any time of the year, with eggs reported from mid-December to early September across North America (Adkisson 1996). Although season and photoperiod play a role in the Red Crossbill's readiness to breed, the presence of abundant food resources largely determines whether it will breed in any given area (Adkisson 1996). The Red Crossbill may only nest in New York when trees have produced "bumper" or excellent cone crops.

During the first Atlas period the Red Crossbill was found predominately in the Adirondacks and the conifer plantations of Chenango, Cortland, Otsego, and adjacent counties of the eastern Appalachian Plateau. Breeding was also confirmed on eastern Long Island, the Delaware Hills, and the Tug Hill Plateau.

Scattered observations were made in other regions across the state. Although reports were made in every year of the first Atlas fieldwork, most came from the invasion year of 1985. During the second Atlas period the Red Crossbill was found in two-thirds fewer blocks. It was reported again primarily from the Adirondacks and along the eastern section of the Appalachian Plateau, although in much lower numbers. Scattered reports again were made across much of the state, but none came from south of the Schoharie Hills. Crossbills were reported in every year of the second Atlas survey, and breeding was confirmed in all years except 2002. Unlike during the first Atlas period, no major invasion took place, which might account for the large decline noted between the two Atlas periods. Red Crossbills in Chenango County were observed feeding on Norway spruce in February 2004, red pine and spruce in April 2005, and unripened white spruce in August 2005. A notable, widespread invasion occurred in 2006–07. Some Red Crossbill types can nest in the same area for successive years, but it is likely that several different types were present during the second Atlas period (Young and Weeks 2005).

No reliable continent-wide Red Crossbill population estimates are available because of the bird's nomadic and opportunistic habits (Adkisson 1996). Breeding Bird Survey methods probably do not sample this species adequately, but the data show a significant decline over the last 25 years (Sauer et al. 2005). Although the Red Crossbill was found in only one-fourth as many blocks as the White-winged Crossbill was during the second Atlas period, and declines appear real, it still occurs in the state from year to year with greater frequency than the White-winged Crossbill. During "big crossbill years," however, the White-winged Crossbill is often the more abundant species.

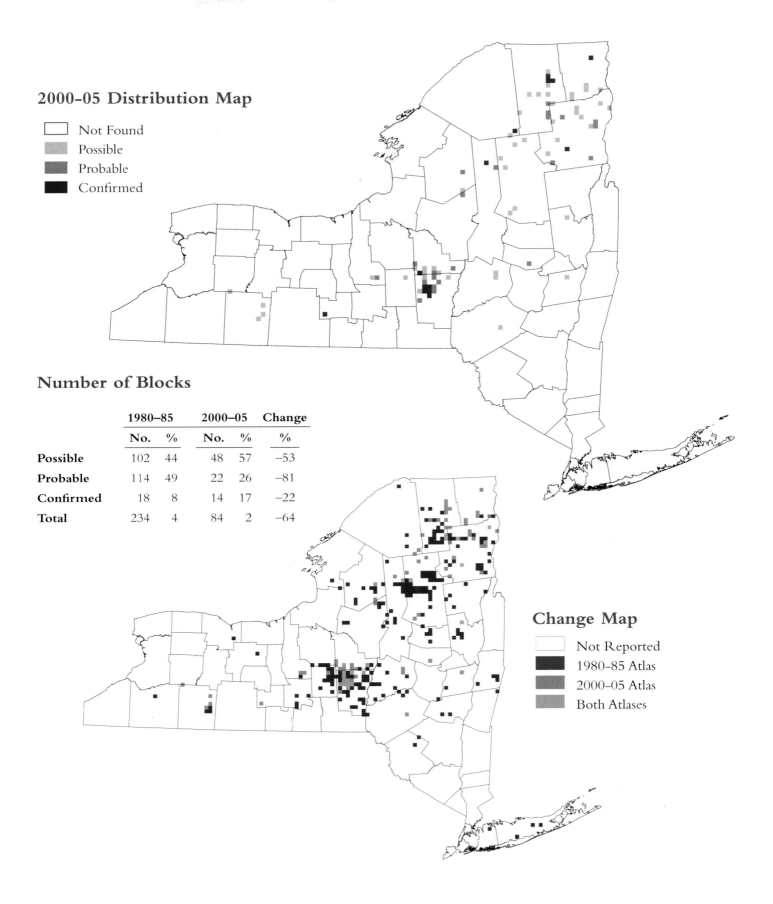

2000–05 Distribution Map

- ☐ Not Found
- Possible
- Probable
- ■ Confirmed

Number of Blocks

	1980–85		2000–05		Change
	No.	%	No.	%	%
Possible	102	44	48	57	−53
Probable	114	49	22	26	−81
Confirmed	18	8	14	17	−22
Total	234	4	84	2	−64

Change Map

- ☐ Not Reported
- ■ 1980–85 Atlas
- 2000–05 Atlas
- Both Atlases

White-winged Crossbill
Loxia leucoptera

MATTHEW A. YOUNG

The handsomely colored, pinkish-red White-winged Crossbill breeds throughout the boreal forest from Alaska across Canada to the Maritime Provinces, and in the very northern United States and rarely in the mountains of the West (Benkman 1992). It is a nomadic and irruptive species that in most years is absent or rare in New York, but appears in numbers during some winters, often becoming more numerous than the Red Crossbill. It has probably always bred irregularly in the Adirondacks and was mentioned as a resident by Merriam (1881). It may never have been common in New York, and good evidence of nesting was only first obtained in February 1975 when a female was discovered building a nest in the Adirondacks at Chubb River Swamp, Essex County (Peterson 1975). At irregular intervals of usually 5–10 years, this species invades the northeastern forests of New York, Maine, New Hampshire, Vermont, and rarely Massachusetts (Petersen and Meservey 2003) to nest. In these forests, the White-winged Crossbill nests primarily in areas of spruce and tamarack (Benkman 1992). A specialized preference for soft cones allows it to nest in the state only when species such as spruce and tamarack produce excellent cone crops. The White-winged Crossbill may nest at nearly any time of the year, but two distinct cycles are recognized: July–October and January–April (Benkman 1992). Emerging, unripened cone crops are used in summer, and ripened cone crops in fall through spring.

During the first Atlas period the White-winged Crossbill was found in the spruce forests of the Central Adirondacks, Adirondack High Peaks, Sable Highlands, and parts of the Western Adirondack Foothills. It was also found breeding in Norway and white spruce plantations of the eastern Appalachian Plateau. A few reports came from the Adirondacks early in the Atlas survey period, but the first Confirmed reports were not until 1984, followed by large numbers in 1985. During 1985, the White-winged Crossbill also nested locally in the Rensselaer Hills and Tug Hill Plateau, with one report coming from the Schoharie Hills and one from the St. Lawrence Plains. It was found in similar numbers and distribution during the second Atlas period, but was reported in far fewer blocks along the eastern section of the Appalachian Plateau and in more blocks in the Adirondacks, especially farther westward in the Western Adirondack Foothills. Outlying reports again came from the Rensselaer Hills, Catskill Highlands, and Tug Hill Plateau, with several reports from the Champlain Valley and one from Allegany County. Most White-winged Crossbill records for the second Atlas were from July 2000 through July 2001. Confirmed reports were made in all months except November and December; all but one were of fledglings or of adults feeding young. Nesting birds were likely missed along the eastern Appalachian Plateau in the winter of 2001 because of lack of coverage. Owing to the crossbill's irruptive nature in the state and its preference for nesting in winter in remote areas with little access, nesting attempts during both Atlas periods were probably missed, making any specific comparisons risky.

White-winged Crossbill populations across the continent fluctuate greatly in response to the availability of cone crops (Benkman 1992). The Breeding Bird Survey probably does not monitor this species well, and BBS data show no significant long-term trends (Sauer et al. 2005). The second Ontario Breeding Bird Atlas reported a modest but significant increase in numbers of White-winged Crossbills breeding in the Canadian Shield portion of that province (Bird Studies Canada et al. 2006). Although this crossbill has been documented breeding in New York multiple times since the first record in the 1970s, it is difficult to assess whether it is actually breeding more frequently here. It is likely to remain an uncommon and irregular breeder in the coniferous forests of this state.

2000-05 Distribution Map

- ☐ Not Found
- ▨ Possible
- ▨ Probable
- ■ Confirmed

Number of Blocks

	1980–85		2000–05		Change
	No.	%	No.	%	%
Possible	78	37	54	23	−31
Probable	114	55	143	60	25
Confirmed	17	8	41	17	141
Total	209	4	238	4	14

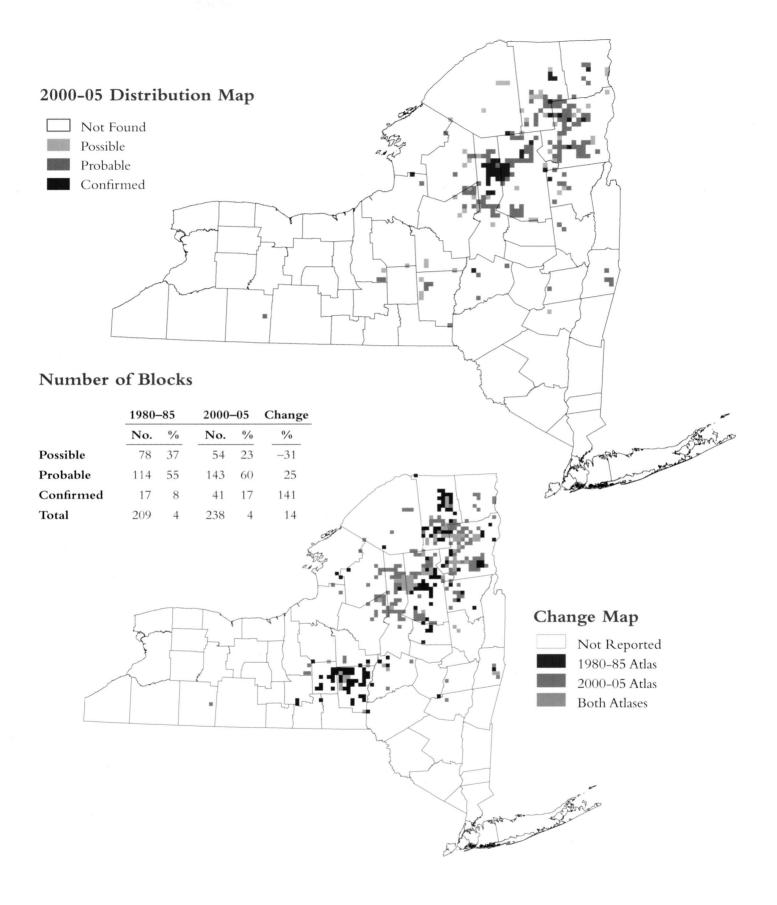

Change Map

- ☐ Not Reported
- ■ 1980-85 Atlas
- ▨ 2000-05 Atlas
- ▨ Both Atlases

Pine Siskin

Carduelis pinus

MATTHEW A. YOUNG

The Pine Siskin breeds throughout the coniferous forests of Alaska, Canada, the upper Great Lakes, and the northeastern states, and the montane coniferous forests of the western United States southward into Central America (Dawson 1997). It also rarely nests following large winter irruptions southward to Georgia in the Appalachians and across the central United States. The Pine Siskin has historically never been a common breeder in New York, but when present during irruptions it can be abundant. Merriam (1881) noted that in the Adirondacks the siskin was an "irregular visitor; sometimes breeding in vast multitudes, and during other seasons not seen at all." Eaton (1914) said that it might possibly occur in the state every year, but it "certainly is rather uncommon except at intervals of a few years." At irregular periods of usually two to five years the Pine Siskin breeds throughout sections of New York, Maine, New Hampshire, Vermont, and rarely Massachusetts, Connecticut, Pennsylvania, and New Jersey, usually following major winter irruptions (Dawson 1997). It nests mainly in areas dominated by soft-coned conifers such as spruce, eastern hemlock, white pine, and to a lesser extent, tamarack or larch. Bull (1974) called the siskin an irregular breeder in the state, even in the Adirondacks, and noted that all 13 known breeding occurrences outside of the mountains were single-year events only. Records were distributed across the state, but none had been recorded in the Coastal Lowlands.

The first Atlas map showed the Pine Siskin nesting primarily in forests of the Adirondacks dominated by spruce, tamarack, white pine, and hemlock, and forests of Chenango, Cortland, Otsego, and adjacent counties of the Appalachian Plateau with European larch, Norway spruce and white spruce plantations, and hemlock. The Pine Siskin also nested, although in significantly lower numbers, across much of the rest of the state. Although the siskin was detected every year of the Atlas survey period, the invasion year of 1985 accounted for 54 percent of all records. Breeding was documented in the Coastal Lowlands for the first time, all in 1982. The second Atlas data also showed the Pine Siskin nesting in the Adirondacks and Appalachian Plateau and in lesser

numbers across the rest of the state. Another invasion occurred in 2001, with most of the siskins nesting in the Adirondacks and in lesser numbers on the Appalachian Plateau, Tug Hill Plateau, and other regions. In 2004 the Pine Siskin settled into the conifer plantations of Chenango, Cortland, Madison, and adjacent counties of the Appalachian Plateau to nest. This nesting event was unusual because in the same year the siskin was noticeably absent in the Adirondacks, its usual stronghold. Documentation of nesting events is made difficult by the species's nature of nesting in late winter and early spring, often in remote areas that are difficult to access. Those habits, together with the siskin's irruptive nature, make a detailed discussion of local changes difficult. It can be noted, however, that unlike during the first Atlas survey, few records came from the Great Lakes Plain during the second Atlas survey, and none were found in the Coastal Lowlands.

As expected for a nomadic and unpredictable breeder, Pine Siskin populations across the continent fluctuate greatly (Dawson 1997). Because nesting often occurs in mid-March to early June (Dawson 1997), the Breeding Bird Survey may not treat this species adequately. BBS data do show a significant decline in Pine Siskin populations across the continent since 1966 (Sauer et al. 2005). Anecdotal evidence suggests that the species has increased as a breeder in New York since the 1980s, but its true status remains difficult to ascertain. For siskins and crossbills alike, it is imperative that plantations be replanted and older-growth conifer forests be maintained, since it is this habitat that produces the most reliable and best conifer cone crops (Benkman 1993).

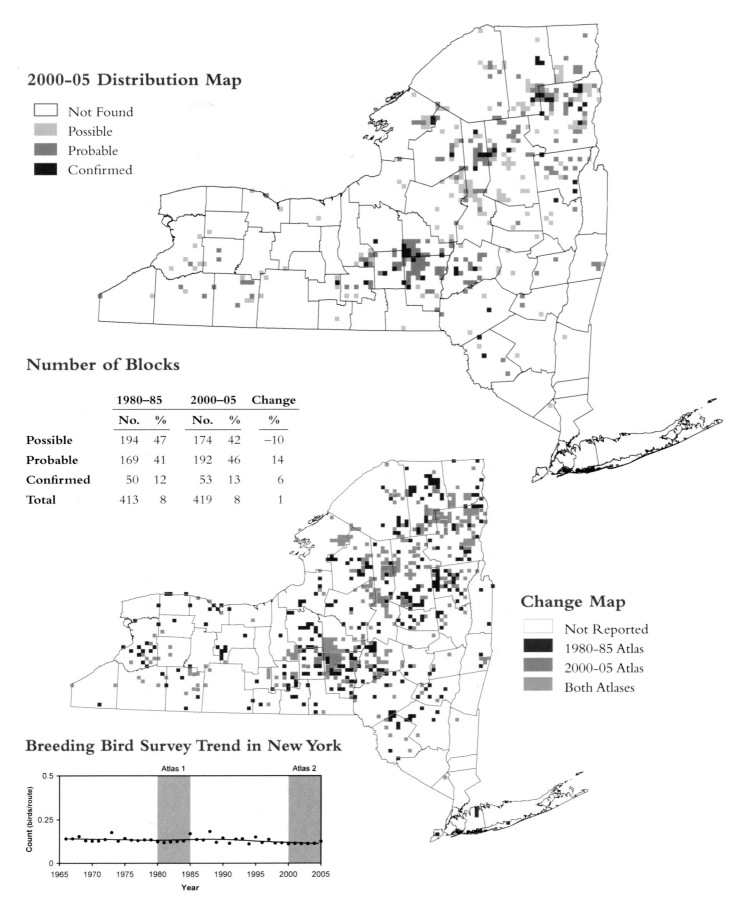

2000–05 Distribution Map

- ☐ Not Found
- Possible
- Probable
- ■ Confirmed

Number of Blocks

	1980–85		2000–05		Change
	No.	%	No.	%	%
Possible	194	47	174	42	−10
Probable	169	41	192	46	14
Confirmed	50	12	53	13	6
Total	413	8	419	8	1

Change Map

- ☐ Not Reported
- ■ 1980–85 Atlas
- 2000–05 Atlas
- Both Atlases

Breeding Bird Survey Trend in New York

American Goldfinch

Carduelis tristis

MATTHEW A. YOUNG

The American Goldfinch is a common, colorful, gregarious bird throughout its range. It breeds across southern Canada and the northern United States southward to Oregon, Colorado, northeastern Texas, and Georgia (Middleton 1993). The American Goldfinch likes open areas where it finds trees for nesting and fields for foraging. This rather general preference allows it to nest in a great variety of habitats such as parks, shrublands, second growth, forest edges, swamps, early-successional fields, orchards, and hedgerows. The goldfinch probably evolved as a bird of river corridors, beaver meadows, swamps, marshes, and fire-maintained open areas, rather than deep forests (Nickell 1951), and was probably not especially common in New York in pre-colonial times (Smith 1988a). It likely reached its peak abundance in the state during the height of the clearing of forests for agriculture, from the mid-1800s to mid-1900s. It was already considered common and widespread in the state by the mid-1800s (DeKay 1844, Giraud 1844, Rathbun 1879) and stayed that way for another 100 years (Bull 1974). One of the latest breeding species in New York, it does not commence nesting until the thistle plant, an introduced species, has matured to seed in late June. It therefore nests from late June through August and occasionally into September. Thistle is used to feed the young and to line the nest.

The first Atlas map showed the American Goldfinch present throughout the state, absent only from parts of the Adirondacks and highly developed areas of New York City and western Long Island. Found in 92 percent of all blocks, it was the 13th most prevalent species. The second Atlas data revealed little change in distribution, if any. A 20 percent increase in the Coastal Lowlands was the largest change noted. The goldfinch was reported in only slightly more blocks overall, now the eighth most common species, but breeding was confirmed in slightly fewer blocks. Confirmation of breeding may have been missed because of the late nesting season when many field workers were perhaps finished with their work.

The survey-wide Breeding Bird Survey trend data describes a relatively stable population across much of its range (Sauer et al. 2007). BBS trend data in New York and the surrounding Northeast show a significant long-term decline since 1966. This decline, however, appears to have occurred predominantly during the 1966–79 period, and the population has not significantly changed since that time (Sauer et al. 2007). The decrease could have been the result of the maturation of forests across the Northeast. Landscaping practices that allow for the presence of weeds could enhance the urban environment for the goldfinch (Middleton 1993). Generally, the future of this bird in New York appears secure.

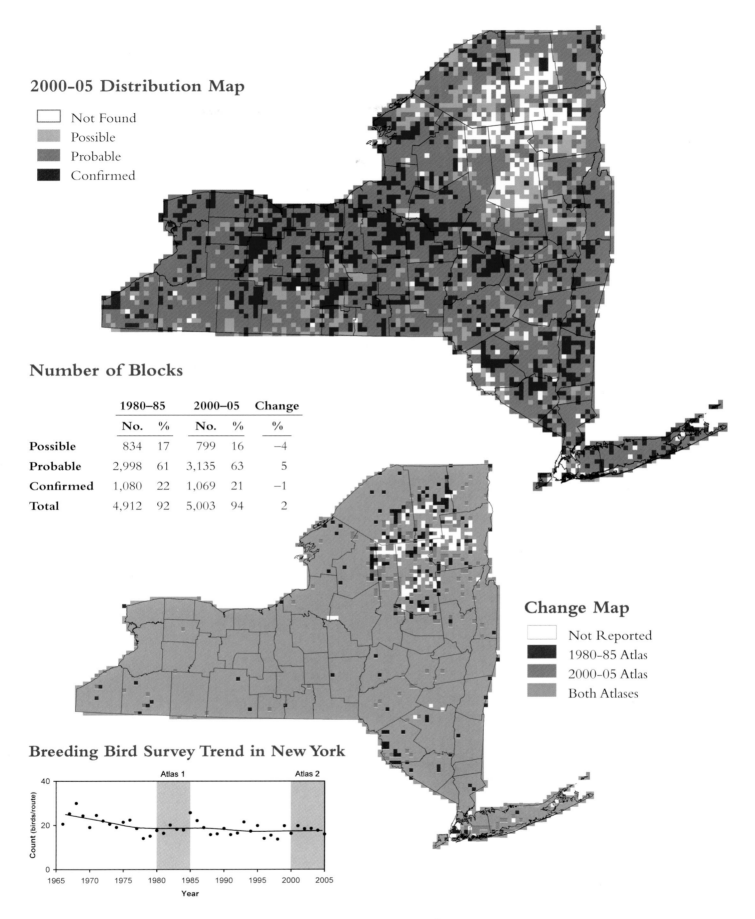

2000-05 Distribution Map

- ☐ Not Found
- Possible
- Probable
- Confirmed

Number of Blocks

	1980–85		2000–05		Change
	No.	%	No.	%	%
Possible	834	17	799	16	−4
Probable	2,998	61	3,135	63	5
Confirmed	1,080	22	1,069	21	−1
Total	4,912	92	5,003	94	2

Change Map

- ☐ Not Reported
- 1980-85 Atlas
- 2000-05 Atlas
- Both Atlases

Breeding Bird Survey Trend in New York

Evening Grosbeak

Coccothraustes vespertinus

MATTHEW A. YOUNG

Before 1900, the beautifully colored Evening Grosbeak was a common and familiar bird across central and western Canada and the western United States, where it nested in montane coniferous and mixed coniferous-deciduous forests (Gillihan and Byers 1997). In the late 1800s to early 1900s the Evening Grosbeak was a rare and casual winter irruptive to the East and New York State (Bull 1974). Winter irruptions became more frequent, and in the 1940s, on one of its great eastward irruptions, the Evening Grosbeak settled in the mixed coniferous-deciduous forests of New York to nest (Bull 1974). Since the 1940s the Evening Grosbeak became an uncommon to locally common breeder throughout east-central Canada, the upper Great Lakes, Maine, New Hampshire, Vermont, and New York, with rare nesting events noted in Massachusetts, Connecticut, and Pennsylvania (Gillihan and Byers 1997). This eastward range expansion has long been attributed to the planting of box elder in the Great Plains, which provided a food source for irruptive flocks (Gillihan and Byers 1997), but the major outbreaks of spruce budworm that occurred in 1945–55 and 1968–88 might have also played a role (Bolgiano 2004). In New York, breeding was primarily restricted to the Adirondacks, but also occurred in scattered locations across the state during the "great" invasion year of 1962 (Bull 1974). The Evening Grosbeak nests in coniferous and mixed-coniferous woods, second growth, and occasionally parks (AOU 1983), often nesting in small villages surrounded by forested areas (J. M. C. Peterson 1988f).

The first Atlas map showed the Evening Grosbeak primarily restricted to the Central Adirondacks, Adirondack High Peaks, and Western and Eastern Adirondack foothills. Isolated nesting events were recorded in the Black River Valley, St. Lawrence Transition, Catskill Peaks, Central Appalachians, Great Lakes Plain, Allegany Hills, Helderberg Highlands, and Rensselaer Hills. This grosbeak was found in 44 percent more blocks during the second Atlas period. Although the center of distribution in the state remained the Adirondacks, some noticeable changes in distribution did occur. Particularly noteworthy were the increases in the Champlain Valley and Eastern Adirondack Foothills. Numbers also increased, and nesting was confirmed, on the St. Lawrence Plains, Central Tug Hill, and Western

Adirondack Foothills. While most records are from heavily forested areas at elevations above 305 m (1,000 ft), the Champlain Valley, where the Evening Grosbeak now commonly nests, is at an elevation below 152 m (500 ft).

It is difficult to accurately estimate populations for a continent-wide nomad such as the Evening Grosbeak, and existing data present conflicting results. The Breeding Bird Survey trend data show significant decreases across much of the grosbeak's range since 1966 (Sauer et al. 2005). BBS trend data for New York and northern New England, however, show significant increases during the same time, with the strongest increases taking place in the last 25 years (Sauer et al. 2005). The second Ontario Atlas reported significant declines across the province (Bird Studies Canada et al. 2006), but preliminary data from the second Vermont Atlas show an apparent increase (R. Renfrew pers. comm.). This species is known to congregate during the nesting season in spruce budworm–infested areas to feed on the caterpillars (Bolgiano 2004). Since the end of the last northeastern spruce budworm outbreak in the mid to late 1980s, Christmas Bird Count data show that the Evening Grosbeak has precipitously declined as a winter visitor in the Northeast, including in New York (National Audubon Society [2007]). These results contrast with the New York BBS and Atlas data. The presence of more feeder stations in New York in hamlets surrounded by forested areas could be a factor contributing to the apparent increase in breeding grosbeaks in the state.

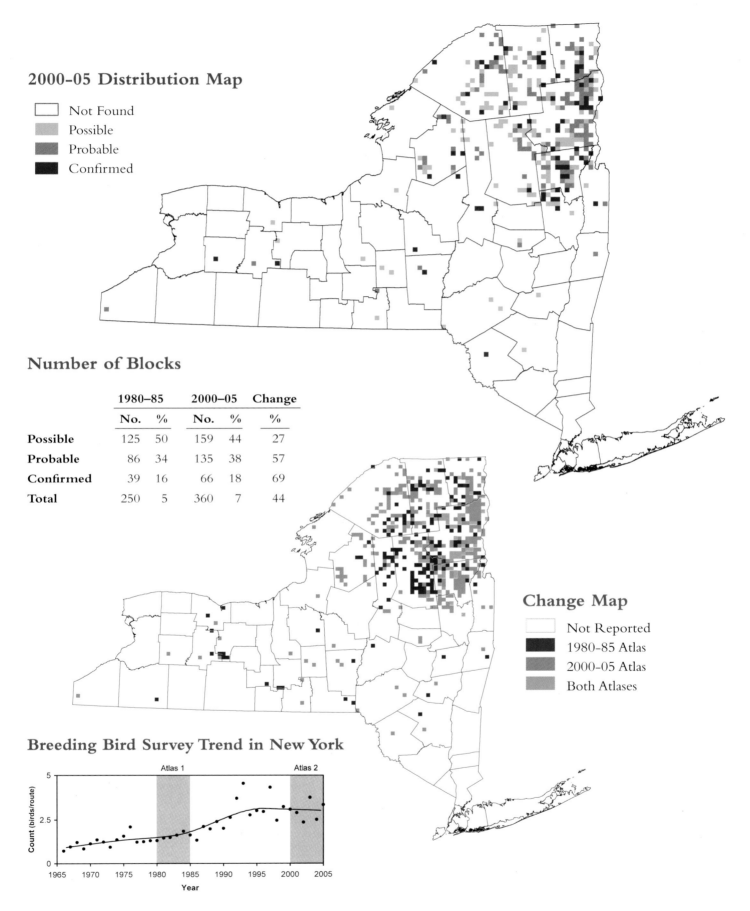

2000–05 Distribution Map

- ☐ Not Found
- Possible
- Probable
- Confirmed

Number of Blocks

	1980–85		2000–05		Change
	No.	%	No.	%	%
Possible	125	50	159	44	27
Probable	86	34	135	38	57
Confirmed	39	16	66	18	69
Total	250	5	360	7	44

Change Map

- ☐ Not Reported
- 1980-85 Atlas
- 2000-05 Atlas
- Both Atlases

Breeding Bird Survey Trend in New York

House Sparrow

Passer domesticus

KEVIN J. MCGOWAN

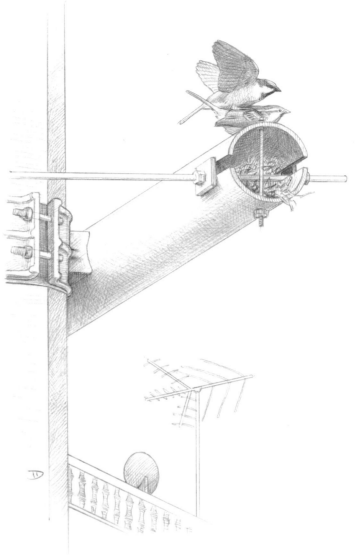

The House Sparrow, introduced from Eurasia, is a common bird in cities and on farms throughout North America. Although it is found in many remote places, this sparrow nearly always stays near people and their buildings. The introduction of the House Sparrow into New York and North America has been well documented. Birds brought from England were released into Brooklyn in the fall of 1851 and the spring of 1852 (Lowther and Cink 2006). The initial expansion in the eastern United States and Canada was aided by transplants from populations already established in North America and from additional introductions from Europe. By 1900 it had spread to the Rocky Mountains. Its spread throughout the West was aided by additional introductions in San Francisco, California, and Salt Lake City, Utah (Lowther and Cink 2006). It is now resident from northern British Columbia to Labrador, and across Canada and the United States southward into Mexico and Central America. It has also been introduced into Hawaii, South America, southern Africa, Australia, and New Zealand. From its introduction in New York City in the 1850s and 1860s, the "English Sparrow" reached all the way to Buffalo by 1879 (Eaton 1914), undoubtedly assisted by introductions into Rochester in 1865–69 (Beardslee and Mitchell 1965). Rathbun (1879) called it abundant in central New York, and Eaton (1914) called it the most common species in the state. Its numbers peaked around 1910–15 and then declined markedly as horses gave way to automobiles (Beardslee and Mitchell 1965, Arbib 1988e). Beardslee and Mitchell (1965) indicated that its numbers increased again in the 1950s. Subsequent declines were apparent in Breeding Bird Survey and Christmas Bird Count data (Windsor 1998a).

The first Atlas map showed the House Sparrow to be abundant and widespread throughout most of the state. It was absent only from forested or sparsely populated areas at higher elevations, especially throughout the Adirondacks and in the Central Tug Hill, Catskill Peaks, Mongaup Hills, and Allegany Hills. The second Atlas survey found similar results, with the same areas of occurrence and absence. Still abundant and widespread, the House Sparrow was sighted in slightly fewer blocks. Declines were noticeable in the regions with an earlier sparse distribution. The number of blocks with records declined 32 percent in the Adirondacks, 34 percent in the Catskill Highlands, and 48 percent in the Catskill Peaks.

Breeding Bird Survey data reveal that the House Sparrow population is declining across most of its North American range. The decline has existed throughout the life of the survey but has been accelerating since 1980 (Sauer et al. 2005). New York BBS data are similar, showing a 2.1 percent yearly decline since 1966 and a 2.9 percent yearly decline since 1980 (Sauer et al. 2005). Data from Christmas Bird Counts also demonstrate a steady decline in the numbers recorded per party-hour since the 1960s (National Audubon Society [2007]). All surrounding states and provinces show similar trends. The second Ontario Breeding Bird Atlas reported a significant decline throughout the province as well (Bird Studies Canada et al. 2006). Populations in Europe also have declined, and explanations for declines in both areas are similar: changing agricultural practices with increased use of pesticides that reduce insect food, and increased efficiency that reduces spillage and weed seeds (Crick et al. 2002, Lowther and Cink 2006). The House Sparrow is still common and widespread in New York, and declines in abundant species are not well monitored by the Atlas project. The next Atlas survey may reveal significant changes, however, if the declines continue.

2000-05 Distribution Map

- ☐ Not Found
- Possible
- Probable
- Confirmed

Number of Blocks

	1980–85		2000–05		Change
	No.	%	No.	%	%
Possible	377	9	387	10	3
Probable	407	10	468	12	15
Confirmed	3,413	81	3,080	78	−10
Total	4,197	79	3,935	74	−6

Change Map

- ☐ Not Reported
- 1980-85 Atlas
- 2000-05 Atlas
- Both Atlases

Breeding Bird Survey Trend in New York

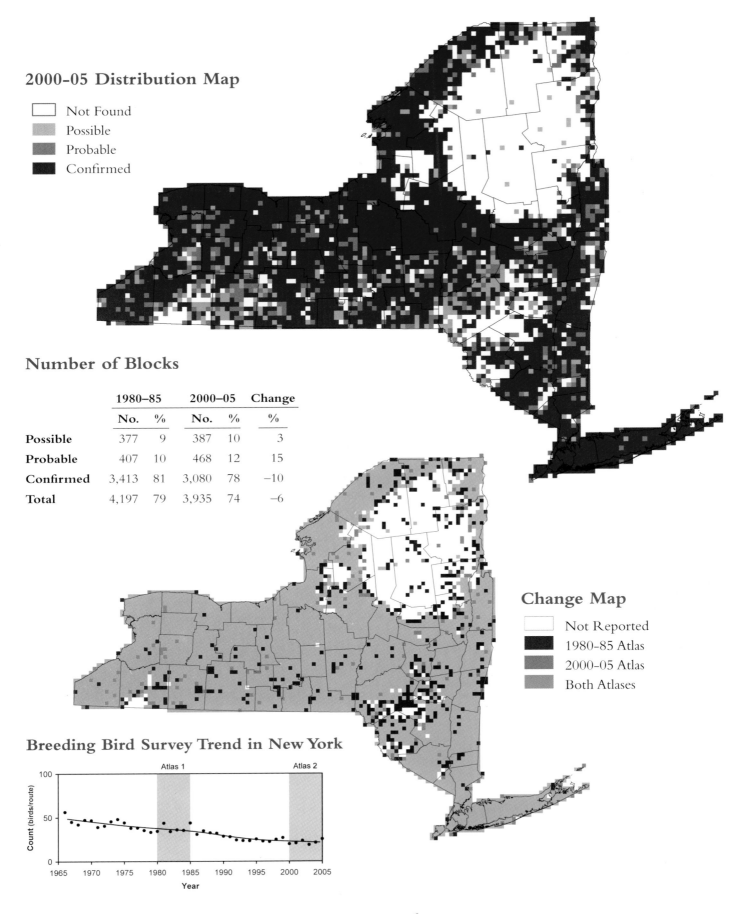

Rare, Improbable, and Historic Breeders

*T*his appendix includes brief accounts for species found but
not confirmed as breeding
during the second Atlas period,
and species known or suspected to have
bred in the state previously.

Greater Scaup, *Aythya marila*

KEVIN J. MCGOWAN

The Greater Scaup is a diving duck
that breeds across northern Canada from
Alaska to Labrador, as well as in scattered
localities across Canada and northern
Eurasia (Kessel et al. 2002). It normally
breeds no closer to New York than the
shore of Hudson Bay or on Prince Edward Island. It is a common migrant and
winter visitor in New York, especially
along Long Island, but has never been
confirmed breeding there. Two individu-
als were reported as Possible breeders in the first Atlas. As stated
in the first Atlas, summering individuals turn up with some regu-
larity but are unlikely to be breeders.

Lesser Scaup, *Aythya affinis*

KEVIN J. MCGOWAN

An abundant diving duck, the Lesser Scaup breeds from
Alaska to western Quebec, and southward to Minnesota, northern Colorado, and very northern California. It breeds primarily
in boreal forests and parklands with small seasonal wetlands and
lakes that have emergent vegetation (Austin et al. 1998). Unlike
other diving ducks in its genus, the Lesser Scaup may place its
nest in uplands away from water and usually selects dry or moist
spots in the wet meadow zone of wetlands (Austin et al. 1998).
New York is well to the southeast of its main breeding range, and
only one breeding record exists: a female with a brood of young
was seen at Tifft Street Marsh, Buffalo, in June 1946 (Beardslee
and Mitchell 1965). Summer reports in New York are regular,
if rare, but most are probably of injured or nonbreeding birds.
Nonbreeding Lesser Scaup are known to summer away from the
breeding grounds (Austin et al. 1998).

The Lesser Scaup was not reported as a Confirmed breeder

in the first Atlas. Pairs were seen in the summer at Braddock Bay,
Monroe County; near Wilson Hill Wildlife Management Area,
St. Lawrence County; and King's Bay WMA, Clinton County.
During the second Atlas period, again no breeding was confirmed, but several sightings were made during the summer in
potential breeding habitat. One sighting was made in June 2000
at the Iroquois National Wildlife Refuge, and a pair was present
on Irondequoit Bay in June 2003.

Although the Lesser Scaup is estimated to be the most abundant diving duck in North America (Austin et al. 1998), continental populations appear to have declined dramatically over the
last 30 years and are currently well below the long-term average
(USFWS 2006c). Reasons for the decline are unclear but may
include contaminant effects on reproduction, habitat alterations
in western boreal forests, and ecosystem changes associated with
climate change on the breeding grounds in Canada. The second
Ontario Breeding Bird Atlas reported the Lesser Scaup still to be
a relatively uncommon nester in the province, located primarily in northern and western regions, but squares with reports
increased significantly in the Southern Shield region and in the
Hudson Bay Lowlands (Bird Studies Canada et al. 2006). It was
rare in southern Ontario, but nesting did take place in several
blocks in the northeastern portion of the province, north of the

2000-05 Distribution Map

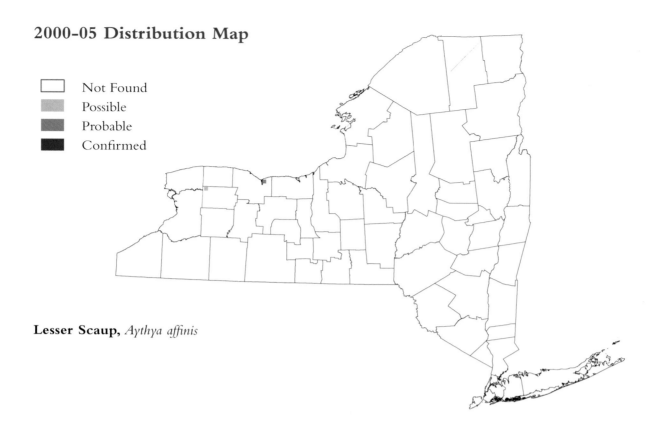

Not Found
Possible
Probable
Confirmed

Lesser Scaup, *Aythya affinis*

St. Lawrence River. Any established population there potentially could spread and lead to nesting events in northern New York. Still, in light of the ongoing continental population decline, sustained breeding by this species in New York seems unlikely.

Bufflehead, *Bucephala albeola*
KEVIN J. McGOWAN

The Bufflehead is a small tree-nesting diving duck that breeds in the boreal forest and aspen parkland from central Alaska throughout Canada to western Quebec, as well as in scattered localities in the Mountain West (Gauthier 1993). Occasional individuals are observed in New York during the summer, and two were reported as Possible breeders in the first Atlas. Such summer reports most likely represent nonbreeders, and Bufflehead has not been confirmed breeding in the state.

Greater Prairie-Chicken (Heath Hen),
Tympanuchus cupido
KEVIN J. McGOWAN

The Greater Prairie-Chicken is a grouse of open grasslands that currently is a resident breeder in scattered locations from South Dakota to Illinois and Texas (Schroeder and Robb 1993). The eastern subspecies *T. c. cupido,* known as the "Heath Hen," inhabited shrubby barrens and scrub oak of the Atlantic states, especially New Jersey, New York, and Massachusetts, before going extinct in 1932 (Schroeder and Robb 1993). Before Eu-

ropean settlement, the species may have been common in the coastal scrub oak and pine barrens on Long Island (Eaton 1910) and possibly other areas in the state as well (Bull 1974). DeKay (1844) noted that the specimen he obtained from Long Island in 1840 was probably the last individual in that region. He mentioned other reports of the Heath Hen possibly remaining in Orange County, as well as parts of Pennsylvania and New Jersey, but by 1870 the only remaining individuals were on Martha's Vineyard, Massachusetts (Schroeder and Robb 1993). Giraud (1844) said that the Heath Hen had been abundant in the brushy plains in Suffolk County only 30 years before his writing, but that hunting for sport and the market resulted in its extinction from Long Island.

American White Pelican, *Pelecanus erythrorhynchos*
KEVIN J. McGOWAN

The American White Pelican is a large colonial-nesting water bird of central and western North America. It breeds on islands in lakes and forages in scattered marshlands (Knopf 2004). Occasional sightings in New York have been documented, occurring not quite annually (Lauro 1998a). Most sightings are of single individuals, and most take place in the spring or fall.

In May of 2005, a pair appeared at Montezuma National Wildlife Refuge. Both were in breeding plumage, with prominent plates or "horns" on the upper bill. Instead of disappearing after a few days, as is the normal pattern, the two remained in the area all through the summer. A single bird stayed until at

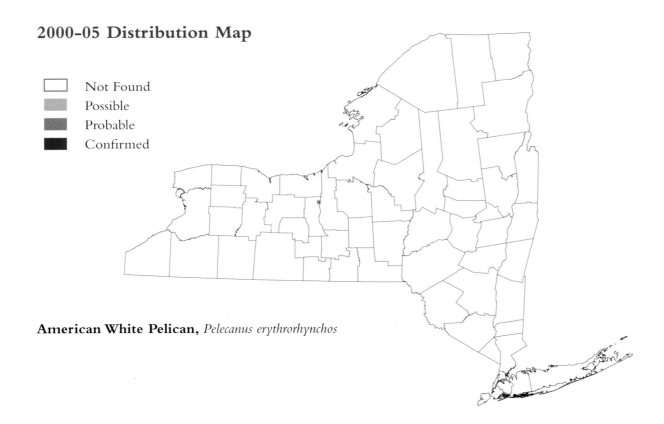

Not Found
Possible
Probable
Confirmed

American White Pelican, *Pelecanus erythrorhynchos*

least mid-October. No nests were seen. Nesting was unlikely but possible. Under Atlas definitions, in fact, breeding was Probable. The Montezuma Wetlands Complex contains a large number of marshes suitable for providing food for young pelicans, and white pelicans are known to nest in marshland in some areas (Knopf 2004). Still, the species is highly social and gregarious, with the smallest colony size reported at eight, although sub-colonies can be as small as two pairs (Evans and Knopf 1993).

American White Pelican populations have been increasing over the last 20 years, and the breeding range is expanding eastward, with new breeding colonies recorded in Wisconsin and western Ontario (King and Anderson 2005). Two new colonies of pelicans were discovered at Cat and Little Gull islands in Lake Michigan in 1997 and 1999 (Cuthbert et al. 2002), only 845 km (525 mi) to the northwest of Montezuma NWR. A breeding expansion to New York is possible in the future.

White-faced Ibis, *Plegadis chihi*

KEVIN J. MCGOWAN

The White-faced Ibis is a long-legged wading bird of western North America. It breeds across the western United States northward to Montana, eastward to western Louisiana, and southward to South America (Ryder and Manry 1994). The species has been known from New York since a specimen was taken on Grand Island in the Niagara River in 1844 (Eaton 1910). It has occurred occasionally during the summer, and the presence of two individuals in 1979, 1980, and 1993 at Jamaica Bay Wild-

life Refuge suggested the possibility of breeding (Burke 1998). It was listed as Possible in the first Atlas, but no breeding has been confirmed in the state yet.

White-winged Tern, *Chlidonias leucopterus*

KIMBERLEY CORWIN

The White-winged Tern's bright white rump, tail, and wing coverts, black underwing, and notably more harsh call clearly distinguish it from the Black Tern, which is the only member of this genus to occur regularly in New York. The presence of a White-winged Tern in the United States causes excitement in the birding community, as it is considered accidental in North America (AOU 1998). This species breeds regularly from eastern Europe to southern Siberia, Mongolia, and northern China (Sibley and Monroe 1990). More than 20 records have been reported in the northeastern United States, where individuals have appeared almost annually since 1975 (Lauro 1998d).

On its breeding grounds, the White-winged Tern associates closely with the Black Tern (Yarrell 1871), and individuals wandering to North America appear to do so as well. Breeding evidence has been documented in North America three times. A female specimen shot on 5 July 1873 in Wisconsin was found to have an egg in the oviduct; it is unknown with what species this female bred (Kumlien and Hollister 1903). The second breeding occurred in Quebec in 1985 when a female White-winged Tern nested with a Black Tern; the pair successfully fledged three young (Yank and Aubry 1985). The third breeding, and

2000-05 Distribution Map

☐ Not Found
▨ Possible
▨ Probable
■ Confirmed

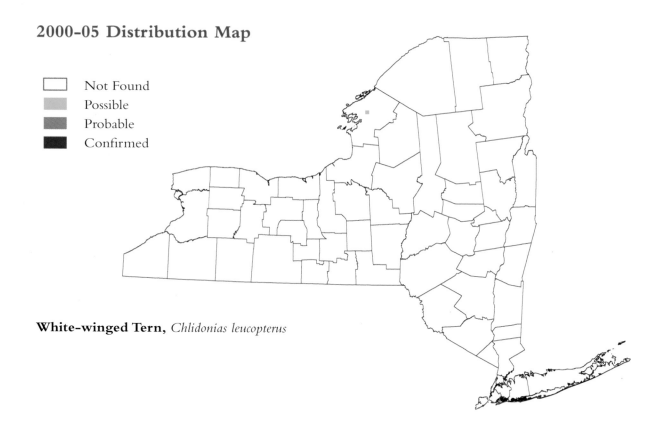

White-winged Tern, *Chlidonias leucopterus*

the first documented in New York, occurred in 1992 at Perch River Wildlife Management Area in Jefferson County, when two chicks were produced as the result of a pairing with a Black Tern (Mazzocchi and Muller 1992, 1993). The chicks, one of which was banded by the observers, did not survive beyond an estimated 10–11 days after hatching.

The first White-winged Tern to be observed in New York was seen on 12 May 1991 among a group of terns in Suffolk County (Schiff and Wollin 1991). Subsequently, in addition to the 1992 breeding attempt, one-time observations were made in Monroe County in 1991 (Skelly 1992) and 1997 (NYSARC 2000b) and at Perch River WMA in May 1994 (Chamberlaine 1994). During the Atlas period, a White-winged Tern was again observed at Perch River WMA during the banding operation at a Black Tern colony. The single bird was seen on 14 June 2000 foraging and mobbing within a group of Black Terns. The observers continued to monitor the site through the season, but the bird was not seen again.

Eurasian Collared-Dove, *Streptopelia decaocto*

KEVIN J. MCGOWAN

A species native to central and southern Eurasia, the Eurasian Collared-Dove was first released in the New World on New Providence, Bahamas, in the mid-1970s and it reached Florida by the 1980s (P. Smith 1987). From there it quickly spread across much of the North American continent, with vagrant individu-

als being observed as far northward as Saskatchewan and isolated pockets of breeding occurring from Montana to Florida (Romagosa 2002). It made a similar expansion across Europe in the mid-1900s (Romagosa 2002). The main, contiguous breeding range in North America in 2002 extended from the Bahamas and Florida to eastern Texas, Arkansas, southern Tennessee, southern South Carolina, and coastal North Carolina (Romagosa 2002). By the end of 2006 that range extended continuously across the southern United States from Florida to California, and northward to Wyoming, Nebraska, southern Wisconsin, Tennessee, and North Carolina (eBird 2006). The species is found in urban, suburban, and agricultural areas where grain is available, and it readily uses bird feeders (Romagosa 2002). It has become one of the most common urban birds in many areas.

Because the species is still commonly kept in captivity, isolated occurrences may well originate from releases and not from expansion of the feral breeding population. Eurasian Collared-Dove was first observed in New York on Long Island in 1996 and then seen again in 2000 (Sherony and Ewald 2003), but these sightings were not evaluated by the New York State Avian Records Committee. The first evaluated sighting was one from the Derby Hill Hawkwatch in Oswego County, on 15 May 2001. That report was not accepted because captive origin could not be ruled out, and the single-observer sighting was not supported by photographic evidence, a requirement for a first state record (NYSARC 2003). The first record accepted by NYSARC was of another individual found on 9 June 2002 on Walker-Lake Ontario

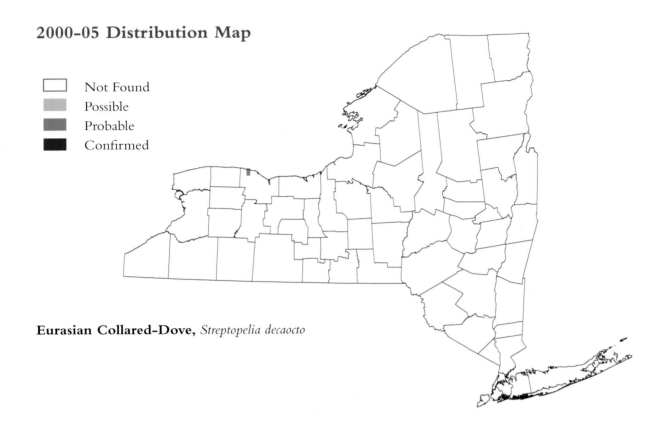

Not Found
Possible
Probable
Confirmed

Eurasian Collared-Dove, *Streptopelia decaocto*

Rd in the town of Hamlin, Monroe County, in the same vicinity where a White-winged Dove was seen (Sherony and Ewald 2003, NYSARC 2004). This bird stayed in the vicinity for a year and called constantly, acting as if it was trying to attract a mate. No second bird was ever seen. Although this bird received an Atlas designation of Probable breeding based on courtship and display, no actual breeding was suspected. Only one individual was involved, but its movements carried it into two adjacent Atlas blocks. A sighting of Eurasian Collared-Dove in Orange County in December 2003 also was accepted by NYSARC (NYSARC 2006), and another individual was again seen in Hamlin, Monroe County, in the summer of 2005 (Tetlow 2005), but reports continue to remain sparse and no known breeding has occurred.

The expansion of the species across North America has proceeded primarily in a northwesterly direction, oddly in almost exactly the same direction as the expansion in Eurasia, and movement up the East Coast has been slow. Although the Eurasian Collared-Dove has been found breeding in a few sites in Pennsylvania (R. Mulvihill pers. comm.), it still has not been found breeding in New Jersey and is barely annual there (P. Lehman pers. comm.). No reasons for its lack of expansion into the Northeast are apparent. Continental populations continue to grow, and it has probably not yet reached the maximum extent of its expansion in North America. The Eurasian Collared-Dove could well become a member of the New York State breeding avifauna in the near future.

Passenger Pigeon, *Ectopistes migratorius*
Kevin J. McGowan

Now extinct, the Passenger Pigeon was once one of the most abundant birds on Earth. Its range extended across eastern North America from the Hudson Bay southward to the Gulf Coast, westward to the Great Plains. By the mid-19th century it was restricted to portions of Canada and the northern border of the United States (AOU 1895). Declines were catastrophic in the 1870s and 1880s, and by the first few years of the 20th century it was gone from the wild (Blockstein 2002). The earliest explorers in New York mentioned the Passenger Pigeon as abundant (Eaton 1910), and the mature forests full of mast would have been much to their liking. DeKay (1844) listed it as a common breeder in New York, although numbers varied from year to year. According to Eaton (1910), the last large pigeon communal nesting recorded in New York occurred in 1868 in Allegany County, with only small and scattered nesting reported from then on. Rathbun (1879) called the Passenger Pigeon common in central New York, but by 1893 Short (1893) listed it as rare in western New York. Reed and Wright (1909) called it "formerly abundant" but noted that none had been recorded since a few were seen in Ithaca in 1892. The latest specimens from New York were collected in 1889 (Eaton 1910), and the last authenticated specimen anywhere was collected in Ohio in 1900 (Blockstein 2002). Although reports of sightings were made here and there for the next decade, no solid evidence was presented for the subsequent

2000-05 Distribution Map

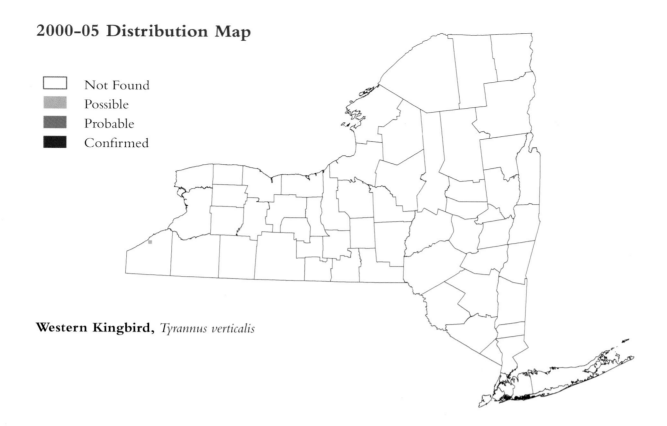

Not Found
Possible
Probable
Confirmed

Western Kingbird, *Tyrannus verticalis*

existence of the pigeon. Judd (1907) noted that the last reports of it in Albany County were of a single bird seen in the summers of 1906 and 1907 in Rensselaerville, and that it had not been common in the county for many years. John Burroughs reported several secondhand sightings in 1906 and 1907 of large flocks in Green and Sullivan counties (Mershon 1907), a flock of 1,000 pigeons in May 1907 in Sullivan County being the very last, but those reports must be suspect.

Black-hooded Parakeet, *Nandayus nenday*

KEVIN J. MCGOWAN

Also known as the Black-headed Parakeet, Nanday Parakeet, or Nanday Conure, this exotic species was confirmed nesting in two blocks and seen in an additional three, all around New York City (Carroll 1988a), during the first Atlas period. It is native to South America, from southern Bolivia and southern Brazil southward to northern Argentina (Collar 1997), and commonly kept in captivity. First discovered nesting in Westchester County in 1980, this species from South America apparently had a hard time with the harsh New York winters; one trapped bird was severely maimed by frostbite (Carroll 1982). After the first Atlas fieldwork was completed, the only additional report was of two birds seen in Orange County in October 1992 (Askildsen 1993). Breeding populations may be established in Florida and southern California (AOU 1998). The New York State Department of Environmental Conservation determined that the Black-hooded

Parakeet was a potential problem for agriculture and native hole-nesting birds, and made the decision in the early 1980s to remove the known individuals from the wild (Carroll 1982). Such actions would preclude this species from establishing itself in the state in the future.

Western Kingbird, *Tyrannus verticalis*

KEVIN J. MCGOWAN

An open-country bird of western North America, the Western Kingbird is a rare to regular visitor to New York. Its normal breeding range extends from eastern British Columbia to southern Manitoba, southward to Minnesota, western Missouri, Texas, and northern Mexico (Gamble and Bergin 1996). The Western Kingbird prefers open habitats, including grassland, desert shrub, pasture, savanna, and urban areas, with trees, shrubs, or tall artificial structures. It occurs annually in small numbers along the Atlantic Coast of New York each fall, but spring and inland records are more uncommon (Marcotte 1998d). Marcotte (1998d) listed six spring sightings: three in Suffolk County, and one each in Richmond, Niagara, and Tompkins counties. Only one additional spring record, from Suffolk County, 25–26 May 2002, has been accepted by the New York State Avian Records Committee since (NYSARC 2006).

No breeding of Western Kingbird is known for New York. During the second Atlas period, on 28 June 2003, a Western Kingbird was observed by an Atlas volunteer near Brocton in

Chautauqua County (Mosher 2004). A report was then received from a nonbirder that the same kind of bird had nested in the same area, near the Brocton Reservoir, earlier that year. The description of the bird and its eggs fit the Western Kingbird, but the nest pointed out was that of an American Robin, located 1.5 m (5 ft) up in a honeysuckle shrub at the edge of a lawn and second-growth woodland. The Western Kingbird is known to rarely use abandoned oriole and Scissor-tailed Flycatcher nests (Gamble and Bergin 1996), as well as old Western Kingbird nests (Bergin 1997), so the use of a robin nest is not impossible. The observer described seeing three blotched, buff-colored eggs and one bird feeding large nestlings, but no further documentation was available (Mosher 2004). Only one gray-headed, yellow-breasted bird was seen attending the nest, so whether a Western Kingbird nested with an Eastern Kingbird mate is not known.

The Western Kingbird has been expanding its breeding range eastward since at least the end of the 19th century as the planting of trees and the erection of telephone poles and other structures in the Great Plains provided nesting sites (Gamble and Bergin 1996). This species occasionally nests east of its regular breeding range, as shown by extralimital breeding records from southern Ontario, southern Wisconsin, northern Illinois, Michigan, central Arkansas, and southwestern Louisiana (Gamble and Bergin 1996). Still, the closest breeding population to western New York is probably central Minnesota, approximately 1,126 km (700 mi) away. Its populations are increasing slightly, though significantly, throughout its range, although its numbers appear to be declining along the eastern edge of the range (Sauer et al. 2005). The open areas that the Western Kingbird prefers are common in the agricultural regions of New York and adjacent states to the west, so just what limits the distribution of this kingbird is not clear. If the Chautauqua County observation was indeed of a nesting Western Kingbird, this event probably represents an isolated occurrence well outside the normal breeding range, not a range extension or harbinger of a future breeding population.

Sky Lark, *Alauda arvensis*

Kevin J. McGowan

A species native to Eurasia, the Sky Lark was introduced in a number of places in North America in the 1800s and early 1900s (Campbell et al. 1997), including the western end of Long Island and the Hudson Valley (Eaton 1914). The Hudson Valley introductions apparently failed, but a breeding population was temporarily established on Long Island. Dutcher (1888) reported on the efforts, at the request of C. Hart Merriam, of Alfred Marshall to look for the Sky Lark in the area of Flatbush, Kings County. He mentioned that Mr. Marshall found the larks to be quite common in the long-grass fields around the town of Flatlands. Marshall collected several young birds and eventually found a nest, establishing the Sky Lark as a breeding species in New York. The lark was still breeding in the Flatbush area by 1895 (Proctor 1895) but had disappeared by the early 1910s (Griscom

1923). Introduced populations are currently established in North America only in Hawaii and on Vancouver Island and the San Juan Islands in the Strait of Georgia, but the species also was recorded breeding naturally in the Pribilof Islands in the Bering Sea off of Alaska (Campbell et al. 1997).

Bewick's Wren, *Thryomanes bewickii*

Kevin J. McGowan

Found primarily in the south-central and western United States and Mexico, Bewick's Wren is a very rare vagrant to New York. A bird of brushy areas and open land with thickets, this wren expanded its range into eastern North America in the 1800s as the forests were cut and turned into farmlands (Kennedy and White 1997). The eastward expansion extended into southwestern Pennsylvania but did not reach New York. Bull (1974) listed only two confirmed records of the species in New York and six additional probable sightings, with the first occurring in 1930. The surprising discovery of a nesting pair on 7 July 1974 in the Shawangunk Mountains at Mohonk Lake, Ulster County, is the only breeding record for New York (Smiley and Stapleton 1974). The pair placed their nest between the rafters and roof of a rustic pagoda and succeeded in fledging three chicks.

The eastern populations of Bewick's Wren began to decline in the 1920s and reached near extinction by 1980 (Kennedy and White 1997, Sauer et al. 2005). The wren disappeared as a breeder from Pennsylvania by the late 1970s (Fingerhood 1992). No sightings have been reported from New York since 1975 (Brooks 1998, NYSARC 2007). The occurrence of a breeding pair in New York was unexpected, and with the continued absence of this species from most of the eastern United States, such an event may not be expected to occur again.

Nelson's Sharp-tailed Sparrow, *Ammodramus nelsoni*

Jon S. Greenlaw

The Nelson's Sharp-tailed Sparrow, recently resurrected as a valid species (AOU 1995), breeds in three disjunct regions in Canada and northeastern New England. Geographic isolation in these regions has led to modest plumage and bill size differentiation and consequent subspecies designations (Greenlaw 1993). The most easterly populations, known as *A. n. subvirgatus*, occur along marine coastlines and inland along some large rivers, from the Gulf of St. Lawrence southward to northern New England. These pale grayish birds can be recognized in the field by experienced observers. Other populations are restricted in the summer to the brackish edges of James Bay and southwestern Hudson Bay (*A. n. alterus*) and to freshwater marshes in the northern Great Plains (*A. n. nelsoni*) (Murray 1969, Greenlaw and Rising 1994). This species is a regular, fairly common to common transient along the New York coast during migration in fall but less common in spring (Griscom 1923; Bull 1964, 1974; J. S. Greenlaw unpubl. data). Some fall migrants from the interior

2000-05 Distribution Map

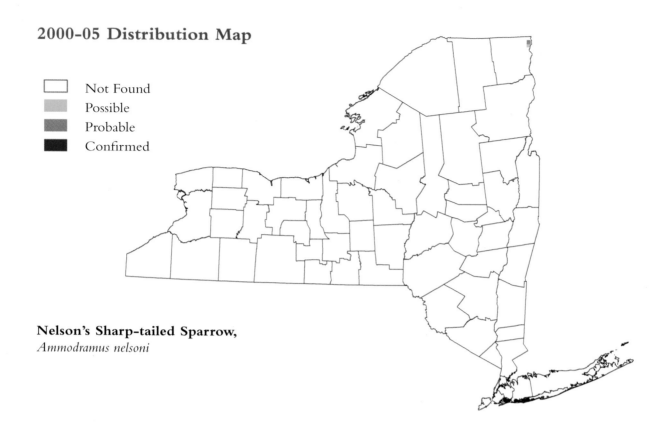

Not Found
Possible
Probable
Confirmed

Nelson's Sharp-tailed Sparrow,
Ammodramus nelsoni

plains and northern bay populations pass southeastward through central New York and reach the southern New England and Long Island coasts before moving southward (Bull 1974). A few northbound birds from these populations pass through western New York (Salzman 1998g, Greenlaw and Woolfenden 2007). Birds that breed in Atlantic Canada and Maine migrate annually through New York along the coast, passing through Long Island from late September through November, and from early May into early June (Bull 1964, J. S. Greenlaw unpubl. data).

The discovery of a singing male *A. n. subvirgatus* on 30 July 2002 in seasonally flooded lowlands along the shore of Lake Champlain in the Chazy Riverlands in Champlain, Clinton County, was one of the great surprises of the second Atlas project. The bird sang irregularly until 9 August but remained in the same wetland until at least 24 August (Krueger 2002). It was observed on seven different dates during this period and was well documented (NYSARC 2004). This notable inland record represents the first documented occurrence in New York north of the lower Hudson Valley (Bull 1964). A single bird was seen again in the same area on 2 and 31 July 2005 (W. Krueger pers. comm.). Elsewhere in the summer, the species occurs inland only along some large coastal rivers (e.g., Erskine 1992). The nearest known summering populations of *A. n. subvirgatus* are on islands in the upper St. Lawrence River near Montreal, at Île aux Fermiers, in the Varennes Archipelago. This location has been occupied since at least 1983 (David 1983) and is about 80 km (129 mi) north of the New York locality. Somewhat farther down-

river near St.-Anne-de-Sorel, Île du Moine (Sorel Archipelago) had one or two males in 1980 (Gosselin and David 1980) and was occupied as early as 1975 (Shaffer et al. 1990, Ouellet 1996). By 1986 the population in the Sorel Islands was estimated to be 25–50 birds (Seutin and Simon 1988). The next nearest breeding population of this subspecies is at Cap-Tourmente, about 200 km (322 mi) northeastward.

Generally *A. n. subvirgatus* occupies brackish and salt marshes, but it uses freshwater marshes on the St. Lawrence islands mentioned above, and in subcoastal locations along rivers elsewhere (Bagg and Emery 1960, Erskine 1992). Outlying, riverine populations, and the male in New York, support the inference that this sparrow is an opportunistic colonizer that readily disperses into potentially suitable habitats, even in inland localities, anywhere from 50 to 200 km (80–322 mi) from existing populations. It is likely that the New York males observed in 2002 and 2005 were solitary colonizers and represented failed founding events. These observations also may provide support for the speculative idea (Bull 1964) that the birds breeding along the St. Lawrence River may migrate to the coast and return inland along the Champlain and Hudson valleys.

Western Meadowlark, *Sturnella neglecta*

KEVIN J. McGOWAN

The Western Meadowlark is a common bird of open country throughout the central and western regions of North America.

2000–05 Distribution Map

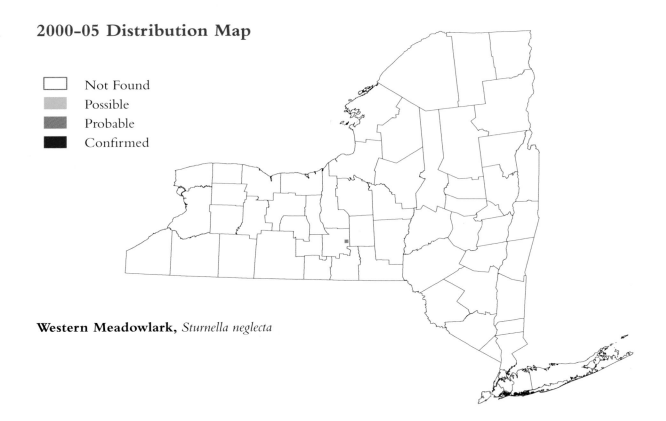

- ☐ Not Found
- ▨ Possible
- ▨ Probable
- ■ Confirmed

Western Meadowlark, *Sturnella neglecta*

Its breeding range barely reaches eastward into southern Ontario. It has been documented breeding in New York only twice, and one of those attempts was with a female Eastern Meadowlark (Lanyon 1998b). The Western Meadowlark extended its breeding range dramatically to the northeast in the first half of the 20th century and became established in southern Ontario by the 1950s (Lanyon 1956). The first New York specimen was collected in Monroe County in 1948 (Klonick 1951), and the first breeding for the state was documented in 1957, also in Monroe County (Miller 1958). Although Lanyon (1998b) reported sightings in western New York as nearly annual, few sightings were made after 1987 (NYSARC 2005a).

The first Atlas reported the presence of singing males in six blocks: four along the Lake Ontario Plain, one in the neighboring Tug Hill Transition, and one in the southern Hudson Valley. During the second Atlas survey, a single singing male was discovered on 8 April 2000 in Dryden, Tompkins County, in the Finger Lakes Highlands. The bird acted territorial and was seen apparently courting a female Eastern Meadowlark. It was observed for several weeks throughout the spring, but not into the summer, and no further indication of breeding was noted.

Western Meadowlark populations are declining throughout the continent, with the largest decline occurring in the northeastern portion of the range (Sauer et al. 2005). This decline may be responsible for the lack of sightings in New York over the last 10 years. The second Ontario Breeding Bird Atlas reported Western Meadowlarks just west of New York, but reports of the species declined throughout the province since the first Atlas work was completed, and they are not common there (Bird Studies Canada et al. 2006). With a source population, albeit a small one, so nearby, further reports of the species in New York can be expected, but it may never become a member of the breeding avifauna of this state.

Brewer's Blackbird, *Euphagus cyanocephalus*

Kevin J. McGowan

The Brewer's Blackbird is a common species of the American West, where it is found in open areas around people, such as farmland, fields, residential lawns, and urban parks. The blackbird took advantage of human activities to expand its range eastward throughout much of the 20th century (Martin 2002). It breeds from southwestern Canada eastward to Ontario, southward in the West to Mexico and in the Midwest to northern Illinois. The first reports of this species in New York began in the 1950s and 1960s, and the first specimen was collected in Erie County in 1966 (Bull 1974). Reports began to increase in the 1980s, especially in the northwestern part of the state. Summer sightings were made in Hamlin, Monroe County, in 1983, 1984, and 1992, but breeding was not established (D'Anna 1998a). During the second Atlas survey, individuals were seen in April 2002 and March 2005 in the same area of Monroe County, but no indication of nesting was noted.

Although the second Ontario Breeding Bird Atlas reported

a number of new breeding areas for Brewer's Blackbird in the southern part of the province, the closest squares to New York in that Atlas were actually farther away than in the first Ontario Atlas (Bird Studies Canada et al. 2006). The distribution shown in Ontario seems to have retreated slightly from the extent of the expansion shown by Stepney and Power (1973), indicating that the 30-year-plus expansion of this species might have come to a halt in the 1970s. The bulk of the eastern Ontario population appears to be located near Lake Huron and Georgian Bay. A failure to spread farther eastward in Ontario may explain the decrease in the number of sightings in New York and the failure to establish a breeding presence in this state.

European Goldfinch, *Carduelis carduelis*

KEVIN J. McGOWAN

Common across Eurasia and a popular cage bird, the European Goldfinch was introduced into North America numerous times in the 19th and 20th centuries. The only introduction that appeared successful was one made in Hoboken, New Jersey, in 1878 (Elliott 1968). European Goldfinches were found in Central Park in New York City the following year, and they quickly spread over the northern portions of Manhattan and its vicinity (Eaton 1914). Eaton (1914) reported some goldfinches building nests in Central Park in 1900 but noted that the species did not seem to be becoming established. Griscom (1923) stated that the introduction had apparently been a failure, as only sporadic reports of the species were made in the New York City area in the 1910s. The goldfinch, however, spread onto Long Island, where a small population maintained itself for a while on the south shore from Baldwin to Babylon, northward to Westbury (Elliott 1968). The birds became relatively common around Massapequa through the 1940s, but by the mid-1950s development destroyed much of the favorable habitat in the area and the species disappeared (Elliott 1968). The European Goldfinch remains a common bird in captivity, and individuals are periodically reported across New York, with 17 reports occurring between 1961 and 1992 (Lincoln 1998a). Most such birds are undoubtedly escapees from captivity, either accidental or intentional. Reports of this and other European bird species in the Midwest and other parts of North America increased in the early 2000s, possibly from large releases by a pet dealer in Chicago in 2002 (Dinsmore and Silcock 2004). Sightings of the European Goldfinch continue, and the large number of individuals involved suggest that successful breeding eventually might occur somewhere on the continent. At this point, though, such an event has not been established, and the New York State Avian Records Committee has not yet accepted any records of this species as of wild origin (NYSARC 2007).

Breeding Season Table

Compiled by Laura A. Sommers

The Breeding Season Table printed as Appendix C (Meade 1988a) in the first Atlas publication is the basis for the table presented here. That first table was compiled by Gordon C. Meade as an aid to the 1980–85 atlasers in their fieldwork and was also provided in the *Handbook for Workers* for the 2000–05 atlasers. The data in the table were derived from Forbush (1929), Bull (1974), and Harrison (1978). Although dates of observations were not formally collected during the 1980–85 Atlas survey, some data from regional coordinators and surveyors were used.

For the 2000–05 project, atlasers were asked to record the dates of all observations. Those dates were incorporated into the Eggs, Nestlings, and Fledglings columns of the table from the first Atlas, and the resulting table is presented here. Dates in the Eggs column are from records with the following codes: ON (occupied nest), NE (nest with eggs), FE (female with egg in oviduct). Dates in the "Nestlings" column are from records with the following codes: FS (carrying fecal sac), NY (nest with young), FY

(feeding young, carrying food for young). Dates in the Fledglings column are from records with the FL (recently fledged young, or downy young of precocial species) code.

The names of new breeding species are printed in red. Information on the number of broods, incubation period, and nestling period for new breeding species was obtained from *The Birds of North America Online* database (see Literature Cited) and may not be specific to New York. Additionally, this reference was consulted to update the table where "no information" was indicated in Meade (1988a).

The breeding dates in red indicate changes from the original table based on records in the 2000–05 Atlas database. Dates were changed when earlier or later dates, or both, were reported for the second Atlas. It is important to note that the ranges of dates are approximations, and some dates may represent only a single record. Also, this table includes data that are currently available to us, and it should not be considered exhaustive or definitive.

Species	Information from literature			Breeding dates for New York (earliest and latest dates reported)		
	No. of broods	Incubation period (days)	Nestling period	Eggs	Nestlings	Fledglings
Canada Goose	1	25–30	Fly @ 9 weeks	3/27–7/24	4/13–7/28	4/12–9/8
Mute Swan	1	34–38	Indep. @ about 4 months	3/25–7/9	4/15–7/29	4/21–8/22
Trumpeter Swan	1 ★	32–37 ★	Fledge @ 90–122 days ★	5/20–6/24	†	6/2–10/28
Wood Duck	1	28–32	Lv. nest in 24–30 hours	3/28–8/20	5/9–8/7	4/9–9/23
Gadwall	1	25–28	Fly @ 7 weeks	5/30–7/25	5/26–8/25	6/13–9/19
American Wigeon	1	24–25	Indep. @ 6–7 weeks	Late May–mid-June	6/24–8/6	6/13–7/26
American Black Duck	1	26–28	Fly @ 7–8 weeks	4/2–6/22	4/28–7/14	4/8–9/13
Mallard	1–2	23–29	Fly @ 7–8 weeks	3/25–7/24	4/17–8/16	4/6–9/28
Blue-winged Teal	1	23–24	Fly @ 7 weeks	5/3–7/4	5/17–8/7	5/11–8/14
Northern Shoveler	1	21–26	Indep. @ 6–7 weeks	5/28–7/8	6/12–7/18	7/2–7/18
Northern Pintail	1	22–26	Fly @ 7 weeks	5/6	†	7/30
Green-winged Teal	1	21–24	Fly @ 6 weeks	5/25–7/15	6/16–7/28	7/5–8/18

Dates from Meade (1988a) in black text; dates from 2000–05 Atlas in red text.

★   Information for North America (*The Birds of North America Online*).

†   No New York data available.

‡   If brood is lost, it usually will be replaced.

§   No information from references checked.

(?)   Probable.

Species	Information from literature			Breeding dates for New York (earliest and latest dates reported)		
	No. of broods	Incubation period (days)	Nestling period	Eggs	Nestlings	Fledglings
Canvasback	1	24–27	Fly @ 10–12 weeks	†	7/3; 7/7	†
Redhead	1	22–24	Fly @ 56–73 days ★	Mid-May–early June	6/4–7/27	6/13–8/2
Ring-necked Duck	1	26	Fledge @ 49–56 days ★	5/20–6/30	5/29–7/11	6/18–8/22
Lesser Scaup	1	21–28	Fly @ 47–61 days ★	Mid-May–June	6/1	†
Common Eider	1 ★	24–26 ★	Fledge @ 60–65 days ★	†	†	8/6
Common Goldeneye	1	27–32	Fly @ 51–60 days	Mid-April–mid-June	†	6/7–9/1
Hooded Merganser	1 †	31	Fledge @ approx. 70 days ★	4/4–6/17	5/9–7/17	5/2–9/10
Common Merganser	1	28–32	Indep. @ 5 weeks	4/4–7/21	5/15–8/18	4/17–9/19
Red-breasted Merganser	1	26–35	Fly by 59 days	5/22	†	6/28–7/25
Ruddy Duck	1	24–30	Fly @ approx. 6–7 weeks ★	June–early July (Ont.)	5/30–9/1	7/18–7/30
Gray Partridge	1–2	21–26	Fly @ 16 days	Late March–early June	†	7/28–8/5
Ring-necked Pheasant	1–2	23–27	Fly @ 12–14 days	4/14–8/16	5/19–7/23	5/10–9/9
Ruffed Grouse	1 †	23–24	Fly @ 10–12 days	4/1–7/8	5/17–7/28	5/7–9/21
Spruce Grouse	1	17–24	Fly @ 10–12 days	5/27	5/18–7/16	5/27–8/22
Wild Turkey	1	28	Fly @ 14 days	4/18–8/10	5/2–8/30	4/15–10/7
Northern Bobwhite	1	23–24	Fly @ 14 days; full grown @ 60 days	5/25–9/14	6/11–9/30	6/3–10/11
Common Loon	1	27–30	Lv. nest soon after hatching	5/15–7/30	6/4–8/22	5/31–9/15
Pied-billed Grebe	1, poss. 2	23–24	Independent @ 25–62 days ★	4/21–7/10	5/14–8/20	5/27–9/23
Double-crested Cormorant	1	25–29	Yg. wander @ 3–4 weeks, fly @ 5–6 weeks, indep. @ 10 weeks	4/11–8/9	5/21–9/19	6/21–8/25
American Bittern	1	24–29	Lv. nest @ 14 days	5/10–7/2	5/26–7/24	6/8–8/14
Least Bittern	1–2	15–19	Lv. nest @ 5–14 days	5/15–7/29	6/10–7/29	7/2–9/4
Great Blue Heron	1	25–29	Yg. fly @ 60 days, lv. nest @ 64–90 days	3/23–7/12	3/24–8/8	5/26–9/1
Great Egret	1	25–28	Yg. fly @ 35–42 days	4/27–7/7	5/21–8/11	6/18–7/25
Snowy Egret	1	21–23	Yg. lv. nest for branches @ 21–28 days	4/16–6/25	5/16–7/14	7/11–9/17
Little Blue Heron	1	21–24	Lv. nest @ 12 days, fly @ 28 days, indep. @ 35–40 days	5/21–6/18	5/26–7/10	6/27–8/1
Tricolored Heron	1	21	Yg. climb @ 11–17 days, fed away from nest @ 24 days	5/15–7/18	5/27–6/4	8/16–9/29
Cattle Egret	1	21–25	Yg. fly @ 40 days, indep. @ 60 days	6/7	5/29–7/10	10/13
Green Heron	1, occ. 2	17–21	Yg. fly @ 21–23 days, indep. @ 35–40 days	4/24–8/4	5/22–8/24	6/1–9/19
Black-crowned Night-Heron	1	24–26	Lv. nest @ 14–21 days, fly @ 6 weeks	4/1–7/23	5/21–7/26	5/26–9/3
Yellow-crowned Night-Heron	1–2	24	Fledge @ approx. 37 days ★	4/29–6/10	5/29–7/15	6/9–8/5
Glossy Ibis	1	21	On branches @ 14 days, fly by 42 days	5/3–7/27	5/29–8/25	7/1–9/14
Black Vulture	1 (?)★	38–39 ★	Fly @ 75–80 days ★	5/5	5/19–6/7	8/11–9/4
Turkey Vulture	1	38–41	Fly @ 11 weeks	4/25–6/20	5/31–8/27	6/6–9/24
Osprey	1	32–33	Fly @ 51–59 days	4/5–7/22	4/9–8/15	6/1–8/22
Bald Eagle	1	28–46	Lv. nest @ 10–11 weeks	3/1–6/30	4/11–7/21	5/20–8/29
Northern Harrier	1	21–36	Fly @ 37 days	4/19–6/25	5/19–8/1	6/25–9/29
Sharp-shinned Hawk	1	21–35	Fly @ 23 days	4/16–7/25	5/10–7/23	6/3–8/20
Cooper's Hawk	1 ‡	21–36	Lv. nest: male @ 30 days, female @ 34 days; indep. @ 8 weeks	3/28–7/10	5/9–7/29	6/3–8/22

Species	Information from literature			Breeding dates for New York (earliest and latest dates reported)		
	No. of broods	Incubation period (days)	Nestling period	Eggs	Nestlings	Fledglings
Northern Goshawk	1	28–41	Fly @ 45 days, hunt @ 50 days, indep. @ 70 days	4/17–6/19	5/9–7/19	5/21–8/13
Red-shouldered Hawk	1 ‡	23–25	Lv. nest @ 5–6 weeks	3/25–7/8	5/2–8/10	5/25–8/30
Broad-winged Hawk	1	23–28	Lv. nest @ 29–30 days	4/27–7/6	5/17–7/27	5/23–8/25
Red-tailed Hawk	1	23–28	Fly @ 45 days	2/25–7/25	3/31–8/4	4/16–8/21
Golden Eagle	1	27–45	Fly @ 9–10 weeks	March–June (U.S.)	7/10	7/24
American Kestrel	1	29–30	Fly @ 30 days	4/5–7/25	5/7–8/2	4/27–9/21
Merlin	1 ★	28–32★	Fly @ about 29 days ★	6/27	6/1–7/20	6/19–8/12
Peregrine Falcon	1	28–29	Fly @ 35–42 days	3/2–6/19	4/19–8/1	5/21–8/31
Black Rail	1 ★ ‡	17–20 ★	§	6/20–7/12	†	†
Clapper Rail	1	20–24	Lv. nest soon after hatching; swim @ 1 day	4/11–8/4	6/6–8/20	6/9–9/3
King Rail	1	21–24	Lv. nest soon after hatching	5/20–7/3	6/16–8/6	8/2–8/31
Virginia Rail	1	20	Lv. nest soon after hatching	5/5–7/13	5/11–8/14	5/26–9/8
Sora	1	14–20	Lv. nest @ 1–2 days, fly @ 36 days	4/30–7/17	5/19–8/8	6/8–9/15
Common Moorhen	1	19–25	Indep. @ 5 weeks	5/14–7/25	6/1–8/27	6/9–9/17
American Coot	1–2	21–24	Indep. @ 8 weeks	4/25–7/14	5/17–8/12	5/31–8/21
Sandhill Crane	1 ★	29–32 ★	Fly @ 67–75 days ★	5/11	†	6/5–6/14
Piping Plover	1 ‡	26–30	Fly @ 30–35 days	4/18–7/23	5/4–8/12	5/27–8/18
Killdeer	1–2	24–28	Fly @ 40 days	3/30–7/20	5/3–7/30	4/9–8/17
American Oystercatcher	1 ‡	24–27	Indep. @ 34–37 days	4/19–7/25	5/12–7/28	5/20–8/19
Spotted Sandpiper	1	18–24	Fly @ 16–18 days	5/6–7/26	5/21–8/19	5/21–9/3
Willet	1	22	Fledge @ approx. 30 days ★	5/17–7/18	6/12–7/18	6/8–8/4
Upland Sandpiper	1	17–21	Full grown @ 30 days	4/23–6/15	5/28–7/18	6/2–8/11
Wilson's Snipe	1	18–20	Fly @ 19–20 days	4/20–7/10	5/19–6/21	6/5–7/28
American Woodcock	1	20–21	Fly @ 14–15 days	3/24–7/7	4/17–7/2	4/20–8/14
Wilson's Phalarope	1 ★	18–27 ★	§	†	†	7/2–7/13
Laughing Gull	1	21–23	Fly @ 4–6 weeks	6/7–6/28	6/27–7/25	6/21–7/16
Ring-billed Gull	1	21–23	Fly @ 35 days	4/26–7/10	5/16–7/10	6/8–8/1
Herring Gull	1	24–28	Fly @ 6 weeks	4/27–7/10	5/17–7/27	6/6–8/31
Great Black-backed Gull	1	26–30	Fed for 7 weeks, then begin to fly	4/25–6/27	5/21–7/6	6/20–8/4
Least Tern	1 ‡	14–22	Fly @ 15–17 days	5/9–7/27	5/30–8/30	7/12–8/29
Gull-billed Tern	1	22–23	Fly @ 4–5 weeks	6/9–6/21	7/22	7/21
Caspian Tern	1 ‡	20–22	Fly @ 25–30 days	5/28–7/6	6/14–7/6	†
Black Tern	1	20–22	Fly @ 3–4 weeks	5/26–7/23	6/4–8/5	7/2–8/25
Roseate Tern	1	21–26	Fledge @ 27–30 days ★	5/20–7/27	6/13–8/31	7/11–9/9
Common Tern	1 ‡	20–23	Fly @ 4 weeks	5/12–8/15	5/20–9/3	6/6–9/9
Forster's Tern	1	23–25	Fly @ 4–5 weeks ★	6/8–6/27	6/16–7/21	7/9–7/21
Black Skimmer	1	23–25 ★	Fly @ 28–30 days ★	5/31–9/3	6/16–9/24	7/14–10/11
Rock Pigeon	2–3	14–19	Indep. @ 30–35 days		All months	
Mourning Dove	2–3	12–15	Fly @ 13–15 days	3/9–9/28	4/6–10/5	4/13–10/26
Monk Parakeet	1–2 ★	24	Lv. nest @ 35–50 days	late April–early July	late May–late August	†
Yellow-billed Cuckoo	1	9–11 ★	Fledge 17 days from start of incubation ★	5/26–8/19	5/25–9/17	6/1–9/23
Black-billed Cuckoo	1	14	Fly @ 21–24 days	5/20–8/28	5/27–9/10	6/1–9/27
Barn Owl	1–2	32–34	Fly @ 60 days, indep. @ 70 days		All months	

Species	Information from literature			Breeding dates for New York (earliest and latest dates reported)		
	No. of broods	Incubation period (days)	Nestling period	Eggs	Nestlings	Fledglings
Eastern Screech-Owl	1	21–26	Lv. nest @ 35 days	3/23–7/8	4/9–7/15	3/25–9/18
Great Horned Owl	1 ‡	30–35	Lv. nest @ 31–35 days	1/22–7/24	2/15–7/9	3/25–12/21
Barred Owl	1 ‡	21–28	Fly @ 6 weeks	3/20–5/4	4/14–7/4	5/4–9/11
Long-eared Owl	1, occ. 2	21–30	Lv. nest @ 23–24 days	3/21–5/23	5/5–6/24	6/1–8/8
Short-eared Owl	1, occ. 2	24–28	Lv. nest @ 12–17 days, fly @ 22–27 days	4/2–5/19	5/7–6/19	6/11–7/13
Northern Saw-whet Owl	1	26–28	Lv. nest @ 36 days, occ. longer	3/31–6/11	4/21–7/16	5/9–8/29
Common Nighthawk	1	16–19	Fly @ 23 days, indep. @ 30 days	5/25–7/25	6/14–8/14	7/7–8/30
Chuck-will's-widow	1 ‡	20	Fly @ 17 days ★	5/23 (Va.)	6/22–6/28	6/29
Whip-poor-will	1	14–20	Fly @ 15–20 days ★	5/6–6/30	6/2–7/14	6/6–8/8
Chimney Swift	1	18–22	Fly @ 24–26 days	5/30–7/27	5/27–8/12	6/12–9/1
Ruby-throated Hummingbird	1–2	14–16	Lv. nest @ 19 days	5/12–8/20	5/20–9/6	7/12–9/30
Belted Kingfisher	1 ‡	17–24	Lv. nest @ 30–35 days	4/28–7/30	5/4–7/19	5/20–9/14
Red-headed Woodpecker	1–2	14	Lv. nest @ 27 days	5/16–6/19	5/31–8/26	6/21–9/15
Red-bellied Woodpecker	1 ‡	12–14	Lv. nest @ 26 days	4/26–6/28	5/3–8/29	5/8–9/1
Yellow-bellied Sapsucker	1 ‡	12–14	Lv. nest @ 25–29 days, depend. 1–2 weeks more	4/29–6/25	5/11–8/24	5/2–9/14
Downy Woodpecker	1	12	Lv. nest @ 20–22 days, depend. 3 weeks more	5/6–6/30	4/11–8/4	4/19–9/2
Hairy Woodpecker	1 ‡	11–14	Lv. nest @ 28–30 days, depend. 2 weeks more	4/23–6/12	5/7–7/15	5/25–9/13
American Three-toed Woodpecker	1	14	§	5/14–6/14	7/2, 7/31	7/9–8/20
Black-backed Woodpecker	1	14	Fly @ about 24 days ★	5/18–6/12	5/30–7/4	6/20–8/15
Northern Flicker	1–2 ‡	11–16	Lv. nest @ 25–28 days	4/20–7/3	5/8–7/26	4/20–9/9
Pileated Woodpecker	1 ‡	18	Lv. nest @ 22–26 days	4/11–6/7	5/10–7/31	6/1–9/1
Olive-sided Flycatcher	1	14–17	Lv. nest @ 15–19 days	6/9–6/27	6/4–6/22	7/6–8/3
Eastern Wood-Pewee	1	12–13	Lv. nest @ 15–18 days	5/30–8/15	5/19–8/13	6/5–9/15
Yellow-bellied Flycatcher	1	12–15	Lv. nest @ 13 days	6/10–6/27	6/12–8/4	6/12–8/9
Acadian Flycatcher	1	12–14	Lv. nest @ 13 days, fed by parents 12 more days	5/24–7/8	6/19–8/21	7/8–8/11
Alder Flycatcher	1	12	Lv. nest @ about 14 days	6/2–7/29	6/9–8/14	6/12–8/24
Willow Flycatcher	1	13–15	Lv. nest @ 12–15 days	6/4–7/29	6/3–8/14	6/18–8/24
Least Flycatcher	1–2	12–16	Lv. nest @ 13–16 days	5/10–7/8	5/31–8/6	5/29–8/22
Eastern Phoebe	1–3	12–16	Lv. nest @ 15–17 days, fed by parents 2–3 weeks more	3/25–8/4	4/22–8/13	4/14–9/6
Great Crested Flycatcher	1	13–15	Lv. nest @ 14–15 days	5/22–7/28	5/9–7/26	5/20–9/14
Eastern Kingbird	1–2	12–16	Lv. nest @ 13–14 days, fed by parents 5 weeks more	5/19–8/1	5/10–8/13	5/3–9/3
Loggerhead Shrike	1–2	13–16	Lv. nest @ 20 days, indep. @ 26–35 days	4/18–6/28	5/18–6/25	5/25–7/26
White-eyed Vireo	1	12–15	Lv. nest @ 9–11 days ★	5/17–7/17	6/3–7/14	6/25–8/28
Yellow-throated Vireo	1	12–14	Lv. nest @ about 13 days ★	5/17–6/20	6/5–7/30	6/1–8/26
Blue-headed Vireo	1	10–11	Lv. nest @ 12–13 days ★	5/10–8/9	5/23–8/13	6/17–9/5
Warbling Vireo	1	12	Lv. nest @ 16 days	5/16–7/11	5/20–7/15	6/1–8/18
Philadelphia Vireo	†	13–14	Lv. nest @ 13–14 days	June–July	6/17–8/2	8/6–8/12
Red-eyed Vireo	1–2	12–14	Lv. nest @ 12 days	5/13–8/1	5/22–8/17	6/2–9/14
Gray Jay	1	16–18	Lv. nest @ about 15 days	3/10–6/5	6/3–7/15	5/19–9/15
Blue Jay	1 ‡	15–18	Lv. nest @ 17–21 days, indep. in 3 weeks more but may be fed longer	4/10–7/14	5/1–8/5	4/28–9/10

Species	Information from literature			Breeding dates for New York (earliest and latest dates reported)		
	No. of broods	Incubation period (days)	Nestling period	Eggs	Nestlings	Fledglings
American Crow	1	16–18	Lv. nest @ about 5 weeks	3/31–7/11	3/27–8/12	3/15–9/9
Fish Crow	1 ‡	16–18	Fledge @ 32–40 days ★	3/20–6/24	4/20–8/4	5/28–8/18
Common Raven	1	19–21	Lv. nest @ 5–6 weeks	3/23–6/22	3/21–7/3	4/17–8/15
Horned Lark	1–3	11–14	Lv. nest @ 9–10 days, fly well @ 20 days	2/28–7/31	3/11–8/4	4/21–9/13
Purple Martin	1, occ. 2	12–20	Lv. nest @ 24–28 days, roost in nest after leaving	5/21–7/16	5/15–8/15	6/12–8/25
Tree Swallow	1–2	13–16	Lv. nest @ 16–14 days	4/16–8/15	4/27–8/10	5/7–8/14
Northern Rough-winged Swallow	1	15–16	Lv. nest @ 18–21 days	5/12–7/5	5/23–7/13	5/21–8/21
Bank Swallow	1–2	12–16	Fly @ 17–18 days, lv. nest 1–2 days later	5/15–7/13	5/23–8/12	5/17–9/1
Cliff Swallow	1–2	12–16	Fly @ 23 days, return to nest for 2–3 days more	5/9–7/31	5/1–8/19	6/15–8/23
Barn Swallow	2–3	13–16	Lv. nest @ 17–24 days	4/29–8/10	4/27–8/28	4/5–9/22
Black-capped Chickadee	1	11–14	Lv. nest @ 16 days	4/1–7/15	5/2–8/8	4/28–9/9
Boreal Chickadee	1 ★	11–16 ★	Fledge @ 18 days ★	6/11–7/17	6/12–7/26	7/2–8/27
Tufted Titmouse	1	12–13	Lv. nest @ 15–16 days	4/14–6/27	4/16–7/20	5/12–8/21
Red-breasted Nuthatch	1	12	Lv. nest @ 18–21 days	4/30–6/17	4/25–7/18	5/10–8/19
White-breasted Nuthatch	1	12 (?)	Fed for 2 weeks after leaving nest	4/13–7/13	4/27–8/30	5/16–9/4
Brown Creeper	1	14–15	Lv. nest @ 14–16 days	4/24–6/30	5/8–7/28	5/30–8/20
Carolina Wren	2–3	12–14	Lv. nest @ 12–14 days	4/1–8/5	4/21–10/2	5/3–9/10
House Wren	1–2	13–15	Lv. nest @ 12–18 days, feed selves @ 13 days	5/9–8/15	5/9–8/28	5/14–9/11
Winter Wren	1–2	14–17	Lv. nest @ 15–20 days	5/22–7/29	5/7–8/4	4/23–9/4
Sedge Wren	1–2	12–14	Lv. nest @ 12–14 days	5/28–7/30	6/15–8/22	6/10–9/15
Marsh Wren	2–3	10–14	Lv. nest @ 13–15 days, fed for 7 more	5/5–8/7	6/13–8/12	6/7–8/31
Golden-crowned Kinglet	1–2	12–17	Lv. nest @ 16–19 days ★	5/28–7/26	5/31–7/25	6/12–9/5
Ruby-crowned Kinglet	1–2	14–15	Lv. nest @ approx. 16 days ★	May–6/29	6/19–7/2	7/2–9/5
Blue-gray Gnatcatcher	1	15	Lv. nest @ 12–13 days, fed for up to 19 days more	5/10–7/11	5/21–7/30	5/12–8/16
Eastern Bluebird	2–3	12	Lv. nest @ 15–18 days, male may continue to feed yg.	4/1–8/18	3/29–9/6	5/1–9/28
Veery	1–2	10–12	Lv. nest @ 10–12 days	5/3–8/2	5/14–7/22	6/10–8/21
Bicknell's Thrush	1	13–14	Lv. nest @ 11–13 days	6/12–6/27	6/27–7/25	7/12–8/7
Swainson's Thrush	1	10–13	Lv. nest @ 10–12 days	5/13–7/11	6/20–7/22	6/23–9/5
Hermit Thrush	2–3	12–13	Lv. nest @ 10 days	5/8–8/24	5/18–8/31	5/15–9/23
Wood Thrush	1–2	12–14	Lv. nest @ 12–13 days	5/12–7/23	5/13–8/8	6/1–8/31
American Robin	2–3	11–14	Lv. nest @ 14–16 days	3/23–9/1	4/12–8/31	4/10–9/25
Gray Catbird	2–3	10–14	Lv. nest @ about 10 days	5/5–8/12	5/8–8/23	5/23–9/21
Northern Mockingbird	2–3	10–14	Lv. nest @ 12–14 days	4/27–7/28	4/26–8/17	5/23–8/30
Brown Thrasher	1–2	11–14	Lv. nest @ 9–12 days	5/6–7/10	5/19–7/29	5/16–8/17
European Starling	1–2	12–16	Fed by parents for 20–22 days	4/10–7/11	4/17–8/20	4/28–9/7
Cedar Waxwing	1–2	12–16	Lv. nest @ 16–18 days	6/2–9/23	5/24–10/1	6/2–10/8
Blue-winged Warbler	1	10–11	Lv. nest @ 8–10 days	5/18–7/25	5/21–7/11	5/27–8/29
Golden-winged Warbler	1	10–11	Lv. nest @ 10 days	5/18–6/16	6/6–7/6	6/19–8/6
Tennessee Warbler	1	11–12 ★	Fledge @ 11–12 days ★	June–July	8/22	†
Nashville Warbler	1	11	Lv. nest @ 11 days	5/19–6/10	5/30–6/22	6/11–8/27
Northern Parula	1–2	12–14	Lv. nest @ 10–11 days ★	5/17–6/27	6/6–7/29	7/4–8/23
Yellow Warbler	1–2	9–15	Lv. nest @ 9–12 days	5/11–7/14	5/18–7/23	5/19–8/15

Species	Information from literature			Breeding dates for New York (earliest and latest dates reported)		
	No. of broods	Incubation period (days)	Nestling period	Eggs	Nestlings	Fledglings
Chestnut-sided Warbler	1, occ. 2	10–13	Lv. nest @ 10–12 days	5/16–7/25	5/17–8/6	5/19–8/30
Magnolia Warbler	1–2	11–13	Lv. nest @ 8–10 days	5/21–7/21	6/3–7/24	6/15–8/29
Cape May Warbler	1	§	§	6/6–6/16	6/18	6/23–7/4
Black-throated Blue Warbler	1–2, occ. 3★	12	Lv. nest @ 10 days	5/26–7/21	6/4–7/29	6/21–9/2
Yellow-rumped Warbler	1	12–13	Lv. nest @ 12–14 days	5/19–7/10	5/17–7/22	6/9–9/9
Black-throated Green Warbler	1–2	12	Lv. nest @ 8–10 days	5/24–7/2	5/13–8/2	6/23–9/12
Blackburnian Warbler	1 ★	12–13 ★	§	6/1–6/25	6/8–7/6	6/7–8/15
Yellow-throated Warbler	1–2(?)★	12–13 ★	§	†	6/21–7/21	†
Pine Warbler	1–2	Est. 10–13 ★	Est. 10-day nestling period ★	5/4–6/20	5/14–6/17	5/20–8/8
Prairie Warbler	1	12–14	Lv. nest @ 8–10 days	5/25–6/29	6/1–7/15	6/2–8/23
Palm Warbler	1–2 (?)	12	Lv. nest @ 12 days	7/8	6/2–7/24	6/25–8/15
Bay-breasted Warbler	1	12–13	Lv. nest @ 11 days	Mid-June	6/25–7/6	7/23–8/10
Blackpoll Warbler	1–2 ★	11	Lv. nest @ 10–11 days	6/5–7/10	6/23–7/4	6/30–9/7
Cerulean Warbler	1	11–12 ★	Lv. nest @ 10–11 days ★	5/19–6/23	6/11–7/6	6/22–7/26
Black-and-white Warbler	1	11–13	Lv. nest @ 8–12 days	5/10–6/30	5/29–7/23	6/8–8/21
American Redstart	1	12	Lv. nest @ 9 days	5/14–7/28	5/24–8/5	5/27–8/25
Prothonotary Warbler	1–2	10–14	Lv. nest @ 10–11 days	5/17–6/29	6/8–7/6	7/10–8/6
Worm-eating Warbler	†	13	Lv. nest @ 10 days	5/24–7/1	6/1–7/15	6/11–8/8
Ovenbird	1–2	12–14	Lv. nest @ 8–10 days	5/5–7/22	5/10–8/8	6/9–9/21
Northern Waterthrush	1	14	Lv. nest @ 9 days ★	5/10–6/28	5/20–7/8	6/4–8/1
Louisiana Waterthrush	1	12–14	Lv. nest @ 10 days, fly @ 16 days	4/25–6/20	5/15–7/6	5/15–8/7
Kentucky Warbler	1	12–13	Lv. nest @ 8–10 days, fed for 17 days more	6/1–6/27	6/20	6/29–7/16
Mourning Warbler	1	12–13	Lv. nest @ 7–9 days, fly 2nd week	5/28–7/7	5/30–7/28	6/21–8/19
Common Yellowthroat	1–2	12	Lv. nest @ 9–10 days	5/9–7/24	5/9–8/22	5/15–9/11
Hooded Warbler	1–2	12	Lv. nest @ 8–9 days	5/25–7/10	6/6–8/12	6/4–9/10
Wilson's Warbler	1	11–13	Lv. nest @ 10–11 days	8/1	†	†
Canada Warbler	1	12 ★	Lv. nest @ 8–10 days (?)★	5/31–7/24	6/8–7/30	6/20–8/20
Yellow-breasted Chat	1	11–15	Lv. nest @ 8–11 days	5/25–7/13	6/8–7/17	6/22
Summer Tanager	1–2 ★	11–12 ★	Lv. nest @ 8–12 days★	†	7/10	†
Scarlet Tanager	1	13–14	Lv. nest @ 15 days	5/20–7/23	5/27–7/29	6/10–9/19
Eastern Towhee	1–2	12–13	Lv. nest @ 8–10 days	5/5–8/4	5/18–9/3	6/2–8/31
Chipping Sparrow	1–2	10–14	Lv. nest @ 9–12 days, fly @ 14 days	5/1–7/26	5/3–9/3	5/15–9/21
Clay-colored Sparrow	1–2	10–11	Lv. nest @ 7–9 days, fed for 8 days more	May–June	6/7–7/26	6/20–7/20
Field Sparrow	2–3	10–13	Lv. nest @ 7–8 days, fly @ 12 days, indep. 18–20 days later	5/16–8/17	5/2–8/20	5/28–9/20
Vesper Sparrow	1–3	11–13	Lv. nest @ 9–13 days, depend. 21 days more	5/5–8/16	6/2–7/16	6/12–8/1
Savannah Sparrow	1–2	12	Lv. nest @ 8–11 days ★	5/11–7/12	5/8–7/23	5/30–8/30
Grasshopper Sparrow	1–3	11–12	Lv. nest @ 9 days	5/17–8/2	6/4–8/19	6/8–9/5
Henslow's Sparrow	1–2	11	Lv. nest @ 9–10 days	5/17–7/5	6/1–7/22	6/19–7/30
Saltmarsh Sharp-tailed Sparrow	1	11	Lv. nest @ 10 days, depend. 20 days more	5/30–7/21	6/5–8/5	7/9–8/23
Seaside Sparrow	1–2	11–12	Lv. nest @ 9 days, depend. 21 days more	5/25–7/10	6/8–7/23	6/26–8/23
Song Sparrow	1–3	12–14	Lv. nest @ 10 days, fly @ 17 days, depend. 18–20 days more	4/14–8/13	4/21–9/3	5/5–9/23

Species	Information from literature			Breeding dates for New York (earliest and latest dates reported)		
	No. of broods	Incubation period (days)	Nestling period	Eggs	Nestlings	Fledglings
Lincoln's Sparrow	1–2	13–14	Lv. nest @ 10–12 days	5/27–6/28	6/5–6/18	7/5–8/2
Swamp Sparrow	1–2	12–15	Lv. nest @ 9–10 days	5/5–7/22	5/20–7/30	6/2–9/9
White-throated Sparrow	1–2 ‡	11–14	Lv. nest @ 7–12 days, fly 3 days later	5/28–7/21	5/28–7/21	5/15–8/31
Dark-eyed Junco	1–3	11–13	Lv. nest @ 10–13 days, depend. 21 days more	4/15–8/1	4/29–9/6	5/13–9/9
Northern Cardinal	2–3	12	Lv. nest @ 9–11 days, fly well @ 19 days, indep. @ 38–45 days	4/8–9/9	4/23–9/23	4/30–9/23
Rose-breasted Grosbeak	1–2	12–14	Lv. nest @ 9–12 days, depend. 3 weeks more	5/6–7/19	5/15–7/26	5/20–9/2
Blue Grosbeak	1–2	11	Lv. nest @ 9–13 days	6/17	6/30	7/1
Indigo Bunting	1–2	12–13	Lv. nest @ 9–13 days	5/20–8/3	5/20–8/17	5/24–9/20
Dickcissel	1–2	11–13	Lv. nest @ 7–10 days, fly @ 11–12 days	May–6/29	6/23	6/18
Bobolink	1	10–13	Lv. nest @ 10–14 days, fly a few days later	5/17–7/12	5/21–8/4	6/2–8/18
Red-winged Blackbird	1–2, occ. 3	10–15	Lv. nest @ 10–11 days, stay near nest 10 days more	4/20–7/30	4/27–7/29	5/10–8/15
Eastern Meadowlark	1–2	13–17	Lv. nest @ 11–12 days	5/9–8/1	5/21–8/13	6/5–8/24
Western Meadowlark	1–2	13–15	Lv. nest @ 12 days, fed for a few days more	May–July	6/23	6/26
Rusty Blackbird	1	14	Lv. nest @ 13 days	5/17–6/22	5/25–7/8	6/11–7/24
Common Grackle	1–2	12–14	Lv. nest @ 10–17 days, near nest only 2–3 days	4/12–8/15	4/22–7/30	5/1–9/5
Boat-tailed Grackle	1–3	13	Lv. nest @ 20–23 days	5/31–7/1	6/5–7/11	6/23–7/29
Brown-headed Cowbird	Not app.★	10–12	Lv. nest @ 10 days, usually before host yg., fed for 2 weeks	4/23–8/6	5/8–8/2	5/5–8/30
Orchard Oriole	1	12–15	Lv. nest @ 11–14 days	5/10–6/28	5/14–7/26	6/11–8/21
Baltimore Oriole	1	14	Lv. nest @ 12–13 days ★	5/7–7/16	4/16–8/16	5/20–8/31
Purple Finch	1	13	Lv. nest @ 14 days	5/13–7/16	5/15–7/24	5/7–9/3
House Finch	2–3	12–14	Lv. nest @ 14–16 days	4/11–8/12	4/15–9/7	5/10–9/5
Red Crossbill	1–2	12–16	Lv. nest @ 17–23 days, depend. 3–4 weeks more	3/30–4/30	4/24–5/27	3/17–10/18
White-winged Crossbill	Variable ★	12–14 (?)★	§	Mid-January– August	1/14–7/31	1/28–11/25
Pine Siskin	1–2	13–14	Lv. nest @ 14–15 days	3/15–5/25	2/20–6/10	2/15–10/18
American Goldfinch	1	12–14	Lv. nest @ 11–17 days	6/13–9/16	5/18–9/30	6/3–10/10
Evening Grosbeak	1, occ. 2 ★	12–14	Lv. nest @ 13–14 days	5/17–6/4	5/31–7/3	6/15–9/5
House Sparrow	2–3	11–14	Lv. nest @ 15 days	3/23–8/10	4/7–8/30	4/23–9/6

Dates from Meade (1988a) in black text; dates from 2000–05 Atlas in red text.

★   Information for North America (*The Birds of North America Online*).

†   No New York data available.

‡   If brood is lost, it usually will be replaced.

§   No information from references checked.

(?)   Probable.

APPENDIX 3

Common and Scientific Names of Plants and Animals Referred to in Text

Plants

Alder	*Alnus* sp.	European larch	*Larix decidua*
Alfalfa	*Medicago sativa*	Gray birch	*Betula populifolia*
American beech	*Fagus grandifolia*	Green arrow-arum	*Peltandra virginica*
American chestnut	*Castanea dentata*	Green ash	*Fraxinus pennsylvanica*
American elm	*Ulmus americana*	Hard maple (sugar maple)	*Acer saccharum*
American larch	*Larix laricina*	Heath / heather (beach)	*Hudsonia* sp.
American sycamore	*Platanus occidentalis*	Hickory	*Carya* sp.
Amur honeysuckle	*Lonicera maackii*	Highbush blueberry	*Vaccinium corymbosum*
Arrowwood	*Viburnum dentatum* var. *lucidulum*	Hobblebush	*Viburnum lantanoides*
		Holly	*Ilex* sp.
Arum (green arrow-arum)	*Peltandra virginica*	Inland saltgrass	*Distichlis spicata*
Arum (water)	*Calla palustris*	Jack pine	*Pinus banksiana*
Ash	*Fraxinus* sp.	Japanese black pine	*Pinus thunbergiana*
Aspen	*Populus* sp.	Larch	*Larix* sp.
Balsam fir	*Abies balsamea*	Laurel	*Kalmia* sp.
Basswood	*Tilia americana* var. *americana*	Marsh elder	*Iva frutescens* ssp. *oraria*
Beech	*Fagus* sp.	Marsh marigold	*Caltha palustris*
Birch	*Betula* sp.	Mountain laurel	*Kalmia latifolia*
Black birch	*Betula lenta*	Mountain-ash	*Sorbus* sp.
Black cherry	*Prunus serotina*	Multiflora rose	*Rosa multiflora*
Black gum	*Nyssa sylvatica*	Narrow-leaf burreed	*Sparganium angustifolium*
Black spruce	*Picea mariana*	Northern white cedar	*Thuga occidentalis*
Blackjack oak	*Quercus marilandica* var. *marilandica*	Norway spruce	*Picea abies*
		Oak	*Quercus* sp.
Blueberry	*Vaccinium* sp.	Old man's beard lichen	*Usnea* sp.
Buckthorn	*Rhamnus cathartica*	Paper birch	*Betula papyrifera*
Bulrush	*Bulboschoenus* sp.	Pickerelweed	*Pontederia cordata*
Bulrush	*Schoenoplectus* sp.	Pitch pine	*Pinus rigida*
Bulrush	*Scirpus* sp.	Poplar	*Populus* sp.
Burreed	*Sparganium* sp.	Post oak	*Quercus stellata*
Buttonbush (common)	*Cephalanthus occidentalis*	Purple loosestrife	*Lythrum salicaria*
Cattail	*Typha* sp.	Red cedar	*Juniperus virginiana* var. *virginiana*
Chestnut	*Castanea* sp.	Red maple	*Acer rubrum*
Chestnut oak	*Quercus montana*	Red oak	*Quercus rubra*
Clover	*Trifolium* sp.	Red pine	*Pinus resinosa*
Common reed	*Phragmites australis* ssp. *australis*	Red spruce	*Picea rubens*
Cottonwood	*Populus deltoides*	Reedgrass	*Calamagrostis* sp.
Dwarf chinquapin oak	*Quercus prinoides*	Saltmeadow cordgrass	*Spartina patens*
Eastern hemlock	*Tsuga canadensis*	Saltwater (smooth) cordgrass	*Spartina alterniflora*
Eelgrass (sea-wrack)	*Zostera marina*	Scotch pine	*Pinus sylvestris* var. *sylvestris*
Elm	*Ulmus* sp.	Scrub chestnut oak	*Quercus prinoides*
Eurasian water milfoil	*Myriophyllum spicatum*	Scrub oak	*Quercus ilicifolia*

Silver maple	*Acer saccharinum*
Skunk cabbage	*Symplocarpus foetidus*
Spanish moss	*Tillandsia usneoides*
Spruce	*Picea* sp.
Sugar maple	*Acer saccharum*
Sweet birch	*Betula lenta*
Sweetgum	*Liquidambar styraciflua*
Tamarack	*Larix laricina*
Tartarian honeysuckle	*Lonicera tatarica*
Thistle	*Cirsium* sp.
Trefoil	*Lotus* sp.
Tulip tree	*Liriodendron tulipifera*
Viburnum	*Viburnum* sp.
Water arum / wild calla	*Calla palustris*
Water chestnut	*Trapa natans*
White ash	*Fraxinus americana*
White birch	*Betula populifolia*
White oak	*Quercus alba*
White pine (Eastern)	*Pinus strobus*
White spruce	*Picea glauca*
Willow	*Salix* sp.

Invertebrates

Balsam woolly adelgid	*Adelges piceae*
Bark beetles	family *Scolytidae*
Black-headed budworm	*Acleris variana*
Eastern spruce budworm	*Choristoneura fumiferana*
Emerald ash borer	*Agrilus planipennis*
Forest tent caterpillar	*Malacosoma disstria*
Hemlock woolly adelgid	*Adelges tsugae*
Karner blue butterfly	*Lycaeides melissa samuelis*
Leaf beetle (Viburnum)	*Pyrrhalta viburni*
Wood-boring beetles	family *Cerambycidae*

Fish

Alewife	*Alosa pseudoharengus*
Round goby	*Neogobius melanostomus*

Reptiles

Bog turtle	*Clemmys muhlenbergii*

Birds

Common Crane	*Grus grus*
Ferruginous Hawk	*Buteo regalis*
Gray-cheeked Thrush	*Catharus minimus*
Swainson's Hawk	*Buteo swainsoni*

Mammals

Beaver (American)	*Castor canadensis*
Eastern chipmunk	*Tamias striatus*
Eastern gray squirrel	*Sciurus carolinensis*
Opossum (Virginia)	*Didelphis virginiana*
Raccoon (common)	*Procyon lotor*
White-tailed deer	*Odocoileus virginianus*

Citations for Map Data

These citations provide source information for the layers that were used to create the maps in Chapter 1 depicting the features of New York State (NYS) and for the coverage maps in Chapter 2.

Figure 1.2 Base Map

New York State Department of Environmental Conservation (NYSDEC). Major Hydrographic Features of New York (ESRI ArcInfo Coverage). Albany, NY, NYSDEC, October 21, 2005. Based on U.S. Geological Survey United States Geological Survey 1:100,000 digital line graph (DLG) files.

New York State Department of Environmental Conservation (NYSDEC). Simplified Municipal, County, DEC Region and State Borders of New York State (ESRI ArcInfo Coverage). Albany, NY, NYSDEC, February 2002. Based on information from NYS Department of Transportation.

Figure 1.4 Cities and Major Roads

Richter, W. Major Roads (ESRI ArcInfo Coverage). Albany, NY, NYSDEC, November 29, 2004. Based on U.S. Geological Survey digital line graph (DLG) files.

Figure 1.5 Population

U.S. Census Bureau and NYS Office of Cyber Security and Critical Infrastructure Coordination (CSCIC). Census Tracts of New York State (Digital Vector Data). Albany, NY, NYSCSCIC, January 1, 2003.

Figure 1.6 Rivers

New York State Department of Environmental Conservation (NYSDEC). Major Hydrographic Features of New York (ESRI ArcInfo Coverage). Albany, NY, NYSDEC, October 21, 2005. Based on U.S. Geological Survey United States Geological Survey 1:100,000 digital line graph (DLG) files.

Figure 1.7 Elevation

New York State Department of Environmental Conservation (NYSDEC). Contours, 500 Foot and 100 Foot (ArcInfo Line Coverage). Albany, NY, NYSDEC, June 2000. Based on U.S. Geological Service 10-m Digital Elevation Models.

New York State Department of Environmental Conservation (NYSDEC). Digital Elevation Model, 70 meter (ESRI ArcInfo GRID). Albany, NY, NYSDEC, August 2000. Derived from U.S. Geological Survey 10-m Digital Elevation Models.

Figure 1.8 Temperature

New York State Department of Environmental Conservation (NYSDEC). Temperature for NYS (ESRI File Geodatabase). Albany, NY, NYSDEC, August 2007. Based on information from National Climatic Data Center. Average Temperatures and Departures from Normal (°F), Climatological Data Annual Summary, NY 2005, vol. 117, no. 13, ISSN 0364-5606 (PDF Report), Ashville, NC.

Figure 1.9 Precipitation

Daly, C., and G. Taylor. Spatial Climate Analysis Service. Average Annual Precipitation, 1961–1990 (ESRI ArcInfo Shapefile). Spatial Climate Analysis Service, Oregon State University, Corvallis; U.S. Department of Agriculture Natural Resources Conservation Service (USDA NRCS) National Water and Climate Center, Portland, OR; USDA NRCS National Cartography and Geospatial Center, Fort Worth, TX, September 2000.

Figure 1.10 Public Lands

Adirondack Park Agency. Adirondack Park Boundary (Vector Digital Data). Ray Brook, NY, NYS Adirondack Park Agency, September 14, 1993.

New York State Department of Environmental Conservation (NYSDEC). Catskill Park Blue Line (ESRI ArcInfo Coverage). Albany, NY, NYSDEC, June 1996. Digitized from NYS regulatory wetland mylars, NYS DOT 7.5-minute planimetric map base.

New York State Department of Environmental Conservation (NYSDEC). DEC Lands (ESRI ArcInfo Coverage). Albany, NY, NYSDEC, July 2006. Original data were digitized from 1:24,000 scale quadrangle DOT (Department of Transportation) maps. Updates come from various sources including NYSDEC Bureau of Real Property and Adirondack Park Agency.

New York State Department of Environmental Conservation (NYSDEC). Wildlife Management Area (ESRI ArcInfo Coverage). Albany, NY, NYSDEC, July 25, 2007.

New York State Department of Transportation (NYSDOT). Recreational and Non-Recreational Land Boundaries of New York State (ESRI ArcInfo Coverage). Albany, NY, NYSDOT, August 2000.

New York State Office of Parks, Recreation and Historic Preservation (NYSOPRHP). State Park (ESRI ArcInfo Coverage). Albany, NY, NYSOPRHP, February 2007.

Figure 1.11 Land Use

U.S. Geological Survey (USGS). New York Land Cover Data Set (Raster Digital Data). Sioux Falls, SD, USGS, January 1, 1997.

Figure 1.12 Forest Types

Ruefenacht, B., M. V. Finco, M. D. Nelson, R. Czaplewski, E. H. Helmer, J. A. Blackard, G. R. Holden, A. J. Lister, D. Salajanu, D. Weyermann, and K. Winterberger. (In Press) Conterminuous US and Alaska forest type mapping using forest inventory and analysis data. Photogrammetric Engineering and Remote Sensing.

Figure 1.13 Ecoregions

The Nature Conservancy (TNC) Eastern Conservation Science, and United States Forest Service, 2002, ecosubsections.

Figure 1.14 Ecozones

New York State Department of Environmental Conservation (NYSDEC). Ecozones (ESRI ArcInfo Coverage). Albany, NY, NYSDEC, May 2000. Digitized from the statewide my-lar map according to specifications from John Ozard of the New York State Department of Environmental Conservation's Significant Habitat Unit during the mid-1980s.

Figure 1.15 Bird Conservation Regions

Environmental Systems Research Institute Inc. (ESRI). ArcView GIS [computer disks]. Version 3.3 for Windows. Redlands, CA, ESRI, 1992–2001.

New York State Department of Environmental Conservation (NYSDEC). Municipal, County, DEC Region and State Borders of New York State (ESRI ArcInfo Coverage). Albany, NY, NYSDEC, November 23, 2004. Based on information from NYS Department of Transportation.

The North American Bird Conservation Initiative (NABCI) Bird Conservation Regions Map. U.S. NABCI Committee, September 2000.

Figure 1.16 Watersheds

U.S. Department of Agriculture Natural Resources Conservation Service (USDA NRCS), New York State Department of Environmental Conservation (NYSDEC), and U.S. Geological Survey. New York State Hydrologic Unit Coverage (ESRI ArcInfo Coverage). Syracuse, NY, USDA NRCS, December 30, 2004.

Figures 2.1, 2.2, 2.3, 2.4, 2.5, 2.6 Block Coverage

Ozard, J. W. Breeding Bird Atlas Block (ESRI ArcInfo Coverage). Albany, NY, NYSDEC, April 1998.

Literature Cited

NOTE: Web site addresses were valid as of 13 February 2008.

Able, K. P. 1998. Black Rail (*Laterallus jamaicensis*). Pages 218–219 *in* Bull's birds of New York State (E. Levine, Ed.). Comstock Publishing Associates, Ithaca, NY.

Adams, R. J. 1991. Wilson's Phalarope (*Phalaropus tricolor*). Page 538 *in* The atlas of breeding birds of Michigan (R. Brewer, G. A. McPeek, and R. J. Adams Jr., Eds.). Michigan State University Press, East Lansing, MI.

Adkisson, C. S. 1996. Red Crossbill (*Loxia curvirostra*). *In* The birds of North America, no. 256 (A. Poole and F. Gill, Eds.). The Academy of Natural Sciences, Philadelphia, PA, and The American Ornithologists' Union, Washington, DC.

Allen, J. A. 1869. Notes on some of the rarer birds of Massachusetts. American Naturalist 3:505–519.

Altman, B., and R. Sallabanks. 2000. Olive-sided Flycatcher (*Contopus cooperi*). *In* The birds of North America, no. 502 (A. Poole and F. Gill, Eds.). The Birds of North America, Inc., Philadelphia, PA.

Alverson, W. S., D. M. Waller, and S. L. Solheim. 1988. Forests too deer: edge effects in northern Wisconsin. Conservation Biology 2:348–358.

American Bird Conservancy. [2007.] ABC WatchList. http://www.abcbirds.org/abcprograms/science/watchlist/index.html.

Ammon, E. M. 1995. Lincoln's Sparrow (*Melospiza lincolnii*). *In* The birds of North America, no. 191 (A. Poole and F. Gill, Eds.). The Academy of Natural Sciences, Philadelphia, PA, and The American Ornithologists' Union, Washington, DC.

Ammon, E. M., and W. M. Gilbert. 1999. Wilson's Warbler (*Wilsonia pusilla*). *In* The birds of North America, no. 478 (A. Poole and F. Gill, Eds.). The Birds of North America, Inc., Philadelphia, PA.

Andersen, D. E., S. DeStefano, M. I. Goldstein, K. Titus, C. Crocker-Bedford, J. J. Keane, R. G. Anthony, and R. N. Rosenfield. 2005. Technical review of the status of Northern Goshawks in the western United States. Journal of Raptor Research 39:192–209.

Andrén, H., and P. Angelstam. 1988. Elevated predation rates as an edge effect in habitat islands: experimental evidence. Ecology 69:544–547.

Andrews, R., Compiler. 1990. Coastal waterbird colonies, Maine to Virginia 1984–85: an update of an atlas based on 1977 data, showing colony locations, species and nesting pairs at both time periods. 2 parts. U.S. Fish and Wildlife Service, Newton Corner, MA.

———. 2003. Northern Shoveler (*Anas clypeata*). Pages 72–73 *in* Massachusetts breeding bird atlas (W. R. Petersen and W. R. Meservey, Eds.). Massachusetts Audubon Society, Lincoln, MA.

Andrle, R. F. 1971. Range extension of the Golden-crowned Kinglet in New York. Wilson Bulletin 83:313–316.

———. 1978. Ruby-crowned Kinglet breeding in Cattaraugus County. Kingbird 28:29–30.

———. 1998. Black Vulture (*Coragyps atratus*). Pages 138–139 *in* Bull's birds of New York State (E. Levine, Ed.). Comstock Publishing Associates, Ithaca, NY.

Andrle, R. F., and J. R., Carroll, Eds. 1988. The atlas of breeding birds in New York State. Cornell University Press, Ithaca, NY.

Angehrn, P. A. M., H. Blokpoel, and P. Courtney. 1979. A review of the status of the Great Black-backed Gull in the Great Lakes area. Ontario Field Biologist 3:27–33.

Ankney, C. D., D. G. Dennis, and R. C. Bailey. 1987. Increasing Mallards, decreasing American Black Ducks: coincidence or cause and effect? Journal of Wildlife Management 51:523–529.

Ankney, C. D., D. G. Dennis, L. N. Wishard, and J. E. Seeb. 1986. Low genic variation between Black Ducks and Mallards. Auk 103:701–709.

AOU (American Ornithologists' Union). 1886. The code of nomenclature and check-list of North American birds adopted by the American Ornithologists' Union. American Ornithologists' Union, New York, NY.

———. 1895. Check-list of North American birds, 2nd ed. American Ornithologists' Union, Washington, DC.

———. 1931. Check-list of North American birds, 4th ed. American Ornithologists' Union, Lancaster, PA.

———. 1973. Thirtieth supplement to the American Ornithologists' Union check-list of North American birds. Auk 90:411–419.

———. 1983. Check-list of North American birds, 6th ed. American Ornithologists' Union, Washington, DC.

———. 1995. Fortieth supplement to the American Ornithologists' Union check-list of North American birds. Auk 112:819–830.

———. 1998. Check-list of North American birds, 7th ed. American Ornithologists' Union, Washington, DC.

Arbib, R. S. Jr. 1963. The Common Loon in New York State. Kingbird 13:132–140.

———. 1988a. Chipping Sparrow (*Spizella passerina*). Pages 438–439 *in* The atlas of breeding birds in New York State (R. F. Andrle and J. R. Carroll, Eds.). Cornell University Press, Ithaca, NY.

———. 1988b. Common Yellowthroat (*Geothlypis trichas*). Pages 416–417 *in* The atlas of breeding birds in New York State (R. F. Andrle and J. R. Carroll, Eds.). Cornell University Press, Ithaca, NY.

———. 1988c. Field Sparrow (*Spizella pusilla*). Pages 442–443 *in* The atlas of breeding birds in New York State (R. F. Andrle and J. R. Carroll, Eds.). Cornell University Press, Ithaca, NY.

———. 1988d. Grasshopper Sparrow (*Ammodramus savannarum*). Pages 448–449 *in* The atlas of breeding birds in New York State (R. F. Andrle and J. R. Carroll, Eds.). Cornell University Press, Ithaca, NY.

———. 1988e. House Sparrow (*Passer domesticus*). Pages 500–501 *in* The atlas of breeding birds in New York State (R. F. Andrle and J. R. Carroll, Eds.). Cornell University Press, Ithaca, NY.

———. 1988f. Purple Finch (*Carpodacus purpureus*). Pages 486–487 *in* The atlas of breeding birds in New York State (R. F. Andrle and J. R. Carroll, Eds.). Cornell University Press, Ithaca, NY.

———. 1988g. Rufous-sided Towhee (*Pipilo erythrophthalmus*). Pages 436–437 *in* The atlas of breeding birds in New York State (R. F. Andrle and J. R. Carroll, Eds.). Cornell University Press, Ithaca, NY.

———. 1988h. Swamp Sparrow (*Melospiza georgiana*). Pages 460–461 *in* The atlas of breeding birds in New York State (R. F. Andrle and J. R. Carroll, Eds.). Cornell University Press, Ithaca, NY.

Arcese, P., M. K. Sogge, A. B. Marr, and M. A. Patten. 2002. Song Sparrow (*Melospiza melodia*). *In* The birds of North America, no. 704 (A. Poole and F. Gill, Eds.). The Birds of North America, Inc., Philadelphia, PA.

Askildsen, J. P. 1993. Region 9—Hudson-Delaware. Kingbird 43:74–79.

———. 1994. Region 9—Hudson-Delaware. Kingbird 44:336–338.

Askins, R. A. 1993. Population trends in grassland, shrubland, and forest birds in eastern North America. Current Ornithology 11:1–34.

———. 2001. Sustaining biological diversity in early successional communities: the challenge of managing unpopular habitats. Wildlife Society Bulletin 29:407–412.

Askins, R. A., F. Chávez-Ramirez, B. C. Dale, C. A. Haas, J. R. Herkert, F. L. Knopf, and P. D. Vickery. 2007. Conservation of grassland birds in North America: understanding ecological processes in different regions. Report of the AOU Committee on Conservation. Ornithological Monographs, no. 64. American Ornithologists' Union, Washington, DC.

Askins, R. A., and M. J. Philbrick. 1987. Effect of changes in regional forest abundance on the decline and recovery of a forest bird community. Wilson Bulletin 99:7–21.

Atwood, J. L., C. C. Rimmer, K. P. McFarland, S. H. Tsai, and L. R. Nagy. 1996. Distribution of Bicknell's Thrush in New England and New York. Wilson Bulletin 108:650–661.

Audubon, J. J. 1835. Ornithological biography, vol. 2. A. Black, Edinburgh, Scotland.

Audubon Vermont. 2003. Lake Champlain Colonial Waterbird Database Project: estimated number of Great Black-backed Gull breeding pairs on Lake Champlain, 1975–2003. http://vt.audubon.org/blackBackedGull.html.

Augustine, D. J., and D. deCalesta. 2003. Defining deer overabundance and threats to forest communities: from individual plants to landscape structure. Ecoscience 10:472–486.

Austin, J. E., C. M. Custer, and A. D. Afton. 1998. Lesser Scaup (*Aythya affinis*). *In* The birds of North America, no. 338 (A. Poole and F. Gill, Eds.). The Birds of North America, Inc., Philadelphia, PA.

Austin, J. E., and M. R. Miller. 1995. Northern Pintail (*Anas acuta*). *In* The birds of North America, no. 163 (A. Poole and F. Gill, Eds.). The Academy of Natural Sciences, Philadelphia, PA, and The American Ornithologists' Union, Washington, DC.

Avery, M. L. 1995. Rusty Blackbird (*Euphagus carolinus*). *In* The birds of North America, no. 200 (A. Poole and F. Gill, Eds.). The Academy of Natural Sciences, Philadelphia, PA, and The American Ornithologists' Union, Washington, DC.

Bagg, A. M., and R. P. Emery. 1960. Regional reports: northeastern maritime region. Audubon Field Notes 14:432–437.

Bagg, A. M., and H. M. Parker. 1951. The Turkey Vulture in New England and eastern Canada up to 1950. Auk 68:315–333.

Bailey, R. G. 1980. Description of the ecoregions of the United States. Miscellaneous Publication 1391. U.S. Department of Agriculture, Washington, DC.

———. 1995. Description of the ecoregions of the United States, 2nd ed. U.S. Department of Agriculture Forest Service, Washington, DC.

Baillie, J. L. Jr., and P. Harrington. 1936. The distribution of breeding birds in Ontario. Pt 1. Transactions of the Royal Canadian Institute 21:1–50.

Baird, S. F., T. M. Brewer, and R. Ridgway. 1874. A history of North American birds. Little, Brown, Boston, MA.

Baird, T. H. 1984. A first record of nesting Yellow-throated Warblers in New York State. Kingbird 34:221–223.

———. 1990. Changes in breeding bird populations between 1930 and 1985 in the Quaker Run Valley of Allegany State Park. New York State Museum Bulletin, no. 477. University of the State of New York, New York State Education Department, Albany, NY.

Baldassarre, G. A., and E. G. Bolen. 2006. Waterfowl ecology and management, 2nd ed. Krieger Publishing Company, Malabar, FL.

Balent, K. L., and C. J. Norment. 2003. Demographic characteristics of a Grasshopper Sparrow population in a highly fragmented landscape of western New York State. Journal of Field Ornithology 74:341–348.

Balgooyen, T. G. 1976. Behavior and ecology of the American Kestrel (*Falco sparverius* L.) in the Sierra Nevada of California. University of California Publications in Zoology 103. University of California Press, Berkeley, CA.

Baltz, M. E., and S. C. Latta. 1998. Cape May Warbler (*Dendroica tigrina*). *In* The birds of North America, no. 332 (A. Poole and F. Gill, Eds.). The Birds of North America, Inc., Philadelphia, PA.

Banko, W. E. 1960. The Trumpeter Swan: its history, habits, and population in the United States. North American Fauna, no. 63. U.S. Fish and Wildlife Service, Washington, DC.

Banks, R. C., R. T. Chesser, C. Cicero, J. L. Dunn, A. W. Kratter, I. J. Lovette, P. C. Rasmussen, J. V. Remsen Jr., J. D. Rising, and D. F. Stotz. 2007. Forty-eighth supplement to the American Ornithologists' Union check-list of North American birds. Auk 124:1109–1115.

Banks, R. C., C. Cicero, J. L. Dunn, A. W. Kratter, P. C. Rasmussen, J. V. Remsen Jr., J. D. Rising, and D. F. Stotz. 2003. Forty-fourth supplement to the American Ornithologists' Union check-list of North American birds. Auk 120:923–931.

Bannor, B. K., and E. Kiviat. 2002. Common Moorhen (*Gallinula chloropus*). *In* The birds of North America, no. 685 (A. Poole and F. Gill, Eds.). The Birds of North America, Inc., Philadelphia, PA.

Barrett, G., A. Silcocks, S. Barry, R. Cunningham, and R. Poulter. 2003. The new atlas of Australian birds. Royal Australasian Ornithologists Union, Hawthorn East, Victoria, Australia.

Bart, J., S. Brown, B. Harrington, and R. I. G. Morrison. 2007. Survey trends of North American shorebirds: population declines or shifting distributions? Journal of Avian Biology 38:73–82.

Bart, J., and S. P. Klosiewski. 1989. Use of presence-absence to measure changes in avian density. Journal of Wildlife Management 53:847–852.

Barton, B. S. 1799. Fragments of the natural history of Pennsylvania. Way and Groff, Philadelphia, PA.

Bauer, P. 2001. Growth in the Adirondack Park: analysis of rates and patterns of development. The Residents' Committee to Protect the Adirondacks, North Creek, NY. http://www.rcpa.org/Library/growthreport.pdf.

Beardslee, C. S. 1932. Prothonotary Warblers nesting near Buffalo, N.Y. Auk 49:91.

Beardslee, C. S., and H. D. Mitchell. 1965. Birds of the Niagara Frontier region: an annotated checklist. Bulletin of the Buffalo Society of Natural Sciences, vol. 22. Buffalo Society of Natural Sciences, Buffalo, NY.

Beason, R. C. 1995. Horned Lark (*Eremophila alpestris*). *In* The birds of North America, no. 195 (A. Poole and F. Gill, Eds.). The Academy of Natural Sciences, Philadelphia, PA, and The American Ornithologists' Union, Washington, DC.

Bednarz, J. C., D. Klem Jr., L. S. Goodrich, and S. E. Senner. 1990. Migration counts at Hawk Mountain, Pennsylvania, as indicators of population trends, 1934–1986. Auk 107:96–109.

Beissinger, S. R., J. M. Reed, J. M. Wunderle Jr., S. K. Robinson, and D. M. Finch. 2000. Report of the AOU Conservation Committee on the Partners in Flight species prioritization plan. Auk 117:549–561.

Belant, J. L., and R. A. Dolbeer. 1993. Population status of nesting Laughing Gulls in the United States 1977–1991. American Birds 47:220–224.

Bellrose, F. C. 1980. Ducks, geese and swans of North America, 3rd ed. Stackpole Books, Harrisburg, PA.

Bellrose, F. C., and D. J. Holm. 1994. Ecology and management of the Wood Duck. Stackpole Books, Mechanicsburg, PA.

Bendire, C. 1895. Life histories of North American birds, from the parrots to the grackles, with special reference to their breeding habits and eggs. U.S. National Museum Special Bulletin, no. 3. Smithsonian Institution, Washington, DC.

Benkman, C. W. 1992. White-winged Crossbill (*Loxia leucoptera*). *In* The birds of North America, no. 27 (A. Poole and F. Gill, Eds.). The Academy of Natural Sciences, Philadelphia, PA, and The American Ornithologists' Union, Washington, DC.

———. 1993. Logging, conifers, and the conservation of crossbills. Conservation Biology 7:473–479.

———. 1999. The selection mosaic and diversifying coevolution between crossbills and lodgepole pine. American Naturalist 153:S75–S91.

Benoit, L. K., and R. A. Askins. 1999. Impact of the spread of phragmites on the distribution of birds in Connecticut tidal marshes. Wetlands 19:194–208.

Benson, D., and S. D. Browne. 1972. Establishing breeding colonies of Redheads in New York by releasing hand-reared birds. New York Fish and Game Journal 19:59–72.

Bent, A. C. 1921. Life histories of North American gulls and terns. U.S. National Museum Bulletin, no. 113. Smithsonian Institution, Washington, DC.

———. 1942. Life histories of North American flycatchers, larks, swallows, and their allies. U.S. National Museum Bulletin, no. 179. Smithsonian Institution, Washington, DC.

———. 1958. Life histories of North American blackbirds, tanagers, orioles and allies. U.S. National Museum Bulletin, no. 211. Smithsonian Institution, Washington, DC.

Benzinger, J. 1994. Hemlock decline and breeding birds. II. Effects of habitat change. Records of New Jersey Birds 20:34–51.

Berger, C., K. Kriedler, and J. Griggs. 2001. The bluebird monitor's guide. HarperResource, New York, NY.

Bergin, T. M. 1997. Nest reuse by Western Kingbirds. Wilson Bulletin 109:735–737.

Berner, A. H. 1988. Federal pheasants—impact of federal agricultural programs on pheasant habitat, 1934–1985. Pages 45–93 *in* Pheasants: symptoms of wildlife problems on agricultural lands (D. L. Hallett, W. R. Edwards, and G. V. Burger, Eds.). North Central Section of The Wildlife Society, Bloomington, IN.

Bernick, A. J. 2005. New York City Audubon harbor herons project: 2005 interim nesting survey. New York City Audubon Society, New York, NY. http://www.nycaudubon.org/projects/harborherons/HHsurveyReports.shtml.

Bevier, L., A. F. Poole, and W. Moskoff. 2004. Veery (*Catharus fuscescens*). *In* The birds of North America online (A. Poole, Ed.). Cornell Lab of Ornithology, Ithaca, NY. http://bna.birds.cornell.edu/BNA/account/Veery/.doi:10.2173/bna.142.

Bielefeldt, J., R. N. Rosenfield, and J. M. Papp. 1992. Unfounded assumptions about diet of the Cooper's Hawk. Condor 94:427–436.

Bildstein, K. L., and K. Meyer. 2000. Sharp-shinned Hawk (*Accipiter striatus*). *In* The birds of North America, no. 482 (A. Poole and F. Gill, Eds.). The Birds of North America, Inc., Philadelphia, PA.

Bird Studies Canada, Canadian Wildlife Service, Ontario Nature, Ontario Field Ornithologists and Ontario Ministry of Natural Resources. 2006. Ontario breeding bird atlas web site. http://www.birdsontario.org/atlas/atlasmain.html.

Blackwell, B. F., and R. A. Dolbeer. 2001. Decline of the Red-winged Blackbird population in Ohio correlated to changes in agriculture (1965–1996). Journal of Wildlife Management 65:661–667.

Blais, J. R., E. G. Kettela, and B. H. Moody. 1981. History of spruce budworm outbreaks in eastern North America with special reference to Newfoundland. Pages 12–17 *in* Review of the spruce budworm outbreak in Newfoundland: its control and forest management implications (J. Hudak and A. G. Raske, Eds.). Newfoundland Forest Research Centre, St. John's, NL.

Blockstein, D. E. 2002. Passenger Pigeon (*Ectopistes migratorius*). *In* The birds of North America, no. 611 (A. Poole and F. Gill, Eds.). The Birds of North America, Inc., Philadelphia, PA.

Blokpoel, H., and G. D. Tessier. 1986. The Ring-billed Gull in Ontario: a review of a new problem species. Canadian Wildlife Service Occasional Paper, no. 57. Canadian Wildlife Service, Hull, QC.

Boag, D. A., and M. A. Schroeder. 1992. Spruce Grouse (*Dendragapus canadensis*). *In* The birds of North America, no. 5 (A. Poole, P. Stettenheim, and F. Gill, Eds.). The Academy of Natural Sciences, Philadelphia, PA, and The American Ornithologists' Union, Washington, DC.

Boarman, W. I., and B. Heinrich. 1999. Common Raven (*Corvus corax*). *In* The birds of North America, no. 476 (A. Poole and F. Gill, Eds.). The Birds of North America, Inc., Philadelphia, PA.

Bochnik, M. 2001. Region 9—Hudson-Delaware. Kingbird 51:813–816.

Bogner, H. E., and G. A. Baldassarre. 2002. Home range, movement, and nesting of Least Bitterns in western New York. Wilson Bulletin 114:297–308.

Böhning-Gaese, K., and N. Lemoine. 2006. Importance of climate change for the ranges, communities and conservation of birds. Pages 211–236 *in* Birds and climate change (A. P. Møller, W. Fiedler, and P. Berthold, Eds.). Academic Press, New York, NY [first published as Advances in Ecological Research, vol. 35, 2004].

Bolgiano, N. C. 2004. Cause and effect: changes in boreal bird irruptions in eastern America relative to the 1970s spruce budworm infestation. American Birds 58:27–33.

Bollinger, E. K. 1995. Successional changes and habitat selection in hayfield bird communities. Auk 112:720–730.

Bollinger, E. K., and T. A. Gavin. 1989. The effects of site quality of breeding-site fidelity in Bobolinks. Auk 106:584–594.

———. 1992. Eastern Bobolink populations: ecology and conservation in an agricultural landscape. Pages 497–506 in Ecology and conservation of Neotropical migrant landbirds (J. M. Hagan III, and D. W. Johnston, Eds.). Smithsonian Institution Press, Washington, DC.

Bonney, R. E. Jr. 1988a. Canada Warbler (Wilsonia canadensis). Pages 422–423 in The atlas of breeding birds in New York State (R. F. Andrle and J. R. Carroll, Eds.). Cornell University Press, Ithaca, NY.

———. 1988b. Fish Crow (Corvus ossifragus). Pages 284–285 in The atlas of breeding birds in New York State (R. F. Andrle and J. R. Carroll, Eds.). Cornell University Press, Ithaca, NY.

———. 1988c. Hermit Thrush (Catharus guttatus). Pages 324–325 in The atlas of breeding birds in New York State (R. F. Andrle and J. R. Carroll, Eds.). Cornell University Press, Ithaca, NY.

———. 1988d. House Wren (Troglodytes aedon). Pages 302–303 in The atlas of breeding birds in New York State (R. F. Andrle and J. R. Carroll, Eds.). Cornell University Press, Ithaca, NY.

———. 1988e. Rose-breasted Grosbeak (Pheucticus ludovicianus). Pages 430–431 in The atlas of breeding birds in New York State (R. F. Andrle and J. R. Carroll, Eds.). Cornell University Press, Ithaca, NY.

———. 1988f. Veery (Catharus fuscescens). Pages 318–319 in The atlas of breeding birds in New York State (R. F. Andrle and J. R. Carroll, Eds.). Cornell University Press, Ithaca, NY.

———. 1988g. White-breasted Nuthatch (Sitta carolinensis). Pages 296–297 in The atlas of breeding birds in New York State (R. F. Andrle and J. R. Carroll, Eds.). Cornell University Press, Ithaca, NY.

———. 1988h. Yellow Warbler (Dendroica petechia). Pages 368–369 in The atlas of breeding birds in New York State (R. F. Andrle and J. R. Carroll, Eds.). Cornell University Press, Ithaca, NY.

Bonter, D. N., and W. M. Hochachka. 2003. Combined data of Project FeederWatch and the Christmas Bird Count indicate declines of chickadees and corvids: possible impacts of West Nile virus. American Birds [103rd CBC issue]:22–25.

Bordage, D. 1996. Common Goldeneye (Bucephala clangula). Pages 328–331 in The breeding birds of Québec: atlas of the breeding birds of southern Québec (J. Gauthier and Y. Aubry, Eds.). Association québécoise des groupes d'ornithologues, Montréal, QC.

Bordage, D., C. Lepage, and S. Orichefsky. 2003. Annual report spring 2003. Black duck joint venture helicopter survey—Québec. Canadian Wildlife Service report, Québec Region, Environment Canada, Sainte-Foy, QC. http://www.qc.ec.gc.ca/faune/faune/pdf/PCCN2003_EN.pdf.

Borgmann, K. L., and A. D. Rodewald. 2004. Nest predation in an urbanizing landscape: the role of exotic shrubs. Ecological Applications 14:1757–1765.

Borror, A. C. 1994. Common Eider (Somateria mollissima). Pages 32–33 in Atlas of breeding birds in New Hampshire (C. R. Foss, Ed.). Chalford Publishing Corporation, Dover, NH.

Bosakowski, T., D. G. Smith, and R. Speiser. 1992. Niche overlap of two sympatric-nesting hawks Accipiter spp. in the New Jersey–New York Highlands. Ecography 15:358–372.

Bosakowski, T., R. Speiser, D. G. Smith, and L. J. Niles. 1993. Loss of Cooper's Hawk nesting habitat to suburban development: inadequate protection for a state-endangered species. Journal of Raptor Research 27:26–30.

Boulet, M., H. L. Gibbs, and K. A. Hobson. 2006. Integrated analysis of genetic, stable isotope, and banding data reveal migratory connectivity and flyways in the northern Yellow Warbler (Dendroica petechia; aestiva group). Ornithological Monographs, no. 61:29–78.

Bouta, R. P. 1991. Population status, historical decline and habitat relationships of Spruce Grouse in the Adirondacks of New York. M.S. thesis, State University of New York College of Environmental Science and Forestry, Syracuse, NY.

Bouta, R. P., and R. E. Chambers. 1990. Status of threatened Spruce Grouse populations in New York: a historical perspective. Pages 82–91 in Ecosystem management: rare species and significant habitats. Proceedings of the 15th Annual Natural Areas Conference (R. S. Mitchell, C. J. Sheviak, and D. J. Leopold, Eds.). New York State Museum Bulletin, no. 471. New York State Museum, Albany, NY.

Brauning, D. W., Ed. 1992. Atlas of breeding birds in Pennsylvania. University of Pittsburgh Press, Pittsburgh, PA.

Brennan, L. A. 1999. Northern Bobwhite (Colinus virginianus). In The birds of North America, no. 397 (A. Poole and F. Gill, Eds.). The Birds of North America, Inc., Philadelphia, PA.

Brennan, L. A., and W. P. Kuvlesky Jr. 2005. Invited papers: North American grassland birds: an unfolding conservation crisis? Journal of Wildlife Management 69:1–13.

Brewster, W. 1881. On the relationship of Helminthophaga leucobronchialis, Brewster, and Helminthophaga lawrencei, Herrick; with some conjectures respecting certain other North American birds. Bulletin of the Nuttall Ornithological Club 6:218–225.

Bridges, J. T. 1998. Black Vulture in New York State—confirmed nesting and observation of early development. Kingbird 48:289–300.

Brinkley, E. S. 1998. Herring Gull (Larus argentatus). Pages 283–284 in Bull's birds of New York State (E. Levine, Ed.). Comstock Publishing Associates, Ithaca, NY.

Brisbin, I. L. Jr., H. D. Pratt, and T. B. Mowbray. 2002. American Coot (Fulica americana) and Hawaiian Coot (Fulica alai). In The birds of North America, no. 697 (A. Poole and F. Gill, Eds.). The Birds of North America, Inc., Philadelphia, PA.

Briskie, J. V. 1994. Least Flycatcher (Empidonax minimus). In The birds of North America, no. 99 (A. Poole and F. Gill, Eds.). The Academy of Natural Sciences, Philadelphia, PA, and The American Ornithologists' Union, Washington, DC.

Brock, R. W. 1998. Ring-billed Gull (Larus delawarensis). Pages 281–282 in Bull's birds of New York State (E. Levine, Ed.). Comstock Publishing Associates, Ithaca, NY.

Brodsky, L. M., C. D. Ankney, and D. G. Dennis. 1988. The influence of male dominance on social interactions in black ducks and Mallards. Animal Behaviour 36:1371–1378.

Brommer, J. E. 2004. The range margins of northern birds shift polewards. Annales Zoologici Fennici 41:391–397.

Brooks, E. W. 1971. A nesting record of the Clay-colored Sparrow in Allegany County. Prothonotary 37:99.

——. 1988. A third post-1875 nesting of Dickcissel in New York State. Kingbird 38:237–239.

——. 1998. Bewick's Wren (*Thryomanes bewickii*). Pages 418–419 *in* Bull's birds of New York State (E. Levine, Ed.). Comstock Publishing Associates, Ithaca, NY.

Brooks, R. T. 2003. Abundance, distribution, trends, and ownership patterns of early-successional forests in the northeastern United States. Forest Ecology and Management 185:65–74.

Brown, C. P. 1954. Distribution of Hungarian Partridge in New York. New York Fish and Game Journal 1:119–129.

Brown, C. P., and S. B. Robeson. 1959. The Ring-necked Pheasant in New York. New York State Division of Conservation Education, Albany, NY.

Brown, C. R. 1997. Purple Martin (*Progne subis*). *In* The birds of North America, no. 287 (A. Poole and F. Gill, Eds.). The Academy of Natural Sciences, Philadelphia, PA, and The American Ornithologists' Union, Washington, DC.

Brown, C. R., and M. B. Brown. 1995. Cliff Swallow (*Petrochelidon pyrrhonota*). *In* The birds of North America, no. 149 (A. Poole and F. Gill, Eds.). The Academy of Natural Sciences, Philadelphia, PA, and The American Ornithologists' Union, Washington, DC.

——. 1999. Barn Swallow (*Hirundo rustica*). *In* The birds of North America, no. 452 (A. Poole and F. Gill, Eds.). The Birds of North America, Inc., Philadelphia, PA.

Brown, K. M., R. M. Erwin, M. E. Richmond, P. A. Buckley, J. T. Tanacredi, and D. Avrin. 2001. Managing birds and controlling aircraft in the Kennedy Airport–Jamaica Bay Wildlife Refuge Complex: the need for hard data and soft opinions. Environmental Management 28:207–224.

Brown, M., and J. J. Dinsmore. 1986. Implications of marsh size and isolation for marsh bird management. Journal of Wildlife Management. 50:392–397.

Brown, S., C. Hickey, B. Harrington, and R. Gill, Eds. 2001. United States Shorebird Conservation Plan, 2nd ed. Manomet Center for Conservation Sciences, Manomet, MA. http://www.fws.gov/shorebirdplan/USShorebird/downloads/USShorebirdPlan2Ed.pdf.

Browne, S. D. 1971. The New York hand-reared duck program. Pages 9–19 *in* Role of hand-reared ducks in waterfowl management, a symposium. Max McGraw Wildlife Foundation, Dundee, IL.

——. 1975. Hooded Mergansers breeding in New York. New York Fish and Game Journal 22:68–70.

Brua, R. B. 2001. Ruddy Duck (*Oxyura jamaicensis*). *In* The birds of North America, no. 696 (A. Poole and F. Gill, Eds.). The Birds of North America, Inc., Philadelphia, PA.

Buckley, F. G., M. Gochfeld, and P. A. Buckley. 1978. Breeding Laughing Gulls return to Long Island. Kingbird 28:202–207.

Buckley, N. J. 1999. Black Vulture (*Coragyps atratus*). *In* The birds of North America, no. 411 (A. Poole and F. Gill, Eds.). The Birds of North America, Inc., Philadelphia, PA.

Buckley, P. A., and F. G. Buckley. 1980. Population and colony-site trends of Long Island waterbirds for five years in the mid-1970s. Transactions of the Linnaean Society of New York 9:23–56.

——. 1981. The endangered status of North American Roseate Terns. Colonial Waterbirds 4:166–173.

——. 1984. Seabirds of the north and middle Atlantic coast of the United States: their status and conservation. Pages 101–133 *in* Status and conservation of the world's seabirds (J. P. Croxall, P. G. H. Evans, and R. W. Schreiber, Eds.). ICBP Technical Publication, no. 2. International Council for Bird Preservation, Cambridge, UK.

Buckley, P. A., F. G. Buckley, and M. Gochfeld. 1975. Gull-billed Tern: New York State's newest breeding species. Kingbird 25:178–183.

Budliger, R. E., and G. Kennedy. 2005. Birds of New York State. Lone Pine Publishing International, Auburn, WA.

Buford, E. W., and D. E. Capen. 1999. Abundance and productivity of forest songbirds in managed, unfragmented landscape in Vermont. Journal of Wildlife Management 63:180–188.

Buidin, C., Y. Rochepault, M. Savard, and J.-P. L. Savard. 2006. Breeding range extension of the Northern Saw-whet Owl in Quebec. Wilson Journal of Ornithology 118:411–413.

Bull, E. L., and J. A. Jackson. 1995. Pileated Woodpecker (*Dryocopus pileatus*). *In* The birds of North America, no. 148 (A. Poole and F. Gill, Eds.). The Academy of Natural Sciences, Philadelphia, PA, and The American Ornithologists' Union, Washington, DC.

Bull, J. 1964. Birds of the New York area. Harper and Row, New York, NY.

——. 1974. Birds of New York State. Doubleday/Natural History Press, Garden City, NY [Reissued with corrections by Cornell University Press, Ithaca, NY, 1985].

——. 1976. Supplement to the Birds of New York State. Special Publication of the Federation of New York State Bird Clubs. Wilkins Printers, Cortland, NY [Reprinted in Birds of New York State by Cornell University Press, Ithaca, NY, 1985].

——. 1981. Double-crested Cormorants breeding at Fishers Island. Kingbird 31:83.

Bump, G. 1941. The introduction and transplantation of game birds and mammals into the state of New York. Transactions of the North American Wildlife Conference 5:409–420.

Bump, G., R. W. Darrow, F. C. Edminster, and W. F. Crissey. 1947. The Ruffed Grouse: life history, propagation, management. New York State Conservation Department, Albany, NY.

Burger, G. V. 1988. 100 years of ringnecks: an historical perspective on pheasants in North America. Pages 1–26 *in* Pheasants: symptoms of wildlife problems on agricultural lands (D. L. Hallet, W. R. Edwards, and G. V. Burger, Eds.). North Central Section of The Wildlife Society, Bloomington, IN.

Burger, J. 1978. The pattern and mechanism of nesting in mixed-species heronries. Pages 45–58 *in* Wading birds (A. Sprunt IV, J. C. Ogden, and S. Winckler, Eds.). National Audubon Society, New York, NY.

——. 1996. Laughing Gull (*Larus atricilla*). *In* The birds of North America, no. 225 (A. Poole and F. Gill, Eds.). The Academy of Natural Sciences, Philadelphia, PA, and The American Ornithologists' Union, Washington, DC.

Burger, J., and J. Shisler. 1978. Nest site selection of Willets in a New Jersey salt marsh. Wilson Bulletin 90:599–607.

Burger, M. F., and J. M. Liner. 2005. Important Bird Areas of New York, 2nd ed. Audubon New York, New York, NY.

Burke, T. A. 1998. White-faced Ibis (*Plegadis chihi*). Pages 136–137 *in* Bull's birds of New York State (E. Levine, Ed.). Comstock Publishing Associates, Ithaca, NY.

Burrill, J. L., and R. E. Bonney Jr. 1988. Eastern Bluebird (*Sialia sialis*). Pages 316–317 *in* The atlas of breeding birds in New York State

(R. F. Andrle and J. R. Carroll, Eds.). Cornell University Press, Ithaca, NY.

Burroughs, J. 1895. The writings of John Burroughs, vol. 1. Wakerobin. Riverside ed. Houghton Mifflin, Boston, MA. http://www.wakerobin.org/pages/WakeRobin.html.

Burtch, V. 1941. Common Tern nesting at Oneida Lake, New York. Auk 58:257–258.

Butcher, G. S., and D. K. Niven. 2007. Combining data from the Christmas Bird Count and the Breeding Bird Survey to determine the continental status and trends of North American birds. http://www.audubon.org/news/pressroom/CBID/Report.pdf.

Butler, R. W. 1992. Great Blue Heron (*Ardea herodias*). *In* The birds of North America, no. 25 (A. Poole, P. Stettenheim, and F. Gill, Eds.). The Academy of Natural Sciences, Philadelphia, PA, and The American Ornithologists' Union, Washington, DC.

Cabe, P. R. 1993. European Starling (*Sturnus vulgaris*). *In* The birds of North America, no. 48 (A. Poole and F. Gill, Eds.). The Academy of Natural Sciences, Philadelphia, PA, and The American Ornithologists' Union, Washington, DC.

———. 1998. The effects of founding bottlenecks on genetic variation in the European Starling (*Sturnus vulgaris*) in North America. Heredity 80:519–525.

Cade, T. J., and W. Burnham, Eds. 2003. Return of the Peregrine: a North American saga of tenacity and teamwork. Peregrine Fund, Boise, ID.

Cade, T. J., J. H. Enderson, C. G. Thelander, and C. M. White, Eds. 1988. Peregrine Falcon populations: their management and recovery. Peregrine Fund, Boise, ID.

Cadman, M. D. 1985. Status report on the Loggerhead Shrike (*Lanius ludovicianus*) in Canada. Unpublished report. COSEWIC (Committee on the Status of Endangered Wildlife in Canada), Ottawa, ON.

———. 1987. Wilson's Phalarope (*Phalaropus tricolor*). Pages 176–177 *in* Atlas of the breeding birds of Ontario (M. D. Cadman, P. F. J. Eagles, and F. M. Helleiner, Eds.). University of Waterloo Press, Waterloo, ON.

———. 1993. Status of the Short-eared Owl (*Asio flammeus*) in Canada. Unpublished report. COSEWIC (Committee on the Status of Endangered Wildlife in Canada), Ottawa, ON.

Cadman, M. D., P. F. J. Eagles, and F. M. Helleiner, Eds. 1987. Atlas of the breeding birds of Ontario. University of Waterloo Press, Waterloo, ON.

Cadman, M. D., and A. M. Page. 1994. Status report on the Short-eared Owl (*Asio flammeus*) in Canada. Unpublished report. COSEWIC (Committee on the Status of Endangered Wildlife in Canada), Ottawa, ON.

Caffrey, C., S. C. R. Smith, and T. J. Weston. 2005. West Nile virus devastates an American Crow population. Condor 107:128–132.

Caffrey, C., T. J. Weston, and S. C. R. Smith. 2003. High mortality among marked crows subsequent to the arrival of West Nile virus. Wildlife Society Bulletin 31:870–872.

Campbell, R. W., L. M. Van Damme, and S. R. Johnson. 1997. Sky Lark (*Alauda arvensis*). *In* The birds of North America, no. 286 (A. Poole and F. Gill, Eds.). The Academy of Natural Sciences, Philadelphia, PA, and The American Ornithologists' Union, Washington, DC.

Canadian Wildlife Service Waterfowl Committee. 2006. Population status of migratory game birds in Canada: November 2006

(and regulation proposals for overabundant species). CWS Migratory Birds Regulatory Report, no. 19. Canadian Wildlife Service, Ottawa, ON. http://www.cws-scf.ec.gc.ca/publications/status/nov06/nov06_e.pdf.

Cannings, R. J. 1993. Northern Saw-whet Owl (*Aegolius acadicus*). *In* The birds of North America, no. 42 (A. Poole and F. Gill, Eds.). The Academy of Natural Sciences, Philadelphia, PA, and The American Ornithologists' Union, Washington, DC.

Carey, M., D. E. Burhans, and D. A. Nelson. 1994. Field Sparrow (*Spizella pusilla*). *In* The birds of North America, no. 103 (A. Poole and F. Gill, Eds.). The Academy of Natural Sciences, Philadelphia, PA, and The American Ornithologists' Union, Washington, DC.

Carleton, G. C. 1935. Notes from Essex County, N.Y. Auk 52:197.

———. 1958. The birds of Central and Prospect parks. Proceedings of the Linnaean Society of New York, nos. 66–70:1–60.

Carleton, G. C., and J. M. C. Peterson. 1999. Birds of Essex County, New York, 3rd ed. High Peaks Audubon Society, Inc., Elizabethtown, NY.

Carleton, G. C., H. H. Poor, and O. K. Scott. 1948. Cape May Warbler breeding in New York State. Auk 65:607.

Carroll, D., and B. L. Swift. 2000. Status of the Trumpeter Swan in New York State. Kingbird 50:232–236.

Carroll, J. P. 1993. Gray Partridge (*Perdix perdix*). *In* The birds of North America, no. 58 (A. Poole and F. Gill, Eds.). The Academy of Natural Sciences, Philadelphia, PA, and The American Ornithologists' Union, Washington, DC.

Carroll, J. R. 1982. Occurrence of the Nanday Conure in Westchester County, New York. New York Fish and Game Journal 29:217.

———. 1988a. Black-hooded Parakeet (*Nandayus nenday*). Pages 194–195 *in* The atlas of breeding birds in New York State (R. F. Andrle and J. R. Carroll, Eds.). Cornell University Press, Ithaca, NY.

———. 1988b. Golden Eagle (*Aquila chrysaetos*). Pages 116–117 *in* The atlas of breeding birds in New York State (R. F. Andrle and J. R. Carroll, Eds.). Cornell University Press, Ithaca, NY.

———. 1988c. King Rail (*Rallus elegans*). Pages 138–139 *in* The atlas of breeding birds in New York State (R. F. Andrle and J. R. Carroll, Eds.). Cornell University Press, Ithaca, NY.

———. 1988d. Mallard x American Black Duck (*Anas platyrhynchos* x *rubripes*). Pages 68–69 *in* The atlas of breeding birds in New York State (R. F. Andrle and J. R. Carroll, Eds.). Cornell University Press, Ithaca, NY.

———. 1988e. Osprey (*Pandion haliaetus*). Pages 98–99 *in* The atlas of breeding birds in New York State (R. F. Andrle and J. R. Carroll, Eds.). Cornell University Press, Ithaca, NY.

———. 1988f. Palm Warbler (*Dendroica palmarum*). Pages 390–391 *in* The atlas of breeding birds in New York State (R. F. Andrle and J. R. Carroll, Eds.). Cornell University Press, Ithaca, NY.

———. 1988g. Status and breeding ecology of the Black Tern (*Chlidonias niger*) in New York. Kingbird 38:159–172.

———. 1988h. Yellow-throated Warbler (*Dendroica dominica*). Pages 384–385 *in* The atlas of breeding birds in New York State (R. F. Andrle and J. R. Carroll, Eds.). Cornell University Press, Ithaca, NY.

Carter, M. F., W. C. Hunter, D. N. Pashley, and K. V. Rosenberg. 2000. Setting conservation priorities for landbirds in the United States: the Partners in Flight approach. Auk 117:541–548.

Case, N. A., and O. H. Hewitt. 1963. Nesting and productivity of the Red-winged Blackbird in relation to habitat. Living Bird 2:7–20.

Caslick, J. W. 1975. Measuring revegetation rates and patterns on abandoned agricultural lands. Search: Agriculture 5(6):1–27.

Cavitt, J. F., and C. A. Haas. 2000. Brown Thrasher (*Toxostoma rufum*). *In* The birds of North America, no. 557 (A. Poole and F. Gill, Eds.). The Birds of North America, Inc., Philadelphia, PA.

Chamberlain, D. E., and R. J. Fuller. 2001. Contrasting patterns of change in the distribution and abundance of farmland birds in relation to farming system in lowland Britain. Global Ecology and Biogeography 10:399–409.

Chamberlaine, L. B. 1994. Region 6—St. Lawrence. Kingbird 44:225–233.

——. 1998a. Common Raven (*Corvus corax*). Pages 394–395 *in* Bull's birds of New York State (E. Levine, Ed.). Comstock Publishing Associates, Ithaca, NY.

——. 1998b. Red-bellied Woodpecker (*Melanerpes carolinus*). Pages 349–350 *in* Bull's birds of New York State (E. Levine, Ed.). Comstock Publishing Associates, Ithaca, NY.

——. 1998c. Sandhill Crane (*Grus canadensis*). Pages 227–228 *in* Bull's birds of New York State (E. Levine, Ed.). Comstock Publishing Associates, Ithaca, NY.

Chapman, F. M. 1908. The Fish Hawks of Gardiner's [sic] Island. Bird-Lore 10:153–159.

Chapman Mosher, B. A. 1986. Factors influencing reproductive success and nesting strategies in Black Terns. Ph.D. dissertation, Simon Fraser University, Burnaby, BC.

Chaulk, K., G. J. Robertson, B. T. Collins, W. A. Montevecchi, and B. Turner. 2005. Evidence of recent population increases in Common Eiders breeding in Labrador. Journal of Wildlife Management 69:805–809.

Ciaranca, M. A., C. C. Allin, and G. S. Jones. 1997. Mute Swan (*Cygnus olor*). *In* The birds of North America, no. 273 (A. Poole and F. Gill, Eds.). The Academy of Natural Sciences, Philadelphia, PA, and The American Ornithologists' Union, Washington, DC.

Cimprich, D. A., and F. R. Moore. 1995. Gray Catbird (*Dumetella carolinensis*). *In* The birds of North America, no. 167 (A. Poole and F. Gill, Eds.). The Academy of Natural Sciences, Philadelphia, PA, and The American Ornithologists' Union, Washington, DC.

Cimprich, D. A., F. R. Moore, and M. P. Guilfoyle. 2000. Red-eyed Vireo (*Vireo olivaceus*). *In* The birds of North America, no. 527 (A. Poole and F. Gill, Eds.). The Birds of North America, Inc., Philadelphia, PA.

Cink, C. L. 2002. Whip-poor-will (*Caprimulgus vociferus*). *In* The birds of North America, no. 620 (A. Poole and F. Gill, Eds.). The Birds of North America, Inc., Philadelphia, PA.

Cink, C. L., and C. T. Collins. 2002. Chimney Swift (*Chaetura pelagica*). *In* The birds of North America, no. 646 (A. Poole and F. Gill, Eds.). The Birds of North America, Inc., Philadelphia, PA.

Clark, A. B., D. A. Robinson Jr., and K. J. McGowan. 2006. Effects of West Nile virus mortality on social structure of an American Crow (*Corvus brachyrhynchos*) population in upstate New York. Ornithological Monographs, no. 60:65–78.

Clark, G. A. Jr. 1994. House Finch (*Carpodacus mexicanus*). Pages 396–397 *in* The atlas of breeding birds of Connecticut (Louis R. Bevier, Ed.). State Geological and Natural History Survey of Connecticut, Hartford, CT.

Clark, K. E., and L. J. Niles. 2000. U.S. Shorebird Conservation Plan: Northern Atlantic regional shorebird plan. Verson 1.0. http://www.fws.gov/shorebirdplan/RegionalShorebird/RegionalPlans.htm.

Clark, R. J. 1975. A field study of the Short-eared Owl *Asio flammeus* (Pontoppidian) in North America. Wildlife Monographs, no. 47:1–67.

Claypoole, K. 1986. Status of the Common Tern population breeding on Oneida Lake, New York, in 1986. Unpublished report. New York Cooperative Fish and Wildlife Research Unit, Cornell University, Ithaca, NY.

——. 1988. First nesting of the Double-crested Cormorant at Oneida Lake, New York. Kingbird 38:235–236.

Cleland, D. T., P. E. Avers, W. H. McNab, M. E. Jensen, R. G. Bailey, T. King, and W. E. Russell. 1997. National hierarchical framework of ecological units. Pages 181–200 *in* Ecosystem management applications for sustainable forest and wildlife resources (M. S. Boyce and A. Haney, Eds.). Yale University Press, New Haven, CT. http://files.dnr.state.mn.us/natural_resources/ecs/nhfeu.pdf.

Clements, R. 1990. Sandhill Crane summers in Chemung County. Kingbird 40:233–234.

Coleman, J. S., and J. D. Fraser. 1989. Black and Turkey vultures. Pages 15–21 *in* Proceedings of the Northeast Raptor Management Symposium and Workshop, 16–18 May 1988, Syracuse, NY (B. Pendleton, M. N. LeFranc Jr., M. B. Moss, C. E. Ruibal, M. A. Knighton, and D. L. Krahe, Eds.). National Wildlife Federation Scientific and Technical Series, no. 13, National Wildlife Federation, Washington, DC.

Coleman, J. T. H., and M. E. Richmond. 2004. Annual report to the N.Y.S. Department of Environmental Conservation. Unpublished report. New York Cooperative Fish and Wildlife Research Unit, Cornell University, Ithaca, NY.

——. 2005. Colonial waterbird nesting and success on Oneida Lake, NY. Annual Report to the New York State Department of Environmental Conservation. Unpublished report. New York Cooperative Fish and Wildlife Research Unit, Cornell University, Ithaca, NY.

Collar, N. J. 1997. Nanday Parakeet. Page 436 *in* Handbook of the birds of the world, vol. 4: sandgrouse to cuckoos (J. del Hoyo, A. Elliott, and J. Sargatal, Eds.). Lynx Editions, Barcelona, Spain.

Colwell, M. A., and J. R. Jehl Jr. 1994. Wilson's Phalarope (*Phalaropus tricolor*). *In* The birds of North America, no. 83 (A. Poole and F. Gill, Eds.). The Academy of Natural Sciences, Philadelphia, PA, and The American Ornithologists' Union, Washington, DC.

Comar, M. C. 1974. Fish Crow in Ithaca, New York. Kingbird 24:124.

Committee on the Status of Pollinators in North America. 2007. Status of pollinators in North America. The National Academies Press, Washington, DC. http://www.nap.edu/catalog/11761.html.

Confer, J. L. 1988a. Blue-winged Warbler (*Vermivora pinus*). Pages 354–355 *in* The atlas of breeding birds in New York State (R. F. Andrle and J. R. Carroll, Eds.). Cornell University Press, Ithaca. NY.

——. 1988b. Downy Woodpecker (*Picoides pubescens*). Pages 232–233 *in* The atlas of breeding birds in New York State (R. F. Andrle and J. R. Carroll, Eds.). Cornell University Press, Ithaca, NY.

——. 1988c. Golden-winged Warbler (*Vermivora chrysoptera*). Pages 356–357 *in* The atlas of breeding birds in New York State (R. F. Andrle and J. R. Carroll, Eds.). Cornell University Press, Ithaca, NY.

——. 1992. Golden-winged Warbler (*Vermivora chrysoptera*). *In* The birds of North America, no. 20 (A. Poole, P. Stettenheim, and F. Gill, Eds.). The Academy of Natural Sciences, Philadelphia, PA, and The American Ornithologists' Union, Washington, DC.

———. 1998. Golden-winged Warbler (*Vermivora chrysoptera*). Pages 453–455 *in* Bull's birds of New York State (E. Levine, Ed.). Comstock Publishing Associates, Ithaca, NY.

———. 2006. Secondary contact and introgression of Golden-winged Warblers (*Vermivora chrysoptera*): documenting the mechanism. Auk 123:958–961.

Confer, J. L., P. E. Allen, and J. L. Larkin. 2003. Effects of vegetation, interspecific competition, and brood parasitism on Golden-winged Warbler nesting success. Auk 120:138–144.

Confer, J. L., and K. Knapp. 1981. Golden-winged Warblers and Blue-winged Warblers: the relative success of a habitat specialist and a generalist. Auk 98:108–114.

Confer, J. L., and S. M. Pascoe. 2003. Avian communities on utility rights-of-ways and other managed shrublands in the northeastern United States. Forest Ecology and Management 85:193–206.

Confer, J. L., and S. K. Tupper. 2000. A reassessment of the status of Golden-winged and Blue-winged warblers in the Hudson Highlands of southern New York. Wilson Bulletin 112:544–546.

Connor, P. F. 1988a. Boat-tailed Grackle (*Quiscalus major*). Pages 476–477 *in* The atlas of breeding birds in New York State (R. F. Andrle and J. R. Carroll, Eds.). Cornell University Press, Ithaca, NY.

———. 1988b. Forster's Tern (*Sterna forsteri*). Pages 180–181 *in* The atlas of breeding birds in New York State (R. F. Andrle and J. R. Carroll, Eds.). Cornell University Press, Ithaca, NY.

———. 1988c. Marsh Wren (*Cistothorus palustris*). Pages 308–309 *in* The atlas of breeding birds in New York State (R. F. Andrle and J. R. Carroll, Eds.). Cornell University Press, Ithaca, NY.

———. 1988d. Orchard Oriole (*Icterus spurius*). Pages 482–483 *in* The atlas of breeding birds in New York State (R. F. Andrle and J. R. Carroll, Eds.). Cornell University Press, Ithaca, NY.

———. 1988e. Pied-billed Grebe (*Podilymbus podiceps*). Pages 28–29 *in* The atlas of breeding birds in New York State (R. F. Andrle and J. R. Carroll, Eds.). Cornell University Press, Ithaca, NY.

Conway, C. J. 1995. Virginia Rail (*Rallus limicola*). *In* The birds of North America, no. 173 (A. Poole and F. Gill, Eds.). The Academy of Natural Sciences, Philadelphia, PA, and The American Ornithologists' Union, Washington, DC.

———. 1999. Canada Warbler (*Wilsonia canadensis*). *In* The birds of North America, no. 421 (A. Poole and F. Gill, Eds.). The Birds of North America, Inc., Philadelphia, PA.

Cook, W. E. 1998. Chipping Sparrow (*Spizella passerina*). Pages 505–506 *in* Bull's birds of New York State (E. Levine, Ed.). Comstock Publishing Associates, Ithaca, NY.

Cooper, D. M., H. Hays, and C. Pessino. 1970. Breeding of the Common and Roseate terns on Great Gull Island. Proceedings of the Linnaean Society of New York, no. 71:83–104.

Courtney, P. A., and H. Blokpoel. 1983. Distribution and numbers of Common Terns on the lower Great Lakes during 1900–1980: a review. Colonial Waterbirds 6:107–120.

Cowardin, L. M., V. Carter, F. C. Golet, and E. T. LaRoe. 1979. Classification of wetlands and deepwater habitats of the United States. U.S. Fish and Wildlife Service, Office of Biological Services, Washington, DC.

Cramp, S., and K. E. L. Simmons, Eds. 1983. Handbook of the birds of Europe, the Middle East and North Africa: the birds of the Western Palearctic, vol. 3: waders to gulls. Oxford University Press, Oxford, UK.

Crewe, T. L., and D. Badzinski. 2006. Red-shouldered Hawk and spring woodpecker survey: 2005 final report. Bird Studies Canada, Port Rowan, ON. http://www.bsc-eoc.org/download/rsha2005.pdf.

Crewe, T. L., S. T. A. Timmermans, and K. E. Jones. 2005. The Marsh Monitoring Program annual report, 1995–2003: annual indices and trends in bird abundance and amphibian occurrence in the Great Lakes Basin. Bird Studies Canada, Port Rowan, ON. http://www.fws.gov/birds/waterbirds/monitoring/2004_MMP_Annual_Report.pdf.

Crick, H. Q. P., R. A. Robinson, G. F. Appleton, N. A. Clark, and A. D. Rickard, Eds. 2002. Investigation into the causes of the decline of Starlings and House Sparrows in Great Britain. BTO (British Trust for Ornithology) Research Report, no. 290. DEFRA (Department for Environment, Food, and Rural Affairs), London, UK. http://www.defra.gov.uk/wildlife-countryside/resprog/findings/sparrow/index.htm.

Crocoll, S. T. 1994. Red-shouldered Hawk (*Buteo lineatus*). *In* The birds of North America, no. 107 (A. Poole, and F. Gill, Eds.). The Academy of Natural Sciences, Philadelphia, PA, and The American Ornithologists' Union, Washington, DC.

———. 1998. Red-shouldered Hawk (*Buteo lineatus*). Pages 191–193 *in* Bull's birds of New York State (E. Levine, Ed.). Comstock Publishing Associates, Ithaca, NY.

Crocoll, S. T., and J. W. Parker. 1989. The breeding biology of Broad-winged and Red-shouldered hawks in western New York. Journal of Raptor Research 23:125–139.

Cruickshank, A. D. 1942. Birds around New York City, when and where to find them. American Museum of Natural History Handbook Series, no. 13. The Museum, New York, NY.

CTDEP (Connecticut Department of Environmental Protection). 1999. Wildlife in Connecticut, endangered and threatened species series, Willet. http://www.ct.gov/dep/lib/dep/wildlife/pdf_files/outreach/fact_sheets/willet.pdf.

Curtis, O. E., R. N. Rosenfield, and J. Bielefeldt. 2006. Cooper's Hawk (*Accipiter cooperii*). *In* The birds of North America online (A. Poole, Ed.). Cornell Lab of Ornithology, Ithaca, NY. http://bna.birds.cornell.edu/BNA/account/Coopers_Hawk/.doi:10.2173/bna.75.

Cuthbert, F. J., J. E. McKearnan, L. R. Wires, and A. R. Joshi. 2002. Distribution and abundance of colonial waterbirds in the U.S. Great Lakes: 1997–1999. Final report to USFWS. Unpublished report. U.S. Fish and Wildlife Service, Fort Snelling, MN.

Cuthbert, F. J., and L. R. Wires. 1999. Caspian Tern (*Sterna caspia*). *In* The birds of North America, no. 403 (A. Poole and F. Gill, Eds.). The Birds of North America, Inc., Philadelphia, PA.

Dabrowski, A., R. Fraser, J. L. Confer, and I. J. Lovette. 2005. Geographic variability in mitochondrial introgression among hybridizing populations of Golden-winged (*Vermivora chrysoptera*) and Blue-winged (*V. pinus*) warblers. Conservation Genetics 6:843–853.

Dahl, T. E. 1990. Wetlands losses in the United States 1780's to 1980's. U.S. Department of the Interior, Fish and Wildlife Service, Washington, DC, and Northern Prairie Wildlife Research Center, Jamestown, ND. http://www.npwrc.usgs.gov/resource/wetlands/wetloss/index.htm.

D'Anna, W. C. 1998a. Brewer's Blackbird (*Euphagus cyanocephalus*).

Pages 550–551 in Bull's birds of New York State (E. Levine, Ed.). Comstock Publishing Associates, Ithaca, NY.

——. 1998b. Chimney Swift (*Chaetura pelagica*). Pages 344–345 in Bull's birds of New York State (E. Levine, Ed.). Comstock Publishing Associates, Ithaca, NY.

David, A. B., II. 2003. Common Eider (*Somateria mollissima*). Pages 80–81 in Massachusetts breeding bird atlas (W. R. Petersen and W. R. Meservey, Eds.). Massachusetts Audubon Society, Lincoln, MA.

David, N. 1983. Québec region. American Birds 37:970–971.

Davis, C. M. 1978. A nesting study of the Brown Creeper. Living Bird 17:237–263.

Davis, M. B., and R. G. Shaw. 2001. Range shifts and adaptive responses to quaternary climate change. Science 292:673–679.

Davis, M. B., T. R. Simons, M. J. Groom, J. L. Weaver, and J. R. Cordes. 2001. The breeding status of the American Oystercatcher on the east coast of North America and breeding success in North Carolina. Waterbirds 24:195–202.

Davis, T. H. 1968. Willet nesting on Long Island, New York. Wilson Bulletin 80:330.

——. 1975. Notes concerning the first New York State nesting of Chuck-will's-widow. Kingbird 25:132–137.

——. 1976. Winter Wren breeding on Long Island. Kingbird 26:200.

——. 1981. Boat-tailed Grackles breeding at Jamaica Bay Wildlife Refuge. Kingbird 31:214.

Davis, W. E. Jr. 1993. Black-crowned Night-Heron (*Nycticorax nycticorax*). In The birds of North America, no. 74 (A. Poole and F. Gill, Eds.). The Academy of Natural Sciences, Philadelphia, PA, and The American Ornithologists' Union, Washington, DC.

Davis, W. E. Jr., and J. Kricher. 2000. Glossy Ibis (*Plegadis falcinellus*). In The birds of North America, no. 545 (A. Poole and F. Gill, Eds.). The Academy of Natural Sciences, Philadelphia, PA.

Davis, W. E. Jr., and J. A. Kushlan. 1994. Green Heron (*Butorides virescens*). In The birds of North America, no. 129 (A. Poole and F. Gill, Eds.). The Academy of Natural Sciences, Philadelphia, PA, and The American Ornithologists' Union, Washington, DC.

Davis, W. H., and P. Roca. 1995. Bluebirds and their survival. University Press of Kentucky, Lexington, KY.

Dawson, W. R. 1997. Pine Siskin (*Carduelis pinus*). In The birds of North America, no. 280 (A. Poole and F. Gill, Eds.). The Academy of Natural Sciences, Philadelphia, PA, and The American Ornithologists' Union, Washington, DC.

DeBenedictis, P. A. 1983. Region 5—Oneida Lake Basin. Kingbird 33:276–279.

deCalesta, D. S. 1994. Effect of white-tailed deer on songbirds within managed forests in Pennsylvania. Journal of Wildlife Management 58:711–718.

DeCandido, R. 2005. History of the Eastern Screech-Owl (*Megascops asio*) in New York City, 1867–2005. Urban Habitats 3:117–133. http://www.urbanhabitats.org/v03n01/urbanhabitats_v03n01_pdf.pdf.

DeGloria, S. D. 1998. Finger Lakes National Forest ecological mapping study. Cornell Institute for Resource Information Systems, Cornell University, Ithaca, NY.

DeGraaf, R. M., G. M. Witman, J. W. Lanier, B. J. Hill, and J. M. Keniston. 1980. Forest habitat for birds of the Northeast. Unpublished report. U.S. Department of Agriculture Forest Service, Washington, DC.

DeGraaf, R. M., and M. Yamasaki. 2001. New England wildlife: habitat, natural history, and distribution. University Press of New England, Hanover, NH.

DeGraff, L. W. 1973. Return of the Wild Turkey. Conservationist 28(Oct–Nov):24–27, 47.

DeGraff, L. W., D. E. Austin, and J. Hauber. 1983. A management plan for Gray Partridge in New York State. Unpublished report. New York State Department of Environmental Conservation, Albany, NY.

De Jong, M. J. 1996. Northern Rough-winged Swallow (*Stelgidopteryx serripennis*). In The birds of North America, no. 234 (A. Poole and F. Gill, Eds.). The Academy of Natural Sciences, Philadelphia, PA, and The American Ornithologists' Union, Washington, DC.

DeKay, J. E. (alternatively spelled De Kay or Dekay) 1844. Zoology of New York, or the New York fauna. Part 2: birds. Carroll and Cook, Albany, NY.

DeLorme [firm]. 2003. New York State atlas and gazetteer, 7th ed. DeLorme, Yarmouth, ME.

Dennis, D. 1987. American Black Duck (*Anas rubripes*). Pages 70–71 in The atlas of breeding birds in Ontario (M. D. Cadman, P. F. J. Eagles, and F. M. Helleiner, Eds.). University of Waterloo Press, Waterloo, ON.

DeOrsey, S., and B. A. Butler. 2006. The Birds of Dutchess County, New York, today and yesterday: a survey of current status with historical changes since 1870. Grinnell and Lawton Publishers, Millbrook, NY, on behalf of The Ralph T. Waterman Bird Club, Inc., Poughkeepsie, NY.

Derrickson, K. C., and R. Breitwisch. 1992. Northern Mockingbird (*Mimus polyglottos*). In The birds of North America, no. 7 (A. Poole, P. Stettenheim, and F. Gill, Eds.). The Academy of Natural Sciences, Philadelphia, PA, and The American Ornithologists' Union, Washington, DC.

DesGranges, J. L., J. Ingram, B. Drolet, C. Savage, J. Morin, and D. Borcard. 2005. Wetland bird response to water level changes in the Lake Ontario–St. Lawrence River hydrosystem. Final report to the International Joint Commission in support of the International Lake Ontario–St. Lawrence River Water Regulation Review Study. Canadian Wildlife Service, Québec and Ontario Regions. Unpublished report. Environment Canada, Sainte-Foy, QC.

Dessecker, D. R., G. W. Norman, and S. J. Williamson, Eds. 2006. Draft Ruffed Grouse conservation plan. Association of Fish and Wildlife Agencies, Washington, DC.

DeStefano, S. 2005. A review of the status and distribution of Northern Goshawks in New England. Journal of Raptor Research 39:342–350.

Dettmers, R. 2003. Status and conservation of shrubland birds in the northeastern US. Forest Ecology and Management 185:81–93.

Dickerman, R. W. 1987. The "old northeastern" subspecies of Red Crossbill. American Birds 41:188–194.

Dickinson, N. R. 1979. A division of southern and western New York State into ecological zones. Unpublished report. New York State Department of Environmental Conservation, Wildlife Resources Center, Delmar, NY.

——. 1983. Physiographic zones of southern and western New York. Unpublished report. New York State Department of Environmental Conservation, Wildlife Resources Center, Delmar, NY.

DiCostanzo, J. 1998. Ruddy Duck (*Oxyura jamaicensis*). Pages 177–178 *in* Bull's birds of New York State (E. Levine, Ed.). Comstock Publishing Associates, Ithaca, NY.

Dilger, W. C. 1956. Adaptive modifications and ecological isolating mechanisms in the thrush genera *Catharus* and *Hylocichla*. Wilson Bulletin 68:170–199.

Dimmick, R. W., M. J. Gudlin, and D. F. McKenzie. 2002. The Northern Bobwhite Conservation Initiative. Miscellaneous publication. Southeastern Association of Fish and Wildlife Agencies, SC. http://www.lmvjv.org/library/nbci_2002.doc.

Dinsmore, S. J., and W. R. Silcock. 2004. The changing seasons: expansions. North American Birds 58:324–330.

Dixon, R. D., and V. A. Saab. 2000. Black-backed Woodpecker (*Picoides arcticus*). *In* The birds of North America, no. 509 (A. Poole and F. Gill, Eds.). The Birds of North America, Inc., Philadelphia, PA.

Dolbeer, R. A., R. B. Chipman, A. L. Gosser, and S. C. Barras. 2003. Does shooting alter flight patterns of gulls: case study at John F. Kennedy International Airport. Pages 546–462 *in* Proceedings of the 26th Annual Meeting of the International Bird Strike Committee, Warsaw, 5–9 May 2003. http://www.int-birdstrike.org/Warsaw_Papers/IBSC26%20WPBB5.pdf.

Dolton, D. D., and R. D. Rau. 2006. Mourning Dove population status, 2006. U.S. Fish and Wildlife Service, Laurel, MD. http://www.fws.gov/migratorybirds/reports/reports.html.

Donald, P. F., and R. J. Fuller. 1998. Ornithological atlas data: a review of uses and limitations. Bird Study 45:129–145. http://www.ingentaconnect.com/content/bto/bird/1998/00000045/00000002/452129.

Donovan, T. M., and C. H. Flather. 2002. Relationships among North American songbird trends, habitat fragmentation, and landscape occupancy. Ecological Applications 12:364–374.

Donovan, T. M., F. R. Thompson, J. Faaborg, and J. R. Probst. 1995. Reproductive success of migratory birds in habitat sources and sinks. Conservation Biology 9:1380–1395.

Downer, R. H. L., and C. E. Liebelt. 1990. 1990 Long Island colonial waterbird and Piping Plover survey. Unpublished report. New York State Department of Environmental Conservation, Stony Brook, NY.

Drilling, N., R. Titman, and F. McKinney. 2002. Mallard (*Anas platyrhynchos*). *In* The birds of North America, no. 658 (A. Poole and F. Gill, Eds.). The Birds of North America, Inc., Philadelphia, PA.

Driscoll, M. J. L., T. Donovan, R. Mickey, A. Howard, and K. K. Fleming. 2005. Determinants of Wood Thrush nest success: a multiscale, model selection approach. Journal of Wildlife Management 69:699–709.

Driscoll, R. S., D. L. Merkel, D. L. Radloff, D. E. Snyder, and J. S. Hagihara. 1984. An ecological land classification framework for the United States. Forest Service Miscellaneous Publication, no. 1439. U.S. Department of Agriculture, Washington, DC.

Droege, S., and J. R. Sauer. 1990. North American Breeding Bird Survey annual summary, 1989. U.S. Fish and Wildlife Service Biological Report, no. 90(8):1–22.

Drury, W. H. 1973. Population changes in New England seabirds. Bird Banding 44:267–313.

DuBowy, P. J. 1996. Northern Shoveler (*Anas clypeata*). *In* The birds of North America, no. 217 (A. Poole and F. Gill, Eds.). The Academy of Natural Sciences, Philadelphia, PA, and The American Ornithologists' Union, Washington, DC.

Dugger, B. D., K. M. Dugger, and L. H. Fredrickson. 1994. Hooded Merganser (*Lophodytes cucullatus*). *In* The birds of North America, no. 98 (A. Poole and F. Gill, Eds.). The Academy of Natural Sciences, Philadelphia, PA, and The American Ornithologists' Union, Washington, DC.

Dunn, E. H., and D. L. Tessaglia. 1994. Predation of birds at feeders in winter. Journal of Field Ornithology 65:8–16.

Dunn, J. L., and K. L. Garrett. 1997. A field guide to warblers of North America. Houghton Mifflin, New York, NY.

Dutcher, W. 1886. Bird notes from Long Island, N.Y. Auk 3:432–444.

———. 1888. Bird notes from Long Island, N.Y. Auk 5:169–183.

Dwyer, C. P. 1992. The breeding ecology of sympatric Mallards and American Black Ducks in the western Adirondacks. M.S. thesis, State University of New York College of Environmental Science and Forestry, Syracuse, NY.

Eadie, J. M., and A. Keast. 1982. Do goldeneye and perch compete for food? Oecologia 55:225–230.

Eadie, J. M., M. L. Mallory, and H. G. Lumsden. 1995. Common Goldeneye (*Bucephala clangula*). *In* The birds of North America, no. 170 (A. Poole and F. Gill, Eds.). The Academy of Natural Sciences, Philadelphia, PA, and the American Ornithologists' Union, Washington, DC.

Eastman, J. 1991. Whip-poor-will (*Caprimulgus vociferus*). Pages 252–253 *in* The atlas of breeding birds of Michigan (R. Brewer, G. A. McPeek, and R. J. Adams Jr., Eds.). Michigan State University Press, East Lansing, MI.

Eaton, E. H. 1910. Birds of New York, pt. 1. University of the State of New York, Albany, NY.

———. 1914. Birds of New York, pt. 2. University of the State of New York, Albany, NY.

———. 1953. Birds of New York 1910 to 1930. Kingbird 3:52–55.

Eaton, S. W. 1959. The Tufted Titmouse invades New York. Kingbird 9:59–62.

———. 1988a. Acadian Flycatcher (*Empidonax virescens*). Pages 250–251 *in* The atlas of breeding birds in New York State (R. F. Andrle and J. R. Carroll, Eds.). Cornell University Press, Ithaca, NY.

———. 1988b. American Coot (*Fulica americana*). Pages 146–147 *in* The atlas of breeding birds in New York State (R. F. Andrle and J. R. Carroll, Eds.). Cornell University Press, Ithaca, NY.

———. 1988c. American Redstart (*Setophaga ruticilla*). Pages 400–401 *in* The atlas of breeding birds in New York State (R. F. Andrle and J. R. Carroll, Eds.). Cornell University Press, Ithaca, NY.

———. 1988d. Black-throated Green Warbler (*Dendroica virens*). Pages 380–381 *in* The atlas of breeding birds in New York State (R. F. Andrle and J. R. Carroll, Eds.). Cornell University Press, Ithaca, NY.

———. 1988e. Canada Goose (*Branta canadensis*). Pages 58–59 *in* The atlas of breeding birds in New York State (R. F. Andrle and J. R. Carroll, Eds.). Cornell University Press, Ithaca, NY.

———. 1988f. Common Snipe (*Gallinago gallinago*). Pages 160–161 *in* The atlas of breeding birds in New York State (R. F. Andrle and J. R. Carroll, Eds.). Cornell University Press, Ithaca, NY.

———. 1988g. Cooper's Hawk (*Accipiter cooperii*). Pages 106–107 *in* The atlas of breeding birds in New York State (R. F. Andrle and J. R. Carroll, Eds.). Cornell University Press, Ithaca, NY.

———. 1988h. Dark-eyed Junco (*Junco hyemalis*). Pages 464–465 *in* The atlas of breeding birds in New York State (R. F. Andrle and J. R. Carroll, Eds.). Cornell University Press, Ithaca, NY.

———. 1988i. Eastern Screech-Owl (*Otus asio*). Pages 202–203 *in* The atlas of breeding birds in New York State (R. F. Andrle and J. R. Carroll, Eds.). Cornell University Press, Ithaca, NY.

———. 1988j. Hooded Warbler (*Wilsonia citrina*). Pages 418–419 *in* The atlas of breeding birds in New York State (R. F. Andrle and J. R. Carroll, Eds.). Cornell University Press, Ithaca, NY.

———. 1988k. Magnolia Warbler (*Dendroica magnolia*). Pages 372–373 *in* The atlas of breeding birds in New York State (R. F. Andrle and J. R. Carroll, Eds.). Cornell University Press, Ithaca, NY.

———. 1988l. Northern Goshawk (*Accipiter gentilis*). Pages 108–109 *in* The atlas of breeding birds in New York State (R. F. Andrle and J. R. Carroll, Eds.). Cornell University Press, Ithaca, NY.

———. 1988m. Northern Waterthrush (*Seiurus noveboracensis*). Pages 408–409 *in* The atlas of breeding birds in New York State (R. F. Andrle and J. R. Carroll, Eds.). Cornell University Press, Ithaca, NY.

———. 1988n. Ring-necked Pheasant (*Phasianus colchicus*). Pages 124–125 *in* The atlas of breeding birds in New York State (R. F. Andrle and J. R. Carroll, Eds.). Cornell University Press, Ithaca, NY.

———. 1988o. Ruddy Duck (*Oxyura jamaicensis*). Pages 94–95 *in* The atlas of breeding birds in New York State (R. F. Andrle and J. R. Carroll, Eds.). Cornell University Press, Ithaca, NY.

———. 1988p. Upland Sandpiper (*Bartramia longicauda*). Pages 158–159 *in* The atlas of breeding birds in New York State (R. F. Andrle and J. R. Carroll, Eds.). Cornell University Press, Ithaca, NY.

———. 1988q. Wild Turkey (*Meleagris gallopavo*). Pages 130–131 *in* The atlas of breeding birds in New York State (R. F. Andrle and J. R. Carroll, Eds.). Cornell University Press, Ithaca, NY.

———. 1988r. Yellow-billed Cuckoo (*Coccyzus americanus*). Pages 198–199 *in* The atlas of breeding birds in New York State (R. F. Andrle and J. R. Carroll, Eds.). Cornell University Press, Ithaca, NY.

———. 1989. Region 1—Niagara Frontier. Kingbird 39:106–109.

———. 1992. Wild Turkey (*Meleagris gallopavo*). *In* The birds of North America, no. 22 (A. Poole, P. Stettenheim, and F. Gill, Eds.). The Academy of Natural Sciences, Philadelphia, PA, and The American Ornithologists' Union, Washington, DC.

———. 1995. Northern Waterthrush (*Seiurus noveboracensis*). *In* The birds of North America, no. 182 (A. Poole and F. Gill, Eds.). The Academy of Natural Sciences, Philadelphia, PA, and The American Ornithologists' Union, Washington, DC.

———. 1998a. Acadian Flycatcher (*Empidonax virescens*). Pages 362–364 *in* Bull's birds of New York State (E. Levine, Ed.). Comstock Publishing Associates, Ithaca, NY.

———. 1998b. Canada Warbler (*Wilsonia canadensis*). Pages 495–496 *in* Bull's birds of New York State (E. Levine, Ed.). Comstock Publishing Associates, Ithaca, NY.

———. 1998c. Eastern Phoebe (*Sayornis phoebe*). Pages 368–369 *in* Bull's birds of New York State (E. Levine, Ed.). Comstock Publishing Associates, Ithaca, NY.

———. 1998d. Hooded Merganser (*Lophodytes cucullatus*). Pages 173–174 *in* Bull's birds of New York State (E. Levine, Ed.). Comstock Publishing Associates, Ithaca, NY.

———. 1998e. Hooded Warbler (*Wilsonia citrina*). Pages 493–495 *in* Bull's birds of New York State (E. Levine, Ed.). Comstock Publishing Associates, Ithaca, NY.

———. 1998f. Red-breasted Merganser (*Mergus serrator*). Pages 176–177 *in* Bull's birds of New York State (E. Levine, Ed.). Comstock Publishing Associates, Ithaca, NY.

———. 1998g. Wild Turkey (*Meleagris gallopavo*). Pages 213–215 *in* Bull's birds of New York State (E. Levine, Ed.). Comstock Publishing Associates, Ithaca, NY.

eBird. 2006. [Eurasian Collared-Dove map.] http://ebird.org/content/ebird/ (accessed 20 Nov 2006).

Eckerle, K. P., and C. F. Thompson. 2001. Yellow-breasted Chat (*Icteria virens*). *In* The birds of North America, no. 575 (A. Poole and F. Gill, Eds.). The Birds of North America, Inc., Philadelphia, PA.

Eddleman, W. R., and C. J. Conway. 1998. Clapper Rail (*Rallus longirostris*). *In* The birds of North America, no. 340 (A. Poole and F. Gill, Eds.). The Birds of North America, Inc., Philadelphia, PA.

Eddleman, W. R., R. E. Flores, and M. Legare. 1994. Black Rail (*Laterallus jamaicensis*). *In* The birds of North America, no. 123 (A. Poole and F. Gill, Eds.). The Academy of Natural Sciences, Philadelphia, PA, and The American Ornithologists' Union, Washington, DC.

Eddleman, W. R., F. L. Knopf, B. Meanley, F. A. Reid, and R. Zembal. 1988. Conservation of North American rallids. Wilson Bulletin 100:458–475.

Edinger, G. J., D. J. Evans, S. Gebauer, T. G. Howard, D. M. Hunt, and A. M. Olivero, Eds. 2002. Ecological communities of New York State, 2nd ed. A revised and expanded edition of Carol Reschke's Ecological communities of New York State (Draft for review). New York Natural Heritage Program, New York State Department of Environmental Conservation, Albany, NY. http://www.dec.ny.gov/animals/29392.html.

Edminster, F. C. 1947. The Ruffed Grouse: its life story, ecology and management. Macmillan, New York, NY.

Elliott, J. E., and P. A. Martin. 1994. Chlorinated hydrocarbons and shell thinning in eggs of (*Accipiter*) hawks in Ontario, 1986–1989. Environmental Pollution 86:189–200.

Elliott, J. J. 1953. The nesting sparrows of Long Island. Long Island Naturalist, no. 2:15–24.

———. 1962. Sharp-tailed and Seaside sparrows on Long Island, New York. Kingbird 12:115–123.

———. 1968. European Goldfinch (*Carduelis carduelis*). Pages 384–385 *in* Life histories of North American cardinals, grosbeaks, buntings, towhees, finches, sparrows, and allies (A. C. Bent). U.S. National Museum Bulletin, no. 237. Smithsonian Institution Press, Washington, DC.

Elliott, J. J., and R. S. Arbib Jr. 1953. Origin and status of the House Finch in the eastern United States. Auk 70:31–37.

Ellison, W. G. 1985a. Cedar Waxwing (*Bombycilla cedrorum*). Pages 258–259 *in* The atlas of breeding birds of Vermont (S. B. Laughlin and D. P. Kibbe, Eds.). University Press of New England, Hanover, NH.

———. 1985b. House Wren (*Troglodytes aedon*). Pages 224–225 *in* The atlas of breeding birds of Vermont (S. B. Laughlin and D. P. Kibbe, Eds.). University Press of New England, Hanover, NH.

———. 1985c. Red-winged Blackbird (*Agelaius phoeniceus*). Pages 160–161 *in* The atlas of breeding birds of Vermont (S. B. Laughlin and D. P. Kibbe, Eds.). University Press of New England, Hanover, NH.

———. 1990. The status and habitat of the Rusty Blackbird in Caledonia and Essex counties. Unpublished report. Vermont Fish and Wildlife Department, Woodstock, VT.

———. 1992. Blue-gray Gnatcatcher (*Polioptila caerulea*). *In* The birds of North America, no. 23 (A. Poole, P. Stettenheim, and F. Gill,

Eds.). The Academy of Natural Sciences, Philadelphia, PA, and The American Ornithologists' Union, Washington, DC.

———. 1993. Historical patterns of vagrancy by Blue-gray Gnatcatchers in New England. Journal of Field Ornithology 64:358–366.

———. 1998a. Hermit Thrush (*Catharus guttatus*). Pages 437–438 *in* Bull's birds of New York State (E. Levine, Ed.). Comstock Publishing Associates, Ithaca, NY.

———. 1998b. Swainson's Thrush (*Catharus ustulatus*). Pages 436–437 *in* Bull's birds of New York State (E. Levine, Ed.). Comstock Publishing Associates, Ithaca, NY.

———. 1998c. Veery (*Catharus fuscescens*). Pages 431–432 *in* Bull's birds of New York State (E. Levine, Ed.). Comstock Publishing Associates, Ithaca, NY.

Enser, R. W. 1992. The atlas of breeding birds in Rhode Island (1982–1987). Rhode Island Department of Environmental Management, West Kingston, RI.

Erskine, A. J. 1992. Atlas of the breeding birds of the Maritime Provinces. Nimbus Publishing and Nova Scotia Museum, Halifax, NS.

Estel, B. L. 1989. Habitat use and nesting success of dabbling ducks in western New York grasslands. M.S. thesis, Cornell University, Ithaca, NY.

Estrada, J., V. Pedrocchi, L. Brontons, and S. Herrando, Eds. 2004. Atles dels ocells nidificants de Catalunya 1999–2002 [Catalan breeding bird atlas 1999–2002]. Institut Català d'Ornitologia (ICO)/Lynx Edicions, Barcelona, Spain.

Evans, R. A. 2002 An ecosystem unraveling? Pages 23–33 *in* Proceedings: Hemlock Woolly Adelgid in the Eastern United States Symposium, February 5–7, 2002, East Brunswick, N.J. (B. Onken, R. Reardon, and J. Lashomb, Eds.). New Jersey Agricultural Experiment Station and Rutgers University, New Brunswick, NJ. http://www.na.fs.fed.us/fhp/hwa/pub/proceedings/eco_unravel.pdf.

Evans, R. M., and F. L. Knopf. 1993. American White Pelican (*Pelecanus erythrorhynchos*). *In* The birds of North America, no. 57 (A. Poole and F. Gill, Eds.). The Academy of Natural Sciences, Philadelphia, PA, and The American Ornithologists' Union, Washington, DC.

Evans Mack, D., and W. Yong. 2000. Swainson's Thrush (*Catharus ustulatus*). *In* The birds of North America, no. 540 (A. Poole and F. Gill, Eds.). The Birds of North America, Inc., Philadelphia, PA.

Evans Ogden, L. J., and B. J. Stutchbury. 1994. Hooded Warbler (*Wilsonia citrina*). *In* The birds of North America, no. 110 (A. Poole and F. Gill, Eds.). The Academy of Natural Sciences, Philadelphia, PA, and The American Ornithologists' Union, Washington, DC.

Evers, D. C. 2007. Status assessment and conservation plan for the Common Loon (*Gavia immer*) in North America. U.S. Fish and Wildlife Service, Divison of Migratory Birds, Hadley, MA. http://www.briloon.org/.

Evers, D. C, and M. Duron. 2006. Developing an exposure profile for mercury in breeding birds of New York and Pennsylvania 2005. Report BRI 2006-11. BioDiversity Research Institute, Gorham, ME.

Ewert, D. 1974. First Long Island, New York, nesting record of the Kentucky Warbler. Proceedings of the Linnaean Society of New York, no. 72:77–79.

Fain, J. J., T. A. Volk, and T. J. Fahey. 1994. Fifty years of change in an upland forest in south-central New York: general patterns. Bulletin of the Torrey Botanical Club 121:130–139.

Falls, J. B., and J. G. Kopachena. 1994. White-throated Sparrow (*Zonotrichia albicollis*). *In* The birds of North America, no. 128 (A. Poole and F. Gill, Eds.). The Academy of Natural Sciences, Philadelphia, PA, and The American Ornithologists' Union, Washington, DC.

Farmer, C. J. 2006. Trends in autumn counts of migratory raptors in U.S. Fish and Wildlife Service Region 5. Raptor Population Index Project technical report. http://rpi-project.org/docs/RPI_USFWS_Region_5_Report.pdf.

Faustino, C. R., C. S. Jennelle, V. Connolly, A. K. Davis, E. C. Swarthout, A. A. Dhondt, and E. G. Cooch. 2004. *Mycoplasma gallisepticum* infection dynamics in a house finch population: seasonal variation in survival, encounter and transmission rate. Journal of Animal Ecology 73:651–669.

Ferren, R. L., and J. E. Myers. 1998. Rhode Island's maritime nesting birds: a history and survey of the state's beach and island breeders—cormorants, gulls, terns, herons, plovers, oystercatchers, and more. Rhode Island Division of Fish and Wildlife, West Kingston, RI.

Feustel, K. 1998. Cedar Waxwing (*Bombycilla cedrorum*). Pages 450–451 *in* Bull's birds of New York State (E. Levine, Ed.). Comstock Publishing Associates, Ithaca, NY.

Ficken, M. S., and R. W. Ficken. 1968. Courtship of Blue-winged Warblers, Golden-winged Warblers, and their hybrids. Wilson Bulletin 80:161–172.

Ficken, M. S., M. A. McLaren, and J. P. Hailman. 1996. Boreal Chickadee (*Parus hudsonicus*). *In* The birds of North America, no. 254 (A. Poole and F. Gill, Eds.). The Academy of Natural Sciences, Philadelphia, PA, and the American Ornithologists' Union, Washington, DC.

Figley, W. K., and L. W. VanDruff. 1982. The ecology of urban Mallards. Wildlife Monographs, no. 81:6–39.

Fingerhood, E. D. 1992. Bewick's Wren (*Thryomanes bewickii*). Pages 435–436 *in* Atlas of breeding birds in Pennsylvania (D. W. Brauning, Ed.). University of Pittsburgh Press, Pittsburgh, PA.

Fischer, J. R., D. E. Stallknecht, M. P. Luttrell, A. A. Dhondt, and K. A. Converse. 1997. Mycoplasmal conjunctivitis in wild songbirds: the spread of a new contagious disease in a mobile host population. Emerging Infectious Diseases 3:69–72.

Fleming, K. K., and W. F. Porter. 2003. Habitat suitability and population structure of Wild Turkeys in New York State: final report to the New York chapter of the National Wild Turkey Federation. SUNY College of Environmental Science and Forestry, Syracuse, NY.

Flinn, K. M., and P. L. Marks. 2004. Land use history and forest herb diversity in Tompkins County, New York, USA. Pages 81–95 *in* Forest biodiversity: lessons from history for conservation (O. Honnay, K. Verheyen, B. Bossuyt, and M. Hermy, Eds.). CABI International, Wallingford, Oxfordshire, UK.

———. 2007. Agricultural legacies in forest environments: tree communities, soil properties, and light availability. Ecological Applications 17:452–463.

Foley, D. D. 1960. Recent changes in waterfowl populations in New York. Kingbird 10:82–89.

Foley, D. D., D. Benson, L. W. DeGraff, and E. R. Holm. 1961. Waterfowl stocking in New York. New York Fish and Game Journal 8:37–48.

Forbush, E. H. 1907. Useful birds and their protection, 2nd ed. Wright and Potter, Boston, MA.

———. 1929. Birds of Massachusetts and other New England states, pts. 2 and 3. Norwood Press, Norwood, MA.

———. 1939. Natural history of the birds of eastern and central North America. Revised and abridged by J. B. May. Houghton Mifflin, Boston, MA.

Forrester, J. A., T. E. Yorks, and D. J. Leopold. 2005. Arboreal vegetation, coarse woody debris, and disturbance history of mature and old-growth stands in a coniferous forested wetland. Journal of the Torrey Botanical Society 132:252–261.

Foss, R., Ed. 1994. Atlas of breeding birds in New Hampshire. Chalford Publishing Corporation, Dover, NH.

Fox, W. F. 1895. The Adirondack black spruce: from the annual report of the New York Forest Commission for 1894. James B. Lyon, Albany, NY.

Frederick, P. C. 1997. Tricolored Heron (*Egretta tricolor*). *In* The birds of North America, no. 306 (A. Poole and F. Gill, Eds.). The Academy of Natural Sciences, Philadelphia, PA, and The American Ornithologists' Union, Washington, DC.

Fritz, R. S. 1977. The distribution and population status of the Spruce Grouse in the Adirondacks. M.S. thesis, State University of New York College of Environmental Science and Forestry, Syracuse, NY.

Gale, G. A., L. A. Hanners, and S. R. Patton. 1997. Reproductive success of Worm-eating Warblers in a forested landscape. Conservation Biology 11:246–250.

Gamble, L. R., and T. M. Bergin. 1996. Western Kingbird (*Tyrannus verticalis*). *In* The birds of North America, no. 227 (A. Poole and F. Gill, Eds.). The Academy of Natural Sciences, Philadelphia, PA, and The American Ornithologists' Union, Washington, DC.

Gardali, T., and G. Ballard. 2000. Warbling Vireo (*Vireo gilvus*). *In* The birds of North America, no. 551 (A. Poole and F. Gill, Eds.). The Birds of North America, Inc., Philadelphia, PA.

Gardali, T., and J. D. Lowe. 2006. Reviving Resident Bird Counts: the 2001 and 2002 Breeding Bird Census. Bird Populations 7:90–95. http://birdpop.net/pubs/birdpopv7.php.

Garrison, B. A. 1999. Bank Swallow (*Riparia riparia*). *In* The birds of North America, no. 414 (A. Poole and F. Gill, Eds.). The Academy of Natural Sciences, Philadelphia, PA, and The American Ornithologists' Union, Washington, DC.

Gaston, K. J. 1998. Ecology: rarity as double jeopardy. Nature 394:229–230.

Gaston, K. J., T. M. Blackburn, J. J. D. Greenwood, R. D. Gregory, R. M. Quinn, and J. H. Lawton. 2000. Abundance-occupancy relationships. Journal of Applied Ecology 37:39–59.

Gauthier, G. 1993. Bufflehead (*Bucephala albeola*). *In* The birds of North America, no. 67 (A. Poole and F. Gill, Eds.). The Academy of Natural Sciences, Philadelphia, PA, and The American Ornithologists' Union, Washington, DC.

Gehlbach, F. R. 1995. Eastern Screech-Owl (*Otus asio*). *In* The birds of North America, no. 165 (A. Poole and F. Gill, Eds.). The Academy of Natural Sciences, Philadelphia, PA, and The American Ornithologists' Union, Washington, DC.

Ghalambor, C. K., and T. E. Martin. 1999. Red-breasted Nuthatch (*Sitta canadensis*). *In* The birds of North America, no. 459 (A. Poole and F. Gill, Eds.). The Birds of North America, Inc., Philadelphia, PA.

Gibbons, D. W., J. B. Reid, and R. A. Chapman, Eds. 1993. The new atlas of breeding birds in Britain and Ireland: 1988–1991. T & AD Poyser [for the] British Trust for Ornithology, Scottish Ornithologists' Club, Irish Wildbird Conservancy, London, UK.

Gibbs, J. P., J. R. Longcore, D. G. McAuley, and J. K. Ringelman. 1991. Use of wetland habitats by selected nongame waterbirds in Maine. U.S. Fish and Wildlife Service Resource Publication, no. 9. U.S. Fish and Wildlife Service, Washington, DC.

Gibbs, J. P., S. Melvin, and F. A. Reid. 1992a. American Bittern (*Botaurus lentiginosus*). *In* The birds of North America, no. 18 (A. Poole, P. Stettenheim, and F. Gill, Eds.). The Academy of Natural Sciences, Philadelphia, PA, and The American Ornithologists' Union, Washington, DC.

Gibbs, J. P., F. A. Reid, and S. M. Melvin. 1992b. Least Bittern (*Ixobrychus exilis*). *In* The birds of North America, no. 17 (A. Poole, P. Stettenheim, and F. Gill, Eds.). The Academy of Natural Sciences, Philadelphia, PA, and The American Ornithologists' Union, Washington, DC.

Gibbs, J. P., S. Woodward, M. L. Hunter, and A. E. Hutchinson. 1987. Determinants of Great Blue Heron colony distribution in coastal Maine. Auk 104:38–47.

Gill, D. E., P. Blank, J. Parks, J. B. Guerard, B. Lohr, E. Schwartzman, J. B. Gruber, G. Dodge, C. A. Rewa, and H. F. Sears. 2006. Plants and breeding bird response on a managed conservation reserve program grassland in Maryland. Wildlife Society Bulletin 34:944–956.

Gill, F. B. 1980. Historical aspects of hybridization between Blue-winged and Golden-winged warblers. Auk 97:1–18.

———. 1997. Local cytonuclear extinction of the Golden-winged Warbler. Evolution 51:519–525.

Gill, F. B., R. A. Canterbury, and J. L. Confer. 2001. Blue-winged Warbler (*Vermivora pinus*). *In* The birds of North America, no. 584 (A. Poole and F. Gill, Eds.). The Birds of North America, Inc., Philadelphia, PA.

Gillihan, S. W., and B. Byers. 1997. Evening Grosbeak (*Coccothraustes vespertinus*). *In* The birds of North America, no. 599 (A. Poole and F. Gill, Eds.). The Birds of North America, Inc., Philadelphia, PA.

Giraud, J. P. Jr. 1844. The birds of Long Island. Wiley and Putnam, New York, NY.

Giroux, J.-F., J. Lefebvre, L. Bélanger, J. Rodrigue, and S. Lapointe. 2001. Establishment of a breeding population of Canada Geese in southern Québec. Canadian Field-Naturalist 115:75–81.

Gochfeld, M. 1983. The Roseate Tern: world distribution and status of a threatened species. Biological Conservation 25:103–125.

Gochfeld, M., and J. Burger. 1981. Boat-tailed Grackles in Hewlettt Bay, Long Island. Kingbird 31:214.

———. 1994. Black Skimmer (*Rynchops niger*). *In* The birds of North America, no. 108 (A. Poole and F. Gill, Eds.). The Academy of Natural Sciences, Philadelphia, PA, and The American Ornithologists' Union, Washington, DC.

Gochfeld, M., J. Burger, and I. C. T. Nisbet. 1998. Roseate Tern (*Sterna dougallii*). *In* The birds of North America, no. 370 (A. Poole and F. Gill, Eds.). The Birds of North America, Inc., Philadelphia, PA.

Godfrey, W. E. 1986. The birds of Canada, rev. ed. National Museums of Canada, Ottawa, ON.

GOMSWG (Gulf of Maine Seabird Working Group). 2005. GOMSWG 2005 annual report. U.S. Fish and Wildlife Service, Milbridge, ME. http://www.fws.gov/northeast/mainecoastal/progsumm05.html.

Good, T. P. 1998. Great Black-backed Gull (*Larus marinus*). *In* The birds of North America, no. 330 (A. Poole and F. Gill, Eds.). The Birds of North America, Inc., Philadelphia, PA.

Goodrich, L. J., S. T. Crocoll, and S. E. Senner. 1996. Broad-winged Hawk (*Buteo platypterus*). *In* The birds of North America, no. 218 (A. Poole and F. Gill, Eds.). The Academy of Natural Sciences, Philadelphia, PA, and The American Ornithologists' Union, Washington, DC.

Gosselin, M., and N. David. 1980. Québec region. American Birds 34:877–878.

Goudie, R. I., G. J. Robertson, and A. Reed. 2000. Common Eider (*Somateria mollissima*). *In* The birds of North America, no. 546 (A. Poole and F. Gill, Eds.). The Birds of North America, Inc., Philadelphia, PA.

Gowaty, P. A., and J. H. Plissner. 1998. Eastern Bluebird (*Sialia sialis*). *In* The birds of North America, no. 381 (A. Poole and F. Gill, Eds.). The Birds of North America, Inc., Philadelphia, PA.

Graham, D., S. Timmermans, and J. McCracken. 2002. A comparison of abundance of colonial marsh birds between 1991 and 2001 in the Canadian portions of Lakes Huron, St. Clair, Ontario, and Erie. Bird Studies Canada, Port Rowan, ON. http://www.bsc-eoc.org/download/marshbirdcomp.pdf.

Greenlaw, J. S. 1983. Microgeographic distribution of breeding Seaside Sparrows on New York salt marshes. Pages 99–114 *in* The Seaside Sparrow, its biology and management (T. L. Quay, J. B. Funderburg Jr., D. S. Lee, E. F. Potter, and C. S. Robbins, Eds.). North Carolina Biological Survey and the North Carolina State Museum of Natural History, Raleigh, NC.

———. 1993. Behavioral and morphological diversification in Sharptailed Sparrows (*Ammodramus caudacutus*) of the Atlantic coast. Auk 110:286–303.

———. 1996. Eastern Towhee (*Pipilo erythrophthalmus*). *In* The birds of North America, no. 262 (A. Poole and F. Gill, Eds.). The Academy of Natural Sciences, Philadelphia, PA, and The American Ornithologists' Union, Washington, DC.

Greenlaw, J. S., and R. F. Miller. 1982. Breeding Soras on a Long Island salt marsh. Kingbird 32:78–84.

Greenlaw, J. S., and J. D. Rising. 1994. Sharp-tailed Sparrow (*Ammodramus caudacutus*). *In* The birds of North America, no. 112 (A. Poole and F. Gill, Eds.). The Academy of Natural Sciences, Philadelphia, PA, and The American Ornithologists' Union, Washington, DC.

Greenlaw, J. S., and G. E. Woolfenden. 2007. Wintering distributions and migration of Saltmarsh and Nelson's sharp-tailed sparrows. Wilson Journal of Ornithology 119:361–377.

Gretch, M. 1988. Common Goldeneye (*Bucephala clangula*). Pages 86–87 *in* The atlas of breeding birds in New York State (R. F. Andrle and J. R. Carroll, Eds.). Cornell University Press, Ithaca, NY.

Griffith, K. C. 1997. Genesee—Region 2. Kingbird 47:295–300.

———. 1998a. Canada Goose (*Branta canadensis*). Pages 144–145 *in* Bull's birds of New York State (E. Levine, Ed.). Comstock Publishing Associates, Ithaca, NY.

———. 1998b. Great Blue Heron (*Ardea herodias*). Pages 124–125 *in* Bull's birds of New York State (E. Levine, Ed.). Comstock Publishing Associates, Ithaca, NY.

———. 1999. Region 2—Genesee. Kingbird 49:329–333.

———. 2004. Region 2—Genesee. Kingbird 54:332–336.

Griscom, L. 1923. Birds of the New York City region. American Mu-

seum of Natural History Handbook Series, no. 9. The Museum, New York, NY.

Gross, D. A. 1992. Cedar Waxwing (*Bombycilla cedrorum*). Pages 282–283 *in* Atlas of breeding birds in Pennsylvania (D. W. Brauning, Ed.). University of Pittsburgh Press, Pittsburgh, PA.

Gross, D. A., and P. E. Lowther. 2001. Yellow-bellied Flycatcher (*Empidonax flaviventris*). *In* The birds of North America, no. 566 (A. Poole and F. Gill, Eds.). The Birds of North America, Inc., Philadelphia, PA.

Groth, J. G. 1993. Evolutionary differentiation in morphology, vocalizations and allozymes among nomadic sibling species in the North American Red Crossbill (*Loxia curvirostra*) complex. University of California Publications in Zoology 127. University of California Press, Berkeley, CA.

———. 1998. Red Crossbill (*Loxia curvirostra*). Pages 564–566 *in* Bull's birds of New York State (E. Levine, Ed.). Comstock Publishing Associates, Ithaca, NY.

Grover, A. M., and G. A. Baldassarre. 1995. Bird species richness within beaver ponds in south-central New York. Wetlands 15:108–118.

Grubb, T. C. Jr., and V. V. Pravosudov. 1994. Tufted Titmouse (*Parus bicolor*). *In* The birds of North America, no. 86 (A. Poole and F. Gill, Eds.). The Academy of Natural Sciences, Philadelphia, PA, and The American Ornithologists' Union, Washington, DC.

Gullion, G. W. 1984. Managing northern forests for wildlife. Ruffed Grouse Society, Caraopolis, PA.

Guzy, M. J., and G. Ritchison. 1999. Common Yellowthroat (*Geothlypis trichas*). *In* The birds of North America, no. 448 (A. Poole and F. Gill, Eds.). The Birds of North America, Inc., Philadelphia, PA.

Hagen, J. M., W. M. Vander Haegen, and P. S. McKinley. 1996. The early development of forest fragmentation effects on birds. Conservation Biology 10:188–202.

Haggerty, T. M., and E. S. Morton. 1995. Carolina Wren (*Thryothorus ludovicianus*). *In* The birds of North America, no. 188 (A. Poole and F. Gill, Eds.). The Academy of Natural Sciences, Philadelphia, PA, and The American Ornithologists' Union, Washington, DC.

Haig, S. M., and E. Elliott-Smith. 2004. Piping Plover (*Charadrius melodus*). *In* The birds of North America online (A. Poole, Ed.). Cornell Lab of Ornithology, Ithaca, NY. http://bna.birds.cornell.edu/BNA/account/Piping_Plover/.doi:10.2173/bna.2.

Haig, S. M., C. L. Ferland, F. J. Cuthbert, J. Dingledine, J. P. Goossen, A. Hecht, and N. McPhillips. 2005. A complete species census and evidence for regional declines in Piping Plovers. Journal of Wildlife Management 69:160–173.

Hale, S. R. 2006. Using satellite imagery to model the distribution and abundance of Bicknell's Thrush (*Catharus bicknelli*) in New Hampshire's White Mountains. Auk 123:1038–1051.

Halkin, S. L., and S. U. Linville. 1999. Northern Cardinal (*Cardinalis cardinalis*). *In* The birds of North America, no. 440 (A. Poole and F. Gill, Eds.). The Birds of North America, Inc., Philadelphia, PA.

Hall, G. A. 1994. Magnolia Warbler (*Dendroica magnolia*). *In* The birds of North America, no. 136 (A. Poole and F. Gill, Eds.). The Academy of Natural Sciences, Philadelphia, PA, and The American Ornithologists' Union, Washington, DC.

———. 1996. Yellow-throated Warbler (*Dendroica dominica*). *In* The birds of North America, no. 223 (A. Poole and F. Gill, Eds.). The Academy of Natural Sciences, Philadelphia, PA., and The American Ornithologists' Union, Washington, DC.

Hamas, M. J. 1994. Belted Kingfisher (*Ceryle alcyon*). *In* The birds of North America, no. 84 (A. Poole, and F. Gill, Eds.). The Academy of Natural Sciences, Philadelphia, PA, and The American Ornithologists' Union, Washington, DC.

Hamel, P. B. 2000. Cerulean Warbler (*Dendroica cerulea*). *In* The birds of North America, no. 511 (A. Poole and F. Gill, Eds.). The Birds of North America, Inc., Philadelphia, PA.

Hames, R. S., J. D. Lowe, S. Barker Swarthout, and K. V. Rosenberg. 2006. Understanding the risk to Neotropical migrant bird species of multiple human-caused stressors: elucidating processes behind the patterns. Ecology and Society 11:Art. 24. http://ecologyand society.org/vol11/iss1/art24/.

Hames, R. S., K. V. Rosenberg, J. D. Lowe, S. E. Barker, and A. A. Dhondt. 2002a. Adverse effects of acid rain on the distribution of the Wood Thrush *Hylocichla mustelina* in North America. Proceedings of the National Academy of Sciences of the United States of America 99:11235–11240.

Hames, R. S., K. V. Rosenberg, J. D. Lowe, S. E. Barker, and A. A. Dhondt. 2002b. Effects of forest fragmentation on tanager and thrush species in eastern and western North America. Studies in Avian Biology, no. 25:81–91.

Hamilton, W. J. Jr. 1933. A late nesting waxwing in central New York. Auk 50:114–115.

Haney, J. C., and C. P. Schaadt. 1996. Functional roles of eastern old growth in promoting forest bird diversity. Pages 76–88 *in* Eastern old-growth forest: prospects for rediscovery and recovery (M. B. Davis, Ed.). Island Press, Washington, DC.

Hanners, L. A., and S. R. Patton. 1998. Worm-eating Warbler (*Helmitheros vermivorus*). *In* The birds of North America, no. 367 (A. Poole and F. Gill, Eds.). The birds of North America, Inc., Philadelphia, PA.

Hansen, P. 1987. Acid rain and waterfowl: the case for concern in North America. Izaak Walton League of America, Arlington, VA.

Hanson, E., C. C. Rimmer, and S. G. Parren. 2006. The 2006 breeding status of Common Loons in Vermont. Vermont Institute of Natural Science, Quechee, VT, and Vermont Fish and Wildlife Department. http://www.vinsweb.org/assets/pdf/LoonReport2006.pdf.

Hardy, Y. J., A. Lafond, and L. Hamel. 1983. The epidemiology of the current spruce budworm outbreak in Quebec. Forest Science 29:715–725.

Harrison, C. 1978. A field guide to the eggs, nests and nestlings of North American birds. William Collins Sons, New York, NY.

Harrison, P. 1983. Seabirds, an identification guide. Houghton Mifflin, Boston, MA.

Hartig, E. K., V. Gornitz, A. Kolker, F. Mushacke, and D. Fallon. 2002. Anthropogenic and climate-change impacts on salt marshes of Jamaica Bay, New York City. Wetlands 22:71–89.

Hartley, M. J., M. F. Burger, and J. Beyea. 2003. Bird, amphibian, and carrion beetle associations with post-harvest stand conditions in northern hardwood forests of New York. Unpublished report. Audubon New York, Albany, NY.

Hatch, J. J., and D. V. Weseloh. 1999. Double-crested Cormorant (*Phalacrocorax auritus*). *In* The birds of North America, no. 441 (A. Poole and F. Gill, Eds.). The Birds of North America, Inc., Philadelphia, PA.

Hawk Creek Wildlife, Inc. 2006. Barn Owl breeding. http://www. hawkcreek.org/.

Hays, H. 1998. Common Tern (*Sterna hirundo*). Pages 299–302 *in* Bull's birds of New York State (E. Levine, Ed.). Comstock Publishing Associates, Ithaca, NY.

Hecht, A. 2005. Preliminary 2005 Atlantic Coast Piping Plover abundance and productivity estimates. U.S. Fish and Wildlife Service, Sudbury, MA. http://www.fws.gov/northeast/pipingplover/status/preliminary.05.pdf.

Heidenreich, D. 2006. Rt. 11 Nestbox Trail. Bluebird News 24(Fall):11.

Hejl, S. J., J. A. Holmes, and D. E. Kroodsma. 2002. Winter Wren (*Troglodytes troglodytes*). *In* The birds of North America, no. 623 (A. Poole and F. Gill, Eds.). The Birds of North America, Inc., Philadelphia, PA.

Hejl, S. J., K. R. Newlon, M. E. McFadzen, J. S. Young, and C. K. Ghalambor. 2002. Brown Creeper (*Certhia americana*). *In* The birds of North America, no. 669 (A. Poole and F. Gill, Eds.). The Birds of North America, Inc., Philadelphia, PA.

Henny, C. J., and N. E. Holgersen. 1974. Range expansion and population increase of the Gadwall in eastern North America. Wildfowl 25:95–101.

Hepp, G. R., and F. C. Bellrose. 1995. Wood Duck (*Aix sponsa*). *In* The birds of North America, no. 169 (A. Poole and F. Gill, Eds.). The Academy of Natural Sciences, Philadelphia, PA, and The American Ornithologists' Union, Washington, DC.

Herbert, C. E., J. Duffe, D. V. Weseloh, E. M. Senese, and G. D. Haffner. 2005. Unique island habitats may be threatened by Double-crested Cormorants. Journal of Wildlife Management 69:68–76.

Herkert, J. R., D. E. Kroodsma, and J. P. Gibbs. 2001. Sedge Wren (*Cistothorus platensis*). *In* The birds of North America, no. 582 (A. Poole and F. Gill, Eds.). The Birds of North America, Inc., Philadelphia, PA.

Herkert, J. R., P. D. Vickery, and D. E. Kroodsma. 2002. Henslow's Sparrow (*Ammodramus henslowii*). *In* The birds of North America, no. 672 (A. Poole and F. Gill, Eds.). The Birds of North America, Inc., Philadelphia, PA.

Heusmann, H. W. 1974. Mallard–black duck relationships in the Northeast. Wildlife Society Bulletin 2:171–177.

——. 2003. Canada Goose (*Branta canadensis*). Pages 58–59 *in* Massachusetts breeding bird atlas (W. R. Petersen and W. R. Meservey, Eds.). Massachusetts Audubon Society, Lincoln, MA.

Heusmann, H. W., T. J. Early, and B. J. Nikula. 2000. Evidence of an increasing Hooded Merganser population in Massachusetts. Wilson Bulletin 112:413–415.

Hickey, J. J. 1942. Eastern population of the Duck Hawk. Auk 59:176–204.

Hickey, J. M. 1997. Breeding biology and population dynamics of the Black Tern in western New York. M.S. thesis, Cornell University, Ithaca, NY.

Hitch, A. T., and P. L. Leberg. 2007. Breeding distributions of North American bird species moving north as a result of climate change. Conservation Biology 21:534–539.

Hobson, K. A., and E. Bayne. 2000. Effects of forest fragmentation by agriculture on avian communities in the southern boreal mixed woods of western Canada. Wilson Bulletin 112:373–387.

Hochachka, W. M., and A. A. Dhondt. 2000. Density-dependent decline of host abundance resulting from a new infectious disease. Proceedings of the National Academy of Sciences of the United States of America 97:5303–5306.

——. 2006. House Finch (*Carpodacus mexicanus*) population-and group-level responses to a bacterial disease. Ornithological Monographs, no. 60:30–43.

Hodgman, T. P., W. G. Shriver, and P. D. Vickery. 2002. Redefining range overlap between the sharp-tailed sparrows of coastal New England. Wilson Bulletin 114:38–43.

Hohman, W. L., and R. T. Eberhardt. 1998. Ring-necked Duck (*Aythya collaris*). *In* The birds of North America, no. 329 (A. Poole and F. Gill, Eds.). The Birds of North America, Inc., Philadelphia, PA.

Holloway, J. E. 2003. Dictionary of birds of the United States: scientific and common names. Timber Press, Portland, OR.

Holmes, R. T. 1990. The structure of a temperate deciduous forest bird community: variability in time and space. Pages 121–139 *in* Biogeography and ecology of forest bird communities (A. Keast, Ed.). SPB Academic Publishing, The Hague, Netherlands.

Holmes, R. T., N. L. Rodenhouse, and T. S. Sillett. 2005. Black-throated Blue Warbler (*Dendroica caerulescens*). *In* The birds of North America online (A. Poole, Ed.). Cornell Lab of Ornithology, Ithaca, NY. http://bna.birds.cornell.edu/BNA/account/Black-throated_Blue_Warbler/.doi:10.2173/bna.87.

Holmes, R. T., and T. W. Sherry 2001. Thirty-year bird population trends in an unfragmented temperate deciduous forest: importance of habitat change. Auk 118:589–609.

Holt, D. W. 1986. Status report: the Short-eared Owl in the Northeast. Eyas 9:3–5.

Holt, D. W., and S. M. Leasure. 1993. Short-eared Owl (*Asio flammeus*). *In* The birds of North America, no. 62 (A. Poole and F. Gill, Eds.). The Birds of North America, Inc., Philadelphia, PA.

Homer, C., C. Huang, L. Yang, B. Wylie, and M. Coan. 2004. Development of a 2001 National Landcover Database for the United States. Photogrammetric Engineering and Remote Sensing 70:829–840. http://www.mrlc.gov/pdfs/July_PERS.pdf.

Hoover, J. P., M. C. Brittingham, and L. J. Goodrich. 1995. Effects of forest patch size on nesting success of Wood Thrushes. Auk 112:146–155.

Hopp, S. L., A. Kirby, and C. A. Boone. 1995. White-eyed Vireo (*Vireo griseus*). *In* The birds of North America, no. 168 (A. Poole and F. Gill, Eds.). The Academy of Natural Sciences, Philadelphia, PA, and The American Ornithologists' Union, Washington, DC.

Horning, E., and J. Williamson. 2001. First breeding record of Common Eider (*Somateria mollissima*) in New York State. Kingbird 51:583–585.

Horsley, S. B., S. L. Stout, and D. S. deCalesta. 2003. White-tailed deer impact on the vegetation dynamics of a northern hardwood forest. Ecological Applications 13:98–118.

Hotopp, K. P. 1986. Status of Common Terns on the Buffalo Harbor and Upper Niagara River. Unpublished report. New York State Department of Environmental Conservation, Buffalo, NY.

Hough, F. N. 1964. The thrushes (*Turdidae*): their occurrence in Ulster County, N.Y. Bulletin of the Research and Records Committee, no. 7. John Burroughs Natural History Society, [n.p.].

Houston, C. S., and D. E. Bowen Jr. 2001. Upland Sandpiper (*Bartramia longicauda*). *In* The birds of North America, no. 580 (A. Poole and F. Gill, Eds.). The Birds of North America, Inc., Philadelphia, PA.

Houston, C. S., D. G. Smith, and C. Rohner. 1998. Great Horned Owl (*Bubo virginianus*). *In* The birds of North America, no. 372 (A. Poole

and F. Gill, Eds.). The Birds of North America, Inc., Philadelphia, PA.

Houston, R. A. 1992. Habitat use and nest success of Mallards in bottomland hardwoods in western New York. M.S. thesis, Cornell University, Ithaca, NY.

Howe, M. A. 1982. Social organization in a nesting population of Eastern Willets (*Catoptrophorus semipalmatus*). Auk 99:88–102.

Howes, P. G. 1926. A Turkey Vulture's nest in the state of New York. Bird-Lore 28:175–180.

Hoyt, S. F. 1957. The ecology of the Pileated Woodpecker. Ecology 38:246–256.

——. 1962. Region 3—Finger Lakes. Kingbird 12:148–150.

Huffman & Associates, Inc. 1999. Wetlands status and trend analysis of New York State—mid-1980s to mid-1990s. Prepared for New York State Department of Environmental Conservation, August 1999. Huffman & Associates, Inc., Larkspur, CA.

Hughes, J. M. 1999. Yellow-billed Cuckoo (*Coccyzus americanus*). *In* The birds of North America, no. 418 (A. Poole and F. Gill, Eds.). The Birds of North America, Inc., Philadelphia, PA.

——. 2001. Black-billed Cuckoo (*Coccyzus erythropthalmus*). *In* The birds of North America, no. 587 (A. Poole and F. Gill, Eds.). The Birds of North America, Inc., Philadelphia, PA.

Hunt, P. D. 2005. 2005 Summary: New England Whip-poor-will surveys. Unpublished report. New Hamphire Audubon, Concord, NH.

Hunt, P. D., and B. C. Eliason. 1999. Blackpoll Warbler (*Dendroica striata*). *In* The birds of North America, no. 431 (A. Poole and F. Gill, Eds.). The Birds of North America, Inc., Philadelphia, PA.

Hunt, P. D., and D. J. Flaspohler. 1998. Yellow-rumped Warbler (*Dendroica coronata*). *In* The birds of North America, no. 376 (A. Poole and F. Gill, Eds.). The Birds of North America, Inc., Philadelphia, PA.

Hustings, F., and J.-W. Vergeer, Eds. 2002. Atlas van de Nederlandse broedvogels 1998–2000: verspreiding, aantallen, verandering. Nederlandse Fauna 5. Nationaal Natuurhistorisch Museum Naturalis, Leiden, KNNV Uitgeverij, Utrecht, and European Invertebrate Survey-Nederland, Leiden, Nederland.

Hyde, A. S. 1939. The ecology and economics of the birds along the northern boundary of New York State. Roosevelt Wildlife Bulletin 7:68–215.

Hyde, D. 2001. Special animal abstract for *Sterna forsteri* (Forster's Tern). Michigan Natural Features Inventory, Lansing, MI. http://web4.msue.msu.edu/mnfi/abstracts/zoology/sterna_forsteri.pdf.

Hyman, J., and S. Pruett-Jones. 1995. Natural history of the Monk Parakeets in Hyde Park, Chicago. Wilson Bulletin 107:510–517.

Ibarzabal, J., and A. Morrier. 1996. Palm Warbler (*Dendroica palmarum*). Pages 900–903 *in* The breeding birds of Québec: atlas of the breeding birds of southern Québec (J. Gauthier and Y. Aubry, Eds.). Association québécoise des groupes d'ornithologues, Montréal, QC.

Imbeau, L., J.-P. L. Savard, and R. Gagnon. 1999. Comparing bird assemblages in successional black spruce stands originating from fire and logging. Canadian Journal of Zoology 77:1850–1859.

Ingold, J. L. 1993. Blue Grosbeak (*Guiraca caerulea*). *In* The birds of North America, no. 79 (A. Poole and F. Gill, Eds.). The Academy of Natural Sciences, Philadelphia, PA, and The American Ornithologists' Union, Washington, DC.

Ingold, J. L., and R. Galati. 1997. Golden-crowned Kinglet (*Regulus satrapa*). *In* The birds of North America, no. 301 (A. Poole and F. Gill,

Eds.). The Academy of Natural Sciences, Philadelphia, PA, and The American Ornithologists' Union, Washington, DC.

Ingold, J. L., and G. E. Wallace. 1994. Ruby-crowned Kinglet (*Regulus calendula*). *In* The birds of North America, no. 119 (A. Poole and F. Gill, Eds.). The Academy of Natural Sciences, Philadelphia, PA, and The American Ornithologists' Union, Washington, DC.

IPCC (Intergovernmental Panel on Climate Change). 2007. Climate change 2007: the physical science basis. Cambridge University Press, Cambridge, UK.

Jackson, B. J. S., and J. A. Jackson. 2000. Killdeer (*Charadrius vociferus*). *In* The birds of North America, no. 517 (A. Poole and F. Gill, Eds.). The Birds of North America, Inc., Philadelphia, PA.

Jackson, C. F., and P. F. Allen. 1932. Additional note on the breeding in Maine of the Great Black-backed Gull. Auk 49:349–350.

Jackson, J. A., and W. E. Davis Jr. 1998. Range expansion of the Red-bellied Woodpecker. Bird Observer 26:4–12.

Jackson, J. A., and H. R. Ouellet. 2002. Downy Woodpecker (*Picoides pubescens*). *In* The birds of North America, no. 613 (A. Poole and F. Gill, Eds.). The Birds of North America, Inc., Philadelphia, PA.

Jackson, J. A., H. R. Ouellet, and B. J. S. Jackson. 2002. Hairy Woodpecker (*Picoides villosus*). *In* The birds of North America, no. 702 (A. Poole and F. Gill, Eds.). The Birds of North America, Inc., Philadelphia, PA.

James, D. A., and J. C. Neal. 1986. Arkansas birds: their distribution and abundance. University of Arkansas Press, Fayetteville, AR.

James, R. D. 1998. Blue-headed Vireo (*Vireo solitarius*). *In* The birds of North America, no. 379 (A. Poole and F. Gill, Eds.). The Birds of North America, Inc., Philadelphia, PA.

Jauvin, D., and P. Lafontaine. 1996. Wilson's Phalarope (*Phalaropus tricolor*). Pages 500–503 *in* The breeding birds of Québec: atlas of the breeding birds of southern Québec (J. Gauthier and Y. Aubry, Eds.). Association québecoise des groupes d'ornithologues, Montréal, QC.

Jenkins, J. C. 1995. Notes on the Adirondack blowdown of July 15th 1995: scientific background, observations, and policy issues. Working paper no. 5. Wildlife Conservation Society, Bronx, NY. http://www.wcs.org/media/file/WCS_WorkingPaper5_Jenkins.pdf.

———. 2004. The Adirondack atlas: a geographic portrait of the Adirondack Park. Syracuse University Press, Syracuse, NY.

Jobes, A. P., E. Nol, and D. R. Voight. 2004. Effects of selection cutting on bird communities in contiguous eastern hardwood forests. Journal of Wildlife Management 68:51–60.

Johnsgard, P. A. 1968. Waterfowl: their biology and natural history. University of Nebraska Press, Lincoln, NE.

———. 1975. North American game birds of upland and shoreline. University of Nebraska Press, Lincoln, NE.

———. 1981. The plovers, sandpipers, and snipes of the world. University of Nebraska Press, Lincoln, NE.

Johnson, D. H., and L. D. Igl. 1995. Contributions of the Conservation Reserve Program to populations of breeding birds in North Dakota. Wilson Bulletin 107:709–718.

Johnson, G., and A. M. Ross. 2003. Distribution of Spruce Grouse populations in New York's Adirondack Mountains: summary and final report 2002–2003. Unpublished report. New York State Department of Environmental Conservation, Albany, NY.

Johnson, K. 1995. Green-winged Teal (*Anas crecca*). *In* The birds of North America, no. 193 (A. Poole and F. Gill, Eds.). The Academy of Natural Sciences, Philadelphia, PA, and The American Ornithologists' Union, Washington, DC.

Johnson, L. S. 1998. House Wren (*Troglodytes aedon*). *In* The birds of North America, no. 380 (A. Poole and F. Gill, Eds.). The Birds of North America, Inc., Philadelphia, PA.

Johnson, N. C., and C. Cicero. 2004. New mitochondrial DNA data affirm the importance of Pleistocene speciation in North American birds. Evolution 58:1122–1130.

Johnston, R. F. 1992. Rock Dove (*Columba livia*). *In* The birds of North America, no. 13 (A. Poole, P. Stettenheim, and F. Gill, Eds.). The Academy of Natural Sciences, Philadelphia, PA., and The American Ornithologists' Union, Washington, DC.

Jones, M. 1980. The New York State Waterfowl Count—a quarter century report. Kingbird 30:210–216.

Jones, P. W., and T. M. Donovan. 1996. Hermit Thrush (*Catharus guttatus*). *In* The birds of North America, no. 261 (A. Poole and F. Gill, Eds.). The Academy of Natural Sciences, Philadelphia, PA, and the American Ornithologists' Union, Washington, DC.

Jones, S. L., and J. E. Cornely. 2002. Vesper Sparrow (*Pooecetes gramineus*). *In* The birds of North America, no. 624 (A. Poole and F. Gill, Eds.). The Birds of North America, Inc., Philadelphia, PA.

Jordan, A. H. B. 1888. A visit to the Four Brothers, Lake Champlain. Ornithologist and Oologist 13:138–139.

Judd, W. W. 1907. The birds of Albany County. Brandow Printing Co., Albany, NY.

Kalm, P. 1773. Travels into North America, 2nd ed., vol. 2. Translated into English by J. R. Forster. T. Lowndes, London, UK. http://www.wisconsinhistory.org.

Keller, J. K. 1980. Species composition and density of breeding birds in several habitat types on the Connecticut Hill Wildlife Management Area. M.S. thesis, Cornell University, Ithaca, NY.

———. 1982. From yellowthroats to woodpeckers: how forest succession affects bird life. Conservationist 37(Jul–Aug):30–35.

Keller, J. K., M. E. Richmond, and C. R. Smith. 2003. An explanation of patterns of breeding bird species richness and density following clearcutting in northeastern USA forests. Forest Ecology and Management 174:541–564.

Keller, J. K., and C. R. Smith. 1983. Birds in a patchwork landscape. Living Bird Quarterly 2(4):20–23.

Kelley, J. R. Jr. 2006. Draft American Woodcock conservation plan. Unpublished report. Woodcock Task Force, Division of Migratory Birds, Washington, DC.

Kelley, J. R. Jr., R. D. Rau, and K. Parker. 2007. American Woodcock population status, 2007. U.S. Fish and Wildlife Service, Laurel, MD. http://www.fws.gov/migratorybirds/reports/status07/woodcock status Report 2007.pdf.

Kelling, S. 1994. Region 3—Finger Lakes. Kingbird 44:304–310.

Kerlinger, P. 2001. New York City Audubon Harbor Herons Project: 2001 nesting survey. New York City Audubon Society, New York, NY.

Kennedy, E. D., and D. W. White. 1997. Bewick's Wren (*Thryomanes bewickii*). *In* The birds of North America, no. 315 (A. Poole and F. Gill, Eds.). The Academy of Natural Sciences, Philadelphia, PA, and The American Ornithologists' Union, Washington, DC.

———. 2002. New York City Audubon Harbor Herons Project: 2002 nesting survey. New York City Audubon Society, New York, NY.

———. 2004. New York City Audubon Harbor Herons Project:

2004 nesting survey. New York City Audubon Society, New York, NY. http://www.nycaudubon.org/projects/harborherons/HH_2004NestingRpt-8-30-04-final.pdf.

Kershner, B., and R. T. Leverett. 2004. Sierra Club guide to the ancient forests of the Northeast. Sierra Club Books, San Francisco, CA.

Kessel, B. 1951. Investigations on the life history and management of the European Starling (*Sturnus vulgaris vulgaris* L.) in North America. Ph.D. dissertation, Cornell University, Ithaca, NY.

Kessel, B., D. A. Rocque, and J. S. Barclay. 2002. Greater Scaup (*Aythya marila*). *In* The birds of North America, no. 650 (A. Poole and F. Gill, Eds.). The Birds of North America, Inc., Philadelphia, PA.

Keys, J. Jr., C. Carpenter, S. Hooks, F. Koenig, W. H. McNab, W. Russell, and M. F. Smith. 1995. Ecological units of the eastern United States—first approximation. CD-ROM. U.S. Department of Agriculture, Forest Service, Atlanta, GA.

Keyser, A. J., G. E. Hill, and E. C. Soehren. 1998. Effects of forest fragment size, nest density, and proximity to edge on the risk of predation to ground-nesting passerine birds. Conservation Biology 12:986–994.

Kibbe, D. P. 1975. Western New York and northwestern Pennsylvania region. American Birds 29:848–850.

——. 1985. Canada Goose (*Branta canadensis*). Pages 46–47 *in* The atlas of breeding birds of Vermont (S. B. Laughlin and D. P. Kibbe, Eds.). University Press of New England, Hanover, NH.

King, D. T., and D. W. Anderson. 2005. Recent population status of the American White Pelican: a continental perspective. Waterbirds 28, Special Publication 1:48–54.

Kinkead, E. 1973. A rumor in the air: the story of the New York state bird. New Yorker 49(24 Dec):50–52.

Kirby, R. E., G. A. Sargeant, and D. Shutler. 2004. Haldane's rule and American Black Duck x Mallard hybridization. Canadian Journal of Zoology 82:1827–1831.

Kirk, D. A., and C. Hyslop. 1998. Population status and recent trends in Canadian raptors: a review. Biological Conservation 83:91–118.

Kirk, D. A., and M. J. Mossman. 1998. Turkey Vulture (*Cathartes aura*). *In* The birds of North America, no. 339 (A. Poole and F. Gill, Eds.). The Birds of North America, Inc., Philadelphia, PA.

Klonick, A. S. 1951. Western Meadowlark, *Sturnella neglecta*, in New York State. Auk 68:107.

Knapton, R. W. 1994. Clay-colored Sparrow (*Spizella pallida*). *In* The birds of North America, no. 120 (A. Poole and F. Gill, Eds.). The Academy of Natural Sciences, Philadelphia, PA, and The American Ornithologists' Union, Washington, DC.

Knopf, F. L. 2004. American White Pelican (*Pelecanus erythrorhynchos*). *In* The birds of North America online (A. Poole, Ed.). Cornell Lab of Ornithology, Ithaca, NY. http://bna.birds.cornell.edu/BNA/account/American_White_Pelican/.doi:10.2173/bna.57.

Knutson, M. G., L. A. Powell, R. K. Hines, M. A. Friberg, and G. J. Niemi. 2006. An assessment of bird habitat quality using population growth rates. Condor 108:301–314.

Koenig, W. D. 2003. European Starlings and their effect on native cavity-nesting birds. Conservation Biology 17:1134–1140.

Komar, N., S. Langevin, S. Hinten, N. Nemeth, E. Edwards, D. Hettler, B. Davis, R. Bowen, and M. Bunning. 2003. Experimental infection of North American birds with the New York 1999 strain of West Nile virus. Emerging Infectious Diseases 9:311–322.

Kozicky, E. L., and F. W. Schmidt. 1949. Nesting habits of the Clapper Rail in New Jersey. Auk 66:355–364.

Kraus, N. 2006. NYSDEC forest tent caterpillar defoliator report 2005. New York State Department of Environmental Conservation, Albany, NY. http://www.dec.ny.gov/docs/lands_forests_pdf/defoliator2005.pdf.

Kress, S. W., and C. S. Hall. 2002. Tern management handbook, coastal northeastern United States and Atlantic Canada. U.S. Fish and Wildlife Service, Hadley, MA.

Kress, S. W., E. H. Weinstein, and I. C. T. Nisbet. 1983. The status of tern populations in the northeastern United States and adjacent Canada. Colonial Waterbirds 6:84–106.

Kricher, J. C. 1995. Black-and-white Warbler (*Mniotilta varia*). *In* The birds of North America, no. 158 (A. Poole and F. Gill, Eds.). The Academy of Natural Sciences, Philadelphia, PA, and The American Ornithologists' Union, Washington, DC.

Kroodsma, D. E., and J. Verner. 1997. Marsh Wren (*Cistothorus palustris*). *In* The birds of North America, no. 308 (A. Poole and F. Gill, Eds.). The Academy of Natural Sciences, Philadelphia, PA, and The American Ornithologists' Union, Washington, DC.

Krueger, W. E. 1993. Wilson's Phalarope, a new nesting species for New York State. Kingbird 43:274–277.

——. 2002. Nelson's Sharp-tailed Sparrow. New York State Breeding Bird Atlas 2000 Newsletter, no. 6:6.

——. 2006. Birds of Clinton County, 2nd ed. 1st Supplement. Available from the author, 40 Colligan Point Rd., Plattsburgh, NY 12901-7112.

Kudish, M. 1979. Catskills soils and forest history. Catskill Center for Conservation and Development, Hobart, NY.

——. 2000. The Catskill forest: a history. Purple Mountain Press, Fleischmanns, NY.

Kumlien, L., and N. Hollister. 1903. The birds of Wisconsin. Bulletin of the Wisconsin Natural History Society, vol. 3:5 [Reprinted with revisions by A. W. Schorger by the Wisconsin Society for Ornithology, Madison WI, 1951].

Kushlan, J. A., M. J. Steinkamp, K. C. Parsons, J. Capp, M. A. Cruz, M. Coulter, I. Davidson, et al. 2002. Waterbird conservation for the Americas: the North American Waterbird Conservation Plan, Version 1. Waterbird Conservation for the Americas. Washington, DC. http://www.waterbirdconservation.org/pubs/complete.pdf.

Kutz, H. L., and D. G. Allen. 1946. The American Pintail breeding in New York. Auk 63:596.

——. 1947. Double-crested Cormorant nesting in New York. Auk 64:137.

Lambert, J. D. 2006. Mountain Birdwatch 2005. Final report to U.S. Fish and Wildlife Service. VINS technical report 06-2. Vermont Institute of Natural Science, Woodstock, VT. http://www.vinsweb.org/assets/pdf/2005_Report.pdf.

Lambert, J. D., and S. D. Faccio. 2005. Canada Warbler: population status, habitat use, and stewardship guidelines for northeastern forests. VINS technical report 05-4. Vermont Institute of Natural Science, Woodstock, VT. http://www.vinsweb.org/assets/pdf/CAWAreport05.pdf.

Lambert, J. D., K. P. McFarland, C. C. Rimmer, S. D. Faccio, and J. L. Atwood. 2005. A practical model of Bicknell's Thrush distribution in the northeastern United States. Wilson Bulletin 117:1–11.

Lanciotti, R. S., J. T. Roehrig, V. Deubel, J. Smith, and M. Parker.

1999. Origin of the West Nile virus responsible for an outbreak of encephalitis in the northeastern United States. Science 286:2333–2337.

Langevin, C. 1996. Lincoln's Sparrow (*Melospiza lincolnii*). Pages 1006–1009 *in* The breeding birds of Québec: atlas of the breeding birds of southern Québec (J. Gauthier and Y. Aubry, Eds.). Association québécoise des groupes d'ornithologues, Montréal, QC.

Langille, J. H. 1884. Our birds in their haunts: a popular treatise on the birds of eastern North America. S. E. Cassino and Co., Boston, MA.

Lanoue, A., and A. Morrier. 1996. Cape May Warbler (*Dendroica tigrina*). Pages 878–879 *in* The breeding birds of Québec: atlas of the breeding birds of southern Québec (J. Gauthier and Y. Aubrey, Eds.). Association québécoise des groupes d'ornithologues, Montréal, QC.

Lanyon, W. E. 1956. Ecological aspects of the sympatric distribution of meadowlarks in the north-central states. Ecology 37:98–108.

———. 1995. Eastern Meadowlark (*Sturnella magna*). *In* The birds of North America, no. 160 (A. Poole and F. Gill, Eds.). The Academy of Natural Sciences, Philadelphia, PA, and The American Ornithologists' Union, Washington, DC.

———. 1997. Great Crested Flycatcher (*Myiarchus crinitus*). *In* The birds of North America, no. 300 (A. Poole and F. Gill, Eds.). The Academy of Natural Sciences, Philadelphia, PA, and The American Ornithologists' Union, Washington, DC.

———. 1998a. Eastern Meadowlark (*Sturnella magna*). Page 547 *in* Bull's birds of New York State (E. Levine, Ed.). Comstock Publishing Associates, Ithaca, NY.

———. 1998b. Western Meadowlark (*Sturnella neglecta*). Pages 547–548 *in* Bull's birds of New York State (E. Levine, Ed.). Comstock Publishing Associates, Ithaca, NY.

Laughlin, S. B., and D. P. Kibbe, Eds. 1985. The atlas of breeding birds of Vermont. University Press of New England, Hanover, NH.

Lauro, A. J. 1998a. American White Pelican (*Pelicanus erythrorhynchos*). Pages 115–116 *in* Bull's birds of New York State (E. Levine, Ed.). Comstock Publishing Associates, Ithaca, NY.

———. 1998b. Little Blue Heron (*Egretta caerulea*). Page 128 *in* Bull's birds of New York State (E. Levine, Ed.). Comstock Publishing Associates, Ithaca, NY.

———. 1998c. Tricolored Heron (*Egretta tricolor*). Page 129 *in* Bull's birds of New York State (E. Levine, Ed.). Comstock Publishing Associates, Ithaca, NY.

———. 1998d. White-winged Tern (*Chlidonias leucopterus*). Page 307 *in* Bull's birds of New York State (E. Levine, Ed.). Comstock Publishing Associates, Ithaca, NY.

———. 1998e. Yellow-crowned Night-Heron (*Nyctanassa violacea*). Pages 133–134 *in* Bull's birds of New York State (E. Levine, Ed.). Comstock Publishing Associates, Ithaca, NY.

Lauro, B., and J. Burger. 1989. Nest-site selection of American Oystercatchers (*Haematopus palliatus*) in salt marshes. Auk 106:185–192.

Lawton, J. H. 1996. Population abundances, geographic ranges and conservation: 1994 Witherby Lecture. Bird Study 43:3–19. http://www.ingentaconnect.com/content/bto/bird/1996/00000043/00000001/431003.

Lazazzero, S. A. 2006. A multi-scale analysis of grassland bird habitat relationships in the St. Lawrence River Valley, NY. M.S. thesis, State University of New York College at Brockport, Brockport, NY.

Lea, R. B. 1942. A study of the nesting habits of the Cedar Waxwing. Wilson Bulletin 54:225–237.

Leichty, E. R., and J. W. Grier. 2006. Importance of facial pattern to sexual selection in Golden-winged Warbler (*Vermivora chrysoptera*). Auk 123:962–966.

Lemoine, N., H. G. Bauer, M. Peintinger, and K. Böhning-Gaese. 2007a. Effects of climate and land-use change on species abundance in a central European bird community. Conservation Biology 21:495–503.

Lemoine, N., and K. Böhning-Gaese. 2003. Potential impact of global climate change on species richness of long-distance migrants. Conservation Biology 17:577–586.

Lemoine, N., H. C. Schaefer, and K. Böhning-Gaese. 2007b. Species richness of migratory birds is influenced by global climate change. Global Ecology and Biogeography 16:55–64.

Lent, R. A. 1988. Laughing Gull (*Larus atricilla*). Pages 164–165 *in* The atlas of breeding birds in New York State (R. F. Andrle and J. R. Carroll, Eds.). Cornell University Press, Ithaca, NY.

Leonard, D. L. Jr. 2001. Three-toed Woodpecker (*Picoides tridactylus*). *In* The birds of North America, no. 588 (A. Poole and F. Gill, Eds.). The Birds of North America, Inc., Philadelphia, PA.

LeSchack, C. R., S. K. McKnight, and G. R. Hepp. 1997. Gadwall (*Anas strepera*). *In* The birds of North America, no. 283 (A. Poole and F. Gill, Eds.). The Academy of Natural Sciences, Philadelphia, PA, and The American Ornithologists' Union, Washington, DC.

Levine, E. 1988a. Blackburnian Warbler (*Dendroica fusca*). Pages 382–383 *in* The atlas of breeding birds in New York State (R. F. Andrle and J. R. Carroll, Eds.). Cornell University Press, Ithaca, NY.

———. 1988b. Hooded Merganser (*Lophodytes cucullatus*). Pages 88–89 *in* The atlas of breeding birds in New York State (R. F. Andrle and J. R. Carroll, Eds.). Cornell University Press, Ithaca, NY.

———. 1988c. Northern Bobwhite (*Colinus virginianus*). Pages 132–133 *in* The atlas of breeding birds in New York State (R. F. Andrle and J. R. Carroll, Eds.). Cornell University Press, Ithaca, NY.

———, Ed. 1998. Bull's birds of New York State. Cornell University Press, Ithaca, NY.

Ley, D. H., J. E. Berkhoff, and J. M. McLaren. 1996. *Mycoplasma gallisepticum* isolated from House Finches (*Carpodacus mexicanus*) with conjunctivitis. Avian Disease 40:480–483.

Ley, D. H., J. E. Berkhoff, and S. Levisohn. 1997. Molecular epidemiologic investigations of *Mycoplasma gallisepticum* conjunctivitis in songbirds by random amplified polymorphic DNA analyses. Emerging Infectious Diseases 3:375–380.

Limoges, B., and S. Gauthier. 1996. Tennessee Warbler (*Vermivora peregrina*). Pages 1006–1009 *in* The breeding birds of Québec: atlas of the breeding birds of southern Québec (J. Gauthier and Y. Aubrey, Eds.). Association québécoise des groupes d'ornithologues, Montréal, QC.

Lincoln, S. R. 1998a. European Goldfinch (*Carduelis carduelis*). Pages 572–573 *in* Bull's birds of New York State (E. Levine, Ed.). Comstock Publishing Associates, Ithaca, NY.

———. 1998b. Federation of New York State Bird Clubs: history of the first fifty years, 1948–1998. Kingbird 48(Supplement 1):1–35.

Lindsay, P. J. 1998. Cerulean Warbler (*Dendroica cerulea*). Pages 478–480 *in* Bull's birds of New York State (E. Levine, Ed.). Comstock Publishing Associates, Ithaca, NY.

Lindsay, P. J., and S. S. Mitra. 2006a. Region 10—Marine. Kingbird 56:289–298.

———. 2006b. Region 10—Marine. Kingbird 56:368–374.

Lindsay, P. J., and T. Vezo. 1994. Cerulean Warbler confirmed breeding and Acadian Flycatcher probable breeding on eastern Long Island. Kingbird 44:108.

Litwin, T. S., and C. R. Smith. 1992. Factors influencing the decline of Neotropical migrants in a northeastern forest fragment: isolation, fragmentation, or mosaic effects? Pages 483–496 in Ecology and conservation of Neotropical migrant landbirds (J. M. Hagan III and D. Johnston, Eds.). Smithsonian Institution Press, Washington, DC.

Lock, A. R. 1988. Recent increases in the breeding population of Ring-billed Gulls, Larus delawarensis, in Atlantic Canada. Canadian Field-Naturalist 102:627–633.

Long Island Sound Study. 2003. Long Island Sound Habitat Restoration Initiative: technical support for coastal habitat restoration. U.S. Environmental Protection Agency, Long Island Sound Office, Stamford, CT. http://longislandsoundstudy.net/habitat/index.htm.

Long, R. E. 1993. Region 6—St. Lawrence. Kingbird 43:330–336.

———. 1994. Region 6—St. Lawrence. Kingbird 44:319–326.

———. 1995. Region 6—St. Lawrence. Kingbird 45:308–313.

Longcore, J. R., D. G. McAuley, G. R. Hepp, and J. M. Rhymer. 2000. American Black Duck (Anas rubripes). In The birds of North America, no. 481 (A. Poole and F. Gill, Eds.). The Birds of North America, Inc., Philadelphia, PA.

Loon Preservation Committee. 2005. Meeting the challenge: thirty years of preserving loons and their habitats in New Hampshire. Unpublished report. Loon Preservation Committee, Moultonborough, NH.

Lor, S. K. 2000. Population status and breeding ecology of marsh birds in western New York. M.S. thesis, Cornell University, Ithaca, NY.

Lorimer, C. G. 2001. Historical and ecological roles of disturbance in eastern North American forests: 9,000 years of change. Wildlife Society Bulletin 29:425–439.

Losito, M. P. 1993. Breeding ecology of female Mallards in the St. Lawrence River Valley, northern New York. Ph.D. dissertation, State University of New York College of Environmental Science and Forestry, Syracuse, NY.

Loucks, B. A. 1998. Peregrine Falcon (Falco peregrinus). Pages 203–206 in Bull's birds of New York State (E. Levine, Ed.). Comstock Publishing Associates, Ithaca, NY.

Loucks, B. A., and C. A. Nadareski. 2005. Back from the brink. New York State Conservationist 59(Apr):19–23.

Lowther, P. E. 1993. Brown-headed Cowbird (Molothrus ater). In The birds of North America, no. 47 (A. Poole and F. Gill, Eds.). The Academy of Natural Sciences, Philadelphia, PA, and The American Ornithologists' Union, Washington, DC.

———. 1999. Alder Flycatcher (Empidonax alnorum). In The birds of North America, no. 446 (A. Poole and F. Gill, Eds.). The Birds of North America, Inc., Philadelphia, PA.

Lowther, P. E., C. Celada, N. K. Klein, C. C. Rimmer, and D. A. Spector. 1999. Yellow Warbler (Dendroica petechia). In The birds of North America online (A. Poole, Ed.). Cornell Lab of Ornithology, Ithaca, NY. http://bna.birds.cornell.edu/BNA/account/Yellow_Warbler/. doi:10.2173/bna.454.

Lowther, P. E., and C. L. Cink. 2006. House Sparrow (Passer domesticus). In The birds of North America online (A. Poole, Ed.). Cornell Lab of Ornithology, Ithaca, NY. http://bna.birds.cornell.edu/BNA/account/House_Sparrow/.doi:10.2173/bna.12.

Lowther, P. E., H. D. Douglas III, and C. L. Gratto-Trevor. 2001. Willet (Catoptrophorus semipalmatus). In The birds of North America, no. 579 (A. Poole and F. Gill, Eds.). The Birds of North America, Inc., Philadelphia, PA.

Ludwig, J. P. 1965. Biology and structure of the Caspian Tern (Hydroprogne caspia) population of the Great Lakes from 1896–1964. Bird-Banding 36:217–233.

Lumsden, H. G. 1984. The pre-settlement breeding of Trumpeter, Cygnus buccinator, and Tundra swans, C. columbianus, in eastern Canada. Canadian Field-Naturalist 98:415–424.

MacNamara, E. E., and H. F. Udell. 1970. Clapper Rail investigations on the south shore of Long Island. Proceedings of the Linnaean Society of New York, no. 71:120–131.

MacWhirter, R. B., and K. L. Bildstein. 1996. Northern Harrier (Circus cyaneus). In The birds of North America, no. 210 (A. Poole and F. Gill, Eds.). The Academy of Natural Sciences, Philadelphia, PA, and The American Ornithologists' Union, Washington, DC.

Mallory, M., and K. Metz. 1999. Common Merganser (Mergus merganser). In The birds of North America, no. 442 (A. Poole and F. Gill, Eds.). The Birds of North America, Inc., Philadelphia, PA.

MANEM (Mid-Atlantic/New England Maritime Region). Waterbird Working Group. 2006. Draft waterbird conservation plan 2006–2010 for the Mid-Atlantic/New England/Maritime region. Waterbird Conservation for the Americas. http://www.fws.gov/birds/waterbirds/MANEM/.

Mank, J. E., J. E. Carlson, and M. C. Brittingham. 2004. A century of hybridization: decreasing genetic distance between American Black Ducks and Mallards. Conservation Genetics 5:395–403.

Manson, H. C. 1991. Region 9—Hudson-Delaware. Kingbird 41:283–286.

Mantlik, F., M. Szantyr, G. Hanisek, J. Hough, and C. Wood. 1998. Eighth report of the Avian Records Committee of Connecticut. Connecticut Warbler 18:162–179.

Marcotte, R. E. 1998a. Black-crowned Night-Heron (Nycticorax nycticorax). Pages 132–133 in Bull's birds of New York State (E. Levine, Ed.). Comstock Publishing Associates, Ithaca, NY.

———. 1998b. Mute Swan (Cygnus olor). Pages 147–148 in Bull's birds of New York State (E. Levine, Ed.). Comstock Publishing Associates, Ithaca, NY.

———. 1998c. Northern Shoveler (Anas clypeata). Pages 157–158 in Bull's birds of New York State (E. Levine, Ed.). Comstock Publishing Associates, Ithaca, NY.

———. 1998d. Western Kingbird (Tyrannus verticalis). Pages 372–373 in Bull's birds of New York State (E. Levine, Ed.). Comstock Publishing Associates, Ithaca, NY.

———. 1998e. Yellow-billed Cuckoo (Coccyzus americanus). Pages 323–324 in Bull's birds of New York State (E. Levine, Ed.). Comstock Publishing Associates, Ithaca, NY.

Marks, J. S., D. L. Evans, and D. W. Holt. 1994. Long-eared Owl (Asio otus). In The birds of North America, no. 133 (A. Poole and F. Gill, Eds.). The Academy of Natural Sciences, Philadelphia, PA, and The American Ornithologists' Union, Washington, DC.

Marks, P. L. 1983. On the origin of the field plants of the northeastern United States. American Naturalist 122:210–228.

Marks, P. L., S. Gardescu, and F. K. Seischab. 1992. Late eighteenth century vegetation of central and western New York State on the basis of original land survey records. New York State Museum Bulletin, no. 484. University of the State of New York, State Education Department, New York State Museum, Biological Survey, Albany, NY.

Marsi, H. T., and G. M. Kirch. 1998. Northern Harrier (*Circus cyaneus*). Pages 186–186 *in* Bull's birds of New York State (E. Levine, Ed.). Comstock Publishing Associates, Ithaca, NY.

Marti, C. D., A. F. Poole, and L. R. Bevier. 2005. Barn Owl (*Tyto alba*). *In* The birds of North America online (A. Poole, Ed.). Cornell Lab of Ornithology, Ithaca, NY. http://bna.birds.cornell.edu/BNA/account.Barn_Owl/.doi:10.2173/bna.1.

Martin, R. P., and P. J. Zwank. 1987. Habitat suitability index models: Forster's Tern (breeding)—Gulf and Atlantic coasts. U.S. Fish and Wildlife Service Biological Report, no. 82 (10.131). http://www.nwrc.usgs.gov/wdb/pub/hsi/hsi-131.pdf.

Martin, S. G. 2002. Brewer's Blackbird (*Euphagus cyanocephalus*). *In* The birds of North America, no. 616 (A. Poole and F. Gill, Eds.). The Birds of North America, Inc., Philadelphia, PA.

Martin, S. G., and T. A. Gavin. 1995. Bobolink (*Dolichonyx oryzivorus*). *In* The birds of North America, no. 176 (A. Poole and F. Gill, Eds.). The Academy of Natural Sciences, Philadelphia, PA, and The American Ornithologists' Union, Washington, DC.

Marzilli, V. 1989. Up on the roof. Maine Fish and Wildlife 31(Summer):25–29.

Mawhinney, K., B. Allen, and B. Benedict. 1999. Status of the American Oystercatcher (*Haematopus palliatus*), on the Atlantic Coast. Northeastern Naturalist 6:177–182.

Mayfield, H. 1965. The Brown-headed Cowbird, with old and new hosts. Living Bird 4:12–28.

Mazur, K. M., and P. C. James. 2000. Barred Owl (*Strix varia*). *In* The birds of North America, no. 508 (A. Poole and F. Gill, Eds.). The Birds of North America, Inc., Philadelphia, PA.

Mazzocchi, I. M., and S. L. Muller. 1992. A White-winged Tern nests in New York State. Kingbird 42:210–212.

———. 1993. Black Tern (*Chlidonias niger*) survey in New York State, 1992. Unpublished report. New York State Department of Environmental Conservation, Albany, NY.

———. 2000. Black Tern (*Chlidonias niger*) investigations in northern New York, 1998. Unpublished report. New York State Department of Environmental Conservation, Division of Fish, Wildlife and Marine Resources, Nongame Unit, Delmar, NY.

McCarty, J. P. 1996. Eastern Wood-Pewee (*Contopus virens*). *In* The birds of North America, no. 245 (A. Poole and F. Gill, Eds.). The Academy of Natural Sciences, Philadelphia, PA, and The American Ornithologists' Union, Washington, DC.

McCrimmon, D. Jr. 1978. Nest-site characteristics among five species of herons on the North Carolina coast. Auk 95:267–280.

———. 1982. Populations of the Great Blue Heron (*Ardea herodias*) in New York State from 1964 to 1981. Colonial Waterbirds 5:87–94.

McCrimmon, D. A. Jr., J. C. Ogden, and G. T. Bancroft. 2001. Great Egret (*Ardea alba*). *In* The birds of North America, no. 570 (A. Poole and F. Gill, Eds.). The Birds of North America, Inc., Philadelphia, PA.

McDonald, M. V. 1998. Kentucky Warbler (*Oporornis formosus*). *In* The birds of North America, no. 324 (A. Poole and F. Gill, Eds.). The Birds of North America, Inc., Philadelphia, PA.

McDonald, R. 1991. Black jewel of the marsh: the precarious existence of the Black Tern. Birder's World 5(Feb):20–23.

McGarigal, K., and W. C. McComb. 1995. Relationships between landscape structure and breeding birds in the Oregon Coast Range. Ecological Monographs, no. 65:235–260.

McGowan, K. J. 2001a. Demographic and behavioral comparisons of suburban and rural American Crows (*Corvus brachyrhynchos*). Pages 365–381 *in* Avian ecology and conservation in an urbanizing world (J. M. Marzluff, R. Bowman, and R. Donnelly, Eds.). Kluwer Academic Publishers, Boston, MA.

———. 2001b. Fish Crow (*Corvus ossifragus*). *In* The birds of North America, no. 589 (A. Poole and F. Gill, Eds.). The Birds of North America, Inc., Philadelphia, PA.

———. 2005. Regional summaries of the 105th Christmas Bird Count: New York. American Birds 59:58–60.

———. 2006. Regional summaries of the 106th Christmas Bird Count: New York. American Birds 60:58–61.

McIlroy, M., Mrs. (Dorothy W.). 1961. Possible hybridization between a Clay-colored Sparrow and a Chipping Sparrow at Ithaca. Kingbird 11:7–10.

McKinney, R. G., and K. C. Parkes. 1998. Yellow Warbler (*Dendroica petechia*). Pages 459–460 *in* Bull's birds of New York State (E. Levine, Ed.). Comstock Publishing Associates, Ithaca, NY.

McMartin, B. 1994. The great forest of the Adirondacks. North Country Books, Utica, NY.

McNicholl, M. K. 1987. Forster's Tern (*Sterna forsteri*). Pages 190–191 *in* Atlas of the breeding birds of Ontario (M. D. Cadman, P. F. J. Eagles, and F. M. Helleiner, Eds.). University of Waterloo Press, Waterloo, ON.

McNicholl, M. K., P. E. Lowther, and J. A. Hall. 2001. Forster's Tern (*Sterna forsteri*). *In* The birds of North America, no. 595 (A. Poole and F. Gill, Eds.). The Birds of North America, Inc., Philadelphia, PA.

McShea, W. J., and J. H. Rappole. 2000. Managing the abundance and diversity of breeding bird populations through manipulation of deer populations. Conservation Biology 14:1161–1170.

McWilliams, G. M., and D. W. Brauning. 2000. The birds of Pennsylvania. Comstock Publishing Associates, Ithaca, NY.

Meade, G. M. 1988a. Appendix C: Breeding season table. Pages 513–518 *in* The atlas of breeding birds in New York State (R. F. Andrle and J. R. Carroll, Eds.). Cornell University Press, Ithaca, NY.

———. 1988b. Great Black-backed Gull (*Larus marinus*). Pages 170–171 *in* The atlas of breeding birds in New York State (R. F. Andrle and J. R. Carroll, Eds.). Cornell University Press, Ithaca, NY.

———. 1988c. Northern Mockingbird (*Mimus polyglottos*). Pages 332–333 *in* The atlas of breeding birds in New York State (R. F. Andrle and J. R. Carroll, Eds.). Cornell University Press, Ithaca, NY.

———. 1988d. White-eyed Vireo (*Vireo griseus*). Pages 342–343 *in* The atlas of breeding birds in New York State (R. F. Andrle and J. R. Carroll, Eds.). Cornell University Press, Ithaca, NY.

Mearns, E. A. 1879. A list of the birds of the Hudson Highlands, with annotations. Bulletin of the Essex Institute 11:193–196.

Melin, C. K. 1998a. Carolina Wren (*Thryothorus lucovicianus*). Pages 417–418 *in* Bull's birds of New York State (E. Levine, Ed.). Comstock Publishing Associates, Ithaca, NY.

———. 1998b. Northern Mockingbird (*Mimus polyglottos*). Pages 444–445 *in* Bull's birds of New York State (E. Levine, Ed.). Comstock Publishing Associates, Ithaca, NY.

Melvin, S. M., and J. P. Gibbs. 1996. Sora (*Porzana carolina*). *In* The birds of North America, no. 250 (A. Poole and F. Gill, Eds.). The Academy of Natural Sciences, Philadelphia, PA, and The American Ornithologists' Union, Washington, DC.

Mendall, H. L. 1938. Ring-necked Duck breeding in eastern North America. Auk 55:401–404.

———. 1958. The Ring-necked Duck in the Northeast. University of Maine Bulletin 60(16). University Press, Orono, ME.

Mendall, H. L., and C. M. Aldous. 1943. The ecology and management of the American Woodcock. Maine Cooperative Wildlife Research Unit. University of Maine, Orono, ME.

Meng, H. K. 1951. The Cooper's Hawk; *Accipiter cooperii* (Bonaparte). Ph.D. dissertation, Cornell University, Ithaca, NY.

———. 1959. Food habits of nesting Cooper's Hawks and Goshawks in New York and Pennsylvania. Wilson Bulletin 71:169–174.

Merriam, C. H. 1881. Preliminary list of birds ascertained to occur in the Adirondack region, northeastern New York. Bulletin of the Nuttall Ornithological Club 6:225–235.

Mershon, W. B. 1907. The Passenger Pigeon. Outing Publishing Co., New York, NY.

Merwin, M. M. 1918. Common Tern nesting at Thousand Islands. Auk 35:74.

Messineo, D. J. 1985. The 1985 nesting of Pine Siskin, Red Crossbill, and White-winged Crossbill in Chenango County, N.Y. Kingbird 35:233–237.

Meyerriecks, A. J. 1957. Louisiana Heron breeds in New York City. Wilson Bulletin 69:184–185.

Middleton, A. L. 1993. American Goldfinch (*Carduelis tristis*). *In* The birds of North America, no. 80 (A. Poole and F. Gill, Eds.). The Academy of Natural Sciences, Philadelphia, PA, and The American Ornithologists' Union, Washington, DC.

———. 1998. Chipping Sparrow (*Spizella passerina*). *In* The birds of North America, no. 334 (A. Poole and F. Gill, Eds.). The Birds of North America, Inc., Philadelphia, PA.

Miga, D. 1999. Region 1—Niagara Frontier. Kingbird 49:324–329.

Millennium Ecosystem Assessment [program]. 2005. Ecosystems and human well-being: current state and trends: findings of the Condition and Trends Working groups of the Millennium Ecosystem Assessment (R. M. Hassan, R. Scholes, and N. Ash, Eds.). Island Press, Washington, DC.

Miller, E. K., A. Vanarsdale, G. J. Keeler, A. Chalmers, L. Poissant, N. C. Kamman, and R. Brulotte. 2005. Estimation and mapping of wet and dry mercury deposition across northeastern North America. Ecotoxicology 14:53–70.

Miller, H. S. 1958. The Western Meadowlark in Monroe County. Kingbird 7:115.

Miller, R. L. 1998. Double-crested Cormorant (*Phalacrocorax auritus*). Pages 118–120 *in* Bull's birds of New York State (E. Levine, Ed.). Comstock Publishing Associates, Ithaca, NY.

Mills, A. 1987. Whip-poor-will (*Caprimulgus vociferus*). Pages 224–225 *in* Atlas of the breeding birds of Ontario (M. D. Cadman, P. F. J. Eagles, and F. M. Helleiner, Eds.). University of Waterloo Press, Waterloo, ON.

Mirarchi, R. E., and T. S. Baskett. 1994. Mourning Dove (*Zenaida macroura*). *In* The birds of North America, no. 117 (A. Poole and F. Gill, Eds.). The Academy of Natural Sciences, Philadelphia, PA, and The American Ornithologists' Union, Washington, DC.

Mitchell, C. D. 1994. Trumpeter Swan (*Cygnus buccinator*). *In* The birds of North America, no. 105 (A. Poole and F. Gill, Eds.). The Acad-

emy of Natural Sciences, Philadelphia, PA, and The American Ornithologists' Union, Washington, DC.

Mitchell, C. W., and W. E. Krueger. 1997. Birds of Clinton County, 2nd ed. High Peaks Audubon Society, Elizabethtown, NY.

Mitchell, L. R., C. R. Smith, and R. A. Malecki. 2000. Ecology of grassland breeding birds in the Northeastern United States—a literature review with recommendations for management. New York Cooperative Fish and Wildlife Research Unit, Department of Natural Resources, Cornell University, Ithaca, NY.

Mitra, S. S. 1999. Ecology and behavior of Yellow Warblers breeding in Rhode Island's Great Swamp. Northeastern Naturalist 6:249–262.

———. 2004. Region 10—Marine. Kingbird 54:367–374.

Mitra, S. S., and P. J. Lindsay. 2005a. Region 10—Marine. Kingbird 55:314–322.

———. 2005b. Region 10—Marine. Kingbird 55:394–402.

Moffatt, K. C., E. E. Crone, K. D. Holl, R. W. Schlorff, and B. A. Garrison. 2005. Importance of hydrologic and landscape heterogeneity for restoring Bank Swallow (*Riparia riparia*) colonies along the Sacramento River, California. Restoration Ecology 13:391–402.

Mohler, C. L., P. L. Marks, and S. Gardescu. 2006. Guide to the plant communities of the Central Finger Lakes Region. New York Agricultural Experiment Station, Geneva, NY.

Moldenhauer, R. R., and D. J. Regelski. 1996. Northern Parula (*Parula americana*). *In* The birds of North America, no. 215 (A. Poole and F. Gill, Eds.). The Academy of Natural Sciences, Philadelphia, PA, and The American Ornithologists' Union, Washington, DC.

Montagna, W. 1942. The Sharp-tailed Sparrows of the Atlantic Coast. Wilson Bulletin 54:107–120.

Montgomery, W. 1992. First record of a Merlin nesting in New York State. Kingbird 42:206–209.

Moore, W. S. 1995. Northern Flicker (*Colaptes auratus*). *In* The birds of North America, no. 166 (A. Poole and F. Gill, Eds.). The Academy of Natural Sciences, Philadelphia, PA, and The American Ornithologists' Union, Washington, DC.

Morgante, M. 2004. Region 1—Niagara Frontier. Kingbird 54:326–332.

———. 2005. Region 1—Niagara Frontier. Kingbird 55:354–360.

———. 2006. Region 1—Niagara Frontier. Kingbird 56:329–335.

Morrison, R. I. G., Y. Aubry, R. W. Butler, G. W. Beyersbergen, G. M. Donaldson, C. L. Gratto-Trevor, P. W. Hicklin, V. H. Johnston, and R. K. Ross. 2001. Declines in North American shorebird populations. Wader Study Group Bulletin 94:34–38.

Morrell, T. E., and R. H. Yahner. 1994. Habitat characteristics of Great Horned Owls in southcentral Pennsylvania. Journal of Raptor Research 28:164–170.

Morse, D. H. 1971. The effects of the arrival of a new species upon habitat utilization by two forest thrushes in Maine. Wilson Bulletin 83:57–65.

———. 1979. Habitat use of the Blackpoll Warbler. Wilson Bulletin 91:234–243.

———. 1980. Foraging and coexistence of spruce-woods warblers. Living Bird 18:7–25.

———. 2004. Blackburnian Warbler (*Dendroica fusca*). *In* The birds of North America online (A. Poole, Ed.). Cornell Lab of Ornithology, Ithaca, NY. http://bna.birds.cornell.edu/BNA/account/ Blackburnian_Warbler/.doi:10.2173/bna.102.

Morse, D. H., and A. F. Poole. 2005. Black-throated Green Warbler (*Dendroica virens*). *In* The birds of North America online (A. Poole,

Ed.). Cornell Lab of Ornithology, Ithaca, NY. http://bna.birds. cornell.edu/bna/species/055/.doi:10.2173/bna.55.

Morton, E. S. 2005. Predation and variation in breeding habitat use in the Ovenbird, with special reference to breeding habitat selection in northwestern Pennsylvania. Wilson Bulletin 117:327–335.

Mosher, J. A., and C. J. Henny. 1976. Thermal adaptiveness of plumage color in screech owls. Auk 93:614–619.

Mosher, T. 2004. One that got away: a possible nesting of Western Kingbird (*Tyrannus verticalis*) in Region 1. Kingbird 54:20–23.

Moskoff, W., and S. K. Robinson. 1996. Philadelphia Vireo (*Vireo philadelphicus*). *In* The birds of North America, no. 214 (A. Poole and F. Gill, Eds.). The Academy of Natural Sciences, Philadelphia, PA, and The American Ornithologists' Union, Washington, DC.

Mostello, C. S. 2002. Least Tern fact sheet. Massachusetts Division of Fisheries and Wildlife. Natural Heritage and Endangered Species Program, Westborough, MA. http://www.mass.gov/dfwele/dfw/ nhesp/species_info/nhfacts/sternaantillarum.pdf.

Mowbray, T. B. 1997. Swamp Sparrow (*Melospiza georgiana*). *In* The birds of North America, no. 279 (A. Poole and F. Gill, Eds.). The Academy of Natural Sciences, Philadelphia, PA, and The American Ornithologists' Union, Washington, DC.

———. 1999a. American Wigeon (*Anas americana*). *In* The birds of North America, no. 401 (A. Poole and F. Gill, Eds.). The Birds of North America, Inc., Philadelphia, PA.

———. 1999b. Scarlet Tanager (*Piranga olivacea*). *In* The birds of North America, no. 479 (A. Poole and F. Gill, Eds.). The Birds of North America, Inc., Philadelphia, PA.

———. 2002. Canvasback (*Aythya valisineria*). *In* The birds of North America, no. 659 (A. Poole and F. Gill, Eds.). The Birds of North America, Inc., Philadelphia, PA.

Mowbray, T. B., C. R. Ely, J. S. Sedinger, and R. E. Trost. 2002. Canada Goose (*Branta canadensis*). *In* The birds of North America, no. 682 (A. Poole and F. Gill, Eds.). The Birds of North America, Inc., Philadelphia, PA.

Mueller, H. 2005. Wilson's Snipe (*Gallinago delicata*). *In* The birds of North America online (A. Poole, Ed.). Cornell Lab of Ornithology, Ithaca, NY. http://bna.birds.cornell.edu/BNA/account/Wilsons_ Snipe/.doi:10.2173/bna.417.

Muller, M. J., and R. W. Storer. 1999. Pied-billed Grebe (*Podilymbus podiceps*). *In* The birds of North America, no. 410 (A. Poole and F. Gill, Eds.). The Birds of North America, Inc., Philadelphia, PA.

Mulvihill, R. S. 1999. Effects of stream acidification on the breeding biology of an obligate riparian songbird, the Louisiana Waterthrush (*Seiurus motacilla*). Pages 51–61 *in* The effects of acidic deposition on aquatic ecosystems in Pennsylvania (W. E. Sharpe and J. R. Drohan, Eds.). Environmental Resources Research Institute, Pennsylvania State University, University Park, PA.

Murphy, M. J. 2005. 2004–05 Farmer pheasant survey. Federal Aid in Wildlife Restoration Grant WE-173-G, Project 6/Job 6.3. Unpublished report. New York State Department of Environmental Conservation, Division of Fish, Wildlife and Marine Resources, Ithaca, NY.

Murphy, M. T. 1996. Eastern Kingbird (*Tyrannus tyrannus*). *In* The birds of North America, no. 253 (A. Poole and F. Gill, Eds.). The Academy of Natural Sciences, Philadelphia, PA, and The American Ornithologists' Union, Washington, DC.

———. 2001a. Habitat-specific demography of a long-distance, Neotropical migrant bird, the Eastern Kingbird. Ecology 82:1304–1318.

———. 2001b. Source-sink dynamics of a declining Eastern Kingbird population and the value of sink habitats. Conservation Biology 15:737–748.

Murray, B. G. Jr. 1969. A comparative study of the Le Conte's and Sharp-tailed sparrows. Auk 86:199–231.

NABCI (North American Bird Conservation Initiative). 2007. Integrated bird conservation in the United States: bird conservation plans. http://www.nabci-us.org/plans.html.

National Audubon Society. 2002. Audubon Watchlist 2002; an early warning system for bird conservation. http://www.audubon.org/ bird/watchlist/.

———. [2007]. The Christmas Bird Count historical results. http:// www.audubon.org/bird/cbc/hr/index.html.

The Nature Conservancy. 2000. Designing a geography of hope: a practitioner's handbook to ecoregional conservation planning, 2nd ed., vol. I. The Nature Conservancy, Arlington, VA. http:// conserveonline.org/docs/2000/11/GOH2-v1.pdf.

NAWMP (North American Waterfowl Management Plan), Plan Committee. 2004. North American Waterfowl Management Plan 2004. Strategic guidance: strengthening the biological foundation. Canadian Wildlife Service, Gatineau, QC; U.S. Fish and Wildlife Service, Arlington, VA; and Secretaria de Medio Ambiente y Recursos Naturales, Colonia Tlacopac, Mexico. http://www.fws.gov/ birdhabitat/NAWMP/files/NAWMP2004.pdf.

Neidermyer, W. J., and J. J. Hickey. 1977. The Monk Parakeet in the United States, 1970–75. American Birds 31:273–278.

New York State Agricultural Statistics Service. 1986–2005. New York agricultural statistics. Annual. New York State Department of Agriculture and Markets, Division of Statistics, Albany, NY.

Nicholson, A. G. 1985. The development of agriculture in New York State. Natural Resources Research and Extension Series, no. 23. Department of Natural Resources, Cornell University, Ithaca, NY.

Nickell, W. P. 1951. Studies of habitats, territory, and nests of the Eastern Goldfinch. Auk 68:447–470.

Nickerson, D. 1978. Wilson's Warbler nests in New York State. Kingbird 28:215–220.

Niering, W. A., G. D. Dreyer, F. E. Egler, and J. P. Anderson Jr. 1986. Stability of a *Viburnum lentago* shrub community after 30 years. Bulletin of the Torrey Botanical Club 113:23–27.

Nisbet, I. C. T. 1978. Recent changes in gull populations in the western North Atlantic. Ibis 120:129–130.

———. 2002. Common Tern (*Sterna hirundo*). *In* The birds of North America, no. 618 (A. Poole and F. Gill, Eds.). The Birds of North America, Inc., Philadelphia, PA.

NJDEP (New Jersey Department of Environmental Protection). [n.d.] [Least Tern fact sheet]. NJDEP, Division of Fish and Wildlife, Endangered and Nongame Species Program. Woodbine, NJ. http:// www.njfishandwildlife.com/ensp/pdf/end-thrtened/leasttern.pdf.

Nol, E., and R. C. Humphrey. 1994. American Oystercatcher (*Haematopus palliatus*). *In* The birds of North America, no. 82 (A. Poole and F. Gill, Eds.). The Academy of Natural Sciences, Philadelphia, PA, and The American Ornithologists' Union, Washington, DC.

Nolan, V. Jr., E. D. Ketterson, and C. A. Buerkle. 1999. Prairie Warbler (*Dendroica discolor*). *In* The birds of North America, no. 455

(A. Poole and F. Gill, Eds.). The Birds of North America, Inc., Philadelphia, PA.

Nolan, V. Jr., E. D. Ketterson, D. A. Cristol, C. M. Rogers, E. D. Clotfelter, R. C. Titus, S. J. Schoech, and E. Snajdr. 2002. Dark-eyed Junco (*Junco hyemalis*). *In* The birds of North America, no. 716 (A. Poole and F. Gill, Eds.). The Birds of North America, Inc., Philadelphia, PA.

Noon, B. R. 1981. The distribution of an avian guild along a temperate elevational gradient: the importance and expression of competition. Ecological Monographs, no. 51:105–124.

Norton, A. H., and R. P. Allen. 1931. Breeding of the Great Black-backed Gull and Double-crested Cormorant in Maine. Auk 48:589–592.

Noss, R. F., E. T. LaRoe III, and J. M. Scott. 1995. Endangered ecosystems of the United States: preliminary assessment of loss and degradation. Technical Report Series. Biological Report 28. U.S. Department of the Interior, National Biological Service, Washington, DC. http://biology.usgs.gov/pubs/ecosys.htm.

Novak, P. G. 1989. Breeding ecology and status of the Loggerhead Shrike in New York State. M.S. thesis, Cornell University, Ithaca, NY.

———. 1998a. Clay-colored Sparrow (*Spizella pallida*). Pages 506–507 *in* Bull's birds of New York State (E. Levine, Ed.). Cornell University Press, Ithaca, NY.

———. 1998b. Dickcissel (*Spiza americana*). Pages 543–544 *in* Bull's birds of New York State (E. Levine, Ed.). Comstock Publishing Associates, Ithaca, NY.

Nye, P. E. 1998a. Bald Eagle (*Haliaeetus leucocephalus*). Pages 182–185 *in* Bull's birds of New York State (E. Levine, Ed.). Comstock Publishing Associates, Ithaca, NY.

———. 1998b. Golden Eagle (*Aquila chrysaetos*). Pages 198–200 *in* Bull's birds of New York State (E. Levine, Ed.). Comstock Publishing Associates, Ithaca, NY.

———. 2005. New York State Bald Eagle report 2005. New York State Department of Environmental Conservation, Albany, NY. http://www.dec.ny.gov/docs/wildlife_pdf/baea2005.pdf.

Nye, P. E., and B. A. Loucks. 1996. Historic and current status of the Golden Eagle in New York State and the eastern United States. Paper presented at the New York Natural History Conference IV, Albany, NY.

NYNHP (New York Natural Heritage Program). 2006. Kentucky Warbler. http://www.acris.nynhp.org/guide.php?id=7074.

NYSARC (New York State Avian Records Committee). 1982. Report of the New York State Avian Records Committee for 1981. Kingbird 32:228–233. http://www.nybirds.org/NYSARC/Reports/NYSARC1981.html.

———. 1987. Report of the New York State Avian Records Committee. Kingbird 37:200–209. http://www.nybirds.org/NYSARC/Reports/NYSARC1985-86.html.

———. 1990. Report of the New York State Avian Records Committee 1988. Kingbird 40:209–212. http://www.nybirds.org/NYSARC/Reports/NYSARC1988.html.

———. 1992. Report of the New York State Avian Records Committee 1990. Kingbird 42:5–9. http://www.nybirds.org/NYSARC/Reports/NYSARC1990.html.

———. 1995. Report of the New York State Avian Records Commit-

tee 1993. Kingbird 45:71–78. http://www.nybirds.org/NYSARC/Reports/NYSARC1993.html.

———. 1996. Report of the New York State Avian Records Committee 1994. Kingbird 46:296–302. http://www.nybirds.org/NYSARC/Reports/NYSARC1994.html.

———. 1999. Report of the New York State Avian Records Committee for 1996. Kingbird 49:114–121. http://www.nybirds.org/NYSARC/Reports/NYSARC1996.html.

———. 2000a. Changes to the NYSARC review list. Kingbird 50:27–33.

———. 2000b. Report of the New York State Avian Records Committee for 1997. Kingbird 50:19–25. http://www.nybirds.org/NYSARC/Reports/NYSARC1997.html.

———. 2003. Report of the NYSARC Committee for 2001. Kingbird 53:280–306. http://www.nybirds.org/NYSARC/Reports/NYSARC2001.html.

———. 2004. Report of the New York State Avian Records Committee for 2002. Kingbird 54:282–313. http://www.nybirds.org/NYSARC/Reports/NYSARC2002.html.

———. 2005. Changes to the NYSARC review list. Kingbird 55:246–247.

———. 2006. Report of the New York State Avian Records Committee for 2003. Kingbird 56:2–41. http://www.nybirds.org/NYSARC/Reports/NYSARC2003.html.

———. 2007. NYSARC reports and decisions summary. http://www.nybirds.org/NYSARC/RecordsSummary.htm.

NYSDEC (New York State Department of Environmental Conservation). 1979. Long range management plan for Ring-necked Pheasants in New York. Unpublished report. New York State Department of Environmental Conservation, Bureau of Wildlife, Delmar, NY.

———. 1999. List of endangered, threatened and special concern fish and wildlife species of New York State. http://www.dec.ny.gov/animals/7494.html.

———. [2001]. Tidal wetlands losses in Nassau and Suffolk counties. New York State Department of Environmental Conservation, Albany, NY. http://www.dec.ny.gov/lands/31989.html.

———. 2004. Management of Double-crested Cormorants to protect public resources in New York, statement of findings. Prepared by Bryan Swift. New York State Department of Environmental Conservation, Albany, NY. http://www.dec.ny.gov/docs/wildlife_pdf/findings04.pdf.

———. 2005a. Comprehensive Wildlife Conservation Strategy (CWCS) plan. New York State Department of Environmental Conservation, Division of Fish, Wildlife and Marine Resources. Albany, NY. http://www.dec.ny.gov/animals/30483.html.

———. 2005b. 2005 New York State 20-year deer book. A contribution to federal aid in Fish and Wildlife Restoration Grant WE-173-G, Job 3aA1. Unpublished report. New York State Department of Environmental Conservation, Albany, NY.

———. 2006. Lower Hudson–Long Island bays basin. Pages 281–321 *in* Comprehensive Wildlife Conservation Strategy (CWCS) for New York State. New York State Department of Environmental Conservation, Division of Fish, Wildlife and Marine Resources. Albany, NY. http://www.dec.ny.gov/docs/wildlife_pdf/lowerhudsontxt.pdf.

———. [2007a]. Freshwater wetlands status and trends. New York State

Department of Environmental Conservation, Albany, NY. http://www.dec.ny.gov/lands/31835.html.

———. 2007b. Nuisance beaver control techniques manual. New York State Department of Environmental Conservation, Division of Fish, Wildlife and Marine Resources. Albany, NY. http://www.dec.ny.gov/animals/6992.html.

NYSDEC (New York State Department of Environmental Conservation). Beaver Management Team. 1992. Beaver management in New York State: history and specification of future program. New York State Department of Environmental Conservation, Bureau of Wildlife, Delmar, NY.

NYSOA (New York State Ornithological Association). 2005. Waterfowl count. Historical waterfowl count data, 1973–2004. http://www.nybirds.org/ProjWaterfowl.htm.

———. [2006]. Checklist of the birds of New York State. http://www.nybirds.org/Publications/ChecklistNYS.htm.

Oatman, G. F. 1985. Spruce Grouse (*Dendragapus canadensis*). Pages 90–91 *in* The atlas of breeding birds of Vermont (S. B. Laughlin and D. P. Kibbe, Eds.). University Press of New England, Hanover, NH.

Ochterski, J. 2005. Enhancing pastures for grassland bird habitat. Cornell Cooperative Extension of Schuyler County, NY. http://scnyat.cce.cornell.edu/grassland/pdf/Pastures&Grassland_Bird.pdf.

———. 2006a. Hayfield management and grassland bird conservation. Cornell Cooperative Extension of Schuyler County, NY. http://scnyat.cce.cornell.edu/grassland/pdf/Hayfields&Grassland_Birds.pdf.

———. 2006b. Transforming fields into grassland bird habitat. Cornell Cooperative Extension of Schuyler County, NY. http://scnyat.cce.cornell.edu/grassland/pdf/Fields&Grassland_Birds.pdf.

O'Connor, R. J. 1981a. Comparisons between migrant and non-migrant birds in Britain. Pages 167–195 *in* Animal migration (D. J. Aidley, Ed.). Cambridge University Press, Cambridge, UK.

———. 1981b. Habitat correlates of bird distribution in British census plots. Studies in Avian Biology, no. 6:533–537.

———. 1986. Dynamical aspects of avian habitat use. Pages 235–240 *In* Wildlife 2000: modeling habitat relationships of terrestrial vertebrates (J. Verner, M. L. Morrison, and C. J. Ralph, Eds.). University of Wisconsin Press, Madison, WI.

———. 1990. Some ecological aspects of migrants and residents. Pages 175–182 *in* Bird migration: physiology and ecophysiology (E. Gwinner, Ed.). Springer Verlag, Berlin, Germany.

Odum, E. P. 1943. The vegetation of the Edmund Niles Huyck Preserve, New York. American Midland Naturalist 29:72–88.

Ollinger, S. V., J. D. Aber, G. M. Lovett, S. E. Millham, R. G. Lathrop, and J. M. Ellis. 1993. A spatial model of atmospheric deposition for the northeastern United States. Ecological Applications 3:459–472.

Omernik, J. M. 1987. Map supplement: ecoregions of the conterminous United States. Annals of the Association of American Geographers 77:118–125.

Orians, G. M. 1961. The ecology of blackbird (*Agelaius*) social systems. Ecological Monographs, no. 31:285–312.

Oring, L. W., E. M. Gray, and J. M. Reed. 1997. Spotted Sandpiper (*Actitis macularia*). *In* The birds of North America, no. 289 (A. Poole and F. Gill, Eds.). The Academy of Natural Sciences, Philadelphia, PA, and The American Ornithologists' Union, Washington, DC.

Ostrander, B. 1998. Region 3—Finger Lakes. Kingbird 48:330–336.

Ouellet, R. 1996. Sharp-tailed Sparrow (*Ammodramus caudacutus*). Pages 994–997 *in* The breeding birds of Québec: atlas of the breeding birds of southern Québec (J. Gauthier and Y. Aubry, Eds.). Association québécoise des groupes d'ornithologues, Montréal, QC.

Palmer, R. S. 1949. Maine birds. Bulletin of the Museum of Comparative Zoology at Harvard College, no. 102. The Museum, Cambridge, MA.

———, Ed. 1976. Handbook of North American birds, vol. 2: waterfowl (first part). Yale University Press, New Haven, CT.

Palmer, W. 1898. Our small eastern shrikes. Auk 15:244–258.

Panjabi, A. O., C. Beardmore, P. J. Blancher, G. Butcher, M. Carter, D. Demarest, E. Dunn, et al. 2001. The Partners in Flight handbook on species assessment and prioritization. Version 1.1. Rocky Mountain Bird Observatory, Brighton, CO. http://www.rmbo.org/pubs/downloads/Handbook.pdf.

Panjabi, A. O., E. H. Dunn, P. J. Blancher, W. C. Hunter, B. Altman, J. Bart, C. J. Beardmore, et al. 2005. The Partners in Flight handbook on species assessment. Version 2005. Partners in Flight Technical Series no. 3. http://www.rmbo.org/pubs/downloads/Handbook2005.pdf.

Panko, D., and G. R. Battaly. 1998. Eastern Screech-Owl (*Otus asio*). Pages 325–328 *in* Bull's birds of New York State (E. Levine, Ed.). Comstock Publishing Associates, Ithaca, NY.

Paradis, S. 1996. Yellow-bellied Sapsucker (*Sphyrapicus varius*). Pages 644–647 *in* The breeding birds of Québec: atlas of the breeding birds of southern Québec (J. Gauthier and Y. Aubry, Eds.). Association québécoise des groupes d'ornithologues, Montréal, QC.

Parchman T. L., C. W. Benkman, and S. C. Britch. 2006. Patterns of genetic variation in the adaptive radiation of New World crossbills. Molecular Ecology 15:1873–1887.

Parker, K. E., and R. L. Miller. 1988. Status of New York's Common Loon population—comparison of two intensive surveys. Pages 145–156 *in* Papers from the 1987 Conference on Common Loon Research and Management, September 18–19, 1987, Laboratory of Ornithology, Ithaca, NY (P. I. V. Strong, Ed.). North American Loon Fund, Meredith, NH.

Parker, K. E., R. L. Miller, and S. Isil. 1986. Status of the Common Loon in New York State. Unpublished report. New York State Department of Environmental Conservation, Non-Game Division, Delmar, NY.

Parkes, K. C. 1951. The genetics of the Golden-winged x Blue-winged warbler complex. Wilson Bulletin 63:4–15.

———. 1952. The birds of New York State and their taxonomy. Ph.D. dissertation, Cornell University, Ithaca, NY.

———. 1954. Traill's Flycatcher in New York. Wilson Bulletin 66:89–92.

Parmesan, C., and G. Yohe. 2003. A globally coherent fingerprint of climate change impacts across natural systems. Nature 421:37–42.

Parnell, J. F., R. M. Erwin, and K. C. Molina. 1995. Gull-billed Tern (*Sterna nilotica*). *In* The birds of North America, no. 140 (A. Poole and F. Gill, Eds.). The Academy of Natural Sciences, Philadelphia, PA, and The American Ornithologists' Union, Washington, DC.

Parnell, J. F., R. N. Needham, R. F. Soots Jr., J. O. Fussell III, and D. M. Dumond. 1986. Use of dredged-material deposition sites by birds in coastal North Carolina, USA. Colonial Waterbirds 9:210–217.

Parsons, K. C. 1994. The Arthur Kill oil spills: biological effects to birds. Pages 215–237 in Before and after an oil spill: the Arthur Kill (J. Burger, Ed.). Rutgers University Press, New Brunswick, NJ.

Parsons, K. C., and T. L. Master. 2000. Snowy Egret (*Egretta thula*). In The birds of North America, no. 489 (A. Poole and F. Gill, Eds.). The Birds of North America, Inc., Philadelphia, PA.

Pashley, D. N., C. J. Beardmore, J. A. Fitzgerald, R. P. Ford, W. C. Hunter, M. S. Morrison, and K. V. Rosenberg. 2000. Partners in Flight: conservation of the land birds of the United States. American Bird Conservancy, The Plains, VA.

Paxton, R. O. 1998a. American Oystercatcher (*Haematopus palliatus*). Page 234 in Bull's birds of New York State (E. Levine, Ed.). Comstock Publishing Associates, Ithaca, NY.

———. 1988b. Blue Grosbeak (*Guiraca caerulea*). Page 540 in Bull's birds of New York State (E. Levine, Ed.). Comstock Publishing Associates, Ithaca, NY.

———. 1998c. Laughing Gull (*Larus atricilla*). Pages 275–277 in Bull's birds of New York State (E. Levine, Ed.). Comstock Publishing Associates, Ithaca, NY.

———. 1998d. Piping Plover (*Charadrius melodus*). Pages 232–233 in Bull's birds of New York State (E. Levine, Ed.). Comstock Publishing Associates, Ithaca, NY.

———. 1998e. Willet (*Catoptrophorus semipalmatus*). Pages 239–240 in Bull's birds of New York State (E. Levine, Ed.). Comstock Publishing Associates, Ithaca, NY.

Paxton, R. O., J. C. Burgiel, B. L. Sullivan, M. Powers, and R. R. Veit. 2005. Hudson-Delaware. North American Birds 59:573–577.

Payne, R. B. 2006. Indigo Bunting (*Passerina cyanea*). In The birds of North America online (A. Poole, Ed.). Cornell Lab of Ornithology, Ithaca, NY. http://bna.birds.cornell.edu/BNA/account/Indigo_Bunting/.doi:10.2173/bna.4.

Pearce, P., D. Peakall, and A. Erskine. 1979. Impacts on forest birds of the 1976 spruce budworm spray operation in New Brunswick. Canadian Wildlife Service Progress Notes, no. 97. Canadian Wildlife Service, Ottawa, ON.

Peck, G. K. 2005. Breeding status and nest site selection of Common Raven in Ontario. Ontario Birds 23:76–86.

Peck, G. K., and R. D. James. 1983. Breeding birds of Ontario: nidiology and distribution, vol. 1: nonpasserines. Royal Ontario Museum, Toronto, ON.

———. 1987. Breeding birds of Ontario: nidiology and distribution, vol. 2: passerines. Royal Ontario Museum, Toronto, ON.

Peer, B. D., and E. K. Bollinger. 1997. Common Grackle (*Quiscalus quiscula*). In The birds of North America, no. 271 (A. Poole and F. Gill, Eds.). The Academy of Natural Sciences, Philadelphia, PA, and The American Ornithologists' Union, Washington, DC.

Pence, D. M., E. Quinn, and C. Alexander. 1990. A continuing investigation of an insular population of Spruce Grouse (*Dendragapus canadensis*) in Essex County, Vermont. Technical Report 17. Vermont Fish and Wildlife Department, Waterbury, VT.

Penhollow, M. E., and D. F. Stauffer. 2000. Large-scale habitat relationships of Neotropical migratory birds in Virginia. Journal of Wildlife Management 64:362–373.

Penrod, B. D., D. E. Austin, and J. W. Hill. 1986. Mortality, productivity and habitat use of hen pheasants in western New York. New York Fish and Game Journal 33:67–123.

Peterjohn, B. G., and D. L. Rice. 1991. The Ohio breeding bird atlas. Ohio Department of Natural Resources, Columbus, OH.

Petersen, W. R. 1999. New England. North American Birds 53:363–366.

———. 2001. New England. North American Birds 55:411–415.

Petersen, W. R., and W. R. Meservey, Eds. 2003. Massachusetts breeding bird atlas. Massachusetts Audubon Society, Lincoln, MA.

Peterson, D. M. 1988a. Glossy Ibis (*Plegadis falcinellus*). Pages 54–55 in The atlas of breeding birds in New York State (R. F. Andrle and J. R. Carroll, Eds.). Cornell University Press, Ithaca, NY.

———. 1988b. Least Tern (*Sterna antillarum*). Pages 182–183 in The atlas of breeding birds in New York State (R. F. Andrle and J. R. Carroll, Eds.). Cornell University Press, Ithaca, NY.

———. 1988c. Piping Plover (*Charadrius melodus*). Pages 148–149 in The atlas of breeding birds in New York State (R. F. Andrle and J. R. Carroll, Eds.). Cornell University Press, Ithaca, NY.

———. 1988d. Roseate Tern (*Sterna dougallii*). Pages 176–177 in The atlas of breeding birds in New York State (R. F. Andrle and J. R. Carroll, Eds.). Cornell University Press, Ithaca, NY.

———. 1988e. Snowy Egret (*Egretta thula*). Pages 40–41 in The atlas of breeding birds in New York State (R. F. Andrle and J. R. Carroll, Eds.). Cornell University Press, Ithaca, NY.

———. 1988f. Yellow-crowned Night-Heron (*Nycticorax violacea*). Pages 52–53 in The atlas of breeding birds in New York State (R. F. Andrle and J. R. Carroll, Eds.). Cornell University Press, Ithaca, NY.

Peterson, D. M., and T. S. Litwin. 1983. 1983 Long Island Least Tern and Piping Plover survey. Unpublished report. Cornell Lab of Ornithology, Seatuck Research Program, Islip, NY.

Peterson, D. M., T. S. Litwin, D. C. MacLean, and R. A. Lent. 1985. 1985 Long Island colonial waterbird and Piping Plover survey. Unpublished report. Cornell Lab of Ornithology, Seatuck Research Program, Islip, NY.

Peterson, J. M. C. 1975. Attempted nesting of the White-winged Crossbill in New York State. Kingbird 25:191–193.

———. 1984a. First record of Palm Warbler nesting in New York State. Kingbird 34:2–7.

———. 1984b. Letter to the editor. Kingbird 34:232.

———. 1988a. Bay-breasted Warbler (*Dendroica castanea*). Pages 392–393 in The atlas of breeding birds in New York State (R. F. Andrle and J. R. Carroll, Eds.). Cornell University Press, Ithaca, NY.

———. 1988b. Black-backed Woodpecker (*Picoides arcticus*). Pages 238–239 in The atlas of breeding birds in New York State (R. F. Andrle and J. R. Carroll, Eds.). Cornell University Press, Ithaca, NY.

———. 1988c. Boreal Chickadee (*Parus hudsonicus*). Pages 290–291 in The atlas of breeding birds in New York State (R. F. Andrle and J. R. Carroll, Eds.). Cornell University Press, Ithaca, NY.

———. 1988d. Cape May Warbler (*Dendroica tigrina*). Pages 374–375 in The atlas of breeding birds in New York State (R. F. Andrle and J. R. Carroll, Eds.). Cornell University Press, Ithaca, NY.

———. 1988e. Caspian Tern (*Sterna caspia*). Pages 174–175 in The atlas of breeding birds in New York State (R. F. Andrle and J. R. Carroll, Eds.). Cornell University Press, Ithaca, NY.

———. 1988f. Evening Grosbeak (*Coccothraustes vespertinus*). Pages 498–499 in The atlas of breeding birds in New York State (R. F. Andrle and J. R. Carroll, Eds.). Cornell University Press, Ithaca, NY.

———. 1988g. Gray Jay (*Perisoreus canadensis*). Pages 278–279 in The atlas of breeding birds in New York State (R. F. Andrle and J. R. Carroll, Eds.). Cornell University Press, Ithaca, NY.

——. 1988h. Herring Gull (*Larus argentatus*). Pages 168–169 *in* The atlas of breeding birds in New York State (R. F. Andrle and J. R. Carroll, Eds.). Cornell University Press, Ithaca, NY.

——. 1988i. Lincoln's Sparrow (*Melospiza lincolnii*). Pages 458–459 *in* The atlas of breeding birds in New York State (R. F. Andrle and J. R. Carroll, Eds.). Cornell University Press, Ithaca, NY.

——. 1988j. Olive-sided Flycatcher (*Contopus borealis*). Pages 244–245 *in* The atlas of breeding birds in New York State (R. F. Andrle and J. R. Carroll, Eds.). Cornell University Press, Ithaca, NY.

——. 1988k. Philadelphia Vireo (*Vireo philadelphicus*). Pages 350–351 *in* The atlas of breeding birds in New York State (R. F. Andrle and J. R. Carroll, Eds.). Cornell University Press, Ithaca, NY.

——. 1988l. Pine Warbler (*Dendroica pinus*). Pages 386–387 *in* The atlas of breeding birds in New York State (R. F. Andrle and J. R. Carroll, Eds.). Cornell University Press, Ithaca, NY.

——. 1988m. Ring-necked Duck (*Aythya collaris*). Pages 84–85 *in* The atlas of breeding birds in New York State (R. F. Andrle and J. R. Carroll, Eds.). Cornell University Press, Ithaca, NY.

——. 1988n. Ruby-crowned Kinglet (*Regulus calendula*). Pages 312–313 *in* The atlas of breeding birds in New York State (R. F. Andrle and J. R. Carroll, Eds.). Cornell University Press, Ithaca, NY.

——. 1988o. Rusty Blackbird (*Euphagus carolinus*). Pages 474–475 *in* The atlas of breeding birds in New York State (R. F. Andrle and J. R. Carroll, Eds.). Cornell University Press, Ithaca, NY.

——. 1988p. Savannah Sparrow (*Passerculus sandwichensis*). Pages 446–447 *in* The atlas of breeding birds in New York State (R. F. Andrle and J. R. Carroll, Eds.). Cornell University Press, Ithaca, NY.

——. 1988q. Swainson's Thrush (*Catharus ustulatus*). Pages 322–323 *in* The atlas of breeding birds in New York State (R. F. Andrle and J. R. Carroll, Eds.). Cornell University Press, Ithaca, NY.

——. 1988r. Tennessee Warbler (*Vermivora peregrina*). Pages 362–363 *in* The atlas of breeding birds in New York State (R. F. Andrle and J. R. Carroll, Eds.). Cornell University Press, Ithaca, NY.

——. 1988s. Three-toed Woodpecker (*Picoides tridactylus*). Pages 236–237 *in* The atlas of breeding birds in New York State (R. F. Andrle and J. R. Carroll, Eds.). Cornell University Press, Ithaca, NY.

——. 1997. Region 7—Adirondack-Champlain. Kingbird 47:320–324.

——. 1999. Region 7—Adirondack-Champlain. Kingbird 49:358–363.

——. 2004. Region 7—Adirondack-Champlain. Kingbird 54:356–360.

——. 2005. Region 7—Adirondack-Champlain. Kingbird 55:382–387.

——. 2006. Birds of Franklin County, New York. County of Franklin, Malone, NY.

Peterson, J. M. C., and C. Fichtel. 1992. Olive-sided Flycatcher *Contopus borealis*. Pages 353–367 *in* Migratory nongame birds of management concern in the Northeast (K. J. Schneider and D. M. Pence, Eds.). U.S. Department of the Interior, Fish and Wildlife Service, Newton Corner, MA.

Peterson, J. M. C., and G. N. Lee. 2004. Birds of Hamilton County, New York. County of Hamilton, Lake Pleasant, NY.

Petit, L. J. 1999. Prothonotary Warbler (*Protonotaria citrea*). *In* The birds of North America, no. 408 (A. Poole and F. Gill, Eds.). The Birds of North America, Inc., Philadelphia, PA.

Petrie, S. A., and C. M. Francis. 2003. Rapid increase in the lower Great Lakes population of feral mute swans: a review and a recommendation. Wildlife Society Bulletin 31:407–416.

Petuh, M. N. 2003. Merlin breeds in Broome County—first historic nesting south of the Adirondacks. Kingbird 53:203–204.

Phillips, J. C. 1915. Experimental studies of hybridization among ducks and pheasants. Journal of Experimental Zoology 18:69–144.

Pickwell, G. B. 1931. The Prairie Horned Lark. Transactions of the Academy of Science, St. Louis, vol. 27 [Originally issued as the author's thesis, Cornell University, 1927].

Pierotti, R. J., and T. P. Good. 1994. Herring Gull (*Larus argentatus*). *In* The birds of North America, no. 124 (A. Poole and F. Gill, Eds.). The Academy of Natural Sciences, Philadelphia, PA, and The American Ornithologist's Union, Washington, DC.

PIF (Partners in Flight). 2000. Draft bird conservation plan for the Adirondack Mountains (Physiographic Area 26). http://www.blm.gov/wildlife/plan/pl_26_10.pdf.

——. Species Assessment Database: scores. 2005. http://www.rmbo.org/pif/scores/scores.html.

——. [n.d.]. Partners in Flight physiographic areas plans. http://www.blm.gov/wildlife/pifplans.htm.

Pitocchelli, J. 1993. Mourning Warbler (*Oporornis philadelphia*). *In* The birds of North America, no. 72 (A. Poole and F. Gill, Eds.). The Academy of Natural Sciences, Philadelphia, PA, and The American Ornithologists' Union, Washington, DC.

Poole, A. F., L. R. Bevier, C. A. Marantz, and B. Meanley. 2005. King Rail (*Rallus elegans*). *In* The birds of North America online (A. Poole, Ed.). Cornell Lab of Ornithology, Ithaca, NY. http://bna.birds.cornell.edu/BNA/account/King_Rail.doi:10.2173/bna.3.

Poole, A. F., R. O. Bierregaard, and M. S. Martell. 2002. Osprey (*Pandion haliaetus*). *In* The birds of North America, no. 683 (A. Poole and F. Gill, Eds.). The Birds of North America, Inc., Philadelphia, PA.

Post, P. W. 1961. The American Oystercatcher in New York. Kingbird 11:3–6.

——. 1962. Glossy Ibis breeding in New York. Auk 79:120–121.

Post, P. W., and G. S. Raynor. 1964. Recent range expansion of the American Oystercatcher into New York. Wilson Bulletin 76:339–346.

Post, W. 1970a. Salt marsh. Audubon Field Notes 24:771–772.

——. 1970b. Ditched salt marsh. Audubon Field Notes 24:772–774.

——. 1974. Functional analysis of space-related behavior in the Seaside Sparrow. Ecology 55:564–575.

——. 1990. Nest survival in a large ibis-heron colony during a three-year decline to extinction. Colonial Waterbirds 13:50–61.

Post, W., and F. Enders. 1969. Reappearance of the Black Rail on Long Island. Kingbird 19:189–191.

——. 1970. Notes on a salt marsh Virginia Rail population. Kingbird 20:61–67.

Post, W., J. P. Poston, and G. T. Bancroft. 1996. Boat-tailed Grackle (*Quiscalus major*). *In* The birds of North America, no. 207 (A. Poole and F. Gill, Eds.). The Academy of Natural Sciences, Philadelphia, PA, and The American Ornithologists' Union, Washington, DC.

Poulin, R. G., S. D. Grindal, and R. M. Brigham. 1996. Common

Nighthawk (*Chordeiles minor*). *In* The birds of North America, no. 213 (A. Poole and F. Gill, Eds.). The Academy of Natural Sciences, Philadelphia, PA, and The American Ornithologists' Union, Washington, DC.

Pranty, B. 2002. The use of Christmas Bird Count data to monitor populations of exotic birds. American Birds [102nd CBC issue]:24–28.

Pranty, B., and K. L. Garrett. 2003. The parrot fauna of the ABA Area: a current look. Birding 35:248–261.

Pravosudov, V. V., and T. C. Grubb Jr. 1993. White-breasted Nuthatch (*Sitta carolinensis*). *In* The birds of North America, no. 54 (A. Poole and F. Gill, Eds.). The Academy of Natural Sciences, Philadelphia, PA, and The American Ornithologists' Union, Washington, DC.

Preston, C. R. 2000. Red-tailed Hawk. Stackpole Books, Mechanicsburg, PA.

Preston, C. R., and R. D. Beane. 1993. Red-tailed Hawk (*Buteo jamaicensis*). *In* The birds of North America, no. 52 (A. Poole and F. Gill, Eds.). The Academy of Natural Sciences, Philadelphia, PA, and The American Ornithologists' Union, Washington, DC.

Proctor, T. 1895. Skylarks nesting on Long Island. Auk 12:390.

Pruitt, L. 2000. Loggerhead Shrike status assessment. U.S. Fish and Wildlife Service, Bloomington, IN. http://www.fws.gov/midwest/eco_serv/soc/birds/LOSH/LOSHSA_entire.pdf.

Puleston, D. 1970. First recorded nesting of the Cattle Egret in New York State. Kingbird 20:178–179.

Putz, F. E., and C. D. Canham. 1992. Mechanisms of arrested succession in shrublands: root and shoot competition between shrubs and tree seedlings. Forest Ecology and Management 49:267–275.

Quinlan, J. L., and J. J. Fritz. 1998. House Wren (*Troglodytes aedon*). Pages 419–420 *in* Bull's birds of New York State (E. Levine, Ed.). Comstock Publishing Associates, Ithaca, NY.

Rackham, O. 1980. Ancient woodland: its history, vegetation, and uses in England. E. Arnold, London, UK.

Raftovich, R. V. 2005. Atlantic Flyway breeding waterfowl plot survey: breeding pair and population size estimates. Draft report. U.S. Fish and Wildlife Service, Laurel, MD.

Rappole, J. H., and M. V. McDonald. 1994. Cause and effect in population declines of migratory birds. Auk 111:652–660.

Rappole, J. H., M. A. Ramos, and K. Winker. 1989. Wintering Wood Thrush movements and mortality in southern Veracruz. Auk 106:402–410.

Raptor Population Index Project. 2006. Eyes on the sky; counting for conservation: the Raptor Population Index 2006 annual report. http://rpi-project.org/docs/RPI_annual_report_2006.pdf.

Rathbun, F. R. 1879. A revised list of birds of central New York. Daily Advertiser and Weekly Journal Printing House, Auburn, NY.

Reed, H. D., and A. H. Wright. 1909. The vertebrates of the Cayuga Lake Basin, N.Y. Proceedings of the American Philosophical Society 48:370–459.

Reid, W. 1992. Common Merganser (*Mergus merganser*). Pages 84–85 *in* Atlas of breeding birds in Pennsylvania (D. W. Brauning, Ed.). University of Pittsburgh Press, Pittsburgh, PA.

Reilly, E. M., and K. C. Parkes. 1959. Preliminary annotated checklist of New York State birds. State Education Department, New York State Museum and Science Service, Albany, NY.

Renfrew, R. 2005. Vermont breeding bird atlas: three years of discovery, two more to go. VINS Field Notes 1(1):6–7. http://www.vinsweb.org/assets/pdf/cbdnews11.pdf.

Renfrow, F. 2005. Range expansion and habitat selection in breeding populations of Red-breasted Nuthatch (*Sitta canadensis*) in the southeastern United States. North American Birds 59:516–523.

Reschke, C. 1990. Ecological communities of New York State. New York Natural Heritage Program, New York State Department of Environmental Conservation, Latham, NY.

———. 1993. Estimated numbers of EOs, acreage, trends, and threats for selected New York natural communities. Unpublished report. New York Natural Heritage Program, New York State Department of Environmental Conservation, Latham, NY (as cited in Noss et al. 1995).

Rich, T. D., C. J. Beardmore, H. Berlanga, P. J. Blancher, M. S. W. Bradstreet, G. S. Butcher, D. W. Demarest, et al. 2004. Partners in Flight North American Landbird Conservation Plan. Cornell Lab of Ornithology, Ithaca, NY.

Richards, T. 1994. Palm Warbler (*Dendroica palmarum*). Page 385 *in* Atlas of breeding birds in New Hampshire (C. R. Foss, Ed.). Chalford Publishing Corporation, Dover, NH.

Richardson, M., and D. W. Brauning. 1995. Chestnut-sided Warbler (*Dendroica pensylvanica*). *In* The birds of North America, no. 190 (A. Poole and F. Gill, Eds.). The Academy of Natural Sciences, Philadelphia, PA, and The American Ornithologists' Union, Washington, DC.

Richmond, M. E. 1993. Status and nesting success of the colonial waterbirds on Oneida Lake. Annual report to the New York State Department of Environmental Conservation. Unpublished report. New York Cooperative Fish and Wildlife Research Unit, Cornell University, Ithaca, NY.

Rimmer, C. C. 1992. Common Loon (*Gavia immer*). Pages 3–30 *in* Migratory nongame birds of management concern in the Northeast (K. J. Schneider and D. M. Pence, Eds.). U.S. Department of the Interior, Fish and Wildlife Service. Newton Corner, MA.

Rimmer, C. C., J. A. Atwood, K. P. McFarland, and L. R. Nagy. 1996. Population density, vocal behavior, and recommended survey methods for Bicknell's Thrush. Wilson Bulletin 108:639–649.

Rimmer, C. C., and K. P. McFarland. 1998. Tennessee Warbler (*Vermivora peregrinus*). *In* The birds of North America, no. 350 (A. Poole and F. Gill, Eds.). The Academy of Natural Sciences, Philadelphia, PA, and the American Ornithologists' Union, Washington, DC.

Rimmer, C. C., K. P. McFarland, W. G. Ellison, and J. E. Goetz. 2001. Bicknell's Thrush (*Catharus bicknelli*). *In* The birds of North America, no. 592 (A. Poole and F. Gill, Eds.). The Birds of North America, Inc., Philadelphia, PA.

Rimmer, C. C., K. P. McFarland, D. C. Evers, E. K. Miller, Y. Aubry, D. Busby, and R. J. Taylor. 2005. Mercury levels in Bicknell's Thrush and other insectivorous passerines in montane forests of northeastern North America. Ecotoxicology 14:223–240.

Ringia, A. M., B. J. Blitvich, H.-Y. Koo, M. Van de Wyngaerde, J. D. Brawn, and R. J. Novak. 2004. Antibody prevalence of West Nile virus in birds, Illinois, 2002. Emerging Infectious Diseases 10:1120–1124.

Rising, G. 1998a. Brown Thrasher (*Toxostoma rufum*). Pages 446–477 *in* Bull's birds of New York State (E. Levine, Ed.). Comstock Publishing Associates, Ithaca, NY.

———. 1998b. Palm Warbler (*Dendroica palmarum*). Pages 474–476 *in* Bull's birds of New York State (E. Levine, Ed.). Comstock Publishing Associates, Ithaca, NY.

Rising, J. D., and N. J. Flood. 1998. Baltimore Oriole (*Icterus galbula*). *In* The birds of North America, no. 384 (A. Poole and F. Gill, Eds.). The Birds of North America, Inc., Philadelphia, PA.

Robbins, C. S., D. Bystrak, and P. H. Geissler. 1986. The Breeding Bird Survey: its first fifteen years, 1965–1979. U.S. Department of the Interior, Fish and Wildlife Service, Washington, DC.

Robbins, C. S., D. K. Dawson, and B. A. Dowell. 1989. Habitat area requirements of breeding forest birds of the middle Atlantic states. Wildlife Monographs, no. 103:3–34.

Roberts, C., and C. J. Norment. 1999. Effects of plot size and habitat characteristics on breeding success of Scarlet Tanagers. Auk 116:73–82.

Roberts, S. D., J. M. Coffey, and W. F. Porter. 1995. Survival and reproduction of female Wild Turkeys in New York. Journal of Wildlife Management 59:437–447.

Robertson, B., and K. V. Rosenberg. 2003. Partners in Flight Bird Conservation Plan: Allegheny Plateau (Physiographic Area 24). http://www.blm.gov/wildlife/plan/pl_24_10.pdf.

Robertson, R. J., B. J. Stutchbury, and R. R. Cohen. 1992. Tree Swallow (*Tachycineta bicolor*). *In* The birds of North America, no. 11 (A. Poole, P. Stettenheim, and F. Gill, Eds.). The Academy of Natural Sciences, Philadelphia, PA, and The American Ornithologists' Union, Washington, DC.

Robinson, T. R., R. R. Sargent, and M. B. Sargent. 1996. Ruby-throated Hummingbird (*Archilochus colubris*). *In* The birds of North America, no. 204 (A. Poole and F. Gill, Eds.). The Academy of Natural Sciences, Philadelphia, PA, and The American Ornithologists' Union, Washington, DC.

Robinson, W. D. 1995. Louisiana Waterthrush (*Seirurus motacilla*). *In* The birds of North America, no. 151 (A. Poole and F. Gill, Eds.). The Academy of Natural Sciences, Philadelphia, PA, and The American Ornithologists' Union, Washington, DC.

———. 1996. Summer Tanager (*Piranga rubra*). *In* The birds of North America, no. 248 (A. Poole and F. Gill, Eds.). The Academy of Natural Sciences, Philadelphia, PA, and The American Ornithologists' Union, Washington, DC.

Rodenhouse, N. L., S. Matthews, K. P. McFarland, J. D. Lambert, L. R. Iverson, T. S. Sillett, and R. T. Holmes. 2008. Potential effects of climate change on birds of the Northeast. Mitigation and Adaptation Strategies for Global Change. [Online first doi:10.1007/s11027-007-9126-1] http://www.springerlink.com/content/n982r6rq51782x63/fulltext.pdf.

Rodewald, P. G., and R. D. James. 1996. Yellow-throated Vireo (*Vireo flavifrons*). *In* The birds of North America, no. 247 (A. Poole and F. Gill, Eds.). The Academy of Natural Sciences, Philadelphia, PA, and The American Ornithologists' Union, Washington, DC.

Rodewald, P. G., J. H. Withgott, and K. G. Smith. 1999. Pine Warbler (*Dendroica pinus*). *In* The birds of North America, no. 438 (A. Poole and F. Gill, Eds.). The Birds of North America, Inc., Philadelphia, PA.

Rodgers, J. A. Jr., and H. T. Smith. 1995. Little Blue Heron (*Egretta caerulea*). *In* The birds of North America, no. 145 (A. Poole and F. Gill, Eds.). The Academy of Natural Sciences, Philadelphia, PA, and The American Ornithologists' Union, Washington, DC.

Rohwer, F. C., W. P. Johnson, and E. R. Loos. 2002. Blue-winged Teal (*Anas discors*). *In* The birds of North America, no. 625 (A. Poole and F. Gill, Eds.). The Birds of North America, Inc., Philadelphia, PA.

Romagosa, C. M. 2002. Eurasian Collared-Dove (*Streptopelia decaocto*). *In* The birds of North America, no. 630 (A. Poole and F. Gill, Eds.). The Birds of North America, Inc., Philadelphia, PA.

Roosevelt, T. R. Jr., and H. D. Minot. 1877. The summer birds of the Adirondacks in Franklin County, N.Y. Privately printed, New York? [Reprinted in the Roosevelt Wild Life Bulletin 1:521–524, 1923, and by The Adirondack Museum, Blue Mountain Lake, NY, 2001]. Available online at http://www.sil.si.edu/digitalcollections/BHL-Collections/BHL_title.cfm?bib_id=SIL-036-005.

Rosche, R. C. 1967. Birds of Wyoming County, New York. Bulletin of the Buffalo Society of Natural Sciences, vol. 23. Buffalo Society of Natural Sciences, Buffalo, NY.

Roscoe, D. R., J. B. Zeh, W. B. Stone, L. P. Brown, and J. L. Renkavinsky. 1973. Observations on the Monk Parakeet in New York State. New York Fish and Game Journal 20:170–173.

Rosenberg, K. V., S. E. Barker, and R. W. Rohrbaugh. 2000. An atlas of Cerulean Warbler populations: final report to USFWS: 1997–2000 breeding seasons. Cornell Lab of Ornithology, Ithaca, NY. http://www.birds.cornell.edu/cewap/cwapresultsdec18.pdf.

Rosenberg, K. V., R. S. Hames, R. W. Rohrbaugh Jr., S. Barker Swarthout, J. D. Lowe, and A. A. Dhondt. 2003. A land manager's guide to improving habitat for forest thrushes. Cornell Lab of Ornithology, Ithaca, NY.

Rosenberg, K. V., R. W. Rohrbaugh Jr., S. E. Barker, R. S. Hames, J. D. Lowe, and A. A. Dhont. 1999. A land manager's guide to improving habitat for Scarlet Tanagers and other forest-interior birds. Cornell Lab of Ornithology, Ithaca, NY.

Rosenfield, R. N., J. Bielefeldt, J. L. Affeldt, and D. J. Beckmann. 1995. Nesting density, nest area reoccupancy, and monitoring implications for Cooper's Hawks in Wisconsin. Journal of Raptor Research 29:1–4.

Roth, R. R. 1976. Spatial heterogeneity and bird species diversity. Ecology 57:773–782.

Roth, R. R., M. S. Johnson, and T. J. Underwood. 1996. Wood Thrush (*Hylocichla mustelina*). *In* The birds of North America, no. 246 (A. Poole and F. Gill, Eds.). The Academy of Natural Sciences, Philadelphia, and The American Ornithologists' Union, Washington, DC.

Rusch, D. H., S. DeStefano, M. C. Reynolds, and D. Lauten. 2000. Ruffed Grouse (*Bonasa umbellus*). *In* The birds of North America, no. 515 (A. Poole and F. Gill, Eds.). The Birds of North America, Inc., Philadelphia, PA.

Ruth, J. M. 2006. Partners in Flight—U.S. web site. Served by the USGS Patuxent Wildlife Research Center, Laurel, MD. http://www.partnersinflight.org.

Ryder, J. P. 1993. Ring-billed Gull (*Larus delawarensis*). *In* The birds of North America, no. 33 (A. Poole, P. Stettenheim, and F. Gill, Eds.). The Academy of Natural Sciences, Philadelphia, PA, and The American Ornithologists' Union, Washington, DC.

Ryder, R. A., and D. E. Manry. 1994. White-faced Ibis (*Plegadis chihi*). *In* The birds of North America, no. 130 (A. Poole and F. Gill, Eds.). The Academy of Natural Sciences, Philadelphia, PA, and The American Ornithologists' Union, Washington, DC.

Sallabanks, R., and F. C. James. 1999. American Robin (*Turdus migratorius*). *In* The birds of North America, no. 462 (A. Poole and F. Gill, Eds.). The Birds of North America, Inc., Philadelphia, PA.

Salzman, E. 1998a. Boat-tailed Grackle (*Quiscalus major*). Pages

553–554 *in* Bull's birds of New York State (E. Levine, Ed.). Comstock Publishing Associates, Ithaca, NY.

——. 1998b. Brown Creeper (*Certhia americana*). Pages 415–416 *in* Bull's birds of New York State (E. Levine, Ed.). Comstock Publishing Associates, Ithaca, NY.

——. 1998c. Fish Crow (*Corvus ossifragus*). Pages 392–394 *in* Bull's birds of New York State (E. Levine, Ed.). Comstock Publishing Associates, Ithaca, NY.

——. 1998d. Great Horned Owl (*Bubo virginianus*). Pages 329–330 *in* Bull's birds of New York State (E. Levine, Ed.). Comstock Publishing Associates, Ithaca, NY.

——. 1998e. Kentucky Warbler (*Oporonis formosus*). Pages 489–490 *in* Bull's birds of New York State (E. Levine, Ed.). Comstock Publishing Associates, Ithaca, NY.

——. 1998f. Monk Parakeet (*Myiopsitta monarchus*). Pages 321–322 *in* Bull's birds of New York State (E. Levine, Ed.). Comstock Publishing Associates, Ithaca, NY.

——. 1998g. Nelson's Sharp-tailed Sparrow (*Ammodramus nelsoni*). Pages 520–521 *in* Bull's birds of New York State (E. Levine, Ed.). Comstock Publishing Associates, Ithaca, NY.

——. 1998h. Pine Warbler (*Dendroica pinus*). Pages 471–473 *in* Bull's birds of New York State (E. Levine, Ed.). Comstock Publishing Associates, Ithaca, NY.

——. 1998i. White-eyed Vireo (*Vireo griseus*). Pages 379–381 *in* Bull's birds of New York State (E. Levine, Ed.). Comstock Publishing Associates, Ithaca, NY.

——. 1998j. Yellow-throated Vireo (*Vireo flavifrons*). Pages 382–383 *in* Bull's birds of New York State (E. Levine, Ed.). Comstock Publishing Associates, Ithaca, NY.

Salzman, E., and K. C. Parkes. 1998. Northern Bobwhite (*Colinus virginianus*). Pages 215–216 *in* Bull's birds of New York State (E. Levine, Ed.). Comstock Publishing Associates, Ithaca, NY.

Sandilands, A. 1987a. Canvasback (*Aythya valisineria*). Pages 86–87 *in* Atlas of the breeding birds of Ontario (M. D. Cadman, P. F. J. Eagles, and F. M. Helleiner, Eds.). University of Waterloo Press, Waterloo, ON.

——. 1987b. Northern Pintail (*Anas acuta*). Pages 74–75 *in* Atlas of the breeding birds of Ontario (M. D. Cadman, P. F. J. Eagles, and F. M. Helleiner, Eds.). University of Waterloo Press, Waterloo, ON.

Sauer, J. R., J. E. Hines, and J. Fallon. 2005. The North American Breeding Bird Survey, results and analysis 1966–2005. Version 6.2.2006. USGS Patuxent Wildlife Research Center, Laurel, MD. http://www.mbr-pwrc.usgs.gov/bbs/bbs2005.html.

Sauer, J. R., J. E. Hines, and J. Fallon. 2007. The North American Breeding Bird Survey, results and analysis 1966–2006. Version 7.23.2007. USGS Patuxent Wildlife Research Center, Laurel, MD. http://www.mbr-pwrc.usgs.gov/bbs/bbs.html.

Sauer, J. R., J. E. Hines, I. Thomas, J. Fallon, and G. Gough. 1999. The North American Breeding Bird Survey, results and analysis 1966–1998. Version 98.1. USGS Patuxent Wildlife Research Center, Laurel, MD. http://www.mbr-pwrc.usgs.gov/bbs/bbs98.html.

Sauer, J. R., S. Schwartz, and B. Hoover. 1996. The Christmas Bird Count home page. Version 95.1. Patuxent Wildlife Research Center, Laurel, MD. http://www.mbr-pwrc.usgs.gov/bbs/cbc.html.

Saunders, A. A. 1923. The summer birds of the Allegany State Park. Roosevelt Wild Life Bulletin 1:239–354 [Reprinted as the New York State Museum Handbook, no. 18, by the University of the State of New York Press, 1942].

——. 1926. The summer birds of central New York marshes. Roosevelt Wild Life Bulletin 3:335–475.

——. 1929. The summer birds of the northern Adirondack Mountains. Roosevelt Wild Life Bulletin 5:327–499.

——. 1936. Ecology of the birds of Quaker Run Valley, Allegany State Park, New York. New York State Museum Handbook, no. 16. University of the State of New York, Albany, NY.

——. 1938. Studies of breeding birds in the Allegany State Park. New York State Museum Bulletin, no. 318. University of the State of New York, Albany, NY.

Sax, D. F., and S. D. Gaines. 2003. Species diversity: from global decreases to local increases. Trends in Ecology and Evolution 18:561–566.

Scharf, W. C., and J. Kren. 1996. Orchard Oriole (*Icterus spurius*). *In* The birds of North America, no. 255 (A. Poole and F. Gill, Eds.). The Academy of Natural Sciences, Philadelphia, PA, and The American Ornithologists' Union, Washington, DC.

Scharf, W. C., G. W. Shugart, W. W. Bowerman, and A. S. Roe. 1998. Distribution and abundance of gull, tern, and cormorant nesting colonies of the U.S. Great Lakes, 1989 and 1990. Gale Gleason Environmental Institute publication, no. 1-2. Lake Superior State University Press, Sault Ste. Marie, MI.

Schiff, S., and A. Wollin. 1990. Region 10—Marine. Kingbird 40:276–279.

——. 1991. Region 10—Marine. Kingbird 41:217–221.

——. 1992. Region 10—Marine. Kingbird 42:278–282.

——. 1997. Region 10—Marine. Kingbird 47:333–336.

——. 1999. Region 10—Marine. Kingbird 49:372–379.

——. 2001a. Region 10—Marine. Kingbird 51:734–740.

——. 2001b. Region 10—Marine. Kingbird 51:817–823.

Schmidt, K. A., and C. J. Whelan. 1999. Effects of exotic *Lonicera* and *Rhamnus* on songbird nest predation. Conservation Biology 13:1502–1506.

Schmidt, K. P. 1938. Herpetological evidence for the postglacial eastward extension of the steppe in North America. Ecology 19:396–407.

Schneider, K. J. 2003. The status and ecology of the Short-eared Owl (*Asio flammeus*) in New York State. Kingbird 53:313–330.

Schneider, K. J., and D. M. Pence, Eds. 1992. Migratory nongame birds of management concern in the Northeast. U.S. Department of the Interior, Fish and Wildlife Service, Newton Corner, MA.

Schoch, N. 2002. The Common Loon in the Adirondack Park: an overview of loon natural history and current research. Working Paper no. 20. Wildlife Conservation Society, Bronx, NY. http://www.wcs.org/media/file/wcswp20.pdf.

Schorger, A. W. 1952. Introduction of the domestic pigeon. Auk 69:462–463.

Schroeder, M. A., and L. A. Robb. 1993. Greater Prairie-Chicken (*Tympanuchus cupido*). *In* The birds of North America, no. 36 (A. Poole, P. Stettenheim, and F. Gill, Eds.). The Academy of Natural Sciences, Philadelphia, PA, and The American Ornithologists' Union, Washington, DC.

Sealy, S. G. 1979. Extralimital nesting of Bay-breasted Warblers: response to forest tent caterpillars? Auk 96:600–603.

Sedgwick, J. A. 2000. Willow Flycatcher (*Empidonax traillii*). *In* The birds of North America, no. 533 (A. Poole and F. Gill, Eds.). The Birds of North America, Inc., Philadelphia, PA.

Sedwitz, W., I. Alperin, and M. Jacobson. 1948. Gadwall breeding on Long Island, New York. Auk 65:610–612.

Serie, J. R., and G. G. Chasko. 1990. Status of Wood Ducks in the Atlantic Flyway. Pages 109–113 in 1988 North American Wood Duck Symposium (L. H. Fredrickson, G. V. Burger, S. P. Havera, D. A. Graber, R. E. Kirby, and T. S. Taylor, Eds.). The Symposium, St. Louis, MO.

Serie, J. R., and B. Raftovich. 2003. Atlantic Flyway final compilation estimates of harvest, hunter activity, and success based on the U.S. Fish and Wildlife Service's Mail Questionnaire Survey, 1961–2001. Unpublished report. U.S. Fish and Wildlife Service, Division of Migratory Bird Management, Laurel, MD.

———. 2006. Atlantic Flyway Waterfowl Harvest and Population Survey data. U.S. Fish and Wildlife Service, Division of Migratory Bird Management, Laurel, MD. http://www.dnr.state.md.us/wildlife/2006_AF_Databook.pdf.

Serrentino, P. 1987. The breeding ecology and behavior of Northern Harriers in Coos County, New Hampshire. M.S. thesis, University of Rhode Island, Kingston, RI.

Seutin, G., and J.-P. Simon. 1988. Protein and enzyme uniformity in a new, isolated population of the Sharp-tailed Sparrow. Biochemical Systematics and Ecology 16:233–236.

Severinghaus, C. W., and D. Benson. 1947. Ring-necked Duck broods in New York State. Auk 64:626–627.

Shackelford, C. E., R. E. Brown, and R. N. Conner. 2000. Red-bellied Woodpecker (Melanerpes carolinus). In The birds of North America, no. 500 (A. Poole and F. Gill, Eds.). The Birds of North America, Inc., Philadelphia, PA.

Shaffer, F., J. P. LeBel, and R. Ouellet. 1990. State of the Sharp-tailed Sparrow (Ammodramus caudacutus subvirgatus) in Québec and Canada. Unpublished report. Department of Recreation, Hunting and Fishing and the Québec Association of Ornithologists' Unions, QC.

Shea, R. E. 2002. Should Trumpeter Swans be re-introduced to the eastern United States and Canada? Yes. Birding 34:341–344, 345.

Sheffield, R., and M. Sheffield. 1963. Nesting of the Philadelphia Vireo in the Adirondacks. Kingbird 13:204–205.

Sheldon, W. G. 1967. The book of the American Woodcock. University of Massachusetts Press, Amherst, MA.

Sherony, D. F. 1998a. Blue-winged Teal (Anas discors). Pages 155–156 in Bull's birds of New York State (E. Levine, Ed.). Comstock Publishing Associates, Ithaca, NY.

———. 1998b. Yellow-throated Warbler (Dendroica dominica). Pages 470–471 in Bull's birds of New York State (E. Levine, Ed.). Comstock Publishing Associates, Ithaca, NY.

Sherony, D. F., and B. M. Ewald. 2003. Eurasian Collared-Dove in New York State. Kingbird 53:98–102.

Sherrod, S. K., C. M. White, and F. S. L. Williamson. 1976. Biology of the Bald Eagle on Amchitka Island, Alaska. Living Bird 15:143–182.

Sherry, T. W., and R. T. Holmes. 1997. American Redstart (Setophaga ruticilla). In The birds of North America, no. 277 (A. Poole and F. Gill, Eds.). The Academy of Natural Sciences, Philadelphia, PA, and The American Ornithologists' Union, Washington, DC.

Shields, W. M., and J. R. Crook. 1987. Barn Swallow coloniality: a net cost for group breeding in the Adirondacks? Ecology 68:1373–1386.

Shoo, L. P., S. E. Williams, and J.-M. Hero. 2006. Detecting climate change induced range shifts: where and how should we be looking? Austral Ecology 31:22–29.

Short, E. H. 1893. Birds of western New York, with notes. A. M. Eddy, Albion, NY.

Sibley, C. G., and B. L. Monroe Jr. 1990. Distribution and taxonomy of birds of the world. Yale University Press, New Haven, CT.

Sibley, S. C. 1988a. American Black Duck (Anas rubripes). Pages 64–65 in The atlas of breeding birds in New York State (R. F. Andrle and J. R. Carroll, Eds.). Cornell University Press, Ithaca, NY.

———. 1988b. Black-capped Chickadee (Parus atricapillus). Pages 288–289 in The atlas of breeding birds in New York State (R. F. Andrle and J. R. Carroll, Eds.). Cornell University Press, Ithaca, NY.

———. 1988c. Blue Jay (Cyanocitta cristata). Pages 280–281 in The atlas of breeding birds in New York State (R. F. Andrle and J. R. Carroll, Eds.). Cornell University Press, Ithaca, NY.

———. 1988d. Blue-winged Teal (Anas discors). Pages 72–73 in The atlas of breeding birds in New York State (R. F. Andrle and J. R. Carroll, Eds.). Cornell University Press, Ithaca, NY.

———. 1988e. Cedar Waxwing (Bombycilla cedrorum). Pages 336–337 in The atlas of breeding birds in New York State (R. F. Andrle and J. R. Carroll, Eds.). Cornell University Press, Ithaca, NY.

———. 1988f. Chimney Swift (Chaetura pelagica). Pages 220–221 in The atlas of breeding birds in New York State (R. F. Andrle and J. R. Carroll, Eds.). Cornell University Press, Ithaca, NY.

———. 1988g. Common Moorhen (Gallinula chloropus). Pages 144–145 in The atlas of breeding birds in New York State (R. F. Andrle and J. R. Carroll, Eds.). Cornell University Press, Ithaca, NY.

———. 1988h. Common Nighthawk (Chordeiles minor). Pages 214–215 in The atlas of breeding birds in New York State (R. F. Andrle and J. R. Carroll, Eds.). Cornell University Press, Ithaca, NY.

———. 1988i. Eastern Wood-Pewee (Contopus virens). Pages 246–247 in The atlas of breeding birds in New York State (R. F. Andrle and J. R. Carroll, Eds.). Cornell University Press, Ithaca, NY.

———. 1988j. Green-backed Heron (Butorides striatus). Pages 48–49 in The atlas of breeding birds in New York State (R. F. Andrle and J. R. Carroll, Eds.). Cornell University Press, Ithaca, NY.

———. 1988k. Hairy Woodpecker (Picoides villosus). Pages 234–235 in The atlas of breeding birds in New York State (R. F. Andrle and J. R. Carroll, Eds.). Cornell University Press, Ithaca, NY.

———. 1988l. Monk Parakeet (Myiopsitta monachus). Pages 192–193 in The atlas of breeding birds in New York State (R. F. Andrle and J. R. Carroll, Eds.). Cornell University Press, Ithaca, NY.

———. 1988m. Purple Martin (Progne subis). Pages 266–267 in The atlas of breeding birds in New York State (R. F. Andrle and J. R. Carroll, Eds.). Cornell University Press, Ithaca, NY.

Siebenheller, N. 1981. Breeding birds of Staten Island, 1881–1981. Staten Island Institute of Arts and Sciences, Staten Island, NY.

Siebenheller, N., and B. Siebenheller. 1982. Blue Grosbeak nesting in New York State: a first record. Kingbird 32:234–238.

Silloway, P. M. 1923. Relation of summer birds to the western Adirondack forest. Roosevelt Wild Life Bulletin 1:397–486.

Sinclair, W. A., H. H. Lyon, and W. T. Johnson. 1987. Diseases of trees and shrubs. Cornell University Press, Ithaca, NY.

Skelly, S. M. 1992. Photographs of New York State rarities 53: White-winged Tern. Kingbird 42:2–4.

———. 1998a. Gull-billed Tern (Sterna nilotica). Page 294 in Bull's birds of New York State (E. Levine, Ed.). Comstock Publishing Associates, Ithaca, NY.

——. 1998b. Least Tern (*Sterna antillarum*). Pages 304–305 *in* Bull's birds of New York State (E. Levine, Ed.). Comstock Publishing Associates, Ithaca, NY.

Slack, R. S., C. B. Slack, R. N. Roberts, and D. E. Emord. 1987. Spring migration of Long-eared Owls and Northern Saw-whet Owls at Nine Mile Point, New York. Wilson Bulletin 99:480–485.

Smallwood, J. A., and D. M. Bird. 2002. American Kestrel (*Falco sparverius*). *In* The birds of North America, no. 602 (A. Poole, and F. Gill, Eds.). The Birds of North America, Inc., Philadelphia, PA.

Smallwood, J. A., and M. W. Collopy. 1993. Management of the threatened Southeastern American Kestrel in Florida: population responses to a regional nest-box program. Abstract of a presentation made at the annual meeting of the Raptor Research Foundation, Inc., Bellevue, WA, Nov. 11–15, 1992. Journal of Raptor Research 27:81.

Smiley, D., and J. Stapleton. 1974. First breeding record of Bewick's Wren in New York State. Kingbird 24:174–175.

Smith, B. E., P. L. Marks, and S. Gardescu. 1993. Two hundred years of forest cover changes in Tompkins County, New York. Bulletin of the Torrey Botanical Club 120:229–247.

Smith, C. R. 1982. What constitutes adequate coverage? New York State Breeding Bird Atlas Newsletter, no. 5:6.

——. 1988a. American Goldfinch (*Carduelis tristis*). Pages 496–497 *in* The atlas of breeding birds in New York State (R. F. Andrle and J. R. Carroll, Eds.). Cornell University Press, Ithaca, NY.

——. 1988b. Scarlet Tanager (*Piranga olivacea*). Pages 426–427 *in* The atlas of breeding birds in New York State (R. F. Andrle and J. R. Carroll, Eds.). Cornell University Press, Ithaca, NY.

——. 1990. Handbook for atlasing North American breeding birds. http://www.bsc-eoc.org/norac/atlascont.htm.

——. 1997. Use of public grazing lands by Henslow's Sparrows, Grasshopper Sparrows, and associated grassland species in central New York State. Pages 171–186 *in* Grasslands of northeastern North America: ecology and conservation of native and agricultural landscapes (P. D. Vickery and P. W. Dunwiddie, Eds.). Massachusetts Audubon Society, Lincoln, MA.

——. 1998a. American Crow (*Corvus brachyrhynchos*). Pages 390–392 *in* Bull's birds of New York State (E. Levine, Ed.). Comstock Publishing Associates, Ithaca, NY.

——. 1998b. Henslow's Sparrow (*Ammodramus henslowii*). Pages 514–516 *in* Bull's birds of New York State (E. Levine, Ed.). Comstock Publishing Associates, Ithaca, NY.

——. 1998c. Red-winged Blackbird (*Agelaius phoeniceus*). Pages 545–546 *in* Bull's birds of New York State (E. Levine, Ed.). Comstock Publishing Associates, Ithaca, NY.

——. 1998d. The role of the Federation in conservation of New York birds: the past twenty years. Pages 42–55 *in* Bull's birds of New York State (E. Levine, Ed.). Cornell University Press, Ithaca, NY.

——. 1998e. Savannah Sparrow (*Passerculus sandwichensis*). Pages 511–512 *in* Bull's birds of New York State (E. Levine, Ed.). Comstock Publishing Associates, Ithaca, NY.

——. 1998f. Upland Sandpiper (*Bartramia longicauda*). Pages 241–243 *in* Bull's birds of New York State (E. Levine, Ed.). Comstock Publishing Associates, Ithaca, NY.

——. 2006. Successful use of artificial nesting structure by Dark-eyed Junco with comments on junco summer distribution in New York. Kingbird 56:122–125.

Smith, C. R., and A. M. Byrne. 1999. An annotated checklist for birds of Cornell Plantations. Cornell University, Ithaca, NY.

Smith, C. R., S. D. DeGloria, M. E. Richmond, S. K. Gregory, M. Laba, S. D. Smith, J. L. Braden, E. H. Fegraus, J. J. Fiore, E. A. Hill, D. E. Ogurcak, and J. T. Weber. 2001. The New York Gap Analysis Project final report. New York Cooperative Fish and Wildlife Research Unit, Cornell University, Ithaca, NY.

Smith, C. R., and S. K. Gregory. 1998. Bird habitats in New York State. Pages 29–41 *in* Bull's birds of New York State (E. Levine, Ed.). Cornell University Press, Ithaca, NY.

Smith, C. R., D. M. Pence, and R. J. O'Connor. 1993. Status of Neotropical migratory birds in the Northeast: a preliminary assessment. Pages 172–188 *in* Status and management of Neotropical migratory birds (D. M. Finch and P. W. Stangel, Eds.). USDA Forest Service general technical report. RM-229. Rocky Mountain Forest and Range Experiment Station, Fort Collins, CO.

Smith, G. A. 1988a. Red-shouldered Hawk (*Buteo lineatus*). Pages 110–111 *in* The atlas of breeding birds in New York State (R. F. Andrle and J. R. Carroll, Eds.). Cornell University Press, Ithaca, NY.

——. 1988b. Sharp-shinned Hawk (*Accipiter striatus*). Pages 104–105 *in* The atlas of breeding birds in New York State (R. F. Andrle and J. R. Carroll, Eds.). Cornell University Press, Ithaca, NY.

Smith, G. A., K. Karwowski, and G. Maxwell. 1984. The current breeding sites of the Common Tern in the international sector of the St. Lawrence River, eastern Lake Ontario, and Oneida Lake. Kingbird 34:18–31.

Smith, K. G., J. H. Withgott, and P. G. Rodewald. 2000. Red-headed Woodpecker (*Melanerpes erythrocephalus*). *In* The birds of North America, no. 518 (A. Poole and F. Gill, Eds.). The Birds of North America, Inc., Philadelphia, PA.

Smith, P. W. 1987. The Eurasian Collared-Dove arrives in the Americas. American Birds 41:1370–1379.

Smith, S. M. 1993. Black-capped Chickadee (*Poecile atricapillus*). *In* The birds of North America, no. 39 (A. Poole, P. Stettenheim, and F. Gill, Eds.). The Academy of Natural Sciences, Philadelphia, PA, and The American Ornithologists' Union, Washington, DC.

Snyder, N. F. R., H. A. Snyder, J. L. Lincer, and R. T. Reynolds. 1973. Organochlorines, heavy metals, and the biology of North American accipiters. BioScience 23:300–305.

Solymár, B. D., and J. D. McCracken. 2002. Draft national recovery plan for the Barn Owl and its habitat: (*Tyto alba*) Ontario population. Recovery of Nationally Endangered Wildlife Committee, Bird Studies Canada. http://www.bsc-eoc.org/baowplan.html.

Sommers, L. A., M. Alfieri, K. Meskill, and R. Miller. 1996. 1995 Long Island colonial waterbird and Piping Plover survey. Unpublished report. New York State Department of Environmental Conservation, Stony Brook, NY.

Sommers, L. A., K. Meskill, R. Miller, and M. Alfieri. 1994. 1992–1993 Long Island colonial waterbird and Piping Plover survey. Unpublished report. New York State Department of Environmental Conservation, Stony Brook, NY.

Sommers, L. A., D. L. Rosenblatt, and M. J. DelPuerto. 2001. 1998–1999 Long Island colonial waterbird and Piping Plover survey. Unpublished report. New York State Department of Environmental Conservation, Albany and Stony Brook, NY.

South, J. M., and S. Pruett-Jones. 2000. Patterns of flock size, diet, and vigilance of naturalized Monk Parakeets in Hyde Park, Chicago. Condor 102:848–854.

Spahn, R. G. 1984. Highlights of the summer season. Kingbird 34:233–235.

———. 1988a. Black Tern (*Chlidonias niger*). Pages 184–185 *in* The atlas of breeding birds in New York State (R. F. Andrle and J. R. Carroll, Eds.). Cornell University Press, Ithaca, NY.

———. 1988b. Loggerhead Shrike (*Lanius ludovicianus*). Pages 338–339 *in* The atlas of breeding birds in New York State (R. F. Andrle and J. R. Carroll, Eds.). Cornell University Press, Ithaca, NY.

———. 1998a. Common Eider (*Somateria mollissima*). Pages 166–167 *in* Bull's birds of New York State (E. Levine, Ed.). Comstock Publishing Associates, Ithaca, NY.

———. 1998b. Gadwall (*Anas strepera*). Pages 151–152 *in* Bull's birds of New York State (E. Levine, Ed.). Comstock Publishing Associates, Ithaca, NY.

———. 1998c. Merlin (*Falco columbarius*). Pages 201–203 *in* Bull's birds of New York State (E. Levine, Ed.). Comstock Publishing Associates, Ithaca, NY.

Spofford, W. R. 1960. The White-headed Eagle in New York State. Kingbird 10:148–152.

———. 1971a. The breeding status of the Golden Eagle in the Appalachians. American Birds 25:3–7.

———. 1971b. The Golden Eagle-rediscovered. Conservationist 26(Aug–Sep):6–8.

Spreyer, M. 1994. Mayor Washington's birds: the legendary Monk Parakeets of Chicago's Hyde Park. Birder's World 8(Dec):40–43.

Spreyer, M. F., and E. H. Bucher. 1998. Monk Parakeet (*Myiopsitta monachus*). *In* The birds of North America, no. 322 (A. Poole and F. Gill, Eds.). The birds of North America, Inc., Philadelphia, PA.

Squires, J. R., and R. T. Reynolds. 1997. Northern Goshawk (*Accipiter gentilis*). *In* The birds of North America, no. 298 (A. Poole and F. Gill, Eds.). The Academy of Natural Sciences, Philadelphia, PA, and The American Ornithologists' Union, Washington, DC.

Stalter, R., D. T. Kincaid, and E. E. Lamont. 1991. Life forms of the flora at Hempstead Plains, New York, and a comparison with four other sites. Bulletin of the Torrey Botanical Club 118:191–194.

Stalter, R., and E. E. Lamont. 1987. Vegetation of Hempstead Plains, Mitchell Field, Long Island, New York. Bulletin of the Torrey Botanical Club 114:330–335.

Stanton, B. F., and N. L. Bills. 1996. The return of agricultural lands to forest: changing land use in the twentieth century. Department of Agricultural, Resource, and Managerial Economics, College of Agriculture and Life Sciences, Cornell University, Ithaca, NY.

Steadman, D. W. 1988. Prehistoric birds of New York State. Pages 19–24 *in* The atlas of breeding birds in New York State (R. F. Andrle and J. R. Carroll, Eds.). Cornell University Press, Ithaca, NY.

Stedman, S. M., and J. Hansen. [n.d.]. Habitat connections: wetlands, fisheries and economics, pt. 5:. Wetlands, fisheries and economics of the mid-Atlantic states. http://www.nmfs.noaa.gov/habitat/ habitatconservation/publications/habitatconections/num5.htm.

Steeves, J. B., and S. Holohan. 1975. Wilson's Phalarope nesting range extended to the St. Lawrence Valley in Québec. Canadian Field-Naturalist 89:185.

Stein, R. C. 1958. The behavioral, ecological and morphological characteristics of two populations of the Alder Flycatcher, *Empidonax*

traillii (Audubon). New York State Museum and Science Service Bulletin, no. 371. University of the State of New York, State Education Department, Albany, NY.

———. 1963. Isolating mechanisms between populations of Traill's Flycatchers. Proceedings of the American Philosophical Society 107:21–50.

Stepney, P. H. R., and D. M. Power. 1973. Analysis of the eastward breeding expansion of Brewer's Blackbird plus general aspects of avian expansions. Wilson Bulletin 85:452–464.

Stoner, D. 1932. Ornithology of the Oneida Lake region: with reference to the late spring and summer seasons. Roosevelt Wild Life Annals 2:271–764.

———. 1936. Studies on the Bank Swallow, *Riparia riparia riparia* (Linnaeus) in the Oneida Lake region. Roosevelt Wild Life Annals 4:126–233.

Stoner, S. J. 1998. Least Bittern (*Ixobrychus exilis*). Pages 123–124 *in* Bull's birds of New York State (E. Levine, Ed.). Comstock Publishing Associates, Ithaca, NY.

Storer, R. J. 1966. Sexual dimorphism and food habits in three North American accipiters. Auk 83:423–436.

Stover, M. E., and P. L. Marks. 1998. Successional vegetation on abandoned cultivated and pastured land in Tompkins County, N.Y. Journal of the Torrey Botanical Society 125:150–164.

Straight, C. A., and R. J. Cooper. 2000. Chuck-will's-widow (*Caprimulgus carolinensis*). *In* The birds of North America, no. 499 (A. Poole and F. Gill, Eds.). The Birds of North America, Inc., Philadelphia, PA.

Strickland, D., and H. Ouellet. 1993. Gray Jay (*Perisoreus canadensis*). *In* The birds of North America, no. 40 (A. Poole, P. Stettenheim, and F. Gill, Eds.). The Academy of Natural Sciences, Philadelphia, PA, and The American Ornithologists' Union, Washington, DC.

Sutton, G. M. 1928. Extension of the breeding range of the Turkey Vulture in Pennsylvania. Auk 45:501–503.

Sydenstricker, K. V., A. A. Dhondt, D. H. Ley, and G. V. Kollias. 2005. Re-exposure of captive house finches that recovered from *Mycoplasma gallisepticum* infection. Journal of Wildlife Diseases 41:326–333.

Tacha, T. C., S. A. Nesbitt, and P. A. Vohs. 1992. Sandhill Crane (*Grus canadensis*). *In* The birds of North America, no. 31 (A. Poole, P. Stettenheim, and F. Gill, Eds.). The Academy of Natural Sciences, Philadelphia, PA, and The American Ornithologists' Union, Washington, DC.

Tarvin, K. A., and G. E. Woolfenden. 1999. Blue Jay (*Cyanocitta cristata*). *In* The birds of North America, no. 469 (A. Poole and F. Gill, Eds.). The Birds of North America, Inc., Philadelphia, PA.

Telfair, R. C., II. 2006. Cattle Egret (*Bubulcus ibis*). *In* The birds of North America online (A. Poole, Ed.). Cornell Lab of Ornithology, Ithaca, NY. http://bna.birds.cornell.edu/BNA/account/Cattle_ Egret/.doi:10.2173/bna.113.

Temple, S. A. 2002. Dickcissel (*Spiza americana*). *In* The birds of North America, no. 703 (A. Poole and F. Gill, Eds.). The Birds of North America, Inc., Philadelphia, PA.

Temple, S. A., and B. L. Temple. 1976. Avian population trends in central New York State, 1935–1972. Bird-Banding 47:238–257.

Tetlow, D. W. 2005. Region 2—Genesee. Kingbird 55:360–364.

Therres, G. D. 1999. Wildlife species of conservation concern in the northeastern United States. Northeast Wildlife 54:93–100.

Thomas, C. D., and J. J. Lennon. 1999. Birds extend their ranges northward. Nature 399:213.

Thomas, C. D., A. M. A. Franco, and J. K. Hill. 2006. Range retractions and extinction in the face of climate warming. Trends in Ecology and Evolution 21:415–416.

Thompson, B. C., J. A. Jackson, J. Burger, L. A. Hill, E. M. Kirsch, and J. L. Atwood. 1997. Least Tern (*Sterna antillarum*). *In* The birds of North America, no. 290 (A. Poole and F. Gill, Eds.). The Academy of Natural Sciences, Philadelphia, PA, and The American Ornithologists' Union, Washington, DC.

Thompson, Z. 1853. Natural history of Vermont. Published by the author, Burlington, VT [Reprinted by Charles E. Tuttle, Rutland, VT, 1971].

Tingley, M. W., D. A. Orwig, R. Field, and G. Motzkin. 2002. Avian response to removal of a forest dominant: consequences of hemlock wooly adelgid infestations. Journal of Biogeography 29:1505–1516.

Titman, R. D. 1999. Red-breasted Merganser (*Mergus serrator*). *In* The birds of North America, no. 443 (A. Poole and F. Gill, Eds.). The Birds of North America, Inc., Philadelphia, PA.

Titus, K., M. R. Fuller, D. F. Stauffer, and J. R. Sauer. 1989. Buteos. Pages 53–64 *in* Proceedings of the Northeast Raptor Management Symposium and Workshop, 16–18 May 1988, Syracuse, NY (B. Pendleton, M. N. LeFranc Jr., M. B. Moss, C. E. Ruibal, M. A. Knighton, and D. L. Krahe, Eds.). National Wildlife Federation Scientific and Technical Series, no. 13. National Wildlife Federation, Washington, DC.

Todd, C. S. 1989. Golden Eagle. Pages 65–70 *in* Proceedings of the Northeast Raptor Management Symposium and Workshop, 16–18 May 1988, Syracuse, NY (B. Pendleton, M. N. LeFranc Jr., M. B. Moss, C. E. Ruibal, M. A. Knighton, and D. L. Krahe, Eds.). National Wildlife Federation Scientific and Technical Series, no. 13. National Wildlife Federation, Washington, DC.

Treacy, E. D. 1973. Region 9—Hudson-Delaware. Kingbird 23:210–213.

Trivelpiece, W., S. Brown, A. Hicks, R. Fekete, and N. J. Volkman. 1979. An analysis of the distribution and reproductive success of the Common Loon in the Adirondack Park, New York. Pages 45–55 *in* The Common Loon: Proceedings of the Second North American Conference on Common Loon Research and Management, January 14–16, 1979, Syracuse, N.Y. (S. Sutcliffe, Ed.). National Audubon Society, New York, NY.

Tuck, L. M. 1972. The Snipes: a study of the genus *Capella*. Canadian Wildlife Service, Ottawa, ON.

Turner, M. G. 2005. Landscape ecology: what is the state of the science? Annual Review of Ecology, Evolution, and Systematics 36:319–344.

Turner, M. G., and R. H. Gardner, Eds. 1991. Quantitative methods in landscape ecology: the analysis and interpretation of landscape heterogeneity. Springer-Verlag, New York, NY.

Tyler, W. M. 1937. Turkey Vulture. Pages 12–28 *in* Life histories of North American birds of prey: order Falconiformes (part 1) (A. C. Bent). U.S. National Museum Bulletin, no. 167. Smithsonian Institution, Washington, DC.

USDI/FWS (U.S. Department of the Interior/Fish and Wildlife Service). 2003. Final environmental impact statement: Double-crested Cormorant management in the United States. U.S. Fish and Wildlife Service, Arlington, VA. http://www.fws.gov/migratorybirds/issues/cormorant/finaleis/cormorantFEIS.pdf.

U.S. Forest Service. 2005. Northeastern forest inventory and analysis—statewide results. http://www.fs.fed.us/ne/fia/states/ny/index.html.

USFWS (U.S. Fish and Wildlife Service). 1987a. Endangered and threatened wildlife and plants; determination: two populations of the Roseate Tern and *Bonamia grandiflora* (Florida bonamia); final rules. U.S. Federal Register 52:211:42064–42071.

———. 1987b. Migratory nongame birds of management concern in the United States: the 1987 list. U.S. Fish and Wildlife Service, Washington, DC.

———. 1996. Piping Plover (*Charadrius melodus*), Atlantic Coast population, revised recovery plan. U.S. Fish and Wildlife Service, Hadley, MA. http://ecos.fws.gov/docs/recovery_plans/1996/960502.pdf.

———. 2002. Birds of conservation concern 2002. Division of Migratory Bird Management, Arlington, VA. http://www.fws.gov/migratorybirds/reports/BCC02/BCC2002.pdf.

———. 2003. Recovery plan for the Great Lakes Piping Plover (*Charadrius melodus*). U.S. Fish and Wildlife Service, Great Lakes–Big River Region, Ft. Snelling, MN. http://ecos.fws.gov/docs/recovery_plans/2003/030916a.pdf.

———. 2004. U.S. Shorebird Conservation Plan. High priority shorebirds—2004. Unpublished report. U.S. Fish and Wildlife Service, Arlington, VA. http://www.fws.gov/shorebirdplan/USShorebird/downloads/ShorebirdPriorityPopulationsAug04.pdf.

———. 2006a. North American Waterfowl Management Plan. http://www.fws.gov/birdhabitat/NAWMP/index.shtm.

———. 2006b. The 2005 North American Trumpeter Swan Survey (T. Moser, compiler). U.S. Fish and Wildlife Service, Division of Migratory Bird Management, Denver, CO. http://library.fws.gov/Bird_Publications/trumpeterswan_survey05.pdf.

———. 2006c. Waterfowl population status, 2006. U.S. Department of the Interior, Washington, DC. http://library.fws.gov/Bird_Publications/waterfowl_population06.pdf.

———. 2007. Removing the Bald Eagle in the lower 48 states from the list of endangered and threatened wildlife; final rule. http://www.fws.gov/migratorybirds/issues/BaldEagle/baldeaglefinaldelisting.pdf.

Vallender, R., R. J. Robertson, V. L. Friesen, and I. J. Lovette. 2007. Complex hybridization dynamics between Golden-winged and Blue-winged warblers (*Vermivora chrysoptera* and *Vermivora pinus*) revealed by AFLP, microsatellite, intron and mtDNA markers. Molecular Ecology 16:2017–2029.

Van Bael, S., and S. Pruett-Jones. 1996. Exponential population growth of Monk Parakeets in the United States. Wilson Bulletin 108:584–588.

Van Horn, M. A., and T. M. Donovan. 1994. Ovenbird (*Seiurus aurocapillus*). *In* The birds of North America, no. 88 (A. Poole and F. Gill, Eds.). The Academy of Natural Sciences, Philadelphia, PA, and The American Ornithologists' Union, Washington, DC.

Van Turnhout, C. A. M., R. P. B. Foppen, R. S. E. W. Leuven, H. Siepel, and H. Esselink. 2007. Scale-dependent homogenization: changes in breeding bird diversity in the Netherlands over a 25-year period. Biological Conservation 134:505–516.

Veit, W. R., and W. R. Petersen. 1993. Birds of Massachusetts. Massachusetts Audubon Society, Lincoln, MA.

Vellend, M. 2002. A pest and an invader: white-tailed deer (*Odocoileus virginianus* Zimm.) as a seed dispersal agent for honeysuckle shrubs (*Lonicera* L.). Natural Areas Journal 22:230–234.

Verbeek, N. A. M., and C. Caffrey. 2002. American Crow (*Corvus brachyrhynchos*). *In* The birds of North America, no. 647 (A. Poole and F. Gill, Eds.). The Birds of North America, Inc., Philadelphia, PA.

Vermeer, K. 1970. Breeding biology of California and Ring-billed gulls: a study of ecological adaptation to the inland habitat. Canadian Wildlife Services Report Series, no. 12. Queen's Printer for Canada, Ottawa, ON.

Vickery, P. D. 1996. Grasshopper Sparrow (*Ammodramus savannarum*). *In* The birds of North America, no. 239 (A. Poole and F. Gill, Eds.). The Academy of Natural Sciences, Philadelphia, PA, and The American Ornithologists' Union, Washington, DC.

Victoria, J. 2005. 2005 Piping Plover/Least Tern nesting season results. Connecticut Department of Environmental Protection press release (10/31/05). http://www.ct.gov/dep/cwp/view.asp?A=27118&Q=324516.

Vierling, K. T. 1999. Habitat quality, population density and habitat-specific productivity of Red-winged Blackbirds (*Agelaius phoeniceus*) in Boulder County, Colorado. American Midland Naturalist 142:401–409.

Walsh, J., V. Elia, R. Kane, and T. Halliwell. 1999. Birds of New Jersey. New Jersey Audubon Society, Bernardsville, NJ.

Walters, E. L., E. H. Miller, and P. E. Lowther. 2002. Yellow-bellied Sapsucker (*Sphyrapicus varius*). *In* The birds of North America, no. 662 (A. Poole and F. Gill, Eds.). The Birds of North America, Inc., Philadelphia, PA.

Walther, G. R., S. Berger, and M. T. Sykes. 2005. An ecological "footprint" of climate change. Proceedings of the Royal Society of London B—Biological Sciences 272:1427–1432.

Warkentin, I. G., N. S. Sodhi, R. H. M. Espie, A. F. Poole, and P. C. James. 2005. Merlin (*Falco columbarius*). *In* The birds of North America online (A. Poole, Ed.). Cornell Lab of Ornithology, Ithaca, NY. http://bna.birds.cornell.edu/BNA/account/Merlin/. doi:10.2173/bna.44.

Washburn, B. E., R. A. Dolbeer, and G. E. Bernhardt. 2005. Laughing Gull nest population in Jamaica Bay, New York, 1992–2005. Special report for the Port Authority of New York and New Jersey John F. Kennedy International Airport. Unpublished report. U.S. Department of Agriculture, National Wildlife Research Center, Sandusky, OH.

Watson, W. 2001. Upstate New York's first Great Egret colony. Kingbird 51:648–660.

Watts, B. D. 1995. Yellow-crowned Night-Heron (*Nyctanassa violacea*). *In* The birds of North America, no. 161 (A. Poole and F. Gill, Eds.). The Academy of Natural Sciences, Philadelphia, PA, and The American Ornithologists' Union, Washington, DC.

Weatherhead, P. J. 2005. Long-term decline in a Red-winged Blackbird population: ecological causes and sexual selection consequences. Proceedings of the Royal Society of London B—Biological Sciences 272:2313–2317.

Weatherhead, P. J., and J. R. Bider. 1979. Management options for blackbird problems in agriculture. Phytoprotection 60:145–155.

Webb, W. L., D. F. Behrend, and B. Saisorn. 1977. Effects of logging on songbird populations in a northeastern hardwood forest. Wildlife Monographs, no. 55:3–35.

Wedgwood, J. A. 1992. Common Nighthawks in Saskatoon. Blue Jay 50:211–217.

Weeks, H. P. Jr. 1994. Eastern Phoebe (*Sayornis phoebe*). *In* The birds of North America online (A. Poole, Ed.). Cornell Lab of Ornithology, Ithaca, NY. http://bna.birds.cornell.edu/BNA/account/Eastern_Phoebe/.doi:10.2173/bna.94.

Weldy, T., and D. Werier. 2005. New York flora atlas. New York Flora Association, Albany, NY. http://atlas.nyflora.org/.

Weller, M. W. 1964. Distribution and migration of the Redhead. Journal of Wildlife Management 28:64–103.

Wells, J. V. 1998. Important Bird Areas in New York State. National Audubon Society, Albany, NY.

———. 2007. Birder's conservation handbook: 100 North American birds at risk. Princeton University Press, Princeton, NJ.

Wells, J. V., and K. J. McGowan. 1991. Range expansion in Fish Crow (*Corvus ossifragus*): the Ithaca, NY, colony as an example. Kingbird 41:73–82.

Welsh, C. J. E., and W. M. Healy. 1993. Effect of even-aged timber management on bird species diversity and composition in northern hardwoods of New Hampshire. Wildlife Society Bulletin 21:143–154.

Whan, B., and G. Rising. 2002. Should Trumpeter Swans be introduced to the eastern United States and Canada? No. Birding 34:338–340.

Wheat, M. C. Jr. 1979. Pronothotary Warbler breeding on Long Island. Kingbird 29:190–191.

Wheelwright, N. T., and J. D. Rising. 1993. Savannah Sparrow (*Passerculus sandwichensis*). *In* The birds of North America, no. 45 (A. Poole and F. Gill, Eds.). The Academy of Natural Sciences, Philadelphia, PA, and The American Ornithologists' Union, Washington, DC.

White, C. M., N. J. Clum, T. J. Cade, and W. G. Hunt. 2002. Peregrine Falcon (*Falco peregrinus*). *In* The birds of North America, no. 660 (A. Poole and F. Gill, Eds.). The Birds of North America, Inc., Philadelphia, PA.

Whitehead, D. R., and T. Taylor. 2002. Acadian Flycatcher (*Empidonax virescens*). *In* The birds of North America, no. 614 (A. Poole and F. Gill, Eds.). The Birds of North America, Inc., Philadelphia, PA.

Whitney, G. G. 1994. From coastal wilderness to fruited plain: a history of environmental change in temperate North America, 1500 to the present. Cambridge University Press, Cambridge, UK.

Whitt, M. B., H. H. Prince, and R. R. Cox Jr. 1999. Avian use of purple loosestrife dominated habitat relative to other vegetation types in a Lake Huron wetland complex. Wilson Bulletin 111:105–114.

Whittaker, R. H., S. A. Levin, and R. B. Root. 1973. Niche, habitat, and ecotope. American Naturalist 107:321–338.

Wiens, J. A. 1969. An approach to the study of ecological relationships among grassland birds. Ornithological Monographs, no. 8:1–93.

Wiese, J. H. 1978. Heron nest-site selection and its ecological effects. Pages 27–34 *in* Wading birds (A. Sprunt, J. Ogden, and S. Winckler, Eds.). National Audubon Society, New York, NY.

Wiggins, D. A. 2004. Short-eared Owl (*Asio flammeus*): a technical conservation assessment. USDA Forest Service, Rocky Mountain Region. http://www.fs.fed.us/r2/projects/scp/assessments/shortearedowl.pdf.

Wilcox, L. 1939. Notes on the life history of the Piping Plover. Birds of Long Island, no. 1:3–13.

——. 1980. Observation on the life history of Willets on Long Island, NY. Wilson Bulletin 92:253–258.

Wilde, S. B., T. M. Murphy, C. P. Hope, S. K. Habrun, J. Kempton, A. Birrenkott, F. Wiley, W. W. Bowerman, and A. J. Lewitus. 2005. Avian vacuolar myelinopathy linked to exotic aquatic plants and a novel cyanobacterial species. Environmental Toxicology 20:348–353.

Will, G. B., R. D. Stumvoll, R. F. Gotie, and E. S. Smith. 1982. The ecological zones of northern New York. New York Fish and Game Journal 29:1–25.

Williams, J. M. 1996. Nashville Warbler (*Vermivora ruficapilla*). *In* The birds of North America, no. 205 (A. Poole and F. Gill, Eds.). The Academy of Natural Sciences, Philadelphia, PA, and The American Ornithologists' Union, Washington, DC.

Wilson, J. E. 1959. The status of the Hungarian Partridge in New York. Kingbird 9:54–57.

Wilson, M. D., and B. D. Watts. 2006. Effect of moonlight on detection of Whip-poor-wills: implications for long-term monitoring strategies. Journal of Field Ornithology 77:207–211.

Wilson, W. H. Jr. 1996. Palm Warbler (*Dendroica palmarum*). *In* The birds of North America, no. 238 (A. Poole and F. Gill, Eds.). The Academy of Natural Sciences, Philadelphia, PA, and The American Ornithologists' Union, Washington, DC.

Windsor, D. A. 1998a. House Sparrow (*Passer domesticus*). Pages 574–576 *in* Bull's birds of New York State (E. Levine, Ed.). Comstock Publishing Associates, Ithaca, NY.

——. 1998b. Sharp-shinned Hawk (*Accipter striatus*). Pages 186–188 *in* Bull's birds of New York State (E. Levine, Ed.). Cornell University Press, Ithaca, NY.

Wires, L. R., and F. J. Cuthbert. 2006. Historic populations of the Double-crested Cormorant (*Phalacrocorax auritus*): implications for conservation and management in the 21st century. Waterbirds 29:9–37.

Wires, L. R., F. J. Cuthbert, D. R. Trexel, and A. R. Joshi. 2001. Status of the Double-crested Cormorant (*Phalacrocorax auritus*) in North America. Final report to the U.S. Fish and Wildlife Service, Nov. 2001. Fort Snelling, MN. http://library.fws.gov/Bird_Publications/cormorant_status01.pdf.

Witmer, M. C., D. J. Mountjoy, and L. Elliott. 1997. Cedar Waxwing (*Bombycilla cedrorum*). *In* The birds of North America, no. 309 (A. Poole, and F. Gill, Eds.). The Academy of Natural Sciences, Philadelphia, PA, and The American Ornithologists' Union, Washington, DC.

Wood, P. B., C. Viverette, L. Goodrich, M. Pokras, and C. Tibbott. 1996. Environmental contaminant levels in Sharp-shinned Hawks from the eastern United States. Journal of Raptor Research 30:136–144.

Woodin, M. C., and T. C. Michot. 2002. Redhead (*Aythya americana*). *In* The birds of North America, no. 695 (A. Poole and F. Gill, Eds.). The Birds of North America, Inc., Philadelphia, PA.

Wootton, J. T. 1996. Purple Finch (*Carpodacus purpureus*). *In* The birds of North America, no. 208 (A. Poole and F. Gill, Eds.). The Academy of Natural Sciences, Philadelphia, PA, and The American Ornithologists' Union, Washington, DC.

Wyatt, V. E., and C. M. Francis. 2002. Rose-breasted Grosbeak (*Pheucticus ludovicianus*). *In* The birds of North America, no. 692 (A. Poole and F. Gill, Eds.). The Birds of North America, Inc., Philadelphia, PA.

Yandik, W. 2005. Region 8—Hudson-Mohawk. Kingbird 55:387–390.

Yank, R., and Y. Aubry. 1985. The nesting season, June 1–July 31, 1985: Quebec region. American Birds 39:889–890.

Yaremych, S. A., R. E. Warner, P. C. Mankin, J. D. Brawn, A. Raim, and R. Novak. 2004. West Nile virus and high death rates in American Crows. Emerging Infectious Diseases 10:709–711.

Yarrell, W. 1871. History of British birds, 4th ed., vol. 1. Revised and enlarged by Alfred Newton and Howard Saunders. J. Fan Voort, London, UK.

Yasukawa, K., and W. A. Searcy. 1995. Red-winged Blackbird (*Agelaius phoeniceus*). *In* The birds of North America, no. 184 (A. Poole and F. Gill, Eds.). The Birds of North America, Inc., Philadelphia, PA, and The American Ornithologists' Union, Washington, DC.

Yosef, R. 1996. Loggerhead Shrike (*Lanius ludovicianus*). *In* The birds of North America, no. 231 (A. Poole and F. Gill, Eds.). The Academy of Natural Sciences, Philadelphia, PA, and The American Ornithologists' Union, Washington, DC.

Young, M. A., and J. Weeks. 2005. Region 4—Susquehanna. Kingbird 55:280–288.

Yunick, R. P. 1984. An assessment of the irruptive status of the Boreal Chickadee in New York State. Journal of Field Ornithology 55:31–37.

Zarudsky, J. D. 1980. Town of Hempstead colonial bird nesting survey, 1980. Unpublished report. Town of Hempstead Department of Conservation and Waterways, Point Lookout, NY.

——. 1981. Forster's Tern breeding on Long Island. Kingbird 31:212–213.

——. 1985. Breeding status of the American Oystercatcher in the town of Hempstead. Kingbird 35:105–113.

Zarudsky, J. D., and R. Miller 1983. Nesting Boat-tailed Grackles on Pearsall's Hassock. Kingbird 33:2–5.

Zeranski, J. D., and T. R. Baptist. 1990. Connecticut birds. University Press of New England, Hanover, NH.

Zerega, L. A. 1882. The nighthawk in cities [Letter to the editor]. Forest and Stream 18(23 Jul):467.

Zuckerberg, B. 2008. Long-term changes in the distributions of breeding birds in response to regional reforestation and climate change in New York State. Ph.D. dissertation, State University of New York College of Environmental Science and Forestry, Syracuse, NY.

Index

COMPILED BY DONALD A. WINDSOR

Bold page numbers indicate location of the
   main species accounts.

Accipiter cooperii 81, **194**, 636
   A. gentilis 81, **196**, 637
   A. striatus **192**, 636
Acid rain 82
   and American Black Duck 100
   and Bicknell's Thrush 442
   and Blackpoll Warbler 506
   and Common Goldeneye 122
   and Hermit Thrush 446
   and Louisiana Waterthrush 522
   and Swainson's Thrush 442
   and Wood Thrush 448
Acknowledgments xi–xxii
Actitis macularius **238**, 637
Adelgid, woolly, degrading habitat 67
   for Black-throated Green Warbler 492
   for Blackburnian Warbler 494
   for Louisiana Waterthrush 522
Adirondacks Ecozone 49
Adirondacks
   Central sub-ecozone 50
   Eastern Foothills sub-ecozone 50
   Eastern Transition sub-ecozone 50
   High Peaks sub-ecozone 50
   Western Foothills sub-ecozone 49
   Western Transition sub-ecozone 49
Aegolius acadicus 298, **302**, 638
Agelaius phoeniceus 66, **590**, 641
Agriculture 38, 44, 45, 48, 49, 50, 51, 52, 59, 60,
   61, 62, 63–65, 66, 68, 76, 81, 82
Airplane collisions with Laughing Gull 252
Aix sponsa **94**, 100, 635
Alauda arvensis 631
Allegany Hills sub-ecozone 44–45
Ammodramus caudacutus 76, 80, **560**, 640
   A. henslowii 3, 6, 28, 76, 81, **558**, 640
   A. maritimus 3, **562**, 640
   A. nelsoni 25, **631**
   A. savannarum 81, **556**, 640
Anas acuta **110**, 635
   A. americana **98**, 635
   A. clypeata **108**, 635
   A. crecca **112**, 635
   A. discors 77, **106**, 635
   A. platyrhynchos 77, 100, **102**, 104, 635
   A. platyrhynchos x *A. rubripes* 104
   A. rubripes 77, 83, **100**, 104, 635
   A. strepera **96**, 635
Appalachian Mountains Bird Conservation
   Region 52
Appalachian Plateau Ecozone 44–45

Appalachians, Central sub-ecozone 45
Aquila chrysaetos 3, **204**, 637
Archilochus colubris **314**, 638
Ardea alba 80, **162**, 164, 636
   A. herodias **160**, 636
Artists, list of xiii–xv
Asio flammeus 3, 81, **300**, 638
   A. otus 3, 81, **298**, 638
Atlantic Northern Forest Bird Conservation
   Region 52
Atlas annual summary reports 4
Atlas methodology, planning, and management 1
Authors, list of xii–xiii
Aythya affinis **625**, 636
   A. americana **116**, 636
   A. collaris **118**, 636
   A. marila 20, **625**
   A. valisineria 20, **114**, 636

Baeolophus bicolor 28, 41, **410**, 434, 639
Bare soil birds 66
Bartramia longicauda 3, 6, 28, **242**, 637
Beaver 62–63
   and American Bittern 156
   and American Black Duck 100
   and Great Blue Heron 160
   and Hooded Merganser 124
   and Lincoln's Sparrow 566
   and Mallard 102
   and Nashville Warbler 476
   and Northern Waterthrush 520
   and Olive-sided Flycatcher 340
   and Pied-billed Grebe 150
   and Red-headed Woodpecker 320
   and Rusty Blackbird 594
   and Wood Duck 94
Biases 4
Bird Banding 72
Bird Conservation Regions 13, 52
Bittern, American 3, 77, 83, **156**, 636
   Least 3, 83, **158**, 636
Black River Valley sub-ecozone 48
Blackbird, Brewer's 20, 633
   Red-winged 37, 66, **590**, 641
   Rusty 82, **594**, 641
Blocks, grid, Atlas 2
Blowfly on Barn Swallow 402
Bluebird, Eastern 28, 63, **438**, 639
Bobolink 66, 81, **588**, 641
Bobwhite, Northern 38, 81, **144**, 636
Bombycilla cedrorum **462**, 639
Bonasa umbellus 138, 636
Books, ornithology 69
Botaurus lentiginosus 3, 77, 83, **156**, 636

Botulism 80
   in Caspian Tern 264
   in Double-crested Cormorant 152
Branta canadensis 28, **88**, 635
Breeding Bird Survey 5–6, 38, 40, 41, 71–72,
   75, 77, 80, 81, 82
Breeding codes 2
Breeding dates, all species 635–641
Broods, number of 635–641
Bubo virginianus 6, 186, **294**, 296, 298, 638
Bubulcus ibis 80, **170**, 636
Bucephala albeola 20, **626**
   B. clangula 77, **122**, 636
Budworm, black-headed, food for Bay-breasted
   Warbler 504
Budworm, spruce 82
   and Bay-breasted Warbler 504
   and Blackpoll Warbler 506
   and Black-throated Green Warbler 492
   and Cape May Warbler 486
   and Evening Grosbeak 620
   and Purple Finch 608
   and Spruce Grouse 140
   and Tennessee Warbler 474
Bufflehead 20, 626
Buildings 57
   as nest site for American Kestrel 206
   as nest site for Barn Owl 290
   as nest site for Barn Swallow 402
   as nest site for Black Vulture 182
   as nest site for Chimney Swift 312
   as nest site for Cliff Swallow 400
   as nest site for Common Nighthawk 306
   as nest site for Killdeer 234
   as nest site for Peregrine Falcon 210
   as nest site for Rock Pigeon 278
   as nest site for Osprey 186
   as nest site for Turkey Vulture 184
Bunting, Indigo 67, **582**, 641
Buteo jamaicensis **202**, 637
   B. lineatus 81, **198**, 202, 637
   B. platypterus **200**, 637
Butorides virescens **172**, 636

Canvasback 20, **114**, 636
Caprimulgus carolinensis 3, **308**, 638
   C. vociferus 3, 81–82, 308, **310**, 638
Cardinal, Northern 67, 434, **576**, 641
Cardinalis cardinalis 67, 434, **576**, 641
Carduelis carduelis 634
   C. pinus **616**, 641
   C. tristis 66, **618**, 636
Carpodacus mexicanus 70, 608, **610**, 641
   C. purpureus **608**, 641

Catbird, Gray 37, **454**, 458, 639
Caterpillar, forest tent, food for
    cuckoos 284, 286
    Bay-breasted Warbler 504
Cathartes aura 28, **184**, 636
Catharus bicknelli 3, 52, 76, 82–83, **442**, 639
    C. fuscescens **440**, 639
    C. guttatus 446, 639
    C. ustulatus 444, 639
Catskill Peaks sub-ecozone 45
Cattaraugus Highlands sub-ecozone 44
Certhia americana 66, 68, **416**, 424, 639
Chaetura pelagica **312**, 638
Champlain Transition sub-ecozone 49
Champlain Valley Ecozone 49
    sub-ecozone 49
Charadrius melodus 76, 80, **232**, 637
    C. vociferus 37, 63, 66, **234**, 637
Chat, Yellow-breasted 3, **536**, 640
Chickadee, Black-capped **406**, 528, 639
    Boreal **408**, 639
"Chicken hawk," *see* Hawk, Cooper's **194**
Chlidonias leucopterus 25, **627**
    C. niger 77, 83, **266**, 627–628, 637
Chordeiles minor 3, **306**, 638
Chuck-will's-widow 3, **308**, 638
Circus cyaneus 3, **190**, 636
Cistothorus palustris 6, **428**, 639
    C. platensis 3, **426**, 639
Citizen Science 70
Climate change 40, 41–42
Coastal Lowlands Ecozone 51–52
Coccothraustes vespertinus **620**, 641
Coccyzus americanus 67, **284**, 286, 637
    C. erythropthalmus 284, **286**, 637
Colaptes auratus **334**, 638
Colinus virginianus 38, 81, **144**, 636
Collared-Dove, Eurasian 25, 628
Columba livia **278**, 637
Competition
    Blue-winged and Golden-winged Warblers
      466
    and Eastern Screech-Owl 292
    with European Starling 292, 320, 334, 438
    and Great Crested Flycatcher 356
    with House Sparrow 392, 422, 438
    and Laughing Gull 252
    Mallard and American Black Duck 77
    Piping Plover and humans 232
Confirmed breeding, definition 2–3
Conjunctivitis, *see* Eye disease, House Finch 610
Conservation of breeding birds, priorities 76
Contopus cooperi 82, **340**, 638
    C. virens 67, **342**, 356, 638
Contributors, list of xvi–xxii
Conure, Nanday, *see* Parakeet, Black-hooded **630**
Coot, American 77, **226**, 637
Coragyps atratus 25, **182**, 636
Cormorant, Double-crested 6, 28, 71, **152**, 186,
    254, 268, 636
Cornell Lab of Ornithology 70
Corvus brachyrhynchos 292, 306, 380, **382**, 384, 639
    C. corax 6, 28, 38, 40, 61, **386**, 639
    C. ossifragus 6, **384**, 639
Coverage 15
Cowbird, Brown-headed 3, **600**, 641

Crane, Sandhill 25, **228**, 637
Creeper, Brown 66, 68, **416**, 424, 639
Crossbill, Red 71, **612**, 614, 641
    White-winged 71, 612, **614**, 641
Crow, American 292, 306, 380, **382**, 384, 639
    Fish 6, **384**, 639
Cuckoo, Black-billed 284, **286**, 637
    Yellow-billed 67, **284**, 286, 637
Cyanocitta cristata **380**, 638
Cygnus buccinator 3, 25, **92**, 635
    C. olor 77, **90**, 635

Data collection 1
    entry and processing 4–5
DDE
    in Cooper's Hawk tissues 194
    in Sharp-shinned Hawk tissues 192
DDT
    and Bald Eagle 188
    and Black-throated Green Warbler 492
    and Cedar Waxwing 462
    and Common Loon 148
    and Cooper's Hawk 194
    and Double-crested Cormorant 152
    and Sharp-shinned Hawk 192
DEC (New York State Department of
    Environmental Conservation) 70
Deer
    and Black Vulture 182
    ecological impact 67, 82
    overbrowsing reduces habitat for Black-and
      white Warbler 510
    overbrowsing reduces habitat for Canada
      Warbler 534
    overbrowsing reduces habitat for Eastern
      Wood-Pewee 342
    overbrowsing reduces habitat for Hooded
      Warbler 530
    overbrowsing reduces habitat for Kentucky
      Warbler 524
    and Turkey Vulture 184
Delaware Hills sub-ecozone 45
Dendroica caerulescens 40, 82, **488**, 640
    D. castanea 3, **504**, 640
    D. cerulea 67, 76, 82, 83, **508**, 640
    D. coronata **490**, 640
    D. discolor 81, **500**, 640
    D. dominica 3, **496**, 640
    D. fusca **494**, 640
    D. magnolia **484**, 640
    D. palmarum 3, 40, **502**, 640
    D. pensylvanica **482**, 640
    D. petechia 25, **480**, 639
    D. pinus **498**, 640
    D. striata **506**, 640
    D. tigrina 3, 25, 82, **486**, 640
    D. virens **492**, 640
Dickcissel 25, **584**, 641
Disease
    effects on American Coot 226
    effects on American Crow 382
    effects on bees and Olive-sided Flycatcher
      340
    effects on Blue Jay 380
    effects on Fish Crow 384
    effects on House Finch 70, 610

    effects on tree species 67
    effects on Wild Turkey 142
DNA analysis of hybrids 470–473
Dolichonyx oryzivorus 66, 81, **588**, 641
Dove, Mourning 25, **280**, 637
Drumlin sub-ecozone 48
Dryocopus pileatus 38, 61, 324, **336**, 638
Duck, American Black 77, 83, **100**, 104, 635
    Mallard x American Black hybrid **104**
    Ring-necked **118**, 636
    Ruddy 3, 77 **130**, 636
    Wood **94**, 100, 635
Dumetella carolinensis 37, **454**, 458, 639

Eagle, Bald 6, 28, 70, 72, 81, **188**, 636
    Golden 3, **204**, 637
Eastern Ontario Plain sub-ecozone 48
Ecological Communities 52–57
    Estuarine 53
    Lacustrine 54
    Marine 53
    Palustrine 54–55
    Riverine 53–54
    Subterranean 57
    Terrestrial 55–57
Ecoregions 43–44
    Great Lakes 43
    High Allegheny Plateau 43
    Lower New England–Northern Piedmont 44
    North Atlantic Coast 44
    Northern Appalachian–Boreal Forest 43
    St. Lawrence–Champlain Valley 44
    Western Allegheny Plateau 43
Ecoregions and Ecozones, difference between
    44
Ecoregions map 12
Ecozones 44–57
    Adirondacks 49
    Appalachian Plateau 44
    Champlain Valley 49
    Coastal Lowlands 51–52
    Great Lakes Plain 45
    Hudson Highlands 51
    Hudson Valley 50
    Manhattan Hills 51
    Mohawk Valley 50
    St. Lawrence Plains 48
    Taconic Highlands 51
    Triassic Lowlands 51
    Tug Hill Plateau 48
Ecozones map 12
Ectopistes migratorius 61, 629
Effort analysis 15
Egg dates, species list 635–641
Egret, Cattle 80, **170**, 636
    Great 80, **162**, 164, 636
    Snowy **164**, 636
Egretta caerulea 80, **166**, 636
    E. thula **164**, 636
    E. tricolor **168**, 636
Eider, Common 25, **120**, 636
Electrocution
    of Golden Eagle 204
    of Osprey 186
Empidonax alnorum **348**, 350, 638
    E. flaviventris **344**, 638

E. minimus 37, 67, **352**, 638
E. traillii 81, 348, **350**, 638
E. virescens **346**, 638
Eremophila alpestris 38, 63, 66, **390**, 639
Erie-Ontario Plain sub-ecozone 48
Estuarine System Ecological Community 53
Euphagus carolinus 82, **594**, 641
    E. cyanocephalus 20, **633**
Eye disease, House Finch 70, 610

Falcipennis canadensis 3, 82, **140**, 196, 636
Falco columbarius 25, 81, **208**, 637
    F. peregrinus 6, 28, 70, 81, **210**, 637
    F. sparverius 63, **206**, 637
Falcon, Peregrine 6, 28, 70, 81, **210**, 637
Farm acreage, land covers 1980–2004 65
Farm acreage 1985–2004 63
Feather-wetting agents to control Red-winged
    Blackbird 590
Federation of New York Bird Clubs, history 69
Fenitrothan affecting Black-throated Green
    Warbler 492
Field cards and surveying 3
Finch, House 70, 608, **610**, 641
    Purple **608**, 641
Finger Lakes Highlands sub-ecozone 45
First reported breeding in New York State
    Black Rail 214
    Black Vulture 182
    Blue Grosbeak 580
    Boat-tailed Grackle 598
    Canvasback 114
    Cape May Warbler 486
    Caspian Tern 264
    Cattle Egret 170
    Chuck-will's-widow 308
    Common Eider 120
    Forster's Tern 272
    Glossy Ibis 178
    Golden Eagle 204
    Great Black-backed Gull 260
    Great Egret 162
    Green-winged Teal 112
    Horned Lark 390
    Little Blue Heron 166
    Merlin 208
    Monk Parakeet 282
    Northern Mockingbird 456
    Northern Rough-winged Swallow 396
    Palm Warbler 502
    Prothonotary Warbler 514
    Redhead 116
    Ring-billed Gull 254
    Ring-necked duck 118
    Ruddy Duck 130
    Sandhill Crane 228
    Snowy Egret 164
    Summer Tanager 538
    Tennessee Warbler 474
    Tricolored Heron 168
    Trumpeter Swan 92
    Turkey Vulture 184
    Willet 240
    Wilson's Phalarope 248
    Yellow-throated Warbler 496
"Fish hawk," *see* Osprey **186**

Fishing line entanglement of Osprey 186
Fledgling dates, species list 635–641
Flicker, Northern **334**, 638
Flycatcher, Acadian **346**, 638
    Alder **348**, 350, 638
    Great Crested 37, **356**, 638
    Least 37, 67, **352**, 638
    Olive-sided 82, **340**, 638
    Willow 81, 348, **350**, 638
    Yellow-bellied **344**, 638
Forest
    old growth 66
    primary 62
    secondary 62
Forests 11, 55–57, 60–62, 64–66
Fort Drum Military Reservation 15, 306, 310,
    534, 548
Fulica americana 77, **226**, 637

Gadwall **96**, 635
Gallinago delicata **244**, 637
Gallinula chloropus **224**, 637
Gavia immer 6, 72, 77, **148**, 636
Gelochelidon nilotica **262**, 637
Geothlypis trichas **528**, 640
Gnatcatcher, Blue-gray **434**, 639
Goldeneye, Common 77, **122**, 636
Goldfinch, American 66, **618**, 636
    European **634**
Goose, Canada 28, **88**, 635
Goshawk, Northern 81, **196**, 637
Grackle, Boat-tailed **598**, 641
    Common 37, **596**, 641
Grassland species 38–39, 63–64, 76, 81, 83
Great Lakes Ecoregion 43
Great Lakes Plain Ecozone 45–46, 48
Grebe, Pied-billed 3, 77, **150**, 636
Grosbeak, Blue **580**, 641
    Evening **620**, 641
    Rose-breasted 25, **578**, 641
Grouse, Ruffed **138**, 636
    Spruce 3, 82, **140**, 196, 636
Grus canadensis 25, **228**, 637
Guild classifications 38
Gull, Great Black-backed **258**, 637
    Herring **256**, 637
    Laughing 80, **252**, 637
    Ring-billed **254**, 637

Habitat, definition 59
Habitat groups 39
Habitats 43–58
Haematopus palliatus 80, **236**, 637
Haliaeetus leucocephalus 6, 28, 70, 72, 81, **188**, 636
Harrier, Northern 3, **190**, 636
Hawk, Broad-winged **200**, 637
    Cooper's 81, **194**, 636
    Red-shouldered 81, **198**, 202, 637
    Red-tailed **202**, 637
    Sharp-shinned **192**, 636
Hawkwatches 72
Heath Hen, *see* Prairie-Chicken, Greater **626**
Helderberg Highlands sub-ecozone 45
Helmitheros vermivorum 25, **516**, 640
Herbivores, overabundant 66–68
Heron, Great Blue **160**, 636

Green **172**, 636
Little Blue 80, **166**, 636
Night, *see* Night-Heron **174**, **176**
Tricolored **168**, 636
High Allegheny Plateau Ecoregion 43
Hirundo rustica 37, **402**, 639
History
    of Federation of NY State Bird Clubs 69
    of land use 60
    of NY State Ornithological Association 69
Hudson, Central sub-ecozone 50
Hudson Highlands Ecozone 51
Hudson Valley Ecozone 50
Hummingbird, Ruby-throated **314**, 638
Hybrids
    Blue-winged x Golden-winged warblers
        470
    DNA analysis 470–473
    Mallard x American Black Duck **104**
    Sparrow, Chipping x Clay-colored **548**
Hydroprogne caspia 25, 80, **264**, 637
Hylocichla mustelina 25, 76, 82, 84, 446, **448**, 639

IBA (Important Bird Area) 72, 270
Ibis, Glossy 80, **178**, 636
    White-faced 20, **627**
Icteria virens 3, **536**, 640
Icterus galbula **604**, 641
    I. spurius **602**, 641
Important Bird Area (IBA) 72, 270
Incubation periods, species list 635–641
Indian River Lakes sub-ecozone 49
Insecticides
    adverse effects on spruce budworm warblers
        474
    and Eastern Screech-Owl 292
    and Tennessee Warbler 474
    and Yellow-throated Vireo 366
Invasive plants, ecological impact 66–67
Ixobrychus exilis 3, 83, **158**, 636

Jay, Blue **380**, 638
    Gray **378**, 638
Junco, Dark-eyed **572**, 641
Junco hyemalis **572**, 641

Kestrel, American 63, **206**, 637
Killdeer 37, 63, 66, **234**, 637
Kingbird, Eastern 25, **358**, 638
    Western 25, **630**
Kingbird, The 69
Kingfisher, Belted 37, **316**, 638
Kinglet, Golden-crowned **430**, 639
    Ruby-crowned **432**, 639

Lacustrine System Ecological Community 54
Land cover class
    Barren Land 46
    Cultivated Crops 47
    Developed 46
    Forest 46–47
    Grassland/Herbaceous 47
    Open Water 46
    Pasture/Hay 47
    Shrub/Scrub 47
    Wetlands 47

Land, private 83–84
Landscape conversion 62
    degradation 62
    succession 62, 66
Land use 59
Land use, history 60
Land use vs land cover, distinction 59
Lanius ludovicianus 3, 20, 72, **360**, 638
Lark, Horned 38, 63, 66, **390**, 639
    Sky **631**
Larus argentatus **256**, 637
    L. atricilla 80, **252**, 637
    L. delawarensis **254**, 637
    L. marinus **258**, 637
Laterallus jamaicensis 3, 76, 80, **214**, 637
Laws adverse to nesting of Bank Swallows 398
Lead poisoning
    of Bald Eagle 188
    of Golden Eagle 204
Lethal control
    of Brown-headed Cowbird 600
    of Red-winged Blackbird 590
    of Rusty Blackbird 594
Limitations 4
Literature cited 647–682
Loon, Common 6, 72, 77, **148**, 636
Loosestrife, purple
    nesting in by Red-winged Blackbird 590
    positive effects on Swamp Sparrow 568
    threats to American Bittern 156
    threats to American Coot 224
    threats to Black Tern 266
Lophodytes cucullatus **124**, 636
Lower Great Lakes/St. Lawrence Plain Bird
    Conservation Region 52
Lower New England–Northern Piedmont
    Ecoregion 44
Loxia curvirostra 71, **612**, 614, 641
    L. leucoptera 71, 612, **614**, 641

Mallard 77, 100, **102**, 104, 635
Malone Plain sub-ecozone 49
Manhattan Hills Ecozone 51
Maps
    base for descriptive maps 6
    Bird Conservation Areas 13
    citations of data sources 645–646
    cities and roads 7
    ecoregions 12
    ecozones and sub-ecozones 12
    elevation 9
    forest types 11
    human population 8
    land use 11
    NYSOA (*Kingbird*) Regions 7
    person-hours 16–19
    precipitation 10
    public lands 10
    river systems 8
    species richness 27–29, 38
    temperature 9
    watersheds 13
Marine System Ecological Community 53
Martin, Purple **392**, 639
"Meadow-hen, freshwater," *see* Rail, King **218**
    "saltwater," *see* Rail, Clapper **216**

Meadowlark, Eastern 81, **592**, 633, 641
    Western **632**, 641
Megaceryle alcyon 37, **316**, 638
Megascops asio 6, **292**, 298, 638
Melanerpes carolinus 28, 41, **322**, 638
    M. erythrocephalus 6, 28, 82, **320**, 638
Meleagris gallopavo 6, 28, **142**, 636
Melospiza georgiana **568**, 641
    M. lincolnii **566**, 641
    M. melodia 564, 584, 640
Mercury accumulation
    in Bicknell's Thrush 442
    in Louisiana Waterthrush 522
Mercury deposition and effects
    on Blackpoll Warbler 506
    on Wood Thrush 448
Mercury poisoning
    of Osprey 186
    of Sharp-shinned Hawk 192
Merganser, Common **126**, 636
    Hooded **124**, 636
    Red-breasted **128**, 636
Mergus merganser **126**, 636
    M. serrator **128**, 636
Merlin 25, 81, **208**, 637
Migratory groups, changes in 39
Mimus polyglottos **456**, 639
Mistakes 5
Mniotilta varia **510**, 640
Mockingbird, Northern **456**, 639
Mohawk Valley Ecozone 50
Molothrus ater 3, **600**, 641
Mongaup Hills sub-ecozone 45
Moorhen, Common **224**, 637
Mowing kills Northern Harrier chicks 190
Mycoplasma gallisepticum in House Finch eyes
    610
Myiarchus crinitus 37, **356**, 638
Myiopsitta monachus 25, **282**, 637

Nandayus nenday **630**
Nest boxes
    use by American Kestrel 206
    use by Barn Owl 290
    use by Common Merganser 126
    use by Eastern Bluebird 438
    use by Hooded Merganser 124
    use by Tree Swallow 394
    use by Wood Duck 94
Nest predation by gulls and crows 306
Nesting material, old man's beard lichen by
    Northern Parula 478
Nestling dates and periods 635–641
Neversink Highlands sub-ecozone 45
New York Birders 69
New York State Avian Records Committee
    (NYSARC) 69
New York State Department of Environmental
    Conservation (DEC) 70
Night-Heron, Black-crowned 80, **174**, 636
    Yellow-crowned **176**, 636
Nighthawk, Common 3, **306**, 638
North Atlantic Coast Ecoregion 44
Northern Appalachin–Boreal Forest Ecoregion
    43–44
Notable species 3

Nuthatch, Red-breasted **412**, 639
    White-breasted **414**, 639
Nyctanassa violacea **176**, 636
Nycticorax nycticorax 80, **174**, 636
NYSARC (New York State Avian Records
    Committee) 69
NYSOA, history 69

Open lands 63
Oporornis formosus 3, 76, 82, **524**, 640
    O. philadelphia **526**, 640
Oriole, Baltimore **604**, 641
    Orchard **602**, 641
Ornithology 69–73
Osprey 6, 28, 81, **186**, 636
Oswego Lowlands sub-ecozone 48
Ovenbird 68, **518**, 640
Owl, Barn 3, 6, **290**, 637
    Barred **296**, 298, 638
    Great Horned 6, 186, **294**, 296, 298, 638
    Long-eared 3, 81, **298**, 638
    Northern Saw-whet 298, **302**, 638
    Screech, *see* Screech-Owl, Eastern 6, **292**,
        298, 638
    Short-eared 3, 81, **300**, 638
Oxyura jamaicensis 3, 77, **130**, 636
Oystercatcher, American 80, **236**, 637

Paint, Cliff Swallow nests slough 400
Palustrine System Ecological Community
    54–55
Pandion haliaetus 6, 28, 81, **186**, 636
Parakeet, Black-headed, *see* Parakeet, Black-
    hooded **630**
    Black-hooded **630**
    Monk 25, **282**, 637
    Nanday, *see* Parakeet, Black-hooded **630**
Parasites
    on Barn Swallow 402
    on Cliff Swallow 400
Partridge, Gray **134**, 636
"Partridge," *see* Grouse, Ruffed **138**
Parula americana **478**, 639
Parula, Northern **478**, 639
Passerculus sandwichensis **554**, 640
Passer domesticus **622**, 641
Passerina caerulea **580**, 641
    P. cyanea 67, **582**, 641
Peer reviewers, list of xii
Pelecanus occidentalis 25, **626**
Pelican, American White 25, **626**
Perdix perdix **134**, 636
Perisoreus canadensis **378**, 638
Person-hours 16
Petrochelidon pyrrhonota **400**, 639
Pewee, *see* Wood-Pewee, Eastern 67, **342**, 356,
    638
Phalacrocorax auritus 6, 28, 71, **152**, 186, 254,
    268, 636
Phalarope, Wilson's 25, **248**, 637
Phalaropus tricolor 25, **248**, 637
Phasianus colchicus **136**, 636
Pheasant, Ring-necked **136**, 636
Pheucticus ludovicianus 25, **578**, 641
Phoebe, Eastern 25, **354**, 638
Phragmites, and Swamp Sparrow 568

Picoides arcticus 330, **332**, 638
  P. dorsalis 3, **330**, 638
  P. pubescens 25, **326**, 638
  P. villosus **328**, 638
Pigeon, Passenger 61, **629**
  Rock **278**, 637
Pintail, Northern **110**, 635
Pipilo erythrophthalmus 66, **544**, 640
Piranga olivacea 82, **540**, 640
  P. rubra 25, **538**, 640
Plants
  invasive 66–68
  scientific names 643–644
Plegadis chihi 20, **627**
  P. falcinellus 80, **178**, 636
Plover, Piping 76, 80, **232**, 637
Podilymbus podiceps 3, 77, **150**, 636
Poecile atricapillus **406**, 528, 639
  P. hudsonica **408**, 639
Poem, "Fiesta" xxiii
Poisoning
  lead, in Bald Eagle 188
  lead, in Golden Eagle 204
  mercury, in Osprey 186
  mercury, in Sharp-shinned Hawk 192
  pesticides, in American Robin 450
  pesticides, in Peregrine Falcon 210
  and Red-winged Blackbird 590
  and Rock Pigeon 278
Poleward shifts in species distribution 41
Polioptila caerulea **434**, 639
Pooecetes gramineus 66, 81, **552**, 640
Population monitoring 40
Porzana carolina **222**, 637
Possible breeding, definition 2
Prairie-Chicken, Greater (Heath Hen) 61, **626**
Predation
  on Common Nighthawk 306
  on Eastern Screech-Owl 292
  in forest interior vs edge 68
  on Gray Partridge 134
  of nests by gulls and crows 292, 306
  of nests in non-native plants 66, 67, 68
  on Osprey 186
  on Piping Plover 232
Predators 66–68
Priorities of bird conservation 76
Private land stewardship 83
Probable breeding, definition 2
Progne subis **392**, 639
Protonotaria citrea 3, 82, **514**, 640

Quality control 4
Quiscalus major **598**
  Q. quiscula **596**

Rail, Black 3, 76, 80, **214**, 637
  Clapper **216**, 637
  King 3, 77, **218**, 637
  Virginia **220**, 637
Rallus elegans 3, 77, **218**, 637
  R. limicola **220**, 637
  R. longirostris **216**, 637
Raven, Common 6, 28, 38, 40, 61, **386**, 639
Records review 4

Redhead **116**, 636
Redstart, American **512**, 640
Regional coordinators, list of xi
Regulus calendula **432**, 639
  R. satrapa **430**, 639
Rensselaer Hills sub-ecozone 51
Results, summary 15–42
Return a Gift to Wildlife ix
Riparia riparia 396, **398**, 639
Riverine System, Ecological Community 53–54
River systems 8
Robin, American 66, 67, **450**, 639
Roof
  gravel, used for nesting by Killdeer 234
  gravel, used for nesting by Common
    Nighthawk 306
  rubberized, unsuitable for nighthawk 306
Rynchops niger 80, **274**, 637

Sable Highlands 49
Sandpiper, Spotted **238**, 637
  Upland 3, 6, 28, **242**, 637
Sapsucker, Yellow-bellied 28, 314, **324**, 460, 638
Sayornis phoebe 25, **354**, 638
Scaup, Greater 20, **625**
  Lesser **625**, 636
Schoharie Hills sub-ecozone 45
Scolopax minor 81, 84, **246**, 637
Screech-Owl, Eastern 6, **292**, 298, 638
Seiurus aurocapilla 68, **518**, 640
  S. motacilla 82, **522**, 640
  S. noveboracensis **520**, 640
Setophaga ruticilla **116**, 636
Shawangunk Hills sub-ecozone 51
Shooting
  of Bald Eagle 188
  of Cooper's Hawk 194
  of Golden Eagle 204
  of Mallard on preserves 102
  of Sharp-shinned Hawk 192
  of Turkey Vulture 184
Shoveler, Northern **108**, 635
Shrike, Loggerhead 3, 20, 72, **360**, 638
Shrublands 64
Sialia sialis 28, 63, **438**, 639
Siskin, Pine **616**, 641
Sitta canadensis **412**, 639
  S. carolinensis **414**, 639
Skimmer, Black 80, **274**, 637
Snipe, Wilson's **244**, 637
Somateria mollissima 25, **120**, 636
Sora **222**, 637
Sparrow, Chipping **546**, 640
  Chipping x Clay-colored hybrids 548
  Clay-colored 3, **548**, 640
  Field **550**, 640
  Grasshopper 81, **556**, 640
  Henslow's 3, 6, 28, 76, 81, **558**, 640
  House **622**, 641
  Lincoln's **566**, 641
  Nelson's Sharp-tailed 25, **631**
  Saltmarsh Sharp-tailed 76, 80, **560**, 640
  Savannah **554**, 640
  Seaside 3, **562**, 640
  Song **564**, 584, 640
  Swamp **568**, 641

  Vesper 66, 81, **552**, 640
  White-throated **570**, 641
"Sparrow hawk," *see* Kestrel, American **206**
Species
  accounts explained 5
  changes adjusted for effort 20–25
  changes and habitat availability 38
  changes in occurrence, ranked 29–34
  Confirmed in only one Atlas 25
  decreases, ranked 36–37
  distribution, poleward shifts 41
  dramatic changes 28
  increases, ranked 35–36
  in only one Atlas 20
  list of, number of blocks, comparison 20–26
  notable 3
  number per block, *see* Species, richness
    18–25, 28
  of greatest conservation need 78–79
  richness 18–25, 28
  top 20 25–26
  trends 28–29, 38–40
Sphyrapicus varius 28, 314, **324**, 460, 638
Spiza americana 25, **584**, 641
Spizella pallida 3, **548**, 640
  S. passerina **546**, 640
  S. pusilla **550**, 640
Spruce budworm, *see* Budworm, spruce
Starling, European 25, **460**, 639
  competition with Eastern Bluebird 438
  competition with Eastern Screech-Owl 292
  competition with Northern Flicker 334
  competition with Purple Martin 392
  competition with Red-headed Woodpecker
    320
Stelgidopteryx serripennis **396**, 639
Sterna dougallii 80, **268**, 637
  S. forsteri 80, **272**, 637
  S. hirundo 70, 80, **270**, 637
Sternula antillarum 80, **260**, 637
St. Lawrence–Champlain Valley Ecoregion 44
St. Lawrence Plains Ecozone 48–49
  sub-ecozone 49
St. Lawrence Transition sub-ecozone 49
Streptopelia decaocto 25, **628**
Strix varia **296**, 298, 638
Sturnella magna 81, **592**, 633, 641
  S. neglecta **632**, 641
Sturnus vulgaris 25, **460**, 639
Sub-ecozones 44–57
Subterranean System Ecological Community 57
Succession, ecological, bird responses to 66
Swallow, Bank 396, **398**, 639
  Barn 37, **402**, 639
  Cliff **400**, 639
  Northern Rough-winged **396**, 639
  Tree **394**, 639
"Swallow, white-bellied," *see* Swallow, Tree **394**
Swan, Mute 77, **90**, 635
  Trumpeter 3, 25, **92**, 635
Swift, Chimney **312**, 638

Tachycineta bicolor **394**, 639
Taconic Foothills sub-ecozone 51
  Highlands Ecozone 51
  Mountains sub-ecozone 51

Tanager, Scarlet 82, **540**, 640
  Summer 25, **538**, 640
Teal, Blue-winged 77, **106**, 635
  Green-winged **112**, 635
Tern, Black 77, 83, **266**, 627–628, 637
  Caspian 25, 80, **264**, 637
  Common 70, 80, **270**, 637
  Forster's 80, **272**, 637
  Gull-billed **262**, 637
  Least 80, **260**, 637
  Roseate 80, **268**, 637
  White-winged 25, **627**
Terrestrial System Ecological Community
    55–57
Thistle, as nest material and food for American
    Goldfinch 618
Thrasher, Brown 28, 66, 81, **458**, 639
Thrush, Bicknell's 3, 52, 76, 82–83, **442**, 639
  Hermit **446**, 639
  Swainson's **444**, 639
  Wood 25, 76, 82, 84, 446, **448**, 639
Thryomanes bewickii 631
Thryothorus ludovicianus 6, 28, 41, **420**, 434,
    639
Titmouse, Tufted 28, 41, **410**, 434, 639
Towhee, Eastern 66, **544**, 640
Toxostoma rufum 28, 66, 81, **458**, 639
"Trap-lining feeders" by Cooper's Hawk 194
Traps lethal for Golden Eagles 204
Tree diseases 67
Tree mortality positive for Brown Creeper 416
Triassic Lowlands Ecozone 51
Tringa semipalmata 80, **240**, 262, 637
Troglodytes aedon **422**, 639
  T. troglodytes **424**, 639
Tug Hill, Central sub-ecozone 48
  Plateau Ecozone sub-ecozone 48
  Transition sub-ecozone 48
Turdus migratorius 66, 67, **450**, 639
Turkey, Wild 6, 28, **142**, 636
Tympanuchus cupido 61, **626**
Tyrannus tyrannus 25, **358**, 638
  T. verticalis 25, **630**
Tyto alba 3, 6, **290**, 637

Usefulness of Atlas data 15

Veery **440**, 639
Vehicle collisions
  with American Kestrel 206
  with Eastern Screech-Owl 292
  with Golden Eagle 204
  with Loggerhead Shrike 360
  with Red-headed Woodpecker 320

Vermivora chrysoptera 76, 81, 82, **468**, 470–473,
    639
  V. peregrina 3, **474**, 640
  V. pinus 82, **466**, 470–473, 639
  V. pinus x *V. chrysoptera* complex 470–473
  V. ruficapilla **476**, 639
Vireo, Blue-headed **368**, 638
  Philadelphia 6, **372**, 638
  Red-eyed **374**, 638
  Warbling **370**, 638
  White-eyed **364**, 638
  Yellow-throated **366**, 638
Vireo flavifrons **366**, 638
  V. gilvus **370**, 638
  V. griseus **364**, 638
  V. olivaceus **374**, 638
  V. philadelphicus 6, **372**, 638
  V. solitarius **368**, 638
Volunteers, number of xvi, 4
Vulture, Black 25, **182**, 636
  Turkey 28, **184**, 636

Warbler, Bay-breasted 3, **504**, 640
  Black-and-white **510**, 640
  Blackburnian **494**, 640
  Blackpoll **506**, 640
  Black-throated Blue 40, 82, **488**, 640
  Black-throated Green **492**, 640
  Blue-winged 82, **466**, 470–473, 639
  Blue-winged x Golden-winged hybrids
    470–473
  Brewster's 470–473
  Canada 28, 76, 82, 84, 342, **534**, 640
  Cape May 3, 25, 82, **486**, 640
  Cerulean 67, 76, 82, 83, **508**, 640
  Chestnut-sided **482**, 640
  Golden-winged 76, 81, 82, **468**, 470–473,
    639
  Hooded **530**, 640
  Kentucky 3, 76, 82, **524**, 640
  Lawrence's 470–473
  Magnolia **484**, 640
  Mourning **526**, 640
  Myrtle, *see* Warbler, Yellow-rumped
    490
  Nashville **476**, 639
  Palm 3, 40, **502**, 640
  Pine **498**, 640
  Prairie 81, **500**, 640
  Prothonotary 3, 82, **514**, 640
  Tennessee 3, **474**, 640
  Wilson's 3, **532**, 640
  Worm-eating 25, **516**, 640
  Yellow 25, **480**, 639

Yellow-rumped **490**, 640
  Yellow-throated 3, **496**, 640
"Warblers, spruce budworm" 474
Waterthrush, Louisiana 82, **522**, 640
  Northern **520**, 640
Waxwing, Cedar **462**, 639
Western Allegheny Plateau Ecoregion 43
West Nile Virus
  in American Crow 382
  in Black-capped Chickadee 406
  in Blue Jay 380
  in Fish Crow 384
Wetlands 43, 48–49, 53–54, 55, 61–62, 68, 77
  and American Bittern 156
  and American Woodcock 226
  and Black Tern 266
  and Common Moorhen 224
  and Great Egret 162
  and Northern Harrier 190
  and Ring-necked Pheasant 136
  and Seaside Sparrow 562
  and Short-eared Owl 300
  and Sora 222
  and Swamp Sparrow 568
  and Virginia Rail 220
  and Wilson's Phalarope 248
  and Yellow-crowned Night-Heron 176
  protection of 83
Whip-poor-will 3, 81–82, 308, **310**, 638
Wigeon, American **98**, 635
Willet 80, **240**, 262, 637
Wilsonia canadensis 28, 76, 82, 84, 342, **534**, 640
  W. citrina **530**, 640
  W. pusilla 3, **532**, 640
Woodcock, American 81, 84, **246**, 637
Woodpecker, American Three-toed 3, **330**, 638
  Black-backed 330, **332**, 638
  Downy 25, **326**, 638
  Hairy **328**, 638
  Pileated 38, 61, 324, **336**, 638
  Red-bellied 28, 41, **322**, 638
  Red-headed 6, 28, 82, **320**, 638
Wood-Pewee, Eastern 67, **342**, 356, 638
Wren, Bewick's **631**
  Carolina 6, 28, 41, **420**, 434, 639
  House **422**, 639
  Marsh 6, **428**, 639
  Sedge 3, **426**, 639
  Winter **424**, 639

Yellowthroat, Common **528**, 640

Zenaida macroura 25, **280**, 637
Zonotrichia albicollis **570**, 641

Breeding Categories and Codes

Breeding was recorded at three levels, indicating increasing certainty: Possible, Probable, and Confirmed. Within each of these categories are breeding codes that describe the specific behavior observed; these codes are the same as those used in the first Atlas. The following descriptions were given to atlasers:

Possible Breeding

X Species observed in possible nesting habitat, but no other indication of breeding noted. Singing male(s) present (or breeding calls heard) in breeding season.

Probable Breeding

S Singing male present (or breeding calls heard) on more than one date at least a week apart in the same place. This is a good indication that a bird has taken up residence if the dates are a week or more apart.

P Pair observed in suitable habitat in breeding season.

T Bird (or pair) apparently holding territory. In addition to territorial singing, chasing of other individuals of same species often marks a territory.

D Courtship and display, agitated behavior, or anxiety calls from adults suggesting probable presence nearby of a nest of young; well-developed brood patch or cloacal protuberance on trapped adult. Includes copulation.

N Visiting probable nest site. Nest building by wrens and woodpeckers. Wrens may build many nests. Woodpeckers, although they usually drill only one nest cavity, also drill holes just for roosting.

B Nest building or excavation of a nest hole.

Confirmed Breeding

DD Distraction display or injury-feigning. Agitated behavior and/or anxiety calls are Probable-D.

UN Used nest found. Caution: these must be carefully identified if they are to be counted as evidence. Some nests (e.g., Baltimore Oriole) are persistent and very characteristic. Most are difficult to identify correctly.

FE Female with egg in the oviduct (by bird bander).

FL Recently fledged young (including downy young of precocious species—waterfowl, shorebirds). This code should be used with caution for species such as blackbirds and swallows, which may move some distance soon after fledging. Recently fledged passerines are still dependent on their parents and are fed by them.

ON Adult(s) entering or leaving nest site in circumstances indicating occupied nest. *Not* generally used for open-nesting birds. It should be used for hole nesters only when a bird enters a hole and remains inside, makes a changeover at a hole, or leaves a hole after having been inside for some time. If you simply see a bird fly into or out of a bush or tree, and do not find a nest, the correct code would be Probable-N.

FS Adult carrying fecal sac.

FY Adult(s) with food for young. Some birds (gulls, terns, and raptors) continue to feed their young long after they are fledged, and even after they have moved considerable distances. Also, some birds (e.g., terns) may carry food over long distances to their young in a neighboring block. Be especially careful on the edge of a block. Care should be taken to avoid confusion with courtship feeding (Probable-D).

NE Identifiable nest and eggs, bird sitting on nest or egg, identifiable eggshells found beneath nest, or identifiable dead nestling(s). If you find a cowbird egg in a nest, the code is NE for cowbird, and NE for the nest's owner.

NY Nest with young. If you find a young cowbird with other young, the code is NY for cowbird and NY for identified nest owner.